STUDY GUIDE

to accompany

ORGANIC CHEMISTRY

Third Edition

T. W. Graham Solomons
Jack Fernandez

University of South Florida
Tampa, Florida

Appendix B developed by

Ronald Starkey

University of Wisconsin, Green Bay

JOHN WILEY & SONS

NEW YORK • CHICHESTER • BRISBANE • TORONTO • SINGAPORE

ISBN 0-471-88826-5

Printed in the United States of America

10 9 8 7 6 5 4

ACKNOWLEDGMENTS

We wish to acknowledge Ronald Starkey of the University of Wisconsin for providing the Molecular Model Set Exercises and Solutions of Appendix B.

We also wish to thank the following persons who graciously read the entire manuscript and who made many helpful suggestions: George R. Wenzinger, University of South Florida; Prof. Darrell Berlin, Oklahoma State University; Prof. John Mangravite, West Chester State College; Prof. J. G. Traynham, Louisiana State University; and Prof. Desmond M. S. Wheeler, University of Nebraska. We are also much indebted to Jeannette Stiefel for proofreading the entire study guide.

T. W. Graham Solomons

Jack E. Fernandez

TO THE STUDENT

This study guide contains several items to aid you in your study of organic chemistry; these include the following.

Answers to the Problems. Solutions are given for all the problems in the text, including the end-of-chapter problems. In many instances we have given not only the answer, but also an explanation of the reasoning that leads to the solution. Although many problems have more than one solution, we have generally given only one. Thus, you should not necessarily assume that your answer is incorrect if it differs from the one given here.

The heart of organic chemistry lies in problem solving. This is as true for the practicing organic chemist as for the beginning student. But, a problem in organic chemistry is like a riddle; once you have seen the answer, it is impossible for you to go through the process of solving it. The essential value of a problem lies in the mental exercise of the problem-solving process, and you cannot get this exercise if you already know the answer. The best way to use this manual, therefore, is to check the problems you have worked, or to find explanations for unsolved problems *only* after you have made serious attempts at working them.

See Tables 13.1, 13.2, and 13.3 inside the front and back covers; they are reproduced to help you solve problems.

Flow Diagrams of Reactions Covered. These flow diagrams should serve to give you a one-page overview of the reactions in the chapter as well as a way to view the interrelations of the reactions. These diagrams should be helpful to you in the early Additional Problems on reactions as well as in the problems that involve multistep syntheses.

Section References to Additional Problems. If you have trouble working the Additional Problems, you may wish to refer to the section in the chapter that deals with the concept being examined. Generally, you should seek help in the chapter before going to the solution in this study guide.

Self-Tests. A Self-Test is given for each chapter of the text. After you think you have mastered the material in each chapter you should then take the Self-Test. When you have finished you can check your answers against those given in Appendix D.

Supplementary Problems. These problems are designed to help you study for tests after you have worked the Additional Problems and Self-Tests.

Answers to Review Problems. Two sets of review problems occur in the text after Chapters 10 and 20. These problems require you to use material covered in the preceeding chapters. These problems should help you review for examinations. The answers to these review problems are given in this study guide.

A Section on the Calculation of Empirical and Molecular Formulas. This topic, usually included in the general chemistry course that precedes the study of organic chemistry, has been included as Appendix A. If you missed it in general chemistry or need a review, you should study it early in the course.

Molecular Model Set Exercises. Appendix B is a set of exercises with solutions. These exercises are designed to help you gain facility with molecular models and to help you understand the relationship between formulas on the page and the three-dimensional molecules that these formulas represent. The chapter corresponding to each exercise is given in Appendix B.

Glossary of Important Terms. Important terms and concepts are collected in Appendix C. These terms and concepts are defined and a reference to the text is given.

CONTENTS

STUDY GUIDE

to accompany

ORGANIC CHEMISTRY

1 CARBON COMPOUNDS AND CHEMICAL BONDS

SOLUTIONS TO PROBLEMS

1.1 Using the elemental symbol to denote the nucleus and inner shell electrons, we account for the formation of an ionic bond, and therefore of ions, by transferring valence shell electrons from the metal atom to the valence shell of the nonmetal atom. The resulting ions will have the electronic structures of an inert gas.

(a) $\cdot Na \cdot + \cdot Cl \colon \longrightarrow Na^+ + \colon Cl \colon^-$

(b) $\cdot Mg \cdot + 2 \cdot F \colon \longrightarrow Mg^{+2} + 2 \colon F \colon^-$

(c) $\cdot K \cdot + \cdot Br \colon \longrightarrow K^+ + \colon Br \colon^-$

1.2 (a) $H \colon \ddot{Br} \colon , H{-}\ddot{Br} \colon$

     (b) $\colon \ddot{Br} \colon \ddot{Br} \colon , \colon \ddot{Br}{-}\ddot{Br} \colon$

     (c) $\colon \ddot{O} \colon \colon C \colon \colon \ddot{O} \colon , \colon \ddot{O}{=}C{=}\ddot{O} \colon$

     (d)
$$H \colon \overset{H}{\underset{H}{C}} \colon H , H{-}\overset{H}{\underset{H}{C}}{-}H$$

(e) $H \colon \ddot{O} \colon \ddot{O} \colon H, H{-}\ddot{O}{-}\ddot{O}{-}H$

(f)
$$H \colon \overset{H}{\underset{H}{Si}} \colon H, H{-}\overset{H}{\underset{H}{Si}}{-}H$$

(g)
$$H \colon \overset{..}{\underset{H}{N}} \colon H, H{-}\overset{..}{\underset{H}{N}}{-}H$$

(h)
$$\colon \ddot{Cl} \colon \overset{..}{\underset{\colon \ddot{Cl} \colon}{P}} \colon \ddot{Cl} \colon , \colon \ddot{Cl}{-}\overset{..}{\underset{\colon \ddot{Cl} \colon}{P}}{-}\ddot{Cl} \colon$$

(i) $:\ddot{F}:N:\ddot{F}:$, $:\ddot{F}-\overset{..}{N}-\ddot{F}:$ (l) $^-:\ddot{O}:H$, $^-:\ddot{O}-H$
          $:\ddot{F}:$ $:\ddot{F}:$

                 H   H
(j) $H:\overset{H}{\underset{H}{C}}:\ddot{Cl}:$, $H-\overset{H}{\underset{H}{C}}-\ddot{Cl}:$ (m) $\left[\,H:\overset{H}{\underset{H}{N}}:H\,\right]^+$ $:\ddot{Cl}:^-$, $\left[\,H-\overset{H}{\underset{H}{N}}-H\,\right]^+$ $:\ddot{Cl}:^-$

(k) $H:\ddot{O}:$, $H-\overset{..}{\underset{H}{O}}:$ (n) $Na^+\ ^-:\ddot{O}:H$, $Na^+\ ^-:\ddot{O}-H$
          H   H

1.3   To calculate formal charge we use the following equation.

Formal charge = group number − [½ (number of shared electrons) + (number of unshared electrons)]

Charge on ion = sum of all formal charges

			Formal Charge	Total Charge
(a)	$\left[\,H-\overset{H}{\underset{H}{B}}-H\,\right]^-$	H	1-[½ (2) + 0] = 0	
		B	3-[½ (8) + 0] = -1	-1
(b)	$:\ddot{O}-H^-$	H	1-[½ (2) + 0] = 0	
		O	6-[½ (2) + 6] = -1	-1
(c)	$\left[\,:\ddot{F}-\overset{\ddot{F}}{\underset{\ddot{F}}{B}}-\ddot{F}:\,\right]^-$	F	7-[½ (2) + 6] = 0	
		B	3-[½ (8) + 0] = -1	-1
(d)	$\left[\,H-\overset{..}{\underset{H}{O}}-H\,\right]^+$	H	1-[½ (2) + 0] = 0	
		O	6-[½ (6) + 2] = +1	+1
(e)	$\left[\,\overset{:\ddot{O}}{\underset{\cdot\ddot{O}\ \ \ddot{O}\cdot}{\overset{\|}{C}}}\,\right]^{2-}$	top O	6-[½ (4) + 4] = 0	
		C	4-[½ (8) + 0] = 0	-2
		bottom O's	6-[½ (2) + 6] = -1	
(f)	$\left[\,H-\overset{..}{\underset{H}{C}}-H\,\right]^-$	H	1-[½ (2) + 0] = 0	
		C	4-[½ (6) + 2] = -1	-1
(g)	$\left[\,H-\overset{}{\underset{H}{C}}-H\,\right]^+$	H	1-[½ (2) + 0] = 0	
		C	4-[½ (6) + 0] = +1	+1
(h)	$H-\overset{\cdot}{\underset{H}{C}}-H$	H	1-[½ (2) + 0] = 0	
		C	4-[½ (6) + 1] = 0	0

(i) H–C̈–H   H $1-[\frac{1}{2}(2) + 0] = 0$
                      C $4-[\frac{1}{2}(4) + 2] = 0$ 0

(j) $\left[\ddot{:}\ddot{N}\text{–H} \atop \quad\overset{|}{\text{H}} \right]^{-}$ H $1-[\frac{1}{2}(2) + 0] = 0$
                      N $5-[\frac{1}{2}(4) + 4] = -1$ -1

1.4   Zero formal charges are not shown.

(a) No formal charges   (d) No formal charges   (g) $CH_3\text{–}\overset{\displaystyle \ddot{O}}{\underset{\displaystyle \ddot{O}:^-}{\overset{\|}{\diagdown C}}}$

(b) No formal charges   (e) No formal charges   (h) $CH_3CH_2\text{–}\overset{+}{\underset{\overset{|}{H}}{\ddot{O}}}\text{–H}$

(c) $CH_3\text{–}\overset{\overset{\displaystyle CH_3}{|}}{\underset{\underset{\displaystyle :\ddot{O}:^-}{|}}{\overset{+}{N}}}\text{–}CH_3$ (f) $CH_3\text{–}\overset{+}{\underset{\underset{\displaystyle :\ddot{O}:^-}{|}}{N}}\text{=}\ddot{O}:$ (i) $CH_3CH\text{–}CHCH_3 \atop \quad\;\; \underset{+}{\overset{\diagdown\diagup}{:\ddot{Br}:}}$

1.5   Any Lewis structure that gives the noble gas structure to each atom is valid.

(a) $^{-}:\ddot{O}\text{–}\overset{+}{\ddot{S}}\text{=}\ddot{O}: \longleftrightarrow :\ddot{O}\text{=}\overset{+}{\ddot{S}}\text{–}\ddot{O}:^{-}$

(b) Yes. Both O–S bonds are hybrids of a single and a double bond. Therefore the two O–S bonds are equivalent and of equal length.

1.6   A bond between two dissimilar atoms is polarized so as to make the more electronegative atom negative and the less electronegative atom positive. A bond between atoms of the same element does not have a dipole moment.

(a) $\overset{\longmapsto}{\text{H–Br}}$ (c) H–H (dipole moment = 0)

(b) $\overset{\longmapsto}{\text{I–Cl}}$ (d) Cl–Cl (dipole moment = 0)

1.7   (a) Yes. Only one tetrahedral structure of CH_2X_2 is possible.

(b) No. Two square planar structures of CH_2X_2 are possible.

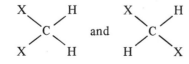

Therefore, if CH_2X_2 had a square planar structure we should observe two compounds (isomers) with the formula CH_2X_2.

1.8   A singly bonded atom that has four pairs of electrons, whether they are involved in bonding or not, will have these four pairs tetrahedrally oriented. An atom that has only three pairs of electrons will have them oriented trigonally in a plane. An atom that has only two pairs of electrons will have them oriented at 180° to one another. The above three cases result from the fact that electron pairs orient themselves so as to minimize their mutual repulsions (VSEPR model).

(a) Tetrahedral   (d) Tetrahedral   (g) Tetrahedral

(b) Tetrahedral   (e) Tetrahedral   (h) Linear

(c) Trigonal planar   (f) Linear   (i) Trigonal planar

1.9   (a) CO_2 has the structure $:\ddot{O}=C=\ddot{O}:$. It has two bonds (both double), therefore they are oriented at 180° to one another and the molecule is linear.

(b) We can draw two resonance structures for SO_2 :

 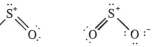

Both structures have three groups of electrons (one single bond, one double bond, and one unshared electron pair) around sulfur. Therefore the molecule is angular as shown. (Because of the space occupied by the unshared electron pair, the three electron groups are oriented at approximately 120° to one another in a plane.)

(c) We can draw three resonance structures for SO_3 :

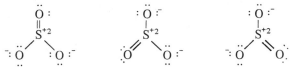

In each case sulfur has three groups of electrons, all of which are in partial multiple bonds, so the molecule is trigonal planar.

1.10   The two C=O bond moments are opposed and cancel each other:

If the bond angle were other than 180°, then the individual bond moments would not cancel. There would be a resultant dipole moment.

1.11   That SO_2 is an angular molecule, . The S–O bond moments do not cancel each other as they would if the molecule were linear.

1.12   The direction of polarity of the N–H bond is opposite to that of the N–F bond.

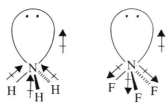

In NH_3, the resultant N–H bond polarities and the polarity of the unshared electron pair are in the same direction.

In NF_3 the resultant N–F bond polarities partially cancel the polarity of the unshared electron pair.

1.13 BF_3 is trigonal planar. The F–B–F bond angles are all equal (120°), and the B–F bonds are all necessarily equal in polarity, so their individual dipole moments cancel each other.

1.14   In drawing the third structural isomer of this molecule we must keep in mind that each carbon atom must have four bonds, each oxygen atom must have two bonds, and each hydrogen atom must have only one bond. Therefore the structure shown below is the third isomer.

```
       H    H H
       |    | |
  H–C–O–C–C–H
       |    | |
       H    H H
```

1.15

(a)

```
     H  :Cl: H  H
     |   |   |  |
H —  C — C — C — C —H
     |   |   |  |
     H  :Cl: H  H
```

```
Cl   Cl
  \  /
   \/
   /\
```

(c)

```
         H
         |
     H H–C–H H  H
     |   |   |  |
H —  C — C — C — C —H
     |   |   |  |
     H H–C–H H  H
         |
         H
```

```
   \   /
    \ /
     X
    / \
```

(b)

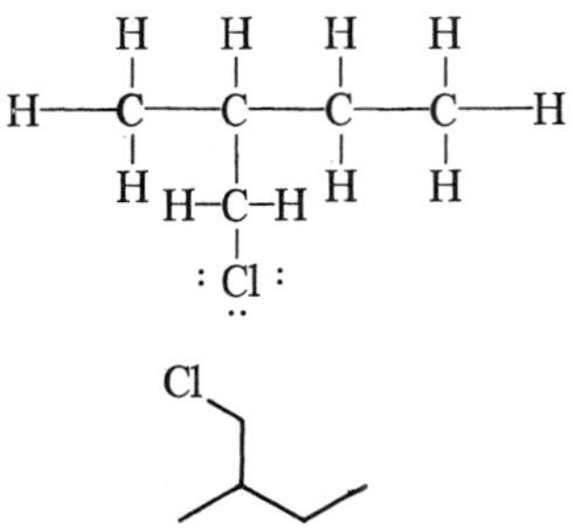

(d)

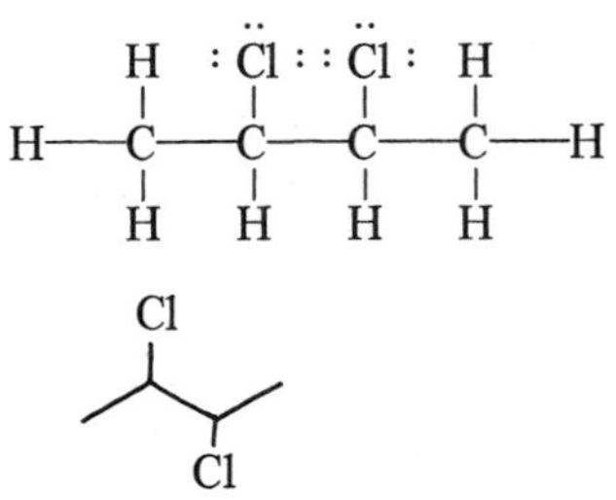

(e)

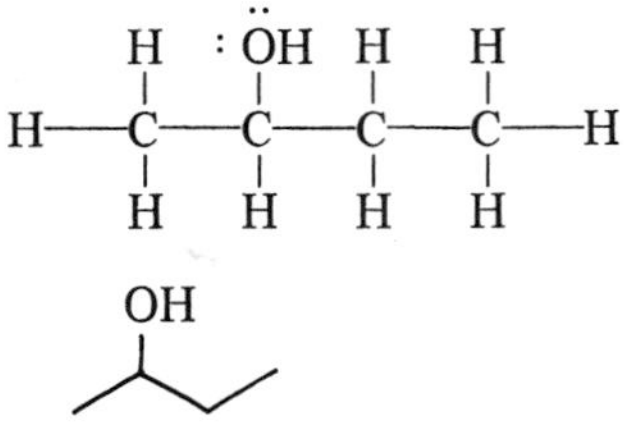

(g)

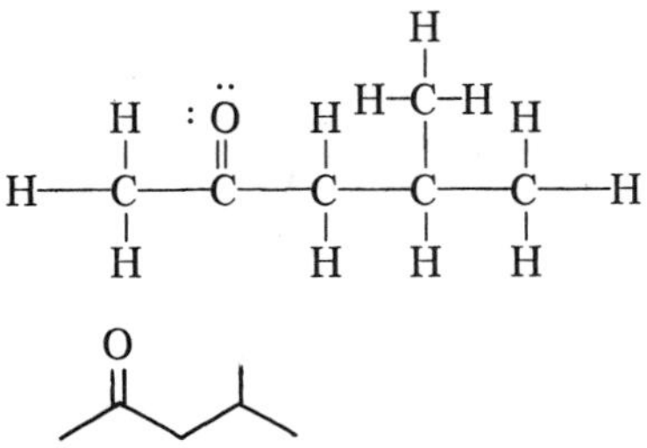

(f)

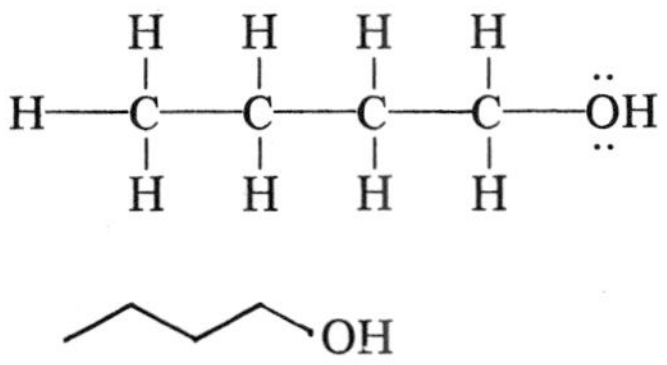

(h)

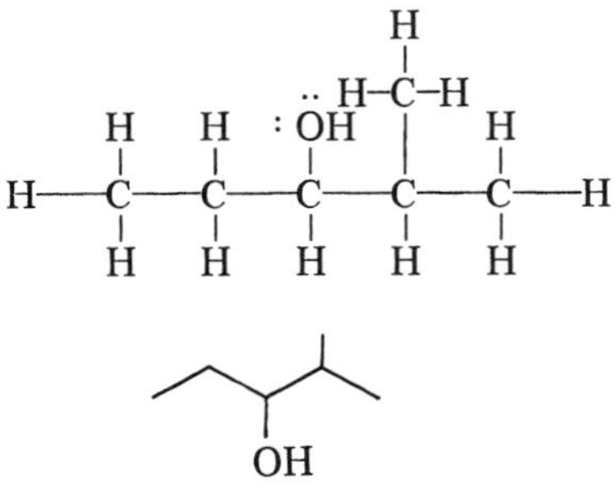

1.16 Recall that structural isomers must have the same molecular formula and must have their atoms connected in a different order. Therefore, (a) and (d) are structural isomers, and (e) and (f) are structural isomers.

1.17

(a)

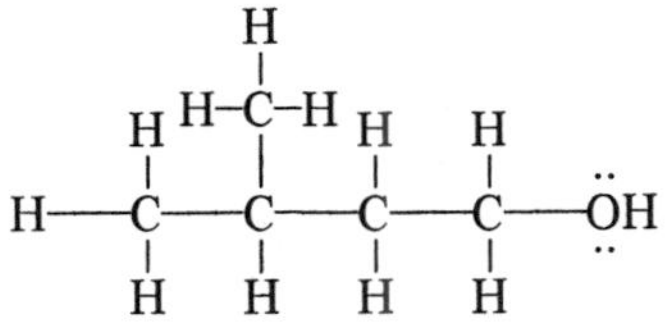

(c)

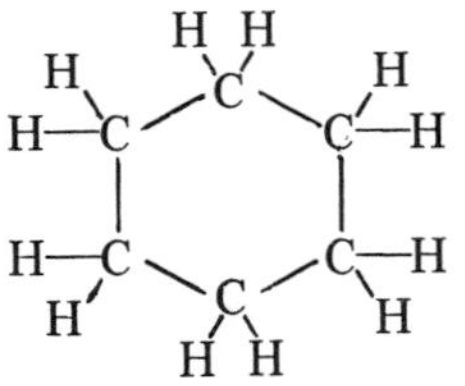

(b)

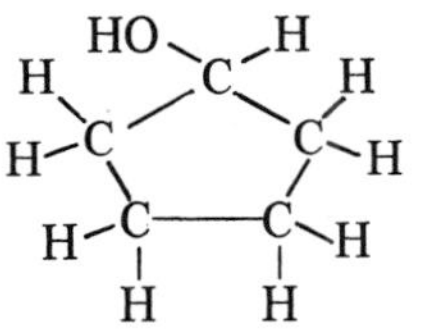

(d)

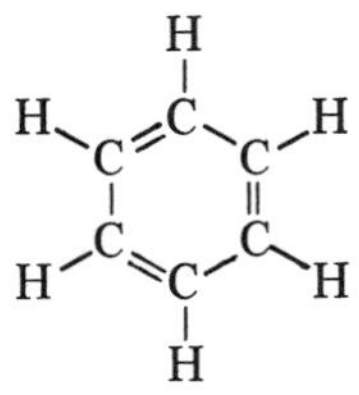

1.18 Each electron experiences less repulsion from other electrons if it is in an orbital by itself because the electrons can be further apart. Consider the three $2p$ orbitals as an example (see Fig. 1.21). With one electron in each $2p$ orbital each electron occupies a different region of space. This would not be true if two electrons were in the same $2p$ orbital.

1.19 (a) Monovalent because only one orbital ($2p$) contains a single electron; the $2s$ orbital is filled. (b) The two p orbitals lie at 90° to one another; the resulting bonds would also lie at 90° to each other. Thus BF_3, based on an excited state of boron, would have the following structure. The angles of 135° result by dividing (360-90) by 2.

$$
\begin{array}{c}
\text{F} \\
90° \quad | \\
\text{F} - \text{B} \quad 135° \\
135° \quad \text{F}
\end{array}
$$

1.20

(a)
$$\text{H} : \overset{\text{H}}{\underset{\text{H}}{\text{C}}} : \ddot{\text{N}} :: \text{C} :: \ddot{\text{S}} :$$

(b)
$$\text{H} : \overset{\text{H}}{\underset{\text{H}}{\text{C}}} : \text{C} ::: \overset{+}{\text{N}} : \ddot{\text{O}} : ^-$$

(c)
$$\text{H} : \overset{\text{H}}{\underset{\text{H}}{\text{C}}} : \ddot{\text{O}} : \overset{:\ddot{\text{O}}}{\underset{+}{\text{N}}} : \ddot{\text{O}} : ^-$$

(d)
$$\text{H} : \overset{\text{H}}{\underset{\text{H}}{\text{C}}} : \ddot{\text{N}} :: \text{C} :: \ddot{\text{O}} :$$

(e)
$$\text{H} : \overset{\text{H}}{\text{C}} :: \text{C} :: \ddot{\text{O}} :$$

(f)
$$\text{H} : \overset{\text{H}}{\text{C}} :: \overset{+}{\text{N}} :: \ddot{\text{N}} : ^-$$

(g) $\text{K}^+ \quad ^-\ddot{\text{N}} : \overset{\text{H}}{\underset{\text{H}}{|}} \text{H}$

(h) $\text{Na}^+ \quad ^-\ddot{\text{N}} :: \overset{+}{\text{N}} :: \ddot{\text{N}} : ^-$

(i)
$$\overset{\text{H}}{\underset{\text{H}}{}} \ddot{\text{C}} :: \ddot{\text{O}} :$$

(j)
$$\text{H} : \overset{:\ddot{\text{O}}:}{\text{C}} : \ddot{\text{O}} : \text{H}$$

1.21 (a) Electron Configuration

(1) Be $1s^2 2s^2$

(2) B $1s^2 2s^2 2p_x^1$

(3) C $1s^2 2s^2 2p_x^1 2p_y^1$

(4) N $1s^2 2s^2 2p_x^1 2p_y^1 2p_z^1$

(5) O $1s^2 2s^2 2p_x^2 2p_y^1 2p_z^1$

(b) Orbital Arrangement

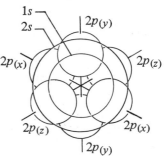

1.22

(a)
$$\text{CH}_3 - \ddot{\text{O}} - \overset{\overset{\ddot{\text{O}}:}{\|}}{\underset{\|}{\text{S}}} - \ddot{\text{O}} : ^-$$
$$\overset{}{\underset{\ddot{\text{O}}:}{}}$$

(b)
$$\text{CH}_3 - \overset{^-:\ddot{\text{O}}:}{\underset{+}{\text{S}}} - \text{CH}_3$$

(c) $:\ddot{O}-\overset{\overset{\textstyle\ddot{O}:}{\|}}{\underset{\underset{\textstyle\ddot{O}:}{\|}}{S}}-\ddot{O}:^{-}$

(d) $CH_3-\overset{\overset{\textstyle\ddot{O}:}{\|}}{\underset{\underset{\textstyle\ddot{O}:}{\|}}{S}}-\ddot{O}:^{-}$

1.23 (a) $(CH_3)_2CHCH_2OH$

(c) $\begin{array}{l} CH-CH_2 \\ \|\quad\ | \\ CH-CH_2 \end{array}$

(b) $(CH_3)_2CH\overset{\overset{\textstyle O}{\|}}{C}CH(CH_3)_2$

(d) $(CH_3)_2CHCH_2CH_2OH$

1.24 (a) $C_4H_{10}O$ (c) C_4H_6

(b) $C_7H_{14}O$ (d) $C_5H_{12}O$

1.25 (a) Different compounds   (i) Different compounds

(b) Structural isomers   (j) Same compound

(c) Same compound   (k) Structural isomers

(d) Same compound   (l) Different compounds

(e) Same compound   (m) Same compound

(f) Structural isomers   (n) Same compound

(g) Different compounds   (o) Same compound

(h) Same compound   (p) Structural isomers

1.26

(a) H C—F with arrow (H, H, H on carbon)

(e) C with H, Cl, H, F and arrow

(b) C with H, H, F, F and arrow

(f) B with Cl, Cl, Cl

No dipole moment

(c) H—C with F, F, F and arrow

(g) F—Be—F

No dipole moment

(d) F—C with F, F, F

No dipole moment

(h) CH_3 $\overset{}{\underset{CH_3}{}}\ddot{O}:$ with arrow

(i) CH_3
       $\overset{+}{\longrightarrow} \ddot{O}$
       H

(j)   H
       $\overset{+}{\longrightarrow}$
       $C = \ddot{O}$:
       H

1.27

(a)   (structure: CH₂CH₂ chain with C=O ketone)

(d)   (structure: branched chain with C–OH and =O, carboxylic acid)

(b)   (branched chain structure)

(e)   (diene chain structure)

(c)   (branched chain with OH)

(f)   (cyclohexenone ring with O)

1.28

(a)
```
      H   H
   H   C      H
     C      C
   H        H
   H        H
     C      C
   H   ·N·   H
        |
        H
```

(c)
```
    H      H  H
    |      |  |
H—C—N—C—C—H
    |   ··  |  |
    H      H  H
       H–C–H
         |
         H
```

(b)
```
        H
        |
   H    C      H
     C      C
   H        ||
     C      C
   H   ·N·   H
```

(d)
```
   H    ··O··    H
  H–C         C–H
   |    ··     |
  H–C—————C–H
   |          |
   H          H
```

1.29 $CH_2=CHCH_2CH_3$ $CH_3CH=CHCH_3$ $CH_2=CCH_3$
                                                            |
                                                           CH_3

$\begin{matrix} CH_2—CH_2 \\ | \quad\quad | \\ CH_2—CH_2 \end{matrix}$ $\begin{matrix} CH_2 \\ \quad \diagdown CH–CH_3 \\ CH_2 \diagup \end{matrix}$

1.30 $\overset{-}{:}\ddot{O}–\ddot{N}=\ddot{O}:$ $:\ddot{O}=\ddot{N}–\ddot{O}:\overset{-}{}$ Yes because the two O–N bonds are equivalent hybrids of a single and a double bond.

1.31   (a) An sp^3 orbital. (b) sp^3 Orbitals. In ammonia and in water the bond angles are close to the tetrahedral angle of 109½°; therefore the N and O atoms must be sp^3 hybridized.

1.32 (a) $e = \dfrac{\mu}{d} = \dfrac{1.08 \times 10^{-18} \text{ esu cm}}{1.27 \times 10^{-8} \text{ cm}}$ (b) $\dfrac{0.85 \times 10^{-10} \text{ esu}}{4.8 \times 10^{-10} \text{ esu/electron}} = 0.18 \text{ electron}$

$e = 0.85 \times 10^{-10} \text{ esu}$

1.33 A carbon-chlorine bond is longer than a carbon-fluorine bond because chlorine is a larger atom than fluorine. Thus in $\overset{\delta+}{C}H_3-\overset{\delta-}{C}l$ the distance, d, that separates the charges is greater than in $\overset{\delta+}{C}H_3-\overset{\delta-}{F}$. The greater value of d for CH_3Cl more than compensates for the smaller value of e and thus the dipole moment ($e \times d$) is larger.

1.34 (a) While the structures differ in the position of their electrons they also differ in the positions of their nuclei and thus *they are not resonance structures*. (In cyanic acid the hydrogen nucleus is bonded to oxygen; in isocyanic acid it is bonded to nitrogen.)

(b) The anion obtained from either acid is a resonance hybrid of the following structures: $^-\!:\!\ddot{O}-C\equiv N:$ $\longleftrightarrow$ $:\ddot{O}=C=\ddot{N}:^-$

1.35 In He_2^+, two electrons are in a bonding molecular orbital, and only one electron is in an antibonding molecular orbital. The resultant He_2^+ ion has a lower energy than the non-bonded $He: + \cdot He^+$.

1.36 (a) BF_3 has an empty orbital which can accommodate the electron pair of $:NH_3$; also, formation of the new B–N bond stabilizes the system. (b) -1, (c) +1, (d) sp^3, (e) sp^3.

1.37 Acid strength increases with increasing (positive) formal charge on the central atom.

Acid Strength: $H_3O^+ > H_2O > OH^-$; $NH_4^+ > NH_3$; and $H_2S > HS^-$.

1.38
(a) $^-\!:\!\ddot{O}\diagup\overset{\overset{\ddot{O}^+}{|}}{\diagdown}\ddot{O}:$ $\longleftrightarrow$ $:\ddot{O}\overset{\overset{\ddot{O}^+}{|}}{\diagup}\diagdown\ddot{O}:^-$

(b) Yes. (c) The ozone molecule is angular, thus the two O–O dipoles do not cancel.
(d) Yes. The unshared electron pair on the central atom occupies space and repels the electrons of the oxygen-oxygen bonds.

1.39 The carbon atom in CH_3^+ utilizes only three of its four valence orbitals; therefore it is sp^2 hybridized. The vacant orbital is a p orbital.

SECTION REFERENCES FOR ADDITIONAL PROBLEMS

If you have trouble solving the Additional Problems refer to the sections in the text next to the problem numbers.

1.20	1.6C, 1.7A		**1.30**	1.8, 1.7A
1.21	1.14		**1.31**	1.16
1.22	1.7A, 1.7B		**1.32**	1.9, 1.11
1.23	1.12B		**1.33**	1.9, 1.11
1.24	1.2B, Appendix A		**1.34**	1.8
1.25	1.3, 1.4, 1.5, 1.12		**1.35**	1.15
1.26	1.9, 1.11, 1.12E		**1.36**	1.15, 1.7A, 1.16
1.27	1.12D		**1.37**	1.7
1.28	1.12A-1.12D		**1.38**	1.8, 1.11, 1.10
1.29	1.12A-1.12D		**1.39**	1.17

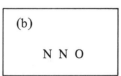

SELF-TEST

1.1   Using the atomic arrangements given below, draw two *different* and valid Lewis dot structures for the nitrous oxide molecule (N_2O). Show all formal charges that are not zero.

(a)	(b)
˙N N O	N N O

1.2   In the spaces provided give (a) the hybridization of the central atom and (b) the overall geometry of each molecule or ion below. In describing geometry take into account the atomic nuclei and the unshared electrons.

Molecule	*Hybridization*	*Geometry*
(a) BCl_3		

(b) $\underline{N}F_3$

(c) $\underline{O}F_2$

1.7   Draw the structural formulas of all the isomers of $C_3H_6Cl_2$.

1.8   Boron reacts with fluorine to form boron trifluoride. Answer the following questions about boron trifluoride. You may refer to the periodic table.

(a) Using vertical arrows to describe electrons, give the electronic configuration of boron in its simplest uncombined state.

$1s$ $2s$ $2p_x$ $2p_y$ $2p_z$

(b) The molecular formula of boron trifluoride is

BF_3

F

(c) Describe the polarity of the B—F bond using the symbols $\delta+$ and $\delta-$

$\overset{+}{\delta}$ $\overset{-}{\delta}$

B—F

(d) The hybridization of the boron atom in boron trifluoride is

SUPPLEMENTARY PROBLEMS

S1.1   Write the dash formulas for all the isomers of $C_2H_3Cl_3$.

S1.2   Given the following electronegativities, explain the difference between the dipole moments of the molecules BF_3 and NF_3.

Electronegativity		μ, D
B = 2.0	BF_3	0
N = 3.0	NF_3	0.23
F = 4.0		

S1.3   Which of the following statements apply *both* to orbital hybridization and to molecular orbital formation?

(1) The process involves the combination of atomic orbitals.

(2) The combination of *n* atomic orbitals produces *n* new orbitals.

(3) The process involves the combination of atomic orbitals on the same atom.

SOLUTIONS TO SUPPLEMENTARY PROBLEMS

S1.1   The essential information here is the number of bonds that each atom must have:

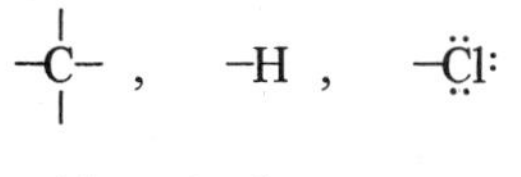

$$-\overset{\displaystyle |}{\underset{\displaystyle |}{C}}-\, ,\quad -H\, ,\quad -\ddot{\underset{\displaystyle \cdot\cdot}{C}}l:$$

The problem is then to assemble molecules that contain 2 C's, 3 H's, and 3 Cl's. Only two isomers are possible:

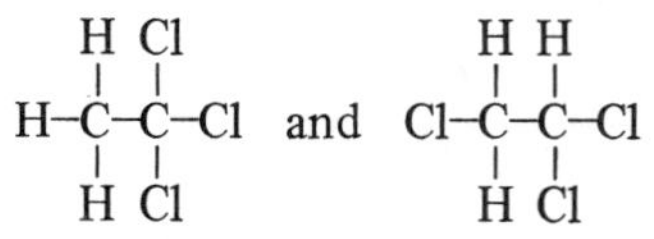

$$\begin{array}{ccc}
\text{H} & \text{Cl} \\
| & | \\
\text{H--C--C--Cl} & \text{and} & \text{Cl--C--C--Cl} \\
| & | \\
\text{H} & \text{Cl}
\end{array}$$

Note that the direction of the bonds in these formulas is unimportant. That is, the following structures are equivalent:

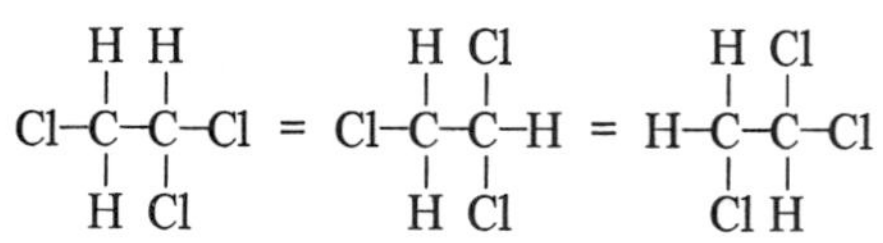

$$\text{Cl--C--C--Cl} = \text{Cl--C--C--H} = \text{H--C--C--Cl}$$

These are equivalent structures because each carbon is tetrahedral and not square planar as drawn.

S1.2   The dipole moment is given by the sum of the individual bond dipole moments. The BF_3 molecule is trigonal planar, and the three bond dipole moments cancel each other. The NF_3 molecule is pyramidal, so the three bond dipole moments do not cancel each other.

S1.3   (1) and (2) are true for both orbital hybridization and molecular orbital formation. (3) is true only for hybridization because molecular orbital formation involves the combination of atomic orbitals on *different* atoms.

2 SOME REPRESENTATIVE CARBON COMPOUNDS

SOLUTIONS TO PROBLEMS

2.1

(a) $CH_3-\overset{\displaystyle H}{\underset{\displaystyle Cl}{C}}-Cl$ and $Cl-CH_2CH_2-Cl$

(b) They differ only by rotation about single bonds. They are therefore interconvertible and are not different compounds.

2.2 (a) $CH_3CH_2CH_2Cl$ and $CH_3\underset{\displaystyle Cl}{CH}CH_3$

(b) $CH_3CH_2CHCl_2$, $CH_3\underset{\displaystyle Cl}{CH}CH_2Cl$, $ClCH_2CH_2CH_2Cl$, and $CH_3\overset{\displaystyle Cl}{\underset{\displaystyle Cl}{C}}CH_3$

(c) $CH_3CH_2CCl_3$, $CH_3\underset{\displaystyle Cl}{CH}CHCl_2$, $ClCH_2CH_2CHCl_2$, $CH_3\overset{\displaystyle Cl}{\underset{\displaystyle Cl}{C}}CH_2Cl$, $ClCH_2\underset{\displaystyle Cl}{CH}CH_2Cl$

2.3 Counting the double bond as two electron pairs located in the region of space between the two carbon atoms, each carbon has three atoms attached to it:

$$\overset{\displaystyle H}{\underset{\displaystyle H}{}}C=C\overset{\displaystyle H}{\underset{\displaystyle H}{}}$$

The maximum separation of the electrons bonding the three atoms about each carbon atom occurs when they are equally spaced about that atom; i.e., when the bond angles are ~ 120°.

2.4 (a) Cis-trans isomers are
not possible

(b) 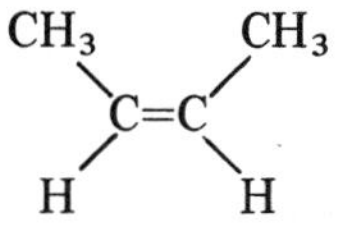 and 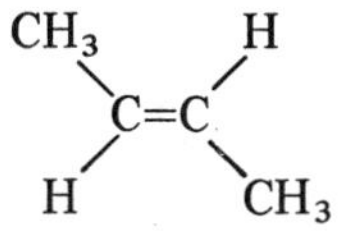

(c) Cis-trans isomers are not possible

(d) 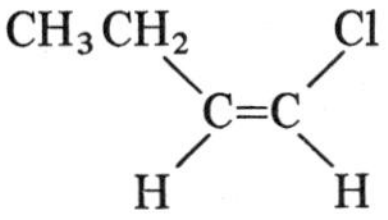 and 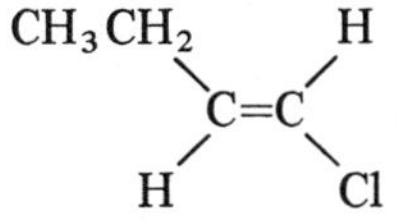

2.5 (a) The C–X bond moments in the trans isomers point in opposite directions and therefore cancel:

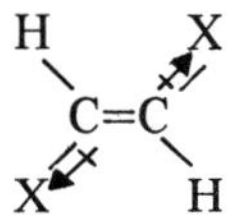

trans

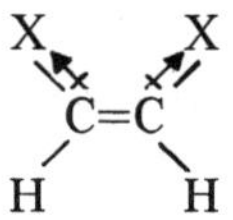

cis

X = Cl or Br

In the cis isomers the bond moments are additive.

(b) The C–Cl bond moment is larger than the C–Br bond moment because Cl is more electronegative than Br, and this effect is not compensated for by greater bond distance. (See Problem 1.33.)

2.6 The structure of propene is

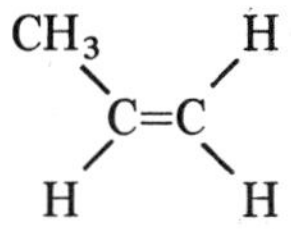

Note that in some cases cis-trans isomers are formed when hydrogens are successively replaced by chlorine.

(a) 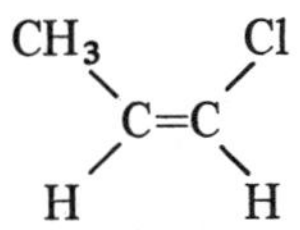 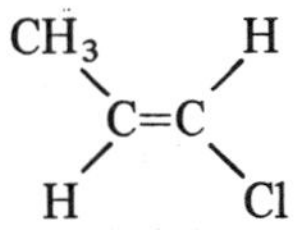 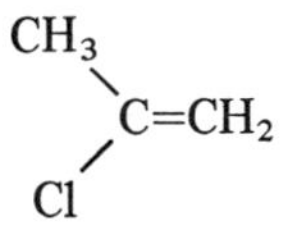 Cl–CH_2CH=CH_2

cis - trans isomers

(b) 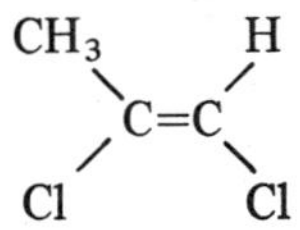 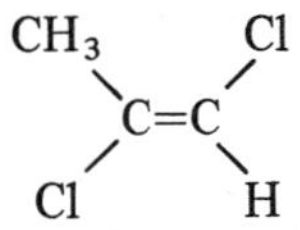 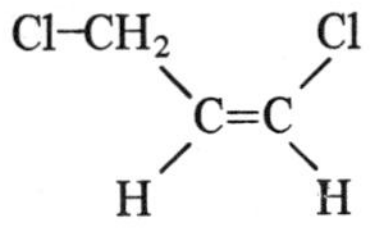 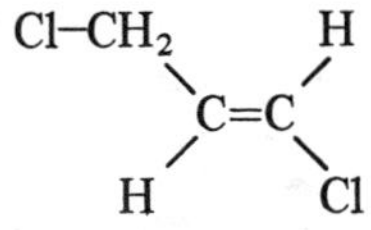

cis - trans isomers   cis - trans isomers

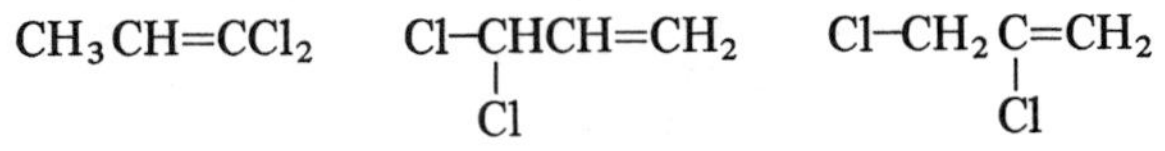

$$CH_3CH=CCl_2 \qquad \underset{\underset{Cl}{|}}{Cl-CHCH}=CH_2 \qquad \underset{\underset{Cl}{|}}{Cl-CH_2C}=CH_2$$

(c) 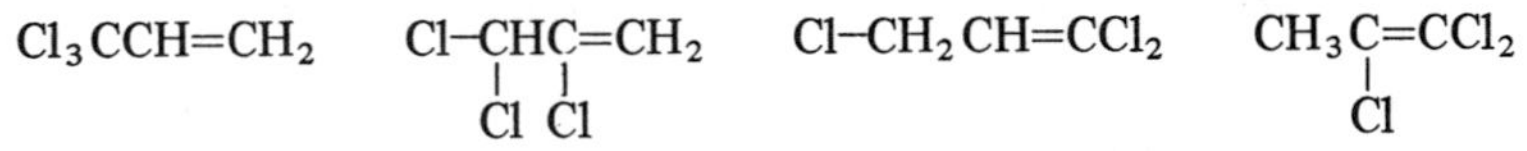 $Cl_3CCH=CH_2 \qquad \underset{\underset{Cl\ \ Cl}{|\ \ |}}{Cl-CHC}=CH_2 \qquad Cl-CH_2CH=CCl_2 \qquad \underset{\underset{Cl}{|}}{CH_3C}=CCl_2$

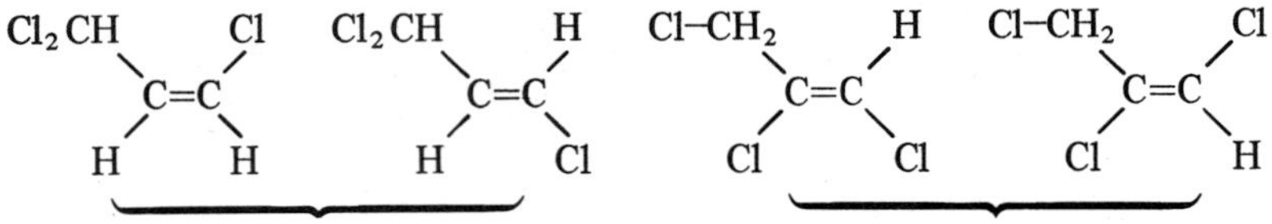

cis - trans isomers   cis - trans isomers

(d) 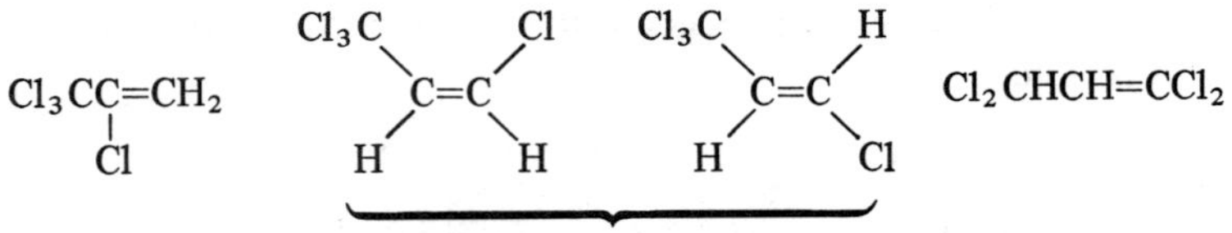 $Cl_3CC=CH_2 \quad$

$\quad Cl_2CHCH=CCl_2$

cis - trans isomers

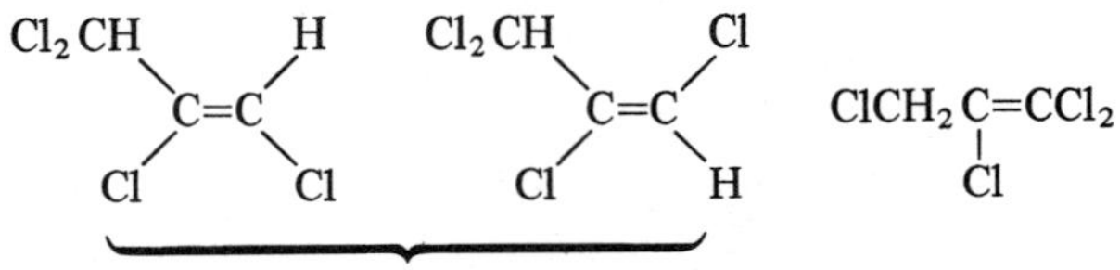

$\quad ClCH_2C=CCl_2$

cis - trans isomers

(e)

$Cl_3CCH=CCl_2 \qquad Cl_2CHC=CCl_2$

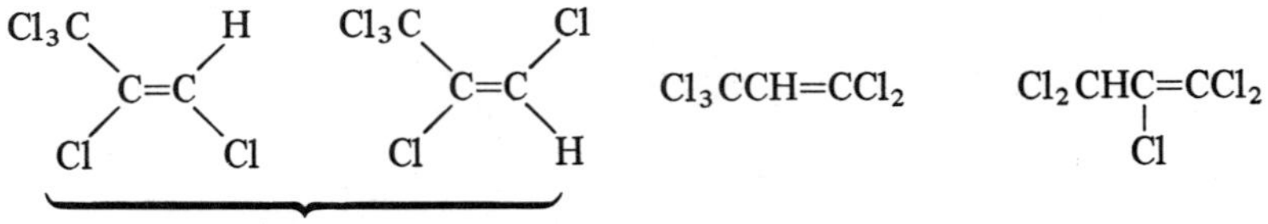

cis - trans isomers

(f) See (a–e) above.

2.7 R stands for the alkyl group, so the general formula is RH.

2.8

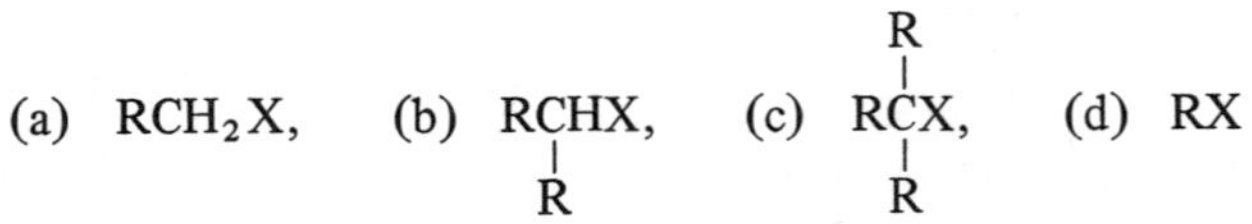

(a) RCH_2X, (b) $\underset{\underset{R}{|}}{RCHX}$, (c) $\underset{\underset{R}{|}}{\overset{\overset{R}{|}}{R}CX}$, (d) RX

2.9 (a) $CH_3CH_2CH_2Cl$, (b) 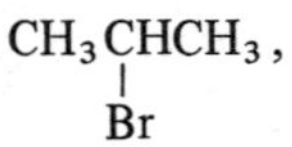 $\underset{\underset{Br}{|}}{CH_3CHCH_3}$, (c) Ethyl fluoride,

(d) Isopropyl iodide, (e) Methyl iodide.

2.10

(a) RCH_2OH,   (b) $\underset{\underset{R}{|}}{R}CHOH$,   (c) $\underset{\underset{R}{|}}{\overset{\overset{R}{|}}{R}}COH$

2.11   (a) $CH_3CH_2CH_2OH$ (b) $CH_3\underset{\underset{OH}{|}}{C}HCH_3$

2.12

(a) $CH_3-O-CH_2CH_3$,   (b) $CH_3CH_2CH_2-O-CH_2CH_2CH_3$,   (c) $CH_3-O-\underset{\overset{|}{CH_3}}{\overset{\overset{CH_3}{|}}{C}}HCH_3$,

(d) Ethyl propyl ether,   (e) Isopropyl propyl ether

2.13   (a) $CH_3-\underset{\underset{CH_3}{|}}{N}-H$,   (b) $CH_3CH_2-\underset{\underset{CH_2CH_3}{|}}{N}-CH_2CH_3$,   (c) $CH_3CH_2-\underset{\underset{CH_3}{|}}{N}-CH_2CH_2CH_3$,

(d) Isopropylmethylamine,   (e) Dipropylmethylamine,   (f) Isopropylamine

2.14   (a) f only,   (b) (a, d),   (c) (b, c, e)

2.15   (a) In each case the oxygen atom has to accommodate eight electrons, so four orbitals are required. To obtain four hybrid orbitals we must mix one $2s$ and three $2p$ atomic orbitals. The result is that four sp^3 orbitals are used.

(b) sp^3 orbitals.

2.16

(a) $K_a = \dfrac{[H_3O^+]\,[CF_3COO^-]}{[CF_3COOH]} = 1$

let $[H_3O^+] = [CF_3COO^-] = X$

then $[CF_3COOH] = 0.1 - X$

$\therefore \quad \dfrac{(X)(X)}{0.1 - X} = 1$ or $X^2 = 0.1 - X$

$X^2 + X - 0.1 = 0$

Using the quadratic formula, $X = \dfrac{-b \pm \sqrt{b^2 - 4ac}}{2a}$,

$X = \dfrac{-1 \pm \sqrt{1 + 0.4}}{2} = \dfrac{-1 \pm \sqrt{1.4}}{2} = \dfrac{-1 \pm 1.183}{2} = \dfrac{+0.183}{2}$

$X = 0.0915$ (We can exclude negative values of X.)

$[H_3O^+] = [CF_3COO^-] = 0.0915$ M

(b) Percentage ionized $= \dfrac{[H_3O^+]}{0.1} \times 100 = \dfrac{(0.0915)(100)}{0.1}$

Percentage ionized $= 91.5\%$

2.17

(a) $HC{\equiv}CH + NaH \xrightarrow{\text{hexane}} HC{\equiv}CNa + H_2$

(b) $HC{\equiv}CNa + D_2O \xrightarrow{\text{hexane}} HC{\equiv}CD + NaOD$

(c) $CH_3CH_2Li + D_2O \xrightarrow{\text{hexane}} CH_3CH_2D + LiOD$

(d) $CH_3CH_2OH + NaH \xrightarrow{\text{hexane}} CH_3CH_2ONa + H_2$

(e) $CH_3CH_2ONa + T_2O \xrightarrow{\text{hexane}} CH_3CH_2OT + NaOT$

(f) $CH_3CH_2CH_2Li + D_2O \xrightarrow{\text{hexane}} CH_3CH_2CH_2D + LiOD$

2.18

(a) $R{-}\overset{..}{\underset{..}{O}}{-}H + \underset{\underset{F}{|}}{\overset{\overset{F}{|}}{B}}{-}F \longrightarrow R{-}\overset{\overset{+}{..}}{\underset{\underset{H}{|}}{O}}{-}\bar{B}F_3$

(b) $\underset{\underset{R}{|}}{\overset{\overset{R}{|}}{R}}{-}N{:} + \underset{\underset{Cl}{|}}{\overset{\overset{Cl}{|}}{Al}}{-}Cl \longrightarrow \underset{\underset{R}{|}}{\overset{\overset{R}{|}}{R}}{-}\overset{+}{N}{-}\bar{Al}Cl_3$

(c) $\underset{R}{\overset{R}{>}}C{=}\overset{..}{\underset{..}{O}}{:} + \underset{\underset{F}{|}}{\overset{\overset{F}{|}}{B}}{-}F \longrightarrow \underset{R}{\overset{R}{>}}C{=}\overset{+}{\underset{..}{O}}{-}\bar{B}F_3$

2.19

(a) $CH_3{-}\overset{..}{\underset{..}{Cl}}{:} + \underset{\underset{Cl}{|}}{\overset{\overset{Cl}{|}}{Al}}{-}Cl \longrightarrow CH_3{-}\overset{+}{\underset{..}{Cl}}{-}\bar{Al}Cl_3$

    Lewis   Lewis
    base   acid

(b) $R{-}\overset{..}{\underset{..}{O}}{-}H + H^+ \longrightarrow R{-}\overset{\overset{H}{\overset{|}{+}}}{\underset{..}{O}}{-}H$

    Lewis   Lewis
    base   acid

(c) $:\overset{..}{\underset{..}{Cl}}:$ + $\overset{\overset{CH_3}{|}}{\underset{\underset{CH_3}{|}}{\overset{+}{C}-CH_3}}$ $\longrightarrow$ $:\overset{..}{\underset{..}{Cl}}-\overset{\overset{CH_3}{|}}{\underset{\underset{CH_3}{|}}{C}-CH_3}$

Lewis   Lewis
base   acid

(d) $H\overset{..}{\underset{..}{O}}:^-$ + $CH_3\overset{\overset{\overset{..}{O}}{||}}{C}-OCH_2CH_3$ $\longrightarrow$ $CH_3\overset{\overset{:\overset{..}{O}:^-}{|}}{\underset{\underset{H\overset{..}{O}:}{|}}{C}}-OCH_2CH_3$

Lewis   Lewis
base   acid

(e) $CH_2\!=\!CH_2$ + H^+ $\longrightarrow$ $\overset{+}{C}H_2-CH_3$

Lewis   Lewis
base   acid

(f) $CH_3CH_2:^-$ + $CH_3-\overset{\overset{\overset{..}{O}}{||}}{C}-H$ $\longrightarrow$ $CH_3\overset{\overset{:\overset{..}{O}:^-}{|}}{\underset{\underset{CH_2CH_3}{|}}{C}}-H$

Lewis   Lewis
base   acid

2.20   Molecules of *N*-propylamine can form hydrogen bonds to each other,

$$CH_3CH_2CH_2N\overset{\overset{\displaystyle H \quad\quad H}{\diagup \quad\quad \diagdown}}{\underset{\underset{\displaystyle H\cdots\cdots H}{\diagdown \quad\quad \diagup}}{}}NCH_2CH_2CH_3,$$

whereas molecules of trimethylamine, because they have no hydrogens attached to nitrogen, cannot form hydrogen bonds to each other.

2.21   Cyclopropane, because its cyclic structure makes it more rigid and symmetrical, permitting stronger crystal lattice forces.

2.22   (a) Alkyne   (b) Carboxylic acid   (c) Alcohol

       (d) Aldehyde   (c) Alkane   (f) Ketone

2.23   (a) Carbon-carbon double bonds, primary alcohol group

       (b) Ketone group, secondary alcohol group, carbon-carbon double bond

(c) Carbon-carbon double bond, ester group

(d) Amide groups

(e) Aldehyde group, primary and secondary alcohol groups

(f) Carbon-carbon double bond, ether linkage

(g) Carbon-carbon double bond, primary alcohol group

(h) Carbon-carbon double bond, aldehyde group

(i) Carbon-carbon double bond, ester groups

2.24 $CH_3CH_2CH_2CH_2Br$
1° Alkyl halide

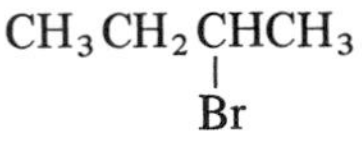

$CH_3CH_2CHCH_3$
|
Br
2° Alkyl halide

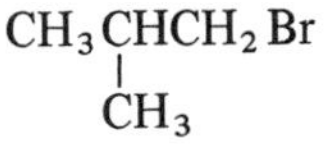

CH_3CHCH_2Br
|
CH_3
1° Alkyl halide

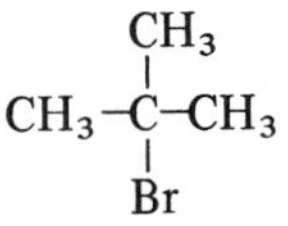

CH_3
|
CH_3-C-CH_3
|
Br
3° Alkyl halide

2.25 $CH_3CH_2CH_2CH_2OH$
1° Alcohol

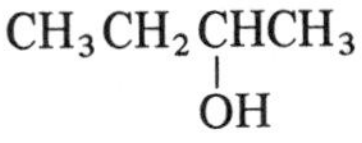

$CH_3CH_2CHCH_3$
|
OH
2° Alcohol

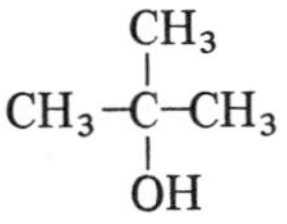

CH_3CHCH_2OH
|
CH_3
1° Alcohol

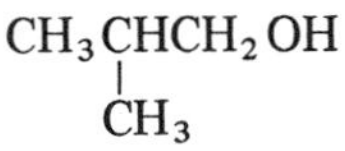

CH_3
|
CH_3-C-CH_3
|
OH
3° Alcohol

$CH_3OCH_2CH_2CH_3$
Ether

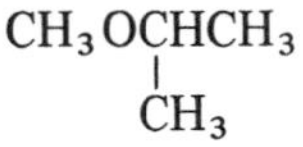

CH_3OCHCH_3
|
CH_3
Ether

$CH_3CH_2OCH_2CH_3$
Ether

2.26 Any four of the following:

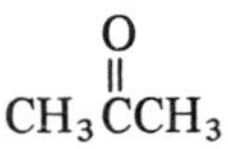

$$\underset{\text{Ketone}}{CH_3\overset{\overset{\displaystyle O}{\|}}{C}CH_3}\qquad \underset{\text{Aldehyde}}{CH_3CH_2\overset{\overset{\displaystyle O}{\|}}{C}H}\qquad \underset{\text{Ether}}{\overset{\displaystyle CH_2-CH_2}{\underset{\displaystyle CH_2-O}{|\qquad|}}}\qquad \underset{\text{Ether}}{CH_3-CH\overset{\displaystyle O}{\diagup\diagdown}CH_2}$$

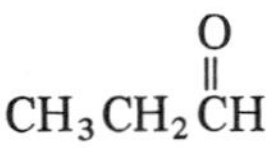

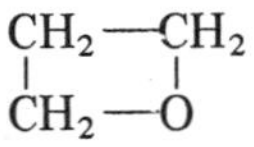

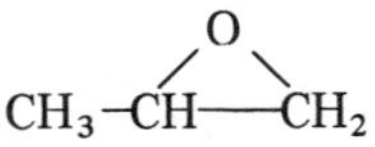

$$CH_2=CHCH_2OH \qquad CH_2=CH-O-CH_3 \qquad \begin{matrix} CH_2 \\ | \\ CH_2 \end{matrix}\!\!\!\!\searrow\!\!\!\nearrow CHOH$$

Alkene, alcohol   Alkene, ether   Alcohol

2.27 (a) Primary   (b) Secondary   (c) Tertiary   (d) Secondary

(e) Secondary   (f) Tertiary

2.28 (a) Secondary   (b) Primary   (c) Tertiary   (d) Primary

(e) Secondary

2.29

(a) $CH_3OCH_2CH_3$ (b) $CH_3CH_2CH_2OH$ (c) $CH_3\overset{\overset{\textstyle OH}{|}}{C}HCH_3$

(d) $CH_3\overset{\overset{\textstyle O}{\|}}{C}OCH_2CH_3 \qquad CH_3CH_2\overset{\overset{\textstyle O}{\|}}{C}OCH_3$ (e) $CH_3CH_2CH_2CH_2X$

(f) $CH_3CH_2CHXCH_3$ (g) $CH_3\overset{\overset{\textstyle CH_3}{|}}{\underset{\underset{\textstyle X}{|}}{C}}CH_3$ (h) $CH_3\overset{\overset{\textstyle CH_3}{|}}{C}H\overset{\overset{\textstyle }{}}{\underset{\underset{\textstyle O}{\|}}{C}}H$ or $CH_3CH_2CH_2\underset{\underset{\textstyle O}{\|}}{C}H$

(i) $CH_3\overset{\overset{\textstyle O}{\|}}{C}CH_2CH_3$ (j) $CH_3CH_2\overset{\overset{\textstyle CH_3}{|}}{C}HNH_2$ (k) $CH_3CH_2CH_2NHCH_3$

(l) $CH_3CH_2N(CH_3)_2$ (m) $CH_3CH_2CH_2\overset{\overset{\textstyle O}{\|}}{C}NH_2$ (n) $CH_3\overset{\overset{\textstyle O}{\|}}{C}NHCH_2CH_3$

(o) ![triangle with CH3 and OH]

2.30 To write *net ionic* equations, our first task is to determine which ions are actually present in the solution.

(a) Both HCl and Na_2CO_3 are completely dissociated in aqueous solution, so the ions are H_3O^+ + Cl^- and Na^+ + CO_3^{2-}. The Cl^- and Na^+ ions are spectator ions because they occur in the same form on both sides of the equation. The net ionic equation is thus

$$2H_3O^+ + CO_3^{-2} \longrightarrow [H_2CO_3] + 2H_2O \longrightarrow 3H_2O + CO_2$$

(b) Here again the ions that interact, excluding the spectator ions Br^- and Na^+, are H_3O^+ and $CH_3\overset{\overset{\textstyle O}{\|}}{C}O^-$

$$H_3O^+ + CH_3\overset{\overset{\textstyle O}{\|}}{C}O^- \longrightarrow H_2O + CH_3\overset{\overset{\textstyle O}{\|}}{C}OH$$

(c)   Here, the base, CO_3^{-2}, reacts with the acid, H_2O

$$CO_3^{-2} + H_2O \longrightarrow HCO_3^- + OH^-$$

(d)   NaH is a very strong base because it releases the very basic $H:^-$

$$:H^- + H_2O \longrightarrow H_2 + OH^-$$

(e)   Here the base is $:CH_3^-$ $:CH_3^- + H_2O \longrightarrow CH_4 + OH^-$

(f)   In this reaction, the acid is $HC{\equiv}CH$

$$:CH_3^- + HC{\equiv}CH \longrightarrow HC{\equiv}C:^- + CH_4$$

(g)   The basic species in aqueous NH_3 is $:NH_3$

$$H_3O^+ + :NH_3 \longrightarrow NH_4^+ + H_2O$$

(h)   The acid is NH_4^+; the base is NH_2^-. As before, Cl^- and Na^+ are spectator ions.

$$NH_4^+ + NH_2^- \longrightarrow 2NH_3$$

(i) $CH_3CH_2O^- + H_2O \longrightarrow CH_3CH_2OH + OH^-$

2.31   Oxygen-containing compounds contain either $={\ddot{O}}:$ or $-{\ddot{O}}-$. Both of these are Brønsted-Lowry bases in the presence of the strong proton donor, sulfuric acid. The equation for the reaction using an ether as an example is

$$R{-}{\ddot{O}}{-}R + H_2SO_4 \;\rightleftarrows\; \underbrace{R{-}\overset{H}{\underset{}{\ddot{O}}}{-}^+R}_{Salt} + HSO_4^-$$

The salt is soluble in the highly polar H_2SO_4.

2.32   (a)   Ethyl alcohol because its molecules can form hydrogen bonds to each other. Methyl ether molecules have no hydrogens attached to oxygen.

(b)   Ethylene glycol because its molecules have more OH groups and will therefore participate in more extensive hydrogen bonding.

(c)   Heptane because it has a higher molecular weight. (Neither compound can form hydrogen bonds.)

(d)   Propyl alcohol because its molecules can form hydrogen bonds to each other. Acetone molecules have no hydrogens attached to oxygen.

(e)   cis-1,2-Dichloroethene because its molecules have a higher dipole moment.

(f)   Propionic acid because its molecules can form hydrogen bonds to each other.

2.33

(a) $CH_3CH_2\overset{\displaystyle O}{\overset{\|}{C}}NH_2$ $CH_3\overset{\displaystyle O}{\overset{\|}{C}}N\underset{\displaystyle H}{CH_3}$ $HC\overset{\displaystyle O}{\overset{\|}{N}}\underset{\displaystyle H}{N}CH_2CH_3$ $H{-}\overset{\displaystyle O}{\overset{\|}{C}}{-}\underset{\displaystyle CH_3}{N}{-}CH_3$

(b) The last one given above [i.e., $\overset{\overset{\displaystyle O}{\|}}{H C} N(CH_3)_2$] because it does not have a hydrogen that is covalently bonded to nitrogen, and, therefore, its molecules cannot form hydrogen bonds to each other. The other molecules all have a hydrogen covalently bonded to nitrogen, and, therefore, hydrogen bond formation is possible. With the first molecule, for example, hydrogen bonds could form in the following way.

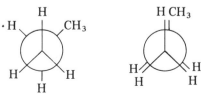

2.34 An acid-base reaction as follows:

$$CH_3CH_2OH + HC\equiv C:^- Na^+ \xrightarrow[NH_3]{liq.} CH_3CH_2O^-Na^+ + HC\equiv CH$$

2.35 (a) $pK_a = -\log K_a$

$pK_a = -\log 1.8 \ -\log 10^{-5}$

$pK_a = -0.25 + 5 = 4.75$

(b) $K_a = 10^{-13}$

2.36 (a) For acid HA, $K_a = 10^{-20}$; for acid HB, $K_a = 10^{-10}$. Because 10^{-10} is larger than 10^{-20}, acid HB is the stronger acid.

(b) Yes because the equilibrium lying to the right (below) yields the weaker acid and weaker base.

HB	+	A :$^-$	$\rightleftharpoons$	HA	+	: B$^-$
Stronger		Stronger		Weaker		Weaker
acid		base		acid		base

2.37

Staggered	Eclipsed

2.38 Basic strength depends upon ability to accept a proton. In $(CF_3)_3N:$, the high electronegativity of fluorine reduces the availability of the lone electron pair on nitrogen. In

$(CH_3)_3N$:, the lone pair is more available to bond with a proton. (An alternative view is that the conjugate acid is rendered less stable by the presence of the electronegative fluorines.)

$$CF_3-\overset{\overset{\displaystyle CF_3}{|}}{\underset{\underset{\displaystyle CF_3}{|}}{N}}: \; + \; HA \; \rightleftharpoons \; CF_3-\overset{\overset{\displaystyle CF_3}{|}}{\underset{\underset{\displaystyle CF_3}{|}}{\overset{+}{N}}}H \; + \; A^-$$

2.39   An ester group,

$$O=\overset{|}{\underset{}{C}}\underset{O}{\diagdown}O\diagup$$

2.40   The attractive forces between hydrogen fluoride molecules are the very strong dipole-dipole attractions that we call *hydrogen bonds*. (The partial positive charge of a hydrogen fluoride molecule is relatively exposed because it resides on the hydrogen nucleus. By contrast, the positive charge of an ethyl fluoride molecule is buried in the ethyl group and is shielded by the surrounding electrons. Thus the positive end of one hydrogen fluoride molecule can approach the negative end of another hydrogen fluoride molecule much more closely with the result that the attractive force between them is much stronger.)

*2.41   Since both molecules are nonpolar, the only intermolecular forces that we need to consider are van der Waals forces. Tetrafluoromethane is a generally spherical, compact molecule and its outer electrons (of the fluorine atoms) are very tightly held. Consequently, it will be difficult for a temporary dipole in one molecule of CF_4 to induce a very large temporary dipole in an adjacent molecule and, as a result, the van der Waals forces acting between them will be small. Hexane is a much larger molecule and the outer electrons are more loosely held. The outer electrons of hexane are more easily distorted—hexane is said to be more *polarizable*—thus the van der Waals forces acting between hexane molecules will be much larger.

*2.42   In the molecules or atoms with greater molecular weight there are not only more electrons, but the outermost electrons are further from the nucleus where they are more loosely held. Thus the temporary dipoles that occur in a given molecule can be larger. Because the outermost electrons of adjacent molecules are also more loosely held, the induced dipoles in the adjacent molecules will also be larger. Consequently the attractive forces between the heavier molecules will be larger and the boiling points will be higher.

SECTION REFERENCES FOR ADDITIONAL PROBLEMS

2.22	2.2, 2.5–2.14	**2.25**	2.10, 2.11
2.23	2.2, 2.5–2.14	**2.26**	2.10, 2.11, 2.13
2.24	2.9	**2.27**	2.10

2.28	2.12	**2.36**	2.15B
2.29	2.5–2.14	**2.37**	2.3
2.30	2.15	**2.38**	1.9, 2.15B
2.31	2.15A	**2.39**	2.14
2.32	2.17	**2.40**	2.17B, 2.17C
2.33	2.14, 2.17C	**2.41**	2.17D
2.34	2.15C	**2.42**	2.17D
2.35	2.15B		

SELF-TEST

2.1   Supply the appropriate formula for each of the following:

(a) The isomer of $C_2H_2Br_2$ that does *not* exhibit cis-trans isomerism.

(b) A hydroxyl group containing compound that is *not* an alcohol.

(c) The bond line formula of a secondary alcohol that has four carbon atoms.

(d) The bond line formula of a tertiary amine that has four carbon atoms.

(e) An ester that has three carbon atoms.

2.2   Classify the following alcohols and amines as primary (1°), secondary (2°), or tertiary (3°).

(a) $CH_3CH_2\overset{\displaystyle CH_3}{\underset{\displaystyle CH_3}{C}}{-}OH$ ▢

(d) ⬡N–H ▢

(b)  $CH_3{-}⬡{-}OH$ ▢

(e) $CH_3CH_2N(CH_3)_2$ ▢

(c) $CH_3CH_2\overset{\displaystyle CH_3}{\underset{\displaystyle CH_3}{C}}CH_2OH$ ▢

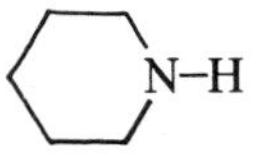

(f) $CH_3\overset{\displaystyle CH_3}{\underset{\displaystyle CH_3}{C}}{-}NH_2$ ▢

2.3   Name the functional groups in the following structure. Give their names in the order in which they occur (left-to-right).

$HOCH_2\overset{\displaystyle O}{\overset{\|}{C}}{-}NHCH{=}CHOCH_3$

2.4   The following equilibrium has $K_{eq} >> 10$:

$$HClO_4 + HNO_3 \rightleftharpoons H_2NO_3^+ + ClO_4^-.$$

What is the strongest base present in the mixture? ▢

2.5   Write and balance the *net ionic equation* for the acid-base reaction in the space provided.

$$HBr(aq.) + CH_3\overset{\displaystyle O}{\overset{\|}{C}}{-}ONa(aq.) \longrightarrow CH_3\overset{\displaystyle O}{\overset{\|}{C}}{-}OH + NaBr(aq.)$$

2.6   A compound $H : \overset{..}{\underset{..}{A}} :$ ($K_a = 10^4$) is dissolved in water. Write the equation for the acid-base reaction that occurs.

2.7 Circle the compound in the pair below that has the higher boiling point and indicate the one that is more soluble in water. Write *same* if they are not significantly different.

(a) $CH_2=CHCH_2OH$

(b) $CH_3\overset{\displaystyle O}{\overset{\|}{C}}CH_3$

SUPPLEMENTARY PROBLEMS

S2.1 Noting the direction in which the following acid-base equilibria are displaced, circle the strongest acid and base in each.

(a) $HA + HB \rightleftharpoons H_2A^+ + B^-$

(b) $HD + HE \rightleftharpoons D^- + H_2E^+$

S2.2 Classify the alcohol and amine groups as primary (1°), secondary (2°), or tertiary (3°) in the compounds below.

(a) NCHCHCH$_2$OH with CH$_3$ and CH$_3$

(b) $CH_3\overset{\displaystyle CH_3}{\underset{\displaystyle CH_3}{C}}NH\overset{\displaystyle CH_3}{\underset{\displaystyle CH_3}{C}}H\,CHOH$

S2.3 Name the functional groups in each of the following molecules.

(a) $CH_3\overset{\displaystyle O}{\overset{\|}{C}}CH_2OH$

(b) $CH_3CH_2\overset{\displaystyle O}{\overset{\|}{C}}OH$

(c) $H\overset{\displaystyle O}{\overset{\|}{C}}CH_2CH_2NH\overset{\displaystyle O}{\overset{\|}{C}}H$

SOLUTIONS TO SUPPLEMENTARY PROBLEMS

S2.1 In any acid-base reaction, the weaker acid and weaker base will predominate at equilibrium.

(a) Since equilibrium is displaced to the right, we know that H_2A^+ is a weaker acid than HB and that HA acts as a base. B^- is a weaker base than HA.

(b) HD is a weaker acid than H_2E^+, and HE is a weaker base than D^-.

S2.2 (a) 3° Amine, 1° alcohol   (b) 2° Amine, 2° alcohol

S2.3 (a) Ketone, 1° alcohol   (b) Carboxyl   (c) Aldehyde, amide

3

ALKANES AND CYCLOALKANES.
GENERAL PRINCIPLES OF
NOMENCLATURE STEREOCHEMISTRY I:
CONFORMATIONAL ANALYSIS

SOLUTION TO PROBLEMS

3.1   The condensed structural formulas are shown below each line-and-circle formula.

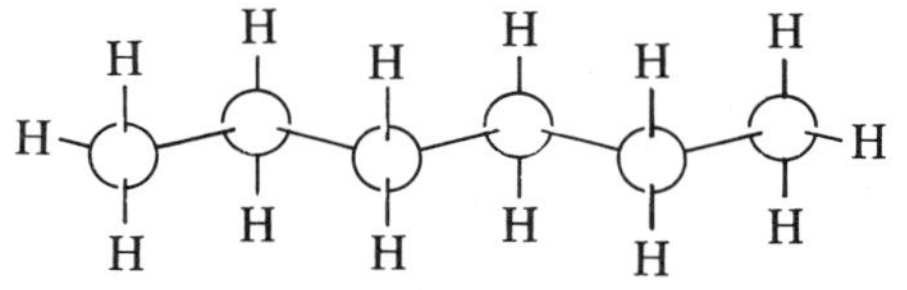

(1) $CH_3CH_2CH_2CH_2CH_2CH_3$

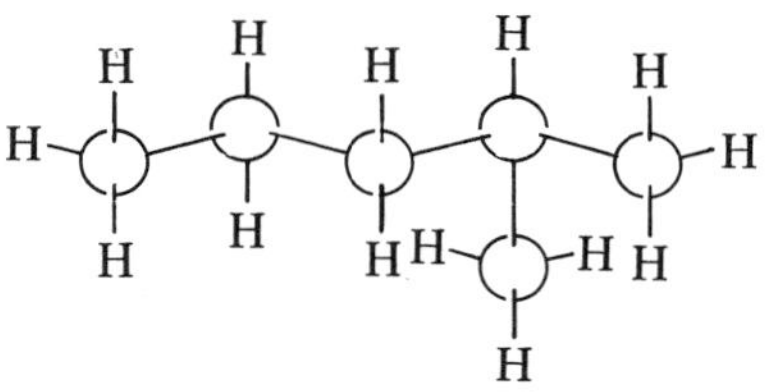

(2) $CH_3CH_2CH_2CHCH_3$
          |
          CH_3

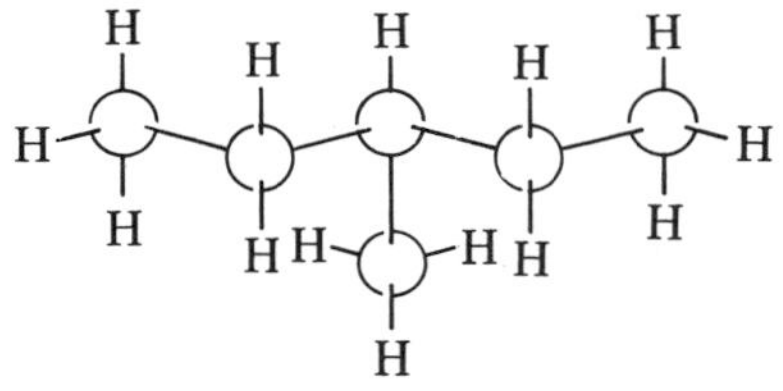

(3) $CH_3CH_2CHCH_2CH_3$
          |
          CH_3

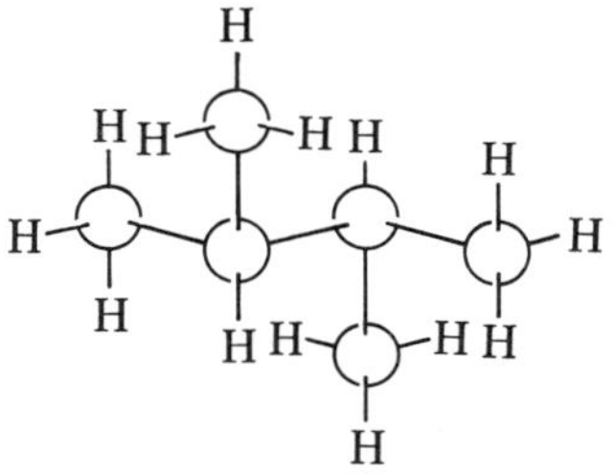

(4) CH_3
          |
       $CH_3CHCHCH_3$ 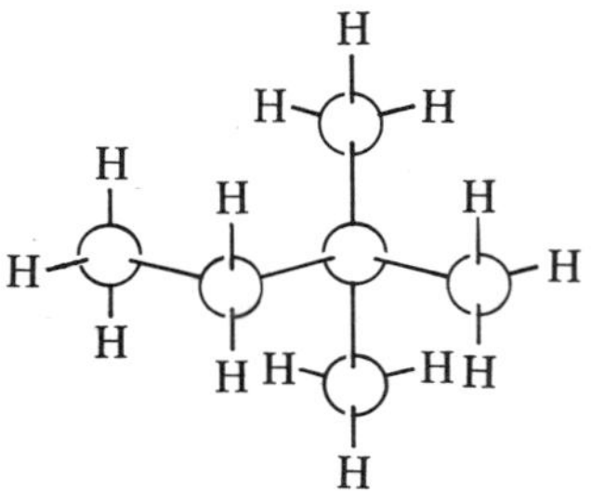
                |
                CH_3

(5) CH_3
          |
       $CH_3CH_2CCH_3$
          |
          CH_3

3.2   (a)   Refer to Problem 3.1 above:

(1)   Hexane,   (2)   2-Methylpentane,   (3)   3-Methypentane,   (4)   2,3-Dimethylbutane,
(5)   2,2-Dimethylbutane.

(b) $CH_3CH_2CH_2CH_2CH_2CH_2CH_3$ Heptane

$CH_3CH_2CH_2CH_2\underset{\underset{\textstyle CH_3}{|}}{C}HCH_3$ 2-Methylhexane

$CH_3CH_2CH_2\underset{\underset{\textstyle CH_3}{|}}{C}HCH_2CH_3$ 3-Methylhexane

$CH_3CH_2CH_2\overset{\overset{\textstyle CH_3}{|}}{\underset{\underset{\textstyle CH_3}{|}}{C}}CH_3$ 2,2-Dimethylpentane

$CH_3CH_2\overset{\overset{\textstyle CH_3}{|}}{C}H\underset{\underset{\textstyle CH_3}{|}}{C}HCH_3$ 2,3-Dimethylpentane

$CH_3\underset{\underset{\textstyle CH_3}{|}}{C}HCH_2\underset{\underset{\textstyle CH_3}{|}}{C}HCH_3$ 2,4-Dimethylpentane

$CH_3CH_2\overset{\overset{\textstyle CH_3}{|}}{\underset{\underset{\textstyle CH_3}{|}}{C}}CH_2CH_3$ 3,3-Dimethylpentane

$CH_3\overset{\overset{\textstyle CH_3}{|}}{C}H-\overset{\overset{\textstyle CH_3}{|}}{\underset{\underset{\textstyle CH_3}{|}}{C}}CH_3$ 2,2,3-Trimethylbutane

$CH_3CH_2\underset{\underset{\textstyle CH_2CH_3}{|}}{C}HCH_2CH_3$ 3-Ethylpentane

3.3   (a) $CH_3CH_2CH_2CH_2Cl$ $CH_3\underset{\underset{\textstyle CH_3}{|}}{C}HCH_2Cl$

     1-Chlorobutane   1-Chloro-2-methylpropane

$CH_3CH_2\underset{\underset{\textstyle Cl}{|}}{C}HCH_3$ $CH_3-\overset{\overset{\textstyle CH_3}{|}}{\underset{\underset{\textstyle Cl}{|}}{C}}-CH_3$

     2-Chlorobutane   2-Chloro-2-methylpropane

(b) $CH_3 CH_2 CH_2 CH_2 CH_2 Br$

1-Bromopentane

$CH_3 CH_2 CH_2 \underset{\underset{\displaystyle Br}{|}}{C}HCH_3$

2-Bromopentane

$CH_3 CH_2 \underset{\underset{\displaystyle Br}{|}}{C}HCH_2 CH_3$

3-Bromopentane

$CH_3 \underset{\underset{\displaystyle CH_3}{|}}{\overset{\overset{\displaystyle CH_3}{|}}{C}}CH_2 Br$

1-Bromo-2,2-dimethyl-
   propane

$CH_3 \underset{\underset{\displaystyle CH_3}{|}}{C}HCH_2 CH_2 Br$

1-Bromo-3-methylbutane

$CH_3 CH_2 \underset{\underset{\displaystyle CH_3}{|}}{C}HCH_2 Br$

1-Bromo-2-methylbutane

$CH_3 \overset{\overset{\displaystyle CH_3}{|}}{\underset{\underset{\displaystyle Br}{|}}{C}}HCHCH_3$

2-Bromo-3-methylbutane

$CH_3 CH_2 \overset{\overset{\displaystyle CH_3}{|}}{\underset{\underset{\displaystyle Br}{|}}{C}}CH_3$

2-Bromo-2-methylbutane

3.4   (a) $CH_3 CH_2 CH_2 CH_2 OH$

1-Butanol

$CH_3 CH_2 \underset{\underset{\displaystyle OH}{|}}{C}HCH_3$

2-Butanol

$CH_3 \underset{\underset{\displaystyle CH_3}{|}}{C}HCH_2 OH$

2-Methyl-1-propanol

$CH_3 \overset{\overset{\displaystyle CH_3}{|}}{\underset{\underset{\displaystyle CH_3}{|}}{C}}OH$

2-Methyl-2-propanol

(b) $CH_3 CH_2 CH_2 CH_2 CH_2 OH$

1-Pentanol

$CH_3 CH_2 CH_2 \underset{\underset{\displaystyle OH}{|}}{C}HCH_3$

2-Pentanol

$CH_3 CH_2 \underset{\underset{\displaystyle OH}{|}}{C}HCH_2 CH_3$

3-Pentanol

$CH_3 \underset{\underset{\displaystyle CH_3}{|}}{C}HCH_2 CH_2 OH$

3-Methyl-1-butanol

$CH_3 CH_2 \underset{\underset{\displaystyle CH_3}{|}}{C}HCH_2 OH$

2-Methyl-1-butanol

$CH_3 \overset{\overset{\displaystyle CH_3}{|}}{\underset{\underset{\displaystyle OH}{|}}{C}}HCHCH_3$

3-Methyl-2-butanol

$$
\begin{array}{c}
\text{CH}_3 \\
| \\
\text{CH}_3\,\text{CCH}_2\,\text{OH} \\
| \\
\text{CH}_3
\end{array}
\qquad\qquad
\begin{array}{c}
\text{CH}_3 \\
| \\
\text{CH}_3\,\text{CH}_2\,\text{CCH}_3 \\
| \\
\text{OH}
\end{array}
$$

2, 2-Dimethyl-1-propanol   2-Methyl-2-butanol

3.5   (a)   1-*tert*-Butyl-3-methylcyclohexane

(b)   1, 3-Dimethylcyclobutane

(c)   1-Butylcyclohexane

(d)   1-Chloro-2, 4-dimethylcyclohexane

(e)   2-Chlorocyclopentanol

(f)   3-*tert*-Butylcyclohexanol

3.6   (a)   Bicyclo[2.2.0]hexane

(b)   Bicyclo[4.4.0]decane

(c)   Bicyclo[2.2.2]octane

(d)   3-Methylbicyclo[3.2.0]heptane

(e)   8-Methylbicyclo[4.2.1]nonane

(f)   Bicyclo[3.1.1]heptane; or

Bicyclo[4.1.0]heptane

3.7

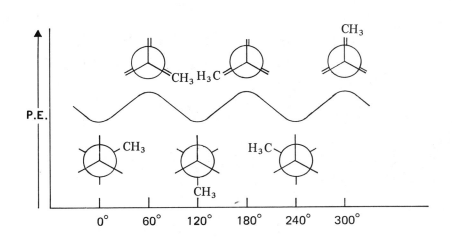

3.8

(a)

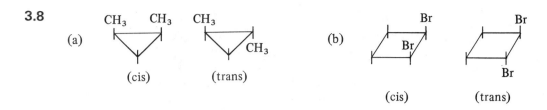

(cis)   (trans)

(b)

(cis)   (trans)

3.9 (a)

(1)   (2)

(b) No. In (1), the methyl group is axial and the *tert*-butyl group is equatorial; in (2) the situation is reversed.

(c) The *tert*-butyl group is larger than the methyl; conformation (1) is more stable because the *tert*-butyl group is equatorial.

(d) The preferred conformation at equilibrium is (1).

3.10 (a) Conformations of cis isomer are equivalent, (e, a) and (a, e).

(a, e)   (e, a)

(b) Conformations of trans isomer are not equivalent, (e, e) and (a, a).

(e, e)   (a, a)

(c) The trans (e, e) conformation is more stable than the trans (a, a).

(d) The trans (e, e) would be more highly populated at equilibrium.

3.11 $CH_3 CH_2 CH=CH_2$ + H_2 $\xrightarrow[C_2H_5OH]{Pt \ or \ Ni}$ $CH_3 CH_2 CH_2 CH_3$

$\underset{H}{\overset{CH_3}{C}}=\underset{H}{\overset{CH_3}{C}}$ + H_2 $\xrightarrow[C_2H_5OH]{Pt \ or \ Ni}$ $CH_3 CH_2 CH_2 CH_3$

$\underset{H}{\overset{CH_3}{C}}=\underset{CH_3}{\overset{H}{C}}$ + H_2 $\xrightarrow[C_2H_5OH]{Pt \ or \ Ni}$ $CH_3 CH_2 CH_2 CH_3$

3.12

$$\underset{\overset{|}{CH_3}}{CH_3\,\underset{\overset{|}{Br}}{CH}CHCH_3} \xrightarrow[Zn]{H^+} \underset{\overset{|}{CH_3}}{CH_3\,CHCH_2\,CH_3}$$

$$\underset{\overset{|}{CH_3}}{CH_3\,\underset{\overset{|}{Br}}{C}CH_2\,CH_3} \xrightarrow[Zn]{H^+} \underset{\overset{|}{CH_3}}{CH_3\,CHCH_2\,CH_3}$$

$$\underset{\overset{|}{CH_3}}{BrCH_2\,CHCH_2\,CH_3} \xrightarrow[Zn]{H^+} \underset{\overset{|}{CH_3}}{CH_3\,CHCH_2\,CH_3}$$

3.13

(a) $CH_3\,CH_2\,Br \xrightarrow[\substack{ether \\ (-LiBr)}]{Li} CH_3\,CH_2\,Li \xrightarrow[(-LiI)]{CuI} (CH_3\,CH_2)_2\,CuLi$

$(CH_3\,CH_2)_2\,CuLi + CH_3\,I \longrightarrow CH_3\,CH_2\,CH_3 + CH_3\,CH_2\,Cu + LiI$

(b) $(CH_3\,CH_2)_2\,CuLi + CH_3\,CH_2\,I \longrightarrow CH_3\,CH_2\,CH_2\,CH_3 + CH_3\,CH_2\,Cu + LiI$

(c)

$$\underset{\overset{|}{CH_3}}{CH_3\,CHCH_2\,Br} \xrightarrow[\substack{ether \\ (-LiBr)}]{Li} \underset{\overset{|}{CH_3}}{CH_3\,CHCH_2\,Li} \xrightarrow[(-LiI)]{CuI} \underset{\overset{|}{CH_3}}{(CH_3\,CHCH_2)_2\,CuLi}$$

$$\xrightarrow{CH_3I} \underset{\overset{|}{CH_3}}{CH_3\,CHCH_2\,CH_3} + \underset{\overset{|}{CH_3}}{CH_3\,CHCH_2\,Cu} + LiI$$

(d) $\underset{\overset{|}{CH_3}}{CH_3\,CHCH_2\,CH_2\,I} \xrightarrow[\substack{ether \\ (-LiI)}]{Li} \underset{\overset{|}{CH_3}}{CH_3\,CHCH_2\,CH_2\,Li} \xrightarrow[(-LiI)]{CuI}$

$$\underset{\overset{|}{CH_3}}{(CH_3\,CHCH_2\,CH_2)_2\,CuLi} \xrightarrow{\underset{\overset{|}{CH_3}}{CH_3\,CHCH_2\,CH_2\,I}} \underset{\overset{|}{CH_3}}{CH_3\,CHCH_2\,CH_2\,CH_2\,CH_2\,\underset{\overset{|}{CH_3}}{CHCH_3}}$$

$$+ \underset{\overset{|}{CH_3}}{CH_3\,CHCH_2\,CH_2\,Cu} + LiI$$

Other syntheses are possible in each part except (a).

3.14 (a) $CH_3\,CH_2\,CH_2\,Br \xrightarrow[\substack{ether \\ (-LiBr)}]{Li} CH_3\,CH_2\,CH_2\,Li \xrightarrow[(-LiI)]{CuI}$

$$(CH_3\,CH_2\,CH_2)_2\,CuLi \xrightarrow{CH_3\,CH_2\,CH_2\,Br} CH_3\,CH_2\,CH_2\,CH_2\,CH_2\,CH_3$$

$$+ CH_3\,CH_2\,CH_2\,Cu + LiBr$$

(b) $CH_3CH_2CH_2CH_2Br$ $\xrightarrow[\substack{\text{ether} \\ (-LiBr)}]{Li}$ $CH_3CH_2CH_2CH_2Li$ $\xrightarrow[(-LiI)]{CuI}$

    $(CH_3CH_2CH_2CH_2)_2CuLi$ $\xrightarrow{CH_3CH_2Br}$ $CH_3CH_2CH_2CH_2CH_2CH_3$

                 $+ \; CH_3CH_2CH_2CH_2Cu \; + \; LiBr$

(c) $CH_3CH_2CH_2CH_2CH_2Br$ $\xrightarrow[\substack{\text{ether} \\ (-LiBr)}]{Li}$ $CH_3CH_2CH_2CH_2CH_2Li$ $\xrightarrow[(-LiI)]{CuI}$

    $(CH_3CH_2CH_2CH_2CH_2)_2CuLi$ $\xrightarrow{CH_3Br}$ $CH_3CH_2CH_2CH_2CH_2CH_3$

                 $+ \; CH_3CH_2CH_2CH_2CH_2Cu \; + \; LiBr$

(d) $CH_3CH_2CH_2CH_2CH_2CH_2Br$ $\xrightarrow[Zn]{H^+}$ $CH_3CH_2CH_2CH_2CH_2CH_3 \; + \; ZnBr_2$

(e) $CH_3CH_2CH=CHCH_2CH_3$ $\xrightarrow[\substack{C_2H_5OH \\ (25°, 50atm)}]{Ni}$ $CH_3CH_2CH_2CH_2CH_2CH_3$

3.15 CH_3CH_2Br $\xrightarrow{Li}$ CH_3CH_2Li $\xrightarrow{CuI}$ $(CH_3CH_2)_2CuI$

or

3.16   (a) $\underset{\underset{Cl \;\; Cl}{|\;\;\;\;|}}{CH_3CHCHCH_2CH_3}$ (b) $\underset{\underset{I}{|}}{\overset{\overset{CH_3}{|}}{CH_3CCH_3}}$ (c) $\underset{\underset{\underset{CH_3}{|}}{CH_2}}{CH_3CH_2CHCH_2CH_3}$

    (d) $\underset{\underset{CH_3\;CH_3\;CH_3}{|\;\;\;\;\;|\;\;\;\;\;|}}{CH_3CH-CH-CHCH_2CH_2CH_2CH_2CH_3}$

    (e) $\underset{\underset{\underset{CH_3 \;\;\;\;\; CH_3}{\diagup \;\;\;\; \diagdown}}{CH}}{|}{CH_3CH_2CH_2CHCH_2CH_2CH_2CH_2CH_3}$

(f)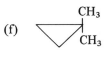

(g)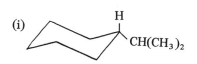

(h) H₃C ... CH₃

(i) H ... CH(CH₃)₂

(j) H ... CH₃ ... H ... CH(CH₃)₂

(k) CH₃CHCH₂CH₂CH₂Cl
         |
         CH₃

(l) CH₃ CH₃
     | |
     CH₃CCH₂CCH₂CH₂CH₂CH₃
     | |
     CH₃ CH₃

(m) CH₃
     |
     CH₃CCH₂Cl
     |
     CH₃

(n) CH₃
     |
     CH₃CHCH₂CH₃

3.17 (a) 3,4-Dimethylhexane   (e) Ethylcyclohexane
         (b) 2-Methylbutane   (f) Cyclopentylcyclopentane
         (c) 2,4-Dimethylpentane   (g) 6-Isobutyl-2-methyldecane
         (d) 3-Methylpentane

3.18 (a) CH₃
              |
              CH₃CCH₃   2,2-Dimethylpropane (neopentane)
              |
              CH₃

         (b) CH₃
              |
              CH₃CHCH₂CH₃   2-Methylbutane (isopentane)

         (c) CH₃CH₂CH₂CH₂CH₃   Pentane

         (d) CH₂—CH₂
              /   \
            CH₂   CH₂   Cyclopentane
               \   /
                CH₂

         (e) CH₃CH₃
              | |
              CH₃CH–CHCH₃   2,3-Dimethylbutane

3.19 Each of the desired alkenes must have the same carbon skeleton as 2-methylbutane,

                 C ←
                 |
            C–C–C–C;

         they are therefore

$$\left. \begin{array}{c} \overset{\displaystyle CH_3}{\underset{\displaystyle |}{CH_2}}=CCH_2CH_3 \\[1em] \overset{\displaystyle CH_3}{\underset{\displaystyle |}{CH_3C}}=CHCH_3 \\[1em] \overset{\displaystyle CH_3}{\underset{\displaystyle |}{CH_3CH}}CH=CH_2 \end{array} \right\} + H_2 \xrightarrow[C_2H_5OH]{Ni} \overset{\displaystyle CH_3}{\underset{\displaystyle |}{CH_3CH}}CH_2CH_3$$

3.20 Only one isomer of C_6H_{14} can be produced from five isomeric hexyl chlorides ($C_6H_{13}Cl$).

The alkane is 2-methylpentane, $CH_3\overset{\displaystyle CH_3}{\underset{\displaystyle |}{CH}}CH_2CH_2CH_3$. The five alkyl chlorides are

$ClCH_2\overset{\displaystyle CH_3}{\underset{\displaystyle |}{CH}}CH_2CH_2CH_3$, $CH_3\overset{\displaystyle CH_3}{\underset{\displaystyle |}{CCl}}CH_2CH_2CH_3$, $CH_3\overset{\displaystyle CH_3}{\underset{\displaystyle |}{CH}}CHClCH_2CH_3$,

$CH_3\overset{\displaystyle CH_3}{\underset{\displaystyle |}{CH}}CH_2CHClCH_3$, and $CH_3\overset{\displaystyle CH_3}{\underset{\displaystyle |}{CH}}CH_2CH_2CH_2Cl$

3.21 $CH_3\overset{\displaystyle CH_3}{\underset{\displaystyle |}{CH}}-\overset{\displaystyle CH_3}{\underset{\displaystyle |}{CH}}CH_3$ 2, 3-Dimethylbutane

From two alkyl chlorides

$$CH_3\overset{\displaystyle CH_3}{\underset{\displaystyle |}{\underset{\displaystyle Cl}{\overset{\displaystyle |}{C}}}}-\overset{\displaystyle CH_3}{\underset{\displaystyle |}{\underset{\displaystyle H}{\overset{\displaystyle |}{C}}}}CH_3$$

$$Cl-CH_2\overset{\displaystyle CH_3}{\underset{\displaystyle |}{CH}}-\overset{\displaystyle CH_3}{\underset{\displaystyle |}{CH}}CH_3$$

$$\xrightarrow[H^+]{Zn} CH_3\overset{\displaystyle CH_3}{\underset{\displaystyle |}{CH}}-\overset{\displaystyle CH_3}{\underset{\displaystyle |}{CH}}CH_3$$

From two alkenes:

$$CH_2=\overset{\displaystyle CH_3}{\underset{\displaystyle |}{C}}-\overset{\displaystyle CH_3}{\underset{\displaystyle |}{CH}}CH_3$$

$$CH_3\overset{\displaystyle CH_3}{\underset{\displaystyle |}{C}}=\overset{\displaystyle CH_3}{\underset{\displaystyle |}{C}}CH_3$$

$$\xrightarrow[Ni]{H_2} CH_3\overset{\displaystyle CH_3}{\underset{\displaystyle |}{CH}}-\overset{\displaystyle CH_3}{\underset{\displaystyle |}{CH}}CH_3$$

3.22

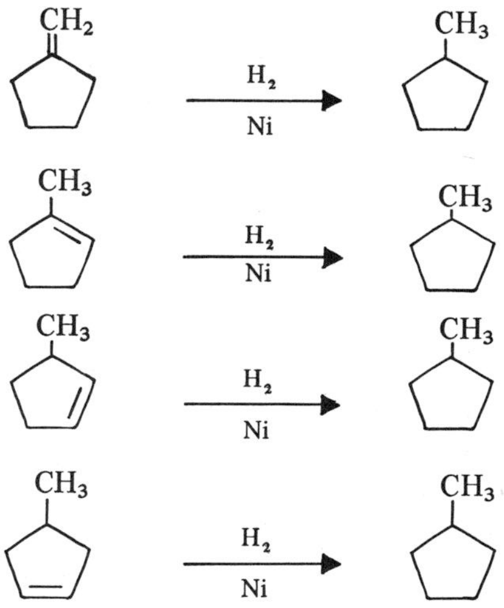

3.23 (a) $CH_3CH_2Br \xrightarrow{Li} CH_3CH_2Li \xrightarrow{CuI} (CH_3CH_2)_2CuLi$

$\xrightarrow{CH_3CH_2CH_2Br} CH_3CH_2CH_2CH_2CH_3$

(b) $(CH_3)_3CBr \xrightarrow{Li} (CH_3)_3CLi \xrightarrow{CuI} [(CH_3)_3C]_2CuLi$

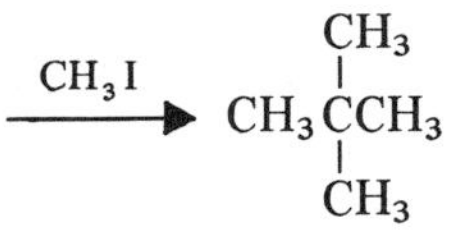

$\xrightarrow{CH_3I} CH_3\underset{\underset{CH_3}{|}}{\overset{\overset{CH_3}{|}}{C}}CH_3$

(c)

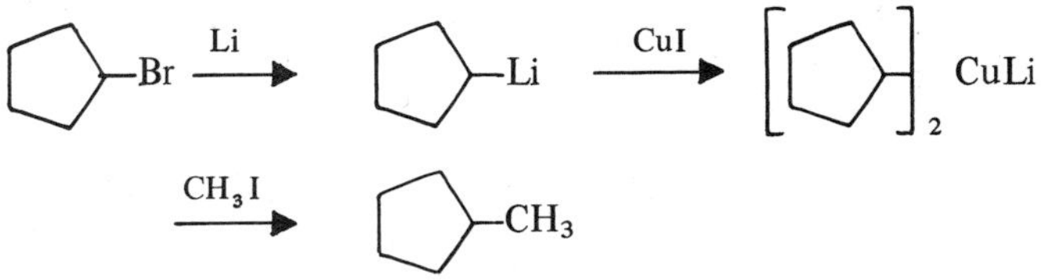

(d) $CH_3\underset{\underset{CH_3}{|}}{\overset{\overset{CH_3}{|}}{C}}CH_2Br \xrightarrow{Li} CH_3\underset{\underset{CH_3}{|}}{\overset{\overset{CH_3}{|}}{C}}CH_2Li \xrightarrow{CuI}$

$\left(CH_3\underset{\underset{CH_3}{|}}{\overset{\overset{CH_3}{|}}{C}}CH_2- \right)_2 CuLi \xrightarrow{BrCH_2\overset{\overset{CH_3}{|}}{C}HCH_3} CH_3\underset{\underset{CH_3}{|}}{\overset{\overset{CH_3}{|}}{C}}CH_2CH_2\overset{\overset{CH_3}{|}}{C}HCH_3$

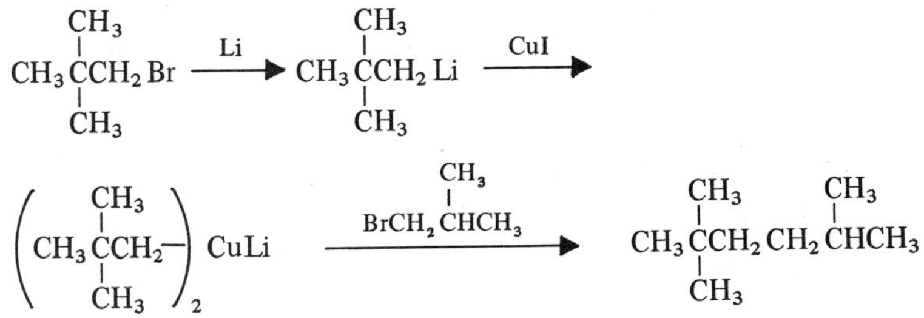

3.24 $(CH_3)_3CCH_3$ is the most stable isomer (i.e., it is the isomer with the lowest potential energy) because it evolves the least amount of heat on a molar basis when subjected to complete combustion.

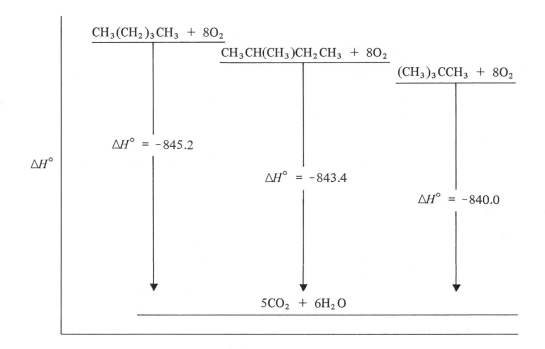

$$CH_3(CH_2)_3CH_3 + 8O_2$$

$$CH_3CH(CH_3)CH_2CH_3 + 8O_2$$

$$(CH_3)_3CCH_3 + 8O_2$$

$$\Delta H^\circ = -845.2$$

$$\Delta H^\circ = -843.4$$

$$\Delta H^\circ = -840.0$$

$$5CO_2 + 6H_2O$$

ΔH°

3.25 A homologous series is one in which each member of the series differs from the one preceding it by a constant amount, usually a CH_2 group. A homologous series of alkyl halides would be the following:

$$CH_3X$$
$$CH_3CH_2X$$
$$CH_3(CH_2)_2X$$
$$CH_3(CH_2)_3X$$
$$CH_3(CH_2)_4X$$
etc.

3.26

This conformation is *less stable* because 1,3-diaxial interactions with the large *tert*-butyl group cause considerable repulsion.

This conformation is *more stable* because 1,3-diaxial interactions with the smaller methyl group are less repulsive.

3.27

Cyclopentane   Methylcyclobutane   *cis*-1, 2-Dimethylcyclopropane

trans-1, 2-Dimethylcyclopropane   1, 1-Dimethylcylopropane

 — CH₂CH₃

Ethylcyclopropane

3.28

(a)   (b)   (c)   (d)

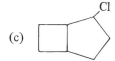

3.29 $CH_3CH_2CH_2Br$ $\xrightarrow{Li}$ $CH_3CH_2CH_2Li$ $\xrightarrow{D_2O}$ $CH_3CH_2CH_2D$

3.30

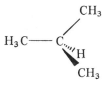

The methyl groups are larger than the hydrogen atom. The resulting mutual repulsions among the methyl groups cause a larger than tetrahedral bond angle.

3.31

(a)

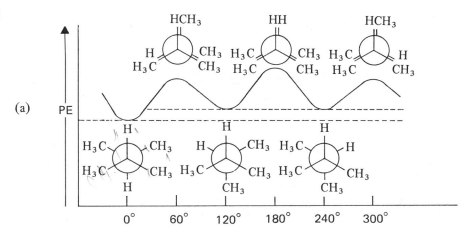

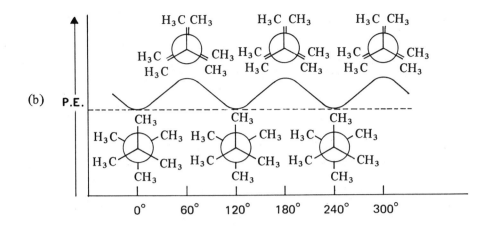

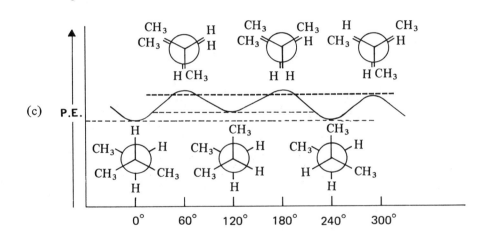

3.32 (a) Hexane. Branched chain hydrocarbons have lower boiling points than their unbranched isomers.

(b) Hexane. Boiling point increases with molecular weight.

(c) Pentane. [See (a) above].

(d) Chloroethane, because it has a higher molecular weight, and is more polar.

(e) Ethyl alcohol because hydrogen bonding causes its molecules to be associated.

3.33 (a) The trans isomer is more stable.

(b) Since they both yield the same combustion products and in the same molar amounts, the one that has the larger heat of combustion has the higher potential energy, and is therefore less stable. The cis isomer is less stable because of the crowding that exists between the methyl groups on the same side of the ring.

3.34

(a)

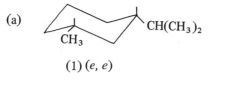

(1) (e, e)

(2) (a, a)

(b)

(3) (a, e)

(4) (e, a)

(c) (1) is more stable than (2) because in (1), both substituents are equatorial. (3) is more stable than (4) because in (3), the larger group [CH(CH₃)₂] is equatorial.

3.35 (a) The trans isomer is more stable because both methyl groups can be equatorial in one conformation (below). In both conformations of *cis*-1, 2-dimethylcyclohexane, one methyl must be axial.

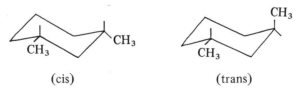

(trans)   (cis)

(b) The cis isomer is more stable because both methyl groups are equatorial in one conformation. In the trans isomer, one methyl must be axial in either conformation.

(cis)   (trans)

(c) The trans isomer is more stable for the same reason as in (a).

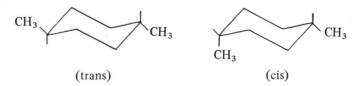

(trans)   (cis)

3.36 In *cis*-1, 3-di-*tert*-butylcyclohexane, the two substituents are both equatorial (see Problem 3.35 b above), whereas in the trans isomer, one of the *tert*-butyl groups must be axial. The instability of a chair conformation with such a large group in an axial position forces the molecule into a less strained twist conformation:

trans *(chair
conformation)*

3.37

β-Glucose

3.38

(a)

(b)   From Table 3.7 we find that this is *cis*-1,2-dimethylcyclohexane.

(c)   Since catalytic hydrogenation produces the cis isomer, both hydrogens must have added from the same side of the double bond. (As we will see in Sect. 6.14A, this type of addition is called a *syn* addition.)

cis—1, 2—Dimethylcyclohexane

The cis isomer is produced when both hydrogens add from the same side.

3.39   (a)   From Table 3.7 we find that this is *trans*-1,2-dichlorocyclohexane.

(b)   Since the product is the trans isomer we can conclude that the chlorine atoms have added from opposite sides of the double bond.

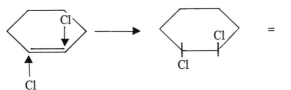

trans—1, 2—Dichlorocyclohexane

The trans isomer is produced when the chlorine atoms add from opposite sides of the double bond.

3.40

(a)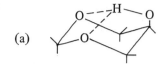

(b) Having the hydroxyl axial allows the formation of a hydrogen bond to either ring oxygen as shown above. The axial conformation is thus stabilized. Intramolecular hydrogen bonding is impossible in the equatorial conformation.

3.41 (a) We can better understand the conformational rigidity of *trans*-decalin if we consider one ring (**A**, below) to be a *trans*-1,2-disubstituted cyclohexane where the 1,2-substituents are the two ends of a four-carbon chain, that is, $-CH_2\,CH_2\,CH_2\,CH_2-$.

Here we consider ring **B** *to be a four-carbon chain. It has no difficulty linking the 1- and 2- positions of ring* **A** *when its ends are diequatorial.*

However if ring **A** of *trans*-decalin were to be flipped into another chair conformation, the carbons of the other ring, **B**, would have to assume a 1,2-diaxial orientation. This is an impossible arrangement for the four carbons of the other ring to assume.

Here we have flipped ring **A** *into another chair conformation. This is an impossible arrangement for the four-carbon chain of ring* **B**, *however, because it cannot link the 1- and 2- positions when its ends are diaxial.*

(b) No. In *cis*-decalin both conformations have one equatorial and one axial bond from ring **A**. This arrangement allows either conformation to span the necessary distance with a four carbon chain.

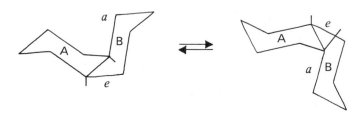

3.42   (a) *cis*-1,2-Dibromocyclohexane must exist in two equivalent conformations with one bromine equatorial and the other axial:

μ = 3.09 D μ = 3.09 D

1-Bromo-*trans*-2-bromo-*cis*-4-*tert*-butylcyclohexane has a similar dipole moment (μ = 3.28 B), and since the presence of the large *tert*-butyl group ensures that the bromines are diequatorial, one can conclude that an equatorial-axial arrangement of the bromines and a diequatorial arrangement have roughly the same dipole moments.

Axial–equatorial bromines   Diequatorial bromines
μ = 3.09 D μ = 3.28 D

Thus were *trans*-1,2-dibromocyclohexane to exist primarily in a diequatorial conformation we would expect it to have a similar dipole moment (i.e., ~ 3.09 *D*). The fact that the dipole moment of *trans*-1,2-dibromocyclohexane is much lower (2.11 *D*) suggests that the diaxial conformation (with $\mu \simeq 0$) is present in appreciable concentration.

$\mu \cong 3.09$ D $\mu \cong 0$

(b) Because of bromine's electronegativity the bromine atoms will be partially negatively charged. In the diequatorial conformation, the bromines are closer together and therefore they repel each other. In the diaxial conformation the bromines are farther apart.

SECTION REFERENCES FOR ADDITIONAL PROBLEMS

If you have trouble solving the Additional Problems refer to the sections in the text next to the problem numbers:

3.26	3.12	**3.35**	3.13
3.27	3.3, 3.4	**3.36**	3.13
3.28	3.4	**3.37**	3.12
3.29	2.15, 3.16	**3.38**	3.16, 3.13
3.30	3.6	**3.39**	2.8, 3.13
3.31	3.6	**3.40**	3.12, 2.17
3.32	3.5	**3.41**	3.14
3.33	3.7, 3.8	**3.42**	3.13
3.34	3.10, 3.12, 3.13		

SELF-TEST

3.1 Give the IUPAC name of the following compound.

$$CH_3 \overset{5}{C}H\overset{4}{C}H\overset{3}{C}H_2 \overset{2}{C}H\overset{1}{C}H_3$$

with CH₃ on the 5-carbon, CH₂–CH₃ (carbons 6 and 7) below, and CH₃ on the 2-carbon.

2,4,5-trimethylheptane

3.2 Draw the Newman projection formula of the molecule below using the partial structure given.

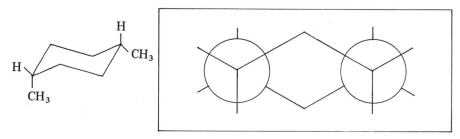

3.3 (a) Give the other chair conformation of molecule I below.

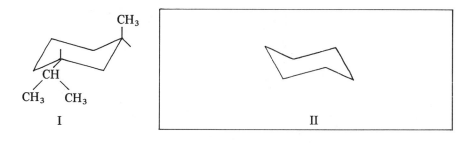

(b) Which conformation (I or II) is present in greater concentration in the equilibrium mixture?

3.4   Write the Newman projection formula for each of the following.

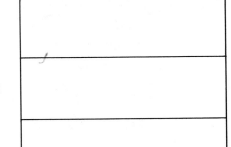

(a)   The *anti* conformation of $ClCH_2CH_2Cl$

(b)   A staggered conformation of $ClCH_2CH_2Cl$

(c)   The most stable conformation of $CH_3CH(CH_3)CH(CH_3)CH_3$

3.5   The following names may be incorrect. Write the correct IUPAC name in the space provided. If the name is correct as given, write OK.

(a)   2-Ethylpentane

(b)   3-Dimethylheptane

(a)   OK.

(b)   3.3 - dimethylheptane

3.6   Complete the line formula given for the most stable conformation of *cis*-1,3-dimethyl-cyclohexane.

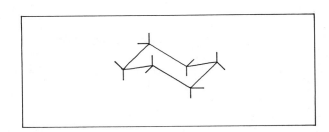

3.7 Consider the formula shown on the right below.

(a) Is the conformation given a cis or trans isomer?

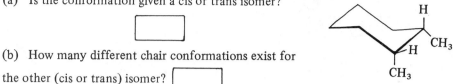

(b) How many different chair conformations exist for the other (cis or trans) isomer?

(c) Draw the Newman projection formula of the structure shown above.

3.8 Give the systematic name of the compound,

3.9 Give the missing organic product(s) or reactant(s) in each of the following reactions. Use the type of formula that shows the appropriate stereochemical features.

(a) $CH_3CH_2Cl + Cl_2$ (1 mole) $\xrightarrow{h\nu}$

(b) $(CH_3CH_2)_2CuLi + CH_3I \longrightarrow$

$CH_3CH_2CH_3 + LiI +$

CH_3CH_2Cu

(c) 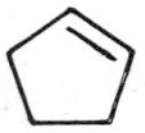 + [ ] $\longrightarrow$ Cyclopentane

(d) $CH_3CH_2CH(Br)CH_3 + Zn + H_3O^+ \longrightarrow$ [ ]

(e) [ ] $+ H_2 \xrightarrow{Pt}$ Cyclohexane

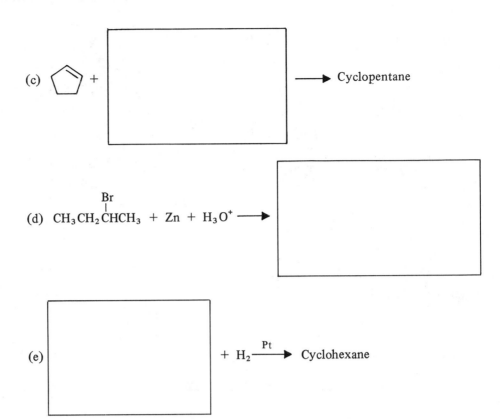

SUPPLEMENTARY PROBLEMS

S3.1 Give the IUPAC name for the compounds below.

(a) 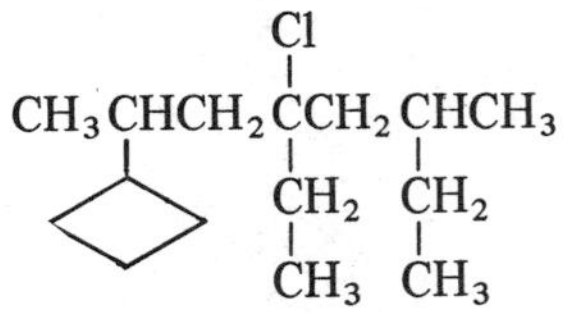

(b) 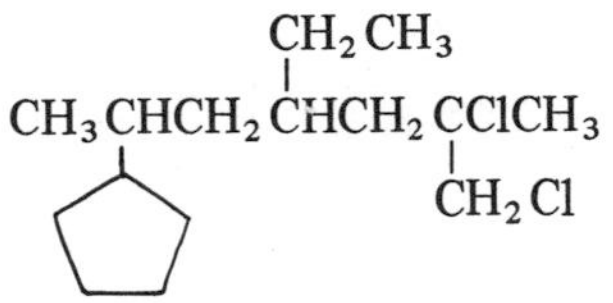

(c) 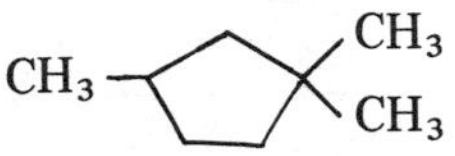

S3.2 Give the Newman projection formula of the (a) highest energy, and (b) lowest energy, staggered conformations of 1,2-dichloroethane.

S3.3 Give the formula of the most stable conformation of (a) *cis*-1,2-dichlorocyclohexane, (b) *cis*-1,3-dichlorocyclohexane.

S3.4 Complete the reaction sequences by giving possible formulas for the missing compounds (A–F).

(a) A $\xrightarrow[\text{ether}]{\text{Li}}$ B + LiBr

$\quad\quad\quad\quad\quad\quad\quad\quad\quad \big\downarrow \text{CuI}$

$\quad\quad\quad\quad\quad\quad\quad\quad\quad\quad\quad$ C + LiI

—CH$_2$CH$_3$ $\xleftarrow{\quad D \quad}$

+ ⋯

(b) Cl—⬠ $\xrightarrow{\quad E \quad}$ ⬠

(c)

CH$_3$ $\qquad\qquad$ CH$_3$

⬠(cyclopentene) $\xrightarrow{\quad F \quad}$ ⬠(cyclopentane)

SOLUTIONS TO SUPPLEMENTARY PROBLEMS

S3.1 (a) (The longest chain is octane.) 4-chloro-2-cyclobutyl-4-ethyl-6-methyloctane

$\quad\quad$ (b) 1,2-dichloro-6-cyclopentyl-4-ethyl-2-methyl-heptane

$\quad\quad$ (c) 1,1,3-trimethylcyclopentane

S3.2

(a) [Newman projection with two Cl groups gauche] The gauche form is higher in energy than the anti form (b).

(b) [Newman projection with two Cl groups anti]

S3.3

(a)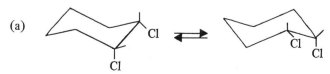

The two cis forms are equivalent because they are both *a, e*.

(b) In this case the *e, e* form shown has lower energy than the *a, a* form.

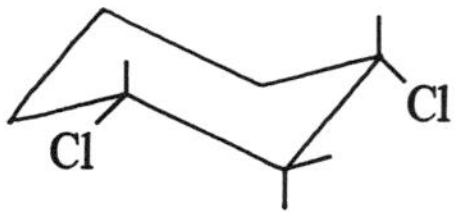

S3.4

(a) A = —Br, B = —Li, C = ($\left(\right.$$\left.\right)_2$ CuLi, D = CH_3CH_2Br

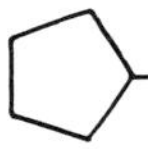

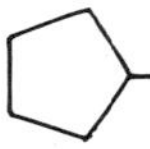

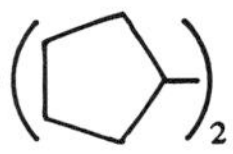

(b) E = Zn/H_3O^+

(c) F = H_2/Ni

4

CHEMICAL REACTIVITY I: FREE RADICAL REACTIONS. REACTIONS OF ALKANES AND CYCLOALKANES

SOLUTIONS TO PROBLEMS

4.1 (a) We answer this question by replacing the hydrogen on C_1 and then by replacing a hydrogen on C_2:

$$\underset{\overset{|}{Cl}}{Cl-CHCH_3} + Cl_2 \longrightarrow \underset{\overset{|}{Cl}}{Cl-\overset{\overset{Cl}{|}}{C}CH_3} + \underset{\overset{|}{Cl}}{Cl-CHCH_2}-Cl$$

1, 1-Dichloroethane $\longrightarrow$ Two trichloroethanes

(b) In this case we obtain the same trichloroethane regardless of which H we replace:

$$Cl-CH_2CH_2-Cl + Cl_2 \longrightarrow \underset{\overset{|}{Cl}}{Cl-CHCH_2}-Cl$$

1, 2-Dichloroethane $\longrightarrow$ One trichloroethane (the same as the second compound above)

(c) See above   (d) Yes, the trichloroethanes are structural isomers.

(e) $$\underset{\overset{|}{Cl}}{Cl-\overset{\overset{Cl}{|}}{C}CH_3} + Cl_2 \longrightarrow \underset{\overset{|}{Cl}}{Cl-\overset{\overset{Cl}{|}}{C}CH_2}-Cl$$

1, 1, 1-Trichloroethane $\longrightarrow$ One tetrachloroethane

$$\underset{\overset{|}{Cl}}{Cl-CHCH_2}-Cl + Cl_2 \longrightarrow \underset{\overset{|}{Cl}}{Cl-\overset{\overset{Cl}{|}}{C}CH_2}-Cl + \underset{\overset{|}{Cl}\;\overset{|}{Cl}}{Cl-CHCH}-Cl$$

1, 1, 2-Trichloroethane $\longrightarrow$ Two tetrachloroethanes, one of which is the same as the one formed from 1, 1, 1-trichloroethane.

Thus there are only two tetrachloroethanes

(f) See (c) above.

(g) Only one pentachloroethane is possible:

$$\begin{array}{c} Cl \\ | \\ Cl-C-CH-Cl \\ | \quad | \\ Cl \quad Cl \end{array}$$

4.2 (a) $CH_3CH_2CH_2Cl$ and $CH_3CHClCH_3$

(b) Boiling points alone would not allow a reliable assignment of structures.

(c) $CH_3CH_2CH_2Cl + Cl_2 \longrightarrow CH_3CH_2CHCl_2$
(bp 46.6°)

$+ CH_3CHClCH_2Cl + ClCH_2CH_2CH_2Cl$

Three isomers with the formula $C_3H_6Cl_2$

$CH_3CHClCH_3 + Cl_2 \longrightarrow CH_3CHClCH_2Cl$
(bp 36.5°)

$+ CH_3CCl_2CH_3$ $\left.\begin{array}{c} \\ \\ \end{array}\right\}$ two isomers with the formula $C_3H_6Cl_2$

The number of isomers produced in each reaction allows us to assign the structures without ambiguity.

(d) See (c) above

4.3

$A = \begin{array}{c} CH_3 \\ | \\ CH_3-C-CH_3 \\ | \\ CH_3 \end{array} + Cl_2 \longrightarrow \begin{array}{c} CH_3 \\ | \\ CH_3-C-CH_2Cl \\ | \\ CH_3 \end{array}$ $\left.\begin{array}{c} \\ \\ \\ \end{array}\right\}$ One isomer of $C_5H_{11}Cl$

$B = CH_3CH_2CH_2CH_2CH_3 + Cl_2 \longrightarrow CH_3CH_2CH_2CH_2CH_2Cl$

$+$

$\begin{array}{c} Cl \\ | \\ CH_3CH_2CH_2CHCH_3 \end{array}$

$+$

$\begin{array}{c} Cl \\ | \\ CH_3CH_2CHCH_2CH_3 \end{array}$

$\left.\begin{array}{c} \\ \\ \\ \\ \\ \\ \\ \end{array}\right\}$ Three isomers of $C_5H_{11}Cl$

$C = \begin{array}{c} CH_3 \\ | \\ CH_3CHCH_2CH_3 \end{array} + Cl_2 \longrightarrow \begin{array}{c} CH_3 \\ | \\ CH_3CHCH_2CH_2Cl \end{array} + \begin{array}{c} CH_3 \\ | \\ CH_3CHCHCH_3 \\ \quad\quad | \\ \quad\quad Cl \end{array}$

$+ \begin{array}{c} CH_3 \\ | \\ CH_3CCH_2CH_3 \\ | \\ Cl \end{array} + \begin{array}{c} CH_3 \\ | \\ Cl-CH_2CHCH_2CH_3 \end{array}$

Four isomers of $C_5H_{11}Cl$

4.4   The chain-initiating step is:

$$Cl_2 \xrightarrow[\text{light}]{\text{heat or}} 2 : \ddot{C}l \cdot$$

The chain propagating steps are:

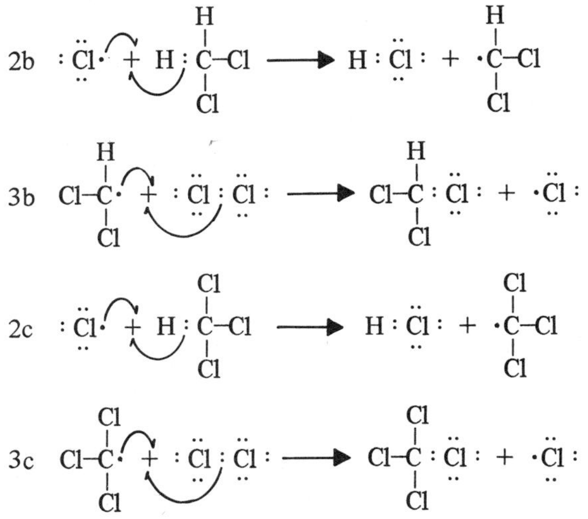

2b $:\ddot{C}l\cdot + H:\underset{Cl}{\overset{H}{C}}-Cl \longrightarrow H:\ddot{C}l: + \cdot\underset{Cl}{\overset{H}{C}}-Cl$

3b $Cl-\underset{Cl}{\overset{H}{C}}\cdot + :\ddot{C}l:\ddot{C}l: \longrightarrow Cl-\underset{Cl}{\overset{H}{C}}:\ddot{C}l: + \cdot\ddot{C}l:$

2c $:\ddot{C}l\cdot + H:\underset{Cl}{\overset{Cl}{C}}-Cl \longrightarrow H:\ddot{C}l: + \cdot\underset{Cl}{\overset{Cl}{C}}-Cl$

3c $Cl-\underset{Cl}{\overset{Cl}{C}}\cdot + :\ddot{C}l:\ddot{C}l: \longrightarrow Cl-\underset{Cl}{\overset{Cl}{C}}:\ddot{C}l: + \cdot\ddot{C}l:$

4.5   A small amount of ethane is formed by the combination of two methyl radicals:

$$2CH_3 \cdot \longrightarrow CH_3 : CH_3$$

This ethane then reacts with chlorine in a substitution reaction (see Sect. 4.10) to form chloroethane.

The significance of this observation is that it is evidence for the proposal that the combination of methyl radicals is one of the chain-terminating steps in the chlorination of methane.

4.6   The use of a large excess of chlorine allows all of the chlorinated methanes (CH_3Cl, CH_2Cl_2, and $CHCl_3$) to react with chlorine.

4.7   (a) $H-H + Br-Br \longrightarrow 2\,H-Br$
$(DH° = 104)\quad (DH° = 46)\qquad 2(DH° = 87.5)$

+ 150 kcal/mole is required for bond cleavage

− 175 kcal/mole is evolved in bond formation

$\Delta H° = +150 - 175 = -25$ kcal/mole (exothermic)

(b) $CH_3CH_2-H + F-F \longrightarrow CH_3CH_2-F + H-F$
$(DH° = 98)\quad (DH° = 38)\quad (DH° = 106)\ (DH° = 136)$
+ 136 kcal/mole   − 242 kcal/mole $\Delta H° = -106$ kcal/mole (exothermic)

(c) $CH_3CH_2-H + I-I \longrightarrow CH_3CH_2-I + H-I$
    $(DH° = 98) (DH° = 36)$ $(DH° = 53.5) (DH° = 71)$
    $+ 134$ kcal/mole -124.5 kcal/mole $\Delta H° = +9.5$ kcal/mole
                                        (endothermic)

(d) $CH_3-H + Cl-Cl \longrightarrow CH_3-Cl + HCl$
    $(DH° = 104) (DH° = 58)$ $(DH° = 83.5) (DH° = 103)$
    $+ 162$ kcal/mole $- 186.5$ kcal/mole $\Delta H° = -24.5$ kcal/mole
                                        (exothermic)

(e) $(CH_3)_3C-H + Cl-Cl \longrightarrow (CH_3)_3C-Cl + H-Cl$
    $(DH° = 91) (DH° = 58)$ $(DH° = 78.5) (DH° = 103)$
    $+ 149$ kcal/mole $- 181.5$ kcal/mole $\Delta H° = -32.5$ kcal/mole
                                        (exothermic)

(f) $(CH_3)_3C-H + Br-Br \longrightarrow (CH_3)_3C-Br + H-Br$
    $(DH° = 91)$ $(DH° = 46)$ $(DH° = 63)$ $(DH° = 87.5)$
    $+ 137$ kcal/mole $- 150.5$ kcal/mole $\Delta H° = -13.5$ kcal/mole
                                        (exothermic)

(g) $CH_3CH_2-CH_3 \longrightarrow CH_3CH_2\cdot + CH_3\cdot$
    $(DH° = 85)$
    $+ 85$ kcal/mole $\Delta H° = +85$ kcal/mole
                                        (endothermic)

(h) $2CH_3CH_2\cdot \longrightarrow CH_3CH_2-CH_2CH_3$
                    $(DH° = 82)$
                    $- 82$ kcal/mole $\Delta H° = -82$ kcal/mole
                                        (exothermic)

4.8 $\Delta H_2° > \Delta H_1°$; therefore isopropyl is more stable than ethyl.

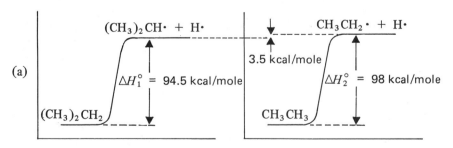

$\Delta H_3° > \Delta H_2°$; therefore ethyl is more stable than methyl.

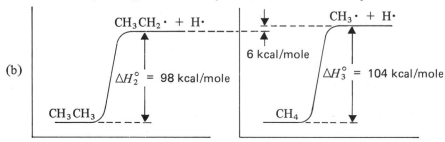

$\Delta H_2^\circ \simeq \Delta H_4^\circ$; therefore the two radicals have nearly equal stabilities.

(c)

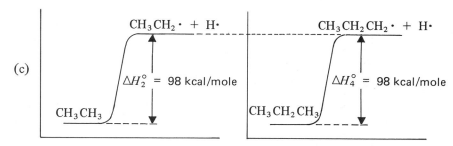

(d) The radicals produced are both primary radicals, and they are otherwise structurally similar, therefore they are of essentially equal stability.

4.9   Homolytic bond dissociation energies of the following C–Cl bonds are:

$$CH_3-Cl \longrightarrow CH_3\cdot + Cl\cdot \qquad\qquad \Delta H^\circ = 83.5 \text{ kcal/mole}$$

$$CH_3CH_2-Cl \longrightarrow CH_3CH_2\cdot + Cl\cdot \qquad \Delta H^\circ = 81.5 \text{ kcal/mole}$$

$$(CH_3)_2CH-Cl \longrightarrow (CH_3)_2CH\cdot + Cl\cdot \quad \Delta H^\circ = 81 \text{ kcal/mole}$$

$$(CH_3)_3C-Cl \longrightarrow (CH_3)_3C\cdot + Cl\cdot \qquad \Delta H^\circ = 78.5 \text{ kcal/mole}$$

Since in each case the same kind of compound (an alkyl chloride) is decomposed into the same kinds of products (an alkyl free radical and a chlorine atom), it follows that the energy required (ΔH°) is a measure of the instability of the radical relative to the alkyl halide. In other words, the less stable the free radical, the more energy will be required to break the bond between it and the chlorine atom. Bond dissociation energies for these alkyl chlorides are, respectively, 83.5, 81.5, 81, and 78.5. They are in the same order as the stabilities of the free radicals produced: $CH_3\cdot < CH_3CH_2\cdot < (CH_3)_2CH\cdot < (CH_3)_3C\cdot$

4.10   Chain-initiating step

$$Br-Br \longrightarrow 2\,Br\cdot \qquad\qquad \Delta H^\circ = +46 \text{ kcal/mole}$$
$$(DH^\circ = 46)$$

Chain-propagating steps

$$Br\cdot + CH_3-H \longrightarrow CH_3\cdot + HBr \qquad \Delta H^\circ = +16.5 \text{ kcal/mole}$$
$$(DH^\circ = 104) \qquad\qquad (DH^\circ = 87.5)$$
$$CH_3\cdot + Br-Br \longrightarrow CH_3-Br + Br\cdot \qquad \Delta H^\circ = -24 \text{ kcal/mole}$$
$$(DH^\circ = 46) \qquad (DH^\circ = 70)$$

Chain-terminating steps

$$CH_3\cdot + Br\cdot \longrightarrow CH_3-Br \qquad\qquad \Delta H^\circ = -70 \text{ kcal/mole}$$
$$(DH^\circ = 70)$$
$$CH_3\cdot + CH_3\cdot \longrightarrow CH_3-CH_3 \qquad \Delta H^\circ = -88 \text{ kcal/mole}$$
$$(DH^\circ = 88)$$
$$Br\cdot + Br\cdot \longrightarrow Br-Br \qquad\qquad \Delta H^\circ = -46 \text{ kcal/mole}$$
$$(DH^\circ = 46)$$

4.11 It would be incorrect to include chain-initiation and chain-termination steps in the calculation of the overall value of $\Delta H°$ because those steps occur only rarely (once for hundreds or thousands of propagation steps).

4.12 (a) E_{act} would equal zero for reactions (3) and (5) because radicals (in the gas phase) are combining to form molecules.

(b) E_{act} would be greater than zero for reactions (1), (2), and (4) because all of these involve bond breaking.

(c) E_{act} **equals** $\Delta H°$ for reaction (1) because this is a gas-phase reaction in which a bond is broken homolytically but no bonds are formed.

4.13 (a) $CH_3\cdot + H{-}Cl \longrightarrow CH_3{-}H + Cl\cdot$ $\Delta H° = -1$ kcal/mole
               $(DH° = 103)$ $(DH° = 104)$ $E_{act} = +2.8$ kcal/mole
                                                          (See text, p. 152; E_{act} for the reverse reaction is 3.8 kcal/mole)

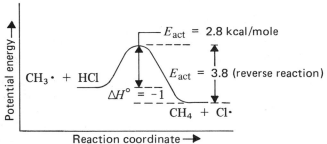

(b) $CH_3\cdot + H{-}Br \longrightarrow CH_3{-}H + Br\cdot$ $\Delta H° = -16.5$ kcal/mole
               $(DH° = 87.5)$ $(DH° = 104)$ $E_{act} = +2.1$ kcal/mole

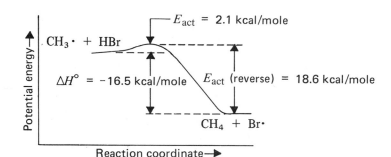

(c) $CH_3-CH_3 \longrightarrow 2 CH_3 \cdot$
 $(DH° = 88)$

$\Delta H° = + 88 \text{ kcal/mole}$
$E_{act} = + 88 \text{ kcal/mole}$

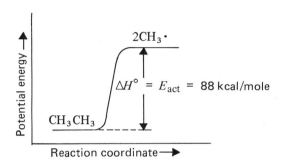

$\Delta H° = E_{act}$ for any reaction in which bonds are broken but no bonds are formed.

(d) $Br-Br \longrightarrow 2 Br\cdot$
 $(DH° = 46)$

$\Delta H° = + 46 \text{ kcal/mole}$
$E_{act} = 46 \text{ kcal/mole}$

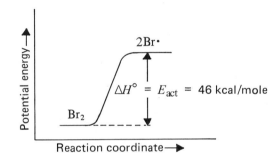
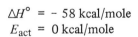

(e) $2 Cl\cdot \longrightarrow Cl-Cl$
 $(DH° = 58)$

$\Delta H° = - 58 \text{ kcal/mole}$
$E_{act} = 0 \text{ kcal/mole}$

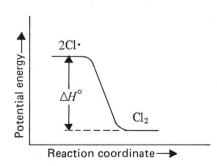

4.14

$$Cl_2 \xrightarrow[\text{or heat}]{h\nu} 2\,Cl\cdot$$

(2a) $Cl\cdot + H\!:\!\underset{\underset{H}{|}}{\overset{\overset{Cl}{|}}{C}}\!-\!CH_3 \longrightarrow H\!:\!Cl + \cdot\underset{\underset{H}{|}}{\overset{\overset{Cl}{|}}{C}}\!-\!CH_3$

(3a) $CH_3\underset{\underset{H}{|}}{\overset{\overset{Cl}{|}}{C}}\!\cdot + Cl\!:\!Cl \longrightarrow CH_3\!-\!\underset{\underset{H}{|}}{\overset{\overset{Cl}{|}}{C}}\!-\!Cl + Cl\cdot$

1,1-Dichloro-
ethane

(2b) $Cl\cdot + H\!-\!CH_2CH_2Cl \longrightarrow H\!:\!Cl + \cdot CH_2CH_2Cl$

(3b) $ClCH_2CH_2\cdot + Cl\!:\!Cl \longrightarrow ClCH_2CH_2Cl + Cl\cdot$

1,2-Dichloro-
ethane

4.15 (a) $CH_3CH_2\!-\!H + Cl\cdot \longrightarrow CH_3CH_2\cdot + H\!-\!Cl$
($DH° = 98$)   ($DH° = 103$)
$\Delta H° = -103 + 98 = -5$ kcal/mole

(b)

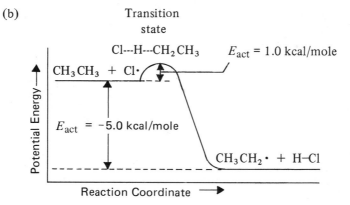

Transition
state

(c) The hydrogen abstraction step, for ethane,

$$CH_3CH_2\!-\!H + Cl\cdot \longrightarrow CH_3CH_2\cdot + HCl \qquad (E_{act} = 1.0 \text{ kcal/mole})$$

has a much lower energy of activation than the corresponding step for methane:

$$CH_3\!-\!H + Cl\cdot \longrightarrow CH_3\cdot + HCl \qquad (E_{act} = 3.8 \text{ kcal/mole})$$

Therefore, ethyl radicals form much more rapidly in the mixture than methyl radicals, and this, in turn, leads to the more rapid formation of ethyl chloride.

4.16 If all 10 hydrogen atoms of isobutane were equally reactive, the relative amounts of reaction at primary hydrogens and at tertiary hydrogens would be 9/1, and the ratio of isobutyl chloride to *tert*-butyl chloride would be 9:1. Since the ratio is instead 63/37 ($\sim$6:4), the tertiary hydrogen atom must be more reactive than the primary hydrogen atoms.

4.17 Laboratory preparation of alkyl halides by direct chlorination can be accomplished in good yield when all hydrogens in the alkane are equivalent. This is true of neopentane, and cyclopentane. (In these cases, the preparation would be practical only for monochlorination, where an excess of hydrocarbon would be employed, or for complete chlorination where an excess of chlorine would be used.)

4.18 (a) $Cl\cdot + CH_3CH_2-H \longrightarrow CH_3CH_2\cdot + H-Cl$
$\qquad\qquad (DH° = 98) \qquad\qquad\qquad\qquad (DH° = 103)$

$\qquad \Delta H° = 98 - 103 = -5$ kcal/mole (exothermic)

$\qquad$ (b) $Cl\cdot + (CH_3)_2CH-H \longrightarrow (CH_3)_2CH\cdot + H-Cl$
$\qquad\qquad (DH° = 94.5) \qquad\qquad\qquad\qquad (DH° = 103)$

$\qquad \Delta H° = 94.5 - 103 = -8.5$ kcal/mole (exothermic)

$\qquad$ (c) $Cl\cdot + CH_3CH_2CH_2-H \longrightarrow CH_3CH_2CH_2\cdot + H-Cl$
$\qquad\qquad (DH° = 98) \qquad\qquad\qquad\qquad (DH° = 103)$

$\qquad \Delta H° = 98 - 103 = -5$ kcal/mole (exothermic)

4.19 The hydrogen abstraction steps in alkane fluorinations are always highly exothermic. Thus the transition states are even more reactant-like in structure and in energy than they are in alkane chlorinations. The type of C–H bond being broken (1°, 2°, or 3°) has practically no effect on the relative rates of the reactions.

4.20

1, 1-Dichlorocyclohexane

cis-1, 2-Dichlorocyclohexane

trans-1, 2-Dichlorocyclohexane

cis-1, 3-Dichlorocyclohexane

trans-1, 3-Dichlorocyclohexane

cis-1, 4-Dichlorocyclohexane

trans-1, 4-Dichlorocyclohexane

4.21   (a) The predominant product is 1-bromo-1-methylcyclopentane.

(b) The greater selectivity of bromine (Sect. 4.10) leads to preferential replacement of the tertiary hydrogen of methylcyclopentane.

4.22   (a) Homolysis is cleavage of a covalent bond in such a way that the electrons of the ruptured bond are divided equally between the atoms involved:

$$: \overset{..}{\underset{..}{Cl}} - \overset{..}{\underset{..}{Cl}} : \longrightarrow : \overset{..}{\underset{..}{Cl}} \cdot \; + \; \cdot \overset{..}{\underset{..}{Cl}} :$$

(b) Heterolysis is cleavage of a covalent bond in such a way that both electrons of the ruptured bond remain with one atom. Ions are formed:

$$H - \overset{..}{\underset{..}{Cl}} : \longrightarrow H^+ \; + \; : \overset{..}{\underset{..}{Cl}} :^-$$

(c) The homolytic bond dissociation energy ($DH°$) is the energy required on a molar basis to dissociate a covalent bond homolytically:

$$H-H \longrightarrow 2 \, H \cdot \quad DH° = 104 \text{ kcal/mole}$$

(d) A free radical is an atom or group that has an unpaired electron.

$$: \overset{..}{\underset{..}{Br}} \cdot \quad \text{or} \quad CH_3 \cdot$$

(e)   A carbocation is an ion that has a trivalent carbon atom that bears a positive charge:

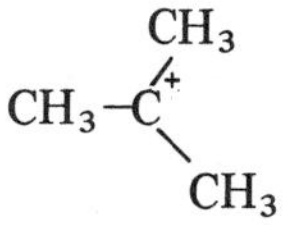

$$CH_3-\overset{\displaystyle CH_3}{\underset{\displaystyle CH_3}{\overset{+}{C}}}$$

(f)   A carbanion is an ion that has a trivalent carbon atom that bears an unshared electron pair and a negative charge.

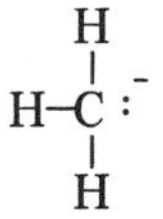

$$H-\overset{\displaystyle H}{\underset{\displaystyle H}{C}}:^-$$

4.23

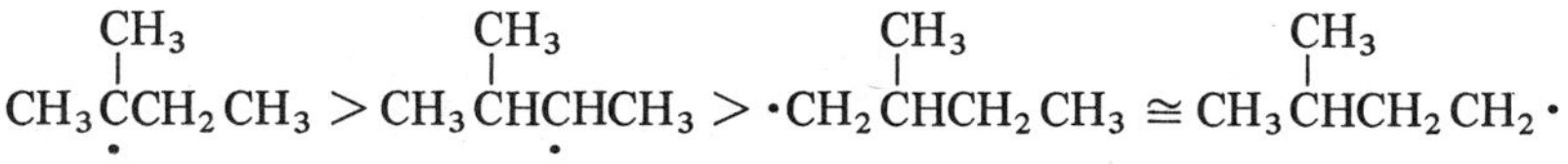

$$CH_3\overset{\displaystyle CH_3}{\underset{\displaystyle \bullet}{C}}CH_2CH_3 > CH_3\overset{\displaystyle CH_3}{\underset{\displaystyle \bullet}{C}}HCHCH_3 > \bullet CH_2\overset{\displaystyle CH_3}{C}HCH_2CH_3 \cong CH_3\overset{\displaystyle CH_3}{C}HCH_2CH_2\bullet$$

4.24

$$CH_3-\overset{\displaystyle CH_3}{\underset{\displaystyle CH_3}{C}}-\overset{\displaystyle CH_3}{\underset{\displaystyle CH_3}{C}}-CH_3$$

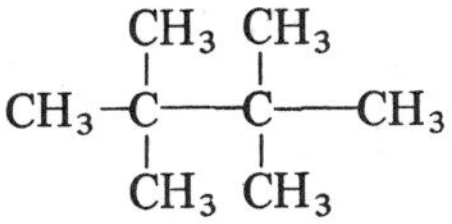

4.25   Six:

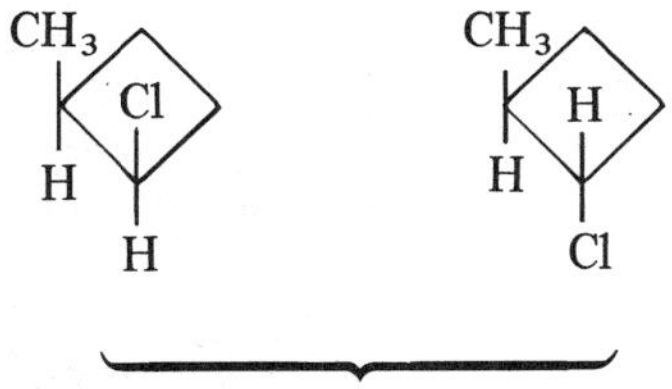

cis-trans isomers

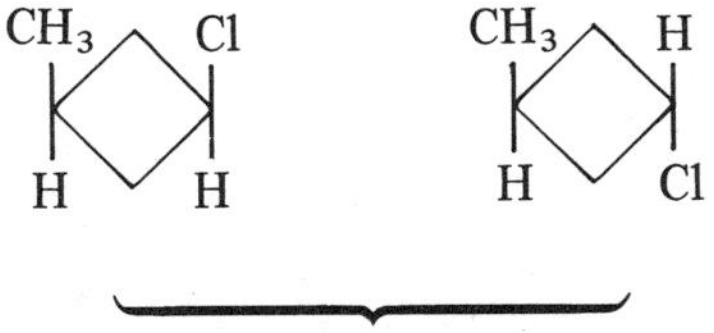

cis-trans isomers

4.26   Five:

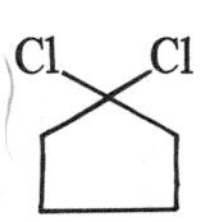

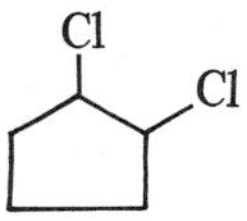

cis and trans 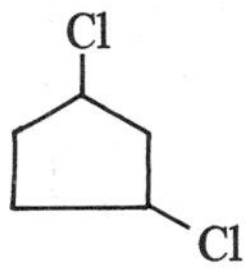   cis and trans

4.27

(a) $CH_3\underset{\underset{CH_3}{|}}{\overset{\overset{Br}{|}}{C}}CH_2CH_3$, because the tertiary hydrogen atom is much more reactive than either the primary or secondary hydrogen atoms.

(b) $CH_3\overset{\overset{CH_3}{|}}{C}HCH_2CH_3 + Cl\cdot \longrightarrow$

$\cdot CH_2\overset{\overset{CH_3}{|}}{C}HCH_2CH_3$

$CH_3-\underset{\underset{\cdot}{}}{\overset{\overset{CH_3}{|}}{C}}-CH_2CH_3$

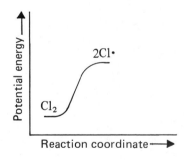

$CH_3-\overset{\overset{CH_3}{|}}{C}H-\underset{\underset{\cdot}{}}{C}HCH_3$

$CH_3-\overset{\overset{CH_3}{|}}{C}H-CH_2CH_2\cdot$

$\xrightarrow{Cl_2}$

$Cl-CH_2\overset{\overset{CH_3}{|}}{C}HCH_2CH_3 + Cl\cdot$

$+$

$CH_3\underset{\underset{Cl}{|}}{\overset{\overset{CH_3}{|}}{C}}-CH_2CH_3 + Cl\cdot$

$+$

$CH_3\overset{\overset{CH_3}{|}}{C}H-\underset{\underset{Cl}{|}}{C}HCH_3 + Cl\cdot$

$+$

$CH_3\overset{\overset{CH_3}{|}}{C}HCH_2CH_2-Cl + Cl\cdot$

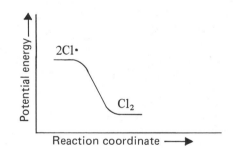

(c) Chlorine is more reactive than bromine and is therefore less selective. See Sect. 4.10.

4.28 (a) $Cl_2 \longrightarrow 2 Cl\cdot$ (b) $2 Cl\cdot \longrightarrow Cl_2$

(c) $H\cdot + Cl_2 \longrightarrow HCl + Cl\cdot$ (d) $I\cdot + CH_4 \longrightarrow HI + CH_3\cdot$

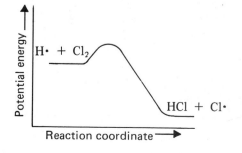

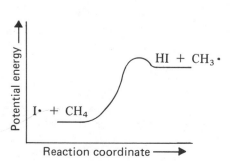

4.29 (a) $Cl_2 \xrightarrow[\text{light}]{\text{heat or}} 2\,Cl\cdot$ Chain-initiating step

(b) $\left\{\begin{array}{l}\Delta H^\circ = -5 \\ \text{kcal/mole}\end{array}\right.$ $\begin{array}{l} Cl\cdot + CH_3CH_2-H \longrightarrow H-Cl + CH_3CH_2\cdot \\ \qquad (DH^\circ = 98) \qquad (DH^\circ = 103)\end{array}$ $\left.\begin{array}{l}\\ \end{array}\right\}$ Chain propagating

$\left.\begin{array}{l}\Delta H^\circ = -23.5 \\ \text{kcal/mole}\end{array}\right\}$ $\begin{array}{l} CH_3CH_2\cdot + Cl_2 \longrightarrow CH_3CH_2-Cl + Cl\cdot \\ \qquad\quad (DH^\circ = 58)\ (DH^\circ = 81.5)\end{array}$ $\left.\begin{array}{l}\\ \end{array}\right\}$ steps

$\left.\begin{array}{l} CH_3CH_2\cdot + Cl\cdot \longrightarrow CH_3CH_2Cl \\ 2CH_3CH_2\cdot \longrightarrow CH_3CH_2CH_2CH_3 \\ 2Cl\cdot \longrightarrow Cl_2 \end{array}\right\}$ Chain-terminating steps

(c) The bond dissociation energy of the CH_3CH_2-H bond (98 kcal/mole) is smaller than that of the CH_3-H bond (104 kcal/mole), therefore ethane reacts with $Cl\cdot$ faster than methane does.

4.30 (a) (2) $Cl\cdot + CH_3-CH_3 \longrightarrow CH_3-Cl + CH_3\cdot$ $\Delta H^\circ = +4.5$ kcal/mole
  $\qquad (DH^\circ=88) \qquad\quad (DH^\circ=83.5)$ $E_{\text{act}} > +4.5$ kcal/mole

(3) $CH_3\cdot + Cl_2 \longrightarrow CH_3-Cl + Cl\cdot$ $\Delta H^\circ = -25.5$ kcal/mole
  $\qquad (DH^\circ=58)\ (DH^\circ=83.5)$ E_{act} is small

In this reaction, step 2 is endothermic ($\Delta H^\circ = +4.5$ kcal/mole) and thus E_{act} must be greater than $+4.5$ kcal/mole. Although we do not know the exact E_{act} of the reaction that yields ethyl chloride (Problem 4.29), we can assume that it is less than 3.8 kcal/mole (E_{act} for the corresponding step in the chlorination of methane). Therefore we conclude that the reaction here, with an E_{act} greater than $+4.5$ kcal/mole, will not compete with the reaction of Problem 4.29.

(b) (1) $F-F \longrightarrow 2F\cdot$ $\Delta H^\circ = +38$ kcal/mole
  $\qquad (DH^\circ = 38)$

(2) $F\cdot + CH_3-CH_3 \longrightarrow CH_3-F + CH_3\cdot$ $\Delta H^\circ = -20$ kcal/mole
  $\qquad (DH^\circ = 88) \qquad\quad (DH^\circ = 108)$ $E_{\text{act}} > 0$

(3) $CH_3\cdot + F-F \longrightarrow CH_3-F + F\cdot$ $\Delta H^\circ = -70$ kcal/mole
  $\qquad (DH^\circ = 38)\ (DH^\circ = 108)$ $E_{\text{act}} > 0$

Since the propagation steps are both highly exothermic it is possible for each E_{act} to be quite small, and therefore for the reaction to take place at a reasonable rate.

4.31 (a) $CH_3-H + F-F \longrightarrow CH_3\cdot + H-F + F\cdot$ $\Delta H^\circ = +6$ kcal/mole
  $\quad (DH^\circ = 104)\ (DH^\circ = 38) \qquad (DH^\circ = 136)$ $E_{\text{act}} > 6$ kcal/mole

$\quad CH_3\cdot + F\cdot \longrightarrow CH_3-F$ $\Delta H^\circ = -108$ kcal/mole
  $\qquad\qquad\qquad (DH^\circ = 108)$ $E_{\text{act}} = 0$

If E_{act} for the first step is not much greater than 6 kcal/mole, this mechanism is likely.

(b) $CH_3-H + Cl-Cl \longrightarrow CH_3\cdot + H-Cl + Cl\cdot$ $\Delta H° = +59$ kcal/mole
   $(DH° = 104)$ $(DH° = 58)$ $(DH° = 103)$ $E_{act} \geq 59$ kcal/mole

   $CH_3\cdot + Cl\cdot \longrightarrow CH_3-Cl$ $\Delta H° = -83.5$ kcal/mole
        $(DH°=83.5)$ $E_{act} = 0$

This mechanism is highly unlikely because the E_{act} for the first step must be ≥ 59 kcal/mole.

4.32

$$CH_3CH_2CH_3 \xrightarrow[h\nu,\ heat]{Br_2} CH_3CH_2CH_2Br + CH_3\underset{Br}{\overset{|}{C}}HCH_3$$

then,

$$CH_3\overset{\overset{CH_3}{|}}{C}HBr \xrightarrow[ether]{Li} CH_3\overset{\overset{CH_3}{|}}{C}HLi \xrightarrow{CuI} \left(CH_3\overset{\overset{CH_3}{|}}{C}H-\right)_2 CuLi$$

$$\xrightarrow{CH_3CH_2CH_2Br} CH_3\overset{\overset{CH_3}{|}}{C}HCH_2CH_2CH_3$$

4.33

$$CH_3CH_3 \xrightarrow[h\nu,\ heat]{Br_2} CH_3CH_2Br \xrightarrow[ether]{Li} CH_3CH_2Li \xrightarrow{CuI}$$

$$(CH_3CH_2)_2CuLi$$

4.34 (a) CH_3-H, $DH° = 104$; CH_3CH_2-H, $DH° = 98$ kcal/mole. (Recall that here, $E_{act} = DH°$.)

CH_3CH_2-H bond rupture requires less energy, therefore spontaneous homolysis (cracking) occurs at a lower temperature.

(b) CH_3-CH_3 $DH° = 88$ kcal/mole $= E_{act}$

C–C bond rupture requires less energy than C–H bond rupture, therefore C–C bond rupture occurs more readily than CH_3CH_2-H bond rupture.

(c) $CH_3CH_2-CH_2CH_3$ $DH° = 82$ kcal/mole $= E_{act}$

   $CH_3CH_2CH_2-CH_3$ $DH° = 85$ kcal/mole $= E_{act}$

Here again the bond with the lower bond dissociation energy will undergo spontaneous homolysis (cracking) more readily.

4.35

(1) $CH_3CH_2CH_3 \longrightarrow CH_3CH_2\cdot + CH_3\cdot$ $DH° = 85$ kcal/mole
(2) $CH_3CH_2CH_3 \longrightarrow CH_3CH_2CH_2\cdot + H\cdot$ $DH° = 98$ kcal/mole
(3) $CH_3CH_2CH_3 \longrightarrow CH_3\overset{\cdot}{C}HCH_3 + H\cdot$ $DH° = 94.5$ kcal/mole

(a) Since E_{act} is equal to $DH°$, we can assume that (1) is the most likely chain-initiating step.

(b) $CH_3\cdot + CH_3CH_2CH_3 \longrightarrow CH_3-H + \cdot CH_2CH_2CH_3$ $\Delta H° = -6$ kcal/mole
$\quad\quad\quad\quad\quad\quad (DH° = 98) \quad\quad\quad\quad (DH° = 104)$

Since $\Delta H°$ is negative, E_{act} need not be large.

(c) $CH_3\cdot + CH_3CH_2CH_3 \longrightarrow CH_4 + CH_3\overset{\cdot}{C}HCH_3$ $\Delta H° = -9.5$ kcal/mole
$\quad\quad\quad\quad\quad\quad (DH° = 94.5) \quad\quad\quad (DH° = 104)$

On the basis of energy requirements, this is a likely alternative to step 1. On the basis of the probability factor, it is less likely because there are only two secondary hydrogen atoms compared with six primary hydrogen atoms.

4.36 **(a)** Oxygen-oxygen single bonds are especially weak, that is,

$$HO-OH \quad\quad DH° = 51 \text{ kcal/mole}$$
$$CH_3CH_2O-OCH_3 \quad DH° = 44 \text{ kcal/mole}$$

This means that a peroxide will dissociate into free radicals at a relatively low temperature.

$$RO-OR \xrightarrow{\text{100-200°}} 2RO\cdot$$

Oxygen-hydrogen single bonds, on the other hand, are very strong. (For HO–H, $DH° = 119$ kcal/mole.) This means that reactions like the following will be highly exothermic.

$$RO\cdot + R-H \longrightarrow RO-H + R\cdot$$

(b) (1) $(CH_3)_3CO-OC(CH_3)_3 \xrightarrow{\text{heat}} 2(CH_3)_3CO\cdot$ ⎫ Chain-
(2) $(CH_3)_3CO\cdot + R-H \longrightarrow (CH_3)_3COH + R\cdot$ ⎬ initiating steps

(3) $R\cdot + Cl-Cl \longrightarrow R-Cl + Cl\cdot$ ⎫ Chain-
(4) $Cl\cdot + R-H \longrightarrow H-Cl + R\cdot$ ⎬ propagating steps

4.37

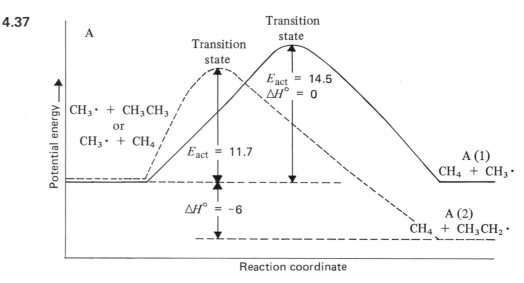

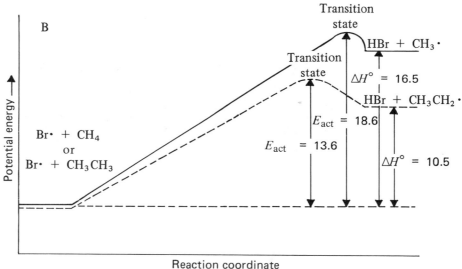

(b)   Reaction **A** (2) since it is most exothermic.

(c)   Reaction **B** (1) since it is most endothermic.

(d)   Since $\Delta H^\circ = 0$, bond breaking should be approximately 50% complete.

(e)   The reactions of set **B**.

(f)   The difference in ΔH° simply reflects the difference in the C–H bond strengths of methane and ethane.

(g)   Because the reactions of set **B** are highly endothermic the transition states show a strong resemblance to products in structure and *in energy,* and the products differ in energy by 6 kcal/mole. (In this instance, since the difference in E_{act} is five-sixths of the difference in ΔH°, we can estimate that bond breaking is about five-sixths complete when the transition states are reached.)

SECTION REFERENCES FOR ADDITIONAL PROBLEMS

If you have trouble solving the Additional Problems refer to the sections in the text next to the problem numbers below.

4.22	4.1, 4.2, 4.6	**4.30**	4.5, 4.7, 4.9
4.23	4.6	**4.31**	4.5, 4.7, 4.9
4.24	4.4	**4.32**	3.16, 4.10
4.25	4.4	**4.33**	3.16, 4.10, 4.12
4.26	4.4	**4.34**	4.6, 4.8
4.27	4.10A	**4.35**	4.8D, 4.3, 4.8C
4.28	4.8D	**4.36**	4.5, 4.6
4.29	4.5, 4.7	**4.37**	4.5, 4.6, 4.10A

SELF-TEST

4.1   Give the structural formula of the *major* organic product in each reaction below.

(a) $CH_3\underset{\underset{\displaystyle CH_3}{|}}{CH}CH_3$ + Br_2 (one mole) $\xrightarrow{\text{light}}$

(b) CH_3CH_2Cl + Cl_2 (one mole) $\longrightarrow$

(more than one product)

4.2   Calculate the $\Delta H°$ of the following reactions.

(a) $CH_3CH_2CH_3$ + Cl_2 $\xrightarrow{\text{light}}$ $CH_3CHClCH_3$ + HCl

(b) CH_3CH_3 + $\cdot Br$ $\longrightarrow$ $CH_3\overset{\displaystyle .}{C}H_2$ + HBr

(c) $CH_3\overset{\displaystyle .}{C}H_2$ + $Br\cdot$ $\longrightarrow$ CH_3CH_2Br

Use the single-bond dissociation energies of Table 4.1:

TABLE 4.1 Single-Bond Dissociation Energies in kcal/mole

	A : B $\longrightarrow$ A· + B· $DH°$		$DH°$
H–H	104	$(CH_3)_2 CH–H$	94.5
D–D	106	$(CH_3)_2 CH–F$	105
F–F	38	$(CH_3)_2 CH–Cl$	81
Cl–Cl	58	$(CH_3)_2 CH–Br$	68
Br–Br	46	$(CH_3)_2 CH–I$	53
I–I	36	$(CH_3)_2 CH–OH$	92
H–F	136	$(CH_3)_2 CH–OCH_3$	80.5
H–Cl	103		
H–Br	87.5	$(CH_3)_3 C–H$	91
H–I	71	$(CH_3)_3 C–Cl$	78.5
$CH_3–H$	104	$(CH_3)_3 C–Br$	63
$CH_3–F$	108	$(CH_3)_3 C–I$	49.5
$CH_3–Cl$	83.5	$(CH_3)_3 C–OH$	90.5
$CH_3–Br$	70	$(CH_3)_3 C–OCH_3$	78
$CH_3–I$	56	$C_6 H_5 CH_2–H$	85
$CH_3–OH$	91.5	$CH_2=CHCH_2–H$	85
$CH_3–OCH_3$	80	$CH_2=CH–H$	103
$CH_3 CH_2–H$	98	$C_6 H_5–H$	103
$CH_3 CH_2–F$	106	$HC≡C–H$	125
$CH_3 CH_2–Cl$	81.5	$CH_3–CH_3$	88
$CH_3 CH_2–Br$	69	$CH_3 CH_2–CH_3$	85
$CH_3 CH_2–I$	53.5	$CH_3 CH_2 CH_2–CH_3$	85
$CH_3 CH_2–OH$	91.5	$CH_3 CH_2–CH_2 CH_3$	82
$CH_3 CH_2–OCH_3$	80	$(CH_3)_2 CH–CH_3$	84
		$(CH_3)_3 C–CH_3$	80
$CH_3 CH_2 CH_2–H$	98	HO–H	119
$CH_3 CH_2 CH_2–F$	106	HOO–H	90
$CH_3 CH_2 CH_2–Cl$	81.5	HO–OH	51
$CH_3 CH_2 CH_2–Br$	69	$CH_3 CH_2 O–OCH_3$	44
$CH_3 CH_2 CH_2–I$	53.5		
$CH_3 CH_2 CH_2–OH$	91.5		
$CH_3 CH_2 CH_2–OCH_3$	80		

From S. W. Benson, "Bond Energies," *J. Chem. Ed., 42*, 502 (1965).

4.3 Draw structures of all the monobromination products of butane (reaction conditions = hν, 25°C).

4.4   Use the bond dissociation energies in Table 4.1 to answer the following questions.

(a) The most likely products of the thermal homolytic cleavage of propane are:

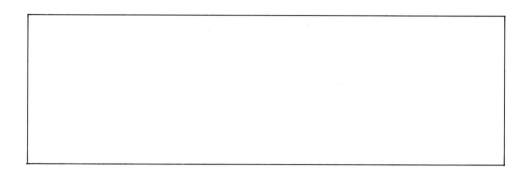

and

(b) The $\Delta H°$ of the reaction above is [ ] kcal/mole.

(c) The most likely monobromination product of propane is: [ ]

(d) The $\Delta H°$ of the reaction (c) above is [ ] kcal/mole.

4.5   When ethane is heated to high temperatures it undergoes thermal cracking. One of the reactions it undergoes is

$$CH_3CH_3 \xrightarrow{\Delta} CH_3\dot{C}H_2 + H\cdot$$

Recombination of the ethyl radicals yields butane.

(a) Assuming that the hydrogen atoms also recombine to produce H_2, calculate the $\Delta H°$ for the overall reaction, $2CH_3CH_3 \longrightarrow CH_3CH_2CH_2CH_3 + H_2$.

$\Delta H° =$

(b) Is this a chain reaction?

SUPPLEMENTARY PROBLEMS

S4.1   The hydrocarbons A–H and B–H have homolytic bond dissociation energies for the bond shown as follows:

$$A–H \quad DH° = 95 \text{ kcal/mole}$$
$$B–H \quad DH° = 99 \text{ kcal/mole}$$

Which hydrocarbon, A–H or B–H, forms the more stable free radical relative to the hydrocarbon from which each is formed?

S4.2   (a) Complete each equation below by supplying the missing species. (b) Label each reaction as a possible initiation, propagation, or termination step. (c) If possible, tell whether each step is endothermic or exothermic.

(1) Br· + _____ ⟶ H–Br + R·

(2) R–X ⟶ R· + _____

(3) R–R ⟶ R· + _____

S4.3   You are assigned the task of preparing 1-halo-1-methylcyclopentane by direct halogenation of methylcyclopentane. Which halogen would you select? Explain your choice. (Hint: See Problem 4.21.)

SOLUTIONS TO SUPPLEMENTARY PROBLEMS

S4.1   The values of $DH°$ refer to the reactions

$$A–H \longrightarrow A· + H·$$
and $$B–H \longrightarrow B· + H·$$

Since the dissociation of A–H requires less energy than that of B–H, the A· radical is more stable than the B· radical.

S4.2   The complete reactions are:

(1) Br· + H–R ⟶ HBr + R·   (propagation)

You cannot tell whether the reaction is endothermic or exothermic without knowing $DH°$ values for the H–R and HBr

(2) R–X ⟶ R· + X·   (initiation)
Endothermic

(3) R–R ⟶ R· + R·   (initiation)
Endothermic

S4.3   The answer is bromine. Of the halogens, only chlorine and bromine are suitable for most direct halogenations; fluorine is too reactive to give predictable products, and iodine is unreactive. Bromine is better than chlorine because it is more selective; i.e., bromination would react to a greater extent at the tertiary carbon than at the primary or secondary carbons. Chlorine, being less selective, would give a more random distribution of products.

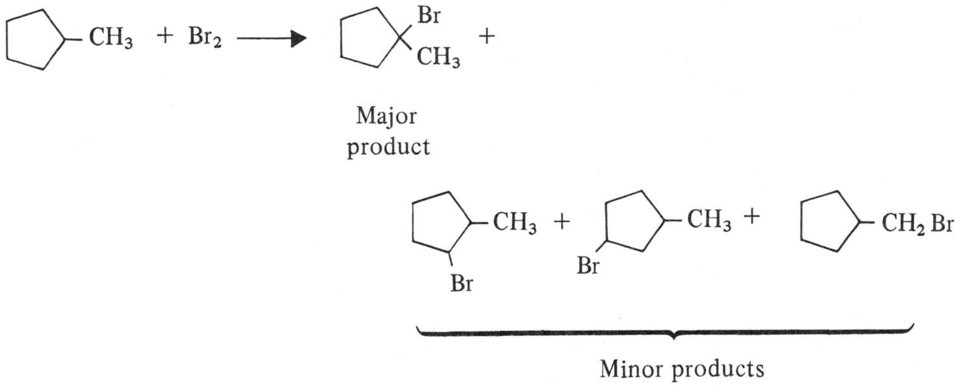

Major
product

Minor products

A

SPECIAL TOPIC
Elementary Thermodynamics: $\triangle H°$, $\triangle S°$, and $\triangle G°$

SOLUTIONS TO PROBLEMS

A.1

(a) $X \longrightarrow Y$, $K_{eq} = \dfrac{[Y]}{[X]} = 10$

Initial $[X] = 1.0$
Equilibrium $[Y] = a$
Equilibrium $[X] = 1.0 - a$

then $K_{eq} = 10 = \dfrac{a}{1.0 - a}$

$10 - 10a = a$
$-11a = -10$
$a = \dfrac{10}{11} = 0.91$ mole/liter

At equilibrium, $[Y] = 0.91$ mole/liter,
$\qquad\qquad\quad [X] = 0.09$ mole/liter,
and 91% of X is converted to product, Y.

(b) If $K_{eq} = 1$, $1 = \dfrac{a}{1.0 - a}$

$1 - a = a$
$-2a = -1$
$a = 0.5$

$\therefore$ At equilibrium, $[Y] = 0.5$ mole/liter,
$\qquad\qquad\qquad [X] = 0.5$ mole/liter,
and 50% of X is converted to product, Y.

(c) If $K_{eq} = 10^{-3}$, $10^{-3} = \dfrac{a}{1 - a}$

$10^{-3} - 10^{-3}a = a$
$-1.001a = -10^{-3}$
$a = \dfrac{10^{-3}}{1.001} \cong 10^{-3}$

At equilibrium, $[Y] = 10^{-3}$ mole/liter,
$\qquad\qquad\quad [X] = 0.999$ mole/liter,
and 0.1% of X is converted to product, Y.

A.2   (a) The majority of the molecules (~99.99%) are in the chair form at equilibrium because the equilibrium, chair $\rightleftharpoons$ boat, has a $\Delta G° = -5$ to -6 kcal/mole. See Table A.1, last column under -5.5 kcal/mole.

(b) For $\Delta G° \sim -1.8$, Table A.1 tells us that 95% of ethylcyclohexane is in the equatorial form.

A.3   (a) $\Delta G° = \Delta H° - T\Delta S°$
$\Delta G° = -41{,}700$ cal/mole $- 300$ deg $(- 26.6$ cal/ deg mole$)$
$\Delta G° = -41{,}700 + 7980 = -33{,}720$ cal/mole
or $\Delta G° = -33.72$ kcal/mole

(b) Yes, because a negative value of $\Delta G°$ tells us that the products are favored at equilibrium.

(c) No, a negative entropy tells us that the products are more ordered, and therefore less favored than the reactants.

(d) There are fewer degrees of freedom in the product molecule, ethene, than in the separate and independent molecules, ethyne and hydrogen.

5

CHEMICAL REACTIVITY II: IONIC REACTIONS. AN INTRODUCTION TO NUCLEOPHILIC SUBSTITUTION AND ELIMINATION REACTIONS OF ALKYL HALIDES

MECHANISM OF S$_N$2 REACTION

$$Nu:^- + \quad \overset{|}{\underset{|}{C}}-L \longrightarrow \overset{\delta-}{Nu} \cdots \overset{|}{\underset{|}{C}} \cdots \overset{\delta-}{L} \longrightarrow Nu-\overset{|}{\underset{|}{C}} + :L^-$$

Transition state

MECHANISM OF E2 REACTION

$$B:^- + \overset{H}{\underset{|}{\overset{|}{C}}}-\overset{|}{\underset{|}{C}}- \longrightarrow B-H + \quad C=C \quad + :L^-$$

MECHANISM OF S$_N$1/E1 REACTION

$$-\overset{H}{\underset{R}{\overset{|}{C}}}-\overset{R}{\underset{|}{\overset{|}{C}}}-L \xrightarrow{-L^-} -\overset{H}{\underset{R}{\overset{|}{C}}}-\overset{R}{\underset{|}{\overset{|}{C}}}^+$$

$$\xrightarrow[S_N1]{R'OH} -\overset{H}{\underset{|}{\overset{|}{C}}}-\overset{R}{\underset{R}{\overset{|}{C}}}-O-R^+$$

$$\xrightarrow[E1]{-H^+} \quad C=C\overset{R}{\underset{R}{}}$$

SUMMARY OF IMPORTANT REACTION PATHWAYS ACCORDING TO THE TYPE OF SUBSTRATE.

CH_3X	RCH_2X	R | RCHX	R | R–C–X | R
Methyl	1°	2°	3°
← ——— Bimolecular reactions only ———→			← $S_N1/E1$ or E2 →
Gives S_N2 reactions.	Gives mainly S_N2 except with a hindered strong base and then gives mainly E2.	Gives mainly S_N2 with weak bases and mainly E2 with strong bases.	No S_N2 reaction. In solvolysis gives S_N1/E_1, and at lower temperatures S_N1 predominates. When a strong base is used, E2 predominates.

SOME SYNTHETICALLY USEFUL S_N2 REACTIONS

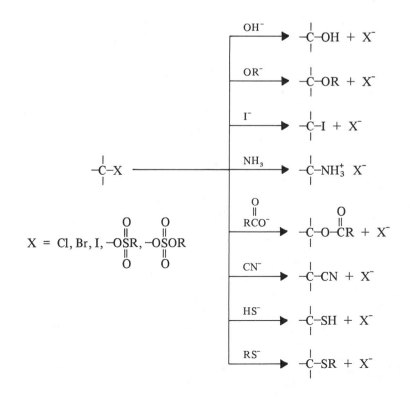

SOLUTIONS TO PROBLEMS

5.1   (a) $CH_3CH_2\overset{\cdot\cdot}{\underset{\cdot\cdot}{O}}$–H ,   (b) $CH_3CH_2\overset{\cdot\cdot}{\underset{\cdot\cdot}{O}}{:}^-$,

(c) $H-\overset{\cdot\cdot}{\underset{|\,H}{N}}-H$,   (d) $CH_3-\overset{\cdot\cdot}{\underset{|\,H}{N}}-H$,

(e) $^-{:}\,CN\,{:}$,   (f) $CH_3\overset{\displaystyle {:}\overset{\cdot\cdot}{O}}{\underset{\|}{C}}-\overset{\cdot\cdot}{\underset{\cdot\cdot}{O}}$–H ,

(g) $CH_3-\overset{\displaystyle {:}\overset{\cdot\cdot}{O}}{\underset{\|}{C}}-\overset{\cdot\cdot}{\underset{\cdot\cdot}{O}}{:}^-$,   (h) $H-\overset{\displaystyle {:}\overset{\cdot\cdot}{O}}{\underset{\|}{C}}-\overset{\cdot\cdot}{\underset{\cdot\cdot}{O}}$–H ,

(i) $H-\overset{\displaystyle {:}\overset{\cdot\cdot}{O}}{\underset{\|}{C}}-\overset{\cdot\cdot}{\underset{\cdot\cdot}{O}}{:}^-$,   (j) $CH_3CH_2-\overset{\cdot\cdot}{\underset{\cdot\cdot}{S}}$–H ,

(k) $CH_3CH_2-\overset{\cdot\cdot}{\underset{\cdot\cdot}{S}}{:}^-$,   (l) $^-{:}\,\overset{\cdot\cdot}{N}{=}\overset{+}{N}{=}\overset{\cdot\cdot}{N}\,{:}^-$

5.2    , *cis*-3-Methylcyclopentanol

5.3   (a)

(b) Because the carbocation is planar, the nucleophile, H_2O, may approach from above or below the plane:

$$\text{CH}_3\overset{}{\diagdown}\!\!\!\diagup\quad\text{CH}_3 \qquad + \qquad \text{CH}_3\overset{}{\diagdown}\!\!\!\diagup\quad\text{OH}$$

CH₃ ⟍ CH₃   +   CH₃ ⟍ OH
  H   OH   H   CH₃

5.4   (a) $CH_3\overset{\displaystyle CH_3}{\underset{\displaystyle CH_3}{\underset{|}{\overset{|}{C}}}}-OCH_2CH_3$

(b) $CH_3\overset{\overset{\displaystyle CH_3}{|}}{\underset{\underset{\displaystyle CH_3}{|}}{C}}-Cl \; \underset{slow}{\rightleftharpoons} \; CH_3\overset{\overset{\displaystyle CH_3}{|}}{\underset{\underset{\displaystyle CH_3}{|}}{C}}+ \;\;\; + \; Cl^-$

$CH_3\overset{\overset{\displaystyle CH_3}{|}}{\underset{\underset{\displaystyle CH_3}{|}}{C}}{}^+ \;\;\; + \; CH_3CH_2\overset{..}{\underset{..}{O}}H \; \underset{}{\overset{fast}{\rightleftharpoons}} \; CH_3\overset{\overset{\displaystyle CH_3\,H}{|\;\;|}}{\underset{\underset{\displaystyle CH_3}{|}}{C}}-\overset{+}{\underset{..}{O}}CH_2CH_3$

$CH_3\overset{\overset{\displaystyle CH_3\,H}{|\;\;|}}{\underset{\underset{\displaystyle CH_3}{|}}{C}}-\overset{+}{\underset{..}{O}}CH_2CH_3 \; + \; CH_3CH_2OH \; \overset{fast}{\rightleftharpoons} \; CH_3\overset{\overset{\displaystyle CH_3}{|}}{\underset{\underset{\displaystyle CH_3}{|}}{C}}-OCH_2CH_3 \; + \; CH_3CH_2\overset{+}{O}H_2$

5.5 **Protic solvents** are those that have an $-H$ bonded to an oxygen or nitrogen (or to another strongly electronegative atom). Therefore, the protic solvents are: Formic acid, $H\overset{\overset{\displaystyle O}{||}}{C}OH$;
formamide $H\overset{\overset{\displaystyle O}{||}}{C}NH_2$; ammonia, NH_3, and ethylene glycol, $HOCH_2CH_2OH$.

Aprotic solvents lack an $-H$ bonded to a strongly electronegative element. Aprotic solvents in this list are: Acetone, $CH_3\overset{\overset{\displaystyle O}{||}}{C}CH_3$; acetonitrile $CH_3C{\equiv}N$; sulfur dioxide, SO_2; and trimethylamine, $N(CH_3)_3$.

5.6 The reaction is an S_N2 reaction. In the polar aprotic solvent (DMF), the nucleophile (CN^-) will be relatively unencumbered by solvent molecules, and, therefore, it will be more reactive than in ethanol. As a result, the reaction will occur faster in dimethylformamide.

5.7 In (a) and (b) the base is a better nucleophile than its conjugate acid. In (c) the determining factor is the size of the atoms in the same group in the periodic table: $P > N$.

(a) NH_2^-,   (b) RS^-,   (c) PH_3

5.8 (a) Increasing the percentage of water in the mixture increases the polarity of the solvent. (Water is more polar than methanol.) Increasing the polarity of the solvent increases the rate of the solvolysis because separated charges develop in the transition state. The more polar the solvent, the more the transition state is stabilized (Sect. 5.11D, page 198).

(b) In an S_N2 reaction of this type, the charge becomes dispersed in the transition state:

$$I^- + CH_3CH_2-Cl \longrightarrow \overset{\overset{\displaystyle CH_3}{|}}{\underset{}{I\text{-}\text{-}\text{-}CH_2\text{-}\text{-}\text{-}Cl}} \longrightarrow ICH_2CH_3 + Cl^-$$

Reactants   Transition state
Charge is   *Charge is dispersed*
concentrated

Increasing the polarity of the solvent increases the stabilization of the reactant I^- more than the stabilization of the transition state, and thereby increases the energy of activation, thus decreasing the rate of reaction.

5.9   In the forward reaction, Cl^- is the leaving group; in the reverse reaction, OH^- would have

$$HO^- + CH_3-Cl \underset{\longleftarrow}{\overset{\longrightarrow}{\;\;\not\;\;}} Cl^- + CH_3OH$$

to be the leaving group. OH^- is very basic and therefore is such a poor leaving group that, for all practical purposes, the reverse reaction does not occur.

5.10   (a)

$$^-OOCCHCH_2CH_2-\overset{..}{\underset{..}{S}}-CH_2$$

$\underset{NH_3^+}{|}$

Adenine

OH   OH

(b)

$$^-OOCCHCH_2CH_2-\overset{..}{\underset{..}{S}}:^-$$

$\underset{NH_3^+}{|}$

(c) The leaving group (a) is a weaker base than (b), therefore (a) is the better leaving group. The reaction with methionine would be much slower than the reaction with S-adenosylmethionine.

5.11   (a) $CH_3CH_2CH_2Br + NaOH \longrightarrow CH_3CH_2CH_2OH + NaBr$

      (b) $CH_3CH_2CH_2Br + NaI \longrightarrow CH_3CH_2CH_2I + NaBr$

      (c) $CH_3CH_2CH_2Br + CH_3CH_2ONa \longrightarrow CH_3CH_2CH_2-O-CH_2CH_3 + NaBr$

      (d) $CH_3CH_2CH_2Br + CH_3SNa \longrightarrow CH_3CH_2CH_2-S-CH_3 + NaBr$

      (e) $CH_3CH_2CH_2Br + CH_3\overset{\overset{\displaystyle O}{\|}}{C}-ONa \longrightarrow CH_3CH_2CH_2-O-\overset{\overset{\displaystyle O}{\|}}{C}CH_3$

      (f) $CH_3CH_2CH_2Br + NaN_3 \longrightarrow CH_3CH_2CH_2N_3 + NaBr$

      (g) $CH_3CH_2CH_2Br + :N(CH_3)_3 \longrightarrow CH_3CH_2CH_2-\overset{\overset{\displaystyle CH_3}{|}}{\underset{\underset{\displaystyle CH_3}{|}}{N^+}}-CH_3 \; Br^-$

      (h) $CH_3CH_2CH_2Br + NaCN \longrightarrow CH_3CH_2CH_2CN + NaBr$

      (i) $CH_3CH_2CH_2Br + NaSH \longrightarrow CH_3CH_2CH_2SH + NaBr$

5.12 (a) $CH_3CH_2CH_2CH_2Br$ because 1° halides are less hindered than 2° halides.

(b) $CH_3CH_2\underset{\underset{\displaystyle Br}{|}}{C}HCH_3$ because 2° halides are less hindered than 3° halides.

(c) $CH_3CH_2CH_2Br$ because a bromide ion is a better leaving group than a chloride ion.

(d) $CH_3\underset{\underset{\displaystyle CH_3}{|}}{C}HCH_2CH_2Br$ because it is less hindered than $CH_3CH_2\underset{\underset{\displaystyle CH_3}{|}}{C}HCH_2Br$

(e) CH_3CH_2Cl because vinyl halides ($CH_2=CHCl$) are very unreactive.

5.13 (a) The second because CH_3O^- is a better nucleophile than CH_3OH.

(b) The second because SH^- is a better nucleophile than OH^-.

(c) The second because CH_3SH is a better nucleophile than CH_3OH.

(d) The second, CH_3S^- (2.0 molar), because the rate is proportional to $[CH_3S^-]$ as well as to $[CH_3CH_2I]$.

5.14 (a) The first because I^- is a better leaving group than Cl^-.

(b) The first because H_2O is a more polar solvent than CH_3OH.

(c) Both the same because $[CH_3O^-]$ does not affect the rate of an S_N1 reaction.

(d) The first because vinylic halides are unreactive.

5.15 Possible methods are given below—

(a) $CH_4 \underset{h\nu,\ heat}{\overset{Cl_2}{\longrightarrow}} CH_3Cl \underset{\substack{CH_3OH \\ (S_N2)}}{\overset{I^-}{\longrightarrow}} CH_3I$
     (excess)

(b) $CH_3CH_3 \underset{h\nu,\ heat}{\overset{Cl_2}{\longrightarrow}} CH_3CH_2Cl \underset{\substack{CH_3OH \\ (S_N2)}}{\overset{I^-}{\longrightarrow}} CH_3CH_2I$
     (excess)

(c) $CH_3Cl \underset{\substack{CH_3OH/H_2O \\ (S_N2)}}{\overset{OH^-}{\longrightarrow}} CH_3OH$

(d) $CH_3CH_2Cl \underset{\substack{CH_3OH/H_2O \\ (S_N2)}}{\overset{OH^-}{\longrightarrow}} CH_3CH_2OH$

(e) $CH_3Cl \underset{\substack{CH_3OH \\ (S_N2)}}{\overset{SH^-}{\longrightarrow}} CH_3SH$

(f) $CH_3CH_2Cl \underset{\substack{CH_3OH \\ (S_N2)}}{\overset{SH^-}{\longrightarrow}} CH_3CH_2SH$

(g) $CH_3Cl \xrightarrow[DMF]{CN^-} CH_3CN$

(h) $CH_3CH_2Cl \xrightarrow[DMF]{CN^-} CH_3CH_2CN$

(i) $CH_3I \xrightarrow{Li} CH_3Li \xrightarrow{CuI} (CH_3)_2CuLi \xrightarrow{CH_3CH_2I} CH_3CH_2CH_3$

(j) $CH_3OH \xrightarrow[(-H_2)]{NaH} CH_3ONa \xrightarrow[CH_3OH]{CH_3I} CH_3OCH_3$

(k) $CH_3CH_2I \xrightarrow{Li} CH_3CH_2Li \xrightarrow{CuI} (CH_3CH_2)_2CuLi \xrightarrow{CH_3CH_2I}$

$CH_3CH_2CH_2CH_3$

(l) $CH_3CH_2OH \xrightarrow[(-H_2)]{NaH} CH_3CH_2ONa \xrightarrow{CH_3I} CH_3CH_2OCH_3$

(m) $\xrightarrow[hv,\ heat]{Cl_2}$ $\xrightarrow[CH_3CH_2OH]{CH_3CH_2ONa}$
(excess)

(n) $\xrightarrow{I^-}$ $\xrightarrow{(CH_3)_2CuLi}$

(o) $\xrightarrow{(CH_3CH_2)_2CuLi}$

(p) $CH_3CH_2CH_3 \xrightarrow[hv,\ heat]{Br_2} CH_3CH_2CH_2Br + CH_3\underset{\underset{Br}{|}}{C}HCH_3 \xrightarrow[CH_3CH_2OH]{CH_3CH_2ONa}$
(excess)

$CH_2=CHCH_3$

5.16

(a) $CH_3\underset{\underset{CH_3}{|}}{C}HCH_3 \xrightarrow[hv,\ heat]{Br_2} CH_3\underset{\underset{Br}{|}}{\overset{\overset{CH_3}{|}}{C}}CH_3 \xrightarrow{Li} CH_3\underset{\underset{Li}{|}}{\overset{\overset{CH_3}{|}}{C}}CH_3 \xrightarrow{CuI} \left[CH_3\underset{\underset{CH_3}{|}}{\overset{\overset{CH_3}{|}}{C}}- \right]_2 CuLi$
(excess)

$\xrightarrow{CH_3I} CH_3\underset{\underset{CH_3}{|}}{\overset{\overset{CH_3}{|}}{C}}CH_3$

(b) $CH_3\overset{\underset{\displaystyle CH_3}{|}}{\underset{\underset{\displaystyle CH_3}{|}}{C}}\!-Br \xrightarrow{Li} CH_3\overset{\underset{\displaystyle CH_3}{|}}{\underset{\underset{\displaystyle CH_3}{|}}{C}}\!-Li \xrightarrow{CuI} \left[CH_3\overset{\underset{\displaystyle CH_3}{|}}{\underset{\underset{\displaystyle CH_3}{|}}{C}}\!- \right]_2 CuLi \xrightarrow{CH_3CH_2I}$

$CH_3\overset{\underset{\displaystyle CH_3}{|}}{\underset{\underset{\displaystyle CH_3}{|}}{C}}\!-CH_2CH_3$

5.17 (a) $H\!:^-$ is a very strong base and therefore is an extremely poor leaving group.

(b) $:CH_3^-$ is a very strong base and therefore is an extremely poor leaving group.

(c) $-\ddot{C}H_2^-$ is a very strong base and an extremely poor leaving group.

(d) With a relatively strong base like CN^-, elimination would predominate to yield $CH_2=C(CH_3)_2 + HCN + Br^-$. S_N2 attack cannot take place at the $3°$ carbon.

(e) Vinylic halides are unreactive in S_N1 and S_N2 reactions.

(f) CH_3O^- is a strong base and therefore a poor leaving group.

(g) $CH_3CH_2\overset{+}{O}H_2$ is a strong acid and would react with NH_3 to convert it to NH_4^+ which is not a nucleophile.

(h) $CH_3:^-$ would react with the acidic proton in CH_3CH_2OH to form $CH_4 + CH_3CH_2O^-$.

5.18 $CH_3CHBrCH_3$ because a $2°$ halide is less likely to give an S_N2 reaction than a $1°$ halide, and therefore an E2 reaction (dehydrohalogenation) would be more likely to predominate.

5.19 Method (2) would be better because the substrate for the S_N2 reaction is a methyl halide. In method (1), because the substrate is a $2°$ halide, considerable (predominant) elimination (E2) would accompany the S_N2 reaction.

5.20 (a) $CH_3CH_2CH_2CH_2OCH_3$ (major) by S_N2; $CH_3CH_2CH=CH_2$ (minor) by E2.

(b) $CH_3CH_2CH_2CH_2-OC(CH_3)_3$ (minor) by S_N2; $CH_3CH_2CH=CH_2$ (major) by E2.

(c) $CH_3-O-C(CH_3)_3$ (only product) by S_N2.

(d) $CH_2=C(CH_3)_2$ (only product) by E2.

(e) (major) by E2; (minor) by S_N2.

(f) + (major products) by S_N1;

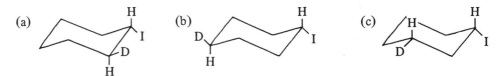

(minor products) by E1 reaction

(g) $CH_3CH=CHCH_2CH_3$ (major) by E2; $CH_3CH_2\underset{\underset{OC_2H_5}{|}}{C}HCH_2CH_3$ (minor) by S_N2.

(h) $CH_2=CHCH_3$ (major) by E2; $CH_3\underset{\underset{OC(CH_3)_3}{|}}{C}HCH_3$ (minor) by S_N2.

5.21   (a), (b), and (c) are all S_N2 reactions and, therefore, proceed with inversion of configuration: The products are:

(a)

(b)

(c)

(d) is an S_N1 reaction. The carbocation that forms can react with either nucleophile (H_2O or CH_3OH) from either the top or bottom side of the molecule. Four substitution products (below) would be obtained. (Considerable elimination by an E1 path would also occur.)

5.22   Isobutyl bromide is more sterically hindered than ethyl bromide because of the methyl groups on the β carbon.

Isobutyl bromide   Ethyl bromide

This steric hindrance causes isobutyl bromide to react more slowly in S_N2 reactions and to give relatively more elimination (by an E2 path) when a strong base is used.

5.23   (a) S_N2 because the substrate is a 1° halide.

(b) Rate $= k$ $[CH_3CH_2Cl]$ $[I^-]$

$= 5 \times 10^{-5}$ liter mole^{-1} sec^{-1} $\times 0.1$ mole liter^{-1} $\times 0.1$ mole liter^{-1}

Rate $= 5 \times 10^{-7}$ mole liter^{-1} sec^{-1}

(c) 1×10^{-6} mole liter^{-1} sec^{-1}

(d) 1×10^{-6} mole liter^{-1} sec^{-1}

(e) 2×10^{-6} mole liter^{-1} sec^{-1}

5.24   (a) CH_3NH^- because it is the stronger base.

(b) CH_3O^- because it is the stronger base.

(c) CH_3SH because sulfur atoms are larger and more polarizable than oxygen atoms.

(d) $(C_6H_5)_3P$ because phosphorus atoms are larger and more polarizable than nitrogen atoms.

(e) H_2O because it is the stronger base.

(f) NH_3 because it is the stronger base.

(g) HS^- because it is the stronger base.

(h) OH^- because it is the stronger base.

5.25

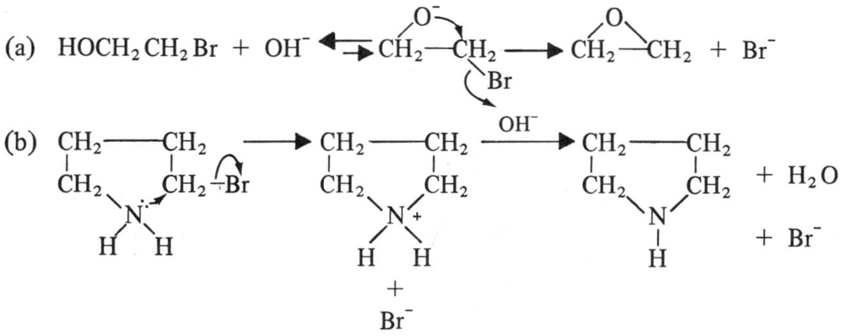

(a) $HOCH_2CH_2Br + OH^- \rightleftharpoons$

(b)

5.26   Iodide ion is a good nucleophile and a good leaving group; it can rapidly convert an alkyl chloride or alkyl bromide into an alkyl iodide, and the alkyl iodide can then react rapidly with another nucleophile. With methyl bromide in water, for example, the following reaction can take place:

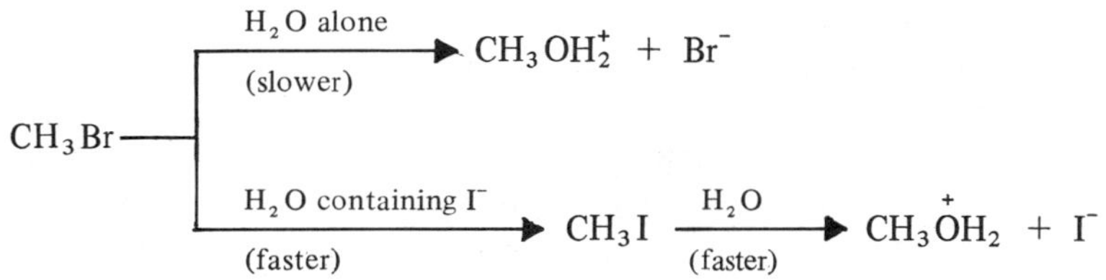

5.27   The rate of formation of *tert*-butyl alcohol does not increase with increasing [OH⁻] because the reaction is S_N1 and is therefore independent of [OH⁻]. Increasing [OH⁻], however, increases the rate of the competing E2 reaction which consumes OH⁻ through the conversion of *tert*-butyl chloride into $CH_2=C(CH_3)_2$.

5.28   (a)   Use a strong, hindered base such as $(CH_3)_3COK$ in a solvent of low polarity in order to bring about an E2 reaction.

(b)   Here we want an S_N1 reaction. We use ethanol as the solvent *and as the nucleophile*, and we carry out the reaction at a low temperature so that elimination will be minimized.

5.29   (a)   Backside attack by the nucleophile is prevented by the cyclic structure. (Notice, too, that the carbon bearing the leaving group is tertiary.)

(b)   The bridged cyclic structure prevents the carbon bearing the leaving group from assuming the planar trigonal conformation required of a carbocation.

5.30   The products are

$$H\!:\!\overset{\overset{\textstyle H}{..}}{\underset{\underset{\textstyle H}{..}}{C}}\!:\!C\!:\!:\!:\!N\!: \quad \text{and} \quad H\!:\!\overset{\overset{\textstyle H}{..}}{\underset{\underset{\textstyle H}{..}}{C}}\!:\!\overset{+}{N}\!:\!:\!:\!\overset{-}{C}\!:$$

The nucleophile can be described by resonance structures that place a pair of electrons and a formal negative charge on either atom: $\;\overset{-}{:}C\!:\!:\!:\!N\!: \longleftrightarrow :C\!:\!:\!\overset{..}{N}\overset{-}{:}$. Thus both atoms are nucleophilic.

5.31   (a)   Since the halides are all primary, these are almost certainly S_N2 reactions with ethanol acting as the nucleophile.

$$C_2H_5\overset{..}{O}H \;+\; \overset{R}{\underset{\underset{\textstyle H}{H}}{C}}\!-\!Br \;\xrightarrow[-HBr]{}\; C_2H_5O\!-\!\overset{R}{\underset{H}{C}}H$$

(b)   Increasing the size of the R group increases steric hindrance to the approaching ethanol molecule and decreases the rate of reaction.

5.32   (a)   This is another example of the relation between reactivity and selectivity that we first encountered in Chapter 4: generally speaking, highly reactive species are relatively unselective while less reactive species are more selective. In an S_N1 reaction the species that reacts with the nucleophile is a *carbocation*—a species that is electron deficient and thus is *highly reactive*. A carbocation, therefore, shows little tendency to discriminate between weak and strong nucleophiles—most often it simply reacts with the first nucleophile that it encounters. In S_N2 reactions, on the other hand, the species that reacts with the nucleophile is an alkyl halide or an alkyl tosylate. Such compounds are far less reactive toward nucleophiles than carbocations and they show much greater nucleophilic selectivities. An alkyl halide molecule, for example, might collide with a weak nucleophile thousands of times before a reaction takes place because few of the collisions will have sufficient energy to allow the weak nucleophile to displace the leaving group. On the other hand, an alkyl halide molecule might collide with a strong nucleophile only a few times before a collison leads to a reaction. This will be true because the strong nucleophile is better able to displace the leaving group and therefore a larger fraction of collisions will have sufficient energy to be fruitful.

(b) The reaction of $CH_3CH_2CH_2CH_2Cl$ is an S_N2 reaction and thus $CH_3CH_2CH_2CH_2Cl$ discriminates very effectively between the strongly nucleophilic CN^- ions and the weakly nucleophilic solvent molecules. By contrast, the reaction of $(CH_3)_3CCl$ is an S_N1 reaction and the carbocation that is formed shows little tendency to discriminate between solvent molecules and CN^- ions. Since solvent molecules are present in a much higher concentration the major product is $(CH_3)_3C\text{-}OCH_2CH_3$.

5.33 The rate-determining step in the S_N1 reaction of *tert*-butyl bromide is the following:

$$(CH_3)_3C\text{-}Br \underset{\text{X}}{\overset{\text{slow}}{\rightleftarrows}} (CH_3)_3C^+ \quad + \quad Br^-$$

$$\xrightarrow[\text{H}_2\text{O}]{} (CH_3)_3COH_2^+$$

$(CH_3)_3C^+$ is so unstable that it reacts almost immediately with one of the surrounding water molecules and, for all practical purposes, no reverse reaction with Br^- takes place. Adding a common ion (Br^- from NaBr) therefore, has no effect on the rate.

Because the $(C_6H_5)_2CH^+$ cation is more stable, a reversible first step occurs and

$$(C_6H_5)_2CHBr \rightleftarrows (C_6H_5)_2CH^+ + Br^-$$

$$\xrightarrow[\text{H}_2\text{O}]{} (C_6H_5)_2CHOH_2^+$$

adding a common ion (Br^-) slows the overall reaction by increasing the rate at which $(C_6H_5)_2CH^+$ is converted back to $(C_6H_5)_2CHBr$.

5.34 Two different mechanisms are involved. $(CH_3)_3CBr$ reacts by an S_N1 mechanism and apparently this reaction takes place fastest. The other three alkyl halides react by an S_N2 mechanism and their reactions are slower because the nucleophile (H_2O) is weak. The reaction rates of CH_3Br, CH_3CH_2Br, and $(CH_3)_2CHBr$ are affected by the steric hindrance and thus their order of reactivity is $CH_3Br > CH_3CH_2Br > (CH_3)_2CHBr$.

SECTION REFERENCES FOR ADDITIONAL PROBLEMS

5.21 5.8A, 5.10A		**5.28** 5.16B	
5.22 5.11		**5.29** 5.11A	
5.23 5.6A, 5.11		**5.30** 1.6	
5.24 5.11B		**5.31** 5.11A	
5.25 5.5		**5.32** 5.8, 5.9, 5.10	
5.26 5.11E		**5.33** 5.9, 5.10, 5.11	
5.27 5.16B		**5.34** 5.11	

SELF-TEST

5.1   Using CF_4 as reactant write equations using Lewis dot formulas to show each of the following.

(a)   Homolytic cleavage

(b)   The most reasonable type of heterolytic cleavage

(c)   The least reasonable type of heterolytic cleavage

5.2   Mark the following statements true or false for each of the four mechanisms shown. (Use + for true, – for false, and 0 for impossible to tell.)

	S_N1	S_N2	E1 (carbocation)	E2
(a) The reaction shows first-order kinetics				
(b) The rate of reaction depends markedly on the nucleophilicity or basicity of the attacking nucleophile				

	S_N1	S_N2	E1 (carbocation)	E2
(c) The mechanism involves one step				
(d) Carbocations are intermediates				
(e) The rate of reaction is proportional to the concentration of the attacking nucleophile or base				
(f) The rate of reaction depends on the nature of the leaving group				

5.3 (a) Give the structural formula of the product of the following S_N2 reaction:

$CH_3CH_2O^-$ +   [structure]   ⟶   [   ]   + Br^-

(b) Complete the table below for the reaction above.

Expt. No.	$[CH_3CH_2O^-]$	$[RBr]$	Initial Rate of Formation of S_N2 Product
1	0.1 Molar	0.1 Molar	0.01 mole/liter/sec.
2	0.2 Molar	0.2 Molar	
3	0.1 Molar	0.2 Molar	

(c) The structural formula of the other organic product in the reaction above is

(d) The favored reaction is

5.4 Mark the following statements true (+) or false (−).

(a) If we want to convert *tert*-butyl chloride into *tert*-butyl alcohol with the least amount of byproducts, we should use a polar solvent like water and a very weak base, preferably water itself. ☐

(b) If we heat 1-bromobutane with NaOH in ethanol as solvent, the major product will be 1-butene. ☐

(c) The conditions described in (a) should encourage the S_N2 mechanism rather than the S_N1 mechanism. ☐

(d) The conditions described in (b) should favor bimolecular mechanisms rather than unimolecular mechanisms. ☐

SUPPLEMENTARY PROBLEMS

S5.1 Which alkyl halide below would you expect to react more rapidly in (a) an S_N2 mechanism, (b) an S_N1 mechanism?

(I)   II

S5.2 Which mechanism (S_N1, S_N2, E1, or E2) would you expect to predominate in the reactions below? Predict the major product in each.

(a) $\xrightarrow[\text{CH}_3\text{CH}_2\text{OH}]{\text{CH}_3\text{CH}_2\text{ONa}}$

(b) $\xrightarrow[\text{CH}_3\text{CH}_2\text{OH}]{\text{H}_2\text{O}}$

S5.3 Which reaction below would you expect to occur at a faster rate? Explain.

(a) $CH_3CH_2CH_2Cl \xrightarrow[\text{C}_2\text{H}_5\text{OH, 25°C}]{\text{C}_2\text{H}_5\text{ONa}} CH_3CH_2CH_2OC_2H_5 + NaCl$

(b) $CH_3CH_2CH_2I \xrightarrow[\text{C}_2\text{H}_5\text{OH, 25°C}]{\text{C}_2\text{H}_5\text{ONa}} CH_3CH_2CH_2OC_2H_5 + NaI$

SOLUTIONS TO SUPPLEMENTARY PROBLEMS

S5.1   The order of reactivity of alkyl halides is different in the two mechanisms:
S_N2: $CH_3X > 1°RX > 2°RX$ (3°RX do not react)
S_N1: 3°RX only. (2°RX and 1°RX do not react appreciably)
The answers are therefore (a) I, (b) II.

S5.2   (a)   The conditions of a strong base (nucleophile) and relatively nonpolar solvent favor the bimolecular mechanism. Since S_N2 does not occur with 3° RX's, the expected reaction is E2 to yield ⬠-CH₃ as the major product.

(b)   The conditions of a weak base (nucleophile) and a highly polar solvent (H_2O) favor the monomolecular mechanism. S_N1 usually predominates over E1, so the major products are ⬠ and ⬠

S5.3   Reaction (b) is faster because I⁻ is a better leaving group than Cl⁻. All other factors are the same in the two reactions.

6
ALKENES: STRUCTURE AND SYNTHESIS

SUMMARY OF SYNTHESES OF ALKENES

SOLUTIONS TO PROBLEMS

6.1 (a) 2-Methyl-2-butene   (c) 1-Bromo-2-methylpropene

(b) *cis*-4-Octene   (d) 4-Methylcyclohexene

6.2 (a), (b), (c), (d), (e)

(f)

CH_3

(g) $CH_3(CH_2)_4CHCH=CH_2$
$\quad\quad\quad\quad\quad\quad |$
$\quad\quad\quad\quad\quad\quad Cl$

(h) CH_3
$\quad\quad CH_3$

(i) CH_3
$\quad\quad\quad CH_3$

(j) Br
$\quad\quad Br$

6.3   Absorption of a photon of the correct frequency can excite a π electron into an anti-bonding orbital. Such an orbital has a nodal plane between the carbon atoms, thus rotation about the C—C bond can occur (see page 221).

6.4   (a) C_6H_{14} = formula of alkane
$\underline{C_6H_{12}}$ = formula of 2-hexene

$\quad H_2$ = difference = 1 pair of hydrogens.
Index of hydrogen deficiency = 1

(b) C_6H_{14} = formula of alkane
$\underline{C_6H_{12}}$ = formula of methylcyclopentane

$\quad H_2$ = difference = 1 pair of hydrogens.
Index of hydrogen deficiency = 1

(c)   No, all isomers of C_6H_{12}, for example, have the same index of hydrogen deficiency.

(d)   No.

(e) C_nH_{2n+2} = formula of alkane
$\underline{C_nH_{2n-2}}$ = formula of alkyne

$\quad H_4$ = difference = 2 pairs of hydrogens.
Index of hydrogen deficiency = 2

(f) $C_{10}H_{22}$ (alkane)
$\underline{C_{10}H_{16}}$ (compound)

$\quad H_6$ = difference = 3 pairs of hydrogens
Index of hydrogen deficiency = 3

The structural possibilities are thus

3 double bonds
1 double bond and one triple bond (See Sect. 9.1)
2 double bonds and 1 ring
1 double bond and 2 rings
3 rings
1 triple bond and one ring (See Sect. 9.1)

6.5   (a) $C_{15}H_{32}$ = formula of alkane

$\underline{C_{15}H_{24}}$ = formula of zingiberene

H_8 = difference = 4 pairs of hydrogens

Index of hydrogen deficiency = 4

(b)   Since one mole of zingiberene absorbs three moles of hydrogen, one molecule of zingiberene must contain three double bonds. (We are told that molecules of zingiberene do not contain any triple bonds.)

(c)   If a molecule of zingiberene has three double bonds and an index of hydrogen deficiency equal to 4, it must have one ring. (The structural formula for zingiberene can be found in Problem 22.3.)

6.6   (a), (b)

$$CH_2{=}\overset{\overset{\displaystyle CH_3}{|}}{C}CH_2CH_3 \xrightarrow[\text{Pt}]{H_2} CH_3\overset{\overset{\displaystyle CH_3}{|}}{C}HCH_2CH_3 \qquad \Delta H° = -28.5 \text{ kcal/mole}$$

2-Methyl-1-butene
(disubstituted)

$$CH_3\overset{\overset{\displaystyle CH_3}{|}}{C}HCH{=}CH_2 \xrightarrow[\text{Pt}]{H_2} CH_3\overset{\overset{\displaystyle CH_3}{|}}{C}HCH_2CH_3 \quad \Delta H° = -30.3 \text{ kcal/mole}$$

3-Methyl-1-butene
(monosubstituted)

$$CH_3\overset{\overset{\displaystyle CH_3}{|}}{C}{=}CHCH_3 \xrightarrow[\text{Pt}]{H_2} CH_3\overset{\overset{\displaystyle CH_3}{|}}{C}HCH_2CH_3 \quad \Delta H° = -26.9 \text{ kcal/mole}$$

2-Methyl-2-butene
(trisubstituted)

(c)   Yes, because hydrogenation converts each alkene to the same product.

(d) $CH_3\overset{\overset{\displaystyle CH_3}{|}}{C}{=}CHCH_3 \;>\; CH_2{=}\overset{\overset{\displaystyle CH_3}{|}}{C}CH_2CH_3 \;>\; CH_3\overset{\overset{\displaystyle CH_3}{|}}{C}HCH{=}CH_2$

(trisubstituted)   (disubstituted)   (monosubstituted)

Notice that this predicted order of stability is confirmed by the heats of hydrogenation. 2-Methyl-2-butene evolves the least heat, therefore, it is the most stable; 3-methyl-1-butene evolves the most heat, therefore, it is the least stable.

(e) $CH_2{=}CHCH_2CH_2CH_3$,

1-Pentene

cis-2-Pentene   trans-2-Pentene

(f)   Heats of combustion, because complete combustion would convert all of the alkenes to the same products. (All of these alkenes have the formula C_5H_{10}.)

$$C_5H_{10} + 7\tfrac{1}{2}O_2 \longrightarrow 5CO_2 + 5H_2O$$

6.7

(a)

$$\underset{\substack{\text{cis-2-Heptene}\\\text{(disubstituted)}\\\textit{More stable}}}{\underset{H}{\overset{CH_3}{}}C=C\underset{H}{\overset{CH_2(CH_2)_2CH_3}{}}} \quad > \quad \underset{\substack{\text{1-Heptene}\\\text{(monosubstituted)}\\\textit{Less stable}}}{CH_2{=}CH(CH_2)_4CH_3}$$

(b)

$$\underset{\substack{\text{trans-2-Heptene}\\\textit{More stable}}}{\underset{H}{\overset{CH_3}{}}C=C\underset{CH_2(CH_2)_2CH_3}{\overset{H}{}}} \quad > \quad \underset{\substack{\text{cis-2-Heptene}\\\textit{Less stable}}}{\underset{H}{\overset{CH_3}{}}C=C\underset{H}{\overset{CH_2(CH_2)_2CH_3}{}}}$$

(c)

$$\underset{\substack{\text{2-Methyl-2-hexene}\\\text{(trisubstituted)}\\\textit{More stable}}}{\underset{CH_3}{\overset{CH_3}{}}C=C\underset{CH_2CH_2CH_3}{\overset{H}{}}} \quad > \quad \underset{\substack{\text{trans-2-Heptene}\\\text{(disubstituted)}\\\textit{Less stable}}}{\underset{H}{\overset{CH_3}{}}C=C\underset{CH_2(CH_2)_2CH_3}{\overset{H}{}}}$$

(d)

$$\underset{\substack{\text{2,3-Dimethyl-2-pentene}\\\text{(tetrasubstituted)}\\\textit{More stable}}}{\underset{CH_3}{\overset{CH_3}{}}C=C\underset{CH_2CH_3}{\overset{CH_3}{}}} \quad > \quad \underset{\substack{\text{2-Methyl-2-hexene}\\\text{(trisubstituted)}\\\textit{Less stable}}}{\underset{CH_3}{\overset{CH_3}{}}C=C\underset{CH_2CH_2CH_3}{\overset{H}{}}}$$

6.8   You could use heats of hydrogenation to determine the relative stabilities of pairs (a) and (b). You would be required to use heats of combustion for pairs (c) and (d) because the members in pairs (c) and (d) give different alkanes on hydrogenation.

6.9   (a) 2-Butene, the more highly substituted alkene.   (b) *trans*-2-Butene.

6.10   An *anti* periplanar transition state allows the molecule to assume the more stable staggered conformation;

whereas, a *syn* periplanar transition state requires the molecule to assume the less stable eclipsed conformation:

6.11   *cis*-1-Bromo-4-*tert*-butylcyclohexane can assume an *anti* periplanar transition state in which the bulky *tert*-butyl group is equatorial:

The conformation (above), because it is relatively stable, is assumed by most of the molecules present, and, therefore, the reaction is rapid.

    On the other hand, for *trans*-1-bromo-4-*tert*-butycyclohexane to assume an *anti* periplanar transition state, the molecule must assume a conformation in which the large *tert*-butyl group is axial:

Such a conformation is of high energy; therefore very few molecules assume this conformation. The reaction, consequently, is very slow.

6.12   (a) *Anti*-periplanar elimination can occur in two ways with the cis isomer.

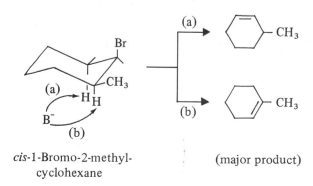

cis-1-Bromo-2-methyl-
cyclohexane
                                            (major product)

(b) *Anti* periplanar elimination can occur in only one way with the trans isomer.

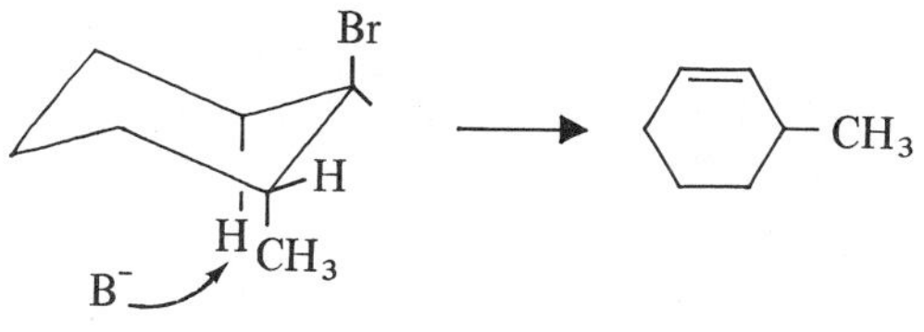

trans-Bromo-2-methyl-
cyclohexane

6.13 (a) Conformation (2) is more stable because in it the groups are more widely separated; therefore there is less repulsion.

(b) Conformation (2) should be more highly populated because it is more stable.

(c) Conformation (1) leads to *cis*-2-butene:

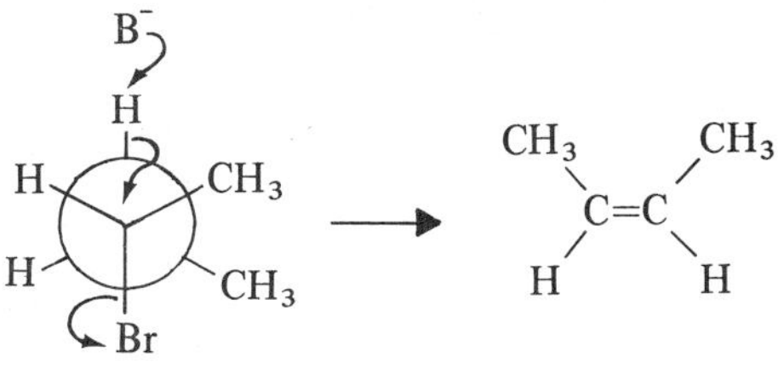

(1)

Conformation (2) leads to *trans*-2-butene:

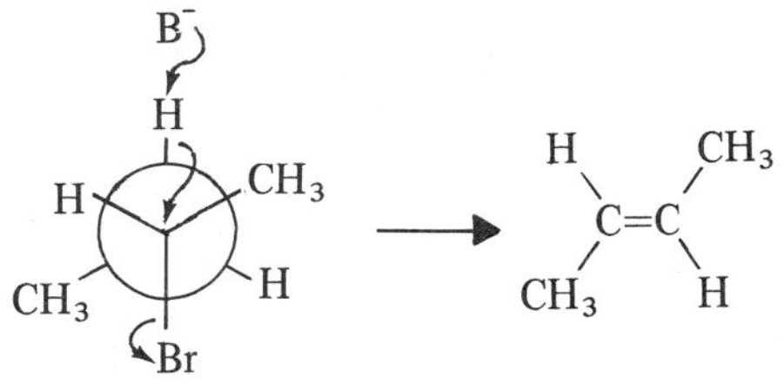

(2)

Because conformation (2) is more highly populated, *trans*-2-butene should be the major product.

6.14 (a) OH^-, a strong base and an extremely poor leaving group. (b) The acid catalyst reacts with the alcohol to form the protonated alcohol $R\overset{+}{O}H_2$. When this ion undergoes dehydration, the leaving group is a weakly basic H_2O molecule—a much better leaving group.

6.15   (1) $CH_3CHCH_2OH + H^+$ ⇌ $CH_3CHCH_2\overset{+}{O}H_2$
          | |
         CH_3 CH_3

(2) $CH_3CHCH_2\overset{+}{O}H_2$ ⇌ $CH_3CH\overset{+}{C}H_2$ $+ H_2O$
    | |
   CH_3 CH_3

1° Carbocation

(3) $CH_3CH\overset{+}{C}H_2$ ⟶ $CH_3CH{-}{-}CH_2$ ⟶ $CH_3\overset{+}{C}H{-}CH_2{-}CH_3$
    | |
   CH_3 CH_3 2° Carbocation

1° Carbocation   Transition state

(4) $CH_3{-}\overset{+}{C}H{-}CH{-}CH_3$ ⟶ $+ H_3\overset{+}{O}$

trans-2-Butene

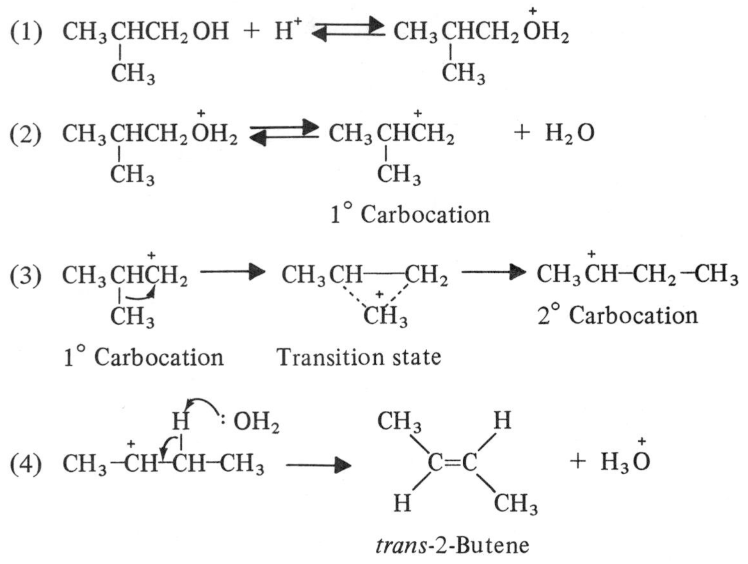

6.16   (a) No rearrangement of the carbon skeleton occurs, but we cannot rule out the occurrence of a hydride shift.

(b) Protonation followed by loss of water gives a secondary carbocation which can lose a proton two different ways:

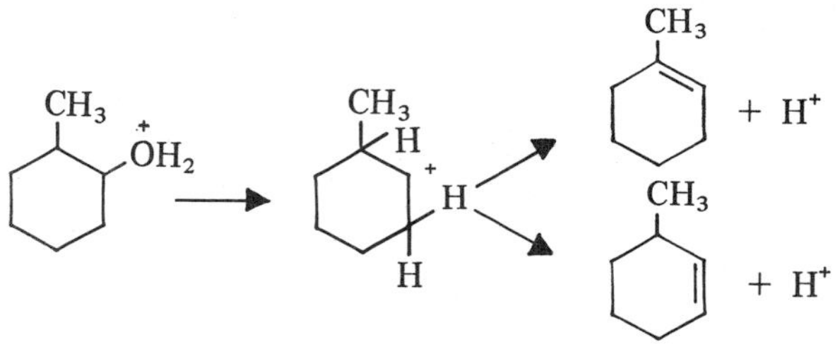

(c)   1-Methylcyclohexene is the major product because it is the more stable (more highly substituted) alkene.

6.17

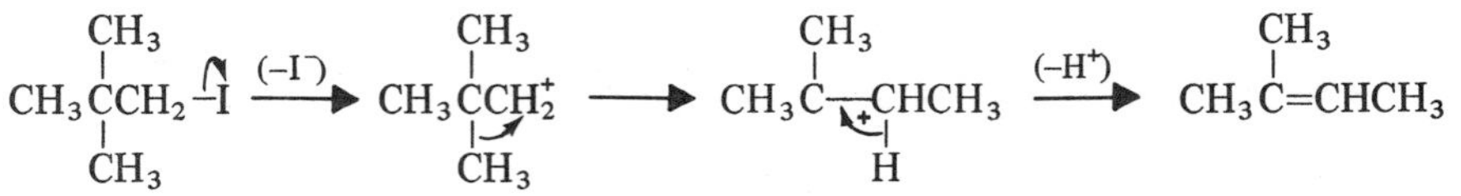

6.18

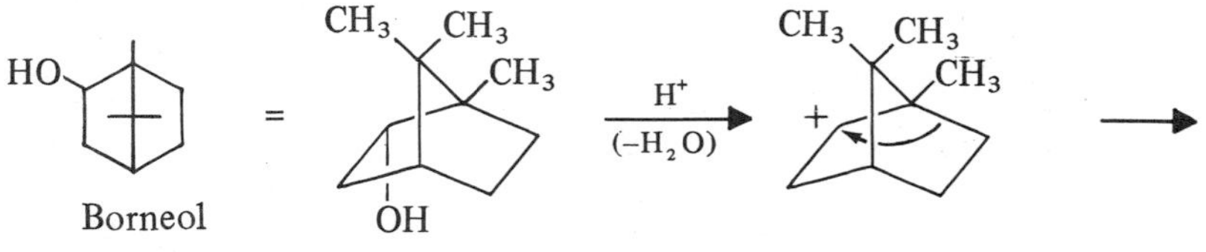

Camphene

6.19 (a) One must use the lower number to designate the location of the double bond.

cis-2-Pentene
(not *cis*-3-pentene)

(b) One must select the longest chain as the base name.

2, 3-Dimethyl-2-butene
(not 1,1,2,2-tetramethylethene)

(c) One must number the ring so as to give the carbons of the double bond numbers 1 and 2 *and to give the substituent the lower number.*

1-Methycycloheptene
(not 2-methycycloheptene)

(d) One must select the longest chain.

$$\begin{array}{cccccccc} 1 & 2 & 3 & 4 & 5 & 6 & 7 & 8 \end{array}$$
$$CH_3CH{=}CHCH_2\,CH_2\,CH_2\,CH_2\,CH_3$$

2-Octene
(not 1-methylheptene)

(e) One must number the chain from the other end. This choice gives the double bond the same number but it gives the methyl group a *lower* number.

$$\begin{array}{c} CH_3 \\ | \\ CH_3CH{=}CCH_3 \end{array}$$
$$\begin{array}{cccc} 4 & 3 & 2\,1 \end{array}$$

2-Methyl-2-butene
(not 3-methyl-2-butene)

(f) One must number the ring the other way. This choice gives the substituents lower numbers while retaining positions 1 and 2 for the double bond.

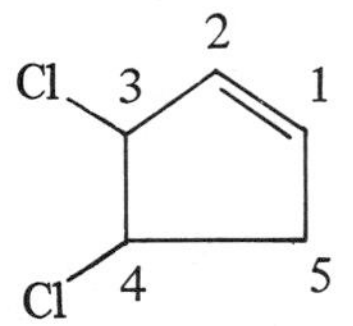

3,4-Dichlorocyclopentene
(not 4,5-dichlorocyclopentene)

6.20

(a)

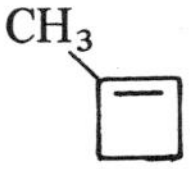

(b)

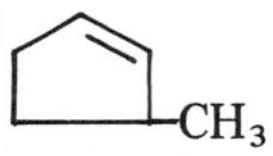

(c) 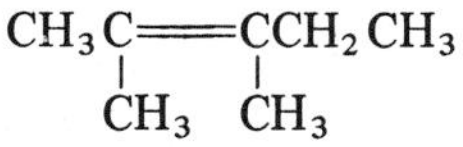 $CH_3C{=\!=\!=}CCH_2CH_3$ with CH_3 CH_3 below

(d)

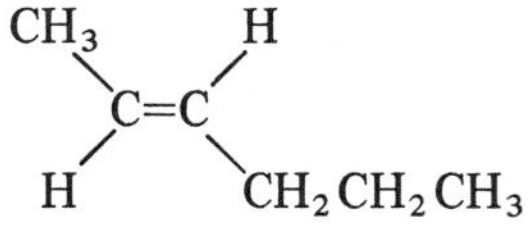

(e)

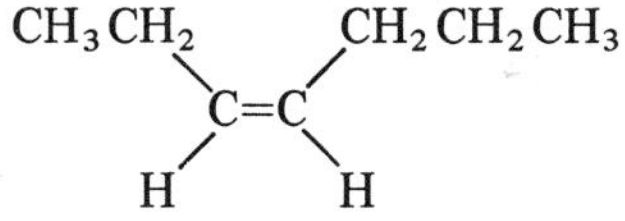

(f) $CH_2{=}CHCCl_3$ (g) 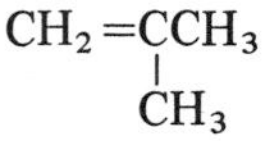 $CH_2{=}CCH_3$ with CH_3 below   (h) $CH_3CH{=}CH_2$

(i) 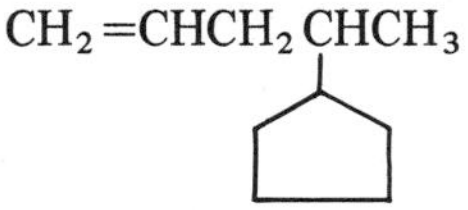 $CH_2{=}CHCH_2CHCH_3$ (j) 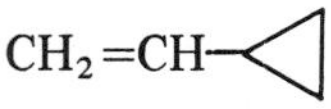 $CH_2{=}CH{-}$

6.21

(a) $CH_2{=}CHCH_2CH_2CH_3$

1-Pentene

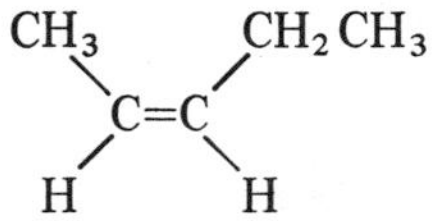

cis-2-Pentene

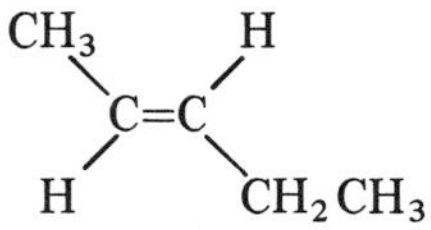

trans-2-Pentene

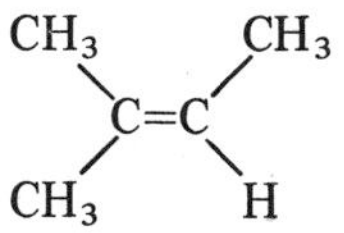

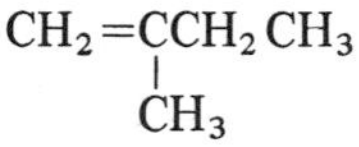

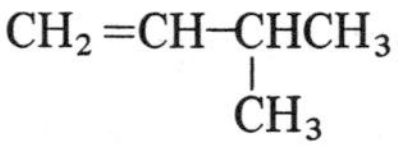

2-Methyl-2-butene

$CH_2{=}CCH_2CH_3$ with CH_3 below

2-Methyl-1-butene

$CH_2{=}CH{-}CHCH_3$ with CH_3 below

3-Methyl-1-butene

(b) $CH_2{=}CHCH_2CH_2CH_2CH_3$

1-Hexene

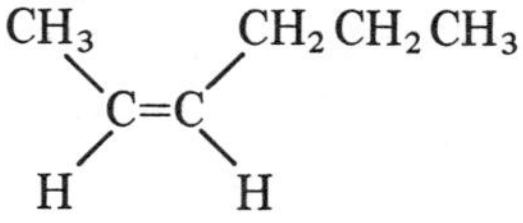

cis-2-Hexene

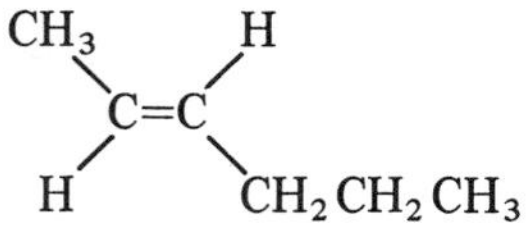

trans-2-Hexene

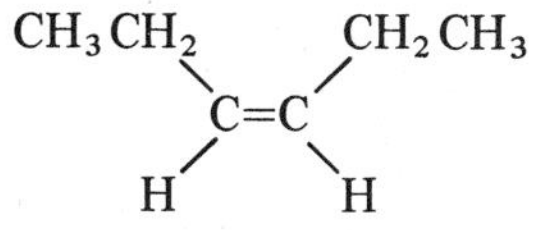
CH3CH2 CH2CH3
C=C
H H

cis-3-Hexene

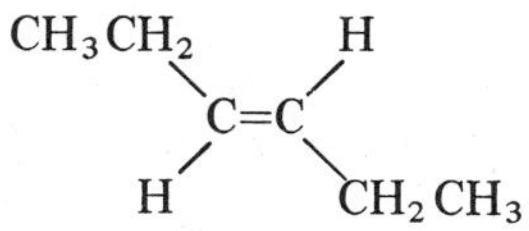
CH3CH2 H
C=C
H CH2CH3

trans-3-Hexene

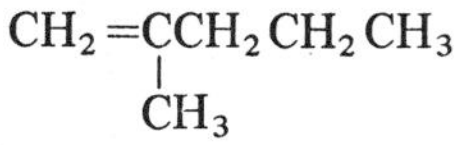
CH2=CCH2CH2CH3
CH3

2-Methyl-1-pentene

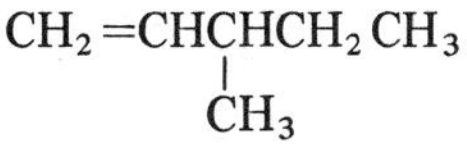
CH2=CHCHCH2CH3
CH3

3-Methyl-1-pentene

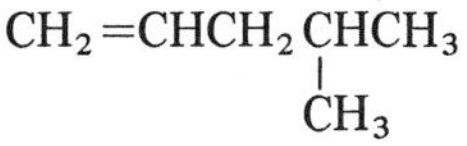
CH2=CHCH2CHCH3
CH3

4-Methyl-1-pentene

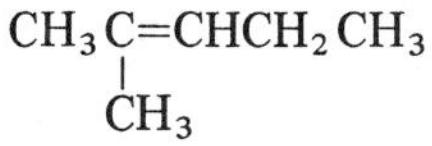
CH3C=CHCH2CH3
CH3

2-Methyl-2-pentene

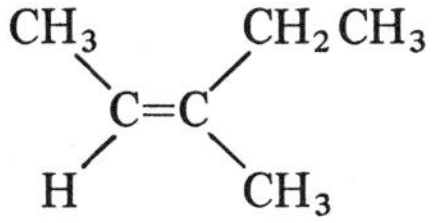
CH3 CH2CH3
C=C
H CH3

trans-3-Methyl-
2-pentene

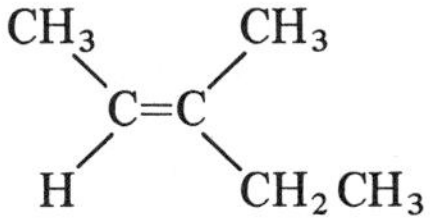
CH3 CH3
C=C
H CH2CH3

cis-3-Methyl-
2-pentene

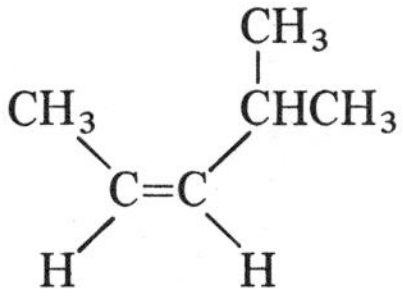
CH3
CH3 CHCH3
C=C
H H

cis-4-Methyl-
2-pentene

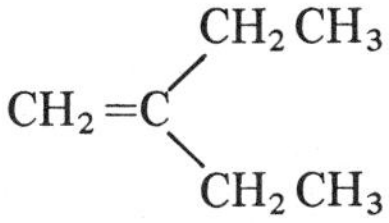
CH2CH3
CH2=C
CH2CH3

2-Ethyl-
1-butene

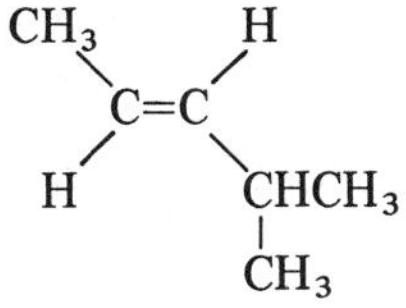
CH3 H
C=C
H CHCH3
CH3

trans-4-Methyl-
2-pentene

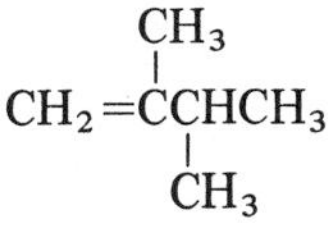
CH3
CH2=CCHCH3
CH3

2,3-Dimethyl-
1-butene

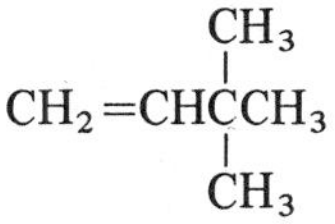
CH3
CH2=CHCCH3
CH3

3, 3-Dimethyl-
1-butene

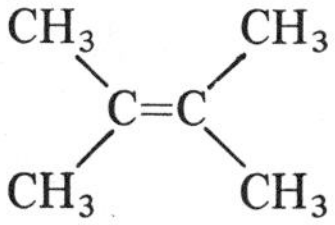
CH3 CH3
C=C
CH3 CH3

2, 3-Dimethyl-
2-butene

(c)

C_5H_{10}:

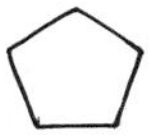

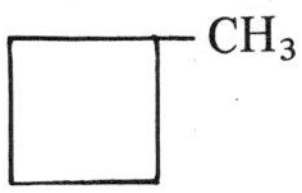
CH3

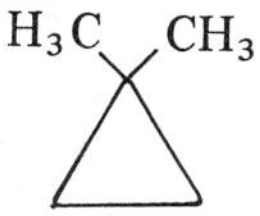
H3C CH3

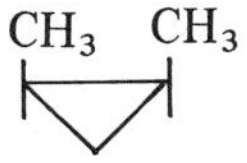
CH3 CH3

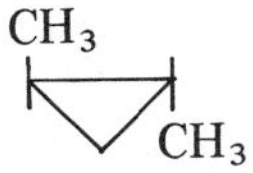
CH3
CH3

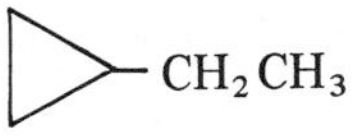
CH2CH3

C_6H_{12}

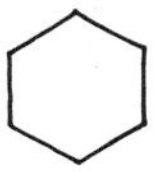

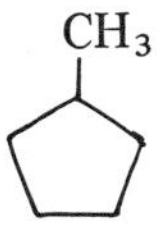
CH3

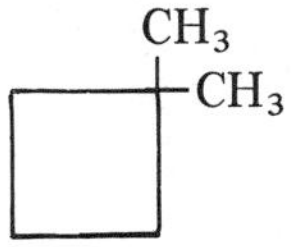
CH3
CH3

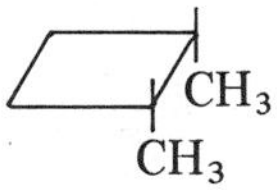
CH3
CH3

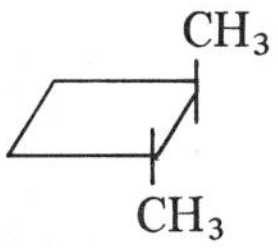
CH3
CH3

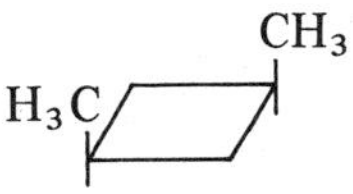
CH3
H3C

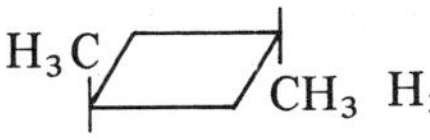
H3C
CH3

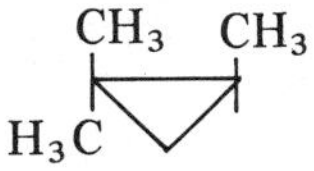
CH3 CH3
H3C

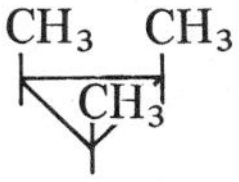
CH3 CH3
CH3

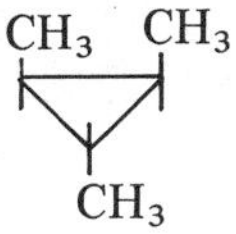
CH3 CH3
CH3

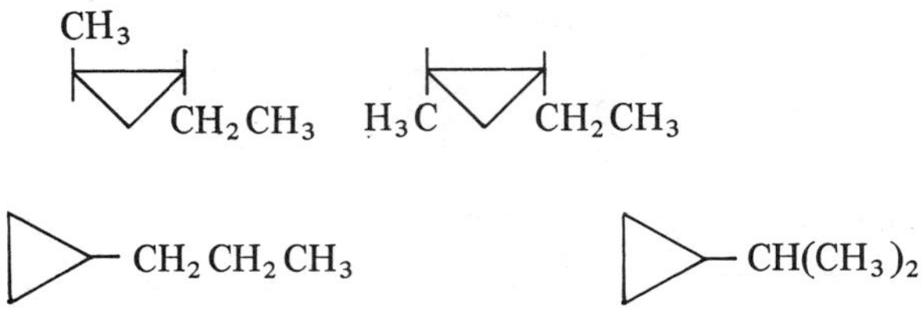

6.22 (a) 1,3-Dimethylcyclohexene, (b) 2-Ethyl-1-pentene, (c) 2-Ethyl-1-pentene,

(d) 1-Ethyl-2-methylcyclopentene

6.23

(a) $CH_3CH_2CH_2Cl$ $\xrightarrow[\text{(CH}_3)_3COH]{\text{(CH}_3)_3CONa}$ $CH_3CH=CH_2$

(b) CH_3CHCH_3 (with Cl below) $\xrightarrow[\text{CH}_3CH_2OH]{\text{CH}_3CH_2ONa}$ $CH_3CH=CH_2$

(c) $CH_3CH_2CH_2OH$ $\xrightarrow{\text{H}^+,\ \text{heat}}$ $CH_3CH=CH_2$

(d) CH_3CHCH_3 (with OH below) $\xrightarrow{\text{H}^+,\ \text{heat}}$ $CH_3CH=CH_2$

(e) CH_3CHCH_2Br (with Br below) $\xrightarrow[\text{acetone}]{\text{Zn}}$ $CH_3CH=CH_2$

6.24

(a) 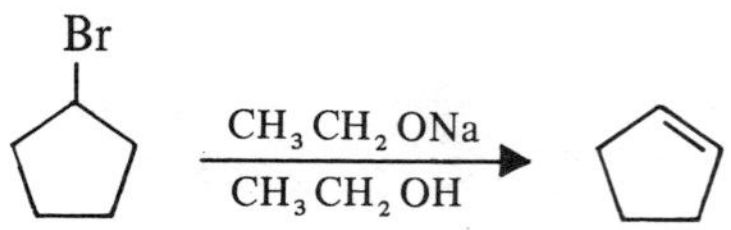 $\xrightarrow[\text{CH}_3CH_2OH]{\text{CH}_3CH_2ONa}$

(b) 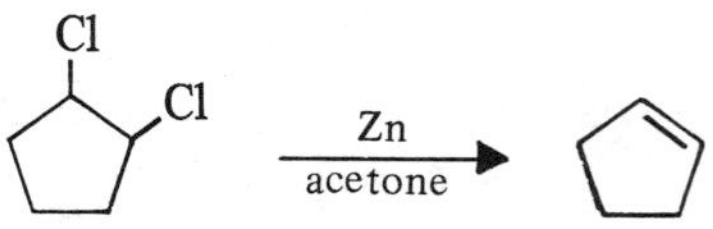 $\xrightarrow[\text{acetone}]{\text{Zn}}$

(c) 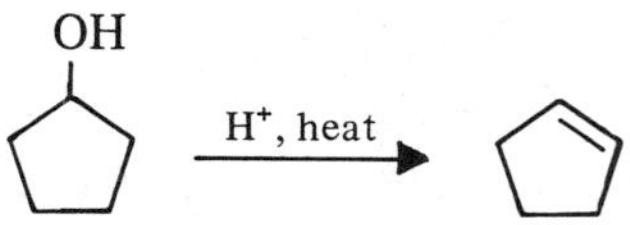 $\xrightarrow{\text{H}^+,\ \text{heat}}$

6.25 Working backward, we can see that to make 2,3-dibromo-2-methylbutane, we need 2-methyl-2-butene:

$$\underset{\text{2-Methyl-2-butene}}{CH_3-\overset{\overset{\displaystyle CH_3}{|}}{C}=CHCH_3} \xrightarrow[\text{CCl}_4]{\text{Br}_2} \underset{\substack{\text{2,3-Dibromo-2-methyl-}\\ \text{butane}}}{CH_3\overset{\overset{\displaystyle CH_3}{|}}{\underset{\underset{\displaystyle Br}{|}}{C}}-\overset{}{\underset{\underset{\displaystyle Br}{|}}{C}}HCH_3}$$

We can make 2-methyl-2-butene by dehydrohalogenation of 2-bromo-2-methylbutane:

$$\underset{\substack{\text{2-Bromo-2-methyl-}\\ \text{butane}}}{CH_3\overset{\overset{\displaystyle CH_3}{|}}{\underset{\underset{\displaystyle Br}{|}}{C}}-CH_2CH_3} \xrightarrow[\text{CH}_3\text{CH}_2\text{OH}]{\text{CH}_3\text{CH}_2\text{ONa}} \underset{\text{2-Methyl-2-butene}}{CH_3\overset{\overset{\displaystyle CH_3}{|}}{C}=CHCH_3}$$

And, we can make 2-bromo-2-methylbutane by treating 2-methylbutane with bromine. Bromine replaces the tertiary hydrogen preferentially (Sect. 4.10)

$$\underset{\text{2-Methylbutane}}{CH_3\overset{\overset{\displaystyle CH_3}{|}}{\underset{\underset{\displaystyle H}{|}}{C}}CH_2CH_3} \xrightarrow{\text{Br}_2} \underset{\substack{\text{2-Bromo-2-methyl-}\\ \text{butane}}}{CH_3\overset{\overset{\displaystyle CH_3}{|}}{\underset{\underset{\displaystyle Br}{|}}{C}}CH_2CH_3}$$

Now we need to make 2-methylbutane from compounds containing no more than 3 carbons. We can do this through a Corey-House synthesis (Sect. 3.16).

$$CH_3\underset{\underset{\displaystyle Br}{|}}{C}HCH_3 \xrightarrow{\text{Li}} CH_3\overset{\overset{\displaystyle CH_3}{|}}{C}HLi \xrightarrow{\text{CuI}} \left(CH_3\overset{\overset{\displaystyle CH_3}{|}}{C}H\right)_2CuLi \xrightarrow{\text{CH}_3\text{CH}_2\text{Br}}$$

$$\underset{\text{2-Methylbutane}}{CH_3\overset{\overset{\displaystyle CH_3}{|}}{C}HCH_2CH_3}$$

6.26 We notice that the deuterium atoms are cis to each other and we conclude, therefore, that we need to choose a method that will cause a *syn* addition of deuterium. One way would be to use D_2 and a metal catalyst (Sect. 6.14)

6.27 Dehydration of *trans* 2-methylcyclohexanol proceeds through the formation of a carbocation (through an El reaction of the protonated alcohol) and leads preferentially to the more stable alkene. 1-Methylcyclohexene (below) is more stable than 3-methylcyclohexene (the minor product of the dehydration) because its double bond is more highly substituted.

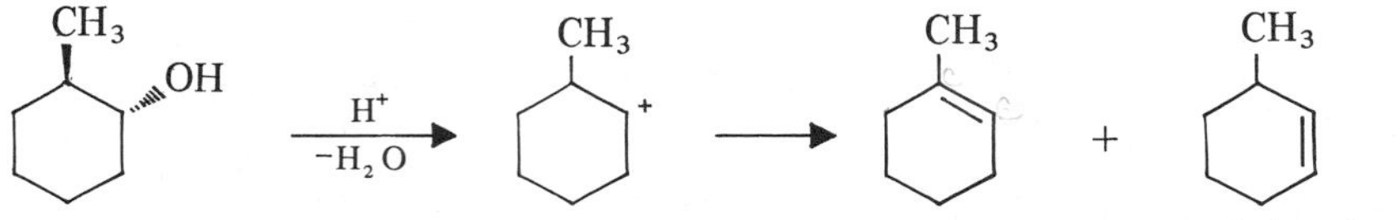

(major)   (minor)
Trisubstituted   Disubstituted
double bond   double bond

Dehydrohalogenation of *trans*-1-bromo-2-methylcyclohexane is an E2 reaction and must proceed through an *anti* periplanar transition state. Such a transition state is possible only for the elimination leading to 3-methylcyclohexene (cf. Problem 6.12).

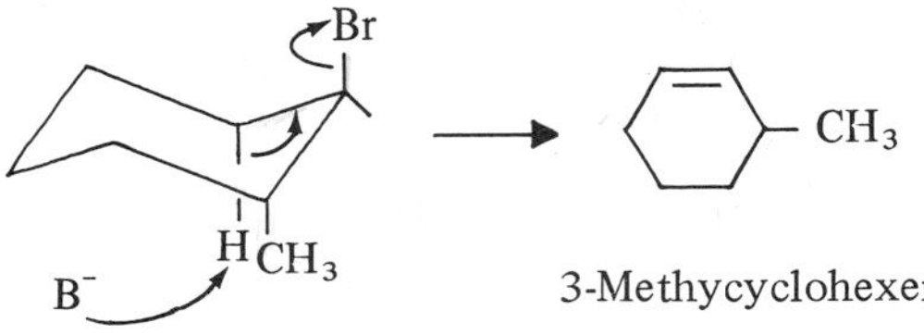

3-Methycyclohexene

6.28 (a) $CH_3\overset{\underset{\displaystyle |}{CH_3}}{C}=CHCH_2CH_3$ $CH_2=\overset{\underset{\displaystyle |}{CH_3}}{C}CH_2CH_2CH_3$

         (major)   (minor)

(b)

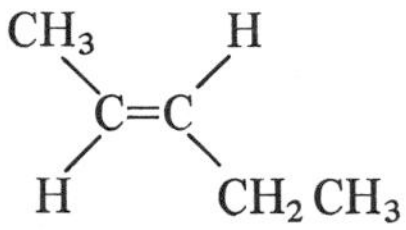

(major) 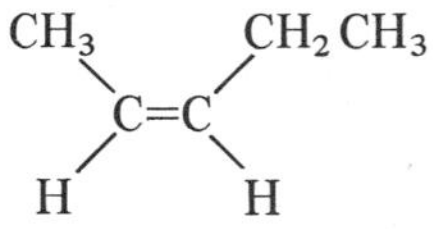   (minor)

$CH_2=CHCH_2CH_2CH_3$
(minor)

(c) $CH_3\overset{\underset{\displaystyle |}{CH_3}}{C}=CHCH_2CH_3$ $CH_2=\overset{\underset{\displaystyle |}{CH_3}}{C}CH_2CH_2CH_3$

       (major)   (minor)

(d)   (e)

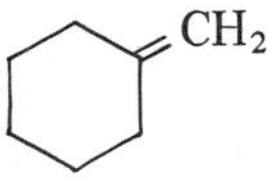

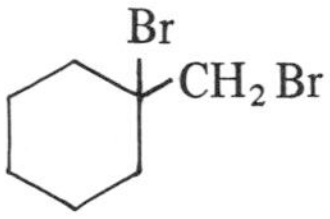

(f) 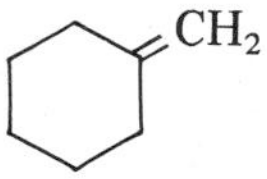   (g)

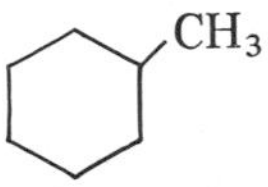

6.29 $CH_2{=}CHCH_2CH_2CH_2CH_3 + Br_2 \xrightarrow[\substack{(dark) \\ R.T.}]{CCl_4}$ $CH_2CHCH_2CH_2CH_2CH_3$ (colorless)

with Br groups: $\underset{Br}{|}\ \underset{Br}{|}$

Cyclohexane does not react with Br_2 in the dark at room temperature, thus the red-brown color of the bromine will persist in the solution.

6.30   (a) No   (b) No

(c) Yes

(d) No

(e) Yes

(f) No

(g) No   (h) No   (i) Yes

6.31   (a) 2,3-Dimethyl-2-butene $>$ 2-methyl-2-pentene $>$ *trans*-3-hexene $>$ *cis*-2-hexene $>$ 1-hexene.

(b) The only alkenes whose relative stabilities could be measured by comparative heats of hydrogenation are those that yield the same hydrogenation product; i.e., *trans*-3-hexene, 1-hexene, *cis*-2-hexene all yield hexane on hydrogenation.

6.32   Although trans molecules are usually more stable than their cis isomers, in the case of cyclooctene, the trans isomer is probably more strained than the cis isomer because the ring is too small to allow a strain-free trans configuration. Therefore we would expect the trans isomer to have the higher heat of hydrogenation.

6.33   (a) Cis-trans isomerization caused by rupture of the π bond.

(b) Equilibrium should favor the trans isomer because it is more stable than the cis isomer.

6.34

(a) $CH_3CH{=}\overset{\overset{\textstyle CH_3}{|}}{C}CH_3$ (major) $+$ $CH_2{=}CH\overset{\overset{\textstyle CH_3}{|}}{C}HCH_3$

(b) $CH_3CH_2\overset{\overset{\displaystyle CH_3}{|}}{C}=CH_2$

(c) $CH_3CH=CHCH_2CH_3$ (trans predominates)

(d) (major) + + $CH_2=CHCH_2CH_2CH_3$

(e)

(f) (major product) +

6.35 (a) $CH_3CH_2CH_2CH_2CH_2Br \xrightarrow[\text{(CH}_3\text{)}_3\text{COH}]{\text{(CH}_3\text{)}_3\text{COK}} CH_3CH_2CH_2CH=CH_2$

(b) $CH_3\overset{\overset{}{\underset{\underset{\displaystyle CH_3}{|}}{C}}}{H}CH_2CH_2Br \xrightarrow[\text{(CH}_3\text{)}_3\text{COH}]{\text{(CH}_3\text{)}_3\text{COK}} CH_3\overset{\underset{\underset{\displaystyle CH_3}{|}}{C}}{H}CH=CH_2$

(c) $CH_3\overset{\overset{\displaystyle CH_3}{|}}{C}H\overset{\underset{\displaystyle CH_3}{|}}{C}HCH_2Br \xrightarrow[\text{(CH}_3\text{)}_3\text{COH}]{\text{(CH}_3\text{)}_3\text{COK}} CH_3\overset{\overset{\displaystyle CH_3}{|}}{C}H\overset{\underset{\displaystyle CH_3}{|}}{C}=CH_2$

(d) $CH_3-$$-Br \xrightarrow[\text{(CH}_3\text{)}_3\text{COH}]{\text{(CH}_3\text{)}_3\text{COK}} CH_3-$

(e) CH_3- $\xrightarrow[\text{CH}_3\text{CH}_2\text{OH}]{\text{CH}_3\text{CH}_2\text{ONa}} CH_3-$

6.36

(a) $CH_3\overset{\overset{\displaystyle OH}{|}}{\underset{\underset{\displaystyle CH_3}{|}}{C}}CH_3$ or $CH_3\overset{\underset{\displaystyle CH_3}{|}}{C}HCH_2OH$

(c)

(b) $CH_3\overset{\overset{\displaystyle OH}{|}}{\underset{\underset{\displaystyle CH_3}{|}}{C}}\text{——}\overset{}{C}HCH_3$ or $CH_3\overset{\overset{\displaystyle CH_3}{|}}{C}\text{——}CH\text{–}CH_3$
$\underset{\displaystyle CH_3}{} \underset{\displaystyle OH}{}$

(d)

(e) $CH_3CH_2\overset{\underset{\underset{\displaystyle OH}{|}}{}}{C}HCH_3$

(f)

6.37

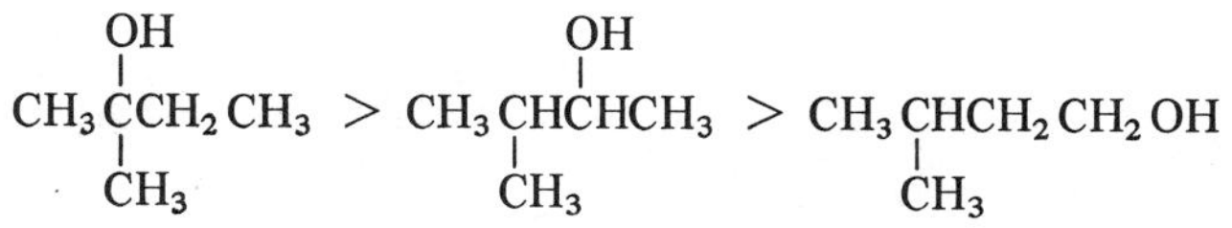

$$\underset{\overset{|}{CH_3}}{\overset{\overset{OH}{|}}{CH_3\overset{|}{C}CH_2\,CH_3}} > \underset{\overset{|}{CH_3}}{\overset{\overset{OH}{|}}{CH_3\,CH\,CHCH_3}} > \underset{\overset{|}{CH_3}}{CH_3\,CHCH_2\,CH_2\,OH}$$

The order of reactivity is dictated by the order of stability of the intermediate carbocations: tertiary > secondary > primary.

6.38 (a) *cis*-1,2-Dimethylcyclopentane

(b) *cis*-1,2-Dimethylcyclohexane

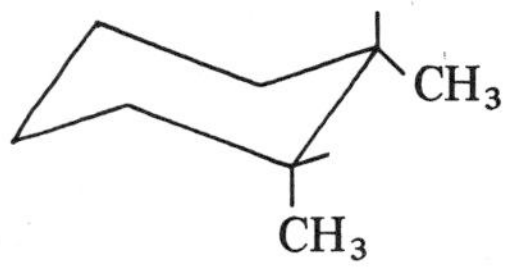

(c) *cis*-1,2-Dideuteriocyclohexane:

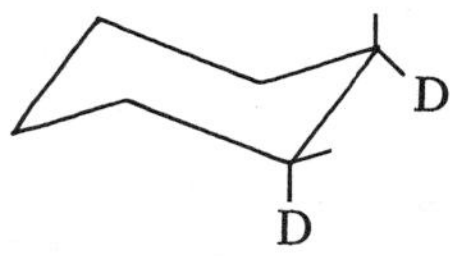

6.39 (a) (1) $\underset{\overset{|}{CH_3}}{\overset{\overset{CH_3}{|}}{CH_3\!-\!\overset{|}{C}\!-\!CH_2\!-\!OH}} + H_3O^+ \rightleftharpoons \underset{\overset{|}{CH_3}}{\overset{\overset{CH_3}{|}}{CH_3\!-\!\overset{|}{C}\!-\!CH_2\!-\!OH_2^+}} + H_2O$

(2) $\underset{\overset{|}{CH_3}}{\overset{\overset{CH_3}{|}}{CH_3\!-\!\overset{|}{C}\!-\!CH_2\!-\!OH_2^+}} \longrightarrow \underset{\overset{|}{CH_3}}{\overset{\overset{CH_3}{|}}{CH_3\!-\!\overset{|}{C}\!-\!CH_2^+}} + H_2O$

(3) $\underset{\overset{|}{CH_3}}{\overset{\overset{CH_3}{|}}{CH_3\!-\!\overset{|}{C}\!-\!CH_2^+}} \longrightarrow \underset{\overset{|}{CH_3}}{\overset{+}{CH_3\!-\!C}\!-\!CH_2\!-\!CH_3}$

(4) $\underset{\overset{|}{CH_3}}{\overset{\overset{H}{|}}{CH_3\!-\!\overset{+}{C}\!-\!CH\!-\!CH_3}} + \;:\!\underset{\overset{|}{H}}{O}\!-\!H \longrightarrow \underset{CH_3}{\overset{CH_3}{\diagdown}}C\!=\!CHCH_3$ (more substituted alkene)

$+\; H_3O^+$

(4a) $\underset{\overset{|}{CH_3}}{\overset{H}{CH_2\!-\!\overset{+}{C}\!-\!CH_2\!-\!CH_3}} + \;:\!\underset{\overset{|}{H}}{O}\!-\!H \longrightarrow CH_2\!=\!C\underset{CH_3}{\overset{CH_2\,CH_3}{\diagup}}$ (less substituted alkene)

$+\; H_3O^+$

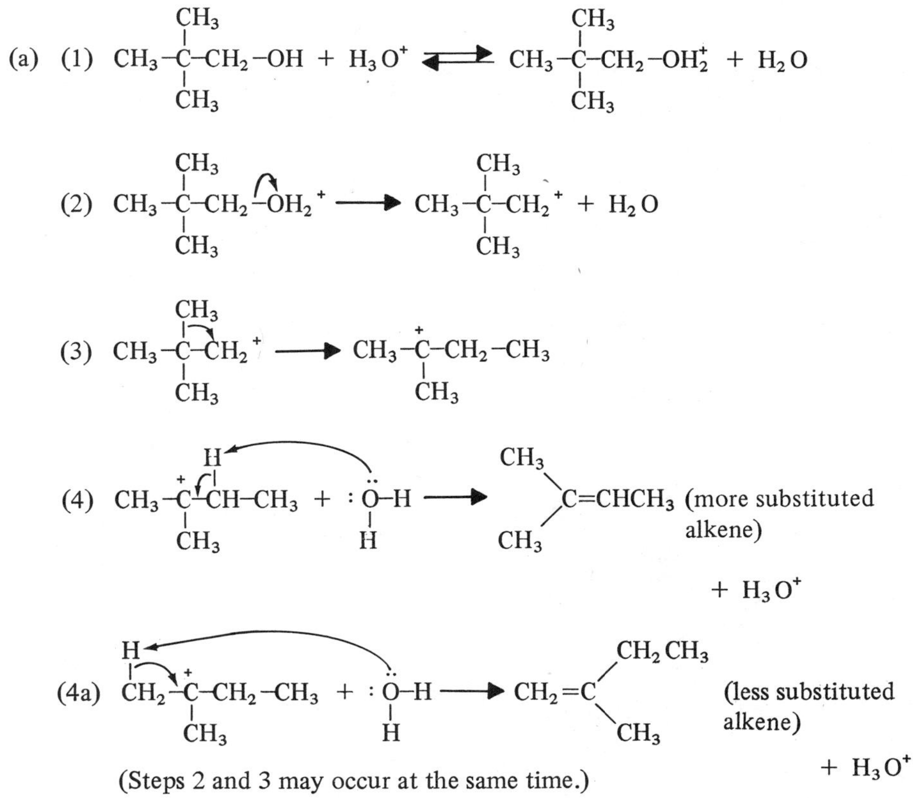

(Steps 2 and 3 may occur at the same time.)

(b)

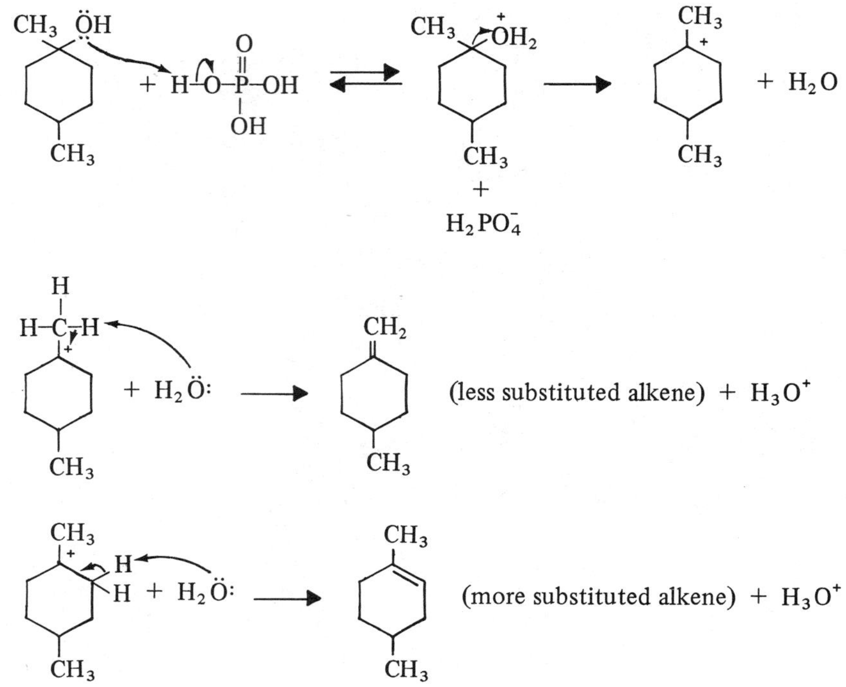

(less substituted alkene) + H_3O^+

(more substituted alkene) + H_3O^+

(c)

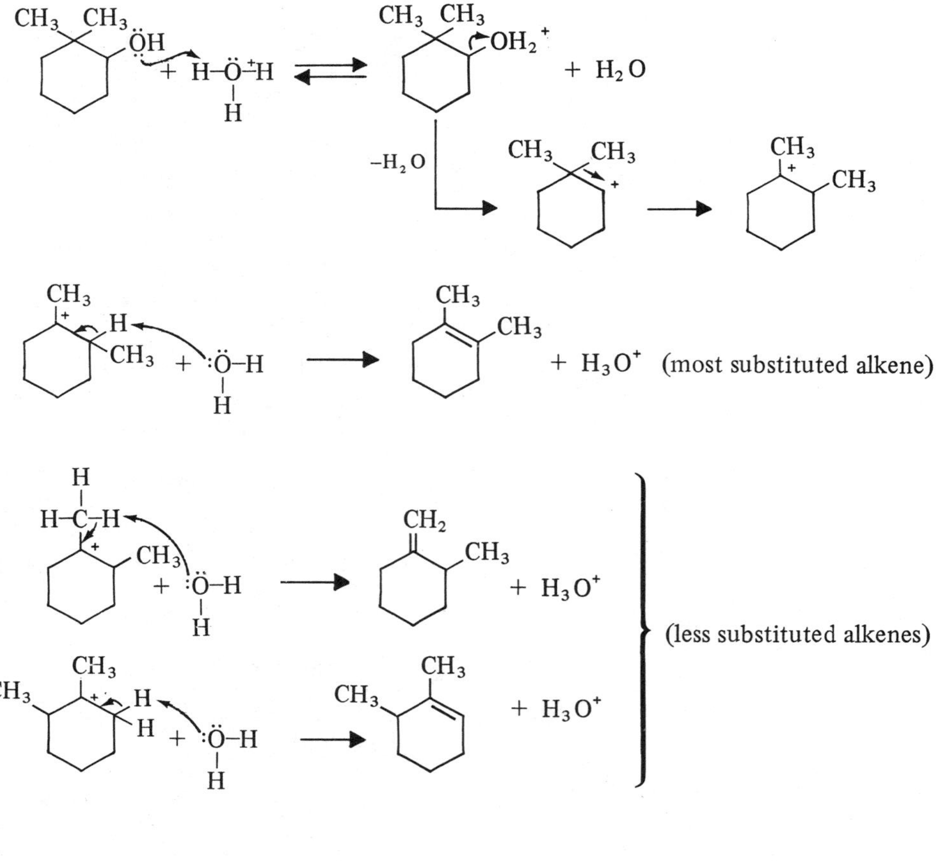

+ H_3O^+ (most substituted alkene)

+ H_3O^+

+ H_3O^+

} (less substituted alkenes)

6.40   The alkyl halide has the structural feature $\diagdown$CHCH$_2$Br. Dehydrobromination gives only

one alkene and no cis-trans isomers, therefore the bromine must be on the end of the chain. The remainder of the molecule may vary, so there are several answers possible. Three of them are

$$CH_3CH_2CH_2CH_2CH_2CH_2CH_2Br , \overset{\overset{\displaystyle CH_3}{|}}{CH_3CHCH_2CH_2CH_2CH_2Br},$$

$$\text{and } CH_3CH_2CH_2CH_2\overset{\overset{\displaystyle CH_3}{|}}{CHCH_2Br}$$

6.41

6.42   (a) Caryophyllene has the same molecular formula as zingiberene (Problem 6.5), thus it, too, has an index of hydrogen deficiency equal to 4. That one mole of caryophyllene absorbs two moles of hydrogen on catalytic hydrogenation indicates the presence of two double bonds per molecule.

(b) Caryophyllene molecules must also have two rings. (See Problem 22.3 for the structure of caryophyllene.)

6.43   (a) $C_{30}H_{62}$ = formula of alkane

$\underline{C_{30}H_{50}}$ = formula of squalene

   H_{12} = difference = 6 pairs of hydrogens

Index of hydrogen deficiency = 6

(b)   Molecules of squalene contain six double bonds.

(c)   Squalene molecules contain no rings. (See Problem 22.3 for the structural formula of squalene.)

6.44   (a)   We are given (on p. 226) the following heats of hydrogenation:

cis-2-Butene $+$ H$_2$ $\longrightarrow$ Butane $\Delta H° = -28.6$ kcal/mole

$trans$-2-Butene $+$ H$_2$ $\longrightarrow$ Butane $\Delta H° = -27.6$ kcal/mole

thus for

cis-2-Butene $\longrightarrow$ $trans$-2-Butene . $\Delta H° = -1.0$ kcal/mole

(b)   Converting cis-2-butene into $trans$-2-butene involves breaking the π bond. Therefore we would expect the energy of activation to be at least as large as the π-bond strength, that is, at least 63 kcal/mole.

(c)

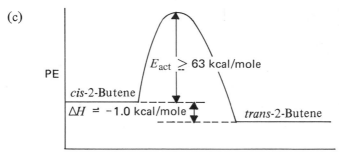

Reaction coordinate

6.45   (a)   An sp^2 hybridized carbon atom has more s character than one that is sp^3 hybridized, thus electrons in these sp^2 orbitals are closer to the nucleus than those in sp^3 orbitals. A bond between and sp^2 hybridized carbon and an sp^3 hybridized carbon is polarized toward the sp^2 hybridized carbon.

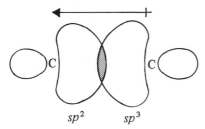

(b)   The greater acidity of ethene can be explained by the greater stability of its conjugate base, CH$_2$=CH$^-$. The greater stability of CH$_2$=CH$^-$ compared with CH$_3$CH$_2$$^-$ can be explained by the greater s character of the sp^2 orbital that holds the unbonded electron pair in CH$_2$=CH$^-$. In CH$_3$CH$_2$$^-$, the electrons are in an sp^3 orbital. Being farther from the nucleus, the sp^3 electrons have a higher potential energy.

6.46

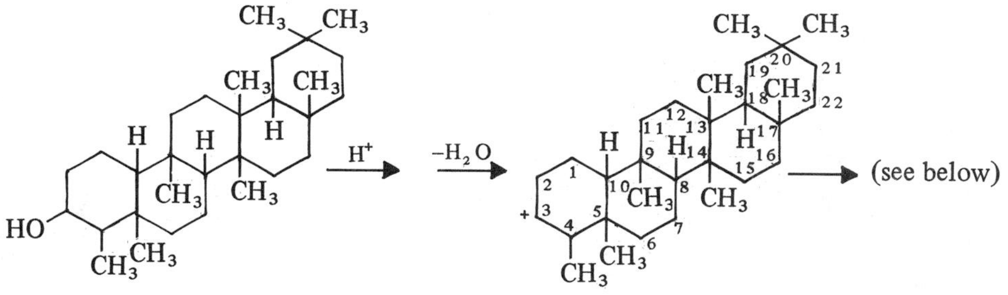

3β-Friedelanol

The migrations occur in the following sequence:

(1) H:$^-$ from C_4 to C_3 leaves (+) at C_4.

(2) CH_3:$^-$ from C_5 to C_4 leaves (+) at C_5.

(3) H:$^-$ from C_{10} to C_5 leaves (+) at C_{10}.

(4) CH_3:$^-$ from C_9 to C_{10} leaves (+) at C_9.

(5) H:$^-$ from C_8 to C_9 leaves (+) at C_8.

(6) CH_3:$^-$ from C_{14} to C_8 leaves (+) at C_{14}.

(7) CH_3:$^-$ from C_{13} to C_{14} leaves (+) at C_{13}.

(8) Loss of H$^+$ from C_{18} leaves double bond at C_{13}–C_{18}

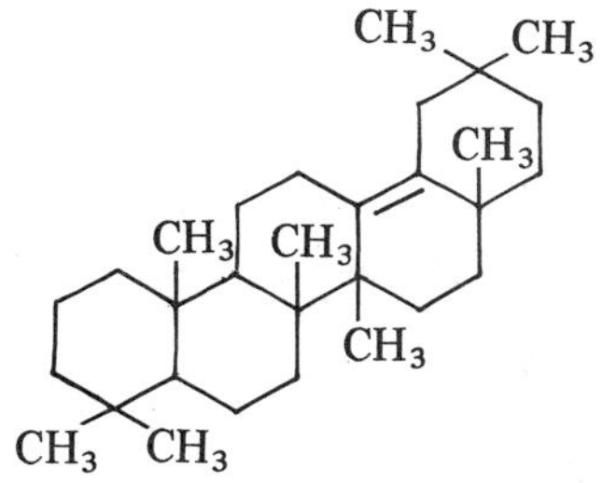

13(18)-Oleanene

The groups which migrate remain on the same face of the molecule after migration as before migration (see page 240 for transition state and see also Corey and Ursprung, *J. Am. Chem. Soc.*, 78, 5041 (1956)).

SECTION REFERENCES FOR ADDITIONAL PROBLEMS

6.19	6.2		**6.33**	6.3
6.20	6.2		**6.34**	6.9
6.21	6.2, 6.5		**6.35**	6.9
6.22	6.2		**6.36**	6.10, 6.11, 6.12
6.23	5.14, 5.15, 6.10, 6.13		**6.37**	6.10
6.24	5.14, 5.15, 6.10, 6.13		**6.38**	6.14
6.25	2.8, 3.16, 4.10, 5.14, 6.9		**6.39**	6.11, 6.12
6.26	6.14		**6.40**	6.9
6.27	6.9–6.12		**6.41**	6.13
6.28	6.9, 6.10, 6.12, 6.13, 6.14		**6.42**	6.5
6.29	6.14		**6.43**	6.5
6.30	6.3, 6.6		**6.44**	6.3
6.31	6.6		**6.45**	6.3
6.32	6.6		**6.46**	6.12

SELF-TEST

6.1   Give an acceptable name for each of the following compounds.

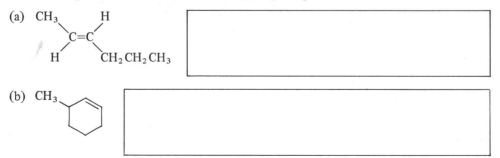

6.2   Supply the formula of the missing reactant(s) or *major* organic product.

(b) 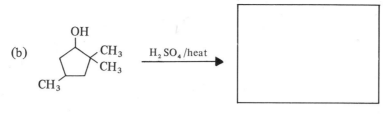 $\xrightarrow{\text{H}_2\text{SO}_4/\text{heat}}$

(c) 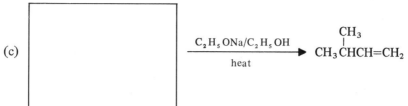 $\xrightarrow[\text{heat}]{\text{C}_2\text{H}_5\text{ONa}/\text{C}_2\text{H}_5\text{OH}}$ $\underset{\text{CH}_3}{\overset{\text{CH}_3}{\text{CH}_3\text{CHCH}=\text{CH}_2}}$

(d)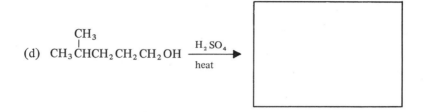

6.3 Which of the following compounds is capable of exhibiting cis-trans isomerism? (**Give the letters only**.)

(a) $CH_2=CHCH_2CH_3$,   (b) $FCH=CHF$,   (c) $F_2C=CH_2$,   (d) 1-Chloro-2-methylpropene,   (e) 2-Pentene,   (f) 1,3-Dimethylcyclobutane   (g) 1,2-Dimethylcyclobutane,   (h) 1,1-Dimethylcyclopropane.

6.4 Arrange the following alkenes in order of increasing stability. Label the *most* stable *3*, the least *1*, etc.

6.5   Compound A whose molecular formula is C_5H_8 undergoes hydrogenation to give C_5H_{10}. A possible structure for compound A is

SUPPLEMENTARY PROBLEMS

S6.1   Name the following compounds

$$CH_2CH=CH_2$$
(a) $CH_3CH_2\overset{|}{C}HCH_2CH_2CH_3$ (b)

S6.2   Compound A has the molecular formula C_7H_{12}. Hydrogenation over a Ni catalyst produces a saturated compound, B, whose molecular formula is C_7H_{14}. How many double bonds and/or rings do A and B possess?

S6.3   Predict the possible products of the reaction below.

(a)   —CH_2Br $\xrightarrow[\text{C}_2\text{H}_5\text{OH, heat}]{\text{NaOC}_2\text{H}_5}$?

SOLUTIONS TO SUPPLEMENTARY PROBLEMS

S6.1   (a)   4-Ethyl-1-heptene,   (b)   2,3-Dimethylcyclopentene

S6.2   Hydrogenation of A produces compound B which has an index of hydrogen deficiency of 1. Therefore B and A each has a ring. Compound A has an index of hydrogen deficiency of 2, so it must also have a double bond. Thus A has a double bond and a ring.

S6.3

(a)

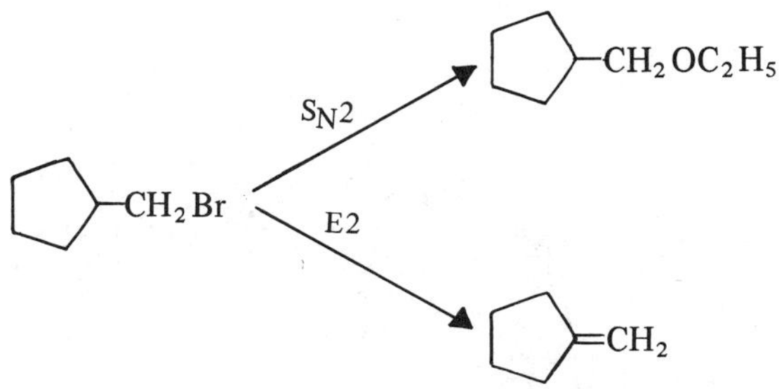

$$\text{(cyclopentyl)}-CH_2Br \quad\xrightarrow[\quad]{S_N2}\quad \text{(cyclopentyl)}-CH_2OC_2H_5$$

$$\xrightarrow[\quad]{E2}\quad \text{(cyclopentylidene)}=CH_2$$

7

ADDITION REACTIONS OF THE CARBON-CARBON DOUBLE BOND: SYNTHESIS OF ALCOHOLS AND ALKYL HALIDES

SUMMARY OF REACTIONS OF ALKENES

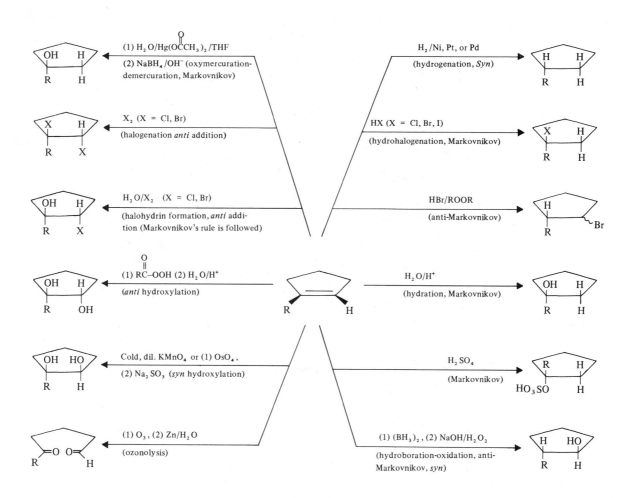

SOLUTIONS TO PROBLEMS

7.1 ICl adds as though it consisted of the ions I^+ and Cl^-:

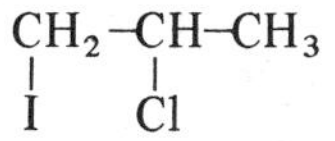

$$\underset{\overset{|}{I}\quad\overset{|}{Cl}}{CH_2-CH-CH_3} \qquad \text{2-Chloro-1-iodopropane}$$

7.2 (a) $CH_3CH_2CH{=}CH_2 \; + \; H{-}\ddot{I}: \;\rightleftharpoons\; CH_3CH_2\overset{+}{C}HCH_3 \; + \; :\ddot{I}:^- \longrightarrow CH_3CH_2\underset{\overset{|}{I}}{C}HCH_3$

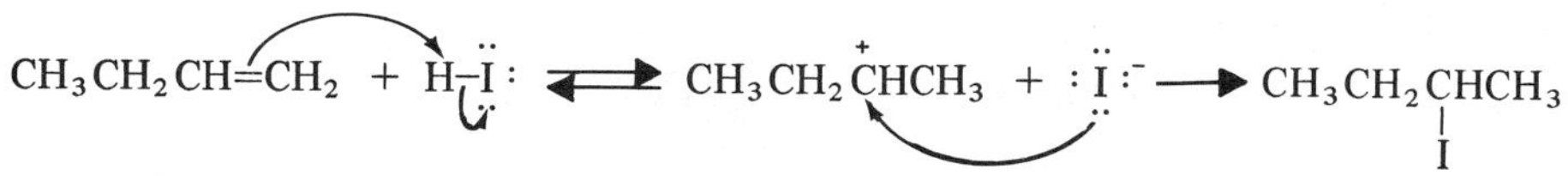

(b)

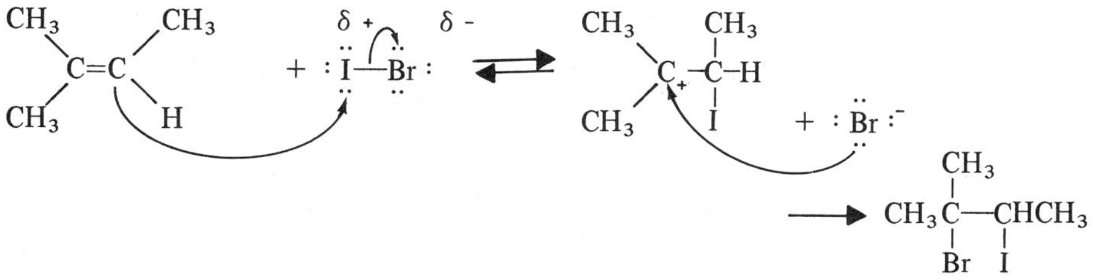

(c)

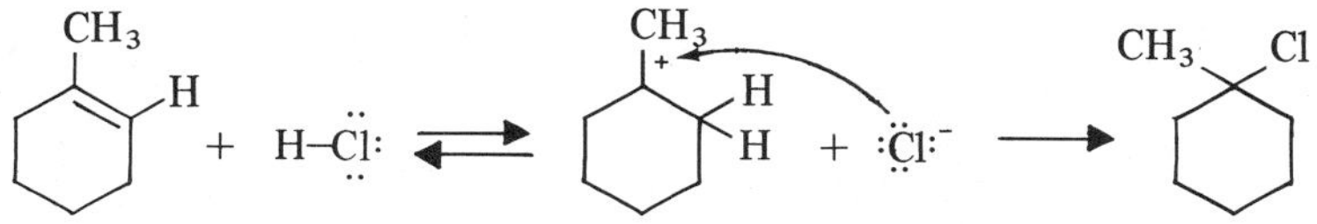

7.3

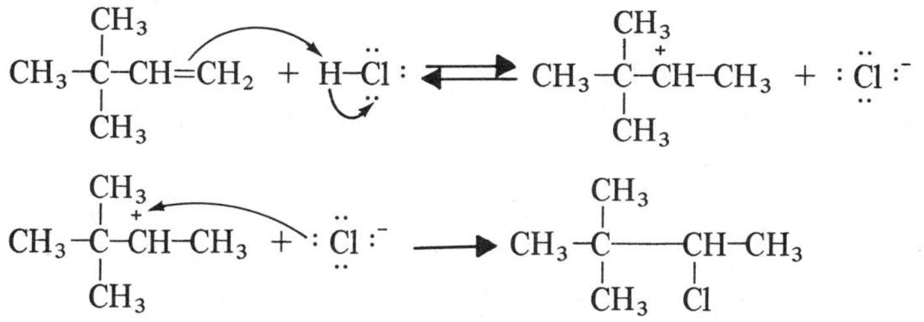

or

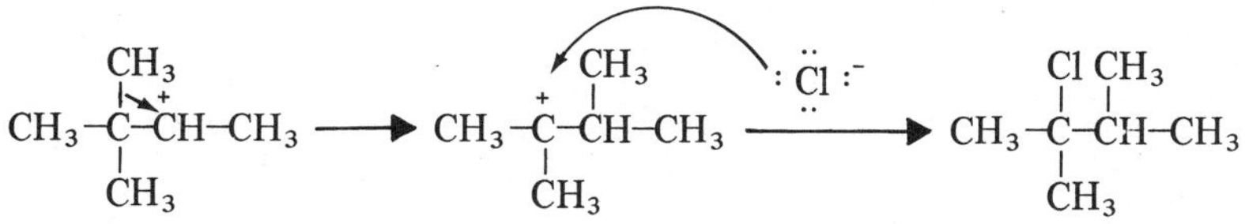

7.4

$$CH_2{=}CH_2 \; + \; H_2SO_4 \longrightarrow CH_3CH_2OSO_3H \xrightarrow[\text{heat}]{H_2O} CH_3CH_2OH \; + \; H_2SO_4$$

7.5 (a) $CH_3{-}CH{=}CH_2 \; + \; \underset{\overset{|}{H}}{H{-}\overset{..+}{O}{-}H} \rightleftharpoons CH_3{-}\overset{+}{C}H{-}CH_3 \; + \; H_2O$

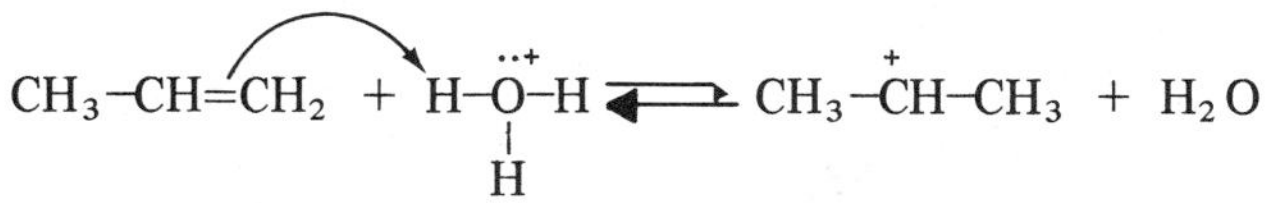

$$CH_3-\overset{+}{C}H-CH_3 \;+\; :\overset{..}{O}-H \;\rightleftharpoons\; CH_3-\overset{\overset{\displaystyle :\overset{+}{O}-H}{|}}{C}H-CH_3$$

$$CH_3-\overset{\overset{\displaystyle :\overset{+}{O}-H}{|}}{C}H-CH_3 \;+\; :\overset{..}{O}-H \;\rightleftharpoons\; CH_3-\overset{\overset{\displaystyle OH}{|}}{C}H-CH_3 \;+\; H_3\overset{+}{O}$$

(b) The product is isopropyl alcohol because the more stable isopropyl carbocation is produced in the first step. The formation of propyl alcohol would require the production of the less stable propyl carbocation.

7.6

$$CH_3-\overset{\overset{\displaystyle CH_3}{|}}{\underset{\underset{\displaystyle CH_3}{|}}{C}}-CH=CH_2 \xrightarrow{H_3O^+} CH_3-\overset{\overset{\displaystyle CH_3}{|}}{\underset{\underset{\displaystyle CH_3}{|}}{C}}-\overset{+}{C}H-CH_3 \xrightarrow[\text{migration}]{\text{methanide}} CH_3-\overset{\overset{\displaystyle CH_3}{|}}{\underset{\underset{\displaystyle CH_3}{|}}{\overset{+}{C}}}-CH-CH_3 \xrightarrow{H_2O}$$

$$CH_3-\overset{\overset{\displaystyle CH_3}{|}}{\underset{\underset{\displaystyle H_2O^+}{|}}{C}}-CH-CH_3 \xrightarrow{-H^+} CH_3-\overset{\overset{\displaystyle CH_3}{|}}{\underset{\underset{\displaystyle HO}{|}}{C}}-CH-CH_3$$

7.7 The order reflects the relative ease with which these alkenes accept a proton and form a carbocation. $(CH_3)_2C=CH_2$ reacts fastest because it leads to a tertiary cation,

$$(CH_3)_2CH=CH_2 \xrightarrow{H^+} CH_3-\overset{\overset{\displaystyle CH_3}{|}}{\underset{\underset{\displaystyle +}{}}{C}}-CH_3 \quad 3° \text{ Carbocation}$$

$CH_3CH=CH_2$ leads to a secondary cation,

$$CH_3CH=CH_2 \xrightarrow{H^+} CH_3\overset{+}{C}HCH_3 \quad 2° \text{ Carbocation}$$

and, $CH_2=CH_2$ reacts most slowly because it leads to a primary carbocation.

$$CH_2=CH_2 \xrightarrow{H^+} CH_3\overset{+}{C}H_2 \quad 1° \text{ Carbocation}$$

Recall that formation of the cation is the rate-limiting step in acid-catalyzed hydration and that the order of stabilities of carbocations is

$$3° > 2° > 1° > \overset{+}{C}H_3$$

7.8

$$CH_3-\overset{\overset{\displaystyle CH_3}{|}}{C}=CH_2 \xrightarrow{H^+} CH_3-\overset{\overset{\displaystyle CH_3}{|}}{\underset{\underset{\displaystyle +}{}}{C}}-CH_3 \xrightarrow{CH_3-\overset{..}{O}-H} CH_3-\overset{\overset{\displaystyle CH_3}{|}}{\underset{\underset{\displaystyle CH_3}{\overset{\displaystyle |}{H-\overset{+}{O}:}}}{C}}-CH_3 \xrightarrow{(-H^+)} CH_3-\overset{\overset{\displaystyle CH_3}{|}}{\underset{\underset{\displaystyle CH_3}{\overset{\displaystyle |}{:\overset{..}{O}:}}}{C}}-CH_3$$

7.9

(a) $CH_3\overset{\overset{\displaystyle CH_3}{|}}{C}{=}CH_2$ $\xrightarrow[\text{THF–H}_2\text{O}]{\text{Hg(OAc)}_2}$ $CH_3-\overset{\overset{\displaystyle CH_3}{|}}{\underset{\underset{\displaystyle HO}{|}}{C}}-CH_2HgOAc$ $\xrightarrow[\text{OH}^-]{\text{NaBH}_4}$ $CH_3-\overset{\overset{\displaystyle CH_3}{|}}{\underset{\underset{\displaystyle OH}{|}}{C}}-CH_3$

(b) $CH_3CH{=}CH_2$ $\xrightarrow[\text{THF–H}_2\text{O}]{\text{Hg(OAc)}_2}$ $CH_3\underset{\underset{\displaystyle OH}{|}}{C}HCH_2HgOAc$ $\xrightarrow[\text{OH}^-]{\text{NaBH}_4}$ $CH_3\underset{\underset{\displaystyle OH}{|}}{C}HCH_3$

(c) $CH_3\overset{}{\underset{\underset{\displaystyle CH_3}{|}}{C}}{=}CHCH_3$ $\xrightarrow[\text{THF–H}_2\text{O}]{\text{Hg(OAc)}_2}$ $CH_3\overset{\overset{\displaystyle HO}{|}}{\underset{\underset{\displaystyle CH_3}{|}}{C}}{-}\overset{\overset{\displaystyle HgOAc}{|}}{C}HCH_3$ $\xrightarrow[\text{OH}^-]{\text{NaBH}_4}$ $CH_3\overset{\overset{\displaystyle OH}{|}}{\underset{\underset{\displaystyle CH_3}{|}}{C}}CH_2CH_3$

7.10

(a) $\underset{}{\overset{}{>}}C{=}C\underset{}{\overset{}{<}}$ $+$ $^+HgO\overset{\overset{\displaystyle O}{\|}}{C}CF_3$ $\longrightarrow$ $-\overset{\overset{\displaystyle |}{}}{\underset{\underset{\displaystyle \delta+}{}}{C}}-\overset{\overset{\displaystyle |}{}}{C}\begin{smallmatrix}|\\ \end{smallmatrix}$ ... $\underset{\underset{\displaystyle \delta+}{}}{HgO\overset{\overset{\displaystyle O}{\|}}{C}CF_3}$ $\xrightarrow{\text{R–O–H}}$ $\overset{\overset{\displaystyle ROH^+}{|}}{-\overset{}{C}}-\overset{}{C}\begin{smallmatrix}|\\ \end{smallmatrix}$ $HgO\overset{\overset{\displaystyle O}{\|}}{C}CF_3$

$\xrightarrow{-H^+}$ $-\overset{\overset{\displaystyle RO}{\underset{}{|}}}{C}-\overset{}{C}\begin{smallmatrix}|\\ \end{smallmatrix}$ $HgO\overset{\overset{\displaystyle O}{\|}}{C}CF_3$

(b) $CH_3-\overset{\overset{\displaystyle CH_3}{|}}{C}{=}CH_2$ $\xrightarrow[\text{solvomercuration}]{\text{Hg(O}\overset{\overset{\displaystyle O}{\|}}{C}CF_3)_2/\text{THF-CH}_3\text{OH}}$ $CH_3-\overset{\overset{\displaystyle CH_3}{|}}{\underset{\underset{\displaystyle CH_3O}{|}}{C}}-CH_2HgO\overset{\overset{\displaystyle O}{\|}}{C}CF_3$

$\xrightarrow[\text{demercuration}]{\text{NaBH}_4/\text{OH}^-}$ $CH_3\overset{\overset{\displaystyle CH_3}{|}}{\underset{\underset{\displaystyle OCH_3}{|}}{C}}CH_3$ $+$ Hg $+$ $CF_3CO_2^-$

7.11

(a) $CH_3CH_2CH{=}CH_2$ $\xrightarrow{\text{THF : BH}_3}$ $(CH_3CH_2CH_2CH_2)_3B$

(b) $CH_3\overset{\overset{\displaystyle CH_3}{|}}{C}{=}CH_2$ $\xrightarrow{\text{THF : BH}_3}$ $(CH_3\overset{\overset{\displaystyle CH_3}{|}}{C}HCH_2)_3B$

(c) $CH_3CH{=}CHCH_3$ $\xrightarrow{\text{THF : BH}_3}$ $(CH_3CH_2\overset{\overset{\displaystyle CH_3}{|}}{C}H)_3B$

(d)

$\xrightarrow[\substack{\textit{syn}\text{ addition}\\\text{anti-Markovnikov}}]{\text{THF:BH}_3}$

7.12

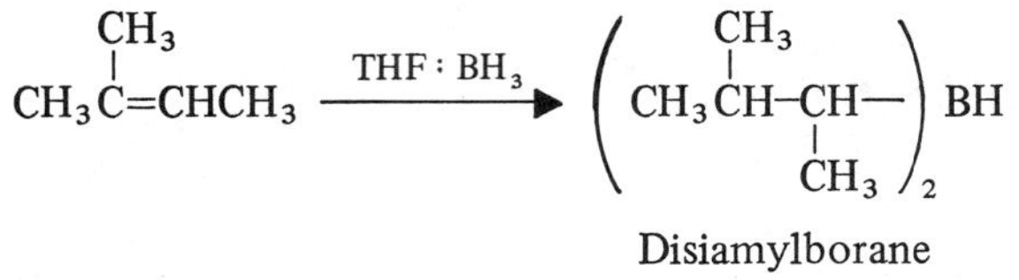

$$CH_3\overset{\overset{\textstyle CH_3}{|}}{C}=CHCH_3 \xrightarrow{\text{THF}:BH_3} \left(CH_3\overset{\overset{\textstyle CH_3}{|}}{CH}-\overset{\underset{\textstyle CH_3}{|}}{CH}-\right)_2 BH$$

Disiamylborane

7.13

$$(CH_3)_3CCH=CHCH_3 \xrightarrow{\text{THF}:BH_3} (CH_3)_3CCH_2\overset{\underset{\textstyle B-}{|}}{C}HCH_3 \; +$$

$$(CH_3)_3C\overset{\underset{\textstyle -B}{|}}{C}HCH_2CH_3 \xrightarrow{160°} (CH_3)_3CCH_2CH_2CH_2-B\diagup$$

$$\xrightarrow[160°]{CH_3(CH_2)_7CH=CH_2} (CH_3)_3CH_2CH=CH_2 \; + \; CH_3(CH_2)_8CH_2B\diagup$$

Distills out   Boils above
at 160°   160°

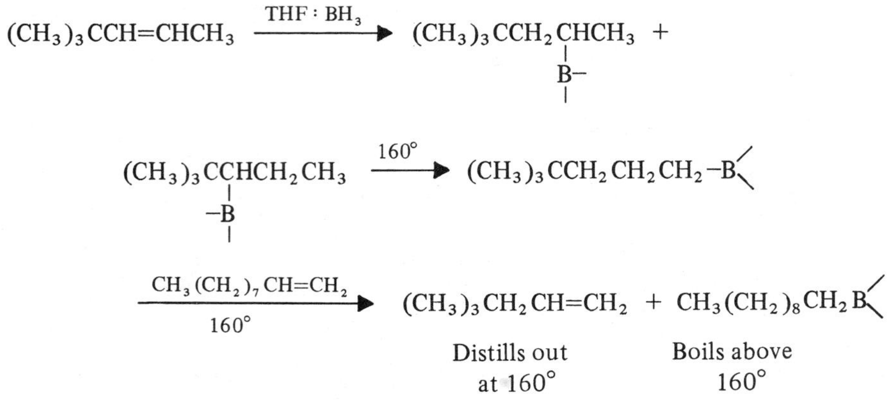

7.14 (a) $3CH_3CH_2CH=CH_2 \; + \; THF:BH_3 \longrightarrow (CH_3CH_2CH_2CH_2)_3B \xrightarrow[OH^-]{H_2O_2}$

$$3CH_3CH_2CH_2CH_2OH \; + \; H_3BO_3$$

(b) $2CH_3-\overset{\overset{\textstyle CH_3}{|}}{C}=CH-CH_3 \; + \; THF:BH_3 \longrightarrow (CH_3-\overset{\overset{\textstyle CH_3}{|}}{C}H-\overset{\overset{\textstyle CH_3}{|}}{C}H)_2BH$

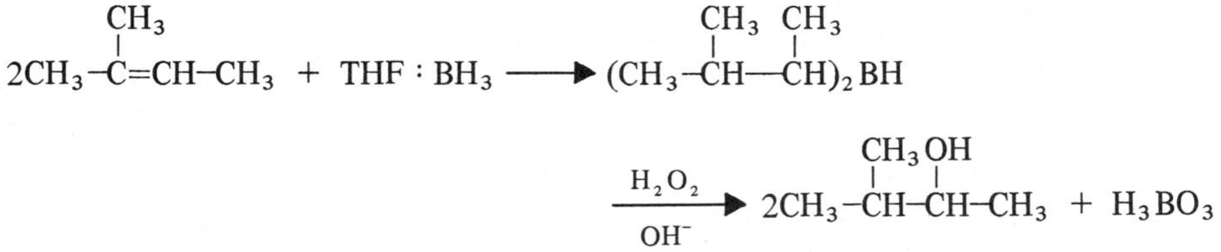

$$\xrightarrow[OH^-]{H_2O_2} 2CH_3-\overset{\overset{\textstyle CH_3}{|}}{C}H-\overset{\overset{\textstyle OH}{|}}{C}H-CH_3 \; + \; H_3BO_3$$

(c) $+ \; H_3BO_3$

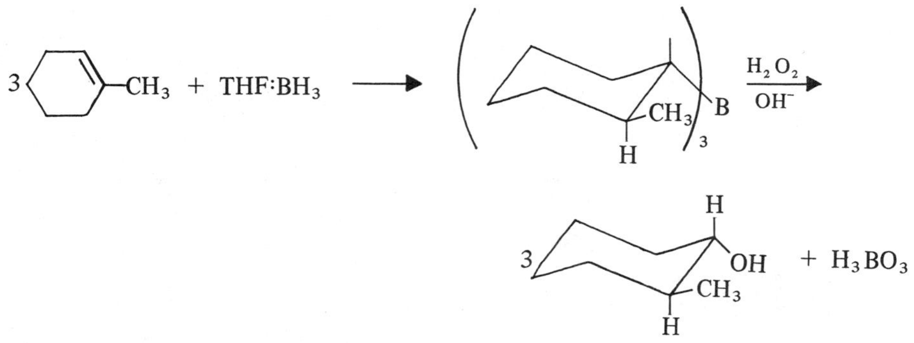

7.15

(a) 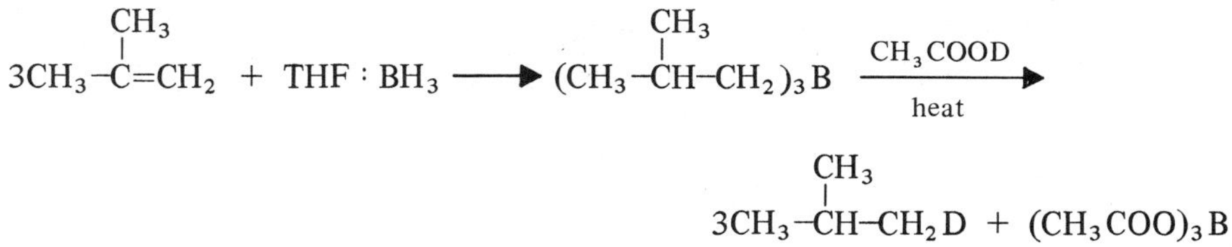 $3CH_3-\overset{\underset{\textstyle CH_3}{|}}{C}=CH_2$ + THF : $BH_3 \longrightarrow (CH_3-\overset{\underset{\textstyle CH_3}{|}}{C}H-CH_2)_3B \xrightarrow[\text{heat}]{CH_3COOD}$

$$3CH_3-\overset{\underset{\textstyle CH_3}{|}}{C}H-CH_2D + (CH_3COO)_3B$$

(b) 3 =CH_2 + THF : $BH_3 \longrightarrow$ $\xrightarrow[\text{heat}]{CH_3COOD}$

3 $-CH_2D + (CH_3COO)_3B$

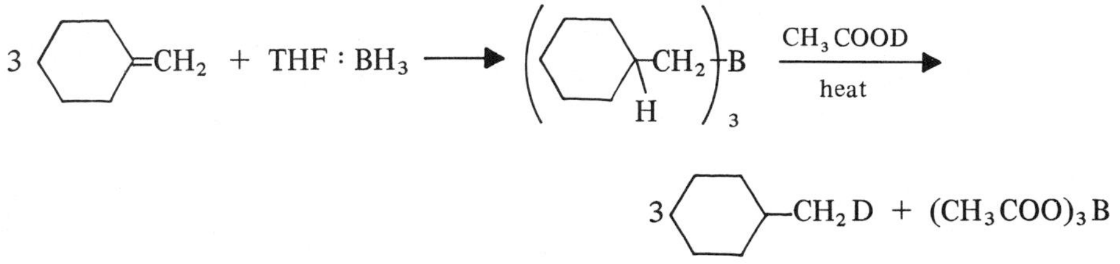

(c) 3 + THF:$BH_3 \longrightarrow$ $\xrightarrow[\text{heat}]{CH_3COOD}$

3 + $(CH_3COO)_3B$

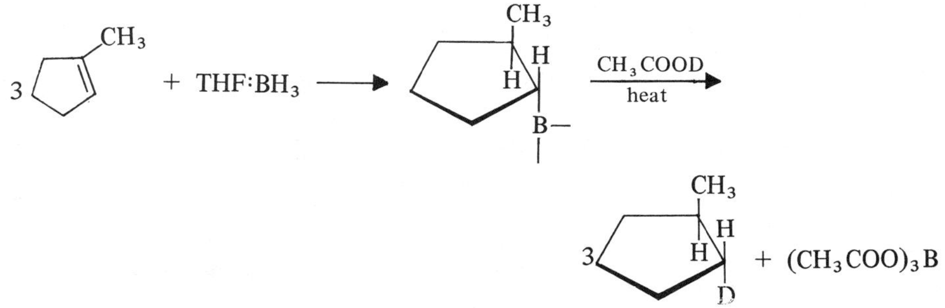

(d) 3 + THF:$BD_3 \longrightarrow$ $\xrightarrow[\text{heat}]{CH_3COOT}$

$\Big\uparrow$ THF

$(BD_3)_2$

3 + $(CH_3COO)_3B$

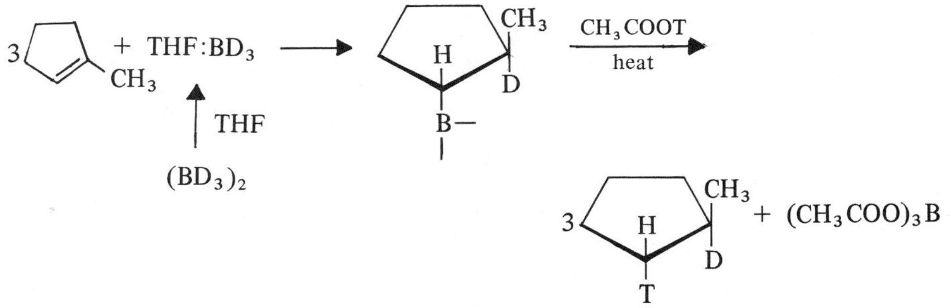

7.16 Using the Corey-House synthesis (Sect. 3.16) we can synthesize the alkane with the required carbon skeleton:

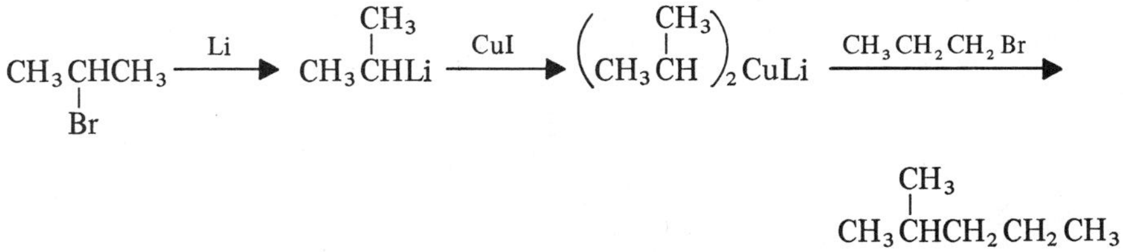

$CH_3\overset{\underset{\textstyle Br}{|}}{C}HCH_3 \xrightarrow{\text{Li}} CH_3\overset{\underset{\textstyle CH_3}{|}}{C}HLi \xrightarrow{\text{CuI}} \Big(CH_3\overset{\underset{\textstyle CH_3}{|}}{C}H\Big)_2CuLi \xrightarrow{CH_3CH_2CH_2Br}$

$$CH_3\overset{\underset{\textstyle CH_3}{|}}{C}HCH_2CH_2CH_3$$

Then bromination (Sect. 4.10A) would lead to preferential replacement of the tertiary hydrogen:

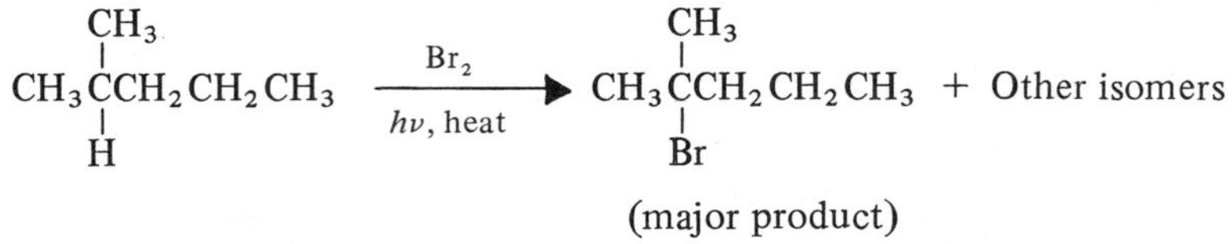

$$\underset{\overset{|}{H}}{\overset{\overset{CH_3}{|}}{CH_3\overset{}{C}CH_2CH_2CH_3}} \xrightarrow[h\nu,\ heat]{Br_2} \underset{\overset{|}{Br}}{\overset{\overset{CH_3}{|}}{CH_3\overset{}{C}CH_2CH_2CH_3}} + \text{Other isomers}$$

(major product)

Dehydrohalogenation (Sect. 6.9) would lead mainly to the following alkene:

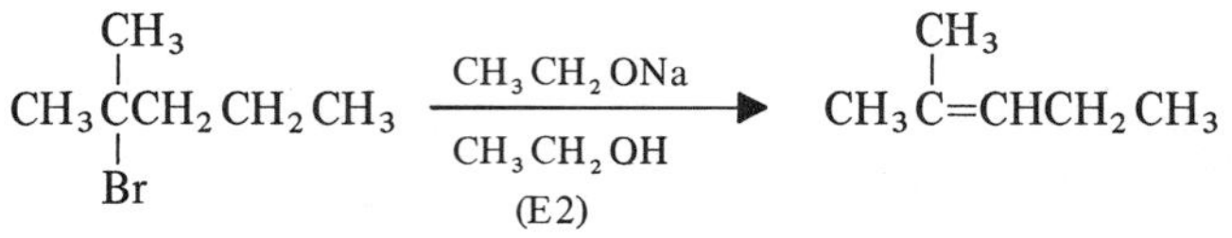

$$\underset{\overset{|}{Br}}{\overset{\overset{CH_3}{|}}{CH_3\overset{}{C}CH_2CH_2CH_3}} \xrightarrow[\underset{(E2)}{CH_3CH_2OH}]{CH_3CH_2ONa} \overset{\overset{CH_3}{|}}{CH_3C=CHCH_2CH_3}$$

Then hydroboration, isomerization, and oxidation would produce the required alcohol.

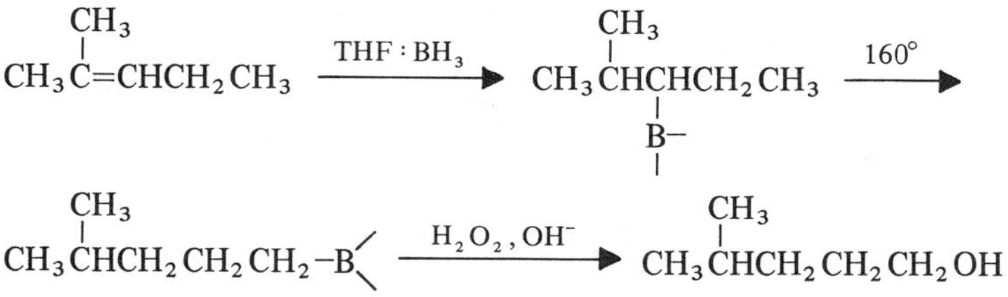

$$\overset{\overset{CH_3}{|}}{CH_3C=CHCH_2CH_3} \xrightarrow{THF\,:\,BH_3} \underset{\overset{|}{B^-}}{\overset{\overset{CH_3}{|}}{CH_3CHCHCH_2CH_3}} \xrightarrow{160°}$$

$$\overset{\overset{CH_3}{|}}{CH_3CHCH_2CH_2CH_2-B\bigg\backslash} \xrightarrow{H_2O_2,\,OH^-} \overset{\overset{CH_3}{|}}{CH_3CHCH_2CH_2CH_2OH}$$

7.17

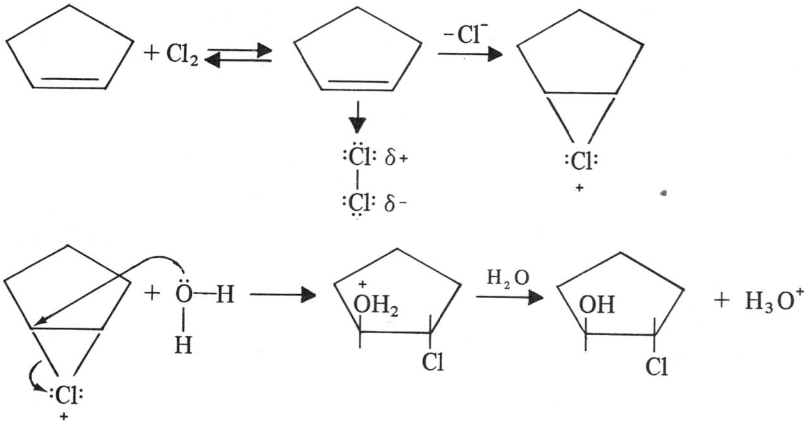

7.18

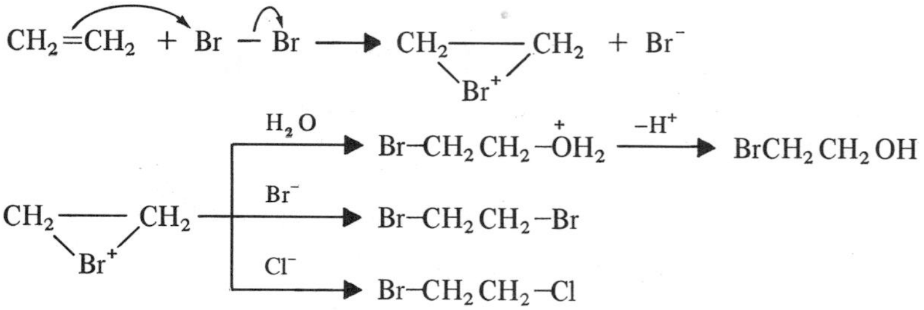

7.19 (a) Nucleophilic substitution by an S_N2 mechanism in which the H_2O molecule is the nucleophile. The acid catalyzes the reaction by protonating the epoxide oxygen to make the leaving group a $-CH_2OH$ rather than the very basic $-CH_2O^-$ which would be a very poor leaving group.

(b) The release in ring strain upon opening the ring helps to counteract the inhibiting effect of the poor leaving group $-CH_2O^-$, therefore the strongly nucleophilic OH^- ion is able to bring about the reaction.

7.20 (a) $CH_3CH_2CH=CHCH_3$

(c) $CH_3CH_2\underset{\underset{CH_3}{|}}{C}HCH=CH_2$

(b) $CH_3\underset{\underset{CH_3}{|}}{C}=\underset{\underset{CH_3}{|}}{C}CH_3$

(d) ⬡ (cyclohexene)

7.21 (a) $CH_3(CH_2)_5\underset{\underset{CBr_3}{|}}{C}HCH_2Br$

(b) This is not the course of the reaction because it requires the formation of a primary radical rather than a secondary one.

7.22 (a) Chain-initiating steps

(1) $R\text{-}\overset{..}{\underset{..}{O}}\text{-}\overset{..}{\underset{..}{O}}\text{-}R \xrightarrow{\text{heat}} 2\ R\text{-}\overset{..}{\underset{..}{O}}\cdot$

(2) $R\text{-}\overset{..}{\underset{..}{O}}\cdot + H\text{-}CCl_3 \longrightarrow R\text{-}\overset{..}{\underset{..}{O}}H + \cdot CCl_3$

Chain-propagating steps

(3) $CH_3CH_2CH_2CH=CH_2 + \cdot CCl_3 \longrightarrow CH_3CH_2CH_2\overset{\cdot}{C}H\text{-}CH_2CCl_3$

(4) $CH_3CH_2CH_2\overset{\cdot}{C}HCH_2CCl_3 + H\text{-}CCl_3 \longrightarrow CH_3CH_2CH_2CH_2CH_2CCl_3$
$+ \cdot CCl_3$

then (3), (4), (3), (4), etc.

(b) Chain-initiating steps

(1) $R\text{-}\overset{..}{\underset{..}{O}}\text{-}\overset{..}{\underset{..}{O}}\text{-}R \xrightarrow{\text{heat}} 2\ R\text{-}\overset{..}{\underset{..}{O}}\cdot$

(2) $R\text{-}\overset{..}{\underset{..}{O}}\cdot + CH_3CH_2\text{-}\overset{..}{\underset{..}{S}}\text{-}H \longrightarrow R\text{-}\overset{..}{\underset{..}{O}}H + CH_3CH_2\text{-}\overset{..}{\underset{..}{S}}\cdot$

Chain-propagating steps

(3) $CH_3\underset{\underset{CH_3}{|}}{C}=CH_2 + \cdot\overset{..}{\underset{..}{S}}CH_2CH_3 \longrightarrow CH_3\underset{\underset{\overset{\cdot}{}}{\underset{CH_3}{|}}}{C}\text{-}CH_2\text{-}\overset{..}{\underset{..}{S}}\text{-}CH_2CH_3$

(4) $CH_3\underset{\underset{\overset{\cdot}{}}{\underset{CH_3}{|}}}{C}CH_2SCH_2CH_3 + HSCH_2CH_3 \longrightarrow CH_3\underset{\underset{CH_3}{|}}{C}HCH_2SCH_2CH_3 + \cdot\overset{..}{\underset{..}{S}}CH_2CH_3$

then (3), (4), (3), (4), etc.

(c)   Chain-initiating steps

(1) $R-\ddot{O}-\ddot{O}-R \xrightarrow{heat} 2\ R-\ddot{O}\cdot$

(2) $R-\ddot{O}\cdot + Cl-CCl_3 \longrightarrow R-\ddot{O}-Cl + \cdot CCl_3$

Chain-propagating steps

(3) $CH_3CH_2\overset{\overset{\displaystyle CH_3}{|}}{C}=CH_2 + \cdot CCl_3 \longrightarrow CH_3CH_2\overset{\overset{\displaystyle CH_3}{|}}{\underset{\cdot}{C}}-CH_2CCl_3$

(4) $CH_3CH_2\overset{\overset{\displaystyle CH_3}{|}}{\underset{\cdot}{C}}CH_2CCl_3 + CCl_4 \longrightarrow CH_3CH_2\overset{\overset{\displaystyle CH_3}{|}}{\underset{\underset{\displaystyle Cl}{|}}{C}}CH_2CCl_3 + \cdot CCl_3$

then (3), (4), (3), (4), etc.

7.23   Rewriting the starting compound, we can better see the required reaction:

7.24   (a) $CH_3CH_2CH_2CHClCH_3$,   (b) $CH_3CH_2CH_2CHBrCH_2Br$,

(c) $CH_3CH_2CH_2CHOHCH_3$,   (d) $CH_3CH_2CH_2\overset{\overset{\displaystyle OSO_2OH}{|}}{C}HCH_3$,

(e) same as (c) ,   (f) $CH_3CH_2CH_2CHBrCH_3$,

(g) same as (c) ,   (h) $CH_3CH_2CH_2CH_2CH_2OH$,

(i) $CH_3CH_2CH_2\overset{\overset{\displaystyle I}{|}}{C}HCH_3$,   (j) $CH_3CH_2CH_2CHDCH_2D$,

(k) $CH_3CH_2CH_2CH=CH_2$,   (l) $CH_3\overset{\cdot}{C}H_2CH_2\overset{\overset{\displaystyle OH}{|}}{C}HCH_2OH$,

(m) same as (l) ,   (n) $CH_3CH_2CH_2\overset{\overset{\displaystyle O}{||}}{C}-OH + CO_2$

(o) $CH_3CH_2CH_2\overset{\overset{O}{\|}}{C}H$ + $H\overset{\overset{O}{\|}}{C}H$,   (p) $CH_3CH_2CH_2CH_2CH_3$,

(q) $CH_3CH_2CH_2CH_2CH_2Br$

7.25 (a) 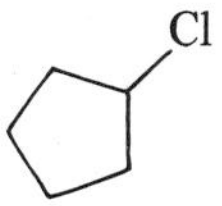 (cyclopentyl-Cl) ,   (b) 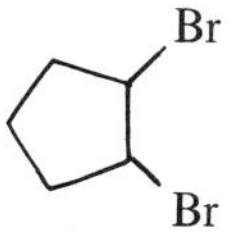 (cyclopentane with two Br) ,   (c) 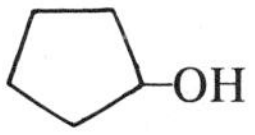 (cyclopentyl-OH) ,

(d) 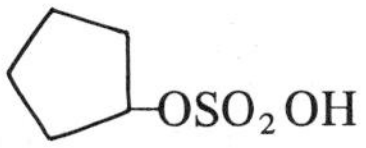 (cyclopentyl-OSO$_2$OH) ,   (e) Same as (c) ,   (f) 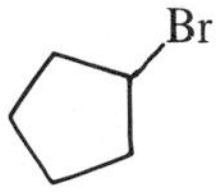 (cyclopentyl-Br) ,

(g) 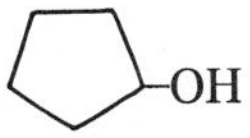 (cyclopentyl-OH) ,   (h) Same as (g),   (i) 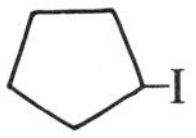 (cyclopentyl-I) ,

(j) 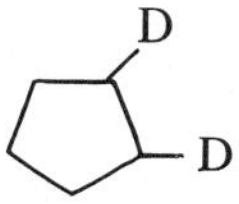 (cyclopentane with two D) ,   (k)  (cyclopentene) ,   (l) 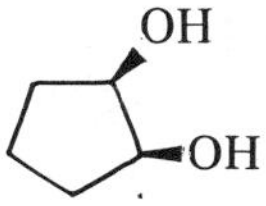 (cyclopentane with two OH) ,   (m) Same as (l) ,

(n) 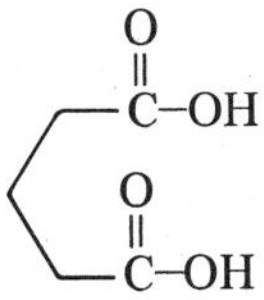 (chain with two C-OH groups) ,   (o) 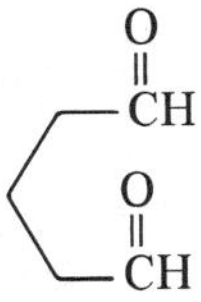 (chain with two CH=O groups) ,   (p)  (cyclopentane) ,

(q) Same as (f)

7.26 (a) $CH_3CH_2\underset{\underset{Br}{|}}{C}HCH_2Br$ (b) 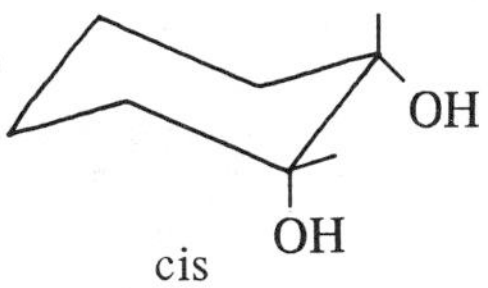 cis   (c) Same as (b)

(d) 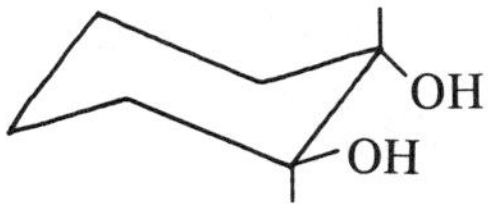 trans   (e) $CH_3CH_2-O-\overset{\overset{O}{\|}}{\underset{\underset{O}{\|}}{S}}-OH$ (f) CH_3CH_2OH

(g) $(CH_3\underset{\underset{CH_3}{|}}{C}HCH_2)_3B$ (h) $CH_3\underset{\underset{CH_3}{|}}{C}HCH_2OH$ (i) 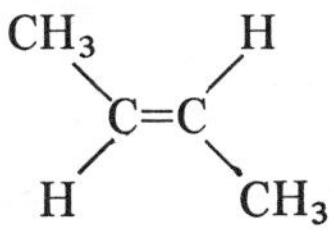 $\underset{H}{\overset{CH_3}{C}}=\underset{CH_3}{\overset{H}{C}}$ (major product)

(j)  (cyclopentene)   (k) $CH_2=CHCH_2CH_2CH_3$ (l) $CH_3\underset{\underset{Br}{|}}{\overset{\overset{CH_3}{|}}{C}}CH(CH_3)_2$

(m) $CH_3\overset{\underset{|}{Cl}}{C}HCH_2CH_2CH_2CH_3$ (n) $BrCH_2CH_2CH_2CH_2CH_2CH_3$

(o) $CH_3CH_2CH\underset{\underset{O\!-\!O}{}}{\overset{\overset{O}{}}{\diagdown\diagup}}CHCH_2CH_3$ (p) $2\ CH_3CH_2CHO$

(q) $2CH_3CH_2\overset{\overset{O}{\|}}{C}-O^-$ (r)   [cyclic structure with CH_3]   (s) $CH_3\overset{\overset{O}{\|}}{C}CH_2CH_2CH_2\overset{\overset{O}{\|}}{C}H$

(t) $CH_3\overset{\overset{O}{\|}}{C}CH_2CH_2CH_2\overset{\overset{O}{\|}}{C}-OH$ (u)   [cyclopentane with CH_3 and OH]   (v)   [cyclopentane with CH_3]

(w) $CH_3\overset{\overset{CH_3}{|}}{\underset{\underset{I}{|}}{C}}CH_2CH_2CH_3$ (x)   [cyclopentane with CH_3, CH_3, Cl]   (y)   [cyclopentane with HO, CH_3, Cl]

7.27   (a) $CH_3CH=CHCH_3 \xrightarrow[CCl_4]{Br_2} CH_3CHBrCHBrCH_3$

(b) $CH_3CH=CHCH_3 \xrightarrow{Br_2/H_2O} CH_3CHBrCH(OH)CH_3$

(c) $CH_3CH=CHCH_3 \xrightarrow[(2)\ Zn/H_2O]{(1)\ O_3} 2CH_3\overset{\overset{O}{\|}}{C}H$

(d) $CH_3CH=CHCH_3 \xrightarrow[heat]{KMnO_4,OH^-} 2\ CH_3\overset{\overset{O}{\|}}{C}O^- \xrightarrow{H^+} 2CH_3\overset{\overset{O}{\|}}{C}OH$

(e) $CH_3CH=CHCH_3 \xrightarrow[(2)\ NaHSO_3]{(1)\ OsO_4} CH_3\underset{\underset{OH}{|}}{C}H-\underset{\underset{OH}{|}}{C}HCH_3$

(f) $CH_3CH=CHCH_3 \xrightarrow[(2)\ NaBH_4,\ OH^-]{(1)\ Hg(OAc)_2,\ THF-H_2O} CH_3CH_2\underset{\underset{OH}{|}}{C}HCH_3$

(g) $CH_3CH=CHCH_3 \xrightarrow{THF:BH_3} CH_3CH_2\underset{\underset{B-}{|}}{C}HCH_3 \xrightarrow{CH_3\overset{\overset{O}{\|}}{C}OD} CH_3CH_2\underset{\underset{D}{|}}{C}HCH_3$

(h) $CH_3CH=CHCH_3 \xrightarrow{THF:BD_3} CH_3\underset{\underset{D}{|}}{C}H-\underset{\underset{B-}{|}}{C}HCH_3 \xrightarrow[OH^-]{H_2O_2} CH_3\underset{\underset{D}{|}}{C}H-\underset{\underset{OH}{|}}{C}HCH_3$

(i) $CH_3CH-CHCH_3$ $\xrightarrow{\overset{\overset{\displaystyle O}{\|}}{CH_3COT}}$ $CH_3CH-CHCH_3$
     $\quad\;$ | | $\qquad\qquad\qquad\qquad\qquad\qquad$ | |
     $\quad\;$ D B– $\qquad\qquad\qquad\qquad\qquad\qquad\;$ D   T
     $\qquad\;\;$ |

(as in part h)

(j) $CH_3CH_2CHCH_3$ $\xrightarrow{160°}$ $CH_3CH_2CH_2CH_2-B-$ $\xrightarrow[OH^-]{H_2O_2}$ $CH_3CH_2CH_2CH_2OH$
     $\qquad\;$ |
     $\qquad\;$ B–
     $\qquad\;$ |
(as in part g)

(k) $CH_3CH_2CH_2CH_2-B-$ $\xrightarrow{\overset{\overset{\displaystyle O}{\|}}{CH_3COD}}$ $CH_3CH_2CH_2CH_2-D$

(as in part j)

(l) $CH_3CH=CHCH_3$ $\xrightarrow{HF}$ $CH_3CH_2CHCH_3$
     $\qquad\qquad\qquad\qquad\qquad\qquad\quad$ |
     $\qquad\qquad\qquad\qquad\qquad\qquad\quad$ F

(m) $CH_3CH=CHCH_3$ $\xrightarrow[Ni]{H_2}$ $CH_3CH_2CH_2CH_3$

(n) $CH_3CH=CHCH_3$ $\xrightarrow[\text{(no peroxides)}]{HBr}$ $CH_3CH_2CHCH_3$
     $\qquad\qquad\qquad\qquad\qquad\qquad\qquad$ |
     $\qquad\qquad\qquad\qquad\qquad\qquad\qquad$ Br

(o) $CH_3CH_2CH_2CH_2-B-$ $\xrightarrow[160°]{CH_3(CH_2)_7CH=CH_2}$ $CH_3CH_2CH=CH_2$

(as in part j)   (distills out)

(p) $CH_3CH_2CH=CH_2$ $\xrightarrow[ROOR]{HBr}$ $CH_3CH_2CH_2CH_2Br$

(as in part o)

(q) $CH_3CH_2CH_2CH_2Br$ $\xrightarrow[(S_N2)]{CN^-}$ $CH_3CH_2CH_2CH_2CN$

(as in part p)

(r) $CH_3CH_2CH_2CH_2Br$ $\xrightarrow[\substack{CH_3OH \\ (S_N2)}]{CH_3ONa}$ $CH_3CH_2CH_2CH_2OCH_3$

(as in part p)

(s) $CH_3CH_2CH_2CH_2Br$ $\xrightarrow{Li}$ $CH_3CH_2CH_2CH_2Li$ $\xrightarrow{CuI}$

(as in part p)

$(CH_3CH_2CH_2CH_2)_2CuLi$ $\xrightarrow{CH_3CH_2CH_2CH_2Br}$ $CH_3(CH_2)_6CH_3$

(t) $CH_3CH_2\overset{\underset{CH_3}{|}}{C}HBr \xrightarrow{\text{Li}} CH_3CH_2\overset{\underset{CH_3}{|}}{C}HLi \xrightarrow{\text{CuI}}$

(as in part n)

$\left(CH_3CH_2\overset{\underset{CH_3}{|}}{C}H-\right)_2 CuLi \xrightarrow{CH_3CH_2CH_2CH_2Br} CH_3CH_2\overset{\underset{CH_3}{|}}{C}H(CH_2)_3CH_3$

7.28 (a) $CH_3\overset{\overset{CH_3}{|}}{C}=CH_2 \xrightarrow{H_3O^+, H_2O} CH_3\overset{\overset{CH_3}{|}}{\underset{\underset{OH}{|}}{C}}CH_3$

(b) $CH_3\overset{\overset{CH_3}{|}}{C}=CH_2 \xrightarrow{HCl} CH_3\overset{\overset{CH_3}{|}}{\underset{\underset{Cl}{|}}{C}}-CH_3$

(c) $CH_3\overset{\overset{CH_3}{|}}{C}=CH_2 \xrightarrow[\text{(no peroxides)}]{HBr} CH_3\overset{\overset{CH_3}{|}}{\underset{\underset{Br}{|}}{C}}CH_3$

(d) $CH_3\overset{\overset{CH_3}{|}}{C}=CH_2 \xrightarrow[\text{ROOR}]{HBr} CH_3\overset{\underset{CH_3}{|}}{C}HCH_2Br$

(e) $CH_3\overset{\underset{CH_3}{|}}{C}H=CH_2 \xrightarrow{\text{THF:BH}_3} CH_3\overset{\underset{CH_3}{|}}{C}HCH_2-B- \xrightarrow[\text{OH}^-]{H_2O_2} CH_3\overset{\underset{CH_3}{|}}{C}HCH_2OH$

(f) $CH_3\overset{\underset{CH_3}{|}}{C}HCH_2-B- \xrightarrow{\overset{\overset{O}{\|}}{CH_3C-OT}} CH_3\overset{\underset{CH_3}{|}}{C}HCH_2T$

(as in part e)

(g) $CH_3\overset{\overset{CH_3}{|}}{C}=CH_2 \xrightarrow{\text{THF:BD}_3} CH_3\overset{\overset{CH_3}{|}}{\underset{\underset{D}{|}}{C}}CH_2-B- \xrightarrow{CH_3COOT} CH_3\overset{\overset{CH_3}{|}}{\underset{\underset{D}{|}}{C}}CH_2T$

(h) $CH_3\overset{\underset{CH_3}{|}}{C}HCH_2Br \xrightarrow[\text{S}_N2]{I^-} CH_3\overset{\underset{CH_3}{|}}{C}HCH_2I$

(as in part d)

(i) $CH_3\overset{\underset{CH_3}{|}}{C}HCH_2Br \xrightarrow[\text{S}_N2]{CN^-} CH_3\overset{\underset{CH_3}{|}}{C}HCH_2CN$

(as in part d)

(j) $CH_3\overset{\overset{\displaystyle CH_3}{|}}{C}=CH_2 \xrightarrow{HF} CH_3\overset{\overset{\displaystyle CH_3}{|}}{\underset{\underset{\displaystyle F}{|}}{C}}CH_3$

(k) $CH_3\overset{\overset{\displaystyle CH_3}{|}}{C}HCH_2OH \xrightarrow{NaH} CH_3\overset{\overset{\displaystyle CH_3}{|}}{C}HCH_2ONa \xrightarrow[S_N2]{CH_3\overset{\overset{\displaystyle CH_3}{|}}{C}HCH_2Br}$

(as in part e)

$CH_3\overset{\overset{\displaystyle CH_3}{|}}{C}HCH_2OCH_2\overset{\overset{\displaystyle CH_3}{|}}{C}HCH_3$

(l) $CH_3\overset{\overset{\displaystyle CH_3}{|}}{C}=CH_2 \xrightarrow{Cl_2,\ H_2O} CH_3\overset{\overset{\displaystyle CH_3}{|}}{\underset{\underset{\displaystyle OH}{|}}{C}}CH_2Cl$

(m) $CH_3\overset{\overset{\displaystyle CH_3}{|}}{C}HCH_2ONa \xrightarrow[S_N2]{CH_3I} CH_3\overset{\overset{\displaystyle CH_3}{|}}{C}HCH_2OCH_3$

(as in part k)

(n) $(CH_3)_3CBr \xrightarrow{Li} (CH_3)_3CLi \xrightarrow{CuI} \left[(CH_3)_3C\right]_2CuLi$

(as in part c)

$\xrightarrow{CH_3\overset{\overset{\displaystyle CH_3}{|}}{C}HCH_2Br} (CH_3)_3CCH_2\overset{\overset{\displaystyle CH_3}{|}}{C}HCH_3$

7.29 (a) $C_{10}H_{22}$ (saturated alkane)
$\underline{C_{10}H_{16}}$ (formula of myrcene)

H_6 = 3 pairs of hydrogen

Index of hydrogen deficiency (IHD) = 3

(b)   Myrcene contains no rings because complete hydrogenation gives $C_{10}H_{22}$ which corresponds to an alkane.

(c)   That myrcene absorbs three molar equivalents of H_2 on hydrogenation indicates that it contains three double bonds.

(d)   Three structures are possible; however, only one gives 2,6-dimethyloctane on complete hydrogenation. Myrcene is therefore

$CH_3\overset{\overset{\displaystyle CH_3}{|}}{C}=CHCH_2CH_2\overset{\overset{\displaystyle CH_2}{||}}{C}CH=CH_2$

(e) $O=CHCH_2CH_2\overset{\overset{\displaystyle O}{||}}{C}CH=O$

7.30 $CH_3CH=CHCH_3 + HCl \rightleftharpoons CH_3CH_2\overset{+}{C}HCH_3 + :\overset{..}{\underset{..}{Cl}}:^-$

$$CH_3CH_2\overset{+}{C}HCH_3 + :\overset{..}{\underset{H}{O}}-CH_2CH_3 \longrightarrow CH_3CH_2\overset{\overset{+\,:\overset{H}{|}}{\overset{|}{O}-CH_2CH_3}}{\underset{}{C}}HCH_3 \xrightarrow{-H^+} CH_3CH_2\overset{\overset{OCH_2CH_3}{|}}{C}HCH_3$$

7.31   The order of reactivity parallels the order of stability of the carbocations produced by the attack of H^+ on each alkene.

$$\overset{R}{\underset{+}{R-\overset{|}{C}-CH_3}} > \underset{+}{R-CH-CH_3} > \underset{+}{CH_2-CH_3}$$

$$3° \qquad\qquad 2° \qquad\qquad 1°$$

7.32   (a)   (b)   (c)

7.33 $2\left(CH_3\overset{\overset{O}{||}}{C}CH_3\right), 4\left(O=CHCH_2CH_2\overset{\overset{CH_3}{|}}{C}=O\right), \quad O=CHCH_2CH=O$

7.34 $\underset{\underset{CH_3}{|}}{CH_3C=CH_2} > CH_3CH=CH_2 > CH_2=CH_2$

The order is the same as the order of stability of the carbocations formed by protonation of the alkenes.

$$\underset{\underset{CH_3}{|}}{CH_3\overset{+}{C}-CH_3} > CH_3\overset{+}{C}H-CH_3 > \overset{+}{C}H_2-CH_3$$

$$3° \qquad\qquad 2° \qquad\qquad 1°$$

7.35   (a) $CH_3CH=CHCH_3 + H^+ \rightleftharpoons CH_3\overset{+}{C}HCH_2CH_3$

(cis or trans)

$$CH_3-CH_2-\overset{+}{CH}\overset{H}{\diagup}CH_2 \longrightarrow CH_3CH_2CH{=}CH_2 + H^+$$

The most stable (most substituted) alkene is formed in greatest amount; i.e., 2-butenes $>$ 1-butene, and *trans*-2-butene $>$ *cis*-2-butene.

(b) 1-Butene, on protonation, gives the same intermediate carbocation: $CH_3CH_2\overset{+}{C}HCH_3$.

(c) The carbocation, $CH_3CH_2\overset{+}{C}HCH_3$, cannot easily rearrange to the branched chain compound because to do so would require the formation of an intermediate primary carbocation, $\overset{+}{C}H_2\underset{\underset{CH_3}{|}}{C}HCH_3$.

7.36

$$CH_3-\underset{\underset{OH}{|}}{CH}-\underset{\underset{CH_3}{|}}{\overset{\overset{CH_3}{|}}{C}}-CH_3 + H-Cl \rightleftharpoons CH_3-\underset{\underset{{}^+OH_2}{|}}{CH}-\underset{\underset{CH_3}{|}}{\overset{\overset{CH_3}{|}}{C}}-CH_3 + :\overset{..}{\underset{..}{Cl}}:^-$$

$$\longrightarrow CH_3-\overset{+}{CH}-\underset{\underset{CH_3}{|}}{\overset{\overset{CH_3}{|}}{C}}-CH_3 + H_2O$$

$$CH_3-\overset{+}{CH}-\underset{\underset{CH_3}{|}}{\overset{\overset{CH_3}{|}}{C}}-CH_3 \longrightarrow CH_3-\underset{\underset{CH_3}{|}}{CH}-\overset{+}{\underset{\underset{CH_3}{|}}{C}}-CH_3 \xrightarrow{:\overset{..}{Cl}:^-} CH_3-\underset{\underset{CH_3}{|}}{CH}-\underset{\underset{CH_3}{|}}{\overset{\overset{CH_3Cl}{|}}{C}}-CH_3$$

7.37 Reassembling the oxidation product as follows we can see where the original double bond was.

About Synthesis

Problems involving syntheses are always intriguing to chemists and students alike. These problems are probably unlike any that you have seen in other courses. In them you are asked to put together a series of reactions that will convert one compound into another. To do this, it is not enough to start your reasoning with the starting materials because you must also keep in mind the desired product. In some instances you can work from both ends simultaneously, and this is best done by trying to find an intermediate that will link the starting materials and products in a sequence of reactions. In many cases, however, a synthesis problem is best solved by reasoning backward, by starting your thinking with the product and by trying to discover a series of reactions that will lead back to the starting compounds. Sherlock Holmes in *A Study in Scarlet* said:

> Most people if you describe a train of events to them, will tell you what the result would be. They can put these events together in their minds, and argue from them that something will come to pass. There are a few people, however, who, if you told them a result, would be able to evolve from their own inner consciousness what the steps were which led up to that result. This power is what I mean when I talk of reasoning backward, or analytically.

This power is what the organic chemistry student must develop.

Let us illustrate this process with the synthesis of the chlorohydrin, $\underset{\underset{OH}{|}}{\overset{\overset{CH_3}{|}}{CH_3CCH_2Cl}}$

from 2-methylpropane. We start by recognizing that we can synthesize the final product from 2-methylpropene:

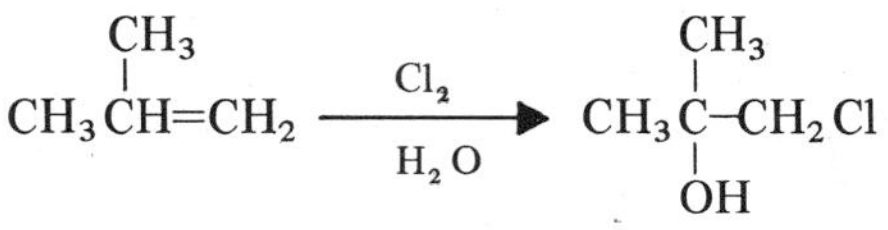

$$\underset{CH_3CH=CH_2}{\overset{\overset{CH_3}{|}}{}} \xrightarrow[H_2O]{Cl_2} \underset{\underset{OH}{|}}{\overset{\overset{CH_3}{|}}{CH_3C-CH_2Cl}}$$

Then our task is to synthesize 2-methylpropene.
This can be done by dehydrohalogenating either of the compounds shown below.

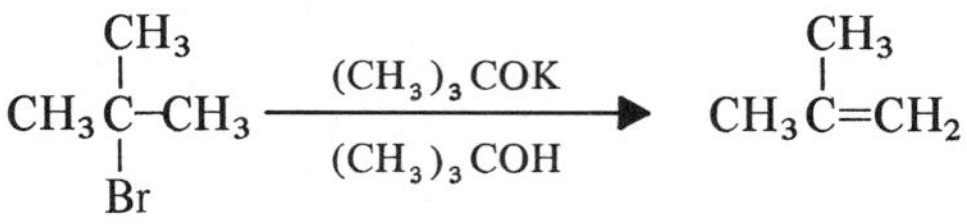

$$\underset{\underset{Br}{|}}{\overset{\overset{CH_3}{|}}{CH_3C-CH_3}} \xrightarrow[(CH_3)_3COH]{(CH_3)_3COK} \overset{\overset{CH_3}{|}}{CH_3C=CH_2}$$

tert-Butyl bromide

or $\quad \overset{\overset{CH_3}{|}}{CH_3CHCH_2Br} \xrightarrow[(CH_3)_3COH]{(CH_3)_3COK} \overset{\overset{CH_3}{|}}{CH_3C=CH_2}$

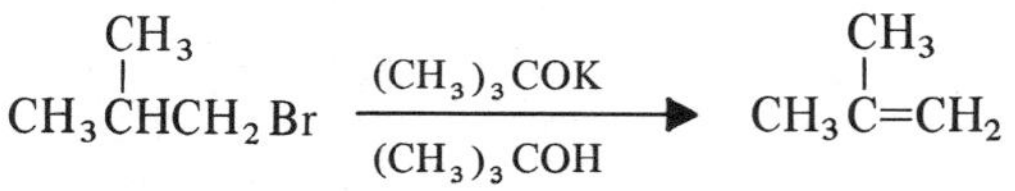

Isobutyl bromide

Both of these compounds can be prepared by brominating isobutane.

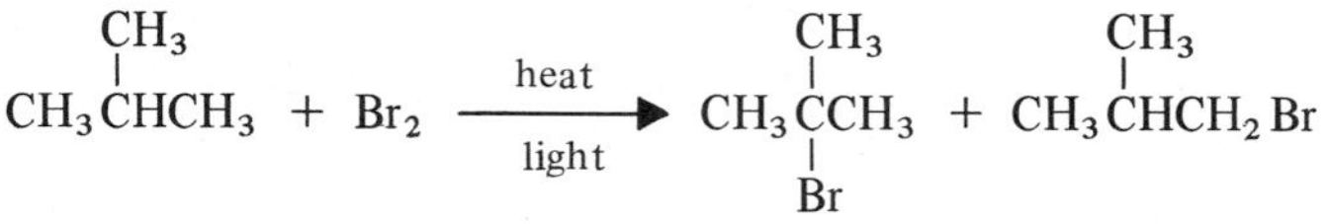

$$\overset{\overset{CH_3}{|}}{CH_3CHCH_3} + Br_2 \xrightarrow[light]{heat} \underset{\underset{Br}{|}}{\overset{\overset{CH_3}{|}}{CH_3CCH_3}} + \overset{\overset{CH_3}{|}}{CH_3CHCH_2Br}$$

That this method yields a mixture of compounds is not a problem in this synthesis because either compound yields 2-methylpropene when subjected to dehydrohalogenation. We need not even separate the components of the mixture. (As we saw in Section 4.10, the mixture formed in this instance is primarily composed of *tert*-butyl bromide.)

7.38 (a) $CH_3CH_2CH_3$ + Br_2 $\xrightarrow[\text{light}]{CCl_4}$ $\left.\begin{array}{l} CH_3CH_2CH_2Br \\ + \\ CH_3\underset{\underset{Br}{|}}{C}HCH_3 \end{array}\right\}$ $\xrightarrow[(CH_3)_3COH]{(CH_3)_3COK}$ $CH_3CH=CH_2$

(excess)

(b) $CH_3CH=CH_2$ (above) + HBr $\xrightarrow[\text{inhibitor}]{\text{free-radical}}$ $CH_3\underset{\underset{Br}{|}}{C}HCH_3$

(c) $CH_3CH=CH_2$ [from (a)] + HBr $\xrightarrow{\text{peroxides}}$ $CH_3CH_2CH_2Br$

(d) $CH_3\underset{\underset{CH_3}{|}}{C}HCH_3$ + Br_2 $\xrightarrow[\text{light}]{\text{heat}}$ $CH_3\underset{\underset{Br}{|}}{\overset{\overset{CH_3}{|}}{C}}CH_3$ $\xrightarrow[CH_3CH_2OH]{CH_3CH_2ONa}$ $CH_3\overset{\overset{CH_3}{|}}{C}=CH_2$

(excess)

(e) $CH_3\overset{\overset{CH_3}{|}}{C}=CH_2$ [from (d)] + H_2O $\xrightarrow{H_3O^+}$ $CH_3\underset{\underset{OH}{|}}{\overset{\overset{CH_3}{|}}{C}}CH_3$

(f) $CH_3CH_2CH_2CH_2Cl$ + $\xrightarrow[(CH_3)_3COH]{(CH_3)_3COK}$ $CH_3CH_2CH=CH_2$ $\xrightarrow[CCl_4]{Cl_2}$

$CH_3CH_2\underset{\underset{Cl}{|}}{C}HCH_2Cl$

(g) CH_3CH_2Br $\xrightarrow[(CH_3)_3COH]{(CH_3)_3COK}$ $CH_2=CH_2$ $\xrightarrow{Br_2 + H_2O}$ $\underset{\underset{OH\ \ Br}{|\ \ \ |}}{CH_2CH_2}$

(h) $CH_3\overset{\overset{CH_3}{|}}{C}=CH_2$ [from (d)] + HBr $\xrightarrow{\text{Peroxides}}$ $CH_3\overset{\overset{CH_3}{|}}{C}HCH_2Br$ $\xrightarrow{Li}$ $CH_3\overset{\overset{CH_3}{|}}{C}HCH_2Li$

$CH_3\overset{\overset{CH_3}{|}}{C}HCH_2CH_2\overset{\overset{CH_3}{|}}{C}HCH_3$ $\xleftarrow{CH_3\overset{\overset{CH_3}{|}}{C}HCH_2Br}$ $(CH_3\overset{\overset{CH_3}{|}}{C}HCH_2)_2CuLi$ $\xleftarrow{CuI}$

(i) + Br_2 $\xrightarrow[\text{light}]{CCl_4}$ —Br $\xrightarrow[CH_3CH_2OH]{CH_3CH_2ONa}$

(excess)

+ Cl_2 + H_2O $\longrightarrow$

(j) $CH_3CH_2CH_2CH_2Br \xrightarrow[\text{(CH}_3)_3\text{COH}]{\text{(CH}_3)_3\text{COK}} CH_3CH_2CH=CH_2 \xrightarrow[\text{peroxides}]{\text{HBr}} \text{no}$

$$CH_3CH_2\underset{\underset{Br}{|}}{C}HCH_3$$

(k) $CH_3CH_2CH_2CH_2Cl \xrightarrow[\text{(CH}_3)_3\text{COH}]{\text{(CH}_3)_3\text{COK}} CH_2CH_2CH=CH_2 \xrightarrow{\text{HCl}} CH_3CH_2\underset{\underset{Cl}{|}}{C}HCH_3$

$\downarrow$ Li

$$CH_3CH_2\underset{\underset{CH_3\;CH_3}{}}{}\ \ \quad \left(CH_3CH_2\overset{\overset{CH_3}{|}}{C}H\right)_2 CuLi \xleftarrow{\text{CuI}} CH_3CH_2\overset{\overset{CH_3}{|}}{C}HLi$$

$$CH_3CH_2\overset{\overset{CH_3}{|}}{C}HCl$$

$$\downarrow$$

$$CH_3CH_2\underset{\underset{CH_3}{|}}{C}H\!-\!\underset{\underset{CH_3}{|}}{C}HCH_2CH_3$$

(l) $CH_3\underset{\underset{CH_3}{|}}{\overset{\overset{CH_3}{|}}{C}}\!-\!OH \xrightarrow[\text{heat}]{H_2SO_4} CH_3\overset{\overset{CH_3}{|}}{C}=CH_2 \xrightarrow{\text{THF:BH}_3} (CH_3\overset{\overset{CH_3}{|}}{C}HCH_2)_3B$

$(CH_3\overset{\overset{CH_3}{|}}{C}HCH_2)_3B \xrightarrow[\text{OH}^-]{H_2O_2} CH_3\overset{\overset{CH_3}{|}}{C}HCH_2OH$

7.39 (a) $\underset{\text{MW=70.12}}{CH_3CH_2CH_2CH=CH_2} + \underset{\text{MW=159.8}}{Br_2} \longrightarrow CH_3CH_2CH_2\underset{\underset{Br}{|}}{C}HCH_2Br$

159.8 g Br_2 will react with 70.12 g pentene. Therefore $\sim$ 16 g Br_2 will react with 7.0 g pentene.

(b) Since bromine and an alkene react in equimolar proportions:

$$\frac{3.20\ g}{160\ g/mole} = 0.02\ \text{mole}\ Br_2 = 0.02\ \text{mole alkene}$$

$$2.24\ g\ \text{alkene} = (0.02\ \text{mole}) (\text{Mol. Wt.})$$

$$\therefore \text{Mol. Wt.} = \frac{2.24\ g}{0.02\ \text{mole}} = 112\ \text{g/mole alkene}$$

7.40

$$CH_3CH_2CH_2CH=CH_2 \ + \ HF \longrightarrow CH_3CH_2CH_2\overset{\overset{\displaystyle F}{|}}{C}HCH_3$$

7.41

(a)

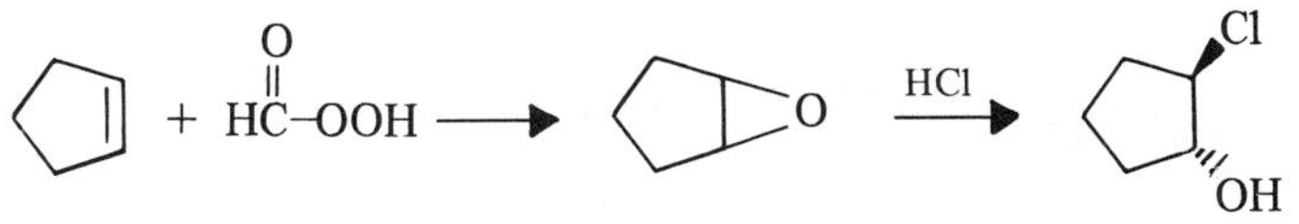

(b) The trans product because the Cl⁻ attacks anti to the epoxide and an inversion of configuration occurs.

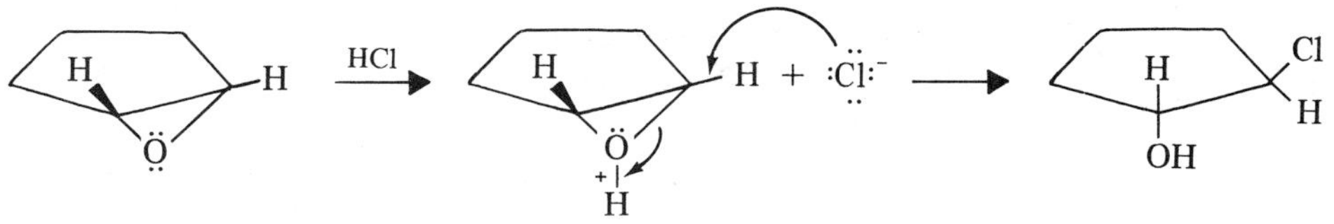

7.42

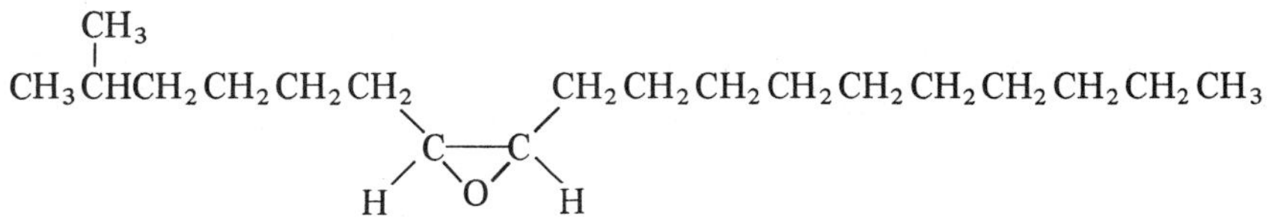

7.43

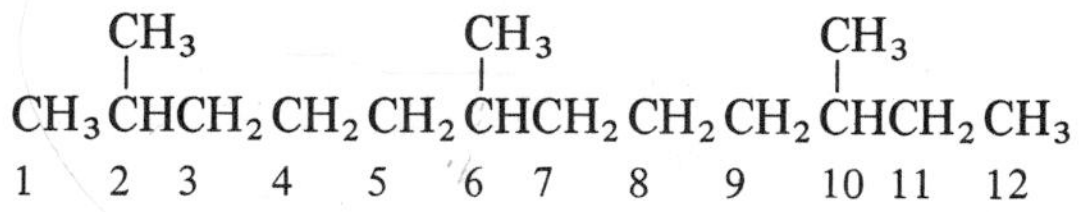

When subjected to ozonolysis followed by treatment with zinc and water one mole of the alarm pheromone produces the following compounds. Identifying the chain atoms as shown above allows us to assign the fragments.

Two moles of formaldehyde, $H-\overset{\overset{\displaystyle O}{||}}{C}-H$, must come from $-\underset{6}{\overset{\overset{\displaystyle O}{||}}{C}}-$, $-\underset{10}{\overset{\overset{\displaystyle CH_2}{||}}{C}}-$, or $-\underset{11\ \ 12}{\overset{\displaystyle CH_2}{C}=CH_2}$

One mole of acetone, $CH_3\overset{\overset{\displaystyle O}{||}}{C}CH_3$, must come from $\underset{1}{CH_3}\underset{2}{\overset{\overset{\displaystyle CH_3}{|}}{C}}=$

One mole of $CH_3\overset{\overset{\displaystyle O}{||}}{\underset{6\ 5}{C}}CH_2\underset{4}{CH_2}\overset{\overset{\displaystyle O}{||}}{\underset{3}{C}}H$ (location in the chain is shown)

$$\overset{\text{O}}{\overset{\|}{\text{HCCH}_2}}\text{CH}_2\overset{\text{O}}{\overset{\|}{\text{C}}}\overset{\text{O}}{\overset{\|}{\text{CH}}}$$

One mole of HCCH$_2$CH$_2$C–CH (location in the chain is shown)

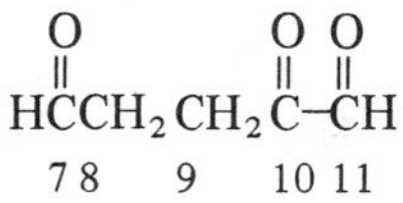

7 8   9   10 11

The assignment for the alarm pheromone is therefore

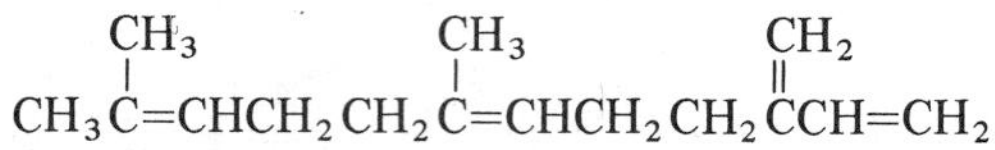

$$\overset{\text{CH}_3}{\underset{|}{\text{CH}_3\text{C}}}=\text{CHCH}_2\text{CH}_2\overset{\text{CH}_3}{\underset{|}{\text{C}}}=\text{CHCH}_2\text{CH}_2\overset{\text{CH}_2}{\overset{\|}{\text{C}}}\text{CH}=\text{CH}_2$$

7.44

(a) 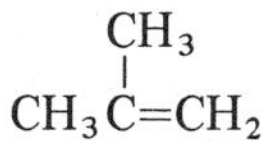 $\overset{\text{CH}_3}{\underset{|}{\text{CH}_3\text{C}}}=\text{CH}_2$

(b) **By** dehydrobromination as shown in (a) above, and then by adding HBr to the resulting alkene, isobutyl bromide can be converted into *tert*-butyl bromide:

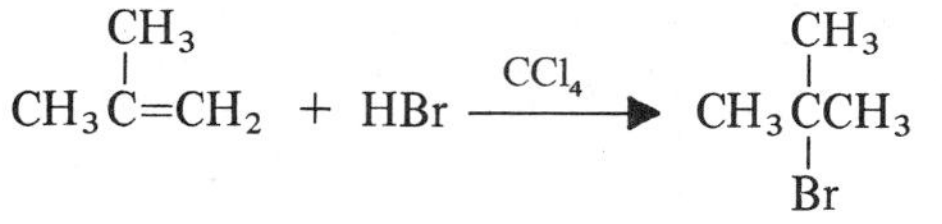

$$\overset{\text{CH}_3}{\underset{|}{\text{CH}_3\text{C}}}=\text{CH}_2 + \text{HBr} \xrightarrow{\text{CCl}_4} \underset{\underset{\text{Br}}{|}}{\overset{\overset{\text{CH}_3}{|}}{\text{CH}_3\text{CCH}_3}} \quad \text{(Markovnikov's rule)}$$

7.45   The intermediate I is competitively attacked by Cl$^-$, Br$^-$, and H$_2$O.

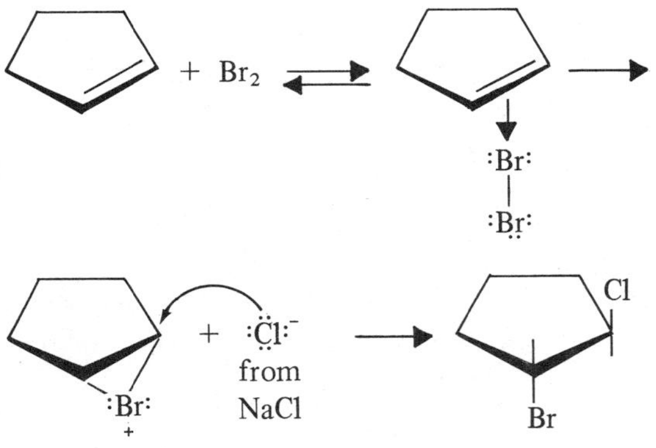

I

7.46

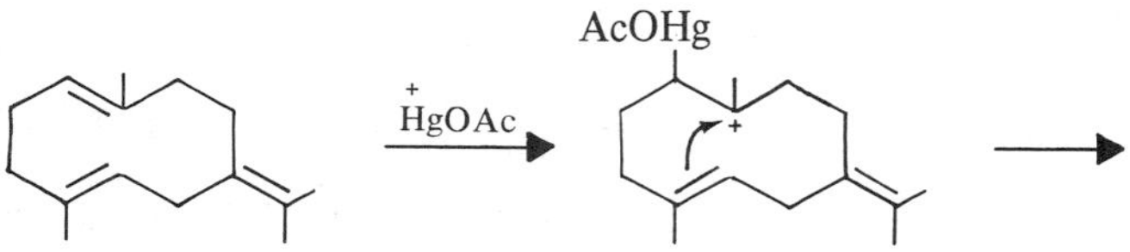

7.47

(a) $H{-}SH \xrightarrow{h\nu} H\cdot + \cdot SH$ **Chain-initiating step**

$R{-}CH{=}CH_2 + \cdot SH \longrightarrow R\overset{\cdot}{C}H{-}CH_2 SH$

$\left. R{-}\overset{\cdot}{C}HCH_2 SH + H{-}SH \longrightarrow RCH_2 CH_2 SH + \cdot SH \right\}$ **Chain-propagating steps**

(b) $R\overset{\cdot}{C}HCH_2 SH + RCH_2 CH_2 SH \longrightarrow RCH_2 CH_2 SH + RCH_2 CH_2 S\cdot$

$RCH{=}CH_2 + \cdot SCH_2 CH_2 R \longrightarrow R\overset{\cdot}{C}HCH_2 SCH_2 CH_2 R$

$R\overset{\cdot}{C}HCH_2 SCH_2 CH_2 R + RCH_2 CH_2 SH \longrightarrow (RCH_2 CH_2)_2 S + RCH_2 CH_2 S\cdot$

7.48 One dimer (the major product) gives the following products on ozonolysis.

The other dimer gives different products.

By isolating and identifying the products of each reaction, Whitmore and his students were able to deduce the structures of the diisobutylenes.

7.49 The isomers are propene tetramers formed by an acid-catalyzed reaction:

$$CH_3 CH{=}CH_2 + H_3 PO_4 \rightleftharpoons CH_3 \overset{+}{C}HCH_3 + H_2 PO_4^-$$

$$CH_3CH^+ + CH_2{=}CHCH_3 \longrightarrow \underset{\underset{CH_3}{|}}{CH}CH_2\underset{\underset{CH_3}{|}}{CH}{}^+$$

$$\underset{\underset{CH_3}{|}}{CH_3CHCH_2CH}{}^+ + CH_2{=}CHCH_3 \longrightarrow CH_3\underset{\underset{CH_3}{|}}{CH}CH_2\underset{\underset{CH_3}{|}}{CH}CH_2CH^+$$

$$CH_3\underset{\underset{CH_3}{|}}{CH}CH_2\underset{\underset{CH_3}{|}}{CH}CH_2\underset{\underset{CH_3}{|}}{CH}{}^+ + CH_2{=}CHCH_3 \longrightarrow CH_3\underset{\underset{CH_3}{|}}{CH}CH_2\underset{\underset{CH_3}{|}}{CH}CH_2\underset{\underset{CH_3}{|}}{CH}CH_2\overset{+}{C}HCH_3$$

$$CH_3\underset{\underset{CH_3}{|}}{CH}CH_2\underset{\underset{CH_3}{|}}{CH}CH_2\underset{\underset{CH_3}{|}}{CH}CH_2\overset{+}{C}HCH_3 \xrightarrow{-H^+} CH_3\underset{\underset{CH_3}{|}}{CH}CH_2\underset{\underset{CH_3}{|}}{CH}CH_2\underset{\underset{CH_3}{|}}{CH}CH{=}CHCH_3$$

$$+$$

$$CH_3\underset{\underset{CH_3}{|}}{CH}CH_2\underset{\underset{CH_3}{|}}{CH}CH_2\underset{\underset{CH_3}{|}}{CH}CH_2CH{=}CH_2$$

*7.50   X = Br is the only case in which both propagation steps are exothermic ($\Delta H°$ is negative). Each of the other reactions has one step with a high E_{act}:

$$\dot{\ddot{X}} = F, E_{act} \geqslant + 38 \text{ kcal/mole (2nd step)}$$
$$\dot{\ddot{X}} = Cl, E_{act} \geqslant + 5 \text{ kcal/mole (2nd step)}$$
$$\dot{\ddot{X}} = I, E_{act} \geqslant + 7 \text{ kcal/mole (1st step)}$$

SECTION REFERENCES FOR ADDITIONAL PROBLEMS

7.29	6.5, 7.13		**7.40**	7.2A
7.30	7.2		**7.41**	7.12A
7.31	7.2		**7.42**	7.12
7.32	6.14, 7.8, 7.9		**7.43**	7.13C
7.33	7.13C		**7.44**	6.9, 7.2
7.34	7.5		**7.45**	7.11
7.35	6.6, 6.12, 7.2, 7.4		**7.46**	7.6
7.36	6.12, 7.2		**7.47**	7.14
7.37	7.13B		**7.48**	7.13C, 7.15
7.38	4.10, 5.14, 6.10, 7.10, 7.11, 7.14		**7.49**	7.15
7.39	7.9		**7.50**	7.14

SELF-TEST

7.1   Supply the missing compounds in the following equations. Show stereochemistry where appropriate. If more than one organic product results, give only the major product. If two steps are required, show them as (1) Step 1, (2) Step 2, etc.

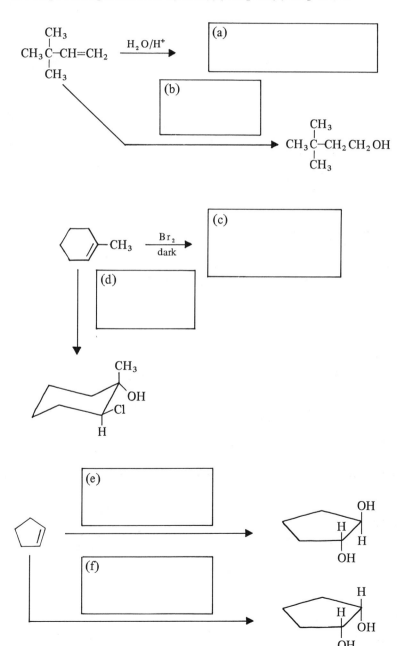

7.2   Give the structural formulas of the missing compounds. Show stereochemistry where appropriate.

Note: **A** and **B** are different

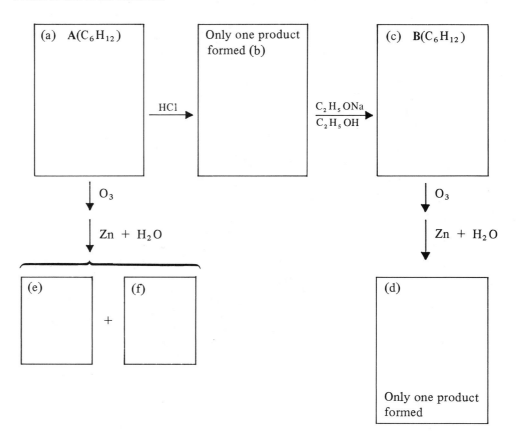

7.3   An unknown hydrocarbon, **A**, has the molecular formula C_7H_{10}. Complete hydrogenation gives **B** whose molecular formula is C_7H_{14}. Ozonolysis of A, followed by $Zn + H_2O$ reduction of the ozonide, gives the following compounds in equal molar amounts.

$$\overset{O}{\overset{\|}{HC}}CH_2\overset{O}{\overset{\|}{C}}CH_3 \quad \text{and} \quad \overset{O}{\overset{\|}{HC}}CH_2\overset{O}{\overset{\|}{C}}H$$

A = _____(a)_____   and **B** = _____(b)_____

SUPPLEMENTARY PROBLEMS

S7.1   Supply the missing compound in each of the following reactions:

(a) 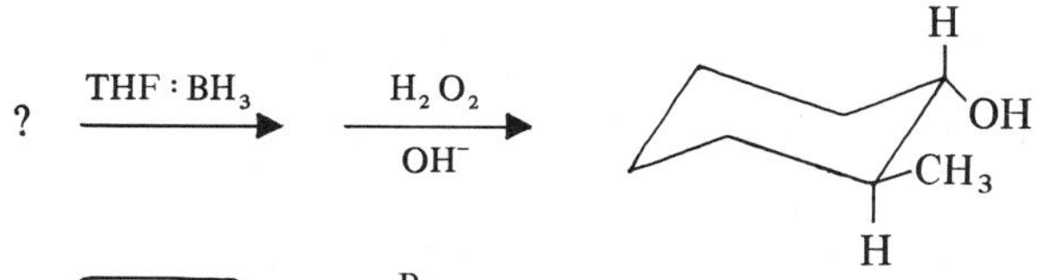 ? $\xrightarrow{\text{THF}\,:\,\text{BH}_3}$ $\xrightarrow[\text{OH}^-]{\text{H}_2\text{O}_2}$

(b) 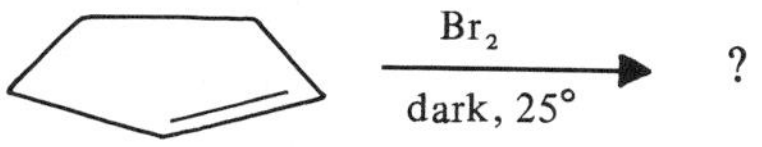 $\xrightarrow[\text{dark, 25°}]{\text{Br}_2}$?

(c) $C_6H_{12}(?)$ $\xrightarrow{O_3}$ $\xrightarrow[\text{H}_2\text{O}]{\text{Zn}}$ $CH_3\overset{\overset{\text{O}}{\|}}{C}CH_3$

S7.2   Show all the steps necessary to convert

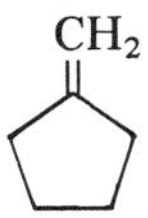

into   (a) 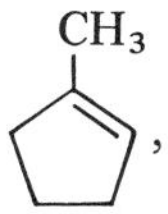 ,   (b) 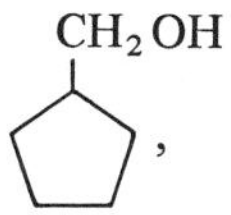 ,   (c)

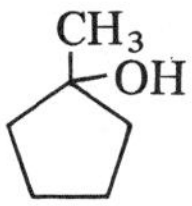

S7.3   A certain compound has the molecular formula C_5H_8. Ozonolysis yields

$$HC\overset{\overset{\text{O}}{\|}}{-}CH_2CH_2\overset{\overset{\text{O}}{\|}}{C}CH_3$$

Give the structural formula of the original compound.

SOLUTIONS TO SUPPLEMENTARY PROBLEMS

S7.1   (a) 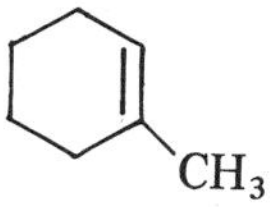   Hydroboration-oxidation involves *syn*-addition of H—and −OH.

(b) 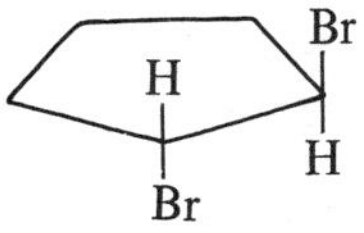   Bromination involves *anti* addition

(c)

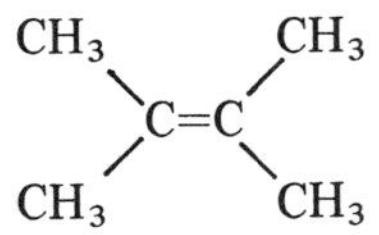

$$\underset{CH_3}{\overset{CH_3}{>}}C=C\underset{CH_3}{\overset{CH_3}{<}}$$

S7.2

(a)

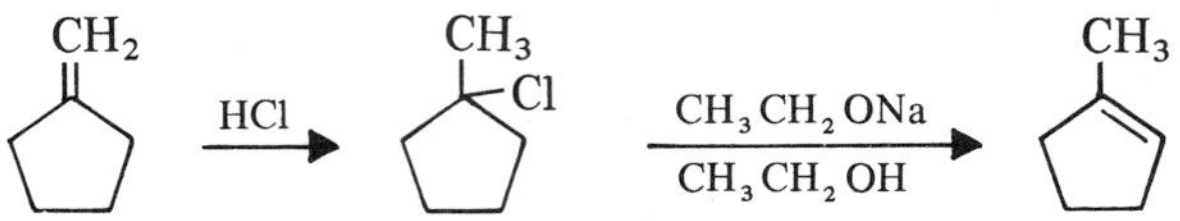

(b)

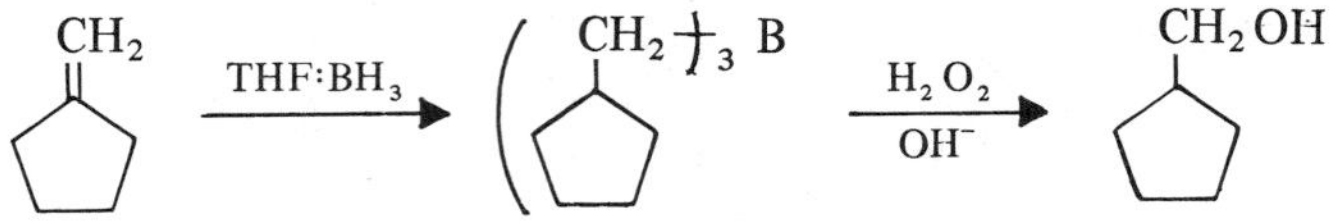

(c)

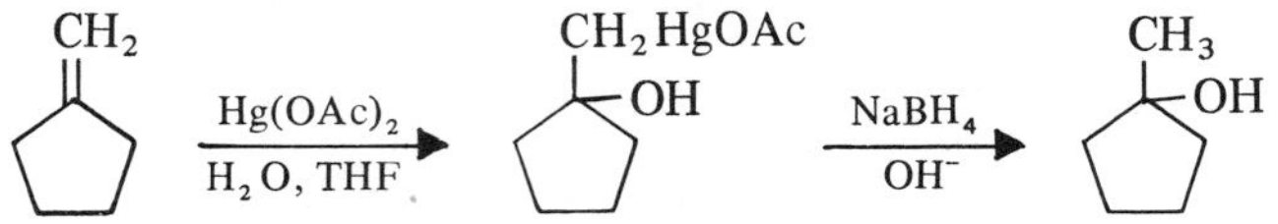

S7.3 Rewriting the ozonolysis product with the carbons of the two carbonyl groups joined together as a double bond reveals the structure of the original C_5H_8:

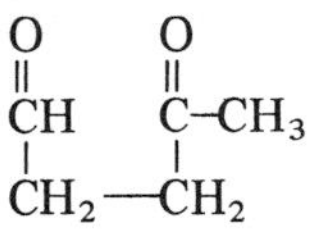

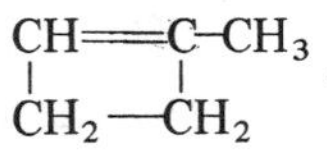

= Original compound

8 STEREOCHEMISTRY II: CHIRAL MOLECULES

SOLUTIONS TO PROBLEMS

8.1 Chiral (a) screw, (e) foot, (f) ear, (g) shoe, (h) spiral staircase
Achiral (b) plain spoon, (c) fork, (d) cup

8.2 (b) Yes (c) No (d) No

8.3 (a) Yes (b) Yes (c) No (d) No

8.4 (a) 1-Chloropropane, (c) 1-chloro-2-methylpropane, (d) 2-chloro-2-methylpropane, (f) 1-chloropentane, and (h) 3-chloropentane are all achiral.

(b) 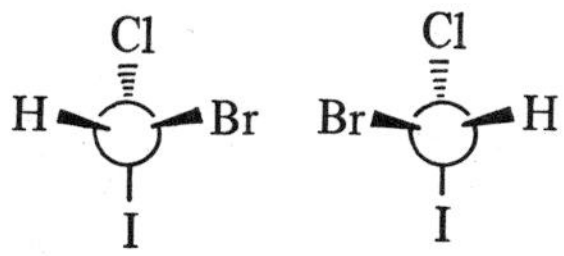

I II

(e) 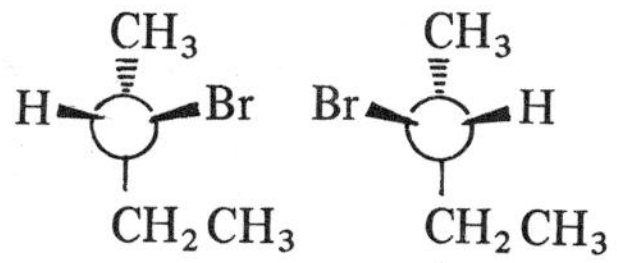

I II

(g) 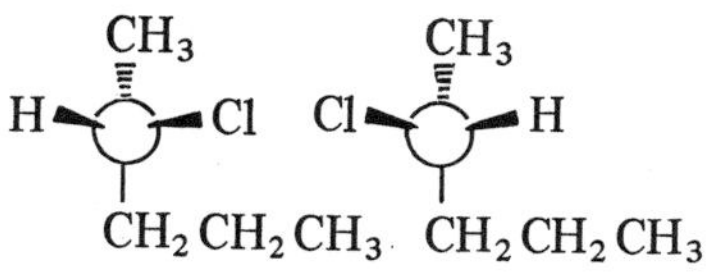

I II

8.5

(a) 1. 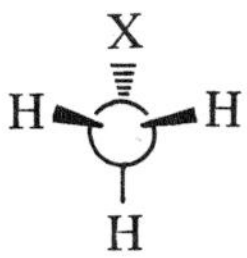

2. 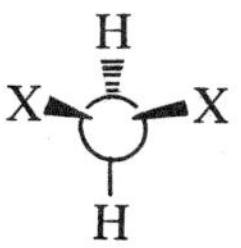

or 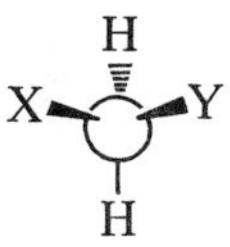

3. 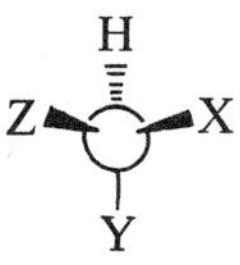

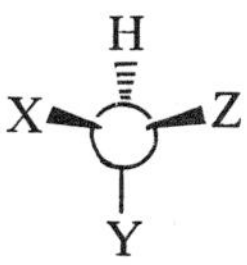

(b) 1. One

2. Two: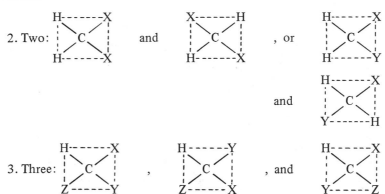

3. Three:

(c) 1. One

2. Three:

3. Six:

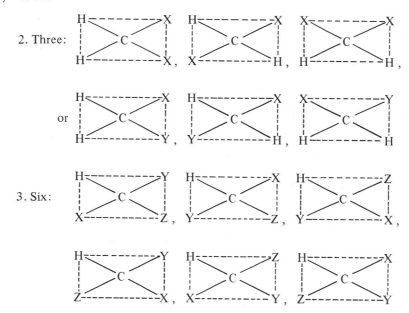

(d) 1. One

2. Two or three:

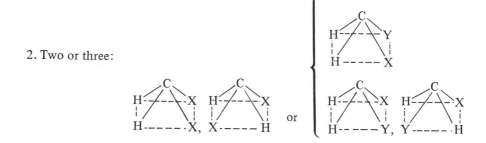

3. Six:

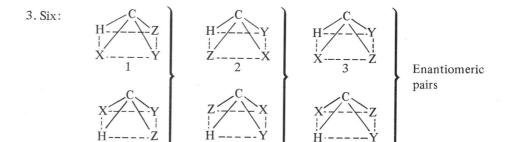

Enantiomeric pairs

8.6   (b) Plain spoon, (c) Fork, (d) Cup all possess a plane of symmetry.

8.7

(a) The plane of symmetry is perpendicular to page and passes through Cl and 3C's

(c) The plane of symmetry is perpendicular to page and passes through Cl and 2C's

(d) A vertical plane perpendicular to page passes through Cl, tertiary C, and CH₃ at bottom

(f) A plane perpendicular to page passes through Cl and 5C's

(h) A plane perpendicular to page passes through Cl, C, and H

8.8

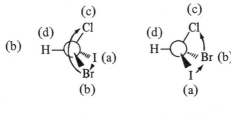

From priority (a) to (b) to (c), the direction is counterclockwise, therefore II is (S)-2-butanol

II

8.9

(b) I = (R)

II = (S)

(e) I = (S)

II = (R)

(g) I = (S)

II = (R)

8.10

CHO
H⎼OH
CH₂OH
(R)

CHO
HO⎼H
CH₂OH
(S)

8.11 (a) (R)   (b) (R)   (c) (R)

8.12 (a) Enantiomers

(b) Two molecules of the same compound

(c) Enantiomers

8.13 The optical purity is 50% (see previous paragraph in text). That means that the sample contains 50% of the (S) enantiomer and 50% of the racemic mixture. The racemic mixture is 50% (S) and 50% (R). Therefore the total percentage of (S) enantiomer in the sample is 75%, the percentage of (R) enantiomer is 25%.

8.14 (a) $CH_3CH_2CH_2CHCH_2CH_3$ (racemic modification because reactants are achiral)
            |
           CH_3

(b) $CH_3CH_2CHOHCH_3$ (racemic modification)   (c) Same as (b)

8.15 (a) Diastereomers   (b) Diastereomers   (c) Diastereomers

(d)

	1	2	3	4
1		enantiomers	diastereomers	diastereomers
2	enantiomers		diastereomers	diastereomers
3	diastereomers	diastereomers		enantiomers
4	diastereomers	diastereomers	enantiomers	

(e) Yes   (f) No

8.16 (a) **A** alone would be optically active.

(b) **B** alone would be optically active.

(c) **C** would be optically inactive because it is a *meso* compound.

(d) An equimolar mixture of **A** and **B** would be optically inactive because it is a racemic modification.

8.17 (1) **C**   (2) **A**   (3) **B**

8.18

(a)

(*meso*)   enantiomers

(b)

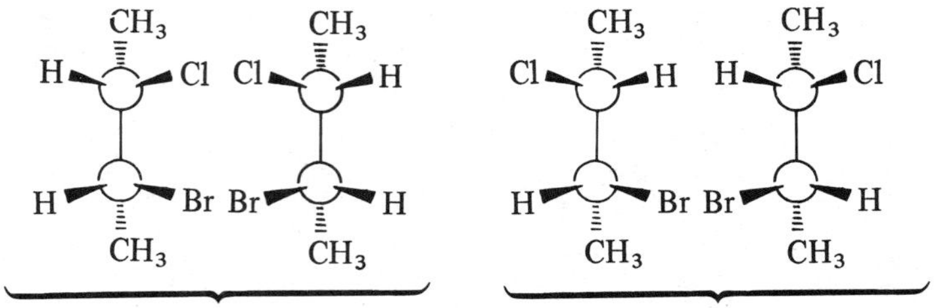

Enantiomers   Enantiomers

I   II   III   IV

(c)

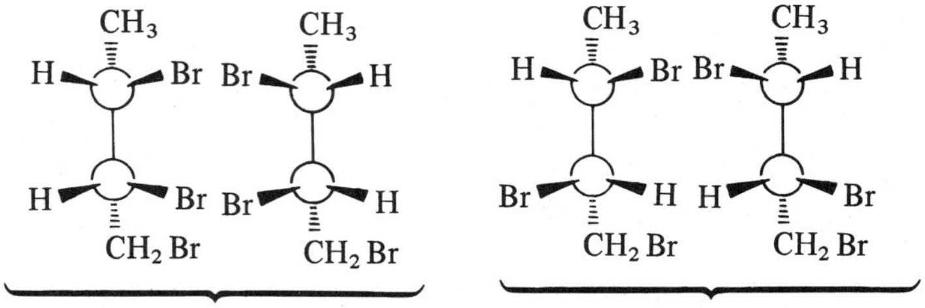

Enantiomers   Enantiomers

(d)

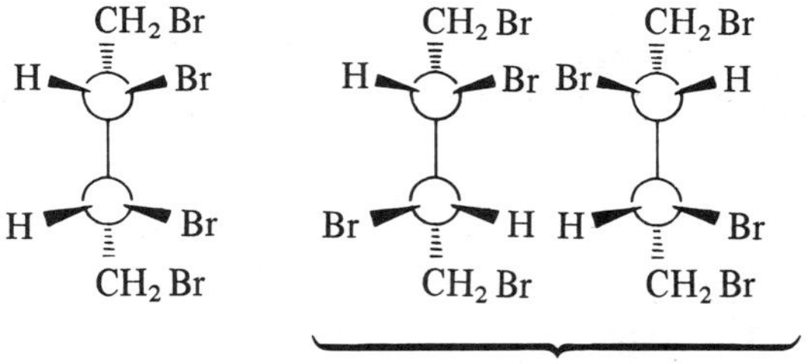

meso   Enantiomers

(e)

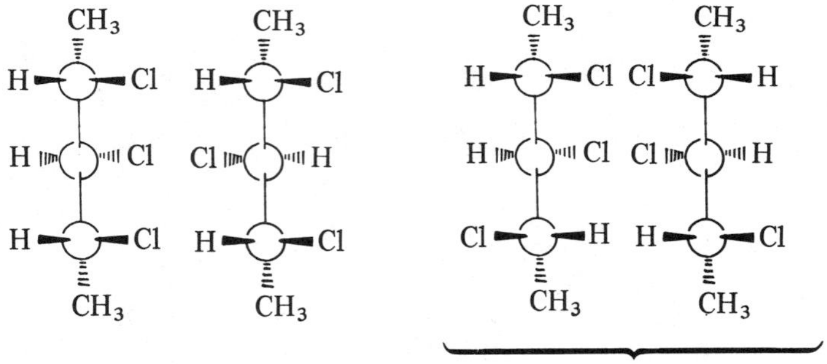

meso   *meso*   Enantiomers

8.19   (a)   Since it is optically inactive and not resolvable, it must be the *meso* form:

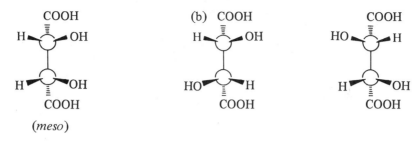

(*meso*)

(c)   No   (d)   A racemic modification

8.20   (a)   No   (b)   Yes   (c)   No   (d)   No   (e)   Diastereomers   (f)   Diastereomers

8.21   (a)   *trans*-1,2-Dibromocyclopentanes   (b)   Racemate

(c)   *cis*-1,2-Dibromocyclopentane (*meso*)

8.22

(a)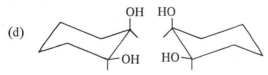

(b)   No they are not superposable.

(c)   No, and they are, therefore, enantiomers of each other.

(d)

(e)   No they are not superposable.

(f)   Yes, and they are, therefore, just different conformations of the same molecule.

(g)

A racemate

(h)

8.23   (a)

(b)   Yes, and therefore *trans*-1,4-cyclohexanediol is achiral.

(c)   No, they are different orientations of the same molecule.

(d)   No, because it does not contain chiral carbons.

(e)   Yes, *cis*-1,4-cyclohexanediol is a stereoisomer (a diastereomer) of *trans*-1,4-cyclo-hexanediol.

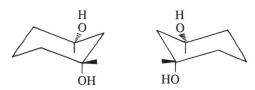

cis-1, 4-Cyclohexanediol

(f)   No, it, too, is superposable on its mirror image. (Notice, too, that the plane of the page constitutes a plane of symmetry for both *cis*-1,2-cyclohexanediol and for *trans*-1,2-cyclohexanediol as we have drawn them.)

(g)   No, because it does not contain chiral carbons.

8.24   *trans*-1,3-Cyclohexanediol can exist in the enantiomeric forms shown below.

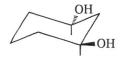

trans-1,3-Cyclohexanediol enantiomers

cis-1,3-Cyclohexanediol consists of achiral molecules and is a *meso* compound. [The plane of the page (below) is a plane of symmetry. Notice, too, that carbons-1 and -3 are chiral carbons. Thus *cis*-1,3-cyclohexanediol fulfills the definition of a *meso* compound: Its molecules are achiral but contain chiral carbons.]

cis-1, 3-Cyclohexanediol
(a *meso* compound)

8.25   (a)   Two stereoisomers would be produced. They are (p. 151) the enantiomers of *trans*-1,2-dibromocyclohexane. The addition of bromine to a double bond is an *anti* addition.

(b) When bromine adds to cyclohexene, the *trans*-1,2-dibromocyclohexane enantiomers are produced initially in their diaxial conformations (Sect. 7.10). These are quickly converted (through ring flips) into a mixture in which the more stable diequatorial conformation predominates. (c) Because attack on the bromonium ion by paths (a) and (b) occur at equal rates, the *trans*-1,2-dibromocyclohexane enantiomers are produced as a racemate.

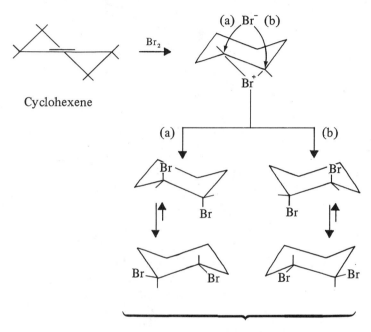

trans-1, 2-Dibromocyclohexane enantiomers
(a racemate)

(d) Distillation cannot separate enantiomers, so one product (an equilibrium mixture of diaxial-diequatorial enantiomers) would result.

(e) No.

8.26 **B**: (2*S*,3*S*)-2,3-Butanediol, **C**: (2*R̶*,3*S̶*)-2,3-butanediol

8.27 (a) The meso compound is (2*S*,3*R*)-2,3-dibromobutane, the two enantiomers are (2*S*,3*S*)-2,3-dibromobutane and (2*R*,3*R*)-2,3-dibromobutane.

(b) I: (2*R*,3*S*)-2-bromo-3-chlorobutane
II: (2*S*,3*R*)-2-bromo-3-chlorobutane
III: (2*R*,3*R*)-2-bromo-3-chlorobutane
IV: (2*S*,3*S*)-2-bromo-3-chlorobutane

8.28 The stereochemistry is consistent with mechanisms involving initial formation of bromonium ions.

cis-2-Butene

Bromonioum ion
(a *meso* compound)

Addition at the other face of *cis*-2-butene yields the same intermediate

Enantiomeric 2, 3-dibromobutanes

Addition at one face of *trans*-2-butene

Addition at the other face of *trans*-2-butene

These bromonium ions are enantiomers of each other

Using the upper enantiomer to illustrate the next step, we find that when the bromide ion attacks either carbon, the reaction produces *meso*-2,3-dibromobutane. Exactly the same result is obtained by use of the other enantiomer of the bromonium ion. (You should prove this for yourself.)

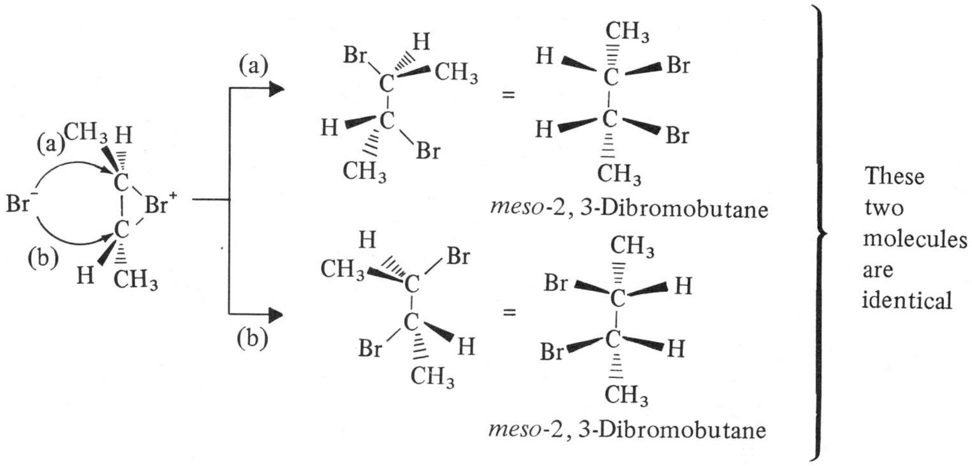

meso-2, 3-Dibromobutane

meso-2, 3-Dibromobutane

These two molecules are identical

8.29

(a)

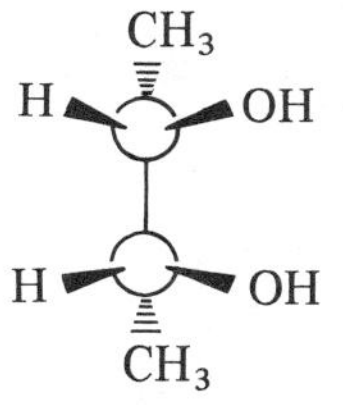

(meso)

(b)

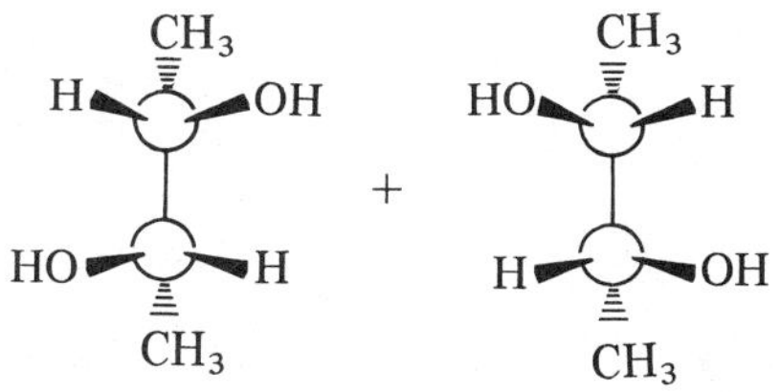

+ (racemate)

8.30

(a) (b)

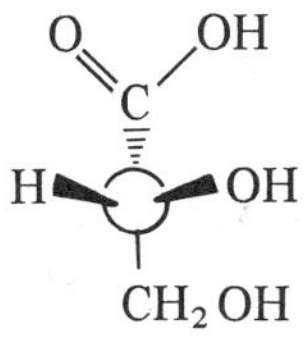

(*R*)-(−)-glyceric acid

(a) (d)

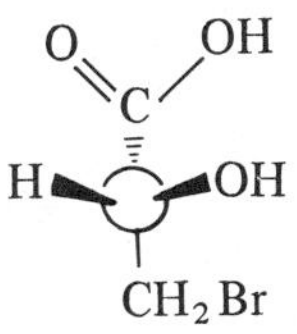

(*S*)-(−)-3-bromo-2-hydroxypropanoic acid

(c)

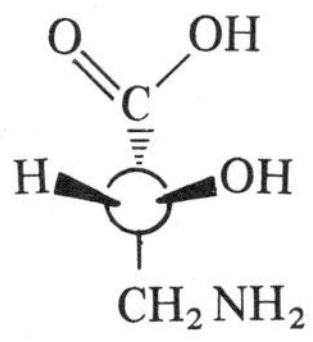

(*R*)-(+)-isoserine

8.31   Reaction to form the ester does not involve the chiral carbon, so the reaction occurs with retention of configuration.

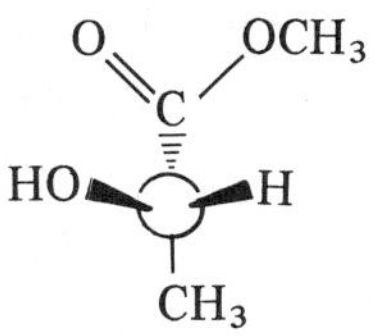

(*S*)-(−)-methyl lactate

8.32 (a) We know that when a secondary alkyl halide reacts with hydroxide ion by substitution, the reaction occurs with *inversion of configuration* because the reaction is S_N2. If we know that the configuration of (–)-2-butanol (from Sect. 8.6C) is that shown below, then we can conclude that (+)-2-chlorobutane has the opposite configuration.

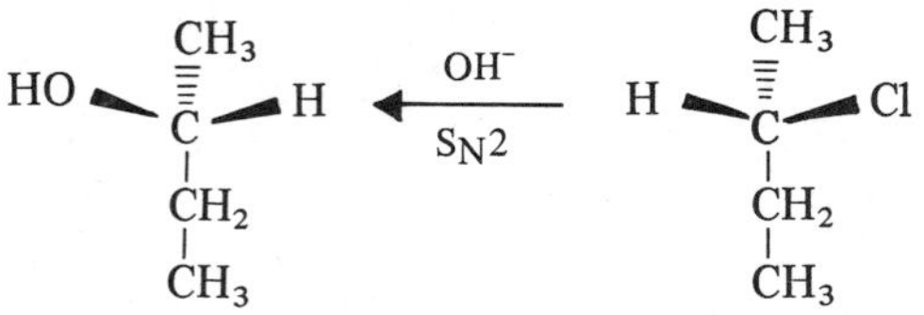

(R)-(–)-2-Butanol (S)-(+)-2-Chlorobutane
$[\alpha]_D^{25°} = -13.52°$ $[\alpha]_D^{25°} = +36.00°$

(b) Again the reaction is S_N2. Because we now know the configuration of (+)-2-chlorobutane to be (S) [cf., part (a)], we can conclude that the configuration of (–)-2-iodobutane is (R).

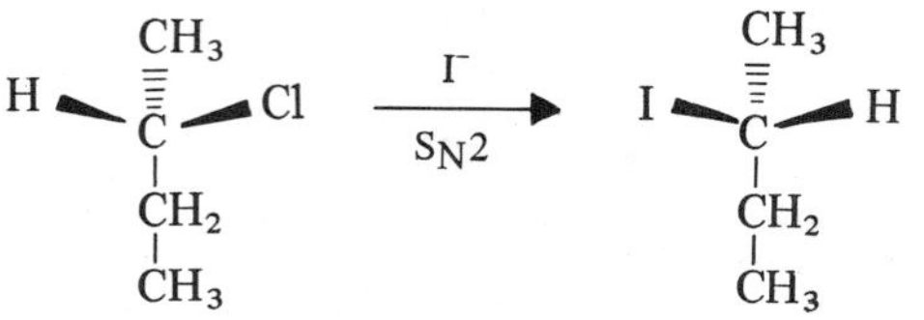

(S)-(+)-2-Chlorobutane (R)-(–)-2-Iodobutane

(+)-2-Iodobutane has the (S) configuration.

8.33 The overall process involves racemization. A possible mechanism involves the formation of an achiral carbocation:

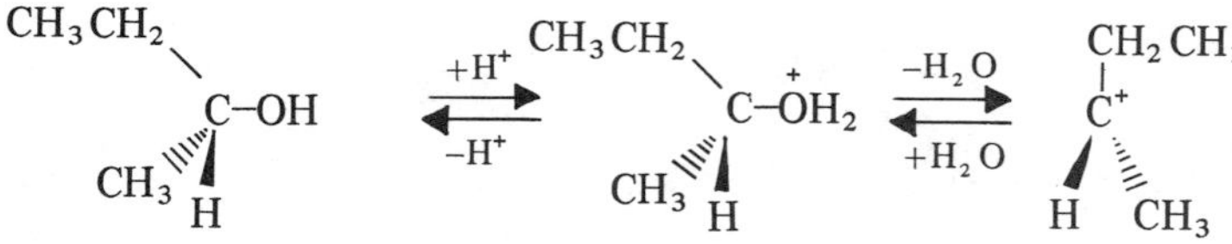

(R)-(–)-2-Butanol   (achiral)

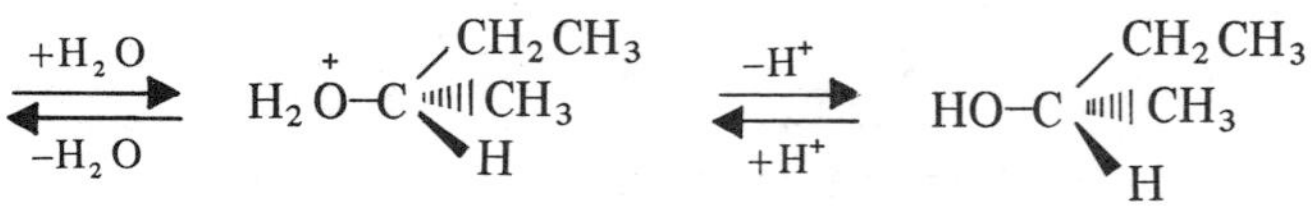

(S)-(+)-2-Butanol

Once formed the carbocation can revert to (R)-(–)-2-butanol or become (S)-(+)-2-butanol. After continued heating a racemate will be produced.

8.34 We know (from Sect. 4.12) that most free radicals are trigonal planar at the carbon bearing the odd electron. Therefore, as free radicals are produced by abstraction of a hydrogen from carbon 2 of (R)-$(-)$-1-chloro-2-methylbutane (below), chiral molecules are converted into an achiral intermediate. The achiral free radical then reacts with chlorine to produce 1,2-dichloro-2-methylbutane as a racemate.

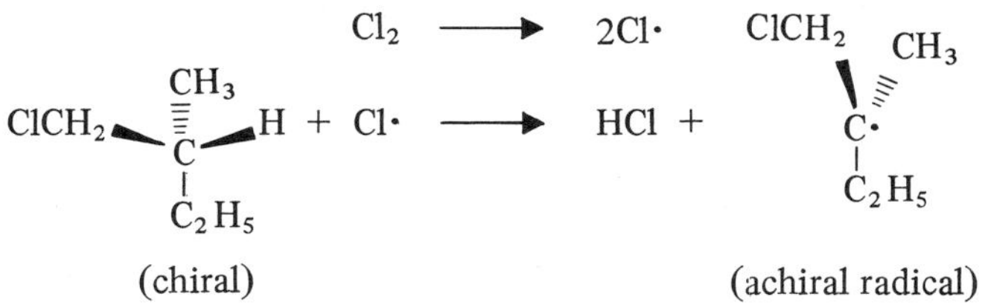

$$Cl_2 \longrightarrow 2Cl\cdot$$

(chiral)   (achiral radical)

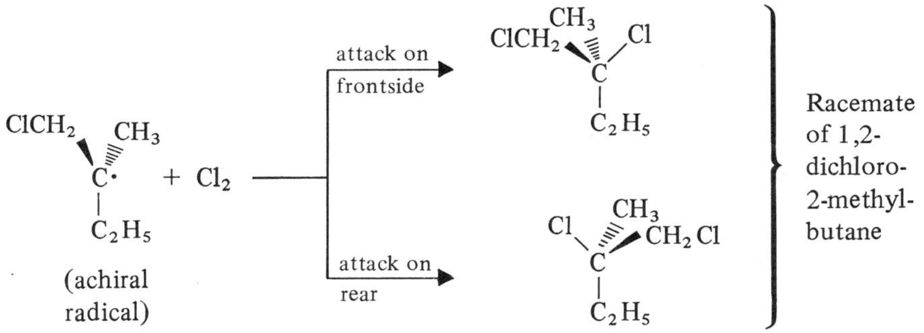

attack on frontside

attack on rear

Racemate of 1,2-dichloro-2-methyl-butane

(achiral radical)

8.35

(a) 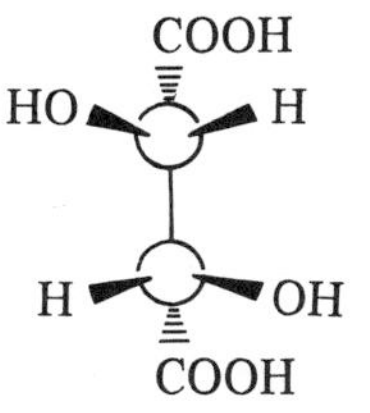   (b)

$(-)$-Tartaric acid $(meso)$-Tartaric acid

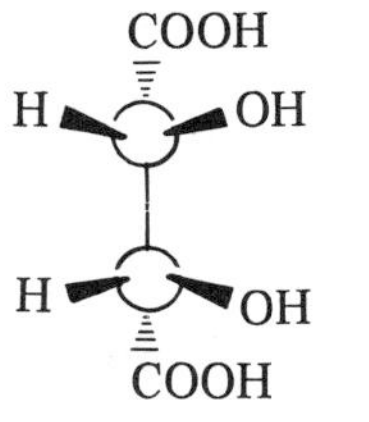

(c) No, *meso*-tartaric acid would *not* be optically active.

8.36 Cis-trans isomers are always diastereomers.

8.37 (a) (Z) - 1-Bromo-1-chloro-1-butene

(b) (Z) - 2-Bromo-1-chloro-1-iodopropene

(c) (*E*) - 3-Ethyl-4-methyl-2-pentene

(d) (*E*) - 1-Chloro-1-fluoro-2-methyl-1-butene

8.38 (a) Isomers are different compounds that have the same molecular formula. C_2H_6O: CH_3CH_2OH and CH_3OCH_3

(b) Structural isomers are isomers that differ because their atoms are joined in a different order. C_4H_{10}: $CH_3CH_2CH_2CH_3$ and $CH_3\overset{|}{C}HCH_3$
$$\overset{|}{C}H_3$$

(c) Stereoisomers are isomers that differ only in the arrangement of their atoms in space: *cis-* and *trans* -2-butene.

(d) Diastereomers are stereoisomers that are not mirror reflections of each other: *cis-* and *trans* -2-butene, or (2 *S*, 3 *S*)- and (2 *S*, 3 *R*)-2, 3-dibromobutane.

(e) Enantiomers are stereoisomers that are nonsuperposable mirror reflections of each other: (2 *S*,3 *S*)-and (2 *R*,3 *R*)- 2, 3-dibromobutane.

(f) A *meso* compound is made up of achiral molecules that contain chiral centers: (2 *S*,3 *R*)- 2, 3-dibromobutane.

(g) A racemate is an equimolar mixture of a pair of enantiomers.

(h) A plane of symmetry is an imaginary plane that bisects a molecule in such a way that the two halves of the molecule are mirror reflections of each other. (See Fig. 8.7.)

(i) A chiral center is any tetrahedral atom that has four different groups attached to it.

(j) A chiral molecule is one that is not superposable on its mirror reflection.

(k) An achiral molecule is superposable on its mirror reflection.

(l) Optical activity is the rotation of the plane of polarization of plane polarized light by a substance placed in the light path.

(m) A dextrorotatory substance is one that rotates the plane of polarization of plane polarized light in a clockwise direction.

(n) A reaction occurs with retention of configuration when all the groups around the chiral atom retain the same relative configuration after the reaction that they had before the reaction.

8.39 (a) Enantiomers (b) Same (c) Enantiomers (d) Diastereomers (e) Same (f) Structural isomers (g) Same (h) Diastereomers (i) Same (j) Enantiomers (k) Same (l) Enantiomers (m) Same (n) Structural isomers (o) Same (p) Diastereomers (q) Enantiomers

8.40 (a)

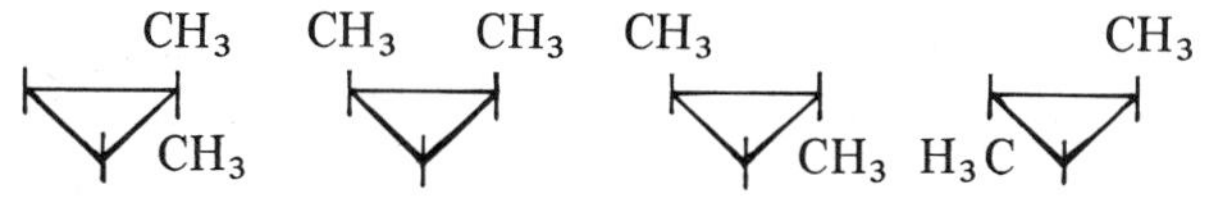

(I)   (II)   (III)   (IV)

meso   Enantiomers

(b) III and IV   (c) II   (d) Three: I, II, and a mixture of III and IV. Enantiomers cannot be separated from one another by distillation.   (e) None, since the only chiral molecules are **III** and **IV**, and they would be obtained in the same amounts as a racemic modification.

8.41

(a) 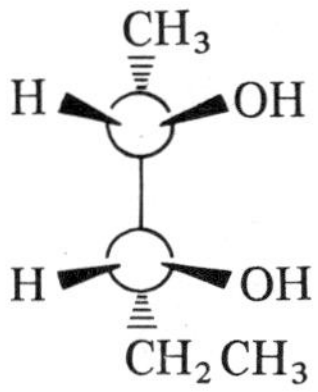 and enantiomer through *syn* addition,

(b) 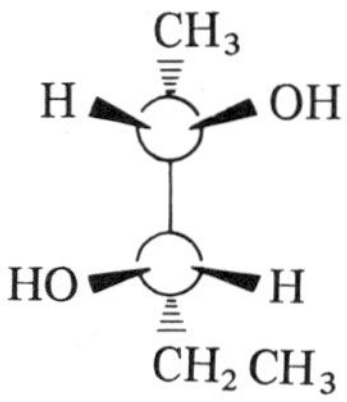 and enantiomer through *anti* addition,

(c) 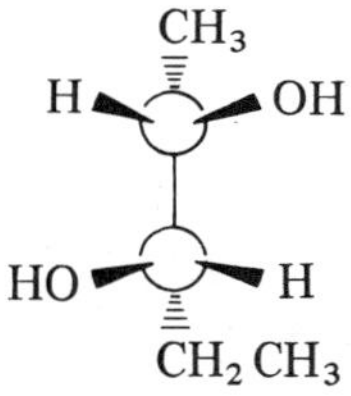 and enantiomer through *syn* addition,

(d) 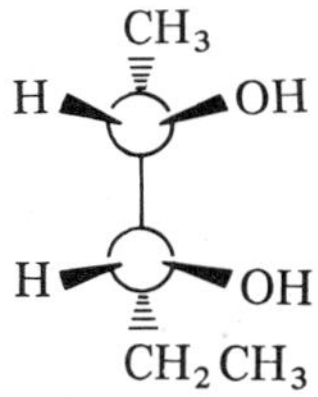 and enantiomer through *anti* addition,

(e) 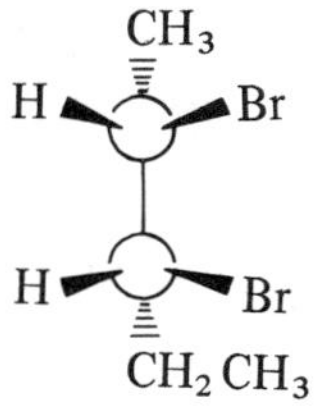 and enantiomer through *anti* addition,

(f) 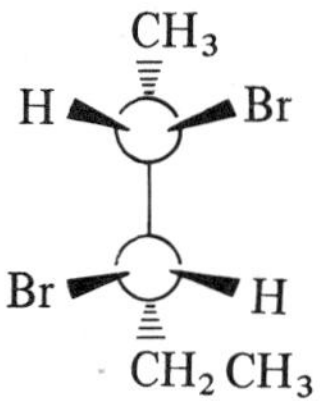 and enantiomer through *anti* addition.

8.42 (a) $(2S,3R)$ - [enantiomer is $(2R,3S)$]   (b) $(2S,3S)$ - [the enantiomer is $(2R,3R)$-]

(c) Same as (b)   (d) Same as (a)   (e) $(2S,3R)$ - [the enantiomer is $(2R,3S)$-]

(f) $(2S,3S)$ - [the enantiomer is $(2R,3R)$-]

8.43 (a) Retention because the chiral carbon is not involved.

(b) Retention because the chiral carbon is not involved.

(c)   Inversion because an S_N2 reaction occurs at the chiral carbon.

(d)   Racemization because proton transfer from H_3O^+ to alcohol is followed by formation of an achiral carbocation (see the answer to Problem 8.33).

(e)   Racemization because an S_N1 reaction occurs at the chiral carbon.

(f)   Inversion because an S_N2 reaction occurs at the chiral carbon.

(g)   Retention because the chiral carbon (the 3° carbon) is not involved. There would be an inversion of configuration at the primary carbon of the CH_2Cl group when it is attacked by OH^-. We would not be able to detect this inversion of configuration because this carbon is not chiral.

8.44

(a) 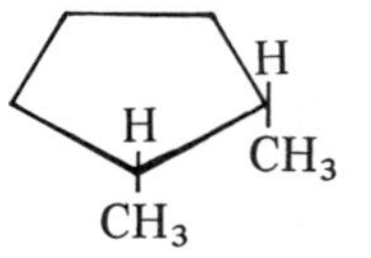   *syn*-addition   (b)   No, it is a *meso* compound.

(c)   No

8.45

(a)

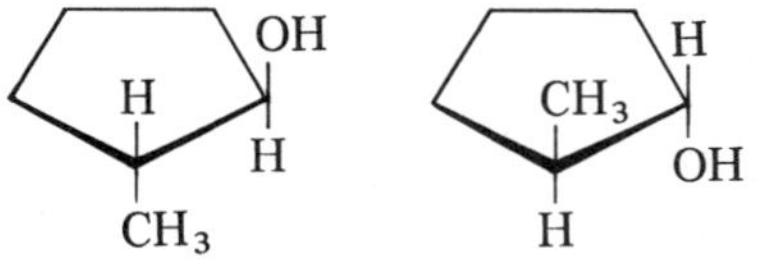

(b)

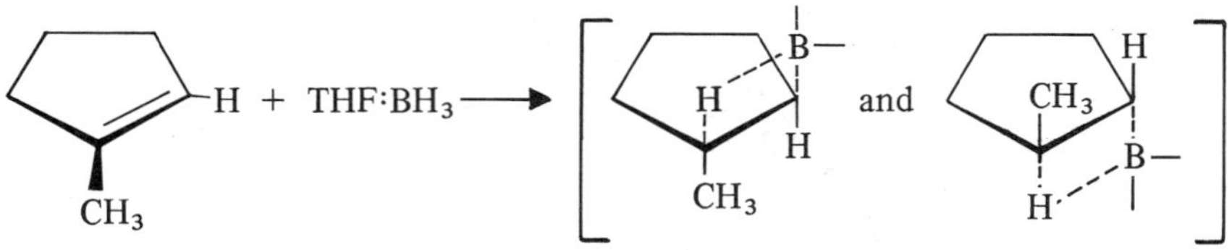

The BH_3 group may attack the double bond from either side of the ring

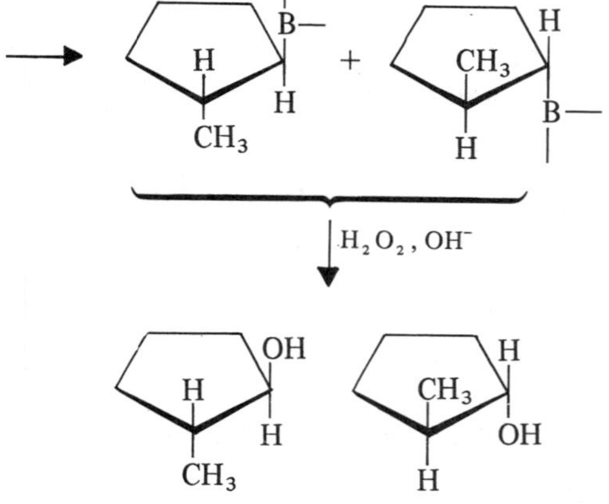

8.46 (a) Four

(b)

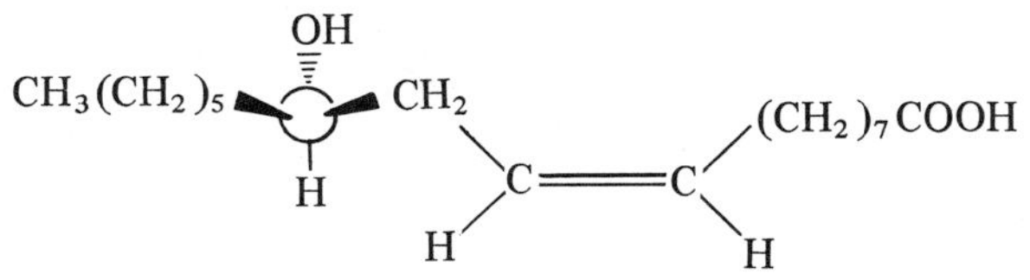

+ Enantiomer

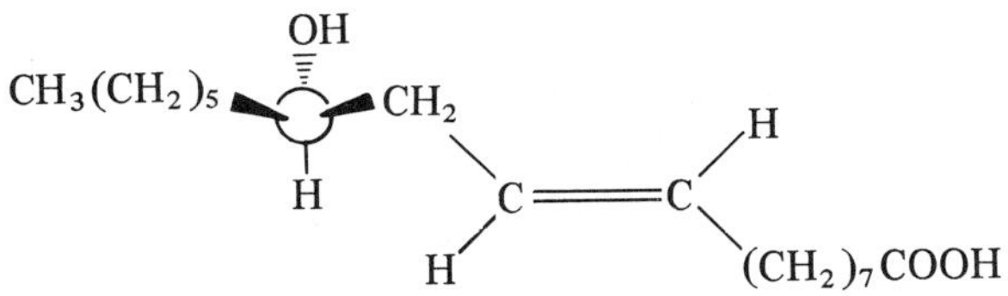

+ Enantiomer

8.47 Hydroxylations by $KMnO_4$ are *syn* hydroxylations (cf Sect. 7.13A). Thus, maleic acid must be the *cis*-dicarboxylic acid:

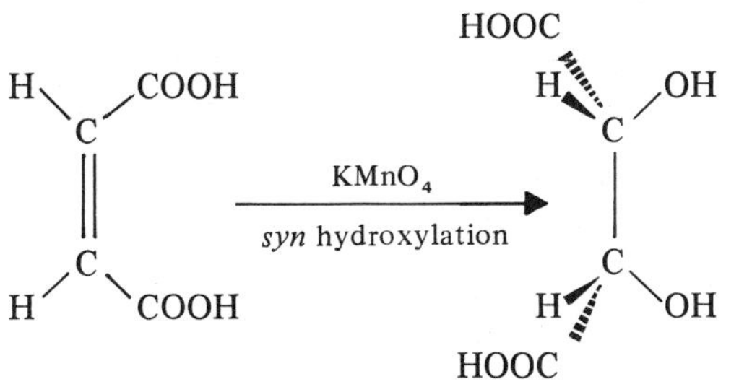

Maleic acid   *meso*-Tartaric acid

Fumaric acid must be the *trans*-dicarboxylic acid:

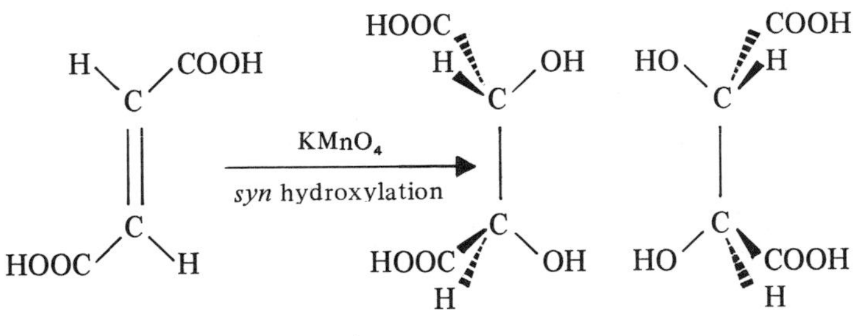

Fumaric acid   (±)-Tartaric acid

8.48 (a) The addition of bromine is an *anti* addition. Thus fumaric acid yields a *meso* compound.

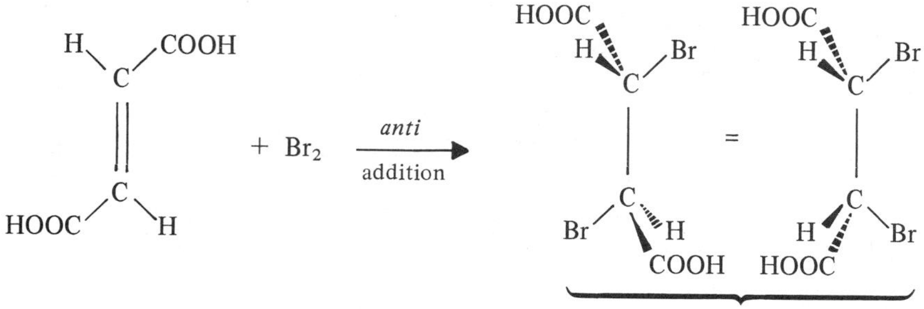

A *meso* compound

(b) Maleic acid adds bromine to yield a racemic modification.

8.49

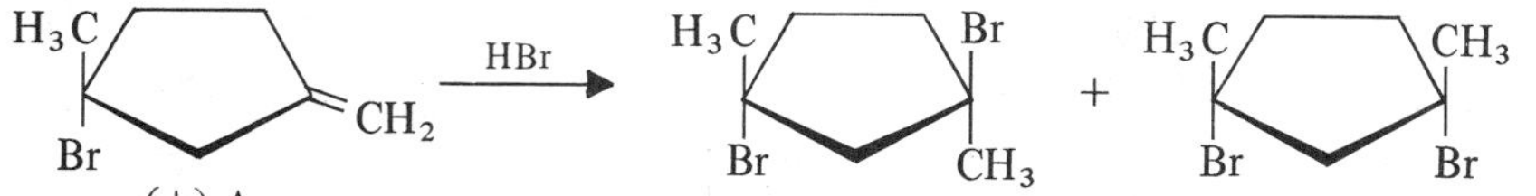

B
(optically active)

C
(a *meso* compound)

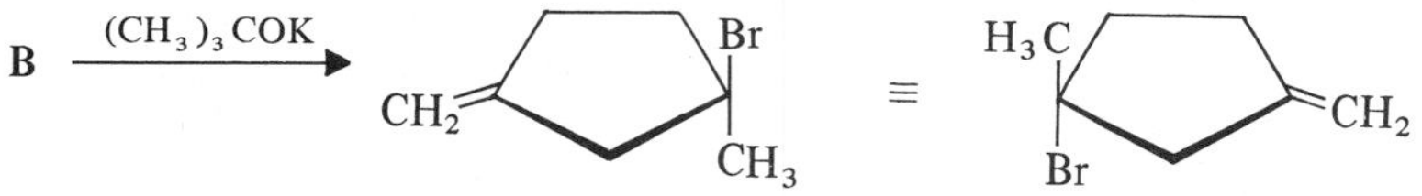

(+) A   (+) A

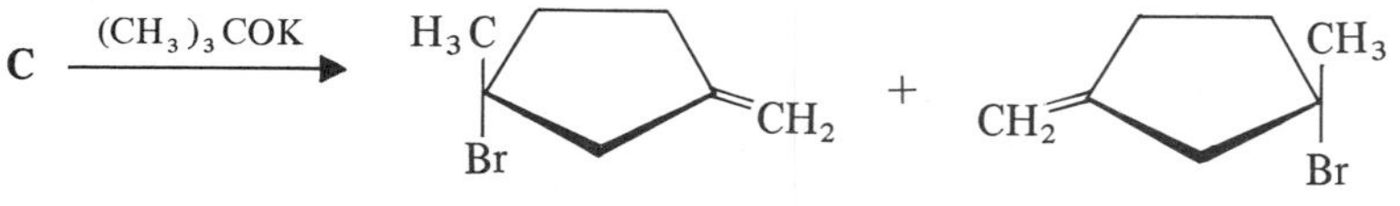

(+) A   (−) A

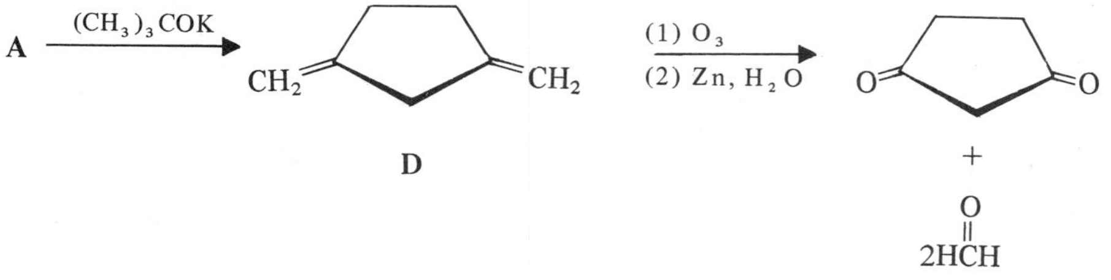

D

$$+$$

$$\underset{\text{2HCH}}{\overset{\text{O}}{\overset{\|}{}}}$$

8.50

(a)

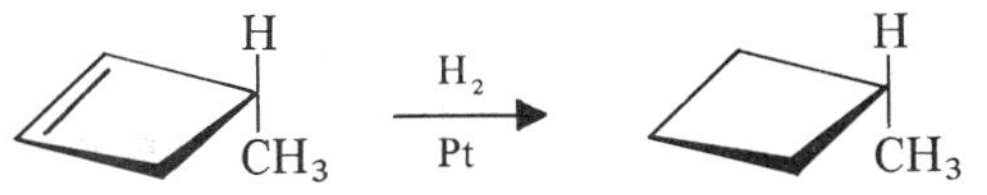

E   **F**

Optically active   Optically inactive and
(the enantiomeric form   nonresolvable
is an equally valid
answer)

(b)

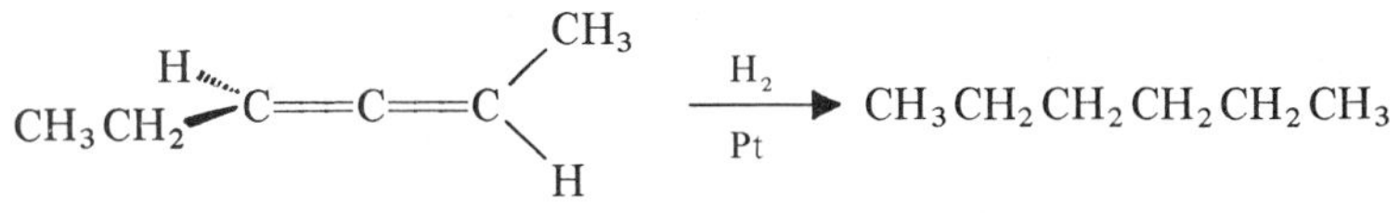

$CH_3CH_2CH_2CH_2CH_2CH_3$

G   **H**

Optically active   Optically inactive and
(the enantiomeric form is   nonresolvable
an equally valid answer)

8.51   That **I** and **J** rotate plane-polarized light in the same direction tells us that **I** and **J** are not enantiomers of each other. Thus, the following are possible structures for **I**, **J**, and **K**. (The enantiomers of **I**, **J**, and **K** would form another set of structures, and other answers are possible as well.)

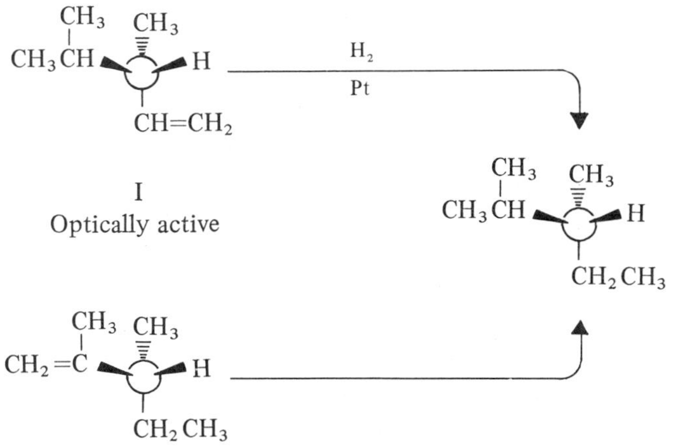

I
Optically active

J
Optically active

K
Optically active

8.52   Possible structures are:

(other answers are possible as well.)

8.53   The reactions proceed through the formation of bromonium ions identical to those formed in the bromination of *trans*- and *cis*-2-butene (see Problem 8.28).

meso-2,3-Dibromobutane

(attack at the other carbon of the bromonium ion gives the same product)

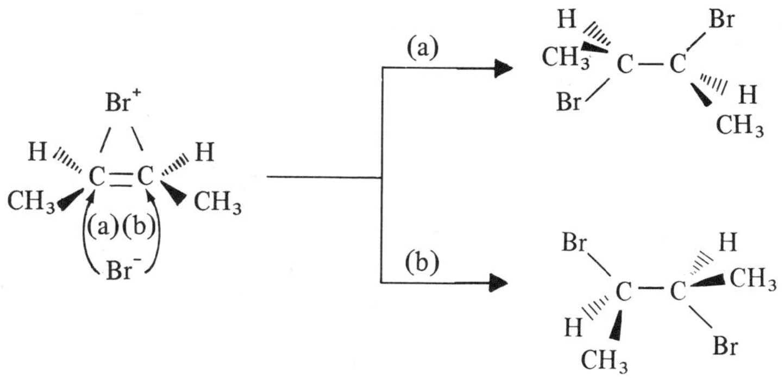

(±)-2,3-Dibromobutane

8.54 (a) If every substitution *involves an inversion*, then racemization will be complete when only *half* the substrate has incorporated radioactive iodine. (At this point there will be an equimolar mixture of the two enantiomers.) Thus, the rate of racemization *should be twice the rate of incorporation of radioactive iodine.*

(b) If an achiral intermediate such as a carbocation were involved, one would expect the rate of racemization to equal the rate of incorporation of radioactive iodine.

SECTION REFERENCES FOR ADDITIONAL PROBLEMS

8.39	8.2, 8.3, 8.4	**8.45**	8.10
8.40	8.9B, 8.6	**8.46**	8.2, 8.3
8.41	8.10	**8.47**	7.13A, 8.10
8.42	8.5	**8.48**	7.10, 8.10
8.43	8.8, 8.10, 8.12	**8.49**	7.2, 6.9, 7.13, 8.13
8.44	8.10	**8.50**	8.9B

SELF-TEST

8.1 Identify the relation between the structures in each of the following pairs. Use the spaces provided and label each pair as follows:

S if they are structural (i.e., constitutional) isomers.
E if they are a pair of enantiomers.
D if they are diastereomers.
I if they are two molecules of the same compound (not isomers).
X if they are different compounds that are not isomers.

(a) 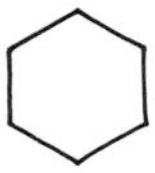 and 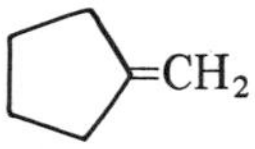

(b) 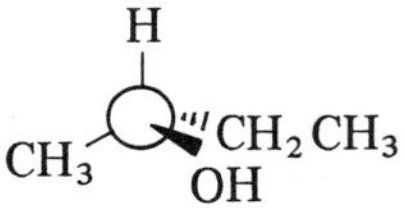 and 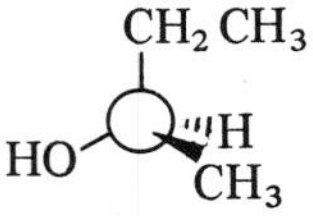

(c) 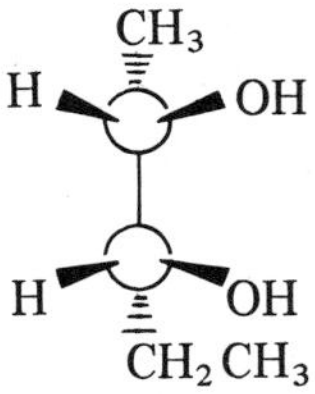 and 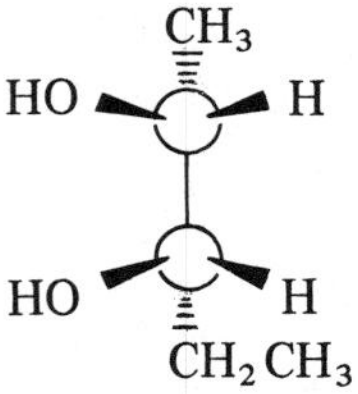

(d) 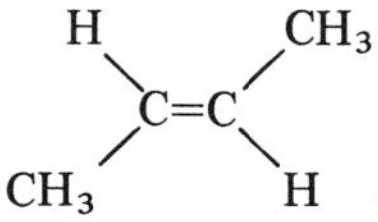 and 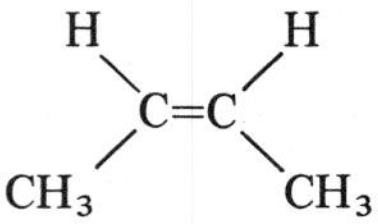

(e) 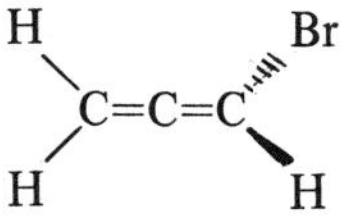 and 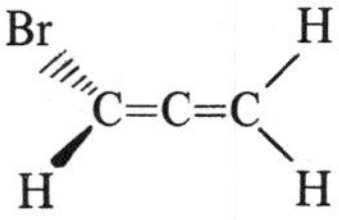

(f) $CH_2{=}C{=}CHCH_3$ and $CH_2{=}CHCH{=}CH_2$

(g) 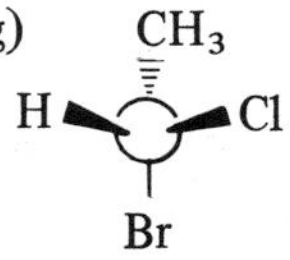 and 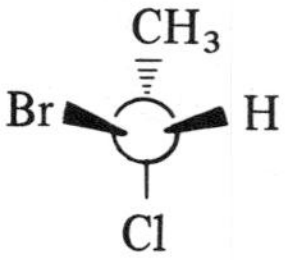

(h) 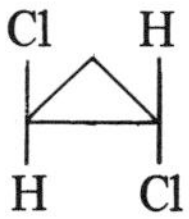 and 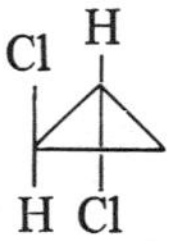

(i) 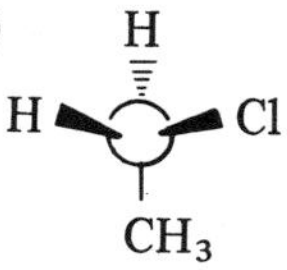 and 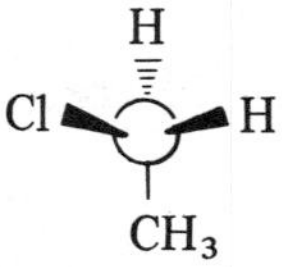

(j)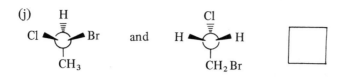

(k)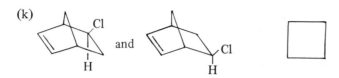

(l)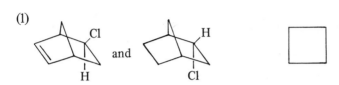

(m)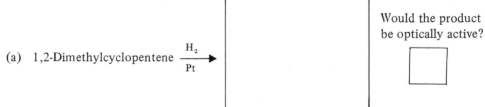

8.2 Give the structural formula of the product of each of the following reactions. If a pair of enantiomers results, draw the structure of only *one* of the enantiomers. Show stereochemistry where appropriate.

(a) 1,2-Dimethylcyclopentene $\xrightarrow[\text{Pt}]{\text{H}_2}$

Would the product be optically active?

(b) Cyclohexene $\xrightarrow[\text{25°, neutral}]{\text{KMnO}_4}$

Would the product be optically active?

(c)　Cyclobutene　$\xrightarrow[\text{CCl}_4]{\text{Br}_2}$

Would the product
be optically active?

8.3　Tell whether each of the following statements is true (+) or false (−).

(a)　If all of the molecules in a sample are chiral, the sample is optically active.

(b)　The terms chiral and optically active mean the same thing.

(c)　A chiral molecule is any molecule that has one or more chiral atoms.

(d)　There are four stereoisomers of 1,1-dibromo-2-methylcyclopentane.

(e)　A pure sample of ⟨structure⟩ is optically active.

(f)　There are three stereoisomers 2,3-diphenylbutane.

(g)　There are two stereoisomers of 1,1-dibromo-1,2-propadiene.

(h)　The formula $CH_2=CH-C$ ⟨with CH_3, NH_2, H⟩ has the (S) configuration.

(i)　The formula ⟨structure⟩ OH has the (R) configuration.

(j)　⟨structures⟩ and ⟨structures⟩ are related as an object and its mirror image, however, they are not enantiomers.

(k)　⟨structure⟩ and ⟨structure⟩ are enantiomers.

SUPPLEMENTARY PROBLEMS

S8.1   Which word best describes the pairs of compounds below: enantiomers, diastereomers, structural isomers, not isomers, identical.

(a)

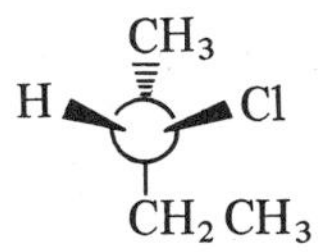

CH_3
H——Cl   and CH_3CH_2——H
CH_2CH_3 Cl

CH_3

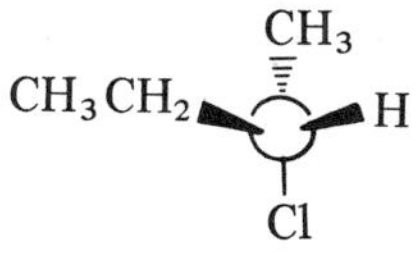

(b)

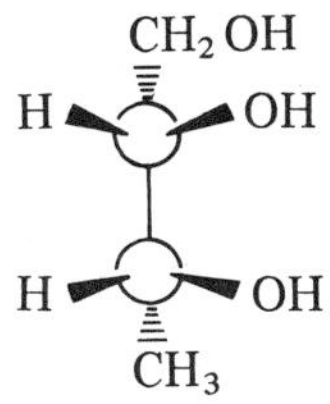

CH_2OH CH_3
H——OH   H——OH
and
H——OH   H——OH
CH_3 CH_2OH

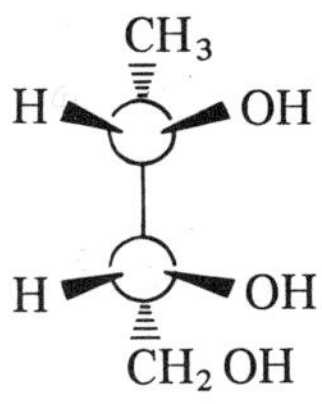

(c)

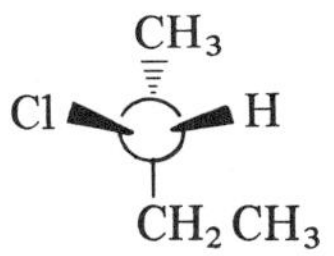

CH_3 CH_3
Cl——H   and CH_3CH_2——H
CH_2CH_3 Cl

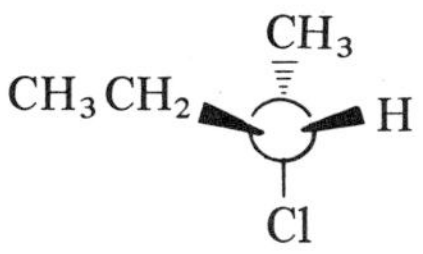

(d)

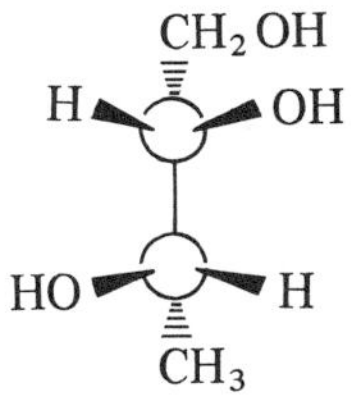

CH_2OH CH_3
H——OH   HO——H
and
HO——H   H——OH
CH_3 CH_2OH

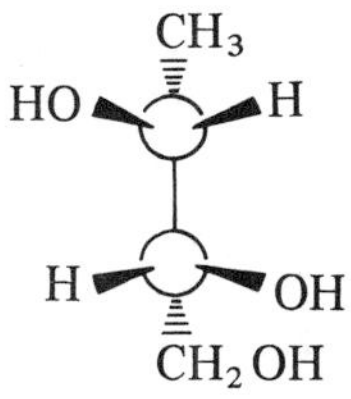

S8.2   Give the (R)-(S) designation of all the chiral atoms in the morphine molecule below.

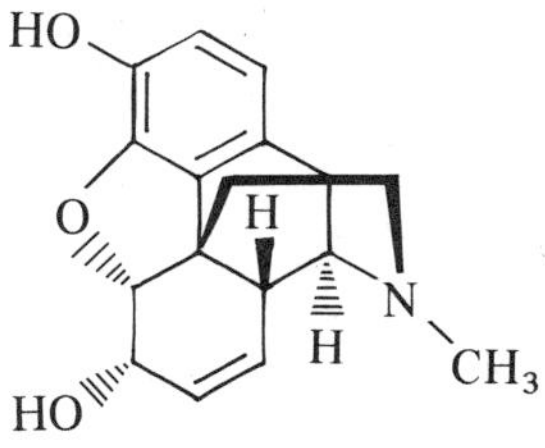

SOLUTIONS TO SUPPLEMENTARY PROBLEMS

S8.1   (a) Identical (b) Enantiomers (c) Enantiomers (d) Enantiomers.

S8.2

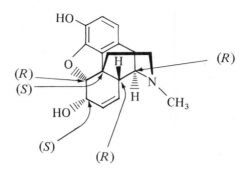

B
SPECIAL TOPIC

Polymerization of Alkenes:
Addition Polymers

SOLUTIONS TO PROBLEMS

B.1 The reaction will proceed through the most stable free radical that can be produced. Head-to-head polymerization, as shown, will lead to a primary radical,

$$R-CH_2-\underset{\underset{CH_3}{|}}{CH}\cdot \;+\; \underset{\underset{CH_3}{|}}{CH}=CH_2 \longrightarrow R-CH_2-\underset{\underset{CH_3}{|}}{CH}-\underset{\underset{CH_3}{|}}{CH}-CH_2\cdot$$

which is less stable than the secondary radical that is produced by head-to-tail polymerization:

$$R-CH_2-\underset{\underset{CH_3}{|}}{CH}\cdot \;+\; CH_2=\underset{\underset{CH_3}{|}}{CH} \longrightarrow R-CH_2-\underset{\underset{CH_3}{|}}{CH}-CH_2-\underset{\underset{CH_3}{|}}{CH}\cdot$$

B.2

(a) $n CH_2=\underset{\underset{F}{|}}{CH} \xrightarrow[\text{peroxide}]{\text{organic}} \underset{\underset{F}{|}}{-(CH_2-CH)-}_n$

(b) $n CF_2=\underset{\underset{Cl}{|}}{CF} \xrightarrow[\text{peroxide}]{\text{organic}} \underset{\underset{Cl}{|}}{-(CF_2-CF)-}_n$

(c) $n CF_2=\underset{\underset{CF_3}{|}}{CF} \;+\; m CH_2=CF_2 \xrightarrow[\text{peroxide}]{\text{organic}} \underset{\underset{CF_3}{|}}{-(CF_2-CF)-}_n \;-(CH_2-CF_2)-_m$

> Note that the units are randomly ordered, and not necessarily joined to their own kind as shown.

B.3 Polymerization will occur to produce the most stable carbocation possible. The scheme shown in this problem involves formation of the primary carbocations,

$$\underset{\underset{CH_3}{|}}{\overset{\overset{CH_3}{|}}{CH}}-CH_2{}^+ \;,\;\; \underset{\underset{CH_3}{|}}{\overset{\overset{CH_3}{|}}{CH}}-CH_2-\underset{\underset{CH_3}{|}}{\overset{\overset{CH_3}{|}}{C}}-CH_2{}^+ \;,\; \text{etc.}$$

instead of the tertiary carbocations,

$$CH_3-\underset{\underset{CH_3}{|}}{\overset{\overset{CH_3}{|}}{C}}-CH_2-\underset{\underset{CH_3}{|}}{\overset{\overset{CH_3}{|}}{C}}\text{+}$$

B.4 (a) By proton transfer from water to the strongly basic carbanion,

$$R-CH_2-\underset{\underset{CN}{|}}{CH}\overset{..}{:}^- + H-\overset{..}{\underset{\underset{H}{|}}{O}}: \longrightarrow R-CH_2-\underset{\underset{CN}{|}}{CH_2} + :\overset{..}{\underset{..}{O}}H^-$$

(b) $\left(CH_2\underset{\underset{R}{|}}{CH}\right)_n\!\!-CH_2\underset{\underset{R}{|}}{CH}\overset{..}{:}^- + (m + 1)\underset{\underset{O}{\diagdown\!\diagup}}{CH_2\!-\!CH_2} \longrightarrow$

$$\left(CH_2\underset{\underset{R}{|}}{CH}\right)_{n+1}\!\!\!\!\!-\left(CH_2-CH_2-O\right)_m\!\!\!-CH_2-CH_2-\overset{..}{\underset{..}{O}}\overset{..}{:}^-$$

$$\xrightarrow{H_2O} \left(CH_2\underset{\underset{R}{|}}{CH}\right)_{n+1}\!\!\!\!\!-\left(CH_2-CH_2-O\right)_m\!\!\!-CH_2-CH_2-OH$$

In this polymer, each chain consists of a long uninterrupted segment of the first repeating unit, $\left(CH_2\underset{\underset{R}{|}}{CH}\right)_{n+1}$ followed by a long uninterrupted segment of the second repeating unit, $\left(CH_2-CH_2-O\right)_m$.

B.5

(a)

(b)

(c)

SPECIAL TOPIC
Divalent Carbon Compounds: Carbenes

SOLUTIONS TO PROBLEMS

C.1

(a)
$$\underset{H}{\overset{CH_3}{>}}C=C\underset{H}{\overset{CH_3}{<}} + HCCl_3 \xrightarrow{KOC(CH_3)_3}$$

(b)
$$\xrightarrow[Zn(Cu)]{CH_2I_2}$$

(c)
$$+ \underset{Cl}{\overset{Cl}{H-C-C(CH_3)_3}} \xrightarrow{KOC(CH_3)_3}$$

(d)
$$+ HCBr_3 \xrightarrow{KOC(CH_3)_3}$$

9 ALKYNES

REACTIONS OF ALKYNES

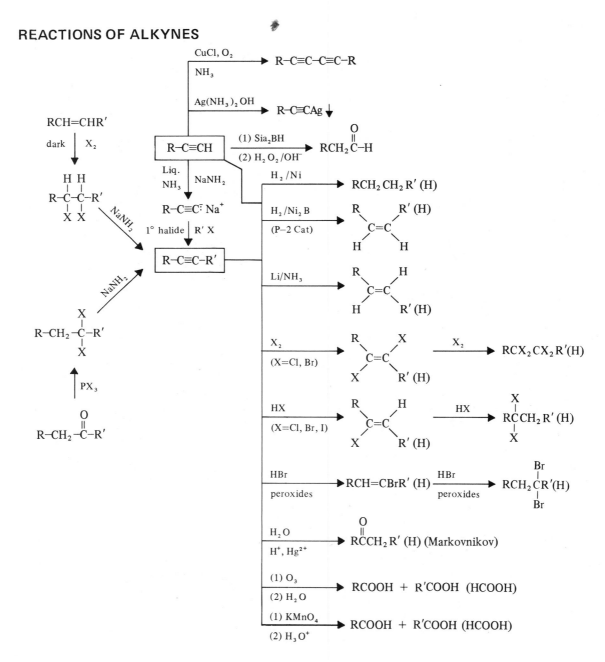

SOLUTIONS TO PROBLEMS

9.1 (a) C_4H_6 : $CH_3CH_2C{\equiv}CH$, $CH_3C{\equiv}CCH_3$

        1-Butyne   2-Butyne

(b) C_5H_8 : $CH_3CH_2CH_2C{\equiv}CH$ $CH_3CH_2C{\equiv}CCH_3$

            1-Pentyne   2-Pentyne

$$\underset{\text{3-Methyl-1-butyne}}{CH_3\underset{\underset{CH_3}{|}}{C}HC{\equiv}CH}$$

(c) $CH_3CH_2CH_2CH_2C{\equiv}CH$ $CH_3CH_2CH_2C{\equiv}CCH_3$

        1-Hexyne   2-Hexyne

$CH_3CH_2C{\equiv}CCH_2CH_3$ $CH_3\underset{\underset{CH_3}{|}}{C}HCH_2C{\equiv}CH$

        3-Hexyne

                                    4-Methyl-1-pentyne

$CH_3C{\equiv}C\underset{\underset{CH_3}{|}}{C}HCH_3$ $HC{\equiv}C\underset{\underset{CH_3}{|}}{C}HCH_2CH_3$

4-Methyl-2-pentyne   3-Methyl-1-pentyne

$$HC{\equiv}C\underset{\underset{CH_3}{|}}{\overset{\overset{CH_3}{|}}{C}}CH_3$$

3,3-Dimethyl-
1-butyne

9.2 The acetylenic carbon is sp-hybridized, whereas the ethylenic carbon is sp^2-hybridized. Because the acetylenic carbon has a greater amount of s-character, it is more electronegative than the sp^2-hybridized ethylenic carbon. The polarity of $-\overset{|}{C}{\rightarrow}C{\equiv}$ is thus greater than the polarity of $-\overset{|}{\underset{|}{C}}{\rightarrow}\overset{|}{C}{=}$.

9.3 Ordinary alkenes *are* more reactive toward electrophilic reagents. But, the alkenes obtained from the addition of an electrophilic reagent to an alkyne have at least one electronegative atom (Cl, Br, etc.) attached to a carbon of the double bond.

$$-C{\equiv}C- \xrightarrow{\text{HX}} \underset{H}{\overset{}{\diagdown}}C{=}C\underset{}{\overset{X}{\diagup}}$$

or

$$-C{\equiv}C- \xrightarrow{X_2} \underset{X}{\overset{X}{\diagdown}}C{=}C\diagup^{X}$$

These alkenes are less reactive than alkynes toward electrophilic addition because the electronegative group makes the double bond "electron poor."

9.4

$$\underset{CH_3}{\overset{CH_3}{|}}\ \underset{}{\overset{CH_3}{|}}$$
$2CH_3CH{-\!-}CH{-}OH$ from the Sia_2B- group.

9.5 (a) $CH_3CH_2C{\equiv}CH \xrightarrow[\substack{HgSO_4 \\ H_2SO_4}]{H_2O} CH_3CH_2\overset{O}{\overset{||}{C}}CH_3$

(b) $C{\equiv}CH + Sia_2BH \longrightarrow$ [cyclopentyl]$CH{=}CH{-}BSia_2 \xrightarrow[OH^-]{H_2O_2}$ [cyclopentyl]$CH_2\overset{O}{\overset{||}{C}}H$

(c) $CH_3C{\equiv}CCH_3 + Sia_2BD \longrightarrow$
$$\underset{D}{\overset{CH_3}{\diagup}}C{=}C\underset{BSia_2}{\overset{CH_3}{\diagdown}} \xrightarrow{CH_3COOD} \underset{D}{\overset{CH_3}{\diagup}}C{=}C\underset{D}{\overset{CH_3}{\diagdown}}$$

$$\underset{CH_3}{\overset{|}{}}$$
$2CH_3C{=}CHCH_3 + (BD_3)_2$ ↑
(cf. Problem 7.12)

or $CH_3C{\equiv}C{-}CH_3 + D_2 \xrightarrow{Ni_2 B(P-2)} \underset{D}{\overset{CH_3}{\diagup}}C{=}C\underset{D}{\overset{CH_3}{\diagdown}}$

(d) $CH_3CH_2C{\equiv}CH + Sia_2BH \longrightarrow \underset{H}{\overset{CH_3CH_2}{\diagup}}C{=}C\underset{BSia_2}{\overset{H}{\diagdown}} \xrightarrow{CH_3COOD} \underset{H}{\overset{CH_3CH_2}{\diagup}}C{=}C\underset{D}{\overset{H}{\diagdown}}$

9.6 (a) $HC{\equiv}CH + :\ddot{N}H_2^- \rightleftharpoons HC{\equiv}C:^- + :NH_3$ (No appreciable amount of reactants are present at equilibrium.)

Stronger acid   Stronger base   Weaker base   Weaker acid

(b) $CH_2{=}CH_2 + :\ddot{N}H_2^- \rightleftharpoons CH_2{=}\ddot{C}H^- + :NH_3$ (No appreciable amount of products are present at equilibrium.)

Weaker acid   Weaker base   Stronger base   Stronger acid

(c) $CH_3CH_3 + :\ddot{N}H_2^- \rightleftharpoons CH_3\ddot{C}H_2^- + :NH_3$ (No appreciable amount of products are present at equilibrium.)

Weaker acid   Weaker base   Stronger base   Stronger acid

(d) $HC \equiv C:^- + CH_3CH_2\overset{\cdot\cdot}{O}H \rightleftharpoons HC \equiv CH + CH_3CH_2\overset{\cdot\cdot}{O}:^-$ $\left(\begin{array}{c}\text{No appreciable amount} \\ \text{of reactants are present} \\ \text{at equilibrium.}\end{array}\right)$

    Stronger   Stronger   Weaker   Weaker

    base   acid   acid   base

(e) $HC \equiv C:^- + H - \overset{\cdot\cdot}{\underset{\underset{H}{|}}{O}}: \rightleftharpoons HC \equiv CH + :\overset{\cdot\cdot}{O}H$ $\left(\begin{array}{c}\text{No appreciable amount of react-} \\ \text{ants are present at equilibrium.}\end{array}\right)$

    Stronger   Stronger   Weaker   Weaker

    base   acid   acid   base

9.7

$$CH_3 - \underset{\underset{CH_3}{|}}{\overset{\overset{CH_3}{|}}{C}} - C \equiv CH + NaNH_2 \longrightarrow CH_3 - \underset{\underset{CH_3}{|}}{\overset{\overset{CH_3}{|}}{C}} - C \equiv C:^- Na^+ + NH_3$$

$$\xrightarrow{CH_3CH_2Br} CH_3 - \underset{\underset{CH_3}{|}}{\overset{\overset{CH_3}{|}}{C}} - C \equiv C - CH_2CH_3$$

A reaction between $CH_3CH_2C \equiv C:^- \overset{+}{Na}$ and $CH_3 - \underset{\underset{CH_3}{|}}{\overset{\overset{CH_3}{|}}{C}} - Br$ would result in elimination to pro-

duce $CH_2 = \underset{\underset{CH_3}{|}}{C} - CH_3 + CH_3CH_2C \equiv CH.$

9.8   By converting the 3-hexyne to *cis*-3-hexene using $H_2/Ni_2B(P-2)$.

Then, addition of bromine to *cis*-3-hexene (Sect. 8.10) will yield $(3R, 4R)$-and $(3S, 4S)$-3,4-dibromohexane as a racemate.

                                 $(3S, 4S)$ $(3R, 4R)$

                                Racemic 3,4-dibromohexane

9.9 (a) [cyclohexyl]—C≡CH $\xrightarrow[\text{H}_2\text{SO}_4]{\text{H}_2\text{O} \atop \text{HgSO}_4}$ [cyclohexyl]—$\overset{\text{O}}{\overset{\|}{\text{C}}}$—CH$_3$

(b) [cyclohexyl]—$\overset{\text{O}}{\overset{\|}{\text{C}}}$—CH$_3$ $\xrightarrow[0°]{\text{PCl}_5}$ [cyclohexyl]—$\overset{\text{Cl}}{\underset{\text{Cl}}{\text{C}}}$—CH$_3$ $\xrightarrow[\text{(2) H}^+]{\text{(1) 3NaNH}_2}$ [cyclohexyl]—C≡CH

[cyclohexyl]—C≡CH + Sia$_2$BH $\longrightarrow$ [cyclohexyl]—CH=CH—BSia$_2$ $\xrightarrow[\text{OH}^-]{\text{H}_2\text{O}_2}$ [cyclohexyl]—CH$_2\overset{\text{O}}{\overset{\|}{\text{C}}}$H

9.10 (a) CH$_3$CHC≡CCH$_2$CH$_3$
　　　　　　|
　　　　　 CH$_3$

2-Methyl-3-hexyne

(b) [cyclooctyne ring structure: C≡C, CH$_2$, CH$_2$, CH$_2$—CH$_2$, CH$_2$, CH$_2$]

Cyclooctyne

(c) HC≡CCH$_2$CH$_2$CH$_2$CH$_3$

1-Heptyne

9.11 (a) 3-Methyl-1-butyne
(b) 2,2-Dimethyl-3-hexyne
(c) 3-Nonyne
(d) 3-Hexyne
(e) 2,2,5,5-Tetramethyl-3-hexyne

(f) 2,5-Dimethyl-3-hexyne
(g) 2-Hexyne
(h) 4-Methyl-2-hexyne
(i) 2,7-Dimethyl-4-octyne
(j) 1-Octyne

9.12 Compounds a and j because they are the only terminal alkynes ($\cdot$RC≡CH).

9.13 (a) Compounds d and g　　(b) None of them

9.14 (a) 3 C + CaO $\xrightarrow{2500°}$ CaC$_2$ + CO
　　　 (coke) (lime)

CaC$_2$ + 2H$_2$O $\xrightarrow[\text{temperature}]{\text{room}}$ HC≡CH + Ca(OH)$_2$

(b) HC≡CH + H$_2$ $\xrightarrow{\text{Ni}_2\text{B (P-2)}}$ CH$_2$=CH$_2$

(c) HC≡CH + NaNH$_2$ $\xrightarrow[\text{NH}_3]{\text{liquid}}$ HC≡C:$^-$Na$^+$ + NH$_3$

CH$_4$ + Br$_2$ $\xrightarrow[\text{heat}]{\text{light}}$ CH$_3$Br + HBr
(excess)

HC≡C:$^-$Na$^+$ + CH$_3$Br $\longrightarrow$ HC≡C–CH$_3$ + NaBr

(d) $CH_3C \equiv CH + H_2 \xrightarrow{Ni_2B \ (P-2)} CH_3CH=CH_2$

(e) $CH_3C \equiv CH + H_2O \xrightarrow[H_2SO_4]{HgSO_4} CH_3\overset{\overset{\displaystyle O}{\|}}{C}CH_3$

(f) $CH_3C \equiv CH + NaNH_2 \xrightarrow[NH_3]{liquid} CH_3C \equiv C:^- Na^+ + NH_3$

$\qquad\qquad\qquad\qquad\qquad\qquad\quad \downarrow CH_3Br$

$\qquad\qquad\qquad\qquad\qquad\qquad\qquad\quad CH_3C \equiv CCH_3 + NaBr$

(g) $CH_2=CH_2 + HBr \longrightarrow CH_3CH_2Br \xrightarrow{HC \equiv C:^- Na^+} HC \equiv CCH_2CH_3 + NaBr$

(h) $CH_3C \equiv CCH_3 + H_2O \xrightarrow[H_2SO_4]{HgSO_4} CH_3\overset{\overset{\displaystyle O}{\|}}{C}CH_2CH_3$

(i) See (g) above.

(j) $CH_3C \equiv C:^- Na^+ + CH_3CH_2Br \longrightarrow CH_3C \equiv CCH_2CH_3 + NaBr$

(k) $CH_2=CH_2 + H_2O \xrightarrow{H_2SO_4} CH_3CH_2OH$

(l) $CH_2=CH_2 + Br_2 \xrightarrow[dark]{CCl_4} CH_2BrCH_2Br$

(m) $CH_3C \equiv CH + 2HCl \longrightarrow CH_3\overset{\overset{\displaystyle Cl}{|}}{\underset{\underset{\displaystyle Cl}{|}}{C}}CH_3$

(n) $CH_3C \equiv CCH_3 + H_2 \xrightarrow{Ni_2B \ (P-2)}$
$\begin{matrix} CH_3 & & CH_3 \\ & \diagdown \ / & \\ & C=C & \\ & / \ \diagdown & \\ H & & H \end{matrix}$

(o) $CH_3C \equiv CCH_3 \xrightarrow[-78°]{Li + C_2H_5NH_2}$
$\begin{matrix} CH_3 & & H \\ & \diagdown \ / & \\ & C=C & \\ & / \ \diagdown & \\ H & & CH_3 \end{matrix}$

(p) $CH_3CH_2C \equiv CH + H_2 \xrightarrow{Ni_2B \ (P-2)} CH_3CH_2CH=CH_2$

(q) $CH_3CH_2CH=CH_2 + HBr \xrightarrow{no \ peroxides} CH_3CH_2\overset{\overset{\displaystyle Br}{|}}{C}HCH_3$

(r) $CH_3CH_2CH=CH_2 + HBr \xrightarrow[peroxide]{} CH_3CH_2CH_2CH_2Br$

(s) $CH_3CH_2CH=CH_2 + THF:BH_3 \longrightarrow (CH_3CH_2CH_2CH_2)_3B \xrightarrow[OH^-]{H_2O_2}$

$\qquad\qquad\qquad\qquad\qquad\qquad\qquad\qquad\qquad\qquad CH_3CH_2CH_2CH_2OH$

(t) $CH_3CH_2CH=CH_2 + Hg(OAc)_2 \longrightarrow$ $CH_3CH_2\underset{\underset{HgOAc}{|}}{C}HCH_3$ $\xrightarrow[OH^-]{NaBH_4}$ $CH_3CH_2\underset{\underset{OH}{|}}{C}HCH_3$

or $CH_3CH_2CH=CH_2 + H_2O \xrightarrow{H_2SO_4}$ $CH_3CH_2\underset{\underset{OH}{|}}{C}H-CH_3$

(u) 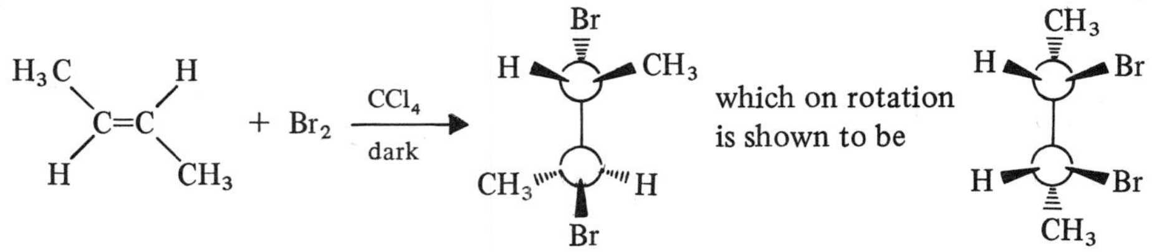   which on rotation is shown to be

(v) 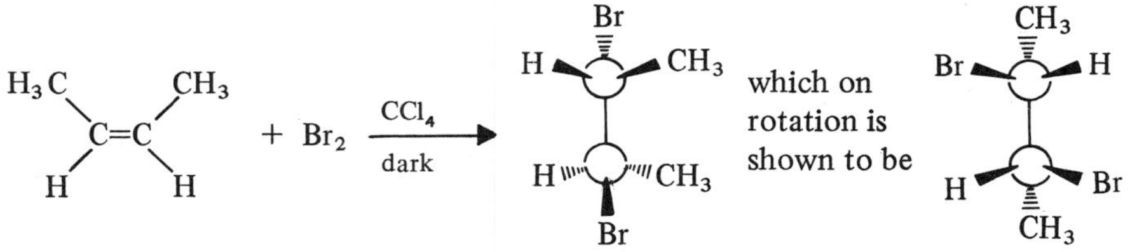   which on rotation is shown to be

\+

enantiomer

(w) $CH_3C{\equiv}CCH_3 + HCl \xrightarrow[CH_3COOH]{Cl^-,\ 25°}$

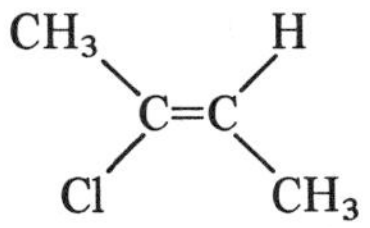

(x) $CH_3CH=CH_2 + HBr \xrightarrow{peroxide} CH_3CH_2CH_2Br$

(y) $CH_3CH_2C{\equiv}CH + NaNH_2 \xrightarrow[NH_3]{liquid} CH_3CH_2C{\equiv}C:^-Na^+ + NH_3$
$\xrightarrow{CH_3CH_2Br} CH_3CH_2C{\equiv}CCH_2CH_3$

(z) $CH_3CH_2C{\equiv}CH + HBr \xrightarrow{peroxide} CH_3CH_2CH=CHBr$

9.15   (a) 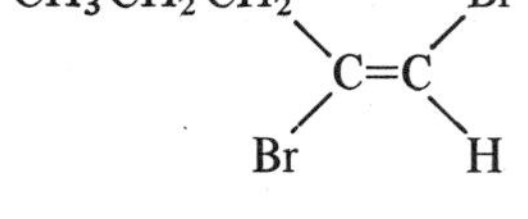   (b) 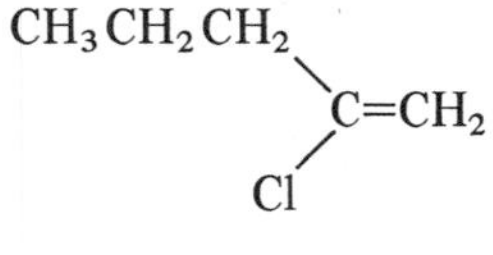   (c) $CH_3CH_2CH_2\underset{\underset{Cl}{|}}{\overset{\overset{Cl}{|}}{C}}CH_3$

(d) $CH_3CH_2CH_2CH=CHBr$ (e) $CH_3CH_2CH_2\overset{\overset{O}{||}}{C}CH_3$ (f) $CH_3CH_2CH_2CH=CH_2$

(g) $CH_3CH_2CH_2CH=CH_2$ (h) $CH_3CH_2CH_2CH_2\overset{\overset{O}{||}}{C}H$ (i) $CH_3CH_2CH_2C{\equiv}C:^-Na^+$

(j) $CH_3CH_2CH_2C{\equiv}CCH_3$ (k) $CH_3CH_2CH_2C{\equiv}CAg$ (l) $CH_3CH_2CH_2C{\equiv}CCu$

9.16   (a)

$$\underset{\underset{Cl}{\displaystyle|}}{\overset{\displaystyle CH_3CH_2}{}}\!\!C\!=\!C\!\!\underset{\displaystyle CH_2CH_3}{\overset{\displaystyle H}{}}$$

(b) $CH_3CH_2\underset{\underset{Cl}{\displaystyle|}}{\overset{\overset{Cl}{\displaystyle|}}{C}}CH_2CH_2CH_3$

(c)

$$\overset{\displaystyle CH_3CH_2}{\underset{\displaystyle Br}{}}\!\!C\!=\!C\!\!\overset{\displaystyle Br}{\underset{\displaystyle CH_2CH_3}{}}$$

(d) $CH_3CH_2\underset{\underset{Br}{\displaystyle|}}{\overset{\overset{Br}{\displaystyle|}}{C}}\!\!-\!\!\underset{\underset{Br}{\displaystyle|}}{\overset{\overset{Br}{\displaystyle|}}{C}}CH_2CH_3$

(e)

$$\overset{\displaystyle CH_3CH_2}{\underset{\displaystyle H}{}}\!\!C\!=\!C\!\!\overset{\displaystyle CH_2CH_3}{\underset{\displaystyle H}{}}$$

(f)

$$\overset{\displaystyle CH_3CH_2}{\underset{\displaystyle H}{}}\!\!C\!=\!C\!\!\overset{\displaystyle Br}{\underset{\displaystyle CH_2CH_3}{}}$$

(g)

$$\overset{\displaystyle CH_3CH_2}{\underset{\displaystyle H}{}}\!\!C\!=\!C\!\!\overset{\displaystyle H}{\underset{\displaystyle CH_2CH_3}{}}$$

(h) $CH_3CH_2\overset{\overset{\displaystyle O}{\parallel}}{C}CH_2CH_2CH_3$

(i)   No reaction   (j)   No reaction   (k)   Same as (e)

(l)   Same as (h)   (m)   No reaction

(n) $CH_3CH_2CH_2CH_2CH_2CH_3$ (o) $2CH_3CH_2COOH$ (p) $2CH_3CH_2COOH$

(q)   No reaction

9.17   (a) $CH_3CH_2CH_2CH\!=\!CH_2 \; + \; Br_2 \longrightarrow CH_3CH_2CH_2\underset{\underset{Br}{\displaystyle|}}{\overset{\overset{}{}}{C}}HCH_2Br$

$$\xrightarrow[\text{(2) }H^+]{\text{(1) 3NaNH}_2} CH_3CH_2CH_2C\!\equiv\!CH$$

(b) $CH_3CH_2CH_2CH_2CH_2Cl \xrightarrow[(CH_3)_3COH]{(CH_3)_3COK} CH_3CH_2CH_2CH\!=\!CH_2$

then proceed as in (a) above.

(c) $CH_3CH_2CH_2CH\!=\!CHCl \xrightarrow[\text{(2) }H^+]{\text{(1) 2NaNH}_2} CH_3CH_2CH_2C\!\equiv\!CH$

(d) $CH_3CH_2CH_2CH_2CHCl_2 \xrightarrow[\text{(2) }H^+]{\text{(1) 3NaNH}_2} CH_3CH_2CH_2C\!\equiv\!CH$

(e) $HC\!\equiv\!CH \xrightarrow[\text{liq. NH}_3]{\text{NaNH}_2} HC\!\equiv\!C\!:^-Na^+ \xrightarrow{CH_3CH_2CH_2Br} HC\!\equiv\!CCH_2CH_2CH_3$

9.18   (a)   Propyne decolorizes Br_2/CCl_4; propane does not.

(b) $Ag(NH_3)_2{}^+OH^-$ gives a precipitate with propyne, not with propene.

(c)   Dilute $KMnO_4$ oxidizes 1-bromopropene and not 2-bromopropane.

(d) $Ag(NH_3)_2{}^+ OH^-$ gives a precipitate with 1-butyne, not with 2-bromo-2-butene.

(e) Sodium fusion followed by acidification with dilute HNO_3 and addition of $AgNO_3$ gives a AgBr precipitate with 2-bromo-2-butene, not with 2-butyne.

(f) Br_2/CCl_4 is decolorized by 2-butyne, not by butyl alcohol.

(g) $AgNO_3/C_2H_5OH$ gives a AgBr precipitate with 2-bromobutane, not with 2-butyne.

(h) Br_2/CCl_4 is decolorized by $CH_3C{\equiv}CCH_2OH$, not by $CH_3CH_2CH_2CH_2OH$.

(i) Br_2/CCl_4 is decolorized by $CH_3CH{=}CHCH_2OH$, not by $CH_3CH_2CH_2CH_2OH$.

(In many cases other tests are possible.)

9.19 Some tentative conclusions are

(1) **A** and **B** have the skeleton C–C–C–C–C (they both yield pentane on hydrogenation.)

(2) **A** has the $HC{\equiv}C-$ group (gives ppt. with ammoniacal $AgNO_3$).

(3) **C** has a ring because hydrogenation yields C_5H_{10} and not C_5H_{12}.

(4) All three compounds have multiple bonds because they all react with Br_2/CCl_4 and Baeyer's reagent, and are soluble in cold, conc. H_2SO_4.

Assignments follow:

(a) **A** = $CH_3CH_2CH_2C{\equiv}CH$, **B** = $CH_3CH_2C{\equiv}CCH_3$, **C** =

(b) Yes, **B** may also be $CH_3CH{=}CH{-}CH{=}CH_2$ or $CH_2{=}CH{-}CH_2{-}CH{=}CH_2$.

C may also be , or , etc.

(c) **B** = $CH_3CH_2C{\equiv}CCH_3$

(d)

9.20 (a) $\underset{\underset{\displaystyle CH_3}{|}}{CH_3CHC{\equiv}CH}$ + HCl (1 molar equivalent) $\longrightarrow$ $\underset{\underset{\displaystyle Cl}{|}}{\overset{\overset{\displaystyle CH_3}{|}}{CH_3CHC}}{=}CH_2$

(b) $\underset{\overset{\displaystyle |}{\displaystyle CH_3}}{CH_3CHC{\equiv}CH}$ $\xrightarrow{H_2/Ni_2 B\ (P\text{-}2)}$ $\overset{\overset{\displaystyle CH_3}{|}}{CH_3CHCH}{=}CH_2$ $\xrightarrow[\text{peroxides}]{HBr}$ $\overset{\overset{\displaystyle CH_3}{|}}{CH_3CHCH_2CH_2Br}$

(c) Product of (a) $\xrightarrow{H_2/Pt}$ $\underset{\underset{\displaystyle Cl}{|}}{\overset{\overset{\displaystyle CH_3}{|}}{CH_3CHCHCH_3}}$

(d) Product of (a) $\xrightarrow[\text{dark}]{Cl_2/CCl_4}$ $CH_3\overset{\overset{\displaystyle CH_3}{|}}{CH}{-}\underset{\underset{\displaystyle Cl}{|}}{\overset{\overset{\displaystyle Cl}{|}}{C}}{-}CH_2Cl$

(e) Product of (a) $\xrightarrow[\text{no peroxides}]{\text{HBr}}$

$$CH_3CH-\underset{\underset{Br}{|}}{\overset{\overset{CH_3}{|}}{C}}-CH_3 \quad (\text{with } Cl \text{ on central } C)$$

(f) $\underset{\overset{|}{CH_3}}{CH_3CHC\equiv CH} \xrightarrow[\text{then H}^+]{\text{KMnO}_4/\text{OH}^-,} \underset{\overset{|}{CH_3}}{CH_3CHCOOH} + CO_2$

9.21 (a) $CH_3CH_2CH_2C\equiv CH + D_2 \xrightarrow{\text{Ni}_2\text{B (P-2)}}$

$$\underset{D}{\overset{CH_3CH_2CH_2}{\diagdown}}C=C\underset{D}{\overset{H}{\diagup}}$$

(b) $CH_3CH_2CH_2C\equiv CH + \text{Sia}_2BH \longrightarrow$

$$\underset{H}{\overset{CH_3CH_2CH_2}{\diagdown}}C=C\underset{BSia_2}{\overset{H}{\diagup}}$$

$\xrightarrow{CH_3COOD}$ $\underset{H}{\overset{CH_3CH_2CH_2}{\diagdown}}C=C\underset{D}{\overset{H}{\diagup}}$

(c) $CH_3CH_2CH_2C\equiv CH + DCl \longrightarrow$ $\underset{Cl}{\overset{CH_3CH_2CH_2}{\diagdown}}C=C\underset{H}{\overset{D}{\diagup}}$

(d) $CH_3CH_2CH_2C\equiv CH + \text{Sia}_2BD \longrightarrow CH_3CH_2CH_2$

$$\underset{D}{\overset{CH_3CH_2CH_2}{\diagdown}}C=C\underset{BSia_2}{\overset{H}{\diagup}}$$

$\xrightarrow[\text{OH}^-]{\text{H}_2\text{O}_2}$ $CH_3CH_2CH_2\underset{\overset{|}{D}}{CHCH}\overset{\overset{O}{||}}{}$

9.22 The syntheses involve combinations of chlorination, dehydrochlorination, and hydrogenation as follows:

(a)-(b) $H-C\equiv C-H \xrightarrow[\text{Cl}^-]{\text{Cl}_2}$ $\underset{Cl}{\overset{H}{\diagup}}C=C\underset{H}{\overset{Cl}{\diagdown}}$ $\xrightarrow[\text{cat.}]{\text{H}_2}$ $Cl-CH_2CH_2-Cl$

$\quad\quad\quad\quad\quad\quad\quad$ *trans*-1, 2-Dichloroethene $\quad\quad\quad\quad$ 1, 2-Dichloroethane

(c)-(e) $H-C\equiv C-H + 2Cl_2 \longrightarrow CHCl_2-CHCl_2$

$\quad\quad\quad\quad\quad\quad\quad\quad$ 1, 1, 2, 2-Tetrachloroethane

$\xrightarrow[(-\text{HCl})]{\text{base}} CHCl=CCl_2 \xrightarrow[\text{cat.}]{\text{H}_2} CH_2ClCHCl_2$

$\quad\quad\quad\quad\quad$ 1, 1, 2-Trichloroethene $\quad\quad$ 1, 1, 2-Trichloroethane (f)–(g) $$CHCl{=}CCl_2 \xrightarrow{Cl_2} CHCl_2CCl_3 \xrightarrow[(-HCl)]{\text{base}} CCl_2{=}CCl_2$$

1, 1, 1, 2, 2-Pentachloroethane — 1, 1, 2, 2-Tetrachloroethene

9.23

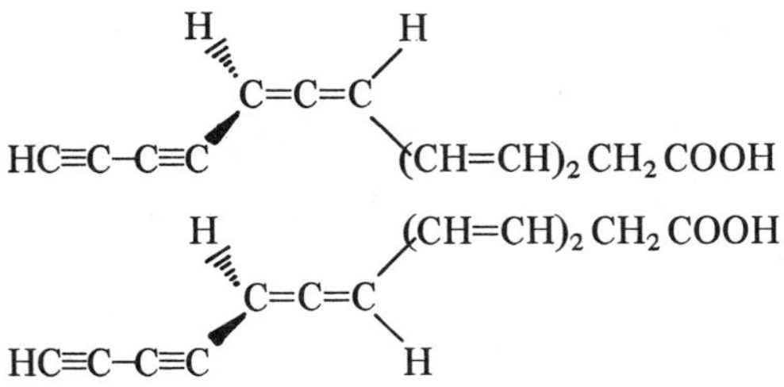

9.24

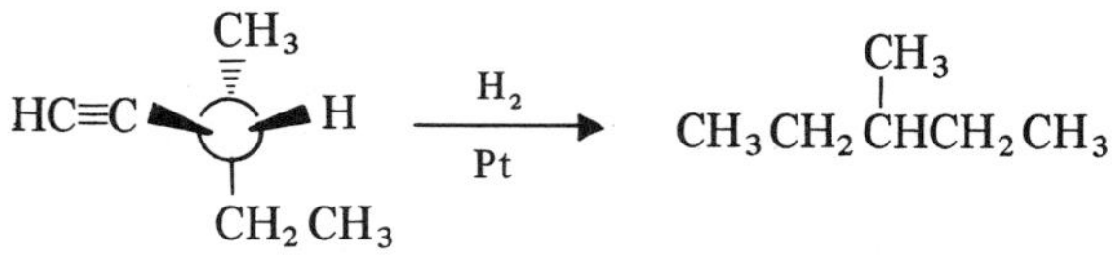

D

Optically active
(the other enantiomer
is an equally valid
answer)

Optically inactive
nonresolvable

SECTION REFERENCES FOR ADDITIONAL PROBLEMS

9.11	9.2A, 9.2B	**9.18**	9.17
9.12	9.14	**9.19**	9.17, 9.18
9.13	9.7	**9.20**	9.18
9.14	9.18	**9.21**	9.18
9.15	9.18	**9.22**	9.8, 9.9
9.16	9.18	**9.23**	8.16
9.17	9.18	**9.24**	9.7, 9.14

SELF-TEST

9.1   Supply the missing reactant or major organic product in each equation below. Show stereochemistry where appropriate. If more than one step is needed, show them as (1), (2), etc. If no reaction occurs, write N.R.

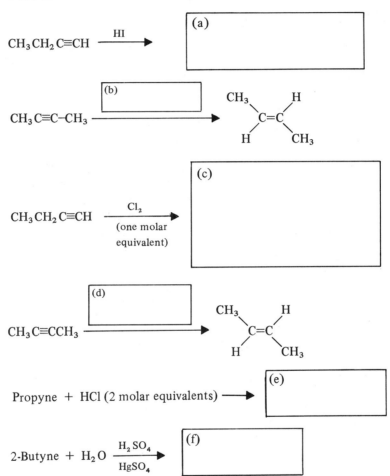

CH$_3$CH$_2$C≡CH $\xrightarrow{\text{HI}}$ (a)

(b)

CH$_3$C≡C–CH$_3$ ⟶ CH$_3$\, , H / C=C / H , CH$_3$

(c)

CH$_3$CH$_2$C≡CH $\xrightarrow[\text{(one molar equivalent)}]{\text{Cl}_2}$

(d)

CH$_3$C≡CCH$_3$ ⟶ CH$_3$\, , H / C=C / H , CH$_3$

(e)

Propyne + HCl (2 molar equivalents) ⟶

(f)

2-Butyne + H$_2$O $\xrightarrow[\text{HgSO}_4]{\text{H}_2\text{SO}_4}$

9.2   Tell whether each of the following statements is true (+) or false (−).

(a)   Carbon 2 of 2-butyne is sp^2 hybridized.

(b)   Carbon 1 of 1-butyne is sp hybridized.

(c) The equilibrium below suggests that acetylene is a stronger acid than water:

$$HC\equiv CH + OH^- \rightleftharpoons HC\equiv C:^- + H_2O$$

⬜

(d) All alkynes can be distinguished from alkenes by the use of $Ag(NH_3)_2^+$.

⬜

(e) Alkynes resemble alkenes in their physical properties.

⬜

SUPPLEMENTARY PROBLEMS

S9.1 Supply the reagents that accomplish each of the following transformations:

(a) Reacts with $CH_3\overset{Cl}{\underset{|}{CH}}\overset{Cl}{\underset{|}{CH}}CH_3$ to form an alkene.

(b) Reacts with $CH_3\overset{Cl}{\underset{|}{CH}}\overset{Cl}{\underset{|}{CH}}CH_3$ to form an alkyne.

(c) Reacts with $CH_3C\equiv CH$ to produce a ketone.

(d) Reacts with $CH_3C\equiv CH$ to produce an aldehyde.

(e) Used to distinguish between 1-butyne and 2-butyne.

S9.2 Supply the structural formulas of compounds **A, B, C,** and **D.**

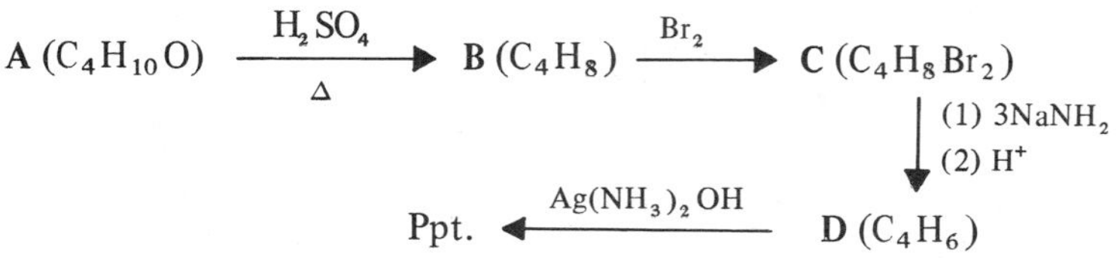

$$A\,(C_4H_{10}O) \xrightarrow[\Delta]{H_2SO_4} B\,(C_4H_8) \xrightarrow{Br_2} C\,(C_4H_8Br_2)$$

$$\text{Ppt.} \xleftarrow{Ag(NH_3)_2OH} D\,(C_4H_6) \xleftarrow[\text{(2) } H^+]{\text{(1) 3NaNH}_2} C$$

SOLUTIONS TO SUPPLEMENTARY PROBLEMS

S9.1   (a)   Zn/heat leads to dechlorination.

(b) $2NaNH_2$ leads to dehydrochlorination.

(c) $H_2O/Hg^{2+}/H_3O^+$ adds H_2O (Markovnikov addition) to the triple bond to give the enol $CH_3\overset{\underset{\textstyle |}{OH}}{C}=CH_2$ which rearranges to the ketone $CH_3\overset{\underset{\textstyle \|}{O}}{C}CH_3$.

(d) Sia_2BH followed by H_2O_2/OH^- gives anti-Markovnikov addition to give the enol $CH_3CH=CHOH$ which rearranges to the aldehyde CH_3CH_2CHO.

(e) $Ag(NH_3)_2OH$ or $Cu(NH_2)_2OH$ gives a precipitate with 1-butyne.

S9.2   **D** gives a precipitate with $Ag(NH_3)_2OH$, so it must be a terminal alkyne: **D** = $RC\equiv CH$.

We conclude from the molecular formula of **D** that the complete formula for **D** is $C_2H_5C\equiv CH$.

A, B, and **C** are deduced from the reactions:

$$CH_3CH_2CH_2CH_2OH \xrightarrow[\Delta]{H_2SO_4} CH_3CH_2CH=CH_2 \xrightarrow{Br_2} CH_3CH_2\overset{\overset{\textstyle Br}{|}}{C}H-\overset{\overset{\textstyle Br}{|}}{C}H_2$$

$$\underset{\textstyle \mathbf{A}}{} \qquad\qquad \underset{\textstyle \mathbf{B}}{} \qquad\qquad \underset{\textstyle \mathbf{C}}{}$$

$$CH_3CH_2C\equiv CAg\downarrow \xleftarrow{Ag(NH_3)_2OH} CH_3CH_2C\equiv CH$$

$$\underset{\textstyle \mathbf{D}}{}$$

(1) $3NaNH_2$
(2) H^+

SOME INTERCONVERSIONS OF ALIPHATIC HYDROCARBONS

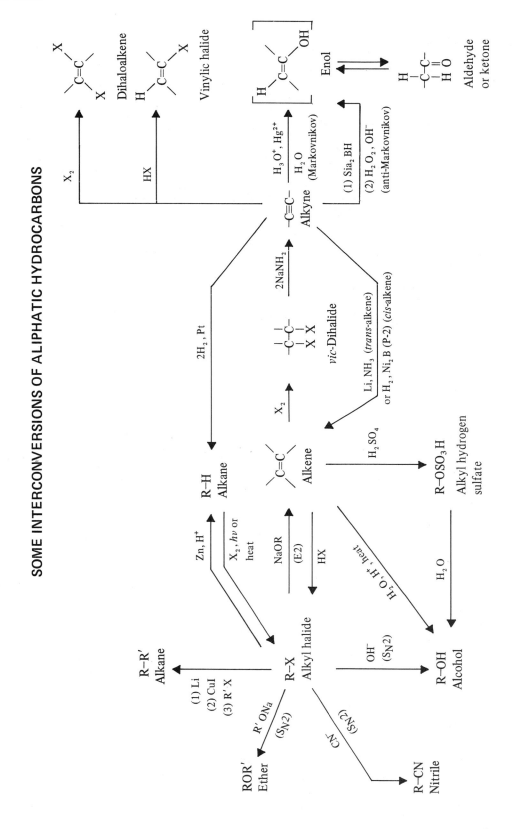

10
CONJUGATED UNSATURATED SYSTEMS: VISIBLE-ULTRAVIOLET SPECTROSCOPY

REACTIONS OF DIENES

1. Allylic Substitution

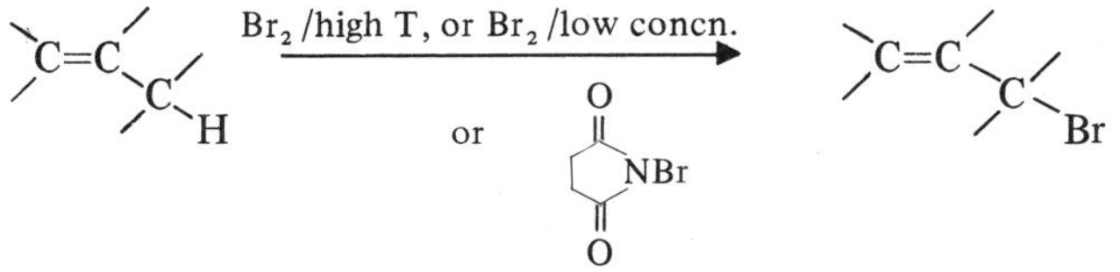

$$\underset{\text{H}}{\overset{}{\text{C}=\text{C}-\text{C}}} \xrightarrow[\text{or}]{\text{Br}_2\,/\text{high T, or Br}_2\,/\text{low concn.}} \underset{\text{Br}}{\overset{}{\text{C}=\text{C}-\text{C}}}$$

with N-bromosuccinimide (NBr)

2. 1,2- and, 1,4-Addition

1, 2-Addition   1, 4-Addition

$$\text{C}=\text{C}-\text{C}=\text{C} + \text{HCl} \longrightarrow \underset{\text{Cl}}{\text{H}-\text{C}-\text{C}-\text{C}=\text{C}} + \underset{\text{C}-\text{C}-\text{Cl}}{\text{H}-\text{C}-\text{C}}$$

HBr:

$$\underset{\text{Br}}{\text{H}-\text{C}-\text{C}-\text{C}=\text{C}} + \underset{\text{C}-\text{C}-\text{Br}}{\text{H}-\text{C}-\text{C}}$$

Br$_2$:

$$\underset{\text{Br}}{\text{Br}-\text{C}-\text{C}-\text{C}=\text{C}} + \underset{\text{C}-\text{C}-\text{Br}}{\text{Br}-\text{C}-\text{C}}$$

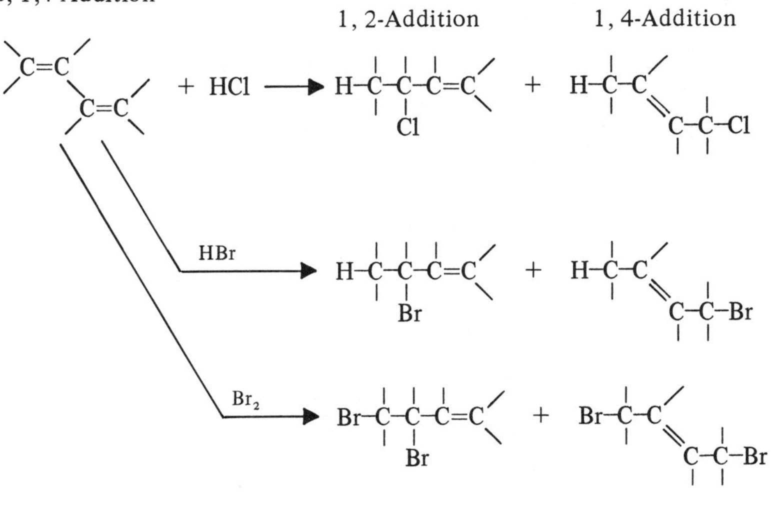

3. Diels-Alder Reaction

SOLUTIONS TO PROBLEMS

10.1   (a) $^{14}CH_2=CHCH_2X$ and $CH_2 = CH - {}^{14}CH_2X$

(b)   The reaction proceeds through the resonance-stabilized free radical,

$$^{14}\overset{\cdot}{CH_2}=CH-CH_2 \longleftrightarrow {}^{14}CH_2-CH=\overset{\cdot}{CH_2} \text{ or } {}^{14}\overset{\overset{\delta\cdot}{}}{CH_2}\text{---}CH\text{---}\overset{\overset{\delta\cdot}{}}{CH_2}$$

Thus attack on X_2 can occur by the carbon at either end of the chain since they are equivalent.

(c)   50:50 because attack at the two ends of the chain are equally probable.

10.2

(a) $\overset{4}{CH_3}-\overset{3}{\underset{+}{CH}}\diagup{}^{\overset{2}{CH}}\diagdown{}_{\overset{1}{CH_2}} \longleftrightarrow \overset{4}{CH_3}-\overset{3}{CH}\diagup{}^{\overset{2}{CH}}\diagdown{}_{\overset{1}{\underset{+}{CH_2}}} \text{ or } \overset{4}{CH_3}-\overset{3}{\underset{\delta+}{CH}}\diagup{}^{\overset{2}{CH}}\diagdown{}_{\overset{1}{\underset{\delta+}{CH_2}}}$

        D   **E**   **F**

(b)   We know that the allylic cation is almost as stable as a tertiary carbocation. Here we find not only the resonance stabilization of an allylic cation but also the additional stabilization that arises from contributor **D** in which the plus charge is on a secondary carbon.

(c) $CH_3-\overset{\overset{Cl}{|}}{CH}-CH=CH_2$ and $CH_3-CH=CH-CH_2-Cl$, because the Cl^- will attack the chain at the two positive centers shown in structure **F**.

10.3   (a)   *cis*-1,3-Pentadiene, *trans, trans*-2,4-hexadiene, *cis*-2-*trans*-4-hexadiene, and 1,3-cyclohexadiene are conjugated dienes.

(b)   1,4-Cyclohexadiene is an isolated diene.

(c)   1-Penten-4-yne is an isolated enyne.

10.4   (a)   Recall that 1,2- and 1,4-addition refer to the conjugated system itself and not the entire carbon chain. $CH_3CH_2\underset{\overset{|}{Cl}}{C}HCH=CHCH_3$ and $CH_3CH_2CH=CH\underset{\overset{|}{Cl}}{C}HCH_3$

(b)   The most stable cation is a hybrid of equivalent forms: $CH_3\underset{+}{C}HCH=CHCH_3 \longleftrightarrow$

$CH_3CH=CH\overset{+}{C}HCH_3$. Thus 1,4- and 1,2-addition yield the same product,

$$CH_3\overset{+}{C}HCH=CHCH_3$$
$$\underset{\overset{|}{Cl}}{}$$

10.5   (a)   Addition of the proton gives the resonance hybrid

$$CH_3-\overset{+}{C}H-CH=CH_2 \longleftrightarrow CH_3-CH=CH-\overset{+}{C}H_2$$
$$\textbf{I} \qquad\qquad\qquad\qquad \textbf{II}$$

The inductive effect of the methyl group in **I** stabilizes the positive charge on the adjacent carbon. Such stabilization of the positive charge does not occur in **II**. Because **I** contributes more heavily to the resonance hybrid than does **II**, C-2 bears a greater positive charge and reacts faster with the bromide ion.

(b) In the 1,4-addition product, the double bond is more highly substituted than in the 1,2-addition product, hence it is the more stable alkene.

10.6

(a) $CH_2=\overset{\overset{\displaystyle CH_3}{|}}{C}-\overset{..}{C}H_2 \longleftrightarrow \overset{.}{C}H_2-\overset{\overset{\displaystyle CH_3}{|}}{C}=CH_2$

(b) $CH_2=CH-\underset{+}{CH}-CH=CH_2 \longleftrightarrow \overset{+}{C}H_2-CH=CH-CH=CH_2 \longleftrightarrow$

$CH_2=CH-CH=CH-\overset{+}{C}H_2$

(c) $\longleftrightarrow$ $\longleftrightarrow$

(d) $\longleftrightarrow$ $\longleftrightarrow$

(e) $CH_3CH=CH-CH=\overset{+}{\overset{..}{O}}H \longleftrightarrow CH_3CH=CH-\overset{+}{C}H-\overset{..}{\overset{..}{O}}H \longleftrightarrow CH_3\overset{+}{C}H-CH=CH-\overset{..}{\overset{..}{O}}H$

(f) $CH_2=CH-\overset{..}{\underset{..}{C}}l: \longleftrightarrow \ ^-:CH_2-CH=\overset{..}{C}l:^+$

(g) $\longleftrightarrow$

(h) $^-:CH_2-\overset{\overset{\displaystyle \overset{..}{O}:}{||}}{C}-CH_3 \longleftrightarrow CH_2=\overset{\overset{\displaystyle :\overset{..}{O}:^-}{|}}{C}-CH_3$

(i) $CH_3-\overset{..}{\underset{..}{S}}-\overset{+}{C}H_2 \longleftrightarrow CH_3-\overset{+}{S}=CH_2$

(j) $CH_3-\overset{+}{N}\overset{\displaystyle :\overset{..}{O}}{\underset{\displaystyle \overset{..}{O}:^-}{\diagdown}} \longleftrightarrow CH_3-\overset{+}{N}\overset{\displaystyle :\overset{..}{O}:^-}{\underset{\displaystyle \overset{..}{O}:}{\diagdown}} \longleftrightarrow CH_3-\overset{2+}{N}\overset{\displaystyle :\overset{..}{O}:^-}{\underset{\displaystyle \overset{..}{O}:^-}{\diagdown}}$

(minor)

10.7

(a) $CH_3CH_2\overset{\overset{\displaystyle CH_3}{|}}{\underset{+}{C}}-CH=CH_2$ because the positive charge is on a tertiary carbon rather than a primary one (rule **8**).

(b) 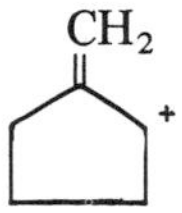 + because the positive charge is on a secondary carbon rather than a primary one (rule **8**).

(c) $CH_2=\overset{+}{N}(CH_3)_2$ because all atoms have a complete octet (rule **b**), and there are more covalent bonds (rule **a**).

(d) $CH_3-\overset{\overset{\textstyle O}{\|}}{C}-OH$ because it has no charge separation (rule **c**).

(e) $CH_2=CH\overset{\cdot}{C}HCH=CH_2$ because the radical is on a secondary carbon rather than a primary one (rule **8**).

10.8 In resonance structures, the positions of the nuclei must remain the same for all structures (rule **2**). The keto and enol forms shown not only differ in the positions of their electrons, they also differ in the position of one of the hydrogen atoms. In the enol form it is attached to an oxygen; in the keto form it has been moved so that it is attached to a carbon.

10.9 (a) (c)

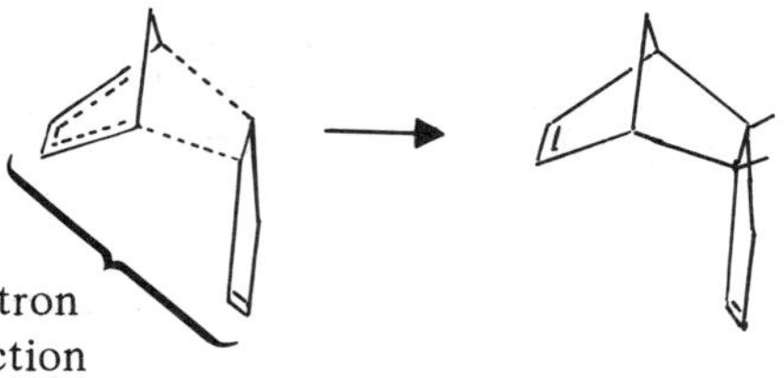

(b) π-Electron interaction occurs here

Endo adduct

10.10

(a)

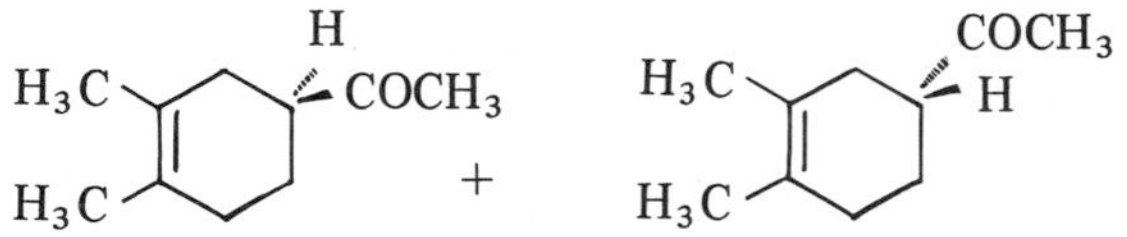

(b)

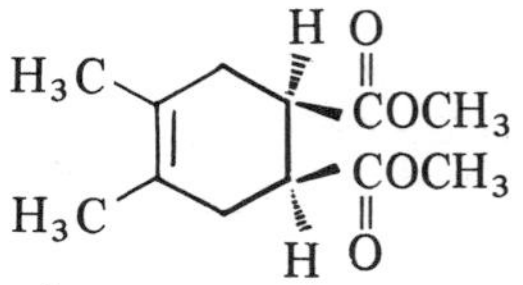

(c)

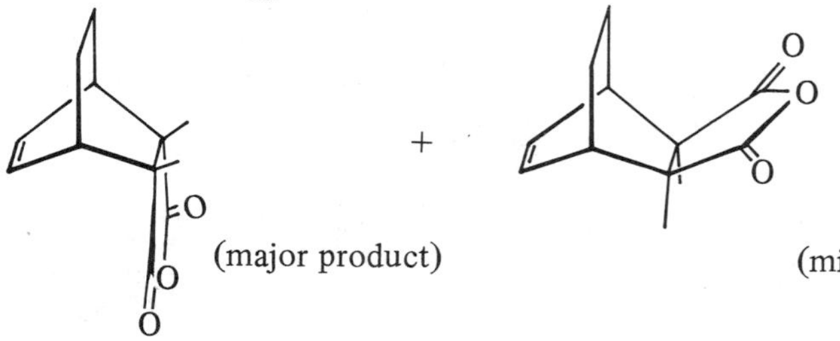

(major product)   (minor product)

10.11 Use the *trans*-diester because the stereochemistry is retained in the adduct.

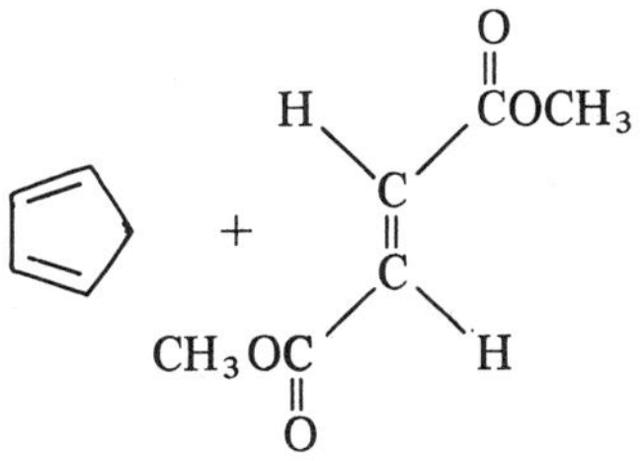

10.12

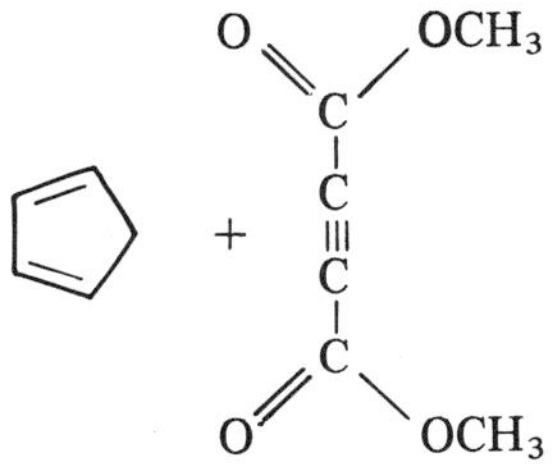

10.13

(a) $BrCH_2CH_2CH_2CH_2Br \xrightarrow[(CH_3)_3COH]{(CH_3)_3COK} CH_2=CH-CH=CH_2$

(b) $HOCH_2CH_2CH_2CH_2OH \xrightarrow[heat]{conc.\ H_2SO_4} CH_2=CH-CH=CH_2$

(c) $CH_2=CH-CH_2CH_2-OH \xrightarrow[heat]{conc.\ H_2SO_4} CH_2=CH-CH=CH_2$

(d) $CH_2=CH-CH_2CH_2-Cl \xrightarrow[(CH_3)_3COH]{(CH_3)_3COK} CH_2=CH-CH=CH_2$

(e) $CH_2=CH-\underset{\underset{Cl}{|}}{CH}-CH_3 \xrightarrow[(CH_3)_3COH]{(CH_3)_3COK} CH_2=CH-CH=CH_2$

(f) $CH_2=CH-\underset{\underset{OH}{|}}{CH}-CH_3 \xrightarrow[heat]{conc.\ H_2SO_4} CH_2=CH-CH=CH_2$

(g) $HC\equiv C-CH=CH_2 + H_2 \xrightarrow{Ni_2B\ (P-2)} CH_2=CH-CH=CH_2$

10.14 $CH_2=\underset{\underset{CH_3}{|}}{C}---\underset{\underset{CH_3}{|}}{C}=CH_2$

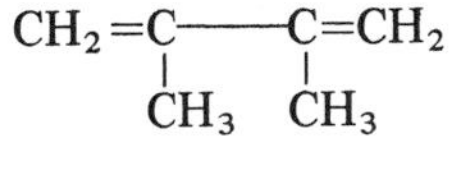

10.15 (a) $Cl-CH_2\underset{\underset{Cl}{|}}{CH}CH=CH_2$ + $Cl-CH_2-CH=CH-CH_2-Cl$

(b) $\underset{\underset{Cl}{|}}{CH_2}-\underset{\underset{Cl}{|}}{CH}-\underset{\underset{Cl}{|}}{CH}-\underset{\underset{Cl}{|}}{CH_2}$ (c) $\underset{\underset{Br}{|}}{CH_2}-\underset{\underset{Br}{|}}{CH}-\underset{\underset{Br}{|}}{CH}-\underset{\underset{Br}{|}}{CH_2}$

(d) $CH_3-CH_2-CH_2-CH_3$ (e) No reaction

(f) $Cl-CH_2-\underset{\underset{OH}{|}}{CH}-CH=CH_2$ + $Cl-CH_2-CH=CH-CH_2-OH$ $(+ ClCH_2\underset{\underset{Cl}{|}}{CH}CH=CH_2$

$+ ClCH_2CH=CHCH_2Cl)$

(g) $4CO_2$ (Note: $KMnO_4$ oxidizes $HOOC-COOH$ to $2CO_2$)

(h) $CH_3-\underset{\underset{OH}{|}}{CH}-CH=CH_2$ + $CH_3-CH=CH-CH_2OH$

10.16

(a) $CH_2=CH-CH_2-CH_3$ + [NBS imide structure] $\xrightarrow{CCl_4}$ $CH_2=CH-\underset{\underset{Br}{|}}{CH}-CH_3$

(+ $CH_2-CH=CH-CH_3$)
      |
      Br

(NBS) $\xrightarrow[{(CH_3)_3COH}]{(CH_3)_3COK}}$ $CH_2=CH-CH=CH_2$

Note: In the second step both allylic halides undergo elimination of HBr to yield 1,3-butadiene and therefore separating the mixture produced in the first step is unnecessary. The $BrCH_2CH=CHCH_3$ undergoes a 1,4-elimination (the opposite of a 1,4-addition).

(b) $CH_2=CH-CH_2CH_2CH_3$ + NBS $\xrightarrow{CCl_4}$ $CH_2=CH-\underset{\underset{Br}{|}}{CH}CH_2CH_3$

(+ $CH_2CH=CHCH_2CH_3$) $\xrightarrow[{(CH_3)_3COH}]{(CH_3)_3COK}}$ $CH_2=CH-CH=CH-CH_3$
      |
      Br

Here again both products undergo elimination of HBr to yield 1,3-pentadiene.

(c) $CH_3CH_2CH_2CH_2OH \xrightarrow[heat]{conc. H_2SO_4}$ $CH_3CH_2CH=CH_2$ $\xrightarrow{[as\ in\ (a)]}$

$\underset{\underset{Br}{|}}{CH_2}-CH=CH-\underset{\underset{Br}{|}}{CH_2}$ $\xleftarrow[heat]{Br_2}$ $CH_2=CH-CH=CH_2$ $\longleftarrow$

(d) $CH_3-CH=CH-CH_3$ + NBS $\xrightarrow{CCl_4}$ $CH_3-CH=CH-CH_2-Br$

+ $CH_2=CH-CHBr-CH_3$

(e) $+ Br_2 \xrightarrow[\text{heat}]{\text{light}}$ $\xrightarrow[(CH_3)_3COH]{(CH_3)_3COK}$ $\xrightarrow[CCl_4]{NBS}$

(excess)

(f) $\xrightarrow[(CH_3)_3COH]{(CH_3)_3COK}$ $\left(\text{same as} \ \text{}\right)$

10.17

$$R-\ddot{O}-\ddot{O}-R \xrightarrow[\text{or heat}]{\text{light}} 2R-\ddot{O}\cdot$$

$$R-\ddot{O}\cdot \ + \ H-\ddot{B}r: \longrightarrow R-\ddot{O}-H \ + \ \cdot\ddot{B}r:$$

$$CH_2=CH-CH=CH_2 \ + \ \cdot\ddot{B}r: \longrightarrow \left[\underset{\overset{|}{Br}}{CH_2=CH-\overset{\bullet}{C}H-CH_2} \longleftrightarrow \underset{\overset{|}{Br}}{\overset{\bullet}{C}H_2-CH=CH-CH_2} \right]$$

$$\xrightarrow{HBr} \underset{\overset{|}{H} \ \ \overset{|}{Br}}{CH_2=CH-CH-CH_2} \ + \ \underset{\overset{|}{H} \ \ \ \ \ \ \ \overset{|}{Br}}{CH_2-CH=CH-CH_2} \ + \ \cdot\ddot{B}r:$$

(cis and trans)

10.18   (a) $Ag(NH_3)_2OH$ gives a precipitate with 1-butyne only.

(b)   1,3-Butadiene decolorizes bromine solution; butane does not.

(c) H_2SO_4 dissolves $CH_2=CHCH_2CH_2OH$. Butane does not dissolve.

(d) $AgNO_3$ in C_2H_5OH gives a AgBr precipitate with $CH_2=CHCH_2CH_2Br$. No reaction with 1,3-butadiene.

(e) $AgNO_3$ in C_2H_5OH gives a AgBr precipitate with $BrCH_2CH=CHCH_2Br$ (it is an allylic bromide), but not with $\underset{\overset{|}{Br} \ \ \overset{|}{Br}}{CH_3CH=CHCH_3}$ (a vinylic bromide).

10.19   (a)   Because a highly resonance-stabilized free radical is formed:

$$CH_2=CH-\overset{\bullet}{C}H-CH=CH_2 \longleftrightarrow CH_2=CH-CH=CH-\overset{\bullet}{C}H_2 \longleftrightarrow \overset{\bullet}{C}H_2-CH=CH-CH=CH_2$$

(b)   Because the carbanion is more stable:

$$CH_2=CH-\overset{\overset{\displaystyle\cdot\cdot}{}}{C}H-CH=CH_2 \longleftrightarrow CH_2=CH-CH=CH-\overset{\overset{\displaystyle\cdot\cdot}{}}{C}H_2 \longleftrightarrow \overset{\overset{\displaystyle\cdot\cdot}{}}{C}H_2-CH=CH-CH=CH_2$$

i.e., we can write more resonance structures of nearly equal energies.

10.20

$$\underset{\overset{|}{CH_3}}{CH_2=C-CH=CH_2} \xrightarrow{H^+}$$

$$\left[\underset{\overset{+}{}}{\overset{\overset{\displaystyle CH_3}{|}}{CH_3\overset{}{C}-CH=CH_2}} \longleftrightarrow \overset{\overset{\displaystyle CH_3}{|}}{CH_3-\overset{+}{C}=CH-\overset{+}{C}H_2} \right] \quad \textbf{I}$$

$$\left[\underset{\overset{+}{}}{\overset{\overset{\displaystyle CH_3}{|}}{CH_2=C-\overset{}{C}H-CH_3}} \longleftrightarrow \overset{\overset{\displaystyle CH_3}{|}}{\overset{+}{C}H_2-C=CH-CH_3} \right] \quad \textbf{II}$$

The resonance hybrid, **I**, has the positive charge, in part, on the tertiary carbon; in **II**, the positive charge is on primary and secondary carbons only. Therefore hybrid **I** is more stable, and will be the intermediate carbocation. 1,4-Addition to **I** gives

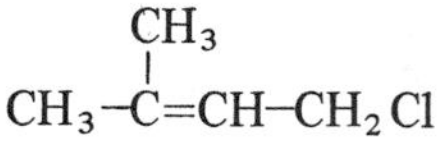

$$CH_3-\overset{\overset{\displaystyle CH_3}{|}}{C}=CH-CH_2\,Cl$$

10.21

(a)

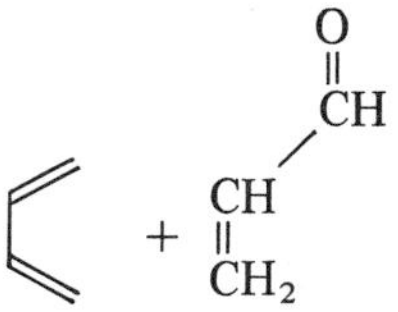

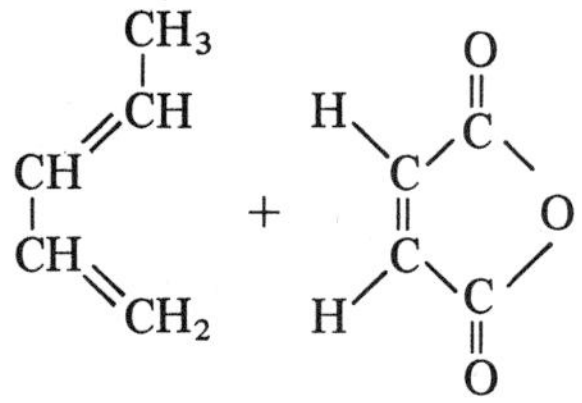

(b)

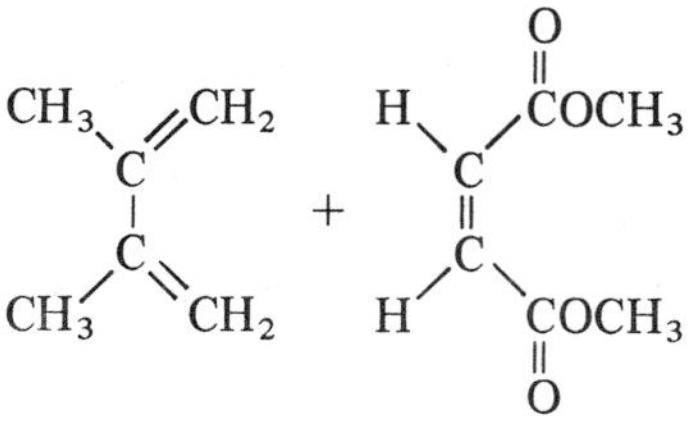

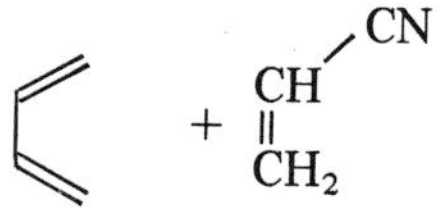

(c)

(d)

(e)

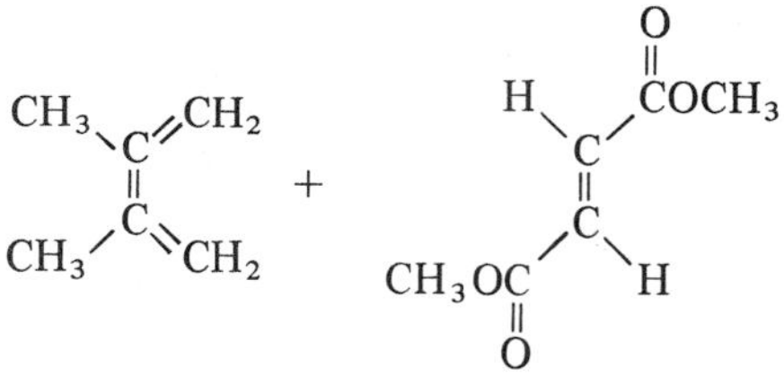

(f)

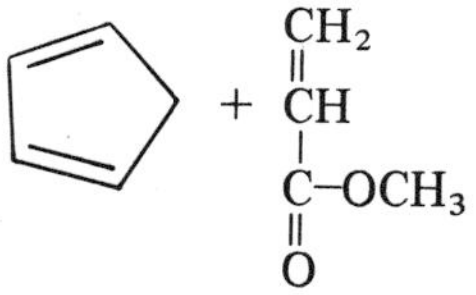

10.22 Neither compound can assume the *s*-cis conformation. 1,3-Butadiyne is linear, and =CH$_2$ is held in an *s*-trans conformation by the requirements of the ring.

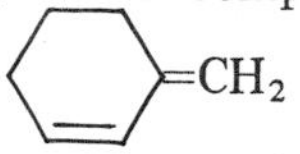

10.23

(a)

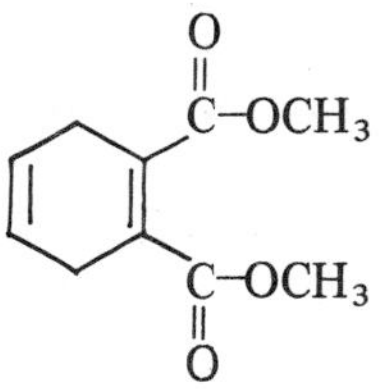

(b)

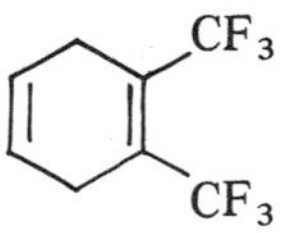

10.24 The formula, C_6H_8, tells us that **A** and **B** have six hydrogens less than an alkane. This unsaturation may be due to three double bonds, one triple bond and one double bond, or combinations of two double bonds and a ring, or one triple bond and a ring. Since both **A** and **B** react with two moles of H_2 to yield cyclohexane, they are either cyclohexyne or cyclohexadienes. The absorption maximum of 256 nm for **A** tells us that it is conjugated. **B**, with no absorption maximum beyond 200, possesses isolated double bonds. We can rule out cyclohexyne because of ring strain caused by the requirement of linearity of the $-C\equiv C-$ system. Therefore **A** is 1,3-cyclohexadiene; **B** is 1,4-cyclohexadiene.

10.25 In the dimer, the remaining double bonds are isolated:

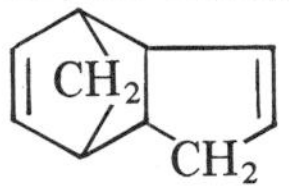

The rate of dimerization can be followed by observing the rate of disappearance of the absorption maximum at 239 nm that is due to the conjugated double bonds in cyclopentadiene (see Table 10.3). The product does not absorb at 239 nm.

10.26 All three compounds have an unbranched five-carbon chain, because the product of hydrogenation is unbranched pentane. The formula, C_5H_6, suggests that they have one double bond and one triple bond. **D**, **E**, and **F** must differ, therefore, in the way the multiple bonds are distributed in the chain. **E** and **F** have a terminal $-C\equiv CH$ [reaction with $Ag(NH_3)_2{}^+OH^-$]. The absorption maximum near 230 nm for **D** and **E** suggests that in these compounds, the multiple bonds are conjugated. The structures are:

$$CH_3-C\equiv C-CH=CH_2 \qquad HC\equiv C-CH=CH-CH_3 \qquad HC\equiv C-CH_2-CH=CH_2$$
$$\textbf{D} \qquad\qquad\qquad \textbf{E} \qquad\qquad\qquad \textbf{F}$$

10.27 The *endo* adduct is less stable than the *exo*, but is produced at a faster rate at 25°. At 90° the Diels-Alder reaction becomes reversible; an equilibrium is established, and the more stable *exo* adduct predominates.

10.28

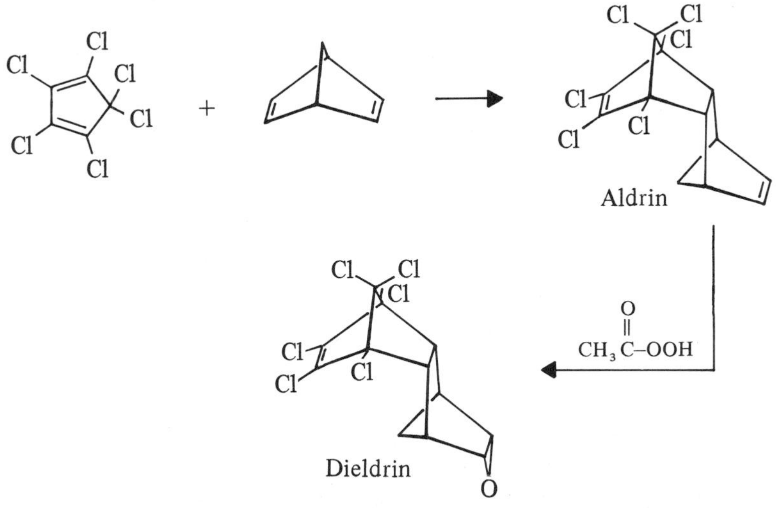

10.29

(a) 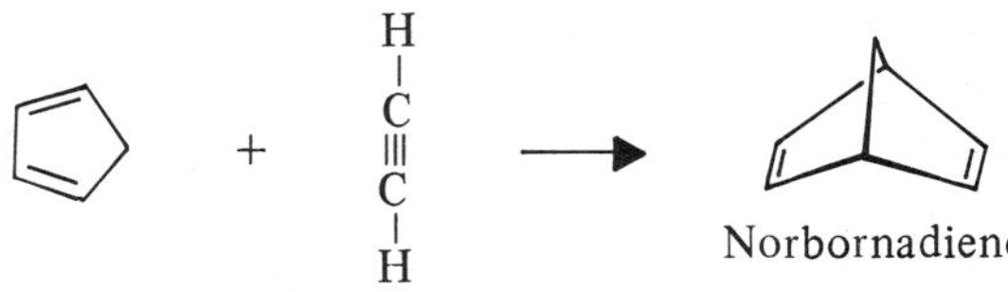 Norbornadiene

(b)

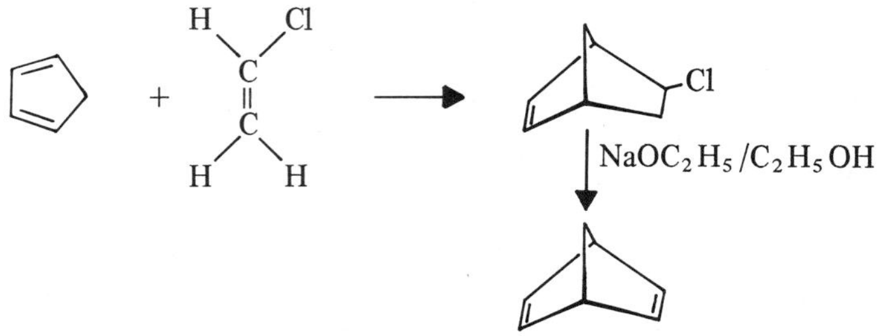

$NaOC_2H_5/C_2H_5OH$

10.30

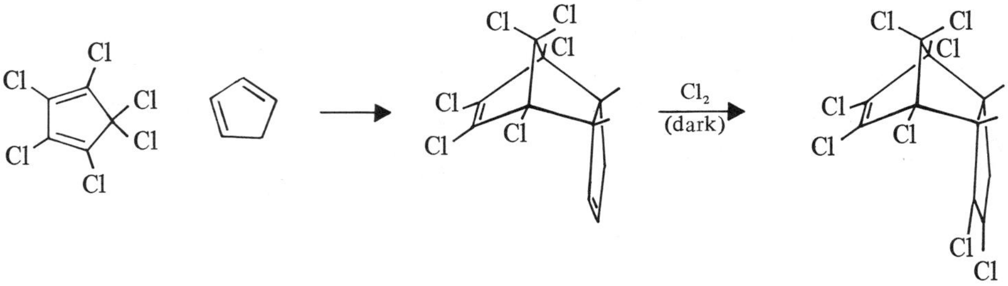

$\dfrac{Cl_2}{(dark)}$

Note: The other double bond is less reactive because of the presence of the two chlorine substituents.

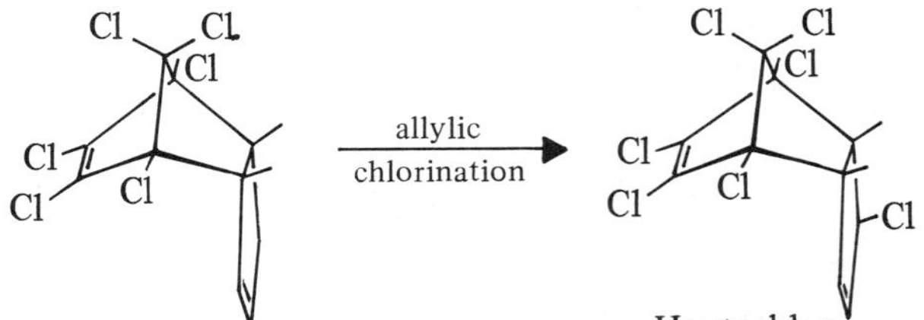

Chlordan

$\dfrac{\text{allylic}}{\text{chlorination}}$

Heptachlor

10.31

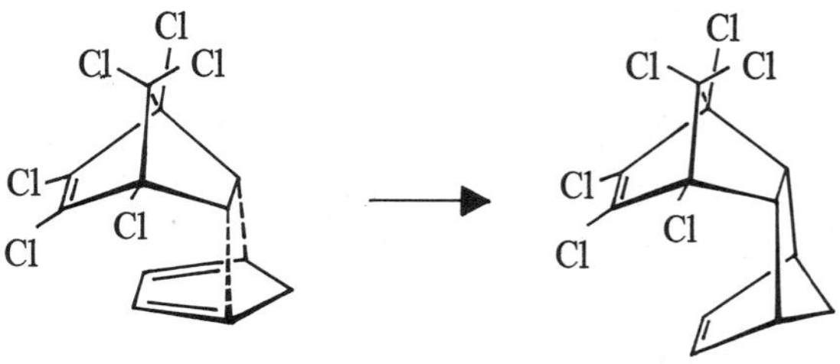

Isodrin

10.32 Protonation of the alcohol leads to an allylic cation that can react with a chloride ion at either carbon-1 or carbon-3.

$$CH_3CH=CHCH_2OH \xrightarrow{H^+} CH_3CH=CHCH_2-\overset{\overset{H}{|}}{O^+}-H \xrightarrow{-H_2O}$$

$$CH_3CH=CHCH_2^+ \longleftrightarrow CH_3\overset{+}{C}HCH=CH_2 \xrightarrow{Cl^-}$$

$$CH_3CH=CHCH_2Cl + CH_3\underset{\underset{Cl}{|}}{C}HCH=CH_2$$

10.33 (1) $CH_2=CH-CH=CH_2 + Cl_2 \longrightarrow ClCH_2-\overset{+}{C}H-CH=CH_2$

$$\updownarrow$$

$$ClCH_2-CH=CH-\overset{+}{C}H_2$$

$$\underbrace{\qquad\qquad\qquad\qquad}$$

$$ClCH_2-\overset{\delta+}{C}H\text{---}CH\text{---}\overset{\delta+}{C}H_2$$

(2) $ClCH_2-\overset{\delta+}{C}H\text{---}CH\text{---}\overset{\delta+}{C}H_2 \xrightarrow[(-H^+)]{CH_3OH} ClCH_2-\underset{\underset{OCH_3}{|}}{C}H-CH=CH_2$

$$+ ClCH_2-CH=CH-CH_2OCH_3$$

10.34 A six-membered ring cannot accommodate a triple bond because of the strain that would be introduced.

10.35 The products are $CH_3CH_2\underset{\underset{Br}{|}}{C}HCH=CH_2$ and $CH_3CH_2CH=CHCH_2Br$. They are formed from an allylic radical in the following way:

$$Br_2 \longrightarrow 2\,Br\cdot$$

(from NBS)

$$Br\cdot \ + \ CH_3CH_2CH_2CH=CH_2 \ \longrightarrow \ CH_3CH_2\overset{\cdot}{C}HCH=CH_2$$

$$+ \ HBr$$

$$CH_3CH_2CH=CH\overset{\cdot}{C}H_2$$

$$CH_3CH_2\overset{\delta\cdot}{CH}\text{---}CH\text{---}\overset{\delta\cdot}{CH_2} \ + \ Br_2 \ \longrightarrow \ CH_3CH_2\overset{|}{\underset{Br}{C}}HCH=CH_2$$

$$+ \ CH_3CH_2CH=CHCH_2Br \ + \ Br\cdot$$

10.36 (a) The same carbocation (a resonance hybrid) is produced in the dissociation step:

$$\underset{CH_3C=CHCH_2Cl}{\overset{CH_3}{|}} \quad \xrightarrow{Ag^+}$$

$$\underset{CH_3\overset{\overset{CH_3}{|}}{\underset{+}{C}}-CH=CH_2}{I} \quad \longleftrightarrow \quad \underset{CH_3\overset{\overset{CH_3}{|}}{C}-CH\underset{+}{-}CH_2}{II} \ + \ AgCl$$

$$\underset{\underset{Cl}{|}}{\overset{\overset{CH_3}{|}}{CH_3C}}-CH=CH_2 \quad \xrightarrow{Ag^+}$$

$$\Big\downarrow H_2O$$

$$\underset{\underset{OH}{|}}{\overset{\overset{CH_3}{|}}{CH_3-C}}-CH=CH_2 \ + \ \overset{\overset{CH_3}{|}}{CH_3-C}=CH-CH_2OH$$

(85%)   (15%)

(b) Structure **I** contributes more than **II** to the resonance hybrid of the carbocation (rule 8). Therefore the hybrid carbocation has a larger positive charge on the tertiary carbon than on the primary carbon. Reaction of the carbocation with water will therefore occur more frequently at the tertiary carbon.

10.37 (a) Propyne. (b) Base ($:B^-$) removes a proton leaving the anion whose resonance structures are shown:

$$CH_2=C=CH_2 \ + \ :B^- \ \rightleftharpoons \ H:B \ + \ \underset{I}{\overset{H}{\underset{H}{C}}=C=\overset{..}{C}\underset{H}{\overset{H}{}}} \ \longleftrightarrow \ \underset{II}{H-\overset{H}{\underset{H}{C}}-C\equiv C}$$

Reaction with H : B may then occur at the CH_2 carbanion. The overall reaction is

$$CH_2=C=CH_2 \ + \ :B^- \ \rightleftharpoons \ [CH_2=C=\overset{..}{C}H \longleftrightarrow \overset{..}{C}H_2-C\equiv CH] \ + \ H:B$$

$$\Big\updownarrow$$

$$CH_3-C\equiv CH \ + \ :B^-$$

10.38   The first crystalline solid is the Diels-Alder adduct below, mp 125°,

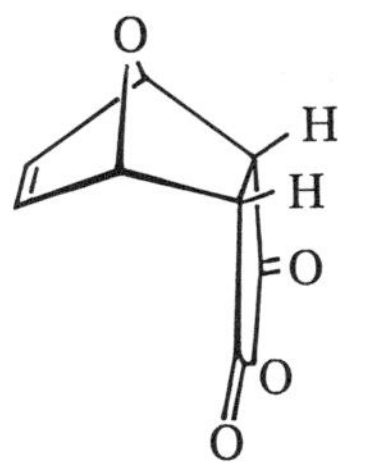

On melting, this adduct undergoes a reverse Diels-Alder reaction yielding furan (which vaporizes) and maleic anhydride, mp 56°.

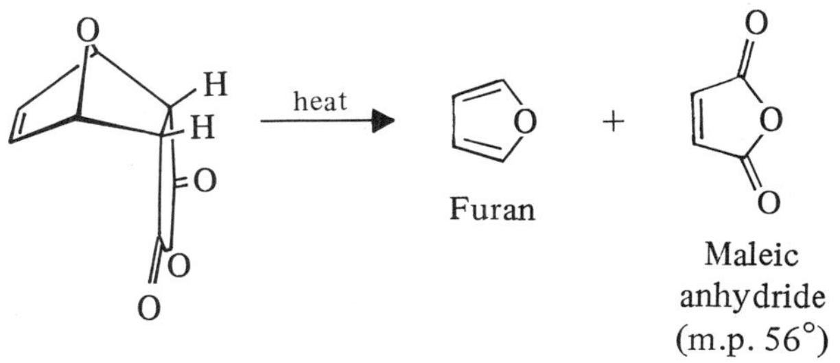

Furan

Maleic
anhydride
(m.p. 56°)

10.39   (a)   *trans*-1,3-Pentadiene assumes the required *s*-cis conformation readily. With *cis*-1,3-pentadiene the concentration of the *s*-cis conformation is much lower because of steric hindrance presented by the internal methyl group.

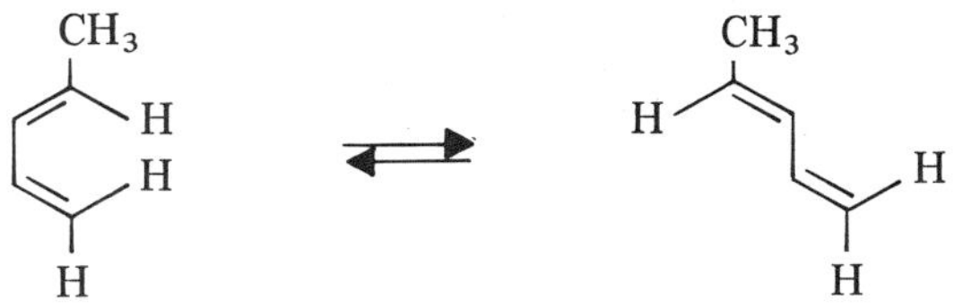

trans-1,3-Pentadiene

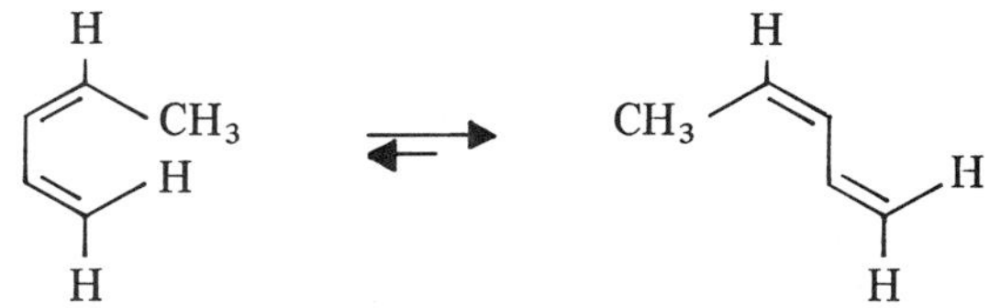

cis-1,3-Pentadiene

(b)   The large *tert*-butyl group at the 2-position of 1,3-butadiene favors the formation of the *s*-cis conformation. (It also increases reactivity by releasing electrons.) On the other hand, a *tert*-butyl group at the 1-position of 1,3-butadiene prevents the formation of significant concentrations of the *s*-cis conformation and thus no Diels-Alder reactions can take place.

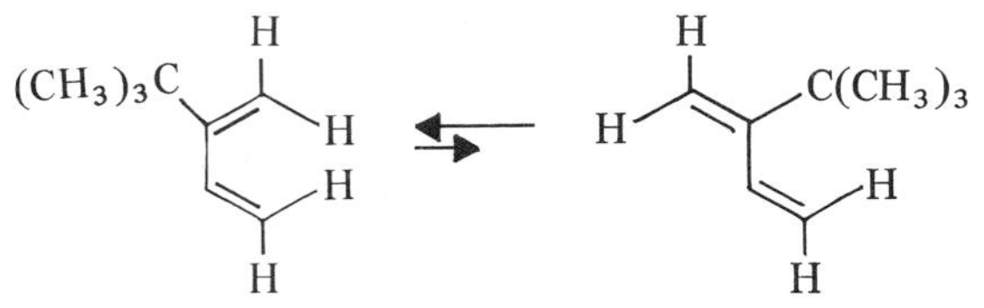

2-*tert*-Butyl-1,3-butadiene

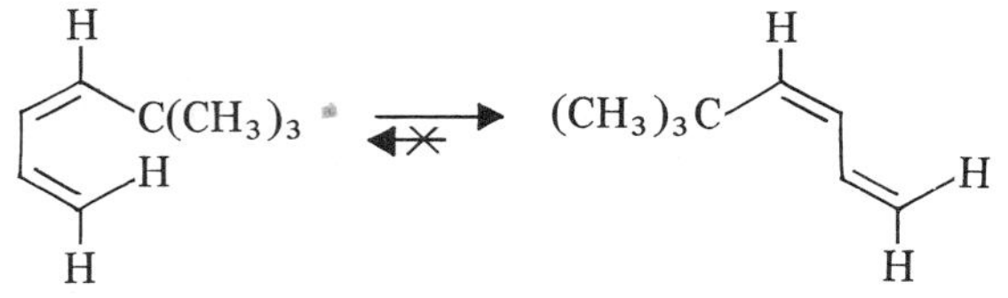

5,5-Dimethyl-*cis*-1,3-hexadiene
(*cis*-1-*tert*-butyl-1,3-butadiene)

10.40 The following reaction takes place:

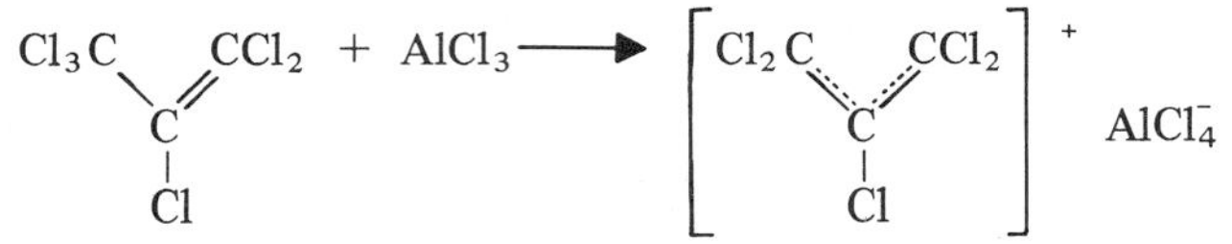

The salt forms because the organic cation is an allylic cation and is, therefore, unusually stable. It is also stabilized by resonance structures involving nonbonding electron pairs of the chlorine atoms such as the second structure below.

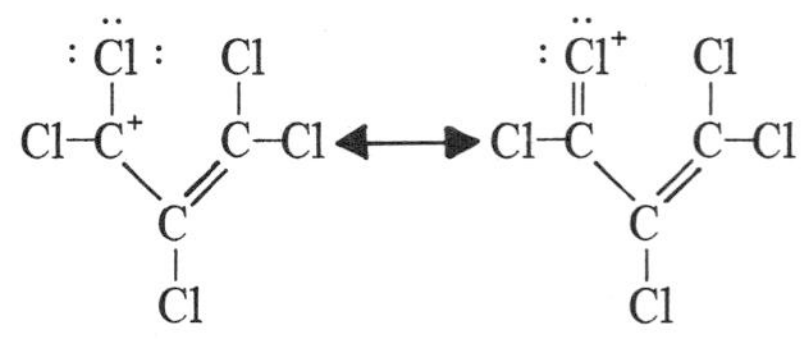

SECTION REFERENCES FOR ADDITIONAL PROBLEMS

10.13	Chapter 6	**10.18**	9.17
10.14	Chapter 6	**10.19**	10.3B
10.15	10.8	**10.20**	10.8, 10.9
10.16	10.2, 10.8	**10.21**	10.10
10.17	10.3B, 10.8	**10.22**	10.10

SELF-TEST

10.1   Supply the missing reactants or major products. Show stereochemistry where applicable. If no reaction occurs write N.R.

(a) $CH_2=CHCH=CH_2$ +

$$\underset{H}{\overset{CH_3}{C}}=\underset{H}{\overset{CH_3}{C}} \xrightarrow{\Delta}$$

C_8H_{14}

(b) $CH_3CH=CHCH=CHCH_3$ + HCl (one mole) $\xrightarrow{\text{(1,4-addition)}}$

(c) $CH_3CH=CHCH=CHCH_3$ + Cl_2 (one molar equivalent) $\longrightarrow$

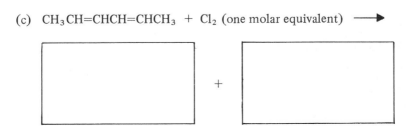

+

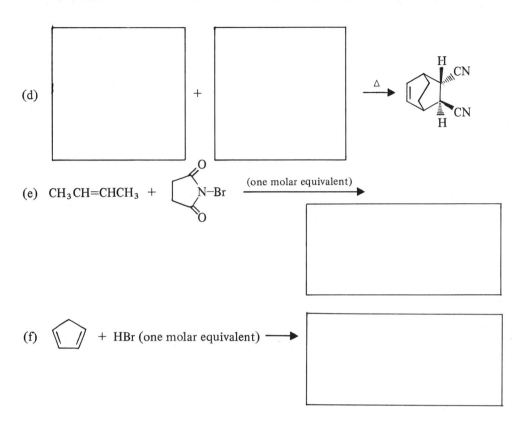

(d) [ ] + [ ] $\xrightarrow{\Delta}$

(e) $CH_3CH=CHCH_3$ + (succinimide N–Br) $\xrightarrow{\text{(one molar equivalent)}}$

(f) (cyclopentadiene) + HBr (one molar equivalent) $\longrightarrow$

10.2 Some of the following pairs represent valid resonance structures and others do not. Place (+) in the space beside those that are valid resonance structures and (0) beside those that are not.

(a) (benzene structure) and (benzene structure) [ ]

(b) (cyclopropene cation) and (cyclopropene cation) [ ]

(c) (piperazine structure) and (piperazine structure) [ ]

(d) $CH_2=CHCH=CH\ddot{C}H_2^-$ and $^-\ddot{C}H_2CH=CHCH=CH_2$ [ ]

10.3   (a) Sketch the relative positions of the energy levels of the π molecular orbitals of the following carbocation. (b) Show the distribution of π-electrons using vertical arrows for electrons. (c) Label the orbitals as bonding, antibonding, or nonbonding.

$$CH_3CH{=}CHCH{=}\overset{+}{C}HCH_3$$

Energy of p atomic orbitals

Increasing Energy

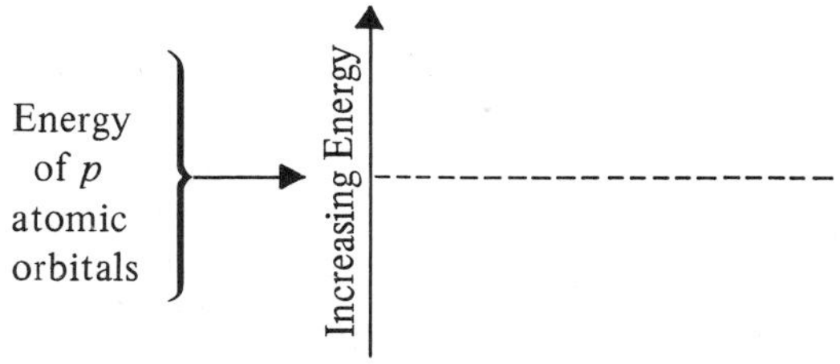

10.4   Which of the following compounds would absorb light at the highest wavelength?

$CH_2{=}CHCH_3$ $CH_2{=}CHCH{=}CH_2$ $CH_3CH{=}CHCH_2CH{=}CH_2$

A   B   C

FIRST REVIEW PROBLEM SET

Following are solutions to the problems that review concepts covered in Chapters 1-10.

1

(a)

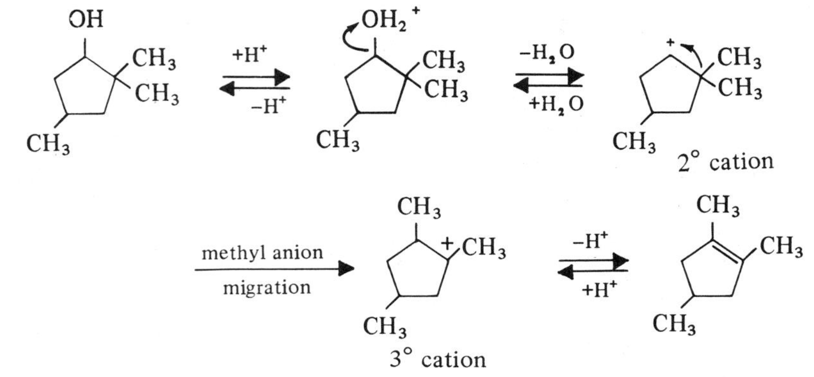

(b)

then,

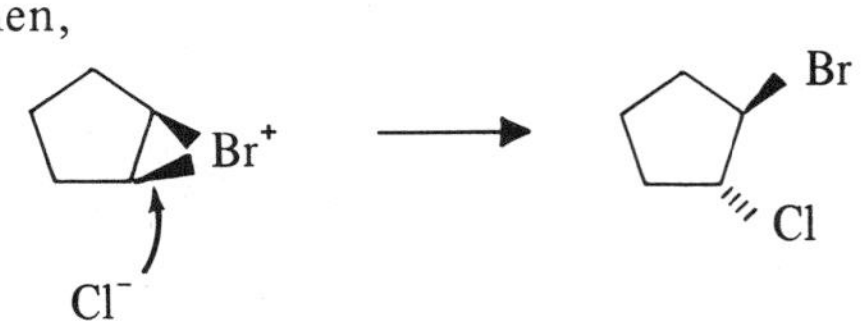

(c) The enantiomer of the product given would be formed in an equimolar amount via the following reaction.

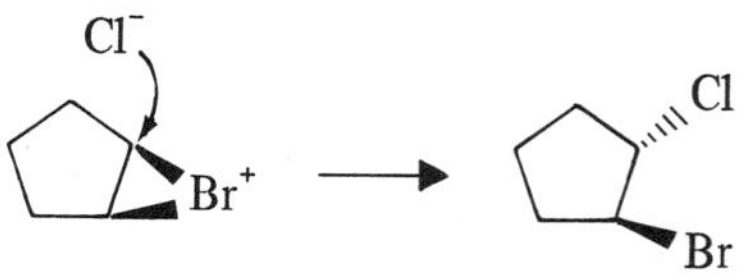

The *trans*-1, 2-dibromocyclopentane would be formed as a racemate via the reaction of the bromonium ion with a bromide ion:

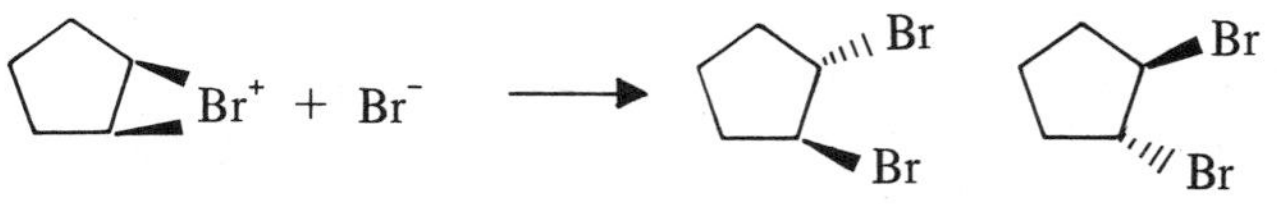

Racemic *trans*-1,2-dibromocyclopentane

And, *trans*-2-bromocyclopentanol (the bromohydrin) would be formed (as a racemate) via the reaction of the bromonium ion with water.

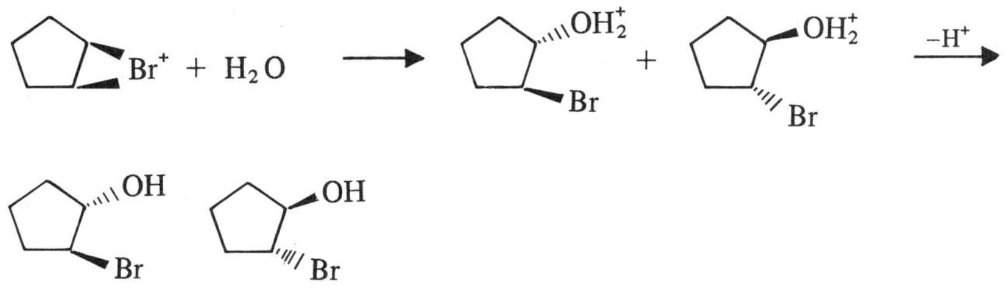

Racemic *trans*-2-bromocyclopentanol

2

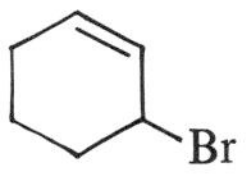

A    B 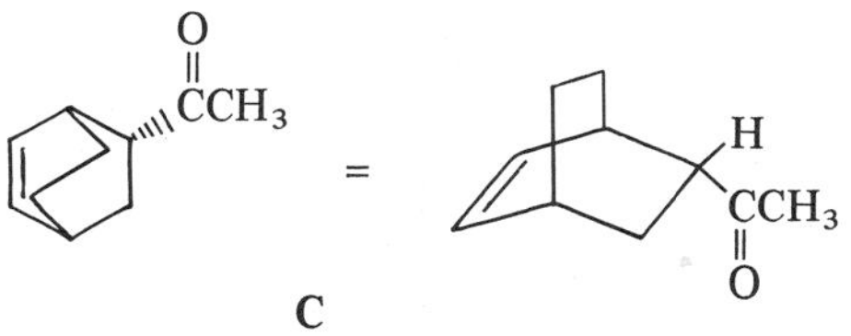   C

A is formed by an allylic bromination. **B** is formed by an E2 elimination. **C** is formed via a Diels-Alder reaction that yield predominantly the *endo* product. Ozonolysis of the double bond then yields the product in which all three substituents are on the same side of the cyclohexane ring.

3   All of these differences can be explained by resonance contribution to the CH_2=CHCl molecule made by **A** and **B** below.

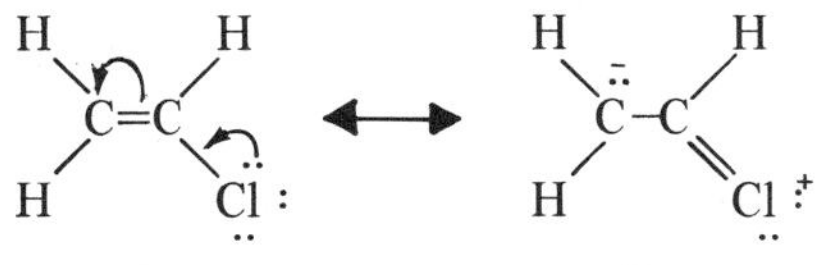

A   B

(a) Because of the contribution made to the hybrid by **B**, the C–Cl bond of CH_2=CH–Cl has some double bond character, and is, therefore, shorter than the "pure" single bond of CH_3CH_2–Cl.

(b) The contribution made to the hybrid by **B** imparts some single bond character to the carbon-carbon double bond of CH_2=CHCl causing it to be longer than the "pure" double bond of CH_2=CH_2.

(c) Electronegativity differences would cause a carbon-chlorine bond to be polarized as follows:

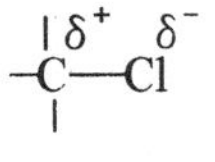

And this effect accounts, almost entirely, for the dipole moment of CH_3CH_2Cl.

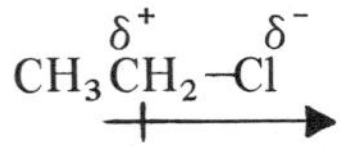

$$\overset{\delta^+}{CH_3CH_2}-\overset{\delta^-}{Cl} \qquad \mu = 2.05 \text{ D}$$

With $CH_2=CH-Cl$, however, the resonance contribution of **B** tends to oppose the polarization of the C—Cl bond caused by electronegativity differences. That is, the resonance effect partially cancels the electronegativity effect causing the dipole moment to be smaller.

4   **A** = $CH_3(CH_2)_{11}CH_2C≡CH$

   B = $CH_3(CH_2)_{11}CH_2C≡CNa$

   C = $CH_3(CH_2)_{11}CH_2C≡CCH_2(CH_2)_6CH_3$

   Muscalure =

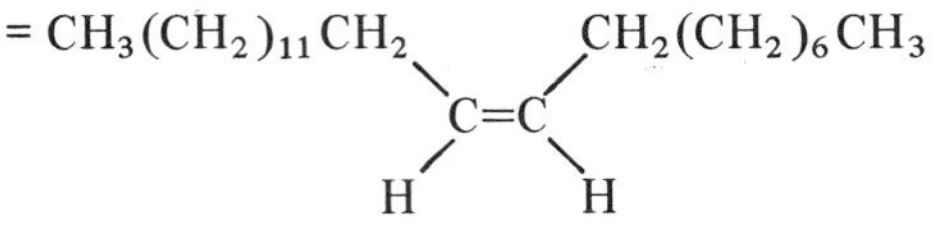

5

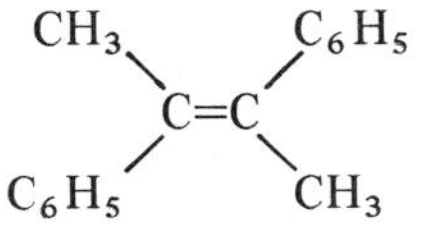

(E)-2,3-Diphenyl-2-   (Z)-2,3-Diphenyl-2-
      butene   butene

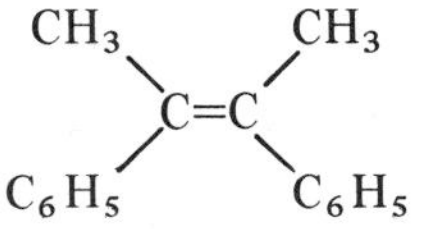

Because catalytic hydrogenation is a *syn* addition, catalytic hydrogenation of the (Z)-isomer would yield a *meso* compound.

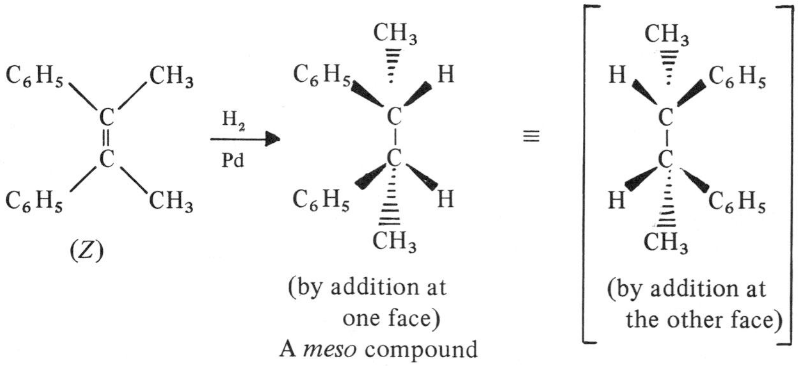

Syn addition of hydrogen to the (E)-isomer would yield a racemate:

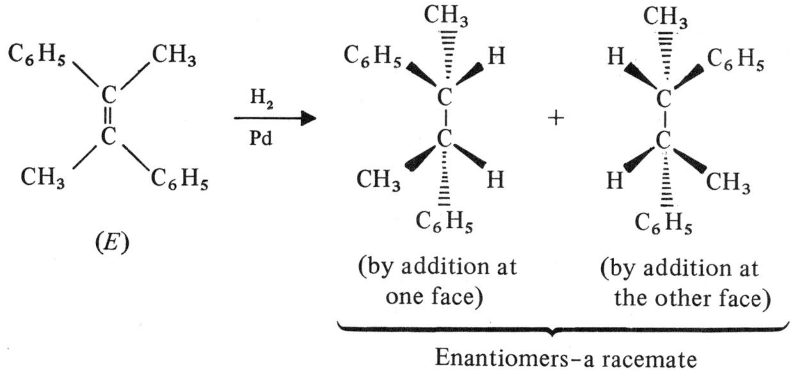

(E)

(by addition at
one face)

(by addition at
the other face)

Enantiomers–a racemate

6   From the molecular formula of **A** and of its hydrogenation product **B** we can conclude that **A** has two rings and a double bond. (**B** has two rings.)

From the product of strong oxidation with $KMnO_4$ and its stereochemistry (i.e., compound **C**) we can deduce the structure of **A**.

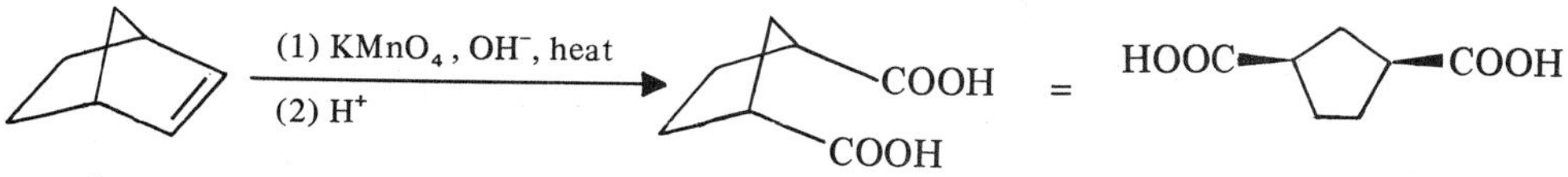

meso-1,3-Cyclopentane-
dicarboxylic acid

Compound **B** is bicycyo [2.2.1] heptane and **C** is a glycol.

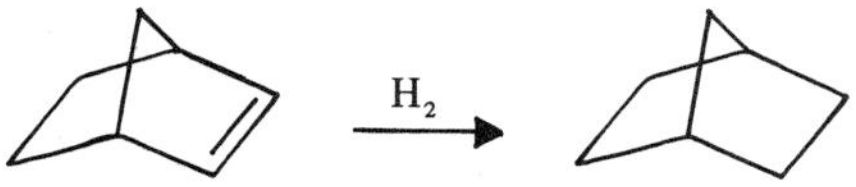

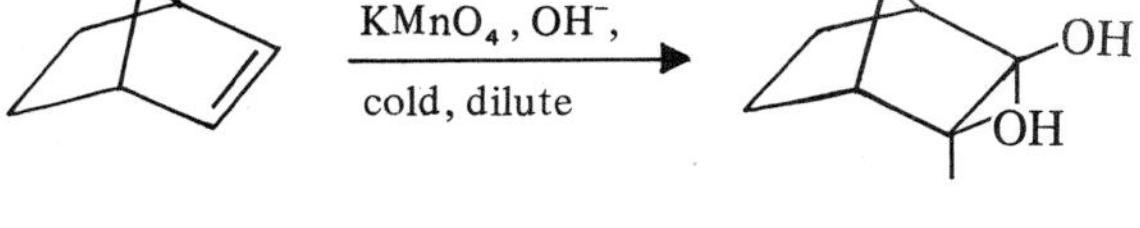

(see page 294 of
the text)

Notice that **C** is a *meso* compound also.

7 (a) $CH_3C{\equiv}CH$ $\xrightarrow{NaNH_2}$ $CH_3C{\equiv}CNa$ $\xrightarrow{CH_3I}$ $CH_3C{\equiv}CCH_3$

(b) $CH_3C{\equiv}CCH_3$ from (a) $\xrightarrow{H_2, Ni_2 B (P-2)}$

$$\begin{array}{c} CH_3 \quad\quad CH_3 \\ C{=}C \\ H \quad\quad\quad H \end{array}$$

(c) $CH_3C{\equiv}CCH_3$ from (a) $\xrightarrow{Li, NH_3}$

$$\begin{array}{c} CH_3 \quad\quad H \\ C{=}C \\ H \quad\quad\quad CH_3 \end{array}$$

(d) $CH_3CH{=}CHCH_3$ from (b) or (c) $\xrightarrow{THF:BH_3}$ $\underset{\underset{|}{\overset{|}{B^-}}}{CH_3CH_2CHCH_3}$ $\xrightarrow[160°]{heat}$

$\underset{|}{CH_3CH_2CH_2CH_2{-}B^-}$ $\xrightarrow[160°]{1\text{-}decene}$ $CH_3CH_2CH{=}CH_2$

(e) $CH_3CH_2CH{=}CH_2$ from (d) $\xrightarrow[CCl_4]{NBS}$ $\left.\begin{array}{c} \underset{\underset{Br}{|}}{CH_3CHCH{=}CH_2} \\ + \\ CH_3CH{=}CHCH_2Br \end{array}\right\}$ $\xrightarrow{(CH_3)_3COK}$

$CH_2{=}CH{-}CH{=}CH_2$

(f) $CH_3CH_2CH{=}CH_2$ from (d) $\xrightarrow[ROOR]{HBr}$ $CH_3CH_2CH_2CH_2Br$

(g) $CH_3CH{=}CHCH_3$ from (b) or (c) $\xrightarrow[\text{no peroxides}]{HBr}$ $\underset{\underset{Br}{|}}{CH_3CH_2CHCH_3}$

or

$CH_3CH_2CH{=}CH_2$ from (d) $\xrightarrow[\text{no peroxides}]{HBr}$ $\underset{\underset{Br}{|}}{CH_3CH_2CHCH_3}$

(h)

$$\begin{array}{c} CH_3 \quad\quad H \\ C{=}C \\ H \quad\quad\quad CH_3 \end{array}$$
from (c) $\xrightarrow[\substack{CCl_4 \\ (anti\ addition)}]{Br_2}$

$$\begin{array}{c} CH_3 \\ Br{-}C{-}H \\ C \\ Br{-}C{-}H \\ CH_3 \end{array}$$
(cf. Sect. 8.10)

(2R, 3S)

A *meso* compound

(i)
from (b)

$\xrightarrow[\text{CCl}_4]{\text{Br}_2}$

(*anti* addition)

(2R, 3R)   (2S, 3S)

A racemate

(j)
from (b)

$\xrightarrow[\text{(2) NaHSO}_3]{\text{(1) OsO}_4}$

(*syn* addition)

(cf. Sect. 8.10)

or

from (c)

$\xrightarrow[\text{(2) H}_3\text{O}^+, \text{ heat}]{\text{(1) RCOOH}}$

(*anti* addition)

(cf. Sect. 8.10)

(k) $CH_3C\equiv C-CH_3$ $\xrightarrow[\text{CH}_3\text{COOH}]{\text{HBr, Br}^-}$

(cf. Sect. 9.9)

8 $CH_3CHCH_2CH_3$ $\xrightarrow{\text{Br}_2, h\nu, \text{ heat}}$ $CH_3CCH_2CH_3$ (cf. Sect. 4.10)
     | |
     CH_3 Br
                                                |
                                                CH_3

(a) $CH_3CCH_2CH_3$ $\xrightarrow[\substack{\text{CH}_3\text{CH}_2\text{OH}\\\text{heat}}]{\text{CH}_3\text{CH}_2\text{ONa}}$ $CH_3C=CHCH_3$
     | |
     Br CH_3
     |
     CH_3

(b) $CH_3C=CHCH_3$ $\xrightarrow{\text{H}_3\text{O}^+, \text{H}_2\text{O}}$ $CH_3CCH_2CH_3$
     | |
     CH_3 OH

from (a)

(c) 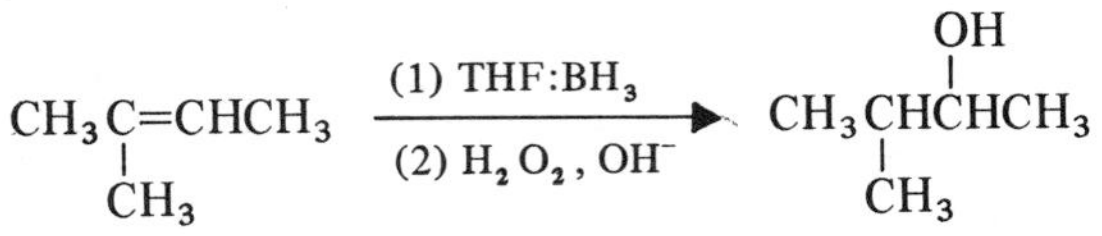 $CH_3C=CHCH_3$ $\xrightarrow[\text{(2) } H_2O_2\text{, } OH^-]{\text{(1) THF:BH}_3}$ $CH_3\overset{OH}{\underset{CH_3}{C}H}CHCH_3$

with CH_3 below on left

from (a)

(d) 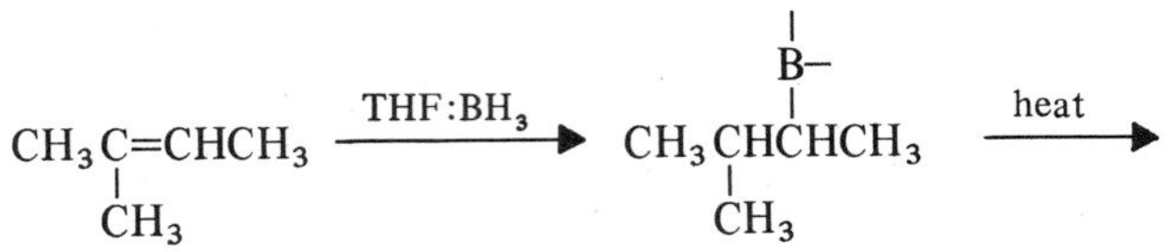 $CH_3C=CHCH_3$ $\xrightarrow{\text{THF:BH}_3}$ $CH_3\overset{B-}{\underset{CH_3}{C}H}CHCH_3$ $\xrightarrow{\text{heat}}$

with CH_3 below on left

from (a)

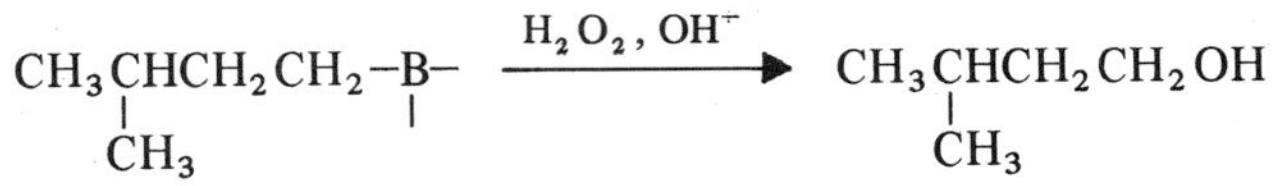

$CH_3CHCH_2CH_2-B-$ $\xrightarrow{H_2O_2\text{, } OH^-}$ $CH_3CHCH_2CH_2OH$

with CH_3 below

(e) 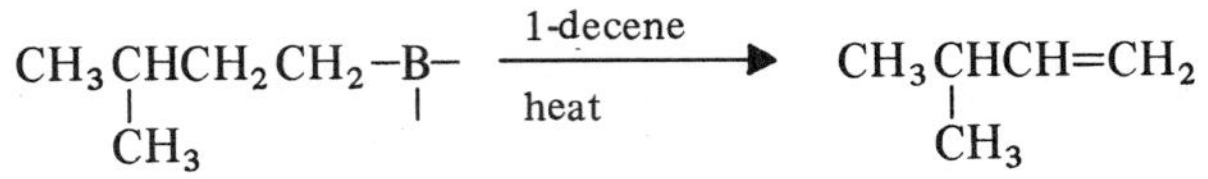 $CH_3CHCH_2CH_2-B-$ $\xrightarrow[\text{heat}]{\text{1-decene}}$ $CH_3CHCH=CH_2$

with CH_3 below

from (d)

(f) 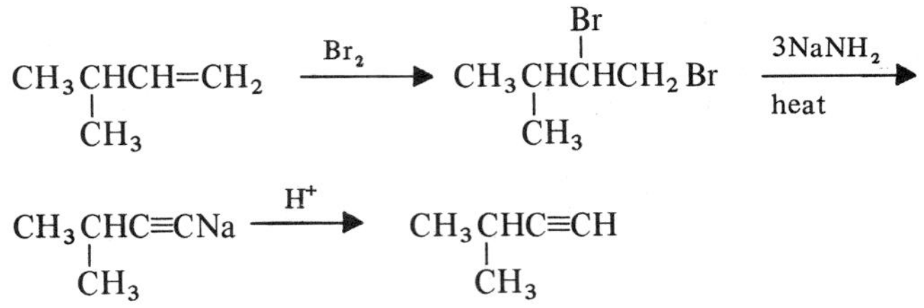 $CH_3CHCH=CH_2$ $\xrightarrow{Br_2}$ $CH_3\overset{Br}{\underset{CH_3}{C}H}CHCH_2Br$ $\xrightarrow[\text{heat}]{\text{3NaNH}_2}$

with CH_3 below on left

$CH_3CHC≡CNa$ $\xrightarrow{H^+}$ $CH_3CHC≡CH$

with CH_3 below

(g) 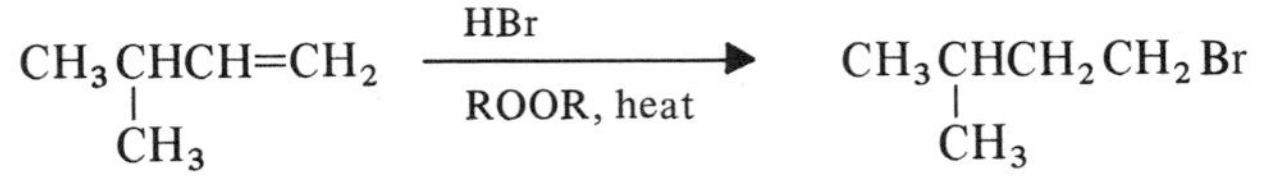 $CH_3CHCH=CH_2$ $\xrightarrow[\text{ROOR, heat}]{\text{HBr}}$ $CH_3CHCH_2CH_2Br$

with CH_3 below

from (e)

(h) 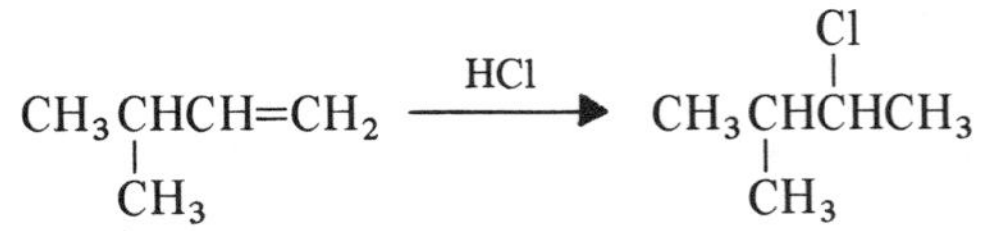 $CH_3CHCH=CH_2$ $\xrightarrow{\text{HCl}}$ $CH_3\overset{Cl}{\underset{CH_3}{C}H}CHCH_3$

with CH_3 below on left

from (e)

(i) 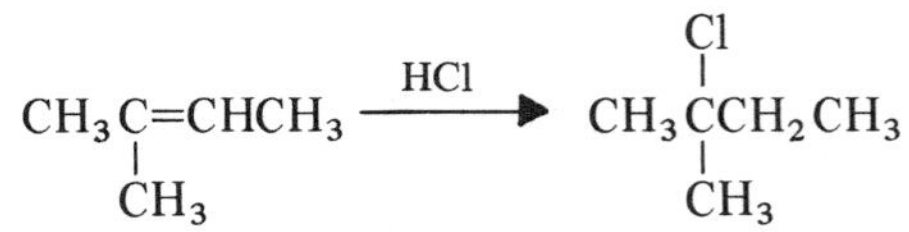 $CH_3C=CHCH_3$ $\xrightarrow{\text{HCl}}$ $CH_3\overset{Cl}{\underset{CH_3}{C}}CH_2CH_3$

with CH_3 below on left

from (a)

(j) 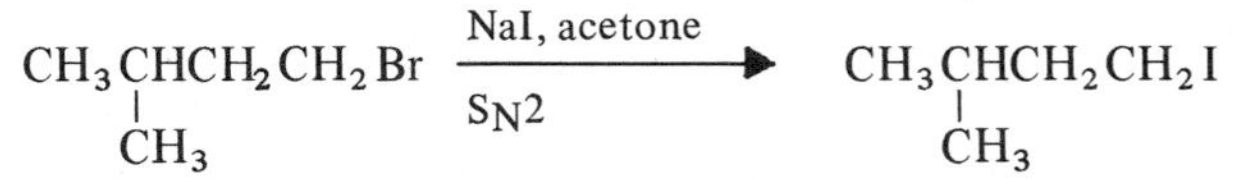 $CH_3CHCH_2CH_2Br$ $\xrightarrow[\text{S}_N2]{\text{NaI, acetone}}$ $CH_3CHCH_2CH_2I$

with CH_3 below

from (g)

(k) 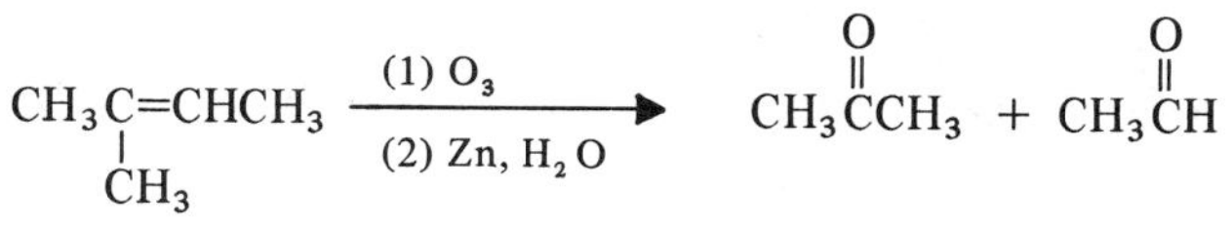 $CH_3C=CHCH_3$ $\xrightarrow[\text{(2) Zn, H}_2\text{O}]{\text{(1) O}_3}$ $CH_3\overset{O}{\overset{\|}{C}}CH_3 + CH_3\overset{O}{\overset{\|}{C}}H$
         |
         CH_3

    from (a)

(1) $CH_3CHCH=CH_2$ $\xrightarrow[\text{(2) Zn, H}_2\text{O}]{\text{(1) O}_3}$ $CH_3\overset{O}{\overset{\|}{C}}HCH + H\overset{O}{\overset{\|}{C}}H$
        |
        CH_3

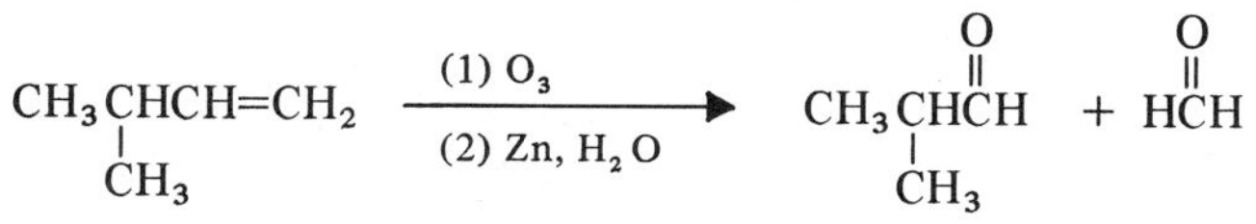

    from (e)

(m) 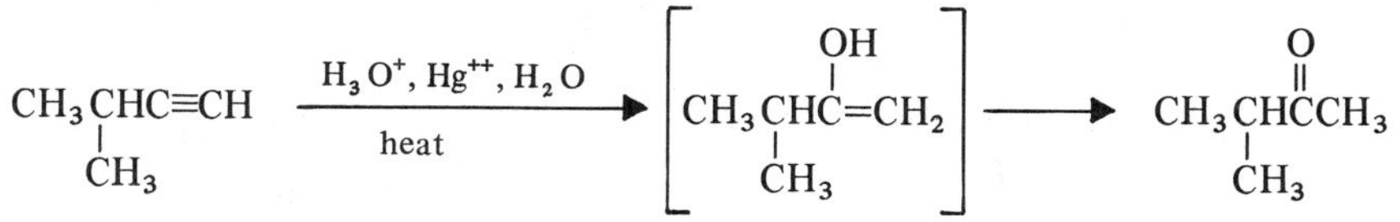 $CH_3CHC{\equiv}CH$ $\xrightarrow[\text{heat}]{\text{H}_3\text{O}^+,\ \text{Hg}^{++},\ \text{H}_2\text{O}}$ $\left[CH_3\underset{\underset{CH_3}{|}}{\overset{\overset{OH}{|}}{C}}HC=CH_2 \right]$ $\longrightarrow$ $CH_3\overset{O}{\overset{\|}{C}}HCCH_3$
        |
        CH_3

    from (f)

9

$$CH_3\underset{\underset{CH_3}{|}}{\overset{\overset{CH_3}{|}}{C}}CH_2CH_3 \xrightarrow{\text{Cl}_2,\ h\nu,\ \text{heat}} CH_3\underset{\underset{CH_3}{|}}{\overset{\overset{CH_2Cl}{|}}{C}}CH_2CH_3 + CH_3\underset{\underset{CH_3}{|}}{\overset{\overset{CH_3}{|}}{C}}CHClCH_3$$

A   **B**   **C**

$$+ CH_3\underset{\underset{CH_3}{|}}{\overset{\overset{CH_3}{|}}{C}}CH_2CH_2Cl$$

D

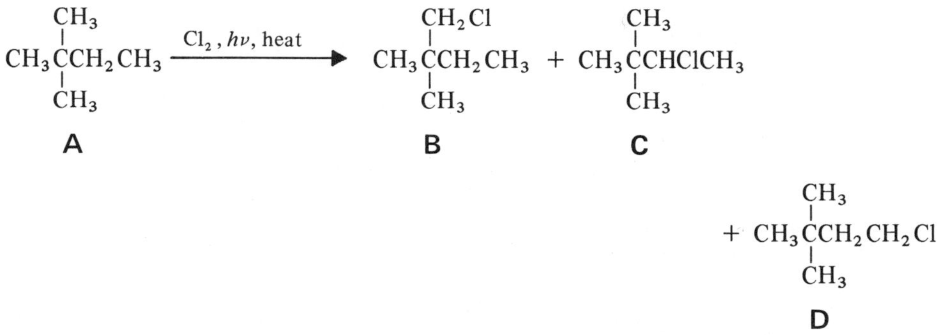

B cannot undergo dehydrohalogenation because it has no β-hydrogen, however **C** and **D** can as shown below.

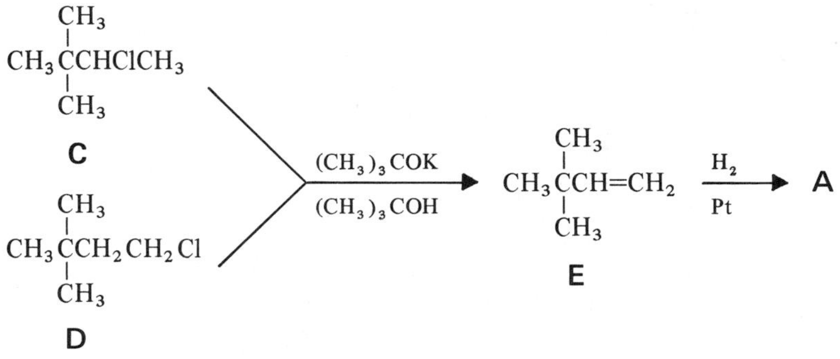

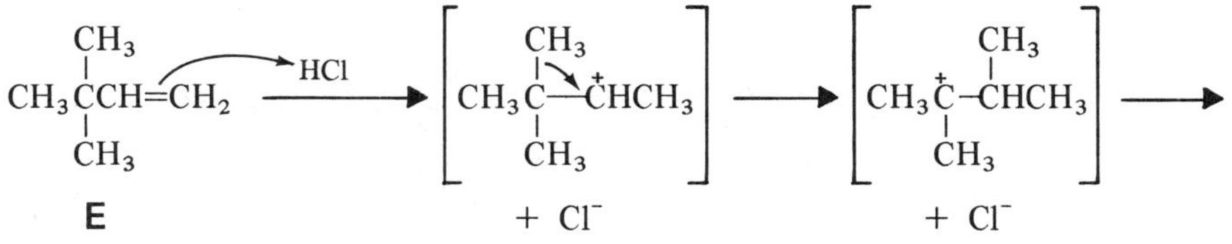

$$CH_3\underset{\underset{CH_3}{|}}{\overset{\overset{CH_3}{|}}{C}}CHClCH_3$$

C

$$CH_3\underset{\underset{CH_3}{|}}{\overset{\overset{CH_3}{|}}{C}}CH_2CH_2Cl$$

D

$\xrightarrow[\text{(CH}_3)_3\text{COH}]{\text{(CH}_3)_3\text{COK}}$ $CH_3\underset{\underset{CH_3}{|}}{\overset{\overset{CH_3}{|}}{C}}CH=CH_2$ $\xrightarrow[\text{Pt}]{\text{H}_2}$ **A**

E

$$CH_3\underset{\underset{CH_3}{|}}{\overset{\overset{CH_3}{|}}{C}}CH=CH_2 \xrightarrow[]{\text{HCl}} \left[CH_3\overset{\overset{CH_3}{|}}{C}{-}\overset{+}{C}HCH_3 \right] \longrightarrow \left[CH_3\overset{\overset{CH_3}{|}}{\overset{+}{C}}{-}CHCH_3 \right] \longrightarrow$$

E $+ Cl^-$ $+ Cl^-$

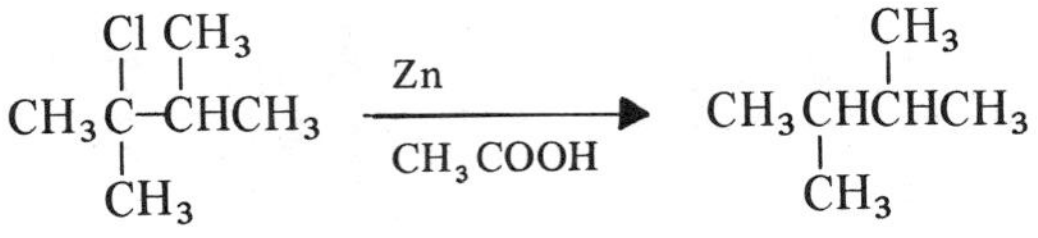

$$CH_3\overset{\overset{\displaystyle Cl}{|}}{\underset{\underset{\displaystyle CH_3}{|}}{C}}-\overset{\overset{\displaystyle CH_3}{|}}{\underset{}{C}}HCH_3 \quad \xrightarrow[CH_3COOH]{Zn} \quad CH_3\overset{\overset{\displaystyle CH_3}{|}}{\underset{\underset{\displaystyle CH_3}{|}}{C}}HCHCH_3$$

F   G

10

$$CH_3C{\equiv}CCH_3$$

$\xrightarrow{H_2 , Pt}$ $CH_3CH_2CH_2CH_3$

$\xrightarrow{Ag(NH_3)_2OH}$ No reaction

A

$\Big\downarrow$ $H_2 , Ni_2 B$ (P-2)

$$\overset{CH_3}{\underset{H}{}}\!\!C{=}C\!\!\overset{CH_3}{\underset{H}{}} \quad \xrightarrow[\substack{(2)\ NaHSO_3 \\ (\textit{syn}\ \text{hydroxylation})}]{(1)\ OsO_4} \quad$$

B

H⫴⫴C⫴⫴OH with CH_3
C—C
H⫴⫴C⫴⫴OH with CH_3

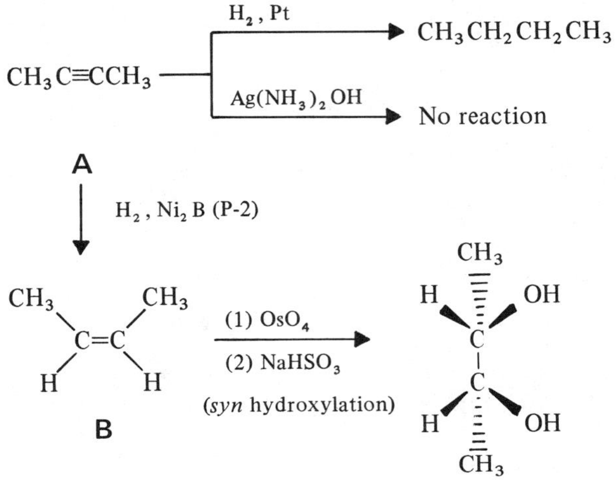

C

(a *meso* compound)

11 The eliminations are *anti* eliminations, requiring an *anti* periplanar arrangement of the bromine atoms.

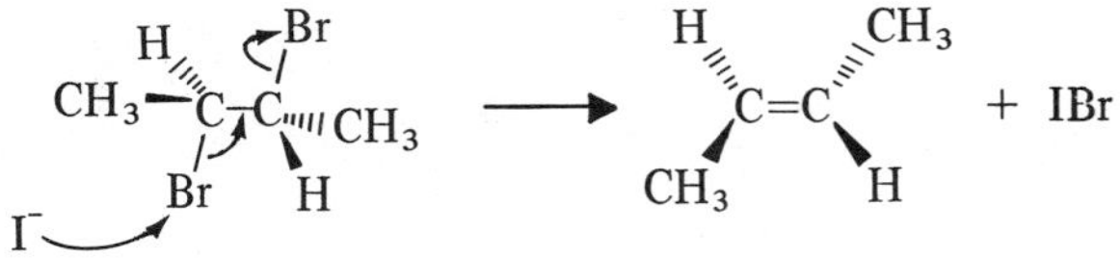

meso-2,3-Dibromo-
butane   *trans*-2-Butene

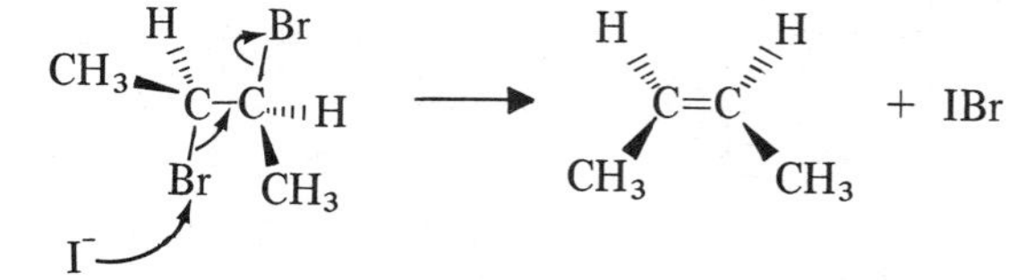

+ IBr

(2*S*, 3*S*)-2,3,-Dibromo-
butane   *cis*-2-Butene

+ IBr

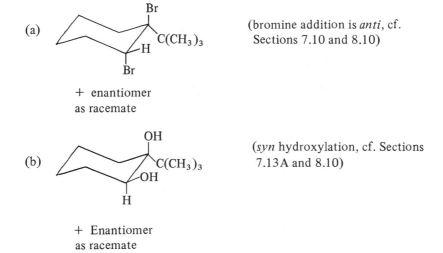

$$\underset{\substack{(2R,3R)\text{-}2,3\text{-Dibromo-}\\ \text{butane}}}{}\longrightarrow \underset{cis\text{-}2\text{-Butene}}{} + \text{IBr}$$

12   The eliminations are *anti* eliminations, requiring an *anti* periplanar arrangement of the —H and —Br.

meso-1, 2-Dibromo-
1, 2-diphenylethane

(*E*)-1-Bromo-1, 2-
diphenylethene

(2*R*, 3*R*) -1, 2-Dibromo-
1, 2-diphenylethane

(*Z*) -1-Bromo-1, 2
diphenylethene

(2*S*, 3*S*)-1, 2-Dibromo-1, 2-diphenylethene will also give (*Z*)-1-bromo-1, 2-diphenylethene in an *anti* elimination.

13   In all structures below, notice that the large *tert*-butyl group is equatorial.

(a)

(bromine addition is *anti*, cf.
Sections 7.10 and 8.10)

+ enantiomer
as racemate

(b)

(*syn* hydroxylation, cf. Sections
7.13A and 8.10)

+ Enantiomer
as racemate

(c)

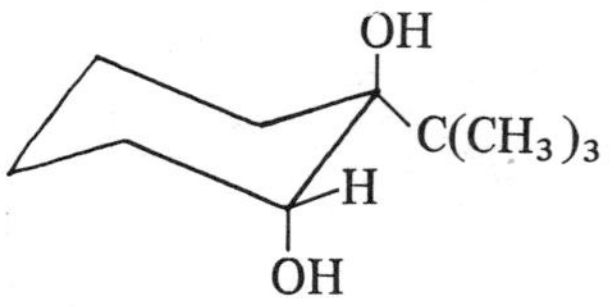

OH
$C(CH_3)_3$
—H
OH

+ Enantiomer
as racemate

(*anti* hydroxylation, cf. Sect.
7.12 and 8.10)

(d)

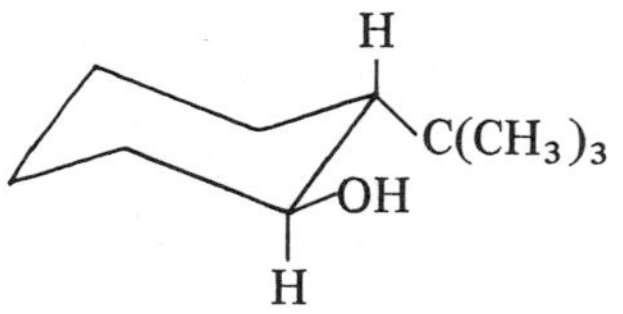

H
$C(CH_3)_3$
OH
H

+ Enantiomer
as racemate

(*syn* and anti-Markovnikov
addition of –H and –OH,
cf. Sect. 7.8)

(e)

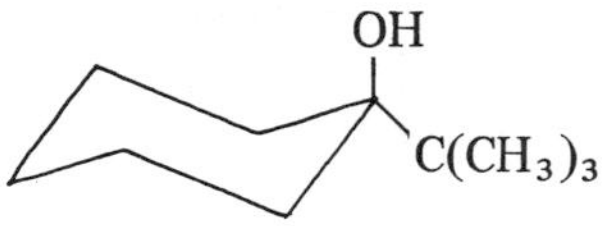

OH
$C(CH_3)_3$

(Markovnikov addition of –H
and –OH, cf. Sect. 7.6)

(f)

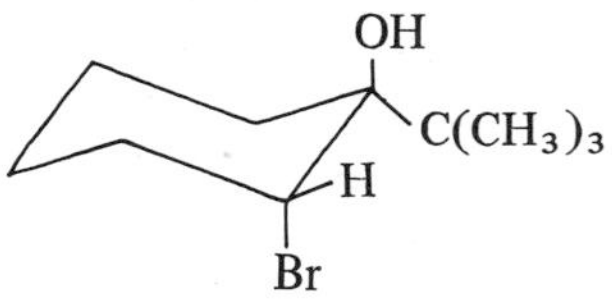

OH
$C(CH_3)_3$
—H
Br

+ Enantiomer
as racemate

(*anti* addition of –Br and –OH, with –Br and
–OH placement resulting from the more
stable partial carbocation in the intermediate
bromonium ion, cf. Sect. 7.11)

(g)

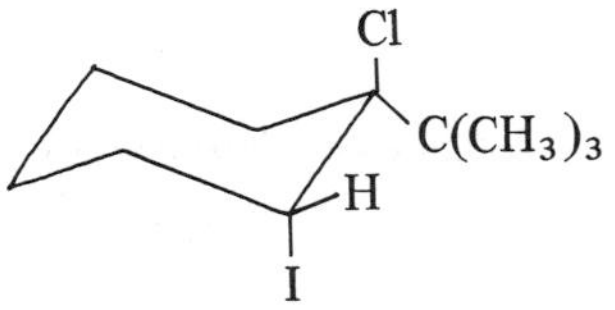

Cl
$C(CH_3)_3$
—H
I

+ Enantiomer
as racemate

(*anti* addition of –I and –Cl, following
Markovnikov's rule, cf. Sect. 7.2C)

(h) $\overset{O}{\overset{\|}{H}C}(CH_2)_4\overset{O}{\overset{\|}{C}}C(CH_3)_3$

(i)

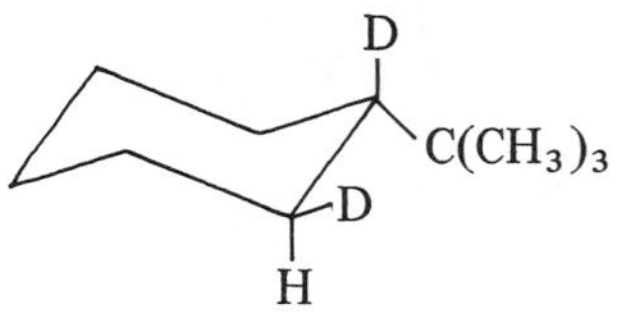

D
$C(CH_3)_3$
—D
H

+ Enantiomer
as racemate

(syn addition of deuterium,
cf. Sect. 6.14)

(j)

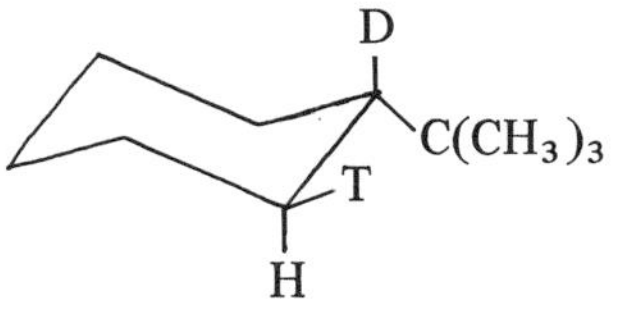

(*Syn*, anti-Markovnikov addition of −D and −B− , with −B− being replaced by −T where it stands, cf. Sect. 7.8B)

+ Enantiomer
as racemate

14   A = $CH_3\overset{\displaystyle CH_3}{\underset{\displaystyle |}{C}}=CHCH_2CH_3$ B = $\left(CH_3\overset{\displaystyle CH_3}{\underset{\displaystyle |}{C}}H\underset{\displaystyle |}{\overset{\displaystyle |}{C}}H\right)_2 BH$ with CH_2 and CH_3

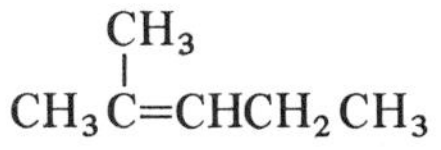

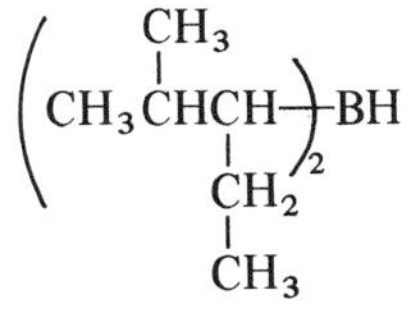

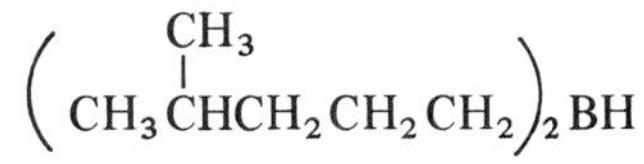

C = $\left(CH_3\overset{\displaystyle CH_3}{\underset{\displaystyle |}{C}}HCH_2CH_2CH_2\right)_2 BH$ D = $CH_3\overset{\displaystyle CH_3}{\underset{\displaystyle |}{C}}HCH_2CH_2CH_2OH$

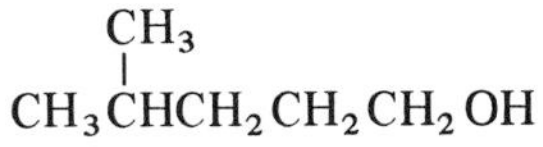

15   (a)   The products (below) are diastereomers. They would have different boiling points and would be in separate fractions. Each fraction would be optically active.

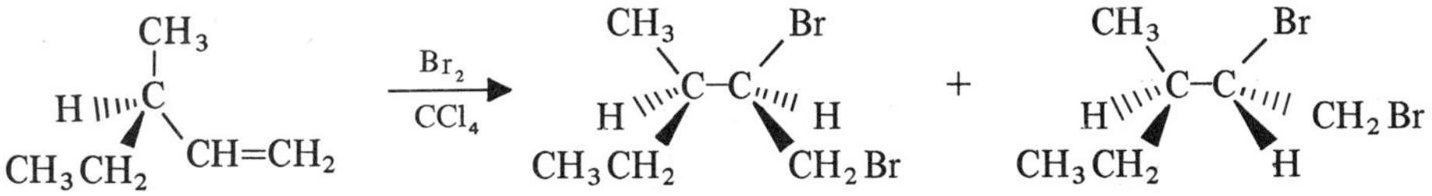

(*R*)-3-Methyl-1-pentene → $\dfrac{Br_2}{CCl_4}$ → (optically active) + (optically active)

Diastereomers

(b)   Only one product is formed. It is achiral, and, therefore, it would not be optically active.

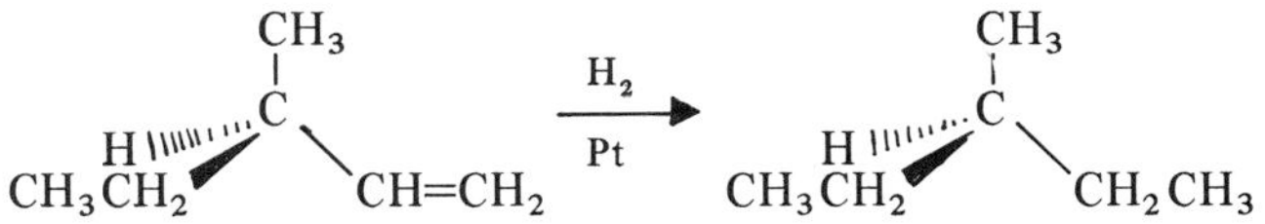

→ $\dfrac{H_2}{Pt}$ → (optically inactive)

(c)   Two diastereomeric products are formed. Two fractions would be obtained. Each fraction would be optically active.

→ (1) OsO$_4$ (2) NaHSO$_3$

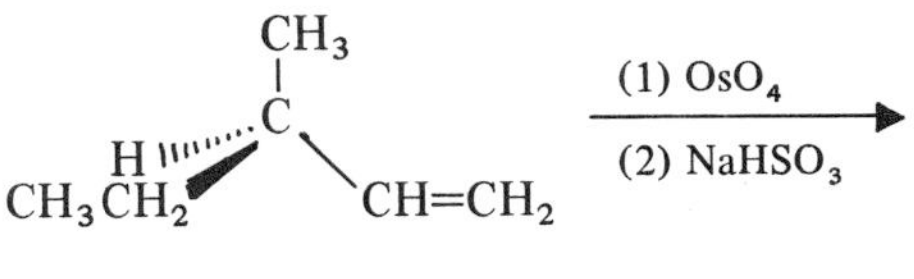

(optically active)   +   (optically active)

Diastereomers

(d) One optically active compound is produced.

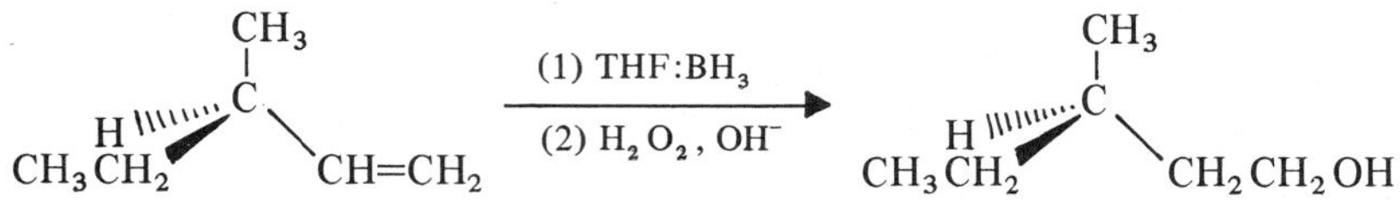

$$\xrightarrow[\text{(2) } H_2O_2, \, OH^-]{\text{(1) THF:BH}_3}$$

(optically active)

(e) Two diastereomeric products are formed. Two fractions would be obtained. Each fraction would be optically active.

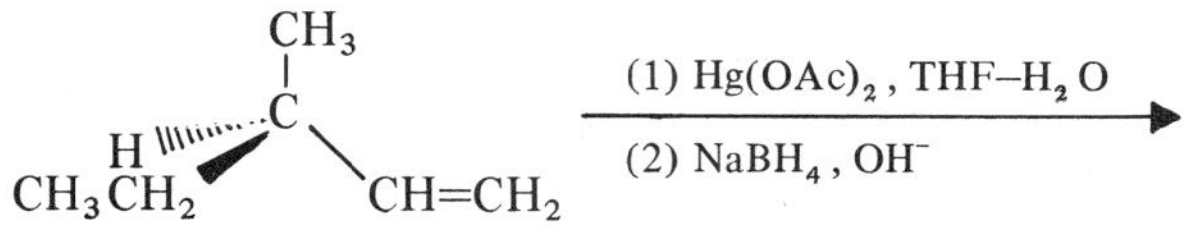

$$\xrightarrow[\text{(2) } NaBH_4, \, OH^-]{\text{(1) } Hg(OAc)_2, \, THF-H_2O}$$

(optically active)   +   (optically active)

Diastereomers

(f) Two diastereomeric products are formed. Two fractions would be obtained. Each fraction would be optically active.

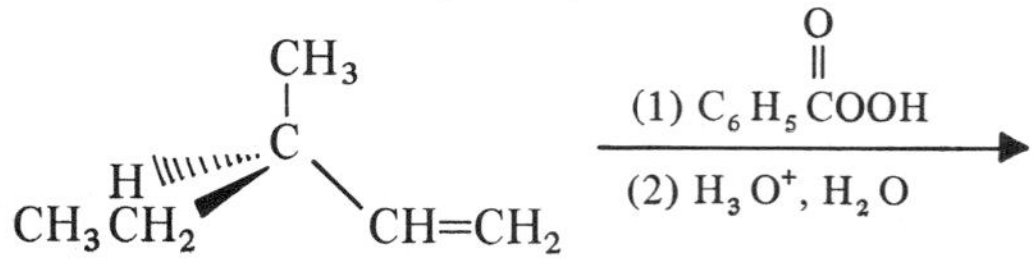

$$\xrightarrow[\text{(2) } H_3O^+, \, H_2O]{\text{(1) } C_6H_5\overset{\overset{O}{\|}}{C}OOH}$$

(optically active)   +   (optically active)

Diastereomers

16

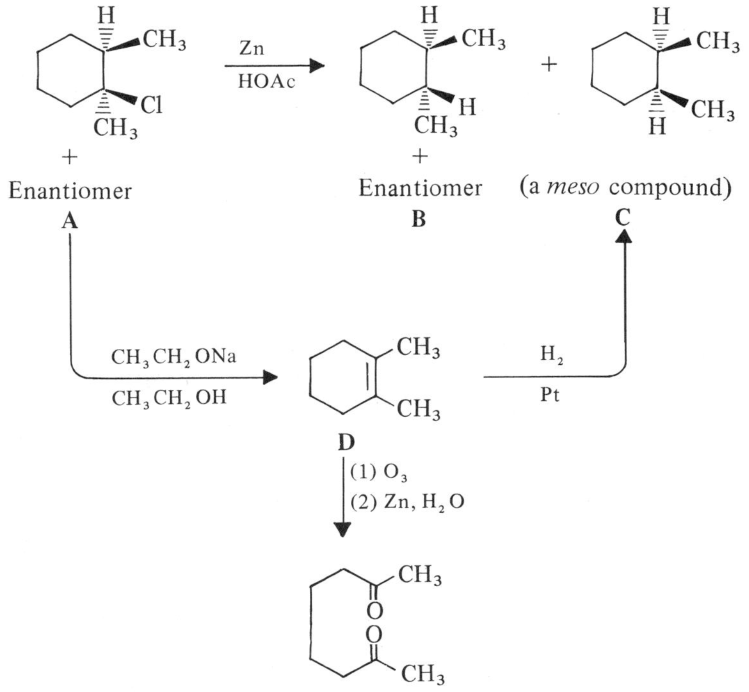

A
+
Enantiomer

Zn / HOAc →

B
+
Enantiomer

+ C
(a *meso* compound)

CH₃CH₂ONa / CH₃CH₂OH →

D (1,2-dimethylcyclohexene)

H₂ / Pt →

(1) O₃
(2) Zn, H₂O

17

(a)

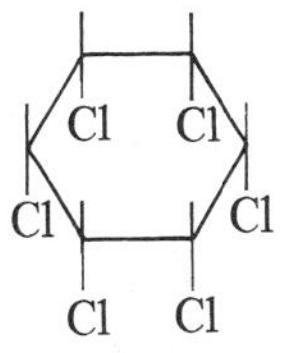

all *cis*
meso
1

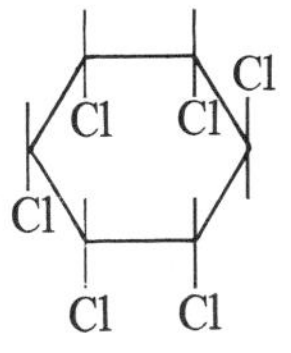

1-*trans*
meso
2

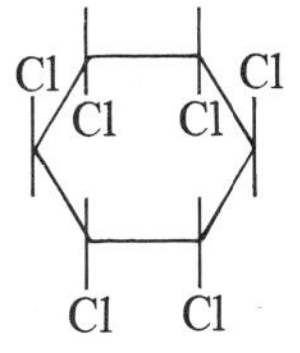

1,4-*trans*
meso
3

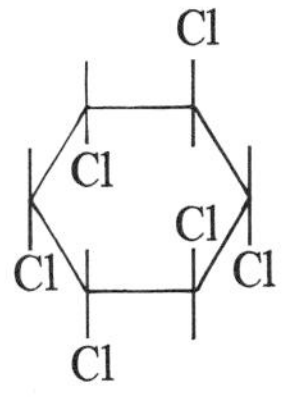

1,3-*trans*
meso
4

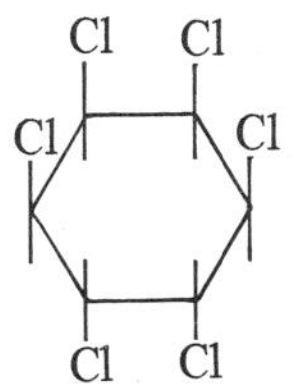

1,2-*trans*
meso
5

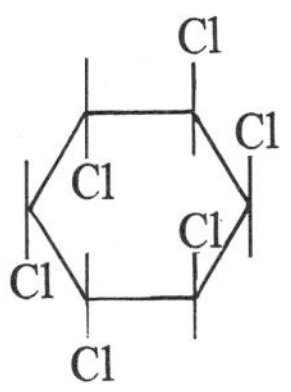

1,2,3-*trans*
meso
6

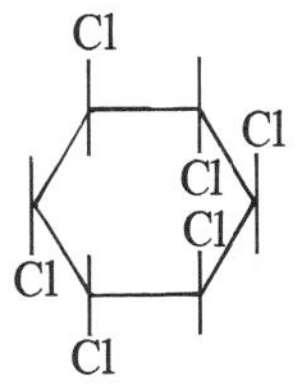

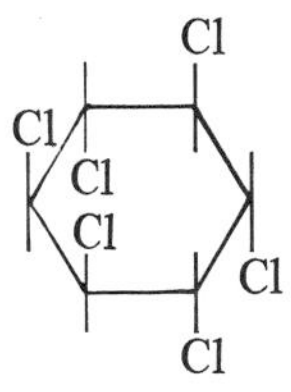

1,2,4-*trans*
enantiomers

7   **8**

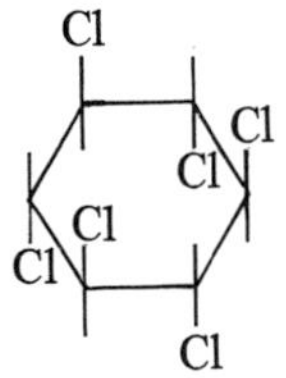

1,3,5-*trans*
meso
9

(b) Isomer **9** is slow to react in E2 reaction because in its more stable conformation (below) all the chlorine atoms are equatorial and an *anti* periplanar transition state cannot be achieved. All other isomers **1-8** can have a —Cl axial and thus achieve an *anti* periplanar transition state.

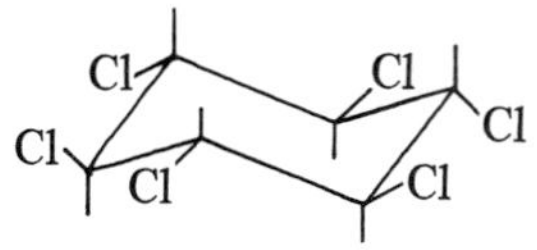

9

18 (a) $CH_3CH(CH_3)CH_2CH_3 \xrightarrow{F_2}$

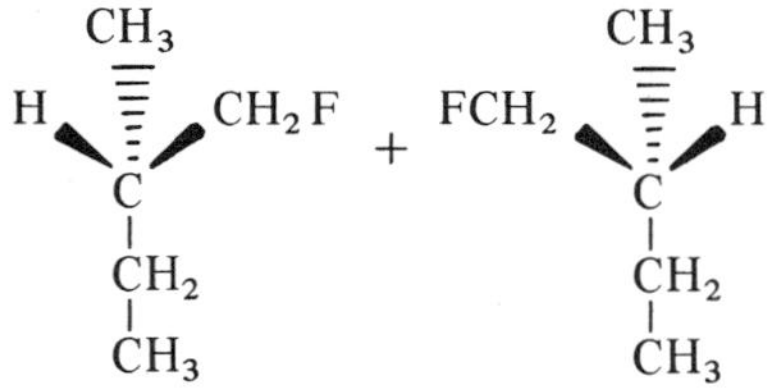

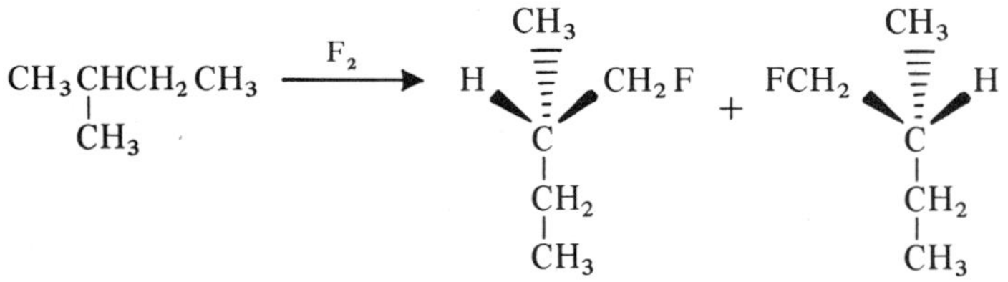

1 + **2**

enantiomers
(obtained in one fraction as an optically inactive racemate)

+ $CH_3CF(CH_3)CH_2CH_3$ +

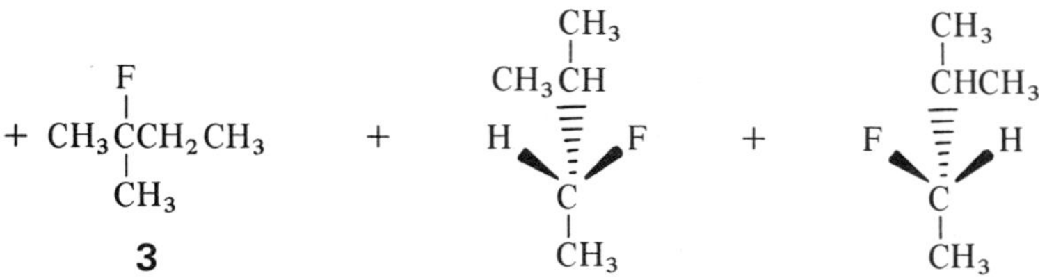

3
(achiral and, therefore, optically inactive)

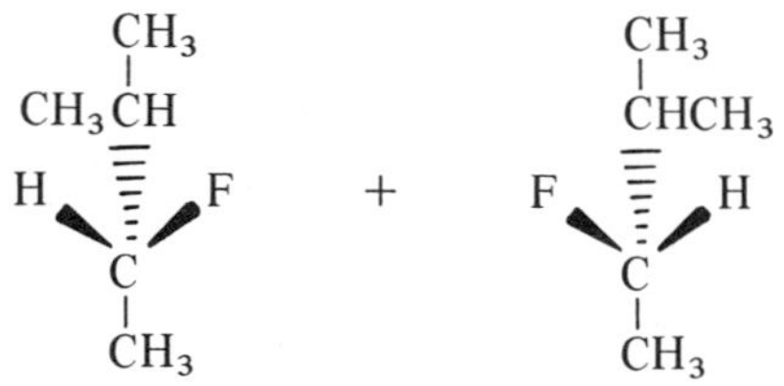

4 + **5**

Enantiomers
(obtained in one fraction as an optically inactive racemate)

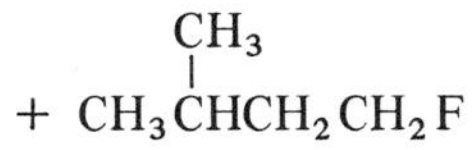

$$CH_3$$
$$+ \ CH_3\overset{|}{C}HCH_2CH_2F$$

6

(achiral and, therefore,
optically inactive)

(b) Four fractions. The enantiomeric pairs would not be separated by fractional distillation because enantiomers have the same boiling points.

(c) All of the fractions would be optically inactive.

(d) The fraction containing **1** and **2** and the fraction containing **4** and **5**.

19

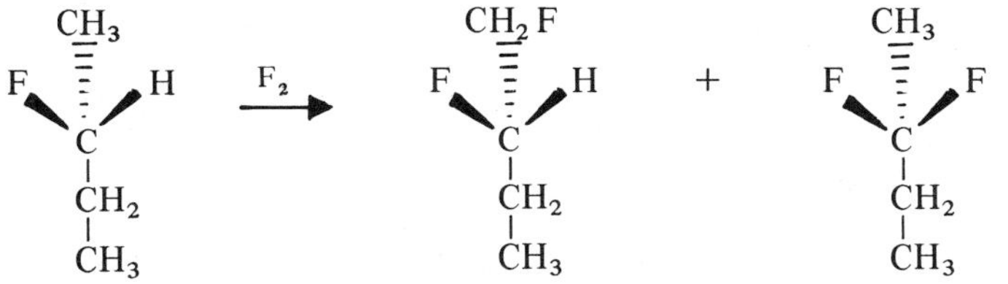

(R)-2-Fluorobutane   (optically active)   (achiral and, therefore, optically inactive)

1   **2**

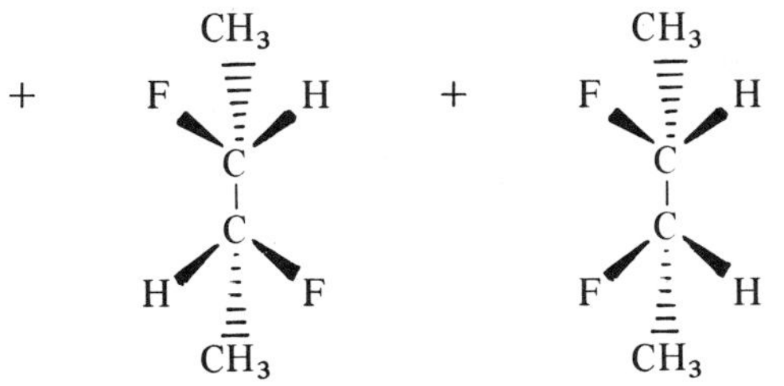

3

(optically active)

4

meso Compound
(optically inactive)

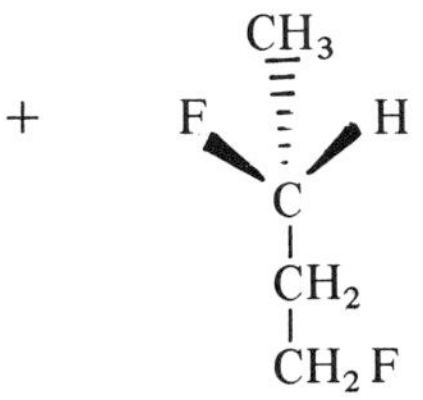

5

(optically active)

(b) Five. Compounds **3** and **4** are diastereomers. All others are structural isomers of each other.

(c) See above.

20

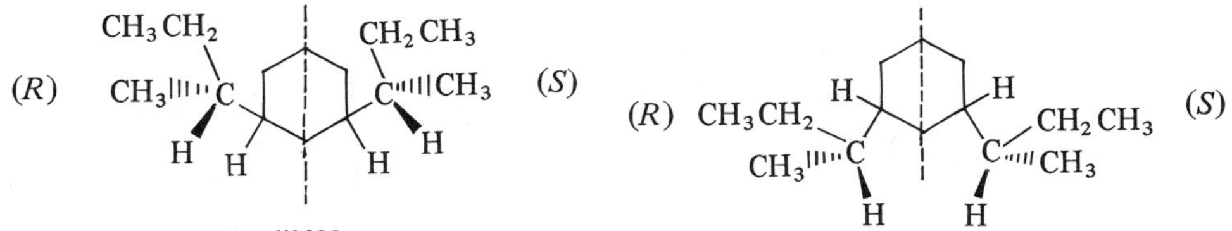

meso

Each of the two structures just given have a plane of symmetry (indicated by the dashed line), and, therefore, each is a *meso* compound. The two structures are not superposable one on the other, therefore they represent molecules of different compounds and are diastereomers.

21   Only a proton or deuteron *anti* to the bromine can be eliminated; that is, the two groups undergoing elimination (H and Br or D and Br) must lie in an *anti* periplanar arrangement. The two conformations of *erythro*-2-bromo-butane-3-*d* in which a proton or deuteron is *anti* periplanar to the bromine are **I** and **II** below.

Conformation **I** can undergo loss of HBr to yield *cis*-2-butene-2-*d*. Conformation **II** can undergo loss of DBr to yield *trans*-2-butene.

11

AROMATIC COMPOUNDS I:
THE PHENOMENON OF AROMATICITY

SOLUTIONS TO PROBLEMS

11.1 (a) None. For example, $H-C{\equiv}C-CH_2CH_2-C{\equiv}C-H$ would yield two different mono-bromo products:

$$Br-C{\equiv}C-CH_2CH_2-C{\equiv}C-H \quad \text{and} \quad H-C{\equiv}C-\underset{\underset{Br}{|}}{C}HCH_2-C{\equiv}C-H$$

(b) None. All of these compounds should undergo addition of bromine.

11.2 Resonance structures may differ *only* in the positions of the electrons. In the two 1,3,5-cyclohexatrienes shown, the carbons are in different positions; therefore they cannot be resonance structures.

11.3

(a)

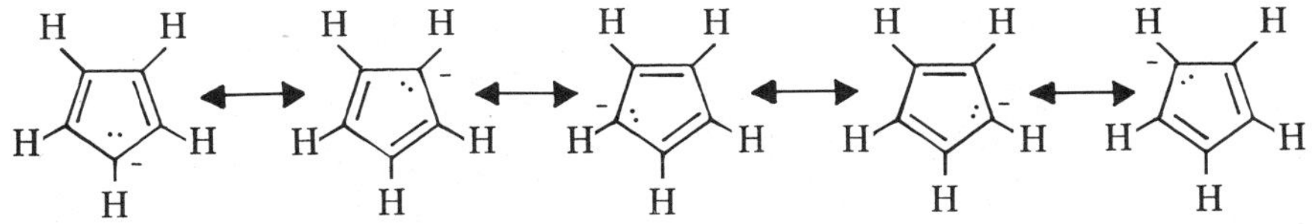

(b) Yes, all of the five resonance structures are equivalent, and all five hydrogen atoms are equivalent.

11.4

(a)

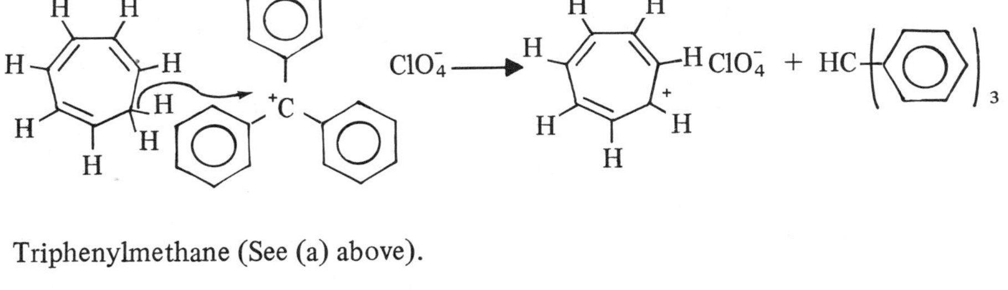

(b) Triphenylmethane (See (a) above).

(c) ClO_4^-

11.5

Tropylium bromide is ionic and has the structure, + Br⁻. The ring is aromatic.

11.6

(a)

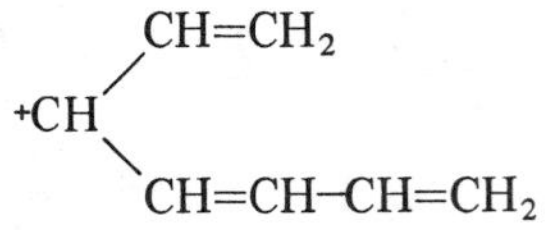

(b) Cycloheptatrienyl cation is aromatic.

11.7

(a)

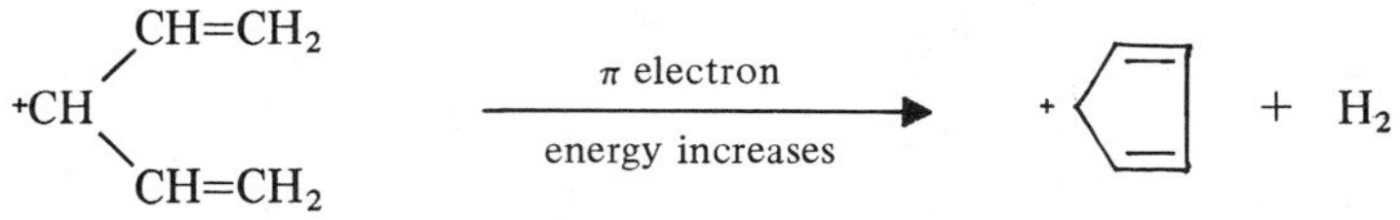

The π-electron energy of cyclopentadienyl cation is higher than that of the open chain counterpart.

(b)

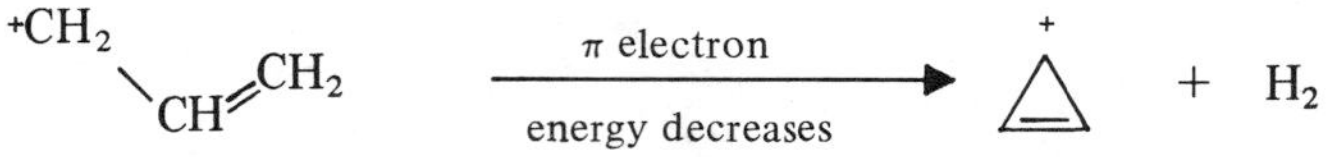

The π electron energy of cyclopropenyl cation is lower than that of the open-chain counterpart.

(c) $4n+2 = 2$ when $n = 0$. Hückel's rule predicts that cyclopropenyl cation is aromatic.

(d) The π-electron energy of cyclopropenyl anion is higher than that of the open-chain counterpart.

11.8

(a)

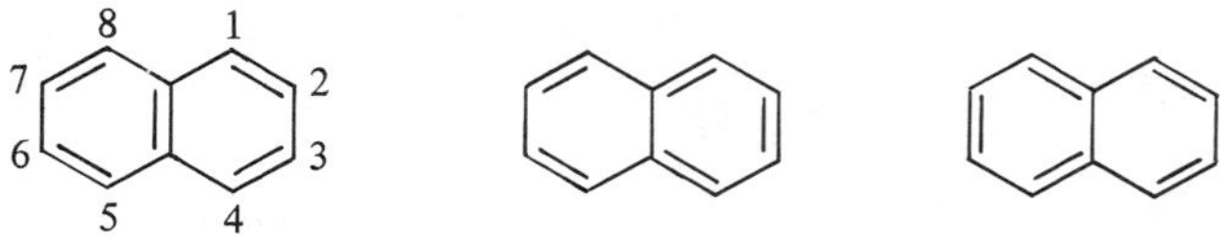

(I)   (II)   (III)

(b) Two of the structures (**I** and **III**) have a double bond between the C_1–C_2 carbons, whereas only structure **II** has a double bond between the C_2–C_3 carbons. If we assume that the three structures contribute nearly equally, the C_1–C_2 bond should be more like a double bond and therefore should be shorter than the C_2–C_3 bond.

11.9

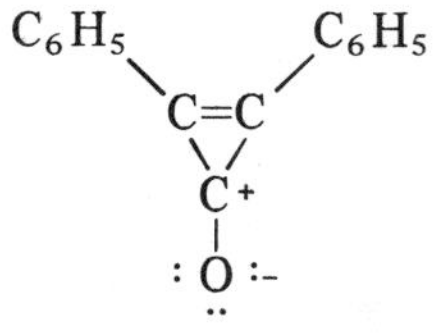

III

III is a more important contributor to the resonance hybrid of **I** than a corresponding ionic structure of **II** is to the hybrid of **II**. **III** is an important contributor to the hybrid of diphenylcyclopropenone because it resembles the aromatic cyclopropenyl cation (cf. Problem 11.7); i.e., the ring in structure **III** has 2 π electrons and is a $4n + 2$ system where $n = 0$.

11.10

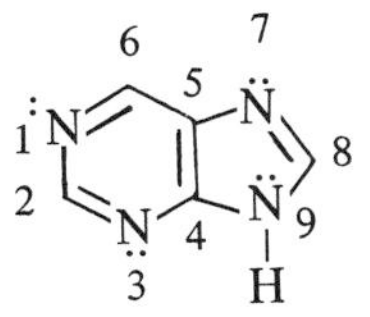

1,3,7 are pyridine-type nitrogens; 9 is a pyrrole-type nitrogen

11.11

(a) 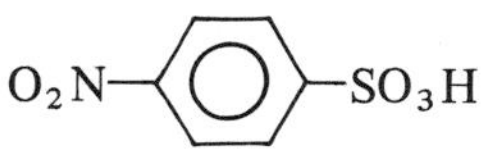 $O_2N-\!\!\!\bigcirc\!\!\!-SO_3H$ (b) 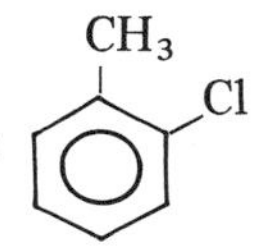 (c) 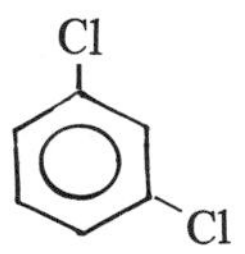 (d)

(e) 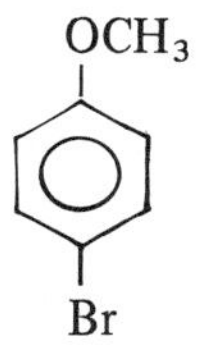 (f) 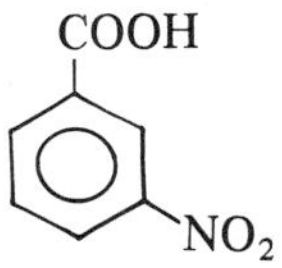 (g)  (h)

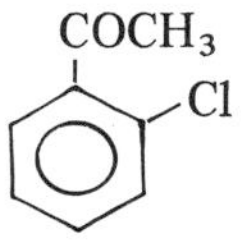

(i) 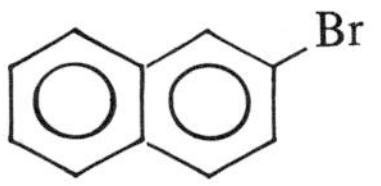 (j) 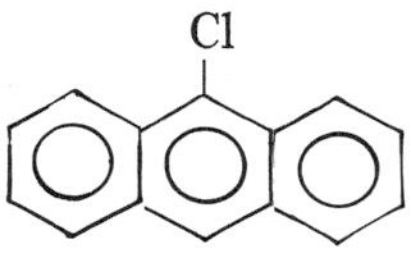 (k) 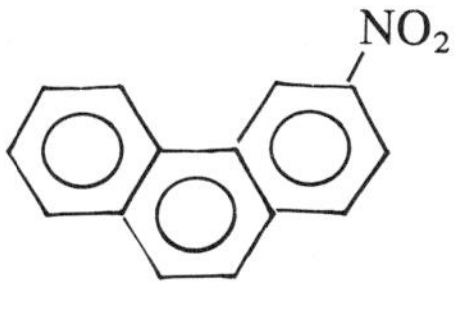 (l)

(m) 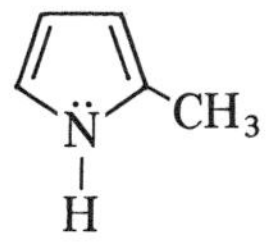 (n) 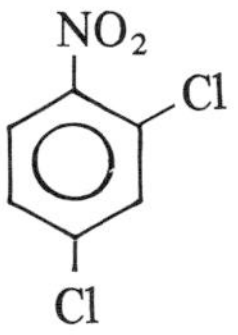 (o) 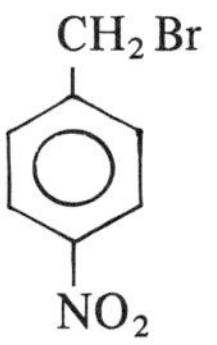 (p)

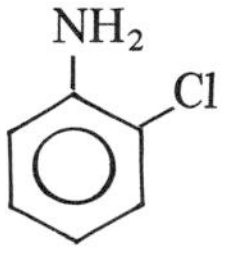

(q) 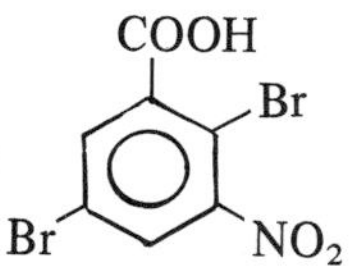 (r) 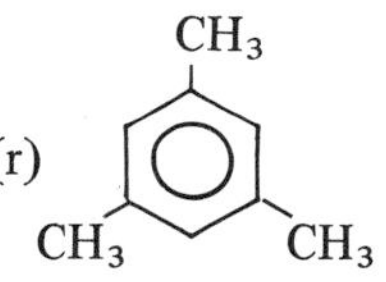 (s) 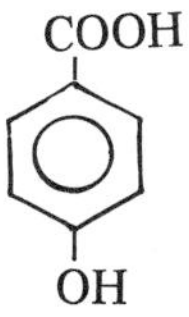 (t)

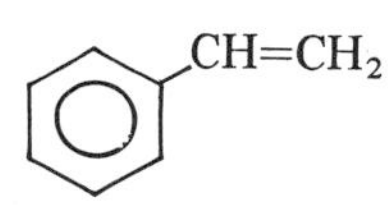

(u)

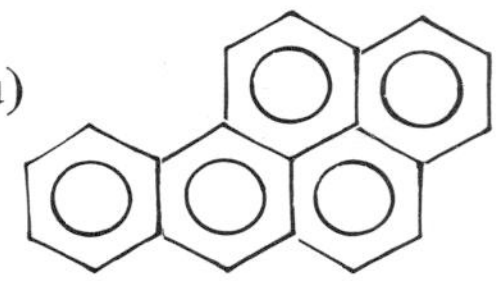

(v)

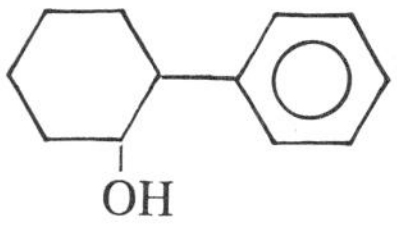

(w)

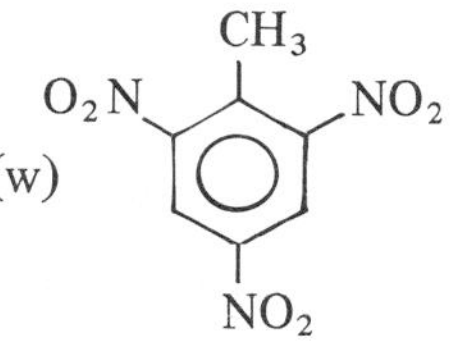

(x)

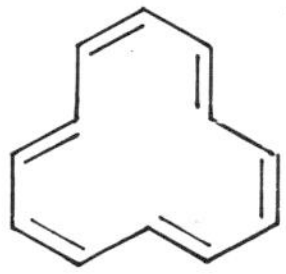

(y)

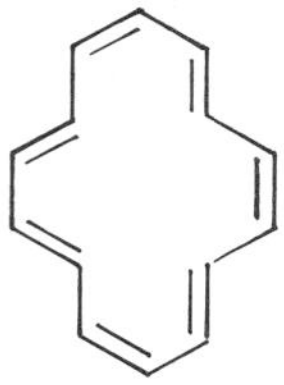

(z)

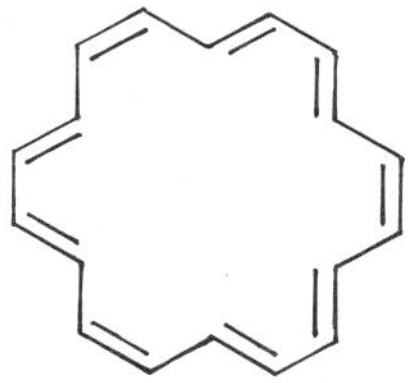

11.12

(a)

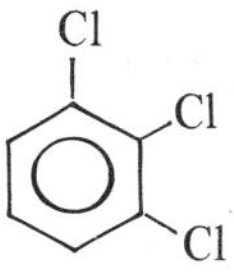

Cl
Cl
Cl

1,2,3-Trichloro-
benzene

Cl
Cl
Cl

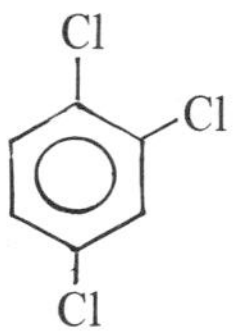

1,2,4-Trichloro-
benzene

Cl
Cl   Cl

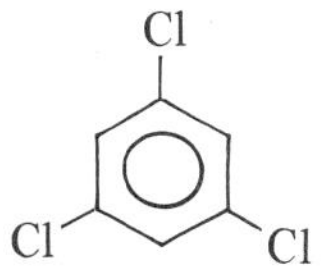

1,3,5-Trichloro-
benzene

(b)

NO₂
Br
Br

2,3-Dibromo-1-
nitrobenzene

NO₂
Br
Br

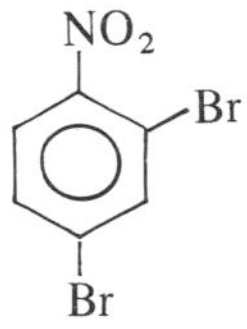

2,4-Dibromo-1-
nitrobenzene

NO₂
Br
Br

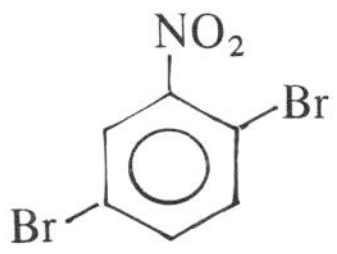

1,4-Dibromo-2-
nitrobenzene

NO₂
Br   Br

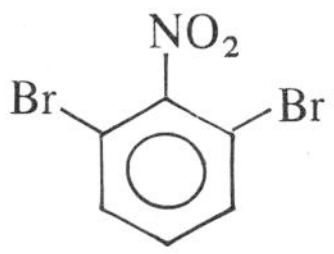

1,3-Dibromo-2-
nitrobenzene

NO₂
Br
Br

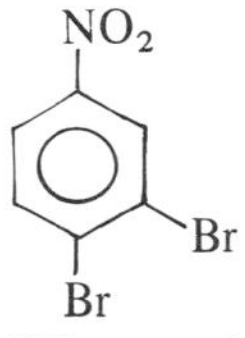

1,2-Dibromo-4-
nitrobenzene

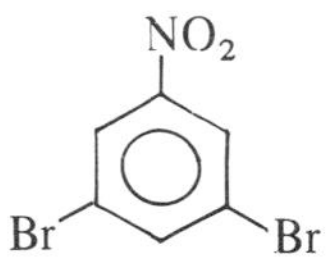

NO₂
Br   Br

3,5-Dibromo-1-nitro-
benzene

(c)

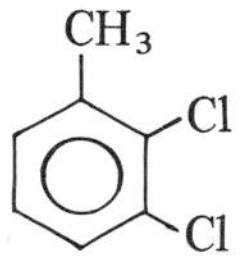

CH₃
Cl
Cl

2,3-Dichloro-
toluene

CH₃
Cl
Cl

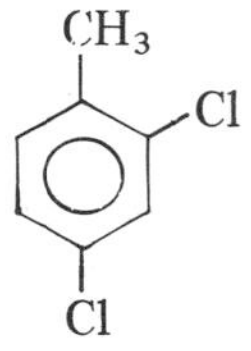

2,4-Dichloro-
toluene

CH₃
Cl
Cl

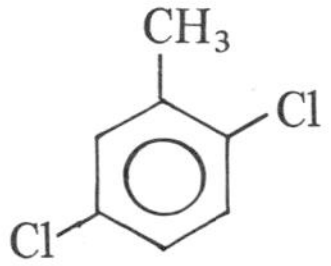

2,5-Dichloro-
toluene

CH₃
Cl   Cl

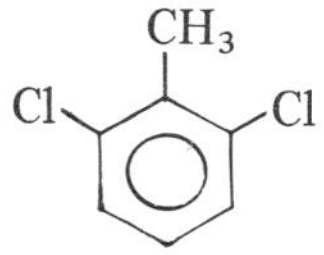

2,6-Dichloro-
toluene

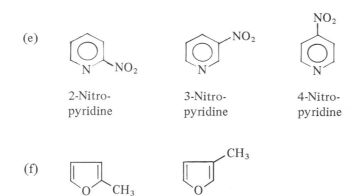

3,4-Dichloro-
toluene

3,5-Dichloro-
toluene

(d)

1-Chloronaphthalene

2-Chloronaphthalene

(e)

2-Nitro-
pyridine

3-Nitro-
pyridine

4-Nitro-
pyridine

(f)

2-Methylfuran

3-Methylfuran

(g)

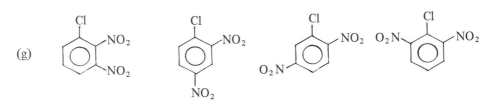

1-Chloro-
2,3-dinitrobenzene

1-Chloro-
2,4-dinitrobenzene

2-Chloro-
1,4-dinitrobenzene

2-Chloro-
1,3-dinitrobenzene

4-Chloro-
1,2-dinitrobenzene

1-Chloro-
3,5-dinitrobenzene

(h)

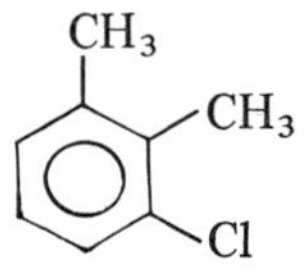

1-Chloro-
2,3-dimethylbenzene

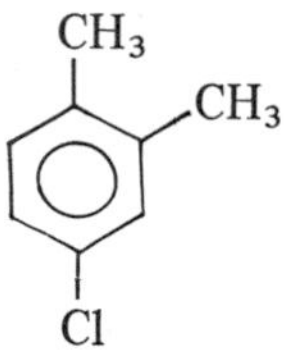

4-Chloro-
1,2-dimethylbenzene

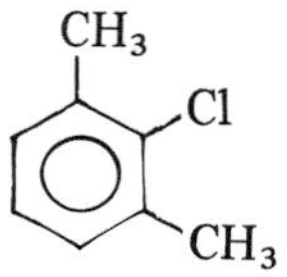

2-Chloro-
1,3-dimethylbenzene

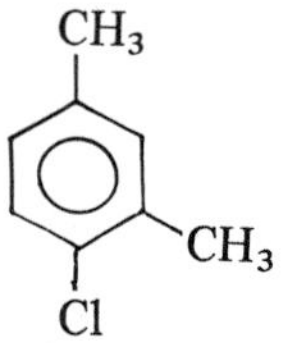

1-Chloro-
2,4-dimethylbenzene

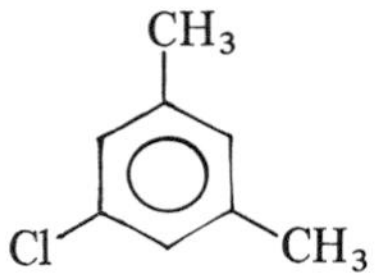

1-Chloro-
3,5-dimethylbenzene

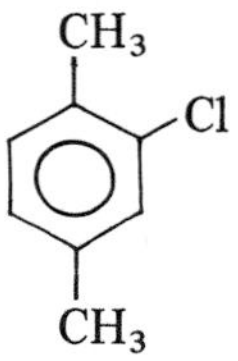

2-Chloro-
1,4-dimethylbenzene

(i)

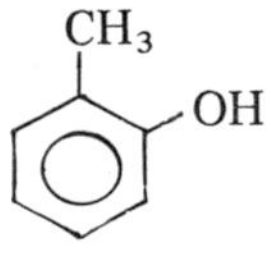

o-Cresol

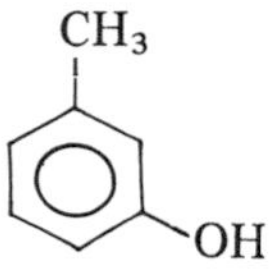

m-Cresol

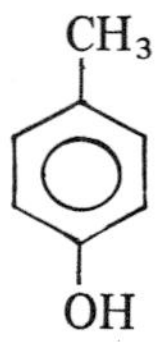

p-Cresol

11.13

(a)

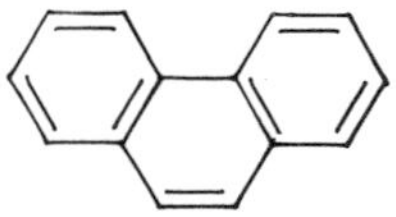

I

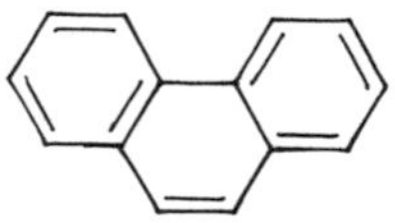

II

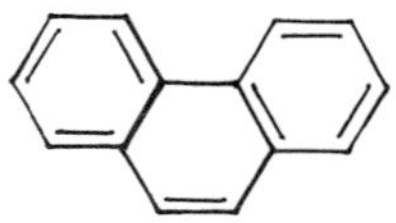

III

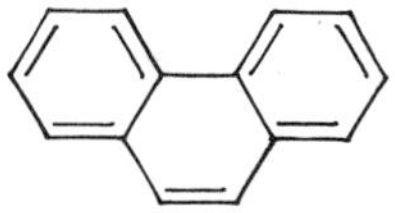

IV

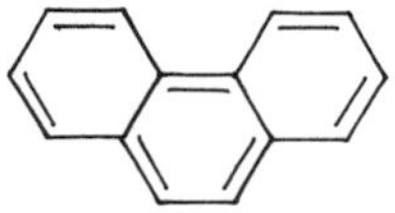

V

(b) The 9,10 bond should be close to that of a double bond, 1.33Å, since in four of the five contributors it is a double bond.

(c) Almost that of an actual double bond.

(d) Bromine adds to the 9,10 double bond because of its large double-bond character and because addition disrupts only one of three aromatic rings.

11.14

(a) 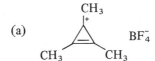 BF$_4^-$

(b) The trimethylcyclopropenyl cation is aromatic.

11.15

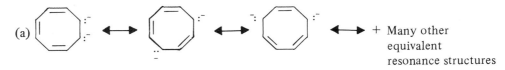

11.16

(a) 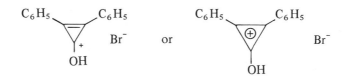 + Many other equivalent resonance structures

(b) It has $4n + 2 = 10$ π electrons ($n = 2$), and is therefore aromatic; i.e., it illustrates Huckel's rule.

11.17 (a) Would not be aromatic; it is a monocyclic system of 12 π electrons and thus does not conform to Hückel's rule.

(b) Would not be aromatic; it is not a conjugated system.

(c) Would not be aromatic; it is an 8 π-electron monocyclic system and thus does not conform to Hückel's rule.

(d) Would not be aromatic; it is a 16 π-electron monocyclic system and thus does not conform to Hückel's rule.

(e) Would be aromatic because of resonance structures (below) that consist of a cyclo-heptatrienyl cation and cyclopentadienyl anion.

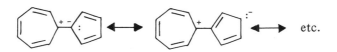 etc.

(f) Would be aromatic; it is a planar monocyclic system of 14 π electrons. (We count only two electrons of the triple bond because only two are in p orbitals that overlap with those of the double bonds on either side.)

(g) Would be aromatic; it is a planar monocyclic system of 10 π electrons.

(h) Would be aromatic; it is a nearly planar monocyclic system of 10 π electrons. (The bridging —CH$_2$— group allows the ring system to be almost planar.)

11.18   Resonance contributors that involve the carbonyl group of **I** resemble the *aromatic* cyclo-heptatrienyl cation and thus stabilize **I**. Similar contributors to the hybrid of **II** resemble the *antiaromatic* cyclopentadienyl cation (see Prob. 11.7) and thus destabilize **II**.

(a)

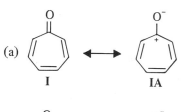

Contributors like **IA** are exceptionally stable because they resemble an aromatic compound. They therefore make large stabilizing contributions to the hybrid.

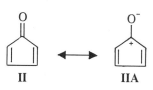

Contributors like **IIA** are exceptionally unstable because they resemble an antiaromatic compound. Any contribution they make to the hybrid is destabilizing.

(b)

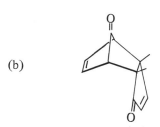

11.19

(a)    (b)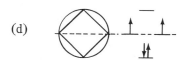

(c)    (d)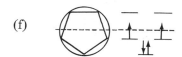

(e) 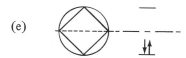   (f)

(g) 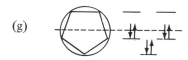   (h)

(i)   (j)

(k) 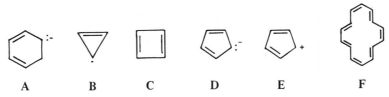   (l)

(m) b, c, d, f, i, j   (n) a, e, g, h, k, l   (o) Same as for (n)

(p) Yes

SECTION REFERENCES FOR ADDITIONAL PROBLEMS

11.11 11.8   **11.16** 11.6B

11.12 11.8   **11.17** 11.6, 11.6A, 11.6B

11.13 11.7A   **11.18** 11.7B

11.14 11.6B   **11.19** 11.6

11.15 11.6B

SELF-TEST

11.1   (a) Which of the following line formulas represent aromatic structures? (*Circle the letters that correspond to your choices.*)

A   B   C   D   E   F

(b) Which of the above formulas represent conjugated systems? (*Circle your choices below.*)

Answers: **A B C D E F**

(c) Draw all the remaining important resonance structures for

11.2   Give an acceptable name for each of the following compounds.

(a)

(b) CH_3CH_2—⌬ _____

(c) $CH_3\overset{\overset{\displaystyle CH_3}{|}}{CH}$—⌬—Br _____

(d) ⌬—$CH_2\overset{\overset{\displaystyle Cl}{|}}{CH}CH_2$—⌬ _____

(e) CH_3—⌬ with NO_2, NO_2, NO_2 _____

11.3   Write the structural formula, **including all hydrogen atoms**, of each of the following:

(a) An aromatic seven-membered carbocyclic ring.

a.

(b) A six-membered carbocyclic ring that is not aromatic.

b.

(c) An aromatic five-membered carbocyclic ring.

c.

(d) A nonaromatic, conjugated five-membered carbocyclic ring.

d.

11.4   (a) How many isomeric trimethylbenzenes are possible?

(b) Which one undergoes ring bromination to give three different monobromotrimethylbenzenes?

(c) The name of the compound above is:

_____

SUPPLEMENTARY PROBLEMS

S11.1   Select the appropriate choice (if any) in each pair of structures below.

(a) Is the higher energy resonance structure

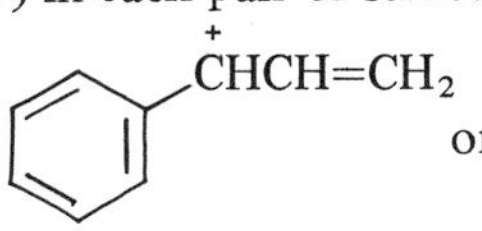

$\overset{+}{C}HCH=CH_2$ or $CH=CH\overset{+}{C}H_2$

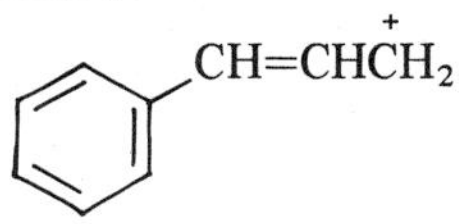

(b) Is an aromatic species

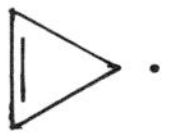

or

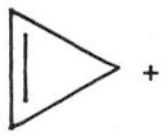

(c) Is an aromatic species

or

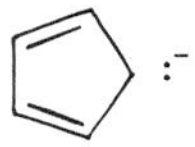

(d) Forms only one tribromo derivative

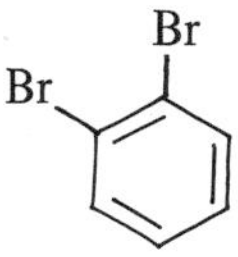

Br, Br   or   Br—⟨⟩—Br

S11.2 Which of the structures in each group is *not* a contributing resonance structure? Explain.

(a)

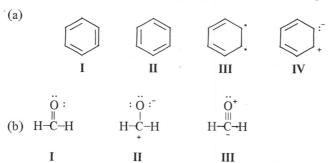

(b)

$$\underset{I}{\text{H}\overset{\overset{\displaystyle\ddot{O}:}{\|}}{\text{C}}\text{H}} \qquad \underset{II}{\text{H}\overset{\overset{\displaystyle :\ddot{O}:^{-}}{|}}{\underset{+}{\text{C}}}\text{H}} \qquad \underset{III}{\text{H}\overset{\overset{\displaystyle\ddot{O}^{+}}{\|}}{\underset{-}{\text{C}}}\text{H}}$$

SOLUTIONS TO SUPPLEMENTARY PROBLEMS

S11.1 (a) Both are allylic cations conjugated with a benzene ring, however the first is 2° and the second is 1°. Therefore the 1° carbocation has higher energy.

(b) ⬡ +, because it has 2π electrons (4n + 2, where n = 0).

(c) Both have 6 π electrons, so both are aromatic.

(d) Br—⬡—Br. Its only tribromo derivative is Br—⬡—Br (with Br).

S11.2 (a) **III**, because it has a different number of unpaired electrons.

(b) **III**, because the carbon has five bonds.

12

AROMATIC COMPOUNDS II: REACTIONS OF AROMATIC COMPOUNDS WITH ELECTROPHILES

REACTIONS OF BENZENE

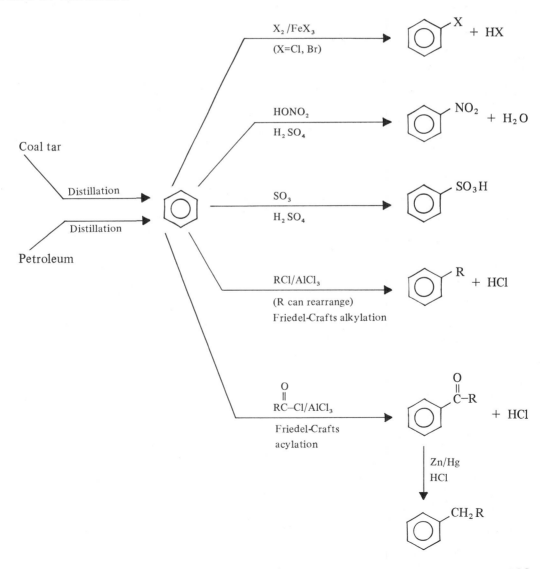

REACTIONS OF ALKYL BENZENES

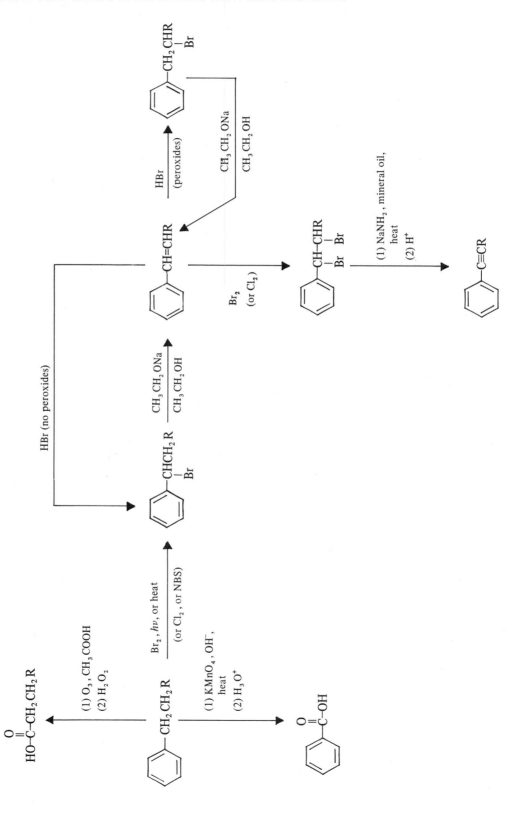

SOLUTIONS TO PROBLEMS

12.1

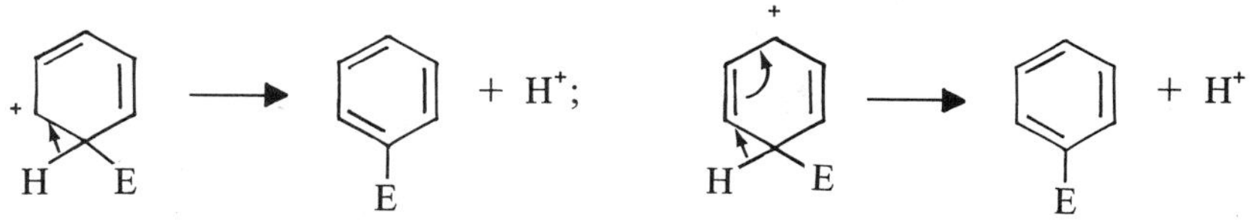

12.2

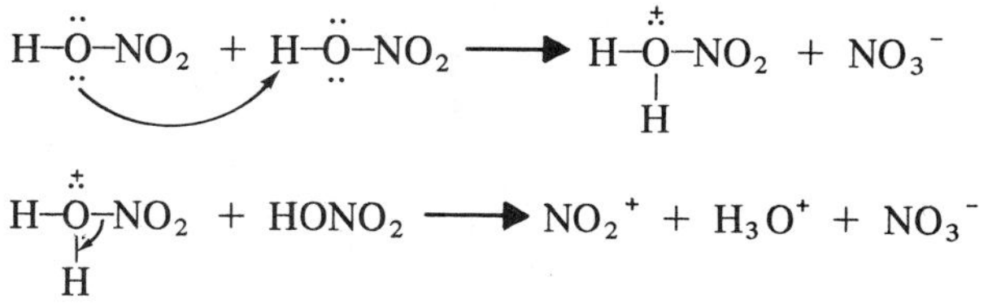

$$H-\ddot{O}-NO_2 + H-\ddot{O}-NO_2 \longrightarrow H-\overset{\pm}{\underset{H}{\ddot{O}}}-NO_2 + NO_3^-$$

$$H-\overset{\pm}{\underset{H}{\ddot{O}}}-NO_2 + HONO_2 \longrightarrow NO_2^+ + H_3O^+ + NO_3^-$$

12.3

(a)

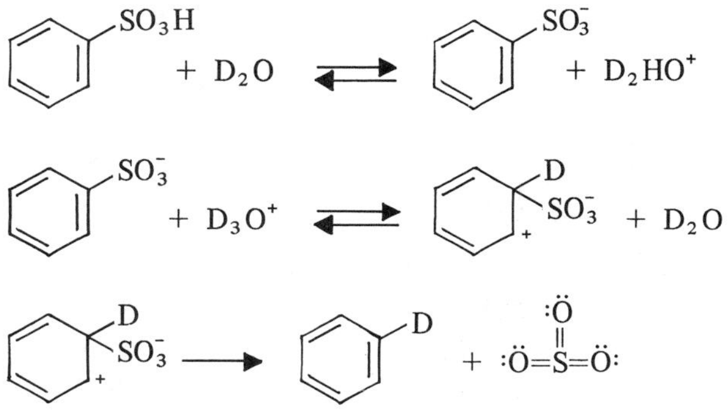

(b) $: \ddot{B}r-\ddot{B}r-\bar{F}eBr_3$ is the electrophile.
$\overset{\delta+}{}\ \overset{\delta+}{}$

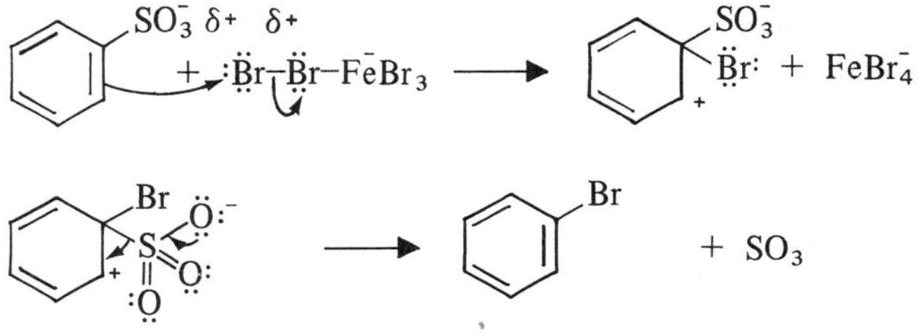

12.4

(a)

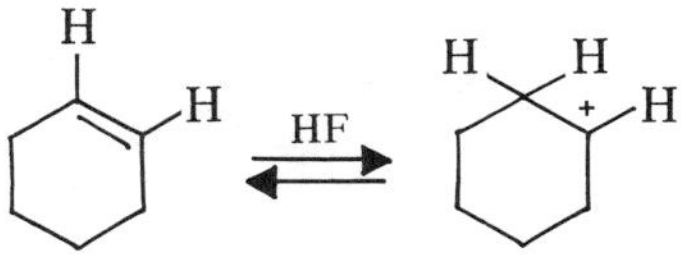

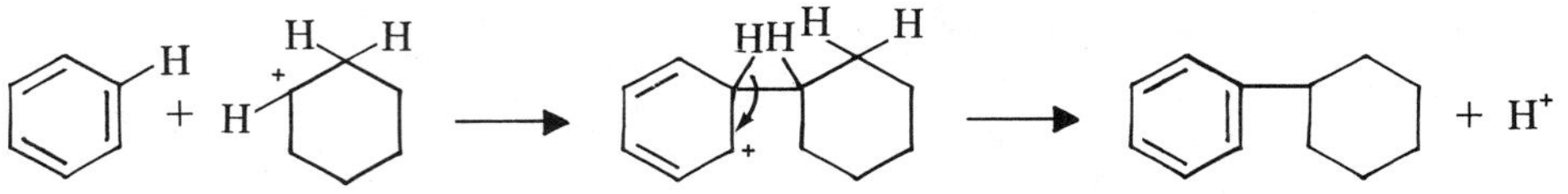

(b)

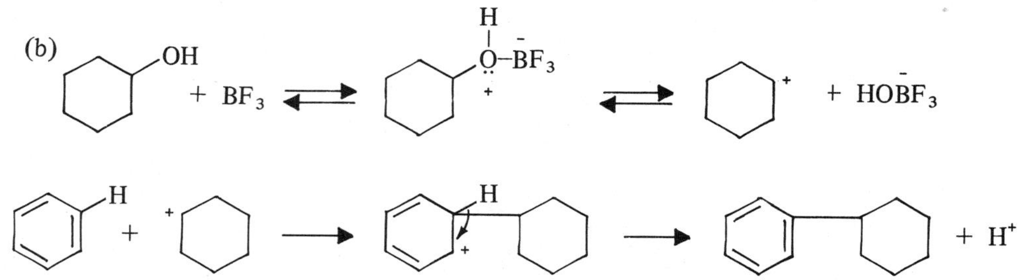

12.5

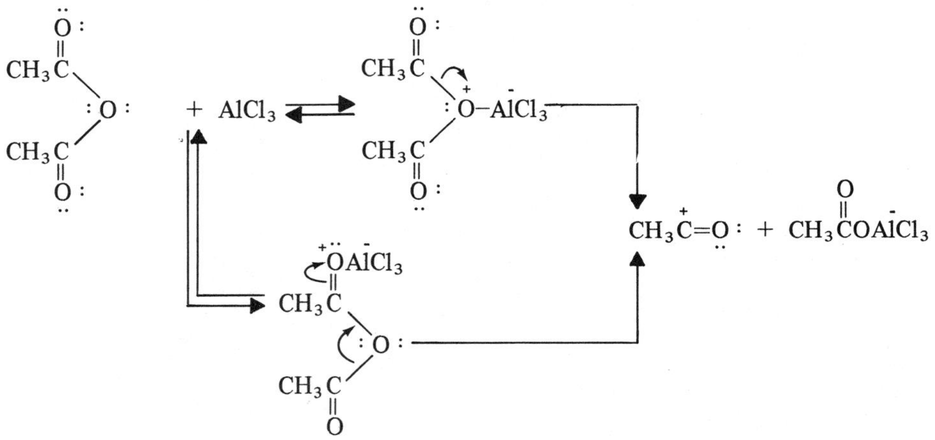

12.6 40% Ortho, 40% meta, 20% para because there are twice as many ortho as para positions.

12.7

(a) 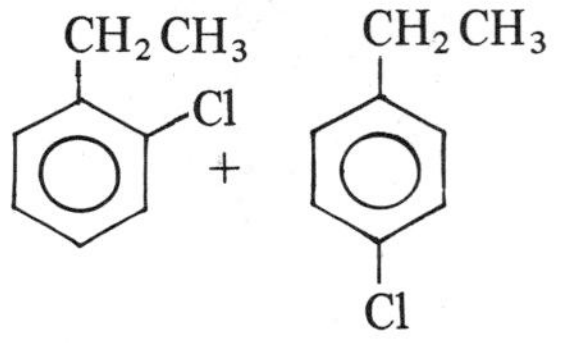 (b) 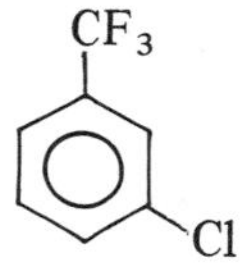 (c) 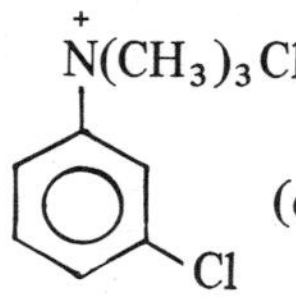 (d) 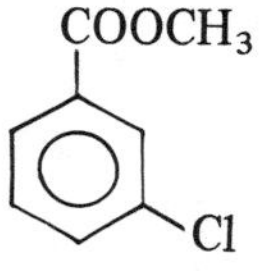

12.8

(a) Ortho: 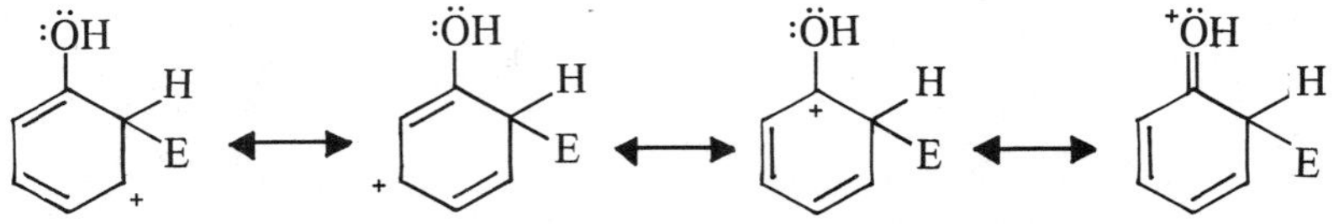

relatively stable

Meta:

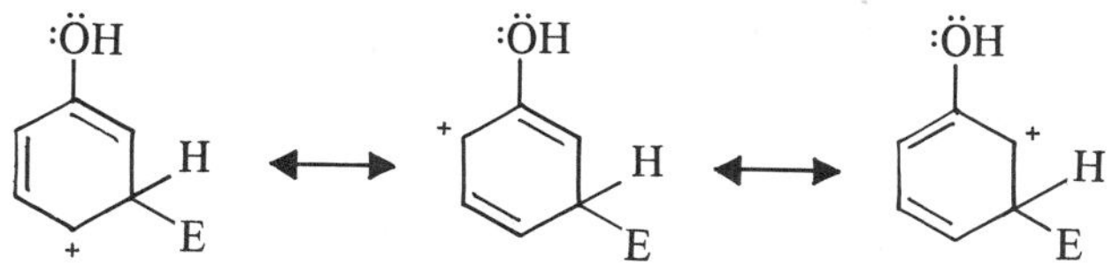

Para:

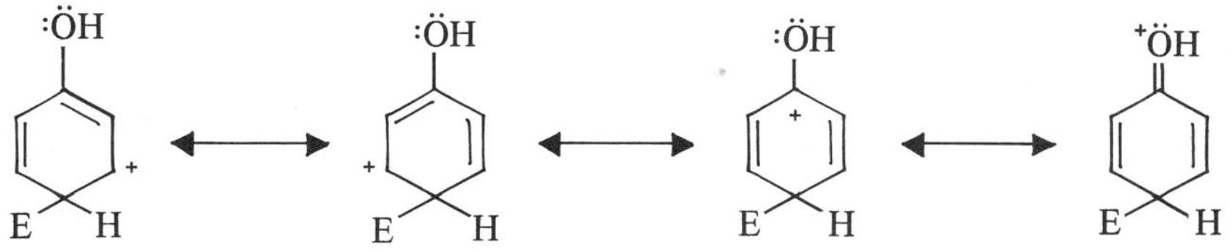

relatively
stable

(b) The electron-releasing ability of the —OH group through resonance increases the electron density of the ring, and it stabilizes the positive charge of the intermediate carbocation.

(c) An extra and relatively stable structure (above) contributes to the intermediate carbocation only when attack is *ortho* or *para*.

(d,e) More reactive because the extra structure (below) does not have a positive charge on its oxygen as is true with phenol.

Ortho:

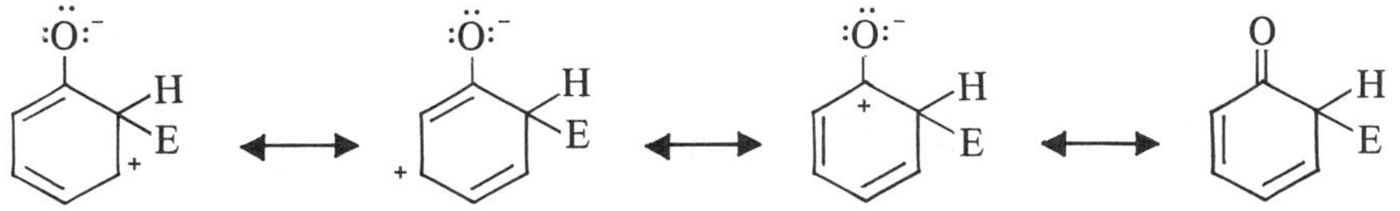

Highly stable

Para:

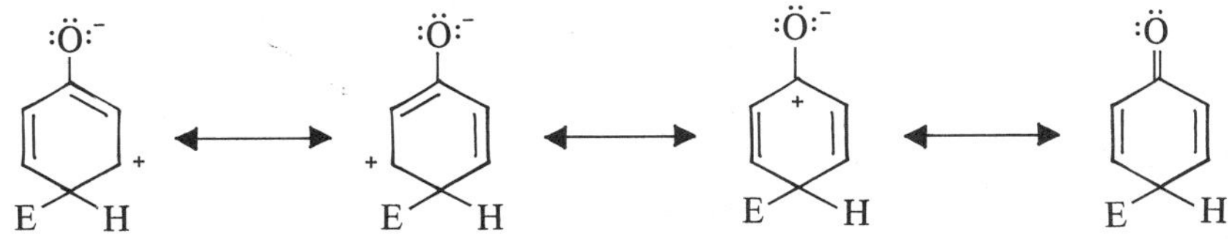

Highly stable

12.9

(a)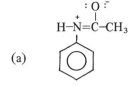

(b) The $-\overset{O}{\overset{\|}{C}}-CH_3$ group competes with the ring for the electron pair on N, therefore stabilization of the intermediate arenium ion is less effective than in aniline.

(c)

A

B

Yes, resonance accounts for an electron release from nitrogen to the ring, and as with aniline (Sect. 12.9D), extra and relatively stable structures (**A** and **B** above) contribute to the arenium ions formed when attack takes place at an *ortho* or *para* carbon.

(d) Phenyl acetate should be less reactive than phenol because the $-COCH_3$ group competes with the ring for electrons on oxygen as shown in the following structure.

Notice that this structure also places a positive charge on the oxygen attached to the ring.

(e) Ortho-para.

(f) More reactive because the $-O-$ group furnishes electrons to the ring in the same way that the nitrogen of acetanilide does [see part (c)].

12.10   The electron-withdrawing inductive effect of the chlorine of chloroethene makes its double bond less electron rich than that of ethene. This causes the rate of reaction of chloroethene with an electrophile (*i.e.*, a proton) to be slower than the corresponding reaction of ethene.

When chloroethene adds a proton, the orientation is governed by a resonance effect. In theory two carbocations can form:

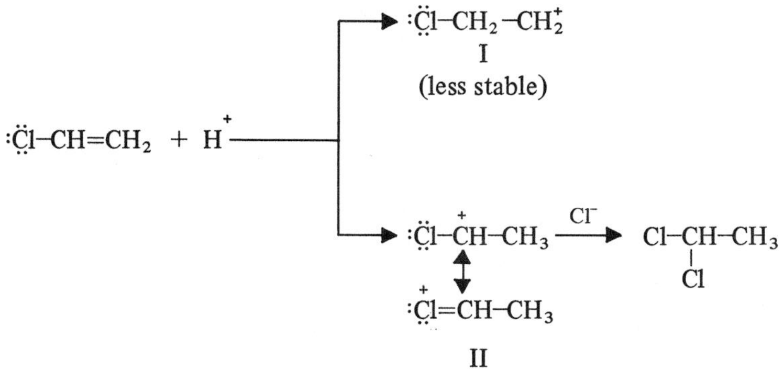

$$:\ddot{C}l-CH=CH_2 \;+\; \overset{+}{H}$$

$$\longrightarrow \quad :\ddot{C}l-CH_2-\overset{+}{CH_2}$$
I
(less stable)

$$\longrightarrow \quad :\ddot{C}l-\overset{+}{C}H-CH_3 \;\; \overset{Cl^-}{\longrightarrow}\;\; Cl-CH-CH_3$$
$$\updownarrow$$
$$:\overset{+}{\ddot{C}l}=CH-CH_3$$

II
(more stable)

Carbocation **II** is more stable than **I** because of the resonance contribution of the extra structure shown above in which the chlorine atom donates an electron pair. (see page 492.)

12.11

Ortho:

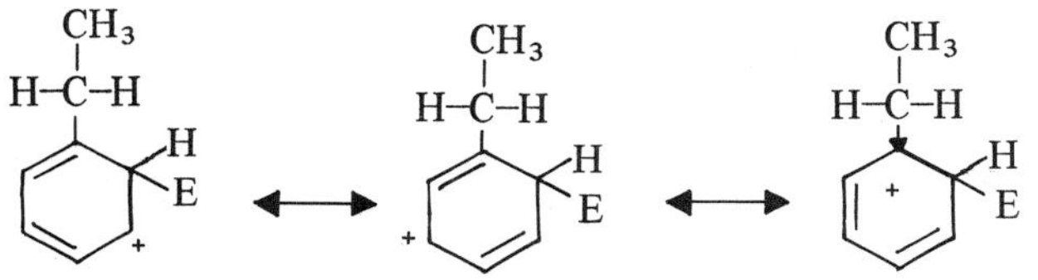

(Relatively stable)

Meta:

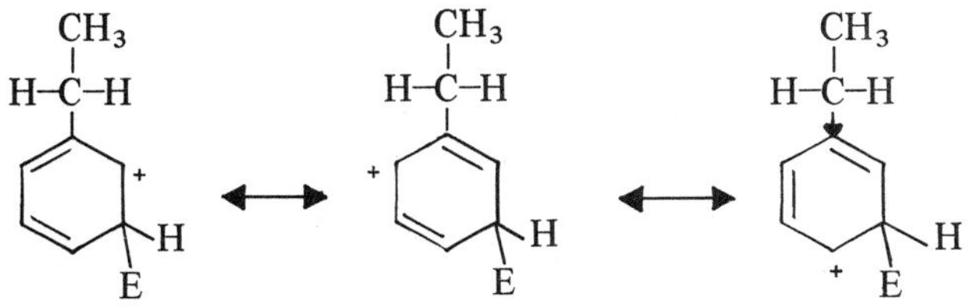

Para:

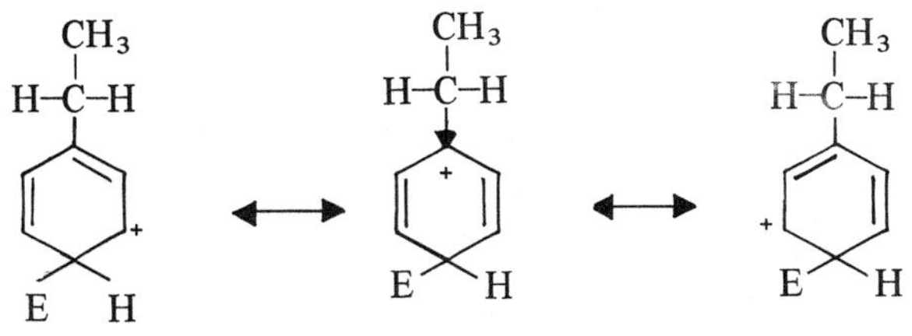

(relatively stable)

12.12

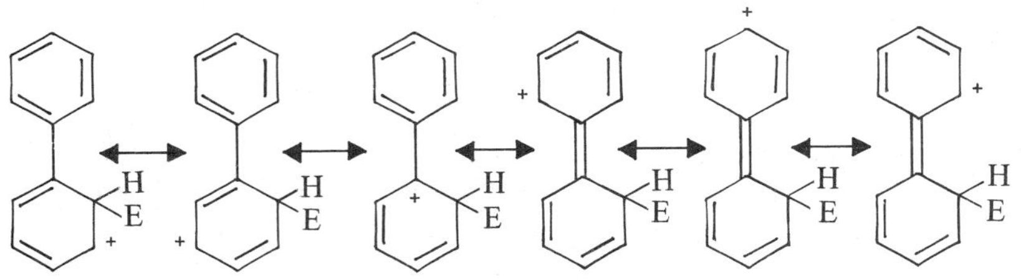

The carbocation above has the positive charge delocalized over both rings and thus it is relatively stable. Similar structures can be drawn for the arenium ions formed when substitution takes place at a para position. However, when electrophilic attack takes place at the meta position it produces a carbocation whose positive charge cannot be delocalized over both rings:

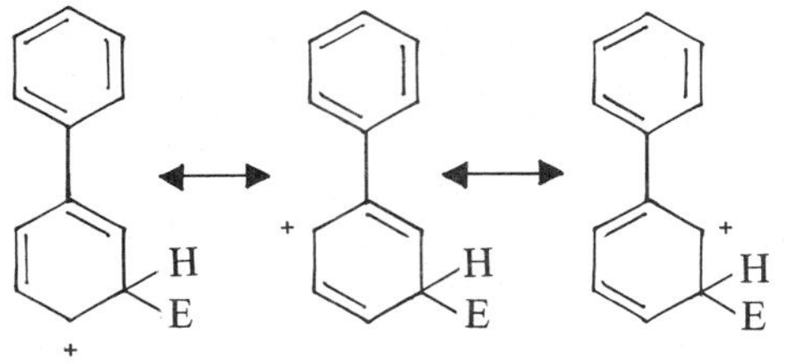

12.13

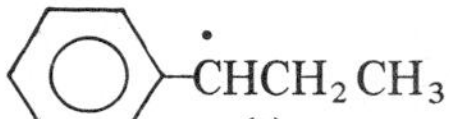

—CHCH$_2$CH$_3$ leads to 1-chloro-1-phenylpropane
   (I)

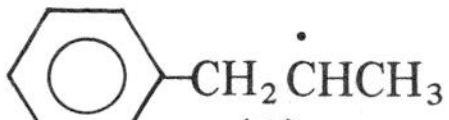

—CH$_2$CHCH$_3$ leads to 2-chloro-1-phenylpropane
   (II)

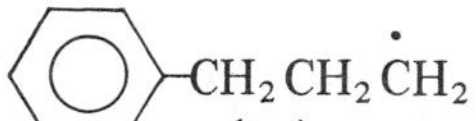

—CH$_2$CH$_2$CH$_2$ leads to 1-chloro-3-phenylpropane
   (III)

The major product is 1-chloro-1-phenylpropane because **I** is the most stable free radical. It is a benzylic radical and therefore is stabilized by resonance.

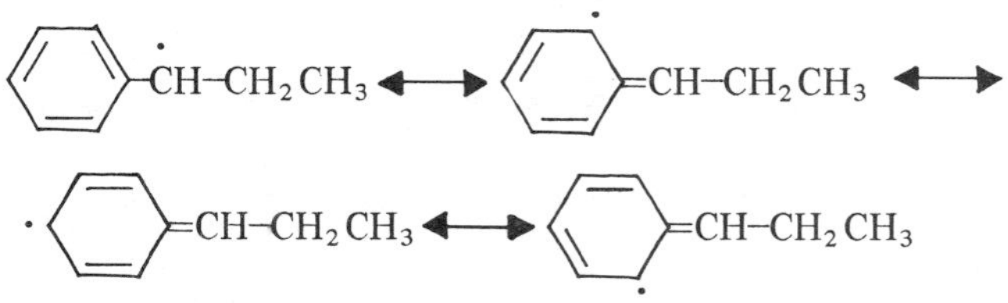

12.14

(a) 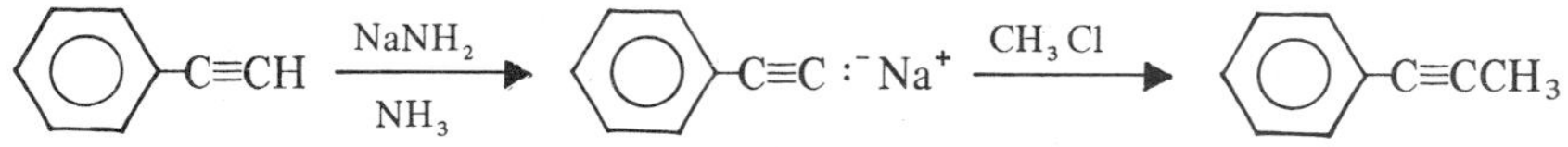 —C≡CH $\xrightarrow[\text{NH}_3]{\text{NaNH}_2}$ —C≡C :$^-$Na$^+$ $\xrightarrow{\text{CH}_3\text{Cl}}$ —C≡CCH$_3$

(b) $C_6H_5-C\equiv CH$ $\xrightarrow[\text{(2) } CH_3CH_2Cl]{\text{(1) } NaNH_2/NH_3}$ $C_6H_5-C\equiv CCH_2CH_3$

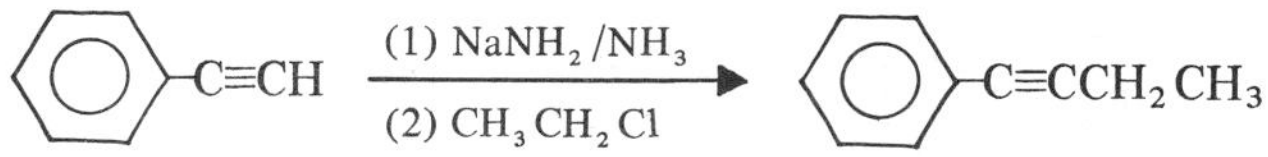

(c) $C_6H_5-C\equiv CCH_3$ $\xrightarrow[H_2]{Ni_2B}$ [alkene product with H, C-H, CH₃]

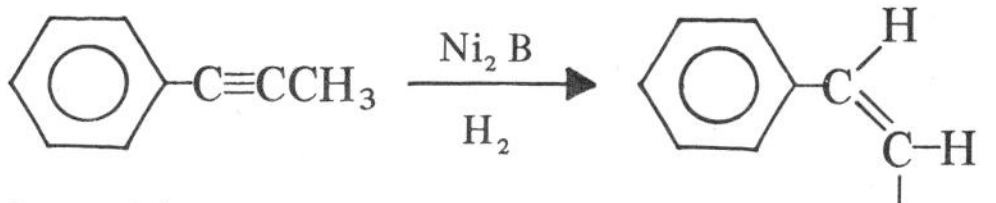

from (a)

(d) 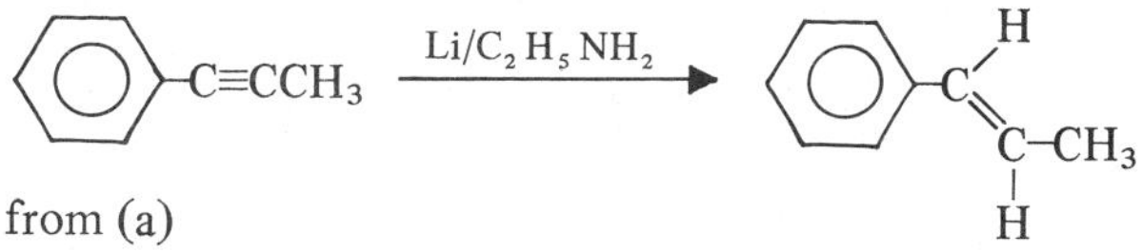 $C_6H_5-C\equiv CCH_3$ $\xrightarrow{Li/C_2H_5NH_2}$ [alkene product with H, C-CH₃, H]

from (a)

12.15

(a)

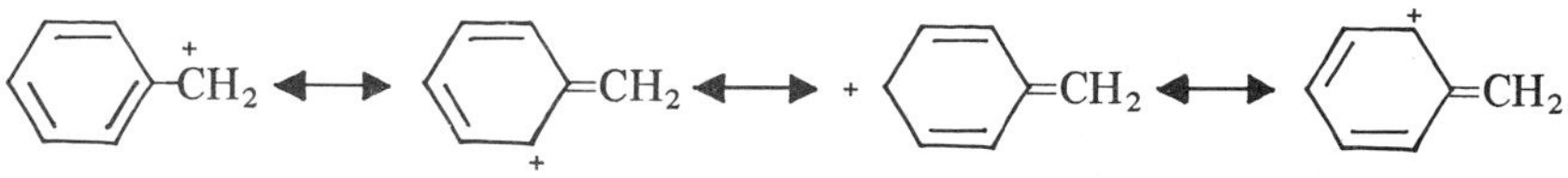

(b) The benzyl cation is stabilized by resonance.

(c) Yes, because the benzyl cation is a hybrid of the structures given in (a).

(d) Over the ortho and para ring carbons and the benzylic carbon.

(e) π_1, π_2, π_3 (see Figure 12.3).

(f) Since π_4 is vacant (see Figure 12.4), molecular orbital theory predicts the same thing as resonance theory that the positive charge is delocalized over the benzylic carbon and the ortho and para ring carbons.

12.16

(a) 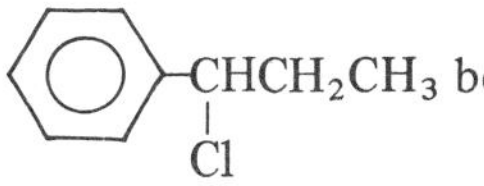 $C_6H_5-\underset{\underset{Cl}{|}}{C}HCH_2CH_3$ because the most stable carbocation intermediate is the benzylic

carbocation, $C_6H_5-\overset{+}{C}HCH_2CH_3$.

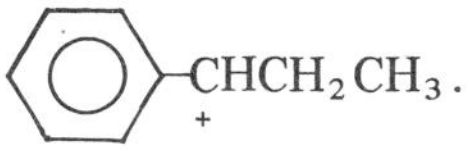

(b) 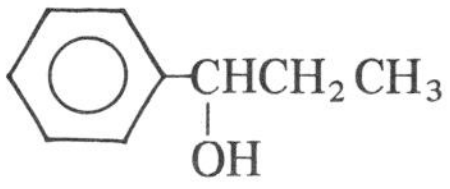 $C_6H_5-\underset{\underset{OH}{|}}{C}HCH_2CH_3$ for the same reason as given in (a).

12.17   Chlorinate the ring first and then introduce the double bond as shown below. If we were to introduce the side-chain double bond first, chlorination of the ring would result in addition of chlorine to the side-chain double bond.

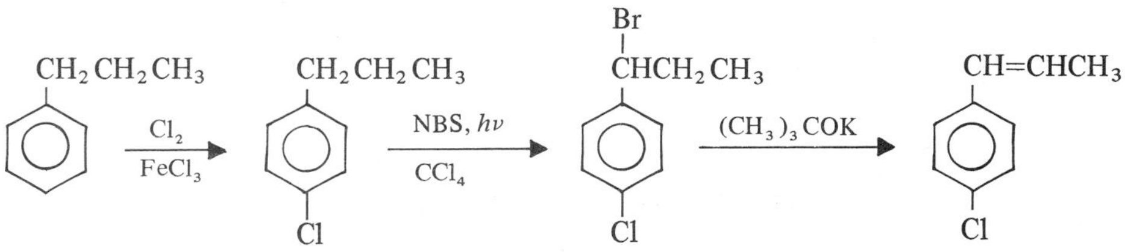

12.18

(a)

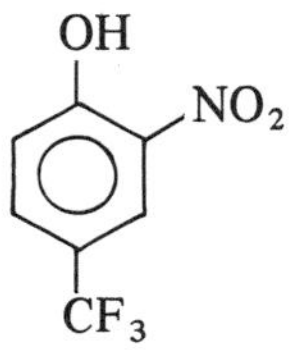

(b)

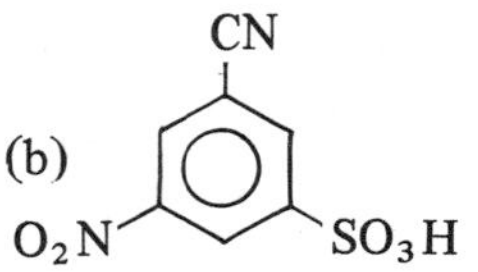

(c)

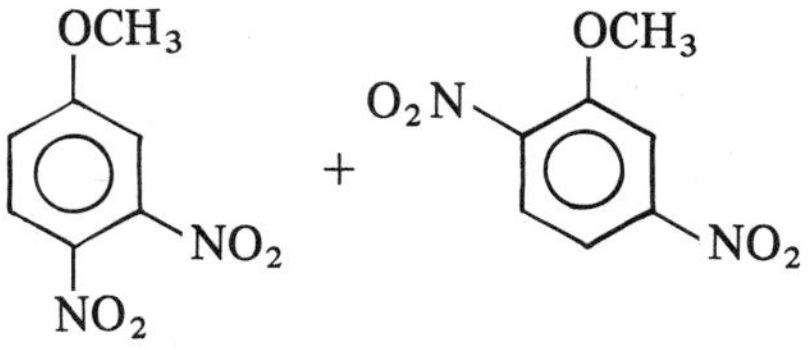

(d)

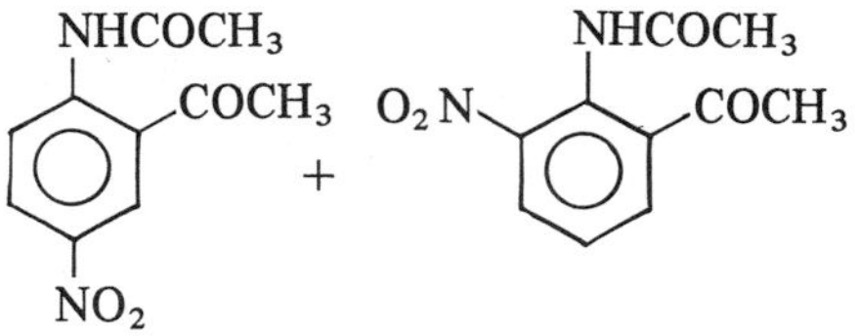

(e)

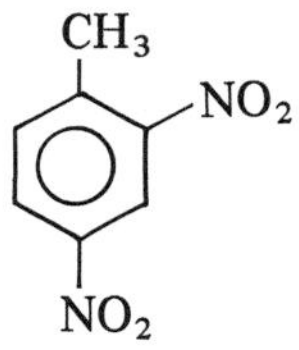

(f)

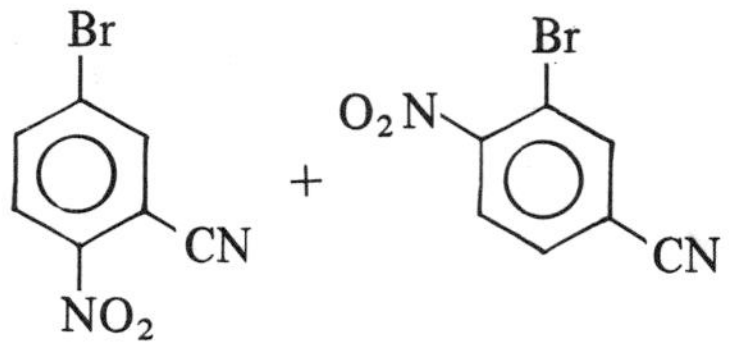

(g)

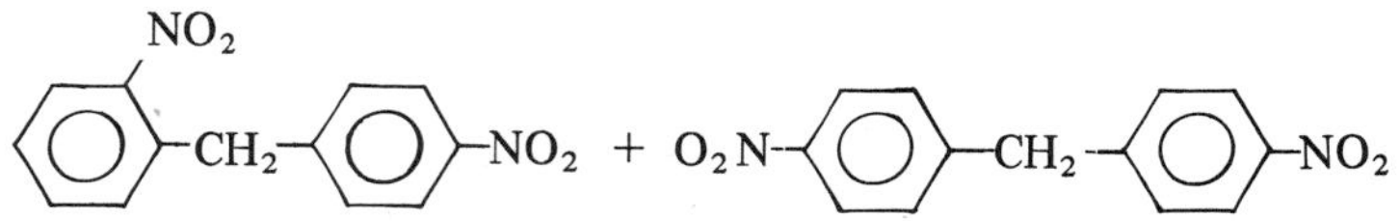

12.19 The carbocation formed by the action of $AlCl_3$ on neopentyl chloride is primary. This carbocation rearranges to the more stable tertiary carbocation before it can react with the benzene ring:

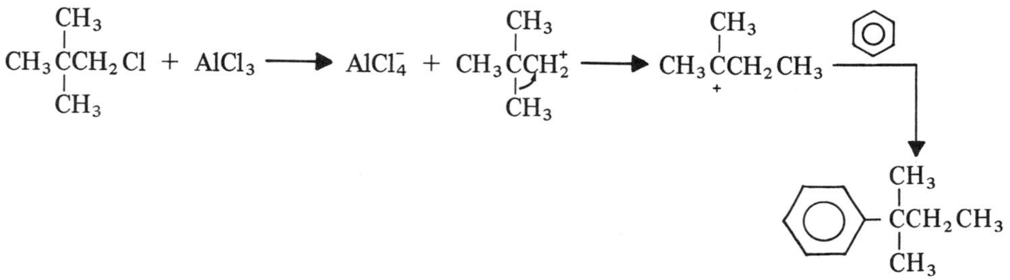

12.20 $CH_3CH_2CH_2-OH + BF_3 \rightleftharpoons CH_3CH_2CH_2^+ + H\overset{..}{O}BF_3$

The propyl cation can rearrange to an isopropyl cation:

$$CH_3CH_2\overset{+}{C}H_2 \xrightarrow[\text{Shift}]{\text{Hydride}} CH_3\overset{+}{C}HCH_3$$

Both cations can then attack the benzene ring.

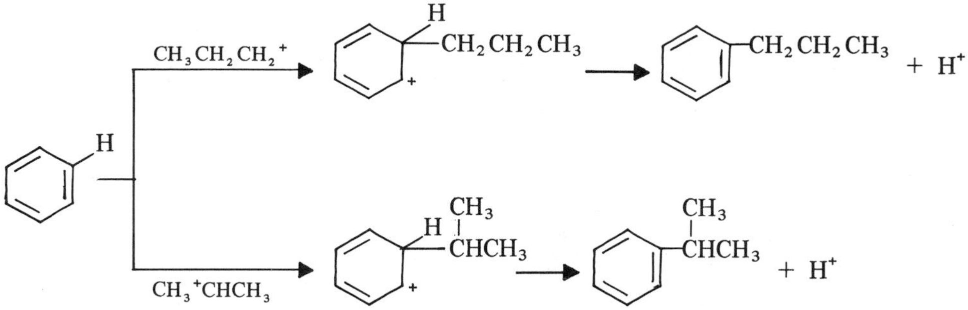

12.21

(a)

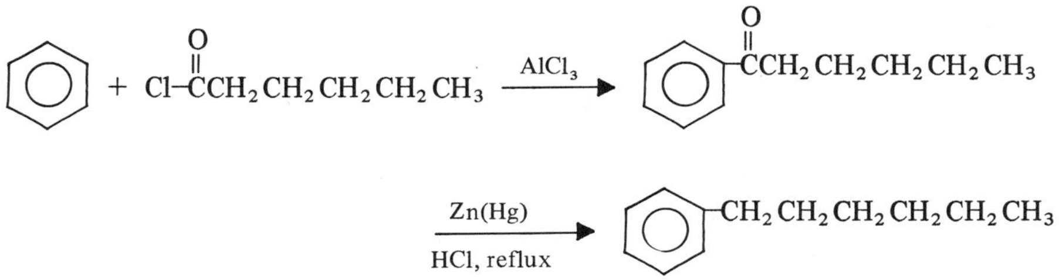

(b)

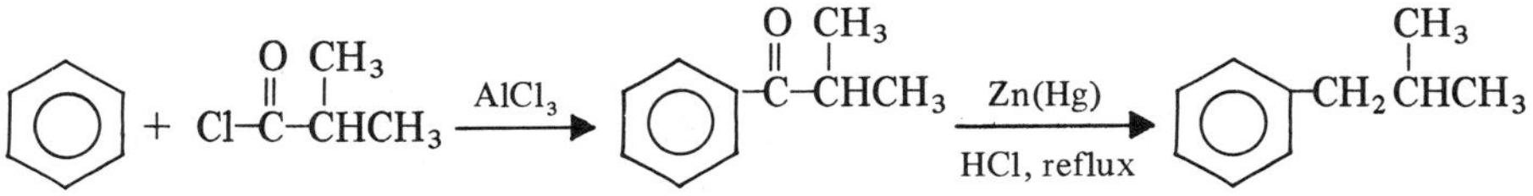

(c)

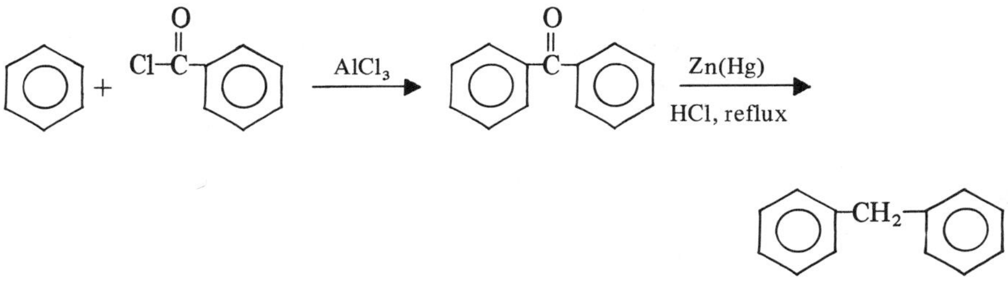

(d)

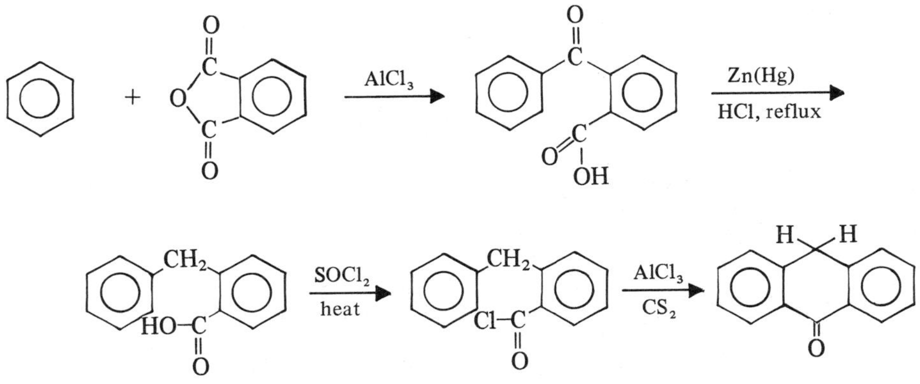

12.22

(a)

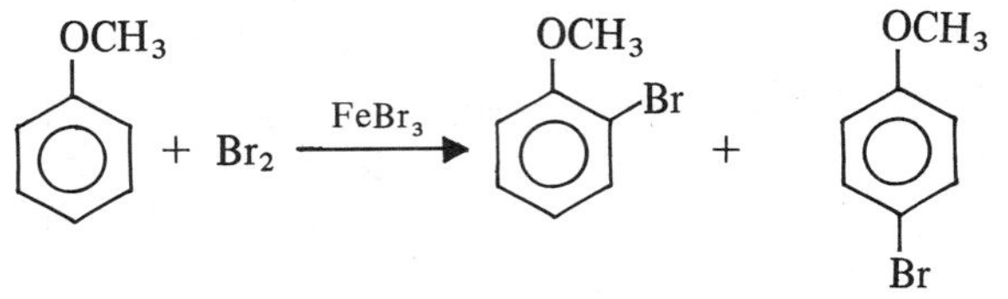

o-Bromoanisole   p-Bromoanisole

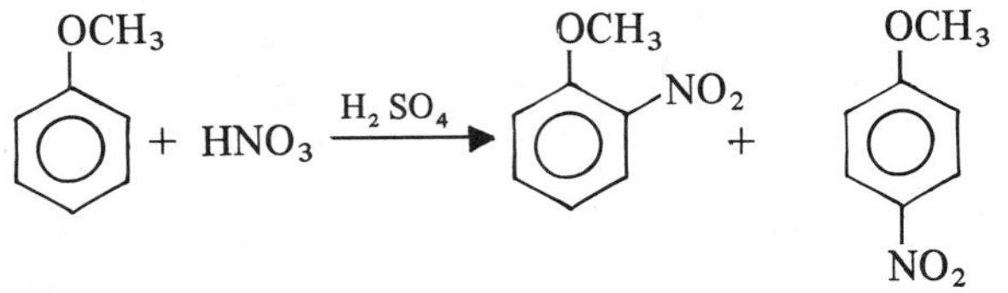

o-Nitroanisole   p-Nitroanisole

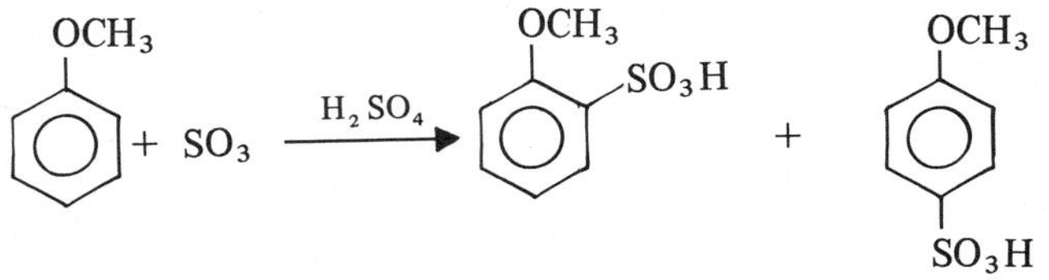

o-Methoxybenzene-   p-Methoxybenzene-
sulfonic acid   sulfonic acid

Reactions are faster than the corresponding reactions of benzene.

(b)

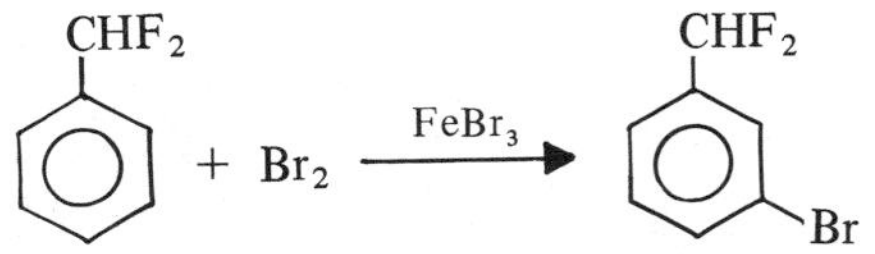

m-(Difluoromethyl)-
bromobenzene

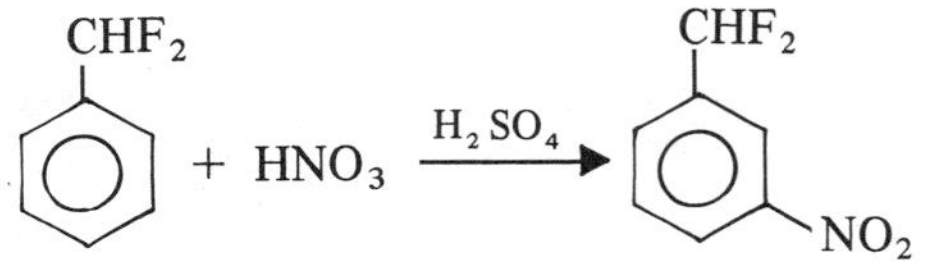

m-(Difluoromethyl)-
nitrobenzene

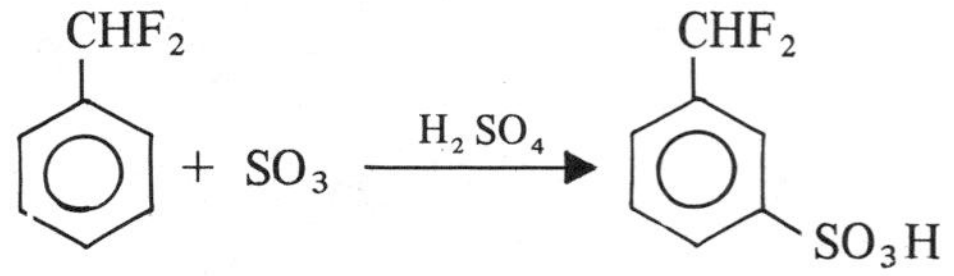

m-(Difluoromethyl)-
benzenesulfonic acid

Reactions are slower than corresponding reactions of benzene.

(c)

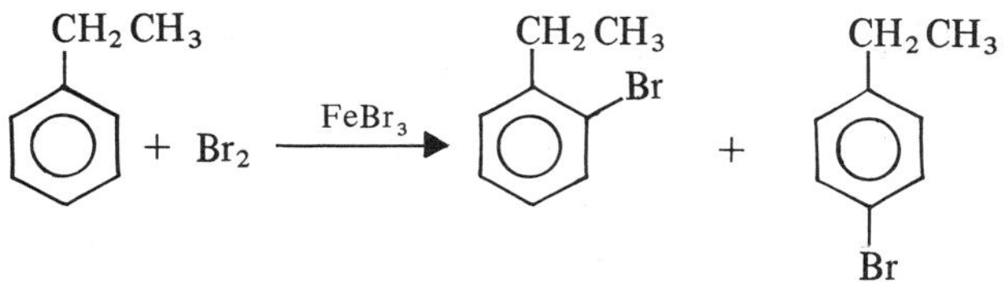

o-Bromoethyl-
benzene

p-Bromoethyl-
benzene

Nitration ⟶ o-Ethylnitrobenzene and p-Ethylnitrobenzene

Sulfonation ⟶ o-Ethylbenzenesulfonic acid and p-Ethylbenzenesulfonic acid.

Reactions are faster than corresponding reactions of benzene.

(d)

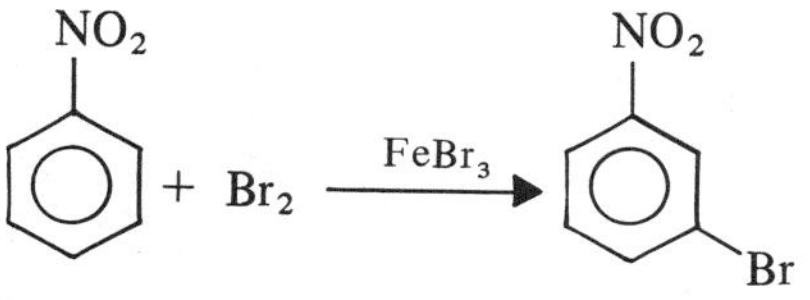

m-Bromonitrobenzene

Nitration ⟶ m-Dinitrobenzene

Sulfonation ⟶ m-Nitrobenzenesulfonic acid

Reactions are slower than corresponding reactions of benzene.

(e)

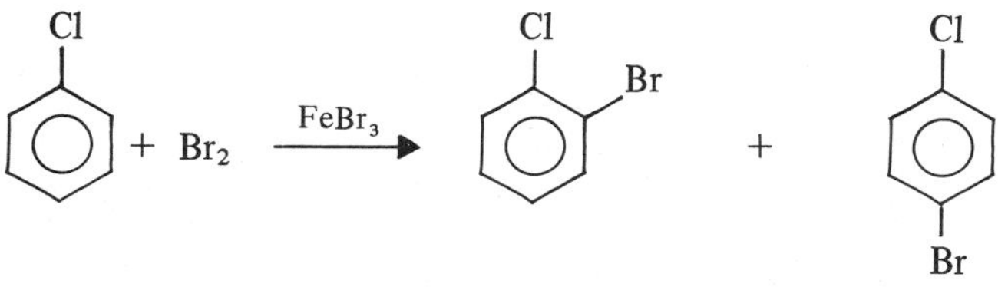

o-Bromochlorobenzene   p-Bromochloro-
benzene

Nitration ⟶ o-Chloronitrobenzene + p-Chloronitrobenzene

Sulfonation ⟶ o-Chlorobenzenesulfonic acid + p-Chlorobenzenesulfonic acid

Reactions are slower than corresponding reactions of benzene.

(f)

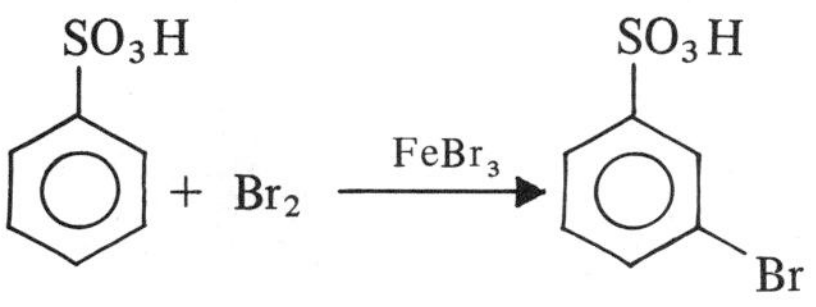

m-Bromobenzenesulfonic acid

Nitration ⟶ m-Nitrobenzenesulfonic acid

Sulfonation ⟶ m-Benzenedisulfonic acid

Reactions are slower than corresponding reactions of benzene.

12.23

(a) 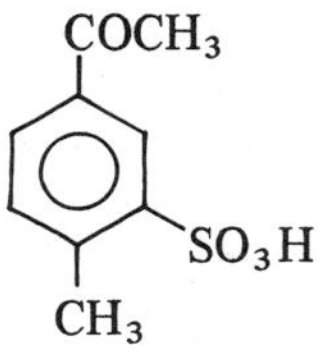

(b) 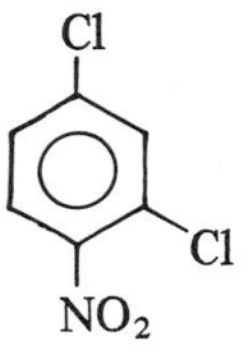

(c) 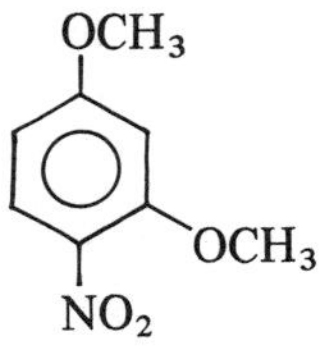

(d) 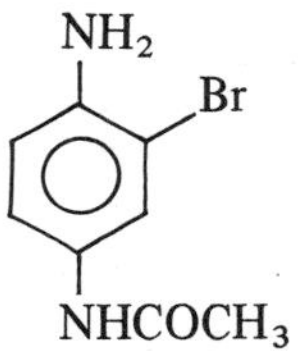

(e) 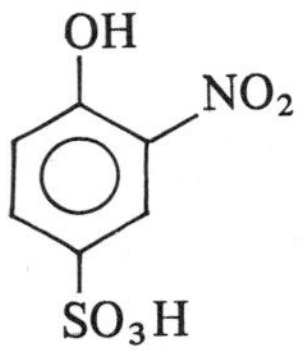

(f) 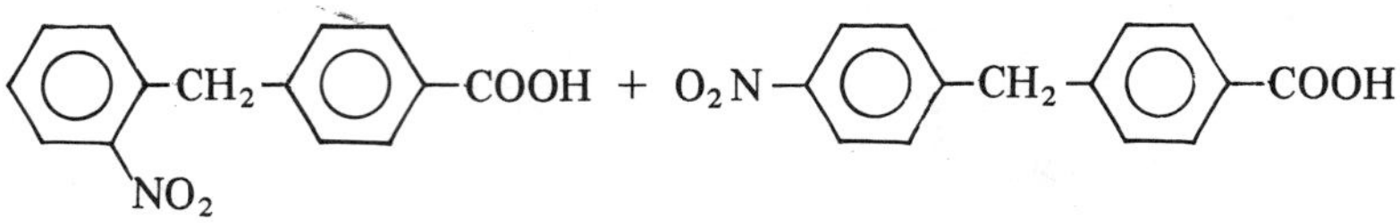

(g) 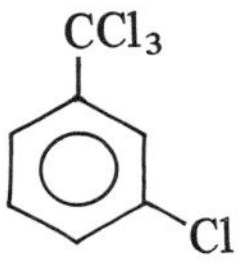

12.24

(a) 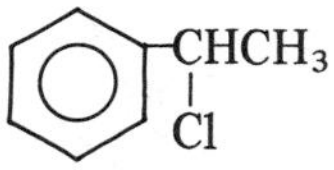

(b) 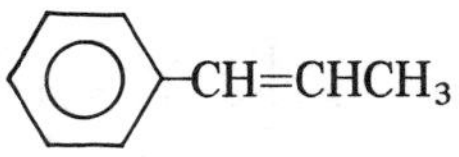

(c) 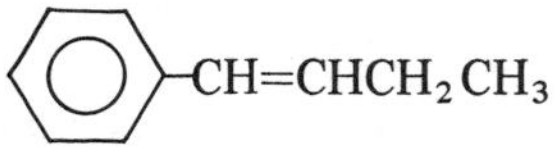

(d) 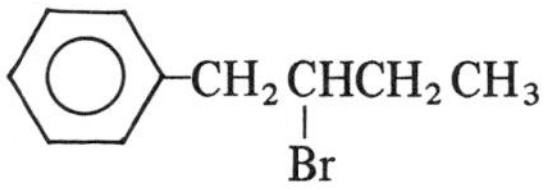

(e) 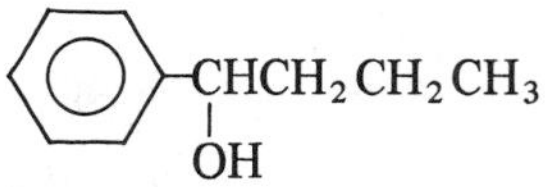

(f) 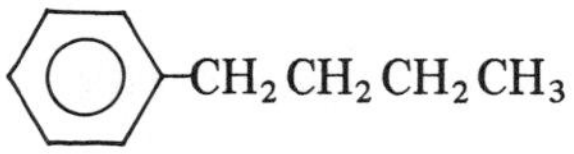

(g) 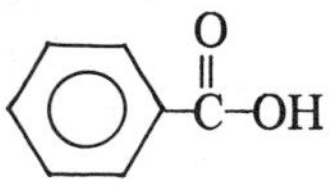

12.25

(a) 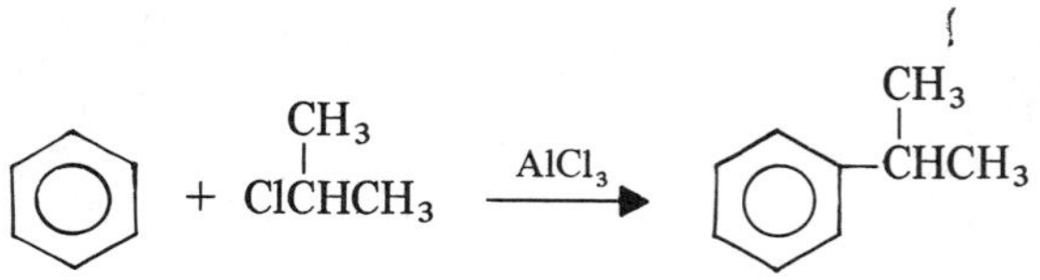

(b) 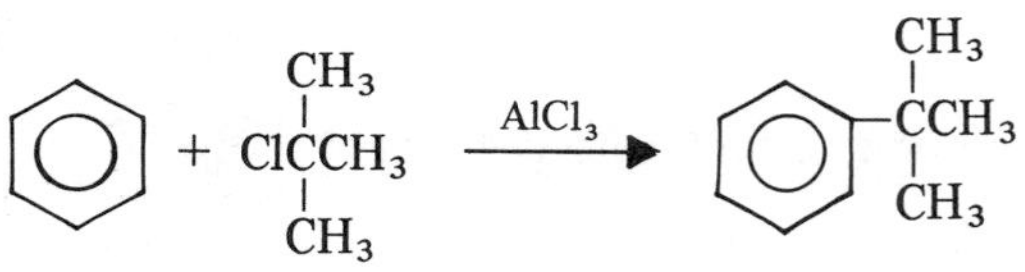

(c)

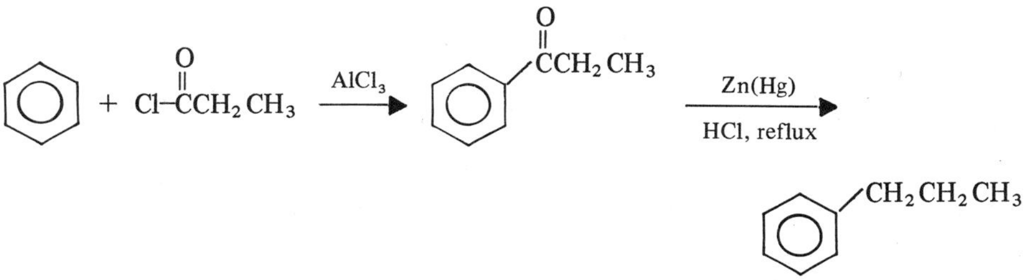

(Note: The use of $Cl-CH_2CH_2CH_3$ in a Friedel-Crafts synthesis gives mainly the rearranged product, isopropylbenzene.)

(d)

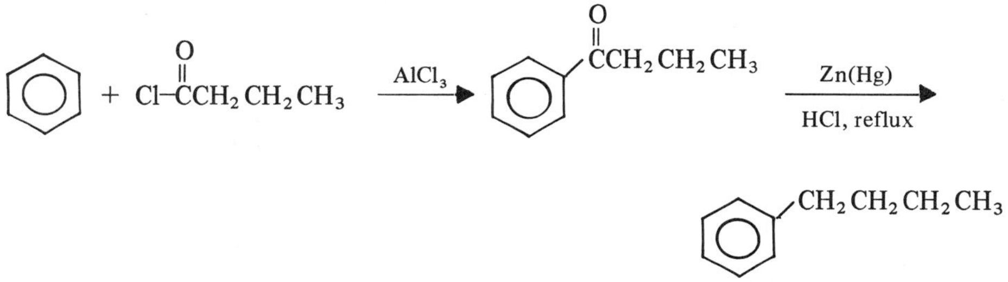

(e)

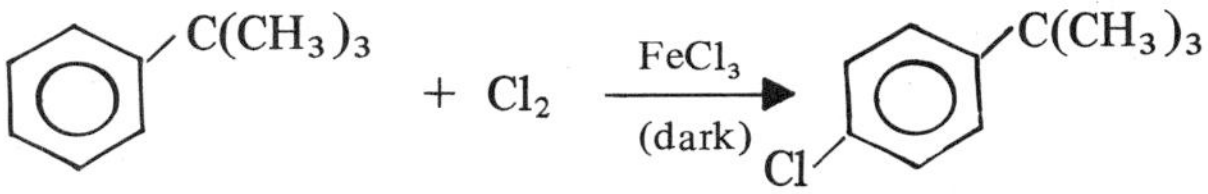

from (b)

(f)

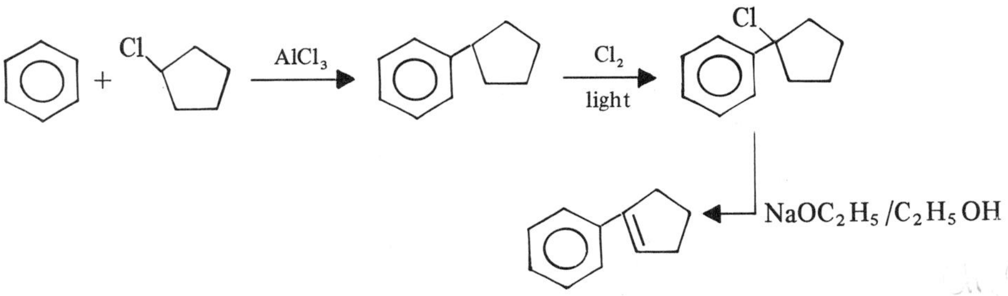

(g)

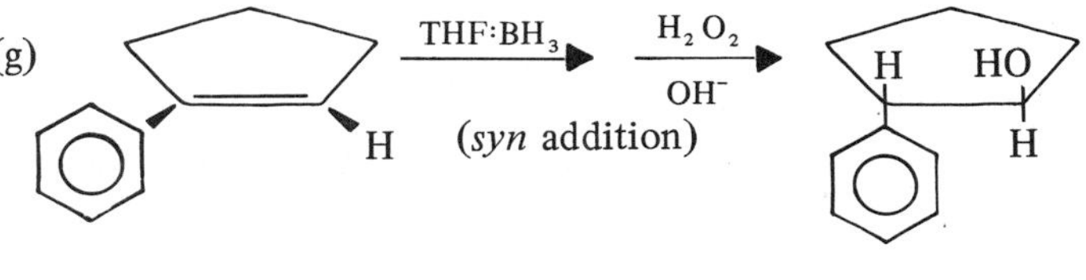

(h)

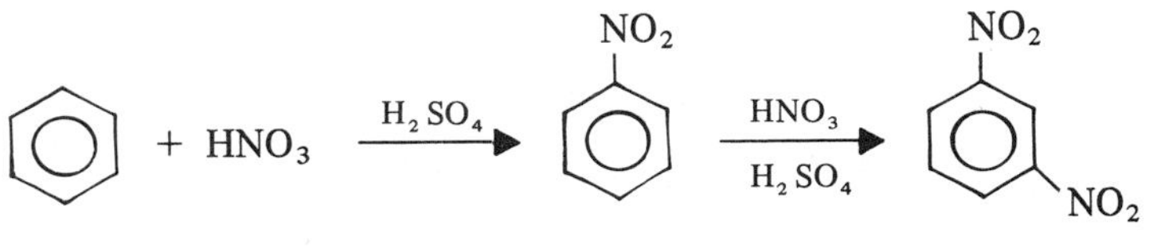

(i)

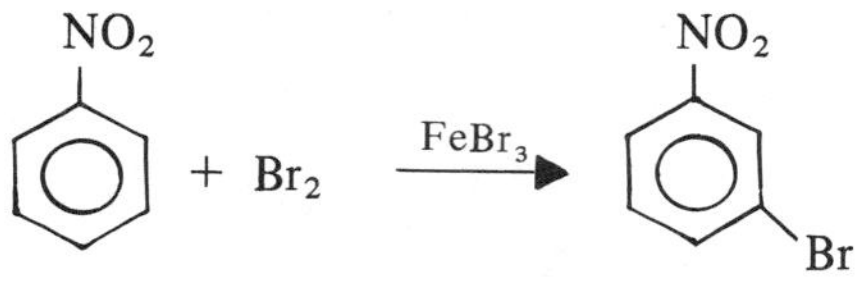

(j)

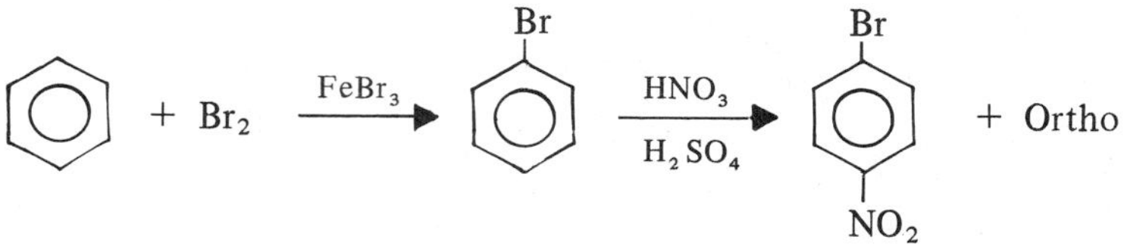

(k)

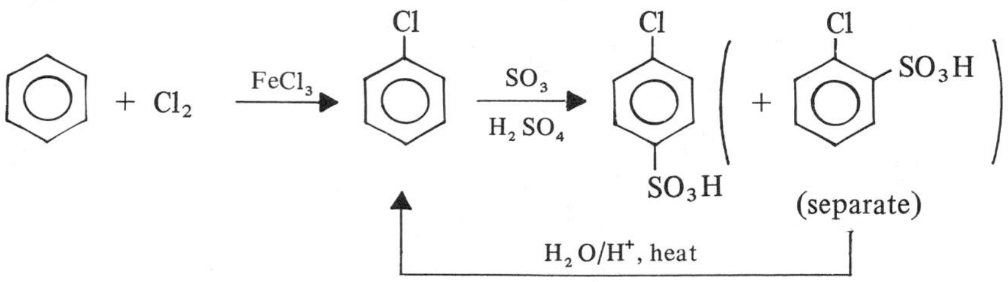

(l)

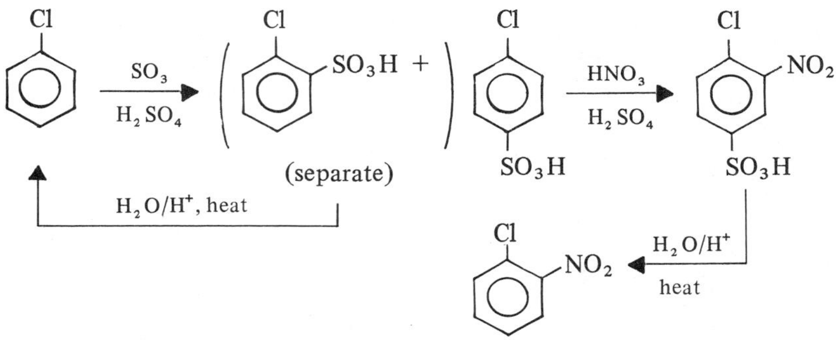

(m)

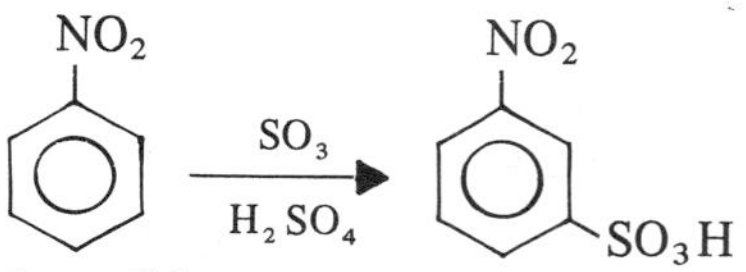

from (h)

(n) 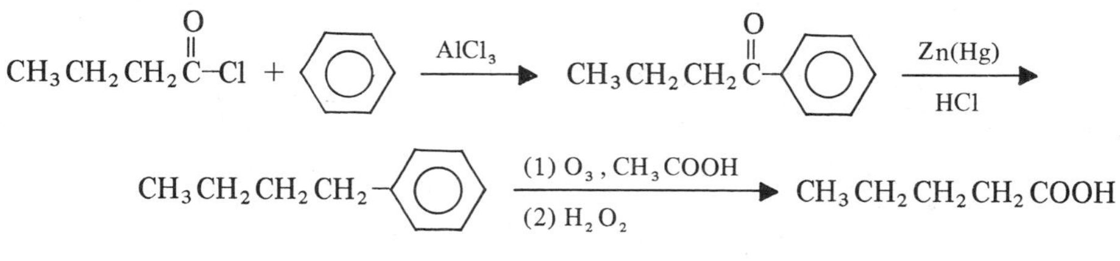 $CH_3CH_2CH_2\overset{O}{\overset{\|}{C}}{-}Cl$ +

$CH_3CH_2CH_2CH_2{-}$ $\xrightarrow[\text{(2) } H_2O_2]{\text{(1) } O_3,\ CH_3COOH}$ $CH_3CH_2CH_2CH_2COOH$

(o) $CH_3CH_2CH_2CH_2{-}$ $\xrightarrow{\text{NBS}}$ $CH_3CH_2CH_2\underset{\underset{\text{Br}}{|}}{CH}{-}$ $\xrightarrow[C_2H_5OH]{NaOC_2H_5}$
from (n)

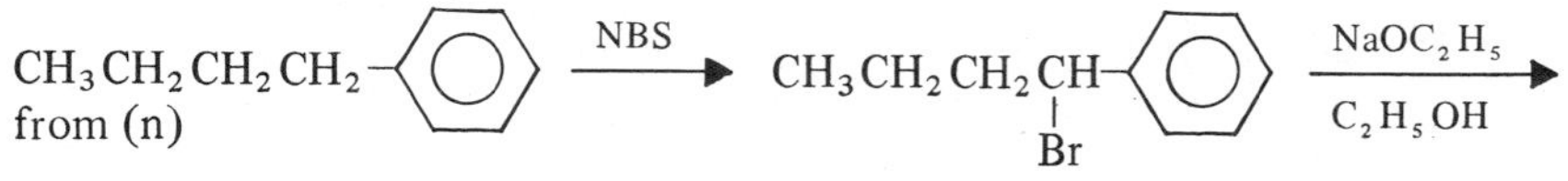

$$CH_3CH_2CH=CH-\bigcirc \xrightarrow{D_2/Ni} CH_3CH_2CHDCHD-\bigcirc \xrightarrow[\text{(2) } H_2O_2]{\text{(1) } O_3, CH_3COOH}$$

$$CH_3CH_2CHDCHDCOOH$$

(p) $CH_3CH_2CH=CH-\bigcirc$ from (o) $\xrightarrow{THF : BH_3} \xrightarrow[160°]{\text{heat}}$ $\rangle BCH_2CH_2CH_2CH_2-\bigcirc$

$$\xrightarrow{CH_3COOD} DCH_2CH_2CH_2CH_2-\bigcirc \xrightarrow[\text{(2) } H_2O_2]{\text{(1) } O_3, CH_3COOH}$$

$$DCH_2CH_2CH_2CH_2COOH$$

12.26

(a) $\bigcirc-CH=CH_2 \xrightarrow{Cl_2} \bigcirc-CHClCH_2Cl$

(b) $\bigcirc-CH=CH_2 \xrightarrow{H_2/Ni} \bigcirc-CH_2CH_3$

(c) $\bigcirc-CH=CH_2 \xrightarrow[25°C]{KMnO_4} \bigcirc-CHOHCH_2OH$

(d) $\bigcirc-CH=CH_2 \xrightarrow[\text{heat}]{KMnO_4} \bigcirc-COOH$

(e) $\bigcirc-CH=CH_2 \xrightarrow[H_2SO_4]{H_2O} \bigcirc-CHOHCH_3$

(f) $\bigcirc-CH=CH_2 \xrightarrow{HBr} \bigcirc-CHBrCH_3$

(g) $\bigcirc-CH=CH_2 \xrightarrow[\text{(2) } H_2O_2/OH^-]{\text{(1) } THF : BH_3} \bigcirc-CH_2CH_2OH$

(h) $\bigcirc-CH=CH_2 \xrightarrow[\text{(2) } CH_3COOD]{\text{(1) } THF : BH_3} \bigcirc-CH_2CH_2D$

(i) $\bigcirc-CH=CH_2 \xrightarrow[\text{peroxides}]{HBr} \bigcirc-CH_2CH_2Br$

(j) $\bigcirc-CH_2CH_2Br + NaI \xrightarrow[H_2O]{\text{acetone}} \bigcirc-CH_2CH_2I$
from (i)

(k) $\bigcirc-CH_2CH_2Br + CN^- \longrightarrow \bigcirc-CH_2CH_2CN$
from (i)

(l)

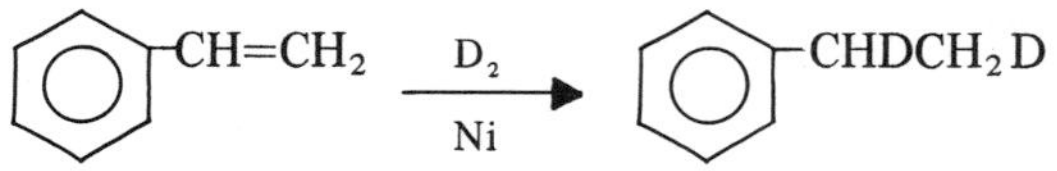

(m)

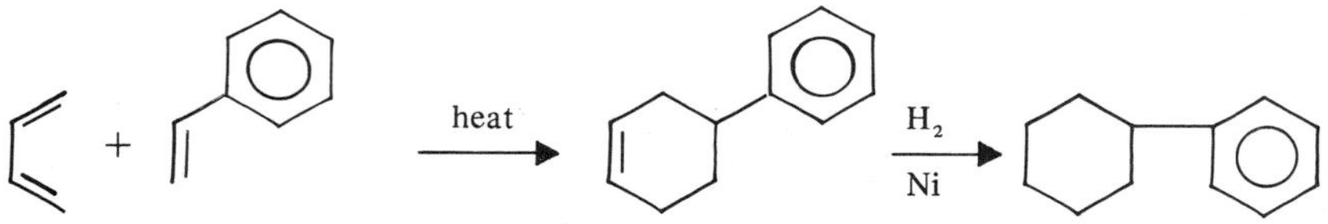

(n)

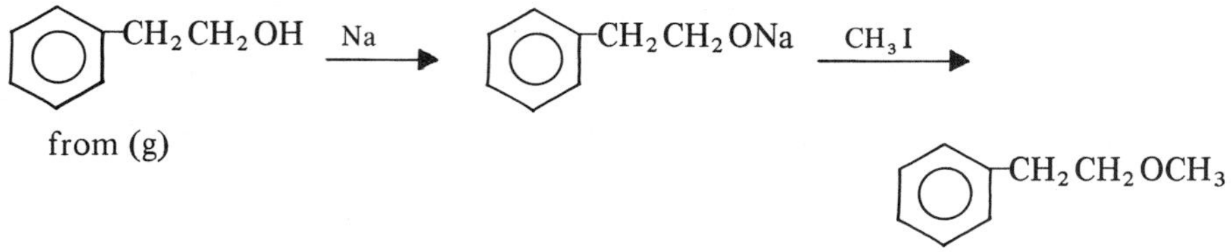

from (g)

12.27

(a)

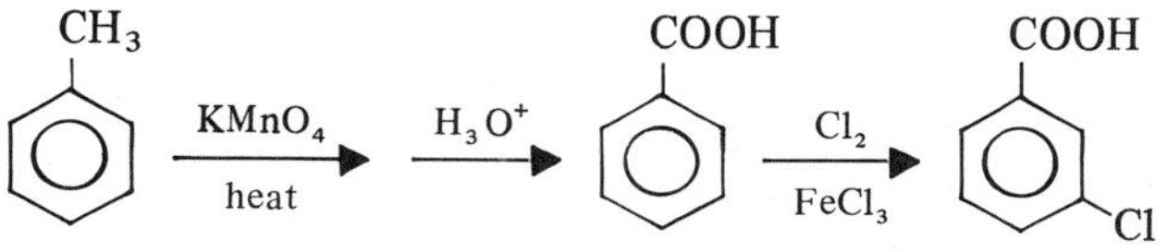

(b)

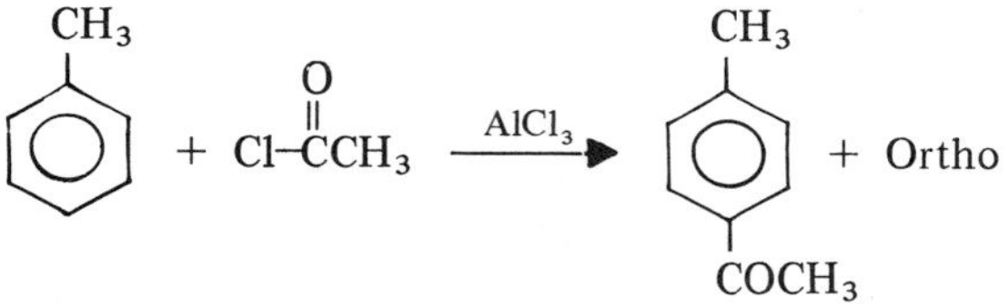

(c)

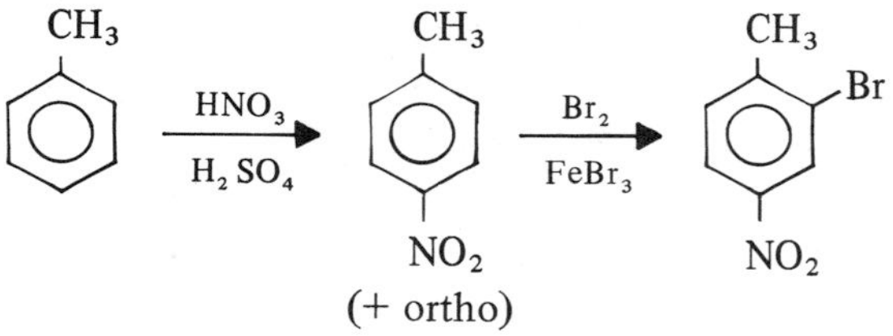

(d)

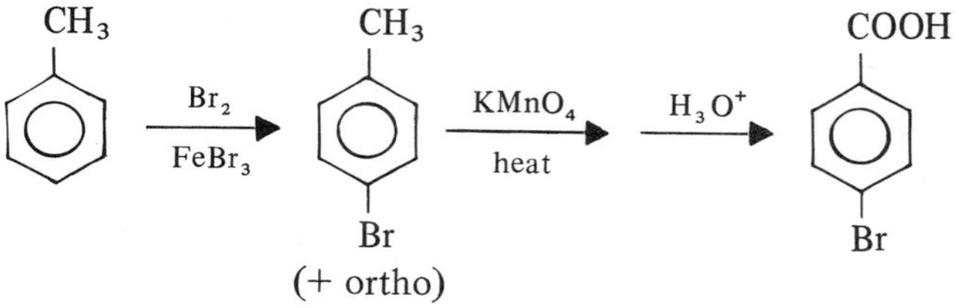

(e)

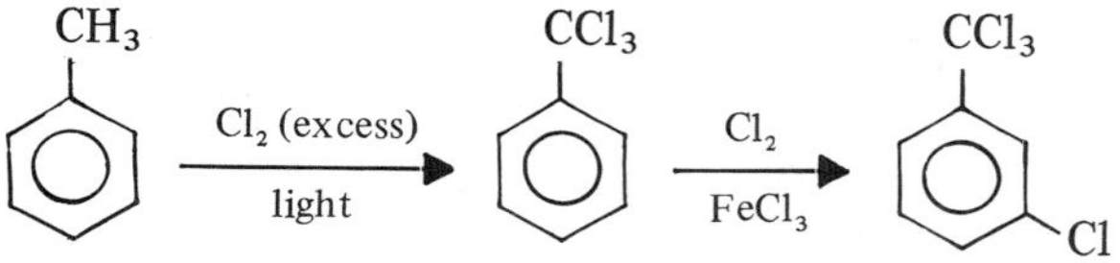

(f)

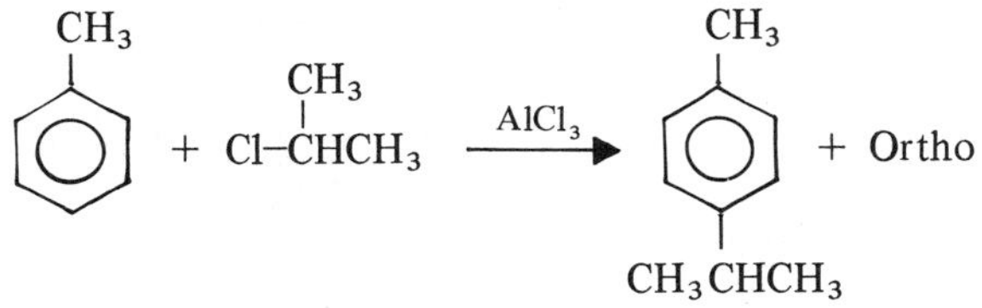

(g)

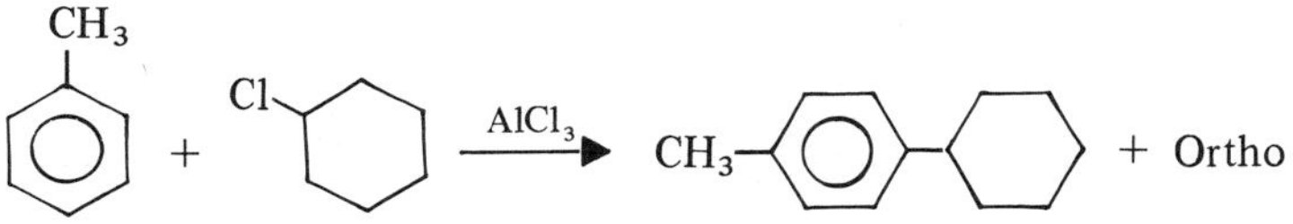

(h)

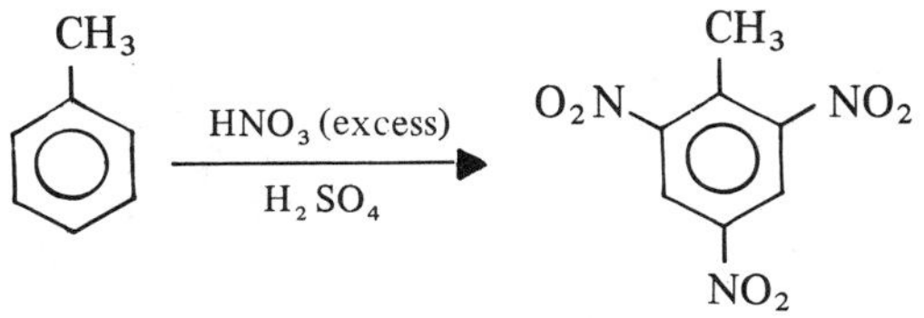

(i)

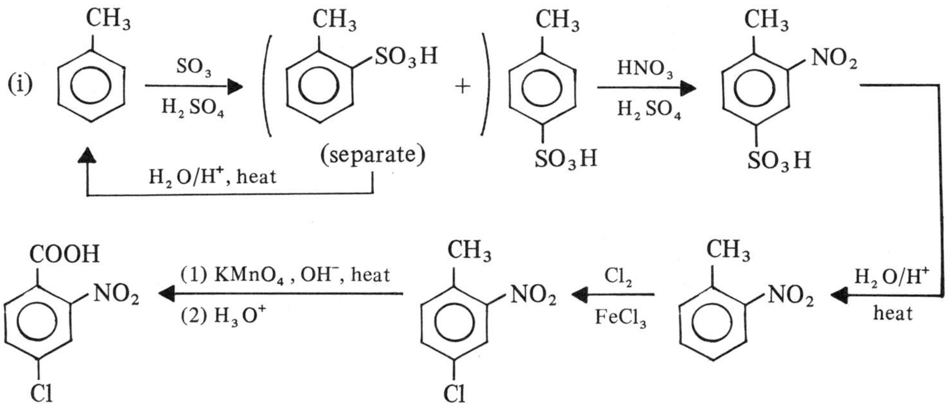

(j)

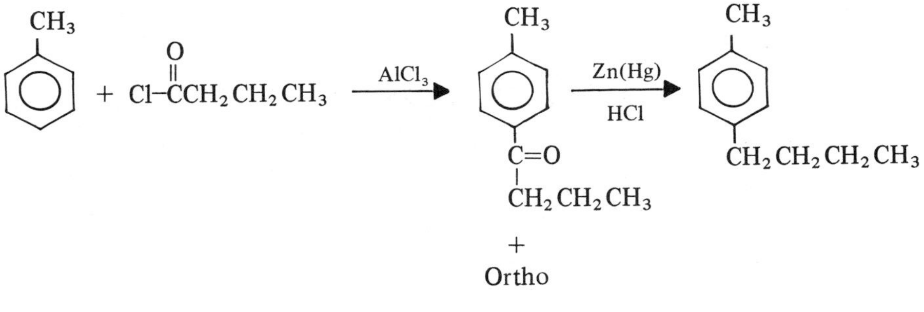

12.28

(a)

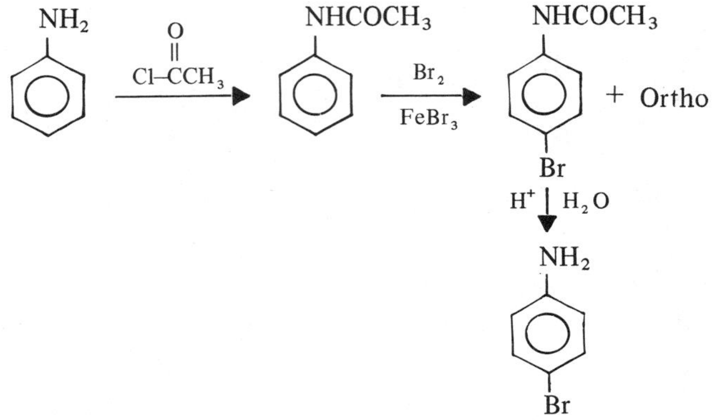

NH2
O
Cl–CCH3
NHCOCH3
Br2
FeBr3
NHCOCH3
+ Ortho
Br
H+
H2O
NH2
Br

(b)

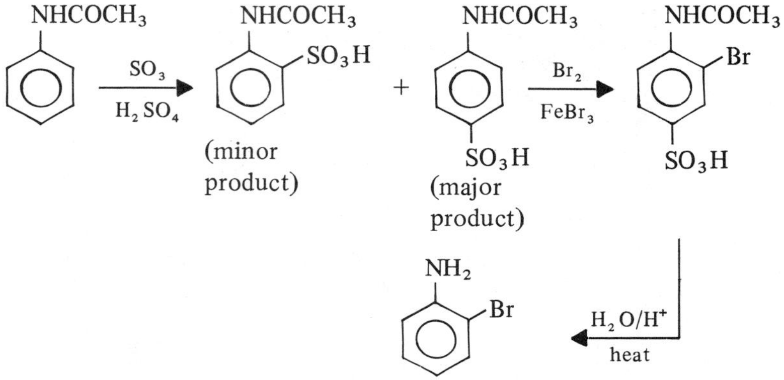

NHCOCH3
SO3
H2SO4
NHCOCH3
SO3H
(minor
product)
+
NHCOCH3
SO3H
(major
product)
Br2
FeBr3
NHCOCH3
Br
SO3H
H2O/H+
heat
NH2
Br

(c)

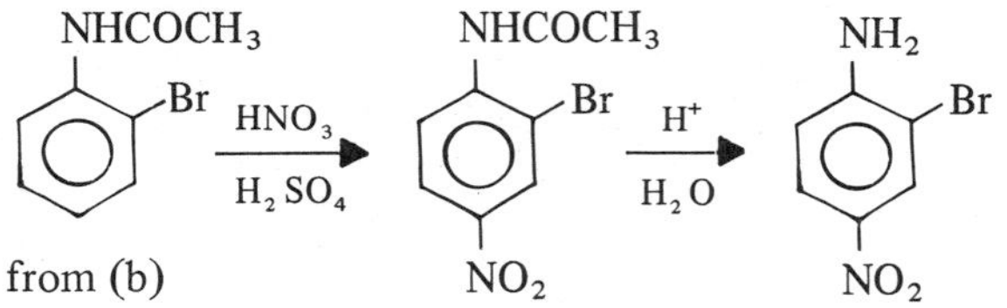

NHCOCH3
Br
from (b)
HNO3
H2SO4
NHCOCH3
Br
NO2
H+
H2O
NH2
Br
NO2

(d)

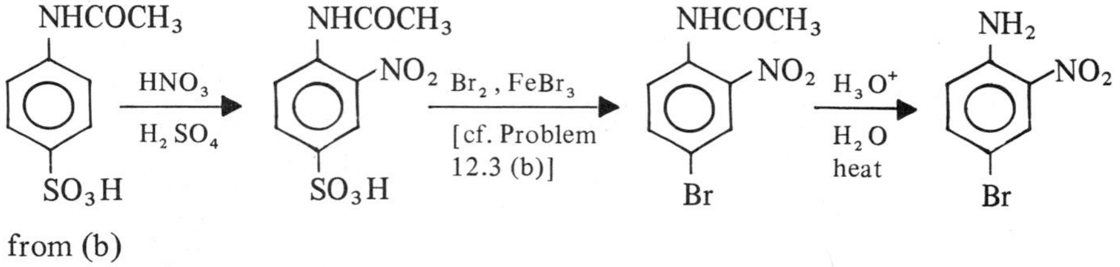

NHCOCH3
SO3H
from (b)
HNO3
H2SO4
NHCOCH3
NO2
SO3H
Br2, FeBr3
[cf. Problem
12.3 (b)]
NHCOCH3
NO2
Br
H3O+
H2O
heat
NH2
NO2
Br

(e)

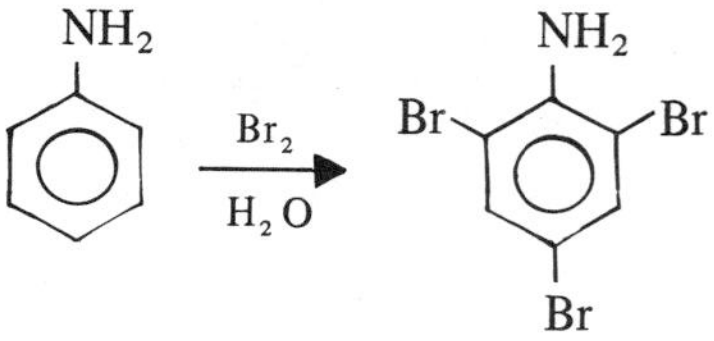

NH2
Br2
H2O
NH2
Br
Br
Br

12.29

(a)

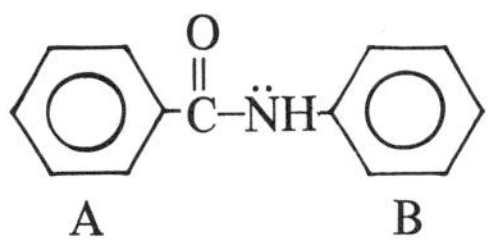

Ring **B** undergoes electrophilic substitution more readily than ring **A**.

(b) Resonance structures such as the one below stabilize the intermediate carbocation:

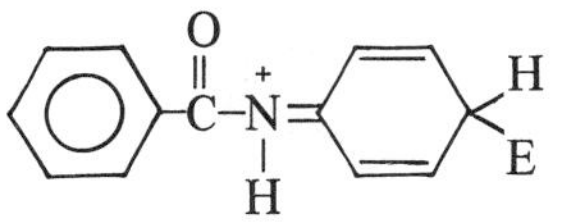

12.30

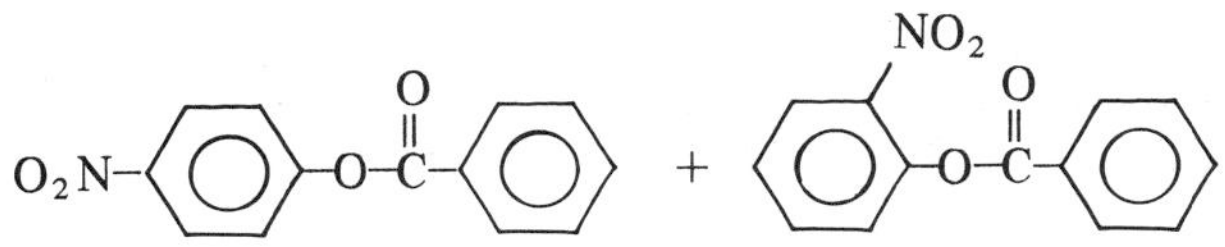

See solution to Problem 12.29

12.31

(a)

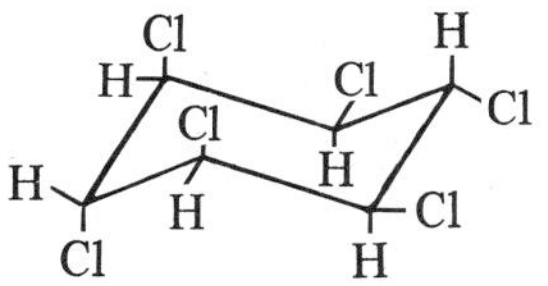

(b) No   (c) Lindane is a *meso* compound.

(d)

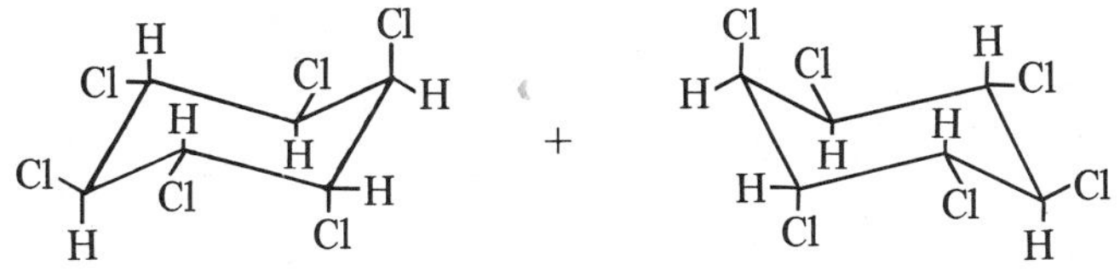

(see also Problem 17 of First Review Problem Set, page 436 of text)

12.32 If we consider resonance structures for the ring that undergoes electrophilic attack, two structures are possible for the arenium ion that forms when attack takes place at the 1-position,

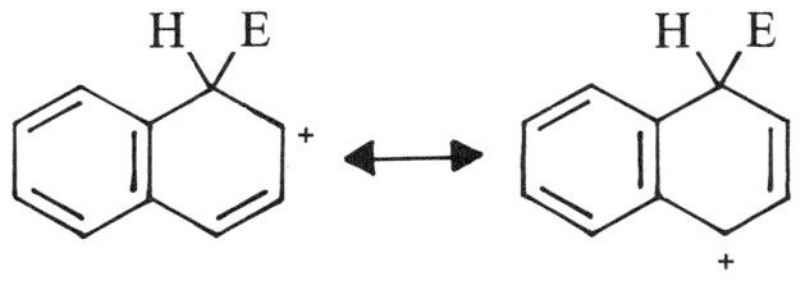

whereas only one is possible when attack takes place at the 2-position,

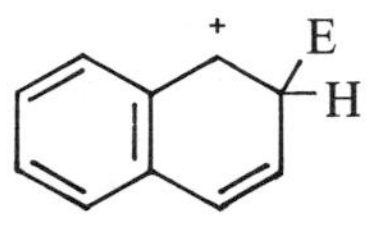

Attack at the 1-position, therefore, takes place faster.

12.33

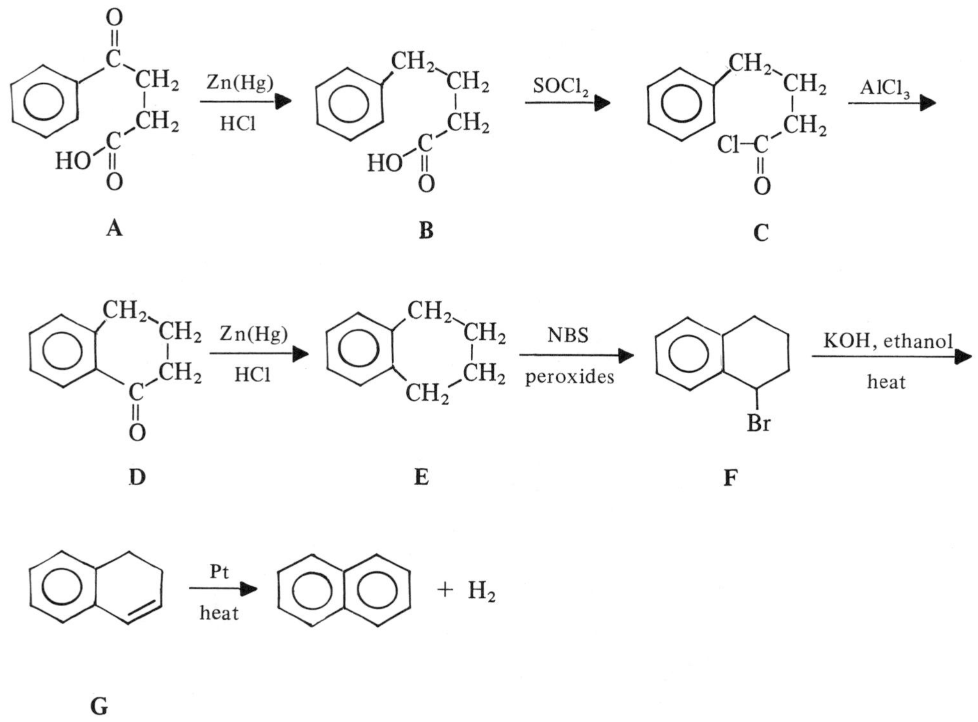

12.34

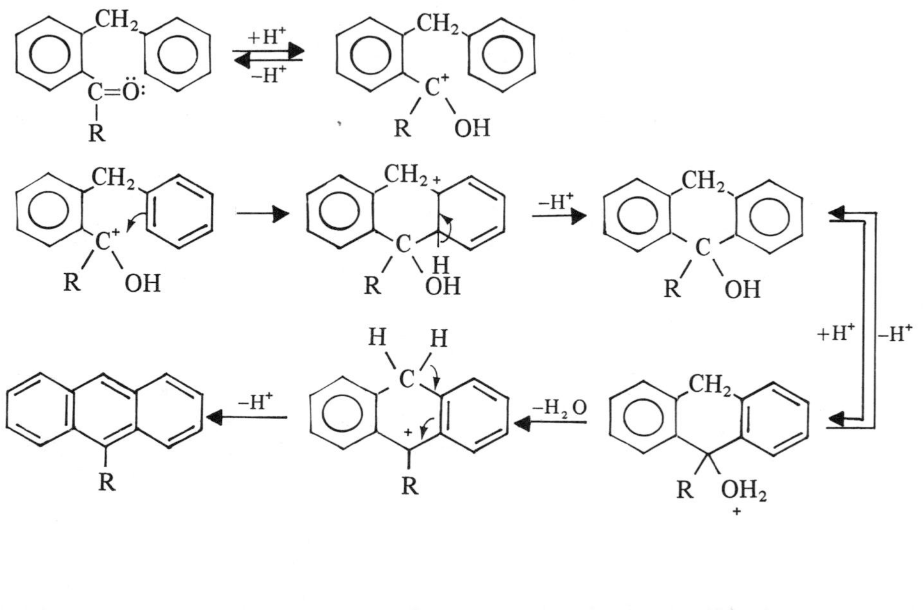

12.35 This problem serves as another illustration of the use of a sulfonic acid group as a blocking group in a synthetic sequence. Here we are able to bring about nitration between two *meta* substituents.

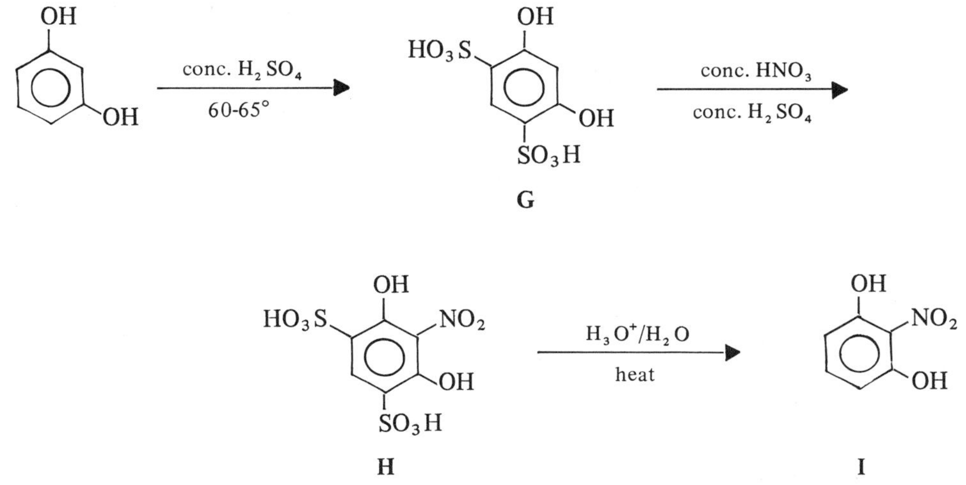

12.36

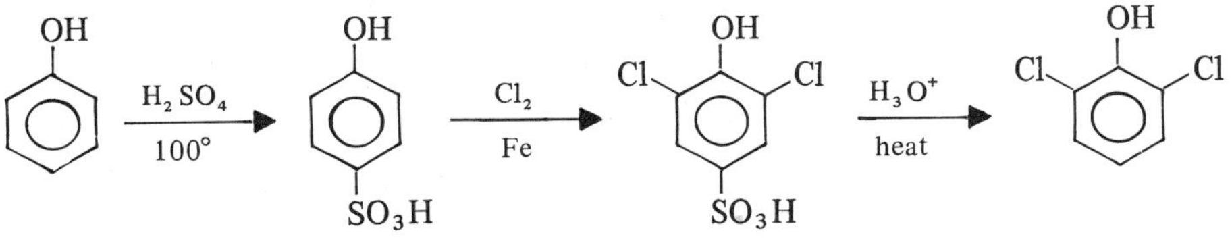

12.37

$$CH_3\overset{\overset{\displaystyle O}{\|}}{C}Cl + AlCl_3 \rightleftharpoons CH_3\overset{+}{C}{=}O + AlCl_4^-$$

$$CH_3\overset{+}{C}{=}O + CH_2{=}CHCH_3 \longrightarrow CH_3\overset{\overset{\displaystyle O}{\|}}{C}CH_2\overset{+}{C}HCH_3$$

$$CH_3\overset{\overset{\displaystyle O}{\|}}{C}CH_2\overset{+}{C}HCH_3 \longrightarrow CH_3\overset{\overset{\displaystyle O}{\|}}{C}CH{=}CHCH_3 + H^+$$

A

$$CH_3\overset{\overset{\displaystyle O}{\|}}{C}CH_2\overset{+}{C}HCH_3 \longrightarrow CH_3\overset{\overset{\displaystyle O}{\|}}{C}CH_2CH{=}CH_2 + H^+$$

B

$$CH_3\overset{\overset{\displaystyle O}{\|}}{C}CH_2\overset{+}{C}HCH_3 \xrightarrow{Cl^-} CH_3\overset{\overset{\displaystyle O}{\|}}{C}CH_2\underset{\underset{\displaystyle Cl}{|}}{C}HCH_3$$

C

12.38 (a)

(1) $C_6H_5\,CH{=}CH{-}CH{=}CH_2 \xrightarrow{\ H^+\ } C_6H_5\,CH{=}CH{-}\overset{+}{C}H{-}CH_3$

$C_6H_5\,\overset{+}{C}H{-}CH{=}CH{-}CH_3$

$C_6H_5\,\overset{\delta+}{C}H{=}\!{=}\!{=}CH{=}\!{=}\!{=}\overset{\delta+}{C}H{-}CH_3$

(2) $C_6H_5\,\overset{\delta+}{C}H{=}\!{=}\!{=}CH{=}\!{=}\!{=}\overset{\delta+}{C}H{-}CH_3 \xrightarrow{\ X^-\ } C_6H_5\,CH{=}CH{-}\underset{\underset{X}{|}}{C}H{-}CH_3$

(b) 1,2-Addition.

(c) Yes. The carbocation given in (a) is a hybrid of *secondary allylic and benzylic* contributors and is therefore more stable than any other possibility; for example,

$C_6H_5\,CH{=}CH{-}CH{=}CH_2 \xrightarrow{\ H^+\ } C_6H_5\,CH_2{-}\overset{+}{C}H{-}CH{=}CH_2$

$C_6H_5\,CH_2{-}CH{=}CH{-}\overset{+}{C}H_2$

A hybrid of allylic contributors only

(d) Since the reaction produces only *the more stable isomer*—that is, the one in which the double bond is conjugated with the benzene ring—the reaction is likely to be under equilibrium control:

$C_6H_5\,\overset{\delta+}{C}H{=}\!{=}\!{=}CH{=}\!{=}\!{=}\overset{\delta+}{C}H{-}CH_3$
$+$
Cl^-

$\longrightarrow\ C_6H_5{-}CH{=}CH{-}\underset{\underset{Cl}{|}}{C}H{-}CH_3$ Actual product
more stable isomer

$\longrightarrow\ C_6H_5\,\underset{\underset{Cl}{|}}{C}H{-}CH{=}CH{-}CH_3$ Not formed
less stable isomer

12.39

(a)

(b) $CH_3-\underset{\underset{C_6H_5}{|}}{C}=CH_2 \xrightarrow{H^+} CH_3-\underset{\underset{C_6H_5}{|}}{\overset{+}{C}}-CH_3 \xrightarrow[C_6H_5]{CH_2=C-CH_3}$

[structure: benzene ring with $C(CH_3)_2$ group and $\overset{+}{CH}(CH_3)C_6H_5$]

[intermediate cation structure with CH_3, CH_3, C_6H_5, H, CH_3] $\xrightarrow{-H^+}$ [indane product structure with CH_3, CH_3, C_6H_5, CH_3]

12.40

[benzene ring] $+$

$CH_3CH{-}\left(CH_2\underset{\underset{CH_3}{|}}{C}{-}\right)_2 CH=CHCH_3$

and

$CH_3CH{-}\left(CH_2\underset{\underset{CH_3}{|}}{CH}\right)_2 CH_2CH=CH_2$

$\underset{\underset{CH_3}{|}}{}$

$\xrightarrow[35\text{-}45°]{AlCl_3}$

$CH_3CH{-}\left(CH_2\underset{\underset{CH_3}{|}}{CH}\right)_2 CH_2\underset{\underset{CH_3}{|}}{CH}{-}$[benzene ring]

and

$CH_3CH{-}\left(CH_2\underset{\underset{CH_3}{|}}{CH}\right)_2{-}\underset{\underset{\underset{CH_3}{|}}{CH_2}}{CH}{-}$[benzene ring]

$\xrightarrow[\text{heat}]{H_2SO_4}$

$CH_3CH{-}\left(CH_2\underset{\underset{CH_3}{|}}{CH}\right)_2 CH_2\underset{\underset{CH_3}{|}}{CH}{-}$[benzene ring]$-SO_3H$

and

$CH_3CH{-}\left(CH_2\underset{\underset{CH_3}{|}}{CH}\right)_2{-}\underset{\underset{\underset{CH_3}{|}}{CH_2}}{CH}{-}$[benzene ring]$-SO_3H$

$\xrightarrow{NaOH}$

$CH_3CH\left(CH_2\underset{\underset{CH_3}{|}}{CH}\right)_2 CH_2\underset{\underset{CH_3}{|}}{CH}{-}$[benzene ring]$-SO_3Na$

and

$CH_3CH\left(CH_2\underset{\underset{CH_3}{|}}{CH}\right)_2{-}\underset{\underset{\underset{CH_3}{|}}{CH_2}}{CH}{-}$[benzene ring]$-SO_3Na$

12.41   (a)   Large *ortho* substituents prevent the two rings from becoming coplanar and prevent rotation about the single bond that connects them. If the correct substitution patterns are present, the molecule as a whole will be chiral. Thus enantiomeric forms are possible even though the molecules do not have a chiral carbon. The compound with 2-NO$_2$, 6-COOH, 2′-NO$_2$, 6′-COOH is an example.

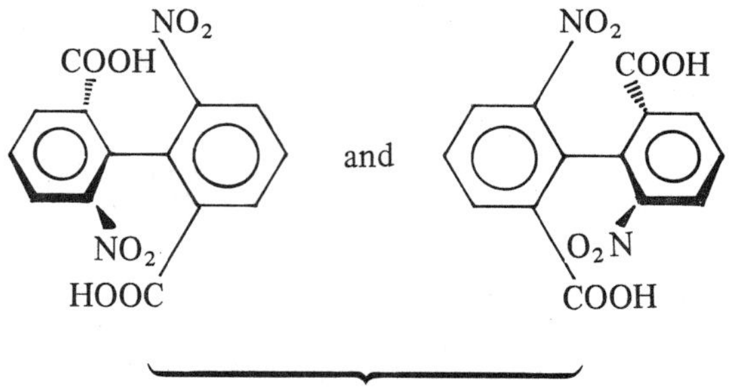

These molecules are nonsuperposable mirror reflections and, thus, are enantiomers.

(b)   Yes

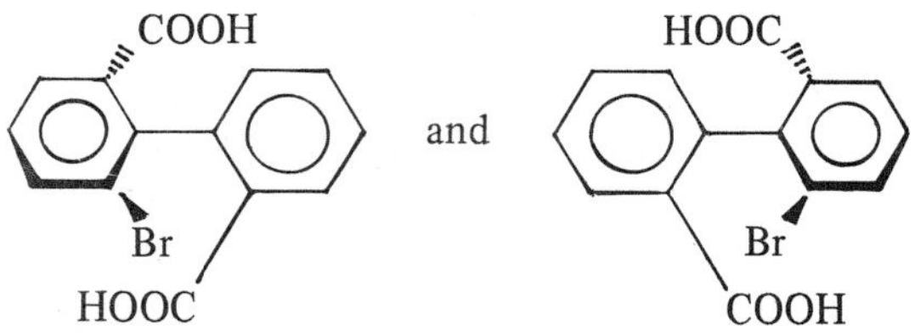

(c)   This molecule has a plane of symmetry.

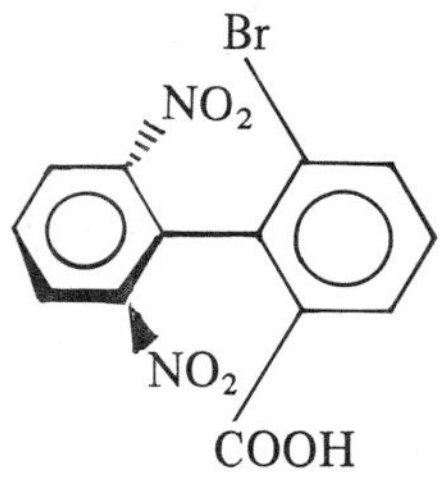

The plane of the page is a plane of symmetry.

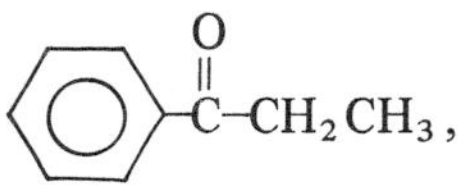

12.42

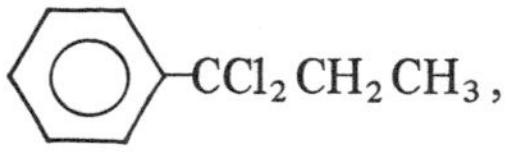

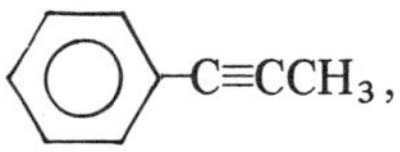

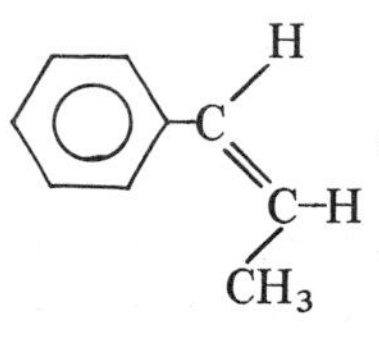

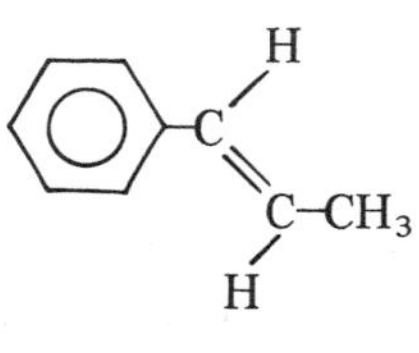

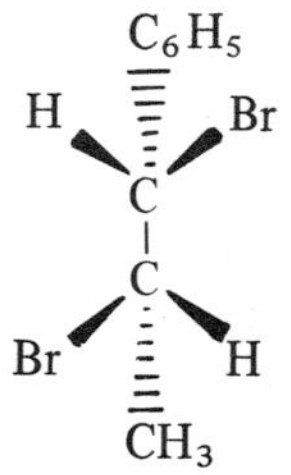

G.

12.43

(a)   (b) This arenium ion is especially stable because its seven-

membered ring is an aromatic cation.   (c)

SECTION REFERENCES FOR ADDITIONAL PROBLEMS

12.22	12.3-12.5, 12.8		**12.33**	12.10, 12.11, 12.12C
12.23	12.8		**12.34**	12.7
12.24	12.10, 12.11		**12.35**	12.8, 12.12
12.25	12.3-12.7		**12.36**	12.12
12.26	12.11		**12.37**	12.7
12.27	12.3-12.7, 12.10		**12.38**	12.11
12.28	12.9D		**12.39**	6.12, 12.7
12.29	12.9D		**12.40**	12.6, 12.5
12.30	12.9D		**12.41**	8.16
12.31	8.9		**12.42**	12.7, 12.10, 12.11
12.32	12.9		**12.43**	12.7

SELF-TEST

12.1   Write the structural formula of the missing reactants or *major* organic products. Give more than one product *only* if they are produced in approximately equal amounts. If more than one step is needed label them (1) step 1, (2) step 2, etc.

(a) [p-methylacetanilide] + HONO₂ $\xrightarrow{\text{H}_2\text{SO}_4}$ [   ]

(b) [benzene] $\xrightarrow{\hspace{3cm}}$ [acetophenone]

(c) [N-phenylbenzamide] + SO₃ $\xrightarrow{\text{H}_2\text{SO}_4}$ [   ]

(d) [ethylbenzene]—CH₂CH₃ + Br₂ $\xrightarrow{h\nu}$ [   ]

(e) [toluene, CH₃] $\xrightarrow{\hspace{3cm}}$ [3-nitrobenzoic acid, CO₂H, NO₂]

(f) [toluene, CH₃] $\xrightarrow{\hspace{3cm}}$ [2,6-dinitrotoluene, O₂N, CH₃, NO₂] (major product)

(g) [benzonitrile, CN] + Br₂ $\xrightarrow{\text{FeBr}_3}$ (C₇H₄BrN) [   ]

(h) Draw the structural formulas of the three principal resonance structures of the inter-mediate (arenium ion) in reaction (g) above.

(i) OCH$_3$ + SO$_3$ $\xrightarrow{\text{H}_2\text{SO}_4}$

(j) CH$_3$ + CH$_3\overset{\overset{\displaystyle O}{\|}}{C}$—Cl $\xrightarrow{\text{AlCl}_3}$

(k) NO$_2$ —CH$_2$— $\xrightarrow[\text{H}_2\text{SO}_4]{\substack{\text{HNO}_3 \text{ (one} \\ \text{molar equivalent)}}}$

(l) —CH$_2$— $\xrightarrow{\text{NBS}}$

12.2   Write the structural formula for the organic ion that serves as the intermediate in the ring bromination of toluene.

12.3 Write two additional resonance structures for the following ion:

12.4 Supply the structural formulas of the missing compounds.

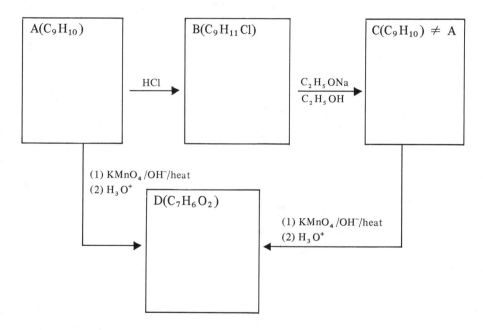

12.5 Outline a practical laboratory synthesis of *o*-nitropropylbenzene starting from benzene and any necessary reagents.

SUPPLEMENTARY PROBLEMS

S12.1   Show all steps in a laboratory synthesis of each compound below starting with phenol, toluene, and any compounds of four carbon atoms or fewer.

(a)

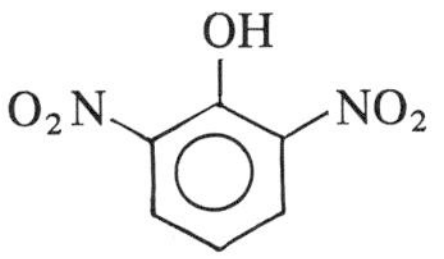

(b)

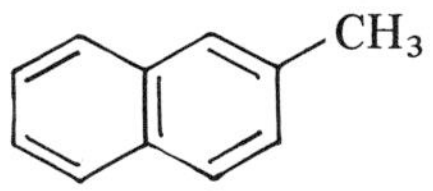

S12.2   Supply the formulas of the unknown compounds.

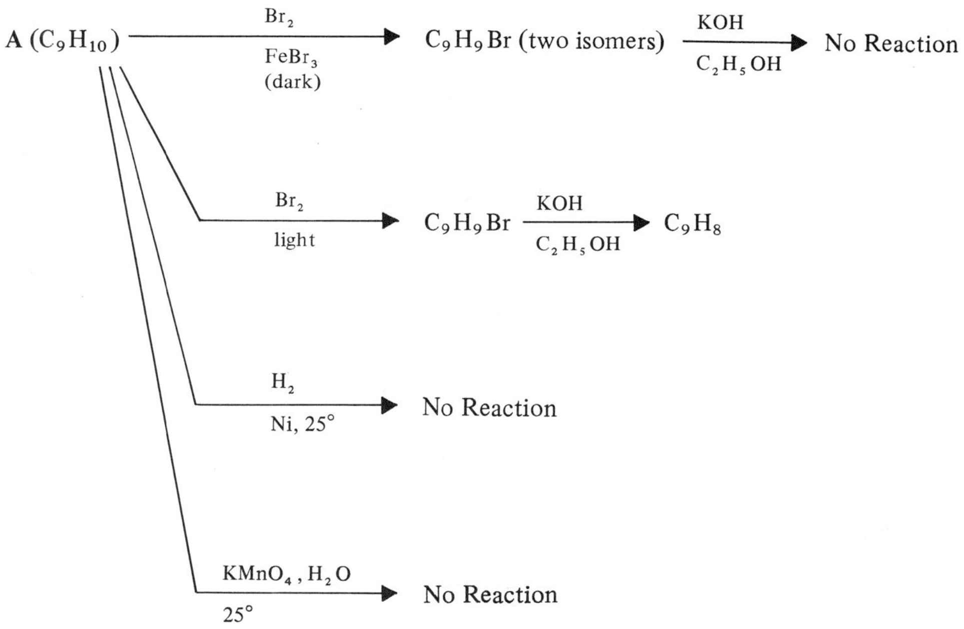

SOLUTIONS TO SUPPLEMENTARY PROBLEMS

S12.1

(a)

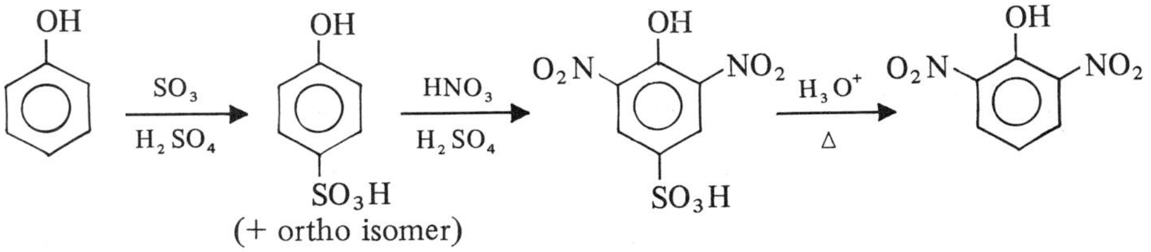

(+ ortho isomer)

(b)

S12.2 The facts that **A** does not add H_2 and does not react with $KMnO_4$ tell us that it has no alkene double bond. The formula C_9H_{10} suggests an aromatic ring. If there were only one alkyl substituent, it would contain: $C_9H_{10} - C_6H_5 = C_3H_5$, which would be unsaturated. The substituent must therefore be a ring. A cyclopropyl ring would have added H_2. We thus conclude that the ring is fused. The remaining reactions are shown:

13

PHYSICAL METHODS OF STRUCTURE DETERMINATION. NUCLEAR MAGNETIC RESONANCE SPECTROSCOPY. INFRARED SPECTROSCOPY

SOLUTIONS TO PROBLEMS

13.1 The methyl protons of 15,16-dimethyldihydropyrene are highly shielded by the induced field in the center of the aromatic system where the induced field opposes the applied field (p 523).

13.2 (a) The six protons (hydrogens) of ethane are equivalent:

$$\underset{CH_3-CH_3}{\overset{(a)\quad(a)}{}}$$

Ethane gives a single signal in its proton nmr spectrum.

(b) Propane has two different sets of equivalent protons:

$$\underset{CH_3-CH_2-CH_3}{\overset{(a)\quad(b)\quad(a)}{}}$$

Propane gives two signals.

(c) The six protons of dimethyl ether are equivalent:

$$\underset{CH_3-O-CH_3}{\overset{(a)\qquad(a)}{}}$$

One signal.

(d) Three different sets of equivalent protons:

Three signals.

(e) Two different sets of equivalent protons:

$$\underset{\underset{\text{Two signals}}{}}{\overset{(a)\qquad\qquad(b)}{CH_3-\overset{\displaystyle O}{\overset{\|}{C}}-O-CH_3}}$$

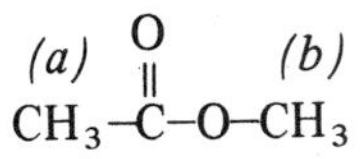

Two signals

(f) Three different sets of equivalent protons:

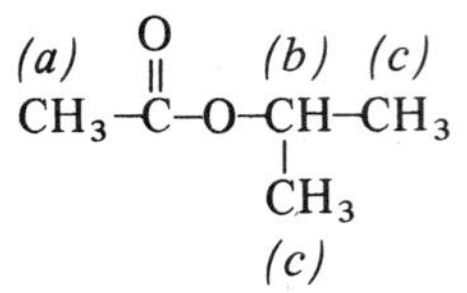

$$\overset{(a)\qquad\qquad(b)\ (c)}{CH_3-\overset{\displaystyle O}{\overset{\|}{C}}-O-\underset{\underset{(c)}{\overset{|}{CH_3}}}{CH}-CH_3}$$

Three signals.

13.3

(a)

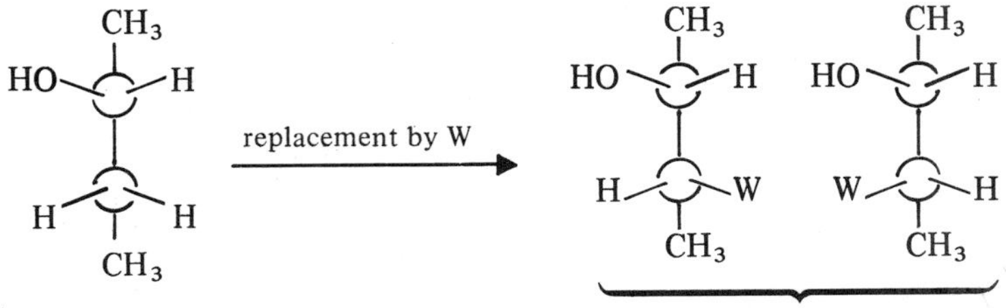

replacement by W

Diastereomers

(b) Six,

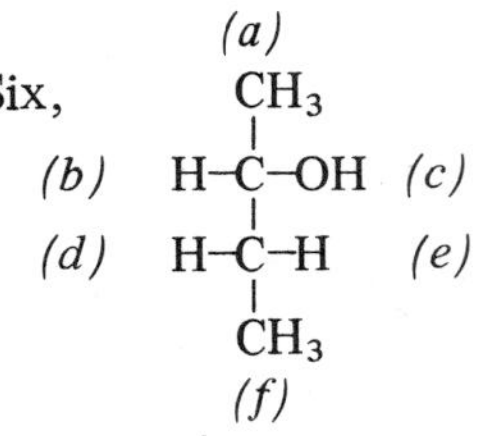

$$\overset{(a)}{\underset{(f)}{\underset{\overset{|}{CH_3}}{\overset{\overset{|}{CH_3}}{\underset{(d)\ \ H-\overset{|}{\underset{|}{C}}-H\ \ (e)}{(b)\ \ H-\overset{|}{C}-OH\ \ (c)}}}}}$$

(c) Six signals.

13.4

(a) Two, $\overset{(a)\ \ (b)\ \ \ (b)\ \ (a)}{CH_3-CH_2-CH_2-CH_3}$

(b) Three, $\overset{(a)\ \ (b)\ \ \ \ (c)}{CH_3-CH_2-O-H}$

(c) Four, $\underset{\underset{(b)\qquad(d)}{H\qquad\qquad H}}{\overset{\overset{(a)\qquad\quad(c)}{CH_3\qquad\ H}}{\diagup C=C\diagdown}}$

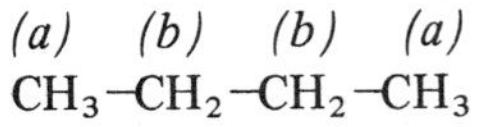

(d) Two, $\underset{\underset{(b)\qquad(a)}{H\qquad\quad CH_3}}{\overset{\overset{(a)\qquad\ (b)}{CH_3\qquad\ H}}{\diagup C=C\diagdown}}$

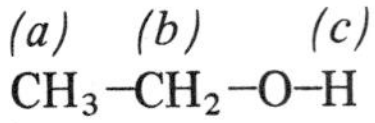

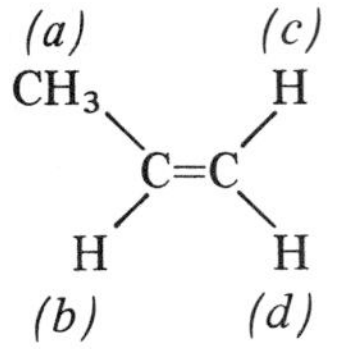

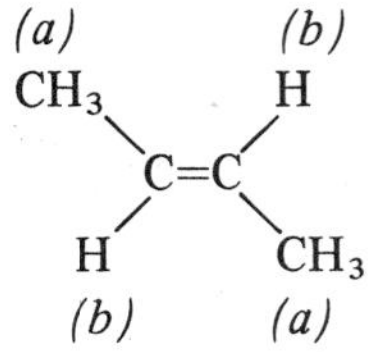

(e) Four,

$$\underset{(a)}{CH_3}-\underset{(b)}{CHBr}-\overset{\overset{\displaystyle H\;(c)}{|}}{\underset{\underset{\displaystyle H\;(d)}{|}}{C}}-Br$$

(f) Two,

(b) H   (a)   H (b)
        CH₃
(b) H   H (b)
        CH₃
        (a)

(g) Three,

(a)   (b)
CH₃(c)   H
    H
H   CH₃
(b) H   (a)
    (c)

(h) Four,

(a)   (a)
CH₃(c)   CH₃
    H
H   H
(b) H   (b)
    (d)

(i) Six,

$$\underset{(a)}{CH_3}-\underset{(b)}{CH_2}-\underset{(c)}{CH_2}$$

C=C, H (e)

H   H (f)
(d)

13.5   The proton nmr spectrum of $CHBr_2CHCl_2$ consists of two doublets. The doublet from the proton of the $-CHCl_2$ group should occur at lowest magnetic field strength because the greater electronegativity of chlorine reduces the electron density in the vicinity of the $-CHCl_2$ proton, and consequently, reduces its shielding relative to $-CHBr_2$.

13.6   The determining factors here are the number of chlorine atoms attached to the carbons bearing protons and the deshielding that results from chlorine's electronegativity. In 1,1,2-trichloroethane the proton that gives rise to the triplet is on a carbon that bears two chlorines, and the signal from this proton is downfield. In 1,1,2,3,3-pentachloropropane the proton that gives rise to the triplet is on a carbon that bears only one chlorine; the signal from this proton is upfield.

13.7 The signal from the three equivalent protons designated *(a)* should be split into a doublet by the proton *(b)*. This doublet, because of the electronegativity of the attached chlorines, should occur downfield.

$$
\begin{array}{cc}
(a) & (b) \\
\end{array}
$$
$$
(Cl_2CH)_3\text{---}CH
$$

The proton designated *(b)* should be split into a quartet by the three equivalent protons *(a)*. The quartet should occur upfield.

13.8

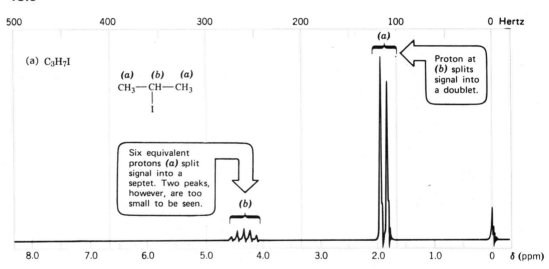

(a) C_3H_7I

$$
\begin{array}{ccc}
(a) & (b) & (a) \\
CH_3\text{---} & CH\text{---} & CH_3 \\
& | & \\
& I & \\
\end{array}
$$

Proton at *(b)* splits signal into a doublet.

Six equivalent protons *(a)* split signal into a septet. Two peaks, however, are too small to be seen.

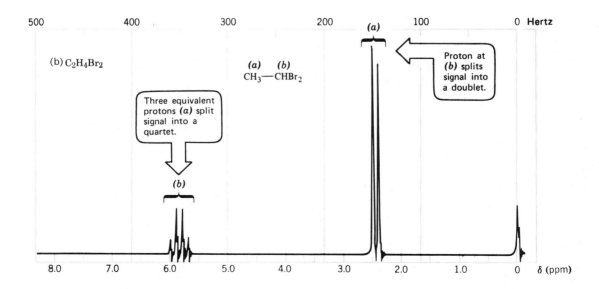

(b) $C_2H_4Br_2$

$$
\begin{array}{cc}
(a) & (b) \\
CH_3\text{---} & CHBr_2 \\
\end{array}
$$

Proton at *(b)* splits signal into a doublet.

Three equivalent protons *(a)* split signal into a quartet.

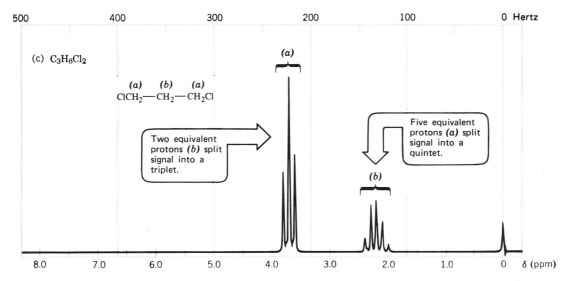

Proton nmr spectra for Problem 13.8. (Spectrum courtesy of Varian Associates, Palo Alto, Calif.)

13.9   (a)

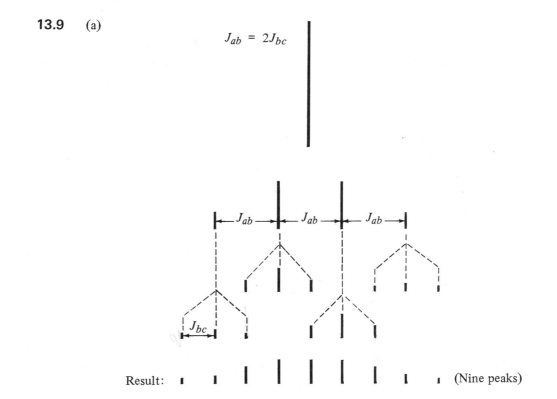

(b) $J_{ab} = J_{bc}$

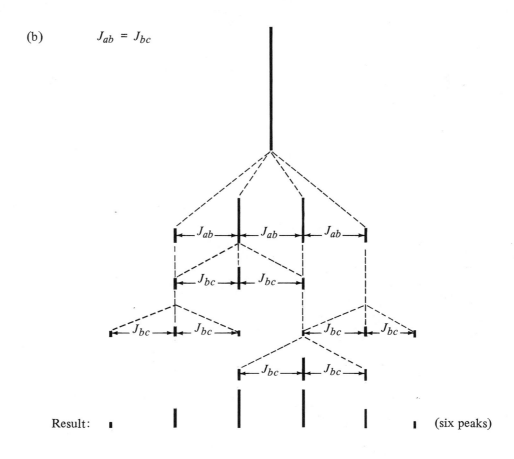

Result: ▎ ▌ ▌ ▌ ▌ ▎   (six peaks)

13.10 (a) $C_6H_5CH(CH_3)_2$

(b) $C_6H_5\underset{\overset{|}{NH_2}}{CH}CH_3$

(c)

Proton nmr spectra for Problem 13.10 are given on page 271.

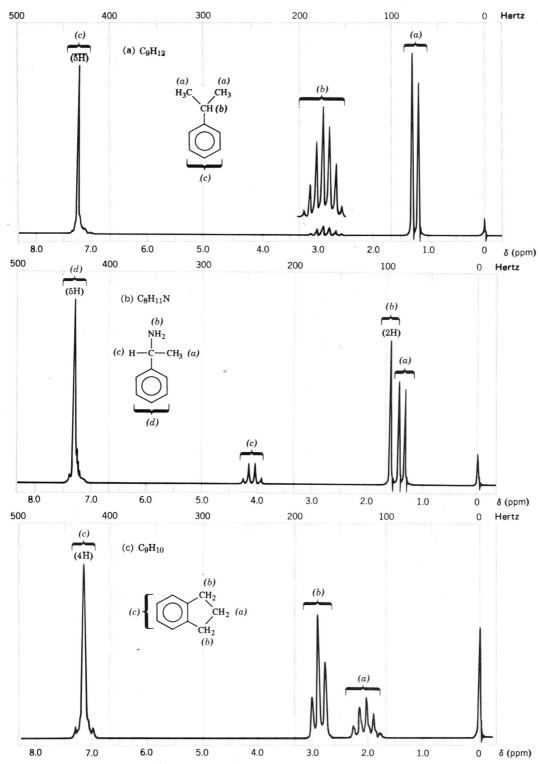

Proton nmr spectra for Problem 13.10 (Spectra courtesy of Varian Associates, Palo Alto, Calif.)

13.11

(a)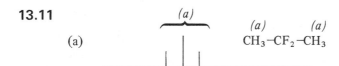

$$CH_3-CF_2-CH_3$$

(b)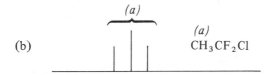

$$CH_3CF_2Cl$$

(c)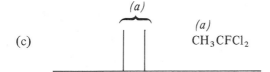

$$CH_3CFCl_2$$

(d)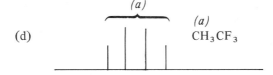

$$CH_3CF_3$$

13.12   A single unsplit signal, because the proton is rapidly shifted from axial to equatorial positions.

13.13

$$C_6H_5\overset{+}{C}\underset{C_6H_5}{\big|}\!\!-\!\!\underset{CH_3}{\overset{\overset{(b)}{H}}{\big|}}\!\!C\!\!-\!\!CH_3$$

(a) Doublet, δ 1.48 (6H)
(b) Multiplet, δ 4.45 (1H)
(c) Multiplet, δ 8.0 (10H)

13.14   Because of their symmetries, *p*-dibromobenzene would give two ^{13}C signals, *o*-dibromobenzene would give three, and *m*-dibromobenzene would give four.

Two signals   Three signals   Four signals

13.15   A is 1-chloro-3-methylbutane. The following are the signal assignments:

$$\underset{\text{(d)}}{\text{ClCH}_2}\underset{\text{(c)}}{\text{CH}_2}\underset{\text{(b)}}{\text{CH}}\underset{\text{(a)}}{(\text{CH}_3)_2}$$

(a) δ 22q

(b) δ 26d

(c) δ 42t

(d) δ 43t

B is 2-chloro-2-methylbutane. The following are the signal assignments:

$$\underset{\text{(a)}}{\text{CH}_3}\underset{\text{(c)}}{\text{CH}_2}\underset{\underset{\text{(d)}}{}}{\overset{\overset{\text{Cl}}{|}}{\text{C}}}\underset{\text{(b)}}{(\text{CH}_3)_2}$$

(a) δ 9q

(b) δ 32q

(c) δ 39t

(d) δ 71s

C is 1-chloropentane. The following are the signal assignments.

$$\underset{\text{(e)}}{\text{ClCH}_2}\underset{\text{(d)}}{\text{CH}_2}\underset{\text{(c)}}{\text{CH}_2}\underset{\text{(b)}}{\text{CH}_2}\underset{\text{(a)}}{\text{CH}_3}$$

(a) δ 14q

(b) δ 22t

(c) δ 29t

(d) δ 33t

(e) δ 45t

13.16

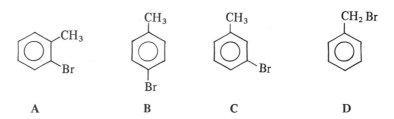

A B C D

A. Strong absorption at 740 cm^{-1} is characteristic of ortho substitution.

B. A very strong absorbtion peak at 795 cm^{-1} is characteristic of para substitution.

C. Strong absorbtion peaks at 680 cm^{-1} and 760 cm^{-1} are characteristic of meta substitution.

D. Strong absorption peaks at 693 cm^{-1} and 765 cm^{-1} are characteristic of a mono-substituted benzene ring.

13.17

(a)

$$\underset{(a)}{CH_3}-\underset{\underset{\underset{(a)}{CH_3}}{|}}{\overset{\overset{(a)}{\overset{CH_3}{|}}}{C}}-OH\,(b)$$

(a)   Singlet, δ 1.28 (9H)
(b)   Singlet, δ 1.35 (1H)

(b)

$$\overset{(a)\ \ (b)\ \ (a)}{CH_3}-\underset{\underset{Br}{|}}{CH}-CH_3$$

(a)   Doublet, δ 1.71 (6H)
(b)   Septet, δ 4.32 (1H)

(c)

$$\overset{(b)\ \ \ \ \ (c)\ \ (a)}{CH_3}-\overset{\overset{O}{||}}{C}-CH_2-CH_3$$

(a)   Triplet, δ 1.05 (3H)
(b)   Singlet, δ 2.13 (3H)
(c)   Quartet, δ 2.47 (2H)
C=O, 1720 cm^{-1}

(d) ⬡—$\overset{(b)\ \ (a)}{CH_2}$—OH
   (c)

(a)   Singlet, δ 2.43 (1H)
(b)   Singlet, δ 4.58 (2H)
(c)   Multiplet, δ 7.28 (5H)
O—H, 3200-3600 cm^{-1}

(e)

$$CH_3-\underset{\underset{(a)}{\underset{CH_3}{|}}}{\overset{(b)\ \ (c)}{CH}}-CH_2\,Cl$$

(a)   Doublet, δ 104 (6H)
(b)   Multiplet, δ 1.95 (1H)
(c)   Doublet, δ 3.35 (2H)

(f)

$$C_6H_5-\underset{\underset{(c)}{\underset{C_6H_5}{|}}}{\overset{(b)\overset{\overset{O}{||}}{\ }(a)}{CH}}-C-CH_3$$

(a)   Singlet, δ 2.20 (3H)
(b)   Singlet, δ 5.08 (1H)
(c)   Multiplet, δ 7.25 (10H)
C=O, near 1720 cm^{-1}

(g)

$$\overset{(a)\ \ \ \ (b)\ \ \ \ (c)\ \ (d)}{CH_3}-CH_2-\underset{\underset{Br}{|}}{CH}COOH$$

(a)   Triplet, δ 1.08 (3H)
(b)   Multiplet, δ 2.07 (2H)
(c)   Triplet, δ 4.23 (1H)
(d)   Singlet, δ 10.97 (1H)
O—H, 2500-3000 cm^{-1}

(h) ⬡—$\overset{(b)\ \ (a)}{CH_2}$—CH$_3$
   (c)

(a)   Triplet, δ 1.25 (3H)
(b)   Quartet, δ 2.68 (2H)
(c)   Multiplet, δ 7.23 (5H)

(a)   (b)   (c)   (d)
(i) $CH_3-CH_2-O-CH_2COOH$

(a)   Triplet, δ 1.27 (3H)
(b)   Quartet, δ 3.66 (2H)
(c)   Singlet, δ 4.13 (2H)
(d)   Singlet, δ 10.95 (1H)
O–H, 2500-3000 cm^{-1}

(a) (b) (a)
(j) $CH_3-CH-CH_3$
          |
          NO_2

(a)   Doublet, δ 1.55 (6H)
(b)   Septet, δ 4.67 (1H)

(a)   (b) (b)   (a)
(k) $CH_3O-CH_2CH_2-OCH_3$

(a)   Singlet, δ 3.25 (6H)
(b)   Singlet, δ 3.45 (4H)

(b)   O (c)
       ‖
(l) $CH_3-C-CH-CH_3$
              |
              CH_3 (a)

(a)   Doublet, δ 1.10 (6H)
(b)   Singlet, δ 2.10 (3H)
(c)   Septet, δ 2.50 (1H)
C=O, near 1720 cm^{-1}

(b) (a)
(m)   ⬡–CH–CH$_3$
           |
           Br
      (c)

(a)   Doublet, δ 2.0 (3H)
(b)   Quartet, δ 5.15 (1H)
(c)   Multiplet, δ 7.35 (5H)

13.18   Compound **E** is phenylacetylene, $C_6H_5C{\equiv}CH$. We can make the following assignments in the infrared spectrum:

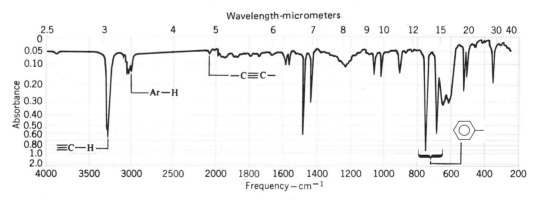

The infrared spectrum of compound **E** *(Problem 13.18). (Spectrum courtesy of Sadtler Research Laboratories Inc., Philadelphia, Pa.)*

13.19   A proton nmr signal this far upfield indicates that cyclooctatetraene is a cyclic polyene and is not aromatic

13.20 Both [14]annulene and dehydro[14]annulene are aromatic as shown by the signals at δ 7.78 (10H) and at δ 8.0, (10H) respectively. [14]Annulene has four "internal" protons (δ −0.61)and dehydro[14]annulene has only two (δ 0.0).

13.21 Compound **F** is *p*-isopropyltoluene. Assignments are shown in the spectra reproduced below.

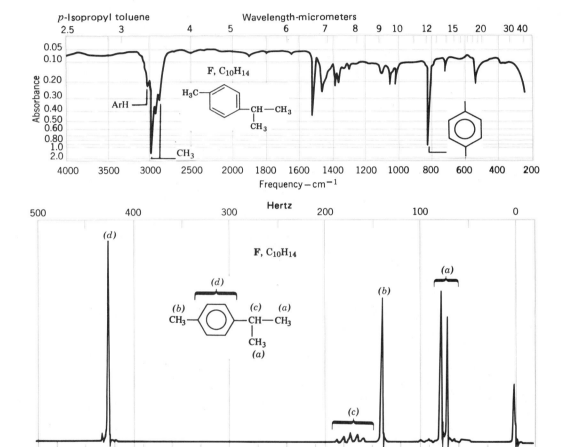

The ir and proton nmr spectra of compound F, Problem 13.21 (Proton nmr spectrum adapted from Varian Associates, Palo Alto, Calif. IR spectrum adapted from Sadtler Research Laboratories, Philadelphia, Pa.)

13.22 (a) In SbF_5 the carbocations formed initially apparently undergo a complex series of rearrangements to the more stable *tert*-butyl cation.

(b) All of the cations formed initially rearrange to the more stable *tert*-pentyl cation,

$$CH_3CH_2\overset{\displaystyle CH_3}{\underset{\displaystyle CH_3}{\overset{|}{\underset{|}{C^+}}}}$$

The spectrum of the *tert*-pentyl cation should consist of a singlet (6H), a quartet (2H), and a triplet (3H). The triplet should be most upfield and the quartet most downfield.

13.23   (a)   Four unsplit signals,

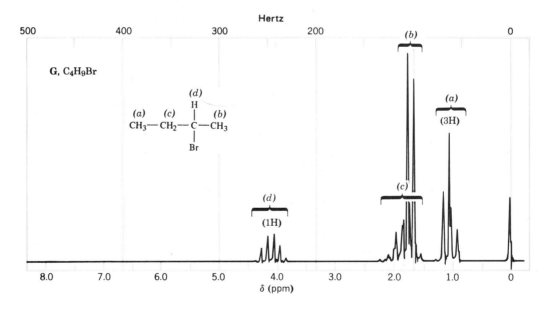

(b)   Absorptions arising from: =C–H, CH$_3$, and C=O groups.

13.24   Compound **G** is 2-bromobutane. Assignments are shown in the spectra reproduced below.

The proton nmr spectrum of compound G (Problem 13.24). (Spectrum courtesy of Varian Associates, Palo Alto, Calif.)

Compound **H** is 2,3-dibromopropene. Assignments are shown in the spectrum on the next page.

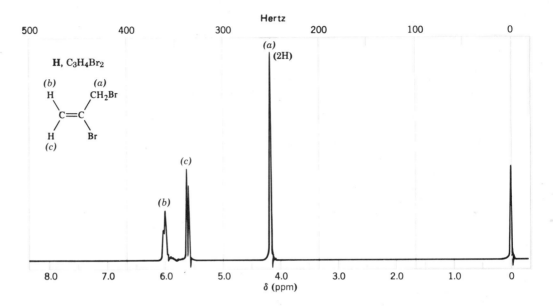

*The proton nmr spectrum of compound **H** (Problem 13.24). (Spectrum courtesy of Varian Associates, Palo Alto, Calif.).*

13.25 Compound **I** is *p*-methoxytoluene. Assignments are shown in the spectra reproduced below.

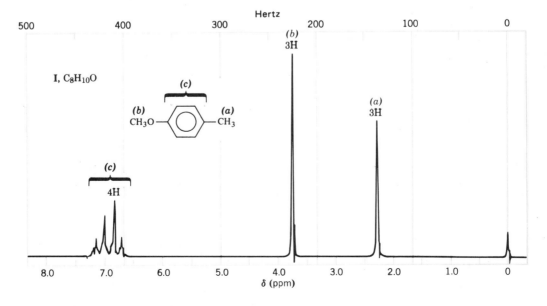

*The proton nmr spectrum of compound **I** (Problem 13.25). (Spectrum courtesy of Varian Associates, Palo Alto, Calif.)*

Wavelength-micrometers

I, $C_8H_{10}O$

ArH

CH₃

*The infrared spectrum of compound **I** (Problem 13.25). (Spectrum courtesy of Sadtler Research Laboratories, Philadelphia, Pa.)*

13.26 Compound **J** is *cis*-1,2-dichloroethene,

We can make the following infrared assignments:

> 3125 cm^{-1}, alkene C–H stretching
> 1625 cm^{-1}, C=C stretching
> 695 cm^{-1}, out-of-plane bending of cis double bond.

13.27 (a) Compound **K** is,

(a) O *(b) (c)*
         ‖
CH₃–C–CH–CH₃
             |
             OH *(d)*

(a) Singlet δ 2.15   *(d)* Singlet δ 3.75
(b) Quartet δ 4.25   C=O, 1720 cm⁻¹
(c) Doublet δ 1.35

(b) When the compound is dissolved in D_2O, the –OH proton *(d)* is replaced by a deuteron and thus the proton nmr absorption peak disappears.

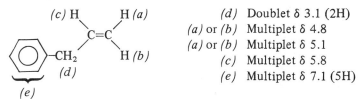

13.28 Compound **L** is allylbenzene,

(c) H   H *(a)*
         \\   /
          C=C
         /   \\
   –CH₂   H *(b)*
   (d)

(d) Doublet δ 3.1 (2H)
(a) or *(b)* Multiplet δ 4.8
(a) or *(b)* Multiplet δ 5.1
(c) Multiplet δ 5.8
(e) Multiplet δ 7.1 (5H)

The following infrared assignments can be made.

3035 cm^{-1}, C–H stretching of benzene ring
3020 cm^{-1}, C–H stretching of –CH=CH$_2$ group
2925 cm^{-1} and 2853 cm^{-1}, C–H stretching of –CH$_2$–group
1640 cm^{-1}, C=C stretching
990 cm^{-1} and 915 cm^{-1}, C–H bendings of –CH=CH$_2$ group
740 cm^{-1} and 695 cm^{-1}, C–H bendings of –C$_6$H$_5$ group

The ultraviolet absorbance maximum at 255 nm is indicative of a benzene ring that is not conjugated with a double bond.

13.29 Run the spectrum with the spectrometer operating at a different magnetic field strength (i.e., at 30 MHz or at 100 MHz). If the peaks are two singlets the distance between them—*when measured in Hertz*— will change because chemical shifts *expressed in Hertz* are proportional to the strength of the applied field (see p. 525). If, however, the two peaks represent a doublet then the distance that separates them, expressed in Hertz, will not change because this distance represents the magnitude of the coupling constant and coupling constants are independent of the applied magnetic field (p. 531).

13.30 Compound **M** is *m*-ethyltoluene. We can make the following assignments in the spectra.

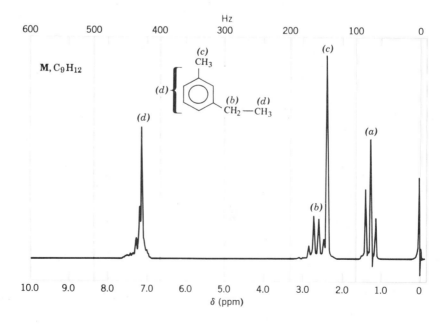

The proton nmr spectrum of compound **M**, Problem 13.30. (Spectrum courtesy of Aldrich Chemical Co., Milwaukee, Wisconsin.)

Meta substitution is indicated by the strong peaks at 690 cm^{-1} and 780 cm^{-1} in the infrared spectrum given on the next page.

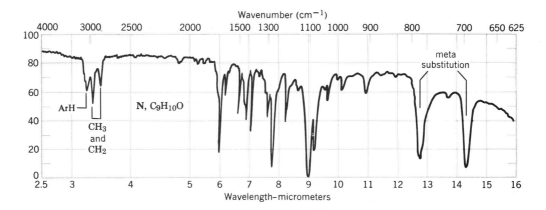

The infrared spectrum of compound N, Problem 13.31. (Spectrum courtesy of Aldrich Chemical Co., Milwaukee, Wis.)

13.31 Compound **N** is $C_6H_5CH=CHOCH_3$. The absence of absorption peaks due to O–H or C=O stretching in the infrared spectrum of **N** suggests that the oxygen atom is present as part of an ether linkage. The (5H) proton nmr multiplet at δ 7.3 strongly suggests the presence of a monosubstituted benzene ring; this is confirmed by the strong peaks at ~690 cm^{-1} and ~770 cm^{-1} in the infrared spectrum.

   We can make the following assignments in the proton nmr spectrum:

     (a) (b) (c) (d)
   C_6H_5–CH=CH–OCH$_3$

   (a) Multiplet δ 7.3
   (c) Doublet δ 6.05
   (b) Doublet δ 5.15
   (d) Singlet δ 3.7

*13.32 That the proton nmr spectrum shows only one signal indicates that all 12 protons of the carbocation are equivalent, and suggests very strongly that what is being observed is the bromonium ion:

$$CH_3 \overset{\overset{\displaystyle Br^+}{\diagup \diagdown}}{\underset{C \!-\! C}{}} CH_3$$

While this experiment does not prove that bromonium ions are intermediates in alkene additions, it does show that bromonium ions are capable of existence and thus makes postulating them as intermediates more plausible.

*13.33 In the presence of SbF$_5$, **I** dissociates first to the cyclic allylic cation, **II**, and then to the aromatic dication, **III**.

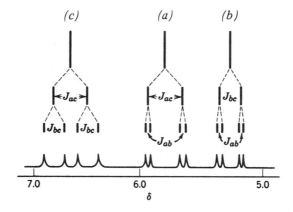

13.34 The vinylic protons of *p*-chlorostyrene should give a spectrum approximately like the following:

13.35 Compound **O** is 1,4-cyclohexadiene and P is cyclohexane.

(a) δ 26.0t

(b) δ 124.5d

13.36 The molecular formula of **Q** (C_7H_8) indicates an index of hydrogen deficiency (Sect. 6.5) of four. The hydrogenation experiment suggests that **Q** contains two double bonds (or one triple bond). **Q**, therefore, must contain two rings.

The ^{13}C spectrum shows that **Q** is 2,5-bicyclo[2.2.1]heptadiene. The following reasoning shows one way to arrive at this conclusion: There is only one signal (δ 143) in the region for a doubly bonded carbon. This fact indicates that the doubly-bonded carbons are all equivalent. That the signal at δ 143 is a doublet in the proton off-resonance decoupled spectrum indicates that each of the doubly bonded carbons bears one hydrogen. Because of their multiplicities in the proton off-resonance spectrum the signal at δ 75 can be assigned to a —CH_2— group and the signal at δ50 to a ⟩C—H group. The molecular formula tells us that the compound must contain two $\geq$C–H groups, and since only one signal occurs in the ^{13}C spectrum, these $\geq$C–H groups must be equivalent. Putting this all together we get the following:

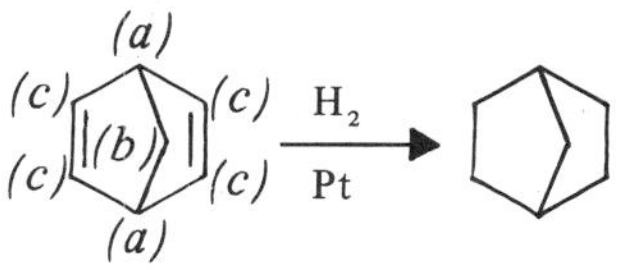

(a) δ 50d

(b) δ 75t

(c) δ 143t

13.37 That S decolorizes bromine indicates that it is unsaturated. The molecular formula of S allows us to calculate an index of hydrogen deficiency equal to one. Therefore, we can conclude that S has one double bond.

The ^{13}C spectrum shows the doubly bonded carbons at δ 130 and δ 135. In the proton off-resonance decoupled spectrum, one of these signals (δ 130) is a singlet indicating a doubly bonded carbon that bears no hydrogens; the other (δ 135) is a doublet indicating that the other doubly bonded carbon bears one hydrogen. We can now arrive at the following partial structure.

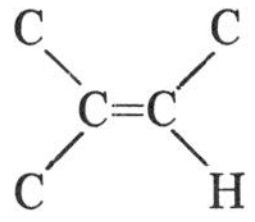

The three most upfield signals (δ19, δ28, and δ31) are all quartets indicating that these signals all arise from methyl groups. The signal at δ32 is a singlet indicating a carbon with no hydrogens. Putting these facts together allows us to arrive at the following structure.

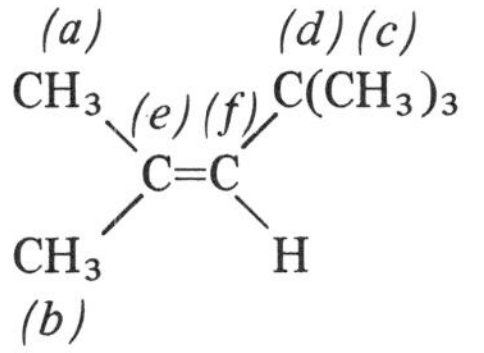

(a) δ 19q

(b) δ 28q

(c) δ 31q

(d) δ 32s

(e) δ 130s

(f) δ 135d

Although the structure given above is the actual compound, other reasonable structures that one might be led to are:

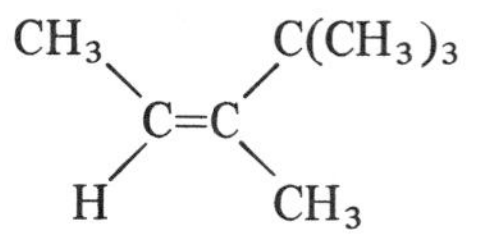

CH$_3$ C(CH$_3$)$_3$ CH$_3$ CH$_3$
   C=C   and   C=C
 H   CH$_3$ H   C(CH$_3$)$_3$

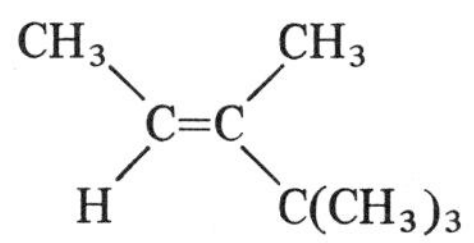

13.38

The infrared absorption band at 1745 cm^{-1} indicates the presence of a $\rangle$C=O group in a five-membered ring, and the signal at δ218.2 can be assigned to the carbon of this carbonyl group.

There are only two other signals in the ^{13}C spectrum; their multiplicities (triplets) in the proton off-resonance decoupled spectrum suggest two equivalent sets of two —CH$_2$— groups each. Putting these facts together, we arrive at cyclopentanone as the structure for **T**.

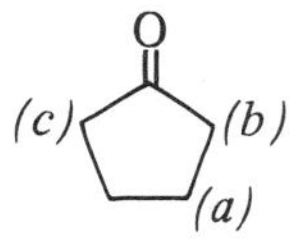

(c) ⟨structure⟩ (b)
       (a)
      T

(a) δ 23.5t

(b) δ 38.0t

(c) δ 218.2t

SECTION REFERENCES FOR ADDITIONAL PROBLEMS

SELF-TEST

13.1   Propose a structure that is consistent with each set of data below.

(a) C_4H_9Br Proton nmr spectrum
                          singlet δ 1.7

(b) $C_4H_7Br_3$ Proton nmr spectrum
                          singlet δ 1.95 (3H)
                          singlet δ 3.9 (4H)

(c) C_8H_{16} Proton nmr spectrum   IR spectrum
                          singlet δ 1.0 (9H)   3040, 2950, 1640 cm^{-1}
                          singlet δ 1.75 (3H)   and other peaks.
                          singlet δ 1.9 (2H)
                          singlet δ 4.6 (1H)
                          singlet δ 4.8 (1H)

(d) $C_9H_{10}O$ Proton nmr spectrum   IR spectrum
                          singlet δ 2.0 (3H)   3100, 3000, 1720,
                          singlet δ 3.75 (2H)   740, 700 cm^{-1}
                          singlet δ 7.2 (5H)   and other peaks.

(e) $C_5H_7NO_2$ Proton nmr spectrum   IR spectrum
                          triplet δ 1.2 (3H)   2980, 2260, 1750 cm^{-1}
                          singlet δ 3.5 (2H)   and other peaks.
                          quartet δ 4.2 (2H)   This compound has a
                                                       nitro group.

SUPPLEMENTARY PROBLEM

S13.1   Explain some advantages of ^{13}C nmr spectroscopy over proton nmr spectroscopy.

SOLUTION TO SUPPLEMENTARY PROBLEM

S13.1   In ^{13}C spectroscopy, we observe the carbon skeleton directly, and, therefore, we observe
          peaks for *all* carbon atoms whether they bear hydrogen atoms or not.
          ^{13}C chemical shifts occur over a greater range than proton nmr chemical shifts.
          We do not observe spin-spin couplings between carbon nuclei in ^{13}C spectra.
          In proton off-resonance decoupled spectra CH_3- groups appear as quartets,

          $-CH_2-$ groups as triplets, $\geq C-H$ groups as doublets, and $-\overset{|}{\underset{|}{C}}-$ groups as singlets.

          (A disadvantage of ^{13}C spectroscopy is that we do not get a quantitative measure
          of the relative number of the different types of carbons.)

E

SPECIAL TOPIC
Mass Spectroscopy

SOLUTIONS TO PROBLEMS

E.1 The compound is methane, CH_4. The molecular ion is at m/e 16. (This peak happens also to be the base peak.)

$$\text{H--C(H)(H)--H} + e^- \longrightarrow \text{H--}\overset{+}{\underset{\cdot}{C}}(H)(H)\text{--H} + 2e^-$$

$$m/e \ 16$$
$$\mathbf{M^{+}}$$

The peaks at m/e 15, 14, 13, and 12 are caused by successive losses of hydrogen atoms.

$$\text{H--}\overset{+}{\underset{\cdot}{C}}(H)(H)\text{--H} \longrightarrow \text{H--}\overset{+}{C}(H)(H) + \text{H}\cdot$$

$$m/e \ 15$$

$$\text{H--}\overset{+}{C}(H)(H) \longrightarrow \text{H--}\overset{+}{\underset{\cdot}{C}}(H) + \text{H}\cdot$$

$$m/e \ 14$$

$$\text{H--}\overset{+}{\underset{\cdot}{C}}(H) \longrightarrow \text{H--C}\overset{+}{:} + \text{H}\cdot$$

$$m/e \ 13$$

$$\text{H--C}\overset{+}{:} \longrightarrow \cdot\text{C}\overset{+}{:} + \text{H}\cdot$$

$$m/e \ 12$$

The small peak at m/e 17 ($M^{+} + 1$) comes mainly from methane molecules that contain ^{13}C.

$$\text{H--}^{13}C(H)(H)\text{--H} + e^- \longrightarrow \text{H--}^{13}\overset{+}{\underset{\cdot}{C}}(H)(H)\text{--H} + 2e^-$$

$$m/e \ 17$$
$$(M^{+} + 1)$$

E.2   The compound is water.

$$H-\ddot{O}-H + e^- \longrightarrow H-\overset{\cdot\,+}{\underset{\cdot\cdot}{O}}-H + 2e^-$$

$$m/e\ 18$$
$$(M^{\ddagger})$$

$$H-\overset{\cdot\,+}{\underset{\cdot\cdot}{O}}-H \longrightarrow H-\ddot{O}^+ + H\cdot$$

$$m/e\ 17$$

$$H-\ddot{O}^+ \longrightarrow \cdot\ddot{O}^+ + H\cdot$$

$$m/e\ 16$$

The peaks at m/e 19 and m/e 20 are due (primarily) to naturally occurring oxygen isotopes.

$$H-^{17}\ddot{O}-H + e^- \longrightarrow H-^{17}\overset{\cdot\,+}{\underset{\cdot\cdot}{O}}-H + 2e^-$$

$$m/e\ 19$$
$$(M^{\ddagger} + 1)$$

$$H-^{18}\ddot{O}-H + e^- \longrightarrow H-^{18}\overset{\cdot\,+}{\underset{\cdot\cdot}{O}}-H + 2e^-$$

$$m/e\ 20$$
$$(M^{\ddagger} + 2)$$

E.3   The compound is methyl fluoride, CH_3F.

$$CH_3-F + e^- \longrightarrow [CH_3F]^{\ddagger} + 2e^-$$

$$m/e\ 34$$
$$(M^{\ddagger})$$

$$[CH_3F]^{\ddagger} \longrightarrow [CH_2F]^+ + H\cdot$$

$$m/e\ 33$$

$$[CH_2F]^+ \longrightarrow [CHF]^{\ddagger} + H\cdot$$

$$m/e\ 32$$

$$[CHF]^{\ddagger} \longrightarrow [CF]^+ + H\cdot$$

$$m/e\ 31$$

$$[CH_3F]^{\ddagger} \longrightarrow [F]^+ + CH_3\cdot$$

$$m/e\ 19$$

$$[CH_3F]^{\ddagger} \longrightarrow [CH_3]^+ + F\cdot$$

$$m/e\ 15$$

$$[CH_3]^+ \longrightarrow [CH_2]^{\ddagger} + H\cdot$$

$$m/e\ 14$$

E.4

(a)

$$CH_3\overset{O}{\underset{\|}{C}}CH_2CH_3 \qquad CH_3CH_2CH_2\overset{O}{\underset{\|}{C}}H \qquad CH_3\underset{\underset{CH_3}{|}}{C}HCH\overset{O}{\underset{\|}{}} \qquad CH_2{=}CHCH_2OCH_3$$

$$CH_3CH{=}CHCH_2OH \qquad CH_2{=}\underset{\underset{CH_3}{|}}{\overset{CH_3}{C}}{-}CH_2OH$$

(b) Only the first three. (The peak at 1730 cm^{-1} is due to a C=O group.)

E.5 First we recalculate the intensities of the peaks so as to base them on the M‡ peak:

m/e		Intensity % of M‡
86 M‡	10.0/10.0 × 100 =	100
87	0.56/10.0 × 100 =	5.6
88	0.04/10.0 × 100 =	0.4

A. Since M‡ is even, the compound must contain an even number of nitrogen atoms (i.e., 0, 2, 4, etc.)

B. The value of the M‡ + 1 peak gives the number of carbon atoms

Number of carbon atoms = 5.6/1.1 ≈ 5

The compound must contain no nitrogen atoms because C_5N_2 = (5 × 12) + (2 × 14) = 88, and the molecular weight of the compound (from the M^{+} peak) is only 86.

C. The very low value of the M‡ + 2 peak (0.4%) tells us that the compound does not contain S, Cl, or Br.

D. If the compound were composed only of C and H it would have to be C_5H_{26}:

H = 86 − (5 × 12) = 26

But C_5H_{26} is impossible.

However, a formula with one oxygen gives a reasonable number of hydrogens,

H = 86 − (5 × 12) − 16 = 10

and thus our compound has the formula $C_5H_{10}O$.

E.6   (a)   The $M^+ + 2$ peak due to $CH_3{}^{37}Cl$ (at m/e 52) should be almost one third (32.5%) as large as the M^+ peak at m/e 50.

(b)   The peaks due to $CH_3{}^{79}Br$ and $CH_3{}^{81}Br$ (at m/e 94 and m/e 96, respectively) should be of nearly equal intensity.

(c)   That the M^+ and $M^+ + 2$ peaks are of nearly equal intensity tells us that the compound contains bromine. C_3H_7Br is therefore a likely molecular formula.

$$C_3 = 36 \qquad\qquad C_3 = 36$$
$$H_7 = 7 \qquad\qquad H_7 = 7$$
$${}^{79}Br = \underline{79} \qquad\qquad {}^{81}Br = \underline{81}$$
$$m/e = 122 \qquad\qquad m/e = 124$$

E.7   Recalculating the intensities to base on M^+

Peak	m/e	% of Base Peak	% of M^+
M^+	73	86.1	100
$M^+ + 1$	74	3.2	3.72
$M^+ + 2$	75	0.2	0.23

These data best fit the formula C_3H_7NO.

E.8   (a)   First recalculating the intensities so as to base them on the M^+ peak:

m/e		Intensity % of M^+
78 M^+	$24/24 \times 100 =$	100
79	$0.8/24 \times 100 =$	3.3
80	$8/24 \times 100 =$	33

A. Since M^+ is even the compound contains an even number of nitrogen atoms.

B. Number of Carbon atoms $= (M^+ + 1)/1.1 = 3.3/1.1 = 3$

C. The intensity of the $M^+ + 2$ peak (33%) tells us that the compound contains one chlorine atom.

D. We use the molecular weight (from the M^+ peak) to calculate the number of hydrogens.

$$H = 78 - (3 \times 12) - 35 = 7$$

Thus the formula for the compound is C_3H_7Cl.

(b) CH_3CHCH_3
          $|$
         Cl

E.9   (a)   A *tert*-butyl cation, $(CH_3)_3C^+$.

$$\left[\begin{array}{c} CH_3 \\ | \\ CH_3-C-CH_3 \\ | \\ CH_3 \end{array}\right]^{\ddagger} \longrightarrow \begin{array}{c} CH_3 \\ | \\ CH_3-\overset{+}{C} \\ | \\ CH_3 \end{array} + CH_3\cdot$$

$$m/e\ 57$$

E.10   A peak at $M^{\ddagger} - 15$ involves the loss of a methyl radical and the formation of a 1° or 2° carbocation.

$$\begin{array}{c} CH_3 \\ | \\ [CH_3CH_2CHCH_2CH_3]^{\ddagger} \end{array} \longrightarrow CH_3CH_2\overset{+}{C}HCH_2CH_3 + CH_3\cdot$$
$$M^{\ddagger} - 15$$

or

$$\begin{array}{c} CH_3 \\ | \\ [CH_3CH_2CHCH_2CH_3]^{\ddagger} \\ M^{\ddagger} \end{array} \longrightarrow \begin{array}{c} CH_3 \\ | \\ CH_3CH_2CHCH_2{}^{+} \\ M^{\ddagger}-15 \end{array} + CH_3\cdot$$

A peak at $M^{\ddagger} - 29$ arises from the loss of an ethyl radical and the formation of a 2° carbocation.

$$\begin{array}{c} CH_3 \\ | \\ [CH_3CH_2CHCH_2CH_3]^{\ddagger} \\ M^{\ddagger} \end{array} \longrightarrow \begin{array}{c} CH_3 \\ | \\ CH_3CH_2\overset{+}{C}H \\ M^{\ddagger}-29 \end{array} + CH_3CH_2\cdot$$

Since a 2° carbocation is more stable, the peak at $M^{\ddagger} - 29$ is more intense.

E.11   Both peaks arise from allylic fragmentations

$$^{+}CH_2-CH\!-\!CH_2\!-\!CHCH_2CH_3 \longrightarrow \overset{\cdot}{C}H_2-CH\!=\!CH_2 + {}^{+}CHCH_2CH_3$$
$$\qquad\qquad\qquad | \qquad\qquad\qquad\qquad\qquad\qquad\qquad\qquad | $$
$$\qquad\qquad\qquad CH_3 \qquad\qquad\qquad\qquad\qquad\qquad\qquad\quad CH_3$$

Allyl radical $m/e\ 57$

$$CH_2{}^{+\cdot}\!CH\!-\!CH_2\!:\!CHCH_2CH_3 \longrightarrow \overset{+}{C}H_2-CH\!=\!CH_2 + \cdot CHCH_2CH_3$$
$$\qquad\qquad\qquad | \qquad\qquad\qquad\qquad\qquad\qquad\qquad\qquad | $$
$$\qquad\qquad\qquad CH_3 \qquad\qquad\qquad\qquad\qquad\qquad\qquad\quad CH_3$$

$m/e\ 41$
Allyl cation

E.12   (a)   Alcohols undergo rapid cleavage of a carbon-carbon bond next to oxygen because this leads to a resonance-stabilized cation.

$$1°\ \text{alcohol}\ R\!:\!CH_2\!-\!\overset{+}{\underset{\cdot\cdot}{O}}H \xrightarrow{-R\cdot} CH_2\!=\!\overset{+}{\underset{\cdot\cdot}{O}}H \longleftrightarrow \overset{+}{C}H_2-\overset{\cdot\cdot}{\underset{\cdot\cdot}{O}}H$$

$$2° \text{ alcohol } R-CH-OH \xrightarrow{-R\cdot} RCH=\overset{+}{O}H \longleftrightarrow RCH-\ddot{O}H$$

$$3° \text{ alcohol } R-\underset{R}{C}-OH \xrightarrow{-R\cdot} R-\underset{R}{C}=\overset{+}{O}H \longleftrightarrow R-\underset{R}{C}-\ddot{O}H$$

The cation obtained from a tertiary alcohol is the most stable (because of the electron-releasing R groups).

(b) Primary alcohols give a peak at m/e 31 due to $CH_2=\overset{+}{O}H$.

(c) Secondary alcohols give peaks at m/e 45, 59, 73, and so forth, because ions like the following are produced.

$$CH_3CH=\overset{+}{O}H \qquad CH_3CH_2CH=\overset{+}{O}H \qquad CH_3CH_2CH_2CH=\overset{+}{O}H$$
$$m/e\ 45 \qquad\qquad m/e\ 59 \qquad\qquad\qquad m/e\ 73$$

(d) Tertiary alcohols give peaks at m/e 59, 73, 87, and so forth, because ions like the following are produced.

$$CH_3\underset{CH_3}{C}=\overset{+}{O}H \qquad CH_3CH_2\underset{CH_3}{C}=\overset{+}{O}H \qquad CH_3CH_2CH_2\underset{CH_3}{C}=\overset{+}{O}H$$
$$m/e\ 59 \qquad\qquad m/e\ 73 \qquad\qquad\qquad m/e\ 87$$

E.13 The spectrum given in Fig. E.12 is that of isopropyl butyl ether. The main clues are the peaks at m/e 101 and m/e 73 due to the following fragmentations.

$$\left[CH_3-\underset{CH_3}{CH}-OCH_2CH_2CH_2CH_3 \right]^{\ddagger} \xrightarrow{-CH_3\cdot} CH_3CH=\overset{+}{O}CH_2CH_2CH_2CH_3$$
$$m/e\ 101$$

$$\left[CH_3\underset{CH_3}{CH}-O-CH_2CH_2CH_2CH_3 \right]^{\ddagger} \xrightarrow{-CH_3CH_2CH_2\cdot} CH_3\underset{CH_3}{CH}O^+=CH_2$$
$$m/e\ 73$$

Propyl butyl ether (Fig. E.13) has no peak at m/e 101 but has a peak at m/e 87 instead.

$$[CH_3CH_2CH_2-O-CH_2CH_2CH_2CH_3]^{\ddagger} \xrightarrow{-CH_3CH_2\cdot} CH_2=\overset{+}{O}CH_2CH_2CH_2CH_3$$
$$m/e\ 87$$

Propyl butyl ether also has a peak at m/e 73.

$$[CH_3CH_2CH_2-O-CH_2CH_2CH_2CH_3]^{\ddagger} \xrightarrow{-CH_3CH_2CH_2\cdot} CH_3CH_2CH_2-\overset{+}{O}=CH_2$$
$$m/e\ 73$$

[Although the observation does not help us decide, it is interesting to notice that both spectra have intense peaks at m/e 43 and m/e 57 corresponding to propyl (or isopropyl) and butyl cations formed by carbon-oxygen bond cleavage.]

E.14   The compound is butanal. The peak at *m/e* 44 arises from a McLafferty rearrangement.

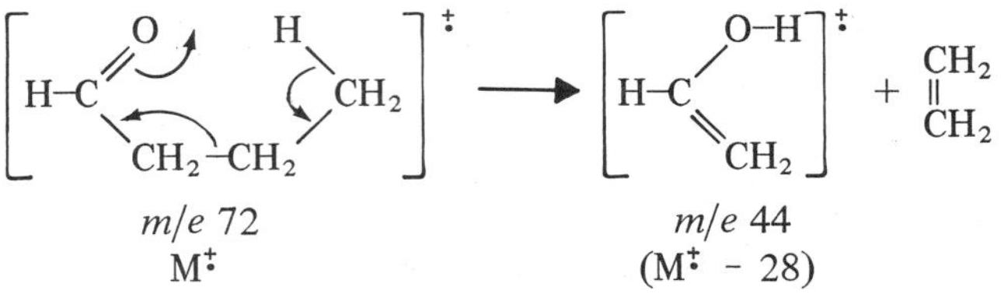

The peak at *m/e* 29 arises from a fragmentation producing an acylium ion.

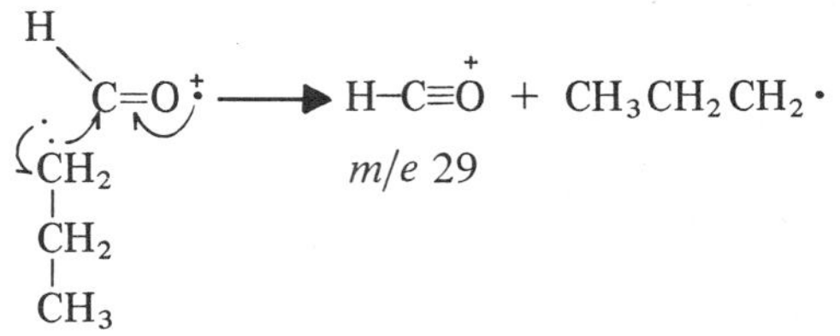

E.15   The ion, $CH_2=\overset{+}{N}H_2$, produced by the following fragmentation.

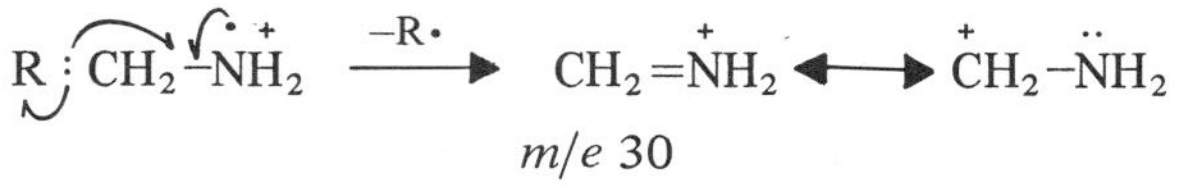

E.16   Compound **A** is *tert*-butylamine. Our first clue is the molecular ion at *m/e* 73 (an odd-numbered mass unit) indicating the presence of an odd number of nitrogen atoms. The base peak at *m/e* 58 is our second important clue. It arises from the following fragmentation.

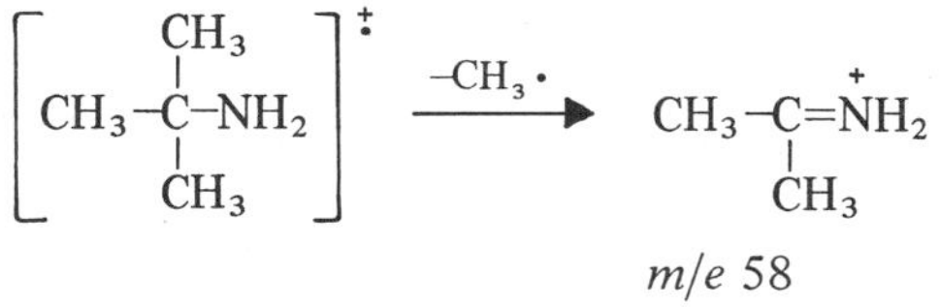

The proton nmr spectrum confirms the structure

(a)   *(b)*
$(CH_3)_3C-NH_2$

(a)   Singlet δ 1.2(9H)

(b)   Singlet δ 1.3(2H)

E.17   The compound is 2-methyl-2-butanol. Although the molecular ion is not discernible, we are given that it is at *m/e* 88. This information gives us the molecular weight of **B** and rules out the possibility of a structure with an odd number of nitrogen atoms.

The infrared absorption (3200-3600 cm^{-1}) suggests the presence of an −OH group.

Two important peaks in the mass spectrum are the intense peaks at m/e 59 and m/e 73. These peaks correspond to fragmentation reactions that produce resonance-stabilized oxonium ions and strongly suggest that we have a tertiary alcohol [see Problem E.12, part (d)].

$$
\begin{bmatrix} \quad CH_3 \quad \\ CH_3CH_2C\text{-}OH \\ \quad CH_3 \quad \end{bmatrix}^{\ddagger} \xrightarrow[-CH_3CH_2\cdot]{} \begin{array}{c} CH_3 \\ | \\ C=^+OH \\ | \\ CH_3 \end{array}
$$

$$m/e\ 59$$

$$\xrightarrow[-CH_3\cdot]{} \begin{array}{c} CH_3CH_2C=\overset{+}{O}H \\ | \\ CH_3 \end{array}$$

$$m/e\ 73$$

The peak at m/e 70 corresponds to the loss of a molecule of water from the molecular ion and the peak at m/e 55 probably arises from a subsequent allylic cleavage

$$
\begin{bmatrix} \quad CH_3 \quad \\ CH_3CH_2C\text{-}OH \\ \quad CH_3 \quad \end{bmatrix}^{\ddagger}
$$

$$\xrightarrow[-H_2O]{} \begin{bmatrix} \quad CH_3 \quad \\ CH_3CH=C\text{-}CH_3 \end{bmatrix}^{\ddagger}$$

$$m/e\ 70$$

$$\xrightarrow[-H_2O]{} \begin{bmatrix} \quad CH_3 \quad \\ CH_3CH_2C=CH_2 \end{bmatrix}^{\ddagger}$$

$$m/e\ 70$$

$$\xrightarrow[-CH_3\cdot]{}$$

$$\begin{array}{c} CH_3 \\ | \\ \overset{+}{C}H_2\text{-}C=CH_2 \end{array}$$

$$m/e\ 55$$

The proton nmr spectrum of **B** confirms that it is 2-methyl-2-butanol

$$
\begin{array}{ccc}
 & & (c) \\
(a) & (b) & CH_3 \\
CH_3 & \text{-}CH_2 & \text{-}C\text{-}CH_3\ (c) \\
 & & OH \\
 & & (d)
\end{array}
$$

(a) Triplet, δ 0.9 (3H)

(b) Quartet, δ 1.6 (2H)

(c) and (d) Overlapping singlets, δ 1.1 (7H)

E.18 Compound **C** is 3-methyl-1-butanol. Here, (because the compound is a primary alcohol) the molecular ion (m/e 88) is small but discernible. Again, the even-numbered mass of the molecular ion rules out a compound with an odd number of nitrogen atoms and the infrared absorption suggests the presence of an —OH group.

An important indication that **C** is a primary alcohol is the peak at m/e 31 corresponding to the following fragmentation [see also Problem E.12, part (b)] .

$$\left[\begin{array}{c} CH_3 \\ | \\ CH_3-CHCH_2CH_2OH \end{array} \right]^{\ddagger} \xrightarrow[- CH_3CHCH_2 \cdot]{CH_3} CH_2=\overset{+}{O}H$$
$$m/e\ 88 \qquad\qquad\qquad\qquad m/e\ 31$$

The peak at m/e 70 ($M^{\ddagger} - 18$) corresponds to the loss of water from the molecular ion.

$$\left[\begin{array}{c} CH_3 \\ | \\ CH_3CHCH_2CH_2OH \end{array} \right]^{\ddagger} \xrightarrow{-H_2O} \left[\begin{array}{c} CH_3 \\ | \\ CH_3CHCH=CH_2 \end{array} \right]^{\ddagger}$$
$$m/e\ 88 \qquad\qquad\qquad\qquad m/e\ 70$$

The peak at m/e 55 probably comes from a subsequent allylic cleavage.

$$\left[\begin{array}{c} CH_3 \\ | \\ CH_3CHCH=CH_2 \end{array} \right]^{\ddagger} \xrightarrow{- CH_3 \cdot} CH_3\overset{+}{C}HCH=CH_2$$
$$m/e\ 70 \qquad\qquad\qquad m/e\ 55$$

The proton nmr spectrum is consistent with this structure. We can make the following assignments.

$$\begin{array}{c} (a) \\ (a)\ CH_3 \\ | \\ CH_3-CH-CH_2-CH_2OH \\ (b)\ (c)\ (d)\ (e) \end{array}$$

(a) Doublet, δ 0.9

(b) and *(c)* Multiplet δ 1.5

(d) Triplet δ 3.7

(e) Singlet δ 2.2

E.19 The compound is 2-pentanone. The infrared absorption at 1710 cm^{-1} strongly indicates the presence of a carbonyl group. In the mass spectrum the molecular ion peak at m/e 86 gives the molecular weight and rules out structures with an odd number of nitrogens. A possible formula is $C_5H_{10}O$. (See Problem E.5.)

The peaks at m/e 71 and m/e 43 correspond to $M^{\ddagger} - 15$ and $M^{\ddagger} - 43$. Fragmentations of 2-pentanone would produce acylium ions with these mass numbers.

$$\left[\begin{array}{c} O \\ \| \\ CH_3CCH_2CH_2CH_3 \end{array} \right]^{\ddagger} \xrightarrow[\displaystyle -CH_3\cdot]{} \overset{+}{O}\equiv CCH_2CH_2CH_3$$

$$m/e\ 71$$

$$m/e\ 86 \qquad \xrightarrow[\displaystyle -CH_3CH_2CH_2\cdot]{} CH_3C\overset{+}{\equiv}O$$

$$m/e\ 43$$

The peak at m/e 58 ($M\overset{+}{\cdot} - 28$) comes from a McLafferty rearrangement.

$$\left[\begin{array}{c} CH_3-C \\ CH_2-CH_2 \end{array} \begin{array}{c} O \\ \\ H \\ CH_2 \end{array} \right]^{\ddagger} \longrightarrow \left[\begin{array}{c} OH \\ CH_3-C \\ CH_2 \end{array} \right]^{\ddagger} + \begin{array}{c} CH_2 \\ \| \\ CH_2 \end{array}$$

$$m/e\ 58$$

The proton nmr spectrum confirms our structure.

$$\underset{\begin{array}{c} (a) \quad (b)\ (c)\ (d) \end{array}}{\overset{\begin{array}{c} O \\ \| \end{array}}{CH_3CCH_2CH_2CH_3}}$$

(a) Singlet, δ 2.2

(b) Triplet, δ 2.4

(c) Multiplet, δ 1.6

(d) Triplet, δ 0.9

E.20   The compound is bromobenzene. That the compound contains bromine is indicated by the $M\overset{+}{\cdot}$ and $M\overset{+}{\cdot} + 2$ peaks of nearly equal intensity at m/e 156 and m/e 158. The peak at m/e 77 (the base peak) strongly suggests the presence of a benzene ring.

$$\langle\!\langle +\cdot \rangle\!\rangle\!-Br \xrightarrow{-Br\cdot} \langle\!\langle + \rangle\!\rangle$$

$$m/e\ 77$$

Putting these facts together with the molecular weight (156) leads us to only one logical conclusion.

SECTION REFERENCES FOR ADDITIONAL PROBLEMS

E.14	E.4C		E.18	E.4B, E.4C
E.15	E.4B		E.19	E.4B, E.4C
E.16	E.4B		E.20	E.3A,
E.17	E.4B, E.4C			

14

ORGANIC HALIDES AND ORGANOMETALLIC COMPOUNDS

SUMMARY OF ORGANIC HALIDES

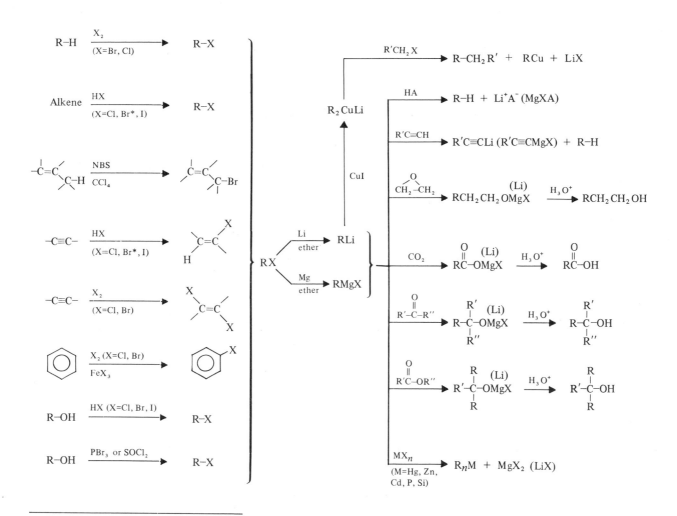

---

*HBr gives anti-Markovnikov addition
when peroxides are present.

SOLUTIONS TO PROBLEMS

14.1 (a) (R)-CH$_3$CHCH$_2$CH$_3$ + NaOH $\xrightarrow[\text{S}_\text{N}2]{\text{H}_2\text{O}}$ (S)-CH$_3$CHCH$_2$CH$_3$ + NaBr
  | |
  Br   OH

(b)

+ NaOH $\xrightarrow[\text{S}_\text{N}2]{\text{H}_2\text{O}}$

+ NaBr

(c) C$_6$H$_5$CHCH$_2$CH$_3$ + NaOC$_2$H$_5$ $\xrightarrow{\text{C}_2\text{H}_5\text{OH}}$ C$_6$H$_5$CH=CHCH$_3$ + NaCl
  |
  Br
                                                           + C$_2$H$_5$OH

          Br
          |
(d) C$_6$H$_5$CCH$_3$ + 2NaNH$_2$ $\xrightarrow{\text{NH}_3}$ C$_6$H$_5$C≡CH + 2NaBr + 2NH$_3$
          |
          Br

                    Br
                    |
(e) C$_6$H$_5$CH$_2$CH$_2$CH + 3NaNH$_2$ $\xrightarrow{(2)\ \text{H}^+}$ C$_6$H$_5$CH$_2$C≡CH
                    |
                    Br

(f) CH$_3$CH$_2$CH$_2$CH$_2$CH$_2$Br + (CH$_3$)$_3$COK $\xrightarrow{(\text{CH}_3)_3\text{COH}}$ CH$_3$CH$_2$CH$_2$CH=CH$_2$
                                                           + NaBr + (CH$_3$)$_3$COH

14.2 (a) In concentrated base and ethyl alcohol (a relatively nonpolar solvent) the S$_\text{N}$2 reaction is favored. Thus the rate depends on the concentration of both the alkyl halide and NaOC$_2$H$_5$. Since no carbocation is formed, the only product is

  CH$_3$CH=CHCH$_2$OCH$_2$CH$_3$.

(b) When the concentration of C$_2$H$_5$O$^-$ ion is small or zero, the reaction occurs through the S$_\text{N}$1 mechanism. The carbocation that is produced in the first step of the S$_\text{N}$1 mechanism is a resonance hybrid.

CH$_3$CH=CHCH$_2$Cl $\rightleftharpoons$ $\left[\begin{array}{c} \text{CH}_3\text{CH=CH}\overset{+}{\text{CH}}_2 \\ \updownarrow \\ \overset{+}{\text{CH}_3\text{CH}}-\text{CH=CH}_2 \end{array}\right]$ + Cl$^-$

This ion reacts with the nucleophile (C$_2$H$_5$O$^-$ or C$_2$H$_5$OH) to produce two isomeric ethers

                                      OCH$_2$CH$_3$
                                      |
CH$_3$CH=CHCH$_2$−OCH$_2$CH$_3$ and CH$_3$CHCH=CH$_2$

(c) In the presence of water, the first step of the S$_\text{N}$1 reaction occurs. The reverse of this reaction produces two compounds because the positive charge on the carbocation is distributed over carbons one and three.

$$\left[\begin{array}{c} CH_3CH=CH\overset{+}{C}H_2 \\ \updownarrow \\ CH_3\overset{+}{C}H-CH=CH_2 \end{array} \right] + Cl^- \longrightarrow \begin{array}{c} CH_3CH=CHCH_2Cl \\ + \\ \underset{CH_3CH-CH=CH_2}{\overset{Cl}{|}} \end{array}$$

14.3   (a)   The carbocation that is produced in the S_N1 reaction is exceptionally stable because one resonance contributor is not only allylic but also tertiary.

$$\underset{CH_3}{\overset{CH_3}{\underset{|}{C}}}=CHCH_2Cl \quad \overset{S_N1}{\underset{\longleftarrow}{\longrightarrow}} \quad \left[\underset{CH_3}{\overset{CH_3}{\underset{|}{C}}}=CH\overset{+}{C}H_2 \longleftrightarrow CH_3-\underset{+}{\overset{CH_3}{\underset{|}{C}}}-CH=CH_2 \right]$$

A 3° allylic carbocation

(b) $\underset{CH_3}{\overset{CH_3}{\underset{|}{C}}}=CHCH_2OH + \underset{\underset{OH}{|}}{\overset{CH_3}{\underset{|}{C}}}CH_3CCH=CH_2$

14.4   Compounds that undergo reactions by an S_N1 path must be capable of forming relatively stable carbocations. Primary halides of the type, $ROCH_2X$ form carbocations that are stabilized by resonance:

$$R-\overset{..}{\underset{..}{O}}-\overset{+}{C}H_2 \longleftrightarrow R-\overset{+}{\underset{..}{O}}=CH_2$$

14.5   The relative rates are in the order of the relative stabilities of the carbocations:

$$C_6H_5\overset{+}{C}H_2 < C_6H_5\overset{+}{C}HCH_3 < (C_6H_5)_2\overset{+}{C}H < (C_6H_5)_3\overset{+}{C}$$

The solvolysis reaction involves a carbocation intermediate.

14.6   (a) $CH_3CH_2CH_2CH=CH_2 + HBr \xrightarrow{\text{peroxides}} CH_3CH_2CH_2CH_2CH_2Br$

(b) $CH_3CH_2CH_2CH=CH_2 + HBr \xrightarrow[\text{inhibitor}]{\text{peroxide}} CH_3CH_2CH_2\underset{\overset{|}{Br}}{\overset{\overset{Br}{|}}{C}}HCH_3$

(c) $CH_3CH_2\underset{}{\overset{CH_3}{\underset{|}{C}}}HCH_3 + Br_2 \xrightarrow[\substack{\text{or} \\ \text{heat}}]{h\nu} CH_3CH_2\underset{\overset{|}{Br}}{\overset{\overset{CH_3}{|}}{C}}CH_3$ (major product)

(d) $CH_3CH_2C\equiv CH + HCl \text{ (1 mole)} \longrightarrow CH_3CH_2\underset{\overset{|}{Cl}}{C}=CH_2$

(e) [cyclohexene] + [N-bromosuccinimide] $\xrightarrow{h\nu}$ [3-bromocyclohexene] + [succinimide NH]

(f) $CH_3CH_2C{\equiv}CH + 2HBr \xrightarrow[\text{inhibitor}]{\text{peroxide}} CH_3CH_2\overset{\displaystyle Br}{\underset{\displaystyle Br}{C}}CH_3$

(g) $CH_3CH{=}CHCH_3 + Br_2 \longrightarrow CH_3\overset{\displaystyle Br}{\underset{\displaystyle Br}{C}HCHCH_3}$

(h) [phenyl]$-CH_2CH_2CH_2CH_2CH_2CH_2CH_3$ + [N-bromosuccinimide] $\xrightarrow[CCl_4]{h\nu}$

[phenyl]$\overset{\displaystyle Br}{C}HCH_2CH_2CH_2CH_2CH_2CH_3$ + [succinimide N–H]

(i) [phenyl]$-C_7H_{15} + Br_2 \xrightarrow{FeBr_3} Br-$[phenyl]$-C_7H_{15} + HBr$

(j) [phenyl]$-CH_3 + Cl_2 \xrightarrow{h\nu}$ [phenyl]$-CH_2Cl + HCl$

(k) [cyclopentene] $+ HF \longrightarrow$ [cyclopentyl]$-F$

(l) [cyclohexene] $+ HI \longrightarrow$ [cyclohexyl]$-I$

14.7

$CH_3\overset{\displaystyle CH_3}{\underset{\displaystyle OH}{C}HCHCH_3} + HBr \rightleftarrows CH_3\overset{\displaystyle CH_3}{\underset{\displaystyle +OH_2}{C}HCHCH_3} + Br^-$

$\updownarrow -H_2O$

$CH_3\overset{\displaystyle CH_3}{\underset{\displaystyle Br}{C}}-CH_2CH_3 \xleftarrow{Br^-} CH_3\overset{\displaystyle CH_3}{\underset{\displaystyle +}{C}}-CH_2CH_3 \longleftarrow CH_3\overset{\displaystyle CH_3}{C}H-\underset{+}{C}HCH_3$

14.8 The protonated phenol ⟨◯⟩—O̊H$_2$⁺ would not dissociate to form the carbocation

because that carbocation is highly unstable.

$$
\begin{array}{c}
\text{H} \qquad \text{H} \\
\text{H}-\!\!\!\underset{\text{H}}{\overset{}{\bigcirc}}\!\!\!\overset{+}{} \\
\text{H} \qquad \text{H}
\end{array}
\qquad \text{(highly unstable carbocation)}
$$

14.9 (a) No. (b) The S$_N$2 reaction of the Cl⁻ ion with the alkyl chlorosulfite would lead to inversion.

$$
\underset{R}{\overset{R'}{\diagdown}}\!\!\text{CH}\ddot{\text{O}}\text{H} + \text{Cl}-\underset{\underset{O}{\|}}{\text{S}}-\text{Cl} \longrightarrow \underset{R}{\overset{R'}{\diagdown}}\!\!\text{CH}-\text{O}-\underset{\underset{O}{\|}}{\text{S}}-\text{Cl} + \text{HCl}
$$

$$
\text{HCl} + (\text{CH}_3)_3\text{N} \longrightarrow (\text{CH}_3)_3\text{NH}^+ + \text{Cl}^-
$$

$$
\text{Cl}^- \!\!\!\curvearrowright\!\! \underset{\underset{R'}{R}}{}\!\!\text{C}-\text{O}-\underset{\underset{O}{\|}}{\text{S}}-\text{Cl} \xrightarrow{\text{inversion}} \text{Cl}-\underset{\underset{R'\,R}{}}{\overset{H}{}}\!\!\text{C} + {}^-\text{O}-\underset{\underset{O}{\|}}{\text{S}}-\text{Cl}
$$

$$
\downarrow
$$

$$
\text{SO}_2 + \text{Cl}^-
$$

14.10 (a) $\text{CH}_3\text{CH}_2\text{CH}_2\text{CH}_2 \overset{\delta-}{:} \overset{\delta+}{\text{Li}} + \text{H} : \ddot{\text{O}}\text{H} \longrightarrow \text{CH}_3\text{CH}_2\text{CH}_2\text{CH}_2-\text{H} + \text{Li}^+ : \ddot{\text{O}}\text{H}^-$

(stronger base) (stronger acid) (weaker acid) (weaker base)

(b) $\text{CH}_3\text{CH}_2\text{CH}_2\text{CH}_2 \overset{\delta-}{:} \overset{\delta+}{\text{Li}} + \text{H} : \ddot{\text{O}}\text{CH}_2\text{CH}_3 \longrightarrow \text{CH}_3\text{CH}_2\text{CH}_2\text{CH}_2-\text{H} + \text{Li}^+ {}^- : \ddot{\text{O}}\text{CH}_2\text{CH}_3$

(stronger base) (stronger acid) (weaker acid) (weaker base)

14.11

$$
\underset{\underset{\text{CH}_3}{|}}{\overset{\overset{\text{CH}_3}{|}}{\text{CH}_3-\text{C}-\text{Br}}} + \text{Mg} \xrightarrow[35°]{\text{ether}} \underset{\underset{\text{CH}_3}{|}}{\overset{\overset{\text{CH}_3}{|}}{\text{CH}_3-\text{C}-\text{MgBr}}} \xrightarrow{\text{D}_2\text{O}} \underset{\underset{\text{CH}_3}{|}}{\overset{\overset{\text{CH}_3}{|}}{\text{CH}_3-\text{C}-\text{D}}}
$$

14.12

C_6H_5—MgBr + $\begin{matrix} Cl \\ | \\ C=O \\ | \\ C_6H_5 \end{matrix}$ ⟶ $\left[\begin{matrix} Cl \\ | \\ C_6H_5-C-O-MgBr \\ | \\ C_6H_5 \end{matrix} \right]$ $\xrightarrow{-MgBrCl}$

$\left[\begin{matrix} C_6H_5 \\ | \\ C=O \\ | \\ C_6H_5 \end{matrix} \right]$ $\xrightarrow{C_6H_5-MgBr}$ $\begin{matrix} C_6H_5 \\ | \\ C_6H_5-C-OMgBr \\ | \\ C_6H_5 \end{matrix}$ $\xrightarrow{H_3O^+}$ $\begin{matrix} C_6H_5 \\ | \\ C_6H_5-C-OH \\ | \\ C_6H_5 \end{matrix}$

14.13 (a) (1) CH_3MgBr + $CH_3\overset{O}{\overset{\|}{C}}CH_3$ $\xrightarrow{\quad\quad} \xrightarrow{(2)\ H_3O^+}$ $\begin{matrix} CH_3 \\ | \\ CH_3-C-OH \\ | \\ CH_3 \end{matrix}$

(2) $2CH_3MgBr$ + $CH_3\overset{O}{\overset{\|}{C}}-OC_2H_5$ $\xrightarrow{\quad\quad} \xrightarrow{(2)\ H_3O^+}$ $\begin{matrix} CH_3 \\ | \\ CH_3-C-OH \\ | \\ CH_3 \end{matrix}$

(b) (1) CH_3MgBr + $CH_3CH_2CH_2\overset{O}{\overset{\|}{C}}H$ $\xrightarrow{\quad\quad} \xrightarrow{(2)\ H_3O^+}$ $CH_3CH_2CH_2\overset{OH}{\overset{|}{C}}HCH_3$

(2) $CH_3CH_2CH_2MgBr$ + $CH_3\overset{O}{\overset{\|}{C}}H$ $\xrightarrow{\quad\quad} \xrightarrow{(2)\ H_3O^+}$ $CH_3CH_2CH_2\overset{OH}{\overset{|}{C}}HCH_3$

(c) (1) C_6H_5MgBr + $CH_3\overset{O}{\overset{\|}{C}}CH_2CH_3$ $\xrightarrow{\quad\quad} \xrightarrow{(2)\ H_3O^+}$ $C_6H_5\overset{CH_3}{\underset{OH}{\overset{|}{\underset{|}{C}}}}CH_2CH_3$

(2) CH_3MgBr + $C_6H_5\overset{O}{\overset{\|}{C}}CH_2CH_3$ $\xrightarrow{\quad\quad} \xrightarrow{(2)\ H_3O^+}$ $C_6H_5\overset{CH_3}{\underset{OH}{\overset{|}{\underset{|}{C}}}}CH_2CH_3$

(3) CH_3CH_2MgBr + $C_6H_5\overset{O}{\overset{\|}{C}}CH_3$ $\xrightarrow{\quad\quad} \xrightarrow{(2)\ H_3O^+}$ $C_6H_5\overset{CH_3}{\underset{OH}{\overset{|}{\underset{|}{C}}}}CH_2CH_3$

(d) (1) $CH_3CH_2CH_2CH_2MgBr$ + $\overset{O}{\overset{\diagup\diagdown}{CH_2-CH_2}}$ $\xrightarrow{\quad\quad} \xrightarrow{(2)\ H_3O^+}$ $CH_3CH_2CH_2CH_2CH_2CH_2OH$

(2) $CH_3CH_2CH_2CH_2CH_2MgBr$ + CH_2O $\xrightarrow{\quad\quad} \xrightarrow{(2)\ H_3O^+}$ $CH_3CH_2CH_2CH_2CH_2CH_2OH$

14.14

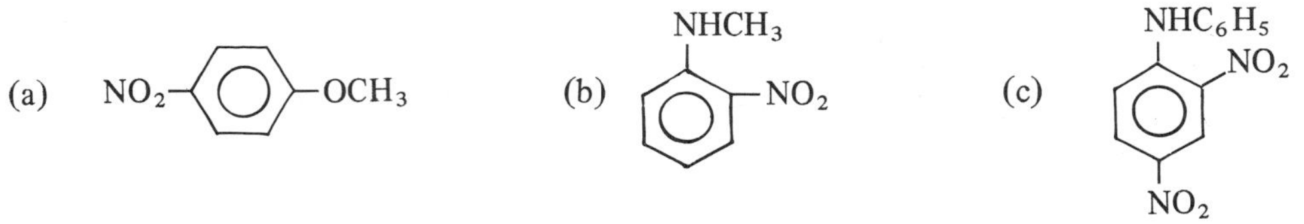

(a) NO_2—⟨benzene ring⟩—OCH_3

(b) ⟨benzene ring with $NHCH_3$ and NO_2⟩

(c) ⟨benzene ring with NHC_6H_5, NO_2, NO_2⟩

14.15

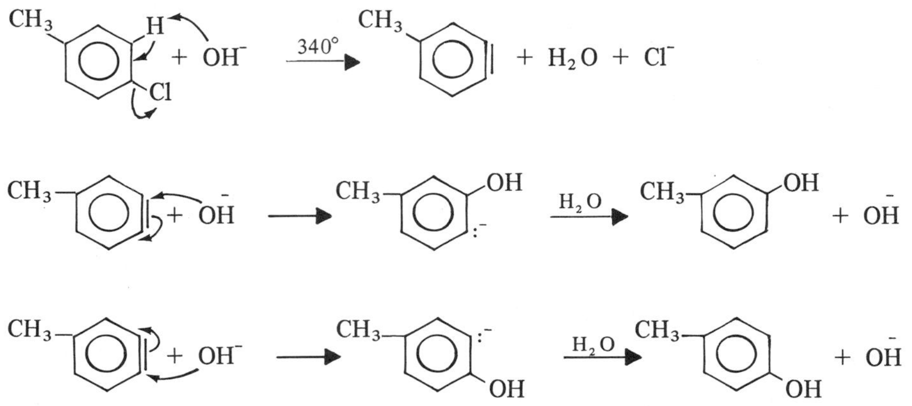

14.16 Since there are no hydrogens *ortho* to the halogen, elimination cannot take place. (Reaction by a bimolecular displacement is not possible either, because the substrate lacks strong electron-withdrawing groups.) Thus the absence of a reaction must be due to the inability of 2-bromo-3-methylanisole to form a benzyne intermediate.

14.17

(a) $3CH_3CH_2CHCH_3 + PBr_3 \longrightarrow 3CH_3CH_2CHCH_3 + H_3PO_3$
       | |
       OH   Br

(b) $CH_3CH_2CH_2CH_2OH \xrightarrow{PBr_3} CH_3CH_2CH_2CH_2Br \xrightarrow{(CH_3)_3COK}$

$CH_3CH_2CH=CH_2 \xrightarrow[\text{(no peroxides)}]{HBr} CH_3CH_2CHCH_3$
                                                        |
                                                        Br

(c) See (b) above.

(d) $CH_3CH_2C{\equiv}CH \xrightarrow{H_2, Ni_2B \text{ (P-2)}} CH_3CH_2CH=CH_2 \xrightarrow[\text{(no peroxides)}]{HBr}$

$CH_3CH_2CHCH_3$
       |
       Br

14.18 (a) $CH_3CH_2CHCH_3$ $\xrightarrow[\text{heat} \\ (-H_2O)]{H^+}$ $CH_3CH=CHCH_3$ $\xrightarrow{THF:BH_3}$ $CH_3CH_2CHCH_3$
|
OH
$+$
$CH_3CH_2CH=CH_2$

$CH_3CH=CHCH_3$ ... B$-$
|
$+$
$CH_3CH_2CH_2CH_2B-$
|

$\xrightarrow{160°}$ $CH_3CH_2CH_2CH_2B-$ $\xrightarrow[\text{OH}^-]{H_2O_2}$ $CH_3CH_2CH_2CH_2OH$ $\xrightarrow{PBr_3}$ $CH_3CH_2CH_2CH_2Br$
|

(b) $CH_3CH_2CH_2CH_2OH$ $\xrightarrow{PBr_3}$ $CH_3CH_2CH_2CH_2Br + H_3PO_3$

(c) $CH_3CH_2CH=CH_2$ $\xrightarrow[\text{(peroxides)}]{HBr}$ $CH_3CH_2CH_2CH_2Br$

(d) $CH_3CH_2C\equiv CH$ $\xrightarrow[\text{peroxides}]{HBr}$ $CH_3CH_2CH=CHBr$ $\xrightarrow[H_2]{Pt}$ $CH_3CH_2CH_2CH_2Br$

14.19 (a) [cyclohexanol] + $SOCl_2$ $\longrightarrow$ [chlorocyclohexane] + SO_2 + HCl

(b) [cyclohexene] + HCl $\longrightarrow$ [chlorocyclohexane]

(c) [1-methylcyclohexene] + HBr $\xrightarrow[\text{peroxides}]{\text{no}}$ [1-bromo-1-methylcyclohexane]

(d) [1-methylcyclohexene] + HBr $\xrightarrow{\text{peroxides}}$ [1-methyl-2-bromocyclohexane]

(e) [1-bromo-1-methylcyclohexane] + Mg $\xrightarrow{\text{ether}}$ [cyclohexyl-MgBr with CH₃] $\xrightarrow{D_2O}$ [1-deuterio-1-methylcyclohexane]

14.20 (a) $(CH_3)_2CHCH_2OH + (CH_3)_2C=CH_2$ (b) $(CH_3)_2CHCH_2CN$

(c) $CH_2=C(CH_3)_2$ (d) $CH_3CHCH_2OCH_3 + (CH_3)_2C=CH_2$
|
CH_3

(e) $(CH_3)_2CHCH_2-\underset{\underset{CH_3}{|}}{\overset{\overset{OH}{|}}{C}}-CH_3$ (f) $(CH_3)_2CHCH_2\overset{\overset{OH}{|}}{C}HCH_3$

(g) $(CH_3)_2CHCH_2\overset{\overset{OH}{|}}{\underset{\underset{CH_3}{|}}{C}}CH_2CH(CH_3)_2$ (h) $(CH_3)_2CHCH_2CH_2CH_2OH$

(i) $(CH_3)_2CHCH_2CH_2OH$ (j) $(CH_3)_2CHCH_3$

(k) $(CH_3)_2CHCH_3 + CH_3C{\equiv}CLi$

14.21   (a) CH_3CH_3 (b) CH_3CH_2D (c) $C_6H_5\underset{\underset{\displaystyle OH}{|}}{CH}CH_2CH_3$

(d) $C_6H_5-\underset{\underset{\displaystyle CH_2CH_3}{|}}{\overset{\overset{\displaystyle OH}{|}}{C}}-C_6H_5$ (e) $C_6H_5-\underset{\underset{\displaystyle CH_2CH_3}{|}}{\overset{\overset{\displaystyle OH}{|}}{C}}-CH_2CH_3$ (f) $C_6H_5-\underset{\underset{\displaystyle CH_3}{|}}{\overset{\overset{\displaystyle OH}{|}}{C}}-CH_2CH_3$

(g) $CH_3CH_3 + CH_3CH_2C{\equiv}C-\underset{\underset{\displaystyle OH}{|}}{CH}CH_3$ (h) $CH_3CH_3 + $ —MgBr

(i) $(CH_3CH_2)_2Hg + 2MgBrCl$ (j) $(CH_3CH_2)_2Cd$ (k) $(CH_3CH_2)_3P$

14.22   (a) $(CH_3)_2CH\underset{\underset{\displaystyle OH}{|}}{CH}CH_2CH_2CH_3$ (b) $(CH_3)_2CH\underset{\underset{\displaystyle CH_3}{|}}{\overset{\overset{\displaystyle OH}{|}}{C}}CH_2CH_2CH_3$

(c) $CH_3CH_2CH_3 + CH_3CH_2CH_2C{\equiv}C-\underset{\underset{\displaystyle CH_3}{|}}{\overset{\overset{\displaystyle OH}{|}}{C}}-CH_3$ (d) $CH_3CH_2CH_3$

(e) $CH_3CH_2CH_2CH_2CH{=}CH_2$ (f) $CH_3CH_2CH_2-$

(g) $\underset{H}{\overset{CH_3CH_2CH_2}{C}}{=}\underset{H}{\overset{CH_3}{C}}$ (h) $CH_3CH_2CH_2CH_3$

(i) $CH_3CH_2CH_2D$ (j) $(CH_3CH_2CH_2)_4Si$ (k) $(CH_3CH_2CH_2)_2Zn$

14.23   (a) (1) $CH_3CH_2MgBr + \underset{\underset{\displaystyle CH_3}{|}}{\overset{\overset{\displaystyle CH_3}{|}}{C}}{=}O \xrightarrow{\text{(2) } H_3O^+} CH_3CH_2\underset{\underset{\displaystyle CH_3}{|}}{\overset{\overset{\displaystyle CH_3}{|}}{C}}-OH$

(2) $CH_3MgBr + CH_3CH_2\underset{\underset{\displaystyle CH_3}{|}}{C}{=}O \xrightarrow{\text{(2) } H_3O^+} CH_3CH_2\underset{\underset{\displaystyle CH_3}{|}}{\overset{\overset{\displaystyle CH_3}{|}}{C}}-OH$

(3) $CH_3CH_2\overset{\overset{\displaystyle O}{\|}}{C}-OCH_3 + 2CH_3MgBr \xrightarrow{\text{(2) } H_3O^+} CH_3CH_2\underset{\underset{\displaystyle CH_3}{|}}{\overset{\overset{\displaystyle CH_3}{|}}{C}}-OH$

(b) (1) CH_3CH_2MgBr + [phenyl]$\overset{O}{\overset{\|}{C}}$–$CH_2CH_3$ $\xrightarrow{(2)\ H_3O^+}$ [phenyl]$\overset{OH}{\underset{CH_2CH_3}{\overset{\|}{C}}}$–$CH_2CH_3$

(2) [phenyl]–$MgBr$ + $CH_3CH_2\overset{O}{\overset{\|}{C}}CH_2CH_3$ $\xrightarrow{(2)\ H_3O^+}$ [phenyl]$\overset{OH}{\underset{CH_2CH_3}{\overset{\|}{C}}}$–$CH_2CH_3$

(3) [phenyl]$\overset{O}{\overset{\|}{C}}$–$OCH_3$ + $2CH_3CH_2MgBr$ $\xrightarrow{(2)\ H_3O^+}$ [phenyl]$\overset{OH}{\underset{CH_2CH_3}{\overset{\|}{C}}}$–$CH_2CH_3$

(c) [cyclohexanone]$=O$ + C_6H_5MgBr $\xrightarrow{(2)\ H_3O^+}$ [cyclohexane]$\overset{OH}{\underset{C_6H_5}{}}$

(d) [cyclopentane]–$MgBr$ + $CH_2\!-\!CH_2$ (epoxide) $\xrightarrow{(2)\ H_3O^+}$ [cyclopentane]–CH_2CH_2OH

(e) (1) [cyclobutane]–$MgBr$ + $CH_3\overset{O}{\overset{\|}{C}}H$ $\xrightarrow{(2)\ H_3O^+}$ [cyclobutane]$\overset{CHCH_3}{\underset{OH}{}}$

(2) [cyclobutane]–$\overset{O}{\overset{\|}{C}}H$ + CH_3MgBr $\xrightarrow{(2)\ H_3O^+}$ [cyclobutane]$\overset{CHCH_3}{\underset{OH}{}}$

14.24 (a) $3(CH_3)_2CHOH$ + PBr_3 $\longrightarrow$ $(CH_3)_2CHBr$ + H_3PO_3

$(CH_3)_2CHBr$ + Mg $\xrightarrow{ether}$ $(CH_3)_2CHMgBr$

$(CH_3)_2CHMgBr$ + $CH_3\overset{O}{\overset{\|}{C}}H$ $\xrightarrow{(2)\ H_3O^+}$ $(CH_3)_2CH\overset{OH}{\overset{\|}{C}}HCH_3$

(b) $(CH_3)_2CHMgBr$ + $H\overset{O}{\overset{\|}{C}}H$ $\xrightarrow{(2)\ H_3O^+}$ $(CH_3)_2CHCH_2OH$
 from (a)

(c) $(CH_3)_2CHMgBr$ + $CH_2\!-\!CH_2$ (epoxide) $\xrightarrow{(2)\ H_3O^+}$ $(CH_3)_2CHCH_2CH_2OH$

$(CH_3)_2CHCH_2CH_2Cl$ $\xleftarrow{SOCl_2}$

(d) $(CH_3)_2CHMgBr$ + $H\overset{O}{\overset{\|}{C}}CH(CH_3)_2$ $\xrightarrow{(2)\ H_3O^+}$ $(CH_3)_2CH\overset{OH}{\overset{\|}{C}}HCH(CH_3)_2$
 from (a)

(e) $(CH_3)_2CHMgBr$ + D_2O $\longrightarrow$ $(CH_3)_2CHD$
 from (a)

(f) $(CH_3)_2CHBr + Li \longrightarrow (CH_3)_2CHLi \xrightarrow{\text{CuI}} [(CH_3)_2CH]_2CuLi$
     from (a)

$(CH_3)_2CH$—⬡

14.25 Ionization of $(C_6H_5)_2CHCl$ yields a carbocation that is highly resonance-stabilized:

etc.

14.26 The Grignard reagent that forms early in the reaction reacts with the allyl halide in an S_N2 reaction:

$$RCH=CHCH_2-CH_2CH=CHR + MgX_2$$

14.27 (a) The carbocation stability is in the order

(b) The methoxy group in the meta position cannot stabilize the carbocation by resonance:

no especially stable structure is possible

The small stabilization resulting from the release of electrons into the ring through resonance is cancelled by oxygen's electron-withdrawing inductive effect.

14.28 (a) (cyclopentyl bromide) $+ (CH_3)_2CuLi \xrightarrow[\text{ether}]{0°}$ (methylcyclopentane) $+ CH_3Cu + LiBr$

(b) (cyclopentenyl bromide) $+ (CH_3)_2CuLi \xrightarrow[\text{ether}]{0°}$ (methylcyclopentene) $+ CH_3Cu + LiBr$

(c) $CH_2{=}CH{-}CH_2Br + (CH_3CH_2)_2CuLi \xrightarrow[\text{ether}]{0°} CH_2{=}CH{-}CH_2{-}CH_2{-}CH_3 +$
$CH_3CH_2Cu + LiBr$

(d)

$$\underset{H}{\overset{CH_3}{|}}C{=}C\underset{I}{\overset{CH_3}{|}} + (CH_3CH_2CH_2CH_2)_2CuLi \xrightarrow[\text{ether}]{0°}$$

$$\underset{H}{\overset{CH_3}{|}}C{=}C\underset{CH_2CH_2CH_2CH_3}{\overset{CH_3}{|}} + CH_3CH_2CH_2CH_2Cu + LiI$$

14.29 (a) (benzene) $+ CH_3COO^-\,Li^+$ (b) (benzene) $+ CH_3O^-\,Li^+$

(c) $CH_4 + MgBrNH_2$ (d) $(CH_3)_4Si + 4MgBrCl$

(e) $\left(\text{phenyl}\right)_3P + 3MgBrCl$ (f) $(CH_3CH_2)_2Cd + 2MgBrCl$

(g) (phenyl)$-CH_2OH + Mg^{++}$

14.30 (a) Allyl bromide decolorizes Br_2/CCl_4 solution; propyl bromide does not.

(b) Benzyl bromide gives an AgBr precipitate with $AgNO_3$ in alcohol; *p*-bromotoluene does not.

(c) Benzyl chloride gives an AgCl precipitate with $AgNO_3$ in alcohol; or vinyl chloride decolorizes Br_2/CCl_4 solution.

(d) Phenyllithium (a small amount) reacts vigorously with water to give benzene and a strongly basic aqueous solution (LiOH). Diphenylmercury does not react in this way.

(e) Bromocyclohexane gives a AgBr precipitate with $AgNO_3$ in alcohol; bromobenzene does not.

14.31   **A** is 3-chloro-2-chloromethyl-1-propene.

(b) H $\quad$ *(a)* CH$_2$–Cl

C=C

(b) H $\quad$ *(a)* CH$_2$–Cl

(a) Singlet δ 4.25 (4H)

(b) Singlet δ 5.35 (2H)

B is 1,3-dichloro-2-butene

(a) CH$_3$ *(c)* –C=CH *(b)* –CH$_2$Cl
$\quad\quad\quad$ |
$\quad\quad\quad$ Cl

(a) Singlet δ 2.2

(b) Doublet δ 4.15

(c) Triplet δ 5.7

14.32   Compound **C** is 1,3-dichlorobutane.

(a) *(b)* *(c)* *(d)*
CH$_3$–CH–CH$_2$–CH$_2$Cl
$\quad\quad$ |
$\quad\quad$ Cl

(a) Doublet δ 1.6

(b) Multiplet δ 4.3

(c) Multiplet δ 2.2 (resembles a quartet)

(d) Multiplet δ 3.7 (resembles a triplet)

Note: the protons labeled *(c)* are actually diastereotopic, but their chemical shifts are approximately the same. Coupling constants J_{bc} and J_{cd} are also approximately the same, and thus the spectrum is fortuitously simple.

14.33   **D** is 3-chloro-2-methylpropene.

(a) H $\quad$ *(c)* CH$_2$–Cl

C=C

(b) H $\quad$ CH$_3$
$\quad\quad\quad$ *(d)*

(a) Singlet, δ 5.1

(b) Singlet, δ 4.9

(c) Singlet, δ 4.0

(d) Singlet, δ 1.9

14.34   **E** is 1,3-butadiene. **F** and **G** are the products of the 1,2- and 1,4-addition of chlorine. **H** is 1,2,3,4-tetrachlorobutane.

$$CH_2\text{=}CH\text{–}CH\text{=}CH_2 \xrightarrow{\ Cl_2\ } CH_2\text{=}CH\text{–}CHCH_2Cl \ + \ ClCH_2CH\text{=}CHCH_2Cl$$

$\quad\quad\quad\quad$ **E** $\quad\quad\quad\quad\quad\quad\quad\quad\quad$ Cl $\quad\quad\quad\quad\quad\quad$ **G**

$\quad\quad\quad\quad\quad\quad\quad\quad\quad\quad\quad\quad\quad\quad\quad$ **F**

$\quad\quad\quad\quad\quad\quad\quad\quad\quad\quad\quad\quad$ (or vice versa)

$$\textbf{F or G} \xrightarrow{\text{Cl}_2} \underset{\underset{\textbf{H}}{}}{\overset{(a)\ (b)\ (b)\ (a)}{\text{ClCH}_2\!-\!\underset{\underset{\text{Cl}}{|}}{\text{CH}}\!-\!\underset{\underset{\text{Cl}}{|}}{\text{CH}}\!-\!\text{CH}_2\text{Cl}}}$$

(a) Doublet δ 3.8

(b) Triplet δ 4.6

SECTION REFERENCES FOR ADDITIONAL PROBLEMS

SELF-TEST

14.1 Give the structural formula of the missing reactant or product, or the molecular formula of the missing reagent. Give only the major product; if ortho and para isomers are produced, show only one. Show stereochemistry where applicable. If no reaction occurs, write N.R.

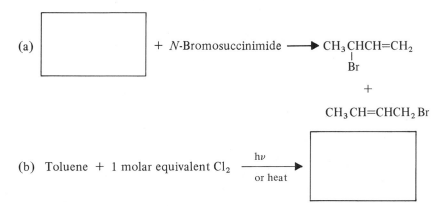

(a) ⬚ + *N*-Bromosuccinimide ⟶ $\underset{\underset{\text{Br}}{|}}{\text{CH}_3\text{CHCH}}=\text{CH}_2$

+

$\text{CH}_3\text{CH}=\text{CHCH}_2\text{Br}$

(b) Toluene + 1 molar equivalent Cl_2 $\xrightarrow[\text{or heat}]{\text{h}\nu}$ ⬚

(c)   ⬡—CH=CHCH$_3$ + HCl(g) ⟶ [ ]

(d) $CH_3\overset{\overset{\displaystyle CH_3}{|}}{C}HCH_2CH_2Li$ $\xrightarrow{CH_3OH}$ [ ]

(e) $CH_3CH_2CH_2Br$ + [ ] ⟶ $CH_3CH_2CH_2Li$ + ...

(f) $CH_3CH=CH_2$ + [ ] ⟶ $CH_3CH_2CH_2Br$ + ···

(g) $CH_3CH=CH_2$ + [ ] ⟶ $CH_3\overset{\overset{}{}}{C}HCH_3$ + ...
       $\overset{|}{\underset{I}{}}$

(h) CH_3CH_2MgBr + $CH_3\overset{\overset{\displaystyle O}{\|}}{C}CH_3$ ⟶ $\xrightarrow{H_3O^+}$ [ ] + ...

(i) $CH_3CH_2CH_2Br$ + [ ] ⟶ $CH_3CH_2CH_2OH$ + ...

14.2   Show how you could carry out the following syntheses by furnishing the necessary organic and/or inorganic reagents over the arrows or by supplying the missing reactant or major product. Show each step separately by using (1), (2), etc.

(a)   Benzene ⟶ ⬡—MgBr

(b)   ⬡—MgBr ⟶ ⬡—CH$_2$CH$_2$OH

(c)   ⬡—MgBr ⟶ ⬡—$\overset{\overset{\displaystyle OH}{|}}{C}HCH_3$

(d) $CH_2=CHCH_3$ ⟶ $CH_2=CHCH=CH_2$

SUPPLEMENTARY PROBLEM

S14.1 Complete each of the following reactions. Show stereochemistry where appropriate.

(a) $CH_2=CHCHCH_2CH_3$ $\xrightarrow[CCl_4]{NBS}$?

(b) 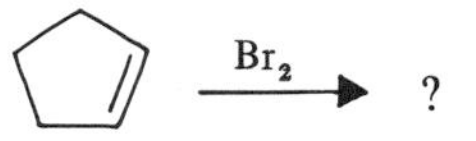 $\xrightarrow{Br_2}$?

(c) 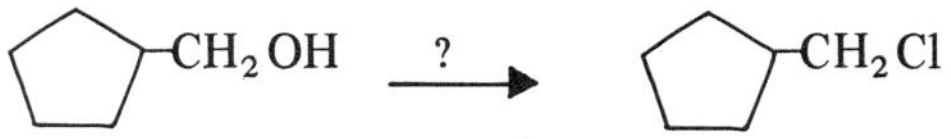 $\xrightarrow{?}$ (with no rearrangement)

(d) ? $\xrightarrow{?}$ $CH_3C\equiv CMgCl$

(e) $CH_3CH_2CH_2Br \xrightarrow{?}$ $CH_3CH_2CH_3$

(f) 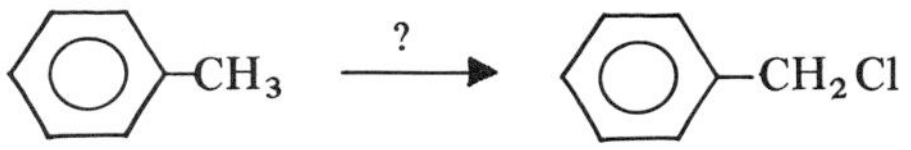 $\xrightarrow{?}$

(g)  $\xrightarrow{?}$

SOLUTION TO SUPPLEMENTARY PROBLEM

S14.1 (a) $CH_2=CHCHCH_2CH_3$ + $BrCH_2CH=CHCH_2CH_3$ (NBS gives allylic substitution)
$\quad\quad\quad\quad\quad\quad\quad\quad$ |
$\quad\quad\quad\quad\quad\quad\quad\quad$ Br

(b) 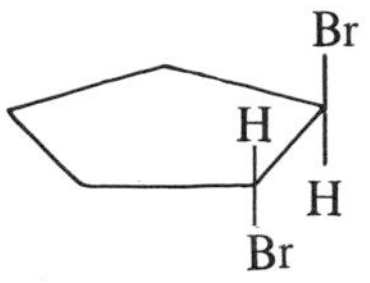 (*anti* addition)

(c) $SOCl_2$. (HCl results in rearrangement of the carbon skeleton to produce 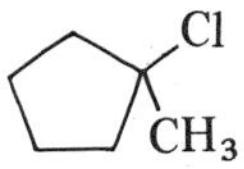).

(d) $RMgCl$ + $CH_3C\equiv CH \longrightarrow RH$ + $CH_3C\equiv CMgCl$

(e) $\xrightarrow{Zn/H^+}$

(f) $Cl_2/h\nu$

(g) $Cl_2/FeCl_3$

F

SPECIAL TOPIC
Organic Halides and Organometallic Compounas in the Environment

SOLUTIONS TO PROBLEMS

F.1

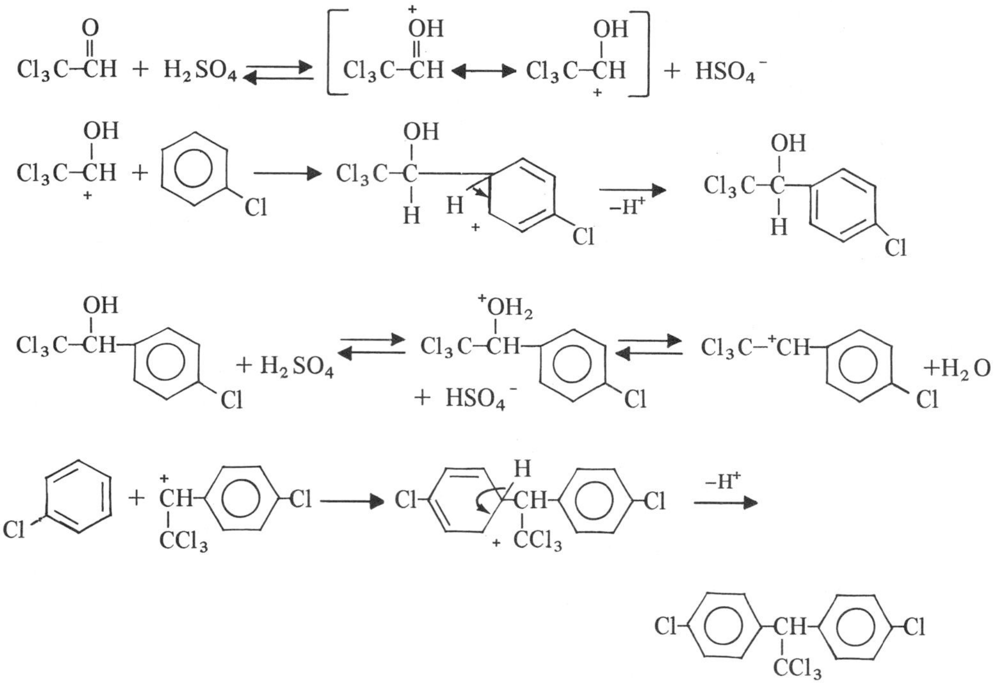

F.2 An elimination reaction.

F.3

(a)

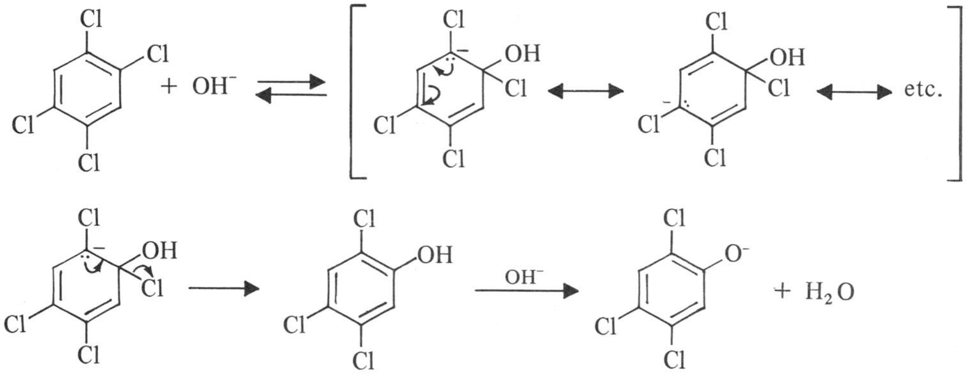

(b)

F.4   An S_N2 reaction:

SOLUTIONS TO PROBLEMS

G.1

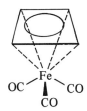

Cyclobutadiene iron
tricarbonyl

$$d^n = \text{Total number of valence electrons (both } s \text{ and } d \text{ electrons) of elemental iron} - \text{Oxidation state of the metal in the complex}$$

$$d^n = 8 - 0 = 8$$

$$\text{Total number of valence electrons of iron in the complex} = d^n + \text{Electrons donated by ligands}$$

$$= 8 + 3(CO) + \text{Cyclobutadiene}$$

$$= 8 + 3(2) + 4 = 18$$

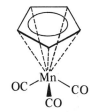

Cyclopentadienylmanganese
tricarbonyl

$$d^n = 7 - 1 = 6$$

$$\text{Total number of valence electrons of Mn in complex} = 6 + 3(CO) + Cp$$

$$= 6 + 3(2) + 6 = 18$$

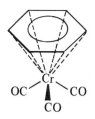

Benzene chromium
tricarbonyl

$d^n = 6 - 0 = 6$

Total number of valence electrons of Cr in complex	=	6 + 3(CO) + Benzene	
	=	6 + 3(2) + 6 = 18	

G.2   A *syn* addition of D_2 to the *trans* alkene would produce the following racemate.

$$\text{H}\underset{\text{EtO}_2\text{C}}{\overset{\text{CO}_2\text{Et}}{\underset{\text{C}}{\overset{\text{C}}{}}}}\text{H} + D_2 \xrightarrow{\text{RhPh}_3\text{Cl}} \cdots + \cdots$$

G.3 $(Ph_3P)_3RhCl + CH_3Li \xrightarrow[\text{exchange}]{\text{ligand}} (Ph_3P)_3RhCH_3 + LiCl$

(16 electrons)   (16 electrons)

Rh^I Rh^I

Oxidative addition

$(Ph_3P)_3Rh(CH_3)I$

(18 electrons)

Rh^{III}

$+ (Ph_3P)_3RhI \xleftarrow[\text{elimination}]{\text{reductive}}$

(16 electrons)

Rh^I

G.4 $(Ph_3P)_2Rh(CO)Cl + CH_3Li \xrightarrow{(a)} (Ph_3P)_2Rh(CO)(CH_3) + LiCl$

$\qquad\qquad$ **1** $\qquad\qquad\qquad\qquad\qquad\qquad\qquad$ **2**

$\qquad\qquad$ (16 electrons) $\qquad\qquad\qquad\qquad\qquad$ (16 electrons)
$\qquad\qquad\quad$ Rh^I $\qquad\qquad\qquad\qquad\qquad\qquad\quad$ Rh^I

$\qquad\qquad\qquad\qquad\qquad\qquad\qquad\qquad\qquad$ (b) $\Big\downarrow$ $C_6H_5\overset{\overset{O}{\|}}{C}Cl$

$(Ph_3P)_2Rh(CO)Cl + C_6H_5\overset{\overset{O}{\|}}{C}CH_3 \xleftarrow{(c)} (Ph_3P)_2Rh(CO)(COC_6H_5)(CH_3)Cl$

$\qquad\qquad\qquad\qquad\qquad\qquad\qquad\qquad\qquad\qquad\qquad\qquad$ **3**

$\qquad$ (16 electrons) $\qquad\qquad\qquad\qquad\qquad\qquad$ (18 electrons)
$\qquad\qquad$ Rh^I $\qquad\qquad\qquad\qquad\qquad\qquad\qquad\qquad$ Rh^{III}

(a)   is a ligand exchange

(b)   is an oxidative addition

(c)   is a reductive elimination

G.5   1. $(Ph_3P)_3Rh(CO)H \xrightarrow{-Ph_3P} (Ph_3P)_2Rh(CO)H$ **Ligand dissociation**

$\qquad\qquad$ (18 electrons, Rh^I) $\qquad\qquad$ (16 electrons, Rh^I)

2. $(Ph_3P)_2Rh(CO)H \xrightarrow{CH_3O\overset{\overset{O}{\|}}{C}C\equiv C\overset{\overset{O}{\|}}{C}OCH_3}$ **Ligand association**

$\qquad\qquad$ (16 electrons, Rh^I)

$\qquad\qquad\qquad\qquad\qquad\qquad\qquad\qquad\qquad\qquad\qquad$ (18 electrons, Rh^I)

3.   **Insertion**

$\qquad$ (18 electrons, Rh^I) $\qquad\qquad\qquad\qquad$ (16 electrons, Rh^I)

4. $\xrightarrow{CH_3-I}$ **Oxidative addition**

$\qquad$ (16 electrons, Rh^I) $\qquad\qquad\qquad\qquad$ (18 electrons, Rh^{III})

5.

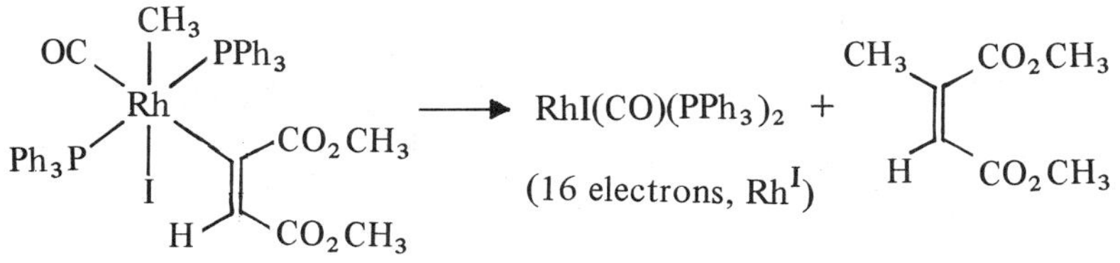

(18 electrons, Rh^{III})

RhI(CO)(PPh$_3$)$_2$ +   **Reductive Elimination**

(16 electrons, Rh^I)

G.6   (CH$_3$)$_2$CuLi +   **Oxidative addition**

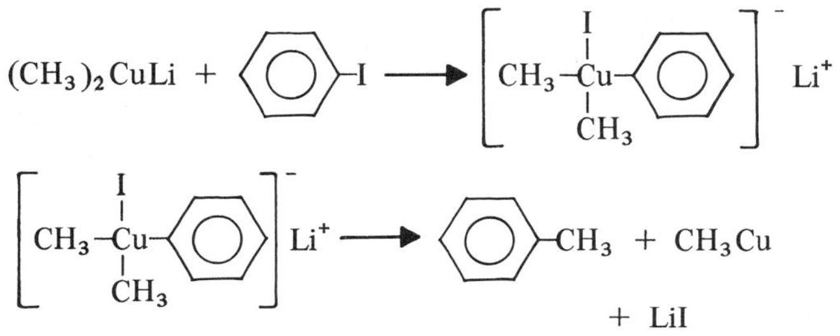

Reductive elimination

+ LiI

G.7   L = Ph$_3$P

1. L$_3$RhCl + C$_6$H$_5$C–H   **Oxidative addition**

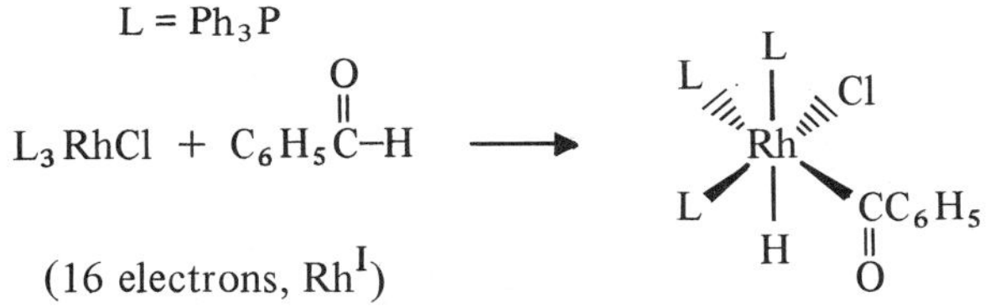

(16 electrons, Rh^I)

(18 electrons, Rh^{III})

2.   **Ligand dissociation**

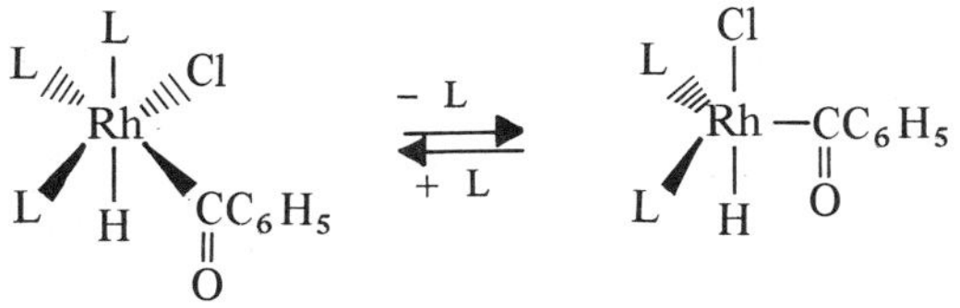

(18 electrons, Rh^{III})   (16 electrons, Rh^{III})

3.   **Deinsertion**

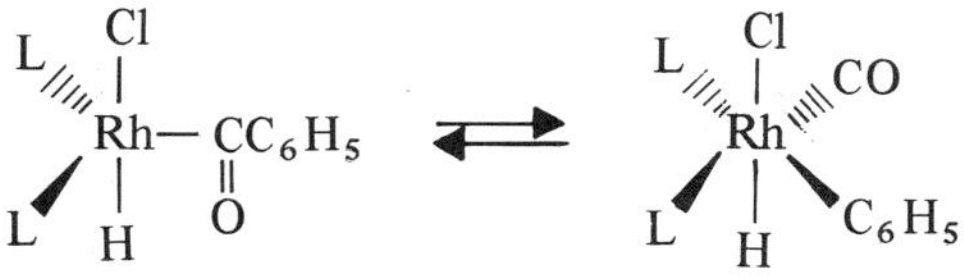

(16 electrons, Rh^{III})   (18 electrons, Rh^{III})

4.

$$\underset{(\text{18 electrons, Rh}^{\text{III}})}{\overset{\displaystyle \text{L}\underset{\text{L}}{\overset{\text{Cl}}{\underset{|}{\underset{\text{H}}{\overset{|}{\text{Rh}}}}}}\overset{\text{CO}}{\underset{\text{C}_6\text{H}_5}{}}} \longrightarrow \underset{(\text{16 electrons, Rh}^{\text{I}})}{\overset{\displaystyle \text{L}\underset{\text{L}}{\overset{}{\text{Rh}}}\overset{\text{CO}}{\underset{\text{Cl}}{}}} + \text{C}_6\text{H}_5\text{--H}$$

Reductive elimination

15 ALCOHOLS, PHENOLS, AND ETHERS

SUMMARY OF ETHERS AND EPOXIDES

$$\text{R–OH} \xrightarrow[\text{(–H}_2\text{O)}]{\text{H}^+} \text{R–O–R}$$

$$\text{R–OH} \xrightarrow{\text{Na}} \text{R–ONa} \xrightarrow[\text{(X=Cl, Br, I)}]{\text{R}'\text{X}} \text{R–O–R}' \xrightarrow{\text{HX}} \text{RX + R}'\text{X}$$

$$\text{R–OH} \xrightarrow[\text{H}_2\text{SO}_4]{\overset{\overset{\text{CH}_3}{|}}{\text{CH}_2\text{=C–CH}_3}} \text{R–O–}\overset{\overset{\text{CH}_3}{|}}{\underset{\underset{\text{CH}_3}{|}}{\text{C}}}\text{–CH}_3$$

EPOXIDES

$$\text{C=C} \xrightarrow{\text{R–C(=O)–O–OH}} \overset{\quad}{\underset{\text{O}}{\text{C}\diagdown\text{C}}}$$

$$\xrightarrow[\text{H}^+]{\text{H}_2\text{O}} -\overset{|}{\underset{|}{\text{C}}}\text{–}\overset{\overset{\text{OH}}{|}}{\underset{\underset{\text{OH}}{|}}{\text{C}}}\text{–}$$

$$\xrightarrow{\text{NH}_3} -\overset{|}{\underset{\underset{\text{OH}}{|}}{\text{C}}}\text{–}\overset{\overset{\text{NH}_2}{|}}{\underset{|}{\text{C}}}\text{–}$$

$$\xrightarrow[\text{ROH}]{\text{RONa}} -\overset{|}{\underset{\underset{\text{OR}}{|}}{\text{C}}}\text{–}\overset{\overset{\text{OH}}{|}}{\underset{|}{\text{C}}}\text{–}$$

SUMMARY OF ALCOHOLS

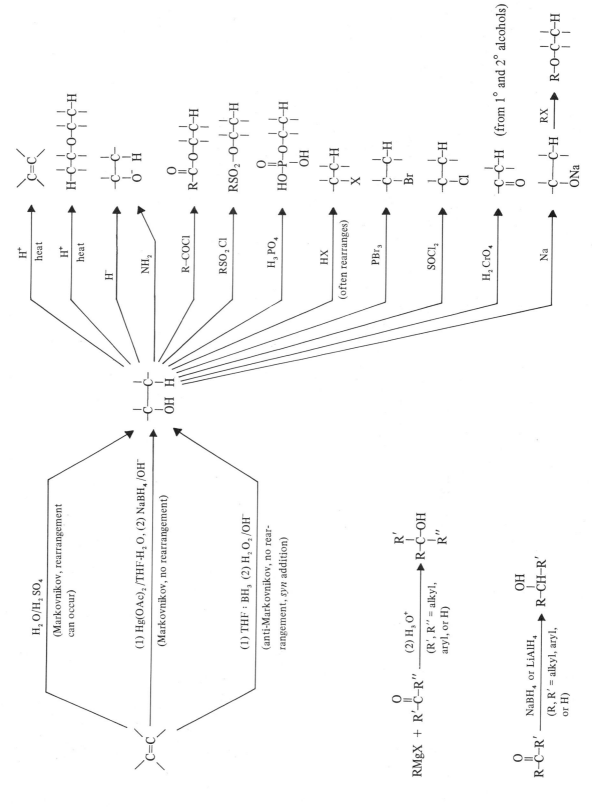

SUMMARY OF PHENOLS

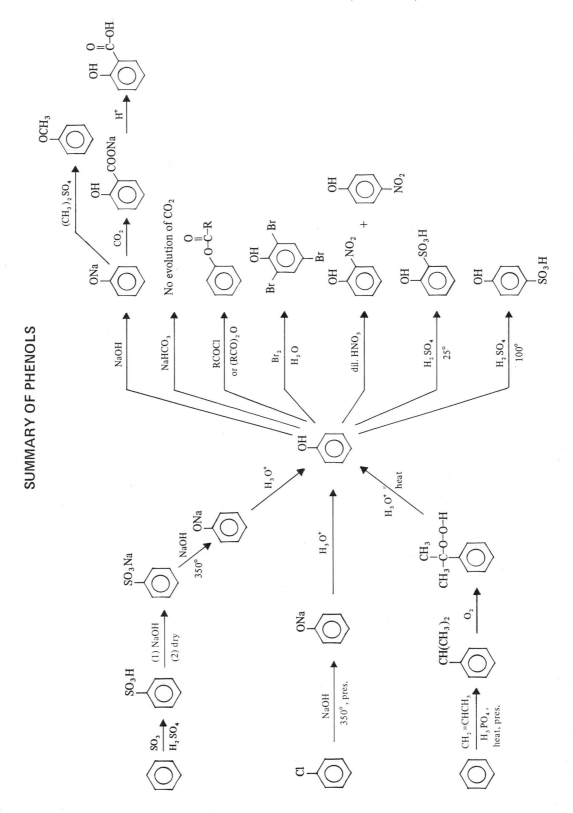

SOLUTIONS TO PROBLEMS

15.1   (a) $CH_3CH_2CH_2OH$, propyl alcohol, 1-propanol.

$$\underset{\underset{\textstyle |}{OH}}{CH_3CHCH_3}, \text{ isopropyl alcohol, 2-propanol}$$

(b) $CH_3CH_2CH_2CH_2OH$, butyl alcohol, 1-butanol

$$\underset{\underset{\textstyle |}{OH}}{CH_3CH_2CHCH_3}, \textit{ sec}\text{-butyl alcohol, 2-butanol}$$

$$\underset{\underset{\textstyle |}{CH_3}}{CH_3CHCH_2OH}, \text{ isobutyl alcohol, 2-methyl-1-propanol}$$

$$CH_3\overset{\overset{\textstyle CH_3}{|}}{\underset{\underset{\textstyle OH}{|}}{C}}CH_3, \textit{ tert}\text{-butyl alcohol, 2-methyl-2-propanol.}$$

15.2

(a) 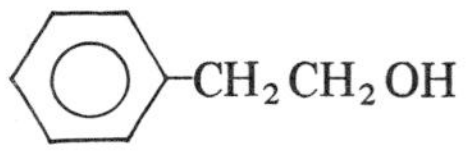   (b) 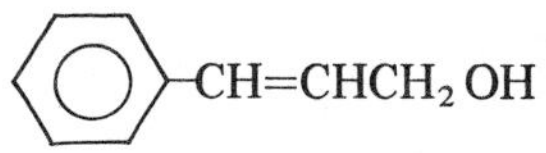   (c)

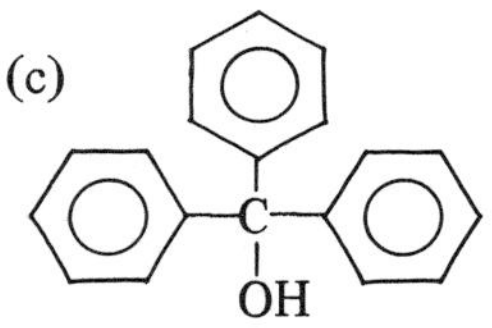

(d)

15.3   (a) Alcohols: $CH_2{=}CHCH_2OH$
          2-Propen-l-ol
          (allyl alcohol)

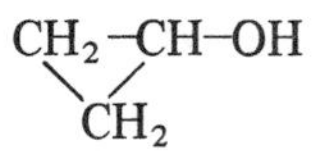

          Cyclopropanol

Ethers: $CH_2{=}CH{-}O{-}CH_3$
          Methoxyethene
          (methyl vinyl ether)

(b) Alcohols: $CH_2{=}CHCH_2CH_2OH$
              3-Buten-1-ol

$$\underset{\underset{\textstyle OH}{|}}{CH_2{=}CHCHCH_3}$$

              3-Buten-2-ol
              $CH_3CH{=}CHCH_2OH$
              2-Buten-1-ol (cis and trans)

$$\underset{\text{2-Methyl-2-propen-1-ol}}{CH_2=\overset{\overset{\displaystyle CH_3}{|}}{C}-CH_2OH}$$

Cyclobutanol   1-Methylcyclopropanol   Cyclopropylmethanol

trans-2-Methylcyclopropanol   *cis*-2-Methylcyclopropanol

Ethers: $CH_3CH=CH-OCH_3$ $CH_2=CHCH_2OCH_3$
       1-Methoxypropene   3-Methoxypropene

$$\underset{\text{2-Methoxypropene}}{CH_2=\overset{\overset{\displaystyle CH_3}{|}}{C}-OCH_3}$$ $\underset{\text{Ethoxyethene}}{CH_2=CHOCH_2CH_3}$

Methoxycyclopropane

(c) Alcohols: $CH_3CH_2CH_2CH_2CH_2OH$ 1-Pentanol

$$\underset{\underset{\displaystyle OH}{|}}{CH_3CH_2CH_2CHCH_3}$$ 2-Pentanol

$$\underset{\underset{\displaystyle OH}{|}}{CH_3CH_2CHCH_2CH_3}$$ 3-Pentanol

$$\overset{\overset{\displaystyle CH_3}{|}}{CH_3CH_2CHCH_2OH}$$ 2-Methyl-1-butanol

$$\overset{\overset{\displaystyle CH_3}{|}}{CH_3CHCH_2CH_2OH}$$ 3-Methyl-1-butanol

$$\underset{\underset{\displaystyle OH}{|}}{\overset{\overset{\displaystyle CH_3}{|}}{CH_3CH_2CCH_3}}$$ 2-Methyl-2-butanol

$$\underset{\underset{\displaystyle OH}{|}}{\overset{\overset{\displaystyle CH_3}{|}}{CH_3CHCHCH_3}}$$ 3-Methyl-2-butanol

$$\underset{\underset{\displaystyle CH_3}{|}}{\overset{\overset{\displaystyle CH_3}{|}}{CH_3-C-CH_2OH}}$$ 2,2-Dimethyl-1-propanol
(neopentyl alcohol)

Ethers:

$CH_3CH_2CH_2CH_2-O-CH_3$ Butyl methyl ether
(1-methoxybutane)

$$CH_3\underset{\underset{CH_3}{|}}{C}HCH_2-O-CH_3$$ Isobutyl methyl ether
(2-methyl-1-methoxypropane)

$$CH_3-\underset{\underset{CH_3}{|}}{\overset{\overset{CH_3}{|}}{C}}-O-CH_3$$ *tert*-Butyl methyl ether
(2-methyl-2-methoxypropane)

$$CH_3CH_2\underset{\underset{CH_3}{|}}{C}H-O-CH_3$$ *sec*-Butyl methyl ether
(2-methoxybutane)

$CH_3CH_2CH_2-O-CH_2CH_3$ Ethyl propyl ether
(1-ethoxypropane)

$$CH_3\underset{\underset{CH_3}{|}}{C}H-O-CH_2CH_3$$ Ethyl isopropyl ether
(2-ethoxypropane)

15.4   The two hydroxyl groups in ethylene glycol allow the formation of more hydrogen bonds than in the monohydroxy alcohols. Thus a single diol molecule can be associated with many neighboring diol molecules.

15.5

(a) $$CH_3\underset{\underset{CH_3}{|}}{C}=CH_2 + H_2O \xrightarrow{H^+} CH_3\underset{\underset{OH}{|}}{\overset{\overset{CH_3}{|}}{C}}CH_3$$

(b) $$CH_3CH_2CH_2CH_2CH=CH_2 + H_2O \xrightarrow{H^+} CH_3CH_2CH_2CH_2\underset{\underset{OH}{|}}{C}HCH_3$$

(c) (cyclopentene) + H_2O $\xrightarrow{H^+}$ (cyclopentanol with OH)

(d) (1-methylcyclohexene) + H_2O $\xrightarrow{H^+}$ (1-methylcyclohexanol with CH₃ and OH)

15.6   Rearrangement of the secondary carbocation to the more stable tertiary carbocation,

$$CH_3\underset{\underset{CH_3}{|}}{\overset{\overset{CH_3}{|}}{C}}-CH=CH_2 \underset{}{\overset{H^+}{\rightleftharpoons}} CH_3-\underset{\underset{CH_3}{|}}{\overset{\overset{CH_3}{|}}{C}}\overset{+}{C}H-CH_3 \longrightarrow CH_3-\overset{+}{\underset{\underset{CH_3}{|}}{C}}-CH-CH_3$$

followed by reaction of the resulting carbocation with water:

$$CH_3-\overset{CH_3}{\underset{CH_3}{\overset{+}{C}}}-CHCH_3 + H_2O \rightleftharpoons CH_3-\overset{+OH_2}{\underset{CH_3}{\overset{|}{C}}}-\overset{}{\underset{CH_3}{\overset{|}{C}}}HCH_3 \rightleftharpoons CH_3-\overset{OH}{\underset{CH_3}{\overset{|}{C}}}-\overset{}{\underset{CH_3}{\overset{|}{C}}}HCH_3$$

$$+ H^+$$

15.7

(a) $CH_3CH_2CH_2CH_2CH=CH_2 \xrightarrow[\text{THF-}H_2O]{Hg(OAc)_2} CH_3CH_2CH_2CH_2\overset{}{\underset{OH}{\overset{|}{C}}}HCH_2-HgOAc$

$\xrightarrow[OH^-]{NaBH_4} CH_3CH_2CH_2CH_2\overset{OH}{\overset{|}{C}}HCH_3$

(b)
$\xrightarrow[\text{(2) }NaBH_4, OH^-]{\text{(1) }Hg(OAc)_2, THF-H_2O}$

(c) $CH_3\overset{CH_3}{\underset{CH_3}{\overset{|}{C}}}CH_2\overset{CH_3}{\overset{|}{C}}=CH_2 \xrightarrow{\text{same as (b)}} CH_3\overset{CH_3}{\underset{CH_3}{\overset{|}{C}}}CH_2\overset{CH_3}{\underset{OH}{\overset{|}{C}}}CH_3$

(d)
$CH_3\overset{}{\underset{}{C}}=CH_2 \xrightarrow{\text{same as (b)}} CH_3\overset{OH}{\overset{|}{C}}CH_3$

15.8

(a) $CH_3-\overset{CH_3}{\underset{CH_3}{\overset{|}{C}}}-CH=CH_2 + THF:BH_3 \longrightarrow (CH_3-\overset{CH_3}{\underset{CH_3}{\overset{|}{C}}}-CH_2CH_2)_3B$

$\xrightarrow[OH^-, H_2O]{H_2O_2} CH_3-\overset{CH_3}{\underset{CH_3}{\overset{|}{C}}}-CH_2CH_2OH$

(b) $CH_3CH_2CH_2CH_2CH=CH_2 \xrightarrow[\text{(2) }H_2O_2, OH^-, H_2O]{\text{(1) }THF:BH_3} CH_3CH_2CH_2CH_2CH_2CH_2OH$

(c)
$-CH=CH_2 \xrightarrow{\text{same as (b)}}$
$-CH_2CH_2OH$

(d) [structure of 1-methylcyclohexene] $\xrightarrow{\text{same as (b)}}$ [chair cyclohexane structure with H, CH₃, OH, H] + Enantiomer

15.9

(a) H–C̈–O–H (with H top and bottom)

3H = 3(−1)
1O = +1
total = −2 = oxidation state of C

$\overset{O}{\underset{\|}{H-C-O-H}}$

1H = −1
3O = +3
total = +2 = oxidation state of C

$\overset{O}{\underset{\|}{H-C-H}}$

2H = −2
2O = +2
total = 0 = oxidation state of C

(b) CH_4, CH_3OH, $\overset{O}{\underset{\|}{HCH}}$, $\overset{O}{\underset{\|}{HCOH}}$, CO_2
   −4   −2   0   +2   +4

(c) a change from −2 to 0

(d) an oxidation, since the oxidation state increases

(e) a reduction from +6 to +3

15.10

(a)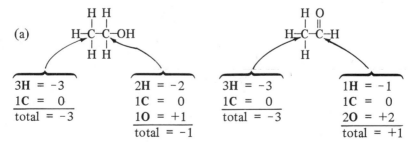

3H = −3
1C = 0
total = −3

2H = −2
1C = 0
1O = +1
total = −1

3H = −3
1C = 0
total = −3

1H = −1
1C = 0
2O = +2
total = +1

(b) Only the carbon of the −CH₂OH group of ethanol undergoes a change in oxidation state. The oxidation state of the carbon in the CH₃− group remains unchanged.

(c)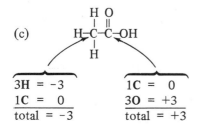

3H = −3
1C = 0
total = −3

1C = 0
3O = +3
total = +3

The oxygen-bearing carbon increases its oxidation state from +1 (in acetaldehyde) to +3 (in acetic acid).

15.11 (a) If we consider the hydrogenation of ethene as an example, we find that the oxidation state of carbon decreases. Thus, because the reaction involves the *addition* of *hydrogen*, it is both an *addition reaction* and a *reduction*.

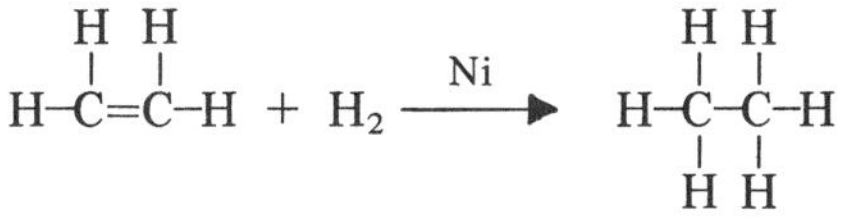

$$\text{H-}\underset{\underset{\displaystyle H}{|}}{\overset{\overset{\displaystyle H}{|}}{C}}\text{=}\underset{\underset{\displaystyle H}{|}}{\overset{\overset{\displaystyle H}{|}}{C}}\text{-H} + \text{H}_2 \xrightarrow{\text{Ni}} \text{H-}\underset{\underset{\displaystyle H}{|}}{\overset{\overset{\displaystyle H}{|}}{C}}\text{-}\underset{\underset{\displaystyle H}{|}}{\overset{\overset{\displaystyle H}{|}}{C}}\text{-H}$$

$$\begin{array}{ll} \text{2H} = -2 & \text{3H} = -3 \\ \underline{\text{2C} = 0} & \underline{\text{1C} = 0} \\ \text{total} = -2 & \text{total} = -3 \end{array}$$

(b) The hydrogenation of acetaldehyde is not only an addition reaction, it is also a *reduction* because the carbon atom of the C=O group goes from a + 1 to a - 1 oxidation state. The reverse reaction (the *dehydrogenation* of ethyl alcohol) is not only an *elimination* reaction, it is also an *oxidation*.

Ion-Electron Half-Reaction Method for Balancing Organic Oxidation Equations

Only two simple rules are needed:

Rule 1: Electrons (e^-) together with protons (H^+) are arbitrarily considered the reducing agents in the half-reaction for the reduction of the oxidizing agent. Ion charges are balanced by *adding electrons to the left-hand side*. (If the reaction is run in neutral or basic solution, add an equal number of OH^- ions to both sides of the balanced half-reaction to neutralize the H^+, and show the resulting $H^+ + OH^-$ as H_2O.

Rule 2: Water (H_2O) is arbitrarily taken as the formal source of oxygen for the oxidation of the organic compound, producing *product, protons*, and *electrons* on the right-hand side. (Again, use OH^- to neutralize H^+ in the *balanced* half-reaction in neutral or basic media.)

EXAMPLE 1

Write a balanced equation for the oxidation of RCH_2OH to RCO_2H by $Cr_2O_7^{-2}$ in acid solution.

Reduction half-reaction:

$$Cr_2O_7^{-2} + H^+ + e^- \longrightarrow 2Cr^{+3} + 7H_2O$$

Balancing atoms and charges:

$$Cr_2O_7^{-2} + 14H^+ + 6e^- = 2Cr^{+3} + 7H_2O$$

Oxidation half-reaction:

$$RCH_2OH + H_2O = RCO_2H + 4H^+ + 4e^-$$

The least common multiple of a 6-electron uptake in the reduction step and a 4-electron loss in the oxidation step is 12, so we multiply the first half-reaction by 2 and the second by 3, and add:

$$3RCH_2OH + 3H_2O + 2Cr_2O_7^{-2} + 28H^+ = 3RCO_2H + 12H^+ + 4Cr^{+3}$$
$$+ 14H_2O$$

Canceling common terms we get:

$$3RCH_2OH + 2Cr_2O_7^{-2} + 16H^+ = 3RCO_2H + 4Cr^{+3} + 11H_2O$$

This shows that the oxidation of 3 moles of a primary alcohol to a carboxylic acid requires 2 moles of dichromate.

EXAMPLE 2

Write a balanced equation for the oxidation of styrene to benzoate ion and carbonate ion by MnO_4^- in alkaline solution.

Reduction: $MnO_4^- + 4H^+ + 3e^- = MnO_2 + 2H_2O$ (in acid)

Since this reaction is carried out in basic solution, we must add $4OH^-$ to neutralize the $4H^+$ on the left side, and, of course, $4OH^-$ to the right side to maintain a balanced equation.

$$MnO_4^- + 4H^+ + 4OH^- + 3e^- = MnO_2 + 2H_2O + 4OH^-$$

or, $MnO_4^- + 2H_2O + 3e^- = MnO_2 + 4OH^-$

Oxidation: $ArCH=CH_2 + 5H_2O = ArCO_2^- + CO_3^{-2} + 13H^+ + 10e^-$

We add $13OH^-$ to each side to neutralize the H^+ on the right side,

$$ArCH=CH_2 + 5H_2O + 13OH^- = ArCO_2^- + CO_3^{-2} + 13H_2O + 10e^-$$

The least common multiple is 30, so we multiply the reduction half-reaction by 10 and the oxidation half-reaction by 3 and add:

$$3ArCH=CH_2 + 39OH^- + 10MnO_4^- + 20H_2O = 3ArCO_2^- + 3CO_3^{-2} +$$
$$24H_2O + 10MnO_2 + 40\ OH^-$$

Canceling:

$$3ArCH=CH_2 + 10MnO_4^- = 3ArCO_2^- + 3CO_3^{-2} + 4H_2O + 10MnO_2$$
$$+ OH^-$$

SAMPLE PROBLEMS

Using the ion-electron half-reaction method, write balanced equations for the following oxidation reactions.

(a)   Cyclohexene $+ MnO_4^- + H^+ \xrightarrow{\text{(hot)}} HOOC(CH_2)_4COOH + Mn^{+2} + H_2O$

(b) Cyclopentene + MnO_4^- + H_2O $\xrightarrow{\text{(cold)}}$ cis-1,2-Cyclopentanediol + MnO_2 + OH^-

(c) Cyclopentanol + HNO_3 $\xrightarrow{\text{(hot)}}$ $HOOC(CH_2)_3COOH$ + NO_2 + H_2O

(d) 1,2,3-Cyclohexanetriol + HIO_4 $\xrightarrow{\text{(cold)}}$ $HOOC(CH_2)_3CHO$ + $HCOOH$ + HIO_3

SOLUTIONS TO SAMPLE PROBLEMS

(a) Reduction:

$$MnO_4^- + 8H^+ + 5e^- = Mn^{+2} + 4H_2O$$

Oxidation:

+ $4H_2O$ = $COOH$ $COOH$ + $8H^+$ + $8e^-$

The least common multiple is 40:

$$8MnO_4^- + 64H^+ + 40e^- = 8Mn^{+2} + 32\,H_2O$$

5 + $20H_2O$ = 5 $COOH$ $COOH$ + $40H^+$ + $40e^-$

Adding and canceling:

5 + $8MnO_4^-$ + $24H^+$ = 5 $COOH$ $COOH$ + $8Mn^{+2}$ + $12H_2O$

(b) Reduction:

$$MnO_4^- + 2H_2O + 3e^- = MnO_2 + 4OH^-$$

Oxidation:

+ $2OH^-$ = OH OH + $2e^-$

The least common multiple is 6:

$$2MnO_4^- + 4H_2O + 6e^- = 2MnO_2 + 8OH^-$$

3 + $6OH^-$ = 3 OH OH + $6e^-$

Adding and canceling:

3 + $2MnO_4^-$ + $4H_2O$ = 3 OH OH + $2MnO_2$ + $2OH^-$

(c) Reduction:

$$HNO_3 + H^+ + e^- = NO_2 + H_2O$$

Oxidation:

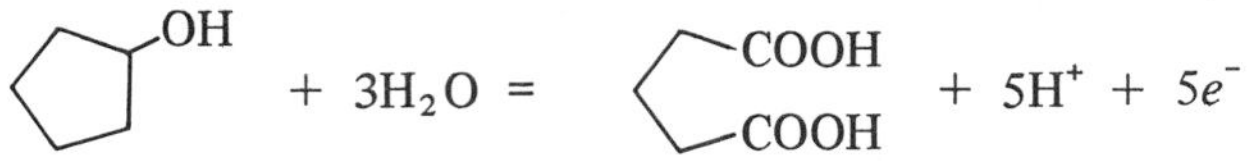

$+ 3H_2O =$ $+ 5H^+ + 5e^-$

The least common multiple is 5:

$$5HNO_3 + 5H^+ + 5e^- = 5NO_2 + 5H_2O$$

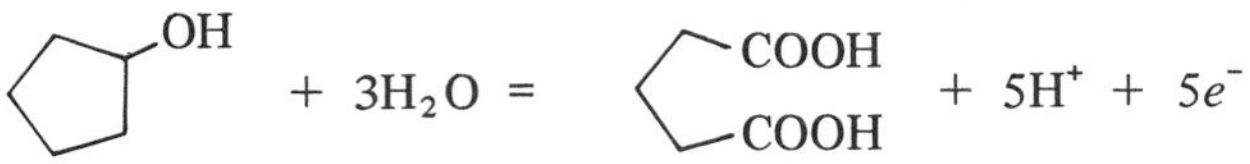

$+ 3H_2O =$ $+ 5H^+ + 5e^-$

Adding and canceling:

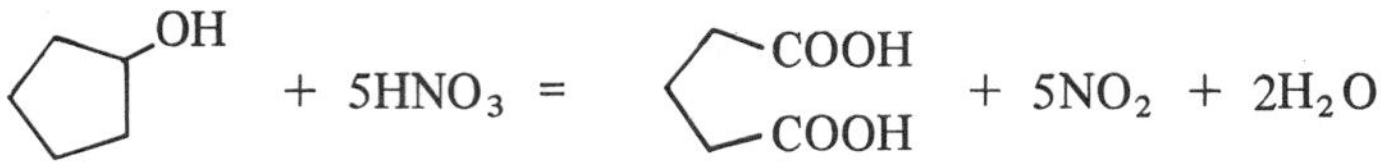

$+ 5HNO_3 =$ $+ 5NO_2 + 2H_2O$

(d) Reduction:

$$HIO_4 + 2H^+ + 2e^- = HIO_3 + H_2O$$

Oxidation:

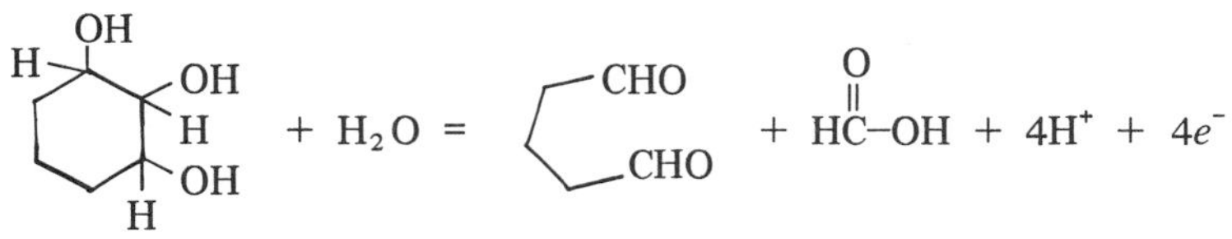

$+ H_2O =$ $+ H\overset{O}{\underset{}{C}}{-}OH + 4H^+ + 4e^-$

The least common multiple is 4:

$$2HIO_4 + 4H^+ + 4e^- = 2HIO_3 + 2H_2O$$

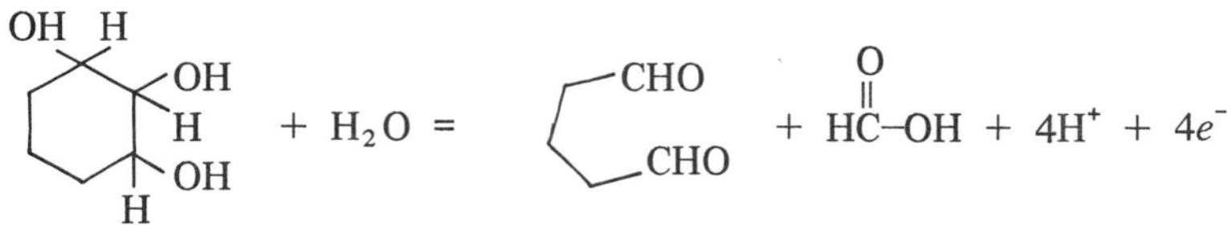

$+ H_2O =$ $+ HC{-}OH + 4H^+ + 4e^-$

Adding and canceling:

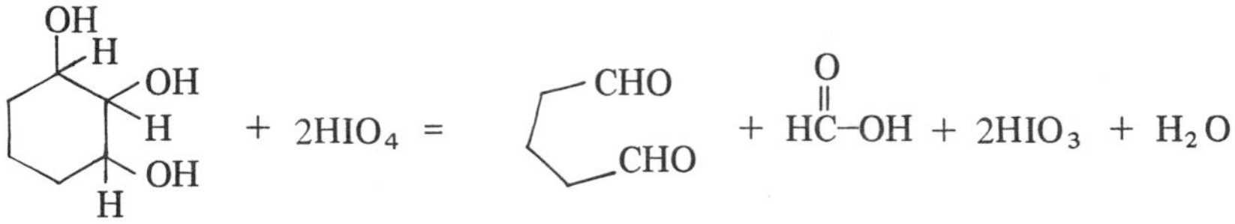

$+ 2HIO_4 =$ $+ HC{-}OH + 2HIO_3 + H_2O$

15.12 (a) $LiAlH_4$ (b) $NaBH_4$ ($LiAlH_4$ would reduce both carbonyl groups.)

(c) $LiAlH_4$

15.13 (a) $CH_3C \equiv C:^- + CH_3CH_2OH \rightleftharpoons CH_3C \equiv CH + CH_3CH_2O^-$

Stronger base   Stronger acid   Weaker acid   Weaker base

(b) $CH_3CH_2CH_2\overset{\delta-}{C}H_2:\overset{\delta+}{Li} + CH_3CH_2OH \rightleftharpoons CH_3CH_2CH_2CH_3 + CH_3CH_2\overset{+}{O}Li$

Stronger base   Stronger acid   Weaker acid   Weaker base

(c) $CH_3\overset{\delta-}{C}H_2:\overset{\delta+}{MgBr} + CH_3CH_2OH \rightleftharpoons CH_3CH_3 + CH_3CH_2\overset{-\ +}{O}MgBr$

Stronger base   Stronger acid   Weaker acid   Weaker base

15.14

$$CH_3CH_2\overset{*}{O}H + Cl\overset{\overset{O}{\|}}{\underset{\underset{O}{\|}}{S}}CH_3 + OH^- \longrightarrow CH_3CH_2\overset{*}{O}\overset{\overset{O}{\|}}{\underset{\underset{O}{\|}}{S}}CH_3 + Cl^- + H_2O$$

If C–O bond cleavage does not occur, then all of the isotopically labeled oxygen (O* = ^{18}O) will be found in the sulfonate ester. Otherwise all or part of the ^{18}O will be found in the water formed in the reaction.

15.15

(a)

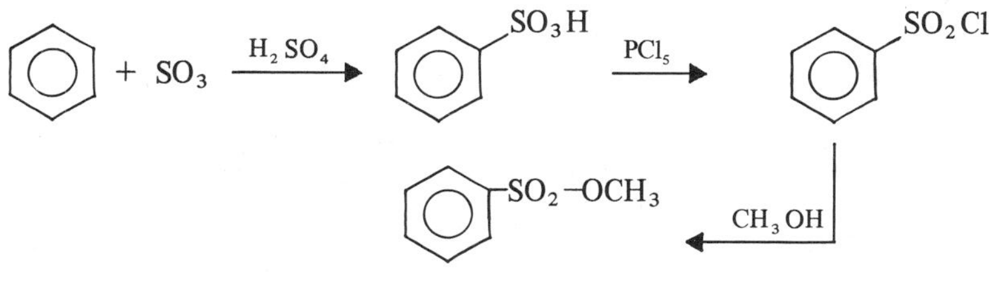

(b)

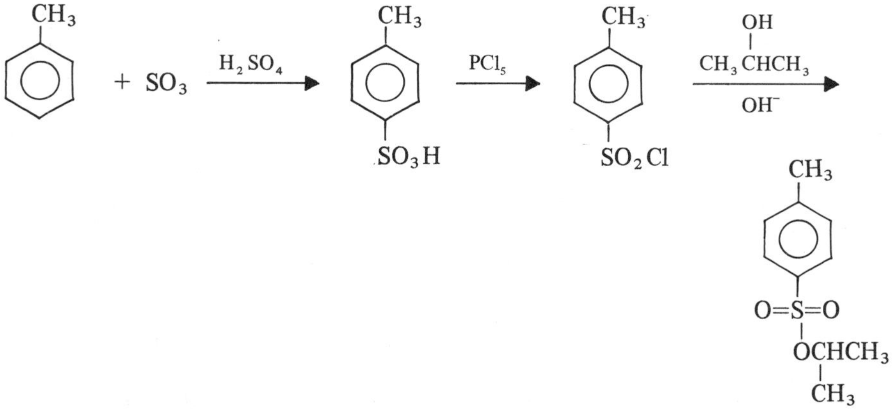

(c)

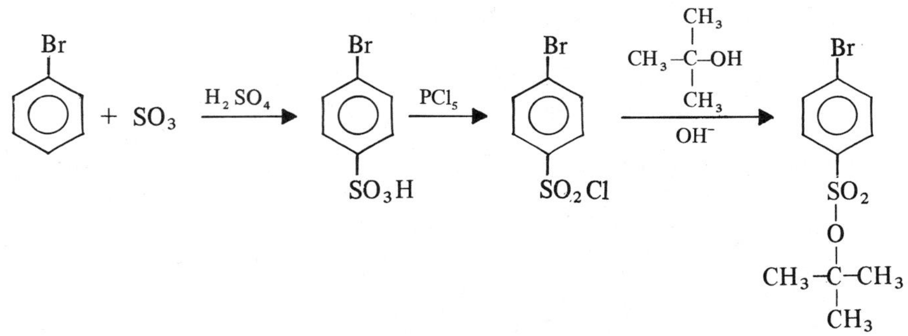

15.16

(a)

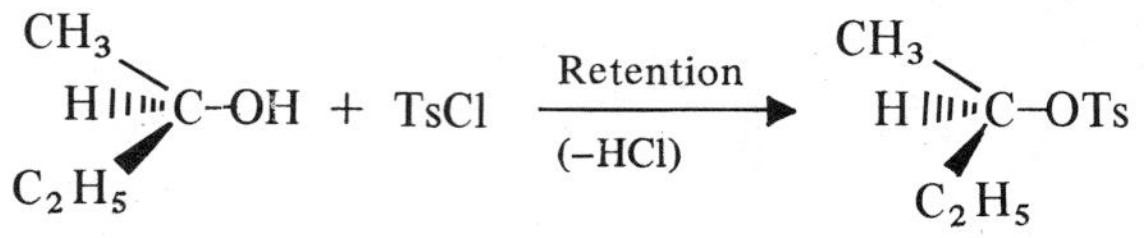

(R)-2-Butanol

(b)

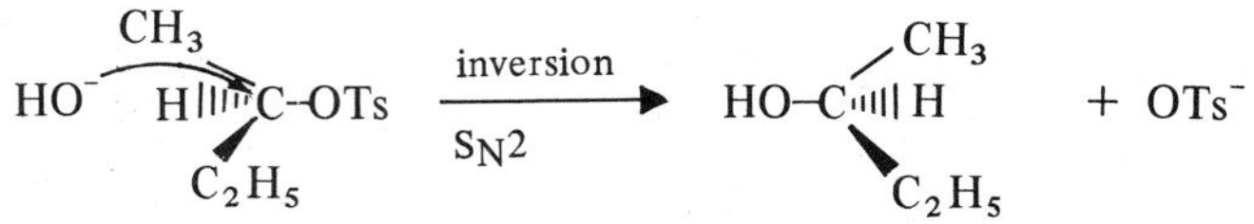

(c)

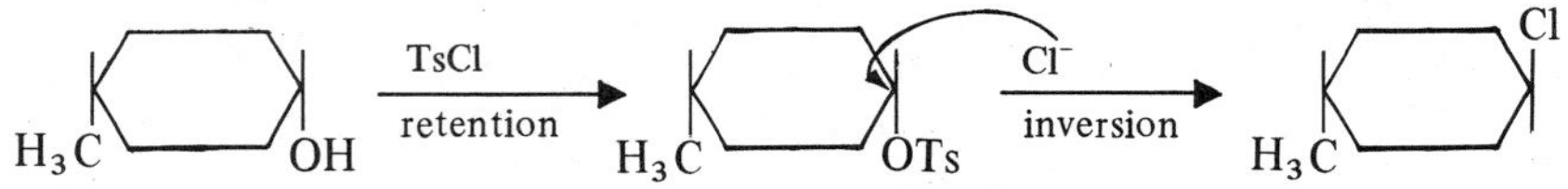

cis-4-Methylcyclohexanol

trans-1-Chloro-4-
methylcyclohexane

15.17 (a) trans-2-Pentene because it is more stable.

(b) 1-Phenylpropene is conjugated and thus is more stable than the unconjugated 3-phenylpropene, and trans-1-phenylpropene is more stable than the cis isomer.

15.18

(a)

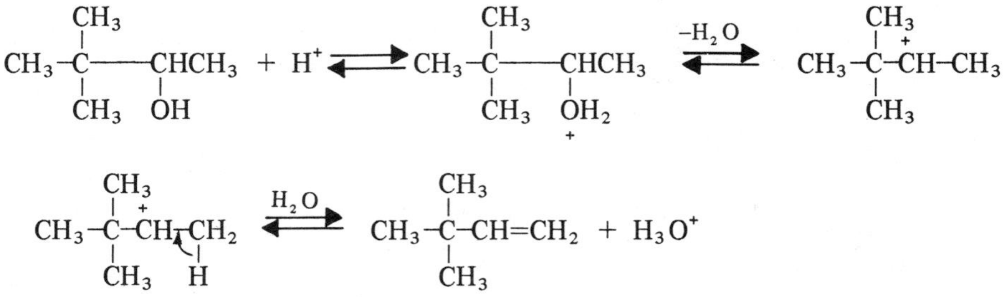

I

But this secondary carbocation can also rearrange to a tertiary carbocation before losing a proton:

(b)   2,3-Dimethyl-2-butene (III) is the most substituted alkene, therefore it is most stable.

15.19

(a)

This reaction succeeds because a 3° carbocation is much more stable than a 1° carbocation. Mixing the 1° alcohol and H_2SO_4, consequently, does not lead to formation of appreciable amounts of a 1° carbocation. However, when the 3° alcohol is added, it is rapidly converted to a 3° carbocation, which then reacts with the 1° alcohol that is present in the mixture.

15.20

(a)   (1)

$$CH_3\overset{CH_3}{\underset{}{C}}HO^-Na^+ + CH_3-L \longrightarrow CH_3\overset{CH_3}{\underset{}{C}}HO-CH_3 + L^- + Na^+$$

(L = X, OSO_2R, or OSO_2OR)

(2)
$$CH_3O^- + CH_3-\overset{CH_3}{\underset{}{C}}H-L \longrightarrow CH_3O-\overset{CH_3}{\underset{}{C}}HCH_3 + L^-$$

(L = X, OSO_2R, or OSO_2OR)

(b)   Both methods involve S_N2 reactions. Therefore, method (1) is better because substitution takes place at an unhindered methyl carbon. In method (2) where substitution must take place at a relatively hindered secondary carbon the reaction would be accompanied by considerable elimination.

15.21   Reaction of the alcohol with K and then of the resulting salt with C_2H_5Br does not break bonds to the chiral carbon, and these reactions therefore occur with retention of configuration at the chiral carbon.

Reaction of the tosylate, $C_6H_5CH_2CHCH_3$, with C_2H_5OH in K_2CO_3 solution, however,

$\qquad\qquad\qquad\qquad\qquad$ OTs

is an S_N2 reaction that takes place at the chiral carbon and thus it occurs with inversion at the chiral carbon.

15.22

$$\underset{\overset{\displaystyle |}{OH}}{\underset{\displaystyle Cl-CH_2}{\overset{\displaystyle CH_2-CH_2}{|\qquad|}}\underset{}{CH_2}} \underset{\longleftarrow}{\overset{OH^-}{\longrightarrow}} \underset{\overset{\displaystyle :O:^-}{}}{\overset{\displaystyle CH_2-CH_2}{Cl-CH_2\quad CH_2}} \longrightarrow \overset{\displaystyle CH_2-CH_2}{\underset{\displaystyle O}{CH_2\quad CH_2}} + Cl^-$$

$$+$$

$$H_2O$$

15.23

(a) $HO^- + HOCH_2-CH_2-Cl \rightleftharpoons H_2O + {}^-O-CH_2-CH_2-Cl \longrightarrow \overset{\displaystyle O}{\underset{}{CH_2-CH_2}}$

(b) The $-\overset{..}{\underset{..}{O}}:^-$ group must displace the Cl^- from the back side,

trans-2-Chloro-
cyclohexanol

Backside attack is not possible with the cis-isomer (below) therefore it does not form an epoxide.

cis-2-Chloro-
cyclohexanol

15.24

(a) $\underset{\overset{\displaystyle |}{CH_3}}{\underset{\displaystyle CH_3}{CH_2=C}} \overset{H^+}{\longrightarrow} \underset{\overset{\displaystyle |}{CH_3}}{\underset{\displaystyle CH_3}{CH_3-C^+}} \overset{R-OH}{\longrightarrow} \underset{\overset{\displaystyle |}{CH_3\ H}}{\underset{\displaystyle CH_3}{CH_3-C\overset{+}{\quad}OR}} \overset{-H^+}{\longrightarrow} \underset{\overset{\displaystyle |}{CH_3}}{\underset{\displaystyle CH_3}{CH_3-C-OR}}$

(b) The *tert*-butyl group is easily removed because, in acid, it is easily converted to a relatively stable, tertiary carbocation.

(c)
$$CH_3-\underset{\underset{CH_3}{|}}{\overset{\overset{CH_3}{|}}{C}}-O-R \xrightarrow{H^+} CH_3-\underset{\underset{CH_3}{|}}{\overset{\overset{CH_3}{|}}{C}}-\underset{\underset{H}{|}}{\overset{+}{O}}R \longrightarrow CH_3-\underset{\underset{CH_3}{|}}{\overset{\overset{CH_3}{|}}{\overset{+}{C}}} + HOR$$

$$CH_3-\underset{\underset{CH_3}{|}}{\overset{\overset{CH_3}{|}}{C}}-OH \xleftarrow{-H^+} CH_3-\underset{\underset{CH_3}{|}}{\overset{\overset{CH_3}{|}}{C}}-\overset{+}{O}H_2 \xleftarrow{H_2O} \qquad \xrightarrow{-H^+} CH_2=\underset{\underset{CH_3}{|}}{C}-CH_3$$

15.25

$$HOCH_2CH_2CH_2Br \xrightarrow[H_2SO_4]{CH_2=C(CH_3)_2} (CH_3)_3COCH_2CH_2CH_2Br \xrightarrow[ether]{Mg}$$

$$(CH_3)_3COCH_2CH_2CH_2MgBr + CH_3\overset{\overset{O}{||}}{C}CH_3 \longrightarrow (CH_3)_3COCH_2CH_2CH_2\underset{\underset{OMgBr}{|}}{C}(CH_3)_2$$

$$(CH_3)_3COH + HOCH_2CH_2CH_2\underset{\underset{OH}{|}}{C}(CH_3)_2 \xleftarrow{H_3\overset{+}{O}/H_2O}$$

15.26

(a)
$$CH_3O-\underset{\underset{CH_2CH_3}{}}{\overset{\overset{H}{|}}{C}}{}_{\prime\prime\prime\prime}CH_3 + HI \longrightarrow I^- + CH_3-\underset{\underset{H}{|}}{\overset{+}{O}}-\underset{\underset{CH_2CH_3}{}}{\overset{\overset{H}{|}}{C}}{}_{\prime\prime\prime\prime}CH_3 \longrightarrow$$

$$ICH_3 + HO-\underset{\underset{CH_2CH_3}{}}{\overset{\overset{H}{|}}{C}}{}_{\prime\prime\prime\prime}CH_3$$

S_N2 attack of the I^- occurs at the methyl carbon because it is less hindered, therefore, the bond between the *sec*-butyl group and the oxygen is not broken.

(b)
$$CH_3-O-C(CH_3)_3 + HI \longrightarrow CH_3-\underset{\underset{H}{|}}{\overset{+}{O}}-C(CH_3)_3 + I^-$$

$$\updownarrow$$

$$CH_3OH + CH_3-\underset{\underset{CH_3}{|}}{\overset{\overset{CH_3}{|}}{\overset{+}{C}}} \xrightarrow{I^-} CH_3-\underset{\underset{CH_3}{|}}{\overset{\overset{CH_3}{|}}{C}}-I$$

In this reaction the much more stable *tert*-butyl cation is produced. It then combines with I^- to form *tert*-butyl iodide.

15.27

(a) 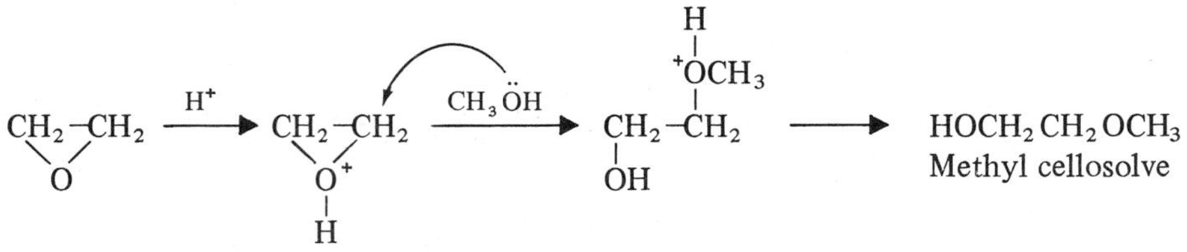
$$CH_2\text{-}CH_2 \xrightarrow{H^+} CH_2\text{-}CH_2 \xrightarrow{CH_3\ddot{O}H} CH_2\text{-}CH_2 \longrightarrow HOCH_2CH_2OCH_3$$

Methyl cellosolve

(b) An analogous reaction yields Ethyl Cellosolve, $HOCH_2CH_2OCH_2CH_3$

(c) 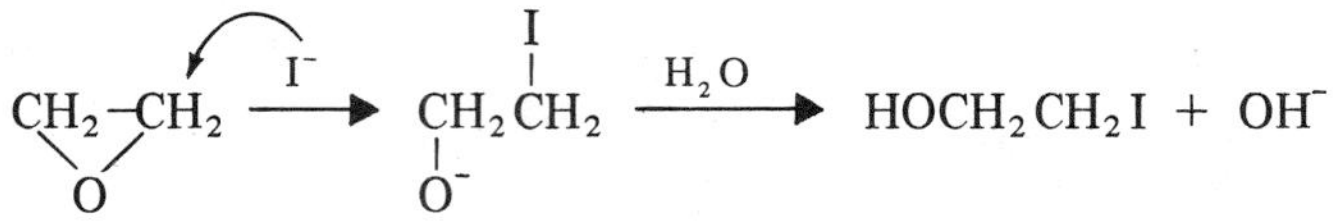
$$CH_2\text{-}CH_2 \xrightarrow{I^-} CH_2CH_2 \xrightarrow{H_2O} HOCH_2CH_2I + OH^-$$

(d) 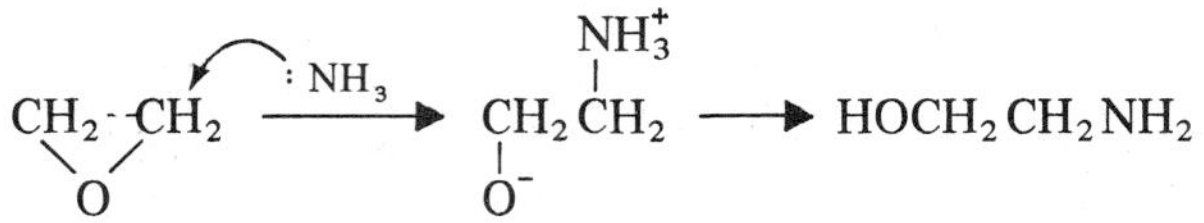
$$CH_2\text{-}CH_2 \xrightarrow{:NH_3} CH_2CH_2 \longrightarrow HOCH_2CH_2NH_2$$

(e) 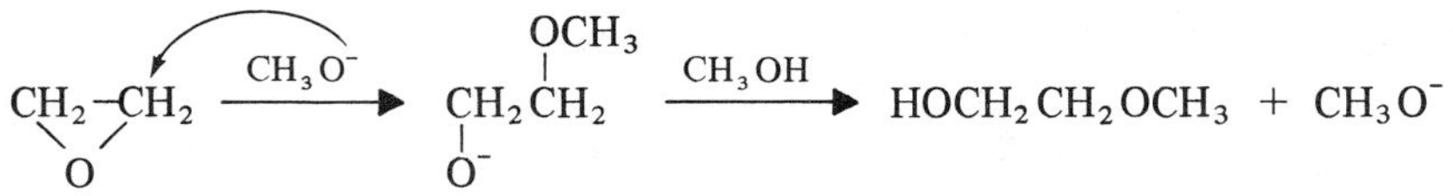
$$CH_2\text{-}CH_2 \xrightarrow{CH_3O^-} CH_2CH_2 \xrightarrow{CH_3OH} HOCH_2CH_2OCH_3 + CH_3O^-$$

15.28 The reaction is an S_N2 reaction and thus nucleophilic attack takes place much more rapidly at the primary carbon than at the more hindered secondary carbon.

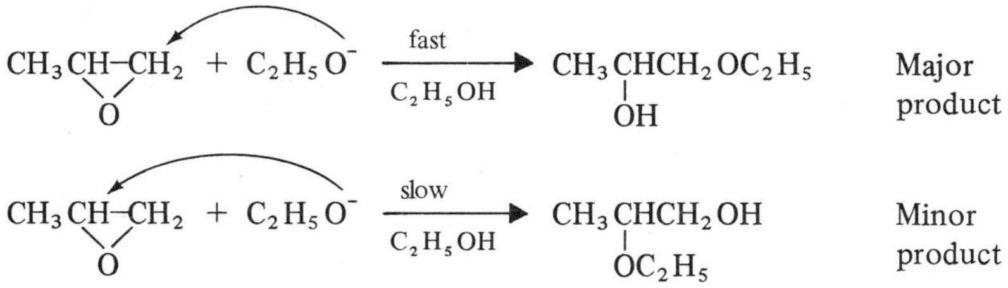

$$CH_3CH\text{-}CH_2 + C_2H_5O^- \xrightarrow[C_2H_5OH]{fast} CH_3CHCH_2OC_2H_5 \quad \text{Major product}$$

$$CH_3CH\text{-}CH_2 + C_2H_5O^- \xrightarrow[C_2H_5OH]{slow} CH_3CHCH_2OH \quad \text{Minor product}$$

15.29 Ethoxide ion attacks the epoxide ring at the primary carbon because it is less hindered and the following reactions take place.

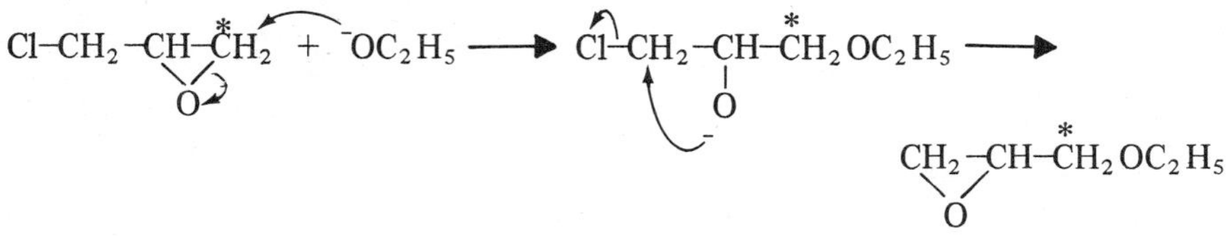

$$Cl\text{-}CH_2\text{-}CH\text{-}\overset{*}{C}H_2 + {}^-OC_2H_5 \longrightarrow Cl\text{-}CH_2\text{-}CH\text{-}\overset{*}{C}H_2OC_2H_5 \longrightarrow$$

$$CH_2\text{-}CH\text{-}\overset{*}{C}H_2OC_2H_5$$

15.30 In structures 2 - 4, page 681, the carbon-oxygen bond is a double bond. Thus we would expect the carbon-oxygen bond of a phenol to be much stronger than that of an alcohol.

2   3   4

The strength of the carbon-oxygen bond is one factor that helps explain the low reactivity of phenol toward conc. HBr. (Another factor is the high energy associated with phenol protonated on oxygen. Structures comparable to 2, 3, and 4 would not contribute appreciably to such a hybrid, because the oxygen would bear a double positive charge.)

15.31   An electron-releasing group (i.e., $-CH_3$) destabilizes the phenoxide anion by intensifying its negative charge. This effect makes the substituted phenol less acidic than phenol itself.

Electron-releasing $-CH_3$ destabilizes the anion more than the acid — K_a is smaller than for phenol.

An electron-withdrawing group such as chlorine can stabilize the phenoxide ion by dispersing its negative charge through an inductive effect. This effect makes the substituted phenol more acidic than phenol itself.

Electron-withdrawing chlorine stabilizes the anion by dispersing its negative charge. K_a is larger than for phenol.

Nitro groups are electron withdrawing by their inductive and resonance effects. The resonance effect is especially important in stabilizing the phenoxide anion. In the 2,4,6-trinitrophenoxide anion, for example, structures, **B**, **C**, and **D** contribute to the resonance hybrid and stabilize it by dispersing the negative charge. These contributions explain why 2,4,6-trinitro phenol (picric acid) is so exceptionally acidic.

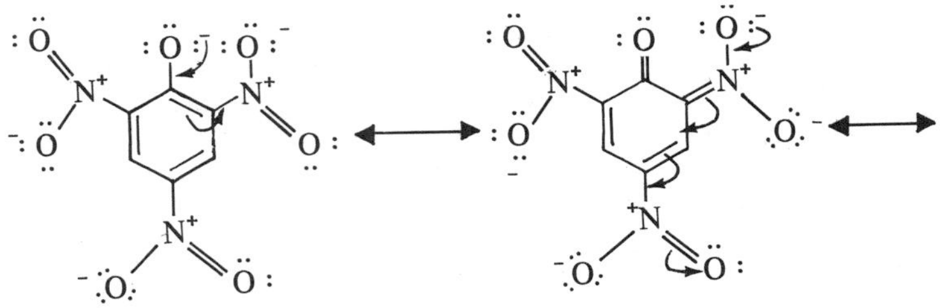

A   B

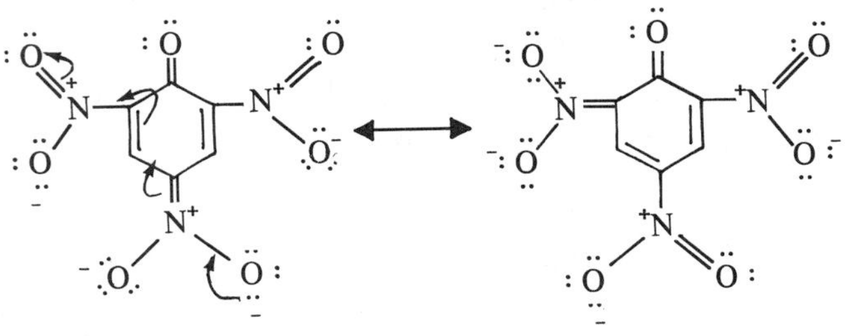

C   D

15.32   (d), (e), (f) All of these are stronger acids than H_2CO_3 (see Table 15.6), thus they would all be converted to their soluble sodium salts when treated with aqueous $NaHCO_3$. With 2,4-dinitrophenol, for example, the following reaction would take place.

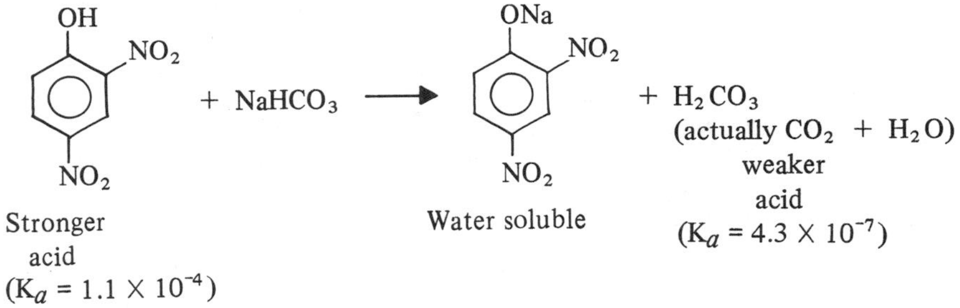

Stronger
acid
$(K_a = 1.1 \times 10^{-4})$

Water soluble

+ H_2CO_3
(actually CO_2 + H_2O)
weaker
acid
$(K_a = 4.3 \times 10^{-7})$

15.33   (a) The para-sulfonated phenol, because it is the major product at the higher temperature—when the reaction is under equilibrium control.

(b) For ortho sulfonation, because it is the major reaction pathway at the lower temperature—when the reaction is under rate control.

15.34

(a) 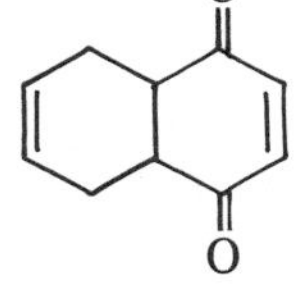   (b) 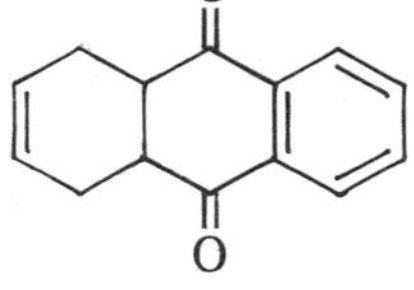   (c)

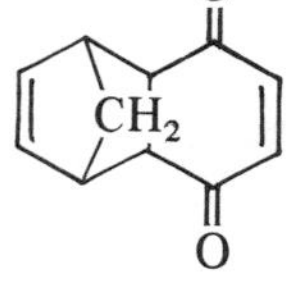

15.35

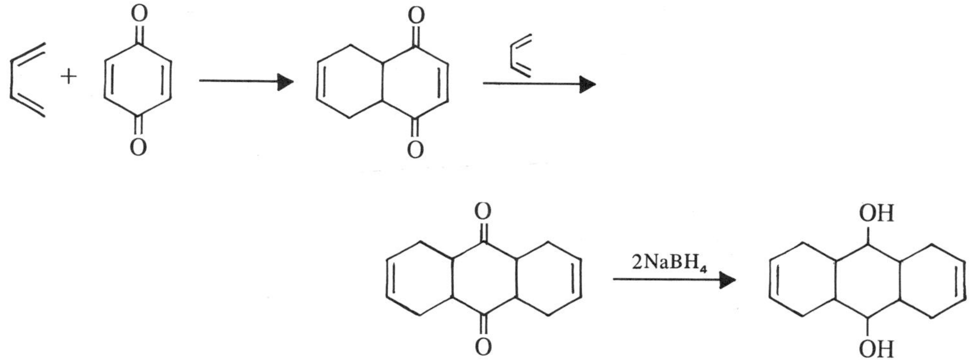

15.36

(a) (1)

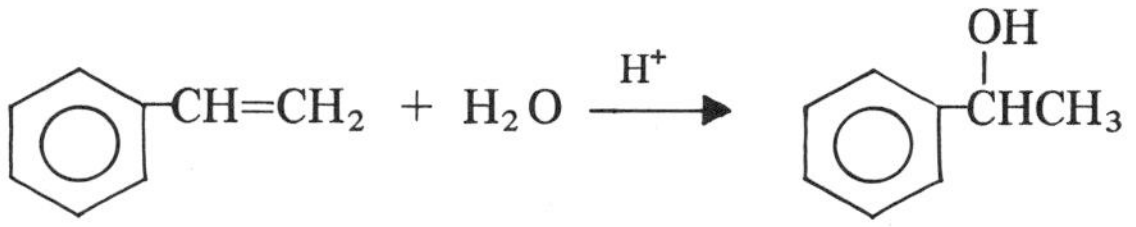

(2)

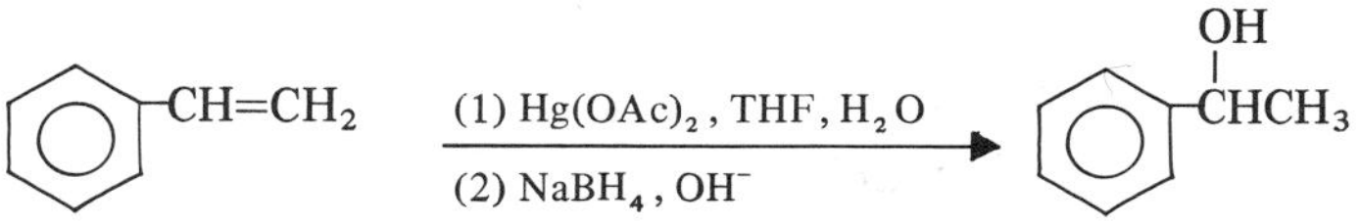

(b)

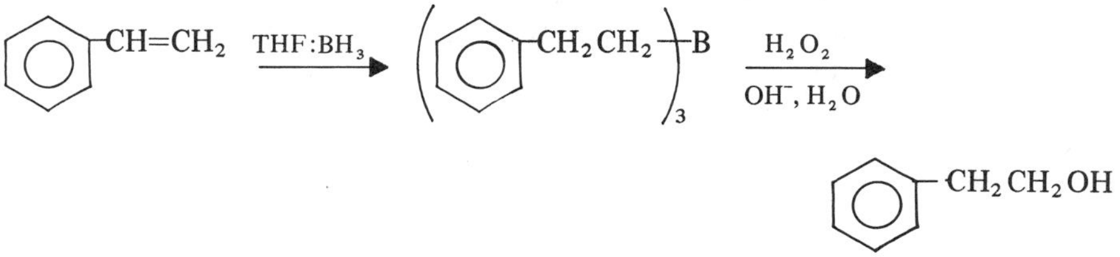

(c)

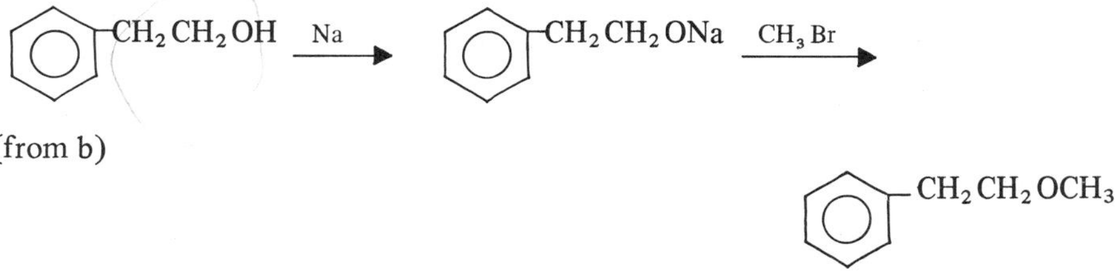

(from b)

(d)

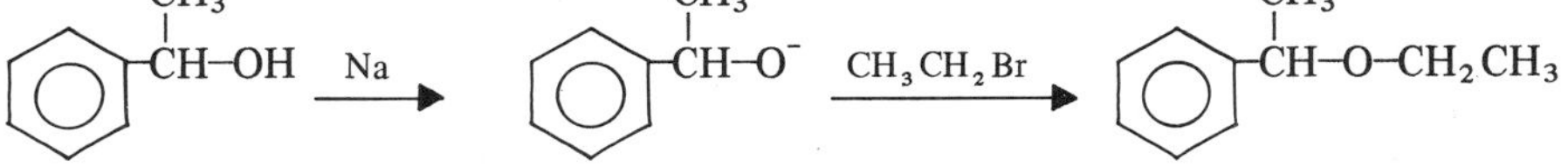

(e)

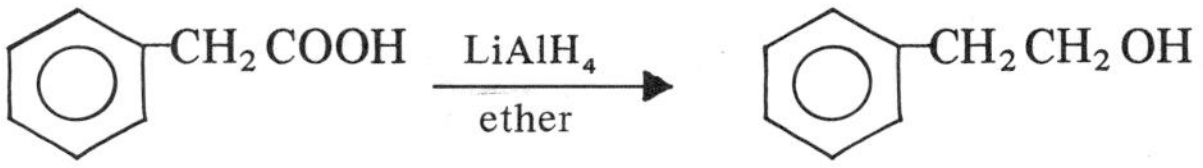

(f) $C_6H_5\!-\!\overset{\overset{\displaystyle O}{\|}}{C}\!-\!CH_3 \xrightarrow[\text{ether}]{\text{LiAlH}_4 \text{ or NaBH}_4} C_6H_5\!-\!\overset{\overset{\displaystyle OH}{|}}{C}H\!CH_3$

(g) $C_6H_5\!-\!CH_3 \xrightarrow[\substack{\text{CCl}_4, \\ \text{light}}]{\text{NBS}} C_6H_5\!-\!CH_2Br \xrightarrow[\text{ether}]{\text{Mg}} C_6H_5\!-\!CH_2MgBr$

$C_6H_5\!-\!CH_2CH_2OH \xleftarrow[\text{(2) H}_3O^+]{\text{(1) CH}_2O}$

(h) $C_6H_6 \xrightarrow[\text{FeBr}_3]{\text{Br}_2} C_6H_5\!-\!Br \xrightarrow[\text{ether}]{\text{Mg}} C_6H_5\!-\!MgBr \xrightarrow[\text{(2) H}_3O^+]{\text{(1) CH}_2\!-\!CH_2 \text{ (epoxide)}}$

$C_6H_5\!-\!CH_2CH_2OH$

(i) $C_6H_5\!-\!CH_2CO_2CH_3 \xrightarrow[\text{ether}]{\text{LiAlH}_4} C_6H_5\!-\!CH_2CH_2OH$

15.37

(a) $CH_3CH_2CH_2CH_2OH \xrightarrow[\text{heat}]{H^+} \begin{array}{c} CH_3CH_2CH=CH_2 \\ + \\ CH_3CH=CHCH_3 \end{array} \xrightarrow{\text{THF:BH}_3} \xrightarrow{160°}$

$CH_3CH_2CH_2CH_2\!-\!\overset{|}{\underset{|}{B}}\!- \xrightarrow[160°]{\text{1-Decene}} CH_3CH_2CH=CH_2 \;(+\; CH_3(CH_2)_9 + \;-\!\overset{|}{\underset{|}{B}}\!-)$
(distills out)

(b) $CH_3CH_2CH=CH_2 \xrightarrow[\text{(2) NaBH}_4,\,OH^-]{\text{(1) Hg(OAc)}_2,\,\text{THF-H}_2O} CH_3CH_2\overset{\overset{\displaystyle OH}{|}}{C}HCH_3$
(from a)

(c) $CH_3CH_2\overset{\overset{\displaystyle OH}{|}}{C}HCH_3 \xrightarrow{\text{H}_2\text{CrO}_4} CH_3CH_2\overset{\overset{\displaystyle O}{\|}}{C}CH_3$

(d) $CH_3CH_2CH_2CH_2OH \xrightarrow{\text{PBr}_3} CH_3CH_2CH_2CH_2Br$

(e) $CH_3CH_2CH=CH_2 + HBr \xrightarrow[\text{(no peroxides)}]{} CH_3CH_2\overset{\overset{\displaystyle Br}{|}}{C}HCH_3$

(f) $CH_3CH_2CH_2CH_2Br \xrightarrow[\text{ether}]{\text{Mg}} CH_3CH_2CH_2CH_2MgBr$

$\xrightarrow[\text{(2) H}_3O^+]{\text{(1) CH}_2O} CH_3CH_2CH_2CH_2CH_2OH$

(g) $CH_3CH_2CH_2CH_2MgBr$ $\xrightarrow[\text{(2) }H_3O^+]{\text{(1) }CH_2\overset{O}{-}CH_2}$ $CH_3CH_2CH_2CH_2CH_2CH_2OH$
(from f)

$\xrightarrow{PBr_3}$ $CH_3CH_2CH_2CH_2CH_2CH_2Br$ $\xrightarrow{(CH_3)_3COK}$ $CH_3CH_2CH_2CH_2CH=CH_2$

(h) $CH_3CH_2CH_2CH_2MgBr$ $+$ $CH_3\overset{O}{\overset{||}{C}}CH_2CH_3$ $\xrightarrow{(2)\,H_3O^+}$ $CH_3CH_2CH_2\overset{OH}{\underset{\underset{CH_3}{|}}{\overset{|}{C}}}CH_2CH_3$
(from f)

(i) $CH_3CH_2CH_2CH_2OH$ $\xrightarrow{CrO_3 \cdot 2C_5H_5N}$ $CH_3CH_2CH_2\overset{O}{\overset{||}{C}}H$

(j) $CH_3CH_2CH_2CH_2MgBr$ $+$ $CH_3CH_2CH_2\overset{O}{\overset{||}{C}}H$ $\xrightarrow{(2)\,H_3O^+}$
(from f)   from (i)

$CH_3CH_2CH_2CH_2\overset{OH}{\overset{|}{C}}HCH_2CH_2CH_3$

(k) $CH_3CH_2\overset{Br}{\overset{|}{C}}HCH_3$ $\xrightarrow[\text{ether}]{Mg}$ $CH_3CH_2\overset{CH_3}{\overset{|}{C}}HMgBr$
(from e)

$\xrightarrow[\text{(2) }H_3O^+]{\text{(1) }CH_3CH_2CH_2\overset{O}{\overset{||}{C}}H}$ $CH_3CH_2\overset{CH_3}{\overset{|}{C}}H-\overset{OH}{\overset{|}{C}}HCH_2CH_2CH_3$

(l) $CH_3CH_2CH_2CH_2MgBr$ $+$ CO_2 $\xrightarrow{(2)\,H_3O^+}$ $CH_3CH_2CH_2CH_2COOH$

(m) $CH_3CH_2\overset{CH_3}{\overset{|}{C}}HOH$ $\xrightarrow{Na}$ $CH_3CH_2\overset{CH_3}{\overset{|}{C}}HONa$
(from b)

$\xrightarrow{CH_3CH_2CH_2CH_2Br}$ $CH_3CH_2\overset{CH_3}{\overset{|}{C}}H-O-CH_2CH_2CH_2CH_3$

or $CH_3CH_2CH=CH_2$ $+$ $Hg(OAc)_2$ $\xrightarrow[CH_3CH_2CH_2CH_2OH]{THF}$ $CH_3CH_2\overset{}{\underset{\underset{OCH_2CH_2CH_2CH_3}{|}}{C}}H-CH_2-HgOAc$

$CH_3CH_2\overset{CH_3}{\overset{|}{C}}H-O-CH_2CH_2CH_2CH_3$ $\xleftarrow[OH^-]{NaBH_4}$

(n) (1) $2CH_3CH_2CH_2CH_2OH$ $\xrightarrow[140°]{H_2SO_4}$ $(CH_3CH_2CH_2CH_2)_2O$

(2) $CH_3CH_2CH_2CH_2OH$ $+$ Na $\longrightarrow$ $CH_3CH_2CH_2CH_2ONa$ $\xrightarrow{CH_3CH_2CH_2CH_2Br}$

$(CH_3CH_2CH_2CH_2)_2O$

(o) $CH_3CH_2CH_2CH_2Br + 2Li \longrightarrow CH_3CH_2CH_2CH_2Li + LiBr$
(from a)

(p) $CH_3CH_2CH_2CH_2Li \xrightarrow{CuI} (CH_3CH_2CH_2CH_2)_2CuLi \xrightarrow{CH_3CH_2CH_2CH_2Br}$
(from o)

$CH_3CH_2CH_2CH_2CH_2CH_2CH_2CH_3$

15.38 (a) $CH_3CH_2CH_2O^-Na^+$ Sodium propoxide

(b) $CH_3CH_2CH_2-O-CH_2CH_2CH_2CH_3$ Butyl propyl ether

(c) $CH_3-\overset{O}{\underset{O}{\overset{\|}{\underset{\|}{S}}}}-OCH_2CH_2CH_3$ Propyl methanesulfonate

(d) $CH_3-\langle\bigcirc\rangle-SO_2-O-CH_2CH_2CH_3$ Propyl p-toluenesulfonate (or propyl tosylate)

(e) $CH_3\overset{O}{\overset{\|}{C}}-O-CH_2CH_2CH_3$ Propyl acetate

(f) $CH_3CH_2\overset{O}{\overset{\|}{C}}-O^-K^+$ Potassium propanoate

(g) $CH_3CH_2CH_2Cl$ 1-Chloropropane

(h) $CH_3CH_2CH_2Cl$ 1-Chloropropane

(i) $CH_3CH_2CH_2-O-CH_2CH_2CH_3$ dipropyl ether

(j) $CH_3CH_2CH_2Br$ 1-Bromopropane

(k) $\langle\bigcirc\rangle-\overset{CH_3}{\underset{CH_3}{CH}}$ Isopropylbenzene (major) $+$ $\langle\bigcirc\rangle-CH_2CH_2CH_3$
      Propylbenzene

15.39

(a) $CH_3\overset{CH_3}{\overset{|}{CHO^-Na^+}}$ Sodium isopropoxide

(b) $CH_3\overset{CH_3}{\overset{|}{CH}}-O-CH_2CH_2CH_2CH_3$ Butyl isopropyl ether

(c) $CH_3SO_2-O-\overset{CH_3}{\overset{|}{CHCH_3}}$ Isopropyl methanesulfonate

(d) $CH_3-\langle\bigcirc\rangle-SO_2-O-\overset{CH_3}{\overset{|}{CHCH_3}}$ Isopropyl p-toluenesulfonate

(e) $CH_3\overset{O}{\overset{\|}{C}}-O-\overset{CH_3}{\overset{|}{CHCH_3}}$ Isopropyl acetate

(f) $CH_3\overset{\overset{\displaystyle O}{\|}}{C}CH_3$ Acetone ($+$ CH_3COOH and CO_2)

(g) $CH_3\overset{\overset{\displaystyle CH_3}{|}}{C}HCl$ 2-Chloropropane

(h) Same as (g)

(i) $CH_3\overset{\overset{\displaystyle CH_3}{|}}{C}H-O-\overset{\overset{\displaystyle CH_3}{|}}{C}HCH_3$ Diisopropyl ether

(j) $CH_3\overset{\overset{\displaystyle CH_3}{|}}{C}HBr$ 2-Bromopropane

(k) 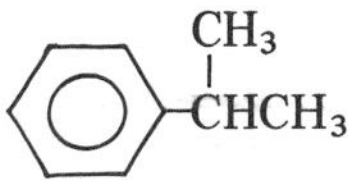 Isopropyl benzene

15.40

(a) 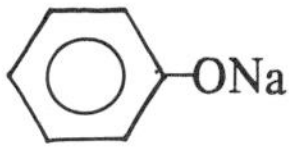 —ONa $+$ CH_3CH_2OH (c) —ONa $+$ H_2O

(b)  $+$ CH_3CH_2OMgBr (d) 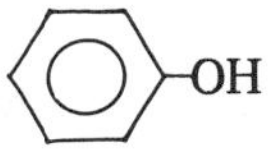 —OH $+$ NaCl

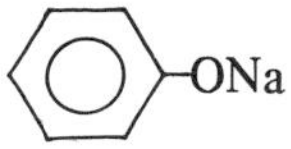

(e) CH_3CH_2OH $+$ NaOH

15.41 (a) CH_3Br $+$ CH_3CH_2Br (c) $Br-CH_2CH_2CH_2CH_2-Br$

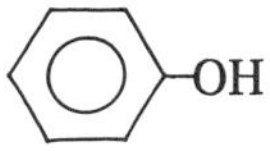

(b) —OH $+$ CH_3CH_2Br (d) $Br-CH_2CH_2-Br$ (2 molar equivalents)

15.42 (a) $CH_3\overset{\overset{\displaystyle }{}}{C}H-CH_2$ (b) $CH_3CH_2-O-CH_2CH_2OH$
           OH OH

(c) $C_6H_5O-CH_2CH_2OH$

(d) 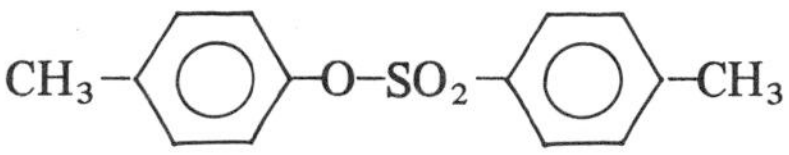 $CH_3-$$-O-SO_2-$$-CH_3$ (e) 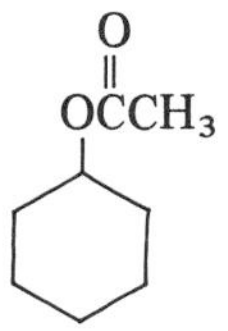   (f)

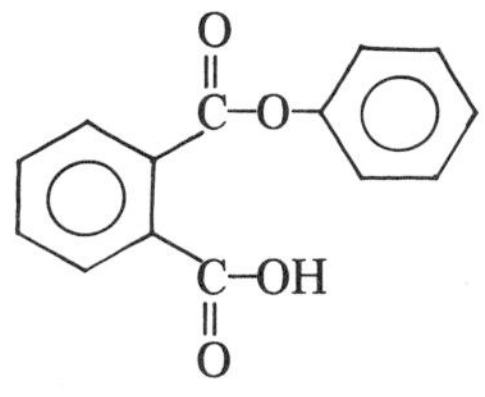

(g) [structure: 2,6-dibromo-4-methylphenol] (h) [structure: benzoate $C-O^- K^+$] (i) [structure: benzaldehyde CH]

(j) [structure: $C_6H_5-CH_2O^- Na^+$] (k) [structure: $C_6H_5-CH_2OCH_3$] (l) [structure: epoxide with CH_3CH_2 and CH_2CH_3, H O H]

(m) [structure with CH_3, CH_2, H—OH, HO—H, CH_2, CH_3] + enantiomer

15.43 (a) *p*-Cresol is soluble in aqueous NaOH; benzyl alcohol is not.

(b) Cyclohexanol is soluble in cold, concentrated H_2SO_4; cyclohexane is not. (Cyclohexanol also gives a positive test with CrO_3 in H_2SO_4, while cyclohexane does not.)

(c) Cyclohexene will decolorize Br_2/CCl_4 solution; cyclohexanol will not.

(d) Allyl propyl ether will decolorize Br_2/CCl_4 solution; dipropyl ether will not.

(e) *p*-Cresol is soluble in aqueous NaOH; anisole is not.

(f) Picric acid is soluble in aqueous $NaHCO_3$: 2,4,6-trimethylphenol is not (cf. Problem 15.32)

15.44

3° Carbocation is more stable.

15.45

(a)

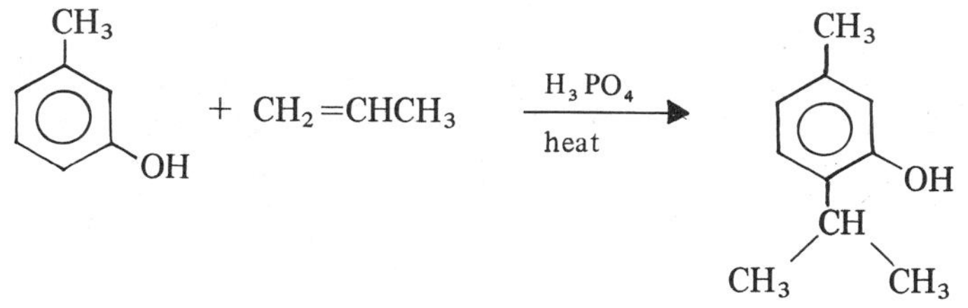

(b)

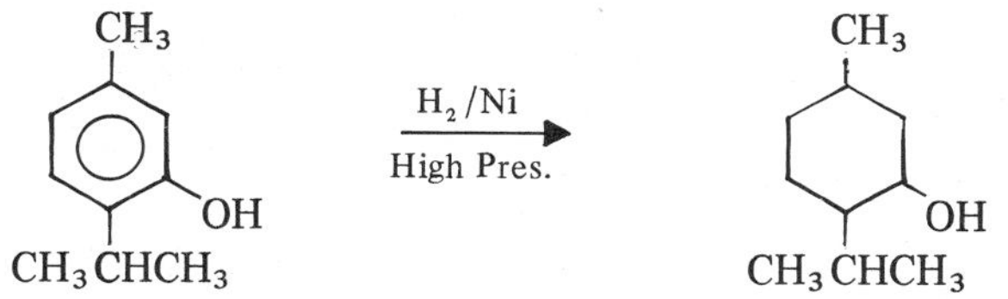

15.46   The position ortho to the isopropyl group is sterically more hindered than the position ortho to the methyl group.

15.47

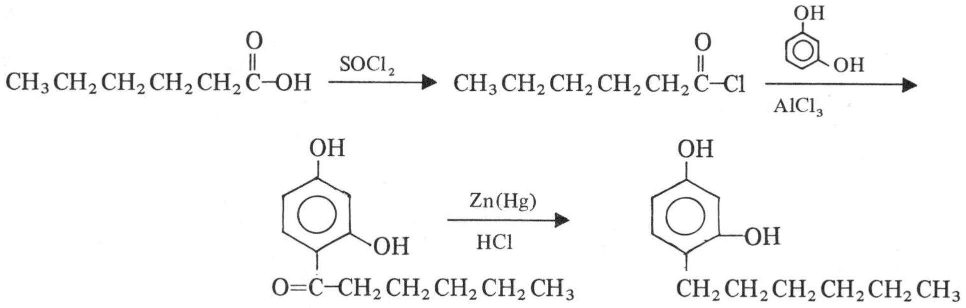

15.48

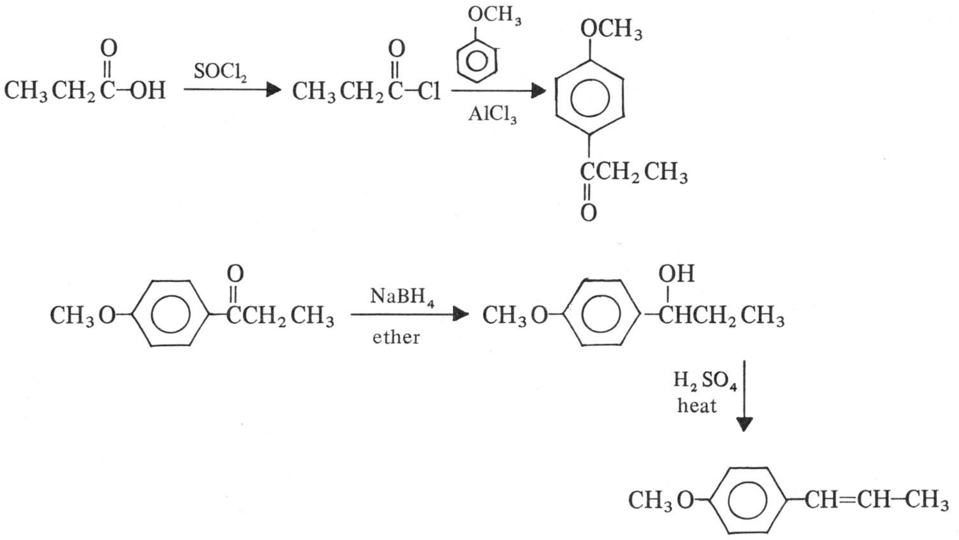

15.49 X is a phenol because it dissolves in aqueous NaOH but not in aqueous $NaHCO_3$. It gives a dibromo derivative, and must therefore be substituted in the ortho or para position. The broad infrared peak at 3250 cm^{-1} also suggests a phenol. The peak at 830 cm^{-1} indicates para substitution. the proton nmr singlet at δ 1.3 (9H) suggests 9 methyl hydrogens which must be a *tert*-butyl group. The structure of X is:

OH

CH$_3$–C–CH$_3$
CH$_3$

15.50 The broad infrared peak at 3400 cm^{-1} indicates a hydroxy group and the two bands at 720 and 770 cm^{-1} suggest a monosubstituted benzene ring. The presence of these groups is also indicated by the peaks at δ 2.7 and δ 7.2 in the proton nmr spectrum. The proton nmr spectrum also shows a triplet at δ 0.7 indicating a –CH$_3$ group coupled with an adjacent –CH$_2$– group. What appears at first to be a quartet at δ 1.9 actually shows further splitting. There is also a triplet at δ 4.35 (1H). Putting these pieces together in the only way possible gives us the following structure for Y.

CHCH$_2$CH$_3$
OH

Analyzed spectra are as follows:

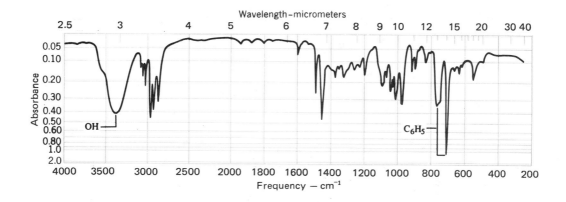

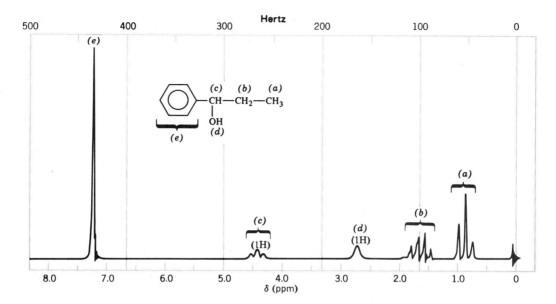

FIG. 15.2. *The infrared and proton nmr spectra of compound Y, problem 15.50 (Spectra courtesy of Sadtler Research Laboratories Inc.)*

15.51

(a) [structure: phenol with OCH₃ para] + CH₂=C(CH₃)–CH₃ →(H⁺) [structure with C(CH₃)₃] + [structure] **BHA**

(b) [structure: p-cresol] + 2 CH₂=C(CH₃)–CH₃ →(H⁺) [structure] **BHT**

Notice that both reactions are Friedel-Crafts alkylations.

15.52 [structure: phenol] →(H₂SO₄, 25°) [structure with SO₃H] →(2Cl₂) [structure with Cl, Cl, SO₃H] →(H₃O⁺, H₂O, (steam))

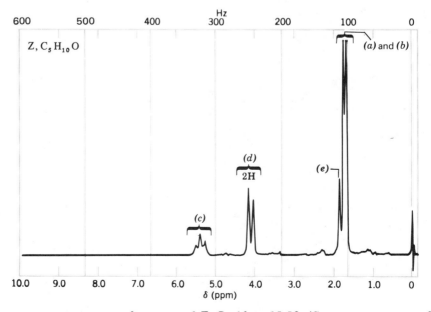

15.53 The broad IR peak at 3200-3600 cm^{-1} suggests a hydroxyl group. The two proton nmr peaks at $\delta 1.7$ and $\delta 1.8$ are not a doublet because their separation is not equal to other splittings; therefore these peaks are singlets. Reaction with Br_2/CCl_4 suggests an alkene. If we put these bits of information together, we conclude that **Z** is 3-methyl-2-buten-1-ol.

The analyzed spectrum is

FIG. 15.3 *The proton nmr spectrum of compound* **Z**, *Problem 15.53. (Spectrum courtesy of Aldrich Chemical Co., Milwaukee, Wis.)*

15.54 That **A** gives a positive test with chromic oxide in aqueous sulfuric acid indicates that **A** is a 1° or 2° alcohol.

The ^{13}C spectrum shows the presence of $-\underset{|}{C}H-$ and $-CH_2-$ groups only (doublet and triplets in the proton off-resonance decoupled spectrum).

These facts when coupled with the molecular formula indicate that **A** is cyclohexanol. The following peak assignments can be made:

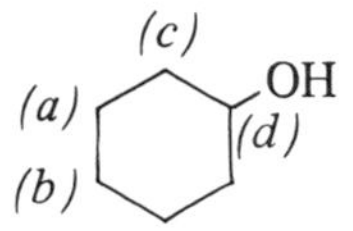

(a) δ 24*t*

(b) δ 26*t*

(c) δ36*t*

(d) δ 70*d*

SECTION REFERENCES FOR ADDITIONAL PROBLEMS

15.36	15.5-15.7, 15.12	**15.45**	15.14
15.37	15.8-15.10	**15.46**	15.14
15.38	15.1, 15.8-15.10	**15.47**	15.14, 15.15D
15.39	15.1, 15.8-15.10	**15.48**	15.14
15.40	15.9A, 15.15A	**15.49**	15.15A, 15.15D, 15.3
15.41	15.13	**15.50**	15.3
15.42	15.13	**15.51**	15.14
15.43	15.9A, 15.15A, 15.13	**15.52**	15.15D, 15.14
15.44	15.10A	**15.53**	15.3
		15.54	13.10

SELF-TEST

15.1 Give the structural formula of the missing reactants or major organic product in each of the following reactions. Write N.R. if no reaction occurs. If two steps are needed, label them (1), (2), etc.

(a) 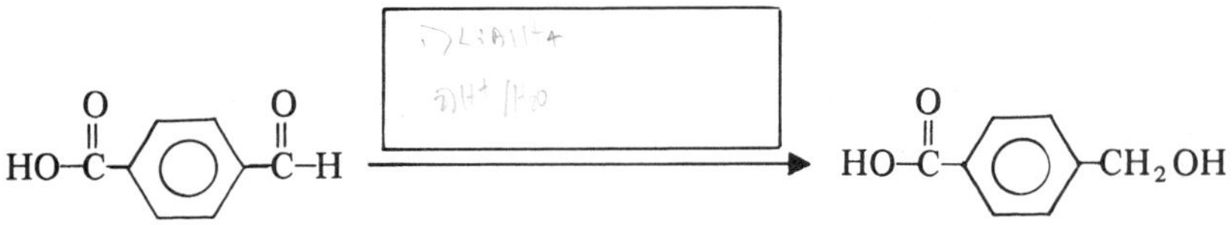

(b)

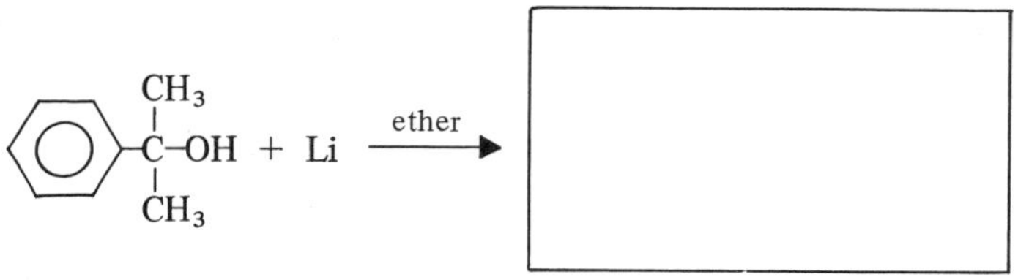

$\text{C}_6\text{H}_5\overset{\overset{\text{CH}_3}{|}}{\underset{\underset{\text{CH}_3}{|}}{\text{C}}}\text{-OH}$ + Li $\xrightarrow{\text{ether}}$

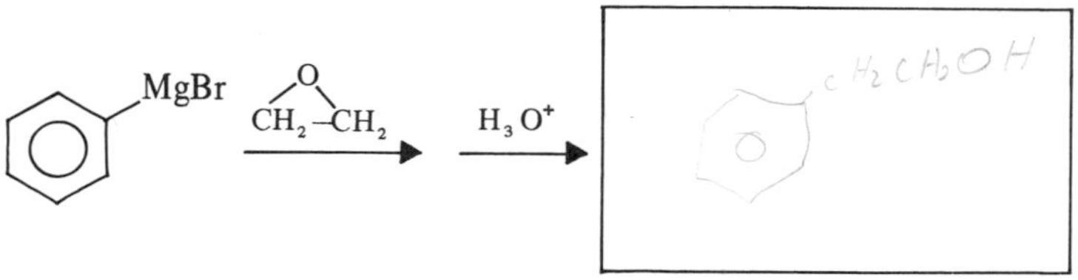

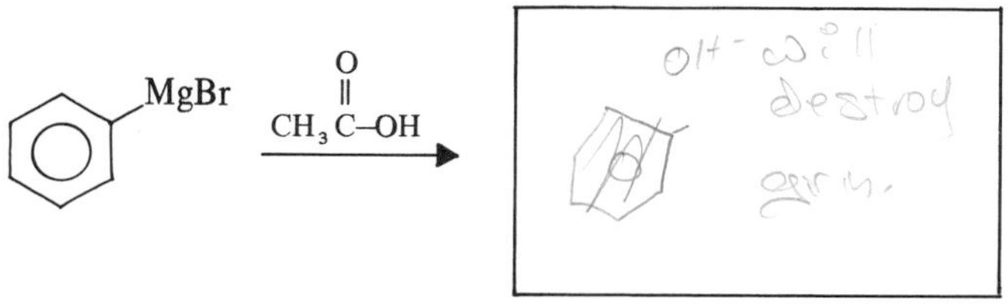

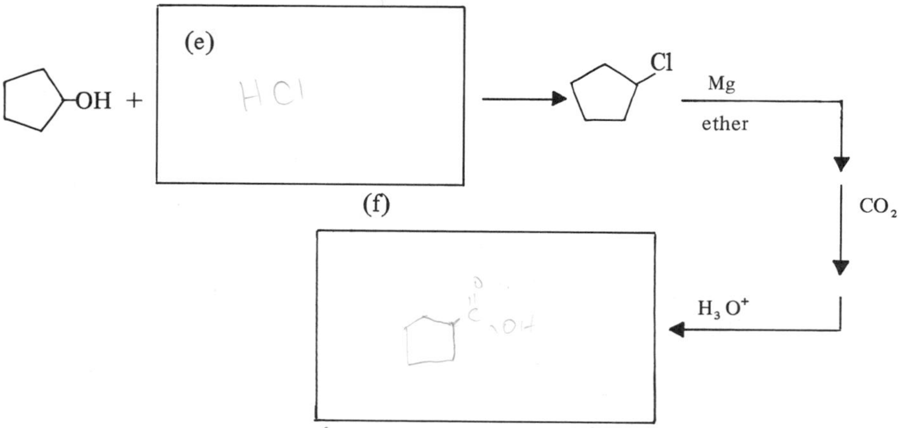

[blank box]

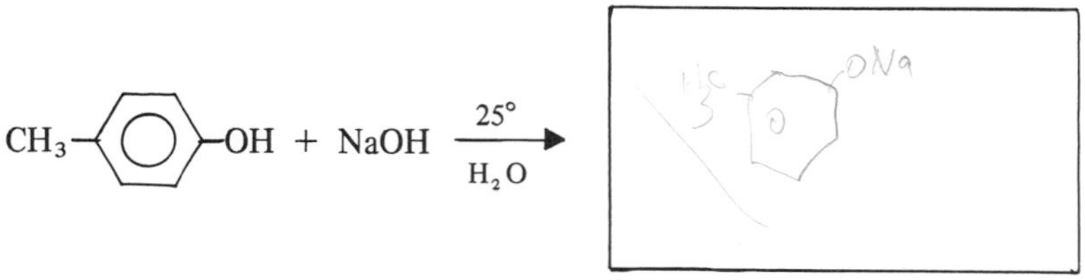

(c)

$\text{C}_6\text{H}_5\text{MgBr}$ $\xrightarrow[\text{CH}_2\text{-CH}_2]{\overset{\text{O}}{\triangle}}$ $\xrightarrow{\text{H}_3\text{O}^+}$

(d)

$\text{C}_6\text{H}_5\text{MgBr}$ $\xrightarrow[\text{CH}_3\overset{\overset{\text{O}}{\|}}{\text{C}}\text{-OH}]{}$

OH⁻ will destroy agrm.

(e)

cyclopentyl-OH + | HCl | $\longrightarrow$ cyclopentyl-Cl $\xrightarrow[\text{ether}]{\text{Mg}}$

(f)

$\downarrow \text{CO}_2$

$\xleftarrow{\text{H}_3\text{O}^+}$

(g)

$\text{CH}_3\text{-C}_6\text{H}_4\text{-OH}$ + NaOH $\xrightarrow[\text{H}_2\text{O}]{25°}$

(h)

$\text{CH}_3\overset{\overset{\text{CH}_3}{|}}{\text{CH}}\text{-O-}\overset{\overset{\text{CH}_3}{|}}{\text{CH}}\text{CH}_3$ + HBr (excess) $\longrightarrow$

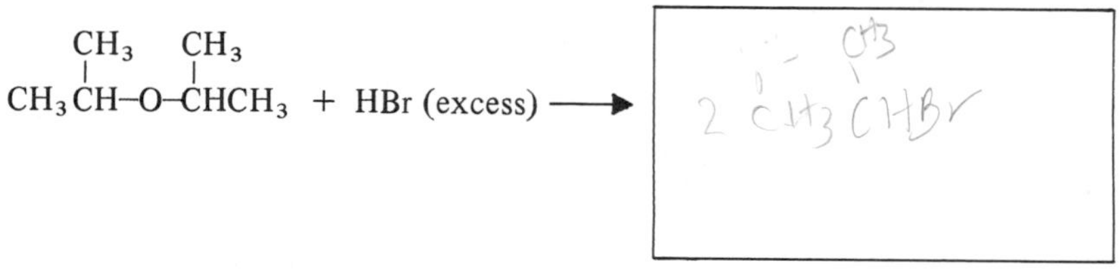

2 CH₃CHBr(CH₃)

(i)   [cyclopentanol structure with OH] + NaOH $\xrightarrow[H_2O]{25°}$ [handwritten: cyclopentyl-ONa]

(j)   [cyclopentanol structure with OH] + [handwritten box: Na⁺ cyclopentyl-ONa + $CH_3CH_2\overset{O}{C}-Br$; cyclopentyl →] ⟶ [cyclopentyl-$O-\overset{\overset{O}{\|}}{C}-CH_2CH_3$]

(k) $CH_3CH_2CH_2OH$ + [empty box] ⟶ $CH_3CH_2CH_2-O-\overset{\overset{O}{\|}}{\underset{\overset{\|}{O}}{S}}-$[benzene ring]

(l) $CH_3CH_2CH_2OH$ + CH_3MgBr ⟶ [handwritten: OH will destroy grn.]

(m) CH_3O-[benzene ring]$-OCH_3$ + HBr (excess) ⟶ [handwritten: $2CH_3Br$; HO-[ring]-OH]

15.2   Supply the structural formula of the missing compounds.

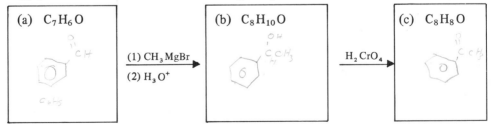

(a) C_7H_6O [handwritten structure: benzaldehyde, C_6H_5-CH=O]
$\xrightarrow[\text{(2) }H_3O^+]{\text{(1) }CH_3MgBr}$
(b) $C_8H_{10}O$ [handwritten structure with OH, CCH₃]
$\xrightarrow{H_2CrO_4}$
(c) C_8H_8O [handwritten structure with CCH₃]

15.3   For each of the following pairs of compounds, tell which has the higher boiling point (write its letter, A or B).

Higher bp

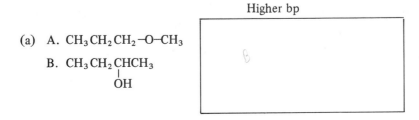

(a) A. $CH_3CH_2CH_2-O-CH_3$

B. $CH_3CH_2\underset{\overset{|}{OH}}{C}HCH_3$

[handwritten: B]

(b) A. $HOCH_2CH_2OH$

B. $CH_3CH_2CH_2OH$

15.4   Give the *intermediate* of the *first step* in the mechanism of the following reaction:

$$CH_3CH_2OH + HBr \longrightarrow CH_3CH_2Br + H_2O$$

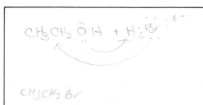

H

SPECIAL TOPIC
Nucleophilic Substitution Reactions—Another Look

SOLUTIONS TO PROBLEMS

H.1   (a) and (b)

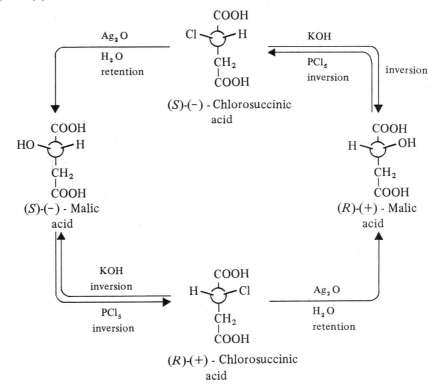

(c)   The reaction takes place with retention of configuration.

(d)

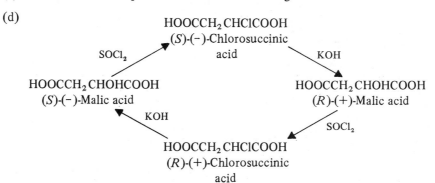

H.2   (a)   Reaction of an alkene with halogen in water solution.

(b) $CH_3CH=CH_2 + Cl_2 \xrightarrow{H_2O} CH_3\underset{\underset{OH}{|}}{C}HCH_2Cl \xrightarrow{NaOH} CH_3CH{-}CH_2$

H.3   2-(*p*-Hydroxyphenyl)-1-chloropropane $>$ 2-(*p*-tolyl)-1-chloropropane $>$ 2-phenyl-1-chloropropane $>$ 2-(*p*-nitrophenyl)-1-chloropropane

H.4   In each case, the reactions apparently involve the participation of the phenyl group and the formation of a phenonium ion as an intermediate. Solvolysis of **A** yields a chiral phenonium ion—one that reacts with solvent at either carbon to produce the same chiral (and thus optically active) acetate.

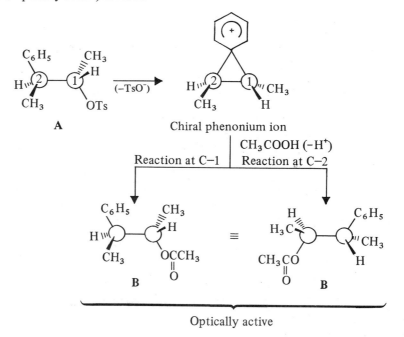

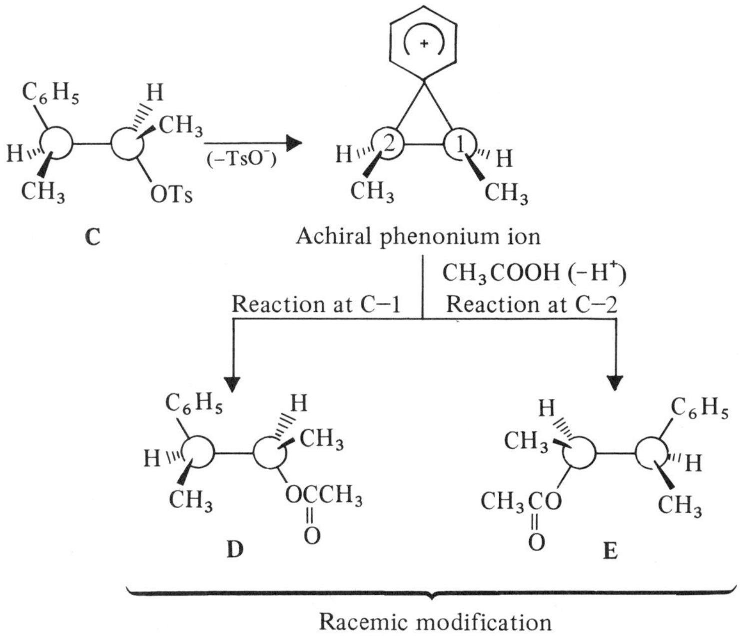

C

Achiral phenonium ion

Reaction at C−1 | CH$_3$COOH (−H$^+$) | Reaction at C−2

D

E

Racemic modification

(For an extensive discussion of this rearrangement, see J. M. Harris and C. C. Wamser, *Organic Reaction Mechanisms.* Wiley, New York, 1976, pp. 166-171.)

SPECIAL TOPIC
Thiols, Thioethers, and Thiophenols

SOLUTIONS TO PROBLEMS

I.1 (a) 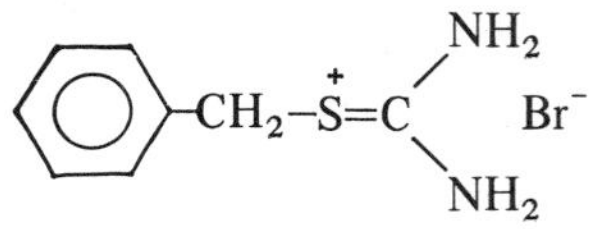 $C_6H_5-CH_2-\overset{+}{S}=C\overset{NH_2}{\underset{NH_2}{\diagup}}$ Br$^-$ (b) $C_6H_5-CH_2SH$

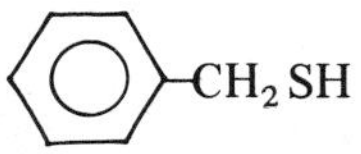

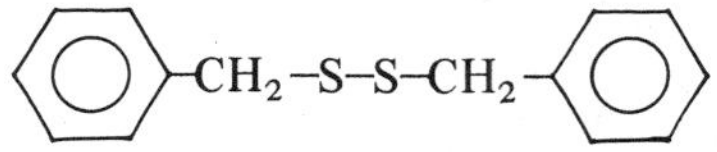

(c) $C_6H_5-CH_2-S-S-CH_2-C_6H_5$ (d) 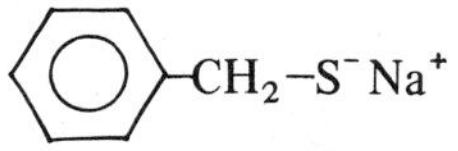 $C_6H_5-CH_2-S^-Na^+$

(e) 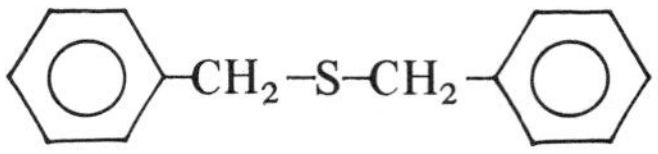 $C_6H_5-CH_2-S-CH_2-C_6H_5$

I.2 $CH_2=CHCH_2Br + S=C\overset{NH_2}{\underset{NH_2}{\diagup}} \xrightarrow[\text{(2) OH}^-\text{, H}_2\text{O}]{\text{(1) CH}_3\text{CH}_2\text{OH}} CH_2=CHCH_2SH$

$\xrightarrow{H_2O_2} CH_2=CHCH_2-S-S-CH_2CH=CH_2$

I.3 $CH_2=CHCH_2OH \xrightarrow{Br_2} CH_2BrCHBrCH_2OH \xrightarrow{NaSH} \underset{\underset{SH}{|}\,\,\underset{SH}{|}}{CH_2-CH-CH_2OH}$

I.4 (a) $ClCH_2CH_2\overset{O}{\overset{||}{C}}(CH_2)_4CO_2C_2H_5$ (this step is the Friedel-Crafts acylation of an alkene)

(b) $SOCl_2$

(c) $2C_6H_5CH_2SH$ and KOH

(d) H_3O^+

(e) 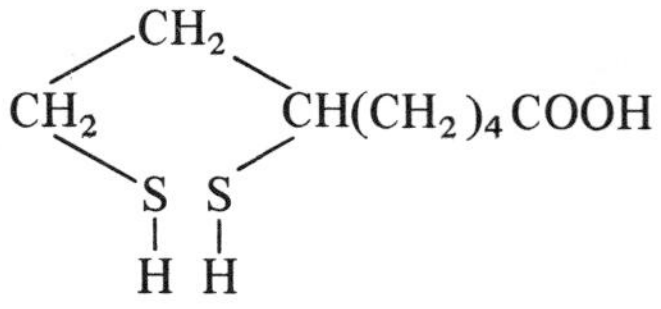 $\underset{\underset{H}{|}\,\,\underset{H}{|}}{\underset{S\,\,\,S}{\overset{\diagup CH_2}{CH_2}\diagdown_{CH(CH_2)_4COOH}}}$

356

I.5 $H_2\ddot{S}: + CH_2\!-\!CH_2 \longrightarrow H\ddot{S}\!-\!CH_2CH_2OH \longrightarrow$
                        $\underset{O}{\diagdown}$ with $CH_2\!-\!CH_2$ over O

$HOCH_2CH_2SCH_2CH_2OH \xrightarrow[\text{ZnCl}_2]{\text{HCl}} ClCH_2CH_2SCH_2CH_2Cl$

$(C_4H_{10}SO_2)$ "Mustard gas"

ALDEHYDES AND KETONES I. NUCLEOPHILIC ADDITIONS TO THE CARBONYL GROUP

PREPARATION AND REACTIONS OF ALDEHYDES

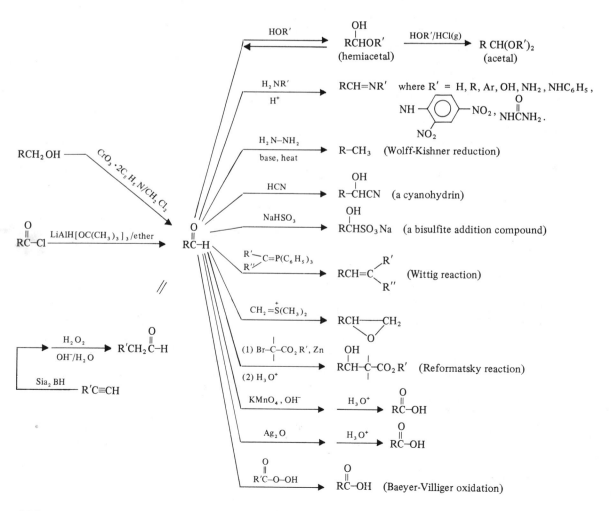

PREPARATION AND REACTIONS OF KETONES

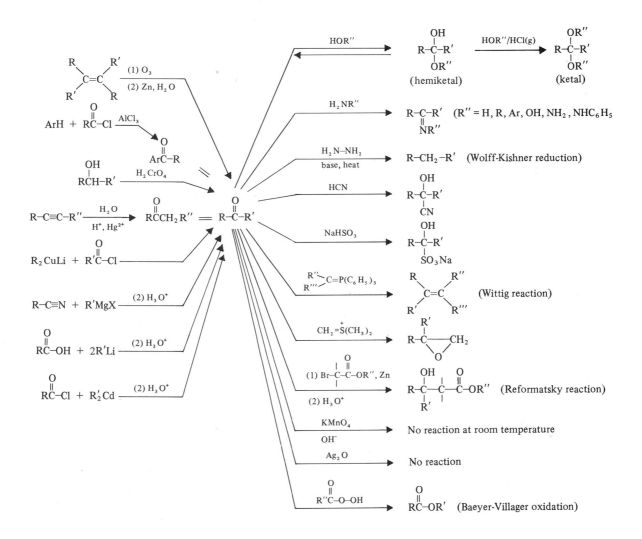

SOLUTIONS TO PROBLEMS

16.1   (a) $\underset{\text{Pentanal}}{CH_3CH_2CH_2CH_2\overset{\displaystyle O}{\overset{\|}{C}}H}$ $\underset{\underset{\displaystyle CH_3}{\displaystyle |}}{CH_3CH_2\overset{\displaystyle O}{\overset{\|}{C}}HCH}$

2-Methylbutanal

$\underset{\underset{\displaystyle CH_3}{\displaystyle |}}{CH_3CHCH_2\overset{\displaystyle O}{\overset{\|}{C}}H}$ $\underset{\underset{\displaystyle CH_3}{\displaystyle |}}{CH_3\overset{\overset{\displaystyle CH_3}{\displaystyle |}}{C}-CHO}$

3-Methylbutanal   2,2-Dimethylpropanal

$CH_3CH_2CH_2\underset{\underset{\displaystyle O}{\|}}{C}CH_3$ $CH_3CH_2\underset{\underset{\displaystyle O}{\|}}{C}CH_2CH_3$

2-Pentanone   3-Pentanone

$\underset{\underset{\displaystyle CH_3}{\displaystyle |}}{CH_3CH\overset{\displaystyle O}{\overset{\|}{C}}CH_3}$

3-Methyl-2-butanone

(b)   and (c)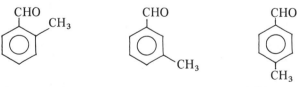

Acetophenone or   Phenylethanal or
methylphenyl ketone   phenylacetaldehyde

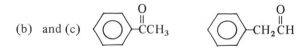

2-Methylbenzaldehyde   3-Methylbenzaldehyde   4-Methylbenzaldehyde
(*o*-tolualdehyde)   (*m*-tolualdehyde)   (*p*-tolualdehyde)

16.2   (a)   1-Pentanol, because its molecules form hydrogen bonds to each other.

(b)   2-Pentanol, because its molecules form hydrogen bonds to each other.

(c)   Pentanal, because its molecules are more polar.

(d)   2-Phenylethanol, because its molecules form hydrogen bonds to each other.

(e)   Benzyl alcohol because its molecules form hydrogen bonds to each other.

16.3 (a) C$_6$H$_6$ $\xrightarrow{\text{Br}_2,\ \text{Fe}}$ C$_6$H$_5$—Br $\xrightarrow[\text{ether}]{\text{Mg}}$ C$_6$H$_5$—MgBr $\xrightarrow[\text{(2) H}^+]{\text{(1) HCHO}}$

C$_6$H$_5$—CH$_2$OH $\xrightarrow[\text{CH}_2\text{Cl}_2]{\text{CrO}_3 \cdot 2\text{C}_5\text{H}_5\text{N}}$ C$_6$H$_5$—CHO

(b) C$_6$H$_5$—CH$_3$ $\xrightarrow[\text{(2) H}^+]{\text{(1) KMnO}_4,\ \text{OH}^-,\ \text{heat}}$ C$_6$H$_5$—COOH $\xrightarrow{\text{SOCl}_2}$

C$_6$H$_5$—COCl $\xrightarrow[\text{ether}]{\text{LiAlH[OC(CH}_3)_3]_3}$ C$_6$H$_5$—CHO

(c) CH$_3$CH$_2$Br $\xrightarrow{\text{HC}\equiv\text{CNa}}$ CH$_3$CH$_2$C$\equiv$CH $\xrightarrow[\text{(2) H}_2\text{O}_2,\ \text{OH}^-]{\text{(1) Sia}_2\text{BH}}$ CH$_3$CH$_2$CH$_2\overset{\displaystyle O}{\overset{\|}{\text{C}}}$H

(d) CH$_3$C$\equiv$CCH$_3$ $\xrightarrow[\text{H}_2\text{O}]{\text{H}_3\text{O}^+,\ \text{Hg}^{++}}$ CH$_3\overset{\displaystyle O}{\overset{\|}{\text{C}}}CH_2CH_3$

(e) C$_6$H$_5$—$\underset{\underset{\displaystyle \text{OH}}{|}}{\text{CH}}CH_3$ $\xrightarrow[\text{H}_2\text{SO}_4]{\text{CrO}_3}$ C$_6$H$_5$—$\overset{\displaystyle O}{\overset{\|}{\text{C}}}CH_3$

(f) C$_6$H$_6$ $\xrightarrow[\text{AlCl}_3]{\text{CH}_3\text{COCl}}$ C$_6$H$_5$—$\overset{\displaystyle O}{\overset{\|}{\text{C}}}CH_3$

(g) C$_6$H$_5$—$\underset{\underset{\displaystyle O}{\|}}{\text{C}}$Cl $\xrightarrow[\substack{\text{or} \\ (\text{CH}_3)_2\text{Cd}}]{(\text{CH}_3)_2\text{CuLi}}$ C$_6$H$_5$—$\underset{\underset{\displaystyle O}{\|}}{\text{C}}CH_3$

(h) C$_6$H$_5$—$\overset{\displaystyle O}{\overset{\|}{\text{C}}}$OH $\xrightarrow{\text{SOCl}_2}$ C$_6$H$_5$—$\overset{\displaystyle O}{\overset{\|}{\text{C}}}$Cl $\xrightarrow{(\text{CH}_3)_2\text{CuLi}}$ C$_6$H$_5$—$\overset{\displaystyle O}{\overset{\|}{\text{C}}}CH_3$

(i) C$_6$H$_5$—CH$_2$Br $\xrightarrow{\text{CN}^-}$ C$_6$H$_5$—CH$_2$CN $\xrightarrow[\text{ether}]{\text{CH}_3\text{CH}_2\text{MgBr}}$ C$_6$H$_5$—CH$_2\overset{\displaystyle \text{NMgBr}}{\overset{\|}{\text{C}}}CH_2CH_3$

$\xrightarrow{\text{H}_3\text{O}^+}$ C$_6$H$_5$—CH$_2\overset{\displaystyle O}{\overset{\|}{\text{C}}}CH_2CH_3$

16.4 (a) The nucleophile is the negatively charged carbon of the Grignard reagent *acting as a carbanion.*

(b) The magnesium portion of the Grignard reagent acts as a Lewis acid and accepts an electron pair of the carbonyl oxygen. This acid-base interaction makes the carbonyl carbon even more positive and, therefore, even more susceptible to nucleophilic attack.

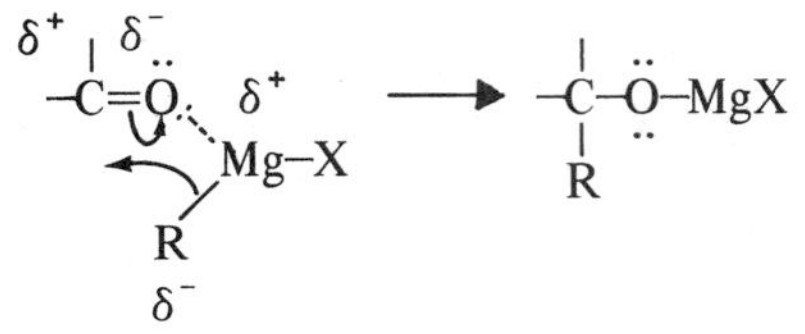

(c) The product that forms initially (above) is a magnesium derivative of an alcohol.

(d) On addition of water, the organic product that forms is an alcohol.

16.5 The nucleophile is a hydride ion.

16.6

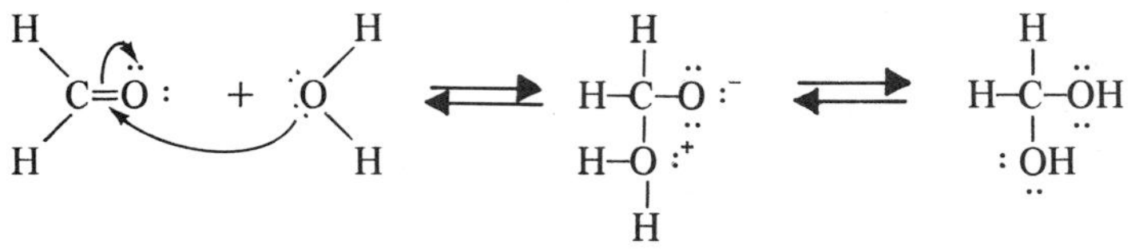

16.7 (a) RCH=$\overset{+}{\underset{..}{O}}$–R ⟷ RCH–$\overset{..}{\underset{..}{O}}$–R

        I   **II**

(b) and (c) Structure I should make a greater contribution because in it both the carbon atom and the oxygen atom have an octet of electrons and because it has one more bond.

16.8

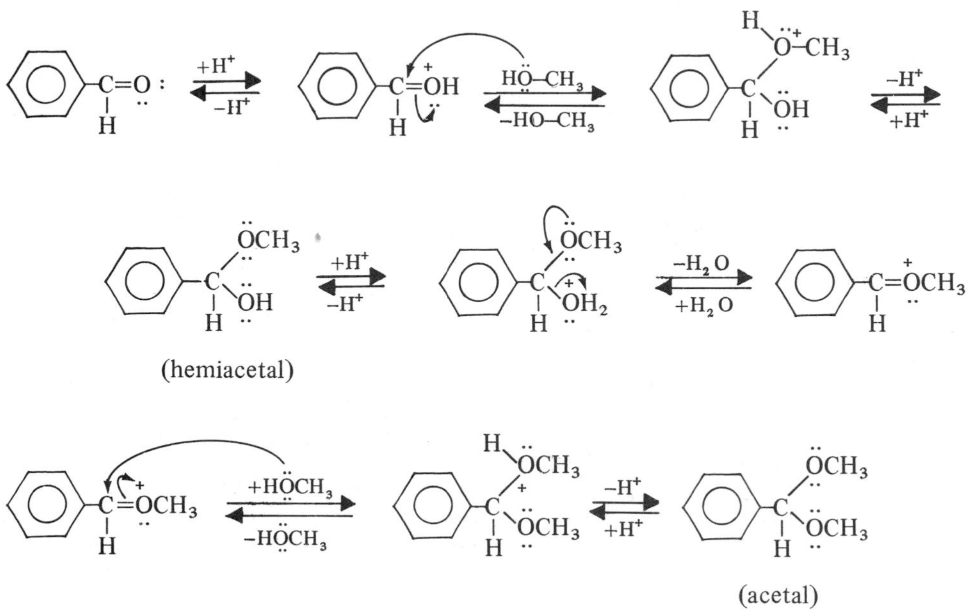

(hemiacetal)

(acetal)

16.9

$$CH_3\text{-}C(CH_3)=O \;\overset{+H^+}{\underset{-H^+}{\rightleftharpoons}}\; CH_3\text{-}\overset{+}{C}(CH_3)=OH \;\overset{+HOCH_2CH_2OH}{\underset{-HOCH_2CH_2OH}{\rightleftharpoons}}\; $$

Structure: CH_3, CH_3 on carbon bonded to $O\text{-}H$ and $\overset{+}{O}CH_2CH_2OH$ with H $\;\overset{-H^+}{\underset{+H^+}{\rightleftharpoons}}$

Structure: CH_3, CH_3 on carbon bonded to $O\text{-}H$ and OCH_2CH_2OH $\;\overset{+H^+}{\underset{-H^+}{\rightleftharpoons}}\;$ protonated $\overset{+}{O}\text{-}H$ form $\;\overset{-H_2O}{\underset{+H_2O}{\rightleftharpoons}}$

$$CH_3\text{-}CH_3\text{-}\overset{+}{C}=OCH_2CH_2\ddot{O}H \;\rightleftharpoons\; $$ five-membered ring with $\overset{+}{O}\text{-}H$ $\;\overset{-H^+}{\underset{+H^+}{\rightleftharpoons}}\;$ cyclic acetal with $O\text{-}CH_2$ / $O\text{-}CH_2$

16.10 *Acid-catalyzed reaction*

$$CH_3\text{-}\overset{O}{\underset{}{C}}\text{-}CH_3 \;\overset{+H^+}{\underset{-H^+}{\rightleftharpoons}}\; CH_3\text{-}\overset{+OH}{\underset{}{C}}\text{-}CH_3 \;\overset{+H_2{}^{18}O}{\underset{-H_2{}^{18}O}{\rightleftharpoons}}\; CH_3\text{-}\overset{OH}{\underset{H_2{}^{18}\overset{+}{O}}{C}}\text{-}CH_3 \;\overset{-H^+}{\underset{+H^+}{\rightleftharpoons}}$$

$$CH_3\text{-}\overset{OH}{\underset{{}^{18}OH}{C}}\text{-}CH_3 \;\overset{+H^+}{\underset{-H^+}{\rightleftharpoons}}\; CH_3\text{-}\overset{+OH_2}{\underset{{}^{18}OH}{C}}\text{-}CH_3 \;\overset{-H_2O}{\underset{+H_2O}{\rightleftharpoons}}\; CH_3\text{-}\overset{}{\underset{{}^{18}\overset{+}{O}H}{C}}\text{-}CH_3 \;\overset{-H^+}{\underset{+H^+}{\rightleftharpoons}}\; CH_3\text{-}\overset{}{\underset{{}^{18}O}{C}}\text{-}CH_3$$

Base-catalyzed reaction

$$OH^- + H_2{}^{18}O \;\rightleftharpoons\; H_2O + {}^{18}OH^-$$

$$CH_3\overset{O}{\underset{}{C}}CH_3 + {}^{18}OH^- \;\rightleftharpoons\; CH_3\overset{O^-}{\underset{{}^{18}OH}{C}}CH_3 \;\overset{H_2O}{\underset{OH^-}{\rightleftharpoons}}\; CH_3\overset{OH}{\underset{{}^{18}OH}{C}}CH_3 \;\overset{OH^-}{\underset{}{\rightleftharpoons}}$$

$$CH_3\overset{OH}{\underset{{}^{18}O}{C}}CH_3 \;\overset{-OH^-}{\underset{+OH^-}{\rightleftharpoons}}\; CH_3\overset{}{\underset{{}^{18}O}{C}}CH_3$$

16.11

(a)

$$A \;\xrightarrow[H^+]{HOCH_2CH_2OH}\; \text{(cyclic ketal-ester)} \;CO_2C_2H_5$$

cyclopentane ring with O= and $CO_2C_2H_5$ (labeled **A**)

$$\xrightarrow{2\,CH_3MgI}\; \text{dioxolane ring with } \overset{OMgI}{\underset{CH_3}{C}}\text{-}CH_3 \;\xrightarrow[H_2O]{H_3O^+}\; O\text{=}\text{cyclopentane-}\overset{OH}{\underset{CH_3}{C}}\text{-}CH_3$$

C

(b) Addition would take place at the ketone group as well as at the ester group. The product (after hydrolysis) would be,

$$
\begin{array}{c}
\underset{CH_3}{\overset{HO}{\diagdown}} \quad \underset{CH_3}{\overset{OH}{\underset{|}{\overset{|}{C}-CH_3}}}
\end{array}
$$

16.12 (a) Cyclohexanone + $HSCH_2CH_2SH \xrightarrow{BF_3}$ dithiolane $\xrightarrow[\text{Ni}]{\text{Raney}} \underset{(H_2)}{}$ cyclohexane $+ CH_3CH_3 + NiS$

(b) $C_6H_5\underset{\parallel}{\overset{O}{C}}H + HSCH_2CH_2SH \xrightarrow{BF_3}$ dithiolane $\xrightarrow[\text{Ni}]{\text{Raney}} \underset{(H_2)}{}$

$C_6H_5CH_3 + NiS + CH_3CH_3$

16.13 (a) $CH_3\underset{\parallel}{\overset{O}{C}}H \xrightarrow{HCN} CH_3\underset{|}{\overset{OH}{C}}HCN \xrightarrow[\text{reflux}]{HCl, H_2O} CH_3\underset{|}{\overset{OH}{C}}HCOOH$

Lactic acid

(b) A racemate.

16.14 (a) cyclopentyl$-Br \xrightarrow{P(C_6H_5)_3}$ cyclopentyl$-P(C_6H_5)_3^+Br^-$

$\xrightarrow{RLi}$ cyclopentylidene$=P(C_6H_5)_3$

(b) $CH_3(CH_2)_4CH_2Br \xrightarrow{(C_6H_5)_3P} CH_3(CH_2)_4CH_2-P(C_6H_5)_3^+Br^-$

$\xrightarrow{RLi} CH_3(CH_2)_4CH=P(C_6H_5)_3$

(c) $BrCH_2CH_2CH_2CH_2Br + 2(C_6H_5)_3P \longrightarrow$

$(C_6H_5)_3{\overset{+}{P}}-CH_2CH_2CH_2CH_2-{\overset{+}{P}}(C_6H_5)_3 \; 2Br^-$

$\xrightarrow{2RLi} (C_6H_5)_3P=CHCH_2CH_2CH=P(C_6H_5)_3$

16.15 (a) CH_3I $\xrightarrow[\text{(2) RLi}]{\text{(1) }(C_6H_5)_3P}$ $CH_2=P(C_6H_5)_3$ $\xrightarrow{C_6H_5\overset{\displaystyle O}{\overset{\|}{C}}CH_3}$ $C_6H_5\underset{\displaystyle CH_3}{\overset{\displaystyle |}{C}}=CH_2$

(b) CH_3CH_2Br $\xrightarrow[\text{(2) RLi}]{\text{(1) }(C_6H_5)_3P}$ $CH_3CH=P(C_6H_5)_3$ $\xrightarrow{C_6H_5\overset{\displaystyle O}{\overset{\|}{C}}CH_3}$ $C_6H_5\underset{\displaystyle CH_3}{\overset{\displaystyle |}{C}}=CHCH_3$

(c) $CH_2=P(C_6H_5)_3$ $\xrightarrow{CH_3\overset{\displaystyle O}{\overset{\|}{C}}CH_3}$ $\underset{\displaystyle CH_3}{\overset{\displaystyle CH_3}{>}}C=CH_2$
(from part a)

(d) $CH_2=P(C_6H_5)_3$ $\longrightarrow$
(from part a)

(e) $CH_3CH_2CH_2Br$ $\xrightarrow[\text{(2) RLi}]{\text{(1) }(C_6H_5)_3P}$ $CH_3CH_2CH=P(C_6H_5)_3$

$\xrightarrow{CH_3\overset{\displaystyle O}{\overset{\|}{C}}CH_2CH_3}$ $CH_3CH_2CH=\underset{\displaystyle CH_2CH_3}{\overset{\displaystyle CH_3}{\overset{\displaystyle |}{C}}}CH_2CH_3$

(f) $CH_2=CHCH_2Br$ $\xrightarrow[\text{(2) RLi}]{\text{(1) }(C_6H_5)_3P}$ $CH_2=CHCH=P(C_6H_5)_3$

$\xrightarrow{C_6H_5\overset{\displaystyle O}{\overset{\|}{C}}H}$ $C_6H_5CH=CHCH=CH_2$

(g) $C_6H_5CH_2Br$ $\xrightarrow[\text{(2) RLi}]{\text{(1) }(C_6H_5)_3P}$ $C_6H_5CH=P(C_6H_5)_3$ $\xrightarrow{C_6H_5\overset{\displaystyle O}{\overset{\|}{C}}H}$

$C_6H_5CH=CHC_6H_5$

16.16

$(C_6H_5)_3P: + C_6H_5\overset{\frown O}{CH}-CHCH_3$ $\longrightarrow$

$\underset{(C_6H_5)_3\overset{+}{P}}{C_6H_5CH-\overset{\displaystyle O^-}{\overset{\displaystyle |}{C}}HC_6H_5}$ $\longrightarrow$ $\underset{(C_6H_5)_3P}{C_6H_5CH}\underset{O}{CHC_6H_5}$

$\longrightarrow$ $C_6H_5CH=CHC_6H_5 + (C_6H_5)_3P=O$

16.17 (a) $CH_3OCH_2Br + (C_6H_5)_3P \xrightarrow{\text{(2) RLi}} CH_3OCH=P(C_6H_5)_3$

(b) Hydrolysis of the ether yields a hemiacetal that then goes on to form an aldehyde:

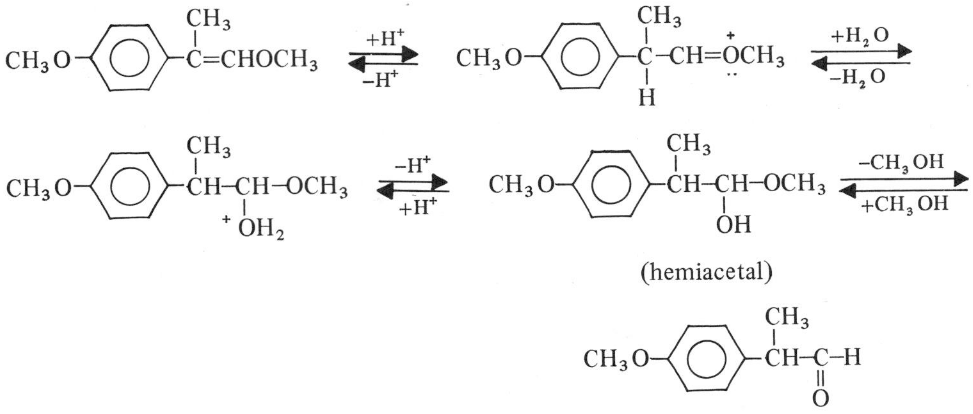

(hemiacetal)

(c)

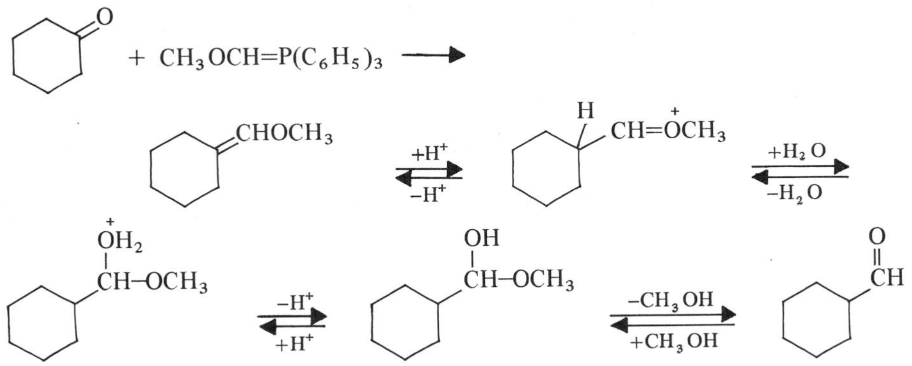

16.18

(a)

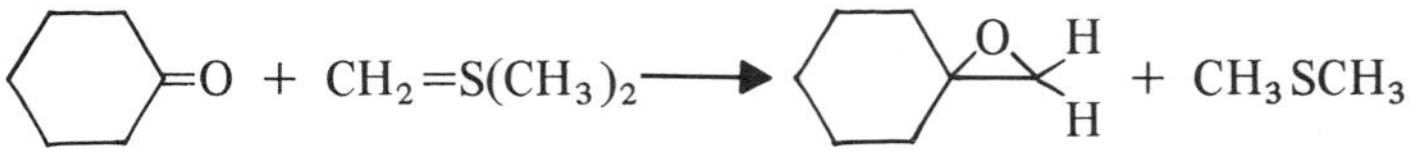

(b)

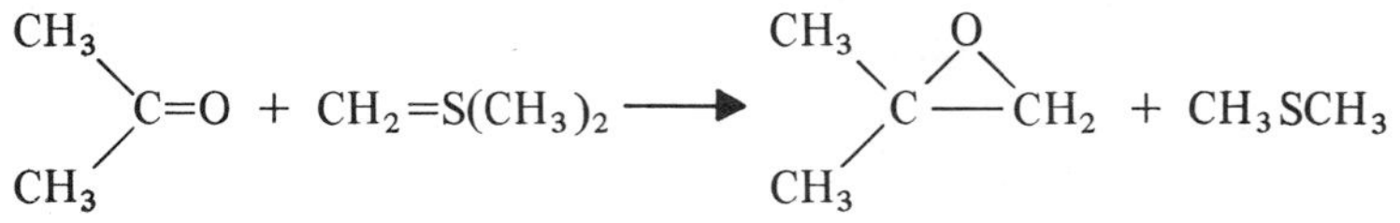

16.19 (a) $(CH_3)_2C=O + BrCH_2CO_2CH_2CH_3 \xrightarrow[\text{benzene}]{\text{Zn}} (CH_3)_2\overset{\displaystyle OZn}{\underset{}{C}}CH_2CO_2CH_2CH_3$

$\xrightarrow{H_3O^+} (CH_3)_2\overset{\displaystyle OH}{\underset{}{C}}CH_2CO_2CH_2CH_3$

(b)

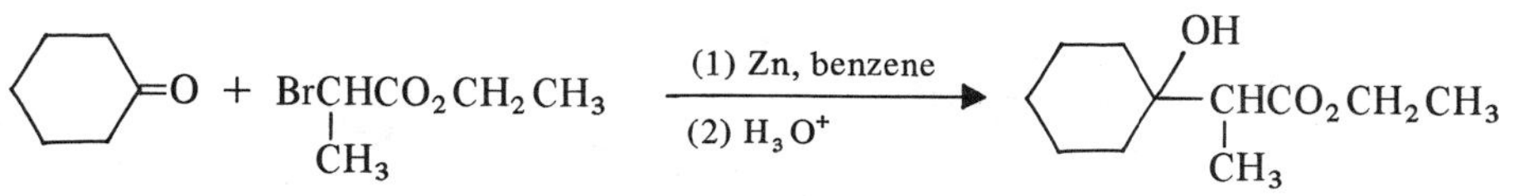

(c)

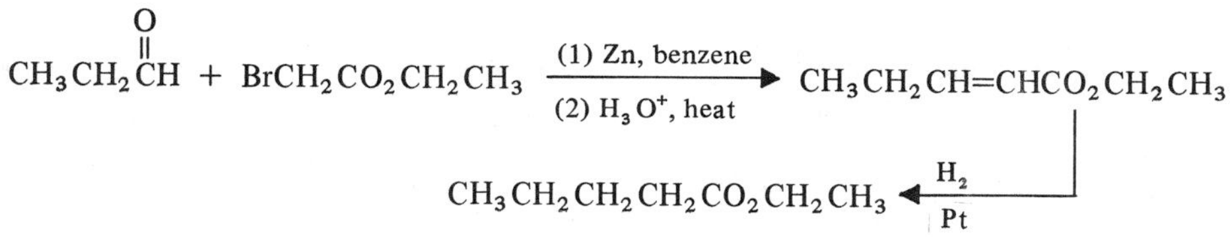

16.20

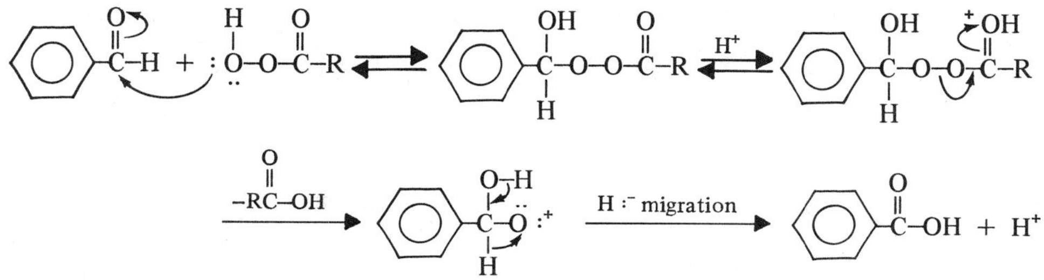

16.21 The product is a lactone, formed as follows.

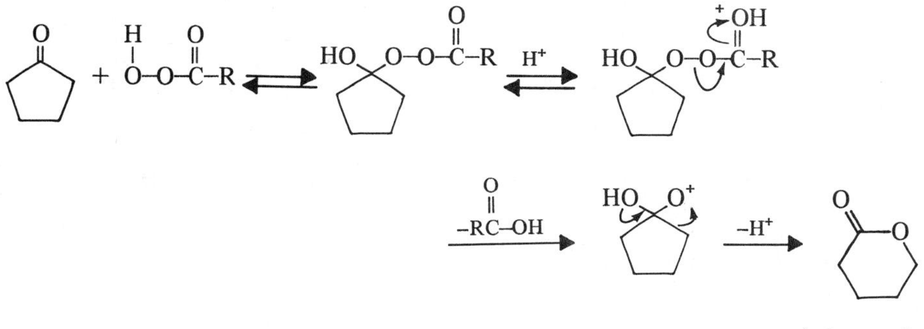

(a lactone)

16.22 $CH_3\overset{O}{\overset{\|}{C}}-O-\underset{\underset{CH_3}{|}}{C}HCH_3$. The isopropyl group has a greater migratory aptitude than the methyl.

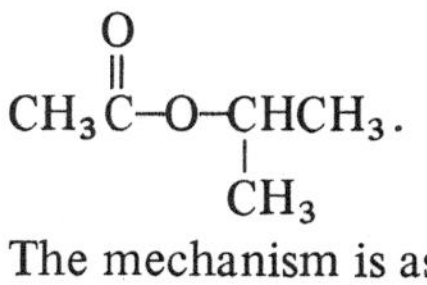

The mechanism is as follows.

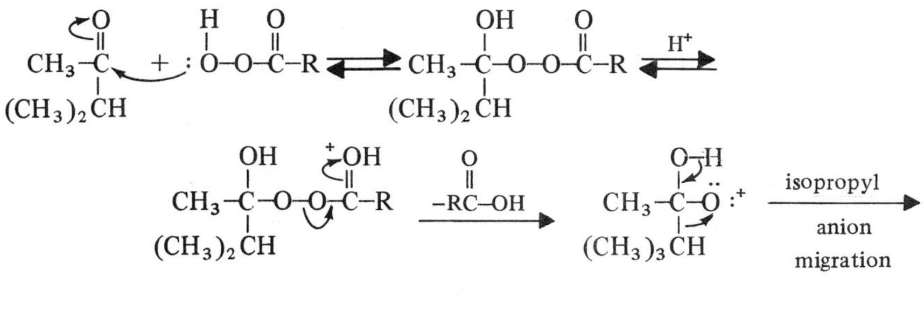

$$CH_3-\overset{\overset{\displaystyle O}{\|}}{C}-O-CH(CH_3)_2 \ + \ H^+$$

16.23 (a) HCHO   Methanal

(b) CH_3CHO Ethanal

(c) $C_6H_5CH_2CHO$ Phenylethanal

(d) CH_3COCH_3 Propanone

(e) $CH_3COCH_2CH_3$ Butanone

(f) $CH_3COC_6H_5$ Methyl phenyl ketone

(g) $C_6H_5COC_6H_5$ Diphenyl ketone

(h) [benzene ring with CHO and OH]   2-Hydroxybenzaldehyde

(i) [benzene ring with CH_3O, CHO, HO]   4-Hydroxy-3-methoxybenzaldehyde

16.24 (a) $CH_3CH_2CH_2OH$ (i) $CH_3CHBrCHO$

(b) $CH_3CH_2CHOHC_6H_5$ (j) $CH_3CH_2COO^-NH_4^+ \ + \ Ag\downarrow$

(c) $CH_3CH_2CH_2OH$ (k) $CH_3CH_2CH{=}NOH$

(d) $CH_3CH_2\overset{\overset{\displaystyle O}{\|}}{C}-O^-$ (l) $CH_3CH_2CH{=}NNHCONH_2$

(e) $CH_3CH_2CH{=}CH_2$ (m) $CH_3CH_2CH{=}NNHC_6H_5$

(f) $CH_3CH_2CH_2OH$ (n) CH_3CH_2COOH

(g) $CH_3CH_2CH{\Big\langle}\begin{matrix}O-CH_2\\ |\\ O-CH_2\end{matrix}$ (o) $CH_3CH_2CH{\Big\langle}\begin{matrix}S-CH_2\\ |\\ S-CH_2\end{matrix}$

(h) $CH_3CH_2CH{=}CHCH_3$ (p) $CH_3CH_2CH_3 \ + \ CH_3CH_3 \ + \ NiS$

(q) CH_3CH_2COOH

16.25 (a) $CH_3CHOHCH_3$ (d) No reaction

(b) $C_6H_5\underset{\underset{\displaystyle CH_3}{|}}{COHCH_3}$ (e) $CH_3\underset{}{\overset{\overset{\displaystyle CH_3}{|}}{C}}{=}CH_2$

(c) $CH_3CHOHCH_3$ (f) $CH_3CHOHCH_3$

(g) 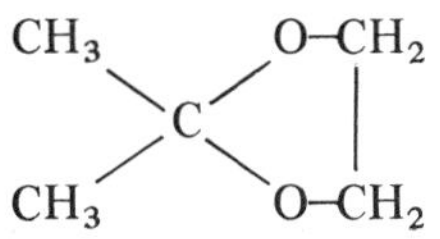 $\begin{array}{c} CH_3 \\ \\ CH_3 \end{array} C \begin{array}{c} O-CH_2 \\ \\ O-CH_2 \end{array}$

(h) $CH_3CH=C(CH_3)_2$

(i) CH_3COCH_2Br

(j) No reaction

(k) $CH_3C=NOH$
      $\quad\ \ |$
      $\quad\ CH_3$

(l) $CH_3C=NNHCONH_2$
      $\quad\ \ |$
      $\quad\ CH_3$

(m) $CH_3C=NNHC_6H_5$
       $\quad\ \ |$
       $\quad\ CH_3$

(n) No reaction

(o) 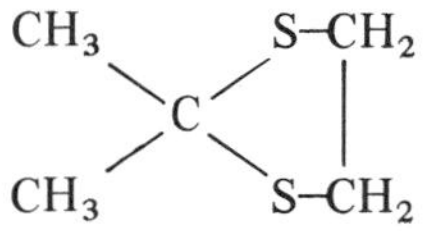 $\begin{array}{c} CH_3 \\ \\ CH_3 \end{array} C \begin{array}{c} S-CH_2 \\ \\ S-CH_2 \end{array}$

(p) $CH_3CH_2CH_3 + CH_3CH_3 + NiS$

(q) $CH_3\overset{\displaystyle O}{\overset{\|}{C}}-OCH_3$

16.26

(a)

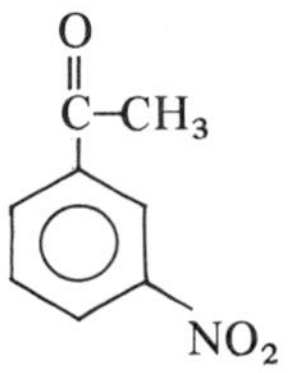

(b)

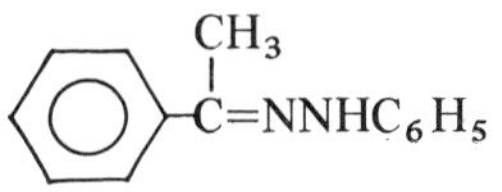

(c)

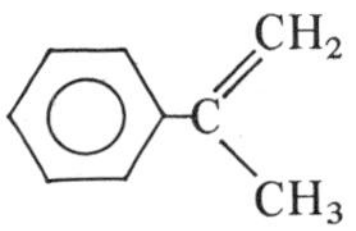

(d)

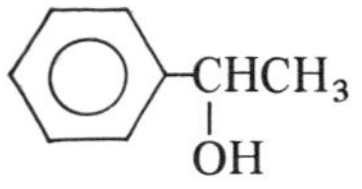

(e)

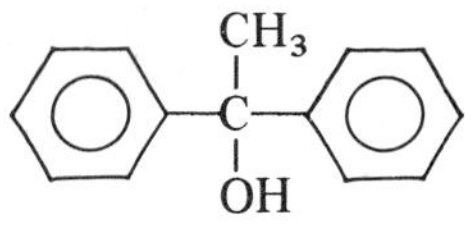

16.27 (a)

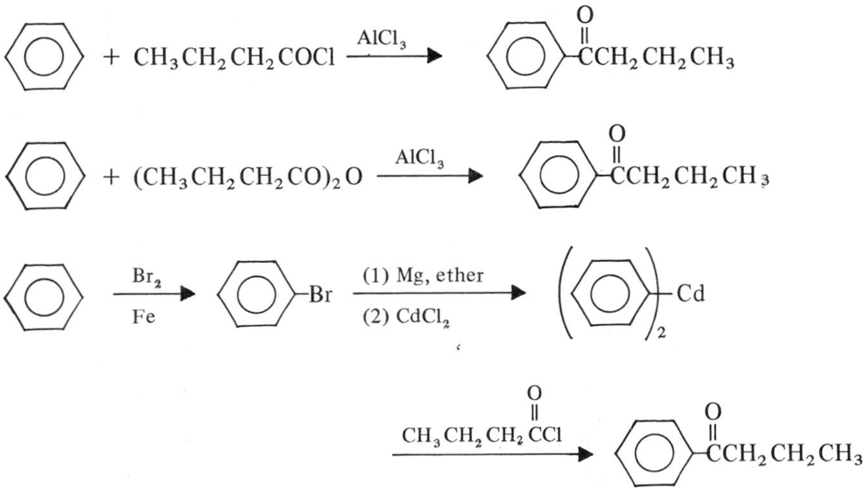

(b)

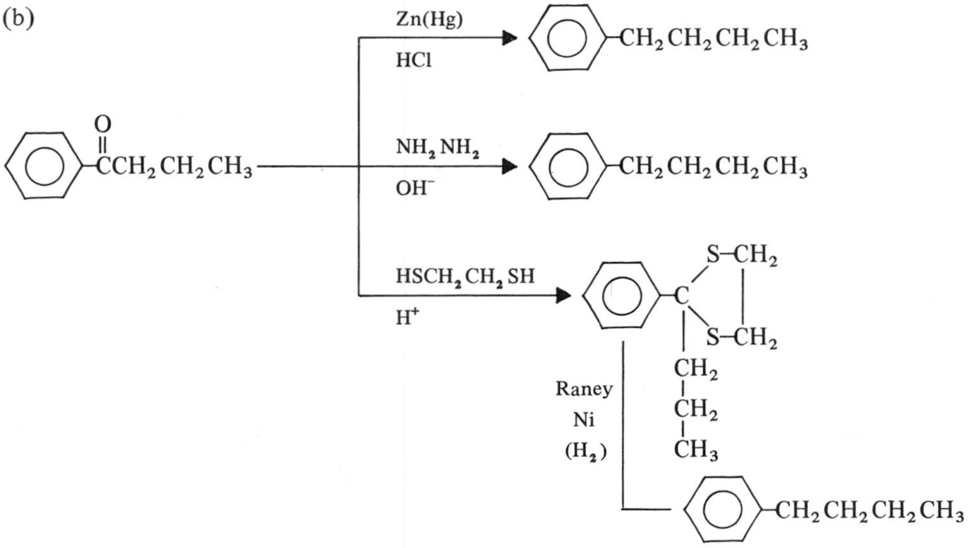

16.28 (a)

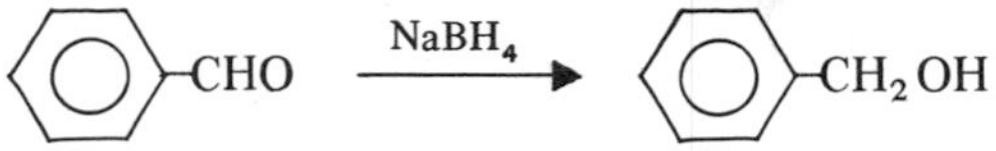

(b)

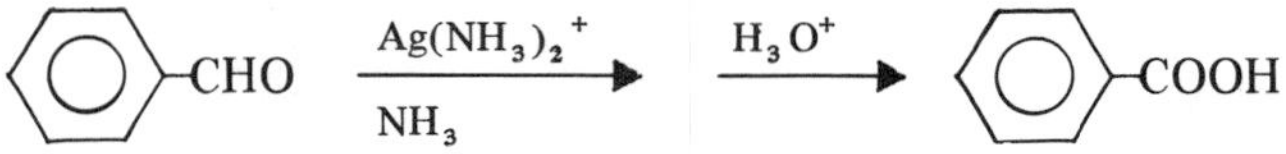

(c)

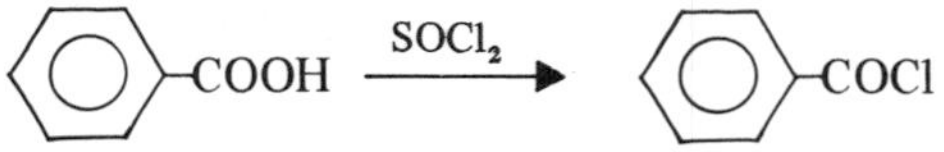

[from (b)]

(d)

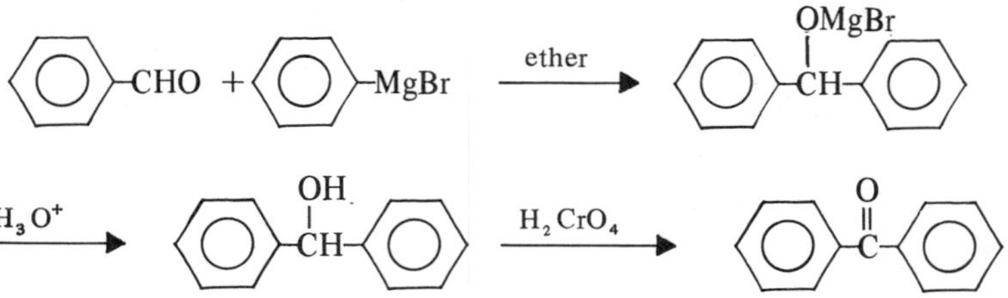

or

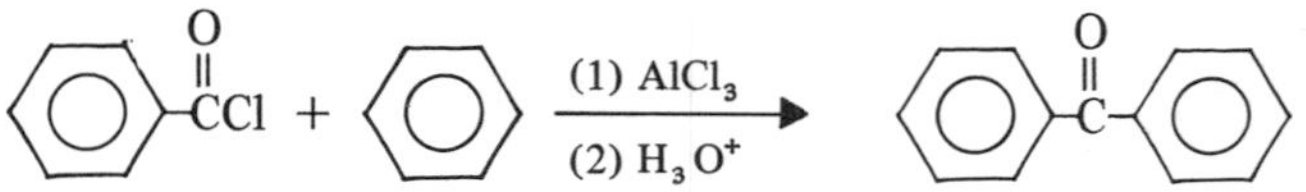

[from (c)]

(e)

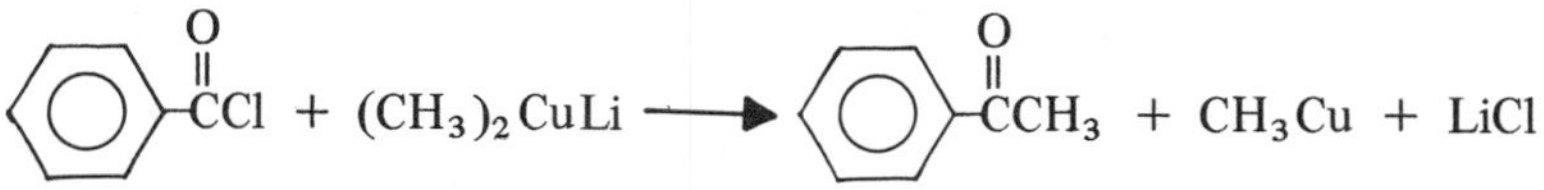

[from (c)]

or

$$C_6H_5\text{-}C(=O)\text{-Cl} + (CH_3)_2Cd \longrightarrow C_6H_5\text{-}C(=O)\text{-}CH_3$$

[from (c)]

(f) $C_6H_5\text{-}C(=O)\text{-H}$ $\xrightarrow[\text{(2) } H_3O^+]{\text{(1) } CH_3MgI}$ $C_6H_5\text{-}CH(OH)CH_3$

(g) $C_6H_5\text{-}C(=O)\text{-H}$ $\xrightarrow[\text{(2) } H_3O^+]{\text{(1) } (CH_3)_2CHCH_2MgBr}$ $C_6H_5\text{-}CH(OH)CH_2CHCH_3$ with CH_3

(h) $C_6H_5\text{-}CH_2OH$ $\xrightarrow{PBr_3}$ $C_6H_5\text{-}CH_2Br$

[from (a)]

(i) $C_6H_5\text{-}CH_2Br$ $\xrightarrow[CH_3COOH]{Zn}$ $C_6H_5\text{-}CH_3$

[from (h)]

or

$$C_6H_5\text{-}CH(=O) \xrightarrow[BF_3]{HSCH_2CH_2SH} C_6H_5\text{-}CH\langle S\text{-}CH_2 / S\text{-}CH_2\rangle \xrightarrow[(H_2)]{\text{Raney Ni}} C_6H_5\text{-}CH_3$$

(j) $C_6H_5\text{-}CH(=O)$ $\xrightarrow{CH_3OH,\ H^+}$ $C_6H_5\text{-}CH(OCH_3)OCH_3$

(k) $C_6H_5\text{-}CH(=O)$ $\xrightarrow[H_3{}^{18}O^+]{H_2{}^{18}O}$ $C_6H_5\text{-}CH(={}^{18}O)$ (see Problem 16.10 for the mechanism)

(l) $C_6H_5\text{-}CH(=O)$ $\xrightarrow[\text{(2) } H_3O^+]{\text{(1) } NaBD_4}$ $C_6H_5\text{-}CHDOH$

(m) $C_6H_5\text{-}CH(=O)$ $\xrightarrow{HCN}$ $C_6H_5\text{-}CH(OH)CN$

(a cyanohydrin)

(n) $C_6H_5\text{-}CH(=O)$ $\xrightarrow{NH_2OH}$ $C_6H_5\text{-}CH=NOH$

(an oxime)

(o) 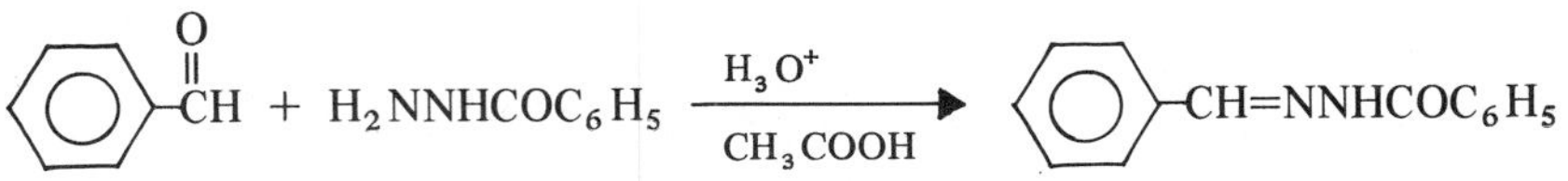 C_6H_5—CH + $H_2NNHCOC_6H_5$ $\xrightarrow[CH_3COOH]{H_3O^+}$ C_6H_5—CH=NNHCOC$_6$H$_5$

(a phenylhydrazone)

(p) 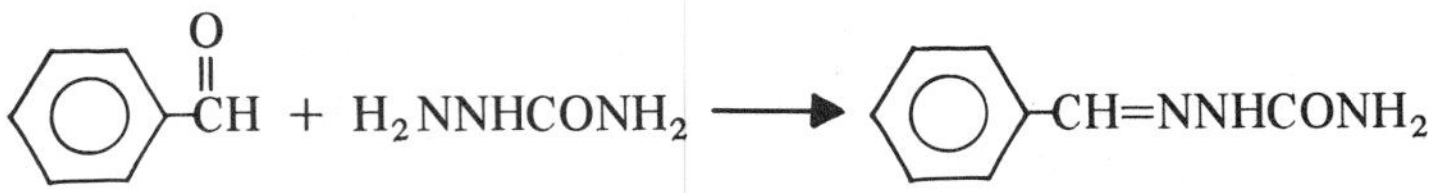 C_6H_5—CH + $H_2NNHCONH_2$ $\longrightarrow$ C_6H_5—CH=NNHCONH$_2$

(a semicarbazone)

(q) 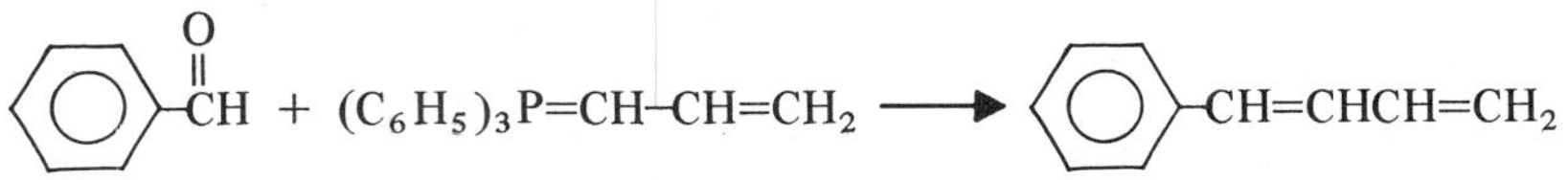 C_6H_5—CH + $(C_6H_5)_3$P=CH—CH=CH$_2$ $\longrightarrow$ C_6H_5—CH=CHCH=CH$_2$

(a Wittig reagent)

(r) 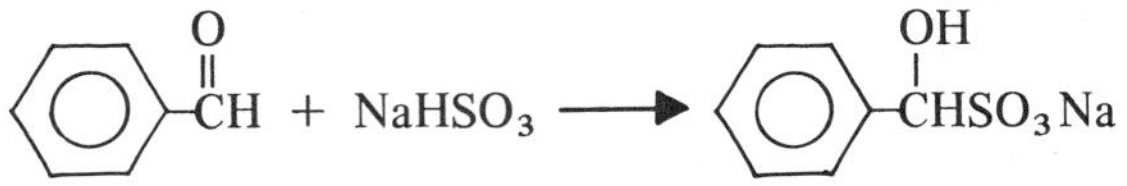 C_6H_5—CH + NaHSO$_3$ $\longrightarrow$ C_6H_5—CHSO$_3$Na (with OH)

16.29

(a) 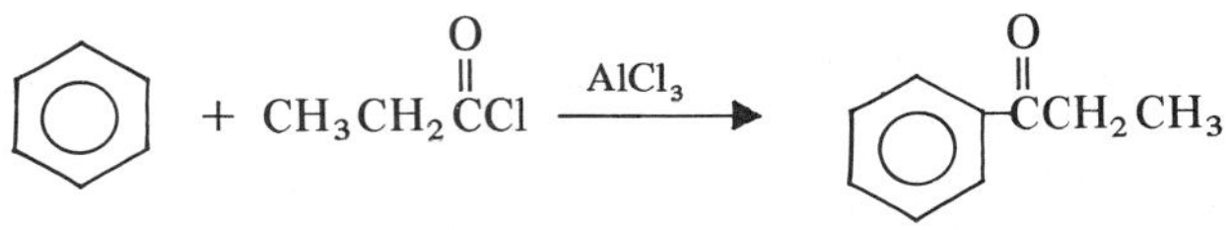 C_6H_6 + CH$_3$CH$_2$CCl $\xrightarrow{AlCl_3}$ C_6H_5—CCH$_2$CH$_3$

(b) C_6H_5—C—Cl + (CH$_3$CH$_2$)$_2$CuLi $\longrightarrow$ C_6H_5—CCH$_2$CH$_3$

(c) C_6H_5—C≡N + CH$_3$CH$_2$Li $\xrightarrow{(2) H_3O^+}$ C_6H_5—C—CH$_2$CH$_3$

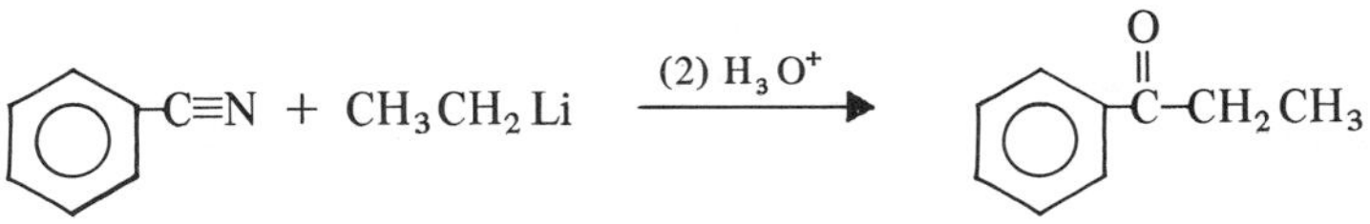

(d) 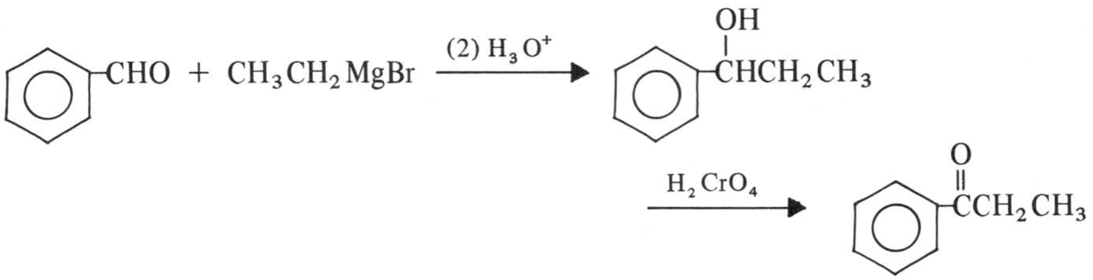 C_6H_5—CHO + CH$_3$CH$_2$MgBr $\xrightarrow{(2) H_3O^+}$ C_6H_5—CHCH$_2$CH$_3$ (with OH)

$\xrightarrow{H_2CrO_4}$ C_6H_5—CCH$_2$CH$_3$

(e) 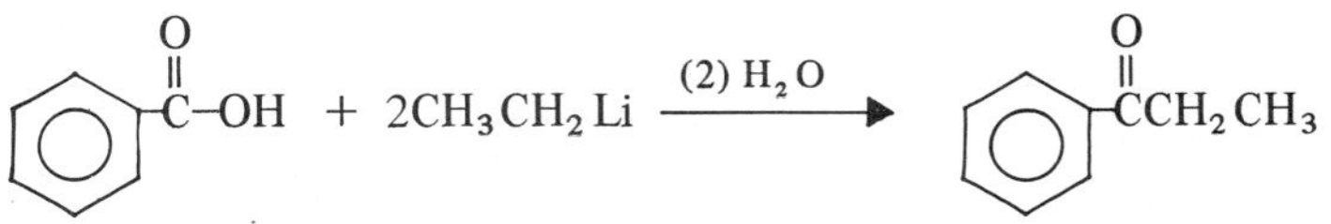 C_6H_5—C—OH + 2CH$_3$CH$_2$Li $\xrightarrow{(2) H_2O}$ C_6H_5—CCH$_2$CH$_3$

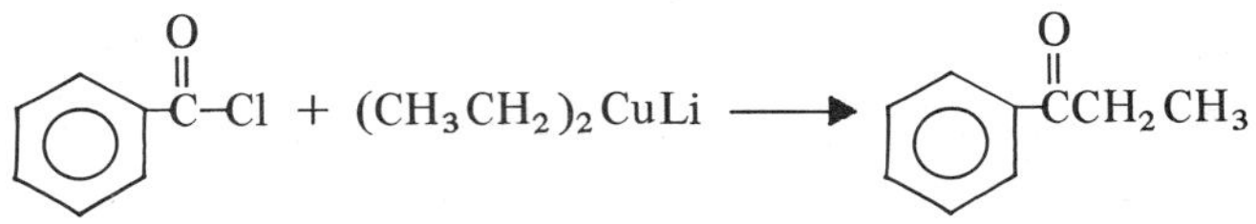

16.30

(a) 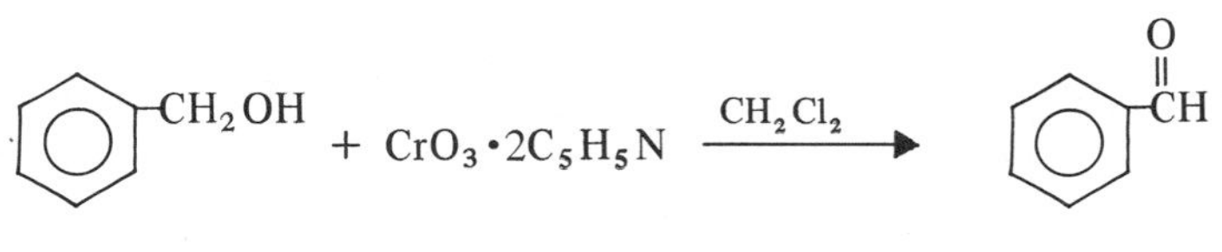 C_6H_5—CH$_2$OH + CrO$_3$·2C$_5$H$_5$N $\xrightarrow{CH_2Cl_2}$ C_6H_5—CH

(b)

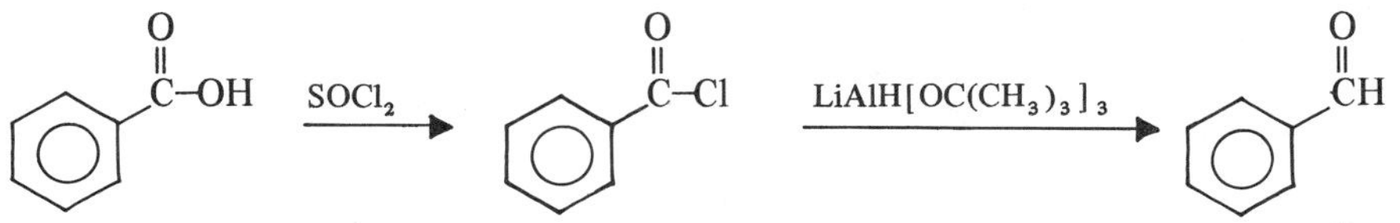

(c)

(d)

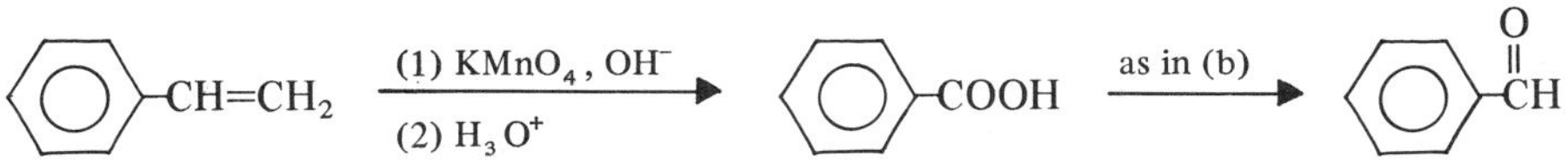

16.31

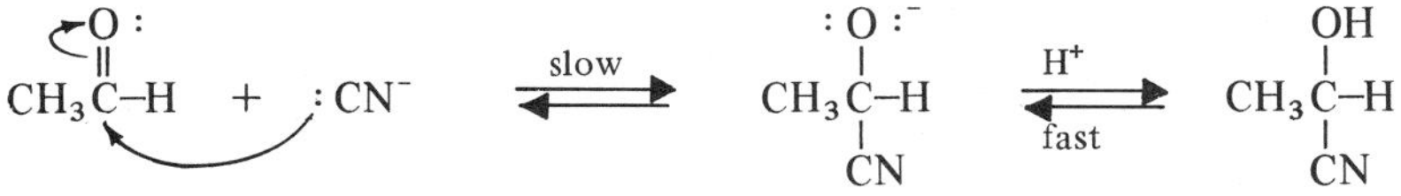

The first step is the slow step. If the second step were slower, then the rate of the reaction would depend also on the concentration of hydrogen ion.

16.32

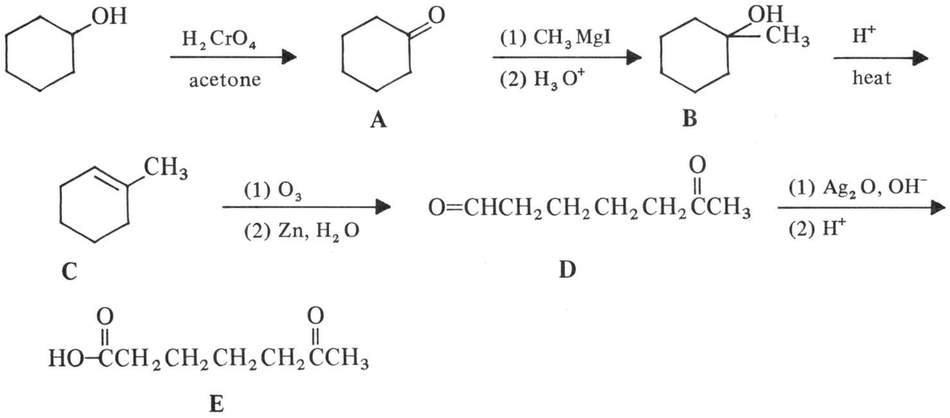

16.33

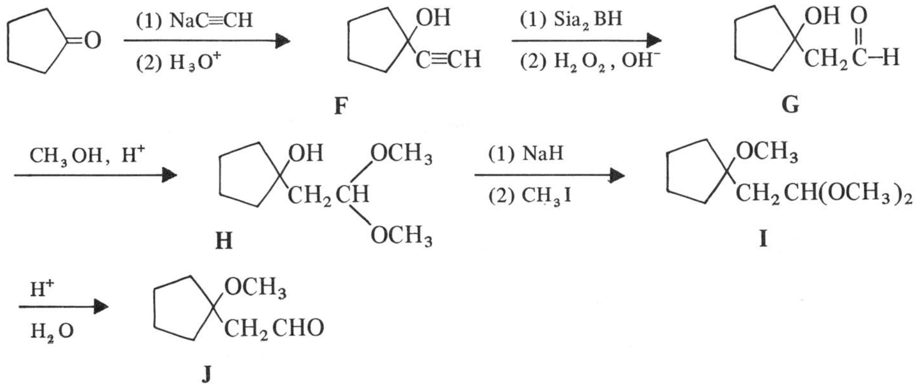

16.34

$$CH_3CH_2\overset{O}{\overset{\|}{C}}H \xrightarrow[Zn]{BrCH_2CO_2Et} \xrightarrow{H_3O^+} \underset{\textbf{K}}{CH_3CH_2\overset{OH}{\overset{|}{C}}HCH_2CO_2Et} \xrightarrow[heat]{H^+}$$

$$\underset{\textbf{L}}{CH_3CH_2CH{=}CHCO_2Et} \xrightarrow{H_2, Pt} \underset{\textbf{M}}{CH_3CH_2CH_2CH_2CO_2Et} \xrightarrow[(2)\ H_2O]{(1)\ LiAlH_4}$$

$$\underset{\textbf{N}}{CH_3CH_2CH_2CH_2CH_2OH} \xrightarrow[CH_2Cl_2]{CrO_3 \cdot 2C_5H_5N} CH_3CH_2CH_2CH_2\overset{O}{\overset{\|}{C}}H$$

16.35

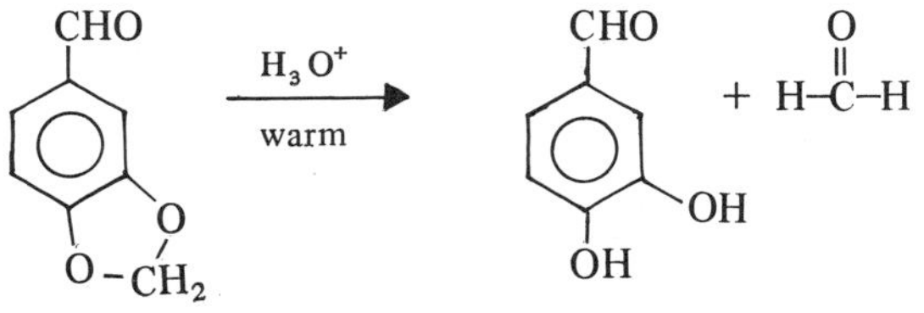

The compound $C_7H_6O_3$ is 3,4-dihydroxybenzaldehyde. The reaction involves hydrolysis of the acetal of formaldehyde.

16.36

(a)

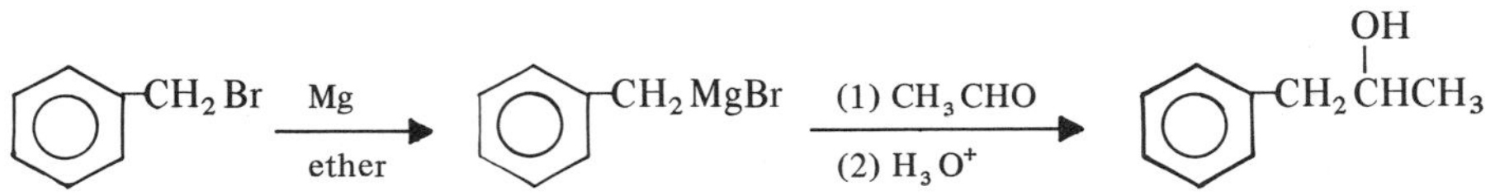

(b)

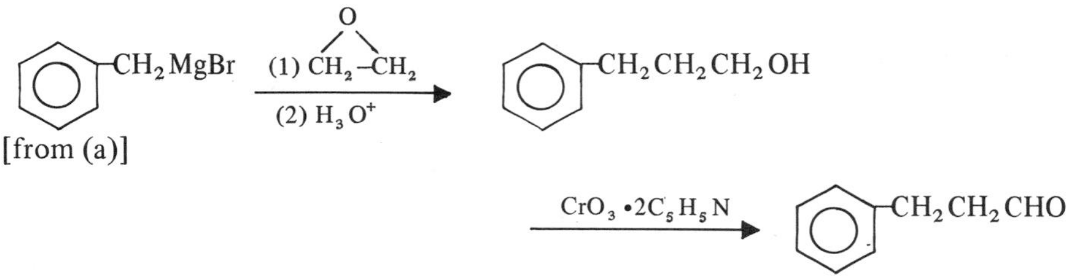

[from (a)]

(c)

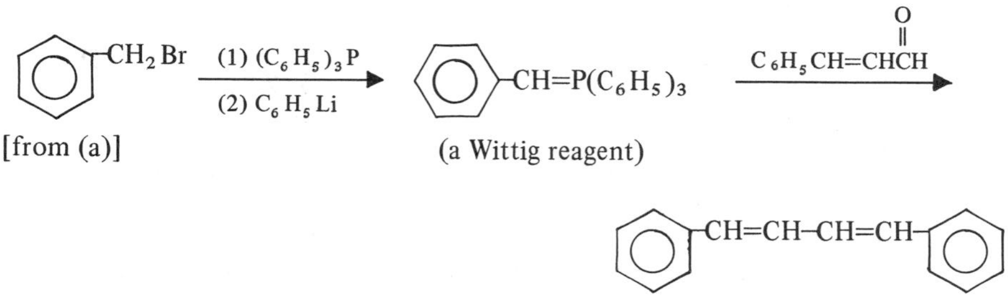

[from (a)]

(a Wittig reagent)

(d) [benzyl]CH_2MgBr + $H{-}\overset{O}{\underset{\|}{C}}CH_2CH_3$ $\xrightarrow{(2)\ H_3O^+}$ [benzyl]$CH_2\overset{OH}{\underset{|}{C}}HCH_2CH_3$

[from (a)]

$\xrightarrow{H_2CrO_4}$ [benzyl]$CH_2\overset{O}{\underset{\|}{C}}CH_2CH_3$

16.37

$BrCH_2CH_2CH_2\overset{O}{\underset{\|}{C}}{-}H$ $\xrightarrow{HO\frown OH,\ H^+}$ $BrCH_2CH_2CH_2CH\overset{O}{\underset{O}{\big\langle}}$ $\xrightarrow{Mg,\ ether}$

A

$BrMgCH_2CH_2CH_2CH\overset{O}{\underset{O}{\big\langle}}$ $\xrightarrow[(2)\ H_3O^+,\ H_2O]{(1)\ CH_3CHO}$ $CH_3\overset{OH}{\underset{|}{C}}HCH_2CH_2CH_2\overset{O}{\underset{\|}{C}}{-}H$

B   **C**

$\rightleftharpoons$ [structure: a hemiacetal with CH_3 and OH] $\xrightarrow[H^+]{CH_3OH}$ [structure: D with CH_3 and OCH_3]

(a hemiacetal)   **D**

(an acetal)

16.38 (a) $(CH_3)_2SO_4$, NaOH or CH_3I, NaOH

(b) (1) $CrO_3 \cdot 2C_5H_5N$, (2) Zn, $Br\overset{CH_3}{\underset{|}{C}}HCOOEt$, (3) H_3O^+

(c) $LiAlH_4$

16.39

$CH_2{=}CHCH_2OH$ $\xrightarrow[CH_2Cl_2]{CrO_3\cdot2C_5H_5N}$ $CH_2{=}CH\overset{O}{\underset{\|}{C}}H$ $\xrightarrow{CH_3OH,\ H^+}$

A

$CH_2{=}CH{-}\overset{OCH_3}{\underset{OCH_3}{C}}H$ $\xrightarrow[cold,\ dilute]{KMnO_4,\ OH^-}$ $\underset{OH\ \ OH\ \ OCH_3}{CH_2CH\overset{OCH_3}{C}H}$ $\xrightarrow[H_2O]{H_3O^+}$ $\underset{OH\ OH}{CH_2CH\overset{O}{\underset{\|}{C}}H}$

B   **C**   Glyceraldehyde

The product would be racemic as no chiral reagents were used.

16.40

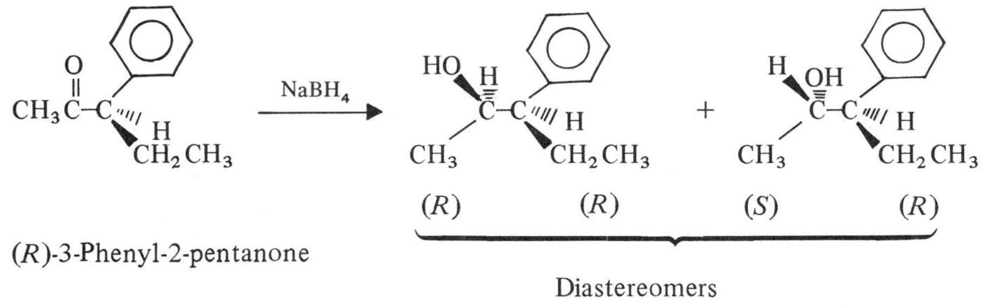

(R)-3-Phenyl-2-pentanone

Diastereomers

16.41

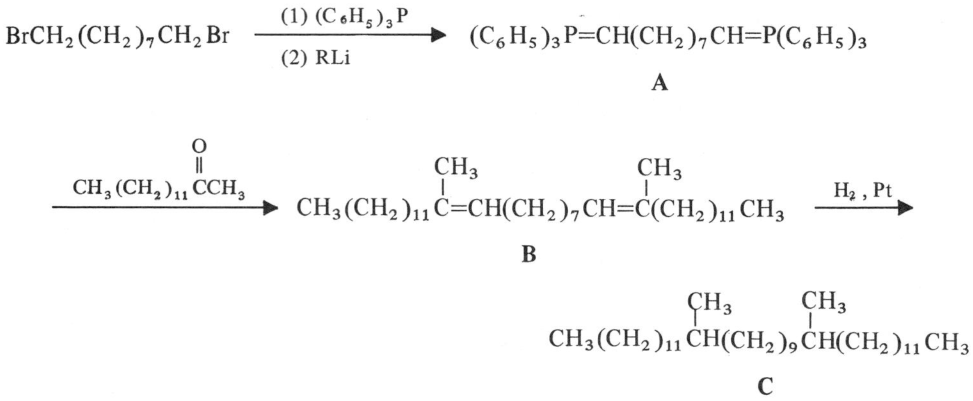

$$BrCH_2(CH_2)_7CH_2Br \xrightarrow[\text{(2) RLi}]{\text{(1) } (C_6H_5)_3P} (C_6H_5)_3P=CH(CH_2)_7CH=P(C_6H_5)_3$$

A

$$CH_3(CH_2)_{11}\overset{O}{\overset{\|}{C}}CH_3$$

$$CH_3(CH_2)_{11}\overset{CH_3}{\overset{|}{C}}=CH(CH_2)_7CH=\overset{CH_3}{\overset{|}{C}}(CH_2)_{11}CH_3 \xrightarrow{H_2, Pt}$$

B

$$CH_3(CH_2)_{11}\overset{CH_3}{\overset{|}{C}}H(CH_2)_9\overset{CH_3}{\overset{|}{C}}H(CH_2)_{11}CH_3$$

C

16.42 (a) $Ag(NH_3)_2{}^+OH^-$ (positive test with benzaldehyde)

(b) $Ag(NH_3)_2{}^+OH^-$ (positive test with hexanal)

(c) Concentrated H_2SO_4 (2-hexanone is soluble)

(d) CrO_3 in H_2SO_4 (positive test with 2-hexanol)

(e) Br_2 in CCl_4 (decolorization with $C_6H_5CH=CHCOC_6H_5$)

(f) $Ag(NH_3)_2{}^+OH^-$ (positive test with pentanal)

(g) Br_2 in CCl_4 (immediate decolorization occurs with enol form)

(h) $Ag(NH_3)_2{}^+OH^-$ (positive test with cyclic hemiacetal)

16.43

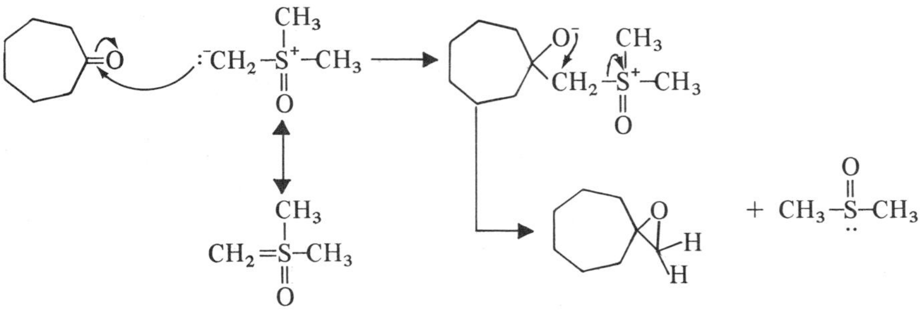

16.44   Compound **W** is:

multiplet, δ 7.3 { ... }—singlet δ 3.4

infrared peak near 1715 cm^{-1}

(1) KMnO$_4$, OH$^-$, heat
(2) H$_3$O$^+$

Phthalic acid

Compound **X** is:

multiplet, δ 7.5 { ... } triplet, δ 2.5

triplet
δ 3.1

16.45   Each proton nmr spectra (Fig. 16.1 and 16.2) has a five hydrogen peak near δ 7.1, suggesting that **Y** and **Z** each have a C_6H_5- group. The infrared spectrum of each compound show a strong peak near 1705 cm^{-1}. This absorption indicates that each compound has a C=O group not adjacent to the phenyl group. We have, therefore, the following pieces,

and $-\overset{\overset{\displaystyle O}{\|}}{C}-$

If we subtract the atoms of these pieces from the molecular formula,

$$C_{10}H_{12}O$$
$$-C_7H_5O \quad (C_6H_5 \; + \; C=O)$$

We are left with, C_3H_7

In the proton nmr spectrum of **Y** we see an ethyl group [triplet, δ 1.0 (3H) and quartet, δ 2.3 (2H)] and an unsplit $-CH_2-$ group [singlet, δ 3.7 (2H)]. This means that **Y** must be,

—$CH_2\overset{\overset{\displaystyle O}{\|}}{C}CH_2CH_3$

1-Phenyl-2-butanone

In the proton nmr spectrum of **Z**, we see an unsplit $-CH_3$ group [singlet, δ 2.0 (3H)] and a multiplet (actually two superimposed triplets) at δ 2.8. This means **Z** must be,

—$CH_2CH_2\overset{\overset{\displaystyle O}{\|}}{C}CH_3$

4-Phenyl-2-butanone

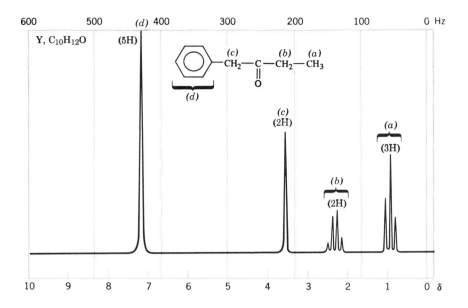

FIG. 16.1 *The proton nmr spectrum of compound Y, problem 16.45. (Spectrum courtesy of Aldrich Chemical Co., Milwaukee, Wis.)*

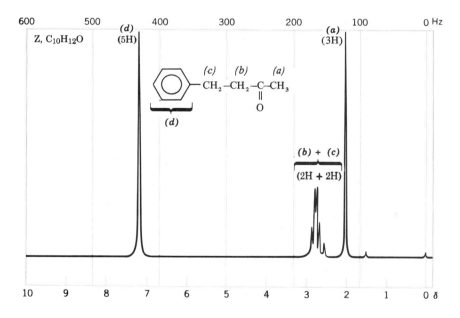

FIG. 16.2. *The proton nmr spectrum of compound Z, problem 16.45. (Spectrum courtesy of Aldrich Chemical Co., Milwaukee, Wis.)*

16.46   The two nitrogens of semicarbazide that are adjacent to the C=O group bear partial positive charges because of resonance contributions made by the second and third structures below,

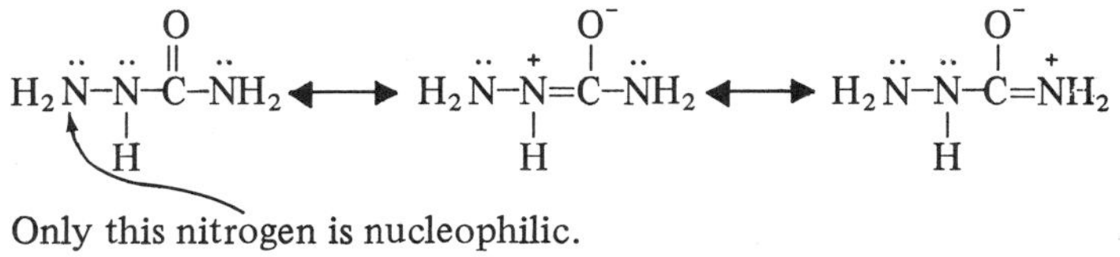

$$H_2\overset{..}{N}-\overset{..}{N}-\overset{O}{\overset{||}{C}}-\overset{..}{N}H_2 \longleftrightarrow H_2\overset{..}{N}-\overset{+}{N}=\overset{..}{C}-\overset{..}{N}H_2 \longleftrightarrow H_2\overset{..}{N}-\overset{..}{N}-\overset{\overset{O^-}{|}}{C}=\overset{+}{N}H_2$$

$$\overset{|}{H} \qquad\qquad\qquad \overset{|}{H} \qquad\qquad\qquad \overset{|}{H}$$

Only this nitrogen is nucleophilic.

16.47

(a)

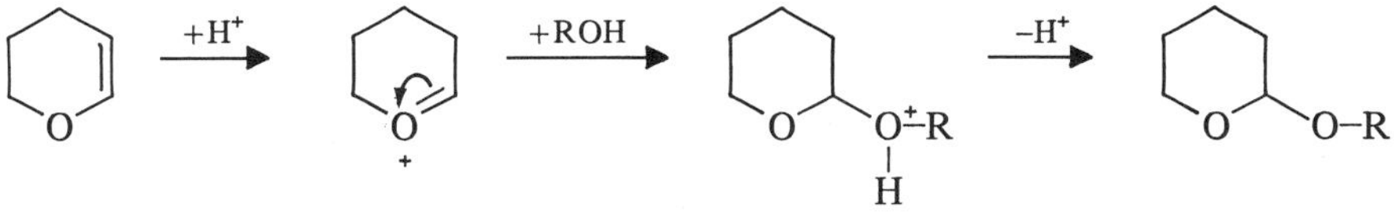

(b) Tetrahydropyranyl ethers are acetals; thus they are stable in aqueous base and hydrolyze readily in aqueous acid.

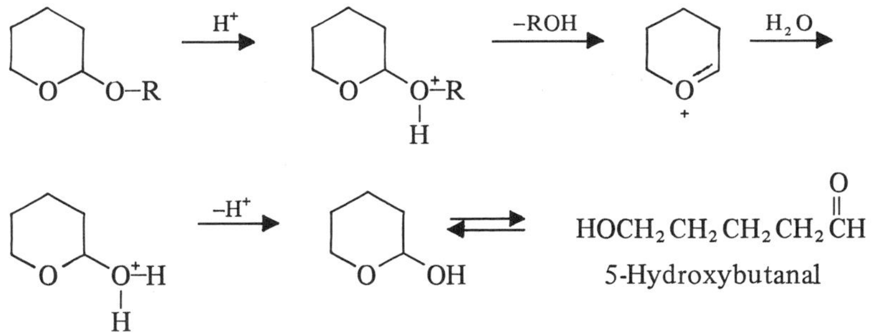

5-Hydroxybutanal

(c) $HOCH_2CH_2CH_2CH_2Cl \xrightarrow[H^+]{} $

$\xrightarrow[\text{ether}]{Mg}$

$\xrightarrow{CH_3\overset{O}{\overset{||}{C}}CH_3}$

$\xrightarrow[H_2O]{H^+} HOCH_2CH_2CH_2CH_2\overset{\overset{CH_3}{|}}{\underset{\overset{|}{CH_3}}{C}}OH$

$$(+ \ HOCH_2CH_2CH_2CH_2\overset{O}{\overset{||}{C}}H)$$

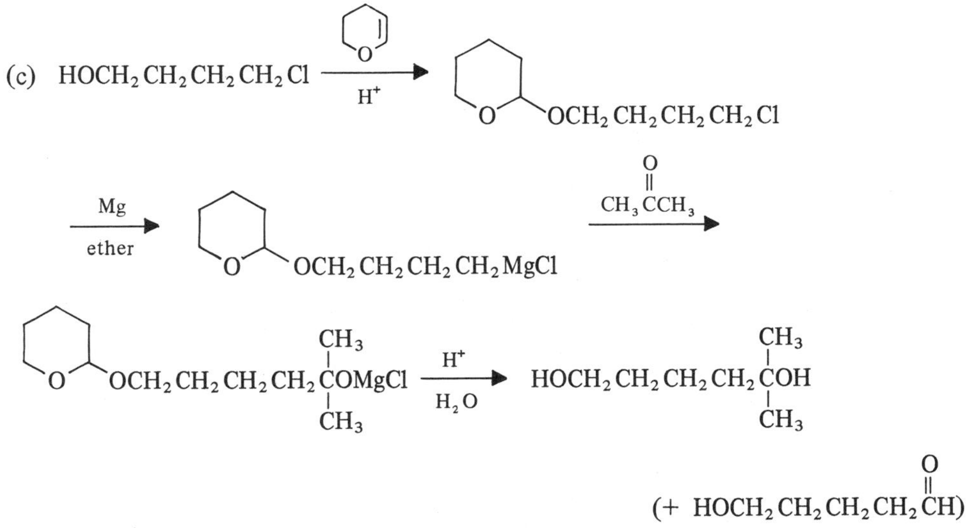

16.48   That compound **A** forms a phenyhydrazone, gives a negative Tollens' test, and gives an infrared band near 1710 cm^{-1} indicates that **A** is a ketone. The ^{13}C spectrum of **A** contains only four signals indicating that **A** has a high degree of symmetry. The splitting patterns of the proton off-resonance decoupled spectrum enable us to conclude that **A** is diisobutyl ketone:

$$\underset{(d)}{(CH_3)_2}\overset{(a)}{\underset{}{}}\overset{(b)\,(c)}{CHCH_2}\overset{O}{\overset{\|}{C}}CH_2CH(CH_3)_2$$

Assignments: *(a)*   quartet δ 22.6

   (b)   doublet δ 24.4

   (c)   triplet δ 52.3

   (d)   singlet δ 210.0

16.49   That the ^{13}C spectrum of **B** contains only three signals indicates that **B** has a highly symmetrical structure. The splitting patterns of the proton off-resonance decoupled spectrum indicate the presence of equivalent methyl groups (quartet at δ 18.8), equivalent $-\overset{|}{\underset{|}{C}}-$ groups (singlet at δ 70.4), and equivalent $\rangle$C=O groups (singlet at δ 215.0). These features allow only one possible structure for **B**:

Assignments: *(a)*   quartet δ 18.8

   (b)   singlet δ 70.4

   (c)   singlet δ 210.0

SECTION REFERENCES FOR ADDITIONAL PROBLEMS

16.23	16.2	**16.28**	16.14, 16.6–16.13
16.24	16.14, 16.6–16.13	**16.29**	16.5
16.25	16.14, 16.6–16.13	**16.30**	16.4
16.26	16.14, 16.6–16.13	**16.31**	16.9
16.27	16.5, 16.8C, 12.12C	**16.32**	16.5, 16.14, 16.6–16.13

16.33 16.14, 16.6–16.13   **16.41** 16.10A

16.34 16.11, 16.4   **16.42** 16.14, 16.17

16.35 16.7A   **16.43** 16.10B

16.36 16.4, 16.14   **16.44** 16.17

16.37 16.17A   **16.45** 16.17

16.38 16.4, 16.14, 16.11   **16.46** 16.8

16.39 16.4, 16.7   **16.47** 16.7

16.40 16.6, 16.14

SELF-TEST

16.1   Give an acceptable name for

$$\underset{\underset{CH_3}{|}}{CH_3\overset{\overset{OH}{|}}{C}HCH_2CHCH_2}\overset{\overset{O}{||}}{C}H$$

16.2   Which of the following compounds has the highest boiling point?

(a) Propanal, (b) Butanal, (c) Butanone, (d) 1-Butanol

16.3   Give a simple chemical test that would serve to distinguish between the compounds in each of the following pairs.

(a)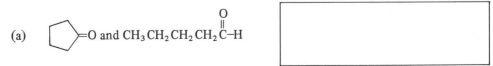

(b)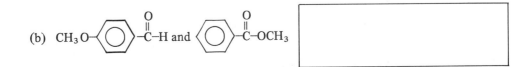

16.4   Give the structural formula of the missing reactant or major organic product. Write NR if no reaction occurs.

(a) [cyclohexanone derivative with methyl and isopropenyl groups] + [   ] ⟶ [methylenecyclohexane derivative with isopropenyl group]

(b) [cyclohexanone] + [   ] $\xrightarrow[\text{heat}]{\substack{\text{conc.}\\ \text{H}_2\text{SO}_4}}$ [cyclohexene carboxylic acid]

(c) [cyclohexene carbonyl chloride] $\xrightarrow{\hspace{2cm}}$ [   ] [cyclohexene carbaldehyde]

(d) $CH_3CHO + CH_3OH \xrightarrow{HCl(g)}$ [   ]

(e) $CH_3\overset{O}{\overset{\|}{C}}CH_3$ + [C$_6$H$_5$]–MgBr $\xrightarrow{\quad} \xrightarrow{H_3O^+}$ [   ]

(f) $CH_3CH_2\overset{O}{\overset{\|}{C}}C_6H_5 \xrightarrow{\overset{\overset{O}{\|}}{RCOOH}}$ [   ]

(g) $CH_3\overset{\overset{O}{\|}}{C}CH_3$ ⟶ $CH_3\underset{\underset{CH_3}{|}}{\overset{\overset{OH}{|}}{C}}CH_2\overset{\overset{O}{\|}}{C}OCH_3$

16.5   Write equations for a reasonable laboratory synthesis of

$H\overset{\overset{O}{\|}}{C}$—⟨O⟩—$CH_2OH$ from $H\overset{\overset{O}{\|}}{C}$—⟨O⟩—$\overset{\overset{O}{\|}}{C}$—OH and any other reagents.

(b)   ⟨⟩=⟨⟩   from cyclopentene and any other reagents.

SUPPLEMENTARY PROBLEMS

S16.1   What major reaction type occurs readily with aldehydes but not as readily with ketones?

S16.2   Many reactions of the carbonyl group of aldehydes and ketones are catalyzed by *both* acids and bases. Explain.

SOLUTIONS TO SUPPLEMENTARY PROBLEMS

S16.1   Oxidation. Ketones do not undergo oxidation with common oxidizing agents such as $KMnO_4$, H_2CrO_4, and Ag_2O. However, ketones may be conveniently oxidized in the Baeyer-Villager oxidation.

S16.2   The carbonyl group is polar:

Reactions occur through a nucleophilic attack at the positive carbon atom. Acid catalysts convert the carbonyl group to the cation,

which is more reactive than the neutral carbonyl group because it has an even greater positive charge on carbon than the neutral carbonyl group.

    Base catalysts often increase the nucleophilicity of the nucleophile by removing a proton; for example,

$$H-C\equiv N: \xrightarrow{\text{base}} {}^-:C\equiv N: + \text{Base-H}^+$$

   (nucleophile)   (better
                    nucleophile)

17

ALDEHYDES AND KETONES II: REACTIONS AT THE α-CARBON. THE ALDOL CONDENSATION

SOLUTIONS TO PROBLEMS

17.1

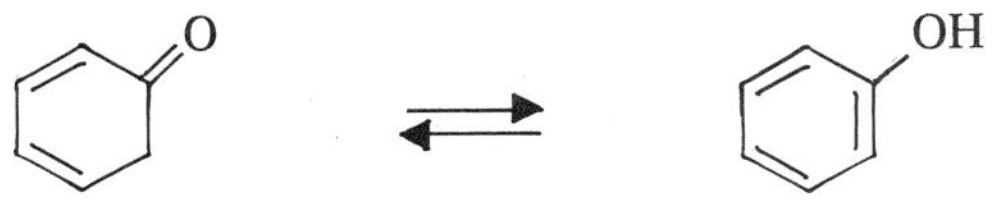

2,4-Cyclohexadien-1-one
(keto form)   ,   Phenol
(enol form)

The enol form is aromatic, and it is therefore stabilized by the resonance energy of the benzene ring.

17.2

No.

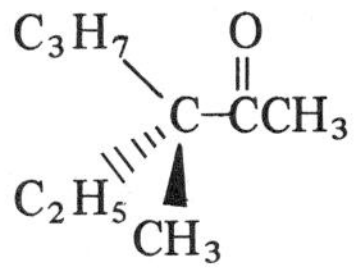

does not have a hydrogen attached to its chiral α carbon and thus enol formation involving the chiral carbon is not possible. With

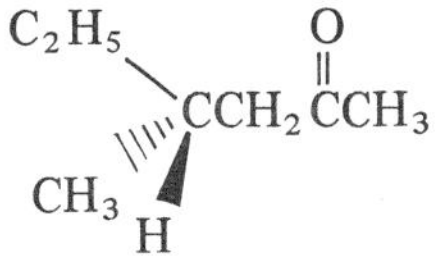

the chiral carbon is a β carbon and thus enol formation does not affect it.

17.3   In OD⁻/D₂O

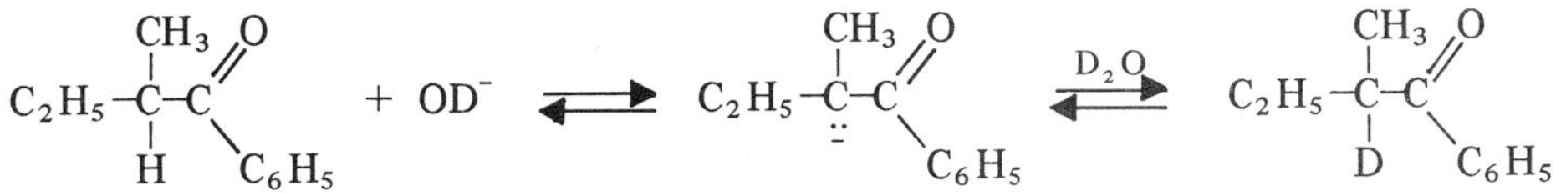

In D₃O⁺/D₂O

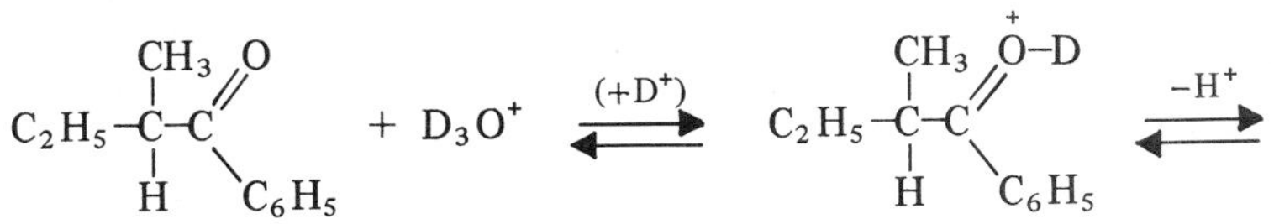

$$CH_3\diagup C=C\diagdown OD \underset{C_2H_5 \diagup \diagdown C_6H_5}{} \quad \xrightleftharpoons{+D^+} \quad C_2H_5-\overset{CH_3}{\underset{D}{C}}-\overset{\overset{+}{O}-D}{C} \diagdown_{C_6H_5} \quad \xrightleftharpoons{-D^+} \quad C_2H_5-\overset{CH_3}{\underset{D}{C}}-\overset{O}{C} \diagdown_{C_6H_5}$$

17.4   The reaction is said to be "base promoted" because base is consumed as the reaction takes place. A catalyst is, by definition, not consumed.

17.5   (a) The slow step in base-catalyzed racemization is the same as that in base-promoted halogenation—*the formation of an enolate ion.* (Formation of an enolate ion from *sec*-butyl phenyl ketone leads to racemization because the enolate ion is achiral. When it accepts a proton it yields a racemic modification.) The slow step in acid-catalyzed racemization is also the same as that in acid-catalyzed halogenation—*the formation of an enol.* (The enol, like the enolate ion, is achiral and tautomerizes to yield a racemic modification of the ketone.)

(b) According to the mechanism given, the slow step for acid-catalyzed iodination (formation of the enol) is the same as that for acid-catalyzed bromination. Thus we would expect both reactions to occur at the same rate.

(c) Again, the slow step for both reactions (formation of the enolate ion) is the same, and consequently, both reactions take place at the same rate.

17.6

(a) Acetone, $CH_3\overset{\overset{O}{\|}}{C}CH_3$

(b) Acetophenone, $C_6H_5\overset{\overset{O}{\|}}{C}CH_3$

(d) 2-Pentanone, $CH_3CH_2CH_2\overset{\overset{O}{\|}}{C}CH_3$

(f) 1-Phenylethanol, $C_6H_5\overset{\overset{OH}{|}}{C}HCH_3$

(h) 2-Butanol, $CH_3CH_2\overset{\overset{OH}{|}}{C}HCH_3$

(i) Methyl 2-naphthyl ketone,

17.7

(a) $\overset{\beta}{C}H_3\overset{\alpha}{C}H_2\overset{\overset{O}{\|}}{C}H + OH^- \rightleftharpoons CH_3\overset{\overset{..}{C}}{H}\overset{\overset{O}{\|}}{C}H + H_2O$

$$CH_3CH_2\overset{\overset{O}{\|}}{C}H + {}^-:CH\overset{\overset{O}{\|}}{C}H \rightleftharpoons CH_3CH_2\overset{\overset{O^-}{|}}{C}HCH\overset{\overset{O}{\|}}{C}H$$
$$\underset{CH_3}{\quad} \qquad\qquad \underset{CH_3}{\quad}$$

$$CH_3CH_2\overset{\overset{O^-}{|}}{C}HCH\overset{\overset{O}{\|}}{C}H + HOH \rightleftharpoons CH_3CH_2\overset{\overset{OH}{|}}{C}HCH\overset{\overset{O}{\|}}{C}H + OH^-$$
$$\underset{CH_3}{\quad} \qquad\qquad\qquad \underset{CH_3}{\quad}$$

(b) For $CH_3CH_2\overset{\overset{OH}{|}}{C}HCH_2CH_2\overset{\overset{O}{\|}}{C}H$ to form, a hydroxide ion would have to remove a β proton in the first step. This does not happen because the anion that would be produced, i.e., $^-:CH_2CH_2CHO$, cannot be stabilized by resonance.

(c) $CH_3CH_2CH{=}\overset{\overset{O}{\|}}{C}H$
$$\underset{CH_3}{\quad}$$

17.8

$$CH_3CHO \xrightarrow[5°]{10\%NaOH} \underset{(aldol)}{CH_3\overset{\overset{OH}{|}}{C}HCH_2CHO} \xrightarrow{heat}$$

$$CH_3CH{=}CHCHO \xrightarrow{H_2,\ Ni} CH_3CH_2CH_2CHO$$

17.9

(a) $2CH_3CH_2CH_2CHO \xrightarrow[H_2O]{OH^-} CH_3CH_2CH_2\overset{\overset{OH}{|}}{C}H\underset{\underset{CH_3}{|}}{\underset{CH_2}{\underset{|}{C}}}HCHO$

(b) Product of (a) $\xrightarrow[(-H_2O)]{H^+} CH_3CH_2CH_2CH{=}\underset{\underset{CH_3}{|}}{\underset{CH_2}{\underset{|}{C}}}CHO$

$$\xrightarrow{NaBH_4} CH_3CH_2CH_2CH{=}\underset{\underset{CH_3}{|}}{\underset{CH_2}{\underset{|}{C}}}CH_2OH$$

(c) Product of (b) $\xrightarrow[Pt]{H_2} CH_3CH_2CH_2CH_2\underset{\underset{CH_3}{|}}{\underset{CH_2}{\underset{|}{C}}}HCH_2OH$

(d) Product of (a) $\xrightarrow{\text{NaBH}_4}$ $\underset{\underset{\underset{CH_3}{|}}{\overset{|}{CH_2}}}{CH_3CH_2CH_2\overset{\overset{OH}{|}}{CH}CHCH_2OH}$

17.10

(a) $CH_3\overset{\overset{O}{\|}}{C}CH_3 + OH^- \rightleftharpoons CH_3\overset{\overset{O}{\|}}{C}CH_2{:}^- + H_2O$

$CH_3\overset{\overset{O}{\|}}{C}CH_2{:}^- + CH_3\overset{\overset{O}{\|}}{C}CH_3 \rightleftharpoons CH_3\overset{\overset{O}{\|}}{C}CH_2\underset{\underset{CH_3}{|}}{\overset{\overset{O^-}{|}}{C}}CH_3$

$CH_3\overset{\overset{O}{\|}}{C}CH_2\underset{\underset{CH_3}{|}}{\overset{\overset{O^-}{|}}{C}}CH_3 + HOH \rightleftharpoons CH_3\overset{\overset{O}{\|}}{C}CH_2\underset{\underset{CH_3}{|}}{\overset{\overset{OH}{|}}{C}}CH_3 + OH^-$

(b) $CH_3\overset{\overset{O}{\|}}{C}CH{=}\underset{\underset{CH_3}{|}}{C}CH_3$

17.11

17.12 Three successive aldol additions occur.

First aldol addition

$CH_3\overset{\overset{O}{\|}}{C}H + OH^- \rightleftharpoons {:}CH_2\overset{\overset{O}{\|}}{C}H + H_2O$

$H\overset{\overset{O}{\|}}{C}H + {:}CH_2\overset{\overset{O}{\|}}{C}H \rightleftharpoons {}^-OCH_2CH_2\overset{\overset{O}{\|}}{C}H$

$^-OCH_2CH\overset{\overset{O}{\|}}{C}H + H_2O \rightleftharpoons HOCH_2CH_2\overset{\overset{O}{\|}}{C}H$

Second aldol addition

$HOCH_2CH_2\overset{\overset{O}{\|}}{C}H + OH^- \rightleftharpoons HOCH_2\overset{..}{C}H\overset{\overset{O}{\|}}{C}H + H_2O$

$H\overset{\overset{O}{\|}}{C}H + HOCH_2\overset{..}{C}H\overset{\overset{O}{\|}}{C}H \rightleftharpoons HOCH_2\underset{\underset{CH_2O^-}{|}}{C}HCHO$

$HOCH_2\underset{\underset{CH_2O^-}{|}}{C}HCHO + H_2O \rightleftharpoons HOCH_2\underset{\underset{CH_2OH}{|}}{C}HCHO + OH^-$

$$
\text{Third aldol addition}
\begin{cases}
\underset{\displaystyle\text{HOCH}_2\text{CH--CHO}}{\overset{\displaystyle\text{CH}_2\text{OH}}{|}} + \text{OH}^- \rightleftharpoons \underset{\displaystyle\text{HOCH}_2\overset{..}{\text{C}}\text{--CHO}}{\overset{\displaystyle\text{CH}_2\text{OH}}{|}} \\[4ex]
\overset{\displaystyle O}{\underset{\displaystyle\text{HCH}}{\|}} + \underset{\displaystyle\text{HOCH}_2\overset{..}{\text{C}}\text{--CHO}}{\overset{\displaystyle\text{CH}_2\text{OH}}{|}} \rightleftharpoons \underset{\displaystyle\underset{\displaystyle\text{CH}_2\text{O}^-}{|}}{\overset{\displaystyle\text{CH}_2\text{OH}}{\underset{\displaystyle\text{HOCH}_2\text{--C--CHO}}{|}}} \\[4ex]
\underset{\displaystyle\underset{\displaystyle\text{CH}_2\text{O}^-}{|}}{\overset{\displaystyle\text{CH}_2\text{OH}}{\underset{\displaystyle\text{HOCH}_2\text{--C--CHO}}{|}}} + \text{H}_2\text{O} \rightleftharpoons \underset{\displaystyle\underset{\displaystyle\text{CH}_2\text{OH}}{|}}{\overset{\displaystyle\text{CH}_2\text{OH}}{\underset{\displaystyle\text{HOCH}_2\text{--C--CHO}}{|}}} + \text{OH}^-
\end{cases}
$$

17.13 (a) $CH_3COOH + BF_3 \rightleftharpoons CH_3COOBF_3^- + H^+$

Pseudoionone

α-Ionone

β-Ionone

(b) In β-ionone both double bonds and the carbonyl group are conjugated, thus it is more stable.

(c) β-Ionone, because it is a fully conjugated unsaturated system.

17.14

(a)

(b) $\overset{\displaystyle O}{\underset{\displaystyle\text{HCH}}{\|}} + CH_3NO_2 \xrightarrow{\text{dil. OH}^-} HOCH_2CH_2NO_2$

(c)

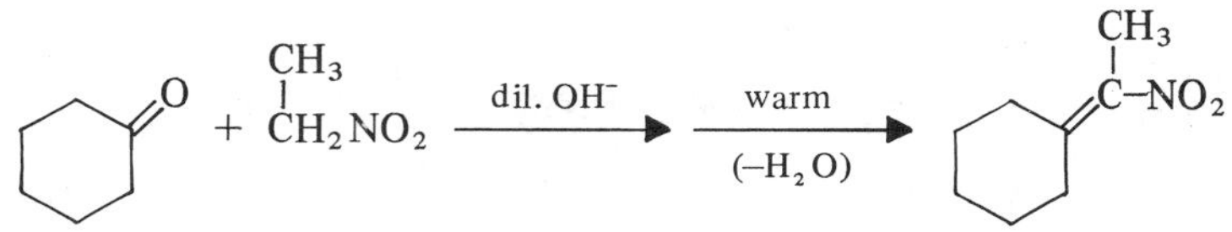

17.15

(a)  $\overset{-}{:}CH_2{-}C{\equiv}N: \longleftrightarrow CH_2{=}C{=}\overset{..}{N}:^{-}$

(b) 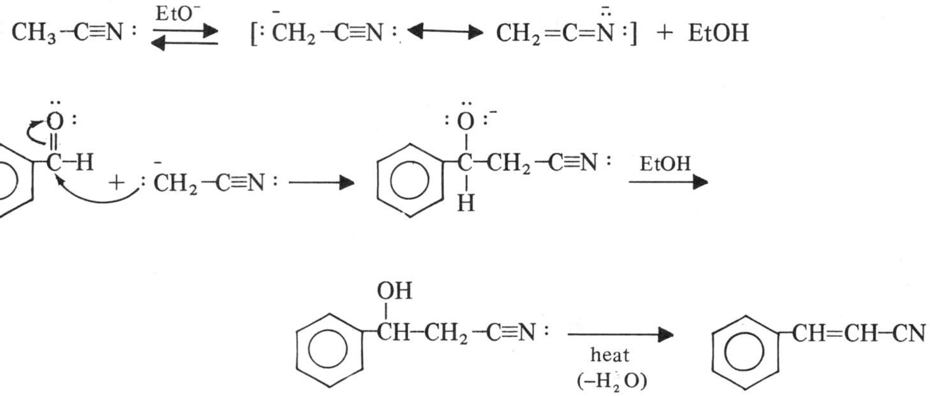 $CH_3{-}C{\equiv}N: \xrightarrow{EtO^-} [\overset{-}{:}CH_2{-}C{\equiv}N: \longleftrightarrow CH_2{=}C{=}\overset{..}{\overset{..}{N}}:] + EtOH$

17.16

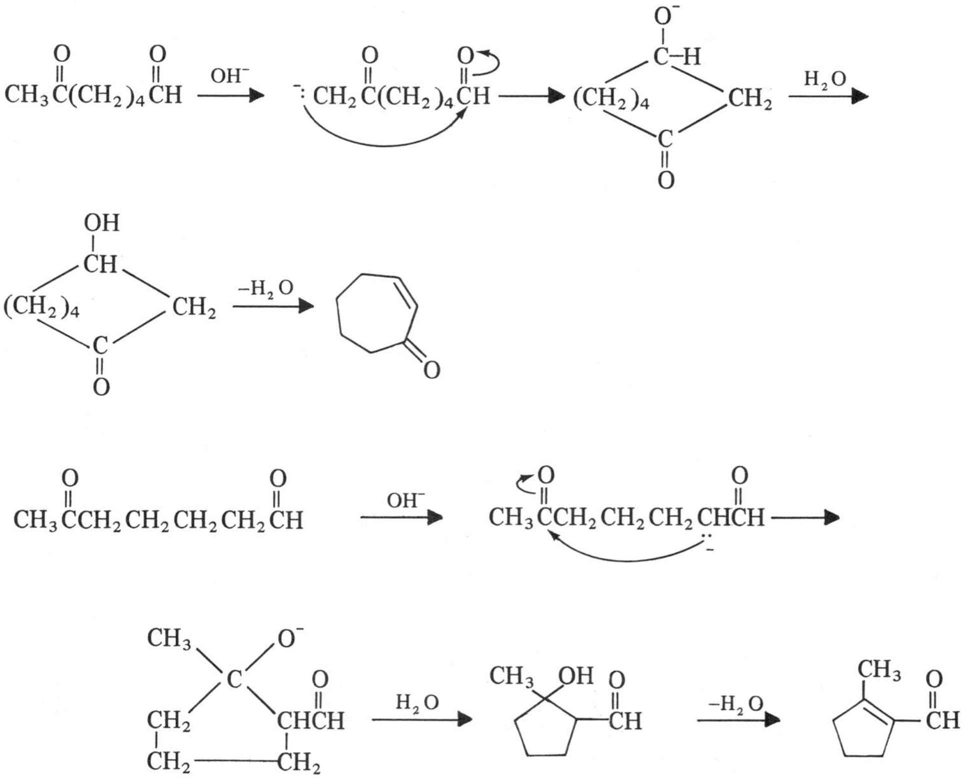

17.17

(a)

(b)

(c)

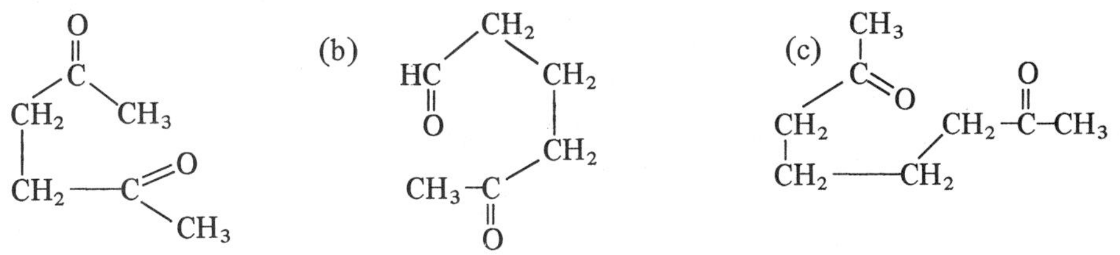

Notice that starting compounds are drawn so as to indicate which atoms are involved in the cyclization reaction.

17.18

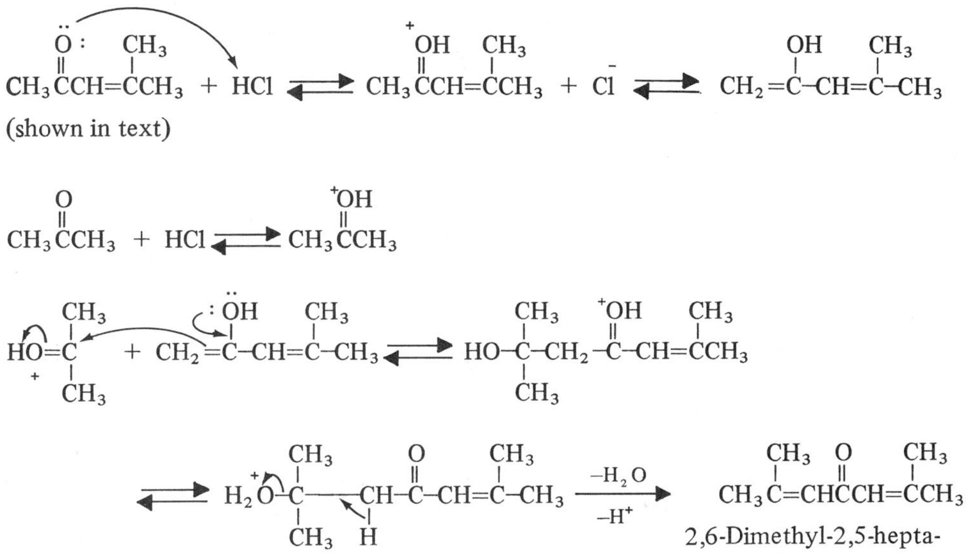

(shown in text)

2,6-Dimethyl-2,5-hepta-
dien-4-one

17.19   Drawing the molecules as they will appear in the final product helps to visualize the necessary steps:

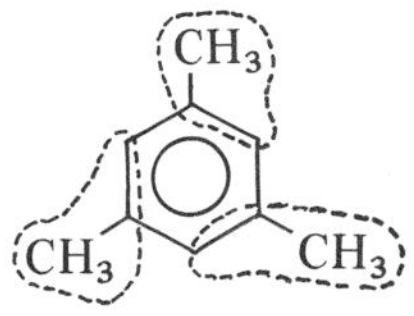

Mesitylene

The two molecules that lead to mesitylene are shown as follows:

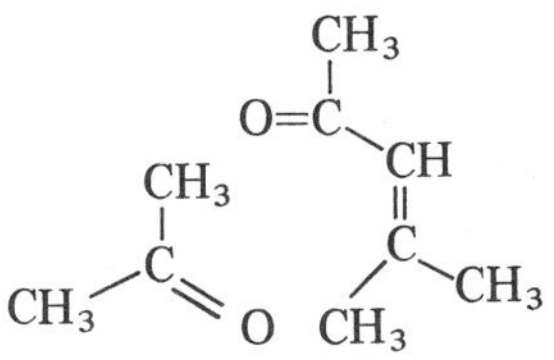

This molecule (4-methyl-3-penten-2-one) is formed by an acid-catalyzed condensation between two molecules of acetone as shown in the text.

The mechanism is,

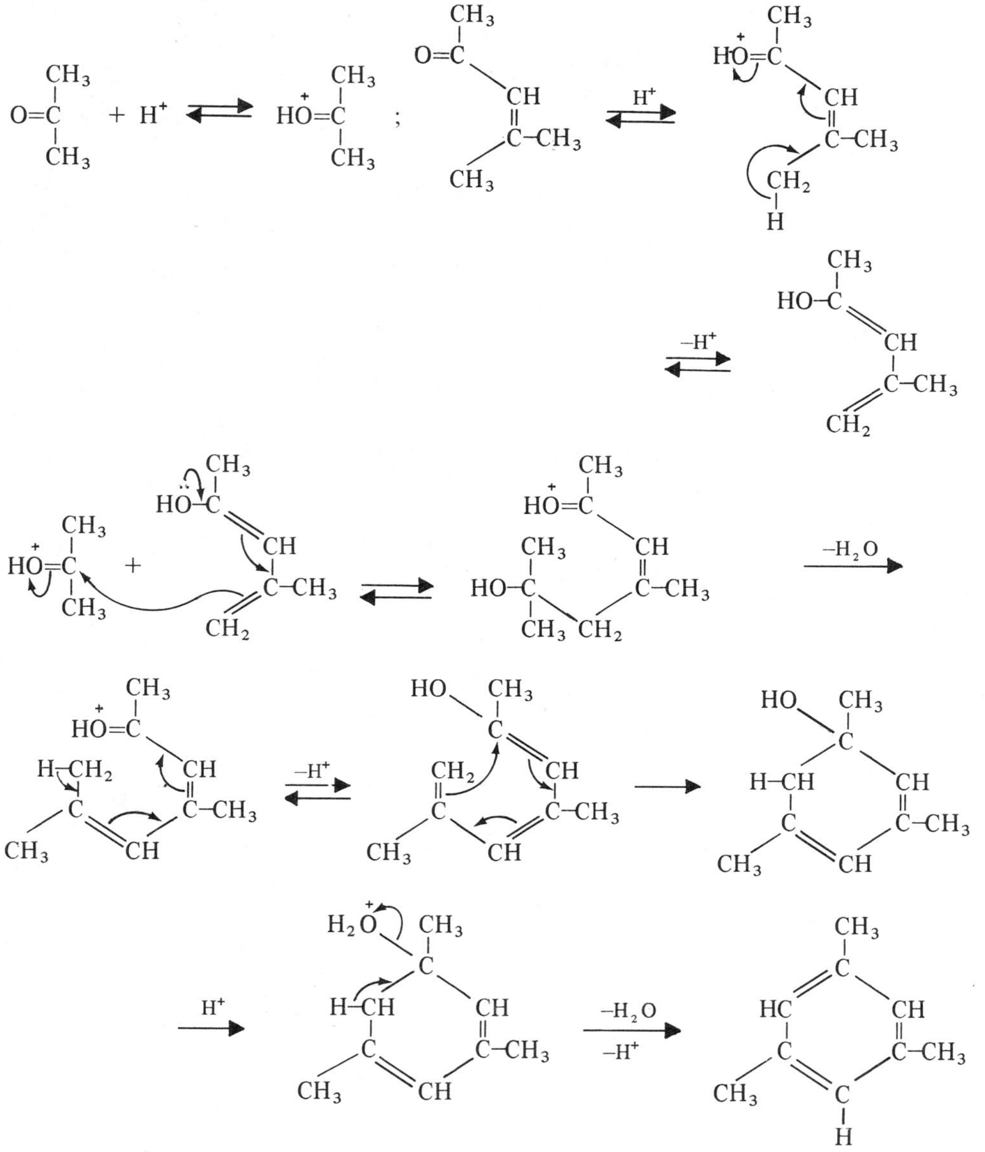

17.20

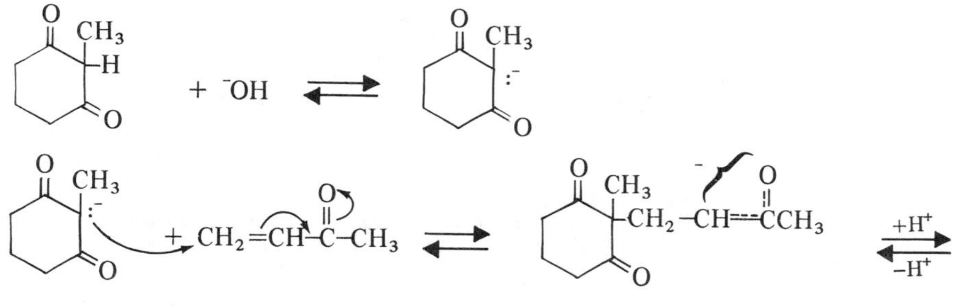

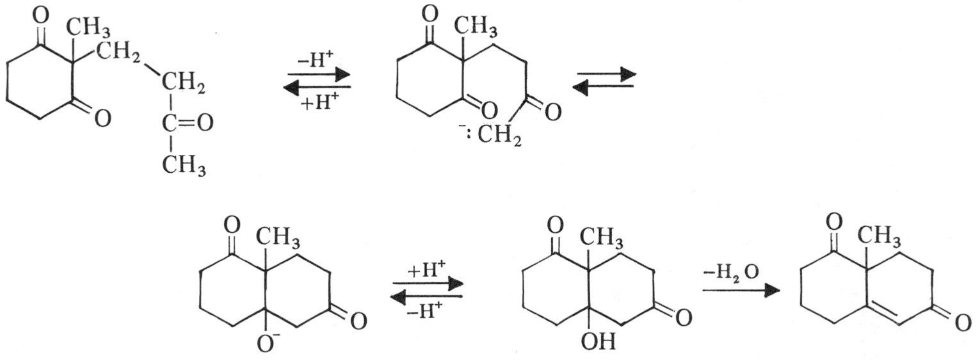

(b) 2-Methyl-1,3-cyclohexanedione is more acidic because its enolate ion is stabilized by an additional resonance structure.

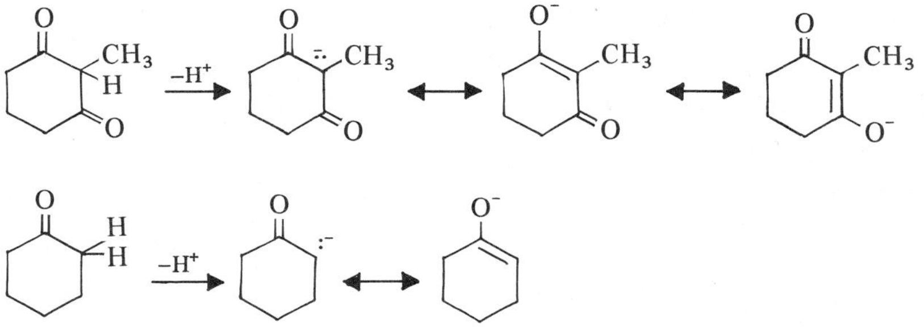

17.21

(a)

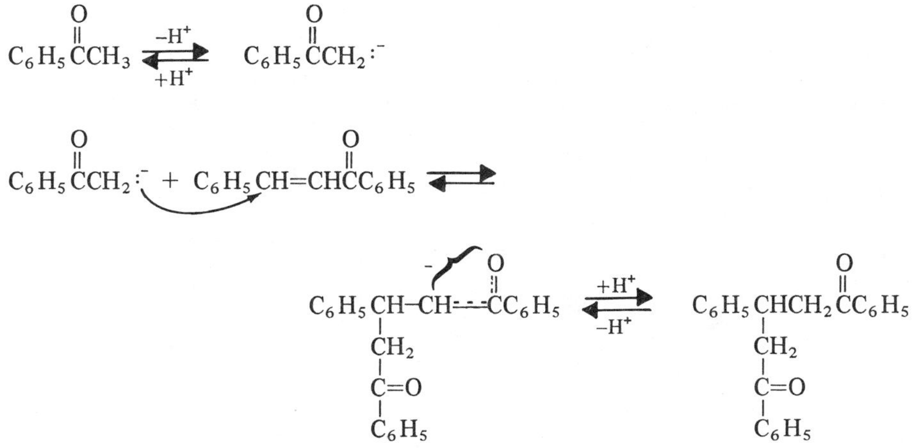

$$C_6H_5\overset{O}{\overset{||}{C}}CH_3 \underset{+H^+}{\overset{-H^+}{\rightleftharpoons}} C_6H_5\overset{O}{\overset{||}{C}}CH_2:^-$$

$$C_6H_5\overset{O}{\overset{||}{C}}CH_2:^- + C_6H_5CH=CH\overset{O}{\overset{||}{C}}C_6H_5 \rightleftharpoons$$

$$C_6H_5CH-CH=\cdot\cdot=\overset{O}{\overset{}{C}}C_6H_5 \underset{-H^+}{\overset{+H^+}{\rightleftharpoons}} C_6H_5CHCH_2\overset{O}{\overset{||}{C}}C_6H_5$$

$$\underset{\underset{C_6H_5}{|}}{\overset{|}{CH_2}}\underset{\underset{C_6H_5}{|}}{\overset{|}{CH_2}}$$

$$\underset{}{C=O}\underset{}{C=O}$$

(b)

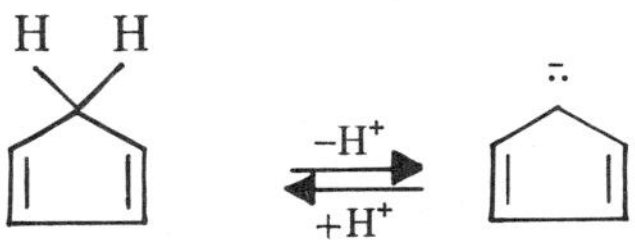

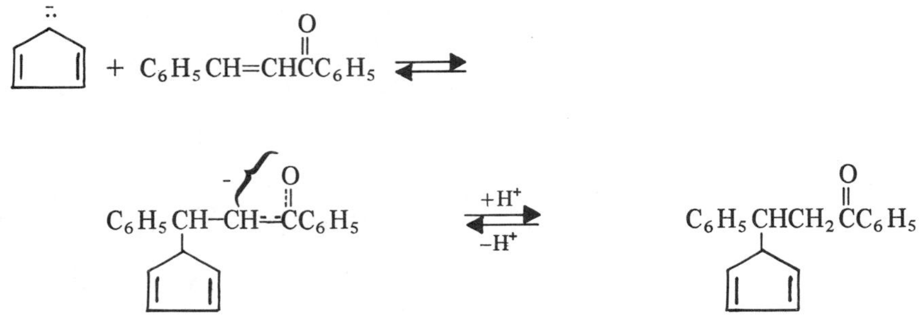

$$C_6H_5CH=CHCC_6H_5$$

$$C_6H_5CH-CH=CC_6H_5 \quad \underset{-H^+}{\overset{+H^+}{\rightleftharpoons}} \quad C_6H_5CHCH_2CC_6H_5$$

17.22

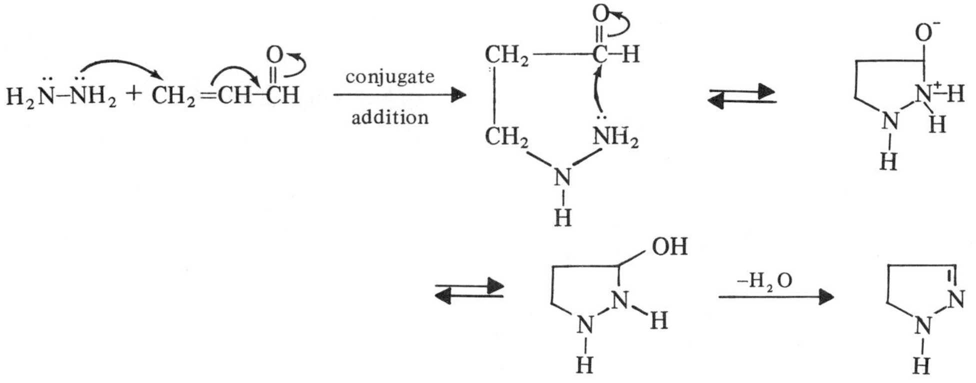

$$H_2\ddot{N}-\ddot{N}H_2 + CH_2=CH-CH \xrightarrow[\text{addition}]{\text{conjugate}}$$

$$\xrightarrow{-H_2O}$$

17.23

$$HCH + OH^- \rightleftharpoons H-\overset{O^-}{\underset{H-O}{C}}-H$$

$$HO^- + H-\overset{O^-}{C}-H + HC \overset{O}{\underset{}{}} -\overset{CH_2OH}{\underset{CH_2OH}{C}}-CH_2OH \longrightarrow$$

(from Prob. 17.12)

$$H_2O + H-\overset{}{\underset{O}{C}}-O^- + H-\overset{O^-}{\underset{H}{C}}-\overset{CH_2OH}{\underset{CH_2OH}{C}}-CH_2OH \rightleftharpoons$$

$$HOCH_2-\overset{CH_2OH}{\underset{CH_2OH}{C}}-CH_2OH + OH^- + HC-O^-\overset{}{\underset{O}{}}$$

Pentaerythritol

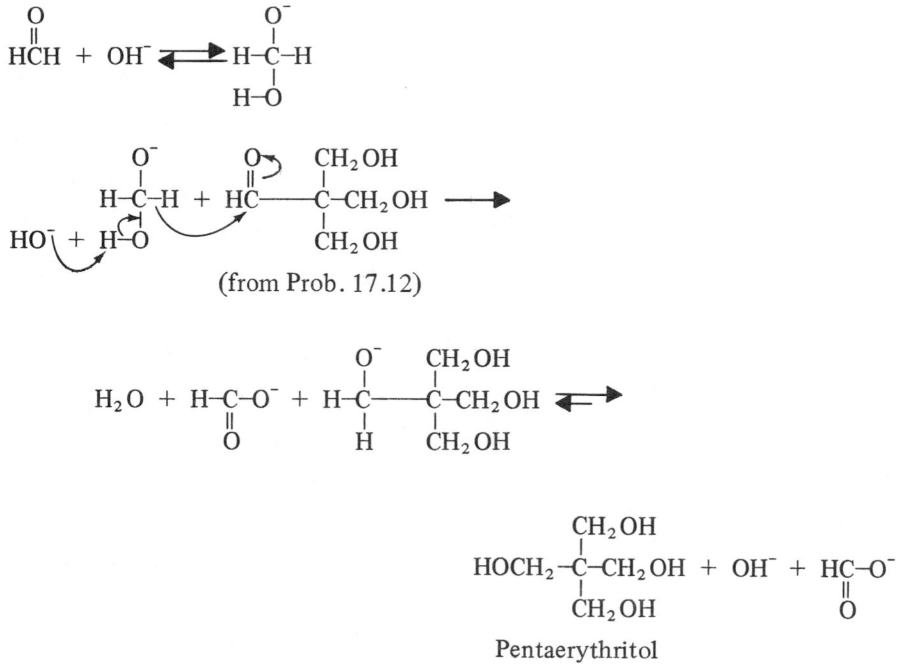

17.24

(a) $CH_3CH_2\underset{\underset{CH_3}{|}}{\overset{\overset{OH}{|}}{CH}}CHCHO$

(b) $\langle\bigcirc\rangle-CH=\underset{\underset{CH_3}{|}}{C}-CHO$

(c) $CH_3CH_2\overset{\overset{OH}{|}}{CH}CN$

(d) $CH_3CH_2CH_2OH$

(e) $CH_3CH_2CH\overset{\overset{O-CH_2}{\diagup}}{\underset{\underset{O-CH_2}{\diagdown}}{}}$

(f) $CH_3CH_2\overset{\overset{O}{\|}}{C}-OH$

(g) $CH_3CH_2\overset{\overset{OH}{|}}{CH}CH_3$

(h) $CH_3CH_2\overset{\overset{O}{\|}}{C}-OH$

(i) $CH_3CH_2CH=NOH$

(j) $CH_3CH_2CH=CHC_6H_5$

(k) $CH_3CH_2\overset{\overset{OH}{|}}{CH}-C_6H_5$

(l) $CH_3CH_2\overset{\overset{OH}{|}}{CH}C\equiv CH$

(m) $CH_3CH_2CH_3$

(n) $CH_3CH_2\underset{\underset{CH_2CH_3}{|}}{\overset{\overset{OH}{|}}{CH}}-CHCO_2Et$

17.25

(a) $CH_3\underset{\underset{OH}{|}}{\overset{\overset{CH_3}{|}}{C}}-CH_2\overset{\overset{O}{\|}}{C}CH_3$

(b) $C_6H_5CH=CH-\overset{\overset{O}{\|}}{C}CH_3$

(c) $CH_3\underset{\underset{CN}{|}}{\overset{\overset{OH}{|}}{C}}CH_3$

(cf. Problem 17.10)

(d) $CH_3\overset{\overset{OH}{|}}{CH}CH_3$

(e) $\underset{\underset{CH_3}{\diagup}}{\overset{\overset{CH_3}{\diagdown}}{}}C\overset{\overset{O-CH_2}{\diagdown}}{\underset{\underset{O-CH_2}{\diagup}}{}}$

(f) No reaction

(g) $CH_3-\underset{\underset{CH_3}{|}}{\overset{\overset{CH_3}{|}}{C}}-OH$

(h) No reaction

(i) $CH_3\overset{\overset{NOH}{\|}}{C}CH_3$

(j) $\underset{\underset{CH_3}{\diagup}}{\overset{\overset{CH_3}{\diagdown}}{}}C=CHC_6H_5$

(k) $CH_3\underset{\underset{CH_3}{|}}{\overset{\overset{OH}{|}}{C}}-C_6H_5$

(l) $CH_3\underset{\underset{CH_3}{|}}{\overset{\overset{OH}{|}}{C}}C\equiv CH$

(m) $CH_3CH_2CH_3$

(n) $CH_3\underset{\underset{CH_3}{|}}{\overset{\overset{HO}{|}}{C}}-\overset{\overset{CH_2CH_3}{|}}{CH}CO_2Et$

17.26

(a) $CH_3-\langle\bigcirc\rangle-CH=CHCHO$

(b) $CH_3-\langle\bigcirc\rangle-\overset{\overset{O}{\|}}{C}-O^- + CH_3-\langle\bigcirc\rangle-CH_2OH$

(c) $CH_3-\langle\bigcirc\rangle-CH_2OH$ (d) $CH_3-\langle\bigcirc\rangle-\overset{\overset{O}{\parallel}}{C}-OH$

(e) $HO-\overset{\overset{O}{\parallel}}{C}-\langle\bigcirc\rangle-\overset{\overset{O}{\parallel}}{C}-OH$ (f) $CH_3-\langle\bigcirc\rangle-CH=CH_2$

(g) $CH_3-\langle\bigcirc\rangle-CH=CH-\overset{\overset{O}{\parallel}}{C}-\langle\bigcirc\rangle$ (h) $CH_3-\langle\bigcirc\rangle-\overset{\overset{OH}{|}}{C}H-CH_2\overset{\overset{O}{\parallel}}{C}-OEt$

17.27

(a) $\langle\bigcirc\rangle-CHO + CH_3-\overset{\overset{O}{\parallel}}{C}-C(CH_3)_3 \xrightarrow{\text{dil. OH}^-} \langle\bigcirc\rangle-CH=CH-\overset{\overset{O}{\parallel}}{C}-C(CH_3)_3$

(b) $\langle\bigcirc\rangle-CHO + \overset{\text{(cyclopentanone)}}{\bigcirc} \xrightarrow{\text{dil. OH}^-} \langle\bigcirc\rangle-CH=\overset{\text{(cyclopentanone)}}{\bigcirc}$

(c) $\langle\bigcirc\rangle-CHO + CH_3CH_2NO_2 \xrightarrow{\text{dil. OH}^-} \langle\bigcirc\rangle-CH=\overset{\overset{}{\underset{\underset{CH_3}{|}}{C}}}{}-NO_2 \xrightarrow{H_2,\,Pt}$

$\langle\bigcirc\rangle-CH_2\overset{\overset{}{\underset{\underset{CH_3}{|}}{C}}}{H}NH_2$

(d) $\overset{CH_3}{\underset{}{}}C=O \overset{CH_2}{\underset{\overset{|}{C}CH_3}{}}_{\overset{\parallel}{O}} \xrightarrow{\text{dil. OH}^-} \overset{}{\underset{CH_3}{}}\overset{}{\underset{\overset{|}{C}-CH_3}{\overset{\parallel}{O}}} \xrightarrow{NaBH_4} \overset{}{\underset{CH_3}{}}\overset{}{\underset{\overset{|}{C}H-CH_3}{\overset{|}{OH}}}$

(e) $CH_3O-\langle\bigcirc\rangle-CHO + CH_3CN \xrightarrow{\text{base}} CH_3O-\langle\bigcirc\rangle-CH=CHCN$

(f) $2CH_3CH_2CH_2CH_2\overset{\overset{O}{\parallel}}{C}H \xrightarrow[5°]{\text{dil. OH}^-} CH_3CH_2CH_2CH_2\overset{\overset{CHO}{|}}{C}H-\overset{\overset{}{\underset{\underset{OH}{|}}{C}}}{H}(CH_2)_2CH_3 \xrightarrow{\text{heat}}$

$CH_3(CH_2)_3CH=\overset{\overset{CHO}{|}}{C}(CH_2)_2CH_3 \xrightarrow{NaBH_4} CH_3(CH_2)_3CH=\overset{\overset{CH_2OH}{|}}{C}(CH_2)_2CH_3$

(g)

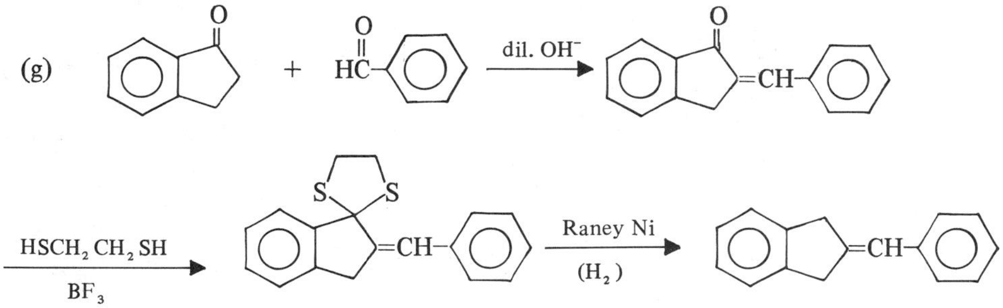

$$\xrightarrow[\text{BF}_3]{\text{HSCH}_2\text{CH}_2\text{SH}}$$

$$\xrightarrow[\text{(H}_2\text{)}]{\text{Raney Ni}}$$

17.28

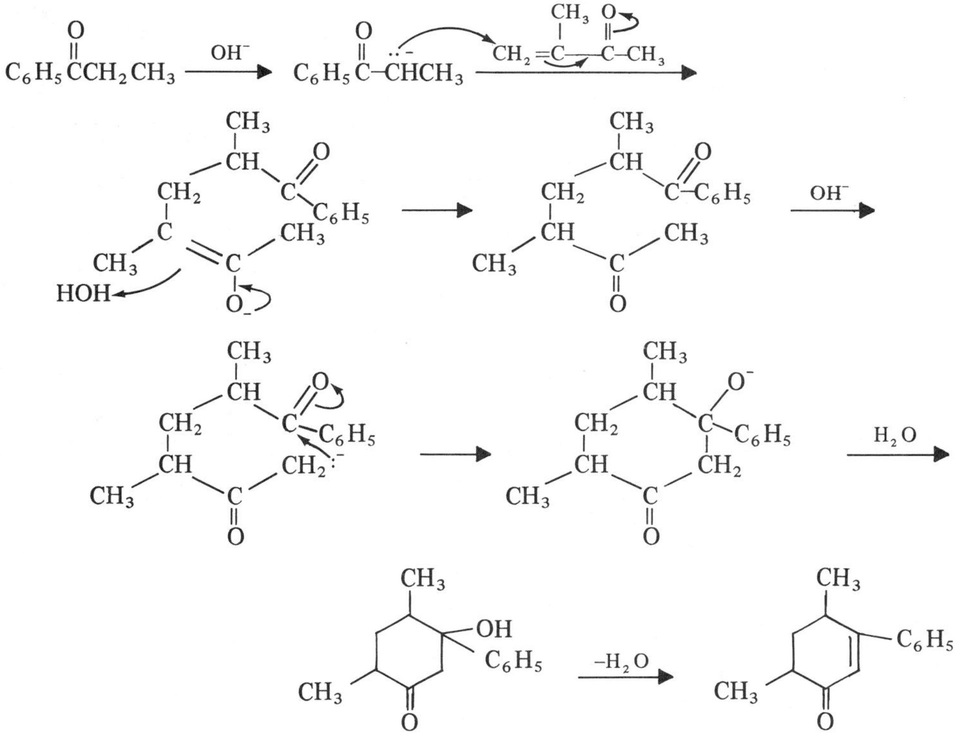

$$\text{C}_6\text{H}_5\overset{\overset{\text{O}}{\|}}{\text{C}}\text{CH}_2\text{CH}_3 \xrightarrow{\text{OH}^-} \text{C}_6\text{H}_5\overset{\overset{\text{O}}{\|}}{\text{C}}\text{–}\overset{\cdot\cdot^-}{\text{C}}\text{HCH}_3 \longrightarrow$$

17.29

$$\text{HC}\equiv\text{CH} \xrightarrow[\substack{(2)\ \text{CH}_3\text{COCH}_3 \\ (3)\ \text{H}^+}]{(1)\ \text{NaNH}_2} \text{HC}\equiv\text{C}\overset{\overset{\text{CH}_3}{|}}{\underset{\underset{\text{CH}_3}{|}}{\text{C}}}\text{–OH} \xrightarrow[\text{H}_2\text{O}]{\text{Hg}^{2+},\ \text{H}_3\text{O}^+} \text{CH}_3\overset{\overset{\text{O}}{\|}}{\text{C}}\overset{\overset{\text{CH}_3}{|}}{\underset{\underset{\text{CH}_3}{|}}{\text{C}}}\text{–OH} \xrightarrow[\text{OH}^-]{\text{C}_6\text{H}_5\text{CHO}}$$

$$\quad\quad\quad\quad\quad\quad\quad\quad\quad\quad\quad\quad\quad\quad \textbf{A} \quad\quad\quad\quad\quad\quad\quad\quad\quad\quad\quad\quad \textbf{B}$$

C

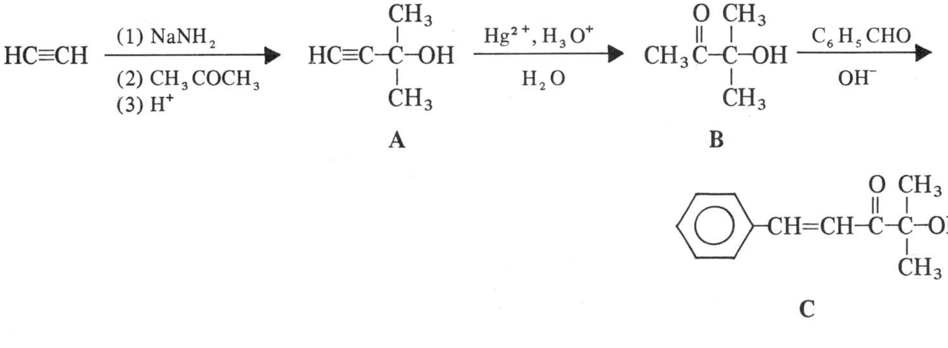

17.30 (a) The conjugate base is a hybrid of the following structures:

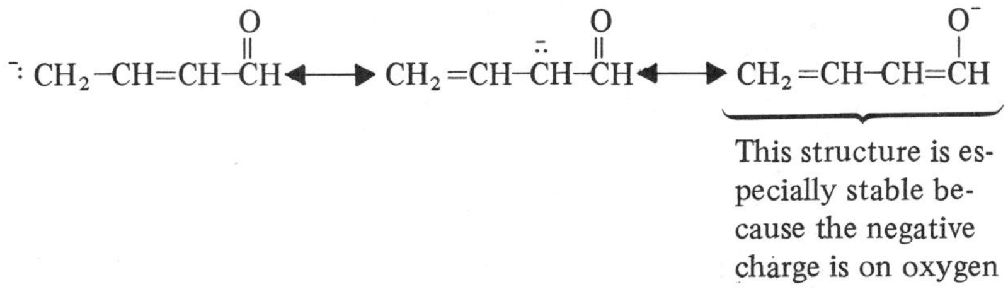

$$:CH_2-CH=CH-\overset{\overset{\displaystyle O}{\|}}{CH} \longleftrightarrow CH_2=CH-\overset{\overset{\displaystyle O}{\|}}{\underset{\cdot\cdot}{C}H-CH} \longleftrightarrow CH_2=CH-CH=\overset{\overset{\displaystyle O^-}{|}}{CH}$$

This structure is especially stable because the negative charge is on oxygen

(b) $CH_3CH=CHCHO \underset{+H^+}{\overset{-H^+}{\rightleftharpoons}} \ ^-:CH_2CH=CHCHO$

$C_6H_5CH=CH\overset{\overset{\displaystyle O}{\|}}{CH} + \ ^-:CH_2CH=CHCHO \rightleftharpoons$

$C_6H_5CH=CH\overset{\overset{\displaystyle O^-}{|}}{CH}-CH_2CH=CHCHO \underset{-H^+}{\overset{+H^+}{\rightleftharpoons}} C_6H_5CH=CH\overset{\overset{\displaystyle OH}{|}}{CH}-CH_2CH=CHCHO$

$\xrightarrow{-H_2O} C_6H_5CH=CHCH=CHCH=CHCHO$

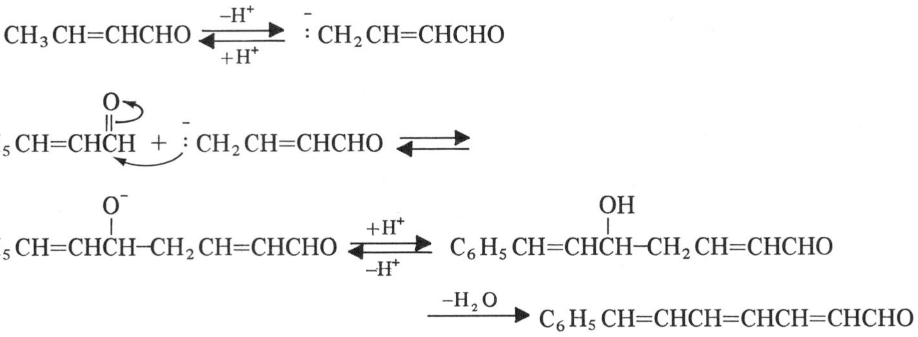

17.31

(a)

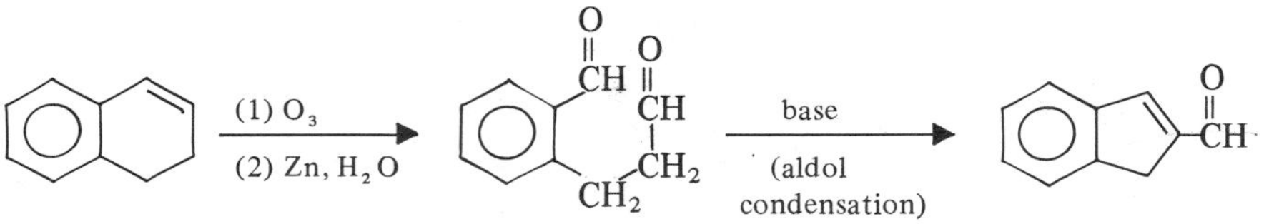

(b)

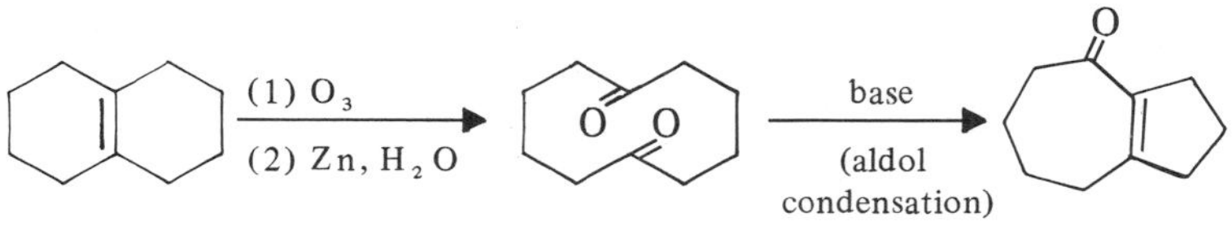

(c)

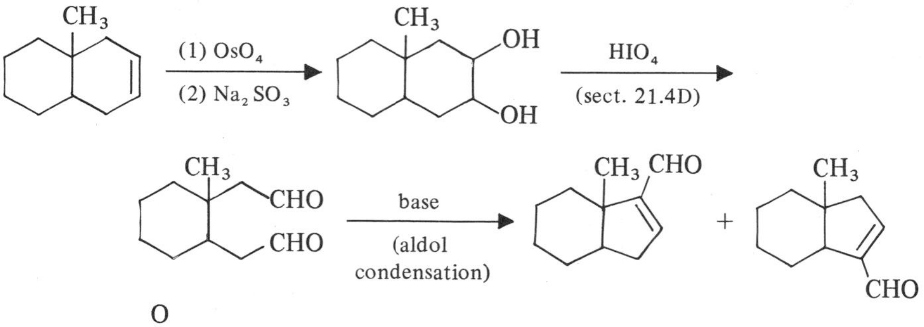

(d)

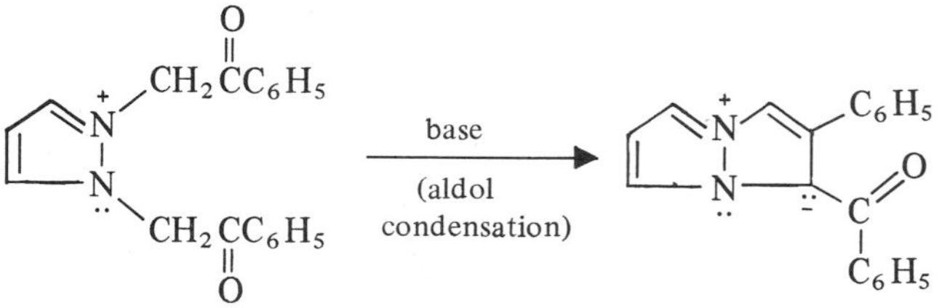

17.32

(a) 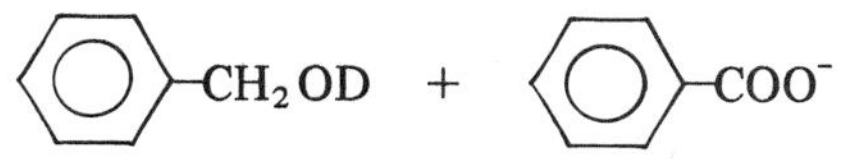 ⟨O⟩—CH₂OD + ⟨O⟩—COO⁻

(b) 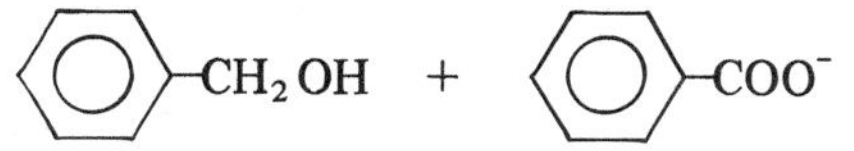 ⟨O⟩—CH₂OH + ⟨O⟩—COO⁻

(c) Yes. In both reactions a hydride ion (rather than a deuteride ion) is transferred to benzaldehyde. This result shows that the hydride ion is transferred from one benzaldehyde molecule to another (as shown on page 771) and not from the solvent to benzaldehyde.

17.33 (a) In simple addition the carbonyl peak (1665-1780 cm^{-1} region) does not appear in the product; in conjugate addition it does.

(b) As the reaction takes place, the long-wavelength absorption arising from the conjugated system should disappear. One could follow the rate of the reaction by following the rate at which this absorption peak disappears.

17.34 (a) Compound **U** is phenyl ethyl ketone: (b) Compound **V** is benzyl methyl ketone:

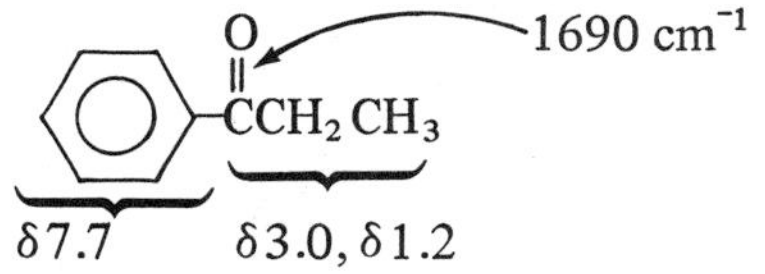

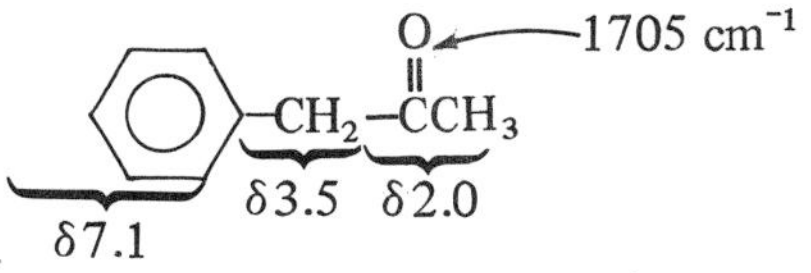

17.35 A is $CH_3\overset{O}{\underset{\|}{C}}CH_2CH(OCH_3)_2$

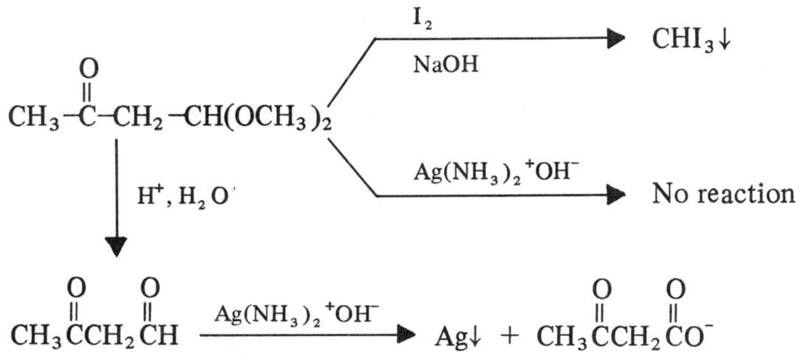

(a) Singlet δ 2.1

(b) Doublet δ 2.6

(c) Singlet δ 3.2

(d) Triplet δ 4.7

17.36 Resonance contributions such as those shown below render the carbonyl groups of 2-hydroxybenzaldehyde and 4-hydroxybenzaldehyde highly unreactive toward nucleophilic attack. Hence no hydride transfer takes place.

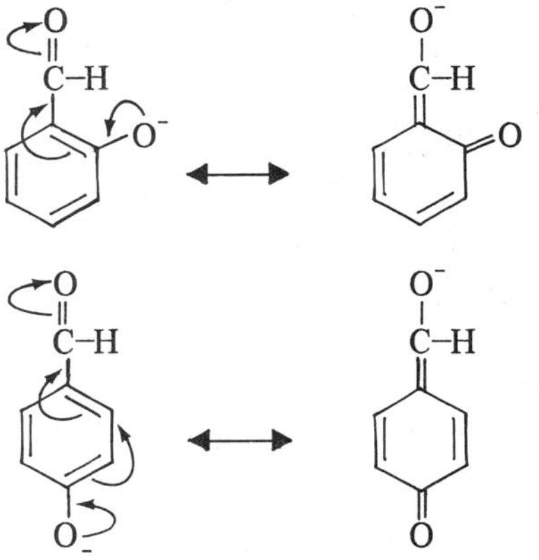

17.37 Abstraction of an α hydrogen at the ring junction yields an enolate ion that can then accept a proton to form either *trans*-1-decalone or *cis*-1-decalone. Since *trans*-1-decalone is more stable, it predominates at equilibrium.

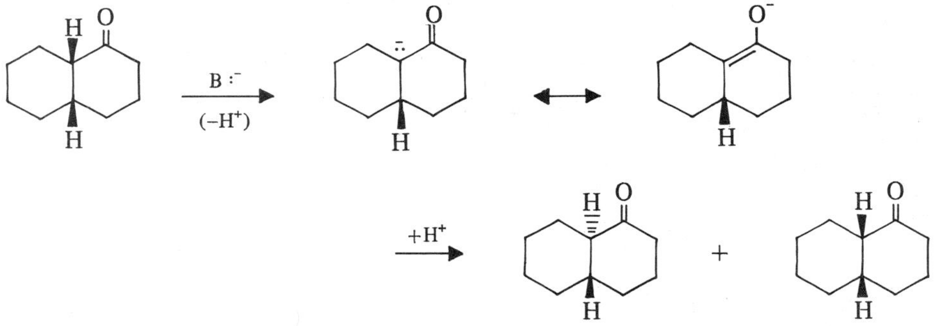

(95%)
trans-1-Decalone
(more stable)

(5%)
cis-1-Decalone
(less stable)

17.38 That compound **B** forms a phenyhydrazone, has an infrared peak near 1715 cm^{-1}, a ^{13}C peak at δ 208, and gives a positive iodoform test indicates that **B** is a methyl ketone,

O
||
R–C–CH$_3$. The ^{13}C nmr spectrum allows us to conclude that **B** is methyl isobutyl ketone:

O
||
$(CH_3)_2CHCH_2CCH_3$
(a)   (b) (d) (e) (c)

(a) quartet δ22.5

(b) doublet δ24.5

(c) quartet δ30.1

(d) triplet δ52.7

(e) singlet δ208.0

17.39 That **C** forms a phenylhydrazone and has a peak near 1715 cm^{-1} indicates the presence of a carbonyl group. That **C** gives a negative Tollens' test indicates that **C** is not an aldehyde; that **C** gives a negative iodoform test indicates that **C** is not a methyl ketone. That the ^{13}C spectrum contains only four signals (with one singlet at δ210.6) indicates that **C** is a highly symmetrical ketone. The splitting patterns of the proton off-resonance decoupled spectrum confirm that **C** is 4-heptanone.

$$\underset{(a)}{CH_3}\underset{(b)}{CH_2}\underset{(c)}{CH_2}\underset{(d)}{\overset{\overset{O}{\|}}{C}}CH_2CH_2CH_3$$

(a) quartet δ13.7

(b) triplet δ 17.4

(c) triplet δ 44.7

(d) singlet δ210.6

SECTION REFERENCES FOR ADDITIONAL PROBLEMS

17.24 Chapters 16 and 17

17.25 Chapters 16 and 17

17.26 16.10, 16.11, 16.12, 17.6, 17.10

17.27 16.7, 16.9, 17.5, 17.6

17.28 17.9B

17.29 9.10, 16.11, 17.6

17.30 17.1, 17.5

17.31 7.13, 17.6

17.32 17.10

17.33 13.11, 16.13, 17.9

17.34 16.13, 17.4

17.35 13.11, 16.12, 16.13, 17.4

17.36 17.10

17.37 3.13, 3.14, 17.1–17.3

17.38 13.10, 16.8, 16.13, 17.4

17.39 13.10, 13.11, 16.8, 16.12, 16.13, 17.4

SELF-TEST

Supply formulas for the missing reagents and intermediates in the following syntheses.

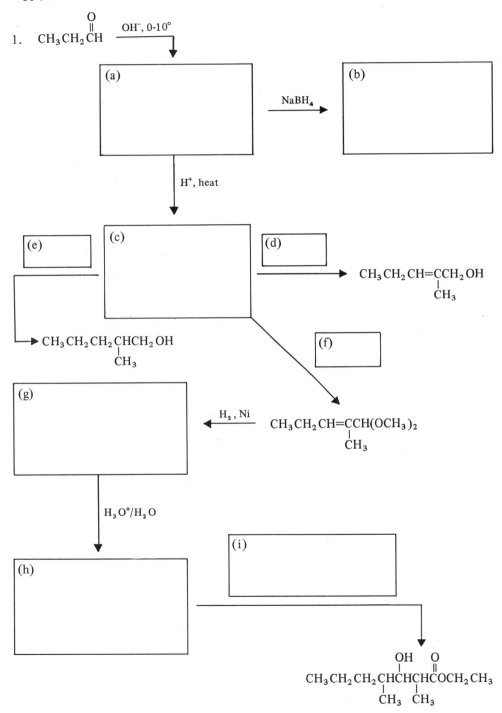

1. $$CH_3CH_2\overset{\displaystyle O}{\overset{\displaystyle \|}{C}}H \xrightarrow{\text{OH}^-,\ 0\text{-}10°}$$

(a)

$\xrightarrow{\text{NaBH}_4}$ (b)

$\downarrow$ H⁺, heat

(e)   (c)   (d)

$$CH_3CH_2CH=\overset{\displaystyle }{\underset{\displaystyle CH_3}{C}}CH_2OH$$

$$CH_3CH_2CH_2\overset{\displaystyle }{\underset{\displaystyle CH_3}{C}}HCH_2OH$$

(f)

(g) $\xleftarrow{\text{H}_2,\ \text{Ni}}$ $$CH_3CH_2CH=\overset{\displaystyle }{\underset{\displaystyle CH_3}{C}}CH(OCH_3)_2$$

$\downarrow$ H₃O⁺/H₂O

(h)

(i)

$$CH_3CH_2CH_2\overset{\displaystyle OH}{\overset{\displaystyle |}{C}}H\overset{\displaystyle }{\underset{\displaystyle CH_3}{C}}H\overset{\displaystyle }{\underset{\displaystyle CH_3}{C}}H\overset{\displaystyle O}{\overset{\displaystyle \|}{C}}OCH_2CH_3$$

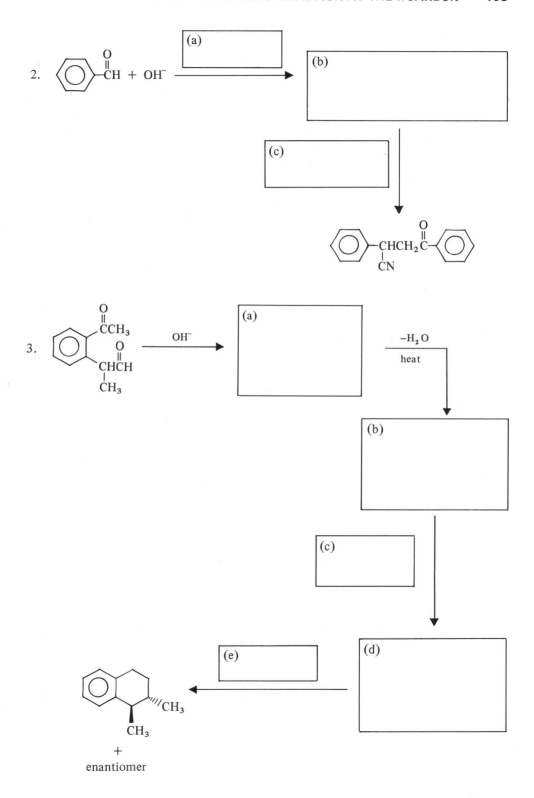

18

CARBOXYLIC ACIDS AND THEIR DERIVATIVES: NUCLEOPHILIC SUBSTITUTION AT ACYL CARBON

REACTIONS OF CARBOXYLIC ACIDS AND THEIR DERIVATIVES

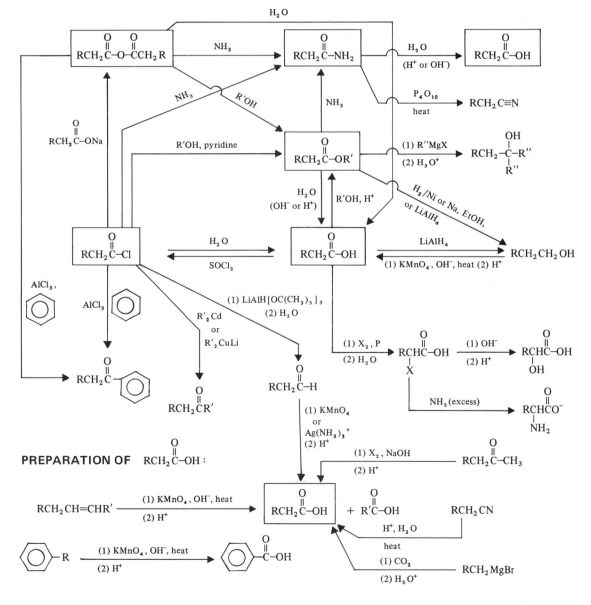

PREPARATION OF $RCH_2C{-}OH$:

SOLUTIONS TO PROBLEMS

18.1   (a)   2-Methylbutanoic acid

(b)   3-Pentenoic acid

(c)   Sodium 4-bromobutanoate

(d)   5-Phenylpentanoic acid

(e)   3-Methyl-3-pentenoic acid

18.2   (a)   Carbon dioxide is an acid; it converts an aqueous solution of the strong base, NaOH, into an aqueous solution of the weaker base, $NaHCO_3$.

$$NaOH_{(aq)} + CO_2 \longrightarrow NaHCO_{3\,(aq)}$$

In this new solution, the more strongly basic p-cresoxide ion accepts a proton and becomes p-cresol,

$$p\text{-}CH_3C_6H_4O^- + HCO_3^- \rightleftharpoons \underset{\text{Water-insoluble}}{p\text{-}CH_3C_6H_4OH} + CO_3^{2-}$$

The more weakly basic benzoate ion remains in solution.

(b)   Dissolve all three compounds in an organic solvent such as ether, then extract with aqueous NaOH. The organic layer will contain cyclohexanol, which can be separated by distillation. The aqueous layer will contain the benzoic acid, as sodium benzoate, and the p-cresol, as sodium p-cresoxide.

   Now pass CO_2 into the aqueous layer; this acidification will cause p-cresol to separate (it can then be extracted into an organic solvent and purified by distillation). After separation of the p-cresol, the aqueous phase can be acidified with aqueous HCl to yield benzoic acid as a precipitate.

18.3   An electron-withdrawing group destabilizes the carboxylic acid and stabilizes the carboxylate ion. It does the latter by assisting in delocalization of the negative charge of the carboxylate ion through an inductive effect.

Electron withdrawing group increases positive charge on $>$C=O and destabilizes acid.

Negative charge is delocalized by the electron-withdrawing chlorine.

Of course, the greater the number of electron-withdrawing groups the greater will be the acid-strengthening effect. Thus dichloroacetic acid is stronger than chloroacetic acid and trichloroacetic acid is stronger yet.

18.4   (a) CH_2FCOOH (F– is more electronegative than H–)

(b) CH_2FCOOH (F– is more electronegative than Cl–)

(c) $CH_2ClCOOH$ (Cl– is more electronegative than Br–)

(d) $CH_3CHClCH_2COOH$ (Cl– is closer to –COOH)

(e) $CH_3CH_2CHClCOOH$ (Cl– is closer to –COOH)

(f) $(CH_3)_3\overset{+}{N}$–⟨◯⟩–COOH [$(CH_3)_3\overset{+}{N}$– is more electronegative than H–]

(g) CF_3–⟨◯⟩–COOH (CF_3– is more electronegative than CH_3–)

18.5   (a)   The carboxyl group is an electron-withdrawing group; thus in a dicarboxylic acid such as those in Table 18.3, one carboxyl group increases the acidity of the other.

(b)   As the distance between the carboxyl groups increases the acid-strengthening, inductive effect decreases.

18.6   (a)   Heptanedioic acid

(b)   Methyl butanoate

(c)   2-Chlorobutanoic acid

(d)   Propanoic anydride

(e)   Butanoyl chloride

(f)   Propanamide

(g)   N-Methylbutanamide

(h)   4-Phenylbutanoyl chloride

18.7

(a) $CH_3CH_2\overset{\overset{\displaystyle O}{\|}}{C}$–$OCH_3$

(b) O_2N–⟨◯⟩–$\overset{\overset{\displaystyle O}{\|}}{C}$–$OCH_2CH_3$

(c) CH_3O–$\overset{\overset{\displaystyle O}{\|}}{C}CH_2$$\overset{\overset{\displaystyle O}{\|}}{C}$–$OCH_3$

(d)   ⟨◯⟩–$\overset{\overset{\displaystyle O}{\|}}{C}$–$N(CH_3)_2$

(e)   ⟨◯⟩ with $\overset{\overset{\displaystyle O}{\|}}{C}$–$OCH_3$ and $\overset{\underset{\displaystyle O}{\|}}{C}$–$OCH_3$

(f) $\underset{H}{\overset{H}{\diagdown\diagup}}$ with $\overset{\overset{\displaystyle O}{\|}}{C}$–$OCH_2CH_2CH_3$ and $\overset{\underset{\displaystyle O}{\|}}{C}$–$OCH_2CH_2CH_3$

(g) H–$\overset{\overset{\displaystyle O}{\|}}{C}$–$N(CH_3)_2$

(h) $CH_3\underset{\underset{\displaystyle Br}{|}}{CH}\overset{\overset{\displaystyle O}{\|}}{C}$–$Br$

18.8   These syntheses are easy to see if we work backward.

(a) $C_6H_5CH_2COOH \xleftarrow[\text{(2) H}^+]{\text{(1) CO}_2} C_6H_5CH_2MgBr$

$\Big\uparrow$ Mg, ether

$C_6H_5CH_2Br$

(b) $CH_3CH_2CH_2\underset{\underset{CH_3}{|}}{\overset{\overset{CH_3}{|}}{C}}COOH \xleftarrow[\text{(2) H}^+]{\text{(1) CO}_2} CH_3CH_2CH_2\underset{\underset{CH_3}{|}}{\overset{\overset{CH_3}{|}}{C}}MgBr$

$\Big\uparrow$ Mg, ether

$CH_3CH_2CH_2\underset{\underset{CH_3}{|}}{\overset{\overset{CH_3}{|}}{C}}Br$

(c) $CH_2{=}CHCH_2COOH \xleftarrow[\text{(2) H}^+]{\text{(1) CO}_2} CH_2{=}CHCH_2MgBr$

$\Big\uparrow$ Mg, ether

$CH_2{=}CHCH_2Br$

(d) $CH_3{-}\bigcirc{-}COOH \xleftarrow[\text{(2) H}^+]{\text{(1) CO}_2} CH_3{-}\bigcirc{-}MgBr$

$\Big\uparrow$ Mg, ether

$CH_3{-}\bigcirc{-}Br$

(e) $CH_3CH_2CH_2CH_2CH_2COOH \xleftarrow[\text{(2) H}^+]{\text{(1) CO}_2} CH_3CH_2CH_2CH_2CH_2MgBr$

$\Big\uparrow$ Mg, ether

$CH_3CH_2CH_2CH_2CH_2Br$

18.9

(a) $C_6H_5CH_2COOH \xleftarrow[\text{(2) H}^+\text{, H}_2\text{O, heat}]{\text{(1) CN}^-} C_6H_5CH_2Br$

$CH_2{=}CHCH_2COOH \xleftarrow[\text{(2) H}^+\text{, H}_2\text{O, heat}]{\text{(1) CN}^-} CH_2{=}CHCH_2Br$

$CH_3CH_2CH_2CH_2CH_2COOH \xleftarrow[\text{(2) H}^+\text{, H}_2\text{O, heat}]{\text{(1) CN}^-} CH_3CH_2CH_2CH_2CH_2Br$

(b) A nitrile synthesis. Preparation of a Grignard reagent from $HOCH_2CH_2CH_2CH_2Br$ would not be possible because of the presence of the acidic hydroxyl group.

18.10

(a) $CH_3COOH + C_6H_5COCl \xrightarrow{\text{pyridine}} CH_3\overset{\overset{\text{O}}{\|}}{C}O\overset{\overset{\text{O}}{\|}}{C}C_6H_5$

(b) $CH_3(CH_2)_4COOH + (CH_3CO)_2O \xrightarrow{\text{heat}}$

$CH_3(CH_2)_4\overset{\overset{\text{O}}{\|}}{C}O\overset{\overset{\text{O}}{\|}}{C}(CH_2)_4CH_3 + 2CH_3COOH$
(remove by distillation)

(c)

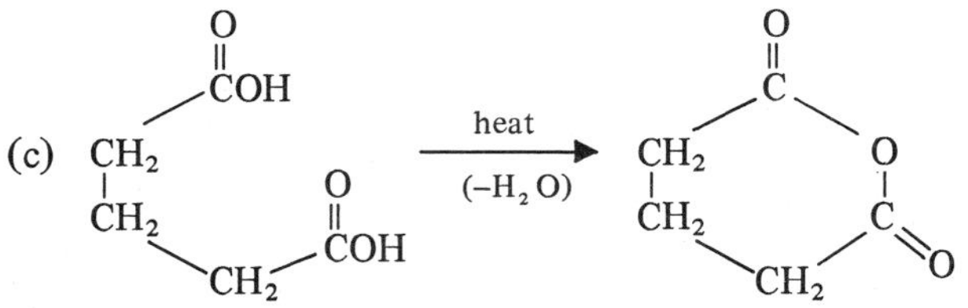

18.11   Since maleic acid is a cis dicarboxylic acid, dehydration occurs readily:

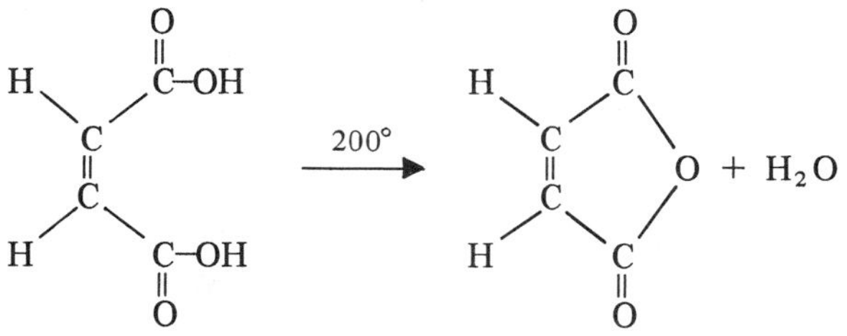

Maleic acid   Maleic anhydride

Being a trans dicarboxylic acid, fumaric acid must undergo isomerization to maleic acid first. This isomerization requires a higher temperature.

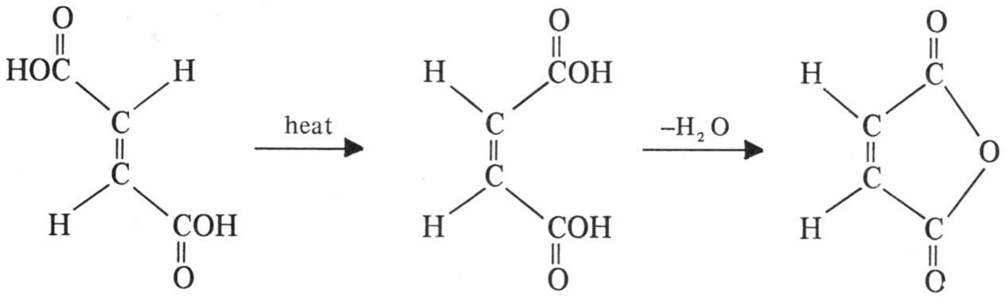

Fumaric acid

18.12   The labeled oxygen should appear in the carboxyl group of the acid. (Follow the reverse steps of the mechanism on page 795 of the text using $H_2{}^{18}O$.)

18.13

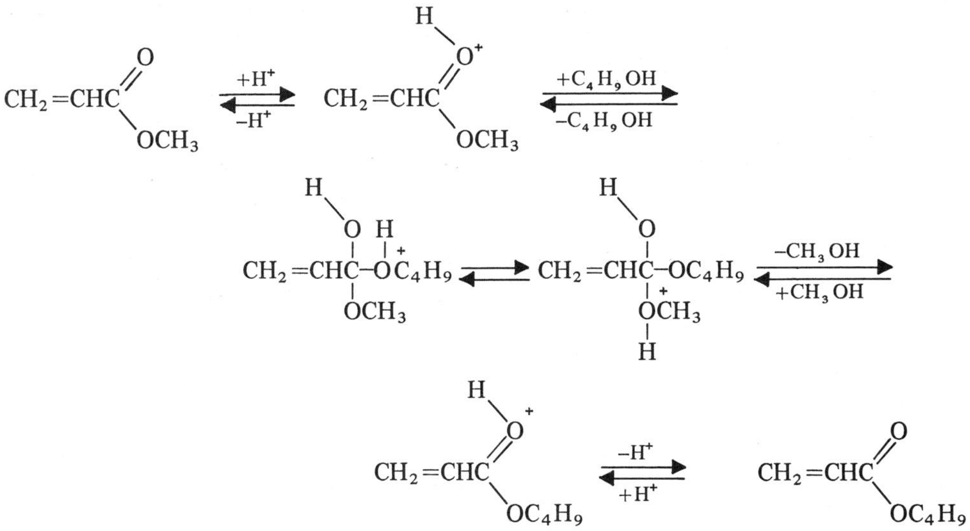

18.14 (a)

(1)

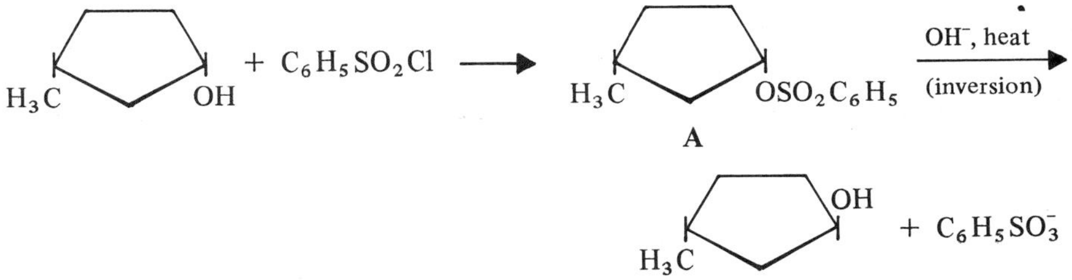

(2)

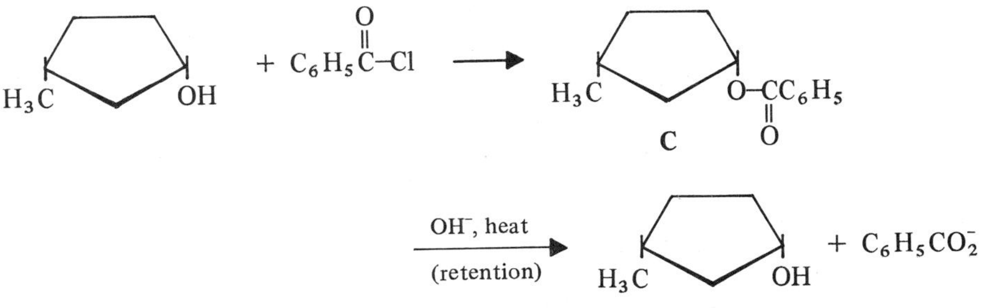

(3)

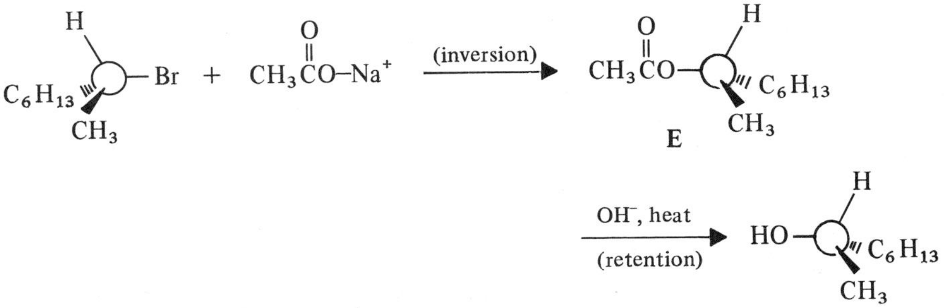

(4)

$$C_6H_{13} \overset{H}{\underset{CH_3}{\diagdown}}\!\!-Br \xrightarrow[\text{(inversion)}]{OH^-,\ heat} HO\!-\!\overset{H}{\underset{CH_3}{\diagup}}C_6H_{13}$$

(b) Method (3) should give a higher yield of **F** than method (4). Since the hydroxide ion is a strong base and since the alkyl halide is secondary, method (4) is likely to be accompanied by considerable elimination. Method (3), on the other hand, employs a weaker base, acetate ion, in the S_N2 step and is less likely to be complicated by elimination. Hydrolysis of the ester **E** that results should also proceed in high yield.

18.15   (a) Steric hindrance presented by the di-ortho methyl groups of methyl mesitoate prevents formation of the tetrahedral intermediate that must accompany attack at the acyl carbon.

(b) Carry out hydrolysis with labeled OH^- in labeled H_2O. The label should appear in the methanol.

18.16

(a) $C_6H_5\overset{O}{\overset{\|}{C}}N(CH_2CH_3)_2$

$\xrightarrow[H_2O]{OH^-} C_6H_5COO^- + (CH_3CH_2)_2NH$

$\xrightarrow[H_2O]{H^+} C_6H_5COOH + (CH_3CH_2)_2\overset{+}{N}H_2$

(b)

$\xrightarrow[H_2O]{OH^-} {}^-O\overset{O}{\overset{\|}{C}}CH_2CH_2CH_2CH_2NH_2$

$\xrightarrow[H_2O]{H^+} HO\overset{O}{\overset{\|}{C}}CH_2CH_2CH_2CH_2\overset{+}{N}H_3$

(c) $HOOCCH\!-\!NH\overset{O}{\overset{\|}{C}}CHNH_2$
       $\underset{CH_3}{|}$ $\underset{\underset{C_6H_5}{|}}{\underset{CH_2}{|}}$

$\xrightarrow[H_2O]{OH^-} {}^-OOCCHNH_2 + {}^-OOCCHNH_2$
       $\underset{CH_3}{|}$ $\underset{\underset{C_6H_5}{|}}{\underset{CH_2}{|}}$

$\xrightarrow[H_2O]{H^+} HOOCC\overset{+}{H}NH_3 + HOOCC\overset{+}{H}NH_3$
       $\underset{CH_3}{|}$ $\underset{\underset{C_6H_5}{|}}{\underset{CH_2}{|}}$

18.17   (a) $(CH_3)_3CCOOH \xrightarrow{SOCl_2} (CH_3)_3CCOCl \xrightarrow{NH_3}$

$$(CH_3)_3CCONH_2 \xrightarrow[\text{heat}]{P_2O_5} (CH_3)_3CC{\equiv}N$$

(b) An elimination reaction would take place.

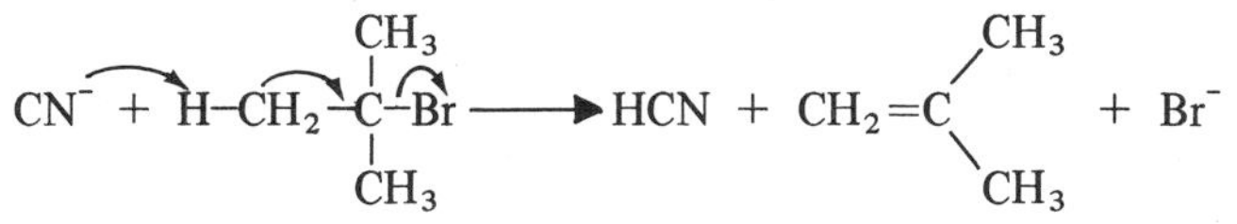

$$CN^- + H-CH_2-\underset{\underset{CH_3}{|}}{\overset{\overset{CH_3}{|}}{C}}-Br \longrightarrow HCN + CH_2{=}C\underset{CH_3}{\overset{CH_3}{<}} + Br^-$$

18.18

(a)

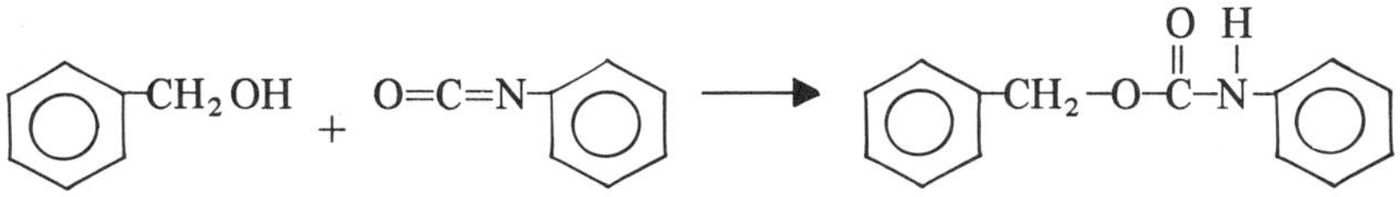

(b) $Cl-\overset{O}{\overset{||}{C}}-Cl + 4CH_3NH_2 \longrightarrow CH_3\underset{H}{\overset{}{N}}-\overset{O}{\overset{||}{C}}-\underset{H}{\overset{}{N}}CH_3 + 2CH_3\overset{+}{N}H_3 + 2Cl^-$

(c)

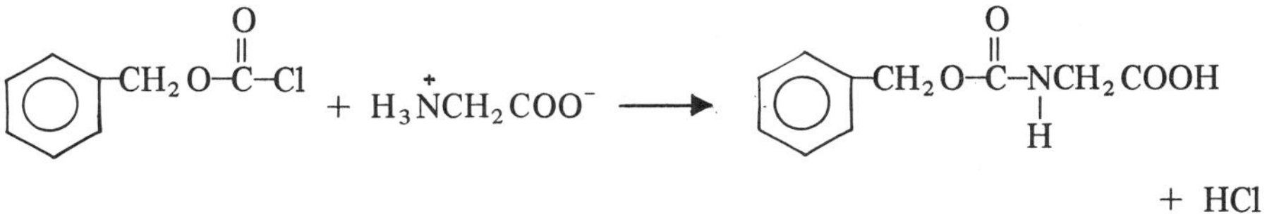

+ HCl

(d) $\xrightarrow{H_2,\ Pd} H_3\overset{+}{N}CH_2COO^- + CO_2 +$

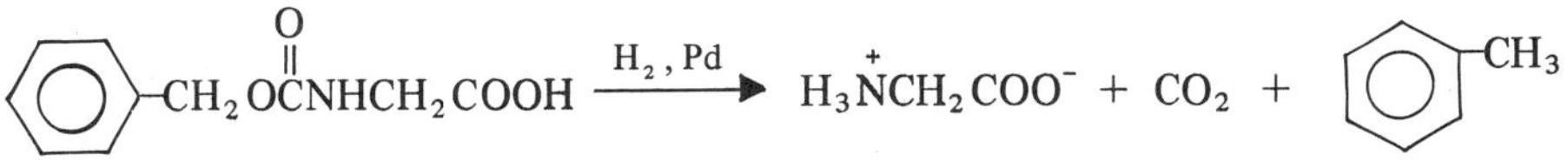

(e) $\xrightarrow{HBr,\ CH_3COOH} H_3\overset{+}{N}CH_2COOH + CO_2 +$

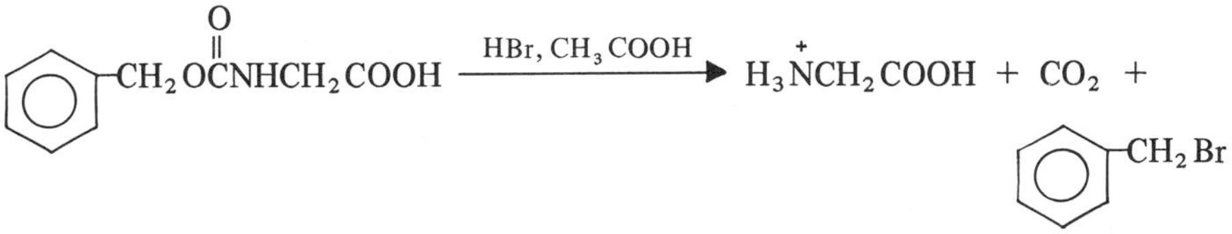

(f) $H_2N-\overset{O}{\overset{||}{C}}-NH_2 \xrightarrow{OH^-,\ H_2O,\ heat} 2\ NH_3 + CO_3{}^{-2}$

18.19 (a) By a Kolbe electrolysis of hexanoic acid:

(1) $CH_3(CH_2)_4\overset{O}{\overset{||}{C}}-O^- \xrightarrow[(-e^-)]{anode} CH_3(CH_2)_4\overset{O}{\overset{||}{C}}-O\cdot$

(2) $CH_3(CH_2)_4\overset{O}{\overset{||}{C}}-O\cdot \longrightarrow CH_3(CH_2)_3CH_2\cdot + CO_2$

(3) $2CH_3(CH_2)_3CH_2\cdot \longrightarrow CH_3(CH_2)_8CH_3$

(b) By decarboxylation of a β-keto acid:

$$CH_3(CH_2)_3\overset{O}{\underset{||}{C}}CH_2\overset{O}{\underset{||}{C}}OH \xrightarrow{100\text{-}150°} CH_3(CH_2)_3\overset{O}{\underset{||}{C}}CH_3 + CO_2$$

(c) By decarboxylation of a substituted malonic acid

$$CH_3CH_2\overset{COOH}{\underset{CH_3}{\overset{|}{\underset{|}{C}}}}COOH \xrightarrow{100\text{-}150°} CH_3CH_2\overset{}{\underset{CH_3}{\overset{|}{\underset{|}{CH}}}}COOH + CO_2$$

(d) By a Hunsdiecker reaction

$$C_6H_5CH_2COOAg + Br_2 \xrightarrow[heat]{CCl_4} C_6H_5CH_2Br + CO_2 + AgBr$$

(e) By decarboxylation of a β-keto acid

$$CH_3CH_2\overset{O}{\underset{||}{C}}CH_2\overset{O}{\underset{||}{C}}OH \xrightarrow{100\text{-}150°} CH_3CH_2\overset{O}{\underset{||}{C}}CH_3 + CO_2$$

(f) By a Hundieker reaction followed by treatment with zinc and acid.

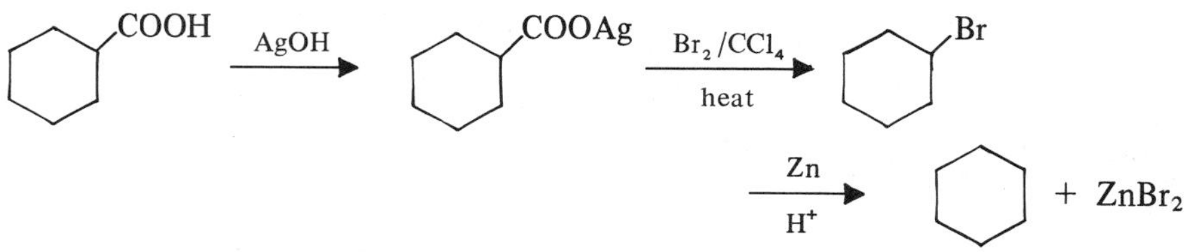

(g) By decarboxylation of a β-keto acid

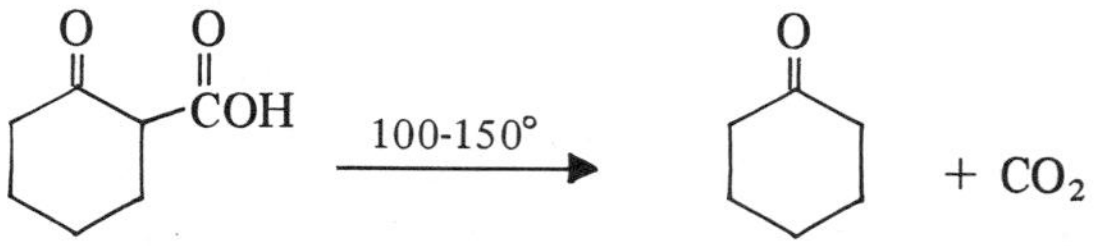

(h) By decarboxylation of a substituted malonic acid.

$$CH_3CH_2CH_2CH\overset{COOH}{\underset{COOH}{<}} \xrightarrow{100\text{-}150°} CH_3CH_2CH_2CH_2COOH + CO_2$$

18.20 (a) The oxygen-oxygen bond of the diacyl peroxide has a low homolytic bond dissociation energy ($DH° \simeq 35$ kcal/mole). This allows the following reaction to occur at a moderate temperature.

$$R\overset{O}{\underset{||}{C}}-O-O-\overset{O}{\underset{||}{C}}R \longrightarrow 2R\overset{O}{\underset{||}{C}}-O\cdot \qquad \Delta H° \simeq 35 \text{ kcal/mole}$$

(b) By decarboxylation of the carboxylate radical produced in part (a).

$$R\overset{O}{\underset{||}{C}}-O\cdot \longrightarrow R\cdot + CO_2$$

(c) (1) $R-\overset{\overset{\displaystyle O}{\|}}{C}-O-O-\overset{\overset{\displaystyle O}{\|}}{C}-R \xrightarrow{\text{heat}} 2R-\overset{\overset{\displaystyle O}{\|}}{C}-O\cdot$ $\Big\}$ Chain Initiating Steps

(2) $R-\overset{\overset{\displaystyle O}{\|}}{C}-O\cdot \longrightarrow R\cdot + CO_2$

(3) $R\cdot + CH_2=CH_2 \longrightarrow RCH_2CH_2\cdot$ $\Big\}$ Chain Propagating Steps

(4) $RCH_2CH_2\cdot + CH_2=CH_2 \longrightarrow RCH_2CH_2CH_2CH_2\cdot$

(3), (4), (3), (4), etc.

ADDITIONAL PROBLEMS

18.21 (a) $CH_3(CH_2)_4COOH$

(b) $CH_3(CH_2)_4CONH_2$

(c) $CH_3(CH_2)_4CONHC_2H_5$

(d) $CH_3(CH_2)_4CON(C_2H_5)_2$

(e) $CH_3CH_2CH=CHCH_2COOH$

(f) $CH_3CH=CHCH_2\underset{\underset{\displaystyle CH_3}{|}}{C}HCOOH$

(g) $HOOCCH_2CH_2CH_2CH_2COOH$

(h) benzene ring with COOH, COOH (ortho)

(i) benzene ring with COOH, COOH (meta)

(j) benzene ring with COOH, COOH (para)

(k) $C_2H_5OOC-COOC_2H_5$

(l) $C_2H_5OOC(CH_2)_4COOC_2H_5$

(m) $CH_3CH_2COOCH_2CH(CH_3)_2$

(n) naphthalene ring with COOH

(o) $\underset{H}{\overset{HOOC}{\diagup}}C=C\underset{H}{\overset{COOH}{\diagdown}}$

(p) $HOOCCHOHCH_2COOH$

(q) $\underset{H}{\overset{HOOC}{\diagup}}C=C\underset{COOH}{\overset{H}{\diagdown}}$

(r) $HOOCCH_2CH_2COOH$

(s) $\overset{\overset{\displaystyle O}{\|}}{\underset{\underset{\displaystyle C}{\underset{\underset{\displaystyle \|}{}}{\underset{\displaystyle O}{}}}}{C}}$ ... five-membered ring: CH_2–CH_2 with two C=O groups and NH

(t) $HOOCCH_2COOH$

(u) $C_2H_5OOCCH_2COOC_2H_5$

18.22

(a) Benzoic acid

(b) Benzoyl chloride

(c) Benzamide

(d) Benzoic anhydride

(e) Benzyl benzoate

(f) Phenyl benzoate

(g) Isopropyl acetate

(h) *N,N*-Dimethylacetamide

(i) Acetonitrile

(j) Maleic anhydride

(k) Phthalic anhydride

(l) Phthalimide

(m) Glyceryl tripalmitate

(n) α-Ketosuccinic acid

(o) Methyl salicylate

18.23

(a)

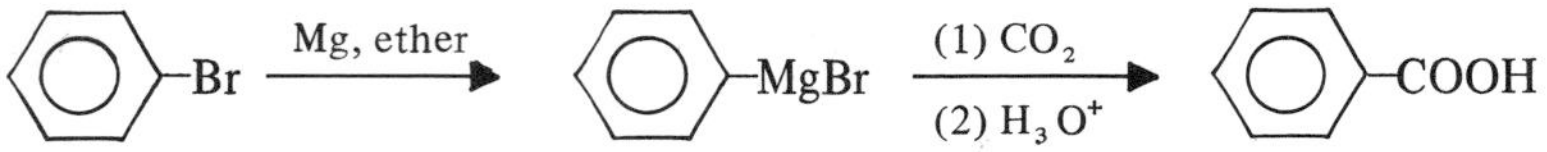

(b)

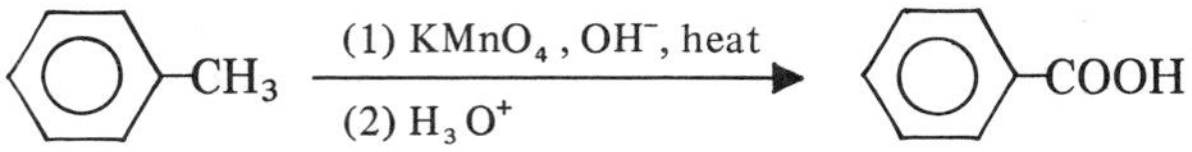

(c)

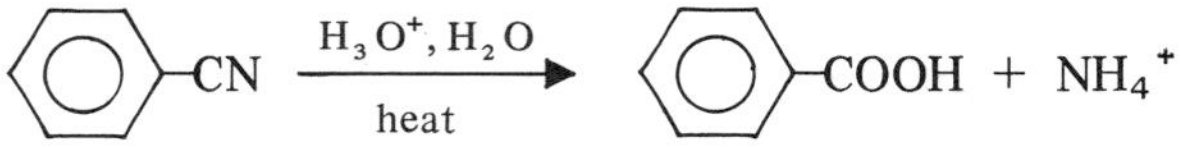

(d)

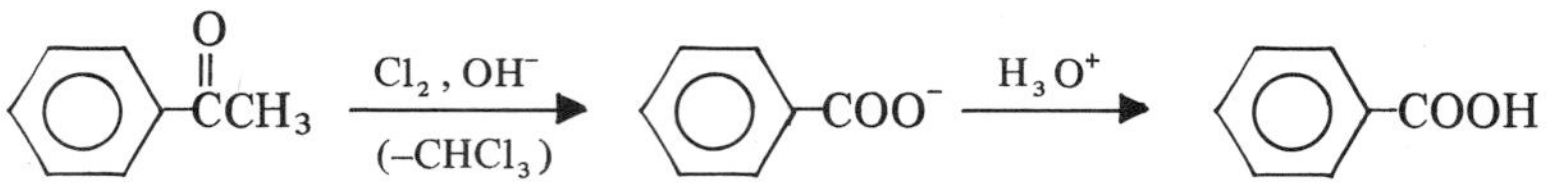

(e)

(f)

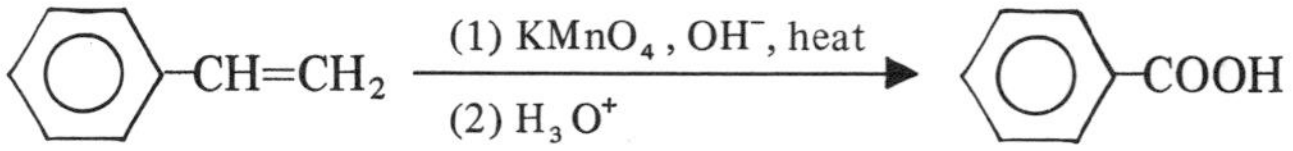

(g)

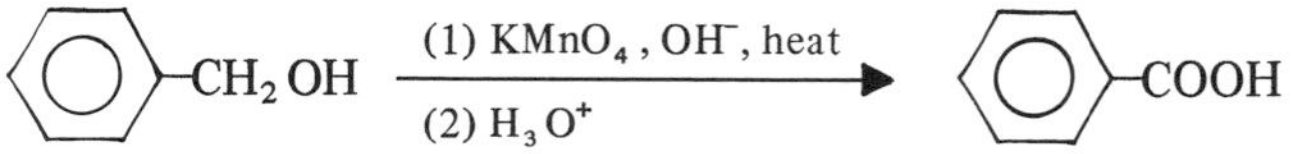

18.24

(a)

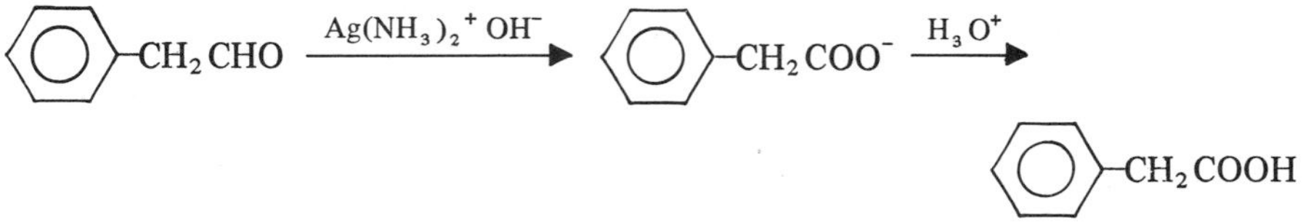

(b) $\underset{\bigcirc}{\big\langle\!\!\!\bigcirc\!\!\!\big\rangle}\!\!-\!CH_2Br \xrightarrow[\text{(2) } CO_2]{\text{(1) Mg, ether}} \underset{\bigcirc}{\big\langle\!\!\!\bigcirc\!\!\!\big\rangle}\!\!-\!CH_2COOMgBr \xrightarrow{H_3O^+}$

$$\underset{\bigcirc}{\big\langle\!\!\!\bigcirc\!\!\!\big\rangle}\!\!-\!CH_2COOH$$

$\underset{\bigcirc}{\big\langle\!\!\!\bigcirc\!\!\!\big\rangle}\!\!-\!CH_2Br \xrightarrow{CN^-} \underset{\bigcirc}{\big\langle\!\!\!\bigcirc\!\!\!\big\rangle}\!\!-\!CH_2CN \xrightarrow[\text{heat}]{H_3O^+, H_2O} \underset{\bigcirc}{\big\langle\!\!\!\bigcirc\!\!\!\big\rangle}\!\!-\!CH_2COOH$

18.25

(a) $CH_3CH_2CH_2CH_2CH_2OH \xrightarrow[\text{(2) } H_3O^+]{\text{(1) } KMnO_4, OH^-, \text{heat}} CH_3CH_2CH_2CH_2COOH$

(b) $CH_3CH_2CH_2CH_2Br \xrightarrow[\text{(2) } CO_2]{\text{(1) Mg, ether}} CH_3CH_2CH_2CH_2COOMgBr \xrightarrow{H_3O^+}$

$$CH_3CH_2CH_2CH_2COOH$$

$CH_3CH_2CH_2CH_2Br \xrightarrow{CN^-} CH_3CH_2CH_2CH_2CN \xrightarrow[\text{heat}]{H_3O^+, H_2O}$

$$CH_3CH_2CH_2CH_2COOH$$

(c) $CH_3CH_2CH_2CH_2\underset{\underset{O}{\|}}{C}CH_3 \xrightarrow[(-CHCl_3)]{Cl_2, OH^-} CH_3CH_2CH_2CH_2COO^- \xrightarrow{H_3O^+}$

$$CH_3CH_2CH_2CH_2COOH$$

(d) $CH_3(CH_2)_3CH{=}CH(CH_2)_3CH_3 \xrightarrow[\text{(2) } H_3O^+]{\text{(1) } KMnO_4, OH^-, \text{heat}} 2CH_3(CH_2)_3COOH$

(e) $CH_3CH_2CH_2CH_2CHO \xrightarrow[\text{(2) } H_3O^+]{\text{(1) } Ag(NH_3)_2{}^+OH^-} CH_3CH_2CH_2CH_2COOH$

18.26

(a) $CH_3COOH + HCl$

(b) $CH_3COOH + AgCl$

(c) $CH_3COOCH_2(CH_2)_2CH_3$

(d) CH_3CONH_2

(e) $\underset{\underset{O}{\|}}{\overset{CH_3}{\big\langle\!\!\!\bigcirc\!\!\!\big\rangle}}\!\!\begin{smallmatrix}CH_3\\ \\ CCH_3\end{smallmatrix} + CH_3\!\!-\!\!\underset{}{\big\langle\!\!\!\bigcirc\!\!\!\big\rangle}\!\!-\!\!\overset{O}{\overset{\|}{C}}CH_3$

(f) CH_3CHO

(g) CH_3COCH_3

(h) $CH_3COCH_2CH_3$

(i) $CH_3CONHCH_3$

(j) $CH_3CONHC_6H_5$

(k) $CH_3CON(CH_3)_2$

(l) $CH_3COOCH_2CH_3$

(m) $(CH_3CO)_2O$

(n) $(CH_3CO)_2O$

(o) $CH_3COOC_6H_5$

18.27 (a) CH_3CONH_2 + CH_3COONH_4

(b) $2CH_3COOH$

(c) $CH_3COOCH_2CH_2CH_3$ + CH_3COOH

(d) $C_6H_5COCH_3$ + CH_3COOH

(e) $CH_3CONHCH_2CH_3$ + $CH_3COO^-CH_3CH_2NH_3{}^+$

(f) $CH_3CON(CH_2CH_3)_2$ + $CH_3COO^-(CH_3CH_2)_2NH_2{}^+$

18.28

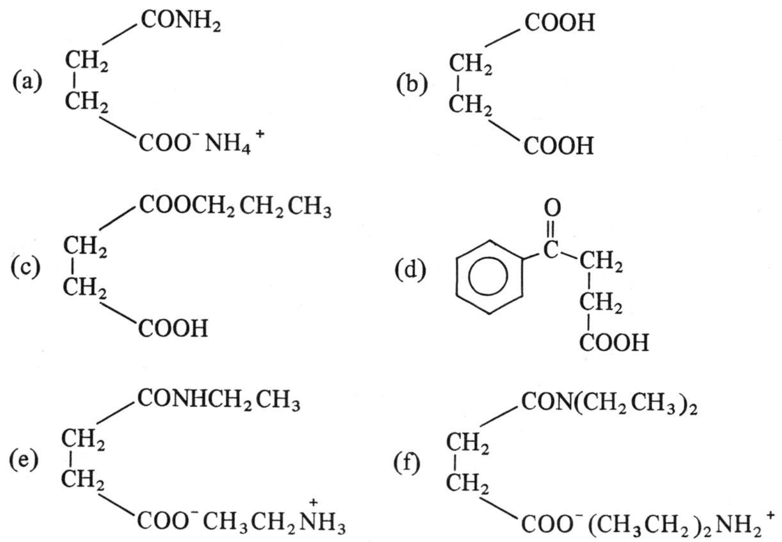

(a)
```
        CONH₂
       /
    CH₂
    |
    CH₂
       \
        COO⁻ NH₄⁺
```

(b)
```
        COOH
       /
    CH₂
    |
    CH₂
       \
        COOH
```

(c)
```
        COOCH₂CH₂CH₃
       /
    CH₂
    |
    CH₂
       \
        COOH
```

(d)

(e)
```
        CONHCH₂CH₃
       /
    CH₂
    |
    CH₂
       \
        COO⁻ CH₃CH₂N⁺H₃
```

(f)
```
        CON(CH₂CH₃)₂
       /
    CH₂
    |
    CH₂
       \
        COO⁻ (CH₃CH₂)₂NH₂⁺
```

18.29

(a)

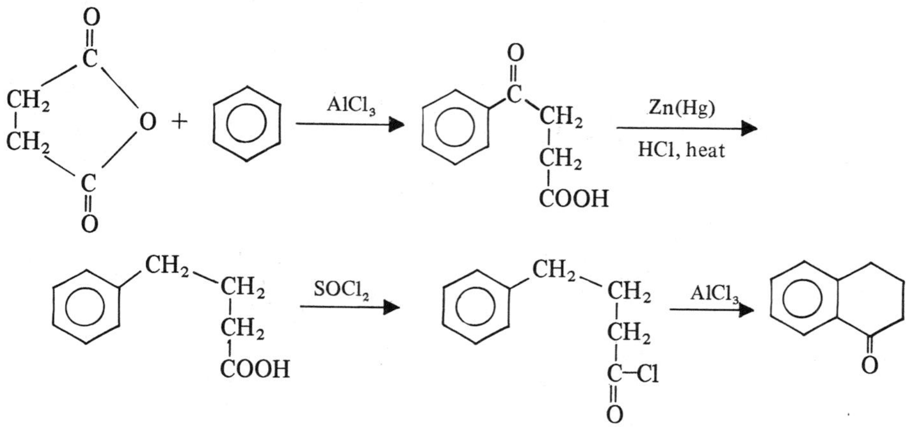

(b)

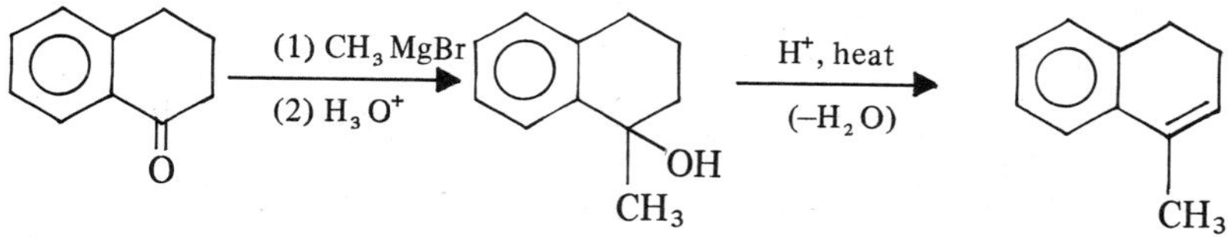

(c)

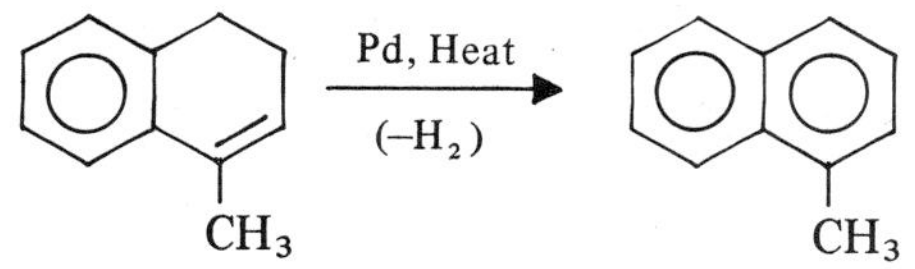

(d)

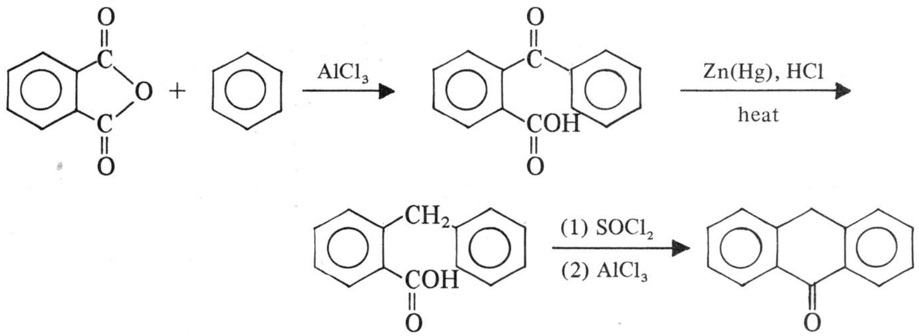

(e)

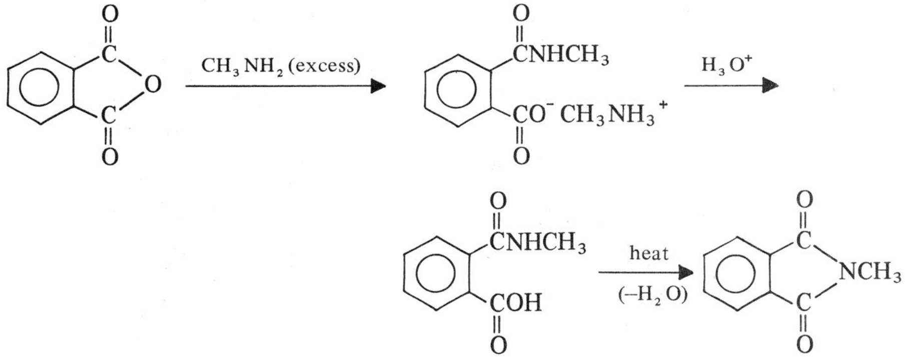

(f)

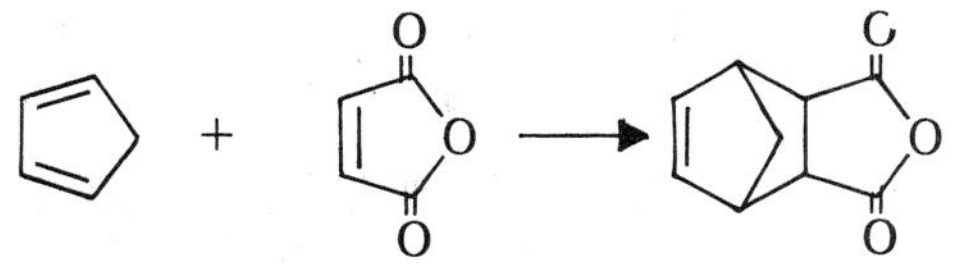

(g)

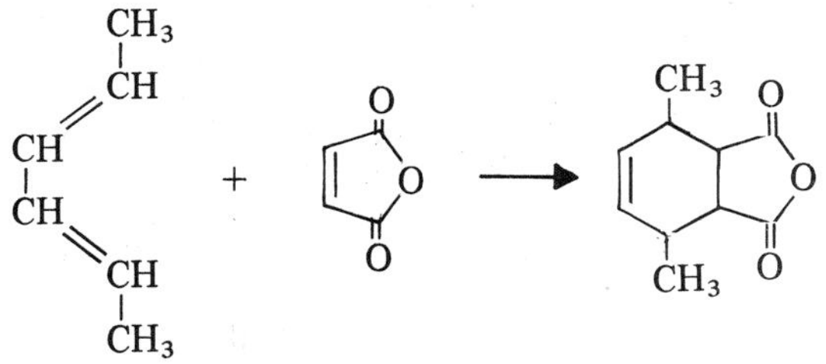

18.30 (a) $CH_3CH_2COOH + CH_3CH_2OH$

(b) $CH_3CH_2COO^- + CH_3CH_2OH$

(c) $CH_3CH_2COO(CH_2)_7CH_3 + CH_3CH_2OH$

(d) $CH_3CH_2CONHCH_3 + CH_3CH_2OH$

(e) $CH_3CH_2CH_2OH + CH_3CH_2OH$

(f) $CH_3CH_2\overset{\displaystyle C_6H_5}{\underset{\displaystyle OH}{C}}-C_6H_5 + CH_3CH_2OH$

18.31 (a) $CH_3CH_2COOH + NH_4^+$

(b) $CH_3CH_2COO^- + NH_3$

(c) CH_3CH_2CN

18.32 (a) Benzoic acid dissolves in aqueous $NaHCO_3$. Methyl benzoate does not.

(b) Benzoyl chloride gives a precipitate (AgCl) when treated with alcoholic $AgNO_3$. Benzoic acid does not.

(c) Benzoic acid dissolves in aqueous $NaHCO_3$. Benzamide does not.

(d) Benzoic acid dissolves in aqueous $NaHCO_3$. *p*-Cresol does not.

(e) Refluxing benzamide with aqueous NaOH liberates NH_3 which can be detected in the vapors with moist red litmus paper. Ethyl benzoate does not liberate NH_3.

(f) Cinnamic acid, because it has a double bond, decolorizes Br_2 in CCl_4. Benzoic acid does not.

(g) Benzoyl chloride gives a precipitate (AgCl) when treated with alcoholic $AgNO_3$. Ethyl benzoate does not.

(h) 2-Chlorobutanoic acid gives a precipitate (AgCl) when treated with alcoholic silver nitrate. Butanoic acid does not.

18.33

(a)
$$\begin{matrix} CH_2-CH_2 \\ | \qquad\quad \\ CH_2-O \end{matrix}\Big\rangle C=O$$

(b) $CH_3CH=CHCOOH$

(c) $CH_3CH_2CH\big\langle\begin{matrix} \overset{O}{\overset{\|}{C}}-O \\ O-\underset{\underset{\displaystyle O}{\|}}{C} \end{matrix}\big\rangle CHCH_2CH_3$

(d)
$$CH_2\Big\langle\begin{matrix} CH_2-\overset{O}{\overset{\|}{C}} \\ \qquad\qquad\Big\rangle O \\ CH_2-\underset{\underset{\displaystyle O}{\|}}{C} \end{matrix}$$

(e)
$$CH_2\Big\langle\begin{matrix} CH_2-\overset{O}{\overset{\|}{C}} \\ \qquad\qquad NH \\ CH_2-\underset{\displaystyle CH_3}{CH} \end{matrix}$$

(f) a benzene ring fused to a ring containing $\overset{O}{\overset{\|}{C}}-NH-CH_2$

18.34

(a)

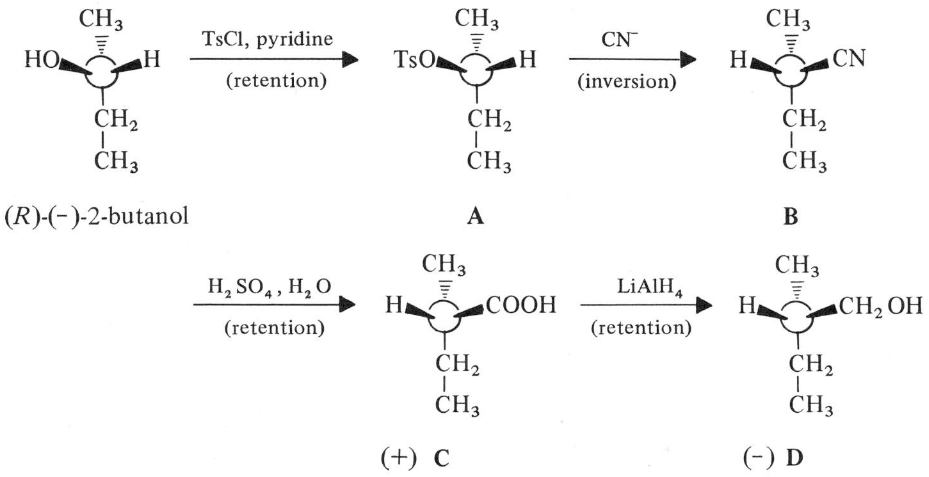
TsCl, pyridine
(retention)
CN⁻
(inversion)
(R)-(−)-2-butanol
A
B
H_2SO_4, H_2O
(retention)
$LiAlH_4$
(retention)
(+) C
(−) D

(b)

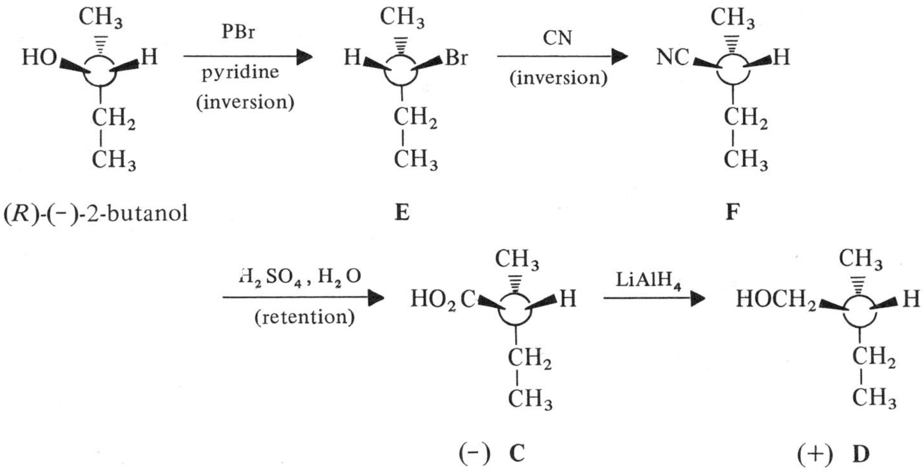
PBr
pyridine
(inversion)
CN
(inversion)
(R)-(−)-2-butanol
E
F
H_2SO_4, H_2O
(retention)
$LiAlH_4$
(−) C
(+) D

(c)

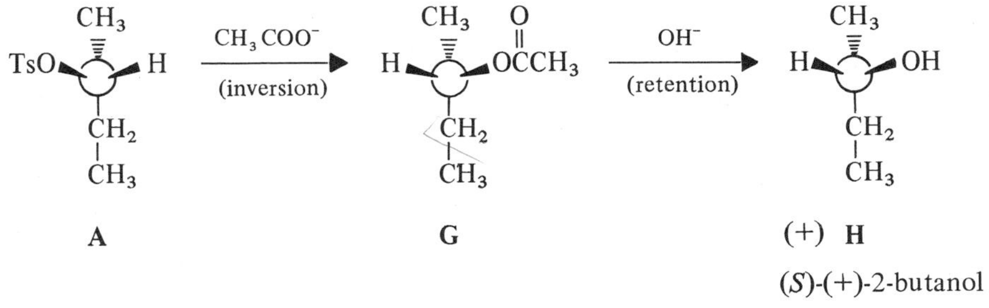
CH_3COO^-
(inversion)
OH⁻
(retention)
A
G
(+) H
(S)-(+)-2-butanol

(d)

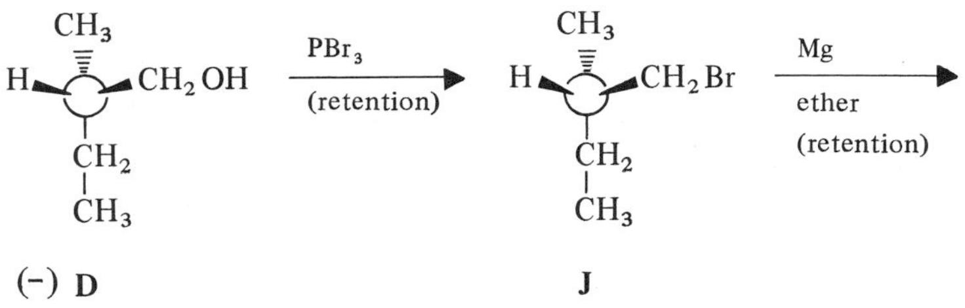
PBr_3
(retention)
Mg
ether
(retention)
(−) D
J

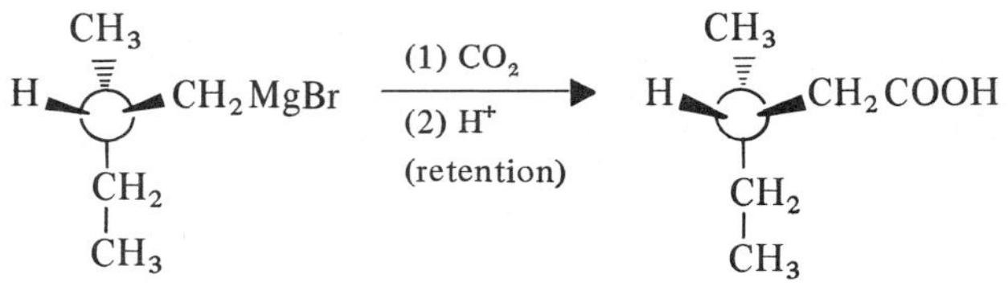

K

L

(e)

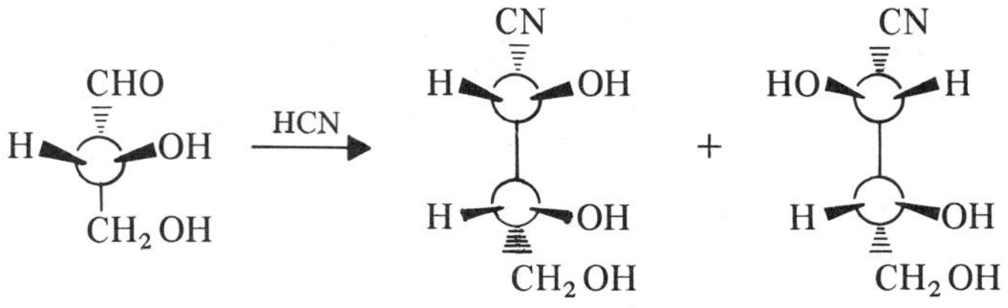

(R)-(+)-Glyceraldehyde   M   N

(f)

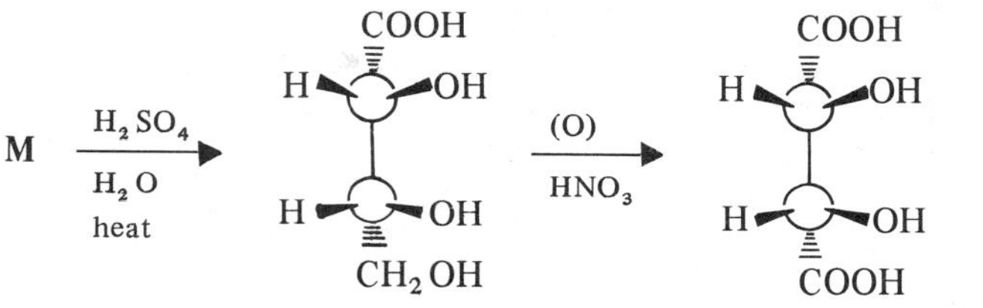

P   meso-Tartaric acid

(g)

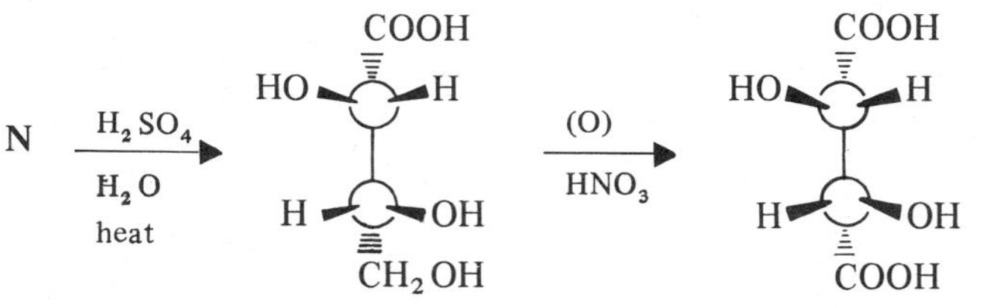

(−)-Tartaric acid

18.35

(a)

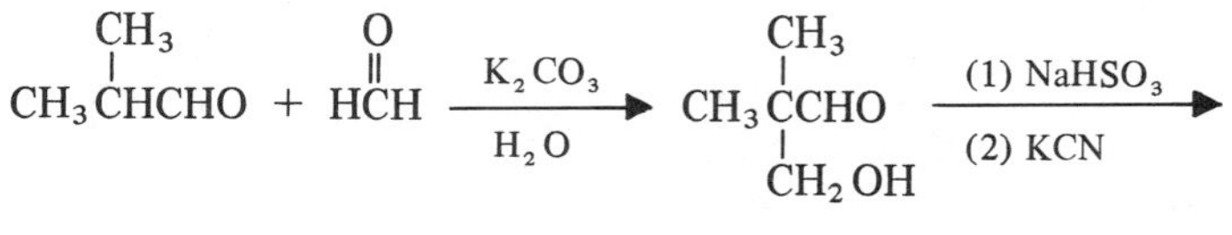

A

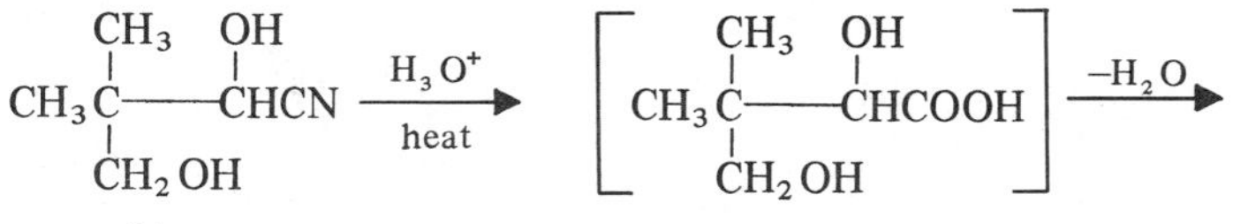

(±)-B   (±)-C

$$\underset{(\pm)\text{-D}}{\text{CH}_3-\underset{\underset{\underset{O}{C=O}}{|}}{\overset{\overset{\text{CH}_3}{|}}{\text{C}}}-\underset{\underset{O}{|}}{\overset{\overset{\text{OH}}{|}}{\text{CH}}}} \quad \xrightarrow{\text{H}_2\text{NCH}_2\text{CH}_2\overset{\overset{O}{||}}{\text{C}}\text{OH}} \quad (\pm)\text{-Pantothenic acid}$$

$$\xrightarrow{\text{H}_2\text{NCH}_2\text{CH}_2\overset{\overset{O}{||}}{\text{C}}\text{NHCH}_2\text{CH}_2\text{SH}} \quad (\pm)\text{-Pantetheine}$$

(b) $(\text{CH}_3)_2\overset{\overset{\text{CH}_2\text{OH}}{|}}{\underset{\underset{\text{H}}{|}}{\text{C}}}\overset{\text{OH}}{\underset{}{\text{C}}}\overset{\overset{O}{||}}{\text{C}}-\text{NHCH}_2\text{CH}_2\overset{\overset{O}{||}}{\text{C}}-\text{NHCH}_2\text{CH}_2\text{SH}$

(c) $\xrightarrow[\text{heat}]{\text{OH}^-,\,\text{H}_2\text{O}}$ $(\text{CH}_3)_2\overset{\overset{\text{CH}_2\text{OH}}{|}}{\underset{\underset{\text{H}}{|}}{\text{C}}}\overset{\text{OH}}{\underset{}{\text{C}}}\text{COO}^- + \text{H}_2\text{NCH}_2\text{CH}_2\text{COO}^- + \text{H}_2\text{NCH}_2\text{CH}_2\text{S}^-$

18.36

$$\underset{\text{Phenacetin}}{\text{CH}_3\text{CH}_2\text{O}-\bigcirc-\text{NH}-\overset{\overset{O}{||}}{\text{C}}-\text{CH}_3} \quad \xrightarrow[\substack{\text{H}_2\text{O} \\ \text{reflux}}]{\text{OH}^-} \quad \underset{\substack{\text{Phenetidine} \\ + \\ \text{CH}_3\text{COO}^-}}{\text{CH}_3\text{CH}_2\text{O}-\bigcirc-\text{NH}_2}$$

An interpretation of the spectral data for phenacetin is given in Fig.

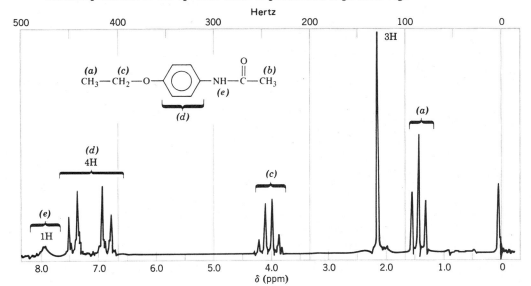

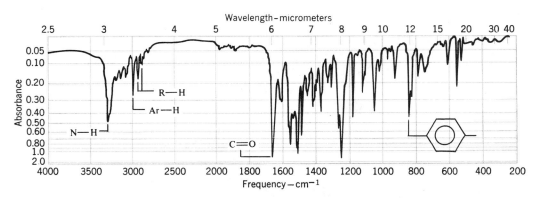

FIG. 18.2. *The proton nmr and infrared spectra of phenacetin. (Proton nmr spectrum courtesy of Varian Associates. IR spectrum courtesy of Sadtler Inc.)*

18.37

(a)
$$CH_3CH_2-O-\overset{\overset{\displaystyle O}{\|}}{C}-CH_2CH_2-\overset{\overset{\displaystyle O}{\|}}{C}-O-CH_2CH_3$$
(a) (c)   (b) (b)   (c) (a)

Interpretation:

(a) Triplet δ1.2 (6H) $2-\overset{\overset{\displaystyle O}{\|}}{C}-$, 1740 cm^{-1}

(b) Singlet δ2.5 (4H)

(c) Quartet δ4.1 (4H)

(b)
$$\text{Ph}-\overset{\overset{\displaystyle O}{\|}}{C}-O-CH_2-\overset{\overset{\displaystyle CH_3 \ (a)}{|}}{CH}-CH_3$$
(c)   (b)   (a)
(d)

Interpretation:

(a) Doublet δ1.0 (6H) $-\overset{\overset{\displaystyle O}{\|}}{C}-$, 1720 cm^{-1}

(b) Multiplet δ2.1 (1H)

(c) Doublet δ4.1 (2H)

(d) Multiplet δ7.8 (5H)

(c)
$$\text{Ph}-CH_2-\overset{\overset{\displaystyle O}{\|}}{C}-O-CH_2CH_3$$
(b)   (c)   (a)
(d)

Interpretation:

(a) Triplet δ1.2 (3H) $-\overset{\overset{\displaystyle O}{\|}}{C}-$, 1740 cm^{-1}

(b) Singlet δ3.5 (2H)

(c) Quartet δ4.1 (2H)

(d) Multiplet δ7.3 (5H)

(d)
$$\overset{\overset{\displaystyle Cl}{|}}{Cl-CH-COOH}$$
    (a)   (b)

Interpretation:

(a) Singlet $\delta 6.0$ $-OH$, 2500-2700 cm^{-1}

(b) Singlet $\delta 11.70$ $\overset{\overset{\displaystyle O}{||}}{-C-}$, 1705 cm^{-1}

(e) $Cl-CH_2-\overset{\overset{\displaystyle O}{||}}{C}-OCH_2CH_3$
        (b)   (c) (a)

Interpretation:

(a) Triplet $\delta 1.3$ $\overset{\overset{\displaystyle O}{||}}{-C-}$, 1745 cm^{-1}

(b) Singlet $\delta 4.0$

(c) Quartet $\delta 4.2$

18.38

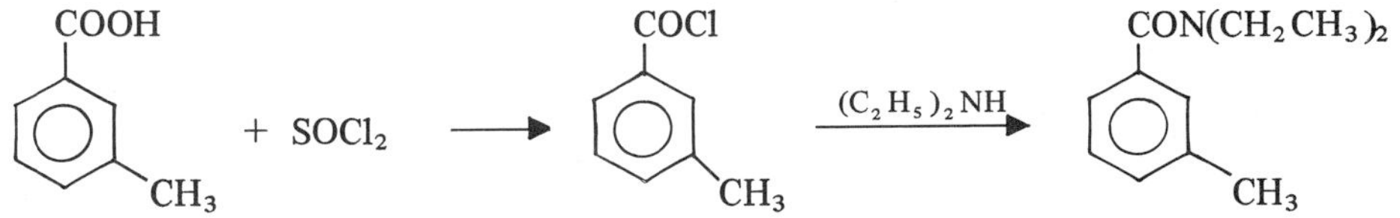

$$\text{COOH (on aryl with } CH_3) + SOCl_2 \longrightarrow \text{COCl (on aryl with } CH_3) \xrightarrow{(C_2H_5)_2NH} \text{CON(CH_2CH_3)_2 (on aryl with } CH_3)$$

18.39 Alkyl groups are electron releasing; they help disperse the positive charge of an alkyl-ammonium salt and thereby help to stabilize it.

$$R\ddot{N}H_2 + H_3O^+ \longrightarrow R \rightarrow NH_3^+ + H_2O$$

*Stabilized by
electron-
releasing
alkyl group*

Alkylamines, consequently, are somewhat stronger bases than ammonia.

Amides, on the other hand, have acyl groups, $R-\overset{\overset{\displaystyle O}{||}}{C}-$, attached to nitrogen, and acyl groups are electron withdrawing. They are especially electron withdrawing because of resonance contributions of the kind shown below,

$$R-\overset{\overset{\displaystyle :\ddot{O}}{||}}{C}-\ddot{N}H_2 \longleftrightarrow R-\overset{\overset{\displaystyle :\ddot{O}:^-}{|}}{C}=\overset{+}{N}H_2$$

This kind of resonance also *stabilizes* the amide. The tendency of the acyl group to be electron withdrawing, however, *destabilizes* the conjugate acid of an amide and reactions such as the following do not take place to an appreciable extent.

$$
\underset{\substack{\text{Stabilized} \\ \text{by} \\ \text{resonance}}}{\overset{\overset{\displaystyle O}{\parallel}}{RC-\ddot{N}H_2}} + H_3O^+ \;\xleftarrow{\;\;\;\;}\;\rightleftharpoons\; \underset{\substack{\text{Destabilized} \\ \text{by electron-} \\ \text{withdrawing} \\ \text{acyl group}}}{\overset{\overset{\displaystyle O}{\parallel}}{RC-NH_3^+}} + H_2O
$$

18.40   (a) The conjugate base of an amide is stabilized by resonance.

$$
\overset{\overset{\displaystyle :\ddot{O}}{\parallel}}{R-C-\ddot{N}H_2} + :B^- \;\rightleftharpoons\; \overset{\overset{\displaystyle :\ddot{O}}{\parallel}}{R-C-\ddot{N}H^-} + BH
$$

$$
\updownarrow
$$

$$
\overset{\overset{\displaystyle :\ddot{O}:^-}{\mid}}{R-C=NH}
$$

*This structure
is especially
stable because the
negative charge is
on oxygen*

(b) The conjugate base of an imide is stabilized by an additional resonance structure,

$$
\overset{\overset{\displaystyle :\ddot{O} \quad \ddot{O}:}{\parallel \quad \parallel}}{RC-\ddot{N}H-CR} + OH^- \;\longrightarrow\; \overset{\overset{\displaystyle :\ddot{O} \quad \ddot{O}:}{\parallel \quad \parallel}}{RC-\ddot{N}-CR} + H_2O
$$

An imide

$$
\updownarrow
$$

$$
\overset{\overset{\displaystyle ^-:\ddot{O} \quad \ddot{O}:}{\parallel \quad \parallel}}{RC=N-CR}
$$

$$
\updownarrow
$$

$$
\overset{\overset{\displaystyle :\ddot{O} \quad :\ddot{O}:^-}{\parallel \quad \mid}}{RC-N=CR}
$$

18.41   (a) (1) $RO-OR \longrightarrow 2\,RO\cdot$ $\left.\begin{array}{c}\\\\\end{array}\right\}$ Chain-initiating steps

(2) $CH_3\overset{\overset{\displaystyle O}{\parallel}}{C}SH + RO\cdot \longrightarrow R\overset{\overset{\displaystyle O}{\parallel}}{C}S\cdot + ROH$

(3) $CH_3\overset{\overset{\displaystyle O}{\parallel}}{C}S\cdot + CH_2{=}CHR \longrightarrow CH_3\overset{\overset{\displaystyle O}{\parallel}}{C}SCH_2\overset{\cdot}{C}HR$ $\left.\begin{array}{c}\\\\\\\\\end{array}\right\}$ Chain-propagating steps

(4) $CH_3\overset{\overset{\displaystyle O}{\parallel}}{C}SCH_2\overset{\cdot}{C}HR + CH_3\overset{\overset{\displaystyle O}{\parallel}}{C}SH \longrightarrow CH_3\overset{\overset{\displaystyle O}{\parallel}}{C}SCH_2CH_2R + CH_3\overset{\overset{\displaystyle O}{\parallel}}{C}S\cdot$

(b) 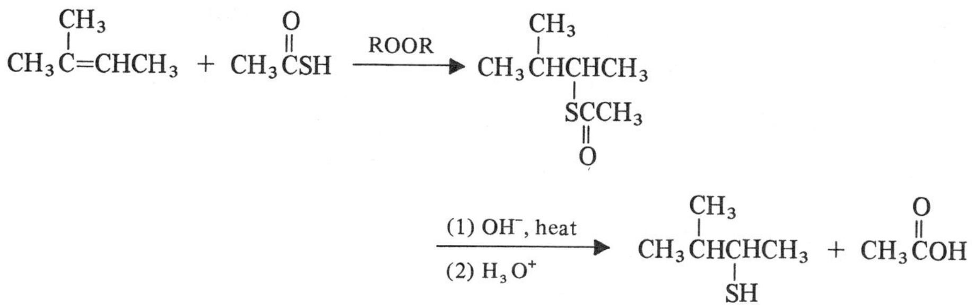
$$CH_3\overset{\underset{\displaystyle |}{CH_3}}{C}=CHCH_3 + CH_3\overset{\underset{\displaystyle \|}{O}}{C}SH \xrightarrow{ROOR} CH_3\overset{\underset{\displaystyle |}{CH_3}}{C}HCHCH_3$$

with $SCCH_3$ (C=O) below

$$\xrightarrow[\text{(2) } H_3O^+]{\text{(1) } OH^-,\text{ heat}} CH_3\overset{\underset{\displaystyle |}{CH_3}}{C}HCHCH_3 + CH_3\overset{\underset{\displaystyle \|}{O}}{C}OH$$

with SH below

18.42 *cis*-4-Hydroxycyclohexane carboxylic acid can assume a boat conformation that permits lactone formation.

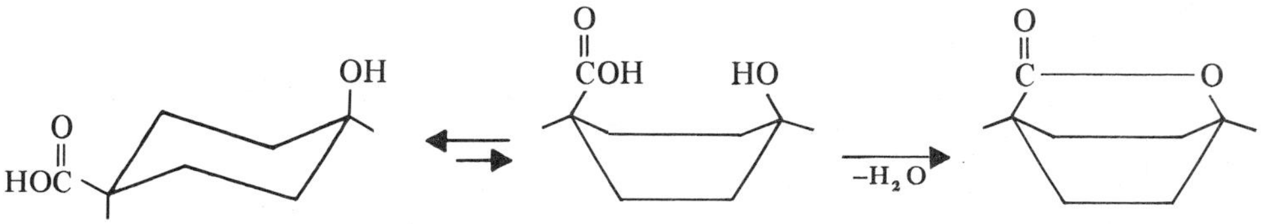

Neither of the chair conformations nor the boat form of *trans*-4-hydroxycyclohexane carboxylic acid places the —OH group and the —COOH group close enough together to permit lactonization.

18.43

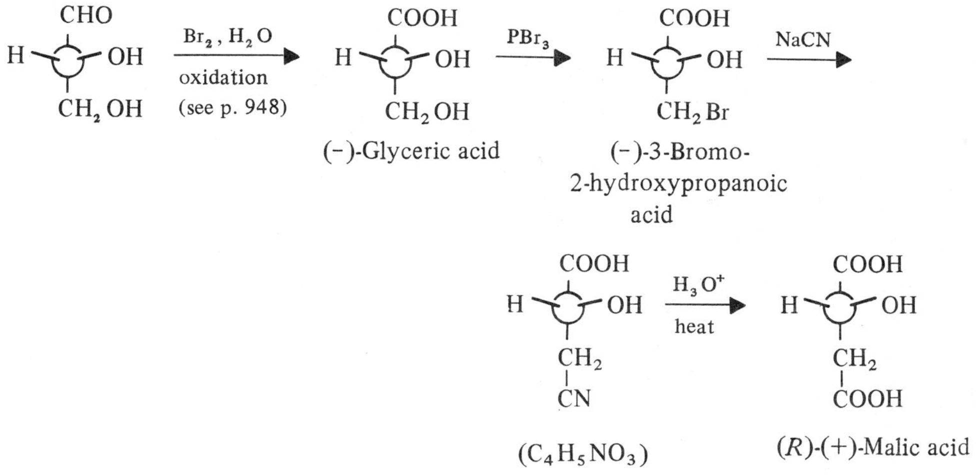

$\xrightarrow[\text{oxidation (see p. 948)}]{Br_2, H_2O}$ (−)-Glyceric acid $\xrightarrow{PBr_3}$ (−)-3-Bromo-2-hydroxypropanoic acid $\xrightarrow{NaCN}$

$\xrightarrow[\text{heat}]{H_3O^+}$ $(C_4H_5NO_3)$ → (*R*)-(+)-Malic acid

18.44

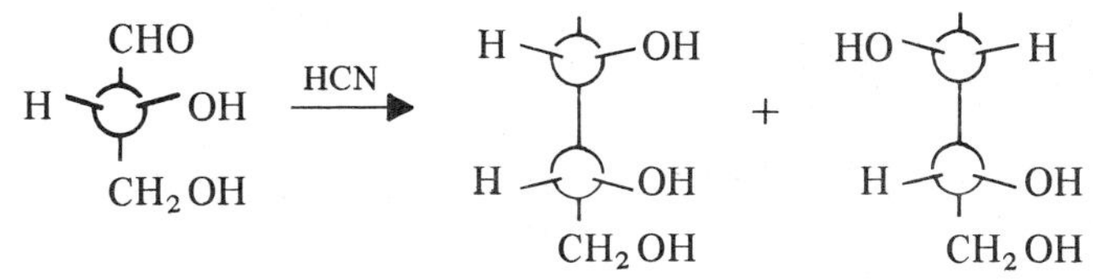

R-(+)-glyceraldehyde $\xrightarrow{HCN}$ M + N   (cf. Problem 18.34e)

N $\xrightarrow[\text{H}_2\text{O}]{\text{H}_2\text{SO}_4}$

COOH
HO—C—H
H—C—OH
CH$_2$OH

$\xrightarrow[\text{HNO}_3]{(\text{O})}$

COOH
HO—C—H
H—C—OH
COOH

$\xrightarrow{\text{PBr}_3}$

COOH
HO—C—H
Br—C—H
COOH

(−)-Tartaric acid

$\xrightarrow[\text{H}^+]{\text{Zn}}$

COOH
HO—C—H
CH$_2$
COOH

(cf. Problem 18.34g)

(b) Replacement of either alcoholic —OH by a reaction that proceeds with inversion produces the same stereoisomer.

COOH
HO—(1)—H
H—(2)—OH
COOH

$\xrightarrow[\substack{\text{(inversion} \\ \text{at C–2)}}]{\text{PBr}_3}$

COOH
HO—C—H
Br—C—H
COOH

$\equiv$

COOH
H—C—Br
H—C—OH
COOH

$\xleftarrow[\substack{\text{(inversion} \\ \text{at C–1)}}]{\text{PBr}_3}$

COOH
HO—(1)—H
H—(2)—OH
COOH

(c) Two. The stereoisomer given in (b) above and the one given below.

COOH
HO—(1)—H
H—(2)—OH
COOH

$\xrightarrow[\substack{\text{(retention} \\ \text{at C–2)}}]{\text{PBr}_3}$

COOH
HO—C—H
H—C—Br
COOH

$\equiv$

COOH
Br—C—H
H—C—OH
COOH

$\xleftarrow[\substack{\text{(retention} \\ \text{at C–1)}}]{\text{PBr}_3}$

COOH
HO—(1)—H
H—(2)—OH
COOH

(d) It would have made no difference because treating either isomer (or both together) with zinc and acid produces (−)-malic acid.

COOH
HO—C—H
Br—C—H
COOH

$\xrightarrow[\text{H}^+]{\text{Zn}}$

COOH
HO—C—H
CH$_2$
COOH

$\equiv$

COOH
HO—C—H
CH$_2$
COOH

$\xleftarrow[\text{H}^+]{\text{Zn}}$

COOH
HO—C—H
H—C—Br
COOH

(−)-Malic acid

18.45   (a) $CH_3O_2C-C\equiv C-CO_2CH_3$. This is a Diels-Alder reaction.

(b) H_2, Pd. The disubstituted double bond is less hindered than the tetrasubstituted double bond and hence is more reactive.

(c) $CH_2=CH-CH=CH_2$. Another Diels-Alder reaction.

(d) $LiAlH_4$

(e) $CH_3\overset{\overset{O}{\|}}{\underset{\underset{O}{\|}}{S}}-Cl$ and pyridine

(f) $CH_3CH_2S^-$

(g) OsO_4

(h)   Raney Ni

(i)   Base. This is an aldol condensation.

(j) C_6H_5Li (or C_6H_5MgBr) followed by H_3O^+

(k) H_3O^+. This is an acid-catalyzed rearrangement of an allylic alcohol.

(l) $CH_3\overset{\overset{O}{\|}}{C}Cl$, pyridine

(m)   Heat. This is an elimination of acetic acid.

(n) O_3 followed by oxidation.

(o)   Heat

18.46

(a)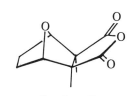

Furan   Dimethylmaleic anhydride

Cantharadin

(b)   Cantharidin apparently undergoes dehydrogenation to the Diels-Alder adduct shown above and then the adduct spontaneously decomposes through a reverse Diels-Alder reaction to furan and dimethylmaleic anhydride. These results suggest that the attempted Diels-Alder synthesis fails because the position of equilibrium favors reactants rather than products.

18.47   That compound **X** does not dissolve in aqueous sodium bicarbonate indicates that **X** is not a carboxylic acid. That **X** has an infrared absorption peak at 1740 cm^{-1} indicates the presence of a carbonyl group, probably that of an ester (Table 18.5). That the molecular formula of **X** ($C_7H_{12}O_4$) contains four oxygen atoms suggests that **X** is a diester.

The ^{13}C spectrum shows only four signals indicating a high degree of symmetry for **X**. The single signal at $\delta 166.7$ is probably that of an ester carbonyl carbon, indicating that both ester groups of **X** are equivalent.

Putting these observations together with the proton off-resonance decoupled spectrum and the molecular formula leads us to the conclusion that **X** is diethyl malonate. The assignments are:

$$\underset{(a)\;(c)\;\;(d)(b)\;\;\;(c)\;\;(a)}{CH_3CH_2\overset{\overset{O}{\|}}{O}CCH_2\overset{\overset{O}{\|}}{C}OCH_2CH_3}$$

(a)   quartet δ 14.2

(b)   triplet δ 41.6

(c)   triplet δ 61.3

(d)   singlet δ 166.7

18.48   The very low hydrogen content of the molecular formula of **Y** ($C_8H_4O_3$) indicates that **Y** is highly unsaturated. That **Y** dissolves slowly in warm aqueous $NaHCO_3$ suggests that **Y** is a carboxylic acid anhydride that hydrolyses, and dissolves because it forms a carboxylate salt:

(insoluble)   (soluble)

The infrared absorption peaks at 1779 cm^{-1} and 1854 cm^{-1} are consistent with those of an aromatic carboxylic anhydride (Table 18.5).

That only four signals appear in the ^{13}C spectrum of **Y** indicates a high degree of symmetry for **Y**. Three of the signals occur in the aromatic region ($\delta 120-\delta 140$) and one signal is downfield ($\delta 163.1$).

These signals and their splitting patterns in the proton off-resonance decoupled spectrum lead us to conclude that **Y** is phthalic anhydride. The assignments are:

(a)   doublet δ 125.3

(b)   singlet δ 131.1

(c)   doublet δ 136.1

(d)   singlet δ 163.1

SECTION REFERENCES FOR ADDITIONAL PROBLEMS

18.21	18.2	**18.35**	16.9, 17.6, 18.3, 18.7c, 18.8
18.22	18.2	**18.36**	18.2I, 18.7B
18.23	18.3	**18.37**	18.2I
18.24	18.3	**18.38**	18.8
18.25	18.3	**18.39**	18.2C
18.26	18.13B	**18.40**	18.2C
18.27	18.13C	**18.41**	7.14
18.28	18.13C	**18.42**	18.7C
18.29	12.12, 14.12	**18.43**	8.12, 8.13, 18.13
18.30	18.13D	**18.44**	8.12, 8.13, 18.13
18.31	18.13E	**18.45**	10.10, 15.7, 15.9B, 7.13A, 17.7
18.32	18.12	**18.46**	10.10
18.33	18.7, 18.13A	**18.47**	18.2C, 18.2I
18.34	8.12, 8.13, 18.3	**18.48**	18.2C, 18.2I

SELF-TEST

18.1   Give an acceptable name for each of the following compounds.

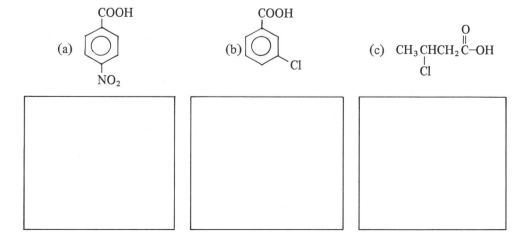

18.2   Use the letters of the appropriate compounds below to answer the following questions.

(a)   The least reactive carboxylic acid derivative toward nucleophilic substitution at the acyl carbon is ▢ .

(b)   The most readily hydrolyzed compound is ▢

(c)   Besides RCOOH itself, the only carboxylic acid derivative that can be prepared directly from all of the others is ▢

A. CH_3COOH

B. CH_3COCl

C. $CH_3COOC_2H_5$

D. CH_3CONH_2

E. $CH_3-\overset{\overset{O}{\|}}{C}-O-\overset{\overset{O}{\|}}{C}-CH_3$

18.3   Supply the structural formula of the missing reactant, reagent, or major product. Show stereochemistry where appropriate. More than one step may be needed.

(a)   *ortho*-Bromotoluene $\xrightarrow[\text{heat}]{\text{KMnO}_4, \text{OH}^-}$ ▢

(b)   ▢ $\xrightarrow[\text{dry ether}]{\text{Mg}}$ $\xrightarrow{\text{CO}_2}$ $\xrightarrow{\text{H}_3\text{O}^+}$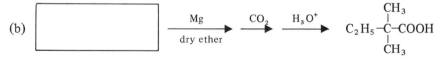

(c)   Butyric acid $\xrightarrow{\text{SOCl}_2}$ ▢

(d)   Benzoic acid + ▢ $\longrightarrow$ Benzoyl chloride

(e)   *m*-Toluic acid + ▢ $\longrightarrow$ *m*-Methylbenzyl alcohol

(f)   Phthalic acid $\xrightarrow{200°}$ ▢

(g)   Ethyl butyrate + $NH_3 \longrightarrow$ ▢ + ▢

(h)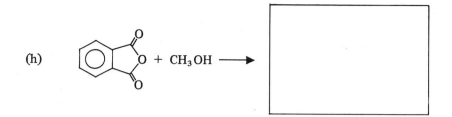

(i) $HOCH_2CH_2CH_2\overset{O}{\overset{\|}{C}}-OH$ $\xrightarrow{H^+}$

(j) [benzene ring]—Cl $\longrightarrow$ [benzene ring]—$\overset{O}{\overset{\|}{C}}$—OH

(k) [benzene ring]—$\underset{OH}{CHCH_2CH_2}\overset{O}{\overset{\|}{C}}$—OH $\xrightarrow[\text{heat}]{H^+}$

(l) [phthalic anhydride] + NH_3(excess) $\xrightarrow[\text{(2) } H_3O^+]{\text{(1) } H_2O, \text{ warm}}$

(m) [phthalic anhydride] + [benzene ring] $\xrightarrow{AlCl_3}$

(n) [   ] $+ (CH_3)_2 NH \xrightarrow{25°}$ [benzene ring]$-\overset{\displaystyle O}{\overset{\displaystyle \|}{C}}-N(CH_3)_2$

18.4   What reagent would distinguish between the compounds in each of the following pairs?

(a) CH_3O-[benzene ring]$-\overset{\displaystyle O}{\overset{\displaystyle \|}{C}}-OH$ and $HO-$[benzene ring]$-\overset{\displaystyle O}{\overset{\displaystyle \|}{C}}-OCH_3$ [   ]

(b) [benzene ring]$-\overset{\displaystyle O}{\overset{\displaystyle \|}{C}}-NH_2$ and [benzene ring]$-\overset{\displaystyle O}{\overset{\displaystyle \|}{C}}-OH$ [   ]

SOME INTERCONVERSIONS OF FUNCTIONAL GROUPS

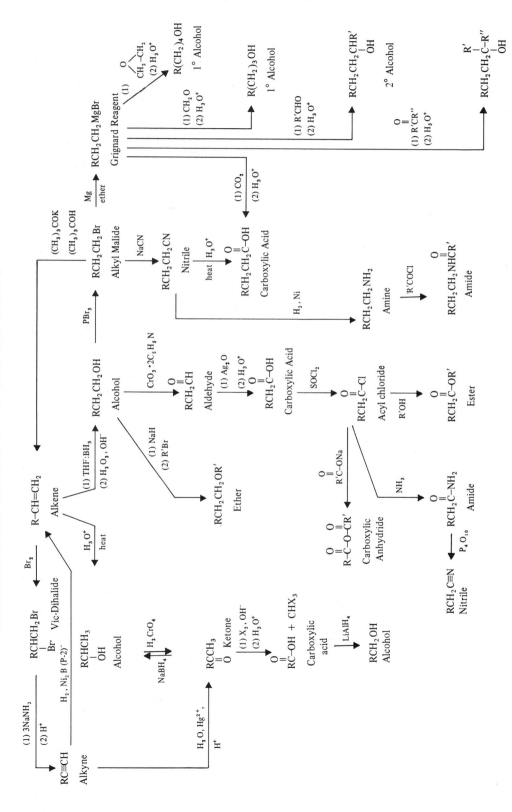

SPECIAL TOPIC
Condensation Polymers

SOLUTIONS TO PROBLEMS

J.1

(a)
$$\text{cyclohexanone} \xrightarrow[\text{H}_2\text{Cr}_2\text{O}_7]{\text{(O)}} \text{HOOC(CH}_2)_4\text{COOH}$$

(b) $\text{HOOC(CH}_2)_4\text{COOH} + 2\text{NH}_3 \longrightarrow \text{NH}_4\text{OOC(CH}_2)_4\text{COONH}_4$

$$\xrightarrow[-2\text{H}_2\text{O}]{\text{heat}} \text{H}_2\overset{\text{O}}{\overset{\|}{\text{N}\text{C}}}(\text{CH}_2)_4\overset{\text{O}}{\overset{\|}{\text{C}}}\text{NH}_2 \xrightarrow[\text{catalyst}]{350°} \text{N}\equiv\text{C(CH}_2)_4\text{C}\equiv\text{N}$$

$$\xrightarrow[\text{catalyst}]{4\text{H}_2} \text{H}_2\text{NCH}_2(\text{CH}_2)_4\text{CH}_2\text{NH}_2$$

(c) $\text{CH}_2=\text{CH}-\text{CH}=\text{CH}_2 \xrightarrow{\text{Cl}_2} \text{ClCH}_2\text{CH}=\text{CHCH}_2\text{Cl} \xrightarrow{2\text{NaCN}}$

$$\text{N}\equiv\text{CCH}_2\text{CH}=\text{CHCH}_2\text{C}\equiv\text{N} \xrightarrow[\text{Ni}]{\text{H}_2} \text{N}\equiv\text{C(CH}_2)_4\text{C}\equiv\text{N}$$

$$\xrightarrow[\text{catalyst}]{4\text{H}_2} \text{H}_2\text{NCH}_2(\text{CH}_2)_4\text{CH}_2\text{NH}_2$$

(d)
$$\text{tetrahydrofuran} \xrightarrow{2\text{HCl}} \text{ClCH}_2\text{CH}_2\text{CH}_2\text{CH}_2\text{Cl} \xrightarrow{2\text{NaCN}}$$

$$\text{N}\equiv\text{C(CH}_2)_4\text{C}\equiv\text{N} \xrightarrow[\text{catalyst}]{4\text{H}_2} \text{H}_2\text{NCH}_2(\text{CH}_2)_4\text{CH}_2\text{NH}_2$$

J.2 (a) $\text{HOCH}_2\text{CH}_2\text{OH} + {}^-:\text{B} \rightleftarrows \text{HOCH}_2\text{CH}_2\text{O}^- + \text{HB}$

$$\text{RO}\overset{\text{O}}{\overset{\|}{\text{C}}}\!\!-\!\!\bigcirc\!\!-\!\!\overset{\text{O}}{\overset{\|}{\text{C}}}\text{OCH}_3 + {}^-\text{OCH}_2\text{CH}_2\text{OH} \rightleftarrows$$

$$\text{RO}\overset{\text{O}}{\overset{\|}{\text{C}}}\!\!-\!\!\bigcirc\!\!-\!\!\underset{\text{OCH}_3}{\overset{\text{O}^-}{\overset{|}{\text{C}}}}\!\!-\!\!\text{OCH}_2\text{CH}_2\text{OH} \rightleftarrows \text{RO}\overset{\text{O}}{\overset{\|}{\text{C}}}\!\!-\!\!\bigcirc\!\!-\!\!\overset{\text{O}}{\overset{\|}{\text{C}}}\text{OCH}_2\text{CH}_2\text{OH}$$

$$+ \text{CH}_3\text{O}^-$$

$$\text{CH}_3\text{O}^- + \text{HB} \rightleftarrows \text{CH}_3\text{OH} + :\text{B}^-$$

$\text{R} = \text{CH}_3-$ or $\text{HOCH}_2\text{CH}_2-$

(b)

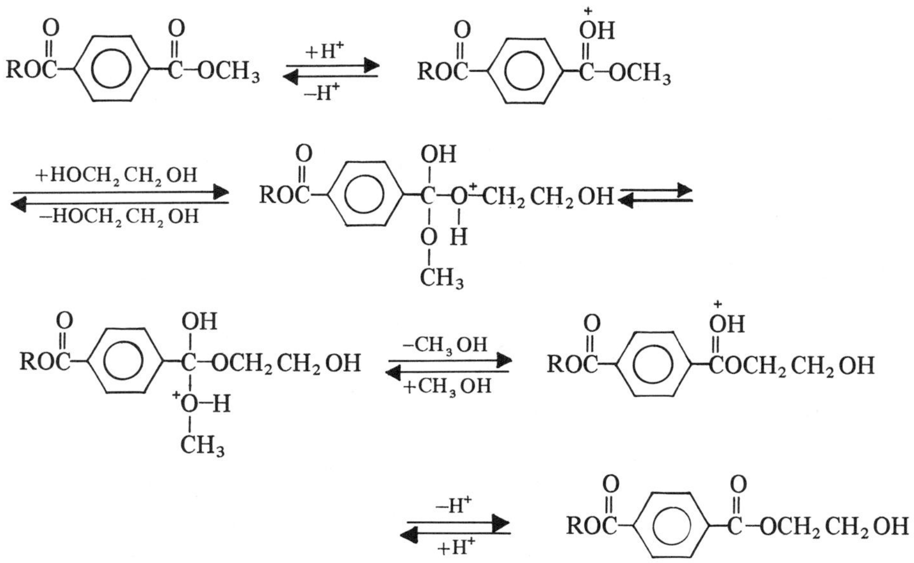

$R = CH_3-$ or $HOCH_2CH_2-$

J.3

(a)

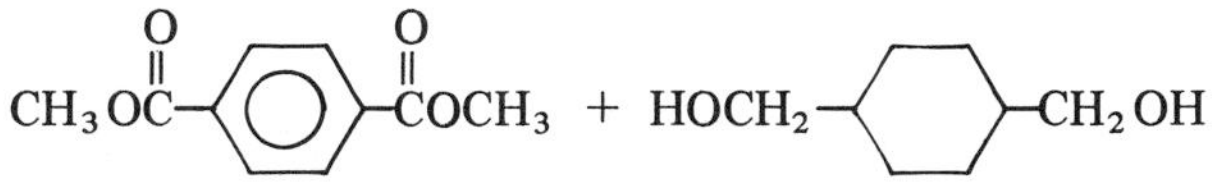

(b) By high-pressure catalytic hydrogenation

J.4

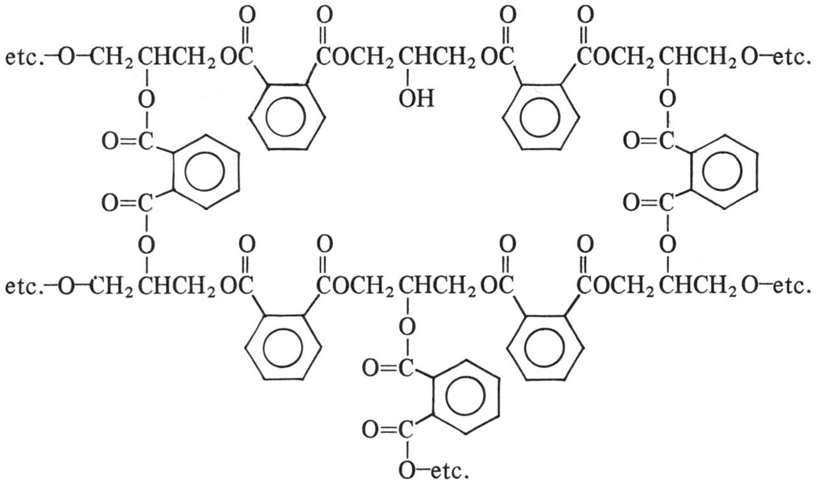

J.5

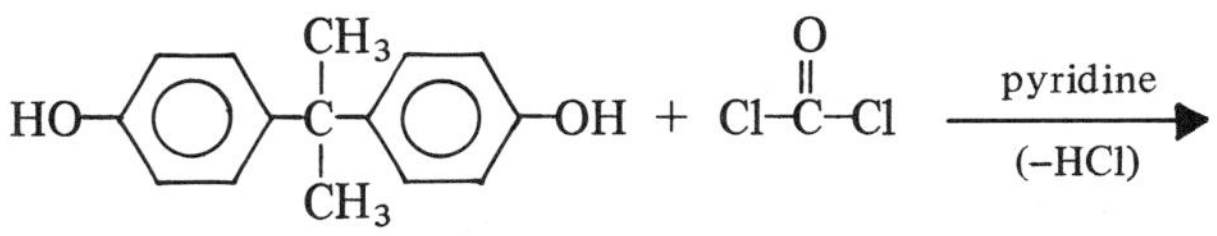

Lexan

J.6   (a)   The resin is probably formed in the following way. Base converts the bisphenol A to a phenoxide ion that attacks a carbon of the epoxide ring of epichlorohydrin:

$$ClCH_2CH{-}CH_2 \; + \; {}^-O{-}[ring]{-}C(CH_3)_2{-}[ring]{-}O^- \; + \; CH_2{-}CHCH_2Cl \longrightarrow$$

$$Cl{-}CH_2{-}CH{-}CH_2{-}O{-}[ring]{-}C(CH_3)_2{-}[ring]{-}OCH_2{-}CH{-}CH_2{-}Cl$$
$$\underset{O^-}{\qquad} \qquad\qquad\qquad \underset{O^-}{\qquad}$$

$$\xrightarrow{-2Cl^-} \; CH_2{-}CHCH_2O{-}[ring]{-}C(CH_3)_2{-}[ring]{-}OCH_2CH{-}CH_2$$
$$\underset{O}{\qquad} \qquad\qquad\qquad\qquad \underset{O}{\qquad}$$

$$^-O{-}[ring]{-}C(CH_3)_2{-}[ring]{-}O^- \qquad CH_2{-}CHCH_2Cl \;(O)$$

$$\xrightarrow{\qquad} then \xrightarrow{\qquad}$$

$$CH_2{-}CHCH_2{-}\left[O{-}[ring]{-}C(CH_3)_2{-}[ring]{-}OCH_2CHCH_2\right]_n{-}O{-}[ring]{-}C(CH_3)_2{-}[ring]{-}OCH_2CH{-}CH_2$$
$$\underset{O}{\qquad}\qquad\qquad\qquad\qquad \underset{OH}{\qquad}\qquad\qquad\qquad\qquad\qquad \underset{O}{\qquad}$$

(b)   The excess of epichlorohydrin limits the molecular weight and insures that the resin has epoxy ends.

(c)   Adding the hardener brings about cross linking by reacting at the terminal epoxide groups of the resin:

$$H_2NCH_2CH_2NHCH_2CH_2NH_2 \; + \; CH_2{-}CHCH_2{-}[polymer]{-}CH_2CH{-}CH_2 \longrightarrow$$
$$\qquad\qquad\qquad\qquad\qquad\qquad\qquad \underset{O}{\qquad}\qquad\qquad\qquad\qquad \underset{O}{\qquad}$$

$$-CH_2{-}CHCH_2{-}NCH_2CH_2{-}N{-}CH_2CH_2{-}N{-}CH_2CHCH_2\,[polymer]\,CH_2CHCH_2{-}etc.$$
$$\underset{OH}{\quad}\quad \underset{H}{\quad}\quad\; \underset{CH_2}{\quad}\quad\; \underset{H}{\quad}\; \underset{OH}{\quad}\qquad\qquad \underset{OH}{\quad}$$
$$\qquad\qquad\qquad\qquad\qquad\quad CHOH$$
$$\qquad\qquad\qquad\qquad\qquad\quad CH_2$$
$$\qquad\qquad\qquad\qquad\quad [polymer]$$
$$\qquad\qquad\qquad\qquad\qquad\quad CH_2$$
$$\qquad\qquad\qquad\qquad\qquad\quad CHOH$$
$$\qquad\qquad\qquad\qquad\qquad\quad CH_2 \qquad\qquad\qquad\qquad etc.$$
$$N{-}CH_2CH_2N{-}CH_2CH_2{-}N{-}CH_2CHCH_2\,[polymer]\,CH_2CHCH_2$$
$$\underset{H}{\quad}\qquad \underset{H}{\quad}\qquad \underset{H}{\quad}\; \underset{OH}{\quad}\qquad\qquad \underset{OH}{\quad}$$

J.7

(a)

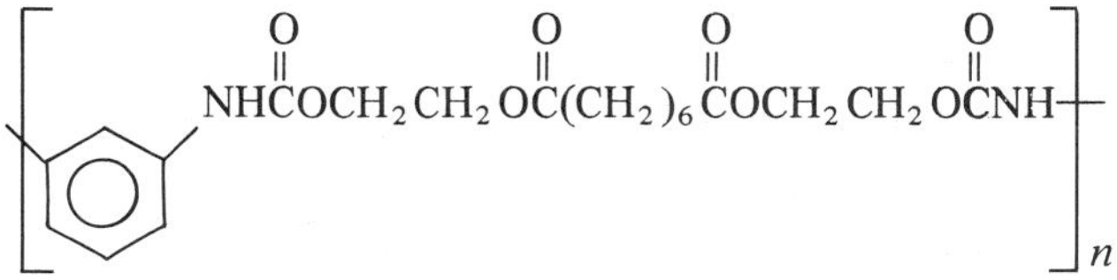

$$\left[\begin{array}{c} \\ \\ \end{array} NHCOCH_2CH_2OC(CH_2)_6COCH_2CH_2OCNH \right]_n$$

(b) To ensure that the polyester chain has $-CH_2OH$ end groups.

J.8   Because the para position is occupied by a methyl group, cross linking does not occur and the resulting polymer remains thermoplastic. (See page 832–833 of text.)

J.9

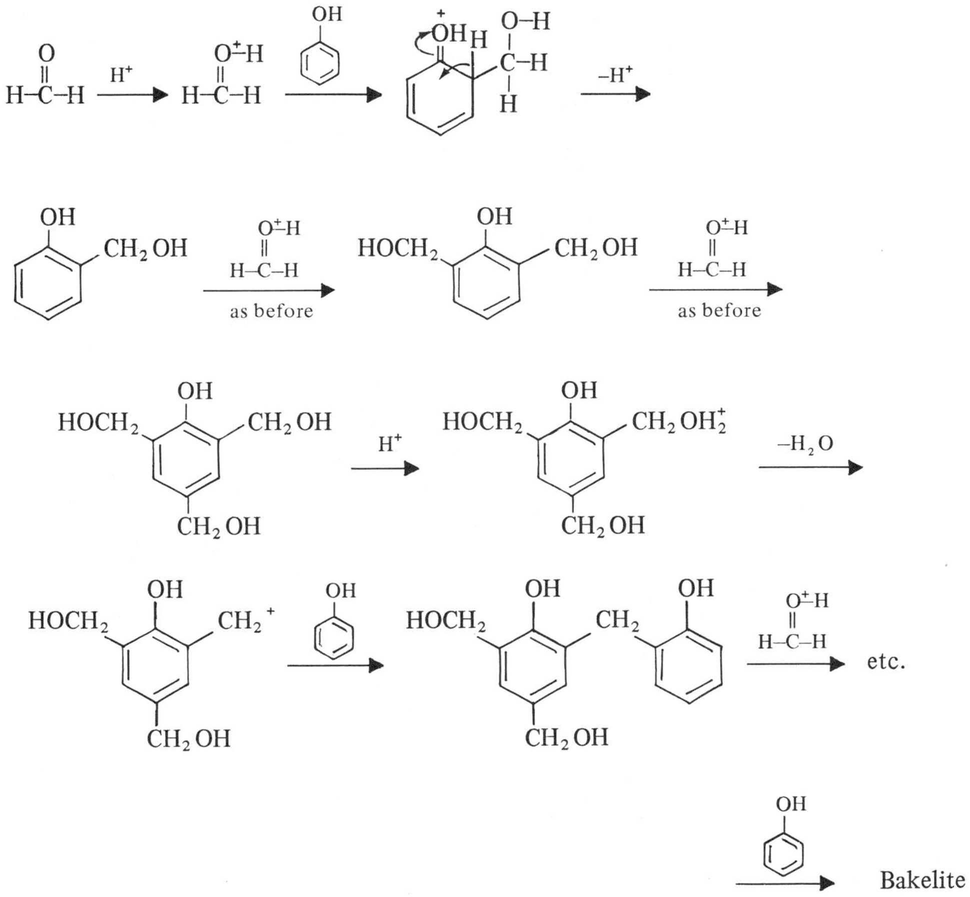

$$H\overset{O}{\underset{}{\overset{\|}{C}}}H \xrightarrow{H^+} H\overset{\overset{+}{O}H}{\underset{}{\overset{\|}{C}}}H \longrightarrow \longrightarrow \xrightarrow{-H^+}$$

CH₂ structures continuing:

$$\xrightarrow[\text{as before}]{\overset{\overset{+}{O}H}{\overset{\|}{\underset{}{C}}}{H-C-H}} \quad \xrightarrow[\text{as before}]{\overset{\overset{+}{O}H}{\overset{\|}{\underset{}{C}}}{H-C-H}}$$

$$\xrightarrow{H^+} \quad \xrightarrow{-H_2O}$$

$$\xrightarrow{} \quad \xrightarrow[\text{H-C-H}]{\overset{\overset{+}{O}H}{\|}} \text{etc.}$$

$$\xrightarrow{} \text{Bakelite}$$

19 AMINES

PREPARATION AND REACTIONS OF AMINES

A. Preparation

(1) Preparation via Nucleophilic Substitution Reactions

$$RCH_2-N_3 \xrightarrow[\text{or LiAlH}_4]{\text{Na/alcohol}} RCH_2NH_2$$

$$RCH_2-N \xrightarrow{NH_2NH_2} RCH_2NH_2 +$$

$$RCH_2Br \xrightarrow{NH_3} RCH_2NH_2 + (RCH_2)_2NH + (RCH_2)_3N \quad \text{(poor method)}$$

(2) Preparation through Reduction of Nitro Compounds

$$\text{benzene} \xrightarrow[\text{H}_2\text{SO}_4]{\text{HNO}_3} \text{NO}_2 \xrightarrow[\text{HCl}]{\text{Fe}} \text{NH}_2$$

(3) Preparation via Reductive Amination

$$\begin{array}{c} R \\ C=O \\ R' \end{array} + NH_3 \xrightarrow{H_2, Ni} \begin{array}{c} R-CHNH_2 \\ | \\ R' \end{array}$$

(4) Preparation of Amines through Reduction of Amides, Oximes, and Nitriles

$$R-CH_2Br \xrightarrow{CN^-} RCH_2CN \xrightarrow{H_2, Ni} RCH_2NH_2$$

$$\begin{array}{c} R \\ C=O \\ R' \end{array} \xrightarrow{NH_2OH} \begin{array}{c} R \\ C=NOH \\ R' \end{array} \xrightarrow{Na/C_2H_5OH} \begin{array}{c} R-CHNH_2 \\ | \\ R' \end{array}$$

$$R-NH_2 + R'\overset{O}{\overset{\|}{C}}Cl \longrightarrow R-NH\overset{O}{\overset{\|}{C}}R' \xrightarrow[(2)\ H_2O]{(1)\ LiAlH_4} RNHCH_2R'$$

(5) Preparation through the Hofmann Degradation of Amides

$$R-\overset{O}{\overset{\|}{C}}OH \xrightarrow{SOCl_2} R\overset{O}{\overset{\|}{C}}Cl \xrightarrow{NH_3} R\overset{O}{\overset{\|}{C}}NH_2 \xrightarrow[(NaOBr)]{Br_2/NaOH} RNH_2 + CO_3^{2-}$$

B. Reactions of Amines

(1) As a Base or a Nucleophile

   As a base

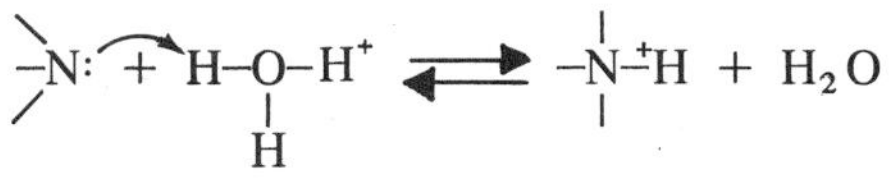

   As a nucleophile in alkylation

   As a nucleophile in acylation

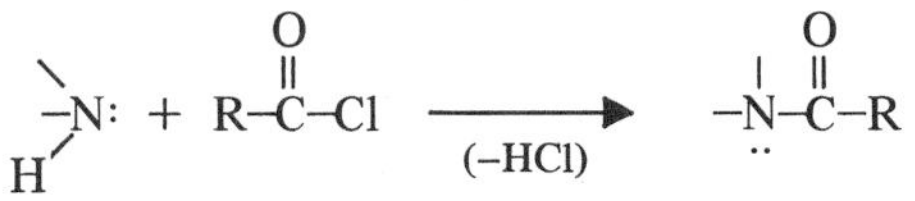

(2) With Nitrous Acid

$$R-NH_2 \xrightarrow[HX]{HONO} R-N_2^+ X^- \xrightarrow{-N_2} R^+ \longrightarrow \text{Alkenes, alcohols, etc.}$$

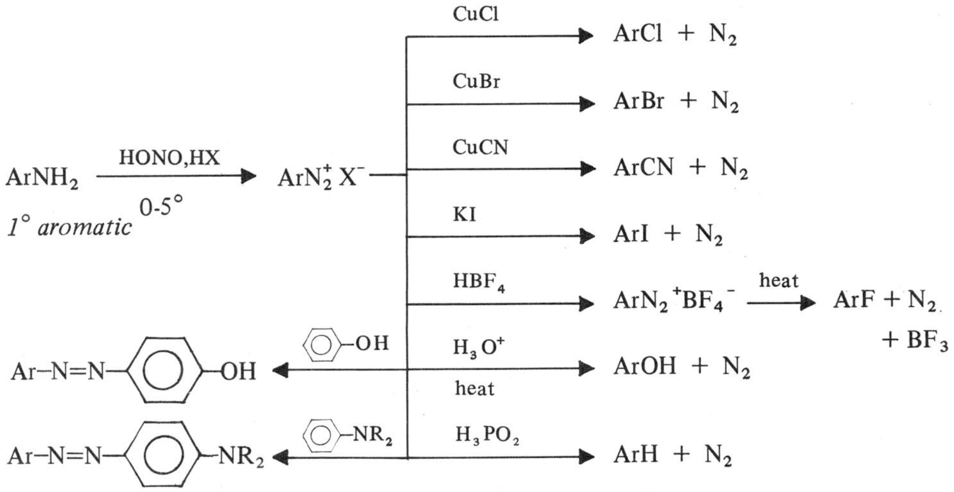

1° aliphatic   (unstable)

$$R_2NH \xrightarrow{\text{HONO}} R_2N-N=O$$

2° aliphatic

$$ArNHR \xrightarrow{\text{HONO}} \underset{\text{Ar}\overset{|}{N}-R}{\overset{N=O}{}}$$

2° aromatic

$$R_3N \xrightarrow{\text{HX, NaNO}_2} R_3NH^+X^- + R_3\overset{+}{N}-N=O\ X^-$$

3° aliphatic

$$R_2N-\langle\bigcirc\rangle \xrightarrow{\text{HONO}} R_2N-\langle\bigcirc\rangle-N=O$$

3° aromatic

(3) With Sulfonyl Chlorides

$$R-NH_2 + ArSO_2Cl \xrightarrow[(-HCl)]{} RNHSO_2Ar \underset{H^+}{\overset{OH^-}{\rightleftarrows}} \left[RNSO_2Ar\right]^- + H_2O$$

1° amine

$$R_2NH + ArSO_2Cl \xrightarrow[(-HCl)]{} R_2NSO_2Ar$$

2° amine

(4) The Hofmann Elimination

$$HO^- + \underset{\underset{+}{N(CH_3)_3}}{-\overset{\overset{H}{|}}{\underset{|}{C}}-\overset{|}{\underset{|}{C}}-} \xrightarrow{\text{heat}} \rangle C=C\langle + (CH_3)_3N + H_2O$$

SOLUTIONS TO PROBLEMS

19.1   Dissolve both compounds in ether and extract with aqueous HCl. This procedure gives an ether layer that contains cyclohexane and an aqueous layer that contains cyclohexylammonium chloride. Cyclohexane may then be recovered from the ether layer by distillation. Cyclohexylamine may be recovered from the aqueous layer by adding aqueous NaOH (to convert cyclohexylammonium chloride to cyclohexylamine) and then by ether extraction and distillation

$$C_6H_{12} + C_6H_{11}NH_2$$
(in ether)

$H_3O^+Cl^-/H_2O$

ether layer   aqueous layer

C_6H_{12} $C_6H_{11}NH_3{}^+Cl^- \xrightarrow{OH^-} C_6H_{11}NH_2$
(evaporate ether   (extract into ether
and distill)   and distill)

19.2   We begin by dissolving the mixture in a water-immiscible organic solvent such as CH_2Cl_2 or ether. Then, extractions with aqueous acids and bases allow us to separate the components. (We separate p-cresol from benzoic acid by taking advantage of benzoic acid's solubility in the more weakly basic aqueous $NaHCO_3$, whereas, p-cresol requires the more strongly basic, aqueous NaOH).

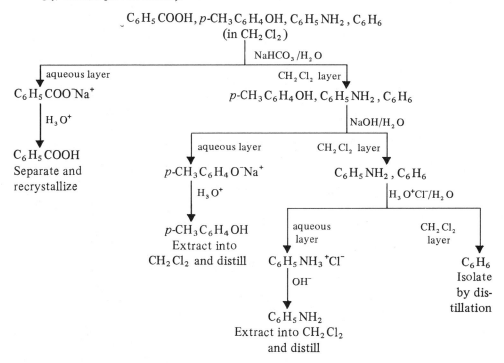

$$C_6H_5COOH, p\text{-}CH_3C_6H_4OH, C_6H_5NH_2, C_6H_6$$
$$(\text{in } CH_2Cl_2)$$

$NaHCO_3/H_2O$

aqueous layer

$C_6H_5COO^-Na^+$

H_3O^+

C_6H_5COOH
Separate and
recrystallize

CH_2Cl_2 layer

$p\text{-}CH_3C_6H_4OH, C_6H_5NH_2, C_6H_6$

$NaOH/H_2O$

aqueous layer

$p\text{-}CH_3C_6H_4O^-Na^+$

H_3O^+

$p\text{-}CH_3C_6H_4OH$
Extract into
CH_2Cl_2 and distill

CH_2Cl_2 layer

$C_6H_5NH_2, C_6H_6$

$H_3O^+Cl^-/H_2O$

aqueous
layer

$C_6H_5NH_3^+Cl^-$

OH^-

$C_6H_5NH_2$
Extract into CH_2Cl_2
and distill

CH_2Cl_2
layer

C_6H_6
Isolate
by dis-
tillation

19.3   (a) Neglecting Kekule forms of the ring, we can write the following resonance structures for the phthalimide anion.

(b) Phthalimide is more acidic than benzamide because its anion is stabilized by resononace to a greater extent than the anion of benzamide. (Benzamide has only one carbonyl group attached to the nitrogen and thus fewer resonance contributors are possible.)

19.4

$\xrightarrow{\text{KOH}}$

$\xrightarrow[(-\text{KBr})]{C_6H_5CH_2Br}$

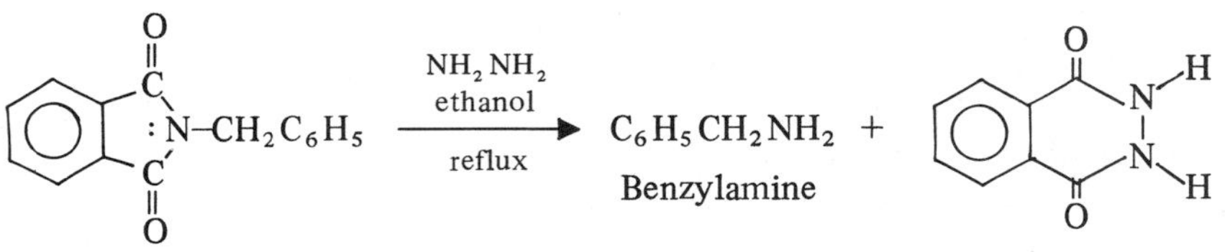

19.5

(a) $CH_3(CH_2)_3CHO + NH_3 \xrightarrow{H_2,\ Ni} CH_3(CH_2)_3CH_2NH_2$

(b) $C_6H_5\overset{\displaystyle O}{\overset{\|}{C}}CH_3 + NH_3 \xrightarrow{H_2,\ Ni} C_6H_5\underset{\displaystyle NH_2}{\underset{|}{C}}HCH_3$

(c) $CH_3(CH_2)_4CHO + C_6H_5NH_2 \xrightarrow[CH_3OH]{LiBH_3CN} CH_3(CH_2)_4CH_2NHC_6H_5$

19.6 The reaction of a secondary halide with ammonia would inevitably be accompanied by considerable elimination thus decreasing the yield.

$$R\overset{\displaystyle R'}{\overset{|}{C}}H\text{—}X + \underset{\text{excess}}{NH_3} \xrightarrow{\text{Substitution}} R\overset{\displaystyle R'}{\overset{|}{C}}HNH_2$$

$$R\overset{\displaystyle R'}{\overset{|}{C}}H\text{—}X + \underset{\text{excess}}{NH_3} \xrightarrow{\text{Elimination}} \text{alkene}$$

19.7

(a) $C_6H_5COOH \xrightarrow{SOCl_2} C_6H_5COCl \xrightarrow{CH_3CH_2NH_2}$

$C_6H_5CONHCH_2CH_3 \xrightarrow{LiAlH_4} C_6H_5CH_2NHCH_2CH_3$

(b) $CH_3CH_2CH_2CH_2CH_2Br \xrightarrow{NaCN} CH_3CH_2CH_2CH_2CH_2CN$

$\xrightarrow{LiAlH_4} CH_3CH_2CH_2CH_2CH_2CH_2NH_2$

(c) $CH_3CH_2COOH \xrightarrow{SOCl_2} CH_3CH_2COCl \xrightarrow{(CH_3CH_2CH_2)_2NH}$

$CH_3CH_2CON(CH_2CH_2CH_3)_2 \xrightarrow{LiAlH_4} (CH_3CH_2CH_2)_3N$

(d) $CH_3\overset{\displaystyle O}{\overset{\|}{C}}CH_2CH_3 \xrightarrow{NH_2OH} CH_3\overset{\displaystyle NOH}{\overset{\|}{C}}CH_2CH_3 \xrightarrow{Na/C_2H_5OH} CH_3\overset{\displaystyle NH_2}{\overset{|}{C}}HCH_2CH_3$

19.8

(a) 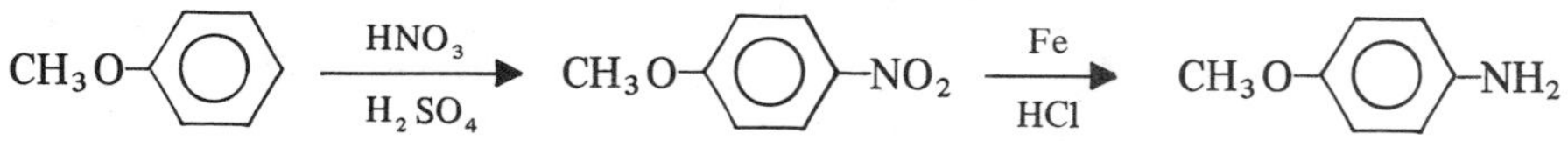

(b) $CH_3O-\langle\bigcirc\rangle$ $\xrightarrow[\text{AlCl}_3]{\text{CH}_3\text{COCl}}$ $CH_3O-\langle\bigcirc\rangle-\overset{\overset{O}{\|}}{C}CH_3$ $\xrightarrow[\text{H}_2,\text{Pt}]{\text{NH}_3}$

$$CH_3O-\langle\bigcirc\rangle-\underset{\underset{NH_2}{|}}{C}HCH_3$$

(c) $\langle\bigcirc\rangle-CH_3$ $\xrightarrow{\text{Cl}_2,\text{h}\nu}$ $\langle\bigcirc\rangle-CH_2Cl$ $\xrightarrow{(\text{CH}_3)_3\text{N}}$ $\langle\bigcirc\rangle-CH_2\overset{+}{N}(CH_3)_3Cl^-$

(d) $O_2N-\langle\bigcirc\rangle-CH_3$ $\xrightarrow[\text{(2) H}_3\text{O}^+]{\text{(1) KMnO}_4,\text{OH}^-}$ $NO_2-\langle\bigcirc\rangle-COOH$ $\xrightarrow{\text{SOCl}_2}$

$O_2N-\langle\bigcirc\rangle-\overset{\overset{O}{\|}}{C}-Cl$ $\xrightarrow{\text{NH}_3}$ $NO_2-\langle\bigcirc\rangle-\overset{\overset{O}{\|}}{C}NH_2$ $\xrightarrow{\text{Br}_2,\text{OH}^-}$ $NO_2-\langle\bigcirc\rangle-NH_2$

(e) $CH_3-\langle\bigcirc\rangle$ + NBS $\xrightarrow{\text{ROOR}}$ $\langle\bigcirc\rangle-CH_2Br$ $\xrightarrow{\text{KCN}}$

$$\langle\bigcirc\rangle-CH_2CN \xrightarrow{\text{LiAlH}_4} \langle\bigcirc\rangle-CH_2CH_2NH_2$$

19.9 An amine acting as a base.

$$CH_3CH_2\overset{..}{N}H_2 + H_3O^+ \rightleftarrows CH_3CH_2NH_3^+ + H_2O$$

An amine acting as a nucleophile in an alkylation reaction.

$$(CH_3CH_2)_3N:\, + CH_3-I \longrightarrow (CH_3CH_2)_3\overset{+}{N}-CH_3I^-$$

An amine acting as a nucleophile in an acylation reaction.

$$(CH_3)_2\overset{..}{N}H + CH_3\overset{\overset{O}{/\!/}}{C}{\underset{Cl}{\diagdown}} \longrightarrow (CH_3)_2N\overset{\overset{O}{\|}}{C}CH_3 + (CH_3)_2NH_2Cl$$
$$\text{(excess)}$$

An amino group acting as an activating group and as an ortho-para director in electrophilic aromatic substitution.

$$\overset{NH_2}{\underset{}{\langle\bigcirc\rangle}} \xrightarrow[\substack{\text{H}_2\text{O}\\\text{room temp.}}]{\text{Br}_2} \overset{NH_2}{\underset{Br}{\underset{}{Br\langle\bigcirc\rangle Br}}}$$

19.10

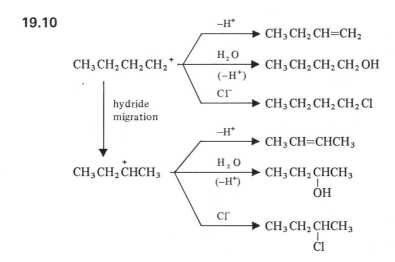

19.11 (a) $^-O-N=O + H_3O^+ \rightleftharpoons HO-N=O + H_2O$

$HO-N=O + H_3O^+ \rightleftharpoons HO^{\pm}_{\underset{H}{|}}N=O + H_2O$

$HO^{\pm}_{\underset{H}{|}}N=O \rightleftharpoons H_2O + \overset{+}{N}=O$

(c)   The $\overset{+}{N}O$ ion is a weak electrophile. For it to react with an aromatic ring, the ring must have a powerful activating group such as $-OH$ or $-NR_2$.

19.12

(a)   benzene $\xrightarrow[\substack{H_2SO_4 \\ heat}]{\text{fuming } HNO_3}$ 1,3-dinitrobenzene (NO$_2$) $\xrightarrow[\text{(2) OH}^-]{\text{(1) Fe, HCl, heat}}$ benzene-1,3-diamine (NH$_2$)

(b)   1,3-dinitrobenzene $\xrightarrow[\substack{NH_3, C_2H_5OH}]{H_2S}$ 3-nitroaniline (NO$_2$, NH$_2$)

(from part a)

(c)

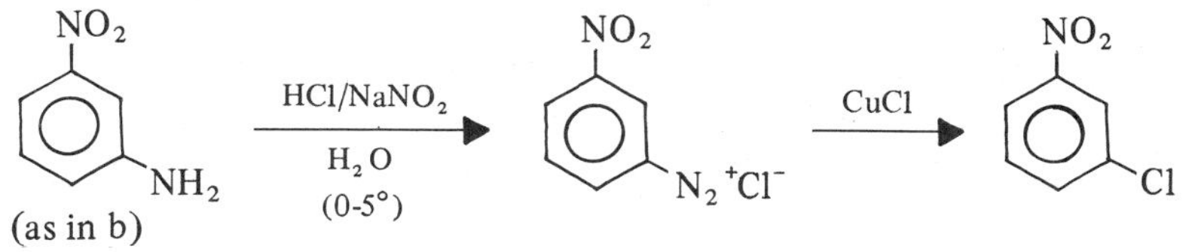
NO2
NH2
(as in b)
HCl/NaNO2
H2O
(0-5°)
NO2
N2+Cl−
CuCl
NO2
Cl

(d)

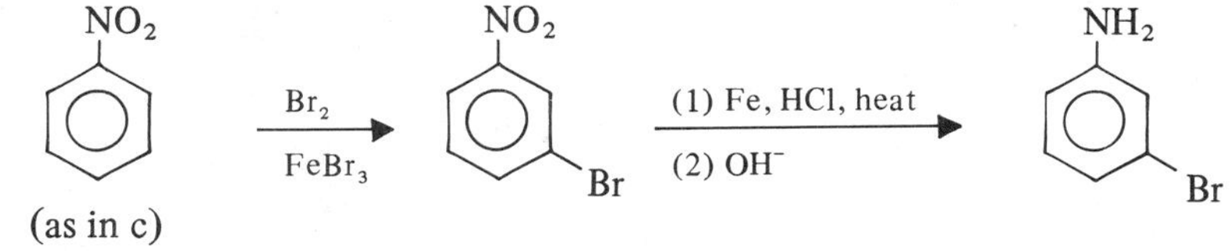
NO2
(as in c)
Br2
FeBr3
NO2
Br
(1) Fe, HCl, heat
(2) OH−
NH2
Br

(e)

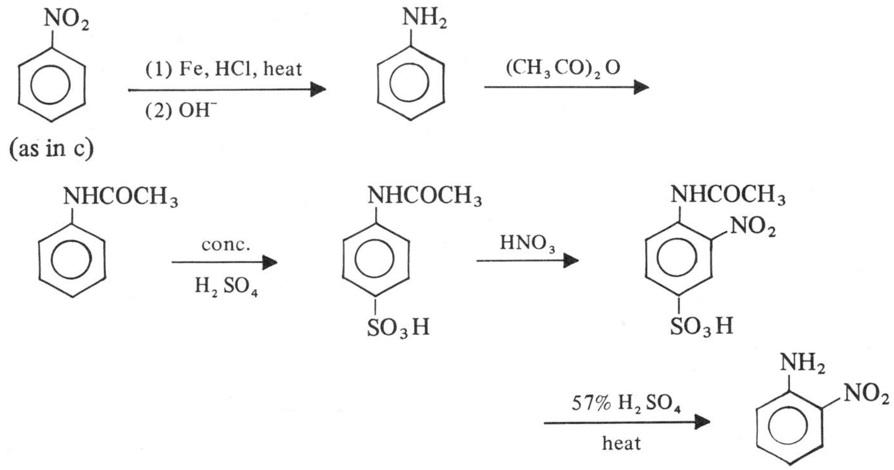
NO2
(as in c)
(1) Fe, HCl, heat
(2) OH−
NH2
(CH3CO)2O
NHCOCH3
conc.
H2SO4
NHCOCH3
SO3H
HNO3
NHCOCH3
NO2
SO3H
57% H2SO4
heat
NH2
NO2

(f)

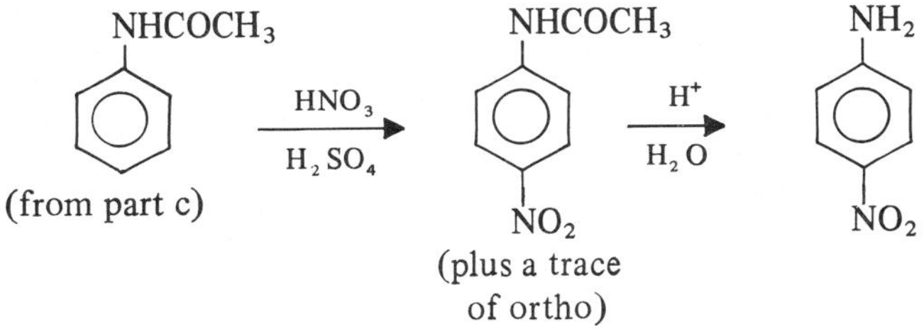
NHCOCH3
(from part c)
HNO3
H2SO4
NHCOCH3
NO2
(plus a trace
of ortho)
H+
H2O
NH2
NO2

19.13

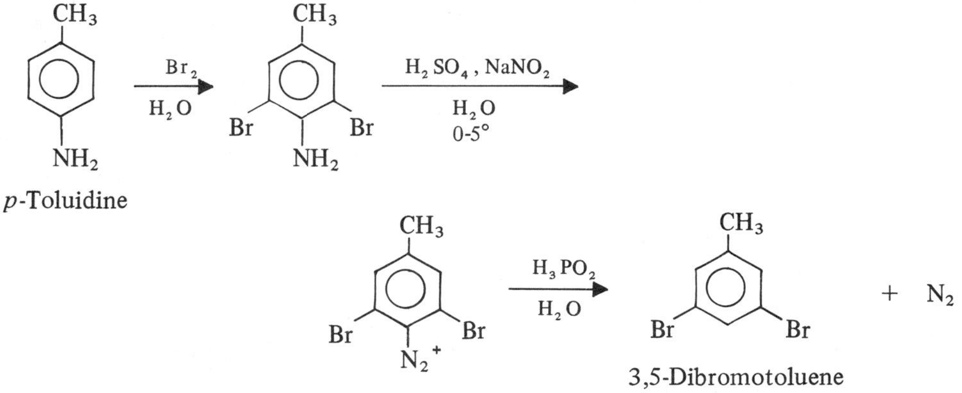
CH3
NH2
p-Toluidine
Br2
H2O
CH3
Br
Br
NH2
H2SO4, NaNO2
H2O
0-5°
CH3
Br
Br
N2+
H3PO2
H2O
CH3
Br
Br
3,5-Dibromotoluene
+ N2

19.14 (a) Toluene $\xrightarrow[\text{H}_2\text{SO}_4]{\text{HNO}_3}$ *p*-Nitrotoluene $\xrightarrow[\text{(2) OH}^-]{\text{(1) Fe, HCl}}$
(+ *o*-nitrotoluene)

(b) CuCl

(c) CuBr

(d) KI

(e) CuCN

(f) $\xrightarrow[\text{H}_2\text{O}]{\text{H}^+}$

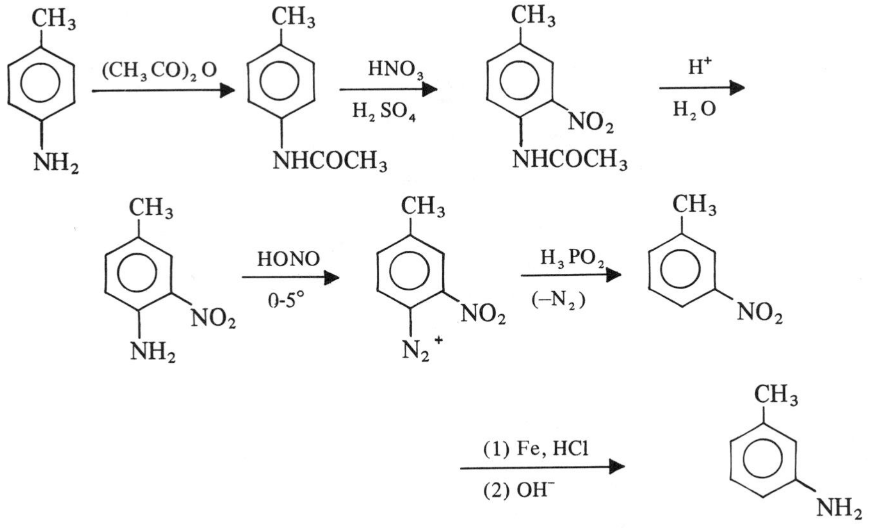

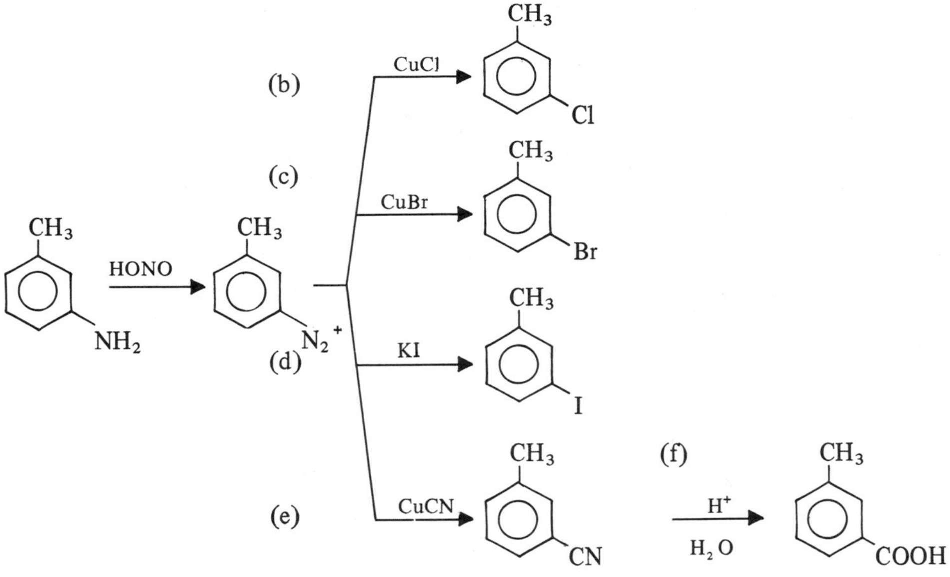

19.15

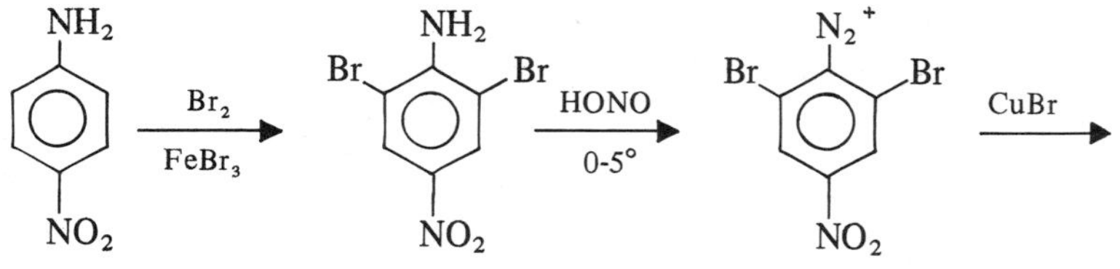

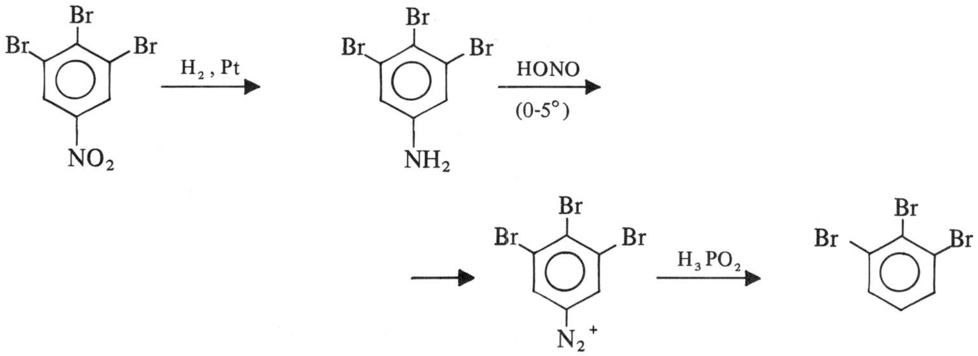

19.16

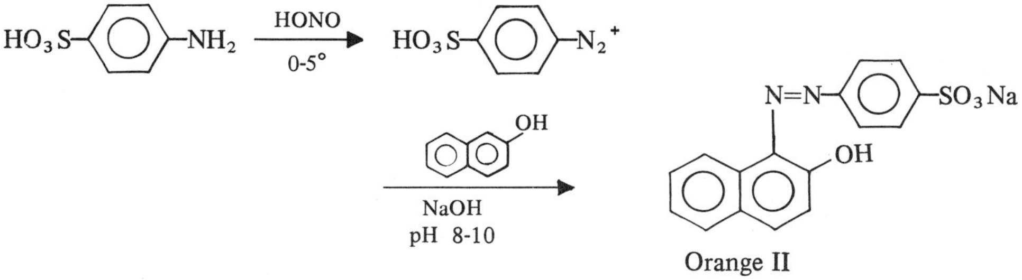

Orange II

19.17

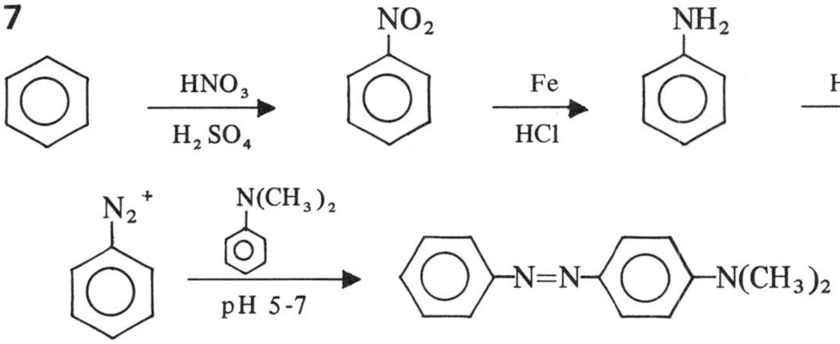

19.18

Phenacetin

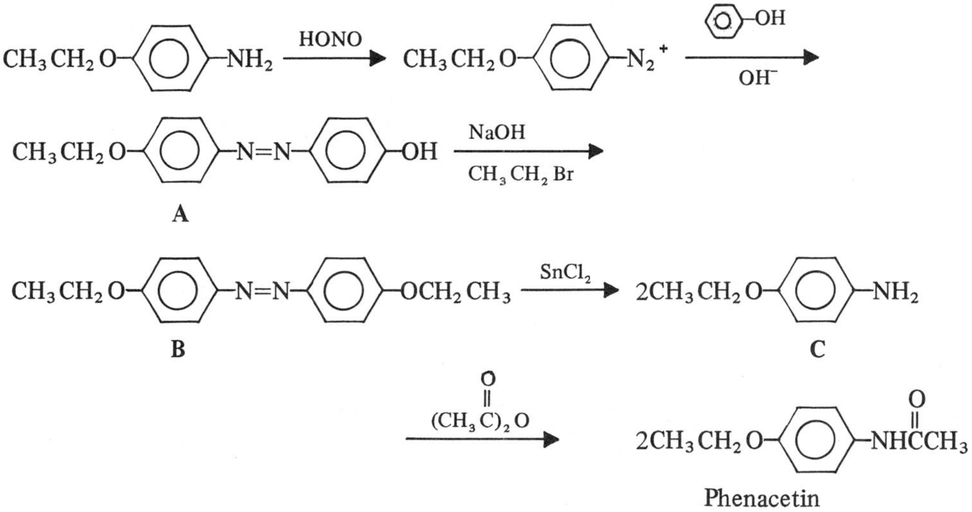

19.19 (1) That **A** reacts with benzenesulfonyl chloride in aqueous KOH to give a clear solution which on acidification yields a precipitate shows that **A** is a primary amine.

(2) That diazotization of **A** followed by treatment with 2-naphthol gives an intensely colored precipitate shows that **A** is a primary aromatic amine; that is, **A** is a substituted aniline.

(3) Consideration of the molecular formula of **A** leads us to conclude that **A** is a toluidine.

$$\frac{\begin{array}{l} C_7H_9N \\ -C_6H_6N \end{array}}{CH_3} = \text{—}\langle O \rangle\text{—}NH_2$$

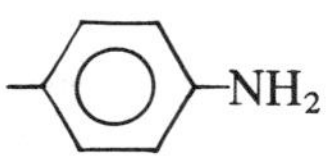

But is **A** *o*-toluidine, *m*-toluidine, or *p*-toluidine?

(4) This question is answered by the infrared data. A single absorption peak in the 680-840 cm^{-1} region at 815 cm^{-1} is indicative of a *para* substituted benzene. Thus **A** is *p*-toluidine.

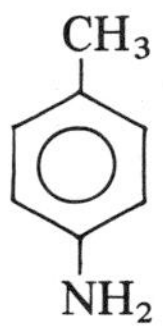

A

19.20 First convert the sulfonamide to its anion, then alkylate the anion with an alkyl halide, then remove the $-SO_2C_6H_5$ group by hydrolysis. For example

19.21 (a)

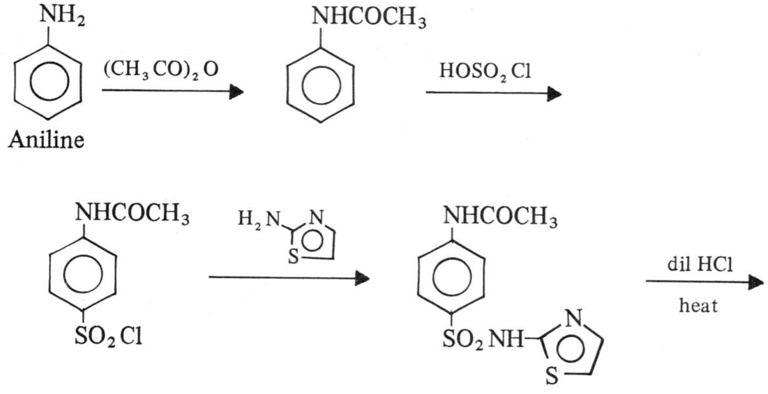

NH$_2$

(b)

Sulfathiazole

SO$_2$NH

$\longrightarrow$

NHCOCH$_2$CH$_2$COOH

SO$_2$NH

Succinoylsulfathiazole

19.22

(a)   CH$_3$Ċ=CH$_2$ + CH$_2$=CH$_2$ (major product)
        CH$_3$

(b)   CH$_3$CH=CH$_2$ + CH$_2$=CH$_2$ (major product)

(c)   (CH$_3$)$_2$NCH$_2$CH$_2$CH$_2$CH=CH$_2$

(d)   CH$_2$=CH–CH=CH$_2$

(e)
D

19.23

(a)   C$_6$H$_5$CH$_2$NHCH$_3$

(b)   (CH$_3$CH)$_3$N
        CH$_3$

(c)
      CH$_3$
  N
      CH$_2$CH$_3$

(d)
  CH$_3$
      NH$_2$

(e)
    CH$_3$
  N
  H

(f)
  N
  CH$_2$CH$_3$

(g)
  N$^+$ Br$^-$
  CH$_2$CH$_3$

(h)
    COOH
 N

(i)
  N
  H

(j)
    O
  NHĊCH$_3$

(k)
    H
CH$_3$–N$^+$H Cl$^-$
    CH$_3$

(l)
  N
    CH$_3$
 N
 H

(m)   H$_2$NCH$_2$CH$_2$CH$_2$OH

(n)   (CH$_3$CH$_2$CH$_2$)$_4$N$^+$ Cl$^-$

(o)
  N
  H

(p)   CH$_3$
        CH$_3$
    N
        CH$_3$

(q) 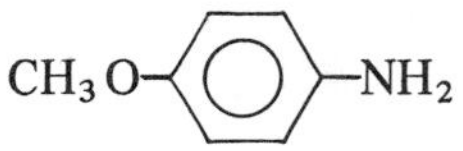 CH_3O—⟨⟩—NH_2

(r) $(CH_3)_4\overset{+}{N}\ OH^-$

(s) 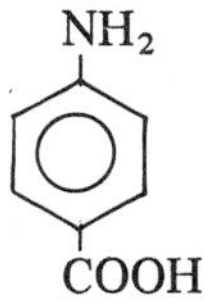 structure with NH_2 on benzene ring and $COOH$

(t)  structure with $NHCH_3$ on benzene ring

19.24

(a) Propylamine

(b) N-methylaniline

(c) Isopropyltrimethylammonium iodide

(d) o-Toluidine

(e) o-Anisidine (or o-methoxyaniline)

(f) Pyrazole

(g) 2-Aminopyrimidine

(h) Benzylammonium chloride

(i) N,N-Dipropylaniline

(j) Benzenesulfonamide

(k) Methylammonium acetate

(l) 3-Aminopropanol

(m) Purine

(n) N-Methylpyrrole

19.25

(a) 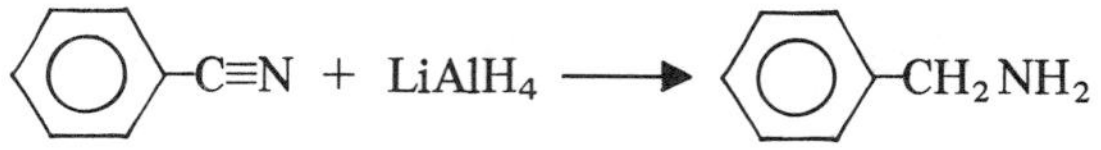 ⟨⟩—$C\equiv N$ + $LiAlH_4$ ⟶ ⟨⟩—CH_2NH_2

(b) ⟨⟩—$\overset{\overset{O}{\|}}{C}$—$NH_2$ + $LiAlH_4$ ⟶ ⟨⟩—CH_2NH_2

(c) ⟨⟩—CH_2Br + NH_3 (excess) ⟶ ⟨⟩—CH_2NH_2

⟨⟩—CH_2Br + (phthalimide)NK ⟶ ⟨⟩—CH_2—N(phthalimide)

$\xrightarrow{NH_2NH_2}$ ⟨⟩—CH_2NH_2 + (phthalhydrazide)

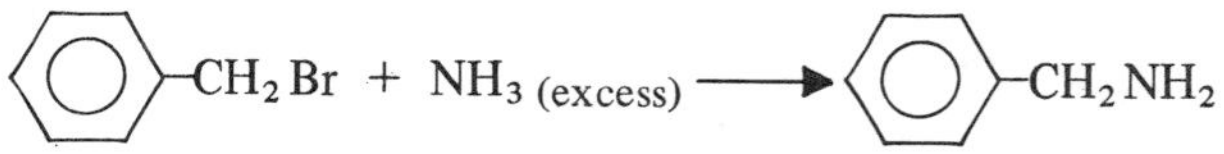

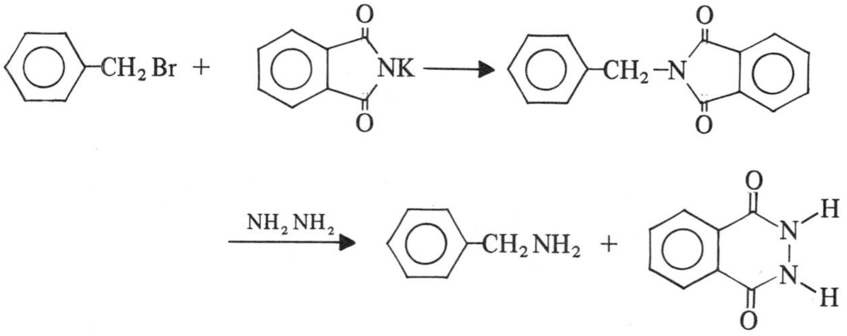

(d) 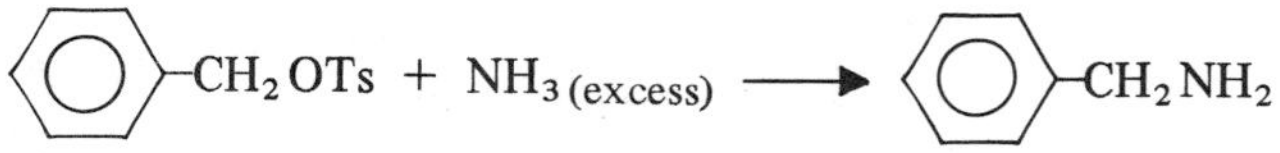 ⟨⟩—CH_2OTs + NH_3 (excess) ⟶ ⟨⟩—CH_2NH_2

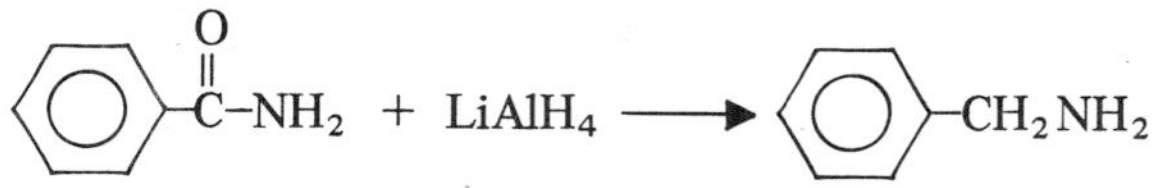

(e) $\langle\text{benzene ring}\rangle\text{—CHO} + NH_3 \xrightarrow{H_2, Ni} \langle\text{benzene ring}\rangle\text{—CH}_2NH_2$

(f) $\langle\text{benzene ring}\rangle\text{—CH}_2NO_2 + 3H_2 \xrightarrow{Pt} \langle\text{benzene ring}\rangle\text{—CH}_2NH_2$

(g) $\langle\text{benzene ring}\rangle\text{—CH}_2\overset{\overset{O}{\|}}{C}NH_2 \xrightarrow{Br_2, OH^-} \langle\text{benzene ring}\rangle\text{—CH}_2NH_2 + CO_3^=$

19.26

(a) $\langle\text{benzene}\rangle \xrightarrow[H_2SO_4]{HNO_3} \langle\text{benzene—NO}_2\rangle \xrightarrow[(2)\ OH^-]{(1)\ Fe,\ HCl,\ heat} \langle\text{benzene—NH}_2\rangle$

(b) $\langle\text{benzene—Br}\rangle \xrightarrow[liq\ NH_3]{NaNH_2} \langle\text{benzene—NH}_2\rangle$

(c) $\langle\text{benzene—CONH}_2\rangle \xrightarrow{Br_2,\ OH^-} \langle\text{benzene—NH}_2\rangle$

19.27

(a) $CH_3(CH_2)_2CH_2OH \xrightarrow{PBr_3} CH_3(CH_2)_2CH_2Br \xrightarrow{\text{(phthalimide NK)}}$

$\langle\text{phthalimide}\rangle NCH_2(CH_2)_2CH_3 \xrightarrow{NH_2NH_2} CH_3(CH_2)_2CH_2NH_2 + \langle\text{phthalhydrazide}\rangle$

(b) $CH_3(CH_2)_2CH_2Br \xrightarrow{NaCN} CH_3(CH_2)_3CN \xrightarrow{LiAlH_4} CH_3(CH_2)_3CH_2NH_2$
(from part a)

(c) $CH_3(CH_2)_2CH_2OH \xrightarrow[(2)\ H_3O^+]{(1)\ KMnO_4,\ OH^-} CH_3CH_2CH_2COOH$

$\xrightarrow[(2)\ NH_3]{(1)\ SOCl_2} CH_3CH_2CH_2CONH_2 \xrightarrow{Br_2,\ OH^-} CH_3CH_2CH_2NH_2$

(d) $CH_3CH_2CH_2CH_2OH$ $\xrightarrow[CH_2Cl_2]{CrO_3 \cdot 2C_5H_5N}$ $CH_3CH_2CH_2CHO$ $\xrightarrow[H_2, Ni]{CH_3NH_2}$

$$CH_3CH_2CH_2CH_2NHCH_3$$

19.28

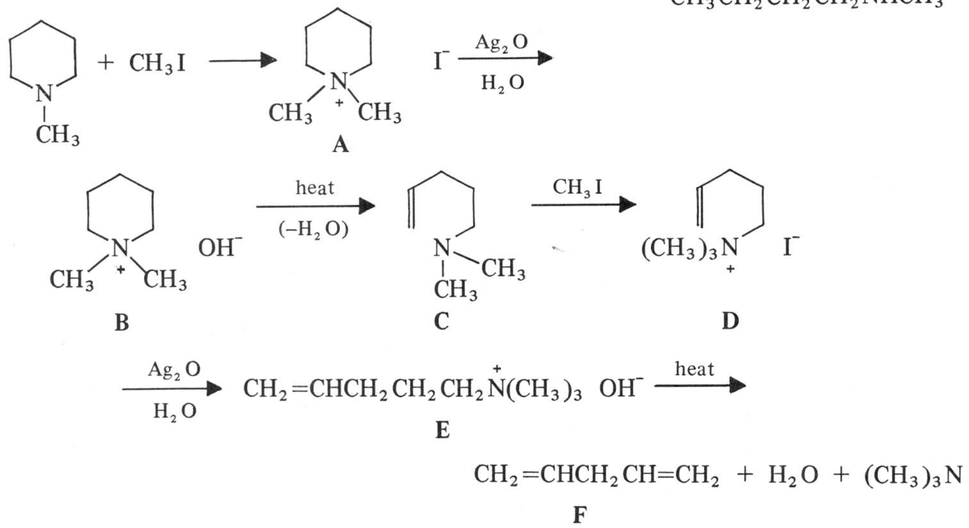

A

B   C   D

$\xrightarrow[H_2O]{Ag_2O}$ $CH_2{=}CHCH_2CH_2CH_2\overset{+}{N}(CH_3)_3$ OH^- $\xrightarrow{heat}$

E

$$CH_2{=}CHCH_2CH{=}CH_2 \ + \ H_2O \ + \ (CH_3)_3N$$

F

19.29

(a)

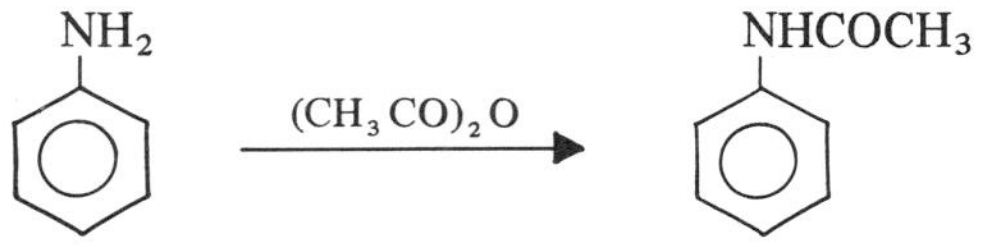

(b)

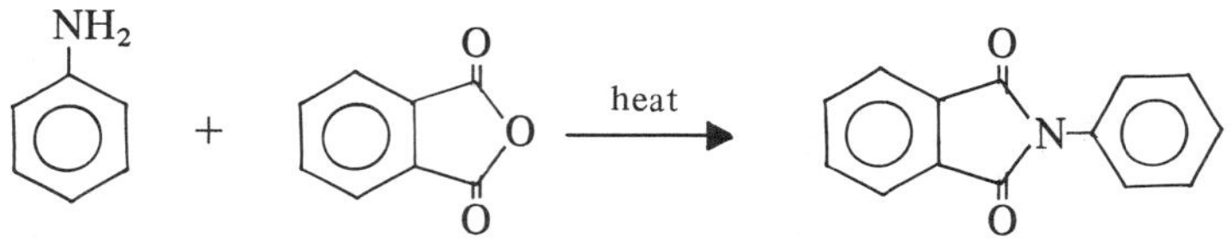

(c)
(from part a)

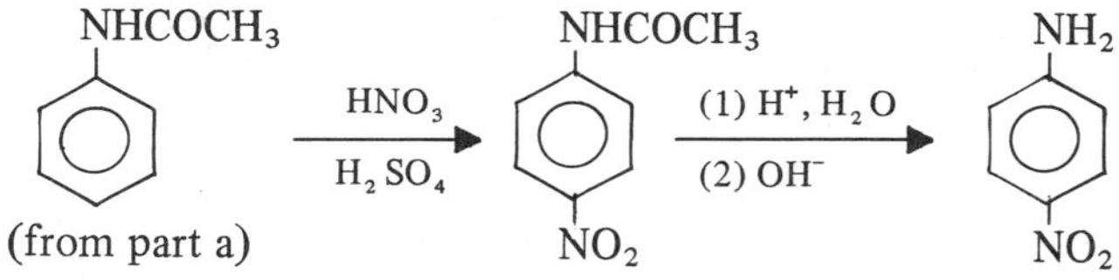

(d)
(from part a)

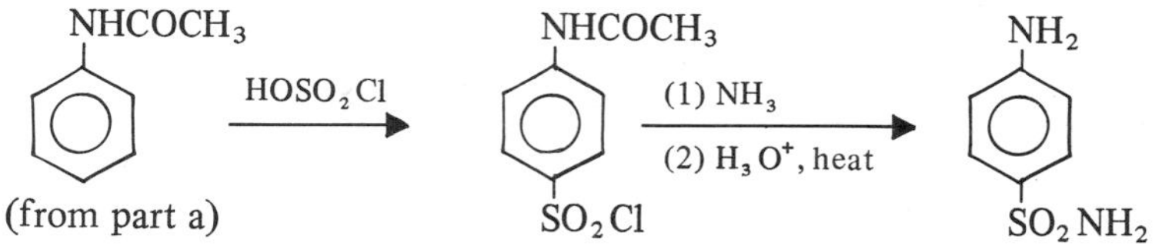

(e)

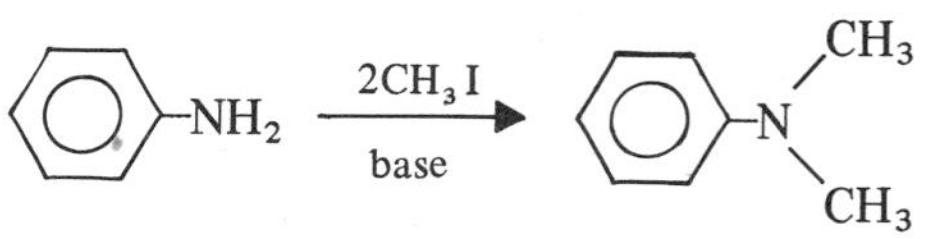

(f)

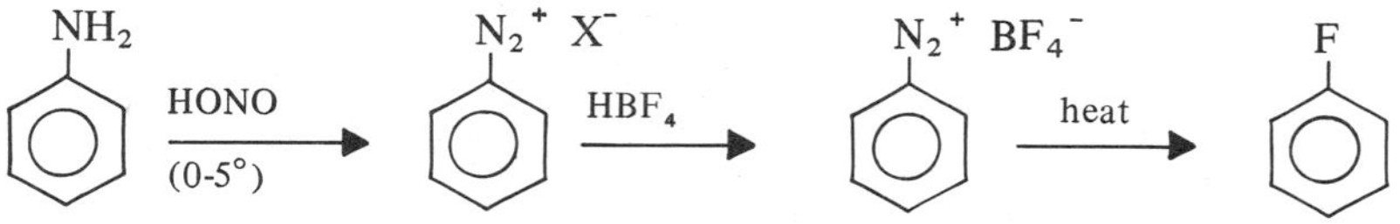

(g)

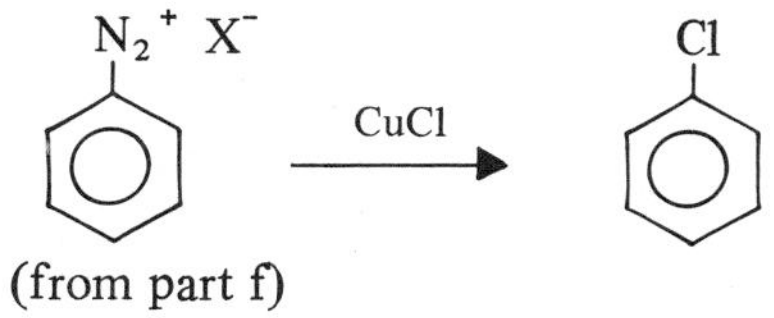

$$\underset{\text{(from part f)}}{\text{N}_2{}^+ \text{ X}^-} \xrightarrow{\text{CuCl}} \text{Cl}$$

(h)

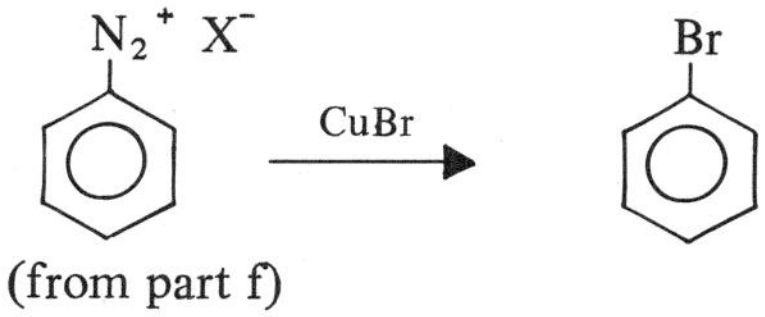

$$\underset{\text{(from part f)}}{\text{N}_2{}^+ \text{ X}^-} \xrightarrow{\text{CuBr}} \text{Br}$$

(i)

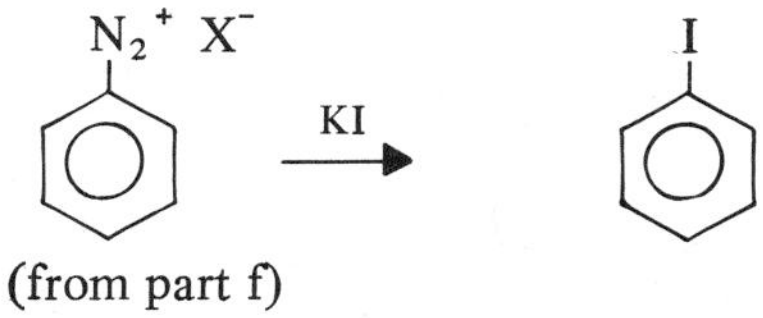

$$\underset{\text{(from part f)}}{\text{N}_2{}^+ \text{ X}^-} \xrightarrow{\text{KI}} \text{I}$$

(j)

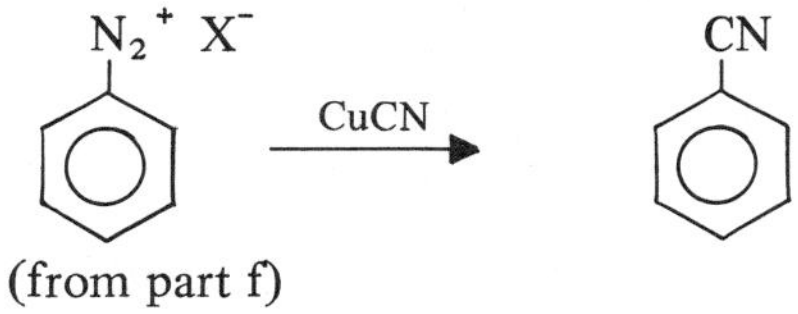

$$\underset{\text{(from part f)}}{\text{N}_2{}^+ \text{ X}^-} \xrightarrow{\text{CuCN}} \text{CN}$$

(k)

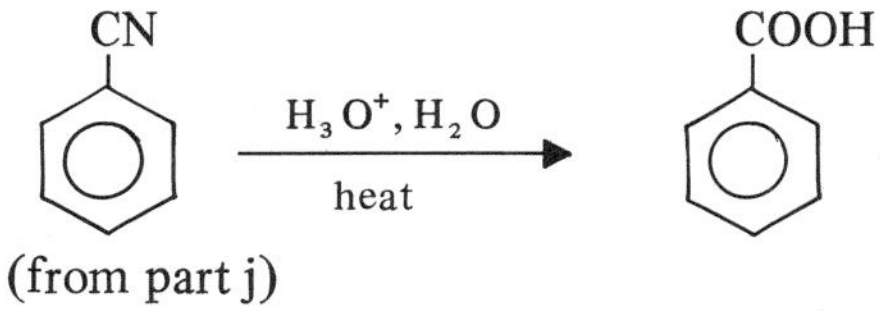

$$\underset{\text{(from part j)}}{\text{CN}} \xrightarrow[\text{heat}]{\text{H}_3\text{O}^+, \text{H}_2\text{O}} \text{COOH}$$

(l)

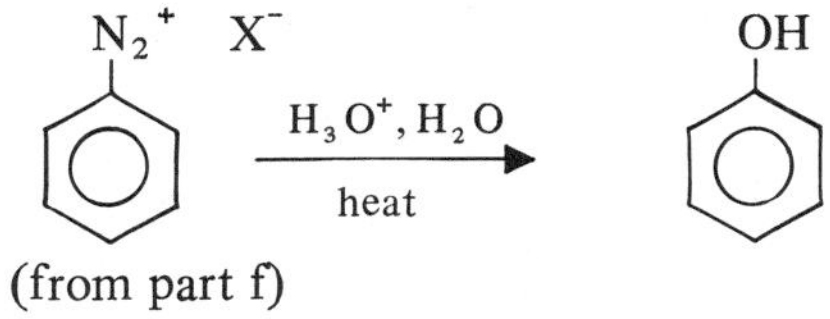

$$\underset{\text{(from part f)}}{\text{N}_2{}^+ \text{ X}^-} \xrightarrow[\text{heat}]{\text{H}_3\text{O}^+, \text{H}_2\text{O}} \text{OH}$$

(m)

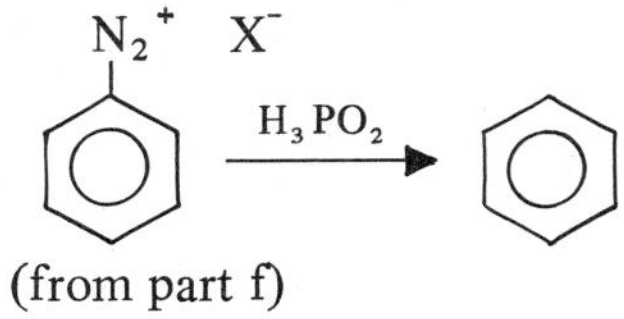

$$\underset{\text{(from part f)}}{\text{N}_2{}^+ \text{ X}^-} \xrightarrow{\text{H}_3\text{PO}_2}$$

(n)

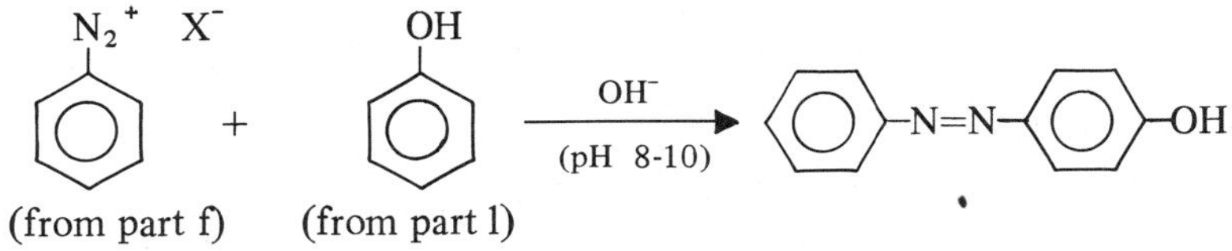

$$\underset{\text{(from part f)}}{\text{N}_2{}^+ \text{ X}^-} + \underset{\text{(from part l)}}{\text{OH}} \xrightarrow[\text{(pH 8-10)}]{\text{OH}^-} \text{—N=N—} \text{OH}$$

(o)

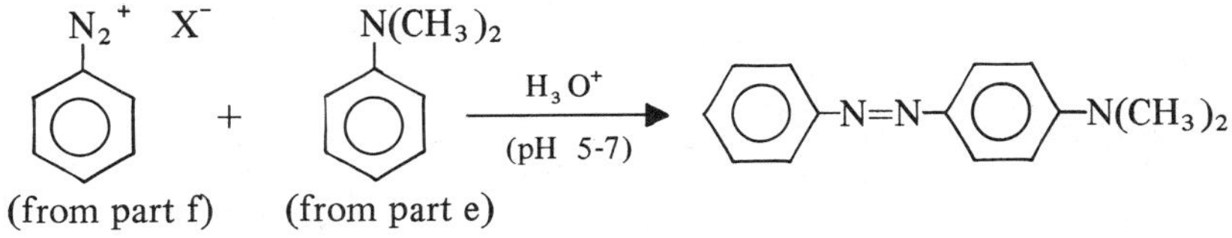

$$\underset{\text{(from part f)}}{\text{N}_2{}^+ \text{ X}^-} + \underset{\text{(from part e)}}{\text{N(CH}_3)_2} \xrightarrow[\text{(pH 5-7)}]{\text{H}_3\text{O}^+} \text{—N=N—} \text{N(CH}_3)_2$$

19.30

(a) $CH_3CH_2CH_2NH_2 \xrightarrow[\text{(NaNO}_2\text{/HCl)}]{\text{HONO}} [CH_3CH_2CH_2N_2{}^+] \xrightarrow{-N_2}$

$[CH_3CH_2CH_2{}^+] \xrightarrow[\text{shift}]{\text{hydride}} [CH_3\overset{+}{C}HCH_3]$

$CH_3CH_2CH_2{}^+$:
- Cl^- → $CH_3CH_2CH_2Cl$
- H_2O → $CH_3CH_2CH_2OH$
- $-H^+$ → $CH_3CH=CH_2$

$CH_3\overset{+}{C}HCH_3$:
- $-H^+$ → $CH_3CH=CH_2$
- H_2O → $CH_3\underset{OH}{C}HCH_3$
- Cl^- → $CH_3\underset{Cl}{C}HCH_3$

(b) $(CH_3CH_2CH_2)_2NH \xrightarrow[\text{(NaNO}_2\text{/HCl)}]{\text{HONO}} (CH_3CH_2)_2N-N=O$

(c) $\underset{\text{C}_6\text{H}_5}{}\text{N}\!\begin{smallmatrix}H\\ \\CH_2CH_2CH_3\end{smallmatrix} \xrightarrow[\text{(NaNO}_2\text{/HCl)}]{\text{HONO}} \text{N}\!\begin{smallmatrix}N=O\\ \\CH_2CH_2CH_3\end{smallmatrix}$

(d) $\text{N}\!\begin{smallmatrix}CH_2CH_2CH_3\\ \\CH_2CH_2CH_3\end{smallmatrix} \xrightarrow[\text{(NaNO}_2\text{/HCl)}]{\text{HONO}} O=N-\!\!\!\text{N}\!\begin{smallmatrix}CH_2CH_2CH_3\\ \\CH_2CH_2CH_3\end{smallmatrix}$

(e) $CH_3CH_2CH_2-\!\!\!\bigcirc\!\!\!-NH_2 \xrightarrow[\text{(NaNO}_2\text{/HCl)}]{\text{HONO, 0-5°}} CH_3CH_2CH_2-\!\!\!\bigcirc\!\!\!-N_2{}^+ \quad Cl^-$

19.31

(a) $CH_3CH_2CH_2NH_2 + C_6H_5SO_2Cl \xrightarrow[\text{H}_2\text{O}]{\text{KOH}} CH_3CH_2CH_2\overset{-}{N}SO_2C_6H_5$
$\underset{K^+}{}$
Clear solution

$\xrightarrow{H_3O^+} CH_3CH_2CH_2NHSO_2C_6H_5$
Precipitate

(b) $(CH_3CH_2CH_2)_2NH + C_6H_5SO_2Cl \xrightarrow[\text{H}_2\text{O}]{\text{KOH}} (CH_3CH_2CH_2)_2NSO_2C_6H_5$
Precipitate

$\xrightarrow{H_3O^+}$ No reaction (precipitate remains)

(c)

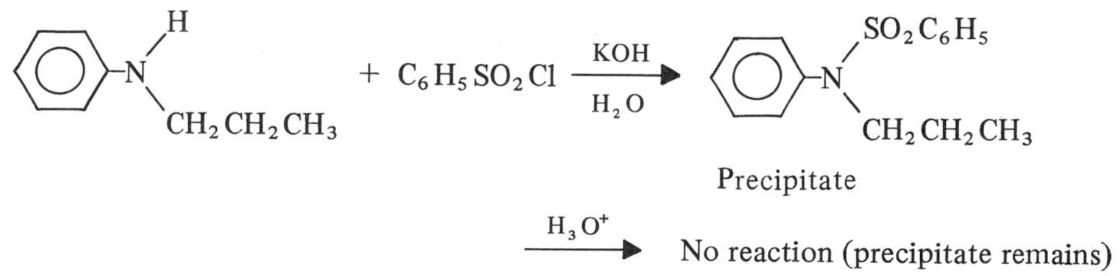

$+ C_6H_5SO_2Cl \xrightarrow[H_2O]{KOH}$

Precipitate

$\xrightarrow{H_3O^+}$ No reaction (precipitate remains)

(d)

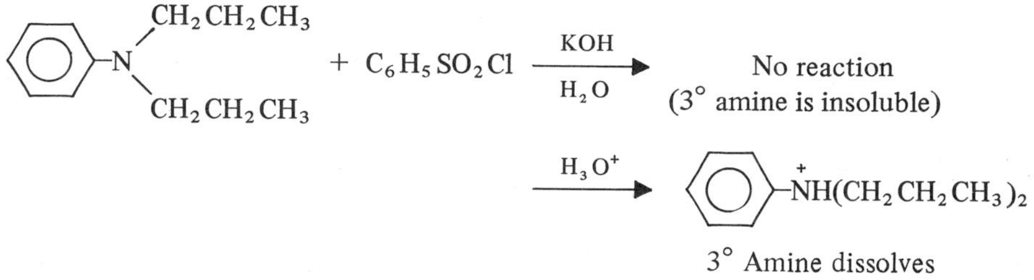

$+ C_6H_5SO_2Cl \xrightarrow[H_2O]{KOH}$ No reaction (3° amine is insoluble)

$\xrightarrow{H_3O^+}$ $\overset{+}{N}H(CH_2CH_2CH_3)_2$

3° Amine dissolves

(e) 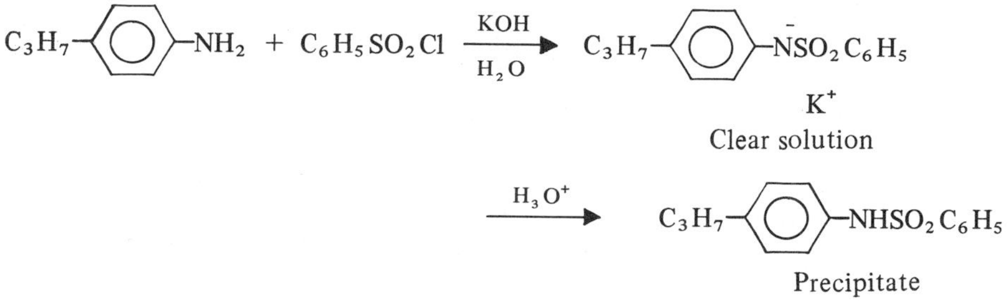 C_3H_7—⬡—$NH_2 + C_6H_5SO_2Cl \xrightarrow[H_2O]{KOH}$ C_3H_7—⬡—$\overset{-}{N}SO_2C_6H_5$

K^+

Clear solution

$\xrightarrow{H_3O^+}$ C_3H_7—⬡—$NHSO_2C_6H_5$

Precipitate

19.32

(a) 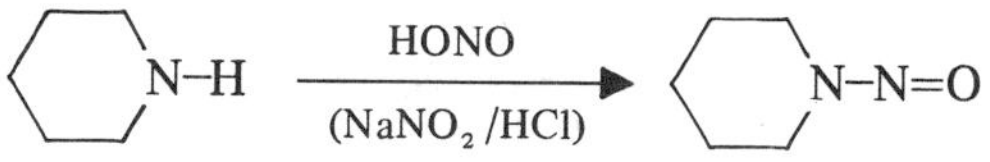 ⬡N–H $\xrightarrow[(NaNO_2/HCl)]{HONO}$ ⬡N–N=O

(b) 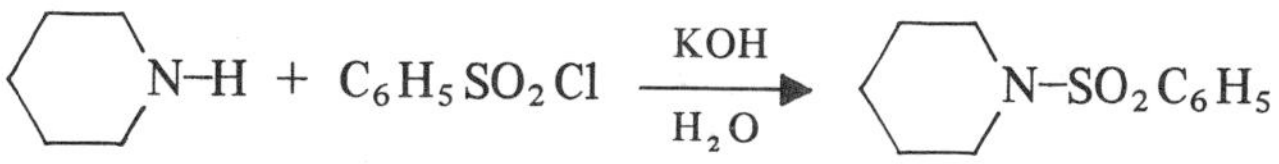 ⬡N–H $+ C_6H_5SO_2Cl \xrightarrow[H_2O]{KOH}$ ⬡N–SO$_2$C$_6$H$_5$

19.33 (a) $2CH_3CH_2NH_2 + C_6H_5COCl \longrightarrow CH_3CH_2NHCOC_6H_5 + CH_3CH_2NH_3^+Cl^-$

(b) $2CH_3NH_2 + (CH_3\overset{O}{\overset{\|}{C}})_2O \longrightarrow CH_3NH\overset{O}{\overset{\|}{C}}CH_3 + CH_3\overset{+}{N}H_3 \ CH_3\overset{O}{\overset{\|}{C}}O^-$

(c)

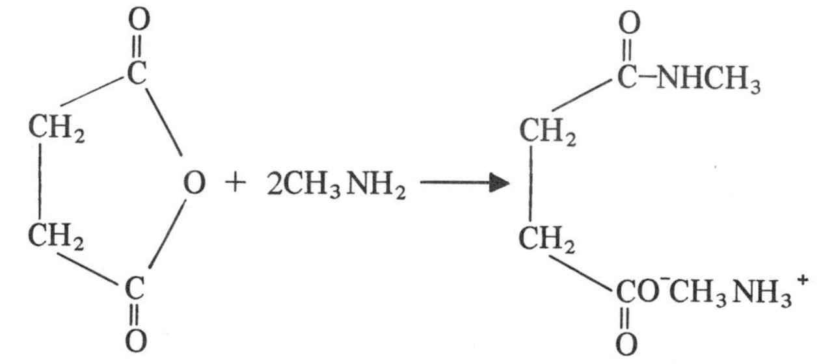

$\begin{matrix} O \\ \| \\ C \\ CH_2 \\ | \quad O \\ CH_2 \\ C \\ \| \\ O \end{matrix} + 2CH_3NH_2 \longrightarrow \begin{matrix} O \\ \| \\ C–NHCH_3 \\ CH_2 \\ | \\ CH_2 \\ CO^-CH_3NH_3^+ \\ \| \\ O \end{matrix}$

(d) 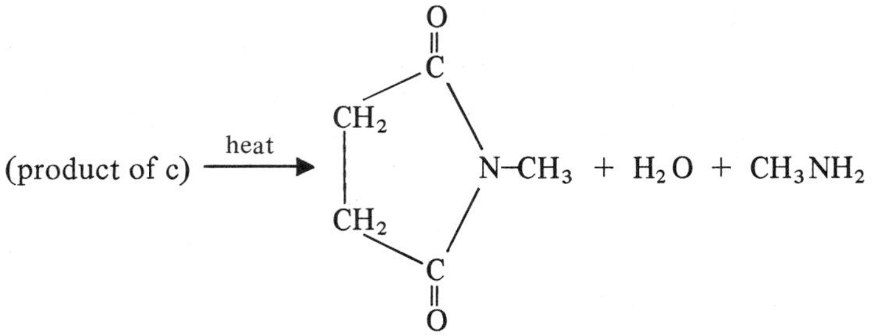 (product of c) $\xrightarrow{\text{heat}}$

$+ H_2O + CH_3NH_2$

(e)

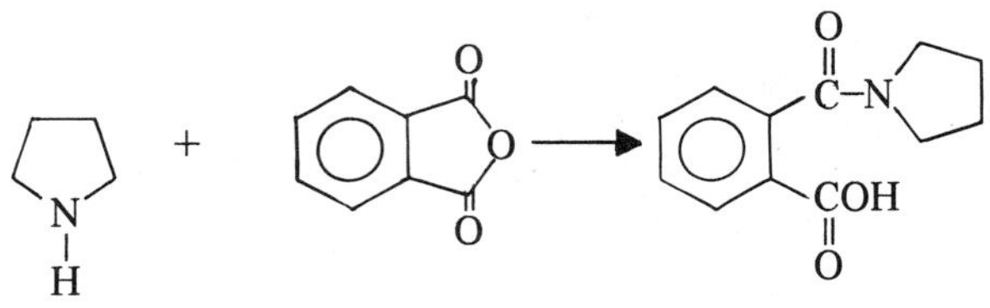

(f)

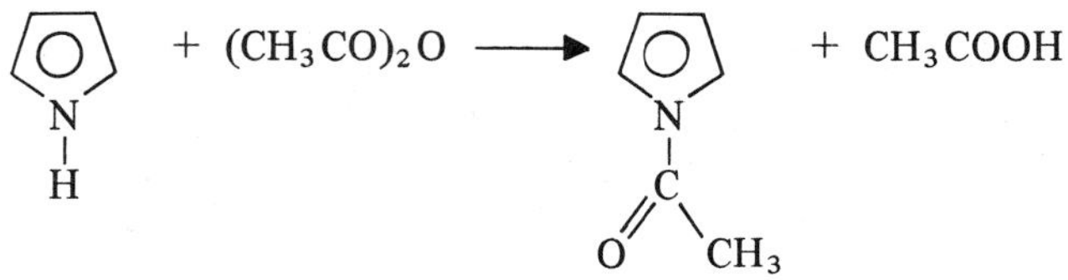

$+ (CH_3CO)_2O \longrightarrow$

$+ CH_3COOH$

(g) 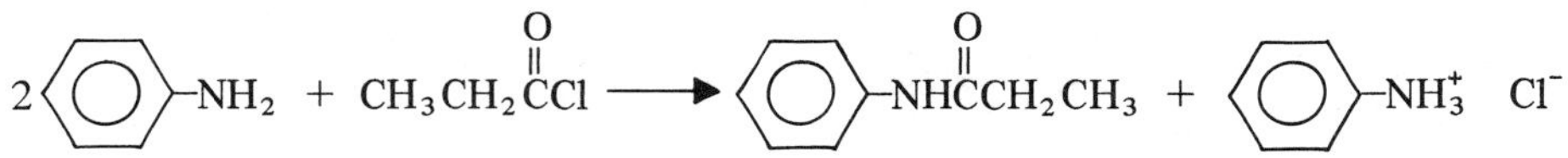 2

$-NH_2 + CH_3CH_2\overset{\overset{O}{\|}}{C}Cl \longrightarrow$

$-NH\overset{\overset{O}{\|}}{C}CH_2CH_3 +$

$-NH_3^+$ Cl^-

(h) $CH_3CH_2-\overset{\overset{\displaystyle CH_2CH_3}{|}}{\underset{\underset{\displaystyle CH_2CH_3}{|}}{N^+}}CH_2CH_3$ $^-OH \longrightarrow CH_2{=}CH_2 + (CH_3CH_2)_3N + H_2O$

(i)

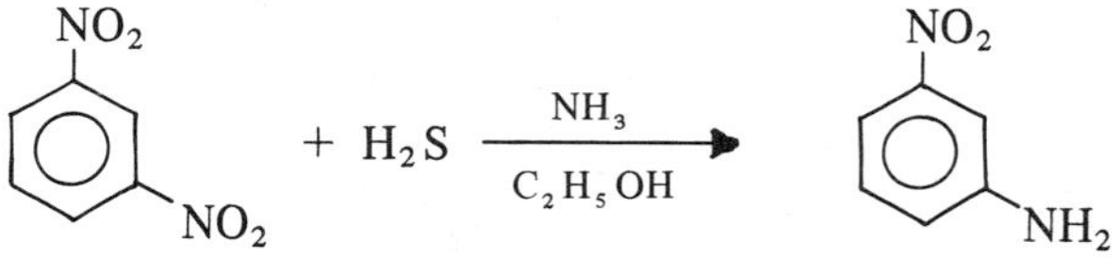

$+ H_2S \xrightarrow[\text{C}_2\text{H}_5\text{OH}]{\text{NH}_3}$

(j)

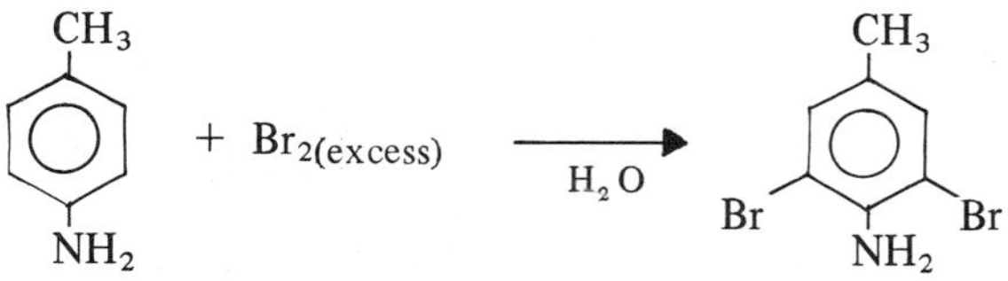

$+ Br_{2(\text{excess})} \xrightarrow{H_2O}$

19.34

(a)

$\xrightarrow[\text{H}_2\text{SO}_4]{\text{HNO}_3}$

$+$

Separate isomers

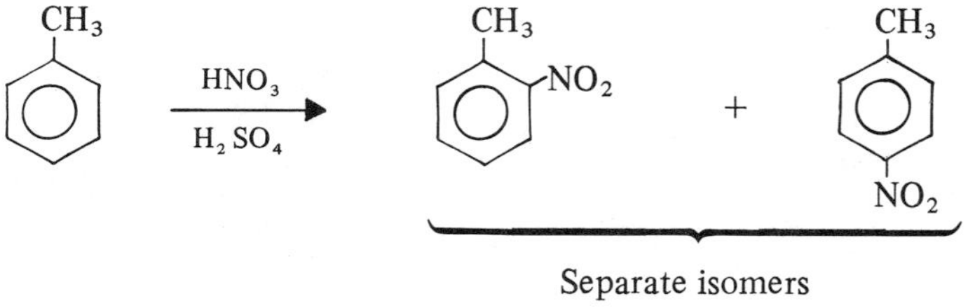

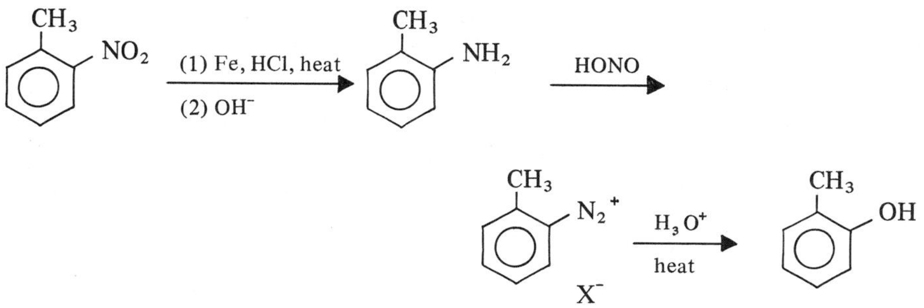

(b)

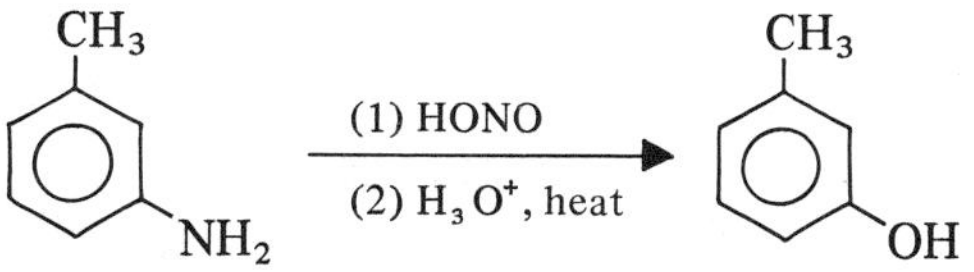

(from Problem 19.14a)

(c)

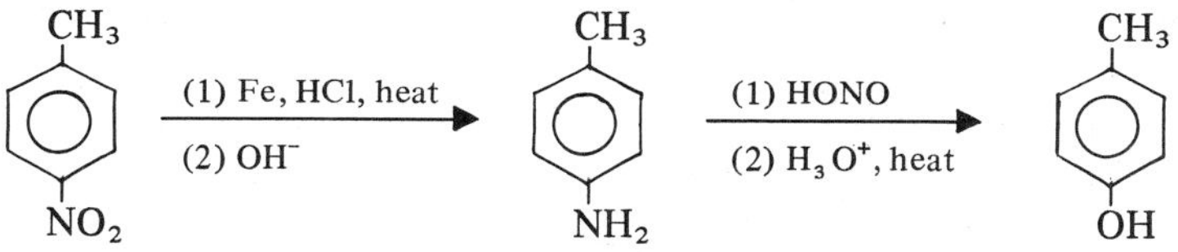

(from part a)

(d)

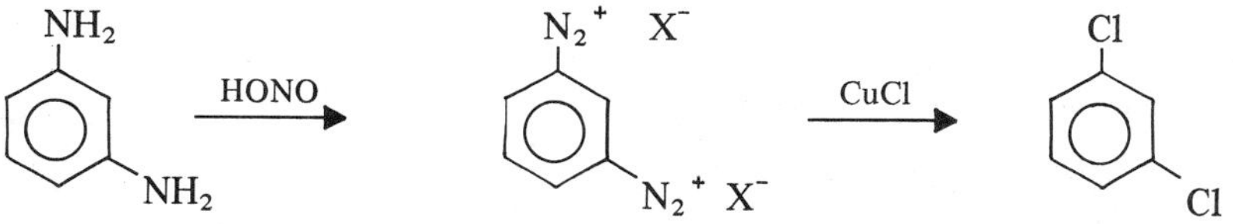

(from Problem 19.12a)

(e)

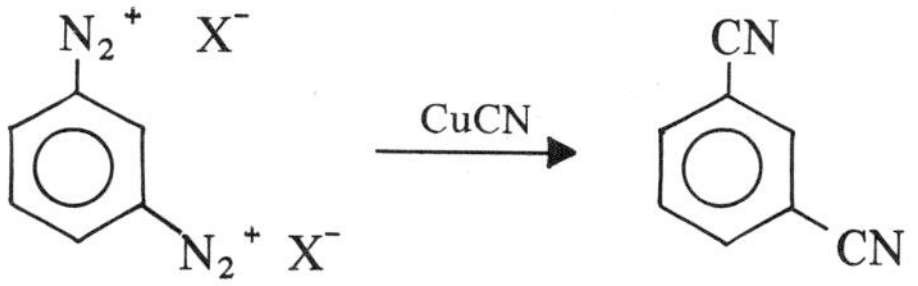

(cf. part d)

(f)

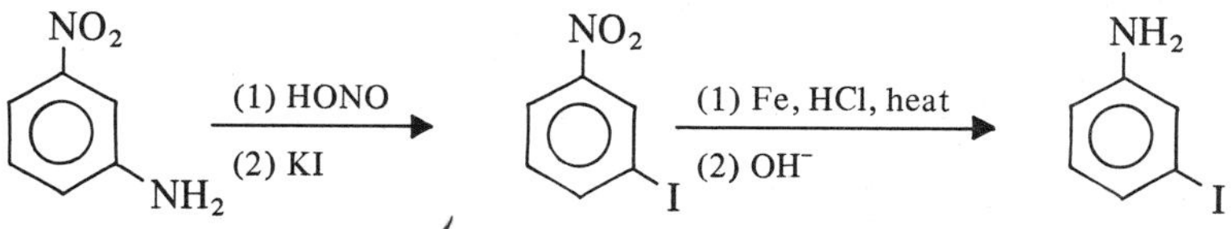

(from Problem 19.12a)

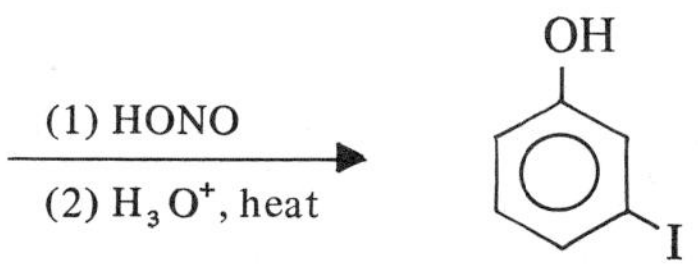

(g)

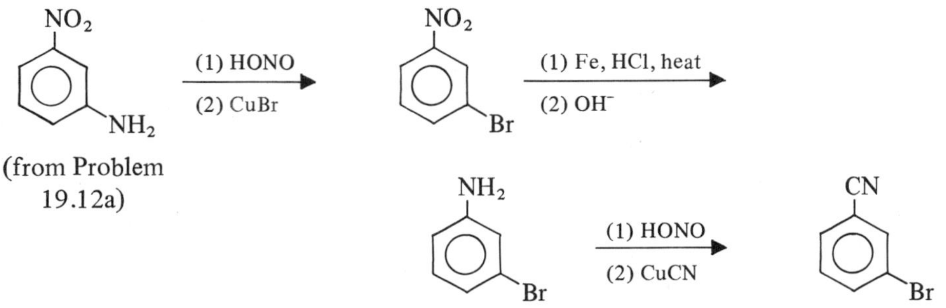

NO$_2$ / NH$_2$ (from Problem 19.12a)

$\xrightarrow[\text{(2) CuBr}]{\text{(1) HONO}}$

NO$_2$ / Br

$\xrightarrow[\text{(2) OH}^-]{\text{(1) Fe, HCl, heat}}$

NH$_2$ / Br

$\xrightarrow[\text{(2) CuCN}]{\text{(1) HONO}}$

CN / Br

(h)

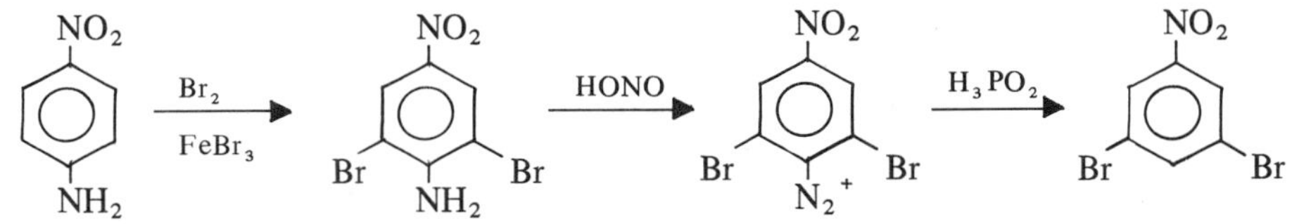

NO$_2$ / NH$_2$ (from Problem 19.12f)

$\xrightarrow[\text{FeBr}_3]{\text{Br}_2}$

NO$_2$ / Br Br / NH$_2$

$\xrightarrow{\text{HONO}}$

NO$_2$ / Br Br / N$_2^+$

$\xrightarrow{\text{H}_3\text{PO}_2}$

NO$_2$ / Br Br

(i)

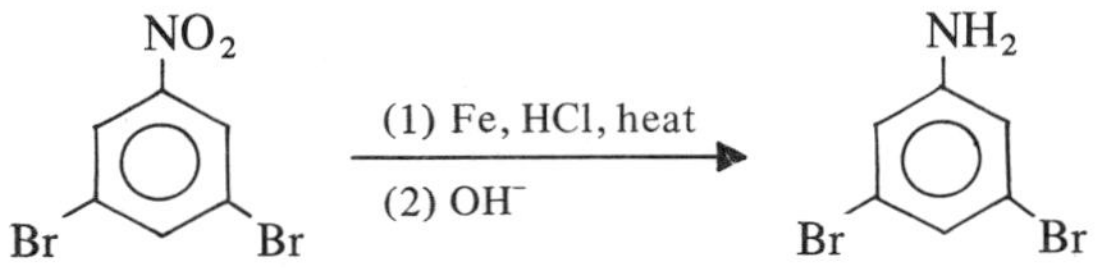

NO$_2$ / Br Br (from part h)

$\xrightarrow[\text{(2) OH}^-]{\text{(1) Fe, HCl, heat}}$

NH$_2$ / Br Br

(j)

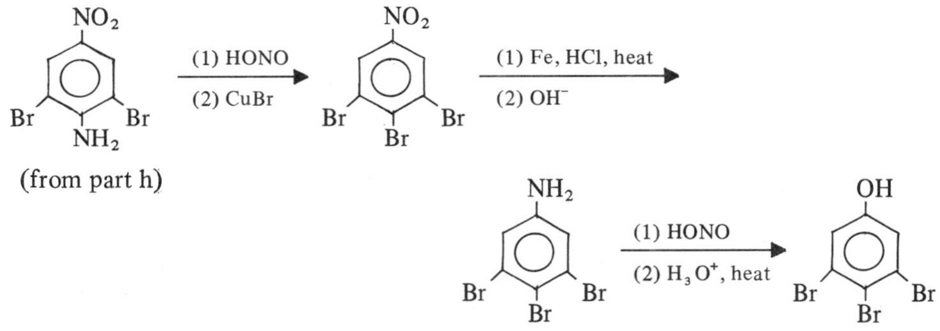

NO$_2$ / Br Br / NH$_2$ (from part h)

$\xrightarrow[\text{(2) CuBr}]{\text{(1) HONO}}$

NO$_2$ / Br Br / Br

$\xrightarrow[\text{(2) OH}^-]{\text{(1) Fe, HCl, heat}}$

NH$_2$ / Br Br / Br

$\xrightarrow[\text{(2) H}_3\text{O}^+, \text{ heat}]{\text{(1) HONO}}$

OH / Br Br / Br

(k)

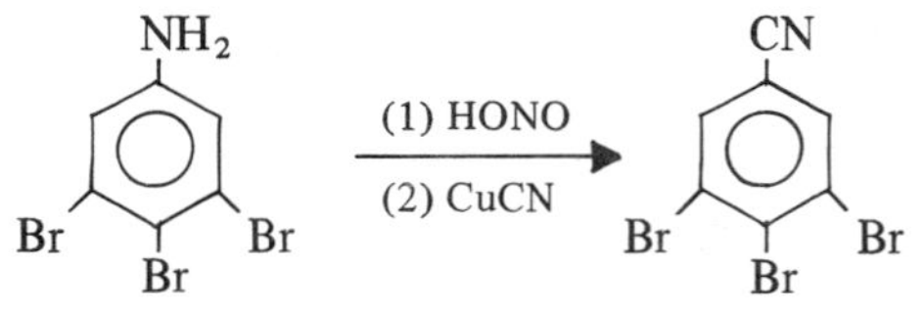

NH$_2$ / Br Br / Br (from part j)

$\xrightarrow[\text{(2) CuCN}]{\text{(1) HONO}}$

CN / Br Br / Br

(l)

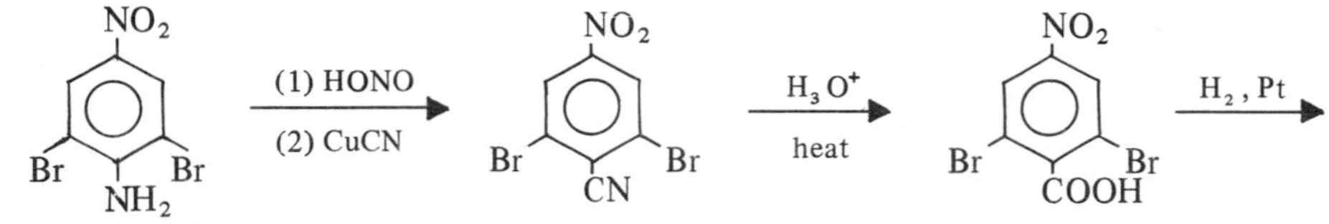

NO$_2$ / Br Br / NH$_2$ (from part h)

$\xrightarrow[\text{(2) CuCN}]{\text{(1) HONO}}$

NO$_2$ / Br Br / CN

$\xrightarrow[\text{heat}]{\text{H}_3\text{O}^+}$

NO$_2$ / Br Br / COOH

$\xrightarrow{\text{H}_2, \text{ Pt}}$

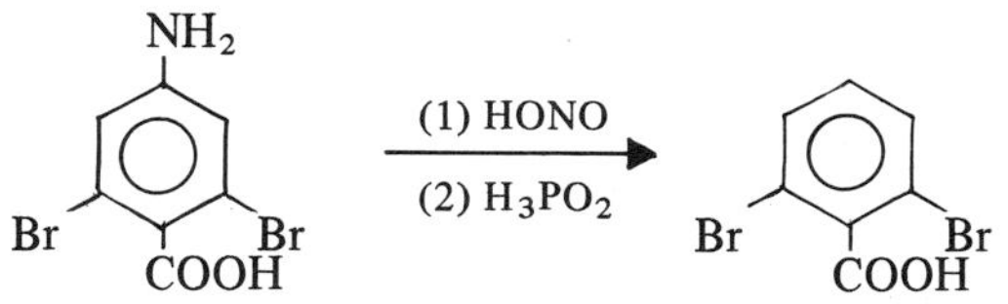

(m)

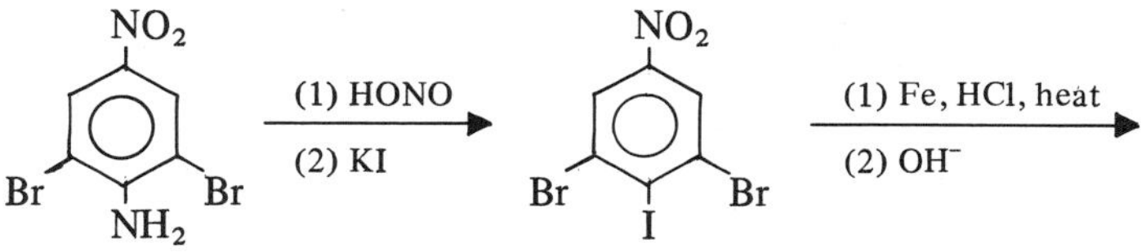

(from part h)

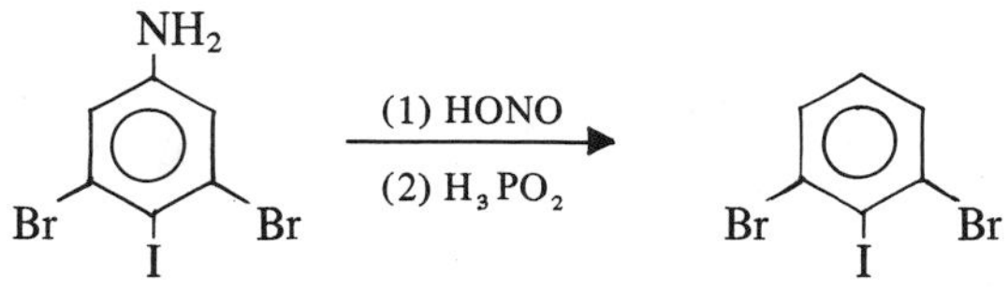

(n)

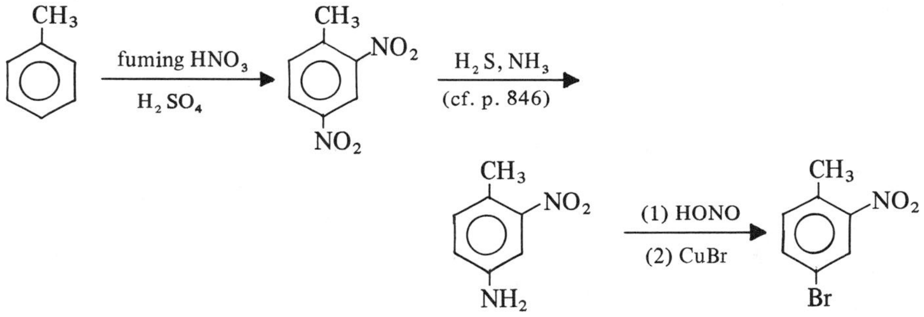

(o)

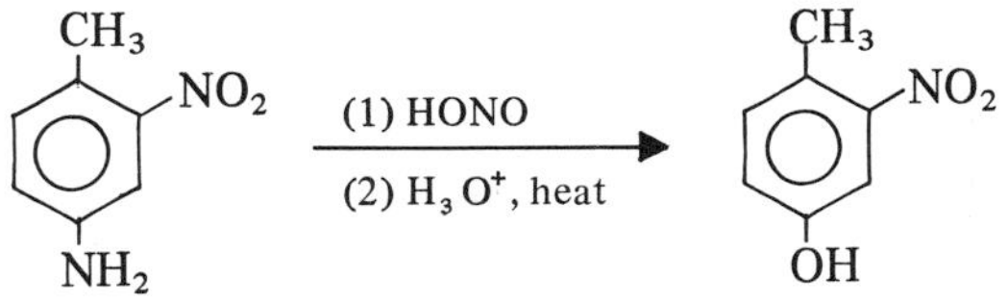

(from part n)

(p)

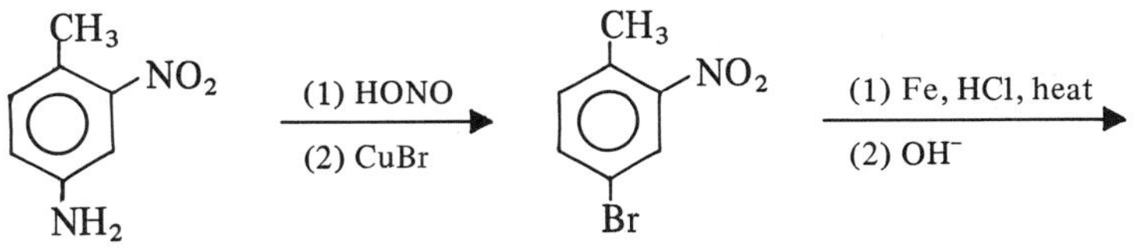

(from part n)

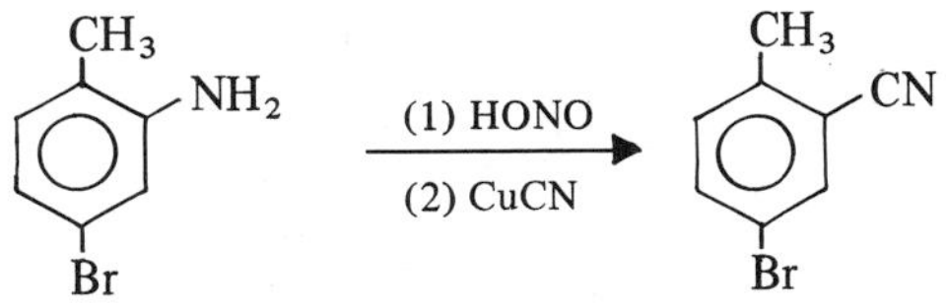

(q)

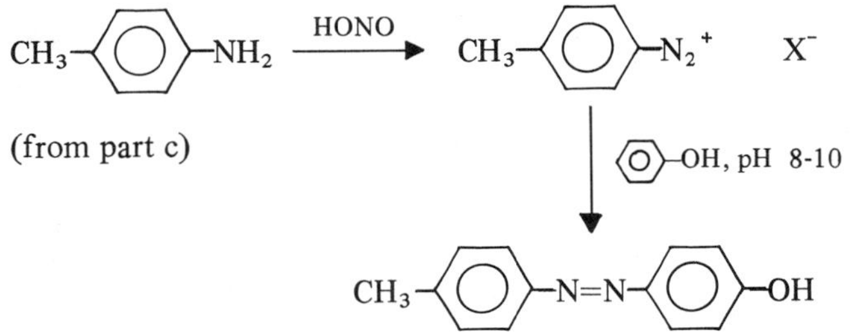

(from part c)

(r)

(from part q)

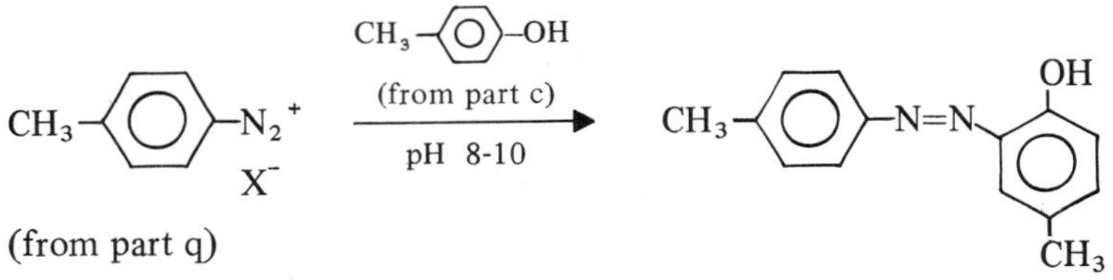

19.35 (a) Benzylamine dissolves in dilute HCl at room temperature,

$$C_6H_5CH_2NH_2 + H_3O^+ + Cl^- \xrightarrow{25°} C_6H_5CH_2\overset{+}{N}H_3Cl^-$$

benzamide does not dissolve:

$$C_6H_5CONH_2 + H_3O^+ + Cl^- \xrightarrow{25°} \text{No reaction}$$

(b) Allylamine reacts with (and decolorizes) bromine in carbon tetrachloride instantly,

$$CH_2{=}CHCH_2NH_2 + Br_2 \xrightarrow{CCl_4} \underset{\overset{|}{Br}\ \ \overset{|}{Br}}{CH_2CHCH_2NH_2}$$

propylamine does not:

$$CH_3CH_2CH_2NH_2 + Br_2 \xrightarrow{CCl_4} \text{No reaction if the mixture is not heated or irradiated.}$$

(c) The Hinsberg test:

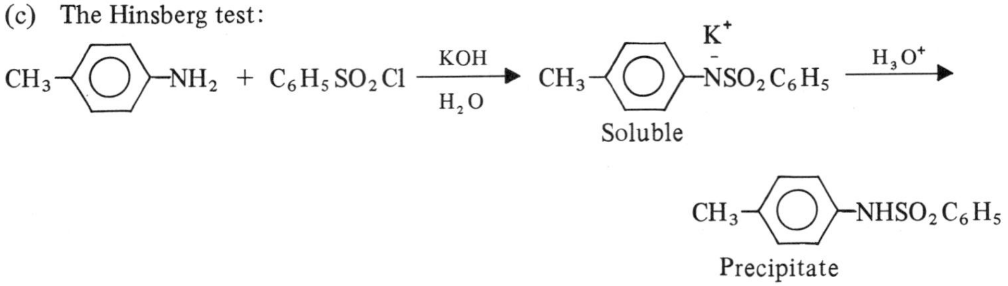

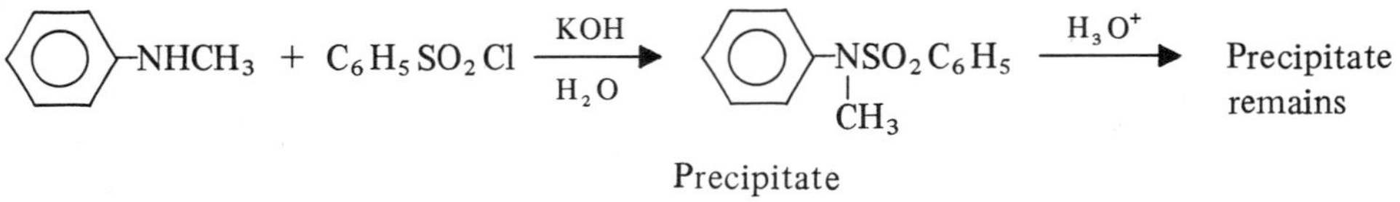

(d) The Hinsberg test:

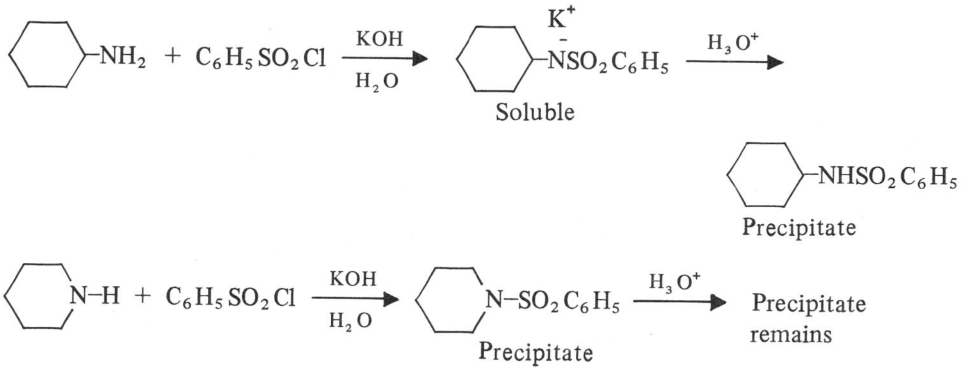

(e) Pyridine dissolves in dilute HCl,

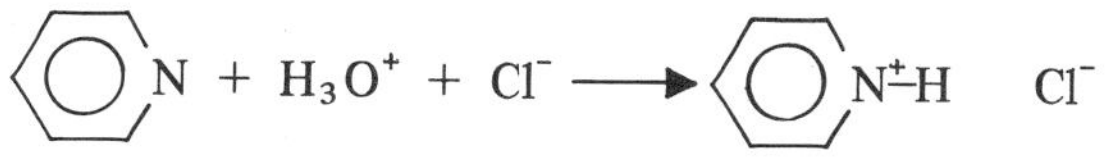

benzene does not:

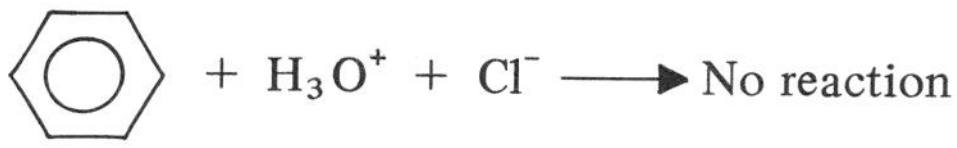

(f) Aniline reacts with nitrous acid at 0-5° to give a stable diazonium salt that couples with 2-naphthol yielding an intensely colored azo compound.

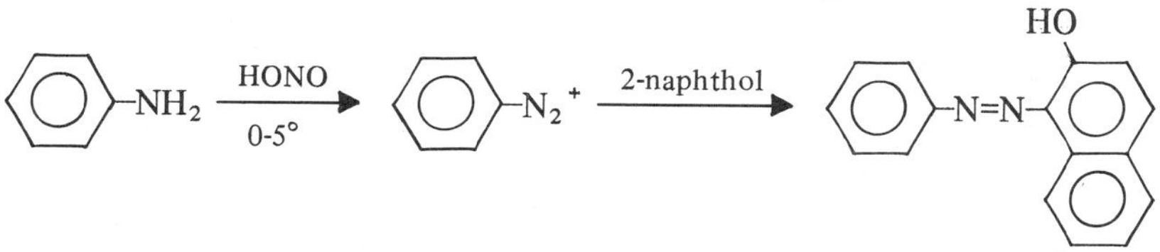

Cyclohexylamine reacts with nitrous acid at 0-5° to yield a highly unstable diazonium salt—one that decomposes so rapidly that the addition of 2-naphthol gives no azo compound.

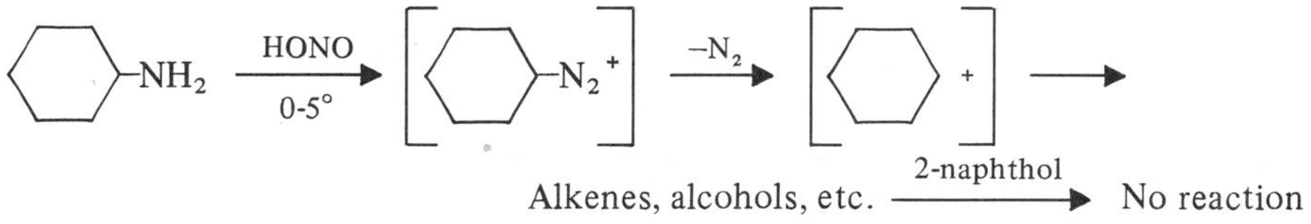

(g) The Hinsberg test:

$(C_2H_5)_3N + C_6H_5SO_2Cl \xrightarrow[H_2O]{KOH}$ No reaction $\xrightarrow{H_3O^+}$ $(C_2H_5)_3\overset{+}{N}H$
Soluble

$(C_2H_5)_2NH + C_6H_5SO_2Cl \xrightarrow[H_2O]{KOH}$ $(C_2H_5)_2NSO_2C_6H_5$ $\xrightarrow{H_3O^+}$ Precipitate remains
Precipitate

(h) Tripropylammonium chloride reacts with aqueous NaOH to give a water insoluble tertiary amine.

$$(CH_3CH_2CH_2)_3\overset{+}{N}H\ Cl^- \xrightarrow[H_2O]{NaOH} (CH_3CH_2CH_2)_3N$$
Water soluble   Water insoluble

Tetrapropylammonium chloride does not react with aqueous NaOH (at room temperature) and the tetrapropylammonium ion remains in solution.

$$(CH_3CH_2CH_2)_4N^+Cl^- \xrightarrow[H_2O]{NaOH} (CH_3CH_2CH_2)_4N^+\ [Cl^-\ or\ OH^-]$$
Water soluble   Water soluble

(i) Tetrapropylammonium chloride dissolves in water to give a neutral solution. Tetrapropylammonium hydroxide dissolves in water to give a strongly basic solution.

19.36 Follow the procedure outlined in the answer to Problem 19.2. Toluene will show the same solubility behavior as benzene.

19.37

$$\xrightarrow[(-CO_3^=)]{Br,\ OH^-} H_2NCH_2CH_2COO^- \xrightarrow{H^+} H_3\overset{+}{N}CH_2CH_2COO^-$$

19.38

(a) $HOCH_2(CH_2)_8CH_2OH \xrightarrow{PBr_3} BrCH_2(CH_2)_8CH_2Br \xrightarrow{2\ (CH_3)_3N}$

$(CH_3)_3\overset{+}{N}CH_2(CH_2)_8CH_2\overset{+}{N}(CH_3)_3\ 2Br^-$

(b) $HOOCCH_2CH_2COOH + 2\ BrCH_2CH_2OH \xrightarrow{H^+}$

$BrCH_2CH_2OOCCH_2CH_2COOCH_2CH_2Br \xrightarrow{2\ (CH_3)_3N}$

$(CH_3)_3\overset{+}{N}CH_2CH_2OOCCH_2CH_2COOCH_2CH_2\overset{+}{N}(CH_3)_3\ 2\ Br^-$

(c) $(CH_3)_3N + CH_2\overset{\diagdown O \diagup}{-}CH_2 \longrightarrow (CH_3)_3\overset{+}{N}CH_2CH_2O^- \xrightarrow{CH_3\overset{O}{\overset{\|}{C}}Cl}$

$(CH_3)_3\overset{+}{N}CH_2CH_2O\overset{O}{\overset{\|}{C}}CH_3\ Cl^-$

19.39 Compound (b) would probably be inactive because of the meta orientation of the groups. Compound (d) would probably be inactive because the distance that separates the —NH₂ from the —SO₂NH— group is too large.

19.40

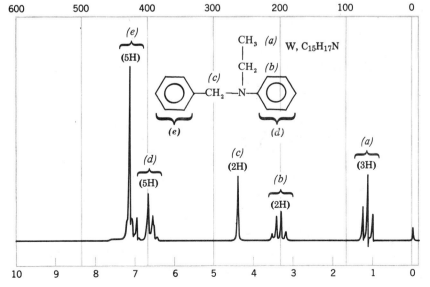

19.41 The results of the Hinsberg test indicate that compound W is a tertiary amine. The proton nmr spectrum provides evidence for the following:

FIG. 19.3. *The proton nmr spectrum of W (Problem 19.41). (Spectrum courtesy of Aldrich Chemical Co.)*

19.42 Compound **X** is benzyl bromide, $C_6H_5CH_2Br$. This is the only structure consistent with the proton nmr and infrared data. (The mono-substituted benzene ring is strongly indicated by the (5H), $\delta 7.3$ proton nmr absorption and is confirmed by the peaks at 690 cm^{-1} and 770 cm^{-1} in the infrared spectrum.)

Compound **Y**, therefore must be phenylacetonitrile, $C_6H_5CH_2CN$, and **Z** must be 2-phenylethylamine, $C_6H_5CH_2CH_2NH_2$.

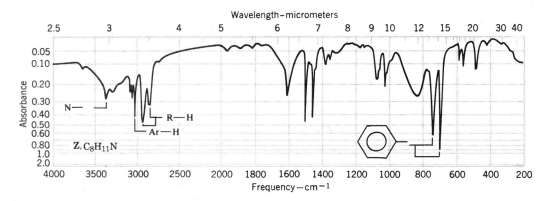

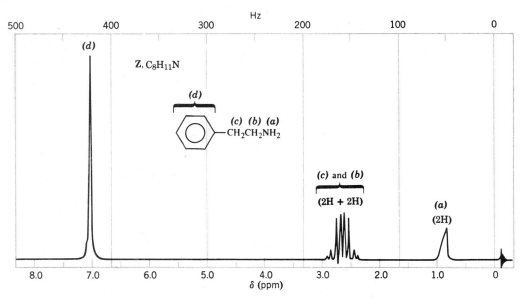

FIG. 19.4. *Infrared and proton nmr spectra for compound Z, Problem 19.42. (Spectra courtesy of Sadtler Inc.)*

(1) Two different C_6H_5- groups (one absorbing at $\delta 7.2$ and one at $\delta 6.7$).
(2) A CH_3CH_2- group (the quartet at $\delta 3.3$ and the triplet at $\delta 1.2$).
(3) An unsplit $-CH_2-$ group (the singlet at $\delta 4.4$).

There is only one reasonable way to put all of this together.

Thus **W** is *N*-benzyl-*N*-ethylaniline.

19.43

19.44   That **A** contains nitrogen and is soluble in dilute HCl suggests that **A** is an amine. The two infrared absorption bands in the 3300-3500 cm^{-1} region suggest that **A** is a primary amine. The ^{13}C spectrum shows only two signals in the upfield aliphatic region. There are four signals downfield in the aromatic region. The splitting patterns of the aliphatic peaks in the proton off-resonance spectrum suggest an ethyl group *or two equivalent ethyl groups*. Assuming the latter, and assuming that **A** is a primary amine, we can conclude from the molecular formula and from the splitting patterns of the aromatic signals that **A** is 2,6-diethylaniline. The assignments are:

(a) quartet δ 12.9   *(d)* doublet δ 125.9

(b) triplet δ 24.2   *(e)* singlet δ 127.4

(c) doublet δ 118.1   *(f)* singlet δ 141.5

(An equally plausible answer would be that **A** is 3,5-diethylaniline.)

19.45   That **B** dissolves in dilute HCl suggests that **B** is an amine. That the infrared spectrum of **B** lacks bands in the 3300-3500 cm^{-1} region suggests that **B** is a tertiary amine. The upfield signals in the ^{13}C spectrum, and the splitting patterns in the proton off-resonance decoupled spectrum suggest two equivalent ethyl groups (as was also true of **A** in the preceding problem.) The splitting of the downfield peaks (in the aromatic region) is consistent with a monosubstituted benzene ring. Putting all of these observations together with the molecular formula leads us to conclude that **B** is *N,N*-diethylaniline. The assignments are:

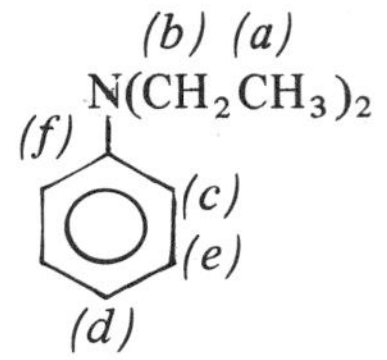

(b) (a)
N(CH₂CH₃)₂
(f)

(c)
(e)
(d)

(a) quartet δ 12.5

(b) triplet δ 44.2

(c) doublet δ 112.0

(d) doublet δ 115.5

(e) doublet δ 128.1

(f) singlet δ 147.8

19.46 That **C** gives a positive Tollens' test indicates the presence of an aldehyde group; the solubility of **C** in aqueous HCl suggests that **C** is also an amine. The absence of bands in the 3300-3500 cm⁻¹ region of the infrared spectrum of **C** suggests that **C** is a tertiary amine. The signal at δ189.7 in the ¹³C spectrum can be assigned to the aldehyde group. The signal at δ39.7 is the only one in the aliphatic region and its splitting (a quartet in the proton off-resonance decoupled spectrum) is consistent with a methyl group or with two equivalent methyl groups. The remaining signals are in the aromatic region. If we

assume that **C** has a benzene ring containing a $-\overset{O}{\overset{\|}{C}}H$ group and a $-N(CH_3)_2$ group then the aromatic signals and their splittings are consistent with **C** being *p*-(*N,N*-dimethylamino)-benzaldehyde. The assignments are:

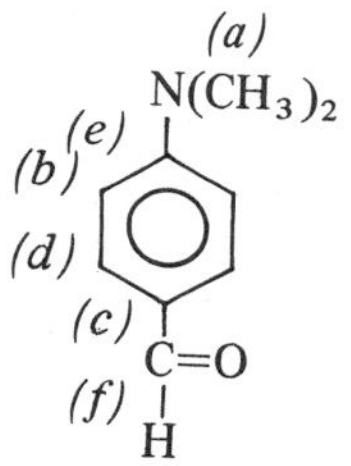

(a)
N(CH₃)₂
(e)
(b)
(d)
(c)
C=O
(f)
H

(a) quartet δ 39.7

(b) doublet δ 110.8

(c) singlet δ 124.9

(d) doublet δ 131.6

(e) singlet δ 154.1

(f) doublet δ 189.7

You should now compare this spectrum with the one given for *p*-(*N,N*-diethylamino)-benzaldehyde given in Figure 13.27 and the analysis of that spectrum given in Section 13.10.

SECTION REFERENCES FOR ADDITIONAL PROBLEMS

19.23	12.12, 17.2, 19.1	**19.26**	12.4, 14.14, 19.5
19.24	19.1	**19.27**	14.7, 15.8, 18.5, 18.8, 19.5
19.25	19.5	**19.28**	19.6, 19.13

19.29	12.12, 18.11, 19.6, 19.7, 19.8, 19.9, 19.10, 19.11	**19.38**	14.7, 15.13, 18.7, 19.5
19.30	19.7	**19.39**	19.11C
19.31	19.10	**19.40**	18.5, 18.6
19.32	19.7, 19.10	**19.41**	13.6, 19.10, 19.12
19.33	12.8, 18.8, 19.5, 19.13	**19.42**	5.5, 13.6, 13.11, 14.2, 19.5, 19.12
19.34	12.8, 19.7, 19.8, 19.9	**19.43**	19.6
19.35	9.17, 18.8, 19.9, 19.11, 19.12	**19.44**	13.10, 19.3, 19.12
19.36	15.15, 17.13, 19.3, 19.12	**19.45**	13.10, 19.3, 19.12
19.37	18.7, 19.6	**19.46**	13.10, 16.13, 19.3, 19.12

SELF-TEST

19.1 Circle the stronger base in each of the following pairs.

(a) ⟨O⟩—NHCOCH₃ and ⟨O⟩—NHCH₂CH₃

(b) ⟨O⟩—NH₂ and ⟨O⟩—CH₂NH₂

(c) CH₃O—⟨O⟩—NH₂ and O₂N—⟨O⟩—NH₂

(d) ⟨O⟩—NH₂ and

19.2 Arrange the following compounds in order of increasing basicity. Place a *1* beside the most basic, and a *4* beside the least basic. Use *2* and *3* for the remaining compounds accordingly. *All four numbers must be correct for this question to be marked correct.*

(a) CH₃NH₂ ▢ , (b) O₂N—⟨O⟩—NH₂ ▢ ,

(c) 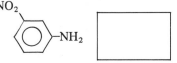 ▢ , (d) NH₃ ▢

19.3   Supply the formulas of the missing reactants, reagents, and products in the following reaction sequences.

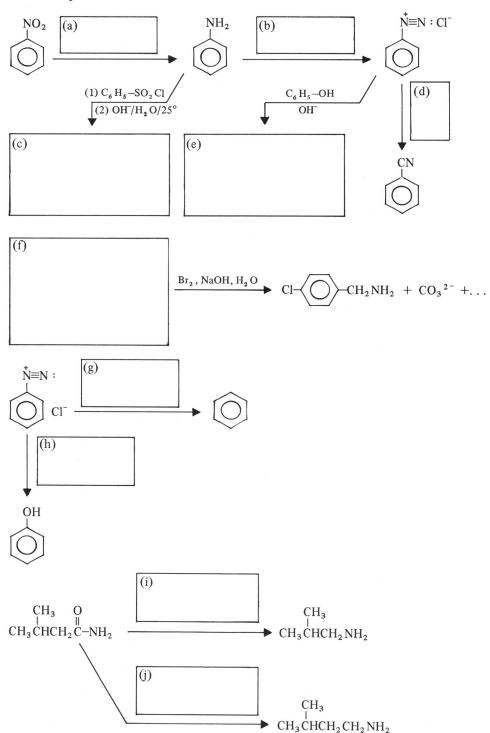

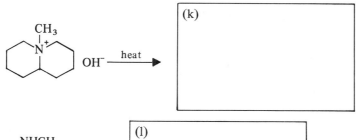

(k)

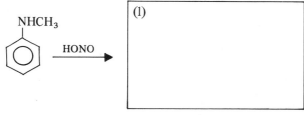

(l)

(m) $C_8H_{11}N$ (insoluble in H_2O)

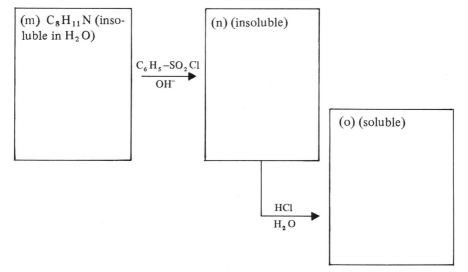

(n) (insoluble)

(o) (soluble)

$\dfrac{C_6H_5-SO_2Cl}{OH^-}$

$\dfrac{HCl}{H_2O}$

19.4   Write equations for a practical laboratory synthesis of each of the following.

(a)   3-Aminopropanoic acid from succinic anhydride

(b) *m*-Nitrotoluene from *p*-nitrotoluene

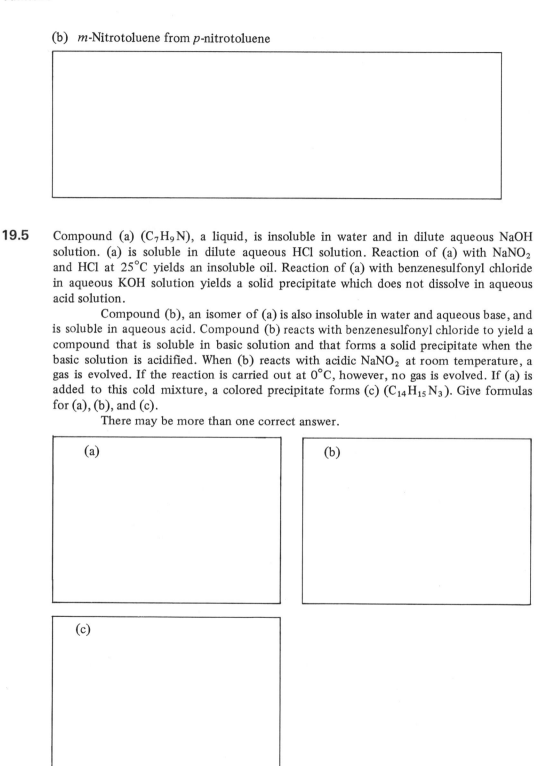

19.5   Compound (a) (C_7H_9N), a liquid, is insoluble in water and in dilute aqueous NaOH solution. (a) is soluble in dilute aqueous HCl solution. Reaction of (a) with $NaNO_2$ and HCl at 25°C yields an insoluble oil. Reaction of (a) with benzenesulfonyl chloride in aqueous KOH solution yields a solid precipitate which does not dissolve in aqueous acid solution.

Compound (b), an isomer of (a) is also insoluble in water and aqueous base, and is soluble in aqueous acid. Compound (b) reacts with benzenesulfonyl chloride to yield a compound that is soluble in basic solution and that forms a solid precipitate when the basic solution is acidified. When (b) reacts with acidic $NaNO_2$ at room temperature, a gas is evolved. If the reaction is carried out at 0°C, however, no gas is evolved. If (a) is added to this cold mixture, a colored precipitate forms (c) ($C_{14}H_{15}N_3$). Give formulas for (a), (b), and (c).

There may be more than one correct answer.

19.6   Complete the following reaction sequence by drawing the correct formulas in the blocks provided

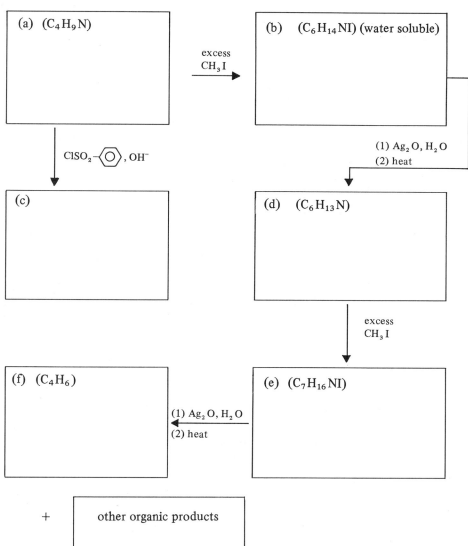

SPECIAL TOPIC
Reactions and Synthesis of Heterocyclic Amines

SOLUTIONS TO PROBLEMS

K.1 (a) [structure: piperidine N–C(=O)–CH₃]   (b) [structure: pyridinium N⁺–CH₃ with I⁻]

(c) [structure: benzene ring with C(=O)–N-pyrrolidine and C–OH with =O below]   (d) [structure: pyrrolidinium N⁺ with two CH₃ groups and I⁻]

(e) $CH_2{=}CHCH_2CH_2N{-}CH_3$ with CH_3 below the N

K.2 (a) The cyclopentadienyl anion.

(b) The pyrrole anion is a resonance hybrid of the following structures:

[resonance structures of pyrrole anion]

The imidazole anion is a hybrid of these:

[resonance structures of imidazole anion]

K.3 A mechanism involving a "pyridyne" intermediate would involve a net loss (of 50%) of the deuterium label.

[mechanism structures: pyridine with D label + :NH₂⁻ → pyridyne + NH₃, −HD]

[further mechanism: pyridine + :NH₂⁻ → anion → 2-aminopyridine]

2-Pyridyne

Since in the actual experiment there was no loss of deuterium this mechanism was disallowed.

The mechanism given on page 883 would not be expected to result in a loss of deuterium, thus it is consistent with the labeling experiment.

K.4   When pyridine undergoes nucleophilic substitution, the leaving group is a hydride ion—an ion that is a strong base and, consequently, a poor leaving group. With 2-halopyridines, on the other hand, the leaving groups are halide ions—ions that are weak bases and thus good leaving groups.

K.5   If we write the reactants in the following way we can better see how the reaction occurs.

$$CH_3\overset{O}{\overset{\|}{C}}CH_2NH_3^+\ Cl^- + OH^- \longrightarrow CH_3\overset{O}{\overset{\|}{C}}CH_2NH_2$$

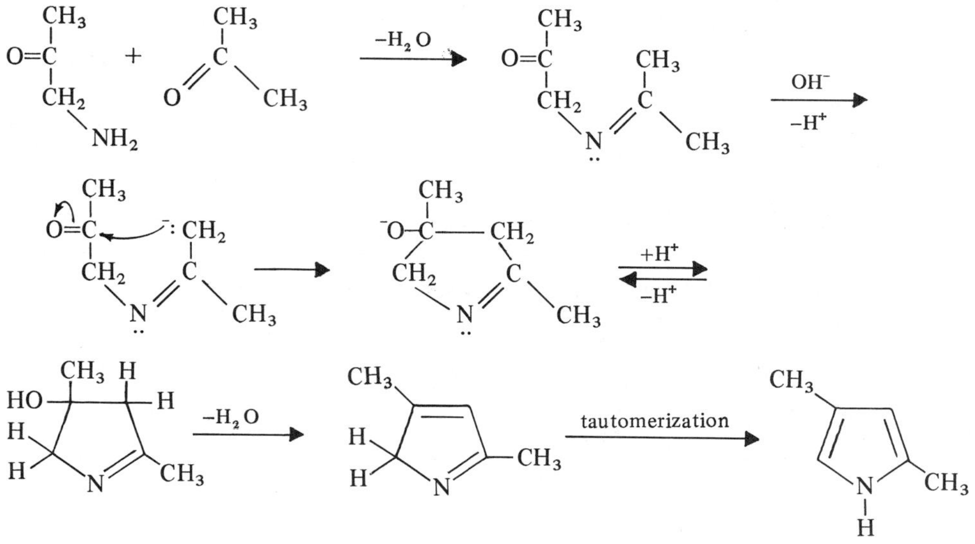

K.6

(a)

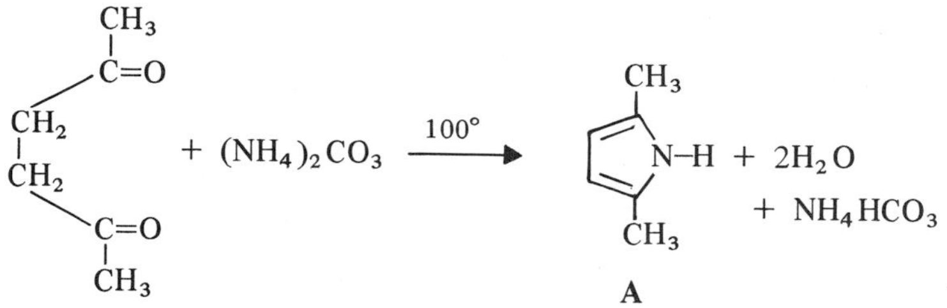

A

(b)

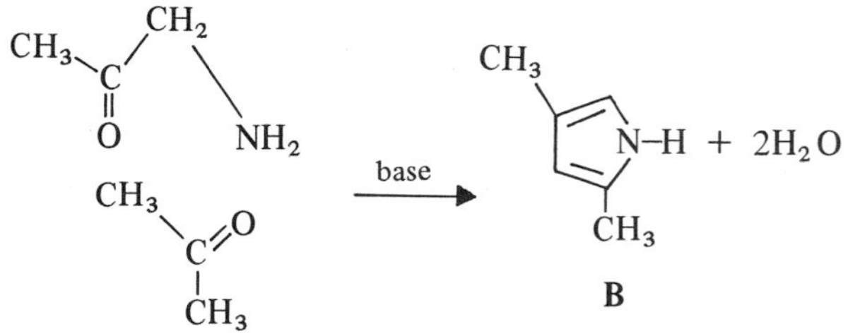

B

(c)

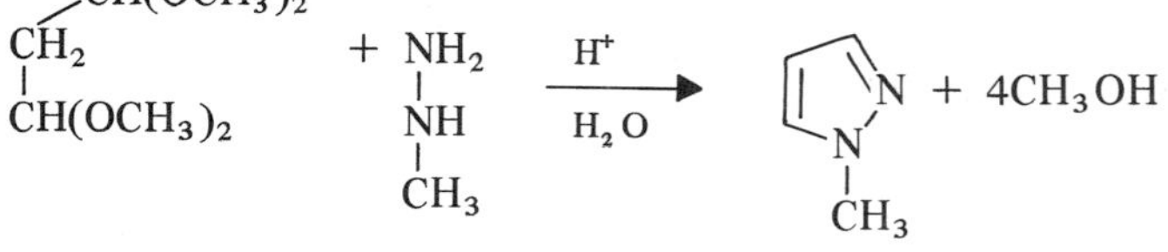

C

(d)

(e)

(f)

SOLUTIONS TO PROBLEMS

L.1 (a) The first step is similar to a crossed-Claisen condensation (see Sect. 20.2A):

(b) This step involves hydrolysis of an amide (lactam) and can be carried out with either acid or base. Here we use acid.

(c) This step is the decarboxylation of a substituted malonic acid; it requires only the application of heat and takes place during the acid hydrolysis of step (b).

(d) This is the reduction of a ketone to a secondary alcohol. A variety of reducing agents can be used, sodium borohydride, for example.

(e) Here we convert the secondary alcohol to an alkyl bromide with hydrogen bromide; this reagent also gives a hydrobromide salt of the aliphatic amine.

(f) Treating the salt with base produces the secondary amine; it then acts as a nucleophile and attacks the carbon bearing the bromine. This reaction leads to the formation of a five-membered ring and (±) nicotine.

L.2 (a) The chiral carbon adjacent to the ester carbonyl group is racemized by base (probably through the formation of an anion that can undergo inversion of configuration, cf. Sect. 17.3).

(b)

L.3

(a)

$C_6H_5CHCOOH$
$\quad\quad |$
$\quad\quad CH_2OH$

($\pm$) tropic acid

Tropine

(b) Tropine is a meso compound; it has a plane of symmetry that passes through the $>CHOH$ group, the $>NCH_3$ group, and between the two $-CH_2-$ groups of the five-membered ring.

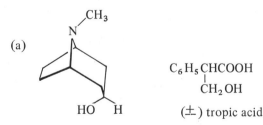

Plane of symmetry

(c)

ψ – Tropine

L.4

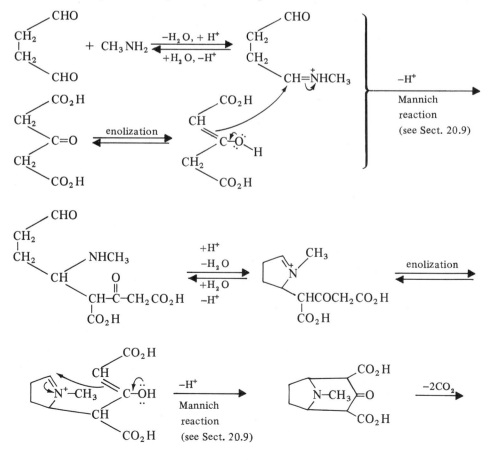

L.5 One possible sequence of steps is the following:

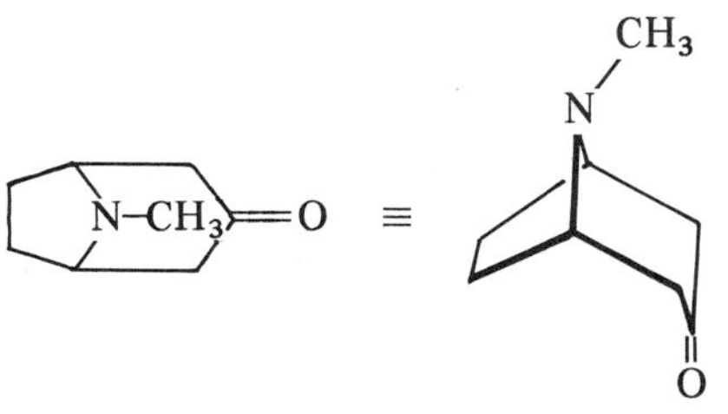

tropinone

L.6

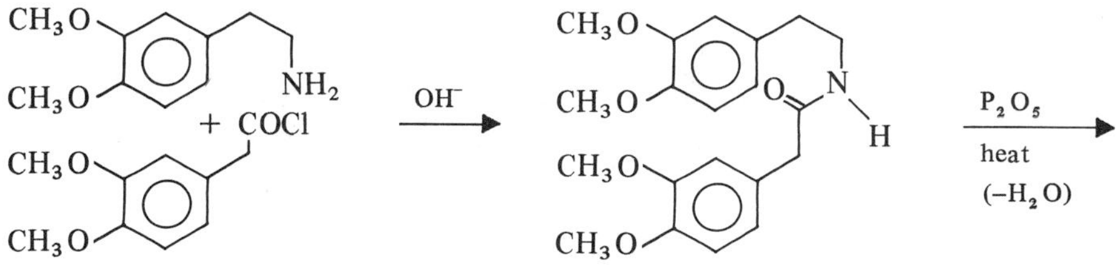

$C_{20}H_{25}NO_5$

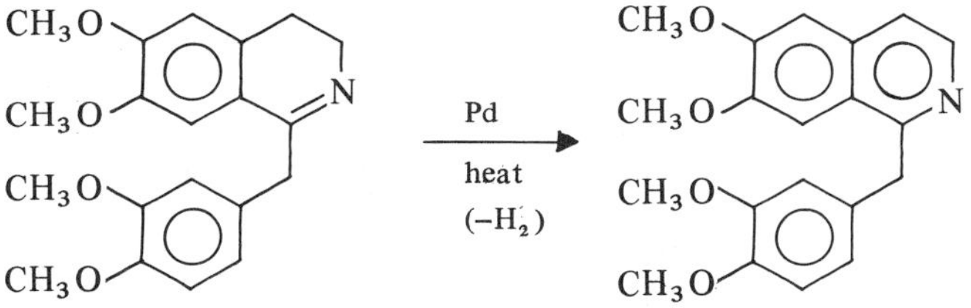

Dihydropapaverine   Papaverine

L.7   A Diels-Alder reaction was carried out using 1,3-butadiene as the diene component.

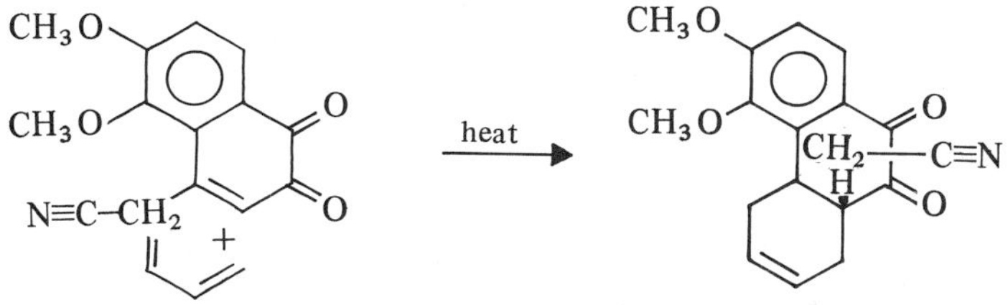

L.8   Acetic anhydride acetylates both —OH groups.

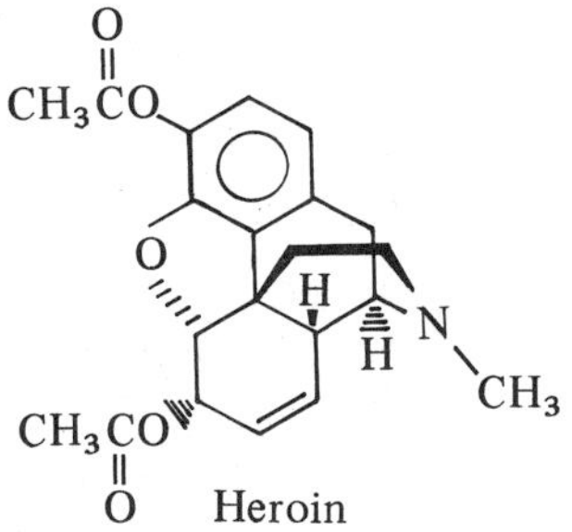

Heroin

L.9 (a) A Mannich reaction (see Sect. 20.9).

(b)

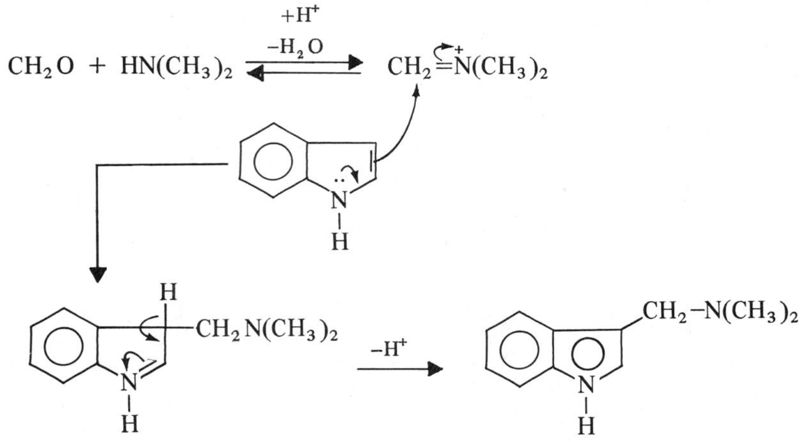

$$CH_2O + HN(CH_3)_2 \underset{-H_2O}{\overset{+H^+}{\rightleftharpoons}} CH_2 = \overset{+}{N}(CH_3)_2$$

Gramine

L.10

Reticulene

ortho-ortho CH₃ coupling → Bulbocapnine

bond rotation

para-ortho CH₃ coupling → Glaucine

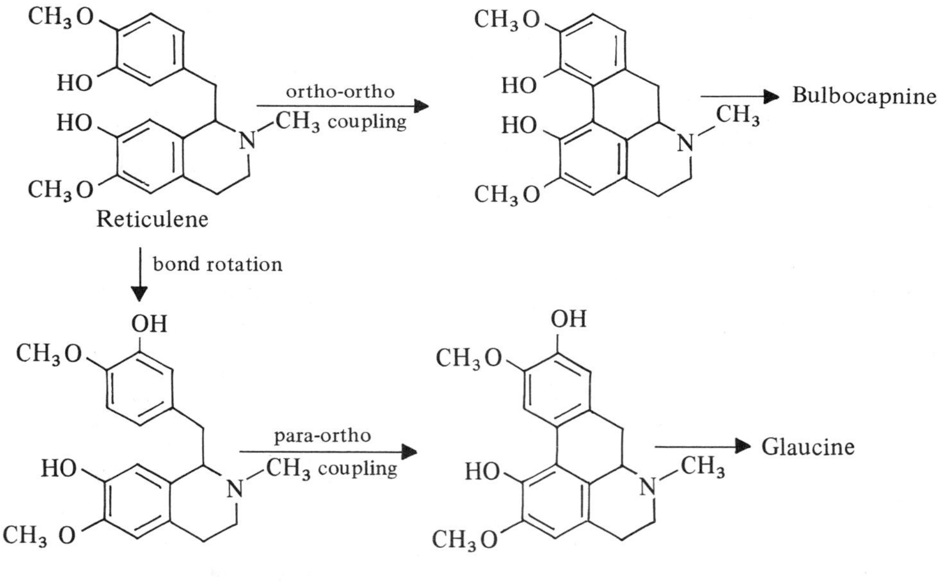

L.11 Yes, because according to the pathway given on pages 893-894, carbons 1 and 3 of papaverine arise from the α-carbons of two molecules of tyrosine.

(b) Yes.

(c) Methylation of the four phenolic hydroxyl groups and dehydrogenation of the nitrogen-containing ring.

L.12

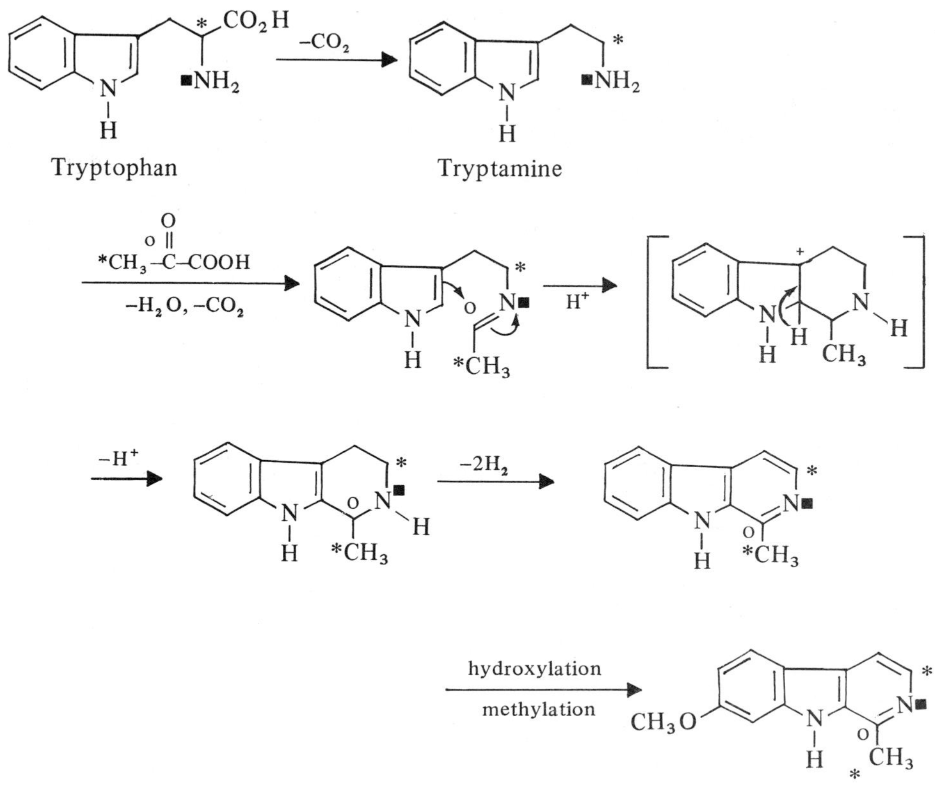

Tryptophan

Tryptamine

Harmine

Cf. T. A. Geissman and D. H. G. Crout, *Organic Chemistry of Secondary Plant Metabolism,* Freeman, Cooper & Co., San Francisco, 1969, pp. 473-474.

20

SYNTHESIS AND REACTIONS OF β-DICARBONYL COMPOUNDS: MORE CHEMISTRY OF ENOLATE IONS

SUMMARY OF ACETOACETIC ESTER AND MALONIC ESTER SYNTHESES

A. Acetoacetic Ester Synthesis

$$CH_3\overset{O}{\overset{||}{C}}CH_2\overset{O}{\overset{||}{C}}OEt \xrightarrow[\text{(2) RX}]{\text{(1) NaOEt}} CH_3\overset{O}{\overset{||}{C}}\overset{O}{\underset{R}{\overset{||}{C}}}HCOEt \xrightarrow[\text{(2) R′X}]{\text{(1) }(CH_3)_3COK}$$

$$CH_3\overset{O}{\overset{||}{C}}\overset{R'}{\underset{R}{\overset{|}{C}}}\overset{O}{\overset{||}{C}}OEt \xrightarrow[\text{(2) }H_3O^+]{\text{(1) OH}^-/H_2O} CH_3\overset{O}{\overset{||}{C}}\overset{R'}{\underset{R}{\overset{|}{C}}}\overset{O}{\overset{||}{C}}OH \xrightarrow[\text{(}-CO_2\text{)}]{\text{heat}} CH_3\overset{O}{\overset{||}{C}}\overset{}{\underset{R}{C}}HR'$$

B. Malonic Ester Synthesis

$$EtO\overset{O}{\overset{||}{C}}CH_2\overset{O}{\overset{||}{C}}OEt \xrightarrow[\text{(2) RX}]{\text{(1) NaOEt}} EtO\overset{O}{\overset{||}{C}}\overset{O}{\underset{R}{\overset{||}{C}}}HCOEt \xrightarrow[\text{(2) R′X}]{\text{(1) }(CH_3)_3COK}$$

$$EtO\overset{O}{\overset{||}{C}}\overset{R'}{\underset{R}{\overset{|}{C}}}\overset{O}{\overset{||}{C}}OEt \xrightarrow[\text{(2) }H_3O^+]{\text{(1) OH}^-/H_2O} HO\overset{O}{\overset{||}{C}}\overset{R'}{\underset{R}{\overset{|}{C}}}\overset{O}{\overset{||}{C}}OH \xrightarrow[\text{(}-CO_2\text{)}]{\text{heat}} HO\overset{O}{\overset{||}{C}}\overset{}{\underset{R}{C}}HR'$$

SOLUTIONS TO PROBLEMS

20.1

(a) Step 1 $CH_3CH\overset{O}{\overset{||}{-C}}OC_2H_5 \quad \overset{-}{}OC_2H_5 \rightleftharpoons CH_3\overset{\cdot\cdot}{CH}\overset{O}{\overset{||}{-C}}OC_2H_5 + C_2H_5OH$

$\overset{|}{H}$

$$CH_3CH=\overset{O^-}{\overset{|}{C}}OC_2H_5$$

482

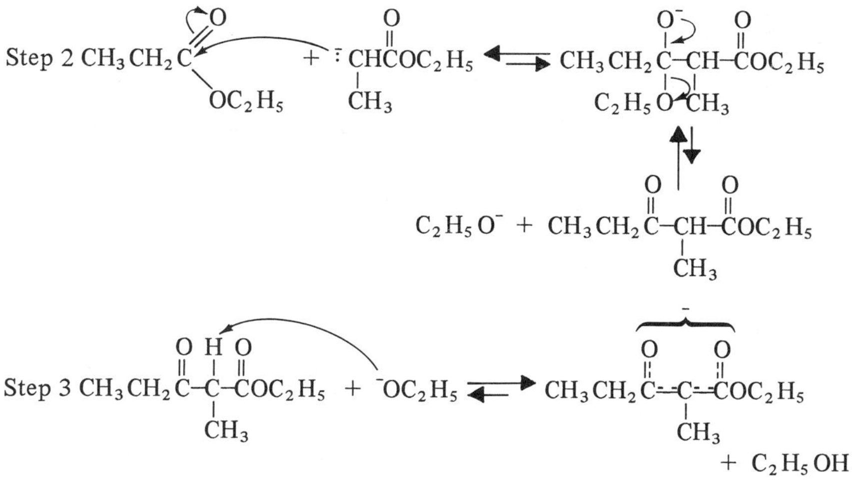

Step 2 CH_3CH_2C ... $+ :CHCOC_2H_5$ ⟶⟵ $CH_3CH_2C-CH-COC_2H_5$

Step 3 $CH_3CH_2C-C-COC_2H_5 + {}^-OC_2H_5$ ⟵⟶ $CH_3CH_2C=C=COC_2H_5$

$+ C_2H_5OH$

(b) 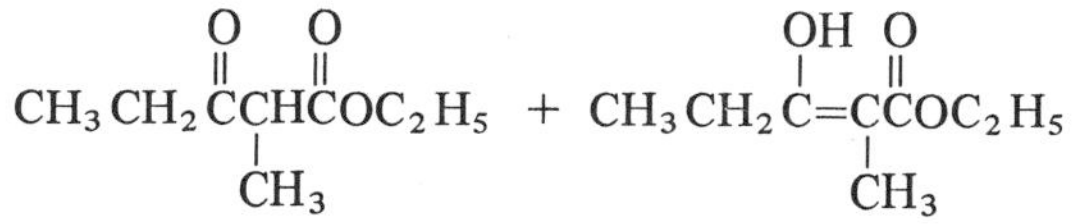 $CH_3CH_2CCHCOC_2H_5 + CH_3CH_2C=CCOC_2H_5$

20.2

(a) 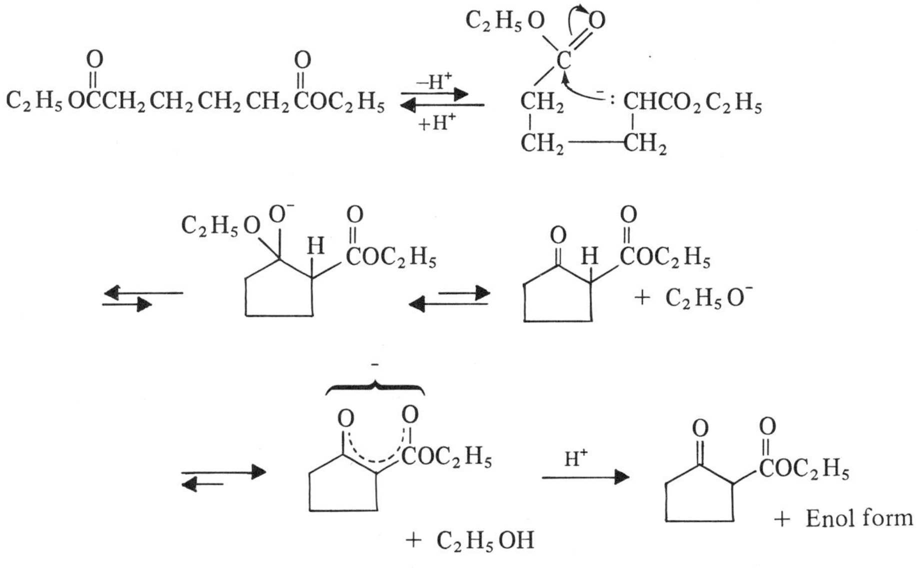 $C_2H_5OCCH_2CH_2CH_2CH_2COC_2H_5$ $\underset{+H^+}{\overset{-H^+}{\rightleftharpoons}}$

$+ C_2H_5O^-$

$+ C_2H_5OH$

$+ \text{Enol form}$

(b)

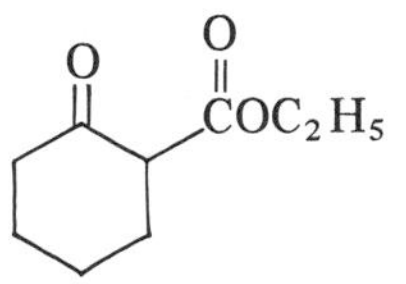

(c) To undergo a Dieckmann condensation, diethyl glutarate would have to form a highly strained four-membered ring.

20.3

$$CH_3\overset{O}{\overset{\|}{C}}OC_2H_5 + C_2H_5O^- \rightleftharpoons {}^{:}CH_2\overset{O}{\overset{\|}{C}}OC_2H_5 + C_2H_5OH$$

$$C_6H_5\overset{O}{\overset{\|}{C}}OC_2H_5 + {}^{:}CH_2\overset{O}{\overset{\|}{C}}OC_2H_5 \rightleftharpoons C_6H_5\overset{O^-}{\underset{OC_2H_5}{\overset{|}{C}}}-CH_2\overset{O}{\overset{\|}{C}}OC_2H_5$$

$$\rightleftharpoons C_6H_5\overset{O}{\overset{\|}{C}}CH_2\overset{O}{\overset{\|}{C}}OC_2H_5 + C_2H_5O^- \rightleftharpoons C_6H_5\overset{O}{\overset{\|}{C}}{=}CH{=}\overset{O}{\overset{\|}{C}}OC_2H_5$$
$$+ C_2H_5OH$$

$$\xrightarrow{H^+} C_6H_5\overset{O}{\overset{\|}{C}}CH_2\overset{O}{\overset{\|}{C}}OC_2H_5$$

$$C_6H_5CH_2\overset{O}{\overset{\|}{C}}OC_2H_5 + C_2H_5O^- \rightleftharpoons C_6H_5\overset{..}{C}H\overset{O}{\overset{\|}{C}}OC_2H_5 + C_2H_5OH$$

$$C_6H_5\overset{..}{C}H\overset{O}{\overset{\|}{C}}OC_2H_5 + C_2H_5O\overset{O}{\overset{\|}{C}}OC_2H_5 \rightleftharpoons C_6H_5\underset{\underset{O}{\overset{\|}{C}}OC_2H_5}{\overset{\overset{O^-}{\overset{|}{C_2H_5O-C-OC_2H_5}}}{\overset{|}{C}H}}$$

$$\rightleftharpoons C_6H_5\underset{\underset{O}{\overset{\|}{C}}OC_2H_5}{\overset{\overset{O}{\overset{\|}{C}}OC_2H_5}{\overset{|}{C}H}} + C_2H_5O^- \rightleftharpoons C_6H_5\underset{\underset{O}{\overset{\|}{C}}OC_2H_5}{\overset{\overset{O}{\overset{\|}{C}}OC_2H_5}{\overset{|}{C}{}^:}} + C_2H_5OH$$

Resonance
stabilized

$$\xrightarrow{H^+} C_6H_5\underset{\underset{O}{\overset{\|}{C}}OC_2H_5}{\overset{\overset{O}{\overset{\|}{C}}OC_2H_5}{\overset{|}{C}H}}$$

20.4

(a) $$CH_3CH_2\overset{O}{\overset{\|}{C}}OC_2H_5 + C_2H_5O\overset{O}{\overset{\|}{C}}-\overset{O}{\overset{\|}{C}}OC_2H_5 \xrightarrow[\text{(2) H}^+]{\text{(1) NaOC}_2\text{H}_5} CH_3\underset{\underset{O\ \ O}{\overset{\|\ \ \|}{C}-\overset{}{C}OC_2H_5}}{\overset{\overset{O}{\overset{\|}{C}}OC_2H_5}{\overset{|}{C}H}}$$

(b) $CH_3\overset{O}{\overset{\|}{C}}OC_2H_5$ + $H\overset{O}{\overset{\|}{C}}OC_2H_5$ $\xrightarrow[\text{(2) H}^+]{\text{(1) NaOC}_2\text{H}_5}$ $H\overset{O}{\overset{\|}{C}}CH_2\overset{O}{\overset{\|}{C}}OC_2H_5$

20.5

(a)

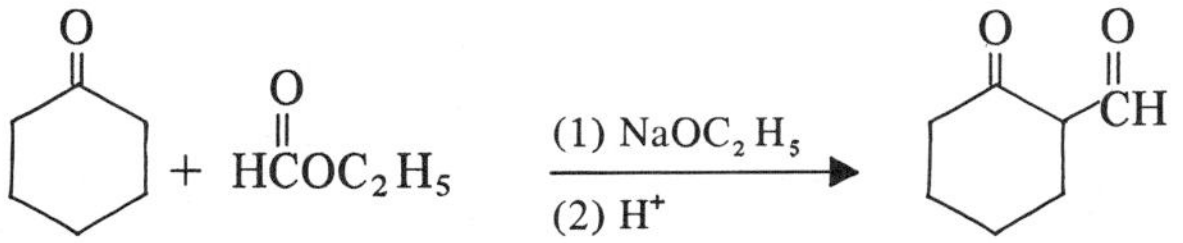

(b) 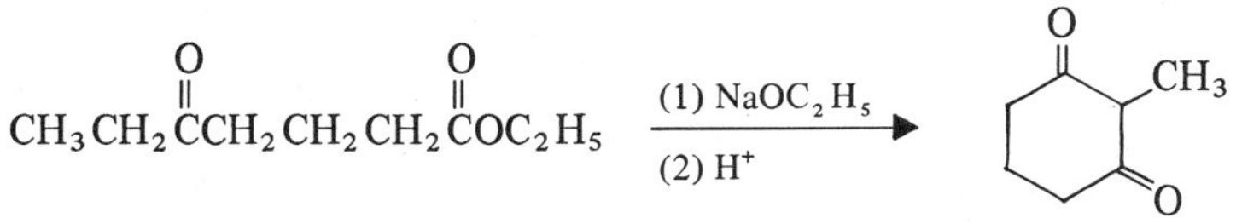 $CH_3CH_2\overset{O}{\overset{\|}{C}}CH_2CH_2CH_2\overset{O}{\overset{\|}{C}}OC_2H_5$ $\xrightarrow[\text{(2) H}^+]{\text{(1) NaOC}_2\text{H}_5}$

(c) $C_2H_5O_2CCH_2\overset{CH_3}{\underset{CH_3}{\overset{|}{\underset{|}{C}}}}CH_2CO_2C_2H_5$ + $C_2H_5O\overset{O}{\overset{\|}{C}}-\overset{O}{\overset{\|}{C}}OC_2H_5$ $\xrightarrow[\text{(2) H}^+]{\text{(1) NaOC}_2\text{H}_5}$

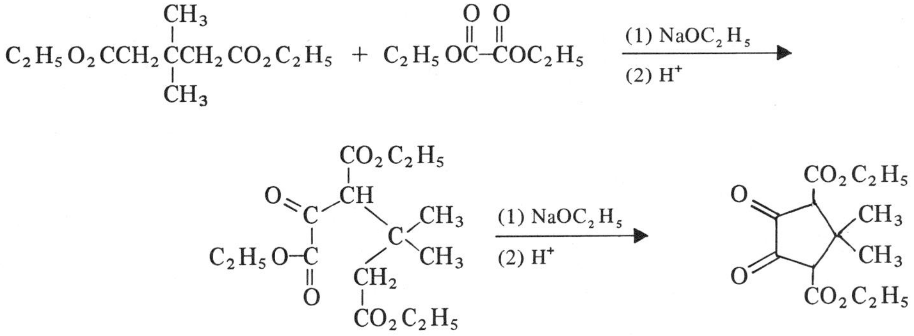

20.6

(a) 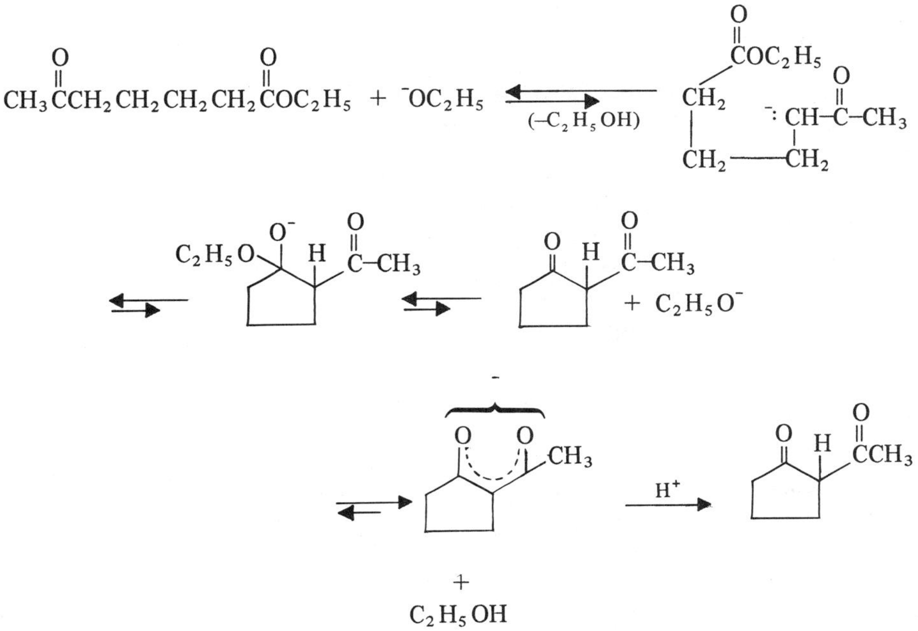 $CH_3\overset{O}{\overset{\|}{C}}CH_2CH_2CH_2CH_2\overset{O}{\overset{\|}{C}}OC_2H_5$ + $^-OC_2H_5$ $\underset{(-C_2H_5OH)}{\rightleftharpoons}$

(b) $CH_3\overset{O}{\overset{\|}{C}}CH_2CH_2CH_2\overset{O}{\overset{\|}{C}}OC_2H_5$ + $^-OC_2H_5$ $\underset{(-C_2H_5OH)}{\longleftrightarrow}$

+ $^-OC_2H_5$

+ C_2H_5OH

$\downarrow H^+$

Ionization of a hydrogen alpha to the ketone group might, in the first step, also yield $CH_3\overset{O}{\overset{\|}{C}}\overset{\cdot\cdot}{C}HCH_2CH_2\overset{O}{\overset{\|}{C}}OC_2H_5$. Cyclization of this enolate anion does not occur to any appreciable extent, however, because to do so it would yield a (highly strained) four-membered ring.

20.7   The partially negative oxygen of sodioacetoacetic ester acts as the nucleophile.

$CH_3\overset{O}{\overset{\|}{C}}-\overset{\cdot\cdot}{C}H-\overset{O}{\overset{\|}{C}}-OC_2H_5$ $\longleftrightarrow$ $CH_3\overset{O^-}{\overset{\|}{C}}=CH-\overset{O}{\overset{\|}{C}}-OC_2H_5$

20.8   Again, working backward,

(a) $CH_3\overset{O}{\overset{\|}{C}}CH_2CH_2CH_3$ $\underset{-CO_2}{\overset{heat}{\longleftarrow}}$ $CH_3\overset{O}{\overset{\|}{C}}\underset{\underset{CH_3}{\overset{|}{CH_2}}}{CH}-\overset{O}{\overset{\|}{C}}OH$ $\underset{(2) H_3O^+}{\overset{(1) \text{ dil. NaOH, heat}}{\longleftarrow}}$

$CH_3\overset{O}{\overset{\|}{C}}\underset{\underset{CH_3}{\overset{|}{CH_2}}}{\overset{O}{C}}H\overset{O}{\overset{\|}{C}}OC_2H_5$ $\underset{(2) CH_3CH_2Br}{\overset{(1) NaOC_2H_5}{\longleftarrow}}$ $CH_3\overset{O}{\overset{\|}{C}}CH_2\overset{O}{\overset{\|}{C}}OC_2H_5$

(b)

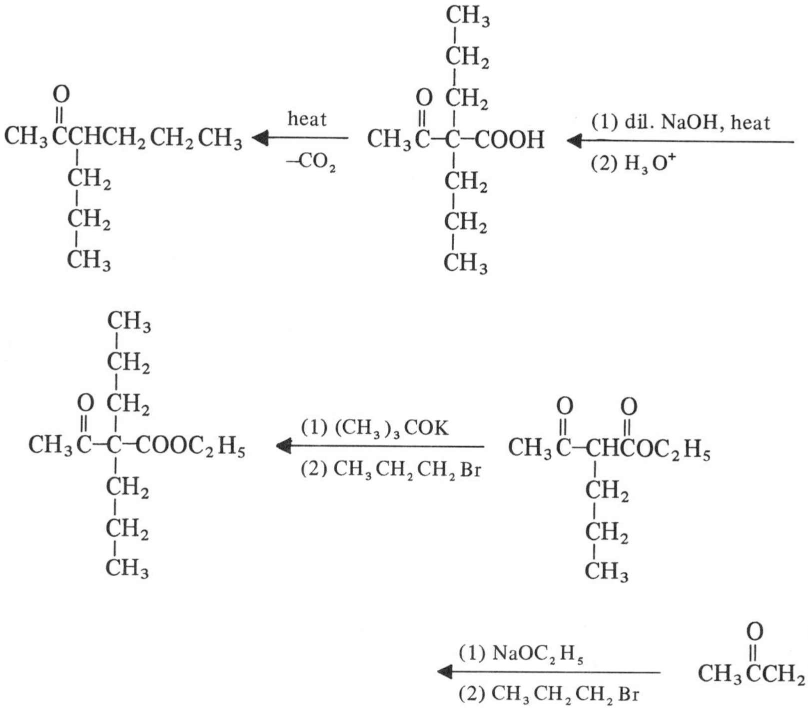

(c)

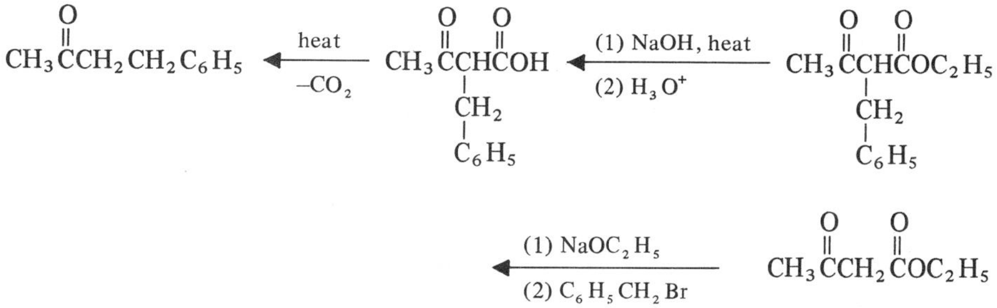

20.9 (a) Reactivity is the same as with any second order reaction. With primary halides substitution is highly favored, with secondary halides elimination competes with substitution, and with tertiary halides elimination is the exclusive course of reaction.

(b) Acetoacetic ester and 2-methylpropene.

(c) Bromobenzene is unreactive toward nucleophilic substitution (cf. Section 14.14 of the text).

20.10

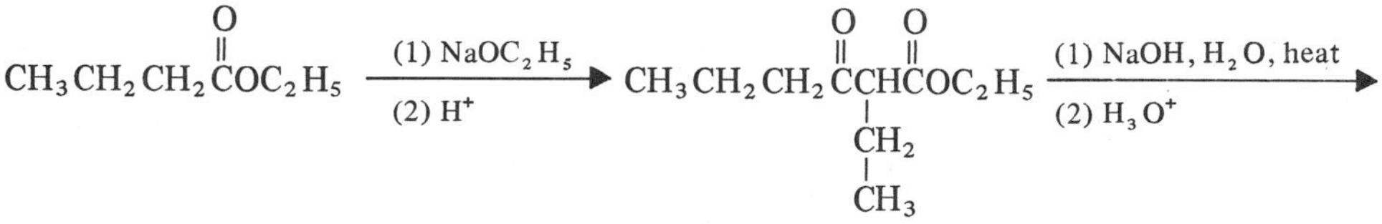

$$CH_3CH_2CH_2\overset{\overset{\displaystyle O}{\|}}{C}\overset{}{\underset{\underset{\underset{\displaystyle CH_3}{|}}{\overset{\displaystyle CH_2}{|}}}{C}}HCOH \xrightarrow[-CO_2]{heat} CH_3CH_2CH_2\overset{\overset{\displaystyle O}{\|}}{C}CH_2CH_2CH_3$$

20.11 The carboxyl group that is lost most readily is the one that is β to the keto group (cf. page 811 of the text).

20.12

$$CH_3\overset{\overset{\displaystyle O}{\|}}{C}CH_2CH_2\overset{\overset{\displaystyle O}{\|}}{C}C_6H_5 \xleftarrow[-CO_2]{heat} CH_3\overset{\overset{\displaystyle O}{\|}}{C}\underset{\underset{\underset{\underset{\displaystyle C_6H_5}{|}}{\overset{\displaystyle C=O}{|}}}{\overset{\displaystyle CH_2}{|}}}{C}HCOH \xleftarrow[\text{(2) } H_3O^+]{\text{(1) } OH^-, H_2O, heat}$$

$$CH_3\overset{\overset{\displaystyle O}{\|}}{C}\underset{\underset{\underset{\underset{\displaystyle C_6H_5}{|}}{\overset{\displaystyle C=O}{|}}}{\overset{\displaystyle CH_2}{|}}}{C}H\overset{\overset{\displaystyle O}{\|}}{C}OC_2H_5 \xleftarrow[\text{(2) } C_6H_5COCH_2Br]{\text{(1) } NaOC_2H_5} CH_3\overset{\overset{\displaystyle O}{\|}}{C}CH_2\overset{\overset{\displaystyle O}{\|}}{C}OC_2H_5$$

20.13

$$CH_3\overset{\overset{\displaystyle O}{\|}}{C}CH_2\overset{\overset{\displaystyle O}{\|}}{C}C_6H_5 \xleftarrow[-CO_2]{heat} CH_3\overset{\overset{\displaystyle O}{\|}}{C}\underset{\underset{\underset{\displaystyle C_6H_5}{|}}{\overset{\displaystyle C=O}{|}}}{C}HCOH \xleftarrow[\text{(2) } H_3O^+]{\text{(1) } OH^-, H_2O, heat}$$

$$CH_3\overset{\overset{\displaystyle O}{\|}}{C}\underset{\underset{\underset{\displaystyle C_6H_5}{|}}{\overset{\displaystyle C=O}{|}}}{C}H\overset{\overset{\displaystyle O}{\|}}{C}OC_2H_5 \xleftarrow[\text{(2) } C_6H_5COCl]{\text{(1) } NaH} CH_3\overset{\overset{\displaystyle O}{\|}}{C}CH_2\overset{\overset{\displaystyle O}{\|}}{C}OC_2H_5$$

20.14 (a) One molar equivalent of $NaNH_2$ converts acetoacetic ester to its anion,

$$CH_3\overset{\overset{\displaystyle O}{\|}}{C}CH_2\overset{\overset{\displaystyle O}{\|}}{C}OEt + NH_2^- \longrightarrow CH_3\overset{\overset{\displaystyle O}{\|}}{C}\overset{..^-}{C}H\overset{\overset{\displaystyle O}{\|}}{C}OEt + NH_3$$

and one molar equivalent of $NaNH_2$ converts bromobenzene to benzyne (cf. Section 14.14B):

Then the anion of acetoacetic ester adds to the benzyne as it forms in the mixture.

This is the end-product of the addition

(b) 1-Phenyl-2-propanone, as follows.

(c) By treating bromobenzene with diethyl malonate and two molar equivalents of NaNH$_2$ to form diethyl phenylmalonate.

[The mechanism for this reaction is analogous to that given in part (a).]

Then hydrolyis and decarboxylation will convert diethyl phenylmalonate to phenylacetic acid

20.15   Here we alkylate the dianion,

$$CH_3-\overset{\overset{O}{\|}}{C}-CH_2-\overset{\overset{O}{\|}}{C}OC_2H_5 \xrightarrow[\text{liq. } NH_3]{2KNH_2} \quad \overset{..}{:}CH_2-\overset{\overset{O}{\|}}{C}-\overset{..}{C}H-\overset{\overset{O}{\|}}{C}OC_2H_5$$

$$\xrightarrow[\text{(2) } NH_4Cl]{\text{(1) } C_6H_5CH_2Cl} \quad C_6H_5CH_2CH_2\overset{\overset{O}{\|}}{C}CH_2\overset{\overset{O}{\|}}{C}OC_2H_5$$

20.16   Working backward,

(a) $CH_3CH_2CH_2CH_2COOH \xleftarrow[-CO_2]{\text{heat}} CH_3CH_2CH_2\overset{\displaystyle COOH}{\underset{\displaystyle COOH}{CH}} \xleftarrow[\text{(2) } H_3O^+]{\text{(1) } OH^-, H_2O, \text{heat}}$

$CH_3CH_2CH_2\overset{\displaystyle COOC_2H_5}{\underset{\displaystyle COOC_2H_5}{CH}} \xleftarrow[CH_3CH_2CH_2Br]{NaOC_2H_5} \overset{\displaystyle COOC_2H_5}{\underset{\displaystyle COOC_2H_5}{\overset{\displaystyle |}{\underset{\displaystyle |}{CH_2}}}}$

(b) $CH_3CH_2CH_2\underset{\displaystyle CH_3}{\overset{\displaystyle |}{CH}}COOH \xleftarrow[-CO_2]{\text{heat}} \overset{CH_3CH_2CH_2}{\underset{CH_3}{C}}\overset{COOH}{\underset{COOH}{}} \xleftarrow[\text{(2) } H_3O^+]{\text{(1) } OH^-, H_2O, \text{heat}}$

$\overset{CH_3CH_2CH_2}{\underset{CH_3}{C}}\overset{COOC_2H_5}{\underset{COOC_2H_5}{}} \xleftarrow[(CH_3)_3COK]{CH_3I} CH_3CH_2CH_2CH\overset{COOC_2H_5}{\underset{COOC_2H_5}{}}$

$\xleftarrow[NaOC_2H_5]{CH_3CH_2CH_2Br} \overset{\displaystyle COOC_2H_5}{\underset{\displaystyle COOC_2H_5}{\overset{\displaystyle |}{\underset{\displaystyle |}{CH_2}}}}$

(c) $CH_3\underset{\displaystyle CH_3}{\overset{\displaystyle |}{CH}}CH_2CH_2COOH \xleftarrow[-CO_2]{\text{heat}} CH_3\underset{\displaystyle CH_3}{\overset{\displaystyle |}{CH}}CH_2\overset{\displaystyle COOH}{\underset{\displaystyle COOH}{CH}} \xleftarrow[\text{(2) } H_3O^+]{\text{(1) } OH^-, H_2O, \text{heat}}$

$CH_3\underset{\displaystyle CH_3}{\overset{\displaystyle |}{CH}}CH_2\overset{\displaystyle COOC_2H_5}{\underset{\displaystyle COOC_2H_5}{CH}} \xleftarrow[\underset{\displaystyle CH_3}{\overset{\displaystyle |}{CH_3CHCH_2Br}}]{NaOC_2H_5} \overset{\displaystyle COOC_2H_5}{\underset{\displaystyle COOC_2H_5}{\overset{\displaystyle |}{\underset{\displaystyle |}{CH_2}}}}$

20.17

(a)   Formaldehyde, $H-\overset{\overset{O}{\|}}{C}-H$

(b)

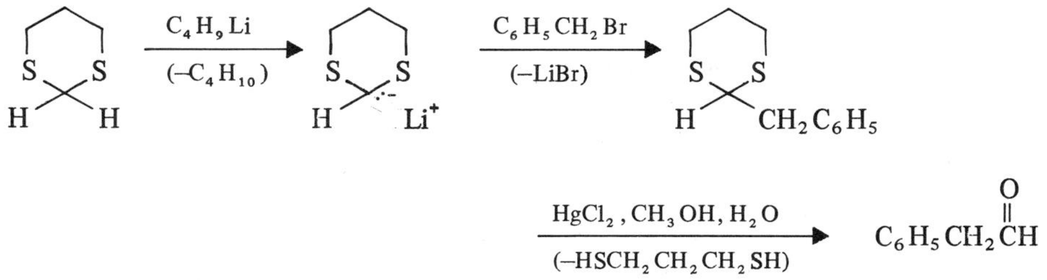

$$C_6H_5CH_2\overset{\overset{\displaystyle O}{\|}}{C}H$$

(c)

$$C_6H_5\overset{\overset{\displaystyle O}{\|}}{C}CH_3 \;+\; HSCH_2CH_2CH_2SH$$

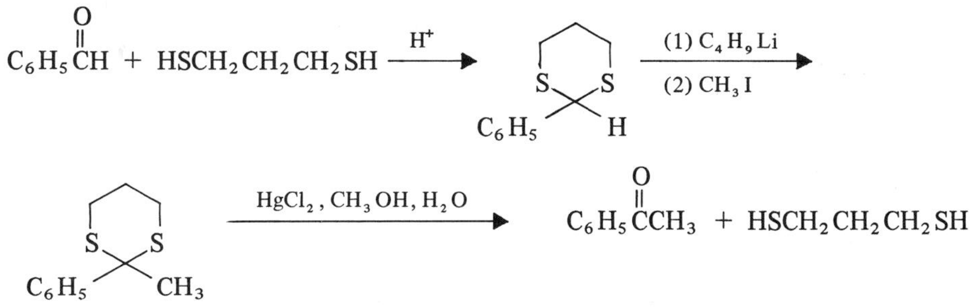

20.18 By treating the thioketal with Raney-nickel.

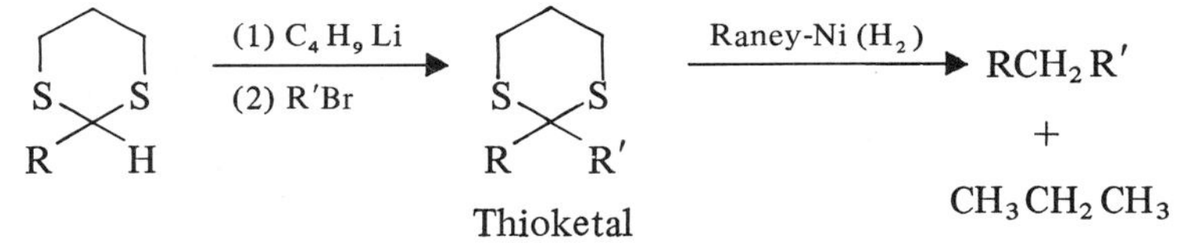

20.19

(a)

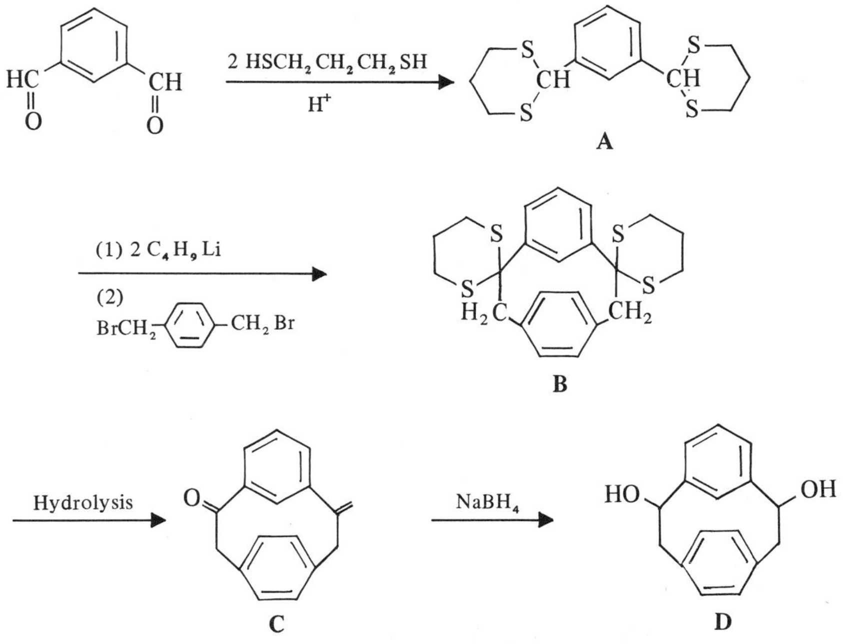

(b)

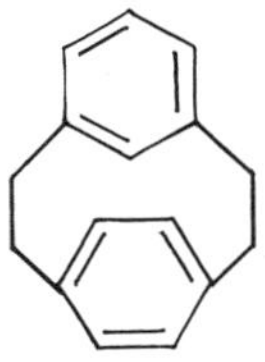

20.20

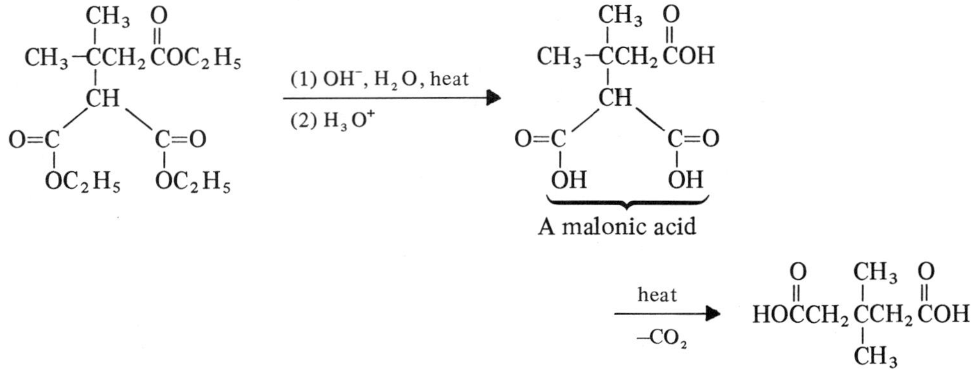

20.21

(a)

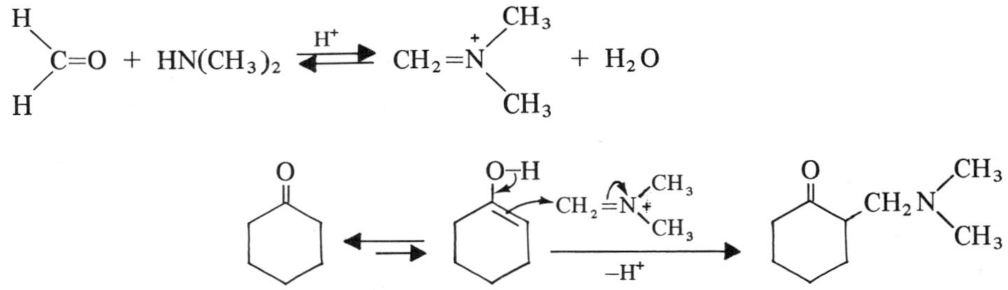

(b)

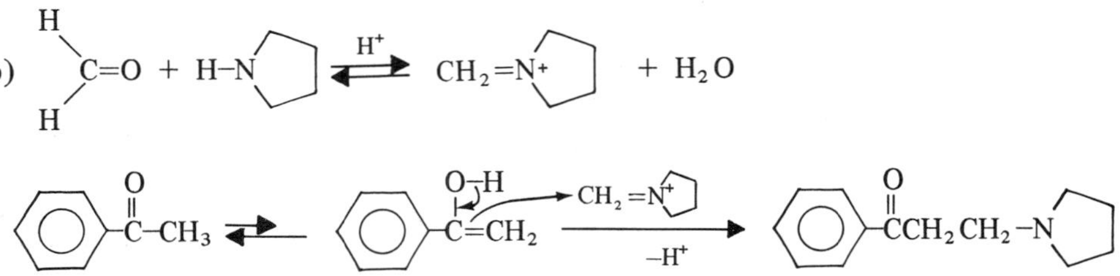

(c)

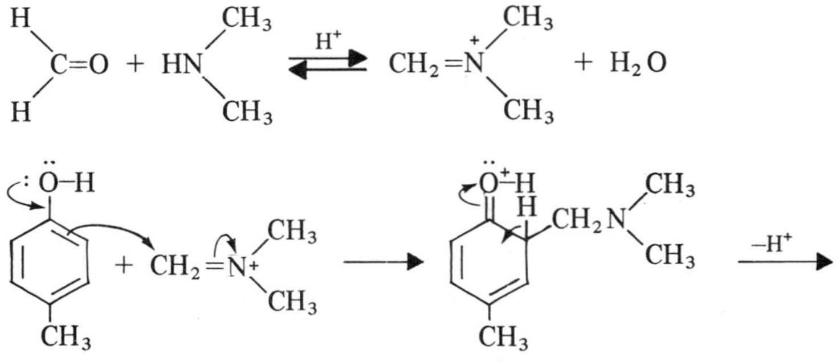

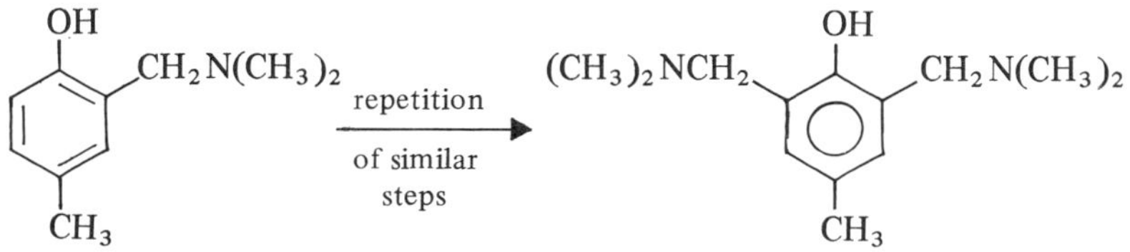

20.22 These syntheses are easy to see if we work backward.

(a)

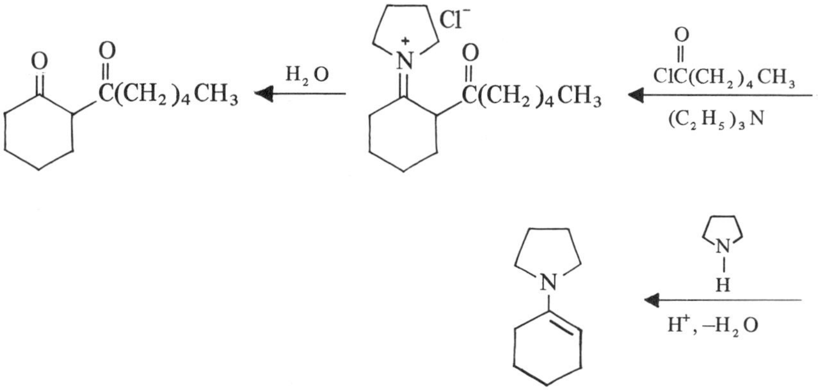

(b)

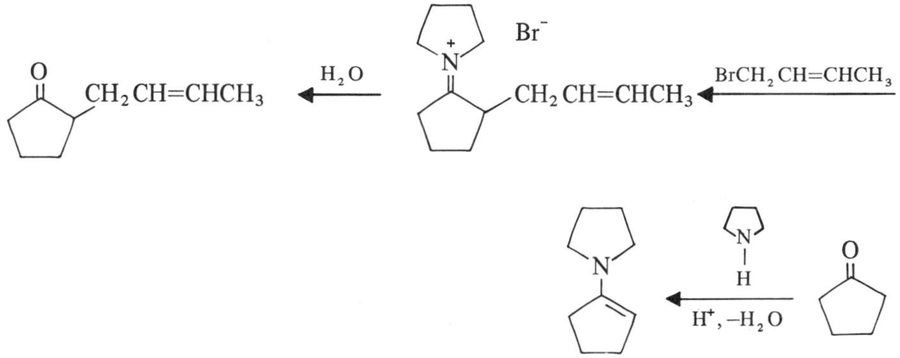

(c)

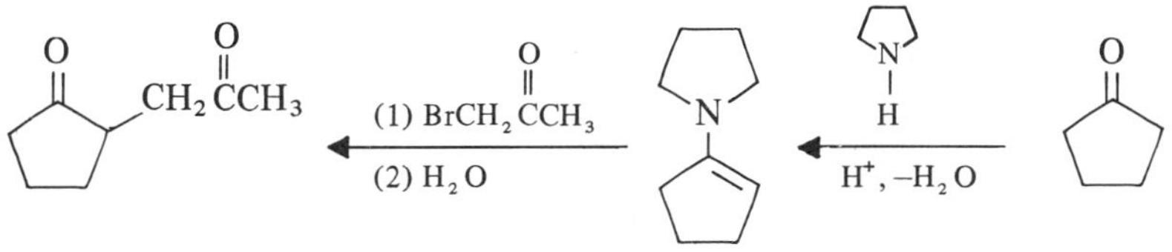

(d)

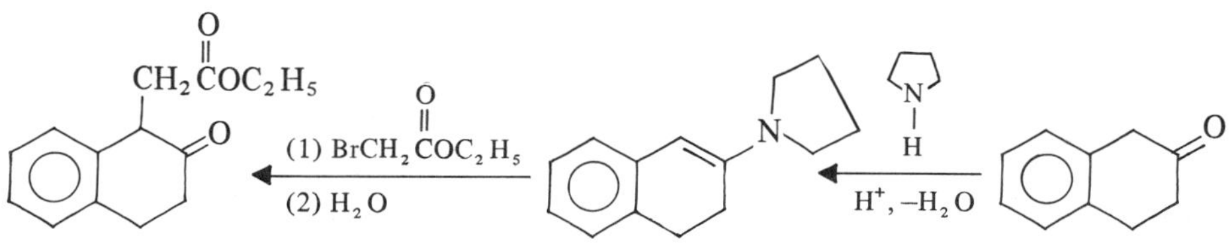

20.23

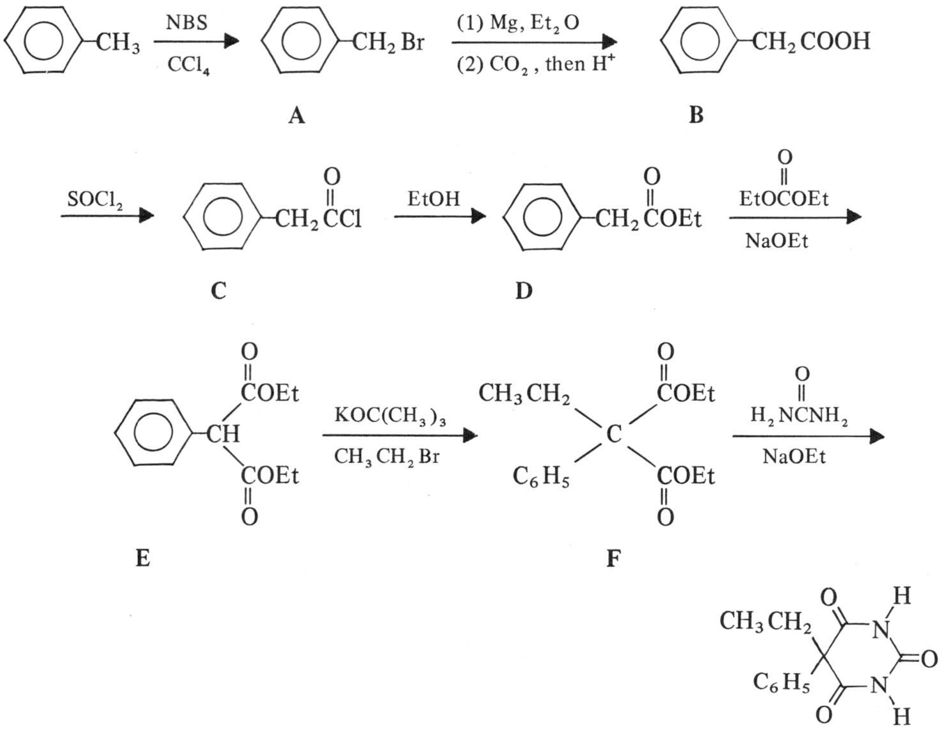

Phenobarbital

20.24

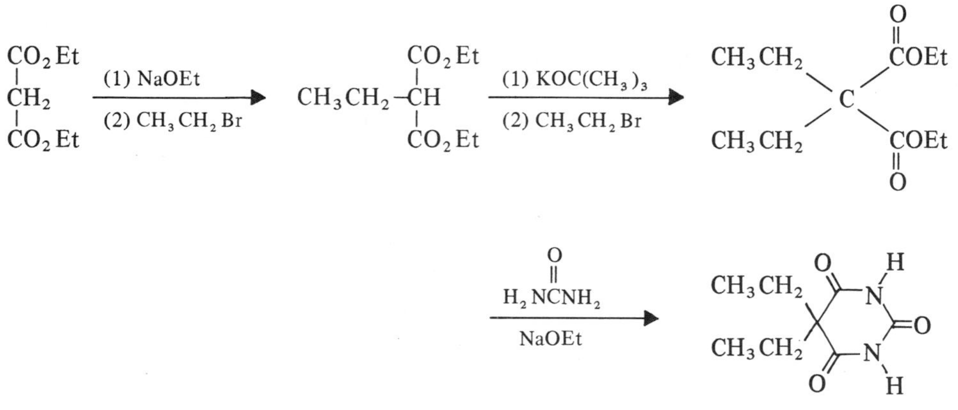

Veronal

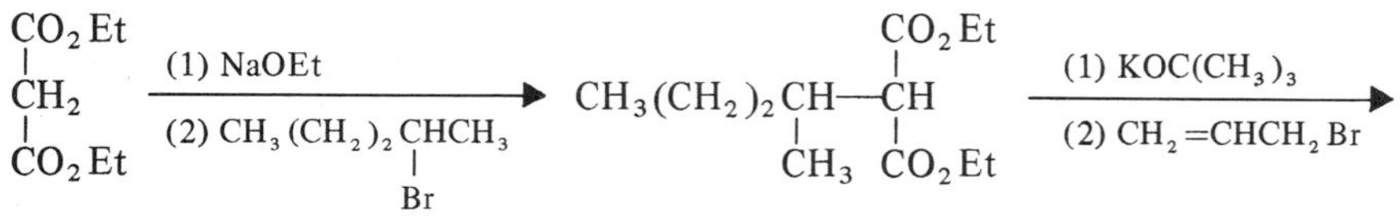

$$CH_2=CHCH_2 \underset{\underset{CH_3}{|}}{\underset{CH_3(CH_2)_2CH}{\big\backslash}} C \underset{\underset{O}{\|}}{\overset{\overset{O}{\|}}{\big/}} \underset{COEt}{\overset{COEt}{}} \quad \xrightarrow[\text{NaOEt}]{\overset{\overset{O}{\|}}{H_2NCNH_2}} \quad$$

Seconal

20.25

(a) $CH_3CH_2CH_2\overset{O}{\overset{\|}{C}}\underset{\underset{CH_3}{\underset{|}{CH_2}}}{CH}\overset{O}{\overset{\|}{C}}OC_2H_5 \xleftarrow[\text{(2) H}^+]{\text{(1) NaOC}_2\text{H}_5} CH_3CH_2CH_2\overset{O}{\overset{\|}{C}}OC_2H_5$

(b) $CH_3CH_2CH_2\overset{O}{\overset{\|}{C}}CH_2CH_2CH_3 \xleftarrow[-CO_2]{\text{heat}} CH_3CH_2CH_2\overset{O}{\overset{\|}{C}}\underset{\underset{CH_3}{\underset{|}{CH_2}}}{CH}\overset{O}{\overset{\|}{C}}OH$

$\xleftarrow[\text{(2) H}_3\text{O}^+]{\text{(1) OH}^-,\ \text{H}_2\text{O, heat}}$ Product of (a)

(c) $C_6H_5\underset{\underset{CH_3}{|}}{CH}COOH \xleftarrow[-CO_2]{\text{heat}} \underset{C_6H_5}{\overset{CH_3}{\big\backslash}}C\underset{COOH}{\overset{COOH}{\big/}} \xleftarrow[\text{(2) H}_3\text{O}^+]{\text{(1) OH}^-,\ \text{H}_2\text{O, heat}}$

$\underset{C_6H_5}{\overset{CH_3}{\big\backslash}}C\underset{COOC_2H_5}{\overset{COOC_2H_5}{\big/}} \xleftarrow[\text{CH}_3\text{I}]{\text{NaOC}_2\text{H}_5} C_6H_5-CH\underset{COOC_2H_5}{\overset{COOC_2H_5}{\big\backslash}}$

$\xleftarrow[\text{(2) H}^+]{\overset{\overset{O}{\|}}{\text{(1) C}_2\text{H}_5\text{OCOC}_2\text{H}_5}}_{\text{NaOC}_2\text{H}_5} C_6H_5CH_2\overset{O}{\overset{\|}{C}}OC_2H_5$

(d) $CH_3CH_2\underset{\underset{O\ O}{\underset{\|\ \|}{C-COC_2H_5}}}{\overset{O}{\overset{\|}{CH}}}COC_2H_5 \xleftarrow[\text{NaOC}_2\text{H}_5 \ \text{(2) H}^+]{\overset{\overset{O\ O}{\|\ \|}}{\text{(1) C}_2\text{H}_5\text{OC-COC}_2\text{H}_5}} CH_3CH_2CH_2\overset{O}{\overset{\|}{C}}OC_2H_5$

(e) $CH_3CH_2CH_2\overset{O\ O}{\overset{\|\ \|}{C-C}}OC_2H_5 \xleftarrow[\text{C}_2\text{H}_5\text{OH}]{\text{H}^+} CH_3CH_2CH_2\overset{O\ O}{\overset{\|\ \|}{C-C}}OH$

$\xleftarrow[-CO_2]{\text{heat}} CH_3CH_2\underset{\underset{O\ O}{\underset{\|\ \|}{C-COH}}}{CH}COOH \xleftarrow[\text{(2) H}_3\text{O}^+]{\text{(1) OH}^-,\ \text{H}_2\text{O, heat}}$ Product of (d)

(f) 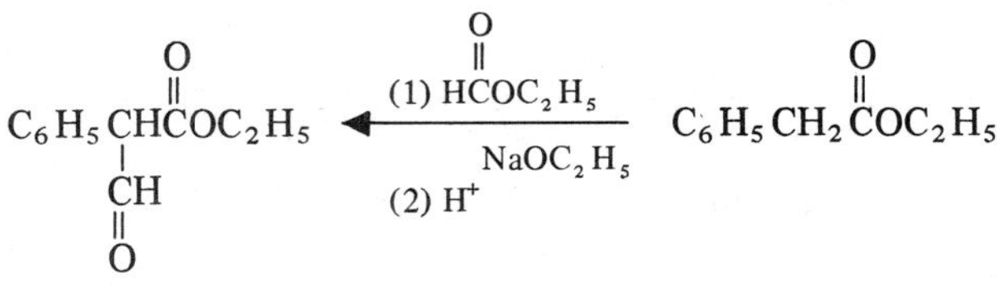

(g) 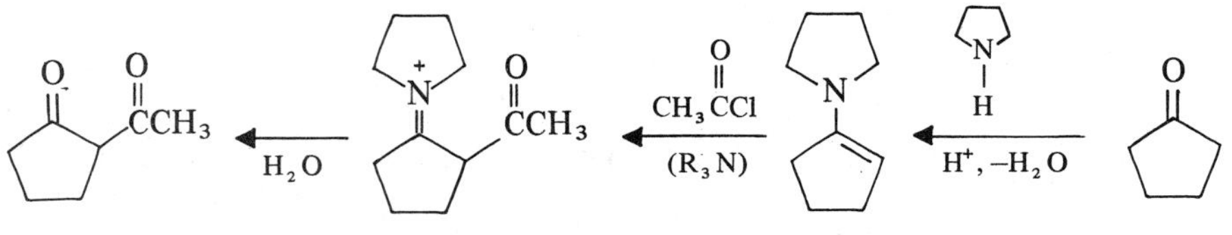

(h) 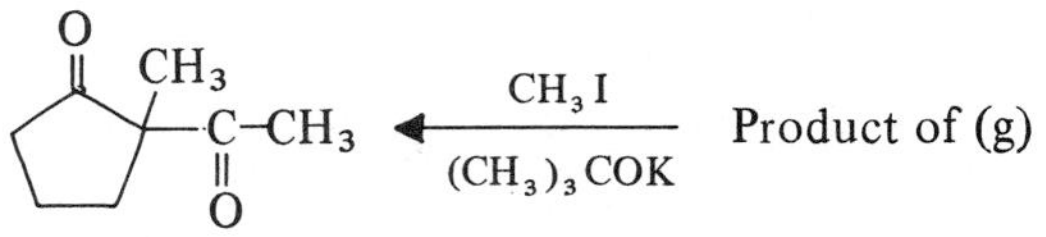

(i) 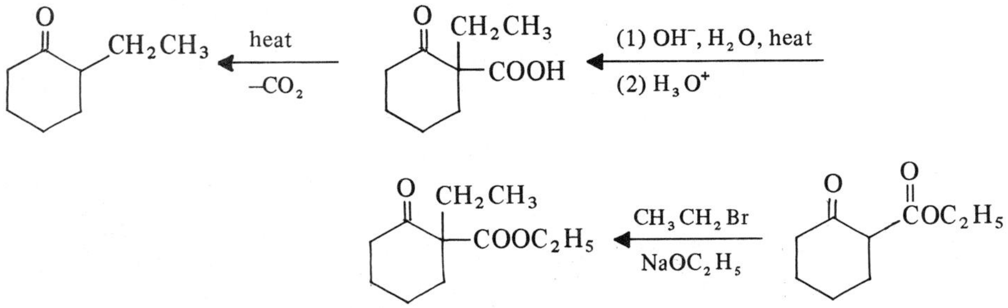

20.26

(a) 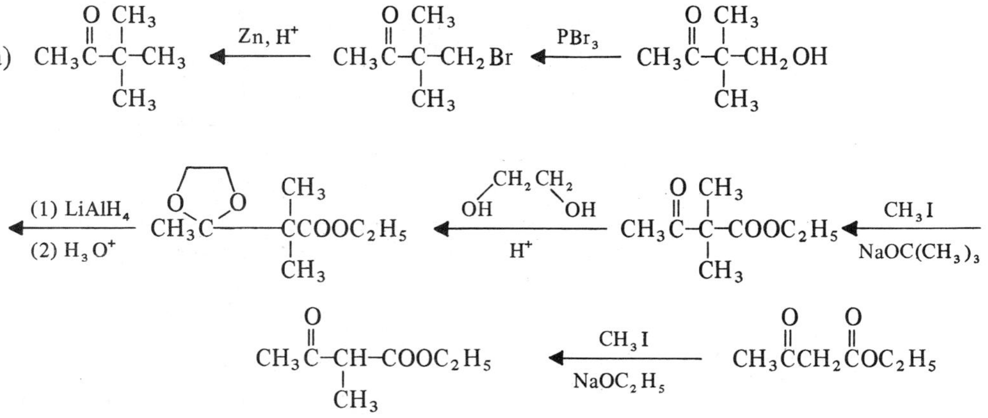

(b) 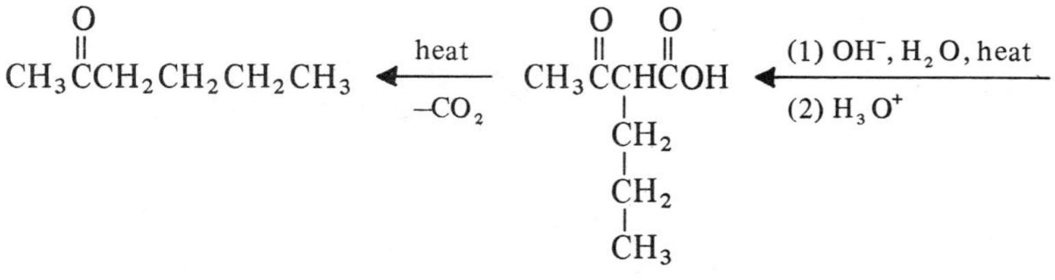

$$CH_3\overset{O}{\overset{||}{C}}\overset{}{\underset{\underset{\underset{CH_3}{|}}{\underset{\underset{CH_2}{|}}{CH_2}}}{CH}}\overset{O}{\overset{||}{C}}OC_2H_5 \xleftarrow[CH_3CH_2CH_2Br]{NaOC_2H_5} CH_3\overset{O}{\overset{||}{C}}CH_2\overset{O}{\overset{||}{C}}OC_2H_5$$

(c) $CH_3\overset{O}{\overset{||}{C}}CH_2CH_2\overset{O}{\overset{||}{C}}CH_3 \xleftarrow[-CO_2]{heat} CH_3\overset{O}{\overset{||}{C}}\overset{}{\underset{\underset{\underset{CH_3}{|}}{\underset{\underset{C=O}{|}}{CH_2}}}{CH}}\overset{O}{\overset{||}{C}}OH \xleftarrow[(2)\ H_3O^+]{(1)\ OH^-,\ H_2O,\ heat}$

$$CH_3\overset{O}{\overset{||}{C}}\overset{}{\underset{\underset{\underset{CH_3}{|}}{\underset{\underset{C=O}{|}}{CH_2}}}{CH}}\overset{O}{\overset{||}{C}}OC_2H_5 \xleftarrow[CH_3COCH_2Br]{NaOC_2H_5} CH_3\overset{O}{\overset{||}{C}}CH_2\overset{O}{\overset{||}{C}}OC_2H_5$$

(d) $\underset{\underset{OH}{|}}{CH_3}CHCH_2CH_2COOH \xleftarrow{NaBH_4} CH_3\overset{O}{\overset{||}{C}}CH_2CH_2\overset{O}{\overset{||}{C}}OH \xleftarrow[-CO_2]{heat}$

$$CH_3\overset{O}{\overset{||}{C}}\overset{}{\underset{\underset{COOH}{|}}{CH_2}}CHOH \xleftarrow[(2)\ H_3O^+]{(1)\ OH^-,\ H_2O,\ heat} CH_3\overset{O}{\overset{||}{C}}\overset{}{\underset{\underset{\underset{O}{||}}{\underset{\underset{COC_2H_5}{|}}{CH_2}}}{CH}}\overset{O}{\overset{||}{C}}OC_2H_5$$

$$\xleftarrow[BrCH_2COOC_2H_5]{NaOC_2H_5} CH_3\overset{O}{\overset{||}{C}}CH_2\overset{O}{\overset{||}{C}}OC_2H_5$$

(e) $\underset{\underset{C_2H_5}{|}}{CH_3}CHCHCH_2OH \xleftarrow[(2)\ H^+]{(1)\ LiAlH_4} CH_3\overset{O}{\overset{||}{C}}\underset{\underset{C_2H_5}{|}}{CH}\overset{O}{\overset{||}{C}}OC_2H_5 \xleftarrow[C_2H_5Br]{NaOC_2H_5} CH_3\overset{O}{\overset{||}{C}}CH_2\overset{O}{\overset{||}{C}}OC_2H_5$

(f) $\underset{\underset{OH}{|}}{CH_3}CHCH_2\underset{\underset{OH}{|}}{CH}C_6H_5 \xleftarrow{NaBH_4} CH_3\overset{O}{\overset{||}{C}}CH_2\overset{O}{\overset{||}{C}}C_6H_5 \longleftarrow$ cf. Problem 20.13

(g) $C_6H_5\underset{\underset{OH}{|}}{CH}CH_2\underset{\underset{OH}{|}}{CH}CH_2CH_2OH \xleftarrow[(2)\ H^+]{(1)\ LiAlH_4} C_6H_5\overset{O}{\overset{||}{C}}CH_2\overset{O}{\overset{||}{C}}CH_2\overset{O}{\overset{||}{C}}OC_2H_5$

cf. Problem 20.15, using
C_6H_5COCl in place of
$C_6H_5CH_2Cl$ in the second
step.

20.27

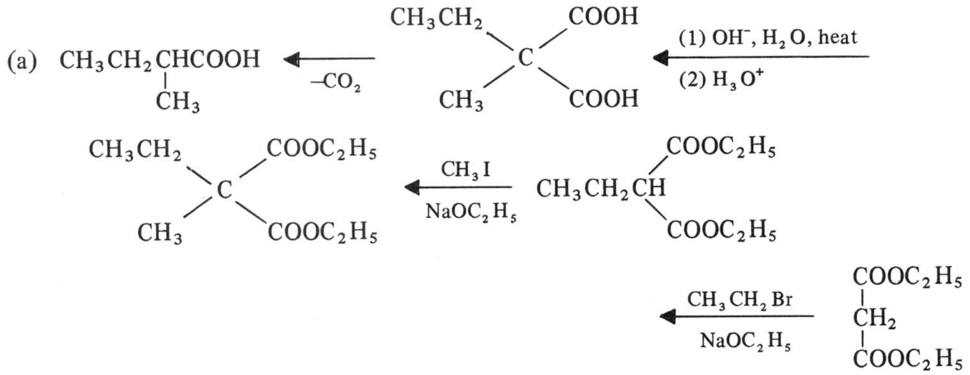

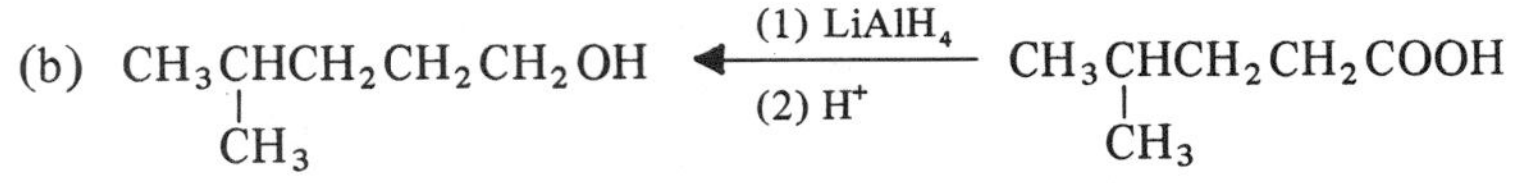

(a)

$$CH_3CH_2\underset{\underset{CH_3}{|}}{CH}COOH \xleftarrow[-CO_2]{} \underset{\underset{COOH}{|}}{\overset{\overset{CH_3CH_2}{|}}{C}}\overset{COOH}{} \xleftarrow[\text{(2) } H_3O^+]{\text{(1) } OH^-, H_2O, \text{heat}}$$

$$\underset{\underset{CH_3}{|}}{\overset{\overset{CH_3CH_2}{|}}{C}}\overset{COOC_2H_5}{\underset{COOC_2H_5}{}} \xleftarrow[\text{NaOC}_2H_5]{CH_3I} CH_3CH_2CH\overset{COOC_2H_5}{\underset{COOC_2H_5}{}}$$

$$\xleftarrow[\text{NaOC}_2H_5]{CH_3CH_2Br} \underset{\underset{COOC_2H_5}{|}}{\overset{\overset{COOC_2H_5}{|}}{CH_2}}$$

(b) $CH_3\underset{\underset{CH_3}{|}}{CH}CH_2CH_2CH_2OH \xleftarrow[\text{(2) } H^+]{\text{(1) LiAlH}_4} CH_3\underset{\underset{CH_3}{|}}{CH}CH_2CH_2COOH$

(from Problem 20.16 c)

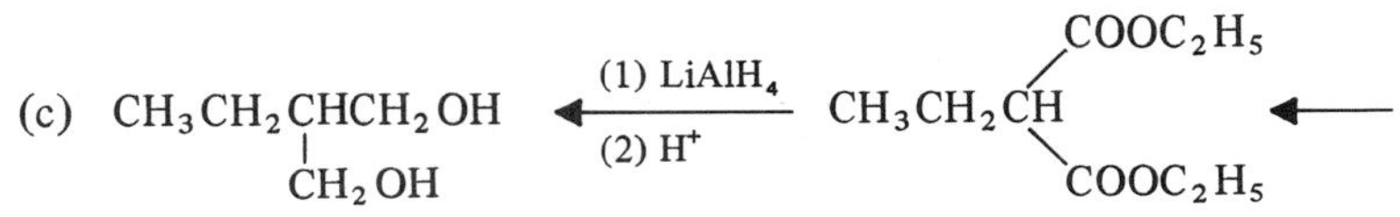

(c) $CH_3CH_2\underset{\underset{CH_2OH}{|}}{CH}CH_2OH \xleftarrow[\text{(2) } H^+]{\text{(1) LiAlH}_4} CH_3CH_2CH\overset{COOC_2H_5}{\underset{COOC_2H_5}{}} \xleftarrow{} \text{cf. p. 911}$

(d) $HOCH_2CH_2CH_2CH_2OH \xleftarrow[\text{(2) } H^+]{\text{(1) LiAlH}_4} HOOCCH_2CH_2COOH \xleftarrow[-CO_2]{\text{heat}}$

$$\underset{HOOC}{\overset{HOOC}{}}CHCH_2COOH \xleftarrow[]{HCl, \text{heat}} \underset{C_2H_5OOC}{\overset{C_2H_5OOC}{}}CHCH_2COOC_2H_5$$

$$\xleftarrow[]{} \underset{\underset{COOC_2H_5}{|}}{\overset{\overset{COOC_2H_5}{|}}{CH_2}} + NaOC_2H_5 + BrCH_2COOC_2H_5$$

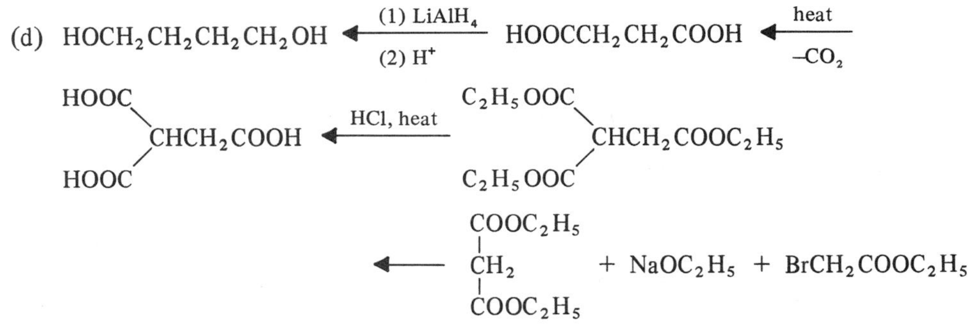

20.28   The following reaction took place,

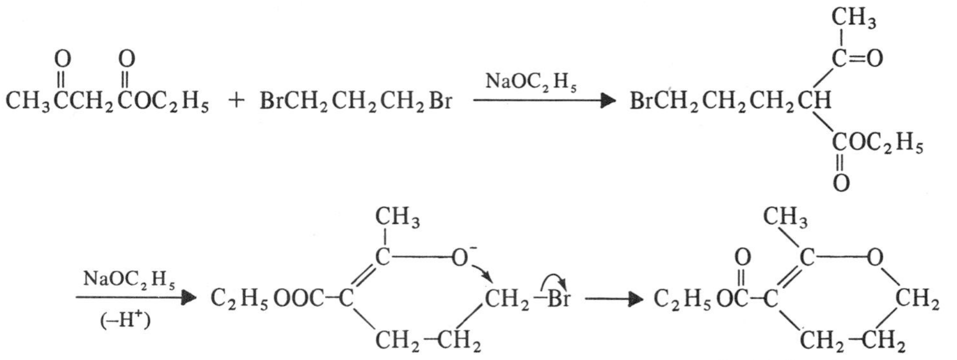

$$CH_3\overset{O}{\overset{||}{C}}CH_2\overset{O}{\overset{||}{C}}OC_2H_5 + BrCH_2CH_2CH_2Br \xrightarrow{\text{NaOC}_2H_5} BrCH_2CH_2CH_2\underset{\underset{\underset{O}{||}}{COC_2H_5}}{\overset{\overset{\overset{CH_3}{|}}{C=O}}{CH}}$$

$$\xrightarrow[(-H^+)]{\text{NaOC}_2H_5} C_2H_5OOC-\underset{\underset{CH_2-CH_2}{}}{\overset{\overset{\overset{CH_3}{|}}{C}}{C}}\overset{O^-}{\underset{CH_2\overset{\curvearrowright}{-}Br}{}} \longrightarrow C_2H_5O\overset{O}{\overset{||}{C}}-\underset{\underset{CH_2-CH_2}{}}{\overset{\overset{\overset{CH_3}{|}}{C}}{C}}\overset{O}{\underset{CH_2}{}}$$

Perkin's ester

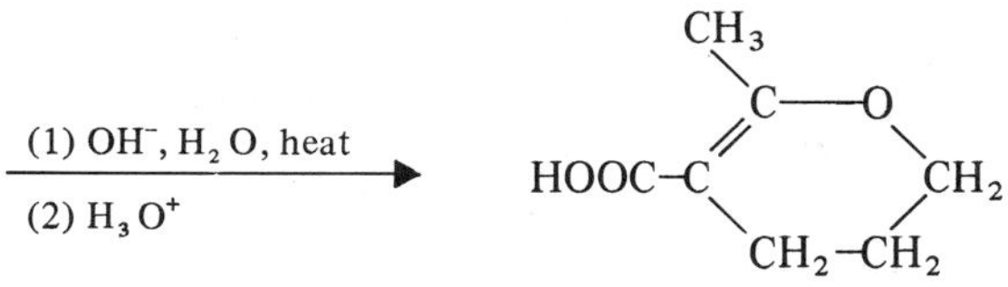

$$\xrightarrow[\text{(2) } H_3O^+]{\text{(1) } OH^-,\ H_2O,\ \text{heat}}$$

Perkin's acid

20.29

(a) $BrCH_2CH_2Br$ + $\underset{\displaystyle COOC_2H_5}{\overset{\displaystyle COOC_2H_5}{CH_2}}$ + $NaOC_2H_5$ ⟶

$$\left[BrCH_2CH_2-\underset{COOC_2H_5}{\overset{COOC_2H_5}{CH}} \right] \xrightarrow[(-H^+)]{NaOC(CH_3)_3} \left[BrCH_2CH_2-\underset{COOC_2H_5}{\overset{COOC_2H_5}{C}}{:}^- \right]$$

⟶ $\xrightarrow[\text{(3) heat, } -CO_2]{\substack{\text{(1) } OH^-,\ H_2O,\ \text{heat} \\ \text{(2) } H_3O^+}}$

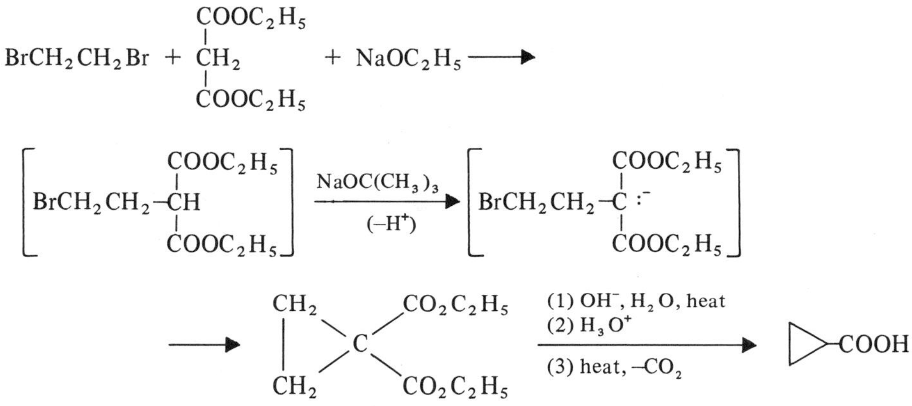

(b) $2NaCH(CO_2C_2H_5)_2$ + $BrCH_2CH_2CH_2Br$ ⟶

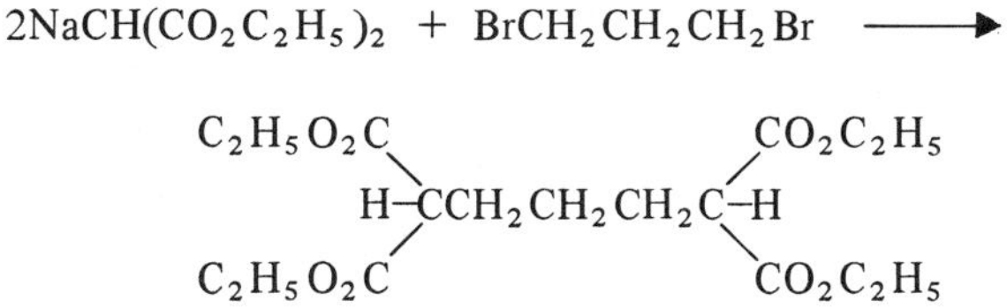

A

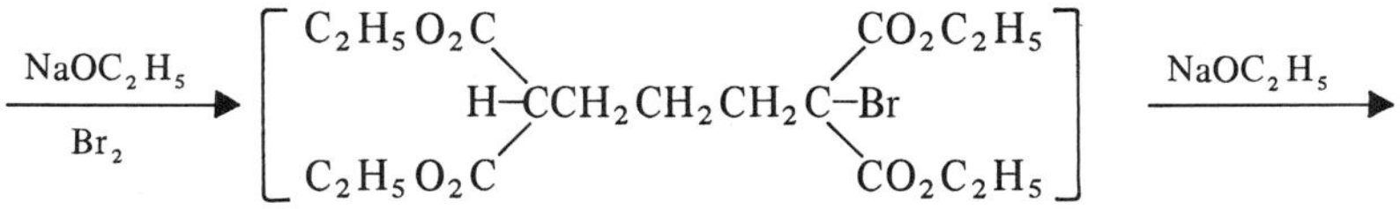

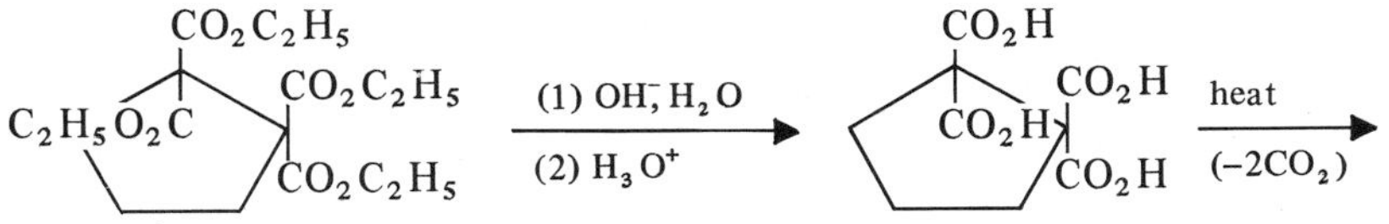

$$\xrightarrow[Br_2]{NaOC_2H_5} \left[\text{} \right] \xrightarrow{NaOC_2H_5}$$

$\xrightarrow[\text{(2) } H_3O^+]{\text{(1) } OH^-,\ H_2O}$ $\xrightarrow[(-2CO_2)]{\text{heat}}$

B   **C**

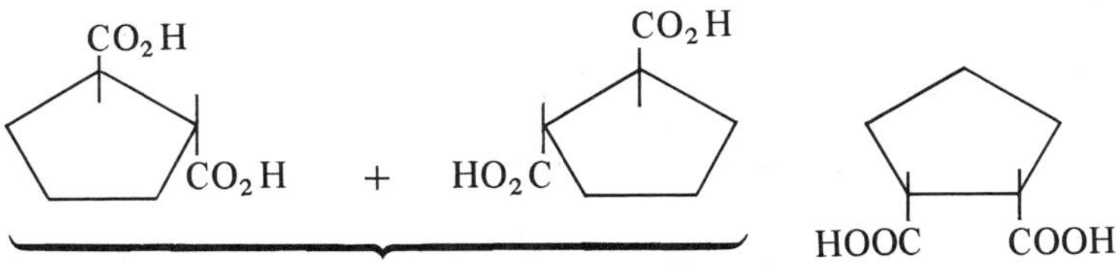

+

D   **E**

racemate   *meso*-compound

(c) $BrCH_2CH_2CH_2CH_2Br$ $\xrightarrow{NaCH(CO_2C_2H_5)_2}$ $BrCH_2CH_2CH_2CH_2\overset{\displaystyle CO_2C_2H_5}{\underset{\displaystyle CO_2C_2H_5}{CH}}$

$\xrightarrow{NaOC(CH_3)_3}$ [cyclopentane ring with $CO_2C_2H_5$ and $CO_2C_2H_5$] $\xrightarrow[\text{(3) heat}]{\overset{\text{(1) OH}^-, H_2O}{\text{(2) } H_3O^+}}$ [cyclopentane ring with —COOH]

20.30 (a) $CH_2(COOC_2H_5)_2 + {}^-OC_2H_5 \rightleftharpoons {}^:CH(COOC_2H_5)_2 + C_2H_5OH$

$C_6H_5CH{=}CH{-}\overset{\displaystyle O}{\overset{\|}{C}}OC_2H_5 + {}^:CH(COOC_2H_5)_2 \rightleftharpoons C_6H_5\overset{\displaystyle CH{-}\overset{\displaystyle O}{\overset{\|}{C}}OC_2H_5}{\underset{\displaystyle CH(COOC_2H_5)_2}{|}}$

$\xrightarrow{{}^-{+}H^+} C_6H_5\overset{\displaystyle CHCH_2\overset{\displaystyle O}{\overset{\|}{C}}OC_2H_5}{\underset{\displaystyle CH(COOC_2H_5)_2}{|}}$

(b) $CH_3\ddot{N}H_2 + CH_2{=}CH{-}\overset{\displaystyle O}{\overset{\|}{C}}OCH_3 \rightleftharpoons CH_3{-}\overset{\displaystyle +}{\underset{\displaystyle H}{N}}{-}CH_2{-}\overset{\displaystyle CH{-}\overset{\displaystyle O}{\overset{\|}{C}}OCH_3}{} \rightleftharpoons$

$CH_3\overset{\displaystyle }{\underset{\displaystyle H}{N}}{-}CH_2{-}CH_2{-}\overset{\displaystyle O}{\overset{\|}{C}}OCH_3 \xrightarrow{CH_2{=}CH{-}\overset{\displaystyle O}{\overset{\|}{C}}OCH_3} CH_3N(CH_2CH_2COOCH_3)_2$

$\xrightarrow{\text{base}} CH_3{-}N\overset{\displaystyle CH_2{-}CH{-}^{COOCH_3}}{\underset{\displaystyle CH_2{-}CH_2{-}\overset{\displaystyle }{C}\overset{OCH_3}{\underset{O}{}}}{}} \xrightarrow[\text{(several steps)}]{\substack{\text{Dieckmann}\\\text{condensation}}} CH_3{-}N$ [piperidinone ring with $COOCH_3$ and $=O$]

(c) $CH_3{-}\overset{\displaystyle CH_3}{\underset{\displaystyle CH(CO_2C_2H_5)_2}{\overset{|}{\underset{|}{C}}}}{-}CH_2{-}\overset{\displaystyle O}{\overset{\|}{C}}OC_2H_5 + C_2H_5O^- \rightleftharpoons CH_3{-}\overset{\displaystyle CH_3}{\underset{\displaystyle CH(CO_2C_2H_5)_2}{\overset{|}{\underset{|}{C}}}}{-}CH{-}\overset{\displaystyle O}{\overset{\|}{C}}OC_2H_5$

$+ C_2H_5OH$

$CH_3{-}\overset{\displaystyle CH_3}{\underset{\displaystyle CH(CO_2C_2H_5)_2}{\overset{|}{\underset{|}{C}}}}{-}CH{-}\overset{\displaystyle O}{\overset{\|}{C}}OC_2H_5 \rightleftharpoons CH_3{-}\overset{\displaystyle CH_3}{\overset{|}{C}}{=}CH{-}\overset{\displaystyle O}{\overset{\|}{C}}OC_2H_5 + {}^:CH(CO_2C_2H_5)_2$

The Michael reaction is reversible and the reaction just given is an example of a reverse Michael reaction.

(d)

(e) This one is a real challenge.

20.31 Two reactions take place. The first is a normal Knoevenagel condensation,

Then the α, β-unsaturated diketone reacts with a second mole of the active methylene compound in a Michael addition.

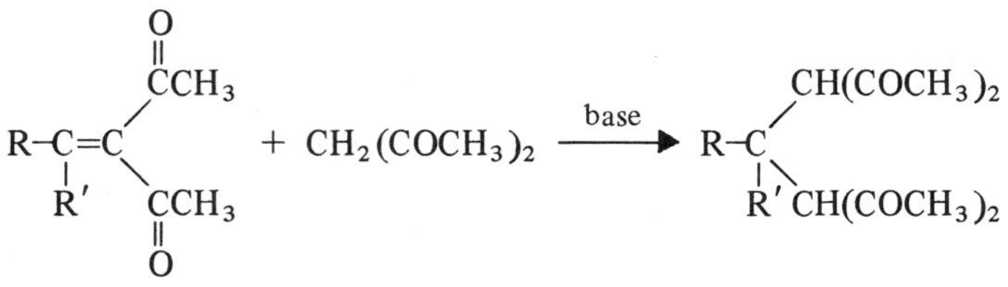

20.32

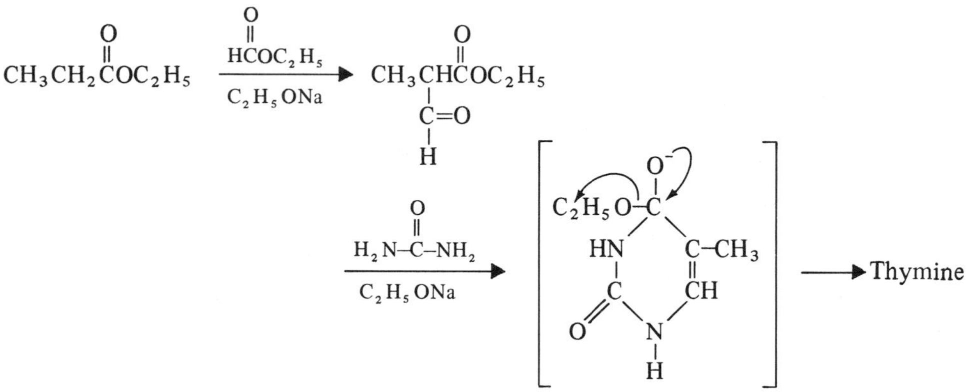

20.33

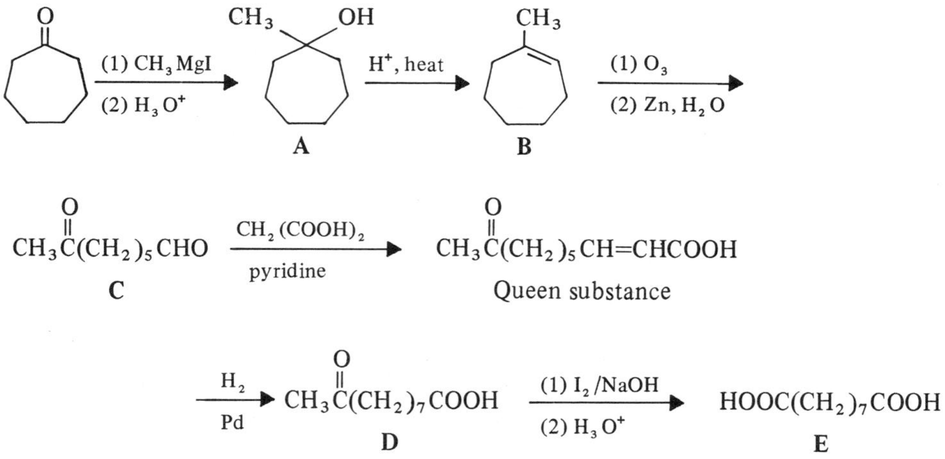

$$CH_3\overset{O}{\overset{\|}{C}}(CH_2)_5CHO \xrightarrow[\text{pyridine}]{CH_2(COOH)_2} CH_3\overset{O}{\overset{\|}{C}}(CH_2)_5CH=CHCOOH$$

C   Queen substance

$$\xrightarrow[\text{Pd}]{H_2} CH_3\overset{O}{\overset{\|}{C}}(CH_2)_7COOH \xrightarrow[(2)\ H_3O^+]{(1)\ I_2/NaOH} HOOC(CH_2)_7COOH$$

D   **E**

20.34

$$CH_2=\underset{CH_3}{\overset{|}{C}}-CH=CH_2 + HBr \longrightarrow CH_3\underset{CH_3}{\overset{|}{C}}=CHCH_2Br$$

F

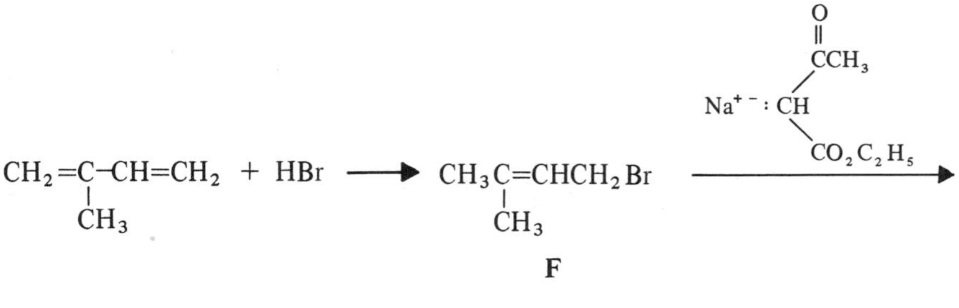

$$CH_3C=CHCH_2\underset{|}{CH}CCH_3 \quad \xrightarrow[\text{(2) } H_3O^+, \text{ (3) heat}]{\text{(1) dil. NaOH}} \quad CH_3C=CHCH_2CH_2CCH_3 \quad \xrightarrow[\text{(2) } H_3O^+]{\text{(1) LiC≡CH}}$$

with CH_3 and $CO_2C_2H_5$ on G; CH_3 on H

G   **H**

$$CH_3C=CHCH_2CH_2\underset{|}{\overset{OH}{C}}C≡CH \quad \xrightarrow[\text{Lindlar's catalyst}]{H_2} \quad \text{Linalool}$$

with CH_3 and CH_3 groups

I

20.35

$$C_2H_5O\overset{O}{\overset{\|}{C}} \quad HC:^-Na^+ + \quad \text{(reaction with 1,3-dibromopropane)} \quad \longrightarrow \quad (C_{10}H_{17}BrO_4)$$

$$\xrightarrow{NaOC_2H_5} \quad (C_{10}H_{16}O_4) \quad \xrightarrow[\text{(2) } H_2O]{\text{(1) LiAlH}_4} \quad \underset{CH_2OH}{\overset{CH_2OH}{}} (C_6H_{12}O_2) \quad \xrightarrow{HBr}$$

$$\underset{CH_2Br}{\overset{CH_2Br}{}} (C_6H_{10}Br_2) \quad \xrightarrow[\text{2NaOC}_2H_5]{CH_2(CO_2C_2H_5)_2} \quad \underset{CO_2C_2H_5}{\overset{CO_2C_2H_5}{}} (C_{13}H_{20}O_4)$$

$$\xrightarrow[\text{(2) } H^+]{\text{(1) OH}^-, H_2O} \quad \underset{COOH}{\overset{COOH}{}} (C_9H_{12}O_4) \quad \xrightarrow{heat} \quad \text{—COOH} + CO_2$$

J

$(C_8H_{12}O_2)$

20.36 (a) $ClCH_2COOC_2H_5 + C_2H_5O^- \rightleftharpoons Cl\overset{..}{\underset{}{C}}HCOOC_2H_5 + C_2H_5OH$

$$\underset{O}{\overset{R'}{R-C}} + :\overset{Cl}{C}HCOOC_2H_5 \rightleftharpoons \left[R-\overset{R'}{\underset{O^-}{C}}-\overset{Cl}{C}HCOOC_2H_5 \right] \longrightarrow R-\overset{R'}{\underset{O}{C}}-CHCOOC_2H_5$$

(b) Decarboxylation of the epoxy acid gives an enol anion which, on protonation, gives an aldehyde.

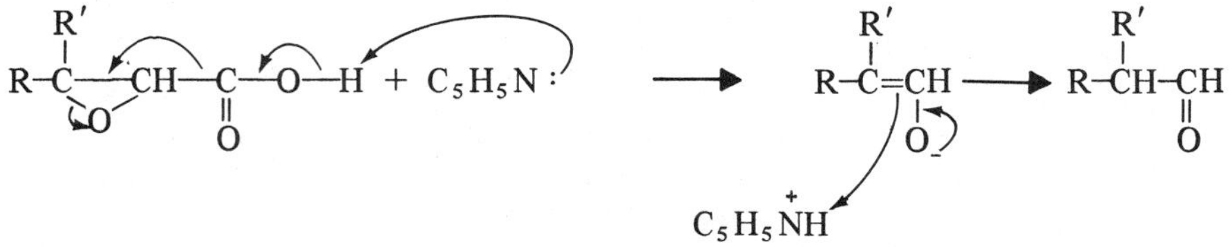

(c)

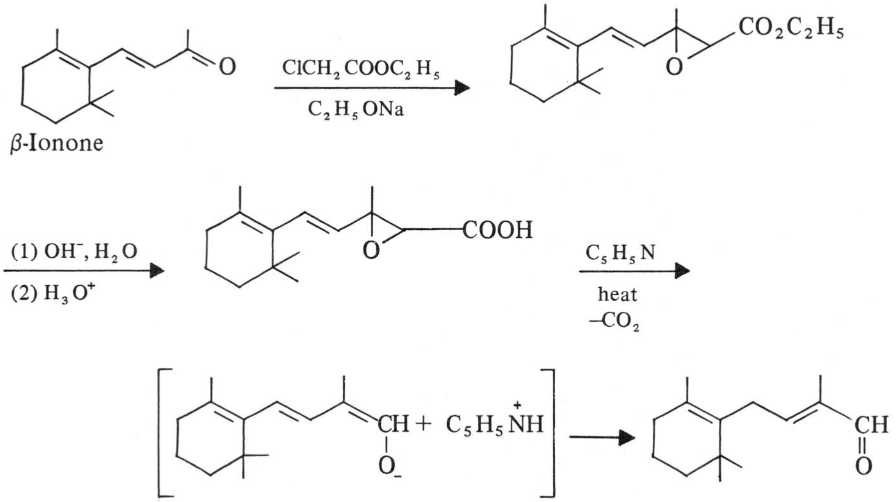

β-Ionone

20.37

(a)

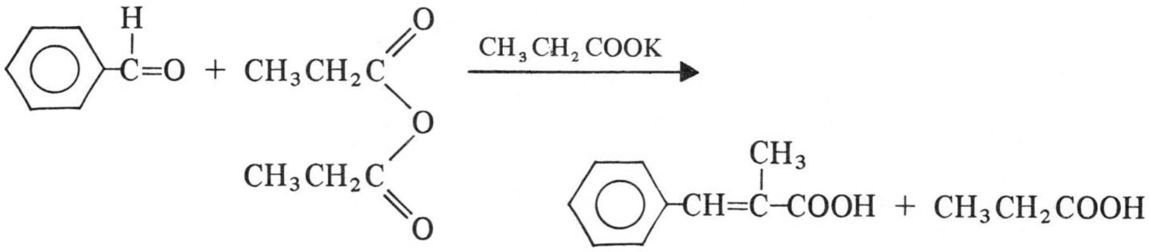

(b)

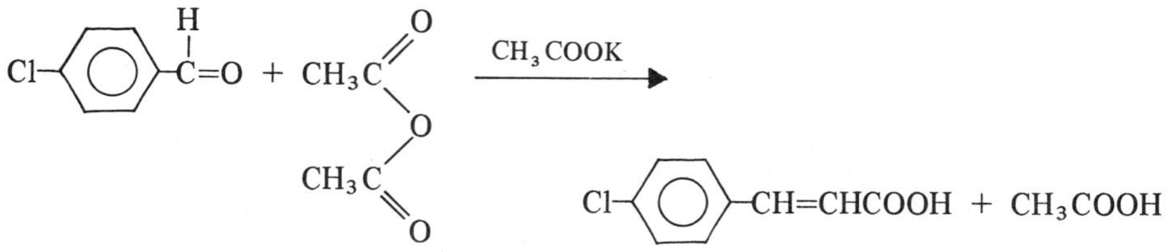

20.38

(a) $CH_2=\overset{\overset{\displaystyle CH_3}{|}}{C}-COOCH_3$

(b) $KMnO_4$, OH^-, then H_3O^+

(c) CH_3OH, H^+

(d) CH_3ONa, then H^+

(e) and (f)

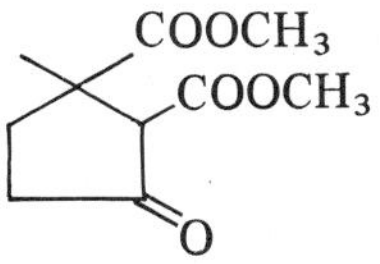

and

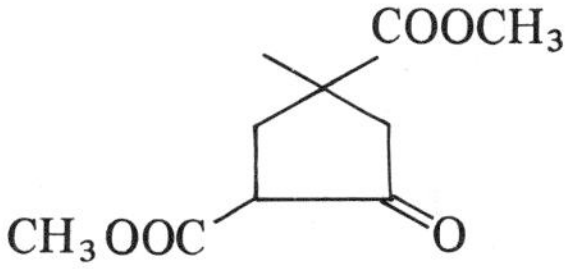

(g) OH^-, H_2O, then H_3O^+

(h)   heat ($-CO_2$)

(i) CH_3OH, H^+

(j) $BrCH_2COOCH_3$, Zn, then H_3O^+

(k)

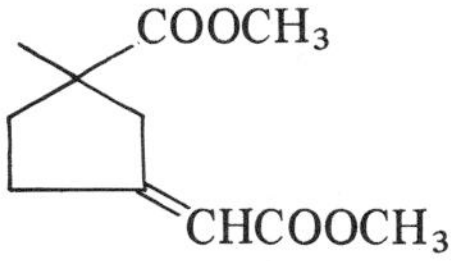

(l) H_2, Pt

(m) CH_3ONa, then H^+

(n) $2\,NaNH_2 + 2\,CH_3I$

20.39   If we look at the molecule as consisting of the following pieces,

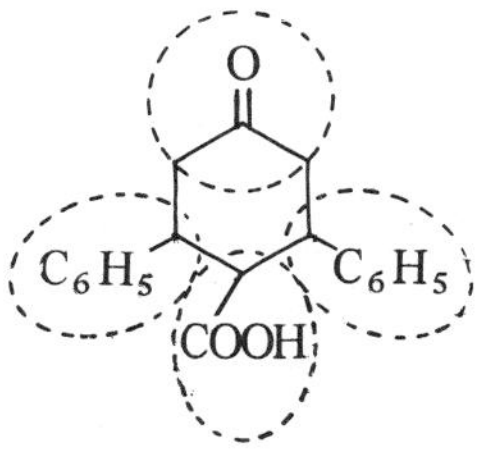

we can begin to see how it might be constructed from acetone, malonic ester, and two moles of benzaldehyde.

We can begin by carrying out a double Claisen-Schmidt condensation using acetone and two moles of benzaldehyde.

$$2\,C_6H_5\overset{H}{\underset{}{C}}{=}O + CH_3-\overset{O}{\underset{}{C}}-CH_3 \xrightarrow{OH^-} C_6H_5CH{=}CH-\overset{O}{\underset{}{C}}-CH{=}CHC_6H_5$$

Then we carry out a double Michael addition, followed by hydrolysis and decarboxylation.

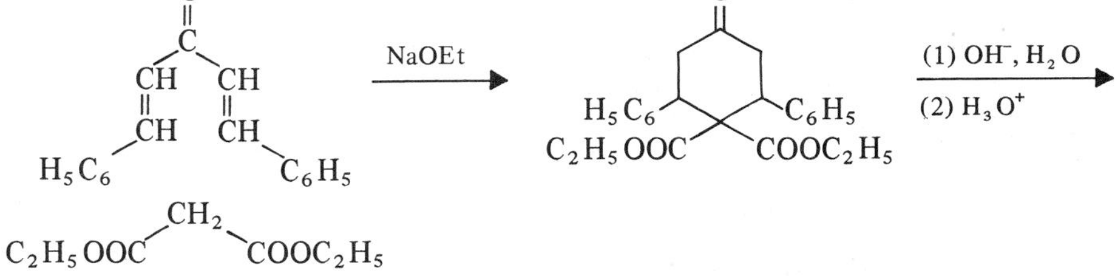

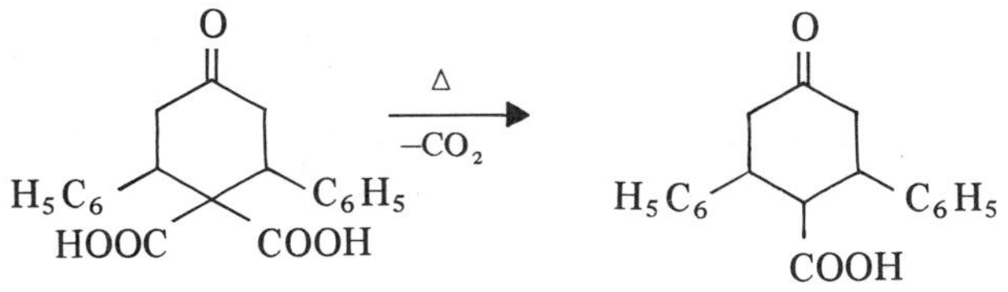

20.40

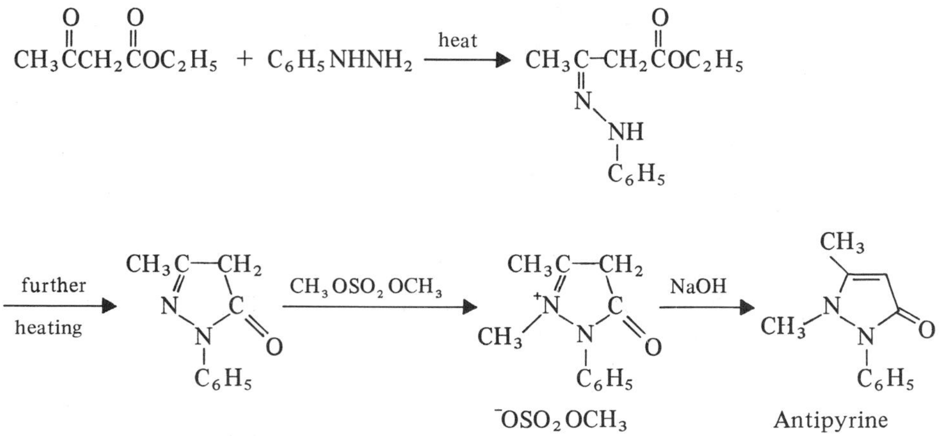

SECTION REFERENCES FOR THE ADDITIONAL PROBLEMS

20.25 15.7, 17.10, 20.2, 20.3, 20.5, 20.10

20.26 15.7, 16.7, 17.10, 20.2, 20.3

20.27 15.7, 17.10, 20.4

20.28 5.5, 20.3

20.29 8.9, 20.4

20.30 17.9, 20.2, 20.8, 20.10

20.31 17.9, 20.7, 20.8

20.32 20.2, 20.11, 24.2

20.33 6.4, 6.10, 7.13, 14.12, 17.4, 20.7

20.34 7.2, 9.7, 16.11, 20.3

20.35 14.6, 15.7, 20.4

20.36 15.12, 17.2, 17.5, 20.2

20.37 18.6, 17.5, 20.2

20.38 6.4, 6.10, 7.13, 10.10, 16.11, 17.1, 18.7, 18.10, 20.2

20.39 17.6, 17.9, 18.10, 20.4, 20.8

20.40 15.10, 16.8, 18.8, 19.5, 19.6

SELF-TEST

20.1   Supply the structural formulas of the missing reactants and major organic products. If no reaction occurs, write N.R.

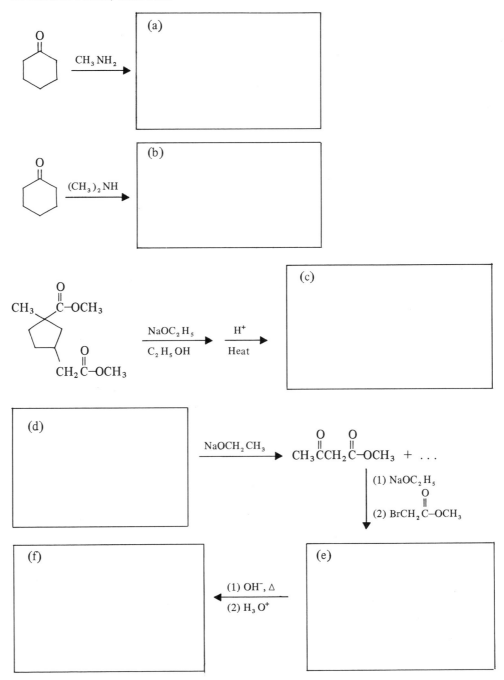

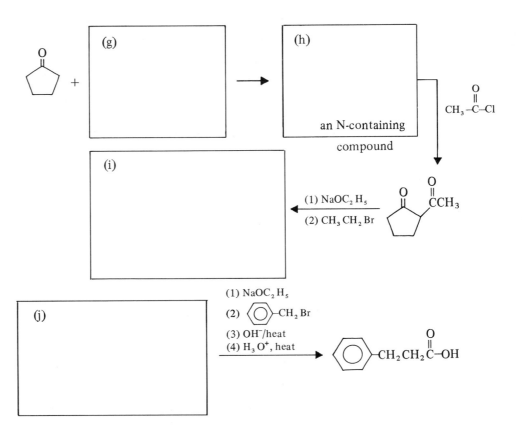

20.2 By circling the appropriate letter tell which of the following reactions you would use to synthesize each of the compounds below.

If your answer is:	*Circle:*
The acetoacetic ester synthesis	A
The malonic ester synthesis	E
An enamine	N
The Knoevenagel condensation	K
A Michael addition	Mi

In the spaces provided give the structural formulas of the reactants (not reagents) needed in the synthesis of each compound shown.

(a) ⟨O⟩—CH₂CH₂$\overset{\overset{\displaystyle O}{\|}}{C}$—OH   A–E–N–K–Mi

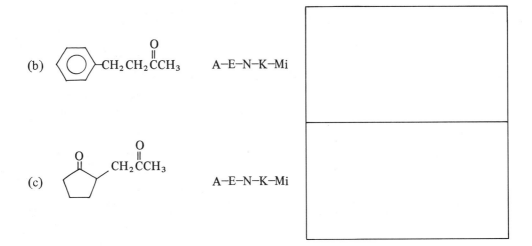

(b) ⟨phenyl⟩—CH₂CH₂CCH₃   A–E–N–K–Mi

(c) (cyclopentanone ring)—CH₂CCH₃   A–E–N–K–Mi

SECOND REVIEW PROBLEM SET

The problems review concepts from Chapters 1-20.

1. | Increasing Acidity ⟶

(a) $CH_3\overset{O}{\overset{\|}{C}}CH_3$ < CH_3CH_2OH < $CH_3O\overset{O}{\overset{\|}{C}}CH_2\overset{O}{\overset{\|}{C}}OCH_3$ < $CH_3\overset{O}{\overset{\|}{C}}OH$

(b) 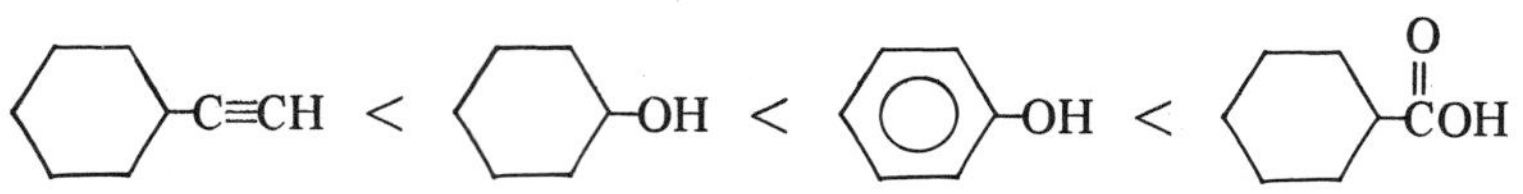 ⬡$-C\equiv CH$ < ⬡$-OH$ < ⬡$-OH$ < ⬡$-\overset{O}{\overset{\|}{C}}OH$

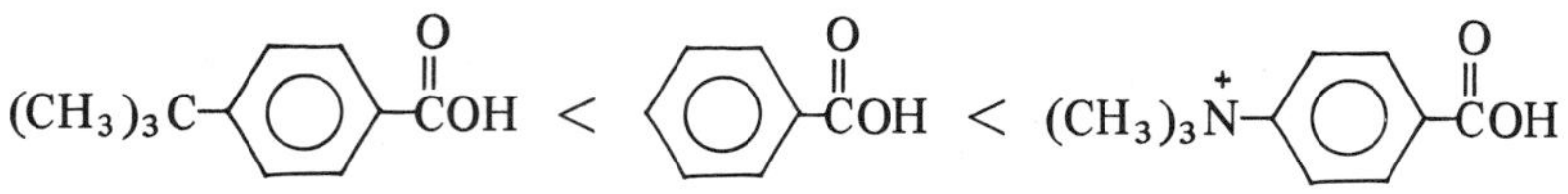

(c) $(CH_3)_3C-$⬡$-\overset{O}{\overset{\|}{C}}OH$ < ⬡$-\overset{O}{\overset{\|}{C}}OH$ < $(CH_3)_3\overset{+}{N}-$⬡$-\overset{O}{\overset{\|}{C}}OH$

(d) $CH_3CH_2\overset{O}{\overset{\|}{C}}OH$ < $CH_3CHCl\overset{O}{\overset{\|}{C}}OH$ < $CH_3CCl_2\overset{O}{\overset{\|}{C}}OH$

(e) 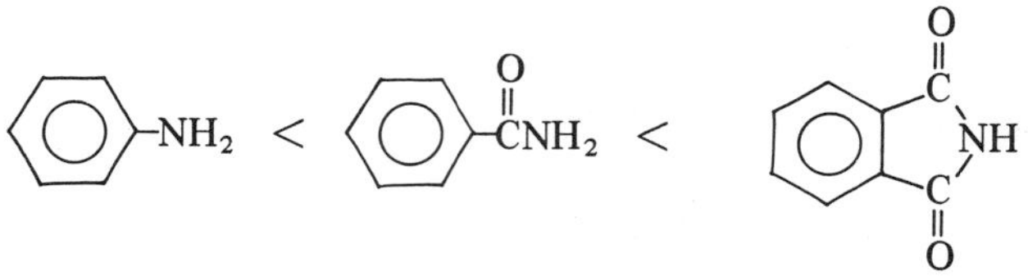 ⬡$-NH_2$ < ⬡$-\overset{O}{\overset{\|}{C}}NH_2$ < (phthalimide structure)

2. | Increasing Basicity ⟶

(a) $CH_3\overset{O}{\overset{\|}{C}}NH_2$ < NH_3 < $CH_3CH_2NH_2$

(b) 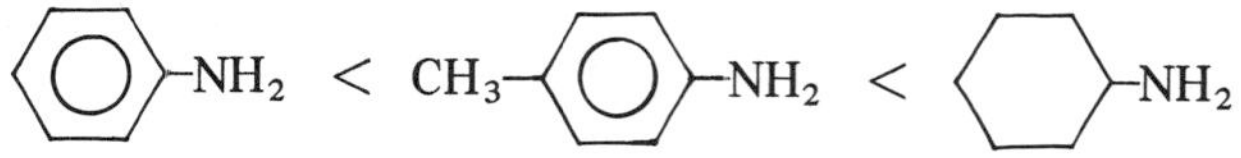 ⬡$-NH_2$ < CH_3-⬡$-NH_2$ < ⬡$-NH_2$

(c) 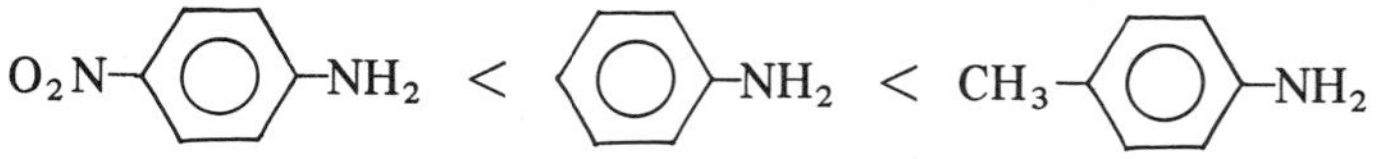 O_2N-⬡$-NH_2$ < ⬡$-NH_2$ < CH_3-⬡$-NH_2$

(d) $CH_3CH_2CH_3$ < CH_3OCH_3 < CH_3NHCH_3

3.

(a) $CH_3(CH_2)_2CH_2OH$ $\xrightarrow[\text{(or HBr)}]{PBr_3}$ $CH_3(CH_2)_2CH_2Br$

(b) $CH_3(CH_2)_2CH_2Br$ $\xrightarrow{\quad}$ $CH_3(CH_2)_2CH_2-N$
[from part (a)]

$\xrightarrow[\text{heat}]{H_2NNH_2}$ $CH_3(CH_2)_2CH_2NH_2$ +

(c) $CH_3(CH_2)_2CH_2Br$ $\xrightarrow{NaCN}$ $CH_3(CH_2)_2CH_2CN$ $\xrightarrow{LiAlH_4}$ $CH_3(CH_2)_3CH_2NH_2$
[from part (a)]

(d) $CH_3(CH_2)_2CH_2OH$ $\xrightarrow[\text{(2) } H_3O^+]{\text{(1) } KMnO_4\text{ , } OH^-\text{, heat}}$ $CH_3(CH_2)_2\overset{O}{\overset{\|}{C}}OH$

(e) $CH_3(CH_2)_2CH_2CN$ $\xrightarrow[\text{H}_2\text{O, heat}]{H_3O^+}$ $CH_3(CH_2)_2CH_2COOH$ + NH_4^+
[from part (c)]

(f) $CH_3(CH_2)_2\overset{O}{\overset{\|}{C}}OH$ $\xrightarrow{SOCl_2}$ $CH_3(CH_2)_2\overset{O}{\overset{\|}{C}}Cl$
[from part (d)]

(g) $CH_3(CH_2)_2\overset{O}{\overset{\|}{C}}Cl$ $\xrightarrow{NH_3}$ $CH_3(CH_2)_2\overset{O}{\overset{\|}{C}}NH_2$
[from part (f)]

(h) $CH_3(CH_2)_2\overset{O}{\overset{\|}{C}}Cl$ $\xrightarrow[\text{base}]{CH_3(CH_2)_2CH_2OH}$ $CH_3(CH_2)_2\overset{O}{\overset{\|}{C}}OCH_2(CH_2)_2CH_3$

(i) $CH_3CH_2CH_2\overset{O}{\overset{\|}{C}}NH_2$ $\xrightarrow[\text{(2) } H_3O^+]{\text{(1) } Br_2\text{ , } OH^-}$ $CH_3CH_2CH_2NH_2$ + $CO_3^=$
[from part (g)]

(j) $CH_3(CH_2)_2\overset{O}{\overset{\|}{C}}Cl$ $\xrightarrow[\text{AlCl}_3]{\text{⬡}}$ $\overset{O}{\overset{\|}{C}}(CH_2)_2CH_3$ $\xrightarrow[\text{HCl}]{Zn(Hg)}$ $CH_2(CH_2)_2CH_3$
[from part (f)]

(k) $CH_3(CH_2)_2\overset{O}{\overset{\|}{C}}Cl$ $\xrightarrow{CH_3(CH_2)_2\overset{O}{\overset{\|}{C}}ONa}$ $[CH_3(CH_2)_2\overset{O}{\overset{\|}{C}}]_2O$
[from part (f)]

(l) $CH_3(CH_2)_2CH_2Br$ [from part (a)] $\xrightarrow{\underset{CO_2Et}{\overset{CO_2Et}{Na:CH}}}$ $CH_3(CH_2)_2CH_2\underset{CO_2Et}{\overset{CO_2Et}{CH}}$ $\xrightarrow[\text{(2) } H_3O^+]{\text{(1) } OH^-, H_2O, \text{ heat}}$

$CH_3(CH_2)_2CH_2\underset{COOH}{\overset{COOH}{CH}}$ $\xrightarrow[-CO_2]{\text{heat}}$ $CH_3(CH_2)_2CH_2CH_2COOH$

4.

(a) CH_3—⬡ $\xrightarrow{Br_2, FeBr_3}$ CH_3—⬡—Br $\xrightarrow{Mg, \text{ ether}}$ CH_3—⬡—MgBr

(separate from ortho isomer)

$\xrightarrow[\text{(2) } H^+]{\text{(1) } CH_2\!-\!CH_2 \text{ (O)}}$ CH_3—⬡—CH_2CH_2OH $\xrightarrow[CH_2Cl_2]{CrO_3 \cdot 2C_5H_5N}$ CH_3—⬡—$CH_2\overset{O}{\overset{\|}{C}H}$

$\xrightarrow[\text{(Aldol condensation)}]{OH^-}$ CH_3—⬡—$CH_2CH{=}C\overset{O}{\overset{\|}{-}}CH$ (with ⬡—CH_3 substituent)

(b) ⬡ $\xrightarrow[HF]{CH_2{=}CHCH_3}$ ⬡—$\underset{CH_3}{\overset{CH_3}{CH}}$ $\xrightarrow[h\nu]{NBS, CCl_4}$ ⬡—$\underset{CH_3}{\overset{CH_3}{C}}$–Br

$\xrightarrow{\text{base}}$ ⬡—$\underset{CH_3}{C}{=}CH_2$ $\xrightarrow[\text{(2) } H_2O_2, OH^-]{\text{(1) } THF:BH_3}$ ⬡—$\underset{CH_3}{CH}CH_2OH$ $\xrightarrow[\text{(2) } CH_3CH_2Br]{\text{(1) } NaH}$

⬡—$\underset{CH_3}{CH}CH_2OCH_2CH_3$

(c) ⬡—NH_2 $\xrightarrow{(CH_3\overset{O}{\overset{\|}{C}})_2O}$ ⬡—$NH\overset{O}{\overset{\|}{C}}CH_3$ $\xrightarrow[\substack{\text{(separate from} \\ \text{ortho isomer)}}]{Cl_2, FeCl_3}$ Cl—⬡—$NH\overset{O}{\overset{\|}{C}}CH_3$

$\xrightarrow[\substack{H_2O \\ \text{heat}}]{OH^-}$ Cl—⬡—NH_2 $\xrightarrow[H_2O]{Br_2}$ Cl—⬡($\overset{Br}{\underset{Br}{}}$)—$NH_2$ $\xrightarrow[\text{(2) } H_3PO_2]{\text{(1) } HONO}$ Cl—⬡($\overset{Br}{\underset{Br}{}}$)

(d) CH$_3$—⟨benzene⟩ $\xrightarrow[\substack{\text{(separate from ortho}\\ \text{isomer)}}]{HNO_3,\ H_2SO_4}$ CH$_3$—⟨benzene⟩—NO$_2$ $\xrightarrow[\text{(2) } H_3O^+]{\text{(1) } KMnO_4,\ OH^-,\ heat}$

O$_2$N—⟨benzene⟩—COOH $\xrightarrow{SOCl_2}$ O$_2$N—⟨benzene⟩—CCl $\xrightarrow[\text{ether}]{LiAlH[OC(CH_3)_3]_3}$

O$_2$N—⟨benzene⟩—CHO $\xrightarrow[OH^-]{CH_3CC_6H_5}$ O$_2$N—⟨benzene⟩—CH=CHC(=O)—⟨benzene⟩

(e) ⟨benzene⟩—CH$_3$ $\xrightarrow[h\nu]{NBS,\ CCl_4}$ ⟨benzene⟩—CH$_2$Br $\xrightarrow{NaC\equiv CH}$ ⟨benzene⟩—CH$_2$C≡CH

$\xrightarrow[H_2O]{Hg^{++},\ H_3O^+}$ ⟨benzene⟩—CH$_2$CCH$_3$ (=O) $\xrightarrow{HCN}$ ⟨benzene⟩—CH$_2$C(OH)(CH$_3$)CN $\xrightarrow[\text{heat}]{H_3O^+}$

[⟨benzene⟩—CH$_2$C(OH)(CH$_3$)COOH] $\xrightarrow{-H_2O}$ ⟨benzene⟩—CH=C(CH$_3$)COOH

5.

CH$_3$—⟨2-methyl-1,3-butadiene⟩ + ⟨diethyl fumarate: EtOC(=O)—CH=CH—COEt(=O)⟩ $\xrightarrow[\text{reaction}]{\text{Diels-Alder}}$ ⟨cyclohexene ring: CH$_3$, COOEt, COOEt⟩ + Enantiomer **A**

2-Methyl-1,3-butadiene   Diethyl fumarate

$\xrightarrow[\text{(2) } H_2O]{\text{(1) LiAlH}_4}$ ⟨ring: CH$_3$, CH$_2$OH, CH$_2$OH⟩ + Enantiomer **B** $\xrightarrow{PBr_3}$ ⟨ring: CH$_3$, CH$_2$Br, CH$_2$Br⟩ + Enantiomer **C** $\xrightarrow[H^+]{Zn}$

⟨ring: CH$_3$, CH$_3$, CH$_3$⟩ + Enantiomer **D**

6.

(a)   A is $CH_2=CHCC\equiv CH$, with CH_3 and OH on the central carbon,   C is $BrMgOCH_2CH=CC\equiv CMgBr$ with CH_3

(b)   **A** is an allylic alcohol and thus forms a carbocation readily. **B** is a conjugated enyne and is therefore more stable than **A**.

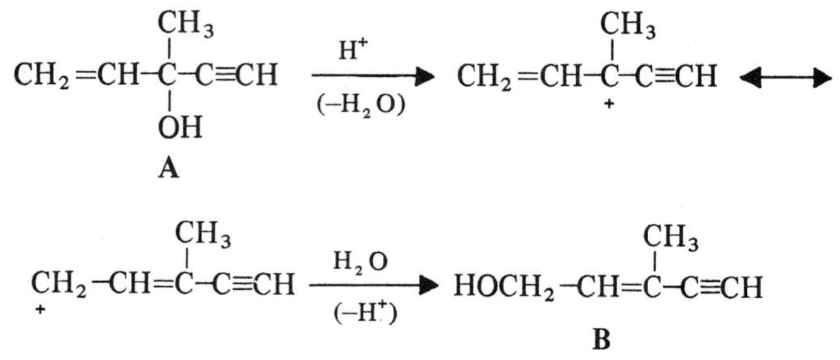

$$CH_2=CH-\underset{\underset{OH}{|}}{\overset{\overset{CH_3}{|}}{C}}-C\equiv CH \xrightarrow[(-H_2O)]{H^+} CH_2=CH-\overset{\overset{CH_3}{|}}{\underset{+}{C}}-C\equiv CH \longleftrightarrow$$

A

$$\underset{+}{CH_2}-CH=\overset{\overset{CH_3}{|}}{C}-C\equiv CH \xrightarrow[(-H^+)]{H_2O} HOCH_2-CH=\overset{\overset{CH_3}{|}}{C}-C\equiv CH$$

B

7.

$$+ \ BrMgOCH_2CH=\overset{\overset{CH_3}{|}}{C}C\equiv CMgBr \xrightarrow{\ \ (2)\ H^+\ }$$

D

$$\xrightarrow{H_2,\ Ni_2\ B(P\text{-}2)}$$

E

$$\xrightarrow{(CH_3C)_2O}$$

F

$$\xrightarrow{-H_2O}$$

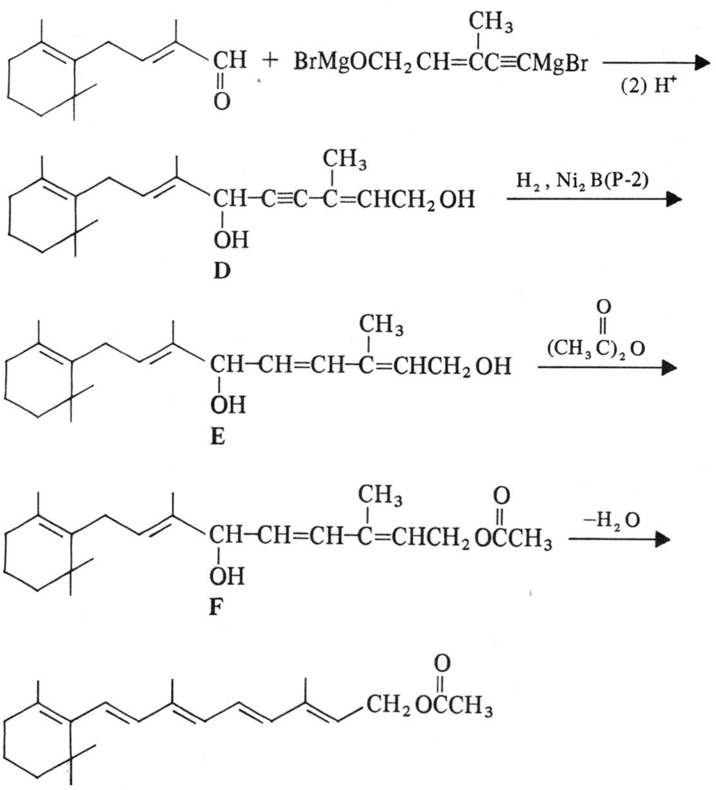

Vitamin A acetate

8.

$$CH_3\overset{\overset{O}{\parallel}}{C}CH_3 + H^+ \rightleftharpoons HO\overset{+}{=}\overset{\overset{CH_3}{|}}{\underset{\underset{CH_3}{|}}{C}} \longleftrightarrow HO-\overset{\overset{CH_3}{|}}{\underset{\underset{CH_3}{|}}{\overset{+}{C}}} \xrightarrow{}$$

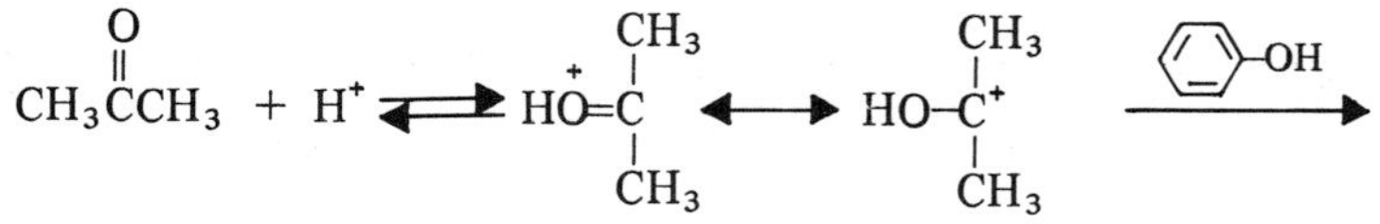

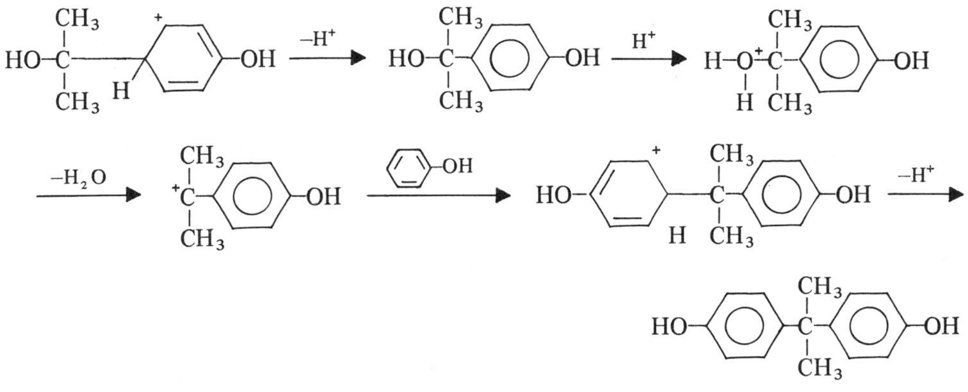

"Bisphenol A"

9.

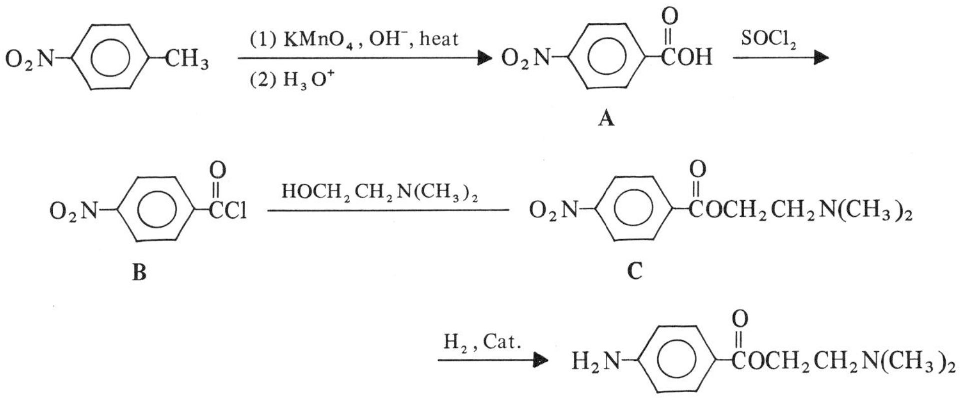

Procaine

10.

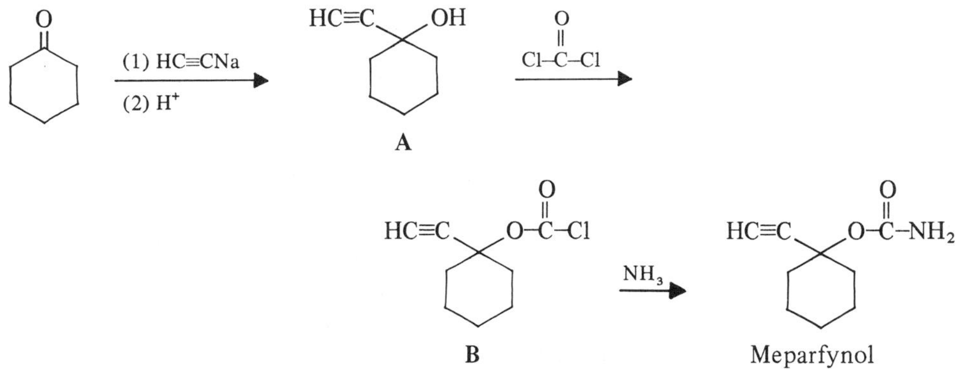

Meparfynol

11.

$$C_6H_5\overset{\overset{O}{\|}}{C}H \xrightarrow[\text{(2) } H_3O^+]{\text{(1) } C_6H_5MgBr} \underset{\underset{A}{\overset{|}{C_6H_5}}}{C_6H_5CHOH} \xrightarrow{PBr_3} \underset{\underset{B}{\overset{|}{C_6H_5}}}{C_6H_5CHBr} \xrightarrow[\text{(−HBr)}]{(CH_3)_2NCH_2CH_2OH}$$

$$C_6H_5\underset{\underset{C_6H_5}{|}}{C}HOCH_2CH_2N(CH_3)_2$$

Diphenhydramine

The last step probably takes place by an S_N1 mechanism. Diphenylmethyl bromide, **B**, ionizes readily because it forms the resonance-stabilized benzylic carbocation,

$$C_6H_5\underset{\underset{C_6H_5}{|}}{C}H^+$$

12. (a) For this synthesis we need to prepare the benzylic halide, $Br\!-\!\langle\bigcirc\rangle\!-\!\underset{\underset{C_6H_5}{|}}{C}HBr$, and

then allow it to react with $(CH_3)_2NCH_2CH_2OH$ as in Problem 11.

This benzylic halide can be made as follows

$$Br\!-\!\langle\bigcirc\rangle\!-\!\overset{\overset{O}{\|}}{C}H \xrightarrow[\text{(2) } H_3O^+]{\text{(1) } C_6H_5MgBr} Br\!-\!\langle\bigcirc\rangle\!-\!\underset{\underset{C_6H_5}{|}}{C}HOH \xrightarrow{PBr_3} Br\!-\!\langle\bigcirc\rangle\!-\!\underset{\underset{C_6H_5}{|}}{C}HBr$$

(b) For this synthesis we can prepare the requisite benzylic halide in two ways:

$$\underset{CH_3}{\langle\bigcirc\rangle}\overset{\overset{O}{\|}}{C}H \xrightarrow[\text{(2) } H_3O^+]{\text{(1) } C_6H_5MgBr} \underset{CH_3}{\langle\bigcirc\rangle}\underset{\underset{C_6H_5}{|}}{C}HOH \xrightarrow{PBr_3} \underset{CH_3}{\langle\bigcirc\rangle}\underset{\underset{C_6H_5}{|}}{C}HBr$$

or

$$C_6H_5\overset{\overset{O}{\|}}{C}H \xrightarrow[\text{(2) } H_3O^+]{\text{(1) } \underset{CH_3}{\langle\bigcirc\rangle}\!-\!MgBr} \underset{CH_3}{\langle\bigcirc\rangle}\underset{\underset{C_6H_5}{|}}{C}HOH \xrightarrow{PBr_3} \underset{CH_3}{\langle\bigcirc\rangle}\underset{\underset{C_6H_5}{|}}{C}HBr$$

We then allow the benzylic halide to react with $(CH_3)_2NCH_2CH_2OH$ as in Problem 11.

13.

$$CH_3\underset{\underset{Br}{|}}{C}HCO_2C_2H_5 \xrightarrow{CH_2(CO_2C_2H_5)_2,\ EtO^-}$$

A

$$\xrightarrow[\text{(Michael addition)}]{CH_2=CHCN,\ EtO^-}$$

B

$$\xrightarrow[\substack{\text{(converts } -C\equiv N \text{ to} \\ -CO_2C_2H_5)}]{C_2H_5OH,\ H^+}$$

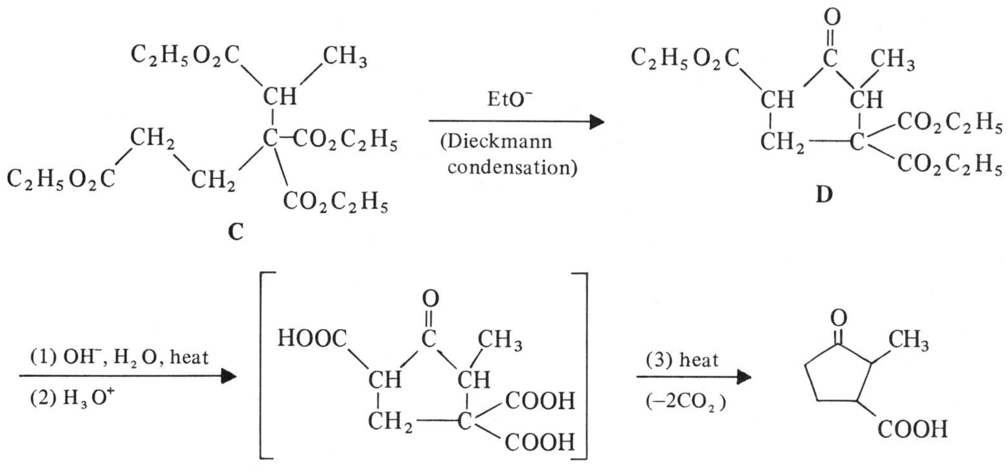

$C_2H_5O_2C$ CH_3
   CH
CH_2 C—$CO_2C_2H_5$
$C_2H_5O_2C$ CH_2 $CO_2C_2H_5$
                    C

$\xrightarrow[\text{condensation)}]{\text{EtO}^-\ \text{(Dieckmann}}$

$C_2H_5O_2C$ O CH_3
   CH CH
   CH_2 C—$CO_2C_2H_5$
                 $CO_2C_2H_5$
                    D

$\xrightarrow[\text{(2) H}_3\text{O}^+]{\text{(1) OH}^-,\ \text{H}_2\text{O, heat}}$

$\left[\ \text{HOOC}\quad \overset{O}{\overset{\|}{C}}\quad CH_3 \right.$
$CH \quad CH$—COOH
$CH_2 \quad C$—COOH
                 COOH $\left. \right]$

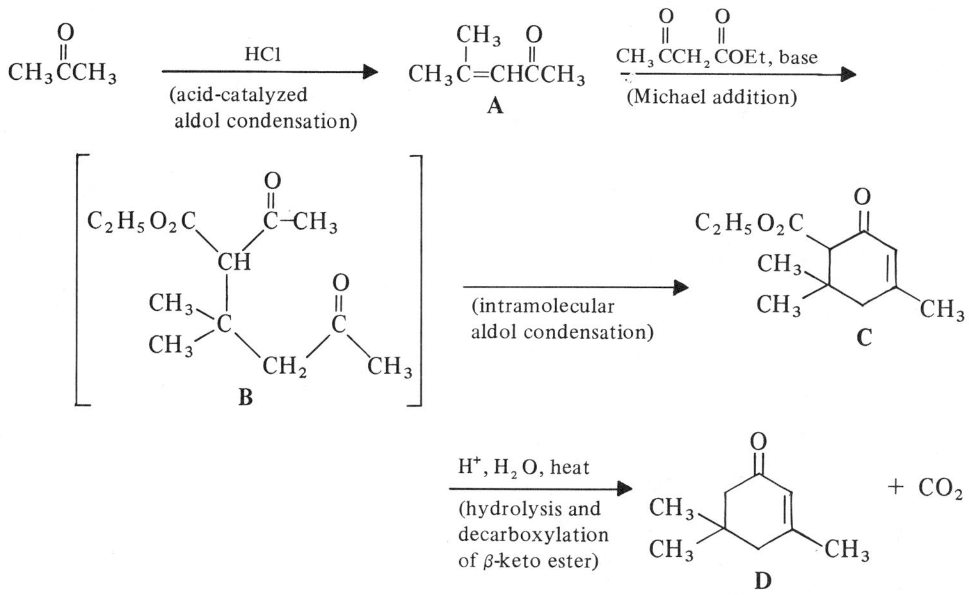

$\xrightarrow[(-2\text{CO}_2)]{\text{(3) heat}}$

(structure: 2-methyl-3-carboxycyclopentanone with O, CH₃, COOH)

14.

$CH_3\overset{O}{\overset{\|}{C}}CH_3$
$\xrightarrow[\substack{\text{(acid-catalyzed}\\ \text{aldol condensation)}}]{\text{HCl}}$
$CH_3\overset{CH_3}{\overset{|}{C}}{=}CH\overset{O}{\overset{\|}{C}}CH_3$
   A

$\xrightarrow[\text{(Michael addition)}]{CH_3\overset{O}{\overset{\|}{C}}CH_2\overset{O}{\overset{\|}{C}}OEt,\ \text{base}}$

$\left[\ C_2H_5O_2C \quad \overset{O}{\overset{\|}{C}}{-}CH_3 \right.$
      CH
$CH_3\quad C$
$CH_3 \quad \overset{O}{\overset{\|}{C}}$
      $CH_2 \quad CH_3$
      $\left. \right]$
         B

$\xrightarrow[\substack{\text{aldol condensation)}}]{\text{(intramolecular}}$

$C_2H_5O_2C$ O
   CH_3
   CH_3 CH_3
              C
(cyclohexenone structure)

$\xrightarrow[\substack{\text{(hydrolysis and}\\ \text{decarboxylation}\\ \text{of }\beta\text{-keto ester)}}]{\text{H}^+,\ \text{H}_2\text{O, heat}}$

CH_3 O
CH_3 CH_3
     D
$+\ CO_2$

15.

(benzaldehyde) $\overset{O}{\overset{\|}{C}}H\ +\ CH_2CH_2OH$ with NO_2
$\xrightarrow[\substack{\text{(aldol-type}\\ \text{addition)}}]{\text{EtO}^-}$
(phenyl) $\overset{OH}{\overset{|}{C}}HCHCH_2OH$ with NO_2
   A
$\xrightarrow{\text{H}_2,\ \text{catalyst}}$

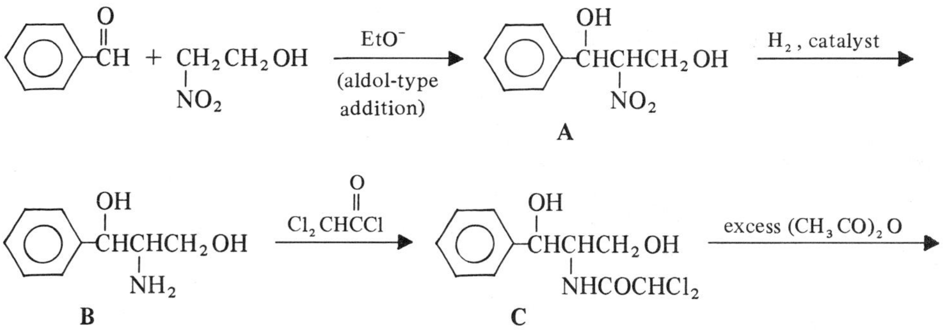

(phenyl) $\overset{OH}{\overset{|}{C}}HCHCH_2OH$ with NH_2
   B
$\xrightarrow{Cl_2CHC\overset{O}{\overset{\|}{}}Cl}$
(phenyl) $\overset{OH}{\overset{|}{C}}HCHCH_2OH$ with $NHCOCHCl_2$
   C
$\xrightarrow{\text{excess (CH}_3\text{CO)}_2\text{O}}$

D $\xrightarrow[\text{H}_2\text{SO}_4]{\text{HNO}_3}$ **E**

$\xrightarrow[\substack{\text{(ester groups}\\ \text{hydrolyze more}\\ \text{rapidly than amide}\\ \text{groups)}}]{\text{OH}^-,\ \text{H}_2\text{O}}$ Chloramphenicol

16.

$\text{CH}_3\text{CH}_2\text{CH}_2\overset{\overset{\text{O}}{\|}}{\text{C}}\underset{\underset{\text{CH}_3}{|}}{\text{CHCH}} \xrightarrow[\text{(aldol addition)}]{\overset{\overset{\text{O}}{\|}}{\text{HCH},\ \text{OH}^-}} \text{CH}_3\text{CH}_2\text{CH}_2\underset{\underset{\text{CH}_3}{|}}{\overset{\overset{\text{CH}_2\text{OH}}{|}}{\text{C}}}\text{CHO} \xrightarrow[\substack{\text{(Cannizzaro}\\ \text{reaction)}}]{\overset{\overset{\text{O}}{\|}}{\text{HCH},\ \text{OH}^-}}$

A

B $\xrightarrow[]{\overset{\overset{\text{O}}{\|}}{\text{ClCCl}}}$ **C** $\xrightarrow{\text{NH}_3}$ Meprobamate

17.

$\xrightarrow{\text{CH}_3\text{CH}_2\text{CH}_2\text{OH}}$ $\text{CH}_3\text{CH}_2\text{CH}_2\text{O}\overset{\overset{\text{O}}{\|}}{\text{C}}\text{CH}_2\text{CH}_2\overset{\overset{\text{O}}{\|}}{\text{C}}\text{OH}$ $\xrightarrow{\text{SOCl}_2}$

A

$\text{CH}_3\text{CH}_2\text{CH}_2\text{O}\overset{\overset{\text{O}}{\|}}{\text{C}}\text{CH}_2\text{CH}_2\overset{\overset{\text{O}}{\|}}{\text{C}}\text{Cl}$ $\xrightarrow{(\text{CH}_3\text{CH}_2)_2\text{NH}}$ $\text{CH}_3\text{CH}_2\text{CH}_2\text{O}\overset{\overset{\text{O}}{\|}}{\text{C}}\text{CH}_2\text{CH}_2\overset{\overset{\text{O}}{\|}}{\text{C}}\text{N}(\text{CH}_2\text{CH}_3)_2$

B   C

18.

$\xrightarrow[\substack{\text{(Diels-Alder}\\ \text{reaction)}}]{}$ A $\xrightarrow{\text{H}_2,\ \text{Pt}}$

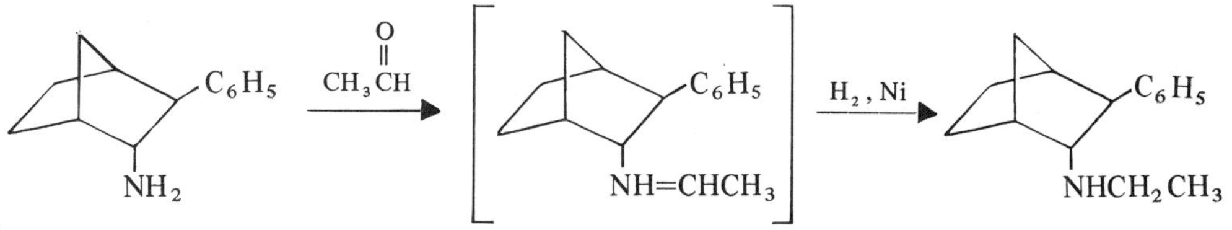

B

C

Fencamfine

19.

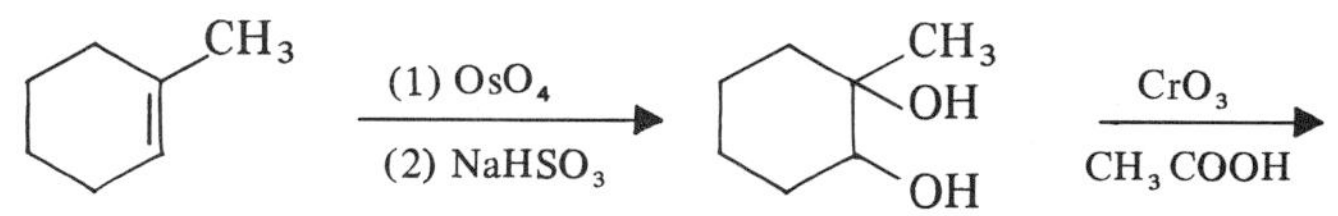

(1) OsO$_4$

(2) NaHSO$_3$

A

CrO$_3$

CH$_3$COOH

infrared band in 3200-3500 cm^{-1} region

infrared band in 1650-1730 cm^{-1} region

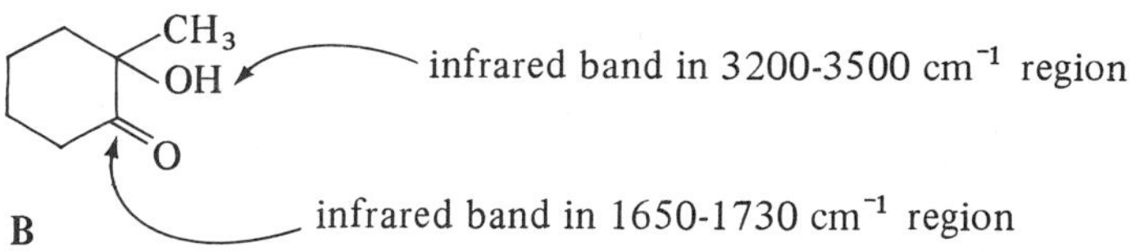

B

Notice that the second step involves the oxidation of a secondary alcohol in the presence of a tertiary alcohol. This selectivity is possible because tertiary alcohols do not undergo oxidation readily (Sect. 15.8).

20. Working backward, we notice that methyl *trans*-4-isopropylcyclohexanecarboxylate has both large groups equatorial and is, therefore, more stable than the corresponding cis isomer. This stability of the trans isomer means that if we were to synthesize the cis isomer or a mixture of both the cis and trans isomers we could obtain the desired trans isomer by a base-catalyzed isomerization:

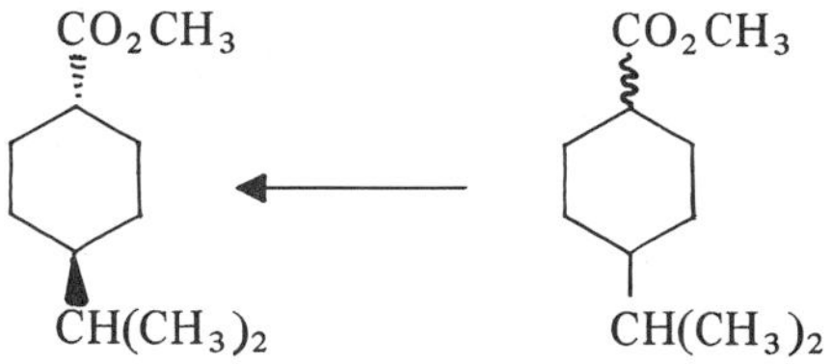

CO$_2$CH$_3$

CH(CH$_3$)$_2$

(more stable trans isomer)

CO$_2$CH$_3$

CH(CH$_3$)$_2$

(cis isomer or mixture of cis and trans isomers)

We could synthesize a mixture of the desired isomers from phenol in the following way.

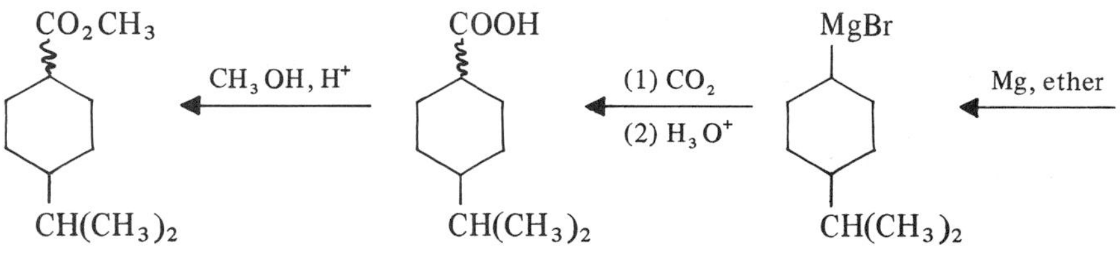

CO$_2$CH$_3$

CH(CH$_3$)$_2$

CH$_3$OH, H$^+$

COOH

CH(CH$_3$)$_2$

(1) CO$_2$

(2) H$_3$O$^+$

MgBr

CH(CH$_3$)$_2$

Mg, ether

21. The positive iodoform test and the strong infrared absorption of **X** indicate that it contains a $-\overset{\overset{\textstyle O}{\textstyle \|}}{C}CH_3$ group. Subtracting this from the molecular formula, $C_5H_{10}O$, leaves only C_3H_7.

$$\begin{array}{r} C_5H_{10}O \\ -C_2H_3O \\ \hline C_3H_7 \end{array}$$

This could be either a propyl group or an isopropyl group. The splitting patterns of the proton off-resonance decoupled spectrum are consistent only with an isopropyl group, hence **X** is isopropyl methyl ketone. The assignments are:

$$\underset{(a)\ \ (c)(d)(b)}{(CH_3)_2\,CH\overset{\overset{\textstyle O}{\textstyle \|}}{C}CH_3}$$

(a) quartet δ 18.1

(b) quartet δ 27.3

(c) doublet δ41.5

(d) singlet δ 211.8

22. That **Y** gives a green opaque solution when treated with CrO_3 in aqueous H_2SO_4 indicates that **Y** is a primary or secondary alcohol. That **Y** gives a negative iodoform test indicates that **Y** does not contain the grouping $-\underset{\underset{\textstyle OH}{\textstyle |}}{C}HCH_3$. The ^{13}C spectrum of **Y** contains only four signals indicating that some of the carbons in **Y** are equivalent. The splitting patterns of the off-resonance decoupled spectrum help us conclude that **Y** is 2-ethyl-1-butanol.

$$\underset{(CH_3CH_2)_2\,CHCH_2OH}{\overset{(a)\ \ (b)\ \ \ \ (c)\,(d)}{}}$$

(a) quartet δ 11.1

(b) triplet δ 23.0

(c) doublet δ 43.6

(d) triplet δ 64.6

Notice that the most downfield signal is a triplet. This fact indicates that the carbon that bears the $-OH$ group also bears two hydrogens and, therefore that **Y** is a primary alcohol. The most upfield signals are a quartet and a triplet indicating the presence of the ethyl groups.

23. That **Z** decolorizes bromine in CCl_4 indicates that **Z** is an alkene. We are told that **Z** is the more stable isomer of a pair of stereoisomers. This fact suggests that **Z** is a trans alkene.

That the ^{13}C spectrum contains only three signals, even though **Z** contains eight carbons, indicates that **Z** is highly symmetric. The splitting patterns of the proton off-resonance decoupled spectrum suggest that the upfield signals of the alkyl groups arise from equivalent isopropyl groups. That the downfield signal is a doublet suggests that each of the equivalent alkenyl carbons bears one hydrogen. We conclude, therefore, that **Z** is *trans*-2,5-dimethyl-3-hexene.

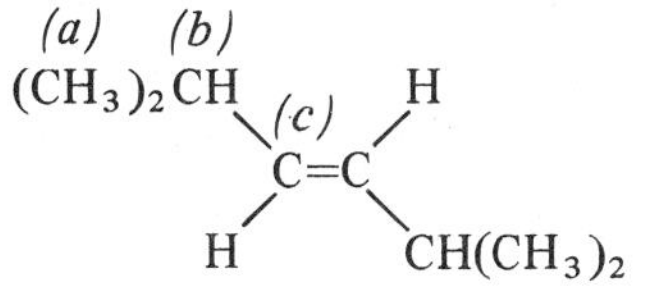

(a) quartet δ 22.8

(b) doublet δ 31.0

(c) doublet δ 134.5

21 CARBOHYDRATES

SUMMARY OF SOME REACTIONS OF MONOSACCHARIDES

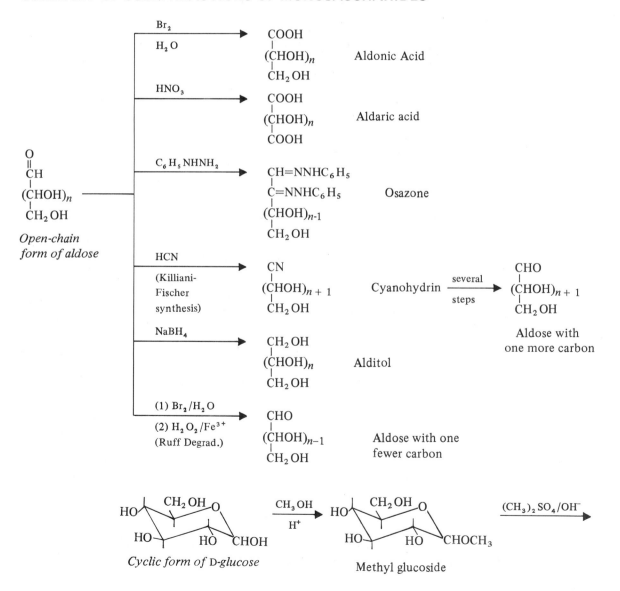

$$\underset{\substack{\text{Open-chain} \\ \text{form of aldose}}}{\overset{\overset{\displaystyle O}{\overset{\|}{CH}}}{\underset{\substack{(CHOH)_n \\ CH_2OH}}{}}}$$

Br$_2$ / H$_2$O →

$$\underset{\substack{(CHOH)_n \\ CH_2OH}}{COOH} \quad \text{Aldonic Acid}$$

HNO$_3$ →

$$\underset{\substack{(CHOH)_n \\ COOH}}{COOH} \quad \text{Aldaric acid}$$

C$_6$H$_5$NHNH$_2$ →

$$\underset{\substack{C=NNHC_6H_5 \\ (CHOH)_{n-1} \\ CH_2OH}}{CH=NNHC_6H_5} \quad \text{Osazone}$$

HCN (Killiani-Fischer synthesis) →

$$\underset{\substack{(CHOH)_{n+1} \\ CH_2OH}}{CN} \quad \text{Cyanohydrin} \xrightarrow[\text{steps}]{\text{several}} \underset{\substack{(CHOH)_{n+1} \\ CH_2OH}}{CHO}$$

Aldose with one more carbon

NaBH$_4$ →

$$\underset{\substack{(CHOH)_n \\ CH_2OH}}{CH_2OH} \quad \text{Alditol}$$

(1) Br$_2$/H$_2$O
(2) H$_2$O$_2$/Fe^{3+} (Ruff Degrad.) →

$$\underset{\substack{(CHOH)_{n-1} \\ CH_2OH}}{CHO} \quad \begin{array}{l}\text{Aldose with one} \\ \text{fewer carbon}\end{array}$$

Cyclic form of D-*glucose* $\xrightarrow[H^+]{CH_3OH}$ Methyl glucoside $\xrightarrow{(CH_3)_2SO_4/OH^-}$

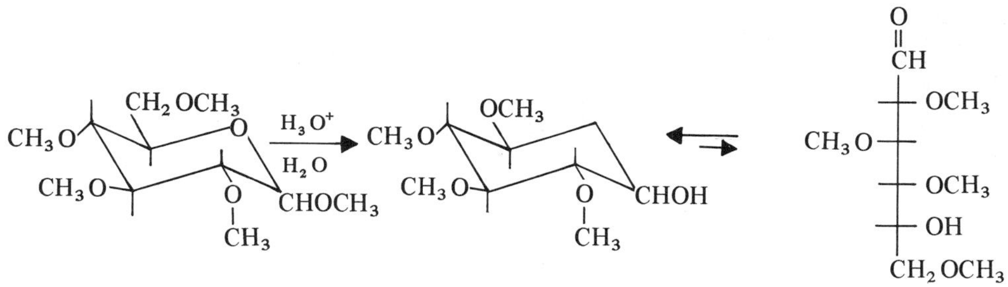

The reaction scheme and Fischer projection shown:

SOLUTIONS TO PROBLEMS

21.1   (a) Two,   CHO
                     |
                    *CHOH
                     |
                    *CHOH
                     |
                    CH$_2$OH

(b) Two,   CH$_2$OH
           |
           C=O
           |
          *CHOH
           |
          *CHOH
           |
          CH$_2$OH

(c) There would be four stereoisomers (two sets of enantiomers) with each general structure: $2^2 = 4$.

21.2

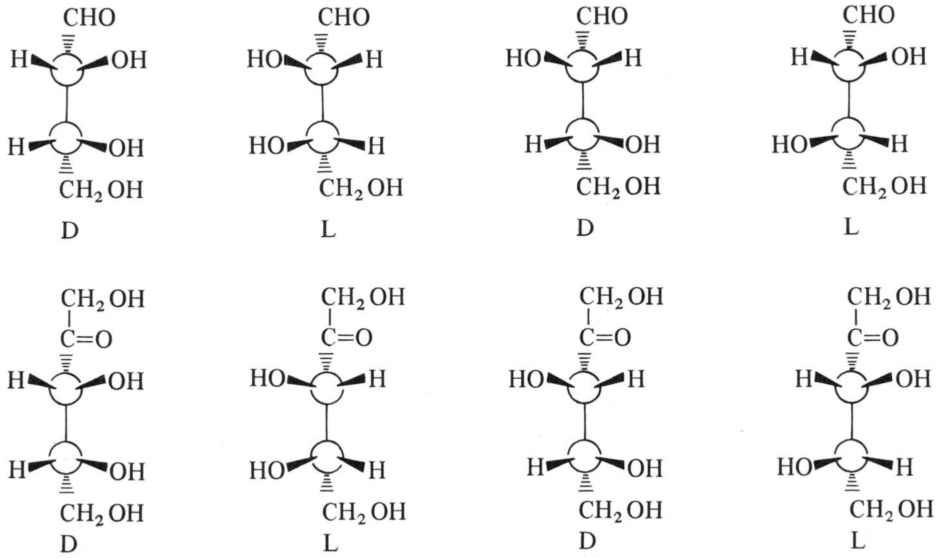

21.3   Since glycosides are acetals they undergo hydrolysis in aqueous acid to form cyclic hemiacetals that then undergo mutarotation.

21.4

Methyl α-D-glucopyranoside   Methyl β-D-glucopyranoside

21.5

Haworth formula   Conformational formula

Methyl-α-D-mannopyranoside

21.6   α-D-Glucopyranose will give a positive test with Benedict's or Tollens' solution because it is a cyclic hemiacetal. Methyl α-D-glucopyranoside, because it is a cyclic acetal, will not.

21.7

$$
\begin{array}{c}
\text{H} \\
\text{C}=\text{O} \\
\text{H–C–OH} \\
\text{HO–C–H} \\
\text{H–C–OH} \\
\text{H–C–OH} \\
\text{CH}_2\text{OH}
\end{array}
\quad \underset{\text{H}_2\text{O}}{\overset{\text{OH}^-}{\rightleftharpoons}} \quad
\begin{array}{c}
\text{H} \\
\text{C}=\text{O} \\
{}^{-}\text{: C–OH} \\
\text{HO–C–H} \\
\text{H–C–OH} \\
\text{H–C–OH} \\
\text{CH}_2\text{OH}
\end{array}
\quad \longleftrightarrow \quad
\begin{array}{c}
\text{H} \\
\text{C–O}^- \\
\text{C–OH} \\
\text{HO–C–H} \\
\text{H–C–OH} \\
\text{H–C–OH} \\
\text{CH}_2\text{OH}
\end{array}
$$

Enolate ion

$\underset{\text{OH}^-}{\overset{\text{H}_2\text{O}}{\rightleftharpoons}}$ $\underset{\text{OH}^-}{\overset{\text{H}_2\text{O}}{\rightleftharpoons}}$

$$
\begin{array}{c}
\text{H} \\
\text{C–OH} \\
\text{C–OH} \\
\text{R}
\end{array}
\qquad\qquad
\begin{array}{c}
\text{H} \\
\text{C}=\text{O} \\
\text{HO–C–H} \\
\text{HO–C–H} \\
\text{H–C–OH} \\
\text{H–C–OH} \\
\text{CH}_2\text{OH}
\end{array}
$$

Enediol   D-Mannose

$\overset{^-\text{OH}}{\underset{\text{H}_2\text{O}}{\updownarrow}}$

(see next page)

(from previous page)

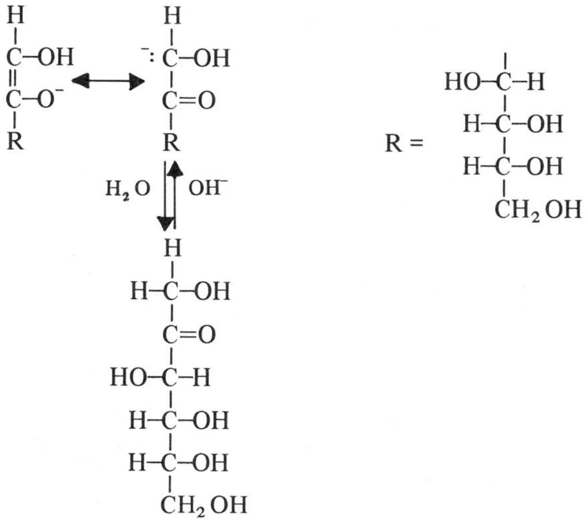

D-Fructose

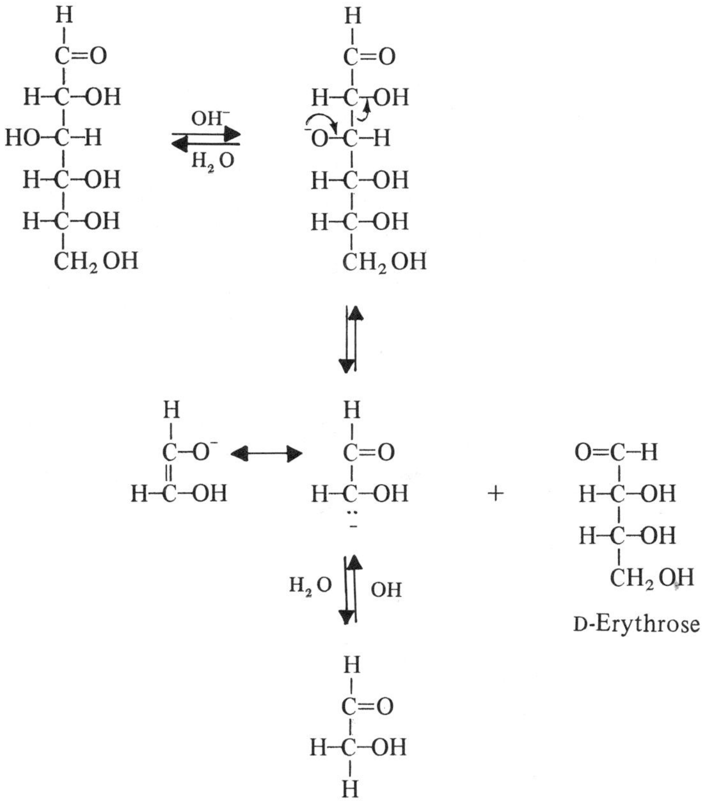

R =

Glycolic
aldehyde

D-Erythrose

21.8

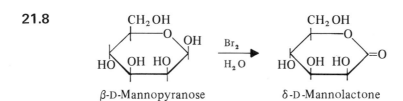

β-D-Mannopyranose $\xrightarrow[\text{H}_2\text{O}]{\text{Br}_2}$ δ-D-Mannolactone

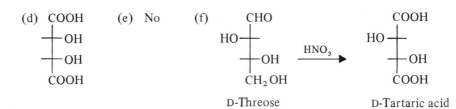

D-Mannonic acid ⇌ γ-D-Mannolactone

21.9   (a) Yes   (b)   COOH   (c) Yes

HO —|
HO —|
     |— OH
     |— OH
     COOH

D-Mannaric acid

(d) COOH   (e) No   (f)   CHO   COOH

|— OH   HO —| HO —|
|— OH |— OH $\xrightarrow{\text{HNO}_3}$ |— OH
COOH   CH₂OH   COOH

                              D-Threose   D-Tartaric acid

(g) The aldaric acid obtained from D-erythrose is *meso*-tartaric acid; the aldaric acid obtained from D-threose is D-tartaric acid.

21.10

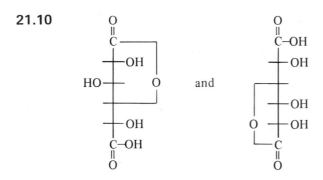

and

21.11 One way of predicting the products from a periodate oxidation is to place an —OH group on each carbon at the point where C—C bond cleavage has occurred:

$$
\begin{array}{c}
-\underset{|}{\overset{|}{C}}-OH \\
-\underset{|}{\overset{|}{C}}-OH
\end{array}
\xrightarrow{\ IO_4^-\ }
\begin{array}{c}
-\underset{|}{\overset{|}{C}}-OH \\
OH \\
+ \\
OH \\
-\underset{|}{\overset{|}{C}}-OH
\end{array}
$$

Then if we recall (Sect. 15.11) that gem-diols are usually unstable and lose water to produce carbonyl compounds, we get the following results:

$$
-\overset{|}{C}\overset{O-H}{\underset{OH}{}} \longrightarrow -\overset{|}{C}=O + H_2O
$$

$$
-\overset{OH}{\underset{|}{C}}\!-O\!-H \longrightarrow -\overset{|}{C}=O + H_2O
$$

Let us apply this procedure to several examples here while we remember that for every C—C bond that is broken one mole of HIO_4 is consumed.

(a)

$$
\begin{array}{c}
CH_3 \\
| \\
H-C-OH \\
------ \\
H-C-OH \\
| \\
CH_3
\end{array}
+ HIO_4 \longrightarrow
\begin{array}{c}
CH_3 \\
| \\
H-C-O-H \\
OH \\
+ \\
OH \\
H-C-O-H \\
| \\
CH_3
\end{array}
\xrightarrow[-2H_2O]{}
\quad 2CH_3\overset{\overset{O}{\|}}{C}-H
$$

(b)

$$
\begin{array}{c}
H \\
| \\
H-C-OH \\
------ \\
H-C-OH \\
------ \\
H-C-OH \\
| \\
CH_3
\end{array}
+ 2HIO_4 \longrightarrow
\begin{array}{c}
H \\
| \\
H-C-O-H \\
OH \\
+ \\
O-H \\
H-C-OH \\
OH \\
+ \\
OH \\
H-C-O-H \\
| \\
CH_3
\end{array}
\xrightarrow[-3H_2O]{}
\begin{array}{c}
H \\
| \\
H-C=O \\
+ \\
O \\
\| \\
H-C-OH \\
+ \\
H-C=O \\
| \\
CH_3
\end{array}
$$

(c)

$$
\begin{array}{c}
\text{H} \\
\text{H–C–OH} \\
\text{------} \\
\text{H–C–OH} \\
\text{H–C–OCH}_3 \\
\text{OCH}_3
\end{array}
+ \text{HIO}_4 \longrightarrow
\begin{array}{c}
\text{H} \\
\text{H–C–OH} \\
\text{OH} \\
+ \\
\text{OH} \\
\text{H–C–OH} \\
\text{H–C–OCH}_3 \\
\text{OCH}_3
\end{array}
\xrightarrow{-2\text{H}_2\text{O}}
\begin{array}{c}
\text{H} \\
\text{H–C=O} \\
+ \\
\text{O} \\
\text{H–C} \\
\text{H–C–OCH}_3 \\
\text{OCH}_3
\end{array}
$$

(d)

$$
\begin{array}{c}
\text{H} \\
\text{H–C–OH} \\
\text{------} \\
\text{H–C–OH} \\
\text{------} \\
\text{C=O} \\
\text{CH}_3
\end{array}
+ 2\text{HIO}_4 \longrightarrow
\begin{array}{c}
\text{H} \\
\text{H–C–OH} \\
\text{OH} \\
+ \\
\text{OH} \\
\text{H–C–OH} \\
\text{OH} \\
+ \\
\text{OH} \\
\text{C=O} \\
\text{CH}_3
\end{array}
\xrightarrow{-2\text{H}_2\text{O}}
\begin{array}{c}
\text{H} \\
\text{H–C=O} \\
+ \\
\text{O} \\
\text{H–C–OH} \\
+ \\
\text{O} \\
\text{CH}_3\text{COH}
\end{array}
$$

(e)

$$
\begin{array}{c}
\text{CH}_3 \\
\text{C=O} \\
\text{------} \\
\text{H–C–OH} \\
\text{------} \\
\text{C=O} \\
\text{CH}_3
\end{array}
+ 2\text{HIO}_4 \longrightarrow
\begin{array}{c}
\text{CH}_3 \\
\text{C=O} \\
\text{OH} \\
+ \\
\text{OH} \\
\text{H–C–OH} \\
\text{OH} \\
+ \\
\text{OH} \\
\text{C=O} \\
\text{CH}_3
\end{array}
\xrightarrow{-2\text{H}_2\text{O}}
2\text{CH}_3\overset{\text{O}}{\overset{\|}{\text{C}}}\text{OH} + \text{H}\overset{\text{O}}{\overset{\|}{\text{C}}}\text{OH}
$$

(f)

$$
\begin{array}{c}
\text{CH}_2 \quad \text{H} \\
\text{CH}_2 \quad \text{C–OH} \\
\text{------} \\
\text{CH}_2 \quad \text{C–OH} \\
\text{H}
\end{array}
+ \text{HIO}_4 \longrightarrow
\begin{array}{c}
\text{H} \\
\text{CH}_2 \quad \text{C–OH} \\
\text{OH} \\
\text{OH} \\
\text{CH}_2 \quad \text{C–OH} \\
\text{H}
\end{array}
\xrightarrow{-2\text{H}_2\text{O}}
$$

$$
\text{H}\overset{\text{O}}{\overset{\|}{\text{C}}}\text{CH}_2\text{CH}_2\text{CH}_2\overset{\text{O}}{\overset{\|}{\text{C}}}\text{H}
$$

(g)

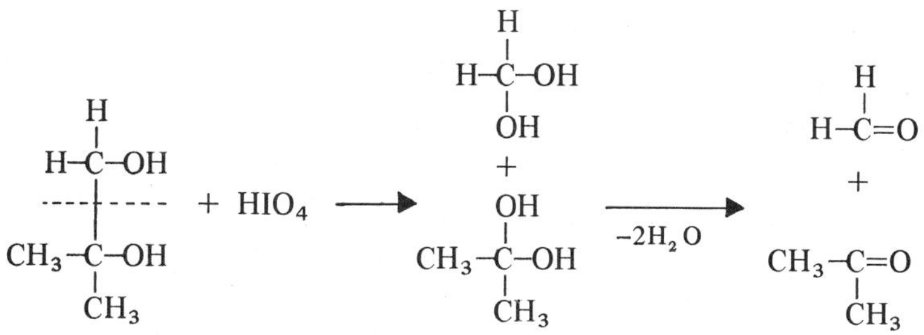

$$\begin{array}{c} H \\ | \\ H-C-OH \\ ---|--- \\ CH_3-C-OH \\ | \\ CH_3 \end{array} \;+\; HIO_4 \;\longrightarrow\; \begin{array}{c} H \\ | \\ H-C-OH \\ | \\ OH \\ + \\ OH \\ | \\ CH_3-C-OH \\ | \\ CH_3 \end{array} \;\xrightarrow[-2H_2O]{}\; \begin{array}{c} H \\ | \\ H-C=O \\ + \\ CH_3-C=O \\ | \\ CH_3 \end{array}$$

(h)

$$\begin{array}{c} O \\ \| \\ H-C \\ ---|--- \\ H-C-OH \\ ---|--- \\ H-C-OH \\ ---|--- \\ H-C-OH \\ | \\ H \end{array} \;+\; 3HIO_4 \;\longrightarrow\; \begin{array}{c} O \\ \| \\ H-C-OH \\ + \\ OH \\ | \\ H-C-OH \\ | \\ OH \\ + \\ OH \\ | \\ H-C-OH \\ | \\ OH \\ + \\ OH \\ | \\ H-C-OH \\ | \\ H \end{array} \;\xrightarrow[-3H_2O]{}\; 3H\overset{O}{\overset{\|}{C}}OH \;+\; H\overset{O}{\overset{\|}{C}}H$$

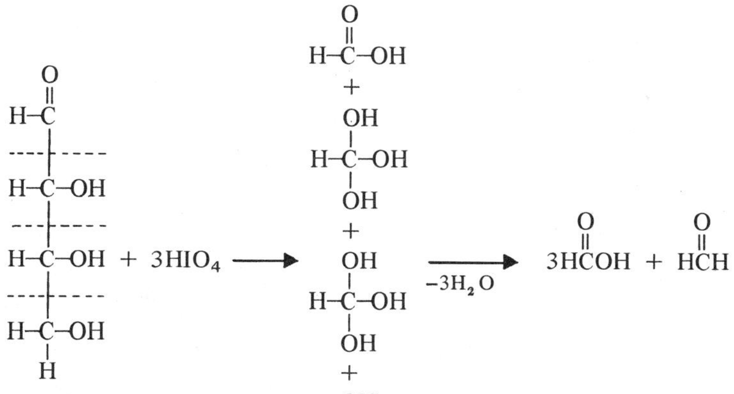

D-Erythrose

21.12 Oxidation of an aldohexose and a ketohexose would each require five moles of HIO_4 but would give different results.

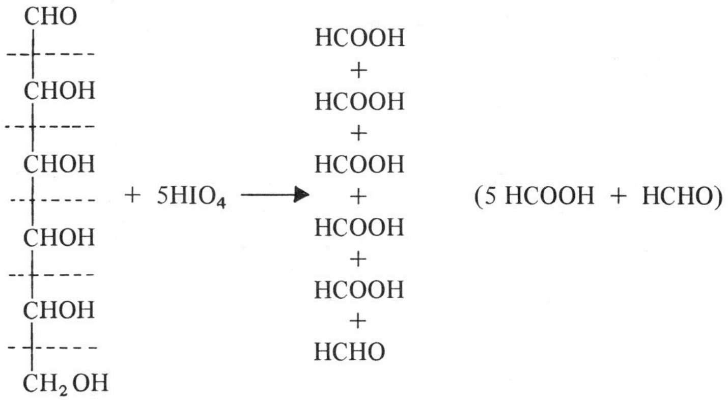

$$\begin{array}{c} CHO \\ --|--- \\ CHOH \\ --|--- \\ CHOH \\ --|--- \\ CHOH \\ --|--- \\ CHOH \\ --|--- \\ CH_2OH \end{array} \;+\; 5HIO_4 \;\longrightarrow\; \begin{array}{c} HCOOH \\ + \\ HCOOH \\ + \\ HCOOH \\ + \\ HCOOH \\ + \\ HCOOH \\ + \\ HCHO \end{array} \qquad (5\ HCOOH \;+\; HCHO)$$

Aldohexose

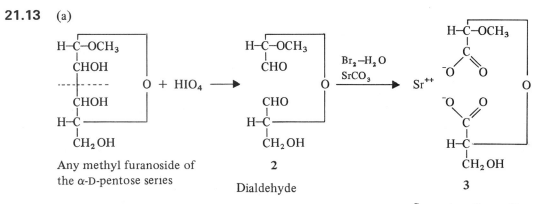

Ketohexose

21.13 (a)

Any methyl furanoside of
the α-D-pentose series

Dialdehyde

2

Same strontium salt

3

(b) Although both compounds yield the same dialdehyde **2** (and Strontium salt **3**), periodate oxidation of a methyl α-D-pentofuranoside consumes only one mole of HIO_4 and produces no formic acid.

21.14 (a)

Glyoxylic
acid

4

D-(−)-Glyceric
acid

5

(b) This relates the configuration of the highest numbered carbon of the aldose to that of D-(+)-glyceraldehyde, and thus allows us to place the aldose in the D-family.

21.15 (a) Yes, D-glucitol would be optically active; only those alditols (p. 531) whose molecules possess a plane of symmetry would be optically inactive.

(b)

$$\begin{array}{c} \text{CHO} \\ \vert \\ \text{H--C--OH} \\ \vert \\ \text{H--C--OH} \\ \vert \\ \text{H--C--OH} \\ \vert \\ \text{H--C--OH} \\ \vert \\ \text{CH}_2\text{OH} \end{array} \xrightarrow{\text{NaBH}_4} \begin{array}{c} \text{CH}_2\text{OH} \\ \vert \\ \text{H--C--OH} \\ \vert \\ \text{H--C--OH} \\ \text{- - - - - -} \\ \text{H--C--OH} \\ \vert \\ \text{H--C--OH} \\ \vert \\ \text{CH}_2\text{OH} \end{array} \quad \text{Plane of symmetry}$$

Optically
inactive

$$\begin{array}{c} \text{CHO} \\ \vert \\ \text{H--C--OH} \\ \vert \\ \text{HO--C--H} \\ \vert \\ \text{HO--C--H} \\ \vert \\ \text{H--C--OH} \\ \vert \\ \text{CH}_2\text{OH} \end{array} \xrightarrow{\text{NaBH}_4} \begin{array}{c} \text{CH}_2\text{OH} \\ \vert \\ \text{H--C--OH} \\ \vert \\ \text{HO--C--H} \\ \text{- - - - - -} \\ \text{HO--C--H} \\ \vert \\ \text{H--C--OH} \\ \vert \\ \text{CH}_2\text{OH} \end{array} \quad \text{Plane of symmetry}$$

Optically inactive

21.16 (a)

$$\begin{array}{c} \text{CH}_2\text{OH} \\ \vert \\ \text{C=O} \\ \vert \\ \text{HO--C--H} \\ \vert \\ \text{H--C--OH} \\ \vert \\ \text{H--C--OH} \\ \vert \\ \text{CH}_2\text{OH} \end{array} \xrightarrow{\text{C}_6\text{H}_5\text{NHNH}_2} \begin{array}{c} \text{CH=NNHC}_6\text{H}_5 \\ \vert \\ \text{C=NNHC}_6\text{H}_5 \\ \vert \\ \text{HO--C--H} \\ \vert \\ \text{H--C--OH} \\ \vert \\ \text{H--C--OH} \\ \vert \\ \text{CH}_2\text{OH} \end{array}$$

(b) This experiment shows that D-glucose and D-fructose have the same configurations at C-3, C-4, and C-5.

21.17 (a)

$$\begin{array}{c} \text{CHO} \\ \vert \\ \text{HO--C--H} \\ \vert \\ \text{HO--C--H} \\ \vert \\ \text{CH}_2\text{OH} \end{array} \qquad \begin{array}{c} \text{CHO} \\ \vert \\ \text{H--C--OH} \\ \vert \\ \text{HO--C--H} \\ \vert \\ \text{CH}_2\text{OH} \end{array}$$

L-Erythrose   L-Threose

(b) L-Glyceraldehyde,

$$\begin{array}{c} \text{CHO} \\ \vert \\ \text{HO--C--H} \\ \vert \\ \text{CH}_2\text{OH} \end{array}$$

21.18 (a)

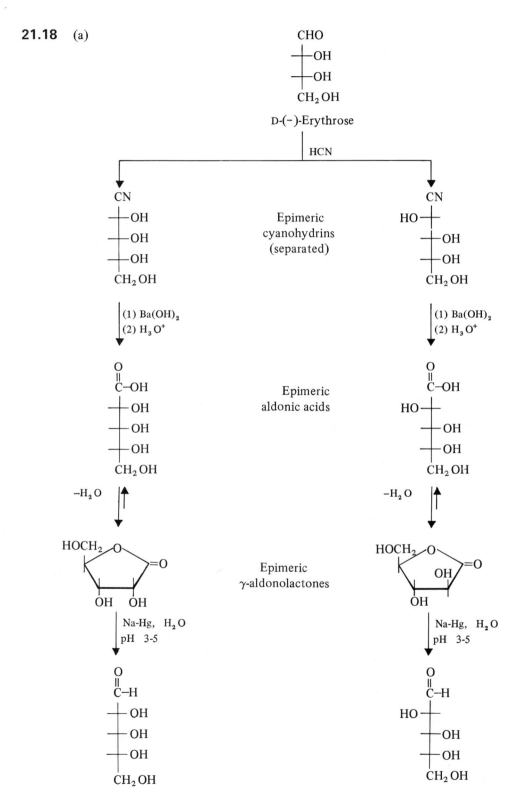

(b)

$$
\begin{array}{c}
\overset{\displaystyle O}{\underset{\displaystyle \|}{C}}-H \\
\text{OH} \\
\text{OH} \\
\text{OH} \\
CH_2OH
\end{array}
\xrightarrow{HNO_3}
\begin{array}{c}
\overset{\displaystyle O}{\underset{\displaystyle \|}{C}}-OH \\
\text{OH} \\
\text{OH} \\
\text{OH} \\
\overset{\displaystyle C}{\underset{\displaystyle \|}{}}-OH \\
O
\end{array}
$$

D-(−)-Ribose   Optically
                      inactive

$$
\begin{array}{c}
\overset{\displaystyle O}{\underset{\displaystyle \|}{C}}-H \\
HO \quad \\
\text{OH} \\
\text{OH} \\
CH_2OH
\end{array}
\xrightarrow{HNO_3}
\begin{array}{c}
\overset{\displaystyle O}{\underset{\displaystyle \|}{C}}-OH \\
HO \quad \\
\text{OH} \\
\text{OH} \\
\overset{\displaystyle C}{\underset{\displaystyle \|}{}}-OH \\
O
\end{array}
$$

D-(−)-Arabinose   Optically
                         active

21.19   A Kiliani-Fischer synthesis starting with D-(−)-threose would yield **I** and **II**.

$$
\begin{array}{c}
CHO \\
\text{OH} \\
HO \quad \\
\text{OH} \\
CH_2OH \\
\textbf{I}
\end{array}
\qquad
\begin{array}{c}
CHO \\
HO \quad \\
HO \quad \\
\text{OH} \\
CH_2OH \\
\textbf{II}
\end{array}
$$

D-(+)-Xylose   D-(−)-Lyxose

I must be D-(+)-xylose because when oxidized by nitric acid, it yields an optically inactive aldaric acid:

$$
\textbf{I} \xrightarrow{HNO_3}
\begin{array}{c}
COOH \\
\text{OH} \\
HO \quad \\
\text{OH} \\
COOH
\end{array}
$$

Optically
inactive

II must be D-(−)-lyxose because when oxidized by nitric acid it yields an optically active aldaric acid:

$$
\text{II} \xrightarrow{\text{HNO}_3}
\begin{array}{c}
\text{COOH} \\
\text{HO}\!-\!\!|\!\!-\! \\
\text{HO}\!-\!\!|\!\!-\! \\
|\!\!-\!\text{OH} \\
\text{COOH}
\end{array}
$$

Optically
active

21.20

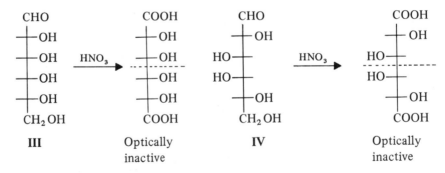

L-(+)-Ribose   L-(+)-Arabinose   L-(−)-Xylose   L-(+)-Lyxose

21.21   Since D-(+)-galactose yields an optically inactive aldaric acid it must have either structure **III** or structure **IV** below.

CHO   COOH   CHO   COOH
|—OH |—OH |—OH |—OH
|—OH $\xrightarrow{\text{HNO}_3}$ |—OH   HO—| HO—|
|—OH |—OH   HO—| $\xrightarrow{\text{HNO}_3}$ HO—|
|—OH |—OH |—OH |—OH
CH₂OH   COOH   CH₂OH   COOH

III   Optically   **IV**   Optically
                        inactive   inactive

A Ruff degradation beginning with **III** would yield D-(−)-ribose

$$
\text{III} \xrightarrow[\text{H}_2\text{O}]{\text{Br}_2} \xrightarrow[\text{Fe}_2(\text{SO}_4)_3]{\text{H}_2\text{O}_2}
\begin{array}{c}
\text{CHO} \\
|\!\!-\!\text{OH} \\
|\!\!-\!\text{OH} \\
|\!\!-\!\text{OH} \\
\text{CH}_2\text{OH}
\end{array}
$$

D-(−)-Ribose

A Ruff degradation beginning with **IV** would yield D-(−)-lyxose: thus D-(+)-galactose must have structure **IV**.

$$\text{IV} \xrightarrow[\text{H}_2\text{O}]{\text{Br}_2} \xrightarrow[\text{Fe}_2(\text{SO}_4)_3]{\text{H}_2\text{O}_2}$$

CHO
HO—
HO—
—OH
CH₂OH

D-(−)-Lyxose

21.22   D-(+)-glucose, as shown below.

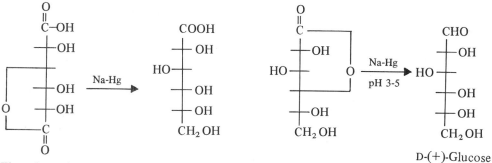

O
‖
C—OH
—OH
—OH
—OH
C
‖
O

$\xrightarrow{\text{Na-Hg}}$

COOH
—OH
HO—
—OH
—OH
CH₂OH

O
‖
C
—OH
HO—   O
—OH
CH₂OH

$\xrightarrow[\text{pH 3-5}]{\text{Na-Hg}}$

CHO
—OH
HO—
—OH
—OH
CH₂OH

D-(+)-Glucose

The other γ-lactone
of D-glucaric acid

21.23   If the methyl glucoside had been a furanoside, hydrolysis of the methylation product would have given:

CHO
—OCH₃
CH₃O—
—OH
—OCH₃
CH₂OCH₃

And, oxidation would have given:

¹CHO
²—OCH₃
CH₃O³—
----
⁴—OH
----
⁵—OCH₃
⁶CH₂OCH₃

$\xrightarrow{\text{HNO}_3}$

¹COOH
²—OCH₃
CH₃O³—
⁴COOH

A dimethoxysuc-
cinic acid

⁴COOH
⁵—OCH₃
+ ⁶CH₂OCH₃

A dimethoxy-
propanoic
acid

¹COOH
+ ²—OCH₃ +
³COOH

Methoxyma-
lonic acid

⁵COOH
⁶CH₂OCH₃

COOH
|
²CH₂OCH₃

Methoxyacetic
acid

$\xleftarrow{-\text{CO}_2}$

21.24

(a)
CHO
|
CHOH
|
CHOH
|
CHOH
|
CH₂OH

(b)
CH₂OH
|
C=O
|
CHOH
|
CHOH
|
CHOH
|
CH₂OH

(c)
CHO
|
(CHOH)ₙ
HO——H
CH₂OH

or

CH₂OH
|
C=O
|
(CHOH)ₙ
HO——H
CH₂OH

(d)
CHOR
|
(CHOH)ₙ   O
|
CH ————
|
CH₂OH

(e)
COOH
|
(CHOH)ₙ
|
CH₂OH

(f)
COOH
|
(CHOH)ₙ
|
COOH

(g)
O
‖
C ————
|
(CHOH)ₙ   O
|
CH ————
|
CH₂OH

(h)
OH
|
CH ————
|
CHOH
|
CHOH   O
|
CHOH
|
CH ————
|
CH₂OH

or

CH₂OH
|
CH ———— O
| |
CHOH   CHOH
| |
CHOH ———— CHOH

(i)
OH
|
CH ————
|
CHOH
|
CHOH   O
|
CH ————
|
CHOH
|
CH₂OH

or

CH₂OH
|
CHOH
| O
CH   CHOH
CHOH–CHOH

(j) Any sugar that has a free aldehyde or ketone group or one that exists as a cyclic hemiacetal or hemiketal. Examples are:

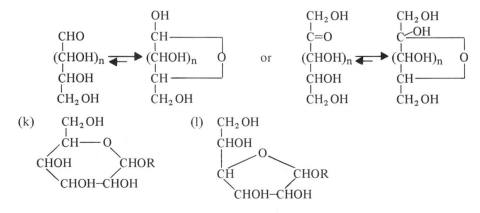

(k)
CH₂OH
|
CH ———— O
| |
CHOH   CHOR
| |
CHOH–CHOH

(l)
CH₂OH
|
CHOH
| O
CH   CHOR
CHOH–CHOH

(m) Any two aldoses that differ only in configuration at C-2. (See also Sect. 21.6 for a broader definition.) D-Erythrose and D-threose are examples.

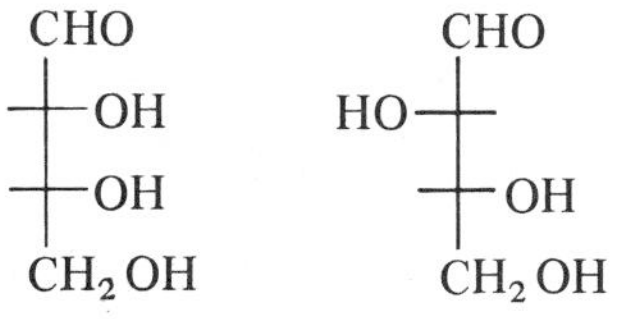

$$\begin{array}{cc}
\text{CHO} & \text{CHO} \\
\hline \text{OH} & \text{HO} \hline \\
\hline \text{OH} & \hline \text{OH} \\
\text{CH}_2\text{OH} & \text{CH}_2\text{OH}
\end{array}$$

D-Erythrose   D-Threose

(n) Cyclic sugars that differ only in the configuration of C-1. Examples are:

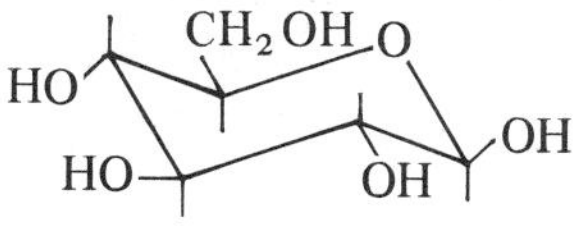

and

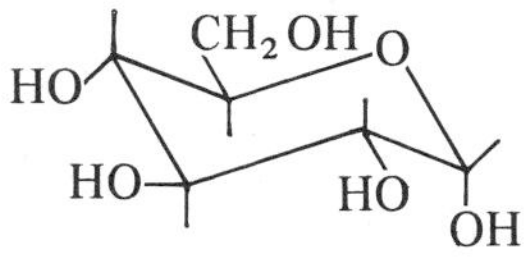

(o) $\text{CH}=\text{NNHC}_6\text{H}_5$
$\;\;\;\;|$
$\;\;\;\text{C}=\text{NNHC}_6\text{H}_5$
$\;\;\;|$
$\;\;(\text{CHOH})_n$
$\;\;\;|$
$\;\;\text{CH}_2\text{OH}$

(p) Maltose is an example:

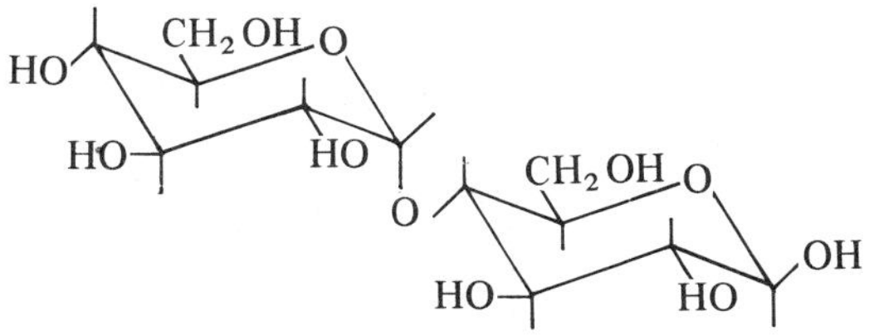

(q) Amylose is an example:

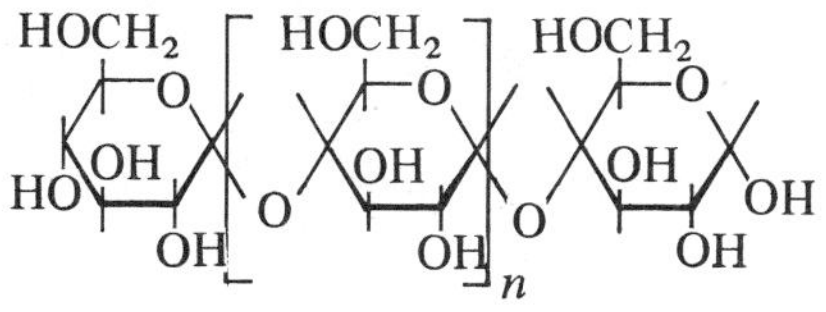

(r) Any sugar in which all potential carbonyl groups are present as acetals or ketals (i.e., as glycosides). Sucrose (Sect. 21.11) is an example of a nonreducing disaccharide; the methyl D-glucopyranosides (Sect. 21.3) are examples of nonreducing monosaccharides.

21.25

(a)

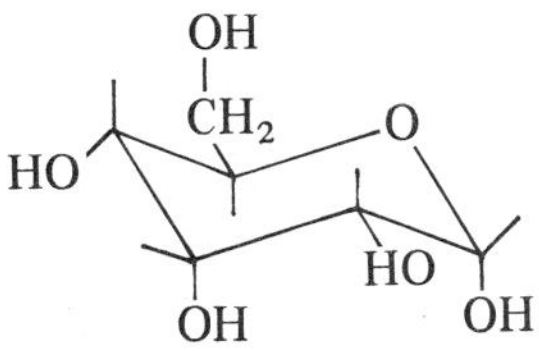

(b)

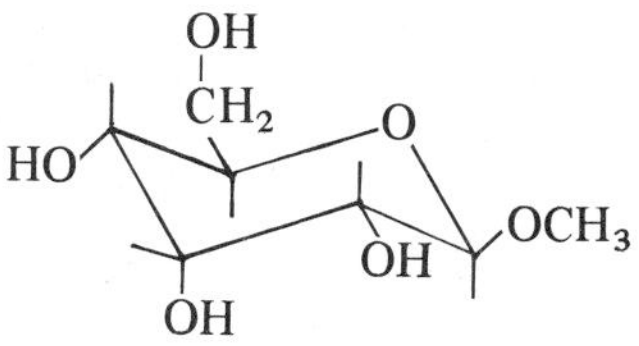

(c)

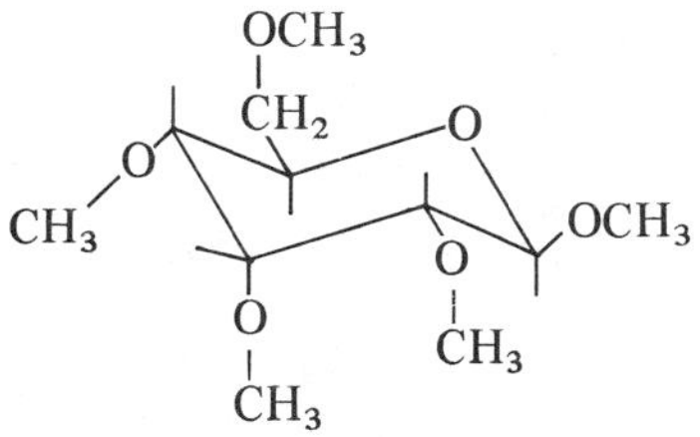

21.26

(a) [structure: HOCH₂ furanose ring] and [structure: pyranose ring]

(b) [structure: HOCH₂ furanose with OCH₃] + HIO₄ ⟶ [dialdehyde product with OCH₃]

[structure: pyranose with OCH₃] + 2HIO₄ ⟶ [product] + HCOH

A methyl ribofuranoside would consume only one mole of HIO₄; a methyl ribopyranoside would consume two moles of HIO₄ and would also produce one mole of formic acid.

21.27   One anomer of D-mannose is dextrorotatory ($[\alpha]_D^{25} = +29.3°$), the other is levorotatory ($[\alpha]_D^{25} = -17.0°$).

21.28   The microorganism selectively oxidizes the —CHOH group of D-glucitol that corresponds to C-5 of D-glucose.

[Fischer projections: D-Glucose → (H₂/Ni) → D-Glucitol → (O₂, Acetobacter suboxydans) → L-Sorbose]

D-Glucose   D-Glucitol   L-Sorbose

21.29   L-Gulose and L-idose would yield the same phenylosazone as L-sorbose.

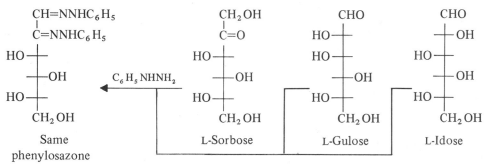

Same phenylosazone   L-Sorbose   L-Gulose   L-Idose

21.30

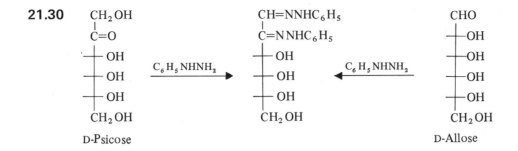

CH₂OH
C=O
──OH
──OH
──OH
CH₂OH
D-Psicose

→ C₆H₅NHNH₂ →

CH=NNHC₆H₅
C=NNHC₆H₅
──OH
──OH
──OH
CH₂OH

← C₆H₅NHNH₂ ←

CHO
──OH
──OH
──OH
──OH
CH₂OH
D-Allose

CH₂OH
C=O
HO──
HO──
──OH
CH₂OH
D-Tagatose

→ C₆H₅NHNH₂ →

CH=NNHC₆H₅
C=NNHC₆H₅
HO──
HO──
──OH
CH₂OH

← C₆H₅NHNH₂ ←

CHO
──OH
HO──
HO──
──OH
CH₂OH
D-Galactose

21.31   **A** is D-altrose, **B** is D-talose, and **C** is D-galactose:

CHO
HO──
──OH
──OH
──OH
CH₂OH
D-Altrose
A

→ H₂ / Ni →

CH₂OH
HO──
──OH
──OH
──OH
CH₂OH

≡

CH₂OH
HO──
HO──
──OH
──OH
CH₂OH

← H₂ / Ni ←

CHO
HO──
HO──
HO──
──OH
CH₂OH
D-Talose
B

Same alditol

↓ C₆H₅NHNH₂

↓ C₆H₅NHNH₂

CH=NNHC₆H₅
C=NNHC₆H₅
──OH
──OH
──OH
CH₂OH

⟨ different phenylosazones ⟩

CH=NNHC₆H₅
C=NNHC₆H₅
HO──
HO──
──OH
CH₂OH

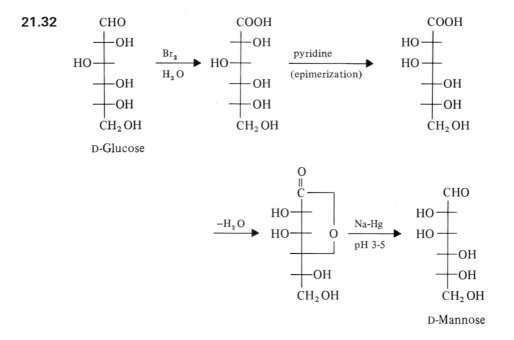

```
        CHO                      CH=NNHC₆H₅                  CHO
      ┌──OH                      C=NNHC₆H₅              HO──┐
  HO──┤         C₆H₅NHNH₂    HO──┤       C₆H₅NHNH₂      HO──┤
  HO──┤        ─────────►    HO──┤      ◄─────────      HO──┤
      ├──OH                      ├──OH                      ├──OH
        CH₂OH                      CH₂OH                      CH₂OH

    D-Galactose              Same phenylosazone            D-Talose
        C                                                      B
```

$$\text{CH}=\text{NNHC}_6\text{H}_5$$

D-Galactose	Same phenylosazone	D-Talose
C		**B**

H₂, Ni   H₂, Ni

```
        CH₂OH                                             CH₂OH
      ┌──OH                                           HO──┐
  HO──┤                 ⟨ different alditols ⟩         HO──┤
  HO──┤                                                HO──┤
      ├──OH                                                ├──OH
        CH₂OH                                               CH₂OH
```

(Note: If we had designated D-talose as **A**, and D-altrose as **B**, then **C** is D-allose)

21.32

```
        CHO                  COOH                    COOH
      ┌──OH               ┌──OH                  HO──┐
  HO──┤        Br₂    HO──┤       pyridine       HO──┤
      │       ────       │      ────────────         │
      ├──OH    H₂O       ├──OH   (epimerization)     ├──OH
      ├──OH               ├──OH                       ├──OH
        CH₂OH               CH₂OH                      CH₂OH

   D-Glucose
```

```
                     O
                     ‖
                     C───┐
             HO──┤          CHO
  -H₂O    HO──┤     O    Na-Hg    HO──┤
  ────►                  ─────         HO──┤
             ├──OH       pH 3-5         ├──OH
               CH₂OH                    ├──OH
                                          CH₂OH

                                       D-Mannose
```

21.33 The conformation of D-idopyranose with four equatorial —OH groups and an axial —CH₂OH group is more stable than the one with four axial —OH groups and an equatorial —CH₂OH group.

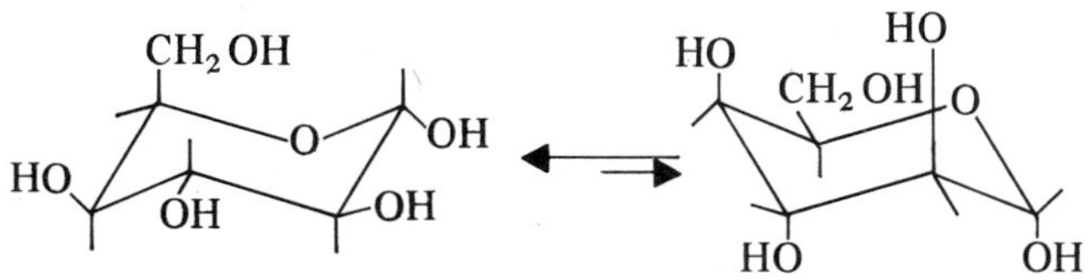

CH₂OH
More stable

Less stable

4 Equatorial –OH groups
1 Axial –CH₂OH

4 Axial –OH groups
1 Equatorial –CH₂OH

21.34 (a) The anhydro sugar is formed when the axial –CH₂OH group reacts with C-1 to form a cyclic acetal.

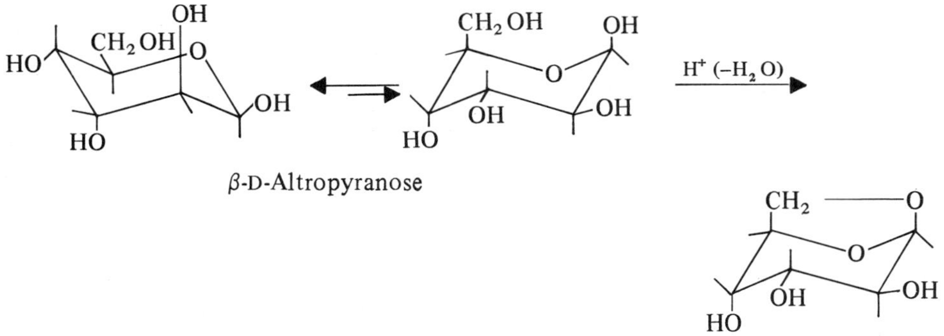

β-D-Altropyranose

H⁺ (–H₂O)

Anhydro sugar

Because the anhydro sugar is an acetal (i.e., an internal glycoside), it is a non reducing sugar.

Methylation followed by acid hydrolysis converts the anhydro sugar to 2,3,4-tri-O-methyl-D-altrose:

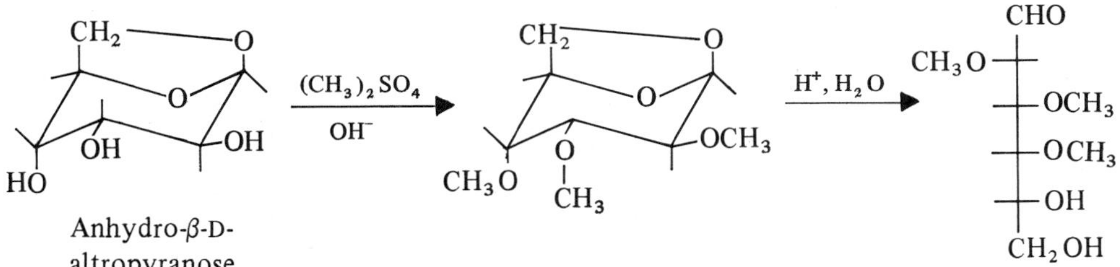

Anhydro-β-D-
altropyranose

(CH₃)₂SO₄
OH⁻

H⁺, H₂O

CHO
CH₃O
OCH₃
OCH₃
OH
CH₂OH

2, 3, 4-Tri-O-
methyl-D-altrose

(b) Formation of an anhydro sugar requires that the monosaccharide adopt a chair conformation with the –CH₂OH group axial. With β-D-altropyranose this requires that two –OH groups be axial as well. With β-D-glucopyranose, however, it requires that all four –OH groups become axial, and thus that the molecule adopt a very unstable conformation:

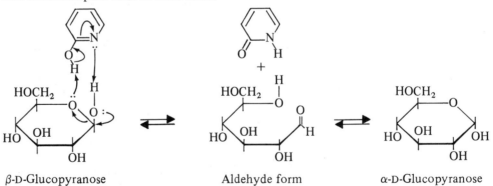

β-D-Glucopyranose

Anhydro-β-D-glucopyranose

21.35   The initial step in mutarotation—ring opening of the cyclic hemiacetal—requires that an acid donate a proton to the ring oxygen and that a base remove a proton from the anomeric hydroxyl. 2-Hydroxypyridine has, in close proximity, acidic and basic groups that can accomplish both of these tasks.

β-D-Glucopyranose   Aldehyde form   α-D-Glucopyranose

21.36   1. The molecular formula and the results of acid hydrolysis show that lactose is a disaccharide composed of D-glucose and D-galactose. The fact that lactose is hydrolyzed by a *β-galactosidase* indicates that galactose is present as a glycoside and that the glycosidic linkage is *beta* to the galactose ring.

2. That lactose is a reducing sugar, forms a phenylosazone, and undergoes mutarotation indicates that one ring (presumably that of D-glucose) is present as a hemiacetal and thus is capable of existing to a limited extent as an aldehyde.

3. This experiment confirms that the D-glucose unit is present as a cyclic hemiacetal and that the D-galactose unit is present as a cyclic glycoside.

4. That 2,3,4,6-tetra-*O*-methyl-D-galactose is obtained in this experiment indicates (by virtue of the free —OH at C-5) that the galactose ring of lactose is present as a pyranoside. That the methylated gluconic acid obtained from this experiment has a free —OH group at C-4 indicates that the C-4 oxygen of the glucose unit is connected in a glycosidic linkage to the galactose unit.

Now only the size of the glucose ring remains in question and the answer to this is provided by experiment 5.

5. That methylation of lactose and subsequent hydrolysis gives 2,3,6-tri-*O*-methyl-D-glucose—that it gives a methylated glucose derivative with a free —OH at C-4 and C-5— demonstrates that the glucose ring is present as a pyranose. (We know already that the oxygen at C-4 is connected in a glycosidic linkage to the galactose unit; thus a free —OH at C-5 indicates that the C-5 oxygen is a part of the hemiacetal group of the glucose unit and that the ring is six-membered.)

21.37 Melibiose has the following structure:

6-*O*-(α-D-galactopyranosyl)-D-glucopyranose

We arrive at this conclusion from the data given:

1. That melibiose is a reducing sugar, that it undergoes mutarotation and forms a phenylosazone indicates that one monosaccharide is present as a cyclic hemiacetal.

2. That acid hydrolysis gives D-galactose and D-glucose indicates that melibiose is a disaccharide composed of one D-galactose unit and one D-glucose unit. That melibiose is hydrolyzed by an α-galactosidase suggests that melibiose is an α-D-galactosyl-D-glucose.

3. Oxidation of melibiose to melibionic acid and subsequent hydrolysis to give D-galactose and D-gluconic acid confirms that the glucose unit is present as a cyclic hemiacetal and that the galactose unit is present as a glycoside. (Had the reverse been true, this experiment would have yielded D-glucose and D-galactonic acid.)

Methylation and hydrolysis of melibionic acid produces 2,3,4,6-tetra-*O*-methyl-D-galactose and 2,3,4,5-tetra-O-methyl-D-gluconic acid. Formation of the first product—a galactose derivative with a free —OH at C-5—demonstrates that the galactose ring is six-membered; formation of the second product—a gluconic acid derivative with a free —OH at C-6—demonstrates that the oxygen at C-6 of the glucose unit is joined in a glycosidic linkage to the galactose unit.

4. That methylation and hydrolysis of melibiose gives a glucose derivative (2,3,4-tri-*O*-methyl-D-glucose) with free —OH groups at C-5 and C-6 shows that the glucose ring is also six-membered. Melibiose is, therefore, 6-*O*-(α-D-galactopyranosyl)-D-glucopyranose.

21.38   Trehalose has the following structure:

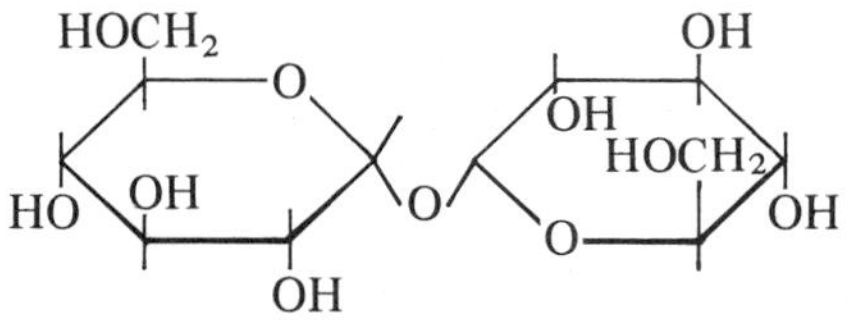

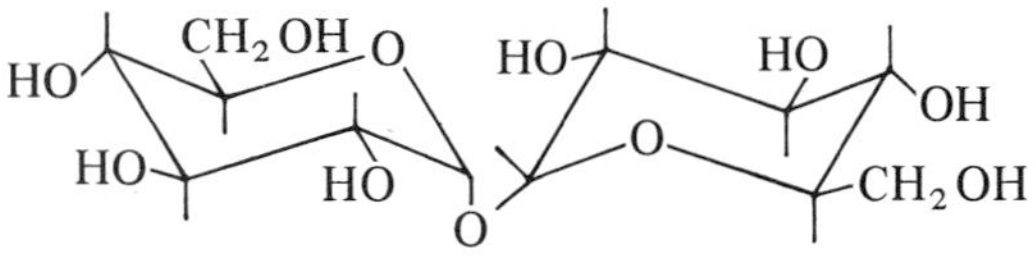

α-D-Glucopyranosyl-α-D-glucopyranoside

or

We arrive at this structure in the following way:

1. Acid hydrolysis shows that trehalose is a disaccharide consisting only of D-glucose units.

2. Hydrolysis by α-glucosidases and not by β-glucosidases shows that the glycosidic linkages are *alpha*.

3. That trehalose is a non reducing sugar, that it does not form phenylosazone, and that it does not react with bromine water indicate that no hemiacetal groups are present. This means that C-1 of one glucose unit and C-1 of the other must be joined in a glycosidic linkage. Fact 2 (above) indicates that this linkage is *alpha* to each ring.

4. That methylation of trehalose followed by hydrolysis yields only 2,3,4,6-tetra-*O*-methyl-D-glucose demonstrates that both rings are six-membered.

21.39   (a) Tollens' reagent or Benedict's reagent will give a positive test with D-glucose but will give no reaction with D-glucitol.

(b) D-Glucaric acid will give an acidic aqueous solution that can be detected with blue litmus paper. D-Glucitol will give a neutral aqueous solution.

(c) D-Glucose will be oxidized by bromine water and the red brown color of bromine will disappear. D-Fructose will not be oxidized by bromine water since it does not contain an aldehyde group.

(d) Nitric acid oxidation will produce an *optically active* aldaric acid from D-glucose but an *optically inactive* aldaric acid will result from D-galactose.

(e) Maltose is a reducing sugar and will give a positive test with Tollens' or Benedict's solution. Sucrose is a nonreducing sugar and will not react.

(f) Maltose will give a positive Tollens' or Benedict's test; maltonic acid will not.

(g) 2,3,4,6-Tetra-*O*-methyl-β-D-glucopyranose will give a positive test with Tollens' or Benedict's solution; methyl β-D-glucopyranoside will not.

(h) Periodic acid will react with methyl α-D-ribofuranoside because it has hydroxyl groups on adjacent carbons. Methyl 2-deoxy-α-D-ribofuranoside will not react.

21.40   That the Schardinger dextrins are nonreducing shows that they have no free aldehyde or hemiacetal groups. This lack of reaction strongly suggests the presence of a *cyclic* structure. That methylation and subsequent hydrolysis yields only 2,3,6-tri-*O*-methyl-D-glucose indicates that the glycosidic linkages all involve C-1 of one glucose unit and C-4 of the next. That α-glucosidases cause hydrolysis of the glycosidic linkages indicates that they are α-glycosidic linkages. Thus we are led to the following general structure.

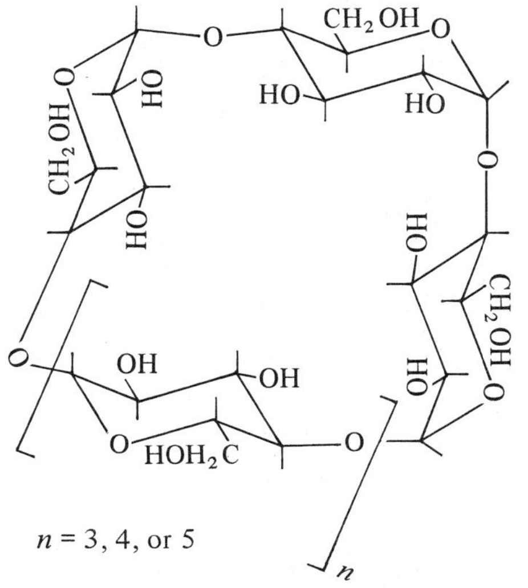

$n = 3, 4,$ or 5

Note: Schardinger dextrins are extremely interesting compounds. They are able to form complexes with a wide variety of compounds by incorporating these compounds in the cavity in the middle of the cyclic dextrin structure. Complex formation takes place, however, only when the cyclic dextrin and the guest molecule are the right size. Anthracene molecules, for example, will fit into the cavity of a cyclic dextrin with eight glucose units but will not fit into one with seven. For more information about these fascinating compounds, see R. J. Bergeron, "Cycloamyloses," *J. Chem. Educ.*, **54**, 204 (1977).

21.41 Isomaltose has the following structure:

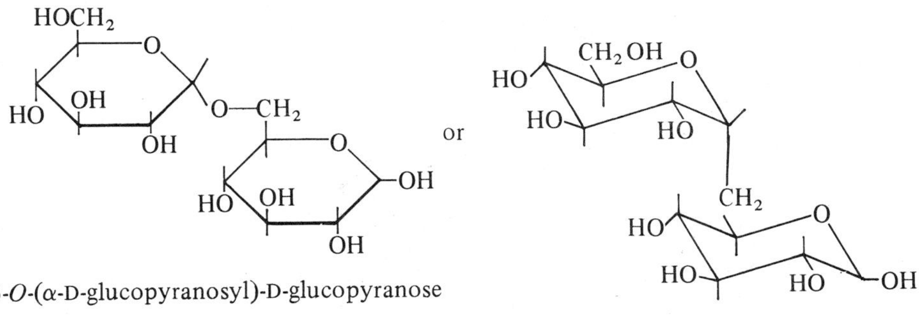

6-*O*-(α-D-glucopyranosyl)-D-glucopyranose   or

(1) The acid and enzymic hydrolysis experiments tell us that isomaltose has two glucose units linked by an α linkage.

(2) That isomaltose is a reducing sugar indicates that one glucose unit is present as a cyclic hemiacetal.

(3) Methylation of isomaltonic acid followed by hydrolysis gives us information about the size of the nonreducing pyranoside ring and about its point of attachment to the reducing ring. The formation of the first product (2,3,4,6-tetra-*O*-methyl-D-glucose)—a compound with an —OH at C-5—tells us that the nonreducing ring is present as a pyranoside. The formation of 2,3,4,5-tetra-*O*-methyl-D-gluconic acid—a compound with an —OH at C-6—shows that the nonreducing ring is linked to C-6 of the reducing ring.

(4) Methylation of maltose itself tells the size of the reducing ring. That 2,3,4-tri-*O*-methyl-D-glucose is formed shows that the reducing ring is also six membered; we know this because of the free —OH at C-5.

21.42 Stachyose has the following structure:

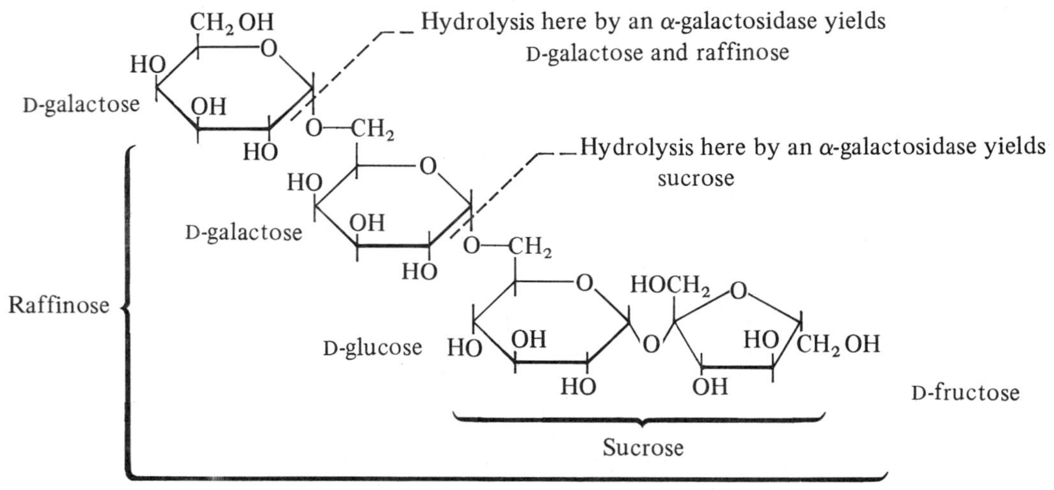

Raffinose has the following structure:

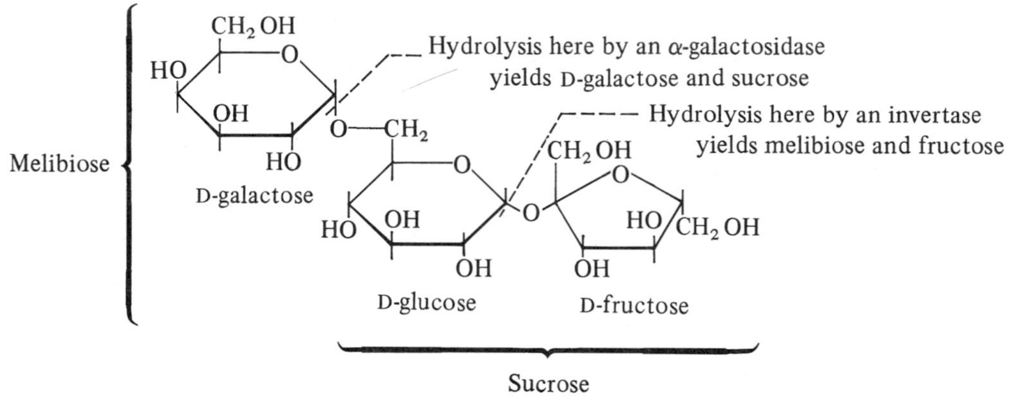

The enzymic hydrolyses (as indicated above) give the basic structure of stachyose and raffinose. The only remaining question is the ring size of the first galactose unit of stachyose. That methylation of stachyose and subsequent hydrolysis yields 2,3,4,6-tetra-*O*-methyl-D-galactose establishes that this ring is a pyranoside.

21.43   Arbutin has the following structure.

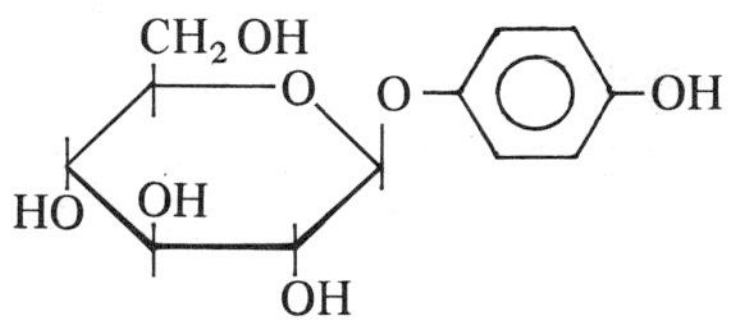

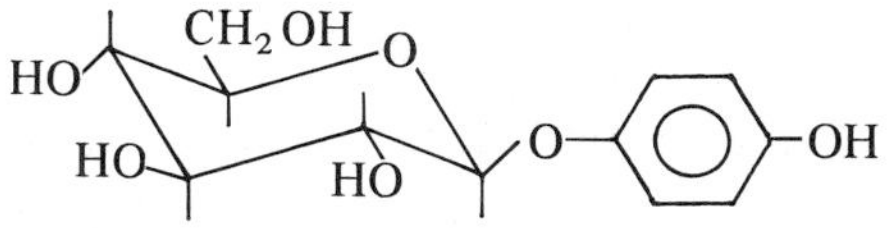

p-Hydroxyphenyl-β-D-glucopyranoside

Compounds **X**, **Y**, and **Z** are hydroquinone, *p*-methoxyphenol, and *p*-dimethoxybenzene respectively.

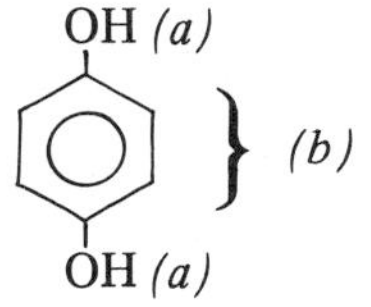

(a)   Singlet δ 7.9 (2H)
(b)   Singlet δ 6.8 (4H)

X
Hydroquinone

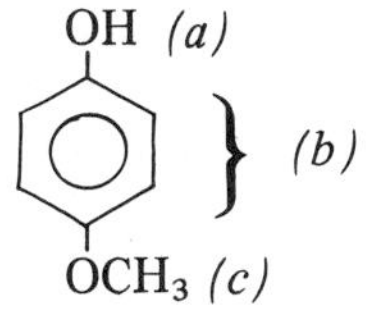

(a)   Singlet δ 4.8 (1H)
(b)   Multiplet δ6.8 (4H)
(c)   Singlet δ 3.9 (3H)

Y
p-Methoxyphenol

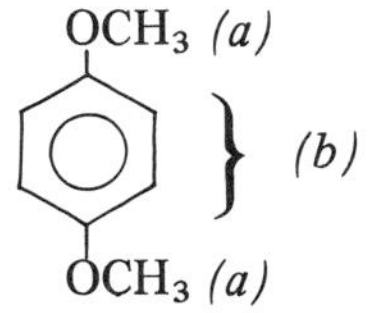

(a)   Singlet δ 3.75 (6H)
(b)   Singlet δ 6.8 (4H)

Z
p-Dimethoxybenzene

The reactions that take place are the following:

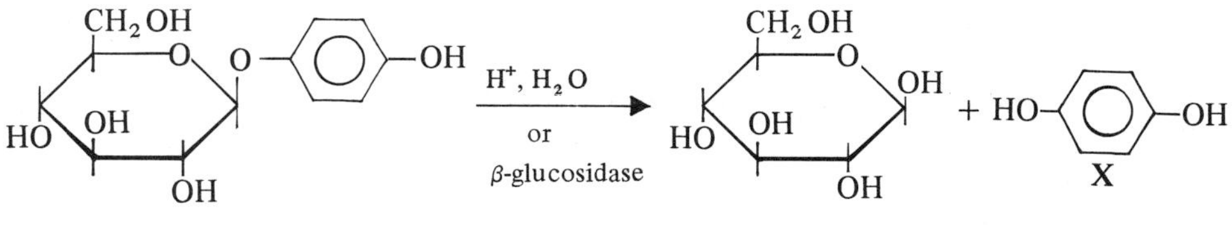

D-Glucose   Hydroquinone

Arbutin $\xrightarrow[\text{OH}^-]{\text{(CH}_3)_2\text{SO}_4 \text{ (excess)}}$

[chemical structure: CH₂OCH₃, OCH₃, CH₃O, OCH₃, OCH₃ glucose with O–O linkage to ring bearing OCH₃]

$\xrightarrow[\text{H}_2\text{O}]{\text{H}^+}$

[chemical structure: CH₂OCH₃, OH, CH₃O, OCH₃, OCH₃ glucose] + HO—⟨ring⟩—OCH₃

Y

2, 3, 4, 6-Tetra-*O*-methyl
D-glucose

p-Methoxyphenol

p-Methoxyphenol $\xrightarrow[\text{OH}^-]{\text{(CH}_3)_2\text{SO}_4}$ CH₃O—⟨ring⟩—OCH₃

Z

p-Dimethoxybenzene

21.44 (a) and (b) Two molecules of acetone react with four hydroxyl groups of D-glucose to yield a compound (below) containing two cyclic ketal linkages. Reaction with cis hydroxyl groups is preferred in reactions like this. Thus D-glucose reacts with acetone preferentially in the furanose form because reaction in the pyranose form would require the formation of a cyclic ketal from the trans hydroxyl groups at C-3 and C-4. This would introduce greater strain into the product.

[chemical structure: α-D-Glucopyranose with HO groups, CH₂OH, O]

⇌

[Fischer projection: CHO, OH, HO, OH, OH, CH₂OH]

α-D-Glucopyranose

[chemical structure: α-D-Glucofuranose furanose ring with OH, CH₂, CH, OH, OH, OH groups]

$\xrightarrow[\text{H}^+]{2\text{CH}_3\overset{\overset{\displaystyle O}{\|}}{\text{C}}\text{CH}_3}$

[chemical structure: "Diacetone glucose" bicyclic structure with OH, CH₃, CH₃ groups]

α-D-Glucofuranose

"Diacetone glucose"

D-Galactose reacts similarly, but it can react in the pyranose form because the hydroxyl groups at C-3 and C-4 are cis (as are those at C-1 and C-2).

α-D-Galactopyranose

SECTION REFERENCES FOR ADDITIONAL PROBLEMS

21.24	21.1, 21.2, 21.3, 21.4, 21.6, 21.11, 21.12	**21.35**	19.3, 21.3
21.25	21.2, 21.3, 21.8, 21.10	**21.36**	21.10, 21.11
21.26	21.4, 21.8	**21.37**	21.10, 21.11
21.27	21.3, 21.8	**21.38**	21.10, 21.11
21.28	15.6, 15.7	**21.39**	17.13, 21.4
21.29	21.6, 21.8, 21.9	**21.40**	21.10, 21.11
21.30	21.6	**21.41**	21.10, 21.11
21.31	21.5, 21.6, 21.8	**21.42**	21.10, 21.11
21.32	19.1, 19.3, 21.4, 21.7, 21.9	**21.43**	13.6, 15.1, 15.17, 21.3, 21.10
21.33	21.3, 21.8	**21.44**	16.7, 21.3, 21.8
21.34	16.7, 21.3, 21.8		

SELF-TEST

21.1   Supply the appropriate structural formula or complete the partial formula for each of the following:

(a)	(b)	(c)	(d)
	CHO | –C– | –C– | –C– | –C– | CH_2OH	CHO | –C– | –C– | –C– | CH_2OH	
a ketotetrose	a D-sugar	an L-sugar	an aldose

(e)	(f)	(g)	(h)
		The compound that gives the same osazone as D-gulose	The compound that gives the same aldaric acid as D-gulose

CHO
H——OH
H——OH
HO——H
H——OH
CH₂OH

D-Gulose

α-D-Gulopyr-anose

β-D-Gulopyr-anose

21.2 Which of the following monosaccharides yields an optically inactive alditol on NaBH₄ reduction?

Answer: [ ]

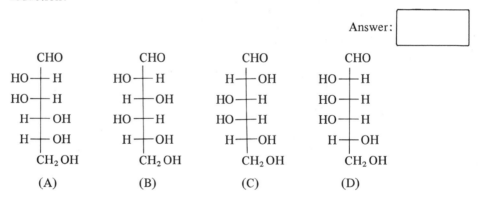

CHO
HO——H
HO——H
H——OH
H——OH
CH₂OH
(A)

CHO
HO——H
H——OH
HO——H
H——OH
CH₂OH
(B)

CHO
H——OH
HO——H
HO——H
H——OH
CH₂OH
(C)

CHO
HO——H
HO——H
HO——H
H——OH
CH₂OH
(D)

21.3 Give the structural formula of the monosaccharide that you could use as starting material in the Kiliani-Fischer synthesis of the compound below:

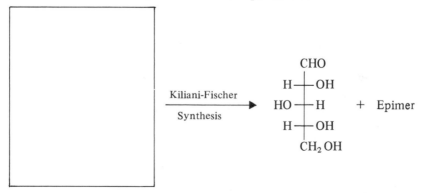

$\xrightarrow[\text{Synthesis}]{\text{Kiliani-Fischer}}$

CHO
H——OH
HO——H
H——OH
CH₂OH
+ Epimer

21.4 The D-aldopentose, (a), is oxidized to an aldaric acid, (b), which is optically active. Compound (a) undergoes a Ruff degradation to form an aldotetrose, (c), which undergoes oxidation to an optically inactive aldaric acid, (d). Supply the reagents for these transformations and the structural formulas of (a), (b), (c), and (d).

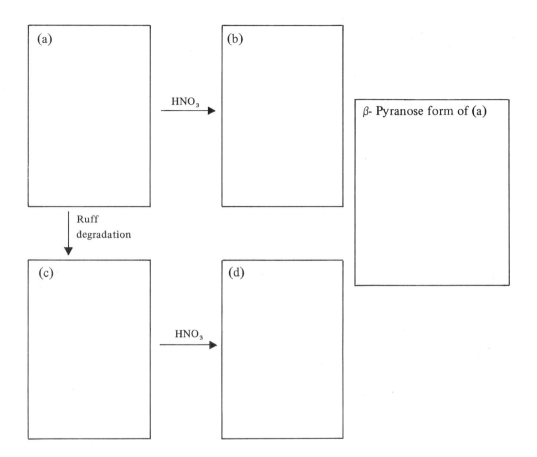

21.5   Give the structural formula of the β-pyranose form of (a) in the space above.

21.6   Complete the skeletal formulas below and complete the statements that follow by filling in the blanks and circling the words that make the statements true.

The Haworth and conformational formulas of the β-cyclic hemiacetal

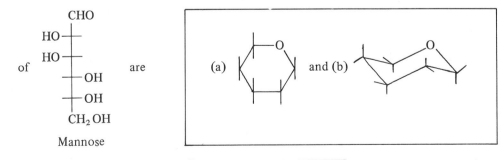

Mannose

The cyclic hemiacetal above is (c) reducing, nonreducing; on reaction with Br_2/H_2O

it gives an optically (d) active, inactive (e) aldaric, aldonic acid. On reaction with dilute HNO_3 it gives an optically $\boxed{\text{(f) active, inactive}}$ $\boxed{\text{(g) aldaric, aldonic}}$ acid. Reaction of the cyclic hemiacetal with $\boxed{\text{(h)}}$ converts it into an optically $\boxed{\text{(i) active, inactive}}$ alditol.

21.7   Outline chemical tests that would allow you to distinguish between:

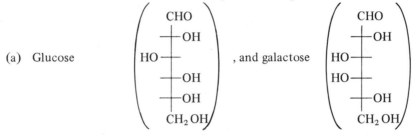

(a) Glucose and galactose

(b) Glucose and fructose

22 LIPIDS

SOLUTIONS TO PROBLEMS

22.1 (a) There are two sets of enantiomers, giving a total of four stereoisomers

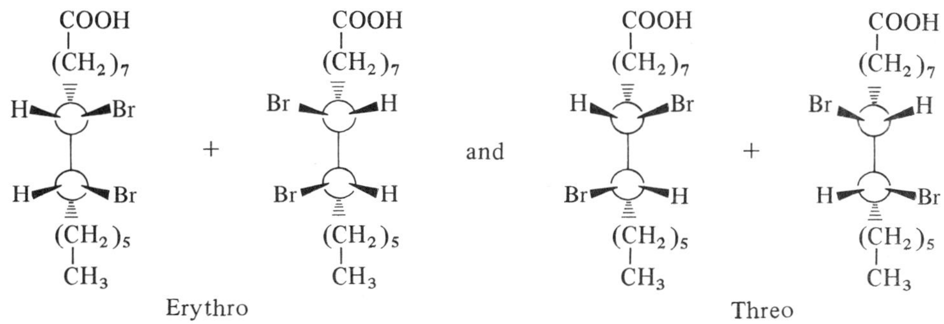

Erythro   Threo

(b)

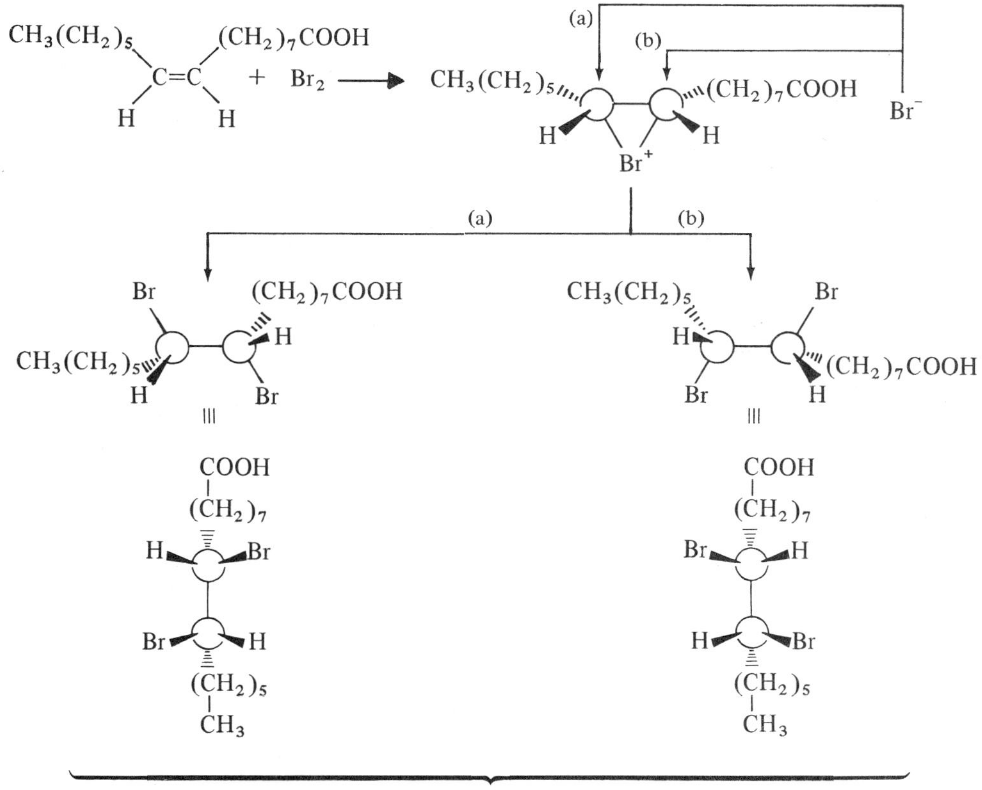

(±)-*threo*-9,10-Dibromohexadecanoic acids

Formation of a bromonium ion at the other face of palmitoleic acid gives a result such that the *threo*-enantiomers are the only products formed (obtained as a racemic modification).

22.2

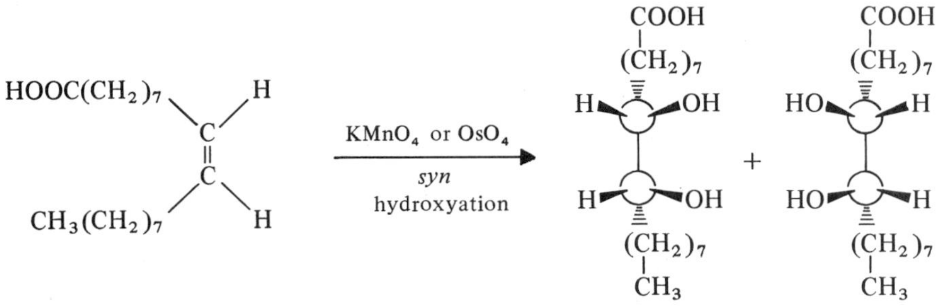

(±)-*erythro*-9, 10-Dihydroxyocta-
decanoic acids

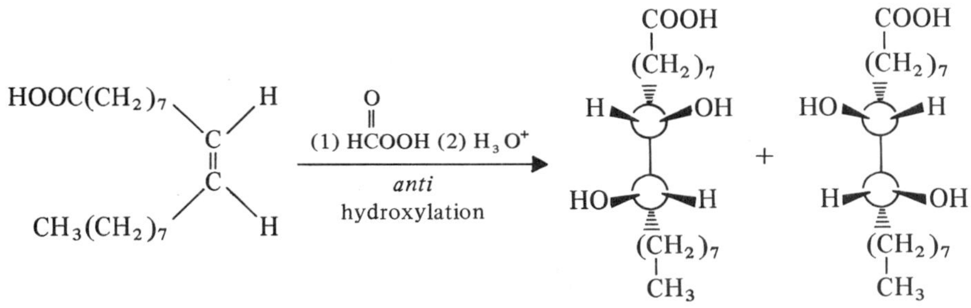

(±)-*threo*- 9, 10-Dihydroxyocta-
decanoic acids

The designations *erythro* and *threo* come from the names of the sugars called *erythrose* and *threose* (Sect. 21.7A).

22.3

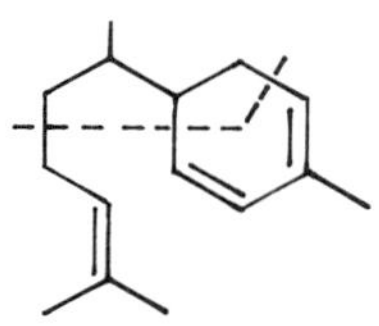

Zingiberene
(a sesquiterpene)

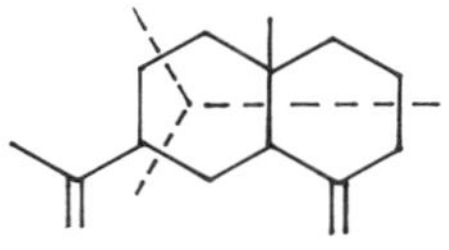

β-Selinene
(a sesquiterpene)

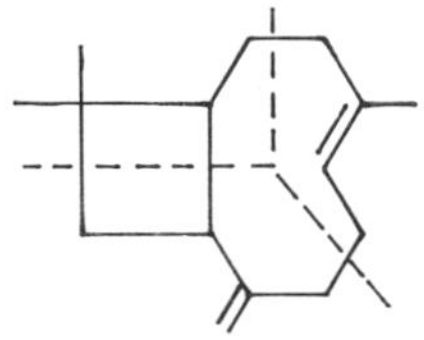

Caryophyllene
(a sesquiterpene)

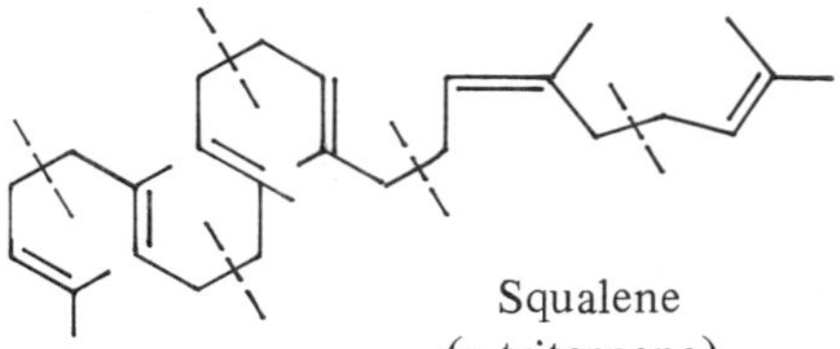

Squalene
(a triterpene)

22.4

(a)

Myrcene $\xrightarrow[\text{(2) Zn, H}_2\text{O}]{\text{(1) O}_3}$

$$\underset{\text{O}}{\overset{\text{HCH}}{\|}} + \text{C} + \text{CH}_3\text{COCH}_3 + \text{HCH}$$

(b)

Limonene $\xrightarrow[\text{(2) Zn, H}_2\text{O}]{\text{(1) O}_3}$

(c) α-Farnesene
(See Sect. 22.3) $\xrightarrow[\text{(2) Zn, H}_2\text{O}]{\text{(1) O}_3}$ $CH_3\overset{O}{\underset{\|}{C}}CH_3 + HC\overset{O}{\underset{\|}{}}CH_2CH_2\overset{O}{\underset{\|}{C}}CH_3$

$+ HC\overset{O}{\underset{\|}{}}CH_2\overset{O}{\underset{\|}{C}}H + HC\overset{O}{\underset{\|}{}}\overset{O}{\underset{\|}{C}}CH_3 + HC\overset{O}{\underset{\|}{}}H$

(d) Geraniol
(See Sect. 22.3) $\xrightarrow[\text{(2) Zn, H}_2\text{O}]{\text{(1) O}_3}$ $CH_3\overset{O}{\underset{\|}{C}}CH_3 + HC\overset{O}{\underset{\|}{}}CH_2CH_2\overset{O}{\underset{\|}{C}}CH_3$

$+ HC\overset{O}{\underset{\|}{}}CH_2OH$

(e) Squalene
(See Sect. 22.3) $\xrightarrow[\text{(2) Zn, H}_2\text{O}]{\text{(1) O}_3}$ $2CH_3\overset{O}{\underset{\|}{C}}CH_3 + HC\overset{O}{\underset{\|}{}}CH_2CH_2\overset{O}{\underset{\|}{C}}H$

$+ 4CH_3\overset{O}{\underset{\|}{C}}CH_2CH_2\overset{O}{\underset{\|}{C}}H$

22.5

(a)

$+ CO_2$

(+ further oxidation
products)

(b)

(c)

(d)

(+ rearranged products)

22.6 Br_2 in CCl_4 or $KMnO_4$ in H_2O. Either reagent would give a positive result with geraniol and a negative result with menthol.

22.7

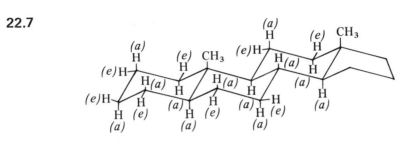

5α-series

5β-Series

22.8

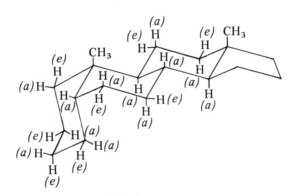

(a)

3α-Hydroxyandrostan-17-one
(androsterone)

(b)

17α-Ethynyl-17β-hydroxy-5(10)-estren-3-one
(norethynodrel)

22.9

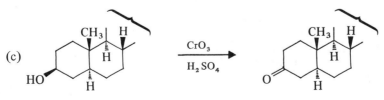

Absolute configuration of cholesterol
(5-cholesten-3β-ol)

22.10 Estrone and estradiol are *phenols* and thus are soluble in aqueous sodium hydroxide. Extraction with aqueous sodium hydroxide separates the estrogens from the androgens.

22.11

(a)

Cholesterol $\xrightarrow[\text{CCl}_4]{\text{Br}_2}$ 5α, 6β-Dibromocholestan-3β-ol

(b)

5α, 6α-Epoxycholestan-3β-ol
(prepared by epoxidation
of cholesterol, cf. Sect. 22.4G) $\xrightarrow[\text{H}_2\text{O}]{\text{H}^+}$ Cholestan-3β, 5α, 6β-triol

(c)

5α-Cholestan-3β-ol
(prepared by hydrogenation
of cholesterol, cf. Sect. 22.4G) $\xrightarrow[\text{H}_2\text{SO}_4]{\text{CrO}_3}$ 5α-Cholestan-3-one

(d)

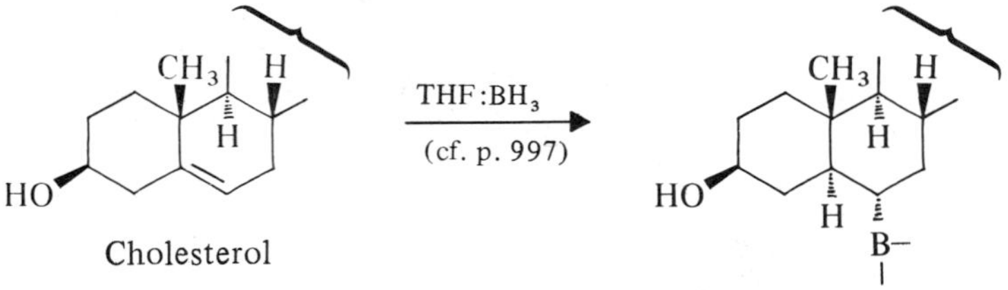

Cholesterol

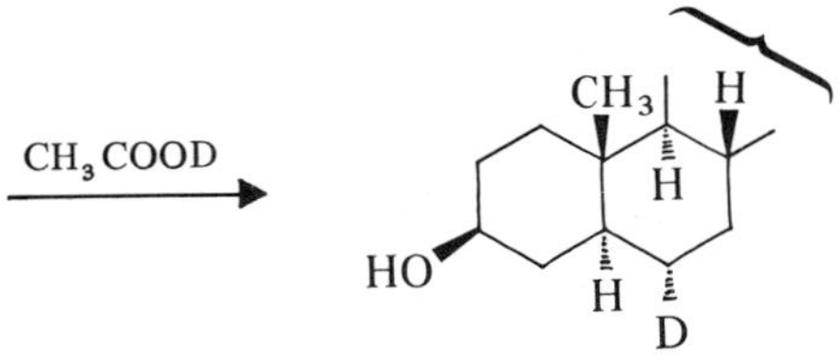

THF:BH$_3$
(cf. p. 997)

CH$_3$COOD

6α-Deuterio-5α-cholestan-3β-ol

(e)

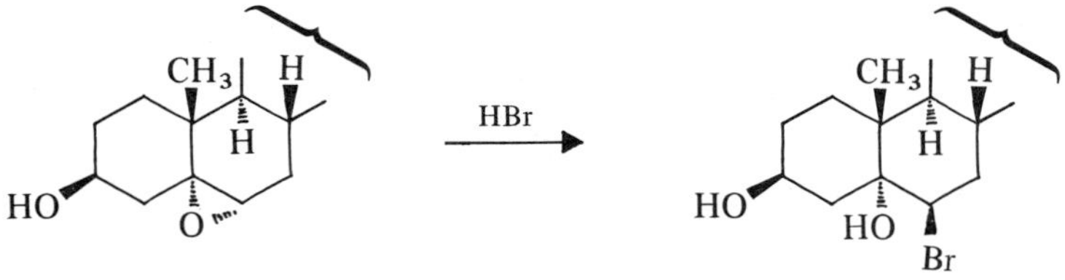

5α, 6α-Epoxycholestan-3β-ol

HBr

6β-Bromocholestan-3β, 5α-diol

22.12

(a)
$$\begin{matrix} CH_2OH \\ | \\ CHOH \\ | \\ CH_2OH \end{matrix} + R\overset{O}{\underset{\|}{C}}OH + R'\overset{O}{\underset{\|}{C}}OH + H_3PO_4 + HOCH_2CH_2\overset{+}{N}(CH_3)_3 \quad X^-$$

(b)
$$\begin{matrix} CH_2OH \\ | \\ CHOH \\ | \\ CH_2OH \end{matrix} + R\overset{O}{\underset{\|}{C}}OH + R'\overset{O}{\underset{\|}{C}}OH + H_3PO_4 + HOCH_2CH_2NH_2$$

(c)
$$\begin{matrix} CH_2OH \\ | \\ CHOH \\ | \\ CH_2OH \end{matrix} + CH_3(CH_2)_nCH_2\overset{O}{\underset{\|}{C}}H + R'\overset{O}{\underset{\|}{C}}OH + H_3PO_4$$

$$+ HOCH_2CH_2\overset{+}{N}(CH_3)_3 \quad X^-$$

22.13

(a) $CH_3(CH_2)_{16}COOH + C_2H_5OH \underset{\overset{H^+}{\rightleftharpoons}}{} CH_3(CH_2)_{16}COOC_2H_5 + H_2O$

$CH_3(CH_2)_{16}COOH \xrightarrow{SOCl_2} CH_3(CH_2)_{16}COCl \xrightarrow{C_2H_5OH} CH_3(CH_2)_{16}COOC_2H_5$

(b) $CH_3(CH_2)_{16}COCl \xrightarrow{(CH_3)_3COH} CH_3(CH_2)_{16}COOC(CH_3)_3$

(c) $CH_3(CH_2)_{16}COCl \xrightarrow{NH_3} CH_3(CH_2)_{16}CONH_2$

(d) $CH_3(CH_2)_{16}COCl \xrightarrow{(CH_3)_2NH} CH_3(CH_2)_{16}CON(CH_3)_2$

(e) $CH_3(CH_2)_{16}CONH_2 \xrightarrow{LiAlH_4} CH_3(CH_2)_{16}CH_2NH_2$

(f) $CH_3(CH_2)_{16}CONH_2 \xrightarrow{Br_2,\ OH^-} CH_3(CH_2)_{15}CH_2NH_2$

(g) $CH_3(CH_2)_{16}COCl \xrightarrow{LiAlH[OC(CH_3)_3]_3} CH_3(CH_2)_{16}CHO$

(h) $CH_3(CH_2)_{16}COOC_2H_5 \xrightarrow{H_2,\ Ni} CH_3(CH_2)_{16}CH_2OH$ ⌉
$CH_3(CH_2)_{16}COCl$ ⌋ $\longrightarrow$
$CH_3(CH_2)_{16}COOCH_2(CH_2)_{16}CH_3$

(i) $CH_3(CH_2)_{16}COOH \xrightarrow[(2)\ H_2O]{(1)\ LiAlH_4} CH_3(CH_2)_{16}CH_2OH$

$CH_3(CH_2)_{16}COOC_2H_5 \xrightarrow{H_2,\ Ni} CH_3(CH_2)_{16}CH_2OH$

(j) $CH_3(CH_2)_{16}COCl + (CH_3)_2Cd \longrightarrow CH_3(CH_2)_{16}COCH_3$
or $(CH_3)_2CuLi$

(k) $CH_3(CH_2)_{16}CH_2OH \xrightarrow{PBr_3} CH_3(CH_2)_{16}CH_2Br$

(l) $CH_3(CH_2)_{16}CH_2Br \xrightarrow[(2)\ H^+,\ H_2O,\ heat]{(1)\ NaCN} CH_3(CH_2)_{16}CH_2COOH$

22.14

(a) $CH_3(CH_2)_{11}CH_2COOH \xrightarrow{Br_2,\ P} CH_3(CH_2)_{11}\underset{\underset{Br}{|}}{CH}COOH$

(b) $CH_3(CH_2)_{11}\underset{\underset{Br}{|}}{CH}COOH \xrightarrow[(2)\ H^+]{(1)\ OH^-,\ heat} CH_3(CH_2)_{11}\underset{\underset{OH}{|}}{CH}COOH$

(c) $CH_3(CH_2)_{11}\underset{\underset{Br}{|}}{CH}COOH \xrightarrow[(2)\ H^+]{(1)\ NaCN} CH_3(CH_2)_{11}\underset{\underset{CN}{|}}{CH}COOH$

(d) $CH_3(CH_2)_{11}\underset{\underset{Br}{|}}{CH}COOH \xrightarrow[(2)\ H^+]{(1)\ NH_3\ (excess)} CH_3(CH_2)_{11}\underset{\underset{NH_2}{|}}{CH}COOH$

or $CH_3(CH_2)_{11}\underset{\overset{+}{\underset{NH_3}{|}}}{CH}COO^-$

22.15

(a) $CH_3(CH_2)_5CH=CH(CH_2)_7COOH \xrightarrow{I_2} CH_3(CH_2)_5CHICHI(CH_2)_7COOH$

(b) $CH_3(CH_2)_5CH=CH(CH_2)_7COOH \xrightarrow{H_2, Ni} CH_3(CH_2)_{14}COOH$

(c) $CH_3(CH_2)_5CH=CH(CH_2)_7COOH \xrightarrow{KMnO_4} CH_3(CH_2)_5CHOHCHOH(CH_2)_7COOH$

(d) $CH_3(CH_2)_5CH=CH(CH_2)_7COOH \xrightarrow{HCl} CH_3(CH_2)_5CH_2CHCl(CH_2)_7COOH$

$+$

$CH_3(CH_2)_5CHClCH_2(CH_2)_7COOH$

22.16 Elaidic acid is *trans*-9-octadecenoic acid:

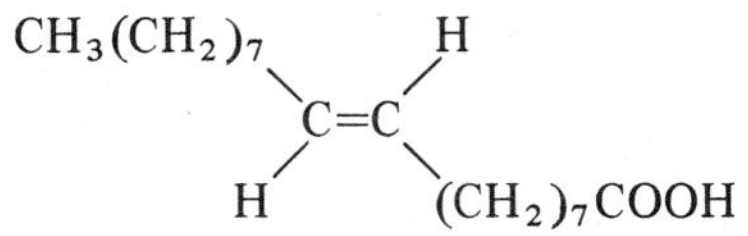

It is formed by the isomerization of oleic acid.

22.17 (a)

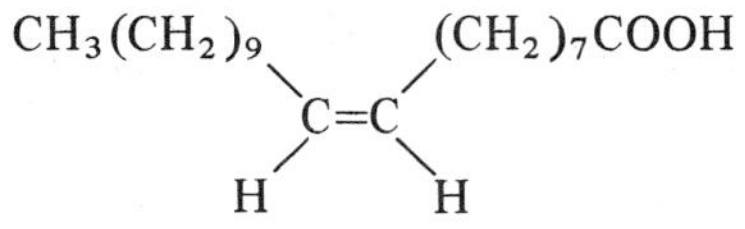

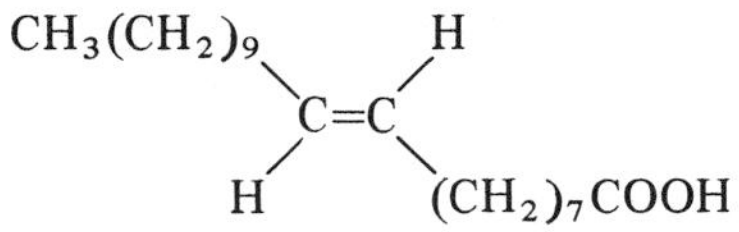

(b) Infrared spectroscopy

(c) A peak in the 675-730 cm^{-1} region would indicate that the double bond is cis; a peak in the 960-975 cm^{-1} region would indicate that it is trans.

22.18 A reverse Diels-Alder reaction takes place.

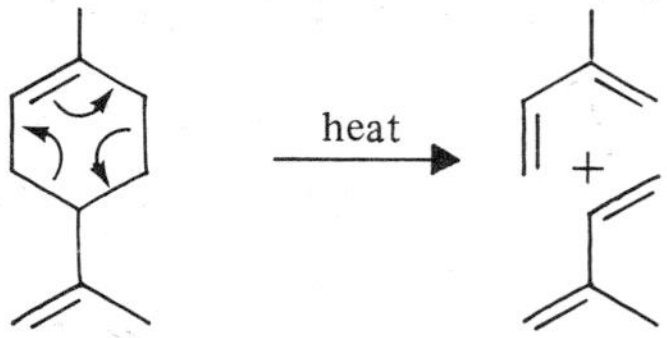

22.19

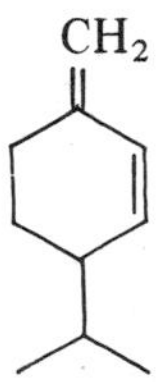

α-Phellandrene β-Phellandrene

Note: On permanganate oxidation, the $=CH_2$ group of β-phellandrene is converted to CO_2 and thus is not detected in the reaction.

22.20 The Diels-Alder reaction requires that the diene units assume an *s-cis* conformation (Sect. 10.10). Vitamin A can do this easily; however, for Neovitamin A steric hindrance is considerable and thus the concentration of the *s-cis* conformation is very small.

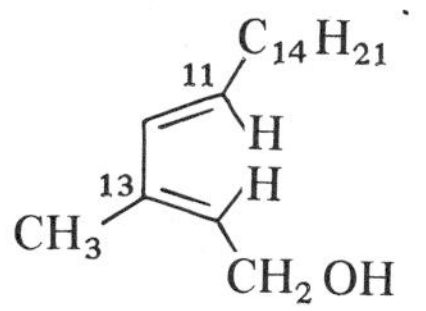

Vitamin A 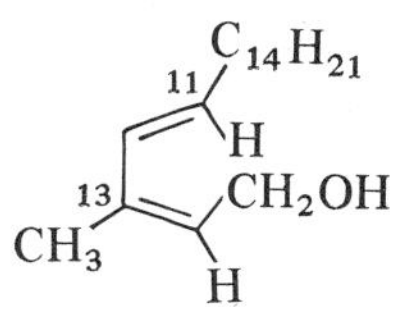   Neovitamin A

22.21 First an elimination takes place,

$$R_3\overset{+}{N}CH_2CH_2\overset{O}{\underset{||}{C}}CH_2CH_3 + NH_2^- \longrightarrow CH_2=CH\overset{O}{\underset{||}{C}}CH_2CH_3 + R_3N + NH_3$$

then a conjugate addition occurs, followed by an aldol addition:

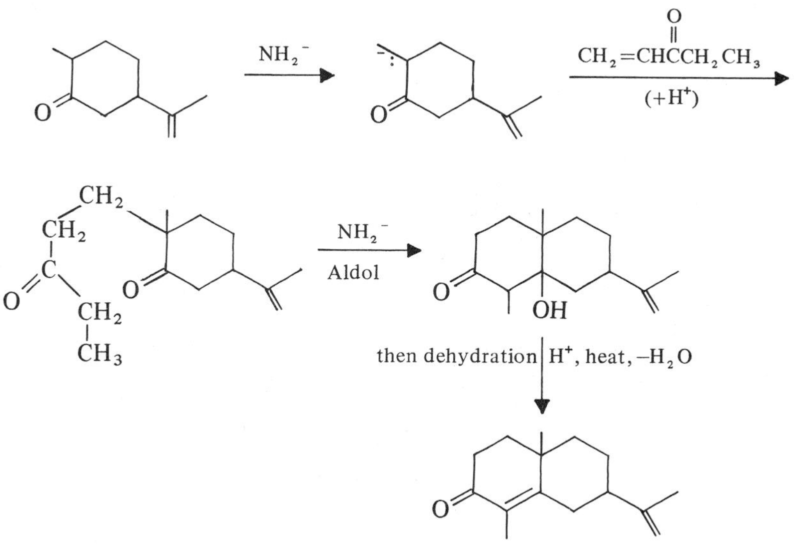

22.22

$$CH_3(CH_2)_5C\equiv CH + NaNH_2 \xrightarrow[NH_3]{} CH_3(CH_2)_5C\equiv CNa$$
$$\text{A}$$

$$\xrightarrow{ICH_2(CH_2)_7CH_2Cl} CH_3(CH_2)_5C\equiv CCH_2(CH_2)_7CH_2Cl \xrightarrow{NaCN}$$
$$\text{B}$$

$$CH_3(CH_2)_5C\equiv CCH_2(CH_2)_7CH_2CN \xrightarrow{KOH, H_2O} CH_3(CH_2)_5C\equiv CCH_2(CH_2)_7CH_2COOK$$
$$\text{C} \qquad\qquad\qquad\qquad \text{D}$$

$$\xrightarrow{H_3O^+} CH_3(CH_2)_5C\equiv CCH_2(CH_2)_7CH_2COOH \xrightarrow{H_2, Pd\text{-}BaSO_4}$$
$$\text{E}$$

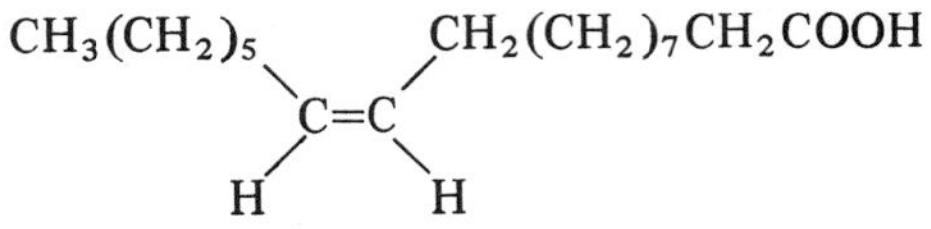

Vaccenic acid

22.23 $FCH_2(CH_2)_6CH_2Br + HC\equiv CNa \longrightarrow FCH_2(CH_2)_6CH_2C\equiv CH$

F

$\xrightarrow[\text{(2) I(CH}_2)_7\text{Cl}]{\text{(1) NaNH}_2} FCH_2(CH_2)_6CH_2C\equiv C(CH_2)_7Cl \xrightarrow[\text{DMSO}]{\text{NaCN}}$

G

$FCH_2(CH_2)_6CH_2C\equiv C(CH_2)_7CN \xrightarrow[\text{(2) H}^+]{\text{(1) KOH}} FCH_2(CH_2)_6CH_2C\equiv C(CH_2)_7COOH$

H   **I**

$\xrightarrow[\text{Ni}_2\text{B (P-2)}]{\text{H}_2} FCH_2(CH_2)_6CH_2 \cdots (CH_2)_7COOH$

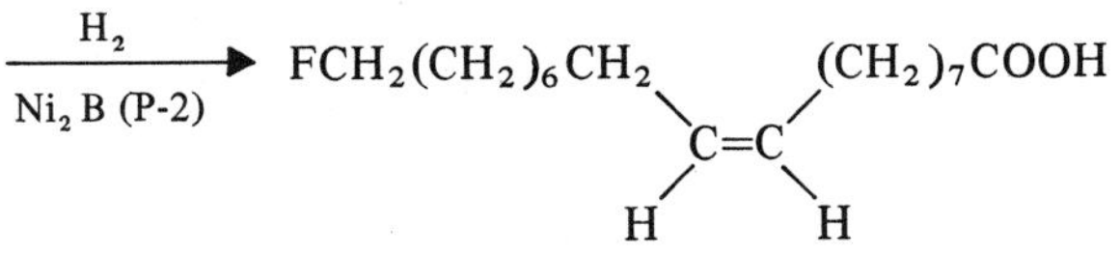

22.24

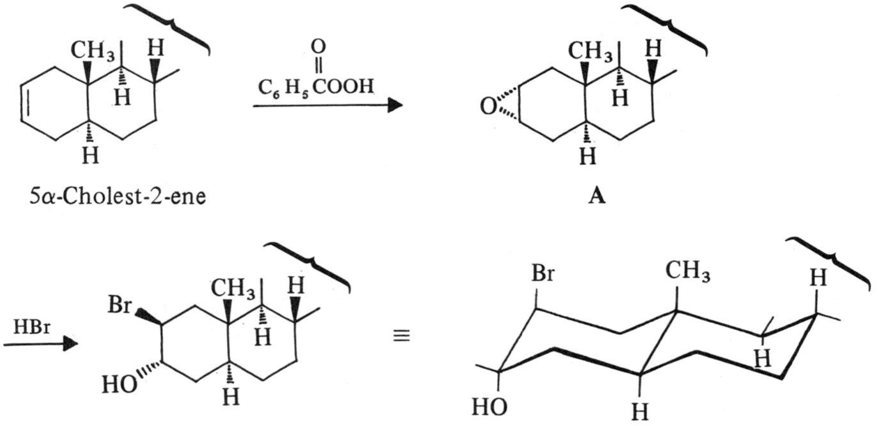

5α-Cholest-2-ene   **A**

B

Here we find that epoxidation takes place at the less hindered α face (cf. Sect. 22.4G). Ring opening by HBr takes place in an *anti* fashion to give a product with diaxial substituents.

22.25

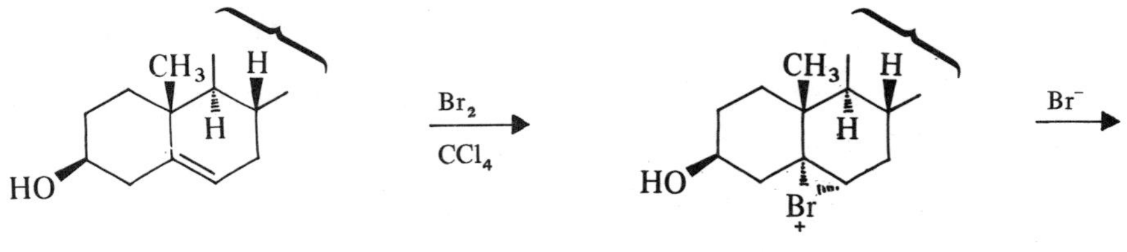

5α, 6α-Bromonium ion

5α, 6β-Dibromocholestan-3β-ol   5β, 6α-Dibromocholestan-3β-ol

Here formation of the bromonium ion takes place preferentially at the α face. Ring opening takes place in an *anti* manner (with a bromide ion attacking the 6-position from above) to give, initially, the 5α,6β-dibromo compound. The 5α,6β-dibromocholestan-3β-ol, however is a *diaxial* dibromide and is, therefore, unstable. It isomerizes to the 5β, 6α-dibromocholestan-3β-ol (below)—a compound in which the bromine substituents are both equatorial.

5α, 6β-Dibromide
(bromines are diaxial)

5β, 6α-Dibromide
(bromines are diequatorial)

This isomerization does not result from a simple "flipping" of the cyclohexane rings; it requires an inversion of configuration at carbons 5 and 6. One mechanism that has been proposed for the isomerization involves the formation of a "bromonium-bromide" ion pair:

Diaxial   Ion pair   Diequatorial

22.26 (a) $CH_2=CH-CH=CH_2$

(b) OH^- (Removal of the α-hydrogen allows isomerization to the more stable compound with a trans ring junction.)

(c) $LiAlH_4$

(d) H_3O^+ and heat. (Hydrolysis of the enol ether is followed by dehydration of one alcohol group.)

(e) $HCOOC_2H_5$, C_2H_5ONa

(f) OsO_4, then $NaHSO_3$

(g) $CH_3\overset{O}{\overset{\|}{C}}CH_3, H^+$

(h) H_2, Pd catalyst

(i) H_3O^+, H_2O

(j) HIO_4

(k) Base and heat. (This reaction is an aldol condensation.)

(l) and (m) Na_2CrO_4, CH_3COOH to oxidize the aldehyde to an acid, followed by esterification.

(n) H_2 and Pt. (Hydrogen addition takes place from the less hindered α-face of the molecule.)

(o), (p), (q) $NaBH_4$ to reduce the keto group; OH^-, H_2O to hydrolyze the ester; and acetic anhydride to esterify the OH at the 3-position.

(r) and (s) $SOCl_2$ to make the acid chloride, followed by treatment with $(CH_3)_2Cd$.

(t) $CH_3\overset{CH_3}{\overset{|}{C}}HCH_2CH_2CH_2MgBr$, followed by H_3O^+.

(u), (v), (w) Acetic acid and heat to dehydrate the tertiary alcohol; followed by acetic anhydride to acetylate the secondary alcohol; followed by H_2, Pt to hydrogenate the double bond.

22.27

(a) $CH_3(CH_2)_4\overset{O}{\overset{\|}{C}}H$

(b) C_4H_9Li

(c) 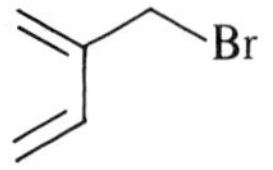

(d) 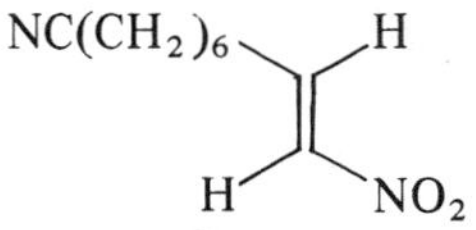

(e) Michael addition using a basic catalyst.

SECTION REFERENCES FOR ADDITIONAL PROBLEMS

22.13 14.7, 15.7, 16.4, 16.5, 18.3, 18.5, 18.7, 18.8, 19.5

22.14 5.6, 18.3, 18.9, 19.5, 22.2

22.15 6.4, 7.2, 7.9, 7.13, 22.2

22.16 6.3, 6.6

22.17 7.13, 13.11, 21.4D

22.18 10.10, 22.3

22.19 6.5, 7.10, 10.11, 22.3

22.20 10.10, 22.3	**22.26** (a) 10.10, (b) 17.1, (c) 15.7,
22.21 17.5, 17.9, 19.13	(d) 17.2, 6.10, (e) 20.2,
22.22 9.7, 9.12, 9.15, 18.3	(f) 7.13, (g) 16.7, (h) 6.4,
22.23 9.7, 9.12, 9.15, 18.3	(i) 16.7, (j) 21.4D, (k) 17.5,
22.24 7.12, 22.4G	(l) 18.3, (m) 18.7, (n) 22.4G,
22.25 7.10, 22.4	(o) 15.7, (p) 18.7, (q) 18.7,
	(r) 18.4, (s) 16.5, (t) 14.12,
	(u) 6.10, (v) 18.7, (w) 6.4,
	22.4G

22.27 16.7, 20.6, 20.8

SELF-TEST

22.1   Write an appropriate formula in each box

(a)

A naturally occurring fatty acid

(b)

A soap

(c)

A solid fat

(d)

An oil

(e)

A synthetic detergent

(f)

5α-Estran-17-one

22.2 Give a reagent that would distinguish between each of the following

(a) Pregnane and 20-pregnanone

(b) Stearic acid and oleic acid

(c) 17α-Ethynyl-1,3,5(10)-estratriene-3,17β-diol (ethynylestradiol) and 1,3,5(10)-estratriene-3,17β-diol (estradiol)

22.3 What product would be obtained by catalytic hydrogenation of 4-androstene.

22.4 Supply the missing compounds

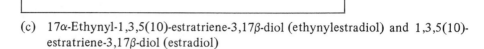

$$CH_3(CH_2)_4CH_2Br \xrightarrow{HC\equiv CNa} \text{(a)}$$

$$\xrightarrow{NaNH_2} \text{(b)} \xrightarrow{ICH_2(CH_2)_5CH_2Cl}$$

$$\text{(c)} \xrightarrow{\text{(d)}} CH_3(CH_2)_5C\equiv C(CH_2)_7CN$$

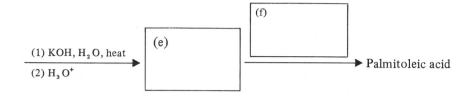

$$\xrightarrow[\text{(2) H}_3\text{O}^+]{\text{(1) KOH, H}_2\text{O, heat}}$$

(e) → (f) → Palmitoleic acid

22.5   Circle the correct answer.

The compound above is a
    monoterpene
    sesquiterpene
    diterpene
    triterpene

22.6   Mark off the isoprene units in the compound above

M SPECIAL TOPIC
Thiol Esters and Lipid Biosynthesis

SOLUTIONS TO PROBLEMS

M.1

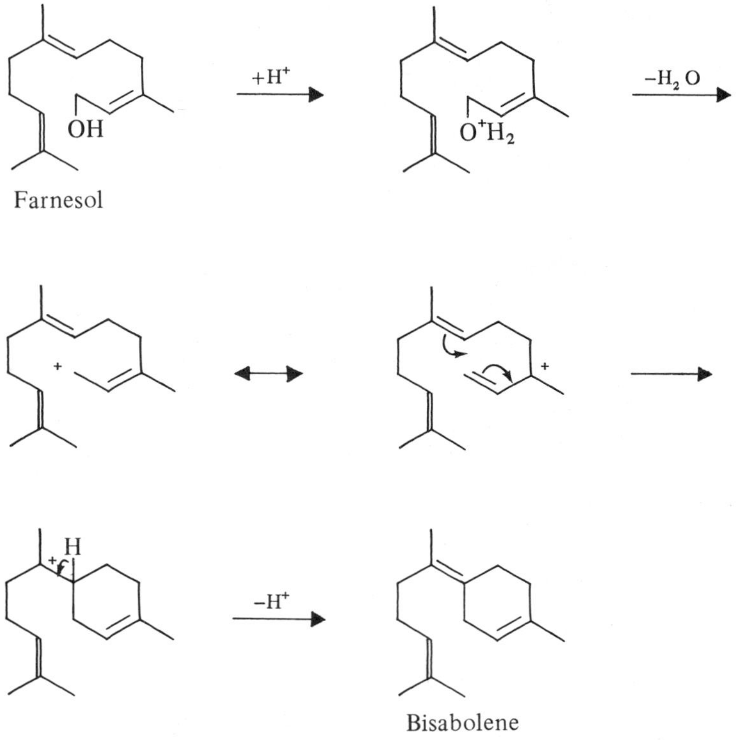

OH
Farnesol
+H⁺
O⁺H₂
−H₂ O
+
+
H
+
−H⁺
Bisabolene

23 AMINO ACIDS AND PROTEINS

SOLUTIONS TO PROBLEMS

23.1 (a) $HOOCCH_2CH_2CHCOOH$
      |
      $\overset{+}{N}H_3$

(b) $^-OOCCH_2CH_2CHCOO^-$
      |
      NH_2

(c) $HOOCCH_2CH_2CHCOO^-$ predominates at the isoelectric point rather than $^-OOCCH_2$-
      |
      $\overset{+}{N}H_3$

$CH_2CHCOOH$ because of the acid-strengthening inductive effect of the α-ammonio group.
   |
   $\overset{+}{N}H_3$

(d) Since glutamic acid is a dicarboxylic acid, acid must be added (i.e., the pH must be made lower) to suppress the ionization of the second carboxyl group and thus achieve the isoelectric point. Glutamine, with only one carboxyl group, is similar to glycine or phenylalanine and has its isoelectric point at a higher pH.

23.2 The conjugate acid is highly stabilized by resonance.

$$\underset{R-NH-\overset{\overset{\displaystyle\overset{..}{N}H}{\|}}{C}-\overset{..}{N}H_2}{} \xrightarrow{H^+} \underset{R-\overset{..}{N}H-\overset{\overset{\displaystyle NH_2{}^+}{\|}}{C}-\overset{..}{N}H_2}{} \longleftrightarrow \underset{R-\overset{..}{N}H-\overset{\overset{\displaystyle \overset{..}{N}H_2}{|}}{C}=NH_2{}^+}{} \longleftrightarrow \underset{R-\overset{+}{N}H=\overset{\overset{\displaystyle NH_2}{|}}{C}-NH_2}{}$$

23.3 (a) $C_6H_5CONHCH(CO_2C_2H_5)_2 \xrightarrow[C_6H_5CH_2Br]{NaOCH_2CH_3}$

$C_6H_5CONHC(CO_2C_2H_5)_2 \xrightarrow[heat]{HBr}$
          |
          CH_2
          |
          C_6H_5

$\left[\begin{array}{c} COOH \\ | \\ H_3\overset{+}{N}-C-COO^- \\ | \\ CH_2 \\ | \\ C_6H_5 \end{array}\right] \xrightarrow{-CO_2}$ $C_6H_5CH_2CHCOO^-$
                                                                          |
                                                                          $\overset{+}{N}H_3$
                                                                      Phenylalanine

(b) $C_6H_5CONHCH(CO_2C_2H_5)_2 \xrightarrow[BrCH_2CO_2C_2H_5]{NaOCH_2CH_3}$

$C_6H_5CONHC(CO_2C_2H_5)_2 \xrightarrow{HBr}$
          |
          CH_2
          |
          $CO_2C_2H_5$

$\left[\begin{array}{c} COOH \\ | \\ H_3\overset{+}{N}-C-COO^- \\ | \\ CH_2 \\ | \\ COOH \end{array}\right] \xrightarrow{-CO_2}$ $HOOCCH_2CHCOO^-$
                                                                          |
                                                                          $\overset{+}{N}H_3$
                                                                      Aspartic acid

(c) $C_6H_5CONHCH(CO_2C_2H_5)_2$ $\xrightarrow[\text{(CH}_3)_2\text{CHBr}]{\text{NaOCH}_2\text{CH}_3}$

$C_6H_5CONHC(CO_2C_2H_5)_2$ $\xrightarrow[\text{heat}]{\text{HBr}}$ $\left[\begin{array}{c} \text{COOH} \\ | \\ H_3\overset{+}{N}-C-COO^- \\ | \\ \text{CHCH}_3 \\ | \\ \text{CH}_3 \end{array} \right]$ $\xrightarrow{-CO_2}$ $CH_3CH-CHCOO^-$
with CHCH_3 / CH_3 below first formula, and $CH_3\overset{+}{NH_3}$ below valine

Valine

23.4

(a) phthalimide-NK $+ BrCH(CO_2C_2H_5)_2 \longrightarrow$

phthalimide $N-CH(CO_2C_2H_5)_2$ $\xrightarrow[\text{(CH}_3)_2\text{CHCH}_2\text{Br}]{\text{NaOCH}_2\text{CH}_3}$

phthalimide $N-\overset{\displaystyle CO_2C_2H_5}{\underset{\displaystyle CO_2C_2H_5}{C}}-CH_2CH(CH_3)_2$ $\xrightarrow[\text{heat}]{\text{NaOH}}$ benzene ring with COO^- and $C-NHCCH_2CH(CH_3)_2$ (O below C, COO^- groups)

$\xrightarrow[\text{Heat}]{\text{HCl}}$ $(CH_3)_2CHCH_2CHCOO^- + CO_2 +$ benzene ring with $COOH$ / $COOH$
with $\overset{+}{NH_3}$ below

Leucine

(b) phthalimide $N-CH(CO_2C_2H_5)_2$ $\xrightarrow[\text{CH}_3\text{I}]{\text{NaOCH}_2\text{CH}_3}$

phthalimide $N-\overset{\displaystyle CO_2C_2H_5}{\underset{\displaystyle CO_2C_2H_5}{C}}-CH_3$ $\xrightarrow[\text{heat}]{\text{NaOH}}$ benzene ring with COO^- and $C-NHCCH_3$ (O below C, COO^- groups)

$\xrightarrow[\text{heat}]{\text{HCl}}$ $CH_3CHCOO^- + CO_2 +$ benzene ring with $COOH$ / $COOH$
with $\overset{+}{NH_3}$ below

Alanine

(c) phthalimide $NCH(CO_2C_2H_5)_2$ $\xrightarrow[\text{C}_6\text{H}_5\text{CH}_2\text{Br}]{\text{NaOCH}_2\text{CH}_3}$ phthalimide $N-\overset{\displaystyle CO_2C_2H_5}{\underset{\displaystyle CO_2C_2H_5}{C}}-CH_2C_6H_5$ $\xrightarrow[\text{heat}]{\text{NaOH}}$

$$C_6H_5CH_2\underset{\overset{|}{\overset{+}{N}H_3}}{C}HCOO^- + CO_2 + $$

Phenylalanine

23.5

(a) $C_6H_5CH_2\overset{\overset{O}{\|}}{C}H \xrightarrow[\text{HCN}]{NH_3} C_6H_5CH_2\underset{\overset{|}{NH_2}}{C}HC\equiv N \xrightarrow{H_3O^+} C_6H_5CH_2\underset{\overset{|}{NH_3{}^+}}{C}HCOO^-$

Phenyl acetaldehyde   D L-Phenylalanine

(b) $CH_3SH + CH_2=CH-\overset{\overset{O}{\|}}{C}H \xrightarrow{\text{base}} CH_3SCH_2CH_2\overset{\overset{O}{\|}}{C}H$

$\xrightarrow[\text{HCN}]{NH_3} CH_3SCH_2CH_2\underset{\overset{|}{NH_2}}{C}HC\equiv N \xrightarrow{H_3O^+} CH_3SCH_2CH_2\underset{\overset{|}{NH_3{}^+}}{C}HCOO^-$

D L-Methionine

23.6   Because of the presence of an electron-withdrawing 2,4-dinitrophenyl group, the labeled amino acid is relatively non-basic and is, therefore, insoluble in dilute aqueous acid. The other amino acids (those that are not labeled) dissolve in dilute aqueous acid.

23.7

(a) $H_3\overset{+}{N}CHCONHCHCONHCH_2COO^- \xrightarrow[HCO_3{}^-]{O_2N-\langle\bigcirc\rangle-F,\ NO_2}$
    $\quad\ \ \underset{\overset{|}{CH_3}}{\overset{|}{C}HCH_3}\quad \overset{|}{CH_3}$

Val·Ala·Gly

$O_2N-\langle\bigcirc\rangle-NHCHCONHCHCONHCH_2COO^- \xrightarrow[\text{heat}]{H_3O^+}$
$\quad\quad\underset{\overset{|}{NO_2}}{}\quad\ \underset{\overset{|}{CH_3}}{\overset{|}{C}HCH_3}\ \overset{|}{CH_3}$

$O_2N-\langle\bigcirc\rangle-NHCHCOOH + H_3\overset{+}{N}CHCOO^- + H_3\overset{+}{N}CH_2COO^-$
$\quad\quad\underset{\overset{|}{NO_2}}{}\quad\ \underset{\overset{|}{CH_3}}{\overset{|}{C}HCH_3}\quad\quad \underset{CH_3}{}$

Labeled valine   Alanine   Glycine
(separate and identify)

(b)

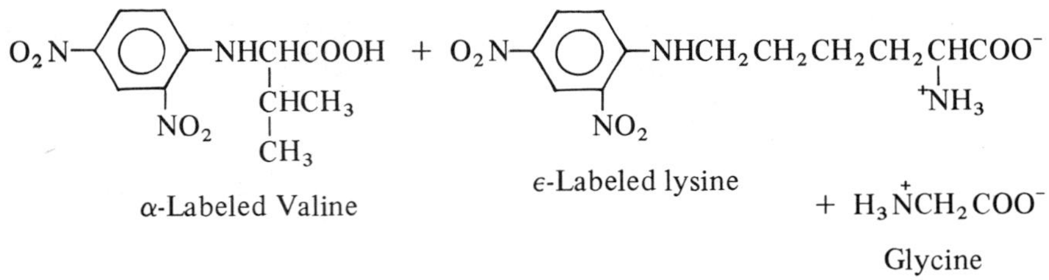

α-Labeled Valine

ε-Labeled lysine

$+ \; H_3 \overset{+}{N}CH_2COO^-$

Glycine

23.8

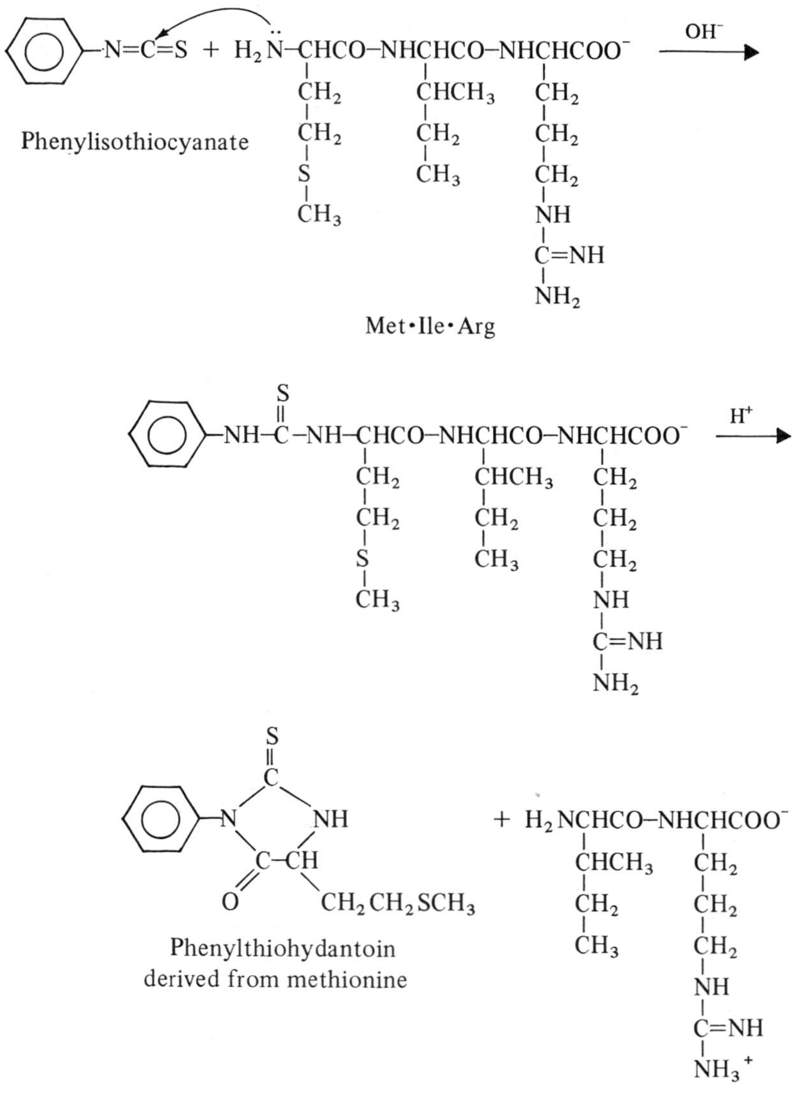

Phenylisothiocyanate

Met·Ile·Arg

Phenylthiohydantoin
derived from methionine

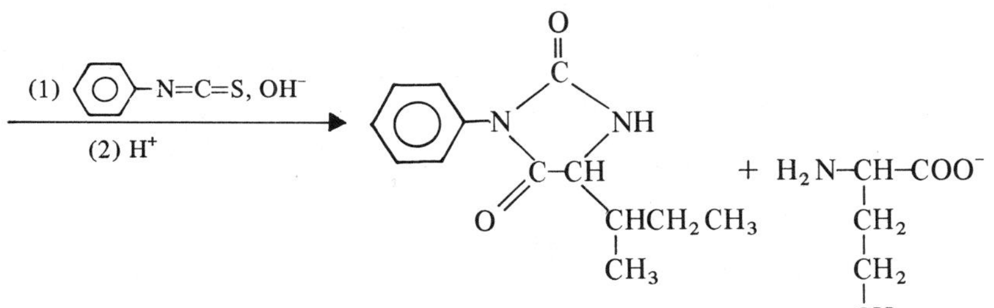

Phenylthiohydantoin
derived from isoleucine

23.9   (a)   Two structures are possible with the sequence Glu·Cys·Gly. Glutamic acid may be linked to cysteine through its α-carboxyl group,

$$HOOCCH_2CH_2CHCO-NHCHCO-NHCH_2COO^-$$
$$^+NH_3 \qquad CH_2SH$$

or through its γ-carboxyl group,

$$H_3\overset{+}{N}CHCH_2CH_2CO-NHCHCO-NHCH_2COO^-$$
$$COO^- \qquad CH_2SH$$

(b)   This result shows that the second structure above is correct, that in glutathione the γ-carboxyl group is linked to cysteine.

23.10   We look for points of overlap to determine the amino acid sequence in each case.

(a)   Ser · Thr
                        Thr · Hyp
        Pro · Ser
        ─────────────────────
        Pro · Ser · Thr · Hyp

(b)   Ala · Cys
                        Cys · Arg
                                    Arg · Val
        Leu · Ala
        ─────────────────────────────
        Leu · Ala · Cys · Arg · Val

23.11   Sodium in liquid ammonia brings about reductive cleavage of the disulfide linkage of oxytocin to two thiol groups, then air oxidizes the two thiol groups back to a disulfide linkage:

See also Special Topic I.

23.12

$$H_3\overset{+}{N}CH_2COO^- + (CH_3)_3CO\overset{O}{\overset{\|}{C}}N_3 \xrightarrow[25°]{OH^-}$$

Glycine   *tert*-Butoxy-
             carbonyl azide

$$(CH_3)_3C-\overset{O}{\overset{\|}{O C}}NHCH_2COOH \xrightarrow[\text{(2) } ClCO_2C_2H_5]{\text{(1) } (C_2H_5)_3N}$$

Boc-Gly

$$(CH_3)_3CO\overset{O}{\overset{\|}{C}}NHCH_2\overset{O}{\overset{\|}{C}}O\overset{O}{\overset{\|}{C}}OC_2H_5 \xrightarrow[(-CO_2, -C_2H_5OH)]{\begin{array}{c} H_3\overset{+}{N}CHCOO^- \\ | \\ CHCH_3 \\ | \\ CH_3 \\ \text{Valine} \end{array}}$$

Mixed anhydride

$$(CH_3)_3CO\overset{O}{\overset{\|}{C}}NHCH_2\overset{O}{\overset{\|}{C}}NHCHCOOH \xrightarrow[\text{(2) } ClCO_2C_2H_5]{\text{(1) } (C_2H_5)_3N}$$

Boc-Gly·Val   CHCH$_3$
                     CH$_3$

$$(CH_3)_3CO\overset{O}{\overset{\|}{C}}NHCH_2\overset{O}{\overset{\|}{C}}NHCHCO\overset{O}{\overset{\|}{C}}OC_2H_5 \xrightarrow[\text{Alanine}]{\begin{array}{c} H_3\overset{+}{N}CHCOO^- \\ | \\ CH_3 \end{array}}$$

Mixed anhydride   CHCH$_3$
                 CH$_3$

$$(CH_3)_3CO\overset{O}{\overset{\|}{C}}NHCH_2\overset{O}{\overset{\|}{C}}NHCH\overset{O}{\overset{\|}{C}}NHCHCOOH \xrightarrow[\substack{CH_3COOH \\ 25°}]{CF_3COOH}$$

Boc-Gly·Val·Ala   CHCH$_3$ CH$_3$
                       CH$_3$

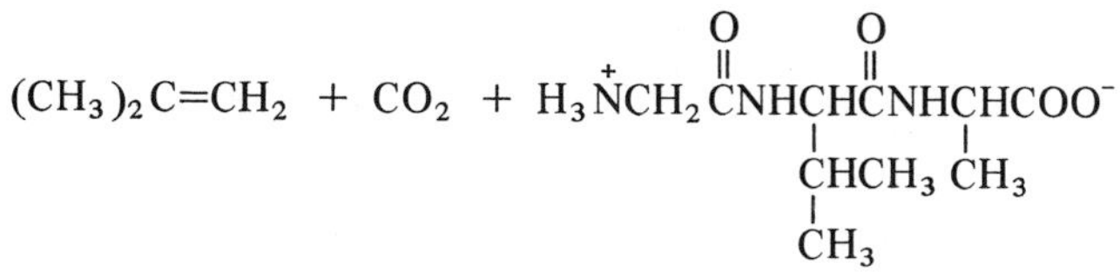

$$(CH_3)_2C=CH_2 \; + \; CO_2 \; + \; H_3\overset{+}{N}CH_2\overset{\overset{O}{\|}}{C}NHCHCHNHCHCOO^-$$

Gly·Val·Ala

23.13

(a) $2C_6H_5CH_2O\overset{\overset{O}{\|}}{C}Cl \; + \; H_2NCH_2CH_2CH_2CH_2CHCOO^- \xrightarrow[25°]{OH^-}$

Benzyl chloro-
carbonate   Lysine

$C_6H_5CH_2O\overset{\overset{O}{\|}}{C}NHCH_2CH_2CH_2CH_2CHCOOH \xrightarrow[(2)\ ClCOOC_2H_5]{(1)\ (C_2H_5)_3N}$

$C_6H_5CH_2O\overset{\overset{O}{\|}}{C}NHCH_2CH_2CH_2CH_2CH\overset{\overset{O}{\|}}{C}\overset{\overset{O}{\|}}{O}COC_2H_5 \xrightarrow[(-CO_2,\ -C_2H_5OH)]{\substack{CH_3CH_2CH-CHCOO^- \\ CH_3\ NH_3^+}}$

$C_6H_5CH_2O\overset{\overset{O}{\|}}{C}NHCH_2CH_2CH_2CH_2CH\overset{\overset{O}{\|}}{C}NHCHCOO^- \xrightarrow[\substack{CH_3COOH \\ cold}]{HBr}$

$2C_6H_5CH_2Br \; + \; 2CO_2 \; + \; H_3\overset{+}{N}CH_2CH_2CH_2CH_2CH\overset{\overset{O}{\|}}{C}NHCHCOO^-$

Lys·Ile

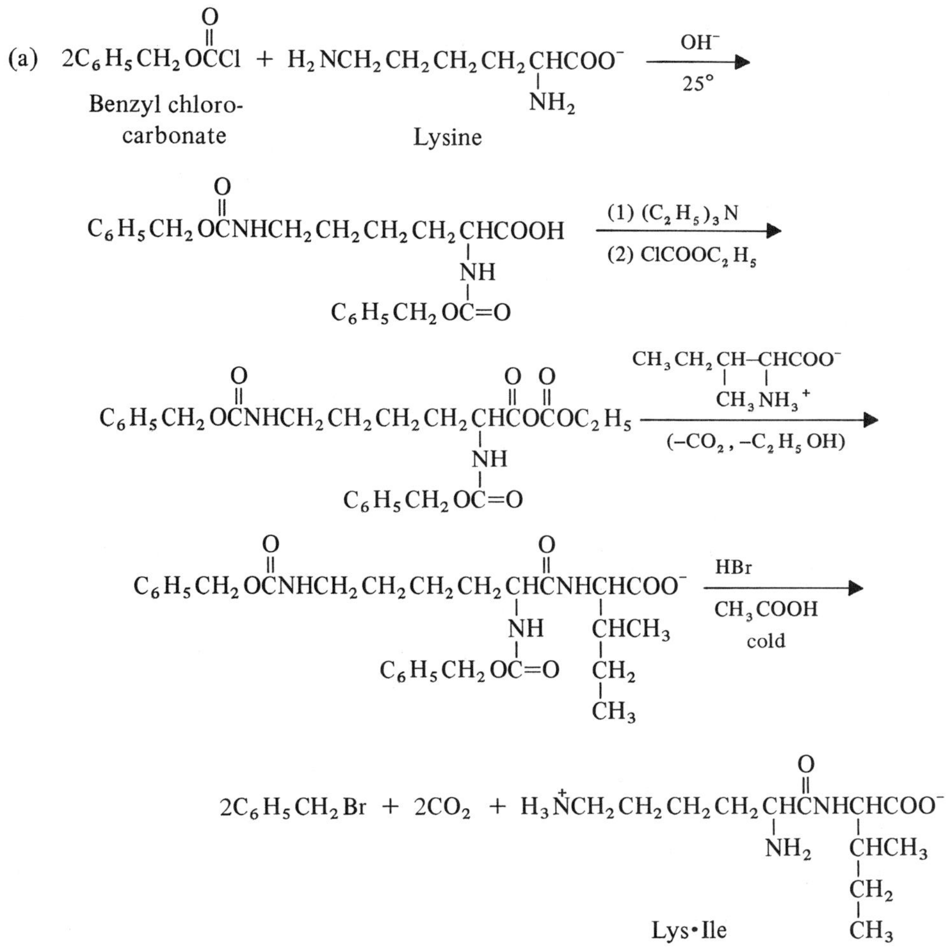

(b) $3C_6H_5CH_2O\overset{\overset{O}{\|}}{C}Cl \; + \; H_2\overset{\overset{NH}{\|}}{C}NHCH_2CH_2CH_2CHCOO^- \xrightarrow[25°]{OH^-}$

$C_6H_5CH_2O\overset{\overset{O}{\|}}{C}NH\overset{\overset{NH}{\|}}{C}NCH_2CH_2CH_2CHCOOH \xrightarrow[(2)\ ClCOOC_2H_5]{(1)\ (C_2H_5)_3N}$

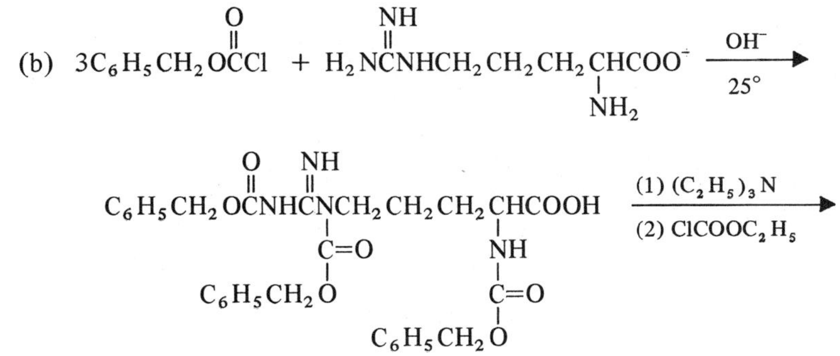

$$C_6H_5CH_2O\overset{O}{\overset{||}{C}}NH\overset{NH}{\overset{||}{C}}NCH_2CH_2CH_2\overset{O}{\overset{||}{C}}HC\overset{O\ O}{\overset{||\ ||}{OC}}OC_2H_5 \xrightarrow[(-CO_2,\ -C_2H_5OH)]{\overset{CH_3\overset{|}{C}HCOO^-}{\overset{+NH_3}{}}}$$

with substituents $\underset{C_6H_5CH_2O}{\overset{C=O}{|}}$ and $\underset{C_6H_5CH_2O}{\overset{NH}{\overset{C=O}{|}}}$

$$C_6H_5CH_2O\overset{O}{\overset{||}{C}}NH\overset{NH}{\overset{||}{C}}NCH_2CH_2CH_2\overset{O}{C}HC\overset{O}{\overset{||}{NH}}CHCOOH \xrightarrow[\underset{cold}{CH_3COOH}]{HBr}$$

with $\overset{C=O}{\underset{C_6H_5CH_2O}{|}}$, CH_3

$$3C_6H_5CH_2Br + 3CO_2 + {}^+H_3N\overset{NH}{\overset{||}{C}}NHCH_2CH_2CH_2\underset{NH_2}{\overset{|}{C}}HCONH\underset{CH_3}{\overset{|}{C}}HCOO^-$$

Arg·Ala

23.14 The weakness of the benzyl-oxygen bond allows these groups to be removed by catalytic hydrogenolysis.

23.15 (a) An electrophilic aromatic substitution reaction:

$$-(CH_2CH)_n- + CH_3OCH_2Cl \xrightarrow{BF_3} -(CH_2CH)_n- + CH_3OH$$

with phenyl groups, product ring bearing CH_2Cl

(b) The linkage between the resin and the polypeptide is a benzylic ester. It is cleaved by HBr in CF_3COOH at room temperature because the carbocation that is formed initially is the relatively stable, benzylic cation.

23.16

$$\bigcirc\!-CH_2Cl + HO\overset{O}{\overset{||}{C}}CHNH\overset{O}{\overset{||}{C}}OC(CH_3)_3$$ with CH_3

↓ base

$$\bigcirc\!-CH_2O\overset{O}{\overset{||}{C}}CHNH\overset{O}{\overset{||}{C}}OC(CH_3)_3$$ with CH_3

↓ CF_3COOH, CH_2Cl_2

1 Add Boc·Ala

2 Purify by washing

3 Remove protecting group

$$\bigcirc\!\!-CH_2OC\overset{\overset{O}{\|}}{}CHNH_2 \qquad \textbf{4}\quad \text{Purify by washing}$$
$$\overset{\underset{CH_3}{|}}{}$$

$$HOC\overset{\overset{O}{\|}}{}CHNHC\overset{\overset{O}{\|}}{}OC(CH_3)_3 \qquad \textbf{5}\quad \text{Add Boc·Phe}$$
$$\overset{\underset{CH_2C_6H_5}{|}}{}$$
$$\text{and}$$
$$\text{dicyclohexylcarbodiimide}$$

$$\bigcirc\!\!-CH_2OC\overset{\overset{O}{\|}}{}CHNHC\overset{\overset{O}{\|}}{}CHNHC\overset{\overset{O}{\|}}{}OC(CH_3)_3 \qquad \textbf{6}\quad \text{Purify by washing}$$
$$\overset{\underset{CH_3}{|}}{}\quad\overset{\underset{CH_2}{|}}{}$$
$$\overset{\underset{C_6H_5}{|}}{}$$

$$CF_3COOH, CH_2Cl_2 \qquad \textbf{7}\quad \text{Remove protecting group}$$

$$\bigcirc\!\!-CH_2OC\overset{\overset{O}{\|}}{}CHNHC\overset{\overset{O}{\|}}{}CHNH_2 \qquad \textbf{8}\quad \text{Purify by washing}$$
$$\overset{\underset{CH_3}{|}}{}\quad\overset{\underset{CH_2}{|}}{}$$
$$\overset{\underset{C_6H_5}{|}}{}$$

$$HOC\overset{\overset{O}{\|}}{}CHCH_2CH_2CH_2CH_2NHC\overset{\overset{O}{\|}}{}OC(CH_3)_3$$
$$\overset{\underset{NH}{|}}{}$$
$$O=COC(CH_3)_3 \qquad \textbf{9}\quad \text{Add protected Lys}$$
$$\text{and}$$
$$\text{dicyclohexylcarbodiimide}$$

$$\bigcirc\!\!-CH_2OC\overset{\overset{O}{\|}}{}CHNHC\overset{\overset{O}{\|}}{}CHNHC\overset{\overset{O}{\|}}{}CHNHC\overset{\overset{O}{\|}}{}OC(CH_3)_3 \qquad \textbf{10}\quad \text{Purify by washing}$$
$$\overset{\underset{CH_3}{|}}{}\quad\overset{\underset{CH_2}{|}}{}\quad\overset{\underset{CH_2}{|}}{}$$
$$\overset{\underset{C_6H_5}{|}}{}\quad\overset{\underset{CH_2}{|}}{}$$
$$\overset{\underset{CH_2}{|}}{}$$
$$\overset{\underset{CH_2}{|}}{}$$
$$NHCOC(CH_3)_3$$
$$\overset{\overset{}{}}{\underset{O}{}}$$

$$CF_3COOH, CH_2Cl_2 \qquad \textbf{11}\quad \text{Remove protecting groups}$$

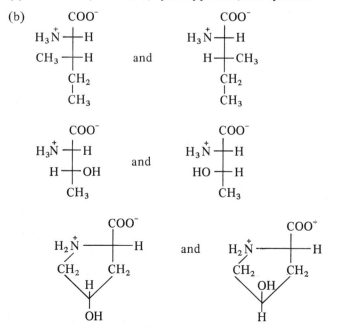

12 Purify by washing

13 Detach tripeptide

14 Isolate Product

Lys·Phe·Ala

23.17 (a) Isoleucine, threonine, hydroxyproline, and cystine.

(b)

(With cystine, both chiral carbons are α-carbons, thus according to the problem, both must have the L-configuration, and no isomers of this type can be written.)

(c) Diastereomers

23.18 (a) Alanine

$$CH_3CHCOO^- + HONO \longrightarrow CH_3CHCOOH + N_2$$
$$\underset{^+NH_3}{|} \qquad\qquad\qquad \underset{OH}{|}$$

(b) Proline and hydroxyproline. All of the other amino acids have at least one primary amino group.

(c) HO—⟨benzene ring with Br at top and Br at bottom⟩—CH_2CHCOO^-
     with $\overset{|}{NH_3{}^+}$

(d) ⟨benzene ring⟩—$CH_2CHCOOC_2H_5$
     with $\overset{|}{NH_3{}^+}$

(e) CH_3CHCOO^-
     $\quad\;\;\underset{|}{NH}$
     $\quad\;\;\underset{|}{C}=O$
     $\quad\;\;C_6H_5$

23.19 (a)

$$\underset{\underset{CH_2OH}{|}}{\overset{\overset{COO^-}{|}}{{}^+H_3N-\!\!\!-H}} \quad\xrightarrow[CH_3OH]{HCl}\quad \underset{\underset{CH_2OH}{|}}{\overset{\overset{COOCH_3}{|}}{{}^+H_3N-\!\!\!-H}} \quad Cl^-$$

L-(−)-Serine

A
$(C_4H_{10}ClNO_3)$

$$\xrightarrow{PCl_5}\quad \underset{\underset{CH_2Cl}{|}}{\overset{\overset{COOCH_3}{|}}{{}^+H_3N-\!\!\!-H}} \quad Cl^- \quad\xrightarrow[(2)\ OH^-]{(1)\ H_3O^+,\ H_2O,\ heat}$$

B
$(C_4H_9Cl_2NO_2)$

$$\underset{\underset{CH_2Cl}{|}}{\overset{\overset{COO^-}{|}}{{}^+H_3N-\!\!\!-H}} \quad\xrightarrow[dil.\ H_3O^+]{Na\text{-}Hg}\quad \underset{\underset{CH_3}{|}}{\overset{\overset{COO^-}{|}}{{}^+H_3N-\!\!\!-H}}$$

C   L-(+)-Alanine
$(C_3H_6ClNO_2)$

(b)

$$\mathbf{B} \quad\xrightarrow{OH^-}\quad \underset{\underset{CH_2Cl}{|}}{\overset{\overset{COOCH_3}{|}}{H_2N-\!\!\!-H}} \quad\xrightarrow{NaSH}\quad \underset{\underset{CH_2SH}{|}}{\overset{\overset{COOCH_3}{|}}{H_2N-\!\!\!-H}} \quad\xrightarrow[(2)\ OH^-]{(1)\ H_3O^+,\ H_2O,\ heat}$$

D   **E**
$(C_4H_8ClNO_2)$ $(C_4H_9NO_2S)$

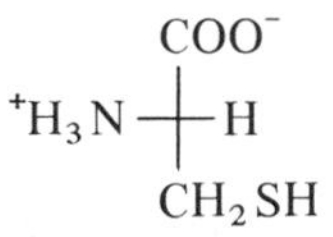

COO⁻ — rendering structures:

$$\overset{COO^-}{\underset{CH_2SH}{\overset{|}{\underset{|}{^+H_3N-\!\!\!-H}}}}$$

L-(+)-Cysteine

(c)

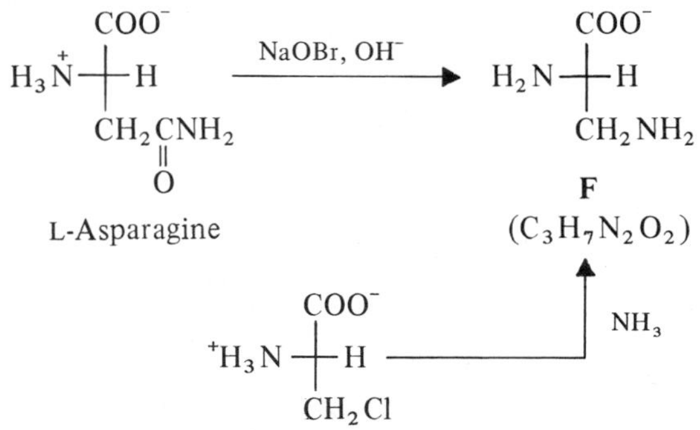

$$\overset{COO^-}{\underset{\underset{\underset{O}{\parallel}}{CH_2CNH_2}}{\overset{|}{\underset{|}{H_3\overset{+}{N}-\!\!\!-H}}}} \xrightarrow{\text{NaOBr, OH}^-} \overset{COO^-}{\underset{CH_2NH_2}{\overset{|}{\underset{|}{H_2N-\!\!\!-H}}}}$$

L-Asparagine

F
($C_3H_7N_2O_2$)

$$\overset{COO^-}{\underset{CH_2Cl}{\overset{|}{\underset{|}{^+H_3N-\!\!\!-H}}}} \xrightarrow{\hspace{1cm}} \quad \text{NH}_3$$

C
(from part a)

23.20

(a) $CH_3\overset{O}{\overset{\parallel}{C}}NHCH(CO_2C_2H_5)_2 \;+\; CH_2{=}CH{-}C{\equiv}N \xrightarrow[C_2H_5OH]{NaOC_2H_5}$

$$CH_3\overset{O}{\overset{\parallel}{C}}NH{-}\underset{CO_2C_2H_5}{\overset{CO_2C_2H_5}{\overset{|}{\underset{|}{C}}}}{-}CH_2CH_2C{\equiv}N \xrightarrow[\text{reflux}]{\text{conc HCl}}$$

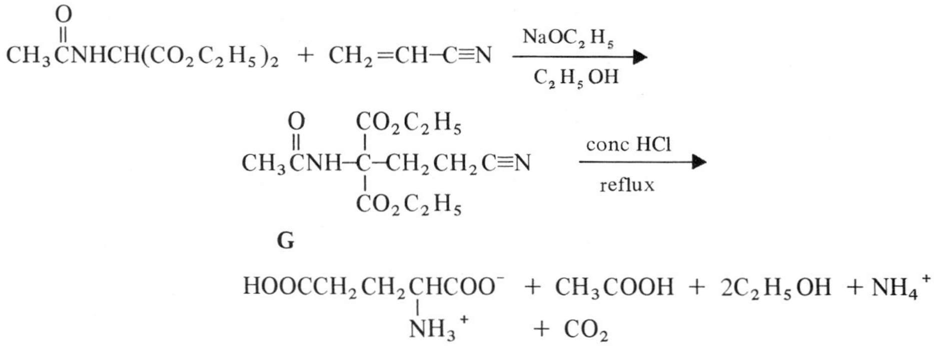

G

$$HOOCCH_2CH_2\underset{\underset{NH_3^+}{|}}{CH}COO^- \;+\; CH_3COOH \;+\; 2C_2H_5OH \;+\; NH_4^+ \;+\; CO_2$$

DL-Glutamic acid

(b)

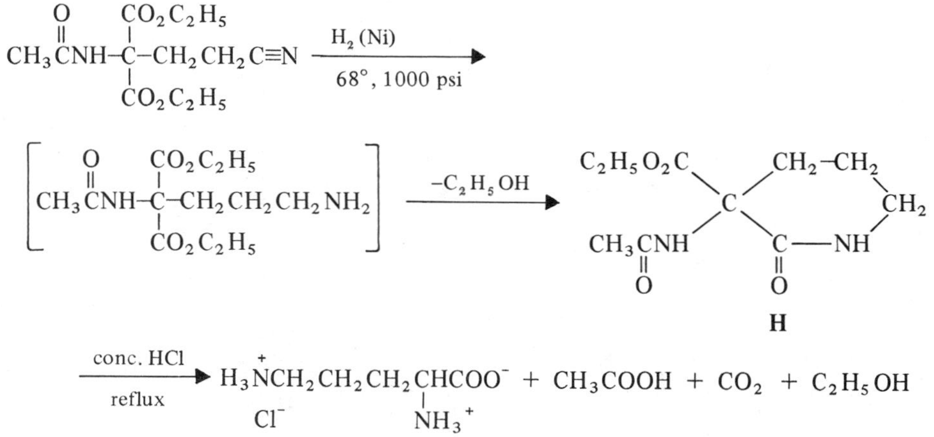

$$CH_3\overset{O}{\overset{\parallel}{C}}NH{-}\underset{CO_2C_2H_5}{\overset{CO_2C_2H_5}{\overset{|}{\underset{|}{C}}}}{-}CH_2CH_2C{\equiv}N \xrightarrow[68°, 1000 \text{ psi}]{H_2 \text{ (Ni)}}$$

$$\left[CH_3\overset{O}{\overset{\parallel}{C}}NH{-}\underset{CO_2C_2H_5}{\overset{CO_2C_2H_5}{\overset{|}{\underset{|}{C}}}}{-}CH_2CH_2CH_2NH_2 \right] \xrightarrow{-C_2H_5OH}$$

(structure **H**)

H

$$\xrightarrow[\text{reflux}]{\text{conc. HCl}} H_3\overset{+}{N}CH_2CH_2CH_2\underset{\underset{NH_3^+}{|}}{CH}COO^- \;+\; CH_3COOH \;+\; CO_2 \;+\; C_2H_5OH$$
$$Cl^-$$

DL-Ornithine hydrochloride

23.21

$$\underset{\underset{NH_3^+}{|}}{C_6H_5CH_2CHCOO^-} + \underset{\underset{O}{\|}}{HOOCCH_2CH_2CCOOH} \xrightleftharpoons{\text{transaminase}}$$

Phenylalanine　　　　　　α-Ketoglutaric acid

$$\underset{\underset{O}{\|}}{C_6H_5CH_2CCOOH} + \underset{\underset{NH_3^+}{|}}{HOOCCH_2CH_2CHCOO^-}$$

Phenylpyruvic acid　　　　Glutamic acid

Then:

$$\underset{\underset{NH_3^+}{|}}{HOOCCH_2CH_2CHCOO^-} + \underset{\underset{O}{\|}}{HOOCCH_2CCOOH} \xrightleftharpoons{\text{transaminase}}$$

Glutamic acid　　　　　　Oxaloacetic acid

$$\underset{\underset{O}{\|}}{HOOCCH_2CH_2CCOOH} + \underset{\underset{NH_3^+}{|}}{HOOCCH_2CHCOO^-}$$

α-Ketoglutaric acid　　　　Aspartic acid

This amounts to:

　Phenylalanine + α-Ketoglutaric acid ⇌ Phenylpyruvic acid + Glutamic acid
　Glutamic acid + Oxaloacetic acid ⇌ α-Ketoglutaric acid + Aspartic acid

Net: Phenylalanine + Oxaloacetic acid ⇌ Phenylpyruvic acid + Aspartic acid

23.22　We look for points of overlap:

```
                              Phe · Ser
                  Pro · Gly · Phe
            Pro · Pro                Ser · Pro · Phe
      Arg · Pro                                  Phe · Arg
      Arg · Pro · Pro · Gly · Phe · Ser · Pro · Phe · Arg
```

Bradykinin

23.23　1. This experiment shows that valine is the *N*-terminal amino acid and that valine is attached to leucine. (Lysine labeled at the ε-amino group is to be expected if lysine is not the *N*-terminal amino acid and if it is linked in the polypeptide through its α-amino group.)

2. This experiment shows that alanine is the *C*-terminal amino acid and that it is linked to glutamic acid.

　　At this point, then, we have the following information about the structure of the heptapeptide.

　　　Val · Leu (Ala, Lys, Phe) Glu · Ala

　　　　　the sequence here is
　　　　　unknown

3. (a) This experiment shows that the dipeptide, **A**, is

   Leu · Lys

(b) The carboxypeptidase reaction shows that the *C*-terminal amino acid of the tripeptide, **B**, is glutamic acid; the DNP labeling experiment shows that the *N*-terminal amino acid is phenylalanine. Thus the tripeptide **B** is:

   Phe · Ala · Glu

Putting these pieces together in the only way possible, we arrive at the following amino acid sequence for the heptapeptide.

Val · Leu

    Leu · Lys

                Phe · Ala · Glu

                               Glu · Ala

———————————————————————————————

Val · Leu · Lys · Phe · Ala · Glu · Ala

23.24 At pH 2-3 the γ-carboxyl groups of polyglutamic acid are uncharged (they are present as —COOH groups). At pH 5 the γ-carboxyl groups ionize and become negatively charged (they become γ-COO⁻ groups). The repulsive forces between these negatively charged groups cause an unwinding of the α-helix and the formation of a random coil.

23.25 The observation that the proton nmr spectrum taken at room temperature shows two different signals for the methyl groups suggests that they are in different environments. This would be true if rotation about the carbon-nitrogen bond was not taking place.

$$\delta 8.05 \; H \qquad CH_3 \; \delta 2.95$$
$$\underset{O}{\overset{}{C}} = N$$
$$O \qquad CH_3 \; \delta 2.80$$

We assign the δ2.80 signal to the methyl group that is on the same side as the electronegative oxygen.

The fact that the methyl signals appear as doublets (and that the formyl signal is a multiplet) indicates that long-range coupling is taking place between the methyl protons and the formyl proton.

That the two doublets are not simply the result of spin-spin coupling is indicated by the observation that the distance that separates one doublet from the other changes when the applied magnetic field strength is lowered. [Remember the magnitude of a chemical shift is proportional to the strength of the applied magnetic field while the magnitude of a coupling constant is not.]

That raising the temperature (to 111°) causes the doublets to coalesce into a single signal indicates that at higher temperatures the molecules have enough energy to surmount the energy barrier of the carbon-nitrogen bond. Above 111°, rotation is taking place so rapidly that the spectrometer is unable to discriminate between the two methyl groups.

SECTION REFERENCES FOR ADDITIONAL PROBLEMS

23.17 8.3, 8.9, 23.2   **23.22** 23.6, 23.7

23.18 23.2, 19.7, 15.15, 18.7, 18.8   **23.23** 23.6, 23.7

23.19 18.7, 14.7, 3.16, 8.12, 5.6, 19.5   **23.24** 23.2, 23.9

23.20 23.2, 20.8, 18.7, 19.3, 18.8   **23.25** 13.6, 23.9

23.21 23.4B

SELF-TEST

23.1   Write the structural formula of the principal ionic species present in aqueous solutions at pH 2, 7, and 12 of isoleucine (2-amino-3-methylpentanoic acid)

at pH = 2   at pH = 7   at pH = 12

(a)	(b)	(c)

23.2   A hexapeptide gave the following products:

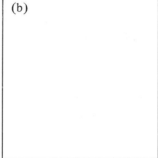

Hexapeptide $\xrightarrow[\text{HCO}_3^-]{}$ $\xrightarrow{\text{H}_3\text{O}^+}$

Hexapeptide $\xrightarrow{\text{3N HCl, 100°}}$ 2-Gly, 1 Leu, 1 Phe, 1 Pro, 1 Tyr

Hexapeptide $\xrightarrow{\text{1 N HCl, 80°}}$ Phe·Gly·Tyr + Gly·Phe·Gly + Pro·Leu·Gly
$+$ Leu·Gly·Phe

The structure of the hexapeptide (using abbreviations such as Gly·Leu·etc) is

24 NUCLEIC ACIDS AND PROTEIN SYNTHESIS

SOLUTIONS TO PROBLEMS

24.1 Adenine:

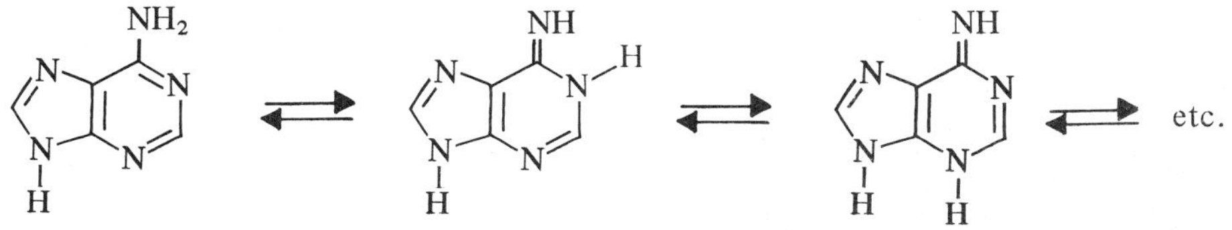

Guanine:

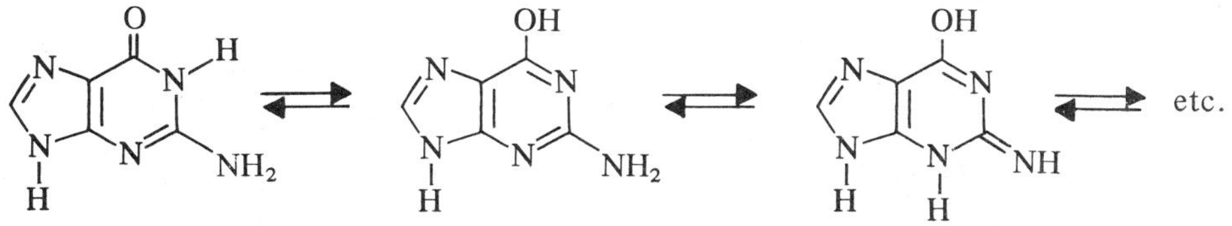

Cytosine:

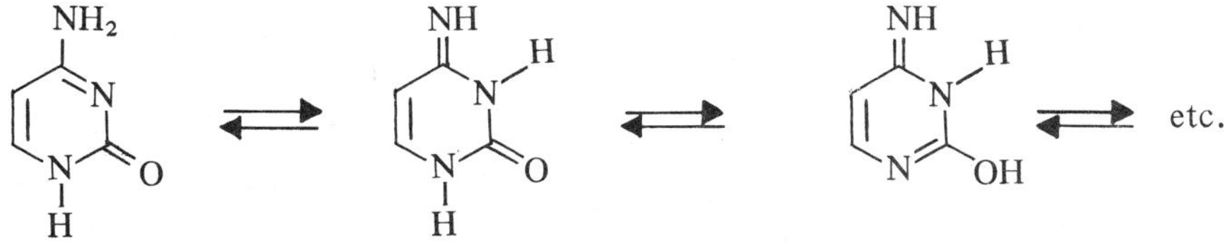

Thymine (R = CH₃) or Uracil (R = H):

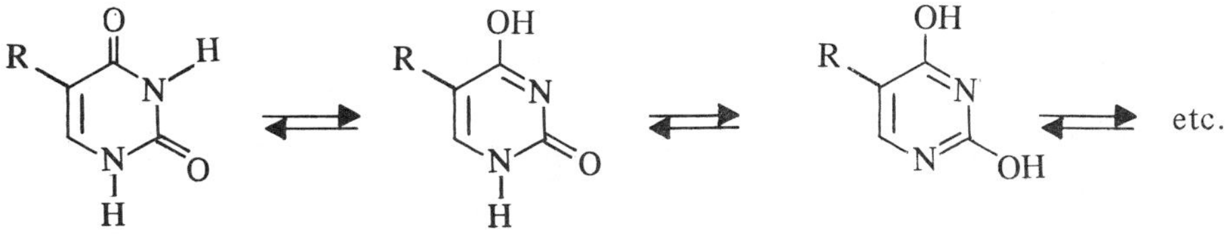

24.2 (a) The nucleosides have an N-glycosidic linkage that (like an O-glycosidic linkage) is rapidly hydrolyzed by aqueous acid but is one that is stable in aqueous base.

(b)

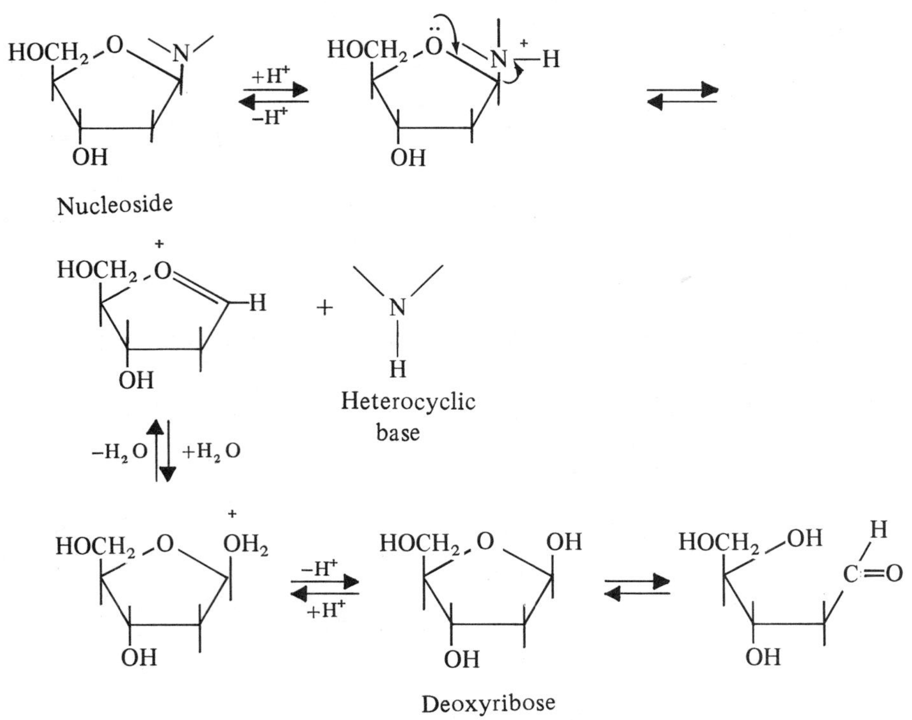
HOCH2
OH
Nucleoside
+H+
-H+
N
H
Heterocyclic base
-H2O
+H2O
OH2
OH
Deoxyribose
C=O

24.3 The reaction appears to take place through an S_N2 mechanism. Attack occurs preferentially at the primary 5′-carbon rather than at the secondary 3′-carbon.

24.4

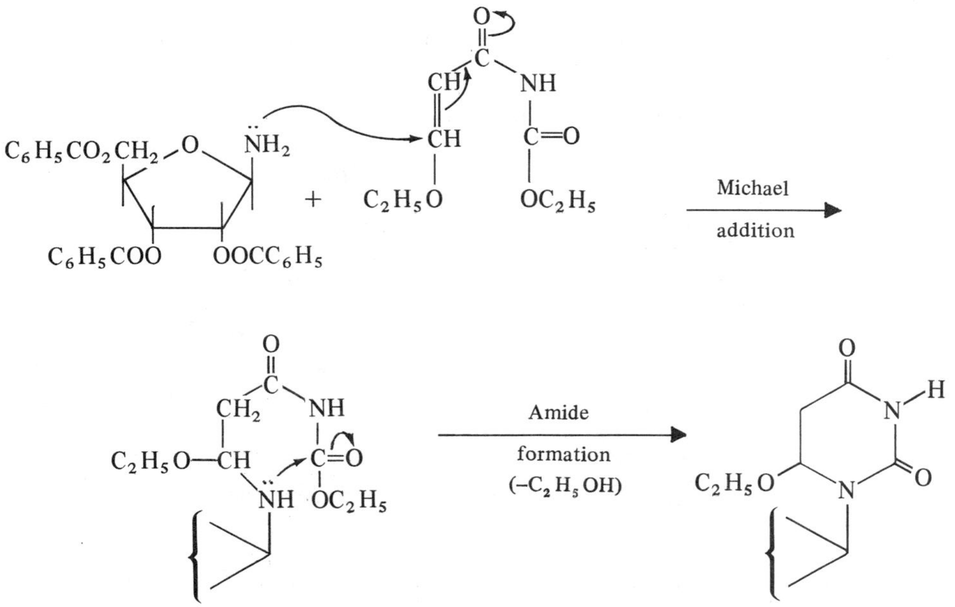
C6H5CO2CH2
NH2
C6H5COO
OOCC6H5
CH
NH
C=O
C2H5O
OC2H5
Michael addition
CH2
C2H5O—CH
Amide formation (–C2H5OH)
N
H

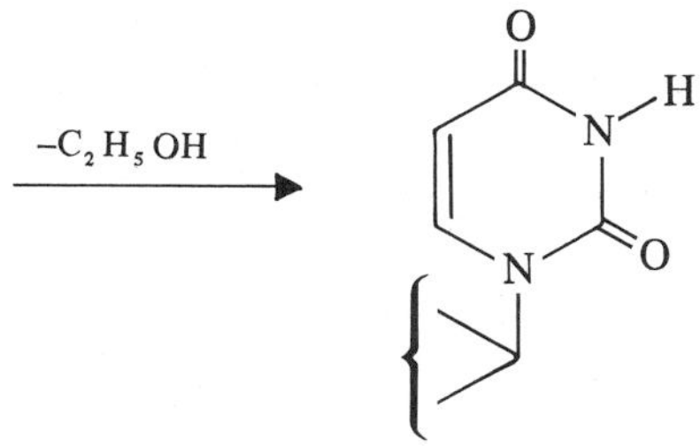

$-C_2H_5OH \longrightarrow$

24.5 (a) The isopropylidene group is part of a cyclic ketal.

(b) It can be installed by treating the nucleoside with acetone and a trace of acid and by simultaneously removing the water that is produced.

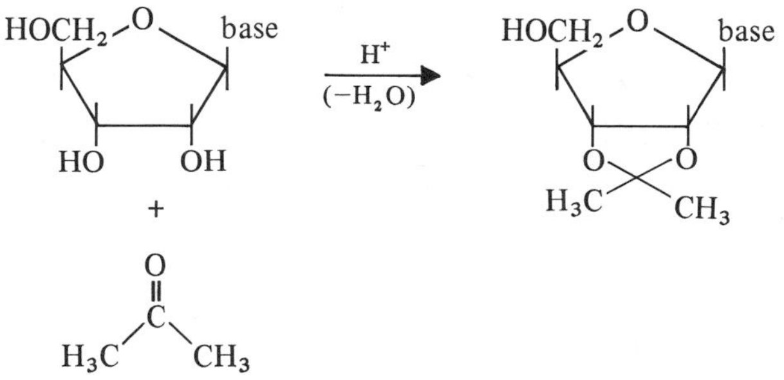

24.6

(a) 6×10^9 base pairs $\times \dfrac{34\text{Å}}{10 \text{ base pairs}} \times \dfrac{10^{-10} \text{ meters}}{\text{Å}} \cong 2$ meters

(b) $6 \times 10^{-12} \dfrac{\text{g}}{\text{ovum}} \times 3 \times 10^9$ ova $= 1.8 \times 10^{-2}$ g

24.7 (a)

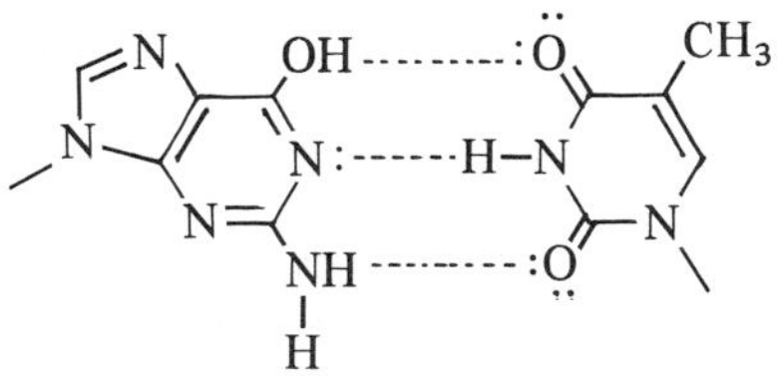

Lactim form   Thymine
of guanine

(b) Thymine would pair with adenine and thus adenine would be introduced into the complementary strand where guanine should occur.

24.8 (a) A diazonium salt and a heterocyclic analog of a phenol.

Hypoxanthine
nucleotide

(b)

Hypoxanthine   Cytosine

(c)   Original double strand

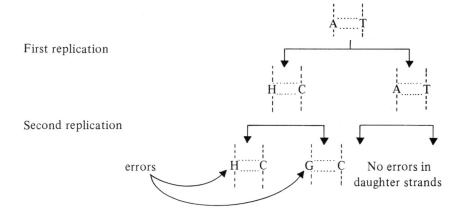

First replication

Second replication

errors

No errors in
daughter strands

24.9

Uracil
(in *m*RNA)

Adenine
(in DNA)

24.10 (a) UGG ¦ GGG ¦ UUU ¦ UAC ¦ AGC   *m*RNA

(b) Tyr ¦ Gly ¦ Phe ¦ Tyr ¦ Ser   Amino acids

(c) ACC ¦ CCC ¦ AAA ¦ AUG ¦ UCG   Anticodons

24.11   Arg · Ile · Cys · Tyr · Val   Amino acids

(a) AGA ¦ AUA ¦ UGC ¦ UGG ¦ GUA ¦   *m*RNA

(b) TCT ¦ TAT ¦ ACG ¦ ACC ¦ CAT ¦   DNA

(c) UCU ¦ UAU ¦ ACG ¦ ACC ¦ CAU ¦   Anticodons

24.12 A change from C–T–T to C–A–T or a change from C–T–C to C–A–C.

N
SPECIAL TOPIC
Reactions Controlled by Orbital Symmetry

SOLUTIONS TO PROBLEMS

N.1   Conrotatory motion of the type shown would lead to increasingly unfavorable interaction of the methyl groups as the transition state is approached. Thus this path is not followed to any appreciable extent.

N.2   According to the Woodward-Hoffmann rule for electrocyclic reactions of $4n$ π electron systems (Sect N.2A), the photochemical cyclization of *cis,trans*-2,4-hexadiene should proceed with *disrotatory motion*. Thus it should yield *trans*-3,4-dimethylcyclobutene:

H— —CH₃ $\xrightarrow[\text{disrotatory}]{hv}$ + enantiomer

cis, trans-2, 4-Hexadiene   *trans*-3, 4-Dimethylcyclobutene

N.3

(a)

ψ_2 of a hexadiene
(p. 1083)

(b) This is a thermal electrocyclic reaction of a $4n$ π electron system; it should, *and does*, proceed with conrotatory motion.

N.4

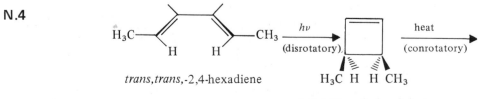

trans,trans,-2,4-hexadiene   H₃C H   H CH₃

cis-3,4-Dimethylcyclobutene

cis, trans-2, 4-Hexadiene

Here we find that two consecutive electrocyclic reactions (the first photochemical, the second thermal), provide a stereospecific synthesis of *cis,trans*-2,4-hexadiene from *trans, trans*-2,4-hexadiene.

N.5 (a) This is a photochemical electrocyclic reaction of an eight π electron system—a $4n$ π system where $n = 2$. It should, therefore, proceed with disrotatory motion.

$$hv \text{ (disrotatory)}$$

cis-7, 8-Dimethyl-1, 3, 5-cyclooctatriene

(b) This is a thermal electrocyclic reaction of the eight π electron system. It should proceed with conrotatory motion.

$$\text{heat (conrotatory)}$$

cis-7, 8-Dimethyl-1, 3, 5-cyclooctatriene

N.6 (a) This is conrotatory motion and since this is a $4n$ π electron system (where $n = 1$) it should occur under the influence of heat.

$$\text{heat (conrotatory)}$$

(b) This is conrotatory motion and since this is also a $4n$ π electron system (where $n = 2$) it should occur under the influence of heat.

(c)   This is disrotatory motion. This, too is a $4n$ π electron system (where $n = 1$), thus it should occur under the influence of light.

N.7   (a)   This is a $(4n + 2)\pi$ electron system (where $n = 1$); a thermal reaction should take place with disrotatory motion:

(b)   This is also a $4n + 2$ π electron system; a photochemical reaction should take place with conrotatory motion.

N.8   Here we need a conrotatory ring opening of *trans*-5,6-dimethyl-1,3-cyclohexadiene (to produce *trans,cis,trans*-2,4,6-octatriene), then we need a disrotatory cyclization to produce *cis*-5,6-dimethyl-1,3-cyclohexadiene.

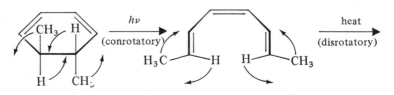

trans-5,6-Dimethyl-1,3-   *trans, cis, trans*-2,4,6-
    cyclohexadiene   Octatriene

cis-5,6-Dimethyl-1,3-
cyclohexadiene

Since both reactions involve $(4n + 2)\pi$ electron systems we apply light to accomplish the first step and heat to accomplish the second. It would also be possible to use heat to produce *trans,cis,cis*-2,4,6-octatriene then use light to produce the desired product.

N.9 The first electrocyclic reaction is a thermal, conrotatory ring opening of a $4n$ π electron system. The second electrocyclic reaction is a thermal, disrotatory ring closure of a $(4n + 2)\pi$ electron system.

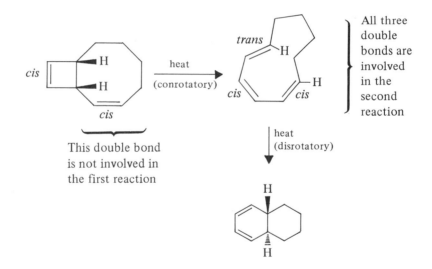

N.10 (a) This reaction involves two π electrons, thus it is a $(4n + 2)\pi$ system where $n = 0$.

(b) An allylic cation is formed by a disrotatory ring opening.

(c) The cyclopropyl anion is a $4n$ π system (where $n = 1$), thus a thermal reaction should take place with conrotatory motion.

N.11 (a) This is a $(4n + 2)\pi$ electron system undergoing disrotatory motion. Heat is required.

(b) This is a $(4n + 2)\pi$ electron system undergoing conrotatory motion. Light is required.

(c) This is a $(4n + 2)\pi$ electron system undergoing conrotatory motion. Light is required.

(d) This is a $(4n + 2)\pi$ electron system undergoing disrotatory motion. Heat is required.

N.12

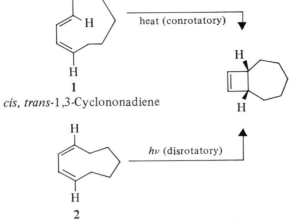

cis, trans-1,3-Cyclononadiene

cis,cis-1,3-Cyclononadiene

N.13

(a)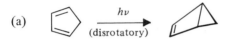

(b) Although the product is highly strained, a concerted thermal reversal of the electro-cyclic reaction would require conrotatory ring opening and the production of an impossibly strained cyclopentadiene ring with one *trans* double bond. The ring opening, therefore, is probably nonconcerted and has a relatively high activation energy.

N.14 (a) There are two possible products that can result from a concerted cycloaddition. They are formed when *cis*-2-butene molecules come together in the following ways:

and

(b) There are two possible products that can be obtained from *trans*-2-butene as well.

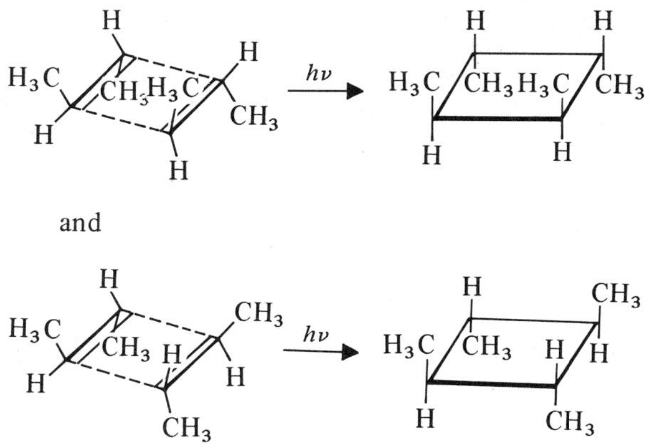

N.15   This is an intramolecular [2 + 2] cycloaddition.

N.16

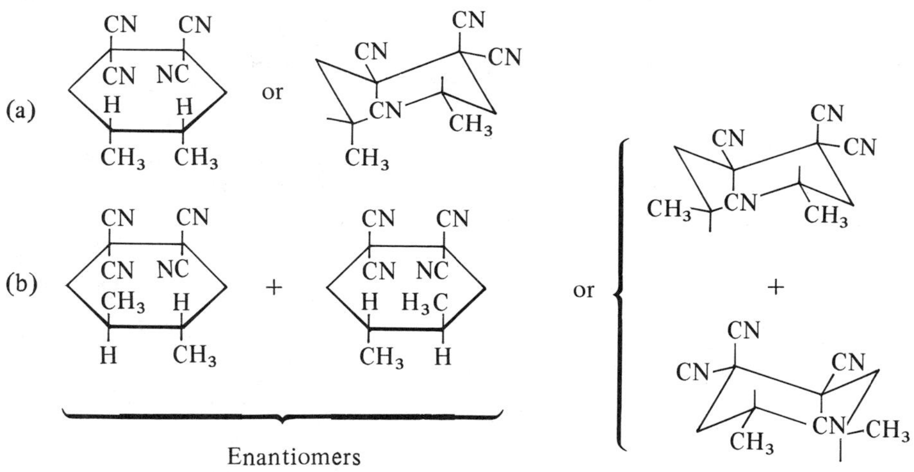

(a)

(b)

Enantiomers

N.17

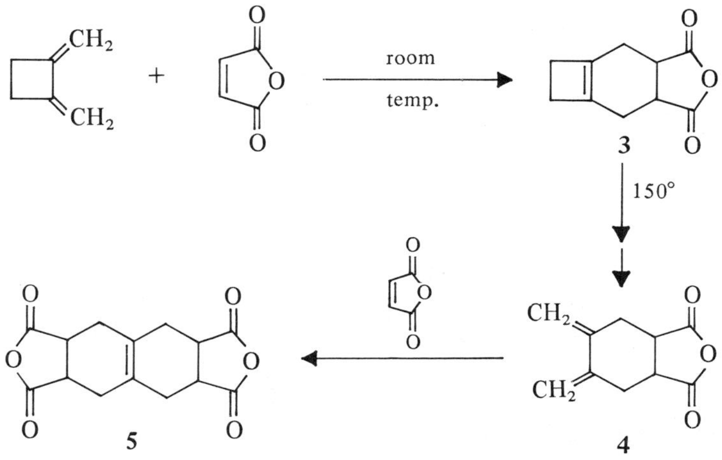

N.18 Compound 7 (below) results from a conrotatory ring opening; it then reacts as the diene component of a Diels-Alder reaction.

7

N.19

A is

B and C are

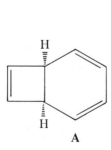 and

N.20 A is the product of a disrotatory thermal electrocyclic reaction involving a 6π electron segment of cyclooctatetraene. B is the Diels-Alder adduct.

A

B

A APPENDIX
Empirical and Molecular Formulas

In Section 1.2, we discussed briefly the pioneering work of Berzelius, Dumas, Liebig, and Cannizzaro in devising methods for determining the formulas of organic compounds. Although the experimental procedures for these analyses have been refined, the basic methods for determining the elemental composition of an organic compound today are not substantially different from those used in the nineteenth century. A carefully weighed quantity of the compound to be analyzed is oxidized completely to carbon dioxide and water. The weights of carbon dioxide and water are carefully measured and used to find the percentages of carbon and hydrogen in the compound. The percentage of nitrogen is usually determined by measuring the volume of nitrogen (N_2) produced in a separate procedure.

Special techniques for determining the percentage composition of other elements typically found in organic compounds have also been developed, but the direct determination of the percentage of oxygen is difficult. However, if the percentage composition of all the other elements is known, then the percentage of oxygen can be determined by difference. The following examples will illustrate how these calculations can be carried out.

EXAMPLE A

A new organic compound is found to have the following elemental analysis.

Carbon	67.95%
Hydrogen	5.69
Nitrogen	26.20
Total:	99.84%

Since the total of these percentages is very close to 100% (within experimental error) we can assume that no other element is present. For the purpose of our calculation it is convenient to assume that we have a 100-g sample. If we did, it would contain the following:

67.95 g of carbon
5.69 g of hydrogen
26.20 g of nitrogen

In other words, we use percents *by weight* to give us the ratios *by weight* of the elements in the substance. To write a formula for the substance, however, we need *ratios by moles*.

We now divide each of these weight-ratio numbers by the atomic weight of the particular element and obtain the number of moles of each element, respectively, in 100 g of the compound. This operation gives us the ratios *by moles* of the elements in the substance:

$$C: \quad \frac{67.95 \text{ g}}{12.01 \text{ g/mole}} = 5.66 \text{ moles}$$

$$H: \quad \frac{5.69 \text{ g}}{1.008 \text{ g/mole}} = 5.64 \text{ moles}$$

$$N: \quad \frac{26.20 \text{ g}}{14.01 \text{ g/mole}} = 1.87 \text{ moles}$$

One possible formula for the compound, therefore, is $C_{5.66}H_{5.64}N_{1.87}$.

By convention, however, we use *whole* numbers in formulas. Therefore, we convert these fractional numbers of moles to whole numbers by dividing each by 1.87, the smallest number.

$$C: \quad \frac{5.66}{1.87} = 3.03 \text{ which is } \sim 3$$

$$H: \quad \frac{5.64}{1.87} = 3.02 \text{ which is } \sim 3$$

$$N: \quad \frac{1.87}{1.87} = 1.00$$

Thus within experimental error, the ratios by moles are 3C to 3H to 1N, and C_3H_3N is the *empirical formula*. By empirical formula we mean the formula in which the subscripts are the smallest integers that give the ratio of atoms in the compound. In contrast, a *molecular* formula discloses the complete composition of one molecule. The molecular formula of this particular compound could be C_3H_3N or some whole-number multiple of C_3H_3N; that is, $C_6H_6N_2$, $C_9H_9N_3$, $C_{12}H_{12}N_4$, and so on. If, in a separate determination, we find that the molecular weight of the compound is 108±3, we can be certain that the *molecular formula* of the compound is $C_6H_6N_2$.

Formula	Molecular Weight
C_3H_3N	53.06
$C_6H_6N_2$	106.13 (which is within the range 108 ± 3)
$C_9H_9N_3$	159.19
$C_{12}H_{12}N_4$	212.26

The most accurate method for determining molecular weights is by mass spectroscopy; this method (which can also be used to determine molecular formulas and structures) is described in Special Topic E. A variety of other methods based on freezing point depression, boiling point elevation, osmotic pressure, and vapor density can also be used to determine molecular weights.

EXAMPLE B

Histidine, an amino acid isolated from protein, has the following elemental analysis:

Carbon	46.38%
Hydrogen	5.90
Nitrogen	27.01
Total:	79.29
Difference	20.71 (assumed to be oxygen)
	100.00%

Since no elements, other than carbon, hydrogen, and nitrogen, are found to be present in histidine the difference is assumed to be oxygen. Again, we assume a 100-g sample and divide the weight of each element by its gram-atomic weight. This gives us the ratio of moles (A).

	(A)	(B)	(C)
C:	$\dfrac{46.38}{12.01} = 3.86$	$\dfrac{3.86}{1.29} = 2.99 \times 2 = 5.98 \sim 6$ carbon atoms	
H:	$\dfrac{5.90}{1.008} = 5.85$	$\dfrac{5.85}{1.29} = 4.53 \times 2 = 9.06 \sim 9$ hydrogen atoms	
N:	$\dfrac{27.01}{14.01} = 1.94$	$\dfrac{1.94}{1.29} = 1.50 \times 2 = 3.00 = 3$ nitrogen atoms	
O:	$\dfrac{20.71}{16.00} = 1.29$	$\dfrac{1.29}{1.29} = 1.00 \times 2 = 2.00 = 2$ oxygen atoms	

Dividing each of the moles (A) by the smallest does not give a set of numbers (B) that is close to a set of whole numbers. Multiplying each of the numbers in column (B) by 2 does, however, as seen in column (C). The empirical formula of histidine is, therefore, $C_6H_9N_3O_2$.

In a separate determination the molecular weight of histidine was found to be 158 ± 5. The empirical formula weight of $C_6H_9N_3O_2$ (155.15) is within this range; thus the molecular formula for histidine is the same as the empirical formula.

PROBLEMS

A.1 What is the empirical formula of each of the following compounds?

(a) Hydrazine, N_2H_4
(b) Benzene, C_6H_6
(c) Dioxane, $C_4H_8O_2$
(d) Nicotine, $C_{10}H_{14}N_2$
(e) Cyclodecane, $C_{10}H_{20}$
(f) Acetylene, C_2H_2

A.2 The empirical formulas and molecular weights of several compounds are given below. In each case calculate the molecular formula for the compound.

Empirical Formula	Molecular Weight
(a) CH_2O	179 ± 5
(b) CHN	80 ± 5
(c) CCl_2	410 ± 10

A.3 The widely used antibiotic, penicillin G, gave the following elemental analysis: C, 57.45%; H, 5.40%; N, 8.45%; S, 9.61%. The molecular weight of penicillin G is 330 ± 10. Assume that no other elements except oxygen are present and calculate the empirical and molecular formulas for penicillin G.

ADDITIONAL PROBLEMS

A.4 Calculate the percentage composition of each of the following compounds.
(a) $C_6H_{12}O_6$
(b) $CH_3CH_2NO_2$
(c) $CH_3CH_2CBr_3$

A.5 An organometallic compound called *ferrocene* contains 30.02% iron. What is the minimum molecular weight of ferrocene?

A.6 A gaseous compound gave the following analysis: C, 40.04%; H, 6.69%. At standard temperature and pressure, 1.00 g of the gas occupied a volume of 746 ml. What is the molecular formula of the compound?

A.7 A gaseous hydrocarbon has a density of 1.251 g/liter at standard temperature and pressure. When subjected to complete combustion, a 1.000-liter sample of the hydrocarbon gave 3.926 g of carbon dioxide and 1.608 g of water. What is the molecular formula for the hydrocarbon?

A.8 Nicotinamide, a vitamin that prevents the occurrence of pellagra, gave the following analysis: C, 59.10%; H, 4.92%; N, 22.91%. The molecular weight of nicotinamide was shown in a separate determination to be 120 ± 5. What is the molecular formula for nicotinamide?

A.9 The antibiotic chloramphenicol gave the following analysis: C, 40.88%; H, 3.74%; Cl, 21.95%; N, 8.67%. The molecular weight was found to be 300 ± 30. What is the molecular formula for chloramphenicol?

SOLUTIONS TO PROBLEMS OF APPENDIX A

A.1   (a) NH_2 (b) CH (c) C_2H_4O (d) C_5H_7N (e) CH_2 (f) CH

A.2

Empirical Formula	Empirical Formula Weight	$\left(\dfrac{\text{Molecular Wt.}}{\text{Emp. Form. Wt.}}\right)$	Molecular Formula
(a) CH_2O	30	$\dfrac{179}{30} \cong 6$	$C_6H_{12}O_6$
(b) CHN	27	$\dfrac{80}{27} \cong 3$	$C_3H_3N_3$
(c) CCl_2	83	$\dfrac{410}{83} \cong 5$	C_5Cl_{10}

A.3   If we assume that we have a 100-g sample, the amounts of the elements are:

	Weight	Moles (A)	B
C	57.45	$\dfrac{57.45}{12.01} = 4.78$	$\dfrac{4.78}{0.300} = 15.9 = 16$
H	5.40	$\dfrac{5.40}{1.008} = 5.36$	$\dfrac{5.36}{0.300} = 17.9 = 18$
N	8.45	$\dfrac{8.45}{14.01} = 0.603$	$\dfrac{0.603}{0.300} = 2.01 = 2$
S	9.61	$\dfrac{9.61}{32.06} = 0.300$	$\dfrac{0.300}{0.300} = 1.00 = 1$
O*	$\dfrac{19.09}{100.00}$	$\dfrac{19.09}{16.00} = 1.19$	$\dfrac{1.19}{0.300} = 3.97 = 4$

(* by difference from 100)

The empirical formula is thus $C_{16}H_{18}N_2SO_4$. The empirical formula weight (334.4) is within the range given for the molecular weight (330 ± 10), thus the molecular formula for Penicillin G is the same as the empirical formula.

A.4   (a) To calculate the percentage composition from the molecular formula, first determine the weight of each element in one mole of the compound. For $C_6H_{12}O_6$,

$C_6 = 6 \times 12.01 = 72.06$ $\dfrac{72.06}{180.2} = 0.400 = 40.0\%$

$H_{12} = 12 \times 1.008 = 12.10$ $\dfrac{12.10}{180.2} = 0.0671 = 6.7\%$

$O_6 = 6 \times 16.00 = 96.00$ $\dfrac{96.00}{180.2} = 0.533 = 53.3\%$

Molecular Wt.   180.16

Then determine the percentage of each element using the formula.

$$\text{Percentage of A} = \frac{\text{Weight of A}}{\text{Molecular Weight}} \times 100$$

(b) $C_2 = 2 \times 12.01 = 24.02$ $\quad \dfrac{24.02}{75.07} = 0.320 = 32.0\%$

$H_5 = 5 \times 1.008 = 5.04$ $\quad \dfrac{5.04}{75.07} = 0.067 = 6.7\%$

$N = 1 \times 14.01 = 14.01$ $\quad \dfrac{14.01}{75.07} = 0.187 = 18.7\%$

$O_2 = 2 \times 16.00 = \underline{32.00}$ $\quad \dfrac{32.00}{75.07} = 0.426 = 42.6\%$

$\text{Total} = 75.07$

(c) $C_3 = 3 \times 12.01 = 36.03$ $\quad \dfrac{36.03}{280.77} = 0.128 = 12.8\%$

$H_5 = 5 \times 1.008 = 5.04$ $\quad \dfrac{5.04}{280.77} = 0.018 = 1.8\%$

$Br_3 = 3 \times 79.90 = \underline{239.70}$ $\quad \dfrac{239.70}{280.77} = 0.854 = 85.4\%$

$\text{Total} = 280.77$

A.5   If the compound contains iron, each molecule must contain at least one atom of iron, and one mole of the compound must contain at least 55.85 grams of iron. Therefore,

$$\text{MW of ferrocene} = 55.85 \frac{\text{grams Fe}}{\text{mole}} \times \frac{1.000 \text{ gram}}{0.3002 \text{ gram Fe}}$$

$$= 186.0 \frac{\text{grams}}{\text{mole}}$$

A.6   First we must determine the empirical formula. Assuming that the difference between the percentages given and 100 percent is due to oxygen, we calculate:

C: 40.04 $\quad \dfrac{40.04}{12.01} = 3.33 \quad \dfrac{3.33}{3.33} = 1$

H: 6.69 $\quad \dfrac{6.69}{1.008} = 6.64 \quad \dfrac{6.64}{3.33} \cong 2$

O: $\underline{53.27}$ $\quad \dfrac{53.27}{16.00} = 3.33 \quad \dfrac{3.33}{3.33} = 1$

       100.00

The empirical formula is thus CH_2O.

To determine the molecular formula we must first determine the molecular weight. At standard temperature and pressure, the volume of one mole of an ideal gas is 22.4 liters. Assuming ideal behavior,

$$\frac{1.00 \text{ g}}{0.746 \text{ liter}} = \frac{M}{22.4 \text{ liters}} \quad \text{Where M = Molecular weight}$$

$$M = \frac{(1.00)(22.4)}{0.746} = 30.0 \text{ g}$$

The empirical formula weight (30.0) equals the molecular weight, thus the molecular formula is the same as the empirical formula.

A.7   As in problem A.6, the molecular weight is found by the equation

$$\frac{1.251 \text{ g}}{1.00 \text{ liter}} = \frac{M}{22.4 \text{ liter}}$$

$$M = (1.251)(22.4)$$
$$M = 28.02$$

To determine the empirical formula, we must determine the amount of carbon in 3.926 g of carbon dioxide, and the amount of hydrogen in 1.608 g of water.

C: $\left(3.926 \text{ g } CO_2\right)\left(\dfrac{12.01 \text{ g C}}{44.01 \text{ g } CO_2}\right) = 1.071 \text{ g carbon}$

H: $\left(1.608 \text{ g } H_2O\right)\left(\dfrac{2.016 \text{ g H}}{18.016 \text{ g } H_2O}\right) = \underline{0.179 \text{ g hydrogen}}$

$$1.250 \text{ g sample}$$

The weight of C and H in a 1.250 g sample is 1.250 g. Therefore there are no other elements present.

To determine the empirical formula we proceed as in problem A.6 except that the sample size is 1.250 instead of 100 g.

C: $\dfrac{1.071}{12.01} = 0.0892$ $\dfrac{0.0892}{0.0892} = 1$

H: $\dfrac{0.179}{1.008} = 0.178$ $\dfrac{0.178}{0.0892} = 2$

The empirical formula is thus CH_2. The empirical formula weight (14) is one-half the molecular weight. Thus the molecular formula is C_2H_4.

A.8   Use the procedure of problem A.3.

C: 59.10 $\dfrac{59.10}{12.01} = 4.92$ $\dfrac{4.92}{0.817} = 6.02 \cong 6$

H: 4.92 $\dfrac{4.92}{1.008} = 4.88$ $\dfrac{4.88}{0.817} = 5.97 \cong 6$

$$\text{N:} \quad 22.91 \quad \frac{22.91}{14.01} = 1.64 \quad \frac{1.64}{0.817} = 2$$

$$\text{O:} \quad \frac{13.07}{100.00} \quad \frac{13.07}{16.00} = 0.817 \quad \frac{0.817}{0.817} = 1$$

The empirical formula is thus $C_6H_6N_2O$. The empirical formula weight is 123.13 which is equal to the molecular weight within experimental error. The molecular formula is thus the same as the empirical formula.

A.9

$$\text{C:} \quad 40.88 \quad \frac{40.88}{12.01} = 3.40 \quad \frac{3.40}{0.619} = 5.5 \quad 5.5 \times 2 = 11$$

$$\text{H:} \quad 3.74 \quad \frac{3.74}{1.008} = 3.71 \quad \frac{3.71}{0.619} = 6 \quad 6 \times 2 = 12$$

$$\text{Cl:} \quad 21.95 \quad \frac{21.95}{35.45} = 0.619 \quad \frac{0.619}{0.619} = 1 \quad 1 \times 2 = 2$$

$$\text{N:} \quad 8.67 \quad \frac{8.67}{14.01} = 0.619 \quad \frac{0.619}{0.619} = 1 \quad 1 \times 2 = 2$$

$$\text{O:} \quad \frac{24.76}{100.00} \quad \frac{24.76}{16.00} = 1.55 \quad \frac{1.55}{0.619} = 2.5 \quad 2.5 \times 2 = 5$$

The empirical formula is thus $C_{11}H_{12}Cl_2N_2O_5$. The empirical formula weight (323) is equal to the molecular weight, therefore the molecular formula is the same as the empirical formula.

B

APPENDIX
Molecular Model Set Exercises

The exercises in this appendix are designed to help you gain an understanding of the three-dimensional nature of molecules. You are encouraged to perform these exercises with a model set as described.

These exercises should be performed as part of the study of the chapters shown below.

Chapter in Text	Accompanying Exercises
3	1, 3, 4, 5, 6, 8, 10, 11, 12, 14, 15, 16, 17, 18, 20, 21
6	9, 19, 22
8	2, 7, 9, 13, 19, 24, 25, 26
9	27
10	30
11	23, 26
22	28
23	29
Special Topic N	31

The following molecular model set exercises were developed by Ronald Starkey for use with the Theta Molecular Model Set (J. Wiley & Sons, Inc.).

Refer to the instruction booklet that accompanies the model set for details of molecular model assembly.

EXERCISE 1 (Chapter 3)

Assemble a molecular model of methane, CH_4. Note that the hydrogens describe the apexes of a regular tetrahedron with the carbon at the center of the tetrahedron. Demonstrate by attempted superposition that two models of methane are identical.

Replace any one hydrogen atom on each of the two methane models with a halogen (a green atom-center in the Theta Molecular Model Set) to form two molecules of CH_3X. Are the two structures identical? Does it make a difference which of the four hydrogens on a methane molecule you replace? How many different configurations of CH_3X are possible?

Repeat the same considerations for two disubstituted methanes with two identical substituents (CH_2X_2), and then with two different substituents (CH_2XY). Two shades of green atom-centers could be used for the two different substituents.

Methane, CH_4

EXERCISE 2 (Chapter 8)

Construct a model of a trisubstituted methane molecule (CHXYZ). Four different colored atom-centers (red, blue, yellow, and white) are attached to a central tetrahedral black carbon atom-center. Note that the carbon now has four different substituents. Compare this model with a second model of CHXYZ. Are the two structures identical (superposable)?

Interchange any two substitutents on one of the carbons. Are the two CHXYZ molecules identical now? Does the fact that interchange of any two substituents on the carbon interconverts the stereoisomers indicate that there are only two possible configurations of a tetrahedral carbon atom?

Compare the two models that were not identical. What is the relationship between them? Do they have a mirror-image relationship? That is, are they related as an object and its mirror reflection?

EXERCISE 3 (Chapter 3)

Make a model of ethane, CH_3CH_3. Does each of the carbon atoms retain a tetrahedral configuration? Can the carbons be rotated with respect to each other without breaking the carbon-carbon bond?

Rotate about the carbon-carbon bond until the carbon-hydrogen bonds of one carbon are aligned with those of the other carbon. This is the eclipsed conformation. When the C—H bond of one carbon bisects the H—C—H angle of the other carbon, the conformation is called staggered. Remember conformations are arrangements of atoms in a molecule that can be interconverted by bond rotations.

In which of the two conformations of ethane you made are the hydrogens of one carbon closer to those of the other carbon?

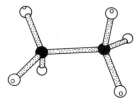

Ethane, CH_3CH_3

EXERCISE 4 (Chapter 3)

Prepare a second model of ethane. Replace one hydrogen, any one, on each ethane model with a substituent such as a halogen (a green atom-center), to form two models of CH_3CH_2X. Are the structures identical? If not, can they be made identical by rotation about the C—C bond? With one of the models demonstrate that there are three equivalent staggered conformations (see Exercise 3) of CH_3CH_2X. How many equivalent eclipsed conformations are possible?

EXERCISE 5 (Chapter 3)

Assemble a model of a 1,2-disubstituted ethane molecule, CH_2XCH_2X. Note how the orientation of and the distance between the X groups changes with rotation of the carbon-carbon bond. The arrangement in which the X substituents are at maximum separation is the *anti*-staggered conformation. The other staggered conformations are called *gauche*. How many *gauche* conformations are possible? Are they energetically equivalent? Are they identical?

EXERCISE 6 (Chapter 3)

Construct two models of butane, $CH_3CH_2CH_2CH_3$. Note that the structures can be viewed as dimethyl substituted ethanes. Show that rotations of the C—2, C—3 bond of butane produce eclipsed, *anti*-staggered, and *gauche*-staggered conformations. Measure the distance between C—1 and C—4 in the conformations mentioned above. The scale of the Theta Molecular Model Set is 3 cm in a model corresponds to approximately 1.0 Angstrom (0.1 nm) on a molecular scale. In which eclipsed conformation are the C—1 and C—4 carbons closest to each other? How many eclipsed conformations are possible?

EXERCISE 7 (Chapter 8)

Using two models of butane verify that the two hydrogens on C—2 are not stereochemically equivalent. Replacement of one hydrogen leads to a product that is not identical to that obtained by replacement of the other C—2 hydrogen. Both replacement products have the same molecular formula $CH_3CHXCH_2CH_3$. What is the relationship of the two products?

EXERCISE 8 (Chapter 3)

Make a model of hexane, $CH_3CH_2CH_2CH_2CH_2CH_3$. Extend the six carbon chain as far as it will go. This puts C—1 and C—6 at maximum separation. Notice that this "straight-chain" structure maintains the tetrahedral bond angles at each carbon and therefore the carbon chain adopts a zig-zag arrangement. Does this extended chain adopt staggered or eclipsed conformations of the hydrogens? How could you describe the relationship of C—1 and C—4?

EXERCISE 9 (Chapter 8)

Prepare models of the four isomeric butenes, C_4H_8. Note that the restricted rotation about the double-bond is responsible for the cis-trans stereoisomerism. Verify this by observing that breaking the *pi*-bond of *cis*-2-butene allows rotation and thus conversion to *trans*-2-butene. Are any of the four isomeric butenes chiral (nonsuperposable with its mirror image)? Indicate pairs of butene isomers that are stuctural (constitutional) isomers. Indicate pairs that are diastereoisomers. How does the distance between the C−1 and C−4 carbons in *trans*-2-butene compare with that of the *anti* conformation of butane? Compare the C−1 to C−4 distance in *cis*-2-butene and the conformation of butane in which the methyls are eclipsed.

$$CH_3CH_2 \diagdown \qquad \diagup H$$
$$C=C$$
$$H \diagup \qquad \diagdown H$$
1-Butene

$$CH_3 \diagdown \qquad \diagup CH_3$$
$$C=C$$
$$H \diagup \qquad \diagdown H$$
cis-2-Butene

$$CH_3 \diagdown \qquad \diagup H$$
$$C=C$$
$$H \diagup \qquad \diagdown CH_3$$
trans-2-Butene

$$CH_3 \diagdown \qquad \diagup H$$
$$C=C$$
$$CH_3 \diagup \qquad \diagdown H$$
2-Methylpropene

EXERCISE 10 (Chapter 3)

Make a model of cyclopropane. The Theta Molecular Model Set requires the use of flexible tubing for the carbon-carbon bonds of the cyclopropane ring. The flexible tubes illustrate quite well the "bent-bond" nature of the ring bonds. It should be apparent that the ring carbons must be coplaner. What is the relationship of the hydrogens on adjacent carbons? Are they staggered, eclipsed, or skewed?

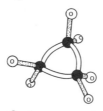

Cyclopropane, △

EXERCISE 11 (Chapter 3)

A model of cyclobutane can easily be assembled in a conformation that has the four carbons coplanar. For this exercise the rigid tubes of the Theta Molecular Model Set should be used for the carbon-carbon bonds of the ring. How many eclipsed hydrogens are there in this conformation? Torsional strain can be relieved at the expense of increased angle strain by a slight folding of the ring. The deviation of one ring carbon from the plane of the other three carbons is about 25°. This folding compresses the C−C−C bond angle to about 88°. Rotate about ring carbon bonds of the planar conformation to obtain the folded conformation. Are the hydrogens on adjacent carbons eclipsed or skewed? Considering both structural and stereoisomers how many dimethylcyclobutane structures are possible? Do deviations of the ring from planarity have to be considered when determining the number of possible dimethyl structures?

Cyclobutane, □

EXERCISE 12 (Chapter 3)

Cyclopentane is a more flexible ring system than cyclobutane or cyclopropane. A model of cyclopentane in a conformation with all the ring carbons coplanar exhibits minimal deviation of the C–C–C bond angles from the normal tetrahedral bond angle. How many eclipsed hydrogen interactions are there in this conformation? If one of the ring carbons is pushed slightly above the plane of the other carbons a model of the envelope conformation is obtained. Does the envelope conformation relieve some of the torsional strain? How many eclipsed hydrogen interactions are there in the envelope conformation?

Cyclopentane

EXERCISE 13 (Chapter 8)

Make a model of 1,2-dimethylcyclopentane. How many stereoisomers are possible for this compound? Identify each of the possible structures as either cis or trans. Is it apparent that cis-trans isomerism is possible in this compound because of restricted rotation? Are any of the stereoisomers chiral? What are the relationships of the 1,2-dimethylcyclopentane stereoisomers?

EXERCISE 14 (Chapter 3)

Assemble the six-membered ring compound cyclohexane. Is the ring flat or puckered? Place the ring in a chair conformation and then in a boat conformation. Demonstrate that the chair and boat are indeed conformations of cyclohexane—that is, they may be interconverted by rotations about the carbon-carbon bonds of the ring.

Chair form   Boat form

Note that in the chair conformation carbons 2, 3, 5, and 6 are in the same plane and carbons 1 and 4 are above and below the plane, respectively. In the boat conformation carbons 1 and 4 are both above (they could also both be below) the plane described by carbons 2, 3, 5, and 6. Is it apparent why the boat is sometimes associated with the flexible form? Are the hydrogens in the chair conformation staggered or eclipsed? Are any hydrogens eclipsed in the boat conformation? Do carbons 1 and 4 have an *anti* or a *gauche* relationship in the chair conformation? (Hint: Look down the C–2, C–3 bond).

A twist conformation of cyclohexane may be obtained by slightly twisting carbons 2 and 5 of the boat conformation as shown:

Boat form   Twist form

Note that the C–2, C–3 and the C–5, C–6 sigma bonds no longer retain their parallel orientation in the twist conformation. If the ring system is twisted too far, another boat conformation results. Compare the nonbonded (van der Waals repulsion) interactions and the torsional strain present in the boat, twist, and chair conformations of cyclohexane. Is it apparent why the relative order of thermodynamic stabilities is chair > twist > boat?

EXERCISE 15 (Chapter 3)

Construct a model of methylcyclohexane. How many chair conformations are possible? How does the orientation of the methyl group change in each chair conformation?

Identify carbons in the chair conformation of methylcyclohexane that have intramolecular interactions corresponding to those found in the *gauche* and *anti* conformations of butane. Which of the chair conformations has the greatest number of *gauche* interactions? How many more? If we assume, as is the case for butane, that the *anti* interaction is 0.8 kcal/mole more favorable than *gauche*, then what is the relative stability of the two chair conformations of methylcyclohexane? Hint: Identify the relative number of *gauche* interactions in the two conformations.

EXERCISE 16 (Chapter 3)

Compare models of the chair conformations of monosubstituted cyclohexanes in which the substituent alkyl groups are methyl, ethyl, isopropyl, and *t*-butyl.

Rationalize the relative stability of axial and equatorial conformations of the alkyl group given in the table for each compound. The chair conformation with the alkyl group equatorial is more stable by the amount shown.

Alkyl Group	ΔH (kcal/mole) Equatorial $\rightleftharpoons$ Axial
CH_3	1.6
CH_2CH_3	1.7
$CH(CH_3)_2$	2.1
$C(CH_3)_3$	5.0 (approx.)

EXERCISE 17 (Chapter 3)

Make a model of 1,2-dimethylcyclohexane. Answer the questions posed in Exercise 13 with regard to 1,2-dimethylcyclohexane.

EXERCISE 18 (Chapter 3)

Compare models of the neutral and charged molecules shown below. Identify the structures that are isoelectronic, that is, those that have the same electronic structure. How do those structures that are isoelectronic compare in their molecular geometry?

CH_3CH_3	CH_3NH_2	CH_3OH
$CH_3CH_2^-$	$CH_3NH_3^+$	$CH_3OH_2^+$

EXERCISE 19 (Chapter 8)

Prepare a model of cyclohexene. Note that chair and boat conformations are no longer possible, as carbons 1, 2, 3, and 6 lie in a plane. Are cis and trans stereoisomers possible for the double bond? Attempt to assemble a model of *trans*-cyclohexene. Can it be done? Are cis and trans stereoisomers possible for 2,3-dimethylcyclohexene? For 3,4-dimethylcyclohexene?

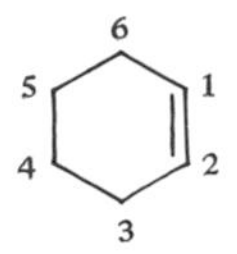

Cyclohexene

Assemble a model of *trans*-cyclooctene. Observe the twisting of the *pi*-bond system. Would you expect the cis stereoisomer to be more stable than *trans*-cyclooctene? Is *cis*-cyclooctene chiral? Is *trans*-cyclooctene chiral?

EXERCISE 20 (Chapter 3)

Construct models of *cis*-decalin (*cis*-bicyclo [4.4.0] decane) and *trans*-decalin. Observe how it is possible to interconvert one conformation of *cis*-decalin in which both rings are in chair conformations to another all chair conformation. This interconversion is not possible in the case of the *trans*-decalin isomer. Suggest a reason for the difference in behavior of the cis and trans isomers. Hint: What would happen to carbons 7 and 10 of *trans*-decalin if the other ring (indicated by carbons numbered 1 to 6) is converted to the alternative chair conformation. Is the situation the same for *cis*-decalin?

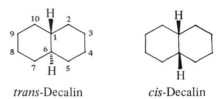

trans-Decalin   *cis*-Decalin

EXERCISE 21 (Chapter 3)

Assemble a model of norbornane (bicyclo [2.2.1] heptane). Observe the two cyclopentane ring systems in the molecule. The structure may also be viewed as a methylene (CH_2) bridge between carbons 1 and 4 of cyclohexane. Describe the conformation of the cyclohexane ring system in norbornane. How many eclipsing interactions are present?

Norbornane

Using a model of twistane identify the cyclohexane ring systems held in twist conformations. In adamantane find the chair conformation cyclohexane systems. How many are present? Evaluate the torsional and angle strain in adamantane. Which of the three compounds in this exercise are chiral?

Twistane   Adamantane

EXERCISE 22 (Chapter 6)

A hypothesis known as "Bredt's Rule" states that a double bond to a bridgehead carbon in a small-ring bridged bicyclic structure is not possible. The basis of this rule can be seen if you attempt to make a model of bicyclo [2.2.1] hept-1-ene, **a**. One approach to the assembly of this model is to try to bridge the number 1 and number 4 carbons of cyclohexene with a methylene (CH_2) unit. Compare this bridging with the ease of installing a CH_2 brige between the 1 and 4 carbons of cyclohexane to form a model of norbornane (See Exercise 21). Explain the differences in ease of assembly of these two models.

A   B

Bridgehead double bonds can be accomodated in larger ring bridged bicyclic compounds such as bicyclo[3.2.2]non-1-ene, *B*. Although this compound has been prepared in the laboratory it is an extremely reactive alkene. The Theta Molecular Model Set model of bicyclo[3.2.2]non-1-ene clearly shows the strained (twisted) double bond system.

EXERCISE 23 (Chapter 11)

Not all cyclic structures with alternating double and single bonds are aromatic. Cyclooctatetraene shows none of the aromatic characteristics of benzene. From examination of molecular models of cyclooctatetraene and benzene explain why there is pi-electron delocalization in benzene but not in cyclooctatetraene. Hint: Can the carbons of the eight-membered ring adopt a planar arrangement?

Benzene   Cyclooctatetraene

Note that benzene can be represented several different ways with the Theta Molecular Model Set. In this exercise the Kekule representation with alternating double and single bonds is appropriate. Alternative representations of benzene are shown in the model set instruction booklet.

EXERCISE 24 (Chapter 8)

Consider the $CH_3CHXCHYCH_3$ system. A butane that has at C–2 and C–3 different shades of green atom-centers is representative. Assemble all possible stereoisomers of this structure. How many are there? Indicate the relationship among them. Are they all chiral?

Repeat the analysis with the $CH_3CHXCHXCH_3$ system. The green atom-centers are suitable for assembly of the models.

EXERCISE 25 (Chapter 8)

Not all molecular chirality is a result of a center of chirality, such as CHXYZ. Cumulated dienes (1,2-dienes or allenes) are capable of generating molecular chirality.

1,2-Propadiene (allene), $H_2C=C=CH_2$

Identify, using models, which of the following cumulated dienes are chiral.

A   B   C

Are the following compounds chiral? How are they structurally related to cumulated dienes?

D   E

Is the cumulated triene shown below chiral? Explain the presence or absence of molecular chirality. More than one stereoisomer is possible for this triene. What are the structures, and what is the relationship between those structures?

F

EXERCISE 26 (Chapters 8 and 11)

Substituted biphenyl systems can produce molecular chirality if the rotation about the bond connecting the two rings is restricted. Which of the three biphenyl compounds indicated here are chiral and would be expected to be optically active?

J. a = f = CH_3 K. a = b = CH_3 L. a = f = CH_3

b = e = $N(CH_3)_3^+$ e = f = $N(CH_3)_3^+$ b = e = H

EXERCISE 27 (Chapter 9)

Assemble a model of ethyne (acetylene). The linear geometry of the molecule should be readily apparent. Note that the Theta Molecular Model Set depicts the sigma and both the pi bonds of the triple bond system. Based on attempts to assemble cycloalkynes, predict the smallest ring cycloalkyne that is stable.

Ethyne, HC≡CH

EXERCISE 28 (Chapter 22)

Construct a model of β-D-glucopyranose. Note that in one of the chair conformations all the hydroxyl groups and the CH_2OH group are in an equatorial orientation. Convert the structure of β-D-glucopyranose to α-D-glucopyranose, to β-D-mannopyranose, and to β-D-galactopyranose. Indicate the number of large ring substituents (OH or CH_2OH) that are axial in the more favorable chair conformation of each of these sugars. Is it reasonable that the β-anomer is more stable than the α-anomer of D-glucopyranose?

Make a model of β-L-glucopyranose. What is the relationship between the D and L configurations? Which is more stable?

β-D-Glucopyranose

D-(+)-Glucose   D-(+)-Mannose   D-(+)-Galactose

EXERCISE 29 (Chapter 23)

Assemble a model of tripeptide A shown below. If the model is made according to the representation of a peptide shown in the Theta Molecular Model Set, you will be able to observe the restricted rotation of the C—N bond in the amide linkage. Note the planarity of the six atoms associated with the amide portions of the molecule. Which bonds along the peptide chain are free to rotate? The amide linkage can either be cisoid or transoid. How does the length (from *N*-terminal nitrogen to *C*-terminal carbon) of the tripeptide chain that is transoid compare with one that is cisoid? Which is more "linear"? Convert a model of tripeptide A in the transoid arrangement to a model of tripeptide B. Which tripeptide has a longer chain?

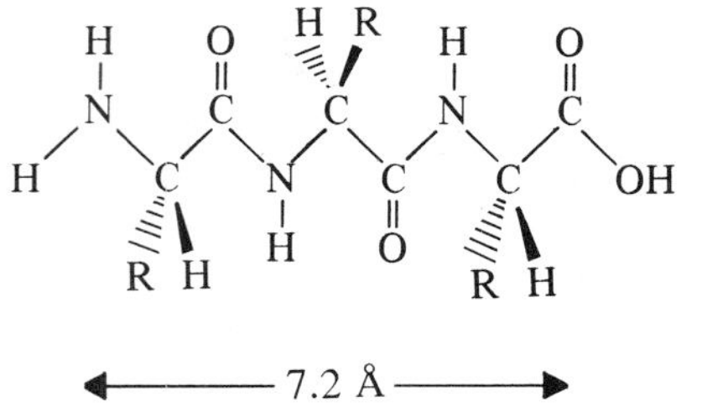

Tripeptide A: R = CH$_3$ (L-alanine)
Tripeptide B: R = CH$_2$OH   (L-serine)

EXERCISE 30 (Chapter 10)

Make models of the π molecular orbitals for the following compounds. Use the phase representation of each contributing atomic orbital shown in the Theta Molecular Model Set instruction booklet. Compare each model with π molecular orbital diagrams shown in the text book.

   A. π_1 and π_2 of ethene (CH$_2$=CH$_2$)

   B. π_1 thru π_4 of 1,3-butadiene (CH$_2$=CH–CH=CH$_2$)

   C. π_1, π_2 and π_3 of the allyl radical (CH$_2$=CH–CH$_2$)

EXERCISE 31 (Special Topic N)

Explain the observed stereochemistry of the pericyclic reactions shown here. The course of the reactions are controlled by orbital symmetry.

A. An electrocyclic reaction.

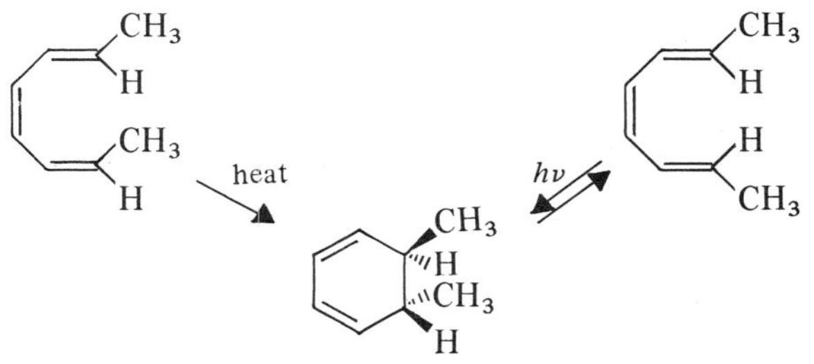

B. A (4+2) cycloaddition reaction.

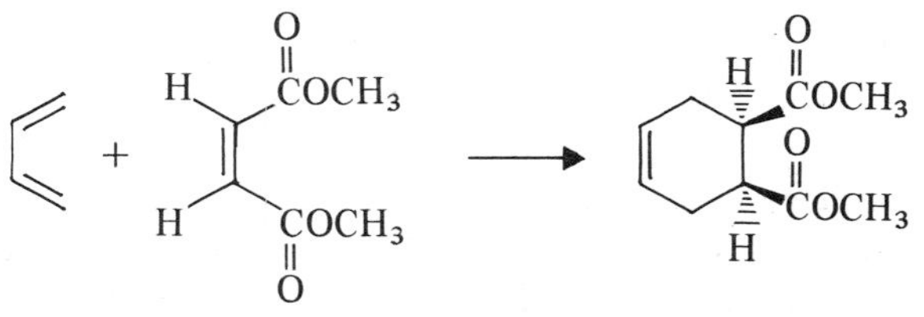

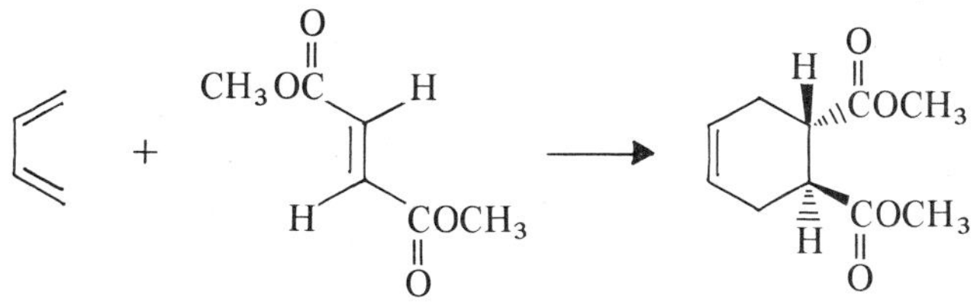

EXERCISE 32

The Theta Molecular Model Set is well suited for the assembly of many fairly complex natural products. Several interesting representative natural products structures, suitable for your model making pleasure, are shown below.

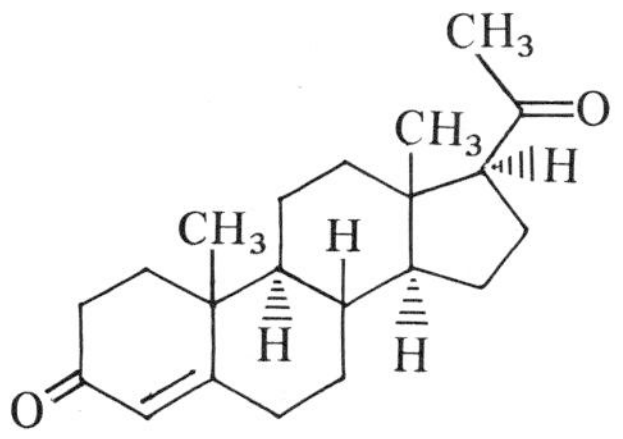

Progesterone

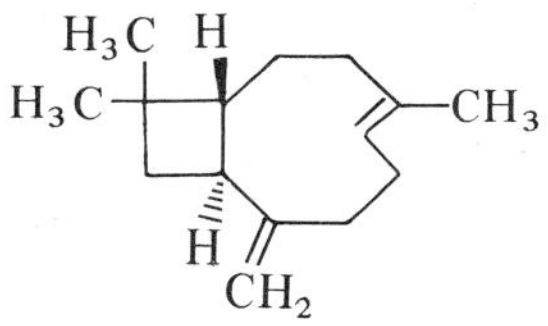

Caryophyllene

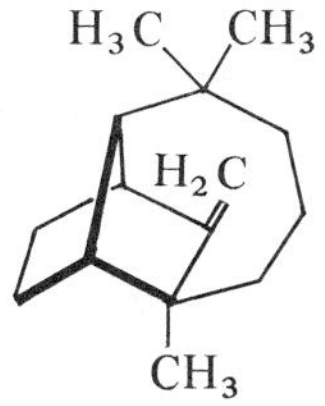

Longifolene

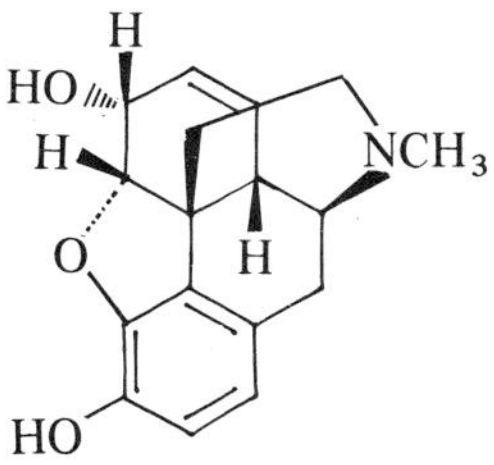

Morphine

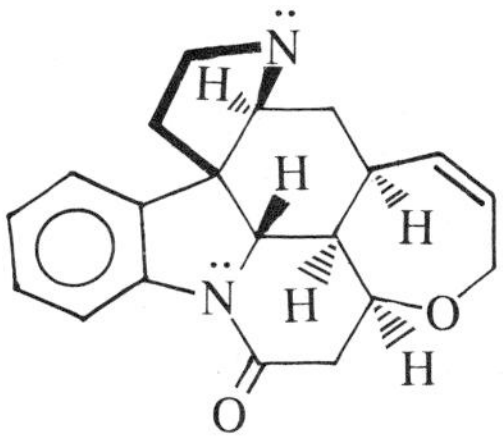

Strychnine

MOLECULAR MODEL SET EXERCISES SOLUTIONS

Solution 1   Replacement of any hydrogen of methane leads to the same monosubstituted product CH_3X. Therefore there is only one configuration of a monosubstituted methane. There is only one possible configuration for a disubstituted methane of either the CH_2X_2 or CH_2XY type.

Solution 2   Interchange of any two substituents converts the configuration of a tetrahedral chiral center to that of its enantiomer. There are only two possible configurations. If the models are not identical, they will have a mirror-image relationship.

Solution 3 The tetrahedral carbons may be rotated without breaking the carbon-carbon bond. There is no change in the carbon-carbon bond orbital overlap during rotation. The eclipsed conformation places the hydrogens closer together than they are in the staggered conformation.

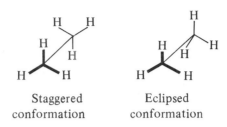

Staggered conformation

Eclipsed conformation

Solution 4 All mono substituted ethanes (CH_3CH_2X) may be rotated to an identical structure. The three energetically equivalent staggered conformations are:

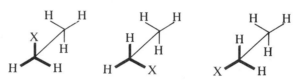

The three equivalent eclipsed conformations are:

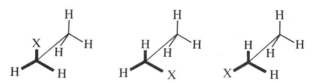

Solution 5 The two gauche conformations are energetically equivalent, but not identical (superposable) since they are conformational enantiomers. They bear a mirror-image relationship and are interconvertible by rotation about the carbon-carbon bond.

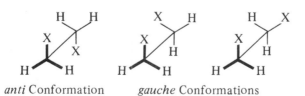

anti Conformation   *gauche* Conformations

Solution 6 There are three eclipsed conformations. The methyl groups (C–1 and C–4) are closest together in the methyl-methyl eclipsed conformation. The carbon-carbon internuclear distances between C–1 and C–4 are shown in the table below. The number of conformations of each type, the model distances, and the corresponding molecular distance in Angstroms are shown.

CONFORMATION	No.	cm	Å
eclipsed (CH_3, CH_3)	1	7.4	2.5
gauche	2	8.5	2.8
eclipsed (H, CH_3)	2	10.0	3.3
anti	1	11.0	3.7

Solution 7   The enantiomers formed from replacement of the C–2 hydrogens of butane are:

$$
\begin{array}{ccc}
CH_3 & \qquad & CH_3 \\
H\blacktriangleright C \blacktriangleleft X & & X \blacktriangleright C \blacktriangleleft H \\
CH_2CH_3 & & CH_2CH_3
\end{array}
$$

Solution 8   The extended chain assumes a staggered arrangement. The relationship of C–1 and C–4 is *anti*.

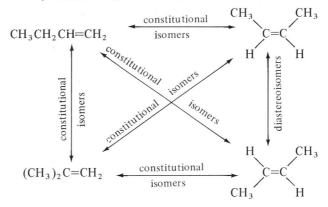

Solution 9   None of the isomeric butenes is chiral. They all have a plane of symmetry. All the isomeric butenes are related as structural (or constitutional) isomers except *cis*-2-butene and *trans*-2-butene, which are diastereomers.

Molecular Model Set C–1 to C–4 distances in centimeters:

cis-1-Butene	6.0 cm
trans-2-Butene	11.0 cm
Butane (*gauche*)	8.5 cm
Butane (*anti*)	11.0 cm

Solution 10   The hydrogens are all eclipsed in Cyclopropane.

Solution 11   All the hydrogens are eclipsed in the planar conformation of cyclobutane. The folded ring system has skew hydrogen interactions. There are six possible isomers of dimethylcyclobutane. Since the ring is not held in one particular folded conformation deviations of the ring planarity need not be considered in determining the number of possible dimethyl structures.

Solution 12   In the planar conformation of cyclopentane all five methylene pairs of hydrogens are eclipsed. That produces ten eclipsed hydrogen interactions. Some torsional strain is relieved in the envelope conformation since there are only six eclipsed hydrogen interactions.

Solution 13   The three configurational stereoisomers of 1,2-dimethylcyclopentane are shown below. Both trans stereoisomers are chiral, while the cis configuration is an achiral meso compound.

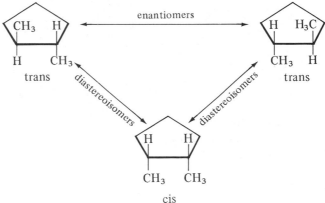

Solution 14   The puckered ring of the chair and the boat conformation may be interconverted by rotation about the carbon-carbon bonds. The chair is more rigid than the boat conformation. All hydrogen atoms in the chair conformation have a staggered arrangement. In the boat conformation there are eclipsed relationships between the hydrogens on C−2 and C−3, and also between those on C−5 and C−6. Carbons that are 1,4 to each other in the chair conformation have a *gauche* relationship. An evaluation of the three conformations confirms the relative stability: chair > twist > boat. The boat conformation has considerable eclipsing strain and nonbonded (van der Waals repulsion) interactions, the twist conformation has slight eclipsing strain, and the chair conformation has a minimum of eclipsing and nonbonded interactions.

Solution 15   Interconversion of the two chair conformations of methylcyclohexane changes the methyl group from an axial to a less crowded equatorial orientation, or the methyl that is equatorial to the more crowded axial position.

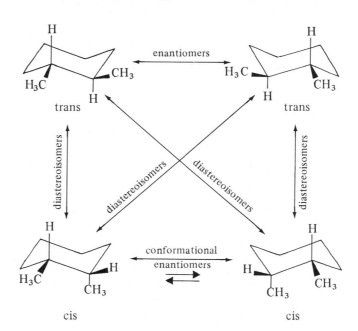

Axial methyl   Equatorial methyl

The conformation with the axial methyl group has two *gauche* (1,3-diaxial) interactions that are not present in the equatorial methyl conformation. These *gauche* interactions are methyl to C−3, and methyl to C−5. The methyl, C−3 and methyl, C−5 relationships with the methyl equatorial is *anti*. Based on two additional *gauche* interactions you would predict the equatorial methyl conformation to be 1.6 kcal/mole (2 × 0.8) more stable.

Solution 16   The $\Delta H°$ value reflects the relative energies of the two chair conformations for each structure. The crowding of the alkyl group in an axial orientation becomes greater as the bulk of the group increases. The increased size of the substituent has little effect on the steric interactions of the conformation that has the alkyl group equatorial. The *gauche* (1,3-diaxial) interactions are responsible for the increased strain for the axial conformation. Since the ethyl and isopropyl groups can rotate to minimize the nonbonded interactions their effective size is less than their actual size. The *t*-butyl group cannot relieve the steric interactions by rotation and thus has a considerably greater difference in potential energy between the axial and equatorial conformation.

Solution 17   All four stereoisomers of 1,2-dimethylcyclohexane are chiral. The *cis*-1,2-dimethylcyclohexane conformations have equal energy and are readily interconverted, as shown below.

Solution 18   The structures that are isoelectronic have the same geometry. Isoelectronic structures are:

$$CH_3CH_3 \qquad \text{and} \qquad CH_3NH_3{}^+$$

$$CH_3NH_2, \qquad CH_3CH_2{}^-, \qquad \text{and} \qquad CH_3OH_2{}^+$$

Structure CH_3NH^- would be isoelectronic to CH_3OH.

Solution 19   Cis-trans stereoisomers are possible only for 3,4-dimethylcyclohexene. The ring size and geometry of the double bond prohibit a trans configuration of the double bond. Two configurational isomers (they are enantiomers) are possible for 2,3-dimethylhexene.

cis-Cyclooctene is more stable because it has less strain than the *trans*-cyclooctene structure. The relative stability of cycloalkene stereoisomers in rings larger than cyclodecane generally favors trans. *trans*-Cyclooctene structure is chiral.

trans-Cyclooctene
(one enantiomer)

Solution 20   The ring fusion in *trans*-decalin is equatorial, equatorial. That is, one ring is attached to the other as 1,2-diequatorial substituents would be. Interconversion of the chair conformations of one ring (carbons 1 thru 6) in *trans*-decalin would require the other ring to adopt a 1,2-diaxial orientation. Carbons 7 and 10 would both become axial substituents to the other ring. The four carbons of the "substituent" ring (carbons 7 thru 10) cannot bridge the diaxial distance. In *cis*-decalin both conformations have an axial, equatorial ring fusion. Four carbons can easily bridge the axial, equatorial distance.

Solution 21   The cyclohexane ring in norbornane is held in a boat conformation, and therefore has four hydrogen eclipsing interactions. All the six-membered ring systems in twistane are in twist conformations. All four of the six-membered ring systems in adamantane are chair conformations.

Solution 22   Bridging the 1 and 4 carbons of cyclohexane is relatively easy since in the boat conformation the flagpole hydrogens (on C–1 and C–4) are fairly close and their C–H bonds are directed toward one another. With cyclohexene the geometry of the double bond and its inability to rotate freely, make it impossible to bridge the C–1, C–4 distance with a single methylene group. Note however, that a cyclohexene ring can accommodate a methylene bridge between C–3 and C–6. This bridged bicyclic system (bicyclo [2.2.1] hept-2-ene) does not have a bridgehead double bond.

Bicyclo[2.2.1]hept-2-ene

Solution 23 The 120° geometry of the double bond is ideal for incorporation into a planar six membered ring, as the internal angle of a regular hexagon is 120°. Cyclooctatetraene can not adopt a planar ring system without considerable angle strain. The eight-membered ring adopts a "tub" conformation that minimizes angle strain and does not allow significant p-orbital overlap other than that of the four double bonds in the system. The cyclooctatetraene thus has four isolated double bonds and is not a delocalized π-electron system.

Cyclooctatetraene (tub conformation)

Solution 24 In the $CH_3CHXCHYCH_3$ system there are four stereoisomers, all of which are chiral.

In the $CH_3CHXCHXCH_3$ system there are three stereoisomers, two of which are chiral. The third stereoisomer (**G** on the next page) is an achiral meso structure.

$$
\begin{array}{ccc}
& CH_3 & \\
X & \!\!-\!\! C \!\!-\!\! H & \\
H & \!\!-\!\! C \!\!-\!\! X & \\
& CH_3 & \\
& \mathbf{E} &
\end{array}
\qquad\xleftrightarrow{\ \text{enantiomers}\ }\qquad
\begin{array}{ccc}
& CH_3 & \\
H & \!\!-\!\! C \!\!-\!\! X & \\
X & \!\!-\!\! C \!\!-\!\! H & \\
& CH_3 & \\
& \mathbf{F} &
\end{array}
$$

diastereoisomers   *diastereoisomers*

$$
\begin{array}{c}
CH_3 \\
H\!\!-\!\!C\!\!-\!\!X \\
H\!\!-\!\!C\!\!-\!\!X \\
CH_3 \\
\mathbf{G}
\end{array}
$$

Solution 25   Structures B and C are chiral. Structure A has a plane of symmetry and is therefore achiral. Compounds D and E are both chiral. The relative orientation of the terminal groups in D and E is perpendicular as is the case in the cumulated dienes.

Cumulated triene F is achiral. It has a plane of symmetry passing thru all six carbon atoms. Structure F has a trans configuration. The cis diastereomer is the only other possible stereoisomer.

Solution 26   Structure J can be isolated as a chiral stereoisomer because of the large steric barrier to rotation about the bond connecting the rings. Biphenyl K has a plane of symmetry and is therefore achiral. The symmetry plane of K is shown below. Compound L has a low energy barrier to rotation and thus would not be optically active. Any chiral conformation of L can easily be converted to its enantiomer by rotation. It is only when a ≠ b and f ≠ e and rotation is restricted by bulky groups that chiral (optically active) stereoisomers can be isolated.

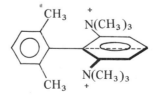

A plane of symmetry

Solution 27   The smallest ring stable cycloalkyne is the nine membered ring cyclononyne. A model of this alkyne can easily be assembled with the Theta Molecular Model Set.

Solution 28   As shown below, the alternative chair conformation of β-D-glucopyranose has all large substituents in an axial orientation. The structures α-D-glucopyranose, β-D-mannopyranose, β-D-galactopyranose all have one large axial substituent in the most favorable conformation. β-L-Glucopyranose is the enantiomer (mirror-image) of β-D-glucopyranose. Enantiomers are of equal thermodynamic stability.

β-D-Glucopyranose

α-D-Glucopyranose

β-D-Galactopyranose

β-D-Mannopyranose

β-L-Glucopyranose

Solution 29   The peptide chain bonds not free to rotate are indicated by the bold lines in the structures shown below. The transoid arrangement produces a more linear tripeptide chain. The length of the tripeptide chain does not change if you change the substituent R groups.

Solution 30   The models of the π molecular orbitals for Ethene are shown below. A diagram of these orbitals can be found in the text on page 221.

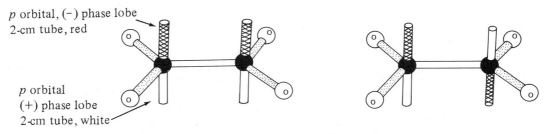

p orbital, (−) phase lobe
2-cm tube, red

p orbital
(+) phase lobe
2-cm tube, white

Ethene, π bonding molecular orbital   Ethene, π* antibonding molecular orbital

The π molecular orbitals for 1,3-butadiene are shown in the text on page 406. A model of one of the π molecular orbitals of 1,3-butadiene is shown in the model set instruction booklet. The phases of the contributing atomic orbitals to the molecular orbitals of the allyl radical can be found in the text on page 399. The π molecular orbital of the allyl radical has a node at C—2. This can be illustrated with the Theta Molecular Model Set by not placing red or white p-orbital tubes on the C—2 atom center prongs. The absence of tubes indicates an orbital phase of zero.

Solution 31   The complete solution to this exercise is given in the text pages 1082–1085 and 1095. The orbitals involved are shown below.

A.

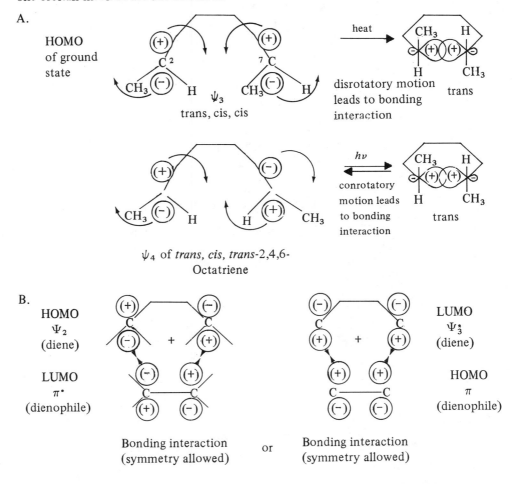

HOMO
of ground
state

ψ_3
trans, cis, cis

heat

disrotatory motion
leads to bonding
interaction

trans

ψ_4 of *trans, cis, trans*-2,4,6-
Octatriene

$h\nu$

conrotatory
motion leads
to bonding
interaction

trans

B.

HOMO
Ψ_2
(diene)

LUMO
π^*
(dienophile)

+

Bonding interaction
(symmetry allowed)

or

+

Bonding interaction
(symmetry allowed)

LUMO
Ψ_3^*
(diene)

HOMO
π
(dienophile)

APPENDIX
Glossary of Important Terms

Acidity Constant (K_a). The acidity constant is a measure of the strength of an acid in water. For the acid HA, the equilibrium is

$$HA + H_2O \rightleftharpoons H_3O^+ + A^-$$

and $K_a = \dfrac{[H_3O^+]\ [A^-]}{[HA]}$

Therefore, the larger K_a is, the stronger the acid is. (Section 2.15B).

Addition Reaction. A reaction in which the product molecule contains all the atoms that were present in the reactant molecules (Section 2.8).
    Example:

$$\underset{\displaystyle }{\text{H–C=C–H}} + \text{Br–Br} \longrightarrow \text{H–C—C–H}$$

Aliphatic Hydrocarbon. A hydrocarbon such as an alkane, alkene, alkyne, cycloalkane, cycloalkene; that is, all hydrocarbons that are not aromatic. (Section 11.1).

Alkyl Group. The molecular fragment that remains when a hydrogen atom is removed from a hydrocarbon (Section 2.8A).
    Example:

Hydrocarbon   Alkyl group

Allylic Hydrogen. A hydrogen on a carbon atom that is adjacent to a C=C double bond (Section 10.2).

Allylic Substitution. Substitution of an allylic hydrogen or group by another atom or group (Section 10.2).

Annulene. A monocyclic compound that can be represented by a structure having alternating single and double bonds. For example, cyclobutadiene is [4] annulene and benzene is [6] annulene (Section 11.6A)

Anti **Addition.** See *Syn* and *Anti* **Addition.**

Antibonding Molecular Orbital. The molecular orbital formed when atomic orbitals of opposite phase sign overlap. The electron probability density of the region between the nuclei is small and it contains a node (Sections 1.15 and 1.19).

Aprotic Solvents. Solvents which lack an −H bonded to a strongly electronegative element. Common aprotic solvents are: acetone, $CH_3\overset{\overset{O}{\|}}{C}CH_3$; acetonitrile $CH_3C\equiv N$; sulfur dioxide, SO_2; dimethylsulfoxide, CH_3SOCH_3; and trimethylamine, $N(CH_3)_3$. (Section 5.11C).

Aromatic Compound. Certain cyclic conjugated compounds. Aromatic compounds have a stability significantly greater than that of a hypothetical resonance structure (e.g., a Kekulé structure). Many aromatic compounds react with electrophilic reagents (Br_2, HNO_3, H_2SO_4) by substitution rather than addition even though they are unsaturated. A modern definition of any aromatic compound compares the energy of the π electrons of the cyclic conjugated molecule or ion with that of its open chain counterpart. If on ring closure the π electron energy *decreases* the molecule is classified as being **aromatic**, if it *increases*, the molecule is classified as being **antiaromatic** and if it remains the same the molecule is classified as being **nonaromatic.** (Section 11.6C)

Atomic Orbital. A region in space where the probability of finding an electron is large. Common atomic orbitals are designated *s, p, d*, etc. (Section 1.14, 1.19).

Aufbau Principle. Orbitals are filled so that those of lowest energy are filled first (Section 1.14).

Axial Group. A group that is attached to a carbon of cyclohexane and that is oriented in a direction that is generally perpendicular to the average plane of the ring (Section 3.12).

Benzenoid. An aromatic compound whose molecules contain benzene rings or fused benzene rings. Examples are benzene, naphthalene, anthracene, and phenanthrene (Section 11.7A).

Boat Conformation. The conformation of cyclohexane (below) in which there is torsional strain but no angle strain:

 (Section 3.10).

Bonding Molecular Orbital. The molecular orbital formed when atomic orbitals with the same phase sign interact. The electron probability density of a bonding molecular orbital is large in the region of space between the two nuclei. (Section 1.15, 1.19).

Bond-Line Formula. Formula that shows only the carbon skeleton. The number of hydrogen atoms necessary to fulfill the carbon atoms' valences are assumed to be present, but we do not write them in. Other atoms are written in (Section 1.12).

Example: $CH_3CHClCH_2CH_3$ is written

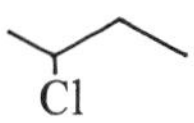

Branched Alkane. Alkane in which at least one carbon atom is bonded to three or four other carbon atoms (Section 3.2).

Brønsted-Lowry Acid-Base Theory. An acid is a substance that can donate a proton. A base is a substance that can accept a proton (Section 2.14A).

Chain Reactions. Reactions whose mechanisms involve a series of steps with each step producing a reactive intermediate that causes the next step to occur. The halogenation of an alkane is a chain reaction (Section 4.5).

Chair Conformation. The most stable conformation of cyclohexane:

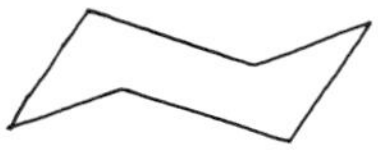

(Section 3.10).

Chirality. Equivalent to "handedness." A chiral molecule is one that is not superposable on its mirror reflection. An *achiral* molecule is one that can be superposed on its mirror reflection. A *chiral carbon* (also called an *asymmetric carbon* or a *chiral center*) is any carbon atom that has four different groups attached to it. A pair of enantiomers will be possible for all molecules that contain *a single* chiral carbon. For molecules with more than one chiral carbon, the number of stereoisomers will not exceed 2^n where n is the number of chiral carbons (Section 8.3).

Circle-and-Line Formula. Three-dimensional formula in which carbon atoms are shown by circles (Section 1.12A).

Example:

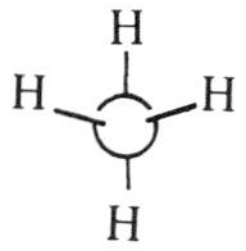

Cis-Trans Isomers. Isomers that differ only in the orientation in space of groups attached to doubly bonded atoms (Section 2.5E) or to rings (Section 3.13).

Example:

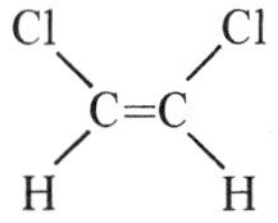

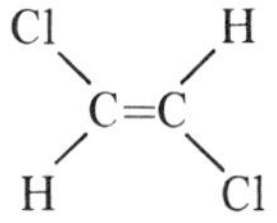

Cis-trans isomerism results because rotation about a carbon-carbon double bond or in a ring is restricted.

Classification of alkadienes. **Cumulated double bonds** are double bonds that share a carbon atom: $C=C=C$. **Conjugated double bonds** are double bonds that are separated by a single bond: $C=C-C=C$.

Isolated double bonds are double bonds that are separated by at least one saturated carbon atom: $C=C-\overset{|}{\underset{|}{C}}-C=C$ (Section 10.5).

Collision Theory. For a chemical reaction to take place, the reacting particles must collide. The rate of a reaction is given by the equation

$$\text{Reaction rate} = Z \times P \times f$$

where Z is the frequency of collision between reacting molecules, P is the probability that the colliding molecules are oriented in a way that allows reaction to take place, and f is the fraction of collisions in which the collision energy is greater than the energy of activation.

In terms of the concentrations of reactants A and B,

$$\text{Reaction rate} = k\,[A]\,[B]$$

where k is a proportionality constant called the rate constant (Section 4.8).

Condensed Formula. A formula in which the atoms that are attached to a particular carbon atom are written immediately after that atom (Section 1.12).
Example: $CH_3CHClCH_2CH_3$

Configuration. The particular arrangement of atoms (or groups) in space that is characteristic of a given stereoisomer. The configuration at each chiral carbon can be designated as *R* or *S* using the rules given in Section 8.5 (Section 8.3).

Conformational Analysis. Analysis of the energy changes that a molecule undergoes as groups rotate about single bonds (Section 2.3).

Conjugated Unsaturated System. A system that has a *p* orbital on an atom adjacent to a double bond—a molecule with delocalized π-bonds. (Section 10.6).

Covalent Bond. A bond that results when atoms share electrons (Sections 1.6 and 1.6A).

Cracking. A process for converting hydrocarbons into other hydrocarbons by heating (thermal cracking) or by heating in the presence of a catalyst (catalytic cracking) (Section 3.15B).

Cycloalkane. Alkanes in which some of the carbon atoms are arranged in a ring (Section 3.1).

Dash Formula. The structural formula in which bonding electron pairs are represented by dashes (Section 1.12).

Example: $H-\overset{\displaystyle H}{\underset{\displaystyle H}{\overset{|}{\underset{|}{C}}}}-H$

Dash-Line-Wedge Formula. Atoms that project out of the plane of the paper are connected by a wedge (➤), those that lie behind the plane are connected with a dash (⫶⫶),

and those atoms in the plane of the paper are connected by a line (Section 1.12E).
   Example:

$$H-\underset{\underset{H}{|}}{\overset{\overset{H}{|}}{C}}\cdots H$$

Debromination.   Elimination of Br_2 from a *vic*-dihalide (Section 6.13).

Dehydration.   Elimination of H_2O from an alcohol (Section 6.10).

Dehydrogenation.   Elimination of H_2 from a molecule (Sections 6.14 and 15.8A).

Dehydrohalogenation.   Elimination of HX (X = Cl, Br, I) from an alkyl halide (Section 6.9).

Diastereomers are stereoisomers that are not enantiomers, that is, they are stereoisomers that are *not* related as an object and its mirror reflection (Section 8.2).

Dielectric Constant.   A measure of the polarity of a solvent. Also described as a measure of the ability of a solvent to insulate charges from each other (Section 5.11).

Dimerization.   The combination of two identical molecules (Section 7.6).

Dipolar Ion.   When a molecule contains both a basic group ($-NH_2$) and an acidic group ($-COOH$), both groups exist primarily in the ionic form; i.e., $-NH_3^+$ and $-COO^-$. Such an ion is called a dipolar ion or **zwitterion** (Section 23.2C)

Dipole-Dipole Forces.   Weakly attractive forces between molecules that possess permanent dipole moments (Section 2.16B).

Dipole Moment.   The product of the magnitude of the charge in electrostatic units and the distance that separates them in centimeter units (Section 1.9).

E1 Reaction.   A unimolecular elimination. The first step of an E1 reaction, formation of a carbocation, is the same as that of an S_N1 reaction, consequently E1 and S_N1 reactions compete with each other. E1 reactions are important when tertiary halides are subjected to solvolysis in polar solvents especially at higher temperatures. The steps in the E1 reaction of *tert*-butyl chloride (section 5.15) are

$$1.\ CH_3-\underset{\underset{CH_3}{|}}{\overset{\overset{CH_3}{|}}{C}}-Cl \xrightarrow{Slow} CH_3-\underset{\underset{CH_3}{|}}{\overset{\overset{CH_3}{|}}{C^+}} + :Cl^-$$

$$2.\ Sol-\overset{..}{O}H + H-CH_2-\underset{\underset{CH_3}{|}}{\overset{\overset{CH_3}{|}}{C^+}} \longrightarrow CH_2=C\overset{CH_3}{\underset{CH_3}{}} + Sol-\overset{+}{O}H_2$$

E2 Reaction.   A bimolecular elimination that often competes with S_N2 reactions. E2 reactions are favored by the use of a high concentration of a strong, bulky, and slightly polarizable base. The order of reactivity of alkyl halides toward E2 reactions is: $3° \gg 2° > 1°$. The mechanism of the E2 reaction (Section 5.14) involves a single step:

$$B: + -\overset{H}{\underset{X}{\overset{|}{C}}}\overset{|}{\underset{|}{C}}- \longrightarrow B-H + \overset{\diagdown}{\underset{\diagup}{C}}=\overset{\diagup}{\underset{\diagdown}{C}} + :X^-$$

Electrical Effect (or **Electronic Effect**). An effect on relative reaction rates when some molecular feature stabilizes the electrical charge on a transition state or an intermediate. The electron-releasing ability of methyl groups stabilizes the transition state and the carbocation formed by ionization of a 3° alkyl halide in the slow step of an S_N1 reaction, for example (Section 5.11).

Electronegativity. The ability of an atom to attract electrons that it is sharing in a covalent bond (Section 1.9).

1,2-Elimination reaction or a **β-Elimination.** A reaction in which the pieces of some molecule are eliminated from adjacent atoms of the reactant leading to the introduction of a multiple bond. Dehydrohalogenation is an elimination reaction in which HX is eliminated from an alkyl halide, leading to the formation of an alkene (Section 5.13).

$$-\overset{H}{\underset{X}{\overset{|}{C}}}\overset{|}{\underset{|}{C}}- + :B^- \longrightarrow \overset{\diagdown}{\underset{\diagup}{C}}=\overset{\diagup}{\underset{\diagdown}{C}} + H:B + :X^-$$

Enantiomers. Enantiomers are stereoisomers that are related as an object and its mirror reflection. Enantiomers only occur with compounds whose molecules are chiral, that is, with molecules that are *not* superposable on their mirror reflections. Separate enantiomers rotate the plane of polarized light and are said to be *optically active.* They have equal but opposite specific rotations (Sections 8.2, 8.3, 8.4, 8.6).

Energy of Activation. The minimum amount of energy (on a molar basis) that must be provided for a reaction to take place. It is the potential energy difference between the reactants and the transition state (Section 4.8D).

Epimers. Isomers that have more than one chiral center and that differ in the configuration of only one of the chiral centers (Section 21.6).

Equatorial Group. A group that is attached to a carbon of cyclohexane and that is oriented in a direction that is generally in the average plane of the ring (Section 3.12).

Formal Charge. Calculated by taking the group number of that atom (from the periodic table) and subtracting the number of electrons associated with it using the formula (Section 1.7A),

Formal Charge = group number − [½ (number of shared electrons)
+ (number of unshared electrons)] .

Free Radicals (also called **Carbon Radicals**). Free radicals are formed by homolysis of a bond to a carbon atom. Carbon radicals have unpaired electrons and show the following order of stabilities (Section 4.1A):

$$\underset{\underset{\displaystyle 3^\circ}{\overset{\displaystyle C}{\underset{|}{C}}}{\overset{C}{\underset{|}{\overset{|}{C}}}}-\overset{\displaystyle \cdot}{C}\cdot \; > \; \underset{\underset{\displaystyle 2^\circ}{\overset{\displaystyle H}{\underset{|}{H}}}{\overset{C}{\underset{|}{\overset{|}{C}}}}-\overset{\displaystyle \cdot}{C}\cdot \; > \; \underset{\underset{\displaystyle 1^\circ}{\overset{\displaystyle H}{\underset{|}{H}}}{\overset{H}{\underset{|}{\overset{|}{C}}}}-\overset{\displaystyle \cdot}{C}\cdot \; > \; \underset{\underset{\displaystyle \text{Methyl}}{\overset{\displaystyle H}{\underset{|}{H}}}{\overset{H}{\underset{|}{\overset{|}{H}}}}-\overset{\displaystyle \cdot}{C}\cdot$$

Functional Group. A grouping of atoms that effectively determines the properties of the compound (Section 2.8).

Halogenations of Alkanes. Substitution reactions in which a halogen replaces one (or more) of the alkane's hydrogens (Section 4.4A).

$$RH + X_2 \longrightarrow RX + HX$$

The reactions occur by a free-radical mechanism (Section 4.5).

1. $\qquad X_2 \longrightarrow 2X\cdot$
2. $RH + X\cdot \longrightarrow R\cdot + HX$
3. $R\cdot + X_2 \longrightarrow RX + X\cdot$

Hammond's Postulate. A postulate which holds that the structure of the transition state of an endothermic step of a reaction resembles the products of that step more than it does the reactants. Conversely, the structure of the transition state of an exothermic step is more like the reactants than the products (Section 4.10A).

Heat of Combustion. The heat evolved on complete combustion of one mole of a substance at 25°C and 1 atm pressure. This heat, called ΔH°, is negative for exothermic reactions and positive for endothermic reactions (Section 2.4A).

Heat of Hydrogenation. The heat of reaction (ΔH°) for the addition of H_2 to one mole of a compound (Section 6.6A).

Heat of Reaction. The enthalpy change (ΔH°) for a chemical reaction equal to $H^\circ_{products} - H^\circ_{reactants}$. For an exothermic reaction ΔH° is negative; for an endothermic reaction ΔH° is positive (Section 4.6).

Heterocyclic Compound. A compound whose molecules have a ring containing an element other than carbon (Section 11.9).

Heterolysis. Cleavage of a covalent bond that leads to ions, i.e., $A{:}B \longrightarrow A^+ + {:}B^-$ (Sect. 4.1A).

Homolysis. Cleavage of a covalent bond that leads to radicals, i.e., $A{:}B \longrightarrow A\cdot + B\cdot$ (Section 4.1A).

Hückel's Rule. A rule that states that planar monocyclic conjugated rings with ($4n + 2$)-π electrons (*i.e.,* with 2, 6, 10, 14, 18, or 22 π electrons) should be aromatic. Hückel's rule has an upper limit. Systems with more than 22 π electrons are not aromatic. (Section 11.6).

Hund's Rule. When we fill orbitals of equal energy (degenerate orbitals) such as the three $2p$ orbitals, we add one electron to each orbital with their spins unpaired until each of the degenerate orbitals contains one electron. Then we begin adding a second electron to each degenerate orbital so that the spins are paired (Section 1.14).

Hybrid Orbitals. Orbitals such as sp^3, sp^2, and sp orbitals that are formed by mixing (hybridizing) the wave functions for orbitals of a different type (i.e., s orbitals and p orbitals) but from the same atom. (Section 1.16 and 1.19).

Hydrocarbon. A compound whose molecules contain only carbon and hydrogen (Section 2.2).

Hydrogenation. Chemical addition of H_2 to an unsaturated compound (Section 3.16).

Hydrogen Bond. The relatively strong dipole-dipole attraction that occurs between a hydrogen that is bonded to a strongly electronegative atom and the nonbonding electron pairs on another electronegative atom (Section 2.17D).

$$X-H \cdots : Y \qquad \text{(X and Y are strongly electronegative usually, O, N, or halogen)}$$

Index of Hydrogen Deficiency. The number of pairs of hydrogen atoms that must be subtracted from the molecular formula of the corresponding alkane to give the molecular formula of the compound under consideration (Section 6.5).

   Example: the index of hydrogen deficiency of C_5H_8 is *two* because it contains two pairs of hydrogen atoms less than the corresponding alkane, C_5H_{12}.

Ionic (or Electrovalent) Bond. A force of attraction between oppositely charged ions formed by the transfer of one or more electrons from one atom to another (Section 1.6 and 1.6A).

Isomers are different compounds that have the same molecular formula. All isomers fall into either of two groups: *structural* isomers or *stereoisomers* (Section 8.2).

Subdivision of Isomers:

ISOMERS
(Different compounds with
same molecular formula)

Structural isomers
or
Constitutional isomers
(Isomers that have their atoms
attached in a different order)

Stereoisomers
(Isomers that differ *only* in the
arrangement of their atoms in space)

Enantiomers
(Stereoisomers that are mirror
reflections of each other)

Diastereomers
(Stereoisomers that are not
mirror reflections of each other)

Leaving Group. The group that is displaced by a nucleophile in a substitution reaction (Section 5.5B).

Lewis Acid-Base Theory. An acid is an electron-pair acceptor. A base is an electron-pair donor (Section 2.16).

Markovnikov's Rule. In the addition of HX to an alkene, the hydrogen adds to the carbon of the double bond with the greater number of hydrogens (Section 7.2).

   Example: $CH_2=CHCH_3 \longrightarrow CH_3CHCH_3$
           $H-Cl$ Cl

Markovnikov's rule may be stated in mechanistic terms: In the ionic addition of an unsymmetrical reagent to a double bond, the positive portion of the adding reagent attaches itself to a carbon atom of the double bond so as to yield the more stable carbocation (Section 7.2B).

   The H^+ ion adds as it does because the carbocation $CH_3\overset{+}{C}HCH_3$ is secondary and is therefore more stable than $\overset{+}{C}H_2CH_2CH_2$ ($1°$) which would be formed if H^+ added to the central carbon atom.

Meso Compound. An optically inactive compound whose molecules are achiral even though they contain chiral carbons (Section 8.9A).

Meta. A prefix used to designate 1,3-disubstituted benzenes (Section 11.8).

Molecular Formula. The formula that shows only the number of each kind of atom in the molecule (Section 1.2B).
   Example: $C_2H_4O_2$.

Molecular Orbitals. Orbitals formed by the combination of atomic orbitals on different bonding atoms. Molecular orbitals encompass all the bonded nuclei (Section 1.15, 1.19).

Molecular Rearrangement. A rearrangement of the carbon skeleton during certain chemical reactions. Such rearrangements occur most commonly in reactions that involve carbocation intermediates (Sections 6.10, 6.12).

Node. The region in space where the probability of finding an electron is zero (Section 1.14)

Nonbenzenoid Aromatic Compounds. Compounds which have a ring that is not six-membered. Examples are [14]annulene, azulene, the cyclopentadienyl anion, and the cycloheptatrienyl cation (Section 11.7B).

Nucleophile. A molecule or negative ion that has an unshared pair of electrons. In a chemical reaction a nucleophile attacks a positive center of some other molecule or ion (Section 5.5A).

Nucleophilic Substitution Reaction (abbreviated as S_N reaction). A substitution reaction brought about when a nucleophile reacts with a *substrate* that bears a *leaving group* (Section 5.5).

Order of Alkene Stability. The stability of an alkene depends on the number of alkyl groups bonded to the $\diagdown C=C\diagup$ group (Section 6.6).
Relative stabilities:

$$
\begin{matrix} R \\ R \end{matrix}\!\!C=C\!\!\begin{matrix} R \\ R \end{matrix} \; > \; \begin{matrix} R \\ R \end{matrix}\!\!C=C\!\!\begin{matrix} R \\ H \end{matrix} \; > \; \begin{matrix} R \\ R \end{matrix}\!\!C=C\!\!\begin{matrix} H \\ H \end{matrix} \; > \; \begin{matrix} R \\ H \end{matrix}\!\!C=C\!\!\begin{matrix} H \\ R \end{matrix} \; >
$$

$$\overset{R}{\underset{H}{}}C=C\overset{R}{\underset{H}{}} \quad > \quad \overset{R}{\underset{H}{}}C=C\overset{H}{\underset{H}{}} \quad > \quad \overset{H}{\underset{H}{}}C=C\overset{H}{\underset{H}{}}$$

Ortho. A prefix used to designate 1,2-disubstituted benzenes (Section 11.8).

Para. A prefix used to designate 1,4-disubstituted benzenes (Section 11.8).

Pauli Exclusion Principle. A maximum of two electrons may be placed in each orbital but only when the spins of the electrons are paired (Section 1.14).

Peptide Linkage. The amide linkages ($-\overset{\overset{\displaystyle O}{\|}}{C}-NH-$) that join α-amino acid residues in proteins (Section 23.5).

Plane of Symmetry. An imaginary plane that bisects a molecule in such a way that the two halves of the molecule are mirror reflections of each other. Any molecule that has a plane of symmetry will be achiral (Section 8.4).

Polar Covalent Bond. A covalent bond between two atoms of unequal electronegativity in which the atom with greater electronegativity draws the electron pair closer to it (Section 1.9).

Polarizability. The ability of electrons in an atom to respond to a changing electric field (Section 2.16B).

Protic Solvents. Solvents that have an $-H$ bonded to an oxygen or nitrogen (or to another strongly electronegative atom). Common protic solvents are: Formic acid, $H\overset{\overset{\displaystyle O}{\|}}{C}OH$; formamide $H\overset{\overset{\displaystyle O}{\|}}{C}NH_2$; water, H_2O; alcohols, ROH; ammonia, NH_3, and ethylene glycol, $HOCH_2CH_2OH$ (Section 5.11C).

Racemic Modification or Racemate. An equimolar mixture of enantiomers (Section 8.7A).

Reaction Mechanism. A description of how a chemical reaction takes place. If the mechanism is multistep, it includes the steps involved and the *intermediates* that form (Section 4.1).

Reaction Rate. The rate at which reactants are converted to products in a chemical reaction. The rate of a reaction can be determined experimentally by measuring the rate at which reactants disappear from the mixture or the rate products form in the mixture (Section 4.8).

Regioselective Reaction. A reaction that yields only one (or a predominance of one) structural isomer when more than one structural isomer can potentially be produced (Section 7.3).

Resolution. The separation of the enantiomers of a racemic modification (Section 8.14).

Resonance Energy of an aromatic compound (sometimes called the **stabilization energy** or **delocalization** energy) is the difference in energy between the actual aromatic compound and that calculated for one of the hypothetical resonance structures, *e.g.* a Kekule structure) (Section 11.4).

Resonance Theory. Whenever a molecule or ion can be represented by two or more Lewis structures that differ only in the positions of the electrons, (a) none of these structures (called resonance structures) is satisfactory, and (b) the actual molecule or ion will be best represented by a hybrid of these structures (Section 1.8).

Ring Strain. The relative instability of three- and four-membered rings due to bond angle strain and torsional strain (Sections 3.7, 3.8). (In larger rings ring strain may also arise from van der Waals repulsions across rings.)

Saturated Compound. A compound whose molecules contain only single bonds (Section 2.2).

S_N1 Reaction. A nucleophilic substitution reaction for which the rate-limiting step is *unimolecular*. The hydrolysis of *tert*-butyl chloride is an S_N1 reaction that takes place in three steps as follows. The rate-limiting step is step (1).

$$1.\ (CH_3)_3CCl \xrightarrow{\text{slow}} (CH_3)_3C^+ + Cl^-$$

$$2.\ (CH_3)_3C^+ + H_2O: \xrightarrow{\text{fast}} (CH_3)_3COH_2^+$$

$$3.\ (CH_3)_3COH_2^+ + H_2O \xrightarrow{\text{fast}} (CH_3)_3COH + H_3O^+$$

S_N1 reactions are important with tertiary halides and with other substrates (benzylic and allylic) that can form relatively stable carbocations (Sections 5.7B, 5.10, 14.2).

S_N2 Reaction. A nucleophilic substitution reaction for which the rate-limiting step is *bimolecular* (i.e., the transition state involves two species). The reaction of methyl chloride with hydroxide ion is an S_N2 reaction. According to the Ingold mechanism it takes place in a *single step* as follows (Sections 5.9, 5.10 and 5.11A).

$$HO:^- + CH_3-Cl \longrightarrow \underset{\substack{H\quad H}}{\overset{\overset{\textstyle H}{|}}{HO\cdots\overset{\delta-}{\underset{}{C}}\cdots\overset{\delta-}{Cl}}} \longrightarrow HO-CH_3 + :Cl^-$$

Transition state

The order of reactivity of alkyl halides in S_N2 reactions is:

$$CH_3-X > RCH_2X > R_2CHX$$

Methyl   1°   2°

Solvolysis. A nucleophilic substitution reaction in which the nucleophile is a molecule of the solvent (Section 5.10B).

Stereochemistry. Chemical studies that take into account the three-dimensional aspects of molecules (Section 8.2).

Stereoisomers. Stereoisomers have their atoms joined in the same order but differ in the way their atoms are arranged in space. Stereoisomers can be subdivided into two categories: *enantiomers* and *diastereomers* (Section 8.2).

Stereoselective Reaction. One that yields exclusively (or predominantly) one of a set of stereoisomers (Section 8.8A).

Stereospecific Reaction. One in which stereoisomerically different reactants give stereoisomerically different products. That is, a reaction in which a given stereoisomeric form of the reactant is converted to a specific stereoisomeric form of product (Section 8.10).

Steric Effect. An effect on relative reaction rates caused by the space-filling properties of those parts of a molecule attached at or near the reacting site. *Steric hindrance* is an important steric effect in S_N2 reactions. It explains why methyl halides are most reactive and tertiary halides are least reactive (Section 5.11).

Structural Isomers (also called **Constitutional Isomers**). Isomers that have their atoms joined in a different order (Section 1.4 and 8.2).

Substitution Reaction. A reaction in which one group replaces another (Section 4.4).

Syn and Anti Addition. Addition of both parts of the adding reagent to the same face of the molecule (*syn* addition), or one part to each of opposite faces (*anti* addition) (Section 6.14A).

Torsional Strain. The energy barrier to rotation about a single bond from one staggered conformation past an eclipsed conformation to another staggered conformation (Section 2.3 and 3.6A).

Unbranched Alkane. Alkane in which each carbon atom is bonded to no more than two other carbon atoms (Section 3.2).

Unsaturated Compound. A compound whose molecules contain multiple bonds (Section 2.2 and 6.4).

Van der Waals Forces. Weakly attractive forces between nonpolar molecules or between parts of the same molecule. These forces are caused by temporary dipoles in one molecule being induced by similar temporary dipoles in surrounding molecules (Section 2.17D and 3.17). If the molecules or parts of the molecule are too close together then the van der Waals forces become repulsive.

VSEPR (Valence Shell Electron Pair Repulsion) Model. Within the confines of the molecule, electron pairs of the valence shell tend to stay as far apart as possible (Section 1.10).

D APPENDIX
Answers to Self-Tests

CHAPTER 1

1. (a) $:\ddot{N}::N::\ddot{O}:$,   (b) $:N:::\overset{+}{N}:\ddot{O}:^-$
   $\quad\overset{-}{}\quad\overset{+}{}$

1.2 (a) sp^2 (planar),   (b) sp^3 (tetrahedral),   (c) sp^3 (tetrahedral)

1.3 (a) 2,   (b) Decrease

1.4 $H:C:::N:$, $H:\overset{+}{C}::\ddot{N}:^-$

1.5 $H:\ddot{N}::C::\ddot{O}:$

1.6 (a) sp^2,   (b) sp^3,   (c) sp^3

1.7
$$\begin{array}{cccc}
\text{H H H} & \text{H H H} & \text{H H H} & \text{H Cl H} \\
\text{H–C–C–C–Cl,} & \text{H–C–C–C–Cl,} & \text{Cl–C–C–C–Cl,} & \text{H–C–C–C–H} \\
\text{H H Cl} & \text{H Cl H} & \text{H H H} & \text{H Cl H}
\end{array}$$

1.8 (a) $\underset{\uparrow\downarrow}{\underline{1s}}\ \underset{\uparrow\downarrow}{\underline{2s}}\ \underset{\downarrow}{\underline{2p_x}}\ \underline{2p_y}\ 2p_z$,   (b) BF_3,   (c) $\overset{\delta+\ \delta-}{B{-}F}$,   (d) sp^2

CHAPTER 2

2.1 (a) $\underset{\underset{H}{}}{\overset{\overset{H}{}}{C}}=\underset{\underset{Br}{}}{\overset{\overset{Br}{}}{C}}$,   (b) $CH_3\overset{O}{\overset{\|}{C}}{-}OH$,   (c) ⌇⌇OH,   (d) $-\overset{\overset{|}{}}{N}\diagdown$,

(e) $CH_3\overset{O}{\overset{\|}{C}}{-}OCH_3$

2.2 (a) 3°,   (b) 2°,   (c) 1°,   (d) 2°,   (e) 3°,   (f) 1°

2.3 Alcohol hydroxyl, amide, alkene, ether

2.4 HNO_3

2.5 $H_3O^+ + CH_3\overset{O}{\overset{\|}{C}}{-}O^- \rightleftharpoons CH_3\overset{O}{\overset{\|}{C}}{-}OH + H_2O$

2.6 $HA + H_2O \rightleftharpoons H_3O^+ + A^-$

2.7 (a)

CHAPTER 3

3.1 2,4,5-Trimethylheptane

3.2

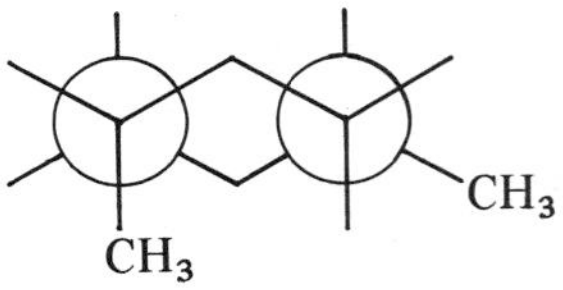

3.3 (a)

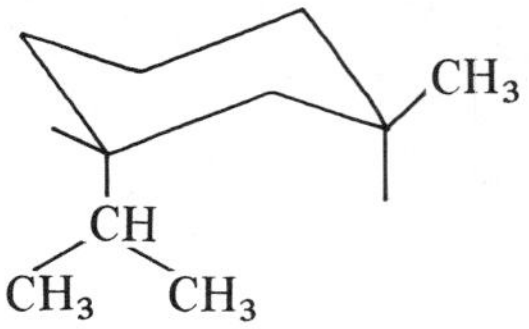

(b) **I**

3.4 (a)

(b)

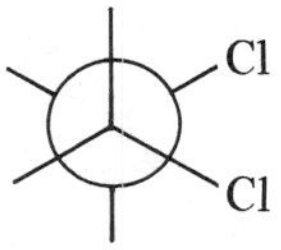

(c)

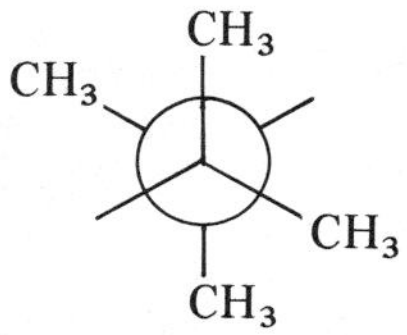

3.5 (a) 3-Methylhexane,   (b) 3,3-Dimethylheptane

3.6

3.7 (a) cis,   (b) 2,   (c)

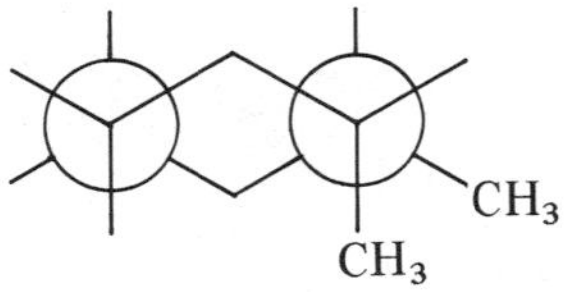

3.8 6-Cyclobutyl-2,3,5-trimethyloctane

3.9 (a) CH_3CHCl_2 + $ClCH_2CH_2Cl$

(b) $CH_3CH_2CH_3$

(c) H_2/Ni

(d) $CH_3CH_2CH_2CH_3$

(e)

CHAPTER 4

4.1 (a)
$$CH_3\overset{\overset{\displaystyle CH_3}{|}}{\underset{\underset{\displaystyle Br}{|}}{C}}CH_3,$$
(b) $CH_3CHCl_2 + ClCH_2CH_2Cl$,

4.2 (a) −31.5,   (b) +11.5,   (c) −69

4.3 $CH_3CH_2CH_2CH_2Br$ and $CH_3CH_2\overset{\overset{\displaystyle }{|}}{\underset{\underset{\displaystyle Br}{|}}{C}}HCH_3$

4.4 (a) $CH_3\overset{\displaystyle \bullet}{C}H_2$ and $\overset{\displaystyle \bullet}{C}H_3$,   (b) +85,   (c) $CH_3\overset{\overset{\displaystyle }{}}{\underset{\underset{\displaystyle Br}{|}}{C}}HCH_3$,   (d) −15.

4.5 (a) + 10 kcal/mole butane,   (b) No

CHAPTER 5

5.1 (a)
$$F:\overset{\overset{\displaystyle F}{..}}{\underset{\underset{\displaystyle F}{}}{C}}:\overset{..}{\underset{..}{F}}: \longrightarrow F:\overset{\overset{\displaystyle F}{..}}{\underset{\underset{\displaystyle F}{}}{C}}\cdot + \cdot\overset{..}{\underset{..}{F}}:$$

(b)
$$F:\overset{\overset{\displaystyle F}{..}}{\underset{\underset{\displaystyle F}{}}{C}}:\overset{..}{\underset{..}{F}}: \longrightarrow F:\overset{\overset{\displaystyle F}{..}}{\underset{\underset{\displaystyle F}{}}{C}}^+ + :\overset{..}{\underset{..}{F}}:^-$$

(c)
$$F:\overset{\overset{\displaystyle F}{..}}{\underset{\underset{\displaystyle F}{}}{C}}:\overset{..}{\underset{..}{F}}: \longrightarrow F:\overset{\overset{\displaystyle F}{..}}{\underset{\underset{\displaystyle F}{}}{C}}:^- + \overset{..}{\underset{..}{F}}:^+$$

5.2

	S_N1	S_N2	E1	E2
(a)	+	−	+	−
(b)	−	+	−	+
(c)	−	+	−	+
(d)	+	−	+	−
(e)	−	+	−	+
(f)	+	+	+	+

5.3 (a)

(b)

Expt. No.	Initial Rate
2	0.04
3	0.02

(c)

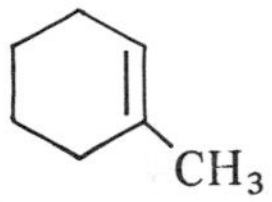

(d) Elimination

5.4 (a) +,   (b) −,   (c) −,   (d) +

CHAPTER 6

6.1 (a) *trans*-2-Hexene,   (b) 3-Methylcyclohexene

6.2 (a) Zn,   (b) 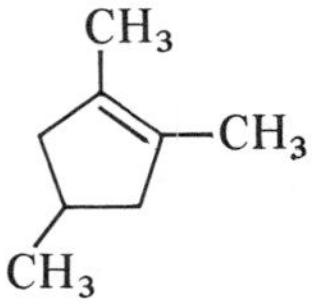   (c) $CH_3CHCH_2CH_2Br$,

(with CH_3 substituent shown on the carbon)

(d) $CH_3CHCH_2CH=CH_2$ (with CH_3 substituent)

6.3 (b), (e), (f), (g)

6.4 1, 3, 2

6.5

CHAPTER 7

7.1 (a) $CH_3C\!\!-\!\!-\!\!CHCH_3$, (with two CH_3 groups and OH)   (b) (1) THF : BH_3 (2) H_2O_2/OH^-,

(c) 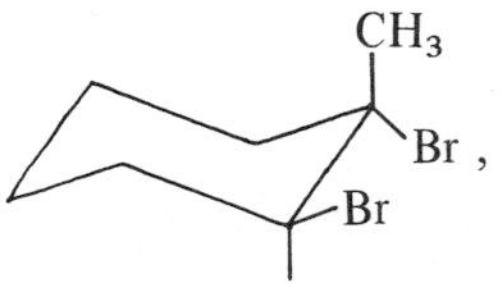 ,

(d) Cl_2/H_2O,   (e) (1) $H\overset{O}{\overset{\|}{C}}\!\!-\!\!O\!\!-\!\!OH$ (2) H_3O^+,   (f) $KMnO_4/25°$

7.2 (a) 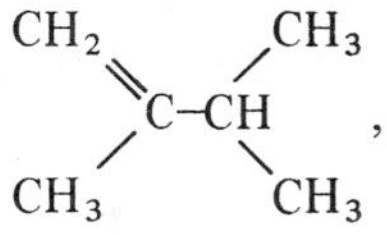 ,   (b) 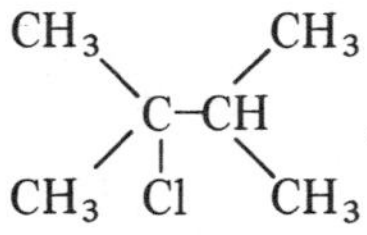 ,   (c) 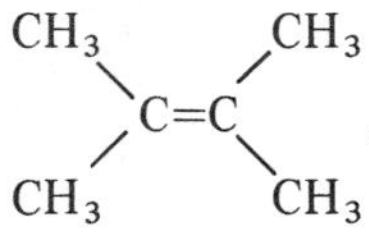 ,

(d) $CH_3\overset{O}{\overset{\|}{C}}CH_3$,   (e) $H\overset{O}{\overset{\|}{C}}H$,   (f) $CH_3\overset{O}{\overset{\|}{C}}CH(CH_3)_2$

7.3 (a) 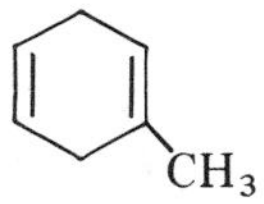 ,   (b)

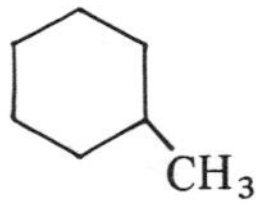

CHAPTER 8

8.1 (a) X,   (b) I,   (c) E,   (d) D,   (e) I,   (f) S,   (g) I,

(h) E,   (i) I,   (j) S,   (k) E,   (l) X,   (m) D

8.2 (a)   No,   (b)   No,   (c)

(plus enantiomer)
No

8.3 (a) −,   (b) −,   (c) −,   (d) −,   (e) +,   (f) +,   (g) −,

(h) +,   (i) +,   (j) +,   (k) −

CHAPTER 9

9.1 (a) $CH_3CH_2\underset{I}{C}=CH_2$,   (b) H_2/Ni_2B (P-2),   (c) ,

(d) $Li/C_2H_5NH_2$,   (e) $CH_3CCl_2CH_3$,   (f) $CH_3\overset{O}{\overset{\|}{C}}CH_2CH_3$

9.2 (a) 0,   (b) +,   (c) 0,   (d) 0,   (e) +

CHAPTER 10

10.1 (a) (cis),   (b) $CH_3CH_2CH=CH\underset{Cl}{C}HCH_3$,

(c) $CH_3\underset{Cl}{C}HCHCH=CHCH_3$ + $CH_3\underset{Cl}{C}HCH=CH\underset{Cl}{C}HCH_3$,

(d) + ,   (e) $CH_3CH=CHCH_2Br$,   (f)

10.2 (a) 0,   (b) +,   (c) 0,   (d) +

10.3

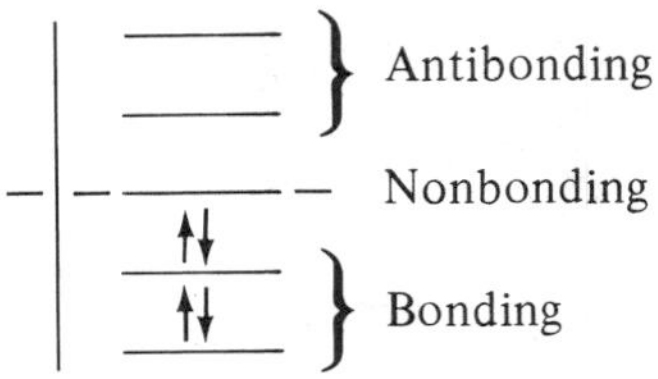

} Antibonding

– – – – – Nonbonding

} Bonding

10.4 B

CHAPTER 11

11.1 (a) D, F,   (b) B, C, D, E, F,   (c)

11.2 (a) *o*-Xylene,   (b) Ethylbenzene,   (c) 4-Bromo-1-isopropylbenzene,

(d) 2-Chloro-1,3-diphenylpropane,   (e) 3,4,5-Trinitrotoluene

11.3 (a) 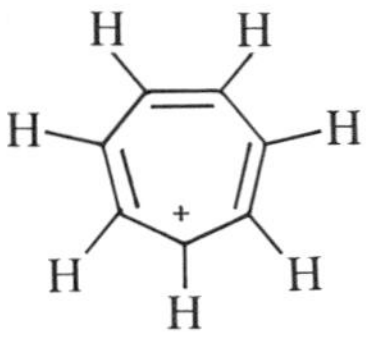 ,   (b) 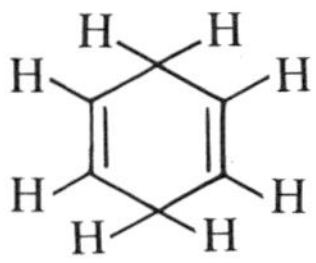 (and others)

(c) 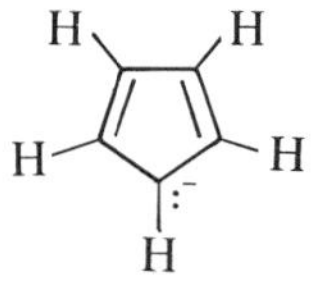 ,   (d)

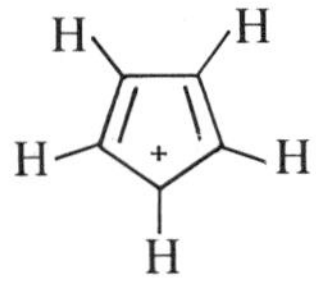

11.4 (a) 3,   (b) 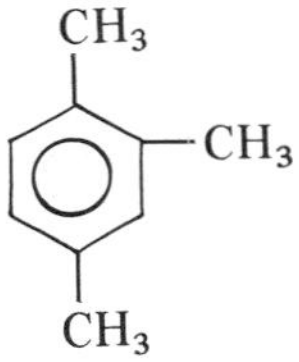 ,   (c) 1,2,4-Trimethylbenzene

CHAPTER 12

12.1 (a) 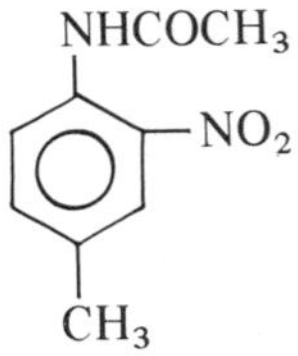 ,   (b) $CH_3\overset{O}{\overset{\|}{C}}-Cl/AlCl_3$,   (c)

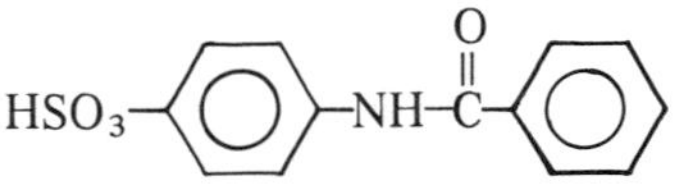

(+ some ortho),   (d) 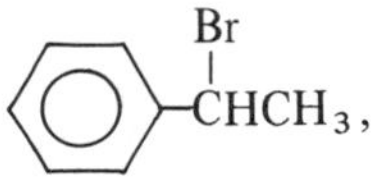 ,   (e) (1) $KMnO_4/OH^-/heat$

(2) H_3O^+ (3) HNO_3/H_2SO_4,   (f) (1) SO_3/H_2SO_4 (2) $HNO_3/H_2SO_4/heat$

(3) H_3O^+/heat,   (g)

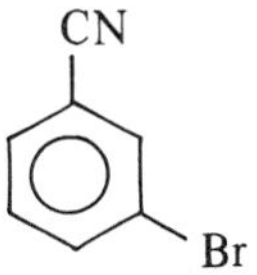

(h)

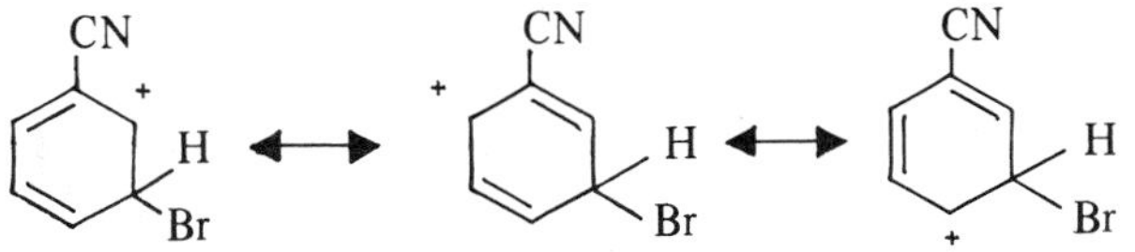

(i)  CH_3O—⟨ ⟩—SO_3H (+ ortho),   (j) 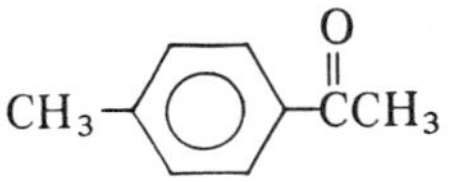 CH_3—⟨ ⟩—$\overset{\overset{O}{\|}}{C}CH_3$ (+ ortho),

(k) 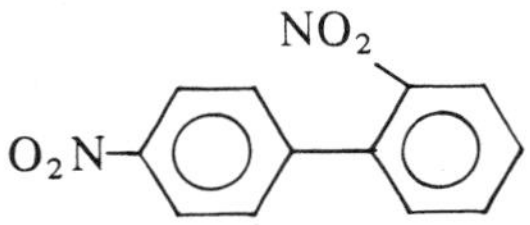 O_2N—⟨ ⟩—⟨ ⟩ NO_2 (+ ortho),   (l) 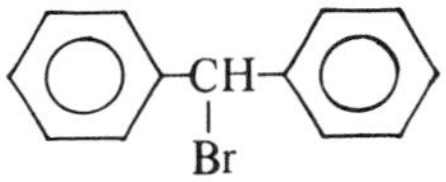 ⟨ ⟩—$\underset{Br}{CH}$—⟨ ⟩

12.2

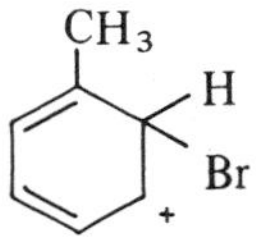

12.3

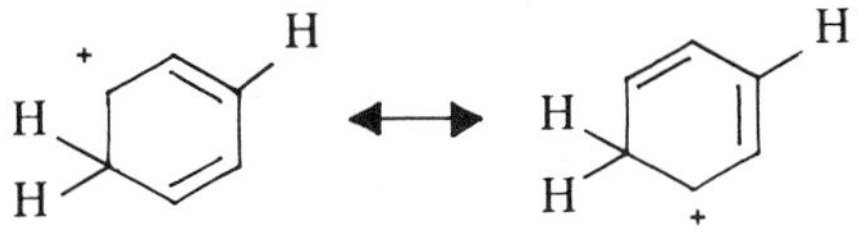

12.4 A: ⟨ ⟩—$CH_2CH=CH_2$,   B: ⟨ ⟩—$CH_2\underset{}{\overset{Cl}{C}}HCH_3$,

C: ⟨ ⟩—$CH=CHCH_3$,   D: ⟨ ⟩—$COOH$

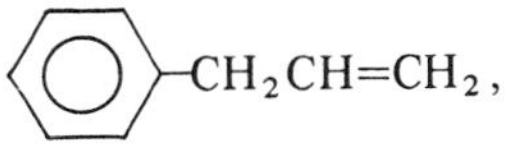

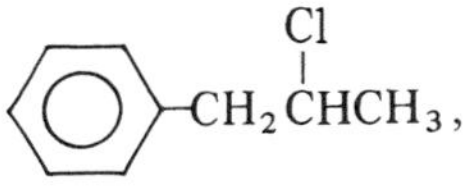

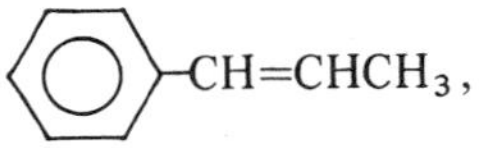

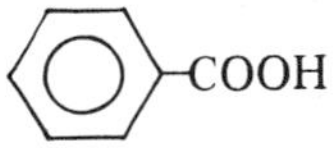

12.5

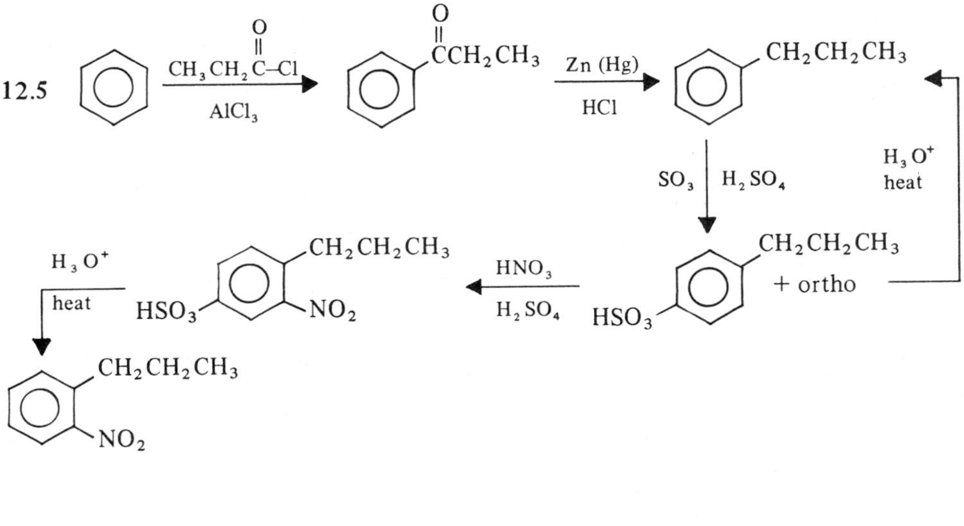

CHAPTER 13

13.1 (a) CH$_3$$\overset{\underset{|}{Br}}{\underset{|}{\underset{}{C}}}$...

13.1 (a) $CH_3\underset{\underset{Br}{|}}{\overset{\overset{CH_3}{|}}{C}}CH_3$, (b) $BrCH_2\underset{\underset{Br}{|}}{\overset{\overset{CH_3}{|}}{C}}CH_2Br$, (c) $CH_2=\overset{\overset{CH_3}{|}}{C}\underset{\underset{CH_3}{|}}{\overset{\overset{}{}}{C}H_2}\underset{\underset{CH_3}{|}}{C}H_3$,

(d) $-CH_2\overset{\overset{O}{\|}}{C}CH_3$, (e) $CH_3CH_2C{\equiv}CCH_2NO_2$

CHAPTER 14

14.1 (a) $CH_3CH_2CH{=}CH_2$, (b) $-CH_2Cl$, (c) $-\underset{\underset{Cl}{|}}{C}HCH_2CH_3$,

(d) $CH_3\overset{\overset{CH_3}{|}}{C}HCH_2CH_3 \ + \ CH_3OLi$, (e) Li, (f) HBr/peroxide,

(g) HI, (h) $CH_3CH_2\underset{\underset{CH_3}{|}}{\overset{\overset{CH_3}{|}}{C}}{-}OH$ (i) NaOH/H$_2$O

14.2 (a) (1) Br$_2$/FeBr$_3$ (2) Mg/ether

(b) (1) $CH_2\overset{O}{\overset{}{{-}}}CH_2$ (2) H$_3$O$^+$

(c) (1) CH$_3$CHO   (2) H$_3$O$^+$

(d) (1) NBS   (2) Mg/ether   (3) $H\overset{\overset{O}{\|}}{C}H$ (4) H$_3$O$^+$ (5) H$_2$SO$_4$/heat

CHAPTER 15

15.1 (a) (1) NaBH$_4$/OH$^-$ (2) H$_3$O$^+$, (b) $-\underset{\underset{CH_3}{|}}{\overset{\overset{CH_3}{|}}{C}}{-}OLi$ (+ H$_2$),

(c) $-CH_2CH_2OH$, (d) , (e) SOCl$_2$,

(f) ^{COOH}, (g) CH_3—$-O^- + Na^+$, (h) 2 $CH_3\overset{\overset{CH_3}{|}}{C}HBr$,

(i) N.R.; i.e., alcohol is insoluble, (j) $Cl{-}\overset{\overset{O}{\|}}{C}CH_2CH_3$, (k) $Cl{-}\overset{\overset{O}{\|}}{\underset{\underset{O}{\|}}{S}}{-}$,

(l) $CH_4 + CH_3CH_2CH_2O^-$,   (m) $2\,CH_3Br + HO\!-\!\langle\bigcirc\rangle\!-\!OH$

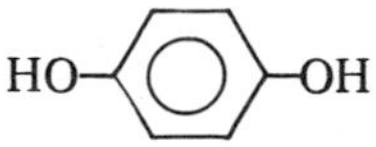

15.2 (a) 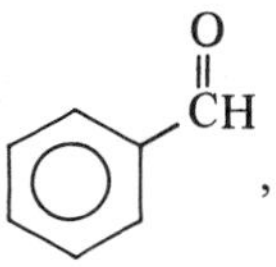 ,   (b) 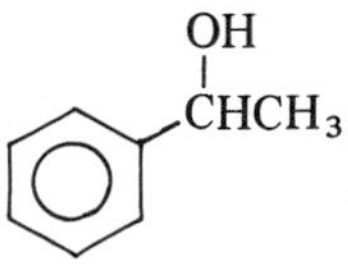 ,   (c)

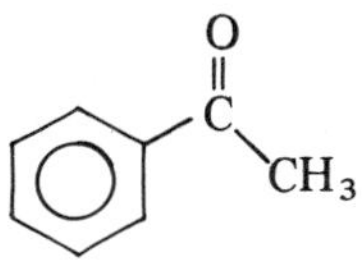

15.3 (a) B,   (b) A

15.4 $CH_3CH_2\overset{+}{O}H_2 + Br^-$

CHAPTER 16

16.1 5-Hydroxy-3-methylheptanal

16.2 (d)

16.3 (a) $Ag(NH_3)_2OH$,   (b) $Ag(NH_3)_2OH$

16.4 (a) $CH_2{=}P(C_6H_5)_3$,   (b) HCN   (c) $LiAlH[OC(CH_3)_3]_3$,

(d) $CH_3CH(OCH_3)_2$,   (e)

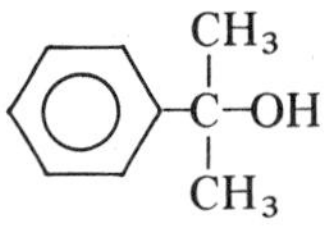

(f) $CH_3CH_2\overset{O}{\overset{\|}{C}}OC_6H_5$ (g) (1) $BrCH_2CO_2CH_3$, Zn   (2) H_3O^+

16.5 (a)

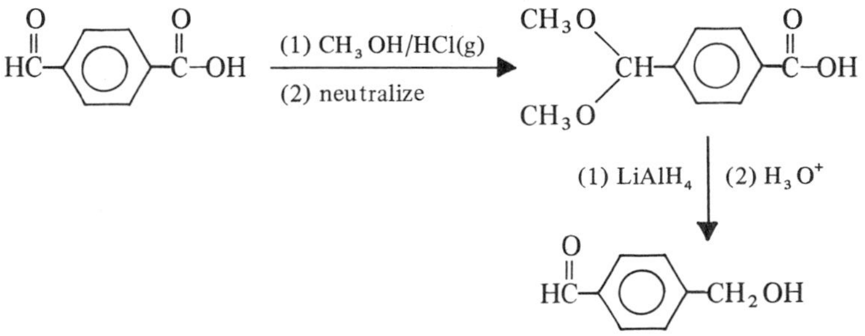

(b)

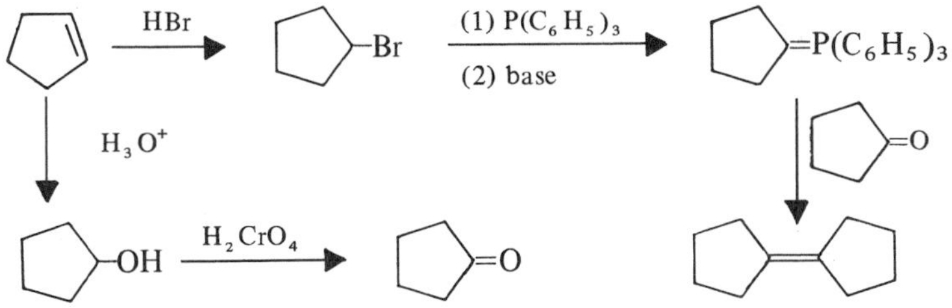

CHAPTER 17

17.1 (a)   (b)   (c)

(d) NaBH$_4$ (e) H$_2$, Ni   (f) CH$_3$OH$_{(excess)}$, H$^+$

(g) CH$_3$CH$_2$CH$_2$CHCH(OCH$_3$)$_2$ (h) CH$_3$CH$_2$CH$_2$CHCH (with C=O above CH, and CH$_3$ below)
    | |
    CH$_3$ CH$_3$

(i) (1) CH$_3$CHBrCO$_2$CH$_2$CH$_3$, Zn   (2) H$_3$O$^+$

17.2 (a) CH$_3$CC$_6$H$_5$ (with O double bond)   (b) C$_6$H$_5$CH=CHCC$_6$H$_5$ (with O double bond)   (c) CN$^-$, CH$_3$COOH, CH$_3$CH$_2$OH

17.3 (a) 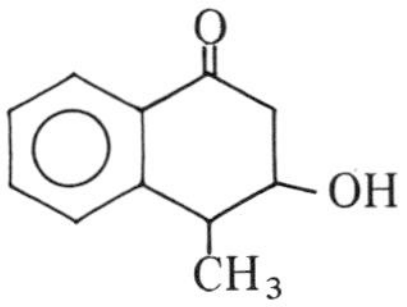   (b)

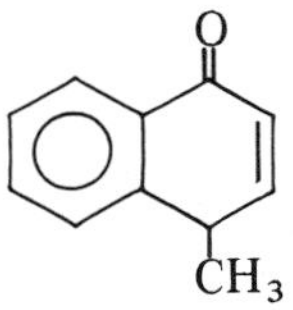

(c) (CH$_3$)$_2$CuLi   (d)

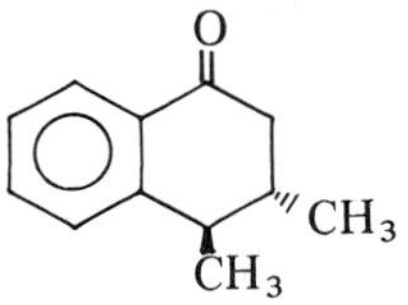

(e) Zn(Hg)/HCl

CHAPTER 18

18.1 (a) 4-Nitrobenzoic acid, (b) 3-Chlorobenzoic acid (c) 3-Chlorobutanoic acid

18.2 (a) D,   (b) B,   (c) D

18.3 (a) 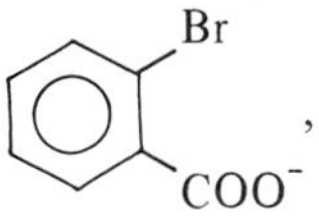 ,   (b) C$_2$H$_5$–C–Br (with CH$_3$ above and CH$_3$ below),   (c) CH$_3$CH$_2$CH$_2$C–Cl (with O double bond),

(d) SOCl$_2$,   (e) LiAlH$_4$,   (f) 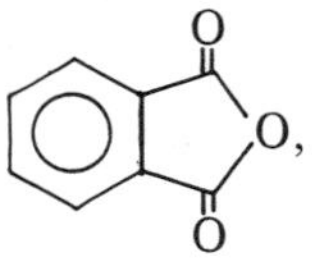 ,   (g) CH$_3$CH$_2$CH$_2$C–NH$_2$ (with O double bond)

+ CH$_3$CH$_2$OH,   (h) 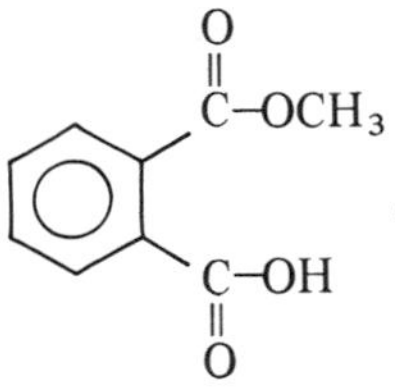 ,   (i) 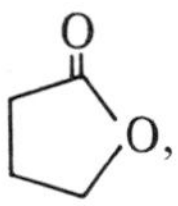 ,

(j) (1) Mg/ether   (2) CO$_2$ (3) H$_3$O$^+$,   (k)

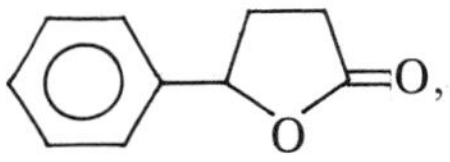

(l) [structure: benzene ring with C(=O)–NH₂ and C(=O)–OH substituents],   (m) [structure: benzene ring with C(=O) bridge to phenyl and C(=O)–OH substituents],   (n) [structure: benzene ring with C(=O)–Cl substituent] (or anhydride)

18.4 (a) Aqueous $NaHCO_3$,   (b) Aqueous $NaHCO_3$

CHAPTER 19

19.1 (a) [phenyl]–$NHCH_2CH_3$,   (b) [phenyl]–CH_2NH_2,

(c) CH_3O–[phenyl]–NH_2,   (d) [cyclohexane ring]–NH_2

19.2 (a) 1,   (b) 4,   (c) 3,   (d) 2

19.3 (a) H_2/Ni,   (b) $NaNO_2/HCl$,   (c) [phenyl]–N–SO₂–[phenyl],   (d) CuCN,

(e) [phenyl]–N=N–[phenyl]–OH,   (f) Cl–[phenyl]–$CH_2\overset{O}{\overset{\|}{C}}$–$NH_2$

(g) H_3PO_2,   (h) H_2O/heat,   (i) $Br_2/NaOH$,   (j) $LiAlH_4$,

(k) [N-methyl piperidine ring with CH₂CH₂CH=CH₂ side chain],   (l) [phenyl with N(CH₃)–N=O],   (m) [phenyl with N(CH₃)₂]

(n) N.R. [same as (m)],   (o) [phenyl with $(CH_3)_2\overset{+}{N}H$]

19.4 (a) [succinic anhydride] $\xrightarrow{NH_3}$ [$\overset{O}{\overset{\|}{C}}$–$NH_2$ with COOH] $\xrightarrow[\text{(2) }H_3O^+]{\text{(1) }Br_2/NaOH}$ $H_2NCH_2CH_2\overset{O}{\overset{\|}{C}}$–$OH$

(b)

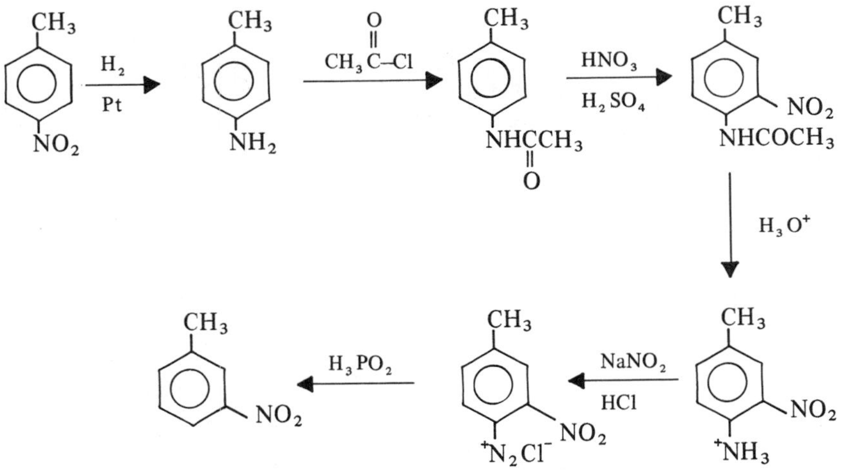

19.5 (a)

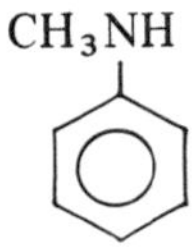

(b)

(or *o* or *m*),

(c) 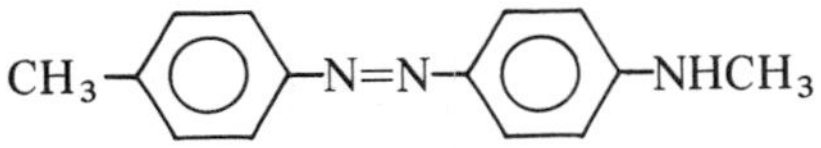 CH_3—〈 〉—$N=N$—〈 〉—$NHCH_3$

19.6 (a)

NH,

(b)

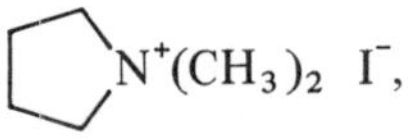

$N^+(CH_3)_2$ I^-,

(c)

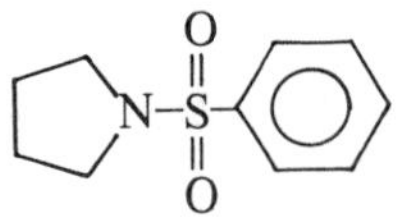

,

(d)

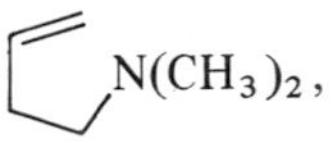

$N(CH_3)_2$,

(e)

$\overset{+}{N}(CH_3)_3$ I^-,

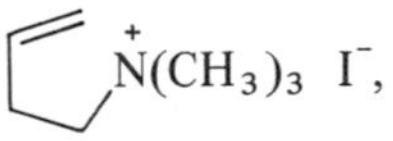

(f) $CH_2=CH-CH=CH_2$
   $+ (CH_3)_3N$

CHAPTER 20

20.1 (a)

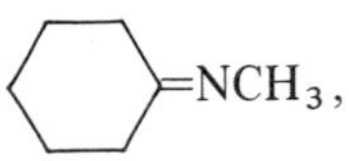

$=NCH_3$,

(b)

$N(CH_3)_2$,

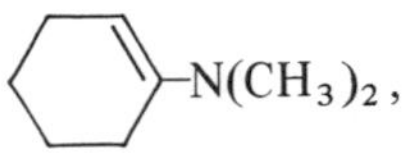

(c)

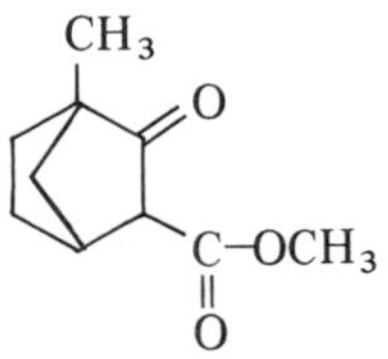

(d) $CH_3\overset{O}{\overset{\|}{C}}-OCH_3$,

(e) $CH_3\overset{O}{\overset{\|}{C}}-\underset{\underset{CH_2CO_2CH_3}{|}}{CH}-\overset{O}{\overset{\|}{C}}-OCH_3$,

(f) $CH_3\overset{O}{\overset{\|}{C}}CH_2CH_2\overset{O}{\overset{\|}{C}}-OCH_3$,

(g)

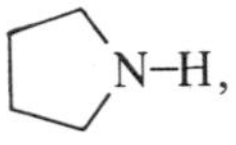

N–H,

(h)

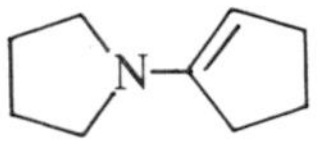

(i) 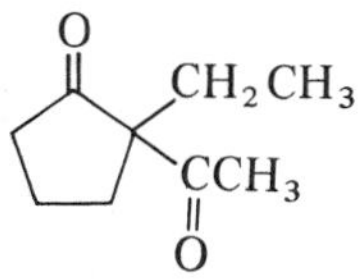 [cyclopentanone structure with CH₂CH₃ and CCH₃ groups] ,   (j) 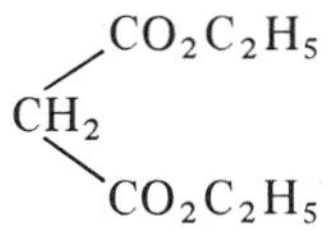 CH₂ with two $CO_2C_2H_5$ groups

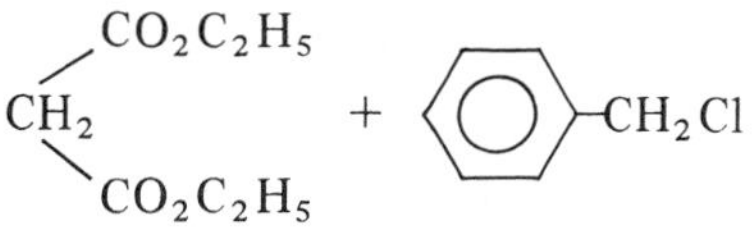

20.2 (a) E, CH_2 with two $CO_2C_2H_5$ groups + [benzene]–CH_2Cl

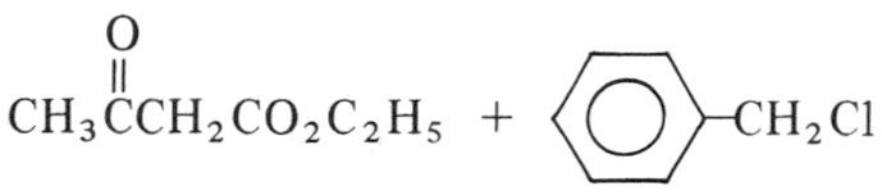

(b) A, $CH_3\overset{O}{\underset{\|}{C}}CH_2CO_2C_2H_5$ + [benzene]–CH_2Cl

(c) N, [pyrrolidine enamine of cyclopentene] + $BrCH_2\overset{O}{\underset{\|}{C}}CH_3$

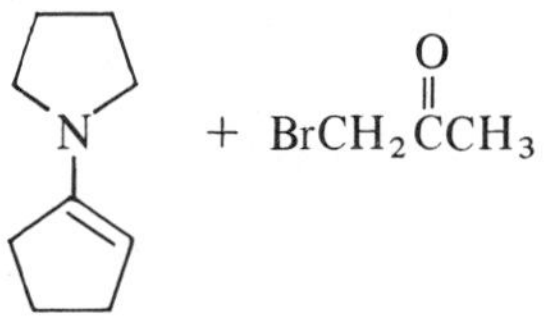

CHAPTER 21

21.1 (a) 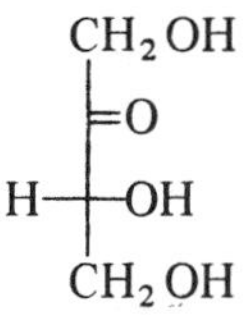
CH_2OH
$C=O$
$H—OH$
CH_2OH

(b)
CHO
$CHOH$
$CHOH$ } OH on either side
$CHOH$
$H—OH$
CH_2OH

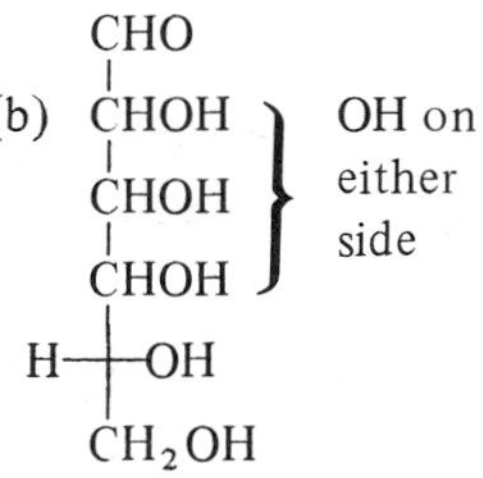

(c)
CHO
$CHOH$
$CHOH$ } OH on either side
$HO—C—H$
CH_2OH

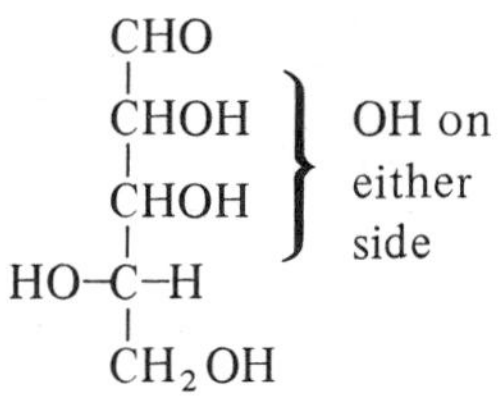

(d) 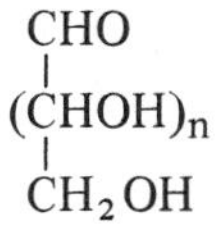 CHO
$(CHOH)_n$
CH_2OH
n = 1,2,3,...

(e) 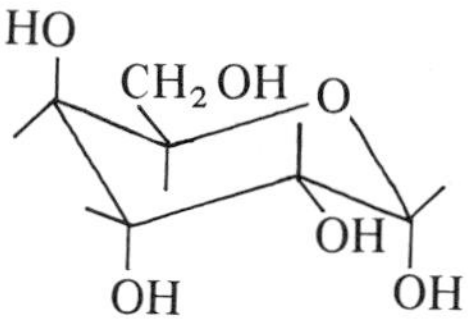 [pyranose ring structure]

(f) 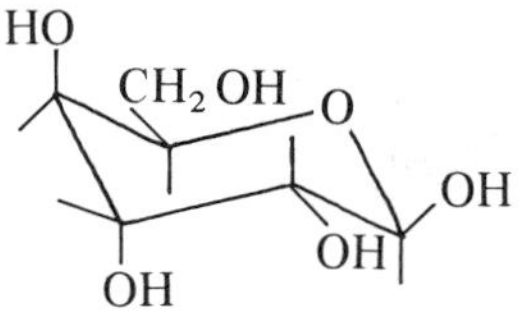 [pyranose ring structure]

(g) 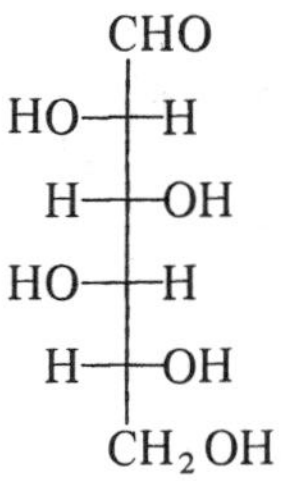
CHO
HO—H
H—OH
HO—H
H—OH
CH_2OH

(h)
CHO
HO—H
H—OH
HO—H
HO—H
CH_2OH

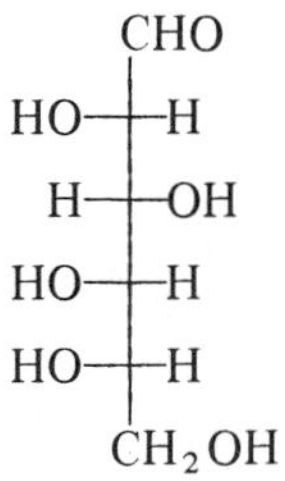

21.2 C

21.3
CHO
HO—H
H—OH
CH_2OH

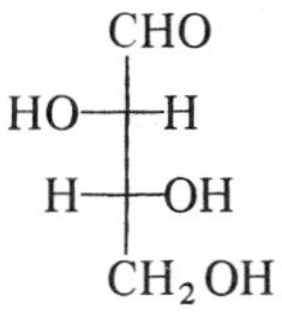

21.4 (a)

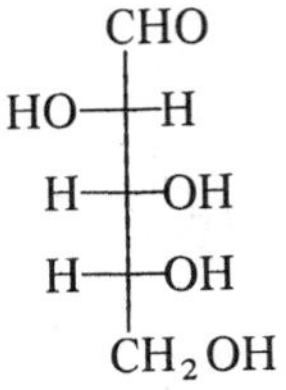

CHO
HO—H
H—OH
H—OH
CH₂OH

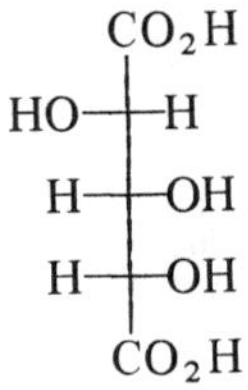

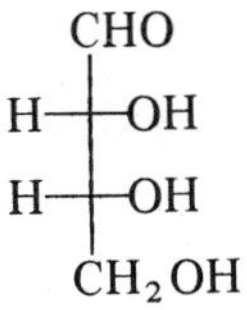

(b)

CO₂H
HO—H
H—OH
H—OH
CO₂H

(c)

CHO
H—OH
H—OH
CH₂OH

(d)

CO₂H
H—OH
H—OH
CO₂H

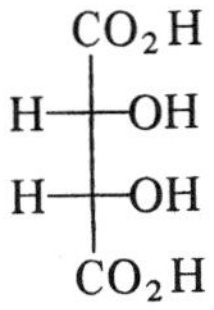

21.5

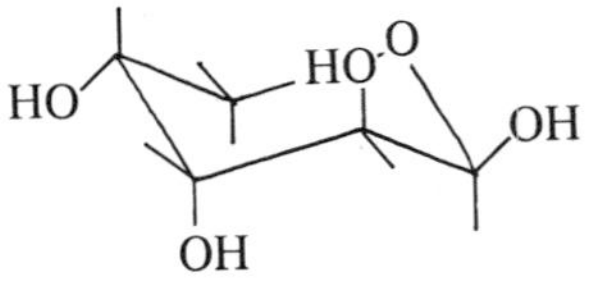

21.6 (a)

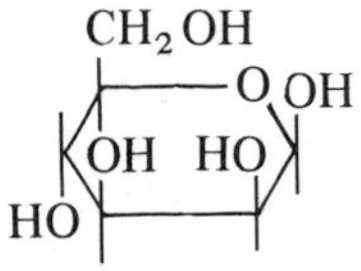

(b)

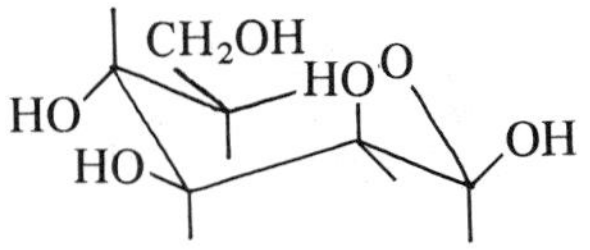

(c) Reducing,

(d) Active, (e) Aldonic, (f) Active, (g) Aldaric, (h) NaBH₄,

(i) Active

21.7 (a) Galactose $\xrightarrow{\text{NaBH}_4}$ Optically *inactive* alditol

(b) HIO₄ oxidation ⟶ Different products:

Fructose ⟶ 2 moles $\overset{O}{\overset{\|}{\text{HCH}}}$ + CO₂ + 3 $\overset{O}{\overset{\|}{\text{HC–OH}}}$

Glucose ⟶ 1 mole $\overset{O}{\overset{\|}{\text{HCH}}}$ + 5 $\overset{O}{\overset{\|}{\text{HC–OH}}}$

CHAPTER 22

22.1 (a) CH₃(CH₂)₁₂CO₂H,

(b) CH₃(CH₂)₁₂$\overset{O}{\overset{\|}{\text{C}}}$–ONa,

(c)

CH₂O$\overset{O}{\overset{\|}{\text{C}}}$(CH₂)₁₂CH₃
|
CHO$\overset{O}{\overset{\|}{\text{C}}}$(CH₂)₁₂CH₃
|
CH₂O$\overset{O}{\overset{\|}{\text{C}}}$(CH₂)₁₂CH₃

(d)

CH₂O$\overset{O}{\overset{\|}{\text{C}}}$(CH₂)₇CH=CH(CH₂)₅CH₃
|
CHO$\overset{O}{\overset{\|}{\text{C}}}$(CH₂)₇CH=CH(CH₂)₅CH₃
|
CH₂O$\overset{O}{\overset{\|}{\text{C}}}$(CH₂)₇CH=CH(CH₂)₅CH₃

(e) CH₃(CH₂)₁₃SO₃Na, (f)

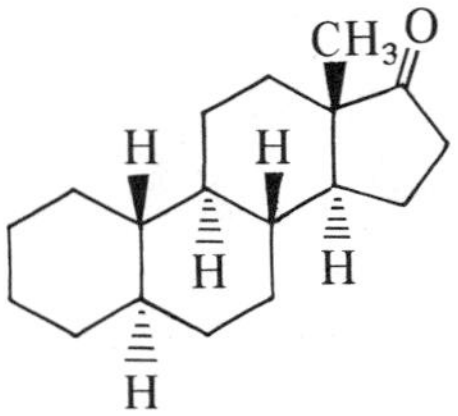

22.2 (a) I_2/OH^- (iodoform test), (b) Br_2/CCl_4, (c) $Ag(NH_3)_2OH$,

22.3 5α-Androstane

22.4 (a) $CH_3(CH_2)_4CH_2C\equiv CH$, (b) $CH_3(CH_2)_5C\equiv CNa$,

(c) $CH_3(CH_2)_5C\equiv C(CH_2)_6CH_2Cl$, (d) KCN

(e) $CH_3(CH_2)_5C\equiv C(CH_2)_7COOH$, (f) H_2/Pd

22.5 Sesquiterpene

22.6

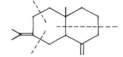

CHAPTER 23

23.1 (a) $CH_3CH_2\overset{\underset{\displaystyle CH_3}{|}}{C}H\overset{\underset{\displaystyle {}^+NH_3}{|}}{C}HCOOH$, (b) $CH_3CH_2\overset{\underset{\displaystyle CH_3}{|}}{C}H\overset{\underset{\displaystyle {}^+NH_3}{|}}{C}HCOO^-$,

(c) $CH_3CH_2\overset{\underset{\displaystyle CH_3}{|}}{C}H\overset{\underset{\displaystyle NH_2}{|}}{C}HCOO^-$

23.2 Pro·Leu·Gly·Phe·Gly·Tyr

NOTES

NOTES

NOTES